Career Readiness

Preparing students for careers is a priority. Now with the Open in Excel functionality in homework problems, students can open data sets directly in Excel and gain experience with the tools they will use in their careers.

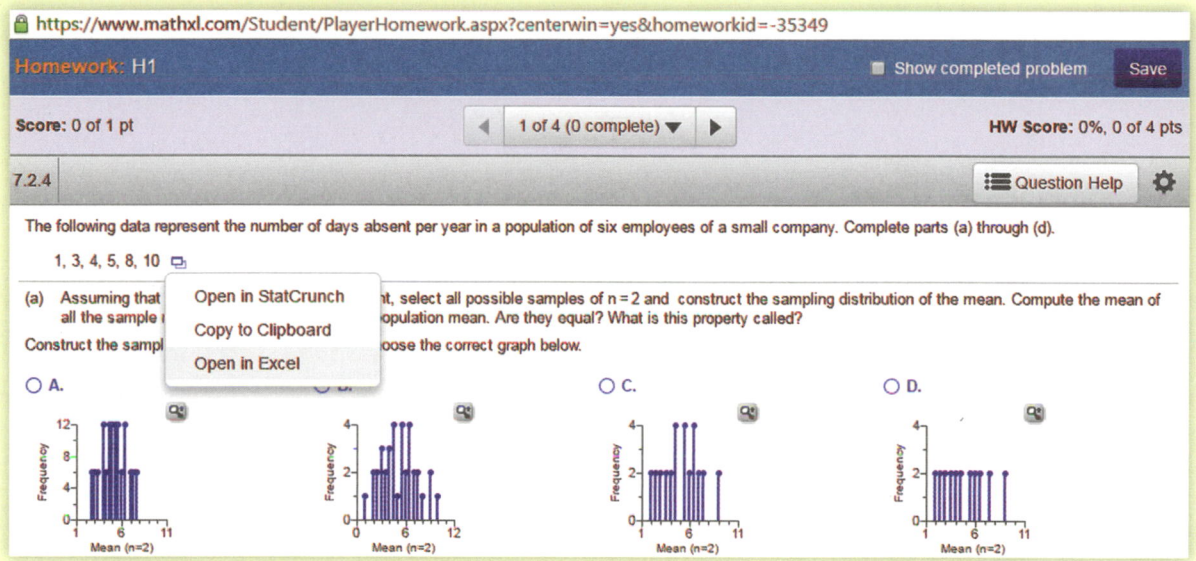

Bring Statistics to Life

Using the StatCrunch Twitter app you can see what people are tweeting about in real time. You can easily load tweets into StatCrunch and construct an interactive word wall showing the most commonly used words.

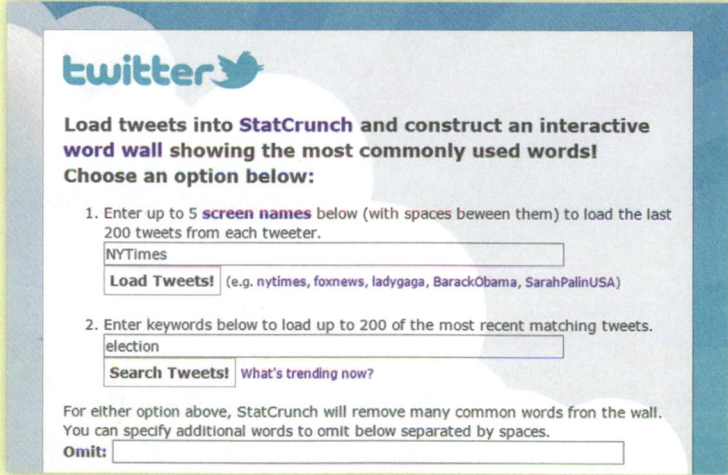

Visit pearson.com/myLab/statistics and click Get Trained to make sure you're getting the most out of MyLab Statistics.

A ROADMAP FOR SELECTING A STATISTICAL METHOD

Data Analysis Task	For Numerical Variables	For Categorical Variables
Describing a group or several groups	Ordered array, stem-and-leaf display, frequency distribution, relative frequency distribution, percentage distribution, cumulative percentage distribution, histogram, polygon, cumulative percentage polygon **(Sections 2.2, 2.4)** Mean, median, mode, geometric mean, quartiles, range, interquartile range, standard deviation, variance, coefficient of variation, skewness, kurtosis, boxplot, normal probability plot **(Sections 3.1, 3.2, 3.3, 6.3)** Index numbers **(online Section 16.8)** Dashboards **(Section 17.2)**	Summary table, bar chart, pie chart, doughnut chart, Pareto chart **(Sections 2.1 and 2.3)**
Inference about one group	Confidence interval estimate of the mean **(Sections 8.1 and 8.2)** *t* test for the mean **(Section 9.2)** Chi-square test for a variance or standard deviation **(online Section 12.7)**	Confidence interval estimate of the proportion **(Section 8.3)** *Z* test for the proportion **(Section 9.4)**
Comparing two groups	Tests for the difference in the means of two independent populations **(Section 10.1)** Wilcoxon rank sum test **(Section 12.4)** Paired *t* test **(Section 10.2)** *F* test for the difference between two variances **(Section 10.4)** Wilcoxon signed ranks test **(online Section 12.8)**	*Z* test for the difference between two proportions **(Section 10.3)** Chi-square test for the difference between two proportions **(Section 12.1)** McNemar test for two related samples **(online Section 12.6)**
Comparing more than two groups	One-way analysis of variance for comparing several means **(Section 11.1)** Kruskal-Wallis test **(Section 12.5)** Randomized block design **(online Section 11.3)** Two-way analysis of variance **(Section 11.2)** Friedman rank test **(online Section 12.9)**	Chi-square test for differences among more than two proportions **(Section 12.2)**
Analyzing the relationship between two variables	Scatter plot, time series plot **(Section 2.5)** Covariance, coefficient of correlation **(Section 3.5)** Simple linear regression **(Chapter 13)** *t* test of correlation **(Section 13.7)** Time-series forecasting **(Chapter 16)** Sparklines **(Section 2.7)**	Contingency table, side-by-side bar chart, PivotTables **(Sections 2.1, 2.3, 2.6)** Chi-square test of independence **(Section 12.3)**
Analyzing the relationship between two or more variables	Colored scatter plots, bubble chart, treemap **(Section 2.7)** Multiple regression **(Chapters 14 and 15)** Dynamic bubble charts **(Section 17.2)** Regression trees **(Section 17.3)** Cluster analysis **(Section 17.5)** Multidimensional scaling **(Section 17.6)**	Multidimensional contingency tables **(Section 2.6)** Drilldown and slicers **(Section 2.7)** Logistic regression **(Section 14.7)** Classification trees **(Section 17.4)** Multiple correspondence analysis **(Section 17.6)**

Basic Business Statistics
Concepts and Applications

Basic Business Statistics
Concepts and Applications

FOURTEENTH EDITION

Mark L. Berenson

Department of Information Management and Business Analytics

School of Business, Montclair State University

David M. Levine

Department of Information Systems and Statistics

Zicklin School of Business, Baruch College, City University of New York

Kathryn A. Szabat

Department of Business Systems and Analytics

School of Business, La Salle University

David F. Stephan

Two Bridges Instructional Technology

Pearson

Director, Portfolio Management: Marcia Horton
Editor in Chief: Deirdre Lynch
Courseware Portfolio Manager: Suzanna Bainbridge
Courseware Portfolio Management Assistant: Morgan Danna
Managing Producer: Karen Wernholm
Content Producer: Sherry Berg and Dana Bettez
Senior Producer: Stephanie Green
Associate Content Producer: Sneh Singh
Manager, Courseware QA: Mary Durnwald
Manager, Content Development: Robert Carroll
Product Marketing Manager: Kaylee Carlson
Product Marketing Assistant: Shannon McCormack
Field Marketing Manager: Thomas Hayward
Field Marketing Assistant: Derrica Moser
Senior Author Support/Technology Specialist: Joe Vetere
Manager, Rights and Permissions: Gina Cheselka
Manufacturing Buyer: Carol Melville, LSC Communications
Composition and Production Coordination: SPi Global
Text Design: Cenveo Publisher Services
Senior Designer and Cover Design: Barbara T. Atkinson
Cover Image: ArtisticPhoto/Shutterstock

Library of Congress CIP data

Names: Berenson, Mark L., author. | Levine, David M., 1946– author. | Szabat, | Kathryn A., author.
Title: Basic business statistics : concepts and applications / Mark L.
  Berenson, Department of Information Management and Business Analytics,
  School of Business, Montclair State University, David M. Levine,
  Department of Information Systems and Business Analytics, Zicklin School
  of Business, Baruch College, City University of New York, Kathryn A.
  Szabat, Department of Business Systems and Analytics, School of Business,
  La Salle University, David F. Stephan, Two Bridges Instructional
  Technology, NY.
Description: Fourteenth Edition. | New York : Pearson Education, [2017]
  Revised edition of the authors' Basic business statistics, [2014]
Identifiers: LCCN 2017050511 | ISBN 9780134684840
Subjects: LCSH: Commercial statistics. | Statistics.
Classification: LCC HF1017 .B38 2017 | DDC 519.5—dc23
LC record available at https://lccn.loc.gov/2017050511

2 18

 **Pearson**

Instructor's Review Copy:
ISBN 13: 978-0-13-468506-9
ISBN 10:   0-13-468506-7

Student Edition:
ISBN 13: 978-0-13-468484-0
ISBN 10:   0-13-468484-2

To our spouses and children,
Rhoda, Marilyn, Mary, Kathy, Lori, Sharyn, and Mark

and to our parents, in loving memory,
Nat, Ethel, Lee, Reuben, Mary, William, Ruth and Francis J.

About the Authors

Kathryn Szabat, David Levine, Mark Berenson, and David Stephan

Mark L. Berenson, David M. Levine, Kathryn A. Szabat, and David F. Stephan are all experienced business school educators committed to innovation and improving instruction in business statistics and related subjects.

Mark L. Berenson is Professor of Information Management and Business Analytics at Montclair State University and also Professor Emeritus of Information Systems and Statistics at Baruch College. He currently teaches graduate and undergraduate courses in statistics and in operations management in the School of Business and an undergraduate course in international justice and human rights that he co-developed in the College of Humanities and Social Sciences.

Berenson received a B.A. in economic statistics and an M.B.A. in business statistics from City College of New York and a Ph.D. in business from the City University of New York. Berenson's research has been published in *Decision Sciences Journal of Innovative Education, Review of Business Research, The American Statistician, Communications in Statistics, Psychometrika, Educational and Psychological Measurement, Journal of Management Sciences and Applied Cybernetics, Research Quarterly, Stats Magazine, The New York Statistician, Journal of Health Administration Education, Journal of Behavioral Medicine,* and *Journal of Surgical Oncology.* His invited articles have appeared in *The Encyclopedia of Measurement & Statistics* and *Encyclopedia of Statistical Sciences.* He has coauthored numerous statistics texts published by Pearson.

Over the years, Berenson has received several awards for teaching and for innovative contributions to statistics education. In 2005, he was the first recipient of the Catherine A. Becker Service for Educational Excellence Award at Montclair State University and, in 2012, he was the recipient of the Khubani/Telebrands Faculty Research Fellowship in the School of Business.

David Levine, Professor Emeritus of Statistics and CIS at Baruch College, CUNY, is a nationally recognized innovator in statistics education for more than three decades. Levine has coauthored 14 books, including several business statistics textbooks; textbooks and professional titles that explain and explore quality management and the Six Sigma approach; and, with David Stephan, a trade paperback that explains statistical concepts to a general audience. Levine has presented or chaired numerous sessions about business education at leading conferences conducted by the Decision Sciences Institute (DSI) and the American Statistical Association, and he and his coauthors have been active participants in the annual DSI Data, Analytics, and Statistics Instruction (DASI) mini-conference. During his many years teaching at Baruch College, Levine was recognized for his contributions to teaching and curriculum development with the College's highest distinguished teaching honor. He earned B.B.A. and M.B.A. degrees from CCNY. and a Ph.D. in industrial engineering and operations research from New York University.

As Associate Professor of Business Systems and Analytics at La Salle University, **Kathryn Szabat** has transformed several business school majors into one interdisciplinary major that better supports careers in new and emerging disciplines of data analysis including analytics. Szabat strives to inspire, stimulate, challenge, and motivate students through innovation and curricular enhancements, and shares her coauthors' commitment to teaching excellence and the continual improvement of statistics presentations. Beyond the classroom she has provided statistical advice to numerous business, nonbusiness, and academic communities, with particular interest in the areas of education, medicine, and nonprofit capacity building. Her research activities have led to journal publications, chapters in scholarly books, and conference presentations. Szabat is a member of the American Statistical Association (ASA), DSI, Institute for Operation Research and Management Sciences (INFORMS), and DSI DASI. She received a B.S. from SUNY-Albany, an M.S. in statistics from the Wharton School of the University of Pennsylvania, and a Ph.D. degree in statistics, with a cognate in operations research, from the Wharton School of the University of Pennsylvania.

Advances in computing have always shaped **David Stephan's** professional life. As an under-graduate, he helped professors use statistics software that was considered advanced even though it could compute *only* several things discussed in Chapter 3, thereby gaining an early appreciation for the benefits of using software to solve problems (and perhaps positively influencing his grades). An early advocate of using computers to support instruction, he developed a prototype of a main-frame-based system that anticipated features found today in Pearson's MathXL and served as special assistant for computing to the Dean and Provost at Baruch College. In his many years teaching at Baruch, Stephan implemented the first computer-based *classroom*, helped redevelop the CIS curriculum, and, as part of a FIPSE project team, designed and implemented a multimedia learning environment. He was also nominated for teaching honors. Stephan has presented at SEDSI and DSI DASI (formerly MSMESB) mini-conferences, sometimes with his coauthors. Stephan earned a B.A. from Franklin & Marshall College and an M.S. from Baruch College, CUNY, and completed the instructional technology graduate program at Teachers College, Columbia University.

For all four coauthors, continuous improvement is a natural outcome of their curiosity about the world. Their varied backgrounds and many years of teaching experience have come together to shape this book in ways discussed in the Preface.

Brief Contents

Brief Contents

Contents

2   Organizing and Visualizing Variables 41

3   Numerical Descriptive Measures 120

4 Basic Probability 168

5 Discrete Probability Distributions 199

6 The Normal Distribution and Other Continuous Distributions 223

7 Sampling Distributions 252

10 Two-Sample Tests 351

11 Analysis of Variance 398

12 Chi-Square and Nonparametric Tests 440

13 Simple Linear Regression 484

14 Introduction to Multiple Regression 536

15 Multiple Regression Model Building 592

16 Time-Series Forecasting 629

17 Business Analytics 678

18 Getting Ready to Analyze Data in the Future 704

19 Statistical Applications in Quality Management (*online*) 19-1

20 Decision Making (*online*) 20-1

Appendices 711

Self-Test Solutions and Answers to Selected Even-Numbered Problems 761

Index 793

Credits 805

Preface

As business statistics evolves and becomes an increasingly important part of one's business education, how business statistics gets taught and what gets taught becomes all the more important.

We, the authors, think about these issues as we seek ways to continuously improve the teaching of business statistics. We actively participate in Decision Sciences Institute (DSI), American Statistical Association (ASA), and Data, Analytics, and Statistics Instruction and Business (DASI) conferences. We use the ASA's Guidelines for Assessment and Instruction (GAISE) reports and combine them with our experiences teaching business statistics to a diverse student body at several universities.

When writing for introductory business statistics students, five principles guide us.

Help students see the relevance of statistics to their own careers by using examples from the functional areas that may become their areas of specialization. Students need to learn statistics in the context of the functional areas of business. We present each statistics topic in the context of areas such as accounting, finance, management, and marketing and explain the application of specific methods to business activities.

Emphasize interpretation and analysis of statistical results over calculation. We emphasize the interpretation of results, the evaluation of the assumptions, and the discussion of what should be done if the assumptions are violated. We believe that these activities are more important to students' futures and will serve them better than focusing on tedious manual calculations.

Give students ample practice in understanding how to apply statistics to business. We believe that both classroom examples and homework exercises should involve actual or realistic data, using small and large sets of data, to the extent possible.

Familiarize students with the use of data analysis software. We integrate using Microsoft Excel, JMP, and Minitab into all statistics topics to illustrate how software can assist the business decision making process. (Using software in this way also supports our second point about emphasizing interpretation over calculation).

Provide clear instructions to students that facilitate their use of data analysis software. We believe that providing such instructions assists learning and minimizes the chance that the software will distract from the learning of statistical concepts.

What's New in This Edition?

This fourteenth edition of *Basic Business Statistics* features many passages rewritten in a more concise style that emphasize definitions as the foundation for understanding statistical concepts. In addition to changes that readers of past editions have come to expect, such as new examples and Using Statistics case scenarios and an extensive number of new end-of-section or end-of-chapter problems, the edition debuts:

- **A First Things First Chapter** that builds on the previous edition's novel Important Things to Learn First Chapter by using real-world examples to illustrate how developments such as the increasing use of business analytics and "big data" have made knowing and understanding statistics that much more critical. This chapter is available as complimentary online download, allowing students to get a head start on learning.

- **JMP Guides** that provide detailed, hands-on instructions for using JMP to illustrate the concepts that this book teaches. JMP provides a starting point for continuing studies in business statistics and business analytics and features visualizations that are easy to construct and that summarize data in innovative ways. The JMP Guides join the Excel and Minitab Guides, themselves updated to reflect the most recent editions of those programs.
- **Tabular Summaries** that state hypothesis test and regression example results along with the conclusions that those results support now appear in Chapters 9 through 15.
- **An All-New Business Analytics Chapter (Chapter 17)** that makes extensive use of JMP and Minitab to illustrate predictive analytics for prediction, classification, clustering, and association as well as explaining what text analytics does and how descriptive and prescriptive analytics relate to predictive analytics. This chapter benefits from the insights the coauthors have gained from teaching and lecturing on business analytics as well as research the coauthors have done for a companion title on business analytics forthcoming for Fall 2018.

Continuing Features that Readers Have Come to Expect

This edition of *Basic Business Statistics* continues to incorporate a number of distinctive features that has led to its wide adoption over the previous editions. Table 1 summaries these carry-over features:

TABLE 1 Distinctive Features Continued in the Fourteenth Edition

Feature	Details
Using Statistics Business Scenarios	A Using Statistics scenario that highlights how statistics is used in a business functional area begins each chapter. Each scenario provides an applied context for learning in its chapter. End-of-chapter "Revisited" sections reinforces the statistical methods that a chapter discusses and apply those methods to the questions raised in the scenario. *In this edition, seven chapters have new or revised Using Statistics scenarios.*
Emphasis on Data Analysis and Interpretation of Results	*Basic Business Statistics* was among the first business statistics textbooks to focus on interpretation of the results of a statistical method and not on the mathematics of a method. This tradition continues, now supplemented by JMP results complimenting the Excel and Minitab results of recent prior editions.
Software Integration	Software instructions in this book feature chapter examples and were personally written by the authors, who collectively have over one hundred years experience teaching the application of software to business. Software usage also features templates and applications developed by the authors that minimize the frustration of using software while maximizing statistical learning
Opportunities for Additional Learning	Student Tips, LearnMore bubbles, and Consider This features extend student-paced learning by reinforcing important points or examining side issues or answering questions that arise while studying business statistics such as "What is so 'normal' about the normal distribution?"
Highly Tailorable Context	With an extensive library of separate online topics, sections, and even two full chapters, instructors can combine these materials and the opportunities for additional learning to meet their curricular needs.
Software Flexibility	With modularized software instructions, instructors and students can switch among Excel, Excel with PHStat, JMP, and Minitab as they use this book, taking advantage of the strengths of each program to enhance learning.

TABLE 1 Distinctive Features Continued in the Fourteenth Edition (*continued*)

Feature	Details
End-of-Section and End-of-Chapter Reinforcements	"Exhibits" summarize key processes throughout the book. "Key Terms" provides an index to the definitions of the important vocabulary of a chapter. "Learning the Basics" questions test the basic concepts of a chapter. "Applying the Concepts" problems test the learner's ability to apply those problems to business problems. For the more quantitatively-minded, "Key Equations" list the boxed number equations that appear in a chapter.
Innovative Cases	End-of-chapter cases include a case that continues through many chapters as well as "Digital Cases" that require students to examine business documents and other information sources to sift through various claims and discover the data most relevant to a business case problem as well as common misuses of statistical information. (Instructional tips for these cases and solutions to the Digital Cases are included in the Instructor's Solutions Manual.)
Answers to Even-Numbered Problems	An appendix provides additional self-study opportunities by provides answers to the "Self-Test" problems and most of the even-numbered problems in this book.
Unique Excel Integration	Many textbooks feature Microsoft Excel, but *Basic Business Statistics* comes from the authors who originated both the Excel Guide workbooks that illustrate model solutions, developed Visual Explorations that demonstrate selected basic concepts, and designed and implemented PHStat, the Pearson statistical add-in for Excel that places the focus on statistical learning. (See Appendix H for a complete summary of PHStat.)

Chapter-by-Chapter Changes Made for This Edition

Because the authors believe in continuous quality improvement, *every* chapter of *Basic Business Statistics* contains changes to enhance, update, or just freshen this book. Table 2 provides a chapter-by-chapter summary of these changes.

TABLE 2
Chapter-by-Chapter
Change Matrix

Chapter	Using Statistics Changed	JMP Guide	Problems Changed	Selected Chapter Changes
FTF	•	•	n.a.	Think Differently About Statistics Starting Point for Learning Statistics
1	•	•	40%	Data Cleaning Other Data Preprocessing Tasks
2		•	60%	Organizing a Mix of Variables Visualizing A Mix of Variables Filtering and Querying Data Reorganized categorical variables discussion. Expanded data visualization discussion. New samples of 379 retirement funds and 100 restaurant meal costs for examples.
3		•	50%	New samples of 379 retirement funds and 100 restaurant meal costs for examples. Updated NBA team values data set.

Chapter	Using Statistics Changed	JMP Guide	Problems Changed	Selected Chapter Changes
4		•	43%	Basic Probability Concepts rewritten. Bayes' theorem example moved online
5		•	60%	Section 5.1 and Binomial Distribution revised. Covariance of a Probability Distribution and The Hypergeometric Distribution moved online.
6	•	•	33%	Normal Distribution rewritten. The Exponential Distribution moved online.
7		•	47%	Sampling Distribution of the Proportion rewritten.
8		•	40%	Confidence Interval Estimate for the Mean revised. Revised "Managing Ashland MultiComm Services" continuing case.
9		•	20%	Chapter introduction revised. Section 9.1 rewritten. New Section 9.4 example.
10	•	•	45%	New Effect Size (online). Using Statistics scenario linked to Chapter 11 and 17. New paired t test and the difference between two proportions examples.
11	•	•	20%	New Using Statistics scenario data. The Randomized Block Design moved online.
12		•	42%	Extensive use of new tabular summaries. Revised "Managing Ashland MultiComm Services" continuing case.
13		•	46%	Chapter introduction revised. Section 13.2 revised.
14		•	30%	Section 14.1 revised. Section 14.3 reorganized and revised. New dummy variable example. Influence Analysis moved online.
15		•	37%	Using Transformations in Regression Models rewritten and expanded. Model Building rewritten
16	•	•	67%	Chapter introduction reorganized and revised. All-new chapter examples.
17	•		42%	All-new chapter. Predictive analytics discussion expanded Uses JMP and Minitab extensively.
18			47%	

Serious About Writing Improvements

Ever review a textbook that reads the same as an edition from years ago? Or read a preface that claims writing improvements but offers no evidence? Among the writing improvements in this edition of *Basic Business Statistics*, the authors have turned to tabular summaries to guide readers to reaching conclusions and making decisions based on statistical information. The authors believe that this writing improvement, which appears in Chapters 9 through 15, not only adds clarity to the purpose of the statistical method being discussed but better illustrates the role of statistics in business decision-making processes. Judge for yourself using the sample from Chapter 10 Example 10.1.

Previously, part of the solution to Example 10.1 was presented as:
You do not reject the null hypothesis because $t_{STAT} = -1.6341 > -1.7341$. The *p*-value (as computed in Figure 10.5) is 0.0598. This *p*-value indicates that the probability that $t_{STAT} < -1.6341$ is equal to 0.0598. In other words, if the population means are equal, the probability that the sample mean delivery time for the local pizza restaurant is at least 2.18 minutes faster than the national chain is 0.0598. Because the *p*-value is greater than a = 0.05, there is insufficient evidence to reject the null hypothesis. Based on these results, there is insufficient evidence for the local pizza restaurant to make the advertising claim that it has a faster delivery time.

In this edition, we present the equivalent solution (on page 357):
Table 10.4 summarizes the results of the pooled-variance *t* test for the pizza delivery data using the calculation above (*not shown in this sample*) and Figure 10.5 results. Based on the conclusions, local branch of the national chain and a local pizza restaurant have similar delivery times. Therefore, as part of the last step of the DCOVA framework, you and your friends exclude delivery time as a decision criteria when choosing from which store to order pizza.

TABLE 10.4
Pooled-variance *t* test summary for the delivery times for the two pizza restaurants

Result	Conclusions
The $t_{STAT} = -1.6341$ is greater than -1.7341.	1. Do not reject the null hypothesis H_0.
The *t* test *p*-value = 0.0598 is greater than the level of significance, $\alpha = 0.05$.	2. Conclude that insufficient evidence exists that the mean delivery time is lower for the local restaurant than for the branch of the national chain.
	3. There is a probability of 0.0598 that $t_{STAT} < -1.6341$.

A Note of Thanks

Creating a new edition of a textbook is a team effort, and we thank our Pearson Education editorial, marketing, and production teammates: Suzanna Bainbridge, Dana Bettez, Kaylee Carlson, Thomas Hayward, Deirdre Lynch, Stephanie Green, and Morgan Danna. Special thanks to the recently-retired Sherry Berg for her design and production oversight in helping to get this edition underway. (Her contributions will be missed!) And we would be remiss not to note the continuing work of Joe Vetere to prepare our screen shot illustrations and the efforts of Julie Kidd of SPi Global to ensure that this edition meets the highest standard of book production quality that is possible.

We also thank Alan Chesen of Wright State University for his diligence in being the accuracy checker for this edition and thank the following people whose comments helped us improve this edition: Mohammad Ahmadi, University of Tennessee-Chattanooga; Sung Ahn,

Washington State University; Kelly Alvey, Old Dominion University; Al Batten, University of Colorado-Colorado Springs; Alan Chesen, Wright State University; Gail Hafer, St. Louis Community College-Meramec; Chun Jin, Central Connecticut State University; Benjamin Lev, Drexel University; Lilian Prince, Kent State University; Bharatendra Rai, University of Massachusetts Dartmouth; Ahmad Vakil, St. John's University (NYC); and Shiro Withanachchi, Queens College (CUNY).

We thank the RAND Corporation and the American Society for Testing and Materials for their kind permission to publish various tables in Appendix E, and to the American Statistical Association for its permission to publish diagrams from the *American Statistician*. Finally, we would like to thank our families for their patience, understanding, love, and assistance in making this book a reality.

Contact Us!

Please email us at **authors@davidlevinestatistics.com** or tweet us **@BusStatBooks** with your questions about the contents of this book. Please include the hashtag #BBS14 in your tweet or in the subject line of your email. We also welcome suggestions you may have for a future edition of this book. And while we have strived to make this book as error-free as possible, we also appreciate those who share with us any perceived problems or errors that they encounter.

If you need assistance using software, please contact your academic support person or Pearson Support at **support.pearson.com/getsupport/**. They have the resources to resolve and walk you through a solution to many technical issues in a way we do not.

As you use this book, be sure to make use of the "Resources for Success" that Pearson Education supplies for this book (described on the following pages). We also invite you to visit **bbs14.davidlevinestatistics.com** (**bit.ly/2xwQoBT**), where we may post additional information or new content as necessary.

Mark L. Berenson
David M. Levine
Kathryn A. Szabat
David F. Stephan

Get the Most Out of
MyLab Statistics

MyLab™ Statistics is the leading online homework, tutorial, and assessment program for teaching and learning statistics, built around Pearson's best-selling content. MyLab Statistics helps students and instructors improve results; it provides engaging experiences and personalized learning for each student so learning can happen in any environment. Plus, it offers flexible and time-saving course management features to allow instructors to easily manage their classes while remaining in complete control, regardless of course format.

Preparedness

One of the biggest challenges in many mathematics and statistics courses is making sure students are adequately prepared with the prerequisite skills needed to successfully complete their course work. Pearson offers a variety of content and course options to support students with just-in-time remediation and key-concept review.

- Build homework assignments, quizzes, and tests to support your course learning outcomes. From *Getting Ready* (GR) questions to the *Conceptual Question Library* (CQL), we have your assessment needs covered from the mechanics to the critical understanding of Statistics. The exercise libraries include technology-led instruction, including new Excel-based exercises, and learning aids to reinforce your students' success.

- Using proven, field-tested technology, auto-graded Excel Projects allow instructors to seamlessly integrate Microsoft® Excel® content into their course without having to manually grade spreadsheets. Students have the opportunity to practice important statistical skills in Excel, helping them to master key concepts and gain proficiency with the program.

Used by more than 37 million students worldwide, MyLab Statistics delivers consistent, measurable gains in student learning outcomes, retention, and subsequent course success.

Resources for Success

MyLab™ Statistics Online Course for Basic Business Statistics
by Berenson/Levine/Szabat/Stephan (requires access code for use)

MyLab™ Statistics is available to accompany Pearson's market leading text offerings. To give students a consistent tone, voice, and teaching method each text's flavor and approach is tightly integrated throughout the accompanying MyLab Statistics course, making learning the material as seamless as possible.

New! Auto- Graded Excel Grader Projects

Using proven, field-tested technology, auto-graded Excel Projects allow instructors to seamlessly integrate Microsoft® Excel® content into their course without having to manually grade spreadsheets.

Students have the opportunity to practice important statistical skills in Excel, helping them to master key concepts and gain proficiency with the program.

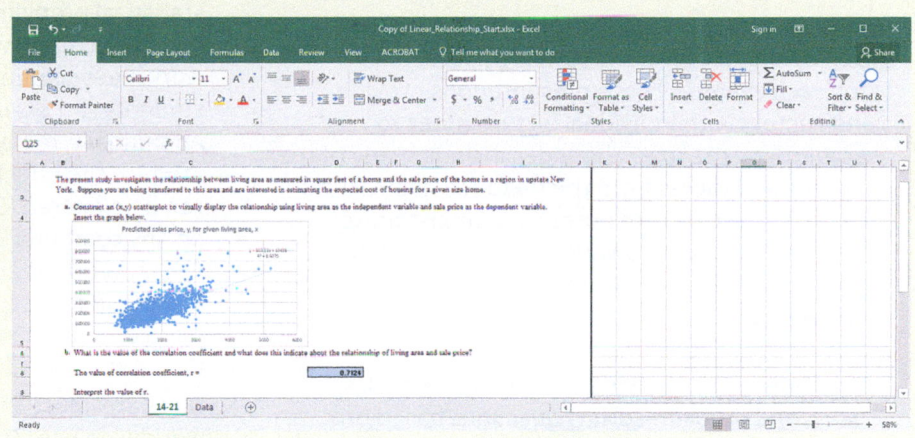

Tutorials and Study Cards for Statistical Software

Tutorials provide brief video walkthroughs and step-by-step instructional study cards on common statistical procedures such as confidence interval estimation, ANOVA, regression, and hypothesis testing. Tutorials and study cards are supplied for Excel 2013 and 2016, Excel with PHStat, JMP, and Minitab.

Diverse Question Libraries

Build homework assignments, quizzes, and tests to support your course learning outcomes. From Getting Ready (GR) questions to the Conceptual Question Library (CQL), we have your assessment needs covered from the mechanics to the critical understanding of Statistics. The exercise libraries include technology-led instruction, including new Excel-based exercises, and learning aids to reinforce your students' success.

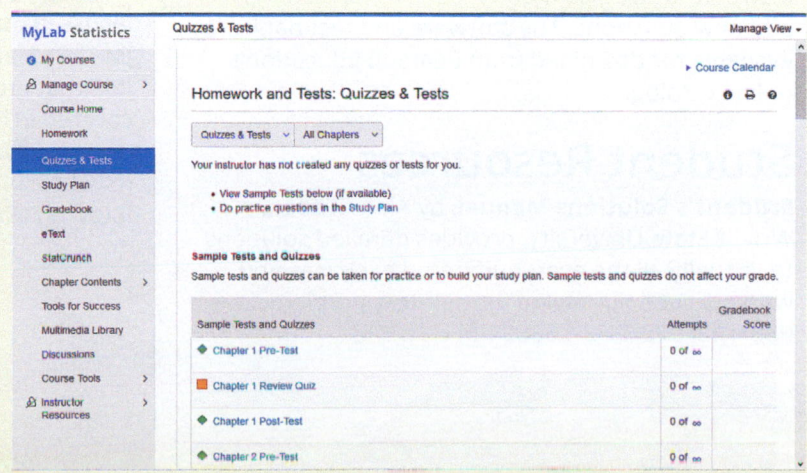

pearson.com/mylab/statistics

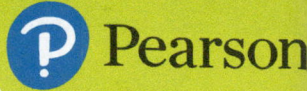

Resources for Success

Instructor Resources

Instructor's Solutions Manual, by Alan Chesen, Wright State University, presents solutions for end-of-section and end-of-chapter problems and answers to case questions, and provides teaching tips for each chapter. The Instructor's Solutions Manual is available for download at **www.Pearson.com** or in MyLab Statistics.

Lecture PowerPoint Presentations, by Patrick Schur, Miami University (Ohio), are available for each chapter. These presentations provide instructors with individual lecture notes to accompany the text. The slides include many of the figures and tables from the textbook. Instructors can use these lecture notes as is or customize them in Microsoft PowerPoint. The PowerPoint presentations are available for download at **www.Pearson.com** or in MyLab Statistics.

Test Bank, contains true/false, multiple-choice, fill-in, and problem-solving questions based on the definitions, concepts, and ideas developed in each chapter of the text. The Test Bank is available for download at **www.Pearson.com** or in MyLab Statistics.

TestGen® (**www.pearsoned.com/testgen**) enables instructors to build, edit, print, and administer tests using a computerized bank of questions developed to cover all the objectives of the text. TestGen is algorithmically based, allowing instructors to create multiple but equivalent versions of the same question or test with the click of a button. Instructors can also modify test bank questions or add new questions. The software and test bank are available for download from Pearson Education's online catalog.

Student Resources

Student's Solutions Manual, by Alan Chesen, Wright State University, provides detailed solutions to virtually all the even-numbered exercises and worked-out solutions to the self-test problems. (ISBN-13: 978-0-13-468504-5)

Online resources complement and extend the study of business statistics and support the content of this book. These resources include **data files** for in-chapter examples and problems, **templates and model solutions**, and **optional topics and chapters**. (See Appendix C for a complete description of the online resources.)

PHStat helps create Excel worksheet solutions to statistical problems. PHStat uses Excel building blocks to create worksheet solutions. These worksheet solutions illustrate Excel techniques and students can examine them to gain new Excel skills. Additionally, many solutions are what-if templates in which the effects of changing data on the results can be explored. Such templates are fully reusable on any computer on which Excel has been installed. PHStat requires an access code and separate download for use. PHStat access codes can be bundled with this textbook using ISBN-13: 978-0-13-468497-0.

Minitab® More than 4,000 colleges and universities worldwide use Minitab software to help students learn quickly and to provide them with a skill-set that's in demand in today's data-driven workforce. Minitab® includes a comprehensive collection of statistical tools to teach beginning through advanced courses. Bundling Minitab software ensures students have the software they need for the duration of their course work. (ISBN-10: 0-13-445640-8; ISBN-13: 978-0-13-445640-9)

JMP® **Student Edition** software is statistical discovery software from SAS Institute Inc., the leader in business analytics software and services. JMP® Student Edition is a streamlined version of JMP that provides all the statistics and graphics covered in introductory and intermediate statistics courses. Available for bundling with this textbook. (ISBN-10: 0-13-467979-2; ISBN-13: 978-0-13-467979-2)

First Things First

▼USING **STATISTICS**
"The Price of Admission"

I t's the year 1900 and you are a promoter of theatrical productions, in the business of selling seats for individual performances. Using your knowledge and experience, you establish a selling price for the performances, a price you hope represents a good trade-off between maximizing revenues and avoiding driving away demand for your seats. You print up tickets and flyers, place advertisements in local media, and see what happens. After the event, you review your results and consider if you made a wise trade-off.

Tickets sold very quickly? Next time perhaps you can charge more. The event failed to sell out? Perhaps next time you could charge less or take out more advertisements to drive demand. If you lived over 100 years ago, that's about all you could do.

Jump ahead about 70 years. You're still a promoter but now using a computer system that allows your customers to buy tickets over the phone. You can get summary reports of advance sales for future events and adjust your advertising on radio and on TV and, perhaps, add or subtract performance dates using the information in those reports.

Jump ahead to today. You're still a promoter but you now have a fully computerized sales system that allows you to constantly adjust the price of tickets. You also can manage many more categories of tickets than just the near-stage and far-stage categories you might have used many years ago. You no longer have to wait until after an event to make decisions about changing your sales program. Through your sales system you have gained insights about your customers such as where they live, what other tickets they buy, and their appropriate demographic traits. Because you know more about your customers, you can make your advertising and publicity more efficient by aiming your messages at the types of people more likely to buy your tickets. By using social media networks and other online media, you can also learn almost immediately who is noticing and responding to your advertising messages. You might even run experiments online presenting your advertising in two different ways and seeing which way sells better.

Your current self has capabilities that allow you to be a more effective promoter than any older version of yourself. Just how much better? Turn the page.

OBJECTIVES

- Statistics is a way of thinking that can lead to better decision making

- Statistics requires analytics skills and is an important part of your business education

- Recent developments such as the use of business analytics and "big data" have made knowing statistics even more critical

- The DCOVA framework guides your application of statistics

- The opportunity business analytics represents for business students

Now Appearing on Broadway ... *and* Everywhere Else

In early 2014, Disney Theatrical Productions woke up the rest of Broadway when reports revealed that its *17*-year-old production of *The Lion King* had been the top-grossing Broadway show in 2013. How could such a long-running show, whose most expensive ticket was less than half the most expensive ticket on Broadway, earn so much while being so old? Over time, grosses for a show decline and, sure enough, weekly grosses for *The Lion King* had dropped about 25% by the year 2009. But, for 2013, grosses were up 67% from 2009 and weekly grosses for 2013 typically exceeded the grosses of opening weeks in 1997, adjusted for inflation!

Heavier advertising and some changes in ticket pricing helped, but the major reason for this change was something else: combining business acumen with the systematic application of *business statistics and analytics* to the problem of selling tickets. As a producer of the newest musical at the time said, "We make educated predictions on price. Disney, on the other hand, has turned this into a science" (see reference 3).

Disney had followed the plan of action that this book presents. It had collected its daily and weekly results, and summarized them, using techniques this book introduces in the next three chapters. Disney then analyzed those results by performing experiments and tests on the data collected (using techniques that later chapters introduce). In turn, those analyses were applied to a new interactive seating map that allowed customers to buy tickets for specific seats and permitted Disney to adjust the pricing of each seat for each performance. The whole system was constantly reviewed and refined, using the semiautomated methods to which Chapter 17 will introduce you. The end result was a system that outperformed the ticket-selling methods others used.

studentTIP

From other business courses, you may recognize that Disney's system uses dynamic pricing.

FTF.1 Think Differently About Statistics

The "Using Statistics" scenario suggests, and the Disney example illustrates, that modern-day information technology has allowed businesses to apply statistics in ways that could not be done years ago. This scenario and example reflect how this book teaches you about statistics. In these first two pages, you may notice

- the lack of calculation details and "math."
- the emphasis on enhancing business methods and management decision making.
- that none of this seems like the content of a middle school or high school statistics class you may have taken.

You may have had some prior knowledge or instruction in *mathematical statistics*. This book discusses *business statistics*. While the boundary between the two can be blurry, business statistics emphasizes business problem solving and shows a preference for using software to perform calculations.

One similarity that you might notice between these first two pages and any prior instruction is *data*. **Data** are the facts about the world that one seeks to study and explore. Some data are unsummarized, such as the facts about a single ticket-selling transaction, whereas other facts, such as weekly ticket grosses, are **summarized**, derived from a set of unsummarized data. While you may think of data as being numbers, such as the cost of a ticket or the percentage that weekly grosses have increased in a year, do not overlook that data can be non-numerical as well, such as ticket-buyer's name, seat location, or method of payment.

Statistics: A Way of Thinking

Statistics are the methods that allow you to work with data effectively. Business statistics focuses on interpreting the results of applying those methods. You interpret those results to help you enhance business processes and make better decisions. Specifically, business statistics provides you with a formal basis to summarize and visualize business data, reach conclusions about that data, make reliable predictions about business activities, and improve business processes.

You must apply this way of thinking correctly. Any "bad" things you may have heard about statistics, including the famous quote "there are lies, damned lies, and statistics" made famous by Mark Twain, speak to the errors that people make when either misusing statistical methods or mistaking statistics as a substitution for, and not an enhancement of, a decision-making process. (Disney Theatrical Productions' success was based on *combining* statistics with business acumen, not *replacing* that acumen.)

DCOVA Framework   To minimize errors, you use a framework that organizes the set of tasks that you follow to apply statistics properly. The five tasks that comprise the **DCOVA framework** are:

- **D**efine the data that you want to study to solve a problem or meet an objective.
- **C**ollect the data from appropriate sources.
- **O**rganize the data collected, by developing tables.
- **V**isualize the data collected, by developing charts.
- **A**nalyze the data collected, to reach conclusions and present those results.

You must always do the **D**efine and **C**ollect tasks before doing the other three. The order of the other three varies and sometimes all three are done concurrently. In this book, you will learn more about the **D**efine and **C**ollect tasks in Chapter 1 and then be introduced to the **O**rganize and **V**isualize tasks in Chapter 2. Beginning with Chapter 3, you will learn methods that help complete the **A**nalyze task. Throughout this book, you will see specific examples that apply the DCOVA framework to specific business problems and examples.

Analytical Skills More Important than Arithmetic Skills   The business preference for using software to automate statistical calculations maximizes the importance of having analytical skills while it minimizes arithmetic skills. With software, you perform calculations faster and more accurately than if you did those calculations by hand, minimizing the need for advanced arithmetic skills. However, with software you can *also* generate inappropriate or meaningless results if you have not fully understood a business problem or goal under study or if you use that software without a proper understanding of statistics.

Therefore, using software to create results that help solve business problems or meet business goals is *always* intertwined with using a framework. And using software does not mean memorizing long lists of software commands or how-to operations, but knowing how to review, modify, and possibly create software solutions. If you can analyze what you need to do and have a general sense of what you need, you can always find instructions or illustrative sample solutions to guide you. (This book provides detailed instructions *as well as* sample solutions for every statistical activity discussed in end-of-chapter software guides and through the use of various downloadable files and sample solutions.)

If you were introduced to using software in an application development setting or an introductory information systems class, do not mistake building applications from scratch as being a necessary skill. A "smart" smartphone user knows how to use apps such as Facebook, Instagram, YouTube, Google Maps, and Gmail effectively to communicate or discover and use information and has no idea how to construct a social media network, create a mapping system, or write an email program. Your approach to using the software in this book should be the same as that smart user. Use your analytical skills to focus on being an effective user and to understand *conceptually* what a statistical method or the software that implements that method does.

Statistics: An Important Part of Your Business Education

Until you read these pages, you may have seen a course in business statistics solely as a required course with little relevance to your overall business education. In just two pages, you have learned that statistics is a way of thinking that can help enhance your effectiveness in business—that is, applying statistics correctly is a fundamental, global skill in your business education.

In the current data-driven environment of business, you need the general analytical skills that allow you to work with data and interpret analytical results regardless of the discipline in which you work. No longer is statistics only for accounting, economics, finance, or other disciplines that directly work with numerical data. As the Disney example illustrates, the decisions you make will be increasingly based on data and not on your gut or intuition supported by past experience. Having a well-balanced mix of statistics, modeling, and basic technical skills as well as managerial skills, such as business acumen and problem-solving and communication skills, will best prepare you for the workplace today … *and* tomorrow (see reference 1).

FTF.2 Business Analytics: The Changing Face of Statistics

Of the recent changes that have made statistics an important part of your business education, the emergence of the set of methods collectively known as business analytics may be the most significant change of all. **Business analytics** combine traditional statistical methods with methods from management science and information systems to form an interdisciplinary tool that supports fact-based decision making. Business analytics include

- statistical methods to analyze and explore data that can uncover previously unknown or unforeseen relationships.
- information systems methods to collect and process data sets of all sizes, including very large data sets that would otherwise be hard to use efficiently.
- management science methods to develop optimization models that support all levels of management, from strategic planning to daily operations.

In the Disney Theatrical Productions example, statistical methods helped determine pricing factors, information systems methods made the interactive seating map and pricing analysis possible, and management science methods helped adjust pricing rules to match Disney's goal of sustaining ticket sales into the future. Other businesses use analytics to send custom mailings to their customers, and businesses such as the travel review site tripadvisor.com use analytics to help optimally price advertising as well as generate information that makes a persuasive case for using that advertising.

Generally, studies have shown that businesses that actively use business analytics and combine that use with data-guided management see increases in productivity, innovation, and competition (see reference 1). Chapter 17 introduces you to the statistical methods typically used in business analytics and shows how these methods are related to statistical methods that the book discusses in earlier chapters.

"Big Data"

Big data are collections of data that cannot be easily browsed or analyzed using traditional methods. Big data implies data that are being collected in huge volumes, at very fast rates or velocities (typically in near real time), and in a variety of forms that can differ from the structured forms such as records stored in files or rows of data stored in worksheets that businesses use every day. These attributes of volume, velocity, and variety (see reference 5) distinguish big data from a "big" (large) set of data that contains numerous records or rows of similar data. When combined with business analytics and the basic statistical methods discussed in this book, big data presents opportunities to gain new management insights and extract value from the data resources of a business (see reference 8).

Unstructured data Big data may also include **unstructured data**, data that has an irregular pattern and contain values which are not comprehensible without additional automated or manual interpretation. Unstructured data takes many forms such as unstructured text, pictures, videos, and audio tracks, with unstructured text, such as social media comments, getting the most immediate attention today for its possible use in customer, branding, or marketing analyses.

Unstructured data can be adapted for use with a number of methods, such as regression, which this book illustrates with conventional, structured files and worksheets. Unstructured data may require one to perform data collection and preparation tasks beyond those tasks that Chapter 1 discusses. While those tasks are beyond the scope of this book, Chapter 17 does include a small example that uses unstructured text to illustrate some of these differences one would face using unstructured data.

FTF.3 Starting Point for Learning Statistics

Statistics has its own vocabulary and learning the precise meanings, or **operational definitions**, of several basic terms provides a start to understanding the statistical methods that this book discusses. For example, *in statistics*, a **variable** defines a characteristic, or property, of an item or individual that can vary among the occurrences of those items or individuals. For example, for the item "book," variables would include the title and number of chapters, as these facts can vary from book to book. For a given book, these variables have a specific value. For *this* book, the value of the title variable would be "Basic Business Statistics," and "20" would be the value for the number of chapters variable. Note that a statistical variable is not an algebraic variable, which serves as a stand-in to represent one value in an algebraic statement and could never take a non-numerical value such as "Basic Business Statistics."

Using the definition of variable, data, in its statistical sense, can be defined as the set of values associated with one or more variables. In statistics, each value for a specific variable is a single fact, not a list of facts. For example, what would be the value of the variable author for this book? Without this rule, you might say that the single list "Berenson, Levine, Szabat, Stephan" is the value. However, applying this rule, one would say that the variable has four separate values: "Berenson", "Levine", "Stephan", and "Szabat". This distinction of using only *single-value data* has the practical benefit of simplifying the task of entering data for software analysis.

Using the definitions of data and variable, the definition of statistics can be restated as the methods that analyze the data of the variables of interest. The methods that primarily help summarize and present data comprise **descriptive statistics**. Methods that use data collected from a small group to reach conclusions about a larger group comprise **inferential statistics**. Chapters 2 and 3 introduce descriptive methods, many of which are applied to support the inferential methods that the rest of the book presents.

Statistic

The previous section uses *statistics* in the sense of a collective noun, a noun that is the name for a collection of things (methods in this case). The word statistics also serves as the plural form of the noun statistic, as in "one uses methods of descriptive statistics (collective noun) to generate descriptive statistics (plural of the singular noun)." In this sense, a **statistic** refers to a value that summarizes the data of a particular variable. (More about this in coming chapters.) In the Disney Theatrical Productions example, the statement "for 2013, weekly grosses were up 67% from 2009" cites a statistic that summarizes the variable weekly grosses using the 2013 data—all 52 values.

When someone warns you of a possible unfortunate outcome by saying, "Don't be a statistic!" you can always reply, "I can't be." *You* always represent one value and a *statistic* always summarizes multiple values. For the statistic "87% of our employees suffer a workplace accident," you, as an employee, will either have suffered or have not suffered a workplace accident. The "have" or "have not" value contributes to the statistic but cannot be the statistic. A statistic can facilitate preliminary decision making. For example, would you immediately accept a position at a company if you learned that 87% of their employees suffered a workplace accident? (Sounds like this might be a dangerous place to work and that further investigation is necessary.)

Can Statistics (*pl.*, statistic) Lie?

The famous quote "lies, damned lies, and statistics" actually refers to the plural form of *statistic* and does not refer to statistics, the field of study. Can any statistic "lie"? No, faulty or invalid statistics can only be produced through willful misuse of statistics or when DCOVA framework tasks are done incorrectly. For example, many statistical methods are valid only if the data being analyzed have certain properties. To the extent possible, you test the assertion that the data have those properties, which in statistics are called *assumptions*. When an assumption is *violated*, shown to be invalid for the data being analyzed, the methods that require that assumption should not be used.

For the inferential methods that this book discusses in later chapters, you must always look for logical causality. **Logical causality** means that you can plausibly claim something directly causes something else. For example, you wear black shoes today and note that the weather is sunny. The next day, you again wear black shoes and notice that the weather continues to be sunny. The third day, you change to brown shoes and note that the weather is rainy. The fourth day, you wear black shoes again and the weather is again sunny. These four days seem to suggest a strong pattern between your shoe color choice and the type of weather you experience. You begin to think if you wear brown shoes on the fifth day, the weather will be rainy. Then you realize that your shoes cannot plausibly influence weather patterns, that your shoe color choice cannot *logically cause* the weather. What you are seeing is mere coincidence. (On the fifth day, you do wear brown shoes and it happens to rain, but that is just another coincidence.)

You can easily spot the lack of logical causality when trying to correlate shoe color choice with the weather, but in other situations the lack of logical causality may not be so easily seen. Therefore, relying on such correlations by themselves is a fundamental misuse of statistics. When you look for patterns in the data being analyzed, you must *always* be thinking of logical causes. Otherwise, you are misrepresenting your results. Such misrepresentations sometimes cause people to wrongly conclude that all statistics are "lies." Statistics (*pl.*, statistic) are not lies or "damned lies." They play a significant role in *statistics*, the way of thinking that can enhance your decision making and increase your effectiveness in business.

FTF.4 Starting Point for Using Software

Because software plays an important role in the application of business statistics, this book uses Excel, JMP, and Minitab to help explain and illustrate statistical concepts and methods. All three programs require knowledge of basic user interface skills, operations, and vocabulary that Table FTF.1 summarizes.

TABLE FTF.1
Basic Computing
Knowledge

Skill or Operation	Specifics
Identify and use standard window objects	Title bar, minimize/resize/close buttons, scroll bars, mouse pointer, menu bars or ribbons, dialog box, window subdivisions such as areas, panes, or child windows
Identify and use common dialog box items	Command button, list box, drop-down list, edit box, option button, check box, tabs (tabbed panels)
Mouse operations	Click, called select in some list or menu contexts and check or clear in some check box contexts; double-click; right-click to make a shortcut menu appear; drag and drag-and-drop

If you found anything new to you in this table, download and review a complimentary copy of the online pamphlet *Basic Computing Skills* and make its study your starting point. (Appendix C discusses how and from where you download online materials.)

Otherwise, a starting point with software begins with review of basic data and document operations. Excel, JMP, and Minitab all use **worksheets** to display the contents of a data set and as the means to enter or edit data. (JMP calls its worksheets **data tables**.) Worksheets are tabular arrangements of data, in which the intersections of rows and columns form **cells**, boxes into which you make individual entries. One places the data for a variable into the cells of a column such that each column contains the data for a different variable, if more than one variable is under study. By convention, one uses the cell in the initial row to enter names of the variables (variable columns). JMP and Minitab provide a special unnumbered row for entering variable names; in Excel, one must use row 1 for this purpose, which can sometimes lead to inadvertent errors. Figure FTF.1 shows the similarities and this key difference among the worksheets of the three programs.

FIGURE FTF.1

Minitab, JMP, and Excel worksheets

student TIP

Many of the Excel solutions as well as selected JMP and Minitab solutions that this book presents exist as templates that simplify the production of results and serve as models for learning more about using formulas in the three programs.

student TIP

Appendix D provides some technical information for add-ins appropriate for use with this book.

Generally, entries in each cell are single data values that can be text or numbers. All three programs also permit **formulas**, instructions to process data, to compute cell values. Formulas can include **functions** that simplify certain arithmetic tasks or provide access to advanced processing or statistical features. Formulas play an important role in designing **templates**, *reusable* solutions that have been previously audited and verified. However, JMP and Minitab allow only *column* formulas that define calculations for all the cells in a column, whereas Excel allows only *cell* formulas that define calculations for individual cells.

All three programs save worksheet data and results as one file, called a **workbook** in Excel and a **project** in JMP and Minitab. JMP and Minitab also allows the saving of individual worksheets or results as separate files, whereas Excel always saves a workbook even if the workbook contains (only) one worksheet. Both JMP and Minitab can open the data worksheets of an Excel workbook, making the Excel workbook a universal format for sharing of files that contain only data, such as the set of data files for use with this book that Appendix C documents. Table FTF.2 summarizes some of the various file formats that the three programs use.

Appendix B discusses the basic document operations of opening, saving, and printing documents, the specifics of which slightly differ among the three programs and further explains file formats as necessary.

TABLE FTF.2

Excel, JMP, and Minitab file formats

File Type	Excel	JMP	Minitab
All-in-one-file	**.xlsx** (workbook)	**.jmpprj** (project)	**.mpj** (project)
Single worksheet	**.xlsx** (see discussion)	**.jmp**	**.mtw**
Results only	**n.a.**	**.jrp** (report), **.jmpappsource** (dashboard)	**.mgf** (graph)
Macro or add-in (simplifies user operations)	**.xlsm**, **.xlam**	**.jsl**, **.jmpaddin**	**.mtb**, **.mac**

student **TIP**
Check the student download web page for this book for more information about PHStat and JMP and Minitab macros and add-ins that may be available for download.

Using Software Properly

Learning to use software *properly* can be hard as software has limited ways to provide feedback for user actions that are invalid operations. In addition, no software will ever know if you are following proper procedures for using that software. The principles that Exhibit FTF.1 list will assist you and should govern your use of software with this book. These principles will minimize your chance of making errors and lessen the frustration that often occurs when these principles are unknown or overlooked by a user.

EXHIBIT   FTF.1

Principles of Using Software Properly

Ensure that software is properly updated.   Many users that manage their own computers often overlook the importance of ensuring that all installed software is up to date.

Understand the basic operational tasks.   Take the time to master the tasks of starting the software, loading and entering data, and how to select or choose commands in a general way.

Understand the statistical concepts that a software procedure uses.   Not understanding those concepts can cause you to make wrong choices in the software and can make interpreting software results difficult.

Know how to review software use for errors.   Review and verify that the proper data preparation procedures (see Chapter 1) have been applied to the data before analysis. Verify that you have selected the correct procedures, commands, and software options. For any information that you entered for results labeling purposes, verify that no typographical errors exist.

Seek reuse of preexisting solutions to solve new problems.   Build solutions from scratch only as necessary, particularly if using Excel in which errors can be most easily made. Some solutions, and almost all Excel solutions that this book presents, exist as models or templates that can *and should* be reused because such reuse models best practice.

Understand how to organize and present information from the results that the software creates.   Think about the best ways to arrange and label your data. Consider ways to enhance or reorganize results that will facilitate communication with others.

Use self-identifying names, especially for the files that you create and save.   Naming files Document 1, Document 2, and so on, will not help you later when you seek to retrieve a file for review and study.

In addition, also look for ways in which you can simplify the user interface of the software you use. If using Excel with this book, consider using PHStat, supplied separately or as part of a bundle by Pearson. PHStat simplifies the user interface by providing a consistent dialog box driven interface that minimizes keystrokes and mouse selections. If using JMP and Minitab, look for macro and add-ins that simplify command sequences or automate repetitive activities.

Software instruction conventions and notation   The instructions that appear in the end-of-chapter software guides and certain appendices use a set of conventions and notation that Table FTF.3 summarizes. These conventions provide a concise and clear way of expressing specific user activities.

TABLE FTF.3 Conventions That This Book Uses

Convention	Example
Names of special keys appear capitalized and in boldface	Press **Enter**. Press **Command** or **Ctrl**.
Key combinations appear in boldface, with key names linked using this symbol:**+**	Enter the formula and press **Ctrl+Enter**. Press **Ctrl+C**.
Menu or Ribbon selections appear in boldface and sequences of consecutive selections are shown using this symbol: **➔**	Select **File ➔ New** Select **PHStat ➔ Descriptive Statistics ➔ Boxplot**.
Target of mouse operations appear in boldface	Click **OK**. Select **Attendance** and then click the **Y button**.
Entries and the location of where entries are made appear in boldface	Enter **450** in cell **B5**. Add **Temperature** to the **Construct Model Effects** list.
Variables in data files that the text names appear capitalized	This file contains the Fund Type, Assets, and Expense Ratio variables.
Placeholders that express a general case appear in italics and may also appear in boldface as part of a function definition	**AVERAGE** (*cell range of variable*) Replace *cell range of variable* with the cell range that contains the Asset variable.
Names of data files that sections or problems refer to explicitly appear in a special font, but names of files in instructions appear in boldface	Retirement Funds Open the **Retirement Funds workbook**.
When current versions of Excel and Minitab differ in their user interface, alternate instructions for older versions appear in a second color immediately following the primary instructions	In the Select Data Source display, click the icon inside the **Horizontal (Category) axis labels** box. Click **Edit** under the **Horizontal (Categories) Axis Labels** heading.

▼REFERENCES

1. Advani, D. "Preparing Students for the Jobs of the Future." *University Business* (2011), **bit.ly/1gNLTJm**.
2. Davenport, T., J. Harris, and R. Morison. *Analytics at Work*. Boston: Harvard Business School Press, 2010.
3. Healy, P. "Ticker Pricing Puts 'Lion King' atop Broadway's Circle of Life." *New York Times, New York edition*, March 17, 2014, p. A1, and **nyti.ms.1zDkzki**.
4. JP Morgan Chase. "Report of JPMorgan Chase & Co. Management Task Force Regarding 2012 CIO Losses," **bit.ly/1BnQZzY**, as quoted in J. Ewok, "The Importance of Excel," *The Baseline Scenario*, **bit.ly/1LPeQUy**.
5. Laney, D. *3D Data Management: Controlling Data Volume, Velocity, and Variety*. Stamford, CT: META Group. February 6, 2001.
6. Levine, D., and D. Stephan. "Teaching Introductory Business Statistics Using the DCOVA Framework." *Decision Sciences Journal of Innovative Education* 9 (Sept. 2011): 393–398.
7. Liberatore, M., and W. Luo. "The Analytics Movement." *Interfaces* 40 (2010): 313–324.
8. "What Is Big Data?" IBM Corporation, **www.ibm.com/big-data/us/en/**.

▼KEY TERMS

big data　4	formula　7	statistics　2
cells　7	function　7	summarized data　2
data　2	inferential statistics　5	template　7
data table　7	logical causality　6	unstructured data　4
business analytics　4	operational definition　5	variable　5
DCOVA framework　3	project (JMP, Minitab)　7	workbook　7
descriptive statistics　5	statistic　5	worksheet　7

EG.1 GETTING STARTED with EXCEL

When you open Excel, you see one window that contains the Office Ribbon user interface on top and a worksheet area that displays the current worksheet of the current workbook, the name of which appears centered in the title bar. At its top, the worksheet area contains a formula bar that allows you to see and edit the contents of the currently selected cell (cell A1 in the illustration). Immediately below the worksheet grid is a sheet tab that identifies the name of current worksheet (DATA). As you use Excel, you can add or generate new sheets, and each sheet will have their own tab that will appear in that same bottom location.

You use Excel with either the Excel Guide workbooks that provide worksheet templates and model solutions or with PHStat that automates using and modifying those templates and model solutions and simplifying Excel operation. Using PHStat requires a separate download and an access code, which may have been bundled with the purchase of this book, as Appendix D fully explains.

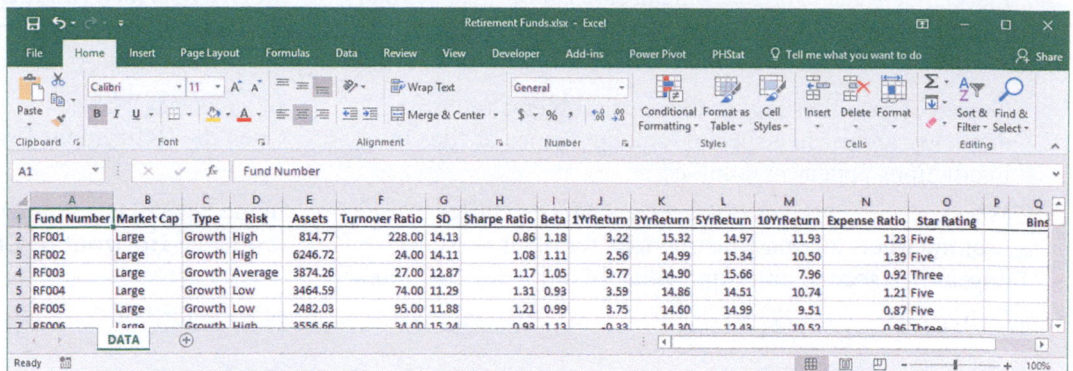

EG.2 ENTERING DATA

In Excel, enter data into worksheet columns, starting with the leftmost, first column, using the cells in row 1 to enter variable names. Avoid skipping rows or columns as such skipping can disrupt or alter the way certain Excel procedures work. Complete a cell entry by pressing **Tab** or **Enter**, or, if using the formula bar to make a cell entry, by clicking the **check mark icon** in the formula bar. To enter or edit data in a specific cell, either use the cursor keys to move the cell pointer to the cell or select the cell directly.

Try to avoid using numbers as row 1 variable headings; if you cannot avoid their use, precede such headings with apostrophes. Pay attention to special instructions in this book that note specific orderings of variable columns that are necessary for some Excel operations. When in doubt, use the DATA worksheets of the Excel Guide Workbooks that Appendix C documents, as your guide for entering and arranging your variable data.

EG.3 OPEN or SAVE a WORKBOOK

Use **File → Open** or **File → Save As**.

Open and **Save As** use similar means to allow you to open or save the workbook by name while specifying the physical

device or network location and folder for that workbook. Save As dialog boxes allow you to save your file in alternate formats for programs that cannot open Excel workbooks (**.xlsx** files) directly. Formats you might use include a simple text file with values delimited with tab characters, **Text (Tab delimited) (*.txt)** that saves the contents of the current worksheet as a simple text file, **CSV (Comma delimited) (*.csv)** that saves worksheet cell values as text values that are delimited with commas, or **Excel 97–2003 Workbook (.xls)** that saves the workbook in the Excel format formerly used. Excels for Mac list these three choices as **Tab Delimited Text (.txt)**, **Windows Comma Separated (.csv)**, and **Excel 97–2004 Workbook (.xls)**, respectively.

The illustration below shows part of the Save As dialog box. In all Windows Excel versions, you can also select a file format in the Open dialog box. If you cannot find a file, select **All Files (*.*)** to see if the file had previously been saved in an unexpected format.

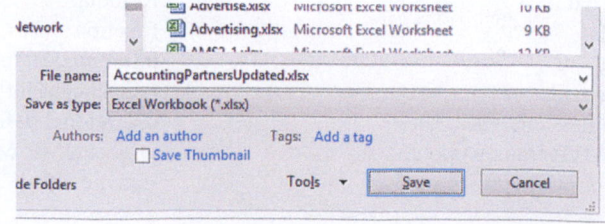

To open a new workbook, select **File ➔ New** (**New Workbook** in Excel for Mac). Excel displays a new workbook with one or more blank worksheets.

EG.4 WORKING WITH a WORKBOOK

Use **Insert** (or **Insert Sheet**), **Delete**, or **Move or Copy**.

You can alter the contents of a workbook by adding a worksheet or by deleting, copying, or rearranging the worksheets and chart sheets that the workbook contains. To perform one of these operations, right-click a sheet tab and select the appropriate choice from the shortcut menu that appears.

To add a worksheet, select **Insert**. In Microsoft Windows Excel, you also click **Worksheet** and then click **OK** in the Insert dialog box. To delete a worksheet or chart sheet, right-click the sheet tab of the worksheet to be deleted and select **Delete**. To copy or rearrange the position of a worksheet or chart sheet, right-click the sheet tab of the sheet and select **Move or Copy**. In the Move or Copy dialog box, first select the workbook and the position in the workbook for the sheet. If copying a sheet, also check **Create a copy**. Then click **OK**.

EG.5 PRINT a WORKSHEET

Use **File ➔ Print**.

In Excel, you print worksheets and chart sheets, not workbooks. When you select **Print**, Excel displays a preview of the currently opened sheet in a dialog box or pane that allows you to select that sheet or other sheets from the workbook. You can adjust the print formatting of the worksheet(s) to be printed by clicking **Page Setup**. Typically, in the Page Setup dialog box, you might click the **Sheet** tab and then check or clear the **Gridlines** and **Row and column headings** checkboxes to add or remove worksheet cell gridlines and the numbered row and lettered column headings that are similar to how a worksheet is displayed onscreen.

EG.6 REVIEWING WORKSHEETS

Follow the best practice of reviewing worksheets before you use them to help solve problems. When you use a worksheet, what you see displayed in cells may be the result of either the recalculation of formulas or cell formatting. A cell that displays 4 might contain the value 4, might contain a formula calculation that results in the value 4, or might contain a value such as 3.987 that has been formatted to display as the nearest whole number.

To display and review all formulas, you press **Ctrl+`** (grave accent). Excel displays the *formula view* of the worksheet, revealing all formulas. (Pressing **Ctrl+`** a second time restores the worksheet to its normal display.) If you use the Excel Guide workbooks, you will discover that each workbook contains one or more FORMULAS worksheets that provide a second way of viewing all formulas.

In the Excel solutions for this book, you will notice cell formatting operations that have changed the background color of cells, changed text attributes such as boldface of cell entries, and rounded values to a certain number of decimal places (typically four). However, if you want to learn more about cell formatting, Appendix B includes a summary of common formatting operations, including those used in the Excel solutions for this book.

EG.7 IF YOU USE the *WORKBOOK* INSTRUCTIONS

Excel Guide *Workbook* instructions enable you to directly modify the template and model worksheet solutions for problems other than the one they help solve. (In contrast, PHStat provides a dialog box interface in which you make entries that PHStat uses to automate such modifications.) *Workbook* instructions express Excel operations in the most universal way possible. For example, many instructions ask you to select (click on) an item from a gallery of items and identify that item selection by name. In some Excel versions, these names may be visible captions for the item; in other versions, you will need to move the mouse over the image to pop up the image name.

Guides also use the word *display* as in the "Format Axis display" to refer to a user interaction that may be presented by Excel in a **task pane** or a **two-panel dialog box** ("Format Axis task pane" or "Format Axis dialog box"). Task panes open to the side of the worksheet and can remain onscreen indefinitely as you do other Excel activities. Initially, some parts of a pane may be hidden and you may need to click on an icon or label to reveal that hidden part to complete a *Workbook* instruction. Two-panel dialog boxes open over the worksheet and must be *closed* before you can do other Excel activities. The left panel of such dialog boxes are always visible and clicking entries in the left panel makes visual one of a set of right panels, only one of which is visible at any given time. (Click the system close button at the top right of a task pane or dialog box to close the display and remove it from the screen.)

Current Excel versions can vary in their menu sequences. Excel Guide instructions show these variations as parenthetical phrases. For example, the menu sequence, "select **Design** (or **Chart Design**) ➔ **Add Chart Element**" tells you to first select **Design** *or* **Chart Design** to begin the sequence and then to continue by selecting **Add Chart Element**. (Microsoft Windows Excels use **Design** and Excel for Mac uses **Chart Design**.)

For the current Excel versions that this book supports (see the FAQs in Appendix G), the *Workbook* Instructions are generally identical. Occasionally, individual instructions may differ significantly for one (or more) versions. In such cases, the instructions that apply for multiple versions (the majority case) appear first, in normal text, and the instructions for the unique version immediately follows in this text color.

JG.1   GETTING STARTED with JMP

When you open JMP, you see the JMP Home Window (shown below) that contains the main menu bar and toolbar through which you make JMP command selections, as well of lists of recent files and any other JMP windows that JMP has been set previously to open. In the illustration below, JMP has opened the Retirement Fund data table window and the Retirement Fund - Chart by Market Cap window and displays those two items in the Window List.

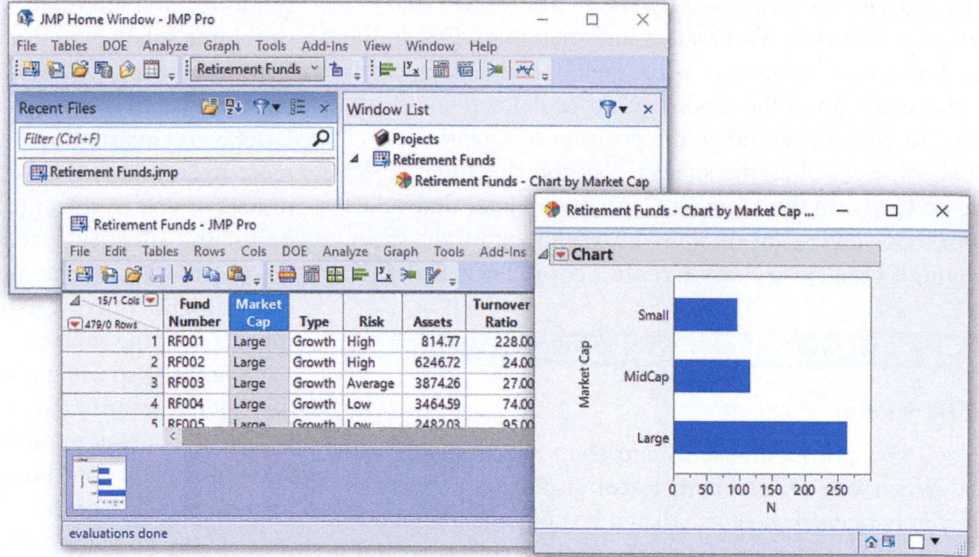

Windows that JMP opens or creates display independently of other windows and can be arranged to overlap, as the illustration shows. Note that JMP displays thumbnails of results windows associated with a data table in an evaluations done panel that appears below the data table. In the Windows List, associated results appear as indented list items under the name of the data table window.

In many windows that JMP creates, JMP hides a copy of the home window's menu bar and tool bar under a "thin blue bar" as shown above. Clicking the **thin blue bar**, seen in the Retirement Fund - Chart by Market Cap window, displays a copy of the home window's user interface. Most results windows also contain a right downward-pointing triangle to the left of a result heading (Chart in the illustration). Clicking this red triangle displays a **red triangle menu** of commands and options appropriate for the results that appear under the heading. Red triangle menus also appear in other contexts, such as in the upper left corner of data tables where they hide various row and column selection, data entry, and formatting commands.

Result headings also include a gray right triangle **disclosure button** that hides or reveals results (to the left of the red triangle in the Chart heading). By using the disclosure button and a combination of red triangle menu selections you can tailor the results, what JMP calls a report, to your specific needs.

Selecting **Help → Books** from the main window's menu bar displays a list of books in PDF format that you can display in JMP or save and read when not using JMP. Consult the books *Discovering JMP* and *Using JMP* as an additional source for getting started with JMP or to discover the JMP features and commands that the instructions in this book do not use.

JG.2   ENTERING DATA

In JMP, enter data into data table (worksheet) columns, starting with the first numbered row and the leftmost, first column. Never skip a cell when entering data because JMP will interpret that skipped cell as a "missing value" (see Section 1.4) that can affect analysis. Complete a cell entry by pressing **Enter**. To enter or edit data in a specific cell, either use the cursor keys to move the cell pointer to the cell or select the cell directly.

As you enter data into columns, JMP assigns default names in the form *Column 1*, *Column 2*, *etc.*, to the column. Change these default names to variable names by double-clicking the name or right-clicking and selecting **Column Info** from the shortcut menu. Either action displays the Column dialog box in which you can enter the variable name and set data type and scale, attributes of the data that Chapter 1 explains.

JG.3   CREATE NEW PROJECT or DATA TABLE

Use **File ➔ New ➔ Project**.

Use **File ➔ New ➔ Data Table**.

While you can open and save the report windows that contain results separately from the data table that provides the data for those results, best practice groups a set of report window and data table files into one project file. To create a project file, select **File ➔ New ➔ Project**. JMP opens a Projects window with a new project named Unititled. Right-click "Untitled" and rename the project. In the illustration below, the project has been renamed Retirement Funds Market Cap Analysis.

To add a window to a project, right-click the project name and select **Add Window**. In the dialog box that appears, select the window to be included and click **OK**. In lieu of selecting **Add Window**, select **Add All Windows** to add all onscreen JMP windows excluding the home window. In the illustration below, the Retirement Funds data table and Chart by Market Cap windows has been added to the renamed project. Project files can be opened and saved as Section JG.4 explains.

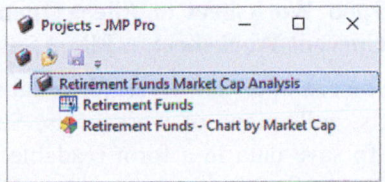

The data table New command opens a blank data table in its own window. Any new data table is not automatically added to the currently open project and you must use the Add Window command if you want a new data table to be part of a project.

JG.4   OPEN or SAVE FILES

Use **File ➔ Open**.

Use **File ➔ Save As**.

In JMP, you can open and save all displayed windows as separate files, as well as open and save special grouping files such as projects. By default, JMP lists all JMP file types in open operations and properly assigns the file type in all save operations. To import an Excel workbook, select **Excel Files (*.xls, *.xlsx, *.xlsm)** from the pull-down list in the Open Data File dialog box. To export a JMP data table as an Excel file, change the **Save as type** in the Save JMP File As dialog box to **Excel Workbook (*.xlsx, *.xls)**.

Report windows can be saved as "interactive HTML" files that allow you or others to use systems on which JMP has not been installed to explore results in an interactive way, using a subset of JMP functionality. To save this type of file, change the **Save as type** in the Save JMP File As dialog box to **Interactive HTML with Data (*.htm;*.html)**.

JG.5   PRINT DATA TABLES or REPORT WINDOWS

Use **File ➔ Print** or **File ➔ Print Preview**.

You select these File commands from the window that contains the object you want to print. For results (report) windows, you must first click the thin blue bar to reveal the menu bar that contains File. If you use Print Preview, JMP opens a new window in which you can preview output and adjust printing options before printing by clicking the leftmost (Print) icon in the window.

JG.6   JMP SCRIPT FILES

JMP script files record many user interface actions and construct or modify JMP objects such as data tables. Using its own JSL scripting language, JMP records your actions as you analyze data in a script file that you can optionally save and play back later to recreate the analysis. Saved script files are text files that can be viewed, edited, and run in their own JMP window or edited by word or texting processing applications.

JSL also includes user interface commands and directives allowing one to construct scripts that simplify and customize the use of the JMP Home window menu bar and toolbar. For selected chapters, JMP scripts created especially for this book can facilitate your use of JMP for those chapters (see Appendix C). JMP scripts are sometimes packaged as a *JMP add-in* that can be "installed" in JMP and directly selected from the JMP Home window menu bar, eliminating the need to open a script and then run the script from inside the script window.

▾MINITAB GUIDE

MG.1 GETTING STARTED WITH MINITAB

When you open Minitab, you see a main window and a number of child windows that cannot be moved outside the boundaries of the main window. You will normally see a blank worksheet and the Session window that records commands and displays results as the child windows. Pictured below is a project with one opened worksheet. Besides the slightly obscured DATA worksheet window and **Session** window, this figure also shows a **Project Manager** that lists the contents of the current project. (Use the keyboard shortcut **Ctrl+I** to display the Project Manager if it is not otherwise visible in the main window.)

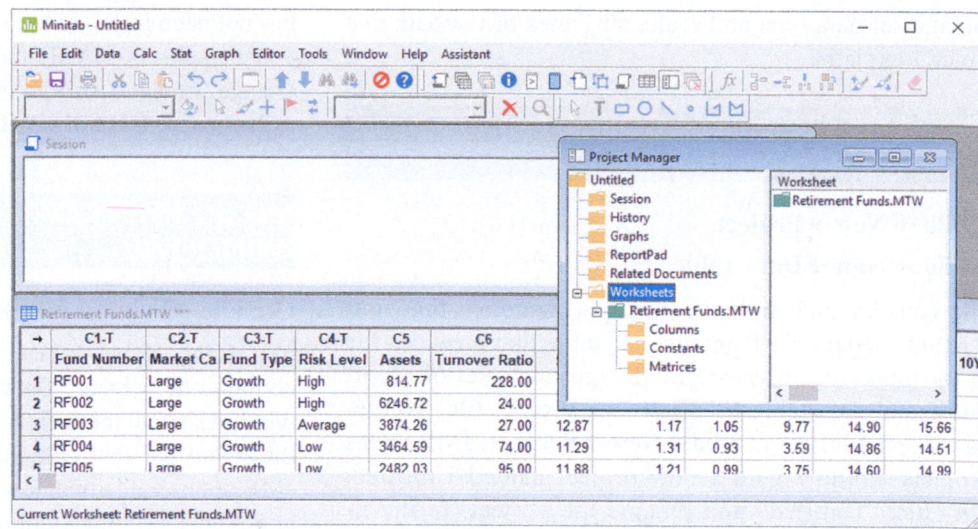

MG.2 ENTERING DATA

In Minitab, enter data into worksheet columns, starting with the first numbered row and leftmost, first column. Minitab names columns using the form Cn, such that the first column is named C1, the second column is C2, and the tenth column is C10. Use the first, unnumbered and shaded row to enter variable names that can be used as a second way to refer to a column by name. If a variable name contains spaces or other special characters, such as **Market Cap**, Minitab will display that name in dialog boxes using a pair of single quotation marks (**'Market Cap'**). You must include those quotation marks any time you enter such a variable name in a dialog box. (With such names, entering the Cn name is the usual choice.)

If a column contains non-numerical data, Minitab displays the column name with an appended **-T** such as C1-T, C2-T, and C3-T in the worksheet shown above. If a column contains data that Minitab interprets as either dates or times, Minitab displays the column name with an appended **-D**. If a column contains data that a column formula (see Chapter 1) computes, Minitab displays a small green check mark above and to the right of the Cn name.

(Neither the appended -D nor the check mark are shown in the worksheet above.)

To enter or edit data in a specific cell, either use the cursor keys to move the cell pointer to the cell or use your mouse to select the cell directly. Never skip a cell in numbered row when entering data because Minitab will interpret a skipped cells as a "missing value" (see Section 1.4).

MG.3 OPEN or SAVE FILES

Use **File→Open Worksheet** or **File→Open Project** and **File→Save Current Worksheet** or **File→Save Project As**.

In Minitab, you can open and save individual worksheets or entire projects, collections of worksheets, Session results, and graphs. To save data in a form readable by Excel, select **Excel** from the **Save as type drop-down list** before you click Save. Other formats you might use include a simple text file, **Text**, or simple text with values delimited with commas, **CSV**.

In Minitab, you can also open and save individual graphs and a project's session window, although these operations are never used in this book.

MG.4   INSERT or COPY WORKSHEETS

Use **File → New** or **File → Open Worksheet**.

To insert a new worksheet, select **File → New** and in the New dialog box click **Minitab Worksheet** and then click **OK**. To insert a copy of a worksheet, select **File → Open Worksheet** and select worksheet to be copied.

MG.5   PRINT WORKSHEETS

Use **File → Print Worksheet** (or **Print Graph** or **Print Session Window**).

Selecting Print Worksheet displays the Data Window Print Options dialog box. In this dialog box, you specify the formatting options for printing and enter a title for the printout. Selecting Print Graph or Print Session Window displays a dialog box that allows you to change the default printer settings.

If you need to change printing attributes, first select **File → Print Setup** and make the appropriate selections in the Print dialog box before you select the Print command.

1

Defining and Collecting Data

OBJECTIVES

- Understand issues that arise when defining variables
- How to define variables
- Understand the different measurement scales
- How to collect data
- Identify the different ways to collect a sample
- Understand the issues involved in data preparation
- Understand the types of survey errors

▼USING **STATISTICS**
Defining Moments

#1 You're the sales manager in charge of the best-selling beverage in its category. For years, your chief competitor has made sales gains, claiming a better tasting product. Worse, a new sibling product from your company, known for its good taste, has quickly gained significant market share at the expense of your product. Worried that your product may soon lose its number one status, you seek to improve sales by improving the product's taste. You experiment and develop a new beverage formulation. Using methods taught in this book, you conduct surveys and discover that people overwhelmingly like the newer formulation, and you decide to use that new formulation going forward, having statistically shown that people prefer the new taste formulation. *What could go wrong?*

#2 You're a senior airline manager who has noticed that your frequent fliers always choose another airline when flying from the United States to Europe. You suspect fliers make that choice because of the other airline's perceived higher quality. You survey those fliers, using techniques taught in this book, and confirm your suspicions. You then design a new survey to collect detailed information about the quality of all components of a flight, from the seats to the meals served to the flight attendants' service. Based on the results of that survey, you approve a costly plan that will enable your airline to match the perceived quality of your competitor. *What could go wrong?*

In both cases, much did go wrong. Both cases serve as cautionary tales that if you choose the wrong variables to study, you may not end up with results that support making better decisions. Defining and collecting data, which at first glance can seem to be the simplest tasks in the DCOVA framework, can often be more challenging than people anticipate.

A s the initial chapter notes, statistics is a way of thinking that can help fact-based decision making. But statistics, even properly applied using the DCOVA framework, can never be a substitute for sound management judgment. If you misidentify the business problem or lack proper insight into a problem, statistics cannot help you make a good decision. Case #1 retells the story of one of the most famous marketing blunders ever, the change in the formulation of Coca-Cola in the 1980s. In that case, Coke brand managers were so focused on the taste of Pepsi and the newly successful sibling Diet Coke that they decided only to define a variable and collect data about which drink tasters preferred in a blind taste test. When New Coke was preferred, even over Pepsi, managers rushed the new formulation into production. In doing so, those managers failed to reflect on whether the statistical results about a test that asked people to compare one-ounce samples of several beverages would demonstrate anything about beverage sales. After all, people were asked which beverage tasted better, not whether they would buy that better-tasting beverage in the future. New Coke was an immediate failure, and Coke managers reversed their decision a mere 77 days after introducing their new formulation (see reference 7).

Case #2 represents a composite story of managerial actions at several airlines. In some cases, managers overlooked the need to state operational definitions for quality factors about which fliers were surveyed. In at least one case, statistics was applied correctly, and an airline spent great sums on upgrades and was able to significantly improve quality. Unfortunately, their frequent fliers still chose the competitor's flights. In this case, no statistical survey about quality could reveal the managerial oversight that given the same level of quality between two airlines, frequent fliers will almost always choose the cheaper airline. While quality was a significant variable of interest, it was not the most significant.

Remember the lessons of these cases as you study the rest of this book. Due to the necessities of instruction, examples and problems presented in all chapters but the last one include pre-identified business problems and defined variables. Identifying the business problem or objective to be considered is always a prelude to applying the DCOVA framework.

student **TIP**

Coke managers also overlooked other issues, such as people's emotional connection and brand loyalty to Coca-Cola, issues better discussed in a marketing book than this book.

1.1 Defining Variables

When a proper business problem or objective has been identified, you can begin to define your data. You define data by defining variables. You assign an **operational definition** to each variable you identify and specify the type of variable and the *scale*, or type of measurement, the variable uses (the latter two concepts are discussed later in this section).

EXAMPLE 1.1

Defining Data at GT&M

You have been hired by Good Tunes & More (GT&M), a local electronics retailer, to assist in establishing a fair and reasonable price for Whitney Wireless, a privately-held chain that GT&M seeks to acquire. You need data that would help to analyze and verify the contents of the wireless company's basic financial statements. A GT&M manager suggests that one variable you should use is monthly sales. What do you do?

SOLUTION Having first confirmed with the GT&M financial team that monthly sales is a relevant variable of interest, you develop an operational definition for this variable. Does this variable refer to sales per month for the entire chain or for individual stores? Does the variable refer to net or gross sales? Do the monthly sales data represent number of units sold or currency amounts? If the data are currency amounts, are they expressed in U.S. dollars? After getting answers to these and similar questions, you draft an operational definition for ratification by others working on this project.

Classifying Variables by Type

You need to know the type of data that a variable defines in order to choose statistical methods that are appropriate for that data. Broadly, all variables are either **numerical**, variables whose data represent a counted or measured quantity, or **categorical**, variables whose data

student TIP

Some prefer the terms **quantitative** and **qualitative** over the terms numerical and categorical when describing variables. These two pairs of terms are interchangeable.

represent categories. Gender with its categories male and female is a categorical variable, as is the variable preferred-New-Coke with its categories yes and no. In Example 1.1, the monthly sales variable is numerical because the data for this variable represent a quantity.

For some statistical methods, you must further specify numerical variables as either being *discrete* or *continuous*. **Discrete** numerical variables have data that arise from a counting process. Discrete numerical variables include variables that represent a "number of something," such as the monthly number of smartphones sold in an electronics store. **Continuous** numerical variables have data that arise from a measuring process. The variable "the time spent waiting on a checkout line" is a continuous numerical variable because its data represent timing measurements. The data for a continuous variable can take on any value within a continuum or an interval, subject to the precision of the measuring instrument. For example, a waiting time could be 1 minute, 1.1 minutes, 1.11 minutes, or 1.113 minutes, depending on the precision of the electronic timing device used.

For some data, you might define a numerical variable for one problem that you wish to study, but define the same data as a categorical variable for another. For example, a person's age might seem to always be a numerical variable, but what if you are interested in comparing the buying habits of children, young adults, middle-aged persons, and retirement-age people? In that case, defining age as categorical variable would make better sense.

Measurement Scales

You identify the **measurement scale** that the data for a variable represent, as part of defining a variable. The measurement scale defines the ordering of values and determines if differences among pairs of values for a variable are equivalent and whether you can express one value in terms of another. Table 1.1 presents examples of measurement scales, some of which are used in the rest of this section.

TABLE 1.1

Examples of Different Scales and Types

Data	Scale, Type	Values
Cellular provider	nominal, categorical	AT&T, T-Mobile, Verizon, Other, None
Excel skills	ordinal, categorical	novice, intermediate, expert
Temperature (°F)	interval, numerical	−459.67°F or higher
SAT Math score	interval, numerical	a value between 200 and 800, inclusive
Item cost (in $)	ratio, numerical	$0.00 or higher

learnMORE

Read the Short Takes for Chapter 1 for more examples of classifying variables as either categorical or numerical.

You define numerical variables as using either an **interval scale**, which expresses a difference between measurements that do not include a true zero point, or a **ratio scale**, an ordered scale that includes a true zero point. If a numerical variable has a ratio scale, you can characterize one value in terms of another. You can say that the item cost (ratio) $2 is twice as expensive as the item cost $1. However, because Fahrenheit temperatures use an interval scale, 2°F does not represent twice the heat of 1°F. For both interval and ratio scales, what the difference of 1 unit represents remains the same among pairs of values, so that the difference between $11 and $10 represents the same difference as the difference between $2 and $1 (and the difference between 11°F and 10°F represents the same as the difference between 2°F and 1°F).

Categorical variables use measurement scales that provide less insight into the values for the variable. For data measured on a **nominal scale**, category values express no order or ranking. For data measured on an **ordinal scale**, an ordering or ranking of category values is implied. Ordinal scales give you some information to compare values but not as much as interval or ratio scales. For example, the ordinal scale poor, fair, good, and excellent allows you to know that "good" is better than poor or fair and not better than excellent. But unlike interval and ratio scales, you do not know that the difference from poor to fair is the same as fair to good (or good to excellent).

PROBLEMS FOR SECTION 1.1

LEARNING THE BASICS

1.1 Four different beverages are sold at a fast-food restaurant: soft drinks, tea, coffee, and bottled water.

a. Explain why the type of beverage sold is an example of a categorical variable.

b. Explain why the type of beverage is an example of a nominal-scaled variable.

1.2 U.S. businesses are listed by size: small, medium, and large. Explain why business size is an example of an ordinal-scaled variable.

1.3 The time it takes to download a video from the Internet is measured.

a. Explain why the download time is a continuous numerical variable.

b. Explain why the download time is a ratio-scaled variable.

APPLYING THE CONCEPTS

 **1.4** For each of the following variables, determine whether the variable is categorical or numerical and determine its measurement scale. If the variable is numerical, determine whether the variable is discrete or continuous.

a. Number of cellphones in the household

b. Monthly data usage (in MB)

c. Number of text messages exchanged per month

d. Voice usage per month (in minutes)

e. Whether the cellphone is used for email

1.5 The following information is collected from students upon exiting the campus bookstore during the first week of classes.

a. Amount of time spent shopping in the bookstore

b. Number of textbooks purchased

c. Academic major

d. Gender

Classify each variable as categorical or numerical and determine its measurement scale.

1.6 For each of the following variables, determine whether the variable is categorical or numerical and determine its measurement scale. If the variable is numerical, determine whether the variable is discrete or continuous.

a. Name of Internet service provider

b. Time, in hours, spent surfing the Internet per week

c. Whether the individual uses a mobile phone to connect to the Internet

d. Number of online purchases made in a month

e. Where the individual accesses social networks to find sought-after information

1.7 For each of the following variables, determine whether the variable is categorical or numerical and determine its measurement scale. If the variable is numerical, determine whether the variable is discrete or continuous.

a. Amount of money spent on clothing in the past month

b. Favorite department store

c. Most likely time period during which shopping for clothing takes place (weekday, weeknight, or weekend)

d. Number of pairs of shoes owned

1.8 Suppose the following information is collected from Robert Keeler on his application for a home mortgage loan at the Metro County Savings and Loan Association.

a. Monthly payments: $2,227

b. Number of jobs in past 10 years: 1

c. Annual family income: $96,000

d. Marital status: Married

Classify each of the responses by type of data and measurement scale.

1.9 One of the variables most often included in surveys is income. Sometimes the question is phrased "What is your income (in thousands of dollars)?" In other surveys, the respondent is asked to "Select the circle corresponding to your income level" and is given a number of income ranges to choose from.

a. In the first format, explain why income might be considered either discrete or continuous.

b. Which of these two formats would you prefer to use if you were conducting a survey? Why?

1.10 If two students score a 90 on the same examination, what arguments could be used to show that the underlying variable—test score—is continuous?

1.11 The director of market research at a large department store chain wanted to conduct a survey throughout a metropolitan area to determine the amount of time working women spend shopping for clothing in a typical month.

a. Indicate the type of data the director might want to collect.

b. Develop a first draft of the questionnaire needed by writing three categorical questions and three numerical questions that you feel would be appropriate for this survey.

1.2 Collecting Data

Collecting data using improper methods can spoil any statistical analysis. For example, Coca-Cola managers in the 1980s (see page 17) faced advertisements from their competitor publicizing the results of a "Pepsi Challenge" in which taste testers consistently favored Pepsi over Coke. No wonder—test recruiters deliberately selected tasters they thought would likely be more favorable to Pepsi and served samples of Pepsi chilled, while serving samples of Coke lukewarm (not a very fair comparison!). These introduced biases made the challenge anything but a proper scientific or statistical test. Proper data collection avoids introducing biases and minimizes errors.

Populations and Samples

You collect your data from either a population or a sample. A **population** contains all the items or individuals of interest that you seek to study. All of the GT&M sales transactions for a specific year, all of the full-time students enrolled in a college, and all of the registered voters in Ohio are examples of populations. A **sample** contains only a portion of a population of interest. You analyze a sample to estimate characteristics of an entire population. You might select a sample of 200 GT&M sales transactions, a sample of 50 full-time students selected for a marketing study, or a sample of 500 registered voters in Ohio in lieu of analyzing the populations identified in this paragraph.

You collect data from a sample when selecting a sample will be less time consuming or less cumbersome than selecting every item in the population or when analyzing a sample is less cumbersome or more practical than analyzing the entire population. Section FTF.3 defines *statistic* as a "value that summarizes the data of a specific variable." More precisely, a **statistic** summarizes the value of a specific variable for sample data. Correspondingly, a **parameter** summarizes the value of a population for a specific variable.

Data Sources

Data sources arise from the following activities:

- Capturing data generated by ongoing business activities
- Distributing data compiled by an organization or individual
- Compiling the responses from a survey
- Conducting a designed experiment and recording the outcomes of the experiment
- Conducting an observational study and recording the results of the study

When you perform the activity that collects the data, you are using a **primary data source**. When the data collection part of these activities is done by someone else, you are using a **secondary data source**.

Capturing data can be done as a byproduct of an organization's transactional information processing, such as the storing of sales transactions at a retailer such as GT&M, or as result of a service provided by a second party, such as customer information that a social media website business collects on behalf of another business. Therefore, such data capture may be either a primary or a secondary source.

Typically, organizations such as market research firms and trade associations distribute complied data, as do businesses that offer syndicated services, such as The Neilsen Company, known for its TV ratings. Therefore, this source of data is usually a secondary source. The other three sources are either primary or secondary, depending on whether you (your organization) are doing the activity. For example, if you oversee the distribution of a survey and the compilation of its results, the survey is a primary data source.

In both observational studies and designed experiments, researchers that collect data are looking for the effect of some change, called a **treatment**, on a variable of interest. In an observational study, the researcher collects data in a natural or neutral setting and has no direct control of the treatment. For example, in an observational study of the possible effects on theme park usage patterns (the variable of interest) that a new electronic payment method might cause, you would take a sample of visitors, identify those who use the new method and those who do not, and then "observe" if those who use the new method have different park usage patterns. In a designed experiment, you permit only those you select to use the new electronic payment method and then discover if the people you selected have different theme park usage patterns (from those who you did not select to use the new payment method). Choosing to use an observational study (or experiment) affects the statistical methods you apply and the decision-making processes that use the results of those methods, as later chapters (10, 11, and 17) will further explain.

learnMORE

Read the SHORT TAKES for Chapter 1 for a further discussion about data sources.

PROBLEMS FOR SECTION 1.2

APPLYING THE CONCEPTS

1.12 The American Community Survey (**www.census.gov/acs**) provides data every year about communities in the United States. Addresses are randomly selected, and respondents are required to supply answers to a series of questions.
a. Which of the sources of data best describe the American Community Survey?
b. Is the American Community Survey based on a sample or a population?

1.13 Visit the website of the Gallup organization at **www.gallup.com**. Read today's top story. What type of data source is the top story based on?

1.14 Visit the website of the Pew Research organization at **www.pewresearch.org**. Read today's top story. What type of data source is the top story based on?

1.15 Transportation engineers and planners want to address the dynamic properties of travel behavior by describing in detail the driving characteristics of drivers over the course of a month. What type of data collection source do you think the transportation engineers and planners should use?

1.16 Visit the home page of the Statistics Portal "Statista" at **statista.com**. Examine one of the "Popular infographic topics" in the Infographics section on that page. What type of data source is the information presented here based on?

1.3 Types of Sampling Methods

When you collect data by selecting a sample, you begin by defining the **frame**. The frame is a complete or partial listing of the items that make up the population from which the sample will be selected. Inaccurate or biased results can occur if a frame excludes certain groups, or portions of the population. Using different frames to collect data can lead to different, even opposite, conclusions.

Using your frame, you select either a nonprobability sample or a probability sample. In a **nonprobability sample**, you select the items or individuals without knowing their probabilities of selection. In a **probability sample**, you select items based on known probabilities. Whenever possible, you should use a probability sample as such a sample will allow you to make inferences about the population being analyzed.

Nonprobability samples can have certain advantages, such as convenience, speed, and low cost. Such samples are typically used to obtain informal approximations or as small-scale initial or pilot analyses. However, because the theory of statistical inference depends on probability sampling, nonprobability samples *cannot be used* for statistical inference and this more than offsets those advantages in more formal analyses.

Figure 1.1 shows the subcategories of the two types of sampling. A nonprobability sample can be either a convenience sample or a judgment sample. To collect a **convenience sample**, you select items that are easy, inexpensive, or convenient to sample. For example, in a warehouse of stacked items, selecting only the items located on the top of each stack and within easy reach would create a convenience sample. So, too, would be the responses to surveys that the websites of many companies offer visitors. While such surveys can provide large amounts of data quickly and inexpensively, the convenience samples selected from these responses will consist of self-selected website visitors. (Read the Consider This essay on page 29 for a related story.)

To collect a **judgment sample**, you collect the opinions of preselected experts in the subject matter. Although the experts may be well informed, you cannot generalize their results to the population.

The types of probability samples most commonly used include simple random, systematic, stratified, and cluster samples. These four types of probability samples vary in terms of cost, accuracy, and complexity, and they are the subject of the rest of this section.

FIGURE 1.1
Types of samples

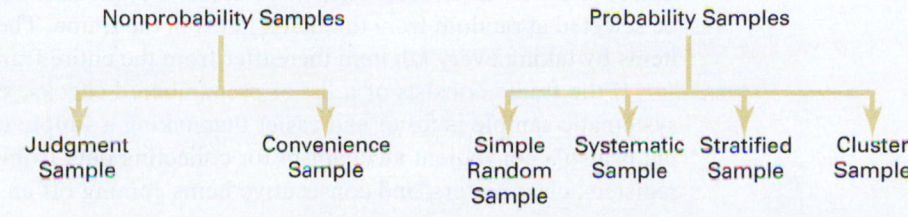

Nonprobability Samples

Probability Samples

Judgment Sample   Convenience Sample   Simple Random Sample   Systematic Sample   Stratified Sample   Cluster Sample

Simple Random Sample

In a **simple random sample**, every item from a frame has the same chance of selection as every other item, and every sample of a fixed size has the same chance of selection as every other sample of that size. Simple random sampling is the most elementary random sampling technique. It forms the basis for the other random sampling techniques. However, simple random sampling has its disadvantages. Its results are often subject to more variation than other sampling methods. In addition, when the frame used is very large, carrying out a simple random sample may be time consuming and expensive.

With simple random sampling, you use n to represent the sample size and N to represent the frame size. You number every item in the frame from 1 to N. The chance that you will select any particular member of the frame on the first selection is $1/N$.

You select samples with replacement or without replacement. **Sampling with replacement** means that after you select an item, you return it to the frame, where it has the same probability of being selected again. Imagine that you have a fishbowl containing N business cards, one card for each person. On the first selection, you select the card for Grace Kim. You record pertinent information and replace the business card in the bowl. You then mix up the cards in the bowl and select a second card. On the second selection, Grace Kim has the same probability of being selected again, $1/N$. You repeat this process until you have selected the desired sample size, n.

Typically, you do not want the same item or individual to be selected again in a sample. **Sampling without replacement** means that once you select an item, you cannot select it again. The chance that you will select any particular item in the frame—for example, the business card for Grace Kim—on the first selection is $1/N$. The chance that you will select any card not previously chosen on the second selection is now 1 out of $N - 1$. This process continues until you have selected the desired sample of size n.

When creating a simple random sample, you should avoid the "fishbowl" method of selecting a sample because this method lacks the ability to thoroughly mix the cards and, therefore, randomly select a sample. You should use a more rigorous selection method.

learnMORE

Learn to use a table of random numbers to select a simple random sample in the **Section 1.3 LearnMore** online topic.

One such method is to use a **table of random numbers**, such as Table E.1 in Appendix E, for selecting the sample. A table of random numbers consists of a series of digits listed in a randomly generated sequence. To use a random number table for selecting a sample, you first need to assign code numbers to the individual items of the frame. Then you generate the random sample by reading the table of random numbers and selecting those individuals from the frame whose assigned code numbers match the digits found in the table. Because the number system uses 10 digits (0, 1, 2, … , 9), the chance that you will randomly generate any particular digit is equal to the probability of generating any other digit. This probability is 1 out of 10. Hence, if you generate a sequence of 800 digits, you would expect about 80 to be the digit 0, 80 to be the digit 1, and so on. Because every digit or sequence of digits in the table is random, the table can be read either horizontally or vertically. The margins of the table designate row numbers and column numbers. The digits themselves are grouped into sequences of five in order to make reading the table easier.

Systematic Sample

In a **systematic sample**, you partition the N items in the frame into n groups of k items, where

$$k = \frac{N}{n}$$

You round k to the nearest integer. To select a systematic sample, you choose the first item to be selected at random from the first k items in the frame. Then, you select the remaining $n - 1$ items by taking every kth item thereafter from the entire frame.

If the frame consists of a list of prenumbered checks, sales receipts, or invoices, taking a systematic sample is faster and easier than taking a simple random sample. A systematic sample is also a convenient mechanism for collecting data from membership directories, electoral registers, class rosters, and consecutive items coming off an assembly line.

To take a systematic sample of $n = 40$ from the population of $N = 800$ full-time employees, you partition the frame of 800 into 40 groups, each of which contains 20 employees. You then select a random number from the first 20 individuals and include every twentieth individual after the first selection in the sample. For example, if the first random number you select is 008, your subsequent selections are 028, 048, 068, 088, 108, ... , 768, and 788.

Simple random sampling and systematic sampling are simpler than other, more sophisticated, probability sampling methods, but they generally require a larger sample size. In addition, systematic sampling is prone to selection bias that can occur when there is a pattern in the frame. To overcome the inefficiency of simple random sampling and the potential selection bias involved with systematic sampling, you can use either stratified sampling methods or cluster sampling methods.

Stratified Sample

learnMORE

Learn how to select a stratified sample in the online in the **Section 1.3 LearnMore** online topic.

In a **stratified sample**, you first subdivide the N items in the frame into separate subpopulations, or **strata**. A stratum is defined by some common characteristic, such as gender or year in school. You select a simple random sample within each of the strata and combine the results from the separate simple random samples. Stratified sampling is more efficient than either simple random sampling or systematic sampling because you are ensured of the representation of items across the entire population. The homogeneity of items within each stratum provides greater precision in the estimates of underlying population parameters. In addition, stratified sampling enables you to reach conclusions about each strata in the frame. However, using a stratified sample requires that you can determine the variable(s) on which to base the stratification and can also be expensive to implement.

Cluster Sample

In a **cluster sample**, you divide the N items in the frame into clusters that contain several items. **Clusters** are often naturally occurring groups, such as counties, election districts, city blocks, households, or sales territories. You then take a random sample of one or more clusters and study all items in each selected cluster.

Cluster sampling is often more cost-effective than simple random sampling, particularly if the population is spread over a wide geographic region. However, cluster sampling often requires a larger sample size to produce results as precise as those from simple random sampling or stratified sampling. A detailed discussion of systematic sampling, stratified sampling, and cluster sampling procedures can be found in references 2, 4, and 6.

PROBLEMS FOR SECTION 1.3

LEARNING THE BASICS

1.17 For a population containing $N = 902$ individuals, what code number would you assign for
a. the first person on the list?
b. the fortieth person on the list?
c. the last person on the list?

1.18 For a population of $N = 902$, verify that by starting in row 05, column 01 of the table of random numbers (Table E.1), you need only six rows to select a sample of $N = 60$ *without* replacement.

1.19 Given a population of $N = 93$, starting in row 29, column 01 of the table of random numbers (Table E.1), and reading across the row, select a sample of $N = 15$
a. *without* replacement.
b. *with* replacement.

APPLYING THE CONCEPTS

1.20 For a study that consists of personal interviews with participants (rather than mail or phone surveys), explain why simple random sampling might be less practical than some other sampling methods.

1.21 You want to select a random sample of $n = 1$ from a population of three items (which are called A, B, and C). The rule for selecting the sample is as follows: Flip a coin; if it is heads, pick item A; if it is tails, flip the coin again; this time, if it is heads, choose B; if it is tails, choose C. Explain why this is a probability sample but not a simple random sample.

1.22 A population has four members (called A, B, C, and D). You would like to select a random sample of $n = 2$, which you decide to do in the following way: Flip a coin; if it is heads, the sample will be items A and B; if it is tails, the sample will be items C and D. Although this is a random sample, it is not a simple random sample. Explain why. (Compare the procedure described in Problem 1.21 with the procedure described in this problem.)

1.23 The registrar of a university with a population of $N = 4,000$ full-time students is asked by the president to conduct a survey to measure satisfaction with the quality of life on campus. The following table contains a breakdown of the 4,000 registered full-time students, by gender and class designation:

GENDER	CLASS DESIGNATION				
	Fr.	**So.**	**Jr.**	**Sr.**	**Total**
Female	700	520	500	480	2,200
Male	560	460	400	380	1,800
Total	1,260	980	900	860	4,000

The registrar intends to take a probability sample of $n = 200$ students and project the results from the sample to the entire population of full-time students.

a. If the frame available from the registrar's files is an alphabetical listing of the names of all $N = 4,000$ registered full-time students, what type of sample could you take? Discuss.
b. What is the advantage of selecting a simple random sample in (a)?
c. What is the advantage of selecting a systematic sample in (a)?
d. If the frame available from the registrar's files is a list of the names of all $N = 4,000$ registered full-time students compiled from eight separate alphabetical lists, based on the gender and class designation breakdowns shown in the class designation table, what type of sample should you take? Discuss.

e. Suppose that each of the $N = 4,000$ registered full-time students lived in one of the 10 campus dormitories. Each dormitory accommodates 400 students. It is college policy to fully integrate students by gender and class designation in each dormitory. If the registrar is able to compile a listing of all students by dormitory, explain how you could take a cluster sample.

✓SELF TEST **1.24** Prenumbered sales invoices are kept in a sales journal. The invoices are numbered from 0001 to 5000.
a. Beginning in row 16, column 01, and proceeding horizontally in a table of random numbers (Table E.1), select a simple random sample of 50 invoice numbers.
b. Select a systematic sample of 50 invoice numbers. Use the random numbers in row 20, columns 05–07, as the starting point for your selection.
c. Are the invoices selected in (a) the same as those selected in (b)? Why or why not?

1.25 Suppose that 10,000 customers in a retailer's customer database are categorized by three customer types: 3,500 prospective buyers, 4,500 first time buyers, and 2,000 repeat (loyal) buyers. A sample of 1,000 customers is needed.
a. What type of sampling should you do? Why?
b. Explain how you would carry out the sampling according to the method stated in (a).
c. Why is the sampling in (a) not simple random sampling?

1.4 Data Cleaning

Even if you follow proper procedures to collect data, that data you collect may contain incorrect or inconsistent data that could affect statistical results. **Data cleaning** corrects such defects and ensures your data contains suitable *quality* for your needs. Cleaning is the most important data preprocessing task you do and must be done before using your data for analysis. Cleaning can take a significant amount of time to do. One survey of big data analysts reported that they spend 60% of their time cleaning data, while only 20% of their time collecting data and a similar percentage for analyzing data (see reference 8).

Data cleaning seeks to correct the following types of irregularities:

- Invalid variable values, including
    - § Non-numerical data for a numerical variable
    - § Invalid categorical values of a categorical variable
    - § Numeric values outside a defined range

- Coding errors, including
    - § Inconsistent categorical values
    - § Inconsistent case for categorical values
    - § Extraneous characters

- Data integration errors, including
    - § Redundant columns
    - § Duplicated rows
    - § Differing column lengths
    - § Different units of measure or scale for numerical variables

With the exception of several examples designed for use with this section, data for the problems and examples in this book have already been properly cleaned, allowing you to focus on the statistical concepts and methods that the book discusses.

By its nature, data cleaning cannot be a fully automated process, even in large business systems that contain data cleaning software components. As this chapter's software guides explain, Excel, JMP, and Minitab have functionality that you can use to lessen the burden of data cleaning. When performing data cleaning, you always first preserve a copy of the original data for later reference.

Invalid Variable Values

Invalid variable values can be identified as being incorrect by simple scanning techniques so long as operational definitions for the variables the data represent exist. For any numerical variable, any value that is not a number is clearly an incorrect value. For a categorical variable, a value that does not match any of the predefined categories of the variable is, likewise, clearly an incorrect value. And for numerical variables defined with an explicit range of values, a value outside that range is clearly an error.

You will most likely semi-automate the finding of invalid variable values and can use various features of Excel, JMP, or Minitab to assist you in this task.

Coding Errors

Coding errors can result from poor recording or entry of data values or as the result of computerized operations such as copy-and-paste or data import. While coding errors are literally invalid values, coding errors may be correctable without consulting additional information whereas the invalid variable values *never* are. For example, for a Gender variable with the defined values F and M, the value "Female" is a *coding error* that can be reasonably changed to F. However, the value "New York" for the same variable is an *invalid variable value* that you cannot reasonably change to either F or M.

Unlike invalid variable values, coding errors may be *tolerated* by analysis software. For example, for the same Gender variable, the values M and m might be treated as the "same" value for purposes of an analysis by software that was tolerant of case inconsistencies, an attribute known as being *insensitive* to case.

Perhaps the most frustrating coding errors are extraneous characters in a value. You may not be able to spot extraneous characters such as nonprinting characters or extra, trailing space characters as you scan data. For example, the value David and the value that is David followed by three space characters may look the same to you as you scan data but may not be treated the same by software. Likewise, values with nonprinting characters may look correct but cause software errors or be reported as invalid by analysis software.

Data Integration Errors

Perhaps not surprising, supplying business systems with automated data interpretation skills that would semi-automate this task is a goal of many companies that provide data analysis software and services.

Data integration errors arise when data from two different computerized sources, such as two different data repositories are combined into one data set for analysis. Identifying data integration errors may be the most time-consuming data cleaning task. Because spotting these errors requires a type of data interpretation that automated processes of a typical business computer systems today cannot supply, you will most likely be spotting these errors using manual means in the foreseeable future.

Some data integration errors occur because variable names or definitions for the same item of interest have minor differences across systems. In one system, a customer ID number may be known as Customer ID, whereas in a different system, the same fact is known as Cust Number. A result of combining data from the two systems may result in having both Customer ID and Cust Number variable columns, a redundancy that should be eliminated.

Duplicated rows also occur because of similar inconsistencies across systems. Consider a Customer Name variable with the value that represents the first coauthor of this book, Mark L. Berenson. In one system, this name may have been recorded as Mark Berenson, whereas in another system, the name was recorded as M L Berenson. Combining records from both systems may result in two records, where only one should exist. Whether "Mark Berenson" is actually the same person as "M L Berenson" requires an interpretation skill that today's software may lack.

Likewise, different units of measurement (or scale) may not be obvious without additional, human interpretation. Consider the variable Air Temperature, recorded in degrees Celsius in one system and degrees Fahrenheit in another. The value 30 would be a plausible value under either measurement system and without further knowledge or context impossible to spot as a Celsius measurement in a column of otherwise Fahrenheit measurements.

Missing Values

Missing values are values that were not collected for a variable. For example, survey data may include answers for which no response was given by the survey taker. Such "no responses" are examples of missing values. Missing values can also result from integrating two data sources which do not have a row-to-row correspondence for each row in both sources. The lack of correspondence creates particular variable columns to be longer, to contain additional rows than the other columns. For these additional rows, *missing* would be the value for the cells in the shorter columns.

Do not confuse missing values with miscoded values. *Unresolved* miscoded values—values that cannot be cleaned by any method—might be changed to *missing* by some researchers or excluded for analysis by others.

Algorithmic Cleaning of Extreme Numerical Values

For numerical variables without a defined range of possible values, you might find **outliers**, values that seem excessively different from most of the other values. Such values may or may not be errors, but all outliers require review. While there is no one standard for defining outliers, most define outliers in terms of descriptive measures such as the standard deviation or the interquartile range that Chapter 3 discusses. Because software can compute such measures, spotting outliers can be automated if a definition of the term that uses a such a measure is used. As later chapters note as appropriate, identifying outliers is important as some methods are *sensitive* to outliers and produce very different results when outliers are included in analysis.

1.5 Other Data Preprocessing Tasks

In addition to data cleaning, there are several other data preprocessing tasks that you might undertake before visualizing and analyzing your data.

Data Formatting

You may need to reformat your data when you collect your data. Reformatting can mean rearranging the structure of the data or changing the electronic encoding of the data or both. For example, suppose that you seek to collect financial data about a sample of companies. You might find these data structured as tables of data, as the contents of standard forms, in a continuous stock ticker stream, or as messages or blog entries that appear on various websites. These data sources have various levels of structure which affect the ease of reformatting them for use.

Because tables of data are highly structured and are similar to the structure of a worksheet, tables would require the least reformatting. In the best case, you could make the rows and columns of a table the rows and columns of a worksheet. Unstructured data sources, such as messages and blog entries, often represent the worst case. You may have to paraphrase or characterize the message contents in a way that does not involve a direct transfer. As the use of business analytics grows (see Chapter 17), the use of automated ways to paraphrase or characterize these and other types of unstructured data grows, too.

Independent of the structure, the data you collect may exist in an electronic form that needs to be changed in order to be analyzed. For example, data presented as a digital picture of Excel worksheets would need to be changed into an actual Excel worksheet before that data could be analyzed. In this example, you are changing the electronic encoding of all the data, from a picture format such as jpeg to an Excel workbook format such as xlsx. Sometimes, individual numerical values that you have collected may need to changed, especially if you collect values that result from a computational process. You can demonstrate this issue in Excel by entering a formula that is equivalent to the expression $1 \times (0.5 - 0.4 - 0.1)$, which should evaluate as 0 but in Excel evaluates to a very small negative number. You would want to alter that value to 0 as part of your data cleaning.

Stacking and Unstacking Data

When collecting data for a numerical variable, you may need to subdivide that data into two or more groups for analysis. For example, if you were collecting data about the cost of a restaurant meal in an urban area, you might want to consider the cost of meals at restaurants in the center city district separately from the meal costs at metro area restaurants. When you want to consider two or more groups, you can arrange your data as either unstacked or stacked.

To use an **unstacked** arrangement, you create separate numerical variables for each group. In the example, you would create a center city meal cost variable and a second variable to hold the meal costs at metro area restaurants. To use a **stacked** arrangement format, you pair the single numerical variable meal cost with a second, categorical variable that contains two categories, such as center city and metro area. If you collect several numerical variables, each of which you want to subdivide in the same way, stacking your data will be the more efficient choice for you.

When you use software to analyze data, you may discover that a particular procedure requires data to be stacked (or unstacked). When such cases arise using Microsoft Excel, JMP, or Minitab for problems or examples that this book discusses, a workbook or project will contain that data in both arrangements. For example, Restaurants, that Chapter 2 uses for several examples, contains both the original (stacked) data about restaurants as well as an unstacked worksheet (or data table) that contains the meal cost by location, center city or metro area.

Recoding Variables

After you have collected data, you may need to reconsider the categories that you defined for a categorical variable or transform a numerical variable into a categorical variable by assigning the individual numeric values to one of several groups. In either case, you can define a **recoded variable** that supplements or replaces the original variable in your analysis.

For example, having already defined the variable class standing with the categories freshman, sophomore, junior, and senior, you decide that you want to investigate the differences between lowerclassmen (freshmen or sophomores) and upperclassmen (juniors or seniors). You can define a recoded variable UpperLower and assign the value Upper if a student is a junior or senior and assign the value Lower if the student is a freshman or sophomore.

When recoding variables, make sure that one and only one of the new categories can be assigned to any particular value being recoded and that each value can be recoded successfully by one of your new categories. You must ensure that your recoding has these properties of being **mutually exclusive** and **collectively exhaustive**.

When recoding numerical variables, pay particular attention to the operational definitions of the categories you create for the recoded variable, especially if the categories are not self-defining ranges. For example, while the recoded categories Under 12, 12–20, 21–34, 35–54, and 55-and-over are self-defining for age, the categories child, youth, young adult, middle aged, and senior each need to be further defined in terms of mutually exclusive and collectively exhaustive numerical ranges.

PROBLEMS FOR SECTIONS 1.4 AND 1.5

APPLYING THE CONCEPTS

1.26 The cellphone brands owned by a sample of 20 respondents were:

Apple, Samsung, Appel, Nokia, Blackberry, HTC, Apple, Samsung, HTC, LG, Blueberry, Samsung, Samsung, APPLE, Motorola, Apple, Samsun, Apple, Samsung

a. Clean these data and identify any irregularities in the data.
b. Are there any missing values in this set of 20 respondents? Identify the missing values.

1.27 The amount of monthly data usage by a sample of 10 cellphone users (in MB) was:

0.4, 2.7MB, 5.6, 4.3, 11.4, 26.8, 1.6, 1,079, 8.3, 4.2

Are there any potential irregularities in the data?

1.28 An amusement park company owns three hotels on an adjoining site. A guest relations manager wants to study the time it takes for shuttle buses to travel from each of the hotels to the amusement park entrance. Data were collected on a particular day that recorded the travel times in minutes.
a. Explain how the data could be organized in an unstacked format.
b. Explain how the data could be organized in a stacked format.

1.29 A hotel management company runs 10 hotels in a resort area. The hotels have a mix of pricing—some hotels have budget-priced rooms, some have moderate-priced rooms, and some have deluxe-priced rooms. Data are collected that indicate the number of rooms that are occupied at each hotel on each day of a month. Explain how the 10 hotels can be recoded into these three price categories.

1.6 Types of Survey Errors

When you collect data using the compiled responses from a survey, you must verify two things about the survey in order to make sure you have results that can be used in a decision-making process. You must evaluate the validity of the survey to make sure the survey does not lack objectivity or credibility. To do this, you evaluate the purpose of the survey, the reason the survey was conducted, and for whom the survey was conducted.

Having validated the objectivity and credibility of such a sample, you then determine if the survey was based on a probability sample (see Section 1.3). Surveys that use nonprobability samples are subject to serious biases that make their results useless for decision-making purposes. In the case of the Coca-Cola managers concerned about the "Pepsi Challenge" results (see page 17), the managers failed to reflect on the subjective nature of the challenge as well as the nonprobability sample that this survey used. Had the managers done so, they might not have been so quick to make the reformulation blunder that was reversed just weeks later.

Even when you verify these two things, surveys can suffer from any combination of the following types of survey errors: coverage error, nonresponse error, sampling error, or measurement error. Developers of well-designed surveys seek to reduce or minimize these types of errors, often at considerable cost.

Coverage Error

The key to proper sample selection is having an adequate frame. **Coverage error** occurs if certain groups of items are excluded from the frame so that they have no chance of being selected in the sample or if items are included from outside the frame. Coverage error results in a **selection bias**. If the frame is inadequate because certain groups of items in the population were not properly included, any probability sample selected will provide only an estimate of the characteristics of the frame, not the *actual* population.

Nonresponse Error

Not everyone is willing to respond to a survey. **Nonresponse error** arises from failure to collect data on all items in the sample and results in a **nonresponse bias**. Because you cannot always assume that persons who do not respond to surveys are similar to those who do, you need to follow up on the nonresponses after a specified period of time. You should make several attempts to convince such individuals to complete the survey and possibly offer an incentive to participate. The follow-up responses are then compared to the initial responses in order to make valid inferences from the survey (see references 2, 4, and 6). The mode of response you use, such as face-to-face interview, telephone interview, paper questionnaire, or computerized questionnaire, affects the rate of response. Personal interviews and telephone interviews usually produce a higher response rate than do mail surveys—but at a higher cost.

Sampling Error

When conducting a probability sample, chance dictates which individuals or items will or will not be included in the sample. **Sampling error** reflects the variation, or "chance differences," from sample to sample, based on the probability of particular individuals or items being selected in the particular samples.

When you read about the results of surveys or polls in newspapers or on the Internet, there is often a statement regarding a margin of error, such as "the results of this poll are expected to be within ±4 percentage points of the actual value." This **margin of error** is the sampling error. You can reduce sampling error by using larger sample sizes. Of course, doing so increases the cost of conducting the survey.

Measurement Error

In the practice of good survey research, you design surveys with the intention of gathering meaningful and accurate information. Unfortunately, the survey results you get are often only a proxy for the ones you really desire. Unlike height or weight, certain information about behaviors and psychological states is impossible or impractical to obtain directly.

When surveys rely on self-reported information, the mode of data collection, the respondent to the survey, and or the survey itself can be possible sources of **measurement error**. Satisficing, social desirability, reading ability, and/or interviewer effects can be dependent on the mode of data collection. The social desirability bias or cognitive/memory limitations of a respondent can affect the results. And vague questions, double-barreled questions that ask about multiple issues but require a single response, or questions that ask the respondent to report something that occurs over time but fail to clearly define the extent of time about which the question asks (the reference period) are some of the survey flaws that can cause errors.

To minimize measurement error, you need to standardize survey administration and respondent understanding of questions, but there are many barriers to this (see references 1, 3, and 12).

Ethical Issues About Surveys

Ethical considerations arise with respect to the four types of survey error. Coverage error can result in selection bias and becomes an ethical issue if particular groups or individuals are purposely excluded from the frame so that the survey results are more favorable to the survey's sponsor. Nonresponse error can lead to nonresponse bias and becomes an ethical issue if the sponsor knowingly designs the survey so that particular groups or individuals are less likely than others to respond. Sampling error becomes an ethical issue if the findings are purposely presented without reference to sample size and margin of error so that the sponsor can promote a viewpoint that might otherwise be inappropriate. Measurement error can become an ethical issue in one of three ways: (1) a survey sponsor chooses leading questions that guide the respondent in a particular direction; (2) an interviewer, through mannerisms and tone, purposely makes a respondent obligated to please the interviewer or otherwise guides the respondent in a particular direction; or (3) a respondent willfully provides false information.

Ethical issues also arise when the results of nonprobability samples are used to form conclusions about the entire population. When you use a nonprobability sampling method, you need to explain the sampling procedures and state that the results cannot be generalized beyond the sample.

CONSIDER THIS

New Media Surveys/Old Survey Errors

Software company executives decide to create a "customer experience improvement program" to record how customers use the company's products, with the goal of using the collected data to make product enhancements. Product marketers decide to use social media websites to collect consumer feedback. These people risk making the same type of survey error that led to the quick demise of a very successful magazine nearly 80 years ago.

By 1935, "straw polls" conducted by the magazine *Literary Digest* had successfully predicted five consecutive U.S. presidential elections. For the 1936 election, the magazine promised its largest poll ever and sent about 10 million ballots to people all across the country. After tabulating more than 2.3 million ballots, the *Digest* confidently proclaimed that Alf Landon would be an easy winner over Franklin D. Roosevelt. The actual results: FDR won in a landslide and Landon received the fewest electoral votes in U.S. history.

(continued)

Being so wrong ruined the reputation of *Literary Digest* and it would cease publication less than two years after it made its erroneous claim. A review much later found that the low response rate (less than 25% of the ballots distributed were returned) and nonresponse error (Roosevelt voters were less likely to mail in a ballot than Landon voters) were significant reasons for the failure of the *Literary Digest* poll (see reference 11).

The *Literary Digest* error proved to be a watershed event in the history of sample surveys. First, the error disproved the assertion that the larger the sample is, the better the results will be—an assertion some people still mistakenly make today. The error paved the way for the modern methods of sampling discussed in this chapter and gave prominence to the more "scientific" methods that George Gallup and Elmo Roper both used to correctly predict the 1936 elections. (Today's Gallup Polls and Roper Reports remember those researchers.)

In more recent times, Microsoft software executives overlooked that experienced users could easily opt out of participating in their improvement program. This created another case of nonresponse error which may have led to the improved product (Microsoft Office) being so poorly received initially by experienced Office users who, by being more likely to opt out of the improvement program, biased the data that Microsoft used to determine Office "improvements."

And while those product marketers may be able to collect a lot of customer feedback data, those data also suffer from nonresponse error. In collecting data from social media websites, the marketers cannot know who chose *not* to leave comments. The marketers also cannot verify if the data collected suffer from a selection bias due to a coverage error.

That you might use media newer than the mailed, dead-tree form that *Literary Digest* used does not mean that you automatically avoid the old survey errors. Just the opposite—the accessibility and reach of new media makes it much easier for unknowing people to commit such errors.

PROBLEMS FOR SECTION 1.6

APPLYING THE CONCEPTS

1.30 A survey indicates that the vast majority of college students own their own smartphones. What information would you want to know before you accepted the results of this survey?

1.31 A simple random sample of $n = 300$ full-time employees is selected from a company list containing the names of all $N = 5,000$ full-time employees in order to evaluate job satisfaction.

a. Give an example of possible coverage error.
b. Give an example of possible nonresponse error.
c. Give an example of possible sampling error.
d. Give an example of possible measurement error.

SELF TEST **1.32** Results of a 2017 Computer Services, Inc. (CSI) survey of a sample of 163 bank executives reveal insights on banking priorities among financial institutions (**goo.gl/mniYMM**). As financial institutions begin planning for a new year, of utmost importance is boosting profitability and identifying growth areas. The results show that 55% of bank institutions note customer experience initiatives as an area in which spending is expected to increase. Implementing a customer relationship management (CRM) solution was ranked as the top most important omnichannel strategy to pursue with 41% of institutions citing digital banking enhancements as the greatest anticipated strategy to enhance the customer experience.

Identify *potential* concerns with coverage, nonresponse, sampling, and measurement errors.

1.33 A recent PwC survey of 1,379 CEOs from a wide range of industries representing a mix of company sizes from Asia, Europe, and the Americas indicated that CEOs are firmly convinced that it is harder to gain and retain people's trust in an increasingly digitalized world (**pwc.to/2jFLzjF**). Fifty-eight percent of CEOs are worried that lack of trust in business would harm their company's growth. Which risks arising from connectivity concern CEOs most? Eighty-seven percent believe that social media could have a negative impact on the level of trust in their industry over the next few years. But they also say new dangers are emerging and old ones are getting worse as new technologies and new uses of existing technologies increase rapidly. CEOs are particularly anxious about breaches in data security and ethics and IT outages and disruptions. A vast majority of CEOs are already taking steps to address these concerns, with larger-sized companies doing more than smaller-sized companies.

What additional information would you want to know about the survey before you accepted the results for the study?

1.34 A recent survey points to tremendous revenue potential and consumer value in leveraging driver and vehicle data in the automobile industry. The 2017 KPMG Global Automotive Executive Study found that automobile executives believe data will be the fuel for future business models and that they will make money from that data (**prn.to/2q9rubN**). Eighty-two percent of automobile executives agree that in order to create value and consequently monetize data, a car needs its own ecosystem/operating system; otherwise the valuable consumer and/or vehicle data will likely be routed through third parties and valuable revenue streams will be lost. What additional information would you want to know about the survey before you accepted the results of the study?

▼ USING **STATISTICS**
Defining Moments, Revisited

The New Coke and airline quality cases illustrate missteps that can occur during the define and collect tasks of the DCOVA framework. To use statistics effectively, you must properly define a business problem or goal and then collect data that will allow you to make observations and reach conclusions that are relevant to that problem or goal.

In the New Coke case, managers failed to consider that data collected about a taste test would not necessary provide useful information about the sales issues they faced. The managers also did not realize that the test used improper sampling techniques, deliberately introduced biases, and were subject to coverage and nonresponse errors. Those mistakes invalidated the test, making the conclusion that New Coke tasted better than Pepsi an invalid claim.

In the airline quality case, no mistakes in defining and collecting data were made. The results that fliers like quality was a valid one, but decision makers overlooked that quality was not the most significant factor for people buying seats on transatlantic flights (price was). This case illustrates that no matter how well you apply statistics, if you do not properly analyze the business problem or goal being considered, you may end up with valid results that lead you to invalid management decisions.

▼ SUMMARY

In this chapter, you learned the details about the Define and Collect tasks of the DCOVA framework which are important first steps to applying statistics properly to decision making. You learned that defining variables means developing an operational definition that includes establishing the type of variable and the measurement scale that the variable uses. You learned important details about data collection as well some new basic vocabulary terms (sample, population, and parameter) and as a more precise definition of statistic. You specifically learned about sampling and the types of sampling methods available to you. Finally, you surveyed data preparation considerations and learned about the type of survey errors you can encounter.

▼ REFERENCES

1. Biemer, P. B., R. M. Graves, L. E. Lyberg, A. Mathiowetz, and S. Sudman. *Measurement Errors in Surveys*. New York: Wiley Interscience, 2004.
2. Cochran, W. G. *Sampling Techniques*, 3rd ed. New York: Wiley, 1977.
3. Fowler, F. J. *Improving Survey Questions: Design and Evaluation, Applied Special Research Methods Series*, Vol. 38, Thousand Oaks, CA: Sage Publications, 1995.
4. Groves R. M., F. J. Fowler, M. P. Couper, J. M. Lepkowski, E. Singer, and R. Tourangeau. *Survey Methodology*, 2nd ed. New York: John Wiley, 2009.
5. Hellerstein, J. "Quantitative Data Cleaning for Large Databases." **http://bit.ly/2q7PGIn**.
6. Lohr, S. L. *Sampling Design and Analysis*, 2nd ed. Boston, MA: Brooks/Cole Cengage Learning, 2010.
7. Polaris Marketing Research. "Brilliant Marketing Research or What? The New Coke Story." **bit.ly/1DofHSM**, posted 20 Sep 2011.
8. Press, G. "Cleaning Big Data: Most Time-Consuming, Least Enjoyable Data Science Task, Survey Says." **bit.ly/2oNCwzh**, posted 23 March 2016.
9. Rosenbaum, D. "The New Big Data Magic." CFO.com, 29 Aug 2011, **bit.ly/1DUMWzv**.
10. Osbourne, J. *Best Practices in Data Cleaning*. Thousand Oaks, CA: Sage Publications, 2012.
11. Squire, P. "Why the 1936 *Literary Digest* Poll Failed." *Public Opinion Quarterly* 52 (1988): 125–133.
12. Sudman, S., N. M. Bradburn, and N. Schwarz. *Thinking About Answers: The Application of Cognitive Processes to Survey Methodology*. San Francisco, CA: Jossey-Bass, 1993.

▼ KEY TERMS

categorical variable 17	collectively exhaustive 27	coverage error 28
cluster 23	continuous variable 18	data cleaning 24
cluster sample 23	convenience sample 21	discrete variable 18

▼ CHECKING YOUR UNDERSTANDING

1.35 What is the difference between a sample and a population?

1.36 What is the difference between a statistic and a parameter?

1.37 What is the difference between a categorical variable and a numerical variable?

1.38 What is the difference between a discrete numerical variable and a continuous numerical variable?

1.39 What is the difference between a nominal scaled variable and an ordinal scaled variable?

1.40 What is the difference between an interval scaled variable and a ratio scaled variable?

1.41 What is the difference between probability sampling and non-probability sampling?

1.42 What is the difference between a missing value and an outlier?

1.43 What is the difference between unstack and stacked variables?

1.44 What is the difference between coverage error and nonresponse error?

1.45 What is the difference between sampling error and measurement error?

▼ CHAPTER REVIEW PROBLEMS

1.46 Visit the official website for Microsoft Excel, **products.office.com/excel** or Minitab (**www.minitab.com**) or JMP (**www.jmp.com**). Review the features of the program you chose and then state the ways the program could be useful in statistical analysis.

1.47 Results of a 2017 Computer Services, Inc. (CSI) survey of a sample of 163 bank executives reveal insights on banking priorities among financial institutions (**goo.gl/mniYMM**). As financial institutions begin planning for a new year, of utmost importance is boosting profitability and identifying growth areas.

The results show that 55% of bank institutions note customer experience initiatives as an area in which spending is expected to increase. Implementing a customer relationship management (CRM) solution was ranked as the top most important omnichannel strategy to pursue with 41% of institutions citing digital banking enhancements as the greatest anticipated strategy to enhance the customer experience.

a. Describe the population of interest.
b. Describe the sample that was collected.
c. Describe a parameter of interest.
d. Describe the statistic used to estimate the parameter in (c).

1.48 The Gallup organization releases the results of recent polls on its website, **www.gallup.com**. Visit this site and read an article of interest.

a. Describe the population of interest.
b. Describe the sample that was collected.
c. Describe a parameter of interest.
d. Describe the statistic used to estimate the parameter in (c).

1.49 A recent PwC survey of 1,379 CEOs from a wide range of industries representing a mix of company sizes from Asia, Europe, and the Americas indicated that CEOs are firmly convinced that it is harder to gain and retain people's trust in an increasingly digitalized world (**pwc.to/2jFLzjF**). Fifty-eight percent of CEOs are worried that lack of trust in business would harm their company's growth. Which risks arising from connectivity concern CEOs most? Eighty-seven percent believe that social media could have a negative impact on the level of trust in their industry over the next few years. But they also say new dangers are emerging and old ones are getting worse as new technologies and new uses of existing technologies increase rapidly. CEOs are particularly anxious about breaches in data security and ethics and IT outages and disruptions. A vast majority of CEOs are already taking steps to address these concerns, with larger-sized companies doing more than smaller-sized companies.

a. Describe the population of interest.
b. Describe the sample that was collected.
c. Describe a parameter of interest.
d. Describe the statistic used to estimate the parameter in (c).

1.50 The American Community Survey (**www.census.gov/acs**) provides data every year about communities in the United States. Addresses are randomly selected and respondents are required to supply answers to a series of questions.
a. Describe a variable for which data is collected.
b. Is the variable categorical or numerical?
c. If the variable is numerical, is it discrete or continuous?

1.51 Download and examine Zarca Interactive's "Sample Survey for Associations/Sample Questions for Surveys for Associations," available at **bit.ly/2p5HlGO**.
a. Give an example of a categorical variable included in the survey.
b. Give an example of a numerical variable included in the survey.

1.52 Three professors examined awareness of four widely disseminated retirement rules among employees at the University of Utah. These rules provide simple answers to questions about retirement planning (R. N. Mayer, C. D. Zick, and M. Glaittle, "Public Awareness of Retirement Planning Rules of Thumb," *Journal of Personal Finance*, 2011 10(1), 12–35). At the time of the investigation, there were approximately 10,000 benefited employees, and 3,095 participated in the study. Demographic data collected on these 3,095 employees included gender, age (years), education level (years completed), marital status, household income ($), and employment category.
a. Describe the population of interest.
b. Describe the sample that was collected.
c. Indicate whether each of the demographic variables mentioned is categorical or numerical.

1.53 Social media provides an enormous amount of data about the activities and habits of people using social platforms like Facebook and Twitter. The belief is that mining that data provides a treasure trove for those who seek to quantify and predict future human behavior. A marketer is planning a survey of Internet users in the United States to determine social media usage. The objective of the survey is to gain insight on these three items: key social media platforms used, frequency of social media usage, and demographics of key social media platform users.
a. For each of the three items listed, indicate whether the variables are categorical or numerical. If a variable is numerical, is it discrete or continuous?
b. Develop five categorical questions for the survey.
c. Develop five numerical questions for the survey.

CHAPTER

1

▾CASES

Managing Ashland MultiComm Services

Ashland MultiComm Services (AMS) provides high-quality telecommunications services in the Greater Ashland area. AMS traces its roots to a small company that redistributed the broadcast television signals from nearby major metropolitan areas but has evolved into a provider of a wide range of broadband services for residential customers.

AMS offers subscription-based services for digital cable television, local and long-distance telephone services, and high-speed Internet access. Recently, AMS has faced competition from other service providers as well as Internet-based, on-demand streaming services that have caused many customers to "cut the cable" and drop their subscription to cable video services.

AMS management believes that a combination of increased promotional expenditures, adjustment in subscription fees, and improved customer service will allow AMS to successfully face these challenges. To help determine the proper mix of strategies to be taken, AMS management has decided to organize a research team to undertake a study.

The managers suggest that the research team examine the company's own historical data for number of subscribers, revenues, and subscription renewal rates for the past few years. They direct the team to examine year-to-date data as well, as the managers suspect that some of the changes they have seen have been a relatively recent phenomena.

1. What type of data source would the company's own historical data be? Identify other possible data sources that the research team might use to examine the current marketplace for residential broadband services in a city such as Ashland.

2. What type of data collection techniques might the team employ?

3. In their suggestions and directions, the AMS managers have named a number of possible variables to study, but offered no operational definitions for those variables. What types of possible misunderstandings could arise if the team and managers do not first properly define each variable cited?

CardioGood Fitness

CardioGood Fitness is a developer of high-quality cardiovascular exercise equipment. Its products include treadmills, fitness bikes, elliptical machines, and e-glides. CardioGood Fitness looks to increase the sales of its treadmill products and has hired The AdRight Agency, a small advertising firm, to create and implement an advertising program. The AdRight Agency plans to identify particular market segments that are most likely to buy their clients' goods and services and then locate advertising outlets that will reach that market group. This activity includes collecting data on clients' actual sales and on the customers who make the purchases, with the goal of determining whether there is a distinct profile of the typical customer for a particular product or service. If a distinct profile emerges, efforts are made to match that profile to advertising outlets known to reflect the particular profile, thus targeting advertising directly to high-potential customers.

CardioGood Fitness sells three different lines of treadmills. The TM195 is an entry-level treadmill. It is as dependable as other models offered by CardioGood Fitness, but with fewer programs and features. It is suitable for individuals who thrive on minimal programming and the desire for simplicity to initiate their walk or hike. The TM195 sells for $1,500.

The middle-line TM498 adds to the features of the entry-level model two user programs and up to 15% elevation upgrade. The TM498 is suitable for individuals who are walkers at a transitional stage from walking to running or midlevel runners. The TM498 sells for $1,750.

The top-of-the-line TM798 is structurally larger and heavier and has more features than the other models. Its unique features include a bright blue backlit LCD console, quick speed and incline keys, a wireless heart rate monitor with a telemetric chest strap, remote speed and incline controls, and an anatomical figure that specifies which muscles are minimally and maximally activated. This model features a nonfolding platform base that is designed to handle rigorous, frequent running; the TM798 is therefore appealing to someone who is a power walker or a runner. The selling price is $2,500.

As a first step, the market research team at AdRight is assigned the task of identifying the profile of the typical customer for each treadmill product offered by CardioGood Fitness. The market research team decides to investigate whether there are differences across the product lines with respect to customer characteristics. The team decides to collect data on individuals who purchased a treadmill at a CardioGood Fitness retail store during the prior three months.

The team decides to use both business transactional data and the results of a personal profile survey that every purchaser completes as their sources of data. The team identifies the following customer variables to study: product purchased—TM195, TM498, or TM798; gender; age, in years; education, in years; relationship status, single or partnered; annual household income ($); mean number of times the customer plans to use the treadmill each week; mean number of miles the customer expects to walk/run each week; and self-rated fitness on a 1-to-5 scale, where 1 is poor shape and 5 is excellent shape. For this set of variables:

1. Which variables in the survey are categorical?
2. Which variables in the survey are numerical?
3. Which variables are discrete numerical variables?

Clear Mountain State Student Survey

The Student News Service at Clear Mountain State University (CMSU) has decided to gather data about the undergraduate students who attend CMSU. They create and distribute a survey of 14 questions and receive responses from 111 undergraduates (stored in StudentSurvey).

Download (see Appendix C) and review the survey document **CMUndergradSurvey.pdf**. For each question asked in the survey, determine whether the variable is categorical or numerical. If you determine that the variable is numerical, identify whether it is discrete or continuous.

Learning with the Digital Cases

Identifying and preventing misuses of statistics is an important responsibility for all managers. The Digital Cases allow you to practice the skills necessary for this important task.

Each chapter's Digital Case tests your understanding of how to apply an important statistical concept taught in the chapter. As in many business situations, not all of the information you encounter will be relevant to your task, and you may occasionally discover conflicting information that you have to resolve in order to complete the case.

To assist your learning, each Digital Case begins with a learning objective and a summary of the problem or issue at hand. Each case directs you to the information necessary to reach your own conclusions and to answer the case questions. Many cases, such as the sample case worked out next, extend a chapter's Using Statistics scenario. You can download digital case files which are PDF format documents that may contain extended features as interactivity or data file attachments. Open these files with a current version of Adobe Reader, as other PDF programs may not support the extended features. (For more information, see Appendix C.)

To illustrate learning with a Digital Case, open the Digital Case file **WhitneyWireless.pdf** that contains summary information about the Whitney Wireless business. Apparently, from the claim on the title page, this business is celebrating its "best sales year ever."

Review the **Who We Are**, **What We Do**, and **What We Plan to Do** sections on the second page. Do these sections contain any useful information? What *questions* does this passage raise? Did you notice that while many facts are presented, no data that would support the claim of "best sales year ever" are presented? And were those mobile "mobilemobiles" used solely for promotion? Or did they generate any sales? Do you think that a talk-with-your-mouth-full event, however novel, would be a success?

Continue to the third page and the **Our Best Sales Year Ever!** section. How would you support such a claim? With a table of numbers? Remarks attributed to a knowledgeable source? Whitney Wireless has used a chart to present "two years ago" and "latest twelve months" sales data by category. Are there any problems with what the company has done? *Absolutely!*

Take a moment to identify and reflect on those problems. Then turn to pages 4 though 6 that present an annotated version of the first three pages and discusses some of the problems with this document.

In subsequent Digital Cases, you will be asked to provide this type of analysis, using the open-ended case questions as your guide. Not all the cases are as straightforward as this example, and some cases include perfectly appropriate applications of statistical methods. And none have annotated answers!

▾EXCEL GUIDE

EG1.1   DEFINING VARIABLES

Classifying Variables by Type

Microsoft Excel infers the variable type from the data you enter into a column. If Excel discovers a column that contains numbers, it treats the column as a numerical variable. If Excel discovers a column that contains words or alphanumeric entries, it treats the column as a non-numerical (categorical) variable.

This imperfect method works most of the time, especially if you make sure that the categories for your categorical variables are words or phrases such as "yes" and "no." However, because you cannot explicitly define the variable type, Excel will allow you to do nonsensical things such as using a categorical variable with a statistical method designed for numerical variables. If you must use categorical values such as 1, 2, or 3, enter them preceded with an apostrophe, as Excel treats all values that begin with an apostrophe as non-numerical data. (To check whether a cell entry includes a leading apostrophe, select the cell and view its contents in the formula bar.)

EG1.2   COLLECTING DATA

There are no Excel Guide instructions for Section 1.2.

EG1.3   TYPES of SAMPLING METHODS

Simple Random Sample

Key Technique Use the **RANDBETWEEN**(*smallest integer, largest integer*) function to generate a random integer that can then be used to select an item from a frame.

Example 1 Create a simple random sample *with* replacement of size 40 from a population of 800 items.

Workbook Enter a formula that uses this function and then copy the formula down a column for as many rows as is necessary. For example, to create a simple random sample with replacement of size 40 from a population of 800 items, open to a new worksheet. Enter **Sample** in cell **A1** and enter the formula **=RANDBETWEEN(1, 800)** in cell **A2**. Then copy the formula down the column to cell **A41**.

Excel contains no functions to select a random sample *without* replacement. Such samples are most easily created using an add-in such as PHStat or the Analysis ToolPak, as described in the following paragraphs.

Analysis ToolPak Use **Sampling** to create a random sample *with replacement*.

For the example, open to the worksheet that contains the population of 800 items in column A and that contains a column heading in cell A1. Select **Data → Data Analysis**. In the

Data Analysis dialog box, select **Sampling** from the **Analysis Tools** list and then click **OK**. In the procedure's dialog box (shown below):

1. Enter **A1:A801** as the **Input Range** and check **Labels**.
2. Click **Random** and enter **40** as the **Number of Samples**.
3. Click **New Worksheet Ply** and then click **OK**.

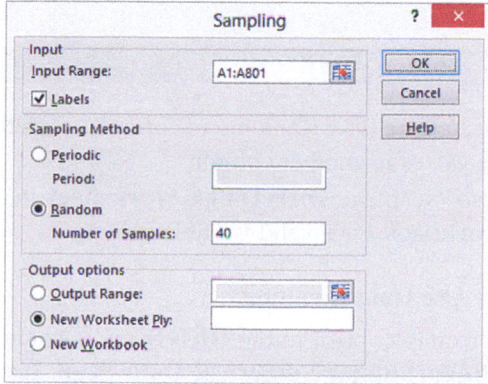

Example 2 Create a simple random sample *without* replacement of size 40 from a population of 800 items.

PHStat Use **Random Sample Generation**.

For the example, select **PHStat → Sampling → Random Sample Generation**. In the procedure's dialog box (shown below):

1. Enter **40** as the **Sample Size**.
2. Click **Generate list of random numbers** and enter **800** as the **Population Size**.
3. Enter a **Title** and click **OK**.

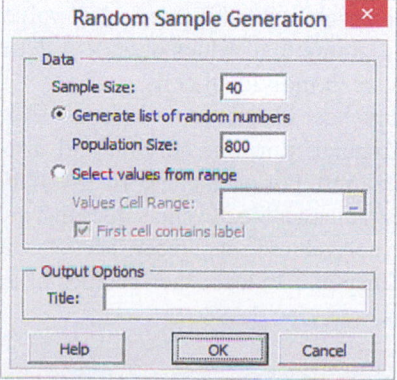

Unlike most other PHStat results worksheets, the worksheet created contains no formulas.

Workbook Use the **COMPUTE worksheet** of the **Random workbook** as a template.

The worksheet already contains 40 copies of the formula **=RANDBETWEEN(1, 800)** in column B. Because the **RANDBETWEEN** function samples *with* replacement as discussed at the start of this section, you may need to add additional copies of the formula in new column B rows until you have 40 unique values.

If your intended sample size is large, you may find it difficult to spot duplicates. Read the SHORT TAKES for Chapter 1 to learn more about an advanced technique that uses formulas to detect duplicate values.

EG1.4   DATA CLEANING

Key Technique Use a column of formulas to detect invalid variable values in another column.

Example Scan the **DirtyDATA worksheet** in the **Dirty Data workbook** for invalid variable values.

PHStat Use **Data Cleaning**.

For the example, open to the **DirtyData worksheet**. Select **Data Preparation→Numerical Data Scan**. In the procedure's dialog box:

1. Enter a column range as the **Numerical Variable Cell Range**.
2. Click **OK**.

The procedure creates a worksheet that contains a column that identifies every data value as either being numerical or non-numerical and states the minimum and maximum values found in the column. To scan for irregularities in categorical data, use the *Workbook* instructions.

Workbook Use the **ScanData worksheet** of the **Data Cleaning workbook** as a model solution to scan for the following types of irregularities: non-numerical data values for a numerical variable, invalid categorical values of a categorical variable, numerical values outside a defined range, and missing values in individual cells.

The worksheet uses several different Excel functions to detect an irregularity in one column and display a message in another column. For each categorical variable scanned, the worksheet contains a table of valid values that are looked up and compared to cell values to spot inconsistencies. Read the SHORT TAKES for Chapter 1 to learn the specifics of the formulas the worksheet uses to scan data.

EG1.5   OTHER DATA PREPROCESSING

Stacking and Unstacking Variables

PHStat Use **Data Preparation→Stack Data** (or **Unstack Data**).

For **Stack Data**, in the Stack Data dialog box, enter an **Unstacked Data Cell Range** and then click **OK** to create stacked data in a new worksheet. For **Unstack Data**, in the Unstack Data dialog box, enter a **Grouping Variable Cell Range** and a **Stacked Data Cell Range** and then click **OK** to create unstacked data in a new worksheet.

Recoding Variables

Key Technique To recode a categorical variable, you first copy the original variable's column of data and then use the find-and-replace function on the copied data. To recode a numerical variable, enter a formula that returns a recoded value in a new column.

Example Using the **DATA worksheet** of the **Recoded workbook**, create the recoded variable UpperLower from the categorical variable Class and create the recoded Variable Dean's List from the numerical variable GPA.

Workbook Use the **RECODED worksheet** of the **Recoded workbook** as a model.

The worksheet already contains UpperLower, a recoded version of Class that uses the operational definitions on page 27, and Dean's List, a recoded version of GPA, in which the value No recodes all GPA values less than 3.3 and Yes recodes all values 3.3 or greater than 3.3. The **RECODED_FORMULAS worksheet** in the same workbook shows how formulas in column I use the IF function to recode GPA as the Dean's List variable.

These recoded variables were created by first opening to the **DATA worksheet** in the same workbook and then following these steps:

1. Right-click column **D** (right-click over the shaded "D" at the top of column D) and click **Copy** in the shortcut menu.
2. Right-click column **H** and click the **first choice** in the **Paste Options** gallery.
3. Enter **UpperLower** in cell **H1**.
4. Select column H. With column H selected, click **Home→Find & Select→Replace**.

In the Replace tab of the Find and Replace dialog box:

5. Enter **Senior** as **Find what**, **Upper** as **Replace with**, and then click **Replace All**.
6. Click **OK** to close the dialog box that reports the results of the replacement command.
7. Still in the Find and Replace dialog box, enter **Junior** as **Find what** and then click **Replace All**.
8. Click **OK** to close the dialog box that reports the results of the replacement command.
9. Still in the Find and Replace dialog box, enter **Sophomore** as **Find what**, **Lower** as **Replace with**, and then click **Replace All**.
10. Click **OK** to close the dialog box that reports the results of the replacement command.
11. Still in the Find and Replace dialog box, enter **Freshman** as **Find what** and then click **Replace All**.
12. Click **OK** to close the dialog box that reports the results of the replacement command.

(This creates the recoded variable UpperLower in column H.)

13. Enter **Dean's List** in cell **I1**.
14. Enter the formula **=IF(G2 < 3.3, "No", "Yes")** in cell **I2**.
15. Copy this formula down the column to the last row that contains student data (row 63).

(This creates the recoded variable Dean's List in column I.)

The RECODED worksheet uses the **IF** function, that Appendix F discusses to recode the numerical variable into two categories. Numerical variables can also be recoded into multiple categories by using the **VLOOKUP** function (see Appendix F).

CHAPTER

▼ JMP GUIDE

JG1.1   DEFINING VARIABLES

Classifying Variables by Type

JMP infers the variable type and scale from the data you enter in a column. To override any inference JMP makes, first right-click a column name and select **Column Info** from the shortcut menu. In the column info dialog box, change the **Data Type** or **Modeling Type** (scale) to the value you want. Shown below is the column information dialog box for the Assets column in the Retirement Funds data table. Contents of this dialog box will vary depending on JMP inferences and the entries you make in the dialog box, but the dialog box will always contain **Column Name** as the JMP Guide in the previous chapter explains. For continuous numerical variables such as Assets, use **Format** to control the display of values. For the format Fixed Dec, the Dec box entry controls the number of decimal places to which values will be rounded in the column.

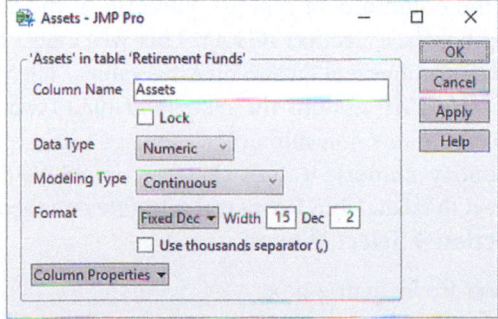

In boxes that lists names of variable columns, JMP uses icons to represent the modeling type of the variable. Below are the icons for nominal (CustomerID), continuous (YTD Spending), ordinal (Texts Sent), and unstructured text (Last Text Message) modeling types, the subset of types that examples use in this book. (Open the Modeling Types data table to explore these choices.)

JG1.2   COLLECTING DATA

There are no JMP Guide instructions for Section 1.2.

JG1.3   TYPES of SAMPLING METHODS

Simple Random Sample and Stratified Sample

Use **Subset**.

To take a simple random sample of data table data, open the data table and select **Tables → Subset**. In the Subset dialog box, click **Random - sample size**, enter the sample size of the sample, enter an **Output table name**, and click **OK**. In the illustration below, 20 has been entered as the sample size and Funds Simple Random Sample as the output table name.

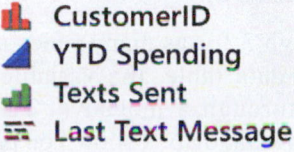

il. **CustomerID**
◢ **YTD Spending**
▮ **Texts Sent**
≡ **Last Text Message**

To specify a stratified sample, check **Stratify**. JMP displays a column list box under this check box from which you choose the variable that will be used to define the strata.

Systematic Sample

Use a formula column to help identify every *kth* item and then use **Subset** to create the sample.

For example, to take a systematic sample of $n = 20$ of the 800 Employees data table that contains 800 rows of data, first determine $k = 40$ (800 divided by 20). With the data table open:

1. Right-click Fund Number (name of first column) and select **Insert Columns**. The new column, Column 1, appears to the left of Fund Number column.
2. Right-click Column 1 heading and select **Formula**.
3. In the large formula composition pane of the Formula dialog box (shown below), enter **Sequence(1, 40)** and then click **OK**.

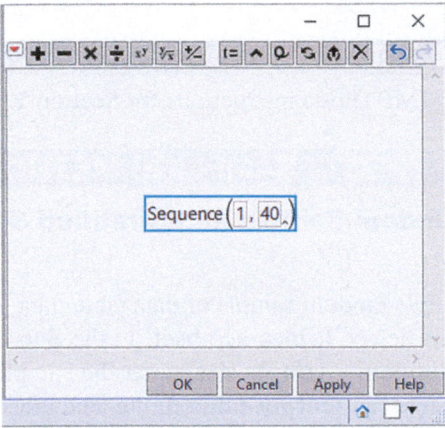

JMP fills Column 1 with the recurring series of 1 to 40 in Column 1. Next choose a random number between 1 and 40 inclusive by any means and:

1. Click the data table **Rows red triangle** and select **Clear Row States**.
2. Click the data table **Rows red triangle** a second time and select **Row Selection → Select Where**.

In the Select Rows dialog box:

3. Select **Column 1** from the column list.
4. Select **equals** from the first pull-down list.
5. Enter the random number that was selected in the edit box to the right of the pull-down and click **OK**.

JMP selects a sample that contains the rows in which the Column 1 value matches the randomly chosen number. Continue to copy the rows to a new data table. With the rows still selected:

6. Select **Tables → Subset**.
7. In the Subset dialog box, click **Selected Rows** and click **OK**.

The sample appears in a new data table in its own window.

JG1.4   DATA CLEANING

Use a variety of techniques including **Recode** and **Row Selection**.

For categorical variables, Recode can be used to spot several kinds of invalid variable names and coding errors. For example, open the **DirtyDATA data table**, select the **Gender column** and:

1. Select **Cols → Recode**.
2. In the Recode dialog box, click the red triangle and select **Group Similar Values**.
3. In the Grouping Options dialog box, check all check boxes and click **OK**.

Back in the Recode dialog box (shown below), JMP attempts to group together similar values. The success of the regrouping by JMP can vary, but regrouping facilitates your review, especially of data the contain many rows. Note that the first entry in the old and new values table for a cell that is blank:

4. Make entries in the **New Values** column as necessary.
5. Click the **Done pull-down list** and select **New Column**.

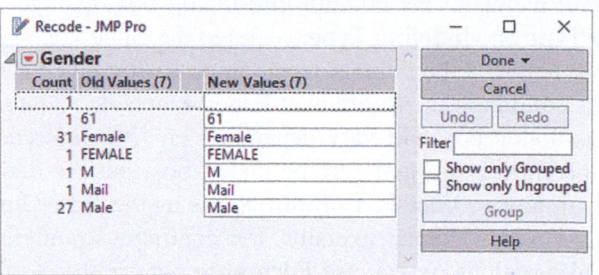

JMP places the corrected data in a new column, preserving the original dirty data in its original column.

To identify non-numerical data in a "numerical" column, changing the column data type to Numeric in the Column Info dialog box (see Section JG1.1). This will cause JMP to change all non-numerical data to missing values. The process works because JMP assigns the *character* data type to any column that contains non-numerical data.

To identify numeric values that are outside a defined range, Select the data table **Rows red triangle** and then select **Row Selection → Select Where**.

In the Select Rows dialog box:

1. Select the variable column to be range-checked.
2. Select a relationship from the pull-down list and enter the appropriated comparison value in the edit box.
3. Click **Add Condition** to add the condition to the Selected Conditions list.

Repeat steps 1 through 3 for as many times as necessary. For the DirtyDATA data table, the variable GPA has a defined range of 0 through 4 inclusive. The conditions listed in the Select Row dialog box shown on page 39 check for GPA values outside that range.

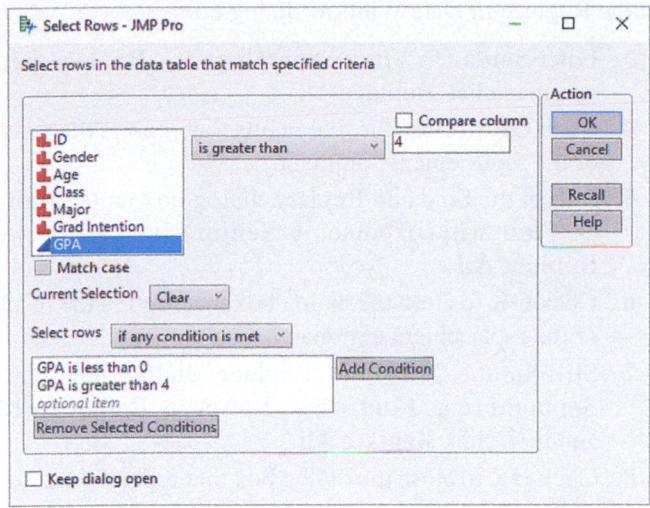

JMP scripts and add-ins exist that semi-automate data cleaning and spot other errors that this section does not address, sometimes using JMP techniques beyond the scope of this book to explain.

JG1.5 OTHER PREPROCESSING TASKS

Stacking and Unstacking Variables

Use **Stack** or **Split**.

To stack data, select **Tables → Stack**. In the Stack dialog box, select the (unstacked) variable columns, click **Stack Columns**, and click **OK**. The stacked data appears in a new column, with the names of columns that were stacked as the values in the Label column.

To unstack data, select **Tables → Split**. In the Split dialog box, select the categorical variable that holds grouping information and click **Split By**, select the numerical column (or columns) to unstack and click **Split Columns** and then click **OK**. The unstacked data appears in a new data table.

Recoding Variables

Use **Recode**.

To recode the values of either a categorical or numerical variable, first select the variable column and then select **Cols → Recode** (in older JMP versions, **Cols → Utilities → Recode**). In the Recode dialog box, JMP lists all unique values found in the column and display form in which you can change one or more of those values. When you finish making changes, click the **Done pull-down** list and select **New Column**. Recoded values appear in a new column.

CHAPTER

▼MINITAB GUIDE

1

MG1.1 DEFINING VARIABLES

Classifying Variables by Type

Minitab infers the variable type from the data you enter into a column as Section MG.2 "Entering Data" explains. Sometimes, Minitab will misclassify a variable, for example, mistaking a numerical variable for a categorical (text) variable. In such cases, select the column, then select **Data → Change Data Type**, and then select one of the choices, for example, **Text to Numeric** for the case of when Minitab has mistaken a numerical variable as a categorical variable.

MG1.2 COLLECTING DATA

There are no Minitab Guide instructions for Section 1.2.

MG1.3 TYPES of SAMPLING METHODS

Simple Random Samples

Use **Sample From Columns**.

For example, to create a simple random sample with replacement of size 40 from a population of 800 items, first create the list of 800 employee numbers in column **C1**.

Select **Calc → Make Patterned Data → Simple Set of Numbers**. In the procedure's dialog box (shown below):

1. Enter **C1** in the **Store patterned data in** box.
2. Enter **1** in the **From first value** box.
3. Enter **800** in the **To last value** box.
4. Verify that the three other boxes contain 1 and then click **OK**.

With the worksheet containing the column C1 list still open:

5. Select **Calc → Random Data → Sample from Columns**.

In the Sample From Columns dialog box (shown below):

6. Enter **40** in the **Number of rows to sample** box.
7. Enter **C1** in the **From columns** box.
8. Enter **C2** in the **Store samples in** box.
9. Click **OK**.

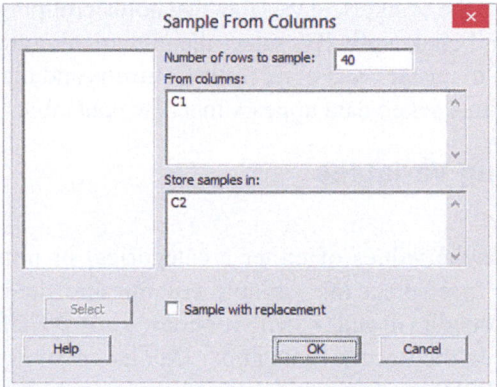

MG1.4 DATA CLEANING

Minitab cleans the data when you import data by opening a file created by another application, such as a workbook file created by Excel. For an existing worksheet, you use a combination of commands and column formulas to count the number of missing values for a variable, change invalid categorical values of a categorical variable to a missing value, and identify numerical values that are outside a defined range.

In the import method, you select data cleaning options in the file open dialog box. The cleaning options vary according the type of file being imported. For an Excel workbook, you can specify which values represent missing values and instruct Minitab to skip a blank row, add missing values to uneven columns, remove nonprintable characters and extra spaces, and correct case mismatches.

Read the SHORT TAKES for Chapter 1 to learn the specifics of the Minitab commands and formulas that you can use to scan data.

MG1.5 OTHER PREPROCESSING TASKS

Recoding Variables

Use the **Replace** command to recode a categorical variable and **Calculator** to recode a numerical variable.

For example, to create the recoded variable UpperLower from the categorical variable Class (C4-T), open to the DATA worksheet of the Recode project and:

1. Select the **Class** column (C4-T).
2. Select **Editor → Replace**.

In the Replace in Data Window dialog box:

3. Enter **Senior** as **Find what, Upper** as **Replace with**, and then click **Replace All**.
4. Click **OK** to close the dialog box that reports the results of the replacement command.
5. Still in the Find and Replace dialog box, enter **Junior** as **Find what** (replacing **Senior**), and then click **Replace All**.
6. Click **OK** to close the dialog box that reports the results of the replacement command.
7. Still in the Find and Replace dialog box, enter **Sophomore** as **Find what, Lower** as **Replace with**, and then click **Replace All**.
8. Click **OK** to close the dialog box that reports the results of the replacement command.
9. Still in the Find and Replace dialog box, enter **Freshman** as **Find what**, and then click **Replace All**.
10. Click **OK** to close the dialog box that reports the results of the replacement command.

To create the recoded variable Dean's List from the numerical variable GPA (C7), with the DATA worksheet of the Recode project still open:

1. Enter **Dean's List** as the name of the empty column **C8**.
2. Select **Calc → Calculator**.

In the Calculator dialog box (shown below):

3. Enter **C8** in the **Store result in variable** box.
4. Enter **IF(GPA < 3.3, "No", "Yes")** in the **Expression** box.
5. Click **OK**.

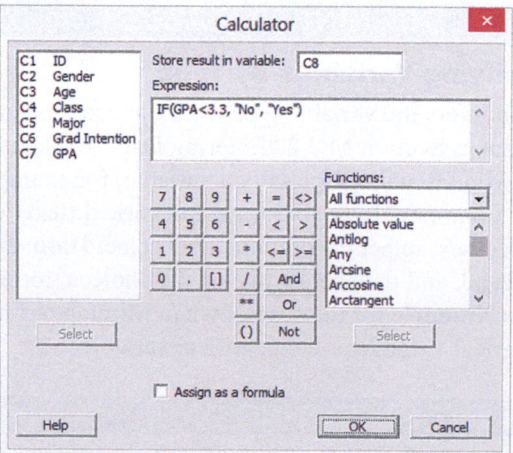

Variables can also be recoded into multiple categories by using the **Data → Code** command. Read the SHORT TAKES for Chapter 1 to learn more about this advanced recoding technique.

2

Organizing and Visualizing Variables

OBJECTIVES

- How to organize and visualize categorical variables

- How to organize and visualize numerical variables

- How to summarize a mix of variables

- How to avoid making common errors when organizing and visualizing variables

▼USING **STATISTICS**
"The Choice Is *Yours"*

Even though he is still in his 20s, Tom Sanchez realizes that you can never start too early to save for retirement. Based on research he has already done, Sanchez seeks to contribute to his 401(k) retirement plan by investing in one or more retirement funds.

Meanwhile, The Choice *Is* Yours investment service has been thinking about being better prepared to counsel younger investors such as Sanchez about retirement funds. To pursue this business objective, a company task force has already selected 479 retirement funds that may prove appropriate for younger investors. You have been asked to define, collect, organize, and visualize data about these funds in ways that could assist prospective clients making decisions about the funds in which they will invest. As a starting point, you think about the facts about each fund that would help customers compare and contrast funds.

You decide to begin by defining the variables for key characteristics of each fund, such as each fund's past performance. You also decide to define variables such as the amount of assets that a fund manages and whether the goal of a fund is to invest in companies whose earnings are expected to substantially increase in future years (a "growth" fund) or invest in companies whose stock price is undervalued, priced low relative to their earnings potential (a "value" fund).

You collect data from appropriate sources and organize the data as a worksheet, placing each variable in its own column. As you think more about your task, you realize that 479 rows of data, one for each fund in the sample, would be hard for prospective clients to review easily.

Is there something else you can do? Can you organize and present these data to prospective clients in a more helpful and comprehensible manner?

learnMORE

The online **Retirement Funds Sample** PDF document defines the variables that the sample of 479 funds uses and discusses retirement funds in general.

Defining your variables of interest and then collecting, preparing, and entering data into worksheets completes the **D**efine and **C**ollect **DCOVA** tasks. In the **DCOVA O**rganize task, you take that prepared data and create summaries that provide initial insights about your variables. These summaries guide you to further exploration of your data as well as sometimes directly facilitate decision making. For example, in the Choice *Is* Yours scenario, creating a summary of the retirement funds sample that would allow a prospective younger investor such as Tom Sanchez to quickly identify funds that were designed for growth and were identified as having moderate risk would be useful.

Methods you use during the Organize step create summaries in the form of various types of tables. Summaries can also take the form of visualizations. Visual summaries can facilitate the rapid review of larger amounts of data as well as show possible significant patterns to the data. For example, for the retirement funds sample, visualizing the ten-year rate of return and the management expense fees charged by each fund would help to identify the funds that would be charging you relatively little in fees for a "good" rate of return as well as the funds whose fees seem excessive given their modest or weak rates of return.

studentTIP

Table 2.15 in the Summary on page 82 lists the methods to organize and visualize variables that this chapter discusses.

Because reviewing tabular *and* visual summaries together can lead to better insights and jumpstart analysis, the DCOVA **V**isualize task is often done concurrent to the **O**rganize task. For that reason, this chapter discusses methods to visualize variables after discussing methods that organize variables. Because the methods used to organize and visualize categorical variables differ from the methods used to organize and visualize numerical variables, this chapter discusses categorical and numerical methods in separate sections.

When you use methods to create tabular and visual summaries you risk making any number of common mistakes. These mistakes distort the information that those summaries present and undermine the usefulness of those summaries for decision making. Section 2.9 discusses the challenges you face in organizing and visualizing your variables.

2.1 Organizing Categorical Variables

You organize a categorical variable by tallying the set of individual values for the variable by categories and placing the results in tables. Typically, you construct a summary table to organize the data for a single categorical variable and you construct a contingency table to organize the data from two or more categorical variables.

The Summary Table

A **summary table** tallies the set of individual values as frequencies or percentages for each category. A summary table helps you see the differences among the categories by displaying the frequency, amount, or percentage of items in a set of categories in a separate column. Table 2.1 presents a summary table that tallies responses to a recent survey that asked *millennials*, those born between the years 1983 and 2001, which devices they used to watch movies or television shows. From this table, stored in Devices , you can conclude that about half of the millennials watch movies and television shows on a television set and half do not.

TABLE 2.1

Percentage of the Time Millennials Watch Movies or Television Shows on Various Devices

Device	Percentage
Laptop/desktop	32%
Smartphone	10%
Tablet	9%
Television set	49%

Source: Data extracted and adapted from A. Sharma, "Big Media Needs to Embrace Digital Shift Not Fight It," *Wall Street Journal,* June 22, 2016, p. 1–2.

EXAMPLE 2.1

Summary Table of Levels of Risk of Retirement Funds

The sample of 479 retirement funds for The Choice *Is* Yours scenario (see page 41) includes the variable Risk Level that has the defined categories low, average, and high. Construct a summary table of the retirement funds, categorized by risk.

SOLUTION In Figure 2.1, the percentages for each category are calculated by dividing the number of funds in each category by the total sample size (479). From Figure 2.1, observe that almost half the funds have an average risk, about 30% have low risk, and less than a quarter have high risk.

FIGURE 2.1

Frequency and percentage summary table of Risk Level for 485 retirement funds

Risk Level	Frequency	Percentage
Low	147	30.69%
Average	224	46.76%
High	108	22.55%
Total	479	100.00%

The Contingency Table

A **contingency table** cross-tabulates, or tallies jointly, the data of two or more categorical variables, allowing you to study patterns that may exist between the variables. Tallies can be shown as a frequency, a percentage of the overall total, a percentage of the row total, or a percentage of the column total. Each tally appears in its own **cell**, and there is a cell for each **joint response**, a unique combination of values for the variables being tallied.

In a contingency table, *both* the rows and the columns represent variables. In the simplest case of a contingency table that summarizes two categorical variables, the rows contain the tallies of one variable and the columns contain the tallies of the other variable. Some use the terms *row variable* and *column variable* to distinguish between the two variables.

For The Choice *Is* Yours scenario, the Fund Type and Risk Levels would be one pair of variables that could be summarized for the sample of 479 retirement funds. Because Fund Type has the defined categories growth and value and the Risk Level has the categories low, average, and high, there are six possible joint responses for this table, forming a two row by three columns contingency table.

Figure 2.2 contains Excel *PivotTable* and JMP versions of this table. (An Excel **PivotTable** generates a table from untallied data.) These summaries show that there are 306 growth and 173 value funds (the row totals) and 147 low risk funds, 224 average risk funds, and 108 high risk funds (the column totals). The tables identify the most frequently encountered joint response in the retirement funds sample as being growth funds with average risk (152).

FIGURE 2.2

Excel (PivotTable) and JMP contingency tables of Fund Type and Risk Level for the sample of the 479 retirement funds.

Fund Type	Low	Average	High	Grand Total
Growth	63	152	91	306
Value	84	72	17	173
Grand Total	147	224	108	479

Fund Type	Low	Average	High	All
Growth	63	152	91	306
Value	84	72	17	173
All	147	224	108	479

Figure 2.3 presents a Minitab contingency table that expresses tallies as a percentage of the row totals (first in a row group), as a percentage of the column totals (second line in a row group), and as a percentage of the overall total (third line in a row group). Expressed as percentages, growth funds comprise 63.88% of the funds in the sample (and value funds comprise 36.12%). Of the growth funds, only 20.59% have low risk, whereas 48.55% of the value funds have low risk. As for the funds with high risk, 84.26% are growth funds (and 15.74% are value funds).

From these contingency tables, you conclude that the pattern of risk for growth funds differs from the pattern for value funds.

student TIP

Remember, each joint response gets tallied into only one cell.

FIGURE 2.3
Minitab contingency table
of Fund Type and Risk
Level for the sample of
the 479 retirement funds,
showing row total, column
total, and overall total
percentages for each joint
response.

Tabulated Statistics: Fund Type, Risk Level
Rows: Fund Type   Columns: Risk Level

	Average	High	Low	All
Growth	49.67	29.74	20.59	100.00
	67.86	84.26	42.86	63.88
	31.73	19.00	13.15	63.88
Value	41.62	9.83	48.55	100.00
	32.14	15.74	57.14	36.12
	15.03	3.55	17.54	36.12
All	46.76	22.55	30.69	100.00
	100.00	100.00	100.00	100.00
	46.76	22.55	30.69	100.00

Cell Contents
  % of Row
  % of Column
  % of Total

PROBLEMS FOR SECTION 2.1

LEARNING THE BASICS

2.1 A categorical variable has three categories, with the following frequencies of occurrence:

Category	Frequency
A	13
B	28
C	9

a. Compute the percentage of values in each category.
b. What conclusions can you reach concerning the categories?

2.2 The following data represent the responses to two questions asked in a survey of 40 college students majoring in business: What is your gender? (M = male; F = female) and What is your major? (A = Accounting; C = Computer Information Systems; M = Marketing):

Gender:	M	M	M	F	M	F	F	M	F	M
Major:	A	C	C	M	A	C	A	A	C	C
Gender:	F	M	M	M	M	F	F	M	F	F
Major:	A	A	A	M	C	M	A	A	A	C
Gender:	M	M	M	M	F	M	F	F	M	M
Major:	C	C	A	A	M	M	C	A	A	A
Gender:	F	M	M	M	M	F	M	F	M	M
Major:	C	C	A	A	A	A	C	C	A	C

a. Tally the data into a contingency table where the two rows represent the gender categories and the three columns represent the academic major categories.
b. Construct contingency tables based on percentages of all 40 student responses, based on row percentages and based on column percentages.

APPLYING THE CONCEPTS

2.3 The following table, stored in Smartphone Sales , represents the annual market share of smartphones, by type, for the years 2011, 2012, 2013, 2014, and 2015.

Type	2011	2012	2013	2014	2015
Android	49.2%	69.0%	78.8%	81.5%	80.7%
iOS	18.8%	18.7%	15.1%	14.8%	17.7%
Microsoft	1.8%	2.5%	3.3%	2.7%	1.1%
Blackberry	10.3%	4.5%	1.9%	0.4%	0.3%
OtherOS	19.8%	5.4%	1.0%	0.6%	0.2%

Source: Data extracted from **www.gartner.com/newsroom/id/3215217**.

a. What conclusions can you reach about the market for smartphones in 2011, 2012, 2013, 2014, and 2015.
b. What differences are there in the 2014 and 2015?

2.4 The Consumer Financial Protection Bureau reports on consumer financial product and service complaint submissions by state, category, and company. The following table, stored in FinancialComplaints1 , represents complaints received from Louisiana consumers by complaint category for 2016.

Category	Number of Complaints
Bank Account or Service	202
Consumer Loan	132
Credit Card	175
Credit Reporting	581
Debt Collection	486
Mortgage	442
Student Loan	75
Other	72

Source: Data extracted from **bit.ly/2pR7ryO**.

a. Compute the percentage of complaints for each category.
b. What conclusions can you reach about the complaints for the different categories?

The following table, stored as FinancialComplaints2 , summarizes complaints received from Louisiana consumers by most-complained-about companies for 2016.

Company	Number of Complaints
Bank of America	42
Capital One	93
Citibank	59
Ditech Financial	31
Equifax	217
Experian	177
JPMorgan	128
Nationstar Mortgage	39
Navient	38
Ocwen	41
Synchrony	43
Trans-Union	168
Wells Fargo	77

c. Compute the percentage of complaints for each company.
d. What conclusions can you reach about the complaints for the different companies?

2.5 In addition to the impact of Big Data, what disruptive technology capability do executives anticipate will have the greatest impact on their firm over the next decade? A survey of 50 Fortune 1000 executives revealed the following:

Disruptive Capability	Percent
Artificial Intelligence/Machine Learning	44.3
Digital Technologies: mobile/social media/IoT	26.2
Fin Tech Solutions	11.5
Cloud Computing	8.2
Blockchain	4.9
Other	4.9

What conclusions can you reach concerning the disruptive technology capabilities that executives anticipate will have greatest impact on their firm over the next decade?

SELF TEST **2.6** This table represents the summer power-generating capacity by energy source in the United States as of July 2016.

Energy Source	Percentage
Coal	26.0
Hydro	7.5
Natural gas	42.0
Nuclear	9.0
Solar	1.5
Wind	7.0
Other	7.0

Source: U.S. Department of Energy.

What conclusions can you reach about the source of energy in July 2016?

2.7 Timetric's 2016 survey of insurance professionals explores the use of technology in the industry. The file Technologies contains the responses to the question that asked what technologies these professionals expected to be most used by the insurance industry in the coming year. Those responses are:

Technology	Frequency
Wearable technology	9
Blockchain technology	9
Artificial Intelligence	17
IoT: retail insurance	23
IoT: commercial insurance	5
Social media	27

Source: Data extracted from **bit.ly/2qxMFRj**.

a. Compute the percentage of responses for each technology.
b. What conclusions can you reach concerning expected technology usage in the insurance industry in the coming year?

2.8 A survey of 1,520 Americans adults asked "Do you feel overloaded with too much information?" The results indicate that 23% of females feel information overload compared to 17% of males. The results are:

| | **GENDER** | | |
OVERLOADED	Male	Female	Total
Yes	134	170	304
No	651	565	1,216
Total	785	735	1,520

Source: Data extracted from **bit.ly/2pR5bHZ**.

a. Construct contingency tables based on total percentages, row percentages, and column percentages.
b. What conclusions can you reach from these analyses?

2.9 A study of selected Kickstarter projects showed that overall a majority were successful, achieving their goal and raising, at a minimum, the targeted amounts. In an effort to identify project types that influence success, selected projects were subdivided into project categories (Film & Video, Games, Music, and Technology). The results are as follows:

| | **OUTCOME** | | |
CATEGORY	Successful	Not Successful	Total
Film & Video	21,759	36,805	58,564
Games	9,329	18,238	27,567
Music	24,285	24,377	48,662
Technology	5,040	20,555	25,595
Total	60,413	99,975	160,388

Source: Kickstarter.com, **kickstarter.com/help/stats**.

a. Construct contingency tables based on total percentages, row percentages, and column percentages.
b. Which type of percentage—row, column, or total—do you think is most informative for these data? Explain.
c. What conclusions concerning the pattern of successful Kickstarter projects can you reach?

2.10 Do social recommendations increase ad effectiveness? A study of online video viewers compared viewers who arrived at an advertising video for a particular brand by following a social media recommendation link to viewers who arrived at the same video by web browsing. Data were collected on whether the viewer could correctly recall the brand being advertised after seeing the video. The results were:

	CORRECTLY RECALLED THE BRAND	
ARRIVAL METHOD	Yes	No
Recommendation	407	150
Browsing	193	91

Source: Data extracted from "Social Ad Effectiveness: An Unruly White Paper," **www.unrulymedia.com**, January 2012, p. 3.

What do these results tell you about social recommendations?

2.2 Organizing Numerical Variables

You create ordered arrays and distribution tables to organize numerical variables. Unless the number of values to organize is very large, you always begin with an **ordered array** that arranges the data for a numerical variable in rank order, from the smallest to the largest value. An ordered array helps you get a better sense of the range of values in your data and is particularly useful when you have more than a few values.

When organizing a numerical variable, you sometimes want to group the data by the value of a categorical variable. For example, in collecting meal cost data as part of a study that reviews the travel and entertainment costs that a business incurs in a major city, you might want to determine if the cost of meals at restaurants located in the center city district differ from the cost at restaurants in the surrounding metropolitan area. As you collect meal cost data for this study, you also note the restaurant location, center city or metro area.

Table 2.2A contains the meal cost data collected from a sample of 50 center city restaurants and 50 metro area restaurants. Table 2.2B presents these two lists of data as two ordered arrays. Note that the ordered arrays in Table 2.2B allow you to make some quick observations about the meal cost data. Using Table 2.2B, you can much more easily see meal costs at center city restaurants range from $23 to $91 and that meal costs at metro area restaurants range from $24 to $81.

TABLE 2.2A
Meal Cost Data for 50 Center City and 50 Metro Area Restaurants

Center City Restaurants Meal Costs

81 28 24 38 45 49 36 60 50 41 84 64 78 57 80 69 89 42 55 32 45 71 50 51 50
66 49 91 66 58 80 58 50 44 53 62 40 45 23 66 52 47 70 56 55 52 49 26 79 40

Metro Area Restaurants Meal Costs at

54 35 29 24 26 31 42 33 25 47 50 59 35 36 43 40 56 34 41 55 42 43 43 64 46
46 81 33 37 39 54 53 41 39 52 52 42 59 39 69 41 51 36 46 44 75 56 36 33 45

TABLE 2.2B
Ordered Array of Meal Costs at 50 Center City and 50 Metro Area Restaurants

Center City Restaurant Meal Costs

23 24 26 28 32 36 38 40 40 41 42 44 45 45 45 47 49 49 49 50 50 50 50 51 52
52 53 55 55 56 57 58 58 60 62 64 66 66 66 69 70 71 78 79 80 80 81 84 89 91

Metro Area Restaurant Meal Costs

24 25 26 29 31 33 33 33 34 35 35 36 36 36 37 39 39 39 40 41 41 41 42 42 42
43 43 43 44 45 46 46 46 47 50 51 52 52 53 54 54 55 56 56 59 59 64 69 75 81

Data for a numerical variable that you intend to group can be stored as stacked or unstacked data, as Section 1.5 discusses. The file Restaurants stores the Table 2.2A data in *both* stacked and unstacked arrangements. As Section 1.5 notes, requirements of specific software procedures often dictate the choice of stacked or unstacked.

When a numerical variable contains a large number of values, using an ordered array to make quick observation or reach conclusions about the data can be difficult. For such a variable, constructing a distribution table would be a better choice. Frequency, relative frequency, percentage, and cumulative distributions are among the types of distribution tables commonly used.

The Frequency Distribution

A **frequency distribution** tallies the values of a numerical variable into a set of numerically ordered **classes**. Each class groups a mutually exclusive range of values, called a **class interval**. Each value can be assigned to only one class, and every value must be contained in one of the class intervals.

To create a useful frequency distribution, you must consider how many classes would be appropriate for your data as well as determine a suitable *width* for each class interval. In general, a frequency distribution should have at least 5 and no more than 15 classes because having too few or too many classes provides little new information. To determine the **class interval width** [see Equation (2.1)], you subtract the lowest value from the highest value and divide that result by the number of classes you want the frequency distribution to have.

DETERMINING THE CLASS INTERVAL WIDTH

$$\text{Interval width} = \frac{\text{highest value} - \text{lowest value}}{\text{number of classes}} \tag{2.1}$$

For the center city restaurant meal cost data shown in Tables 2.2A and 2.2B, between 5 and 10 classes are acceptable, given the size (50) of that sample. From the center city restaurant meal costs ordered array in Table 2.2B, the difference between the highest value of $91 and the lowest value of $23 is $68. Using Equation (2.1), you approximate the class interval width as follows:

$$\frac{68}{10} = 6.8$$

This result suggests that you should choose an interval width of $6.80. However, your width should always be an amount that simplifies the reading and interpretation of the frequency distribution. In this example, such an amount would be either $5 or $10, and you should choose $10, which creates 8 classes, and not $5, which creates 15 classes, too many for the sample size of 50.

Having chosen a class interval, you examine your data to establish **class boundaries** that properly and clearly define each class. In setting class boundaries, you are looking to establish classes that are simple to interpret and include all values being summarized. With the meal cost data, having decided on $10 as the class interval, you note that the cost of a center city meal ranges from $23 to $91 and the cost of a metro area meal ranges from $24 to $81. You then conclude that the lower class boundary of the first class must be no more than $23 and that the upper boundary of the last class must include $91. You set the lower class boundary of the first class to $20 (for ease of readability) and define the first class as $20 but less than $30, the second class as $30 but less than $40, and so on, ending with the class $90 but less than $100. Table 2.3 uses these class intervals to present frequency distributions for the sample of 50 center city restaurant meal costs and the sample of 50 metro area restaurant meal costs.

Frequency distributions allow you to more easily make observations about your data that support preliminary conclusions about your data. For example, Table 2.3 shows that the cost of center city restaurant meals is concentrated between $40 and $60, while the cost of metro area restaurant meal is concentrated between $30 and $60.

For some charts discussed later in this chapter, class intervals are identified by their **class midpoints**, the values that are halfway between the lower and upper boundaries of each class. For the frequency distributions shown in Table 2.3, the class midpoints are $25, $35, $45, $55, $65, $75, $85, and $95. Note that well-chosen class intervals lead to class midpoints that are simple to read and interpret, as in this example.

TABLE 2.3
Frequency Distributions
for Cost of a Meal at 50
Center City Restaurants
and 50 Metro Area
Restaurants

Meal Cost ($)	Center City Frequency	Metro Area Frequency
20 but less than 30	4	4
30 but less than 40	3	14
40 but less than 50	12	16
50 but less than 60	14	12
60 but less than 70	7	2
70 but less than 80	4	1
80 but less than 90	5	1
90 but less than 100	1	0
Total	50	50

If the data you have collected do not contain a large number of values, different sets of class intervals can create different impressions of the data. Such perceived changes will diminish as you collect more data. Likewise, choosing different lower and upper class boundaries can also affect impressions.

EXAMPLE 2.2

Frequency Distributions of the Three-Year Return Percentages for Growth and Value Funds

As a member of the company task force in The Choice *Is* Yours scenario (see page 41), you are examining the sample of 479 retirement funds stored in Retirement Funds . You want to compare the numerical variable 3YrReturn, the three-year percentage return of a fund, for the two subgroups that are defined by the categorical variable Type (Growth and Value). You construct separate frequency distributions for the growth funds and the value funds.

SOLUTION   The three-year return for the growth funds is concentrated between 2.5 and 15, while the three-year return for the value funds is concentrated between 2.5 and 10.

TABLE 2.4
Frequency Distributions
of the Three-Year
Return Percentage
for Growth and Value
Funds

Three-Year Return Percentage	Growth Frequency	Value Frequency
−5.00 but less than −2.50	1	1
−2.50 but less than 0	0	1
0 but less than 2.50	14	8
2.50 but less than 5.00	27	20
5.00 but less than 7.50	60	69
7.50 but less than 10.00	109	67
10.00 but less than 12.50	68	7
12.50 but less than 15.00	26	0
15.00 but less than 17.50	1	0
Total	306	173

In the solution for Example 2.2, the total frequency is different for each group (306 and 173). When such totals differ among the groups being compared, you cannot compare the distributions directly as was done in Table 2.3 because of the chance that the table will be misinterpreted. For example, the frequencies for the class interval "5.00 but less than 7.50" look similar—60 and 69—but represent two very different parts of a whole: 60 out of 306 and 69 out of 173 or 19.61% and 39.88%, respectively. When the total frequency differs among the groups being compared, you construct either a relative frequency distribution or a percentage distribution.

Classes and Excel Bins

Microsoft Excel creates distribution tables using *bins* rather than classes. A **bin** is a range of values defined by a bin number, the upper boundary of the range. Unlike a class, the lower boundary is not explicitly stated but is deduced by the bin number that defines the preceding bin. Consider the bins defined by the bin numbers 4.99, 9.99, and 14.99. The first bin represents all values up to 4.99, the second bin all values greater than 4.99 (the preceding bin number) through 9.99, and the third bin all values greater than 9.99 (the preceding bin number) through 14.99.

Note that when using bins, the lower boundary of the first bin will always be negative infinity, as that bin has no explicit lower boundary. That makes the first Excel bin always much larger than the rest of the bins and violates the rule having equal-sized classes. When you translate classes to bins to make use of certain Excel features, you must include an extra bin number as the first bin number. This extra bin number will always be a value slightly less than the lower boundary of your first class.

You translate your classes into a set of bin numbers that you enter into a worksheet column in ascending order. Tables 2.3 through 2.7 use classes stated in the form "*valueA* but less than *valueB*." For such classes, you create a set of bin numbers that are slightly lower than each *valueB* to approximate each class. For example, you translate the Table 2.4 classes on page 48 as the set of bin numbers −5.01 (the "extra" first bin number that is slightly lower than −5, the lower boundary value of the first class), −2.51 (slightly less than −2.5 the *valueB* of the first class), −0.01, 2.49, 4.99, 7.49, 9.99, 12.49, 14.99, and 17.49 (slightly less than 17.50, the *valueB* of the eighth class).

For classes stated in the form "all values from *valueA* to *valueB*," you can approximate classes by choosing a bin number slightly more than each *valueB*. For example, you can translate the classes stated as 0.0 through 4.9, 5.0 through 9.9, 10.0 through 14.9, and 15.0 through 19.9, as the bin numbers: −0.01 (the extra first bin number), 4.99 (slightly more than 4.9), 9.99, 14.99, and 19.99 (slightly more than 19.9).

The Relative Frequency Distribution and the Percentage Distribution

Relative frequency and percentage distributions present tallies in ways other than as frequencies. A **relative frequency distribution** presents the relative frequency, or proportion, of the total for each group that each class represents. A **percentage distribution** presents the percentage of the total for each group that each class represents. When you compare two or more groups, knowing the proportion (or percentage) of the total for each group better facilitates comparisons than a table of frequencies for each group would. For example, for comparing meal costs, using Table 2.5 is better than using Table 2.3 on page 48, which displays frequencies.

TABLE 2.5
Relative Frequency Distributions and Percentage Distributions of the Meal Costs at Center City and Metro Area Restaurants

MEAL COST ($)	CENTER CITY		METRO AREA	
	Relative Frequency	Percentage	Relative Frequency	Percentage
20 but less than 30	0.08	8%	0.08	8%
30 but less than 40	0.06	6%	0.28	28%
40 but less than 50	0.24	24%	0.32	32%
50 but less than 60	0.28	28%	0.24	24%
60 but less than 70	0.14	14%	0.04	4%
70 but less than 80	0.08	8%	0.02	2%
80 but less than 90	0.10	10%	0.02	2%
90 but less than 100	0.02	2%	0.00	0%
Total	1.00	100.0%	1.00	100.0%

student TIP

Relative frequency columns always sum to 1.00. Percentage columns always sum to 100%.

The **proportion**, or **relative frequency**, in each group is equal to the number of *values* in each class divided by the total number of values. The percentage in each group is its proportion multiplied by 100%.

COMPUTING THE PROPORTION OR RELATIVE FREQUENCY

The proportion, or relative frequency, is the number of *values* in each class divided by the total number of values:

$$\text{Proportion} = \text{relative frequency} = \frac{\text{number of values in each class}}{\text{total number of values}} \quad \textbf{(2.2)}$$

If there are 80 values and the frequency in a certain class is 20, the proportion of values in that class is

$$\frac{20}{80} = 0.25$$

and the percentage is

$$0.25 \times 100\% = 25\%$$

You construct a relative frequency distribution by first determining the relative frequency in each class. For example, in Table 2.3 on page 48, there are 50 center city restaurants, and the cost per meal at 14 of these restaurants is between $50 and $60. Therefore, as shown in Table 2.5, the proportion (or relative frequency) of meals that cost between $50 and $60 at center city restaurants is

$$\frac{14}{50} = 0.28$$

You construct a percentage distribution by multiplying each proportion (or relative frequency) by 100%. Thus, the proportion of meals at center city restaurants that cost between $50 and $60 is 14 divided by 50, or 0.28, and the percentage is 28%. Table 2.5 on page 49 presents the relative frequency distribution and percentage distribution of the cost of meals at center city and metro area restaurants. From Table 2.5, you conclude that meal cost is higher at center city restaurants than at metro area restaurants. You note that 14% of the center city

---

EXAMPLE 2.3

Relative Frequency Distributions and Percentage Distributions of the Three-Year Return Percentage for Growth and Value Funds

As a member of the company task force in The Choice *Is* Yours scenario (see page 41), you want to compare the three-year return percentages for the growth and value retirement funds. You construct relative frequency distributions and percentage distributions for these funds.

SOLUTION From Table 2.6, you conclude that the three-year return percentage is higher for the growth funds than for the value funds. For example, 19.61% of the growth funds have returns between 5.00 and 7.50 as compared to 39.88% of the value funds, while 22.22% of the growth funds have returns between 10.00 and 12.50 as compared to 4.05% of the value funds.

TABLE 2.6
Relative Frequency Distributions and Percentage Distributions of the Three-Year Return Percentage for Growth and Value Funds

THREE-YEAR RETURN PERCENTAGE	GROWTH Relative Frequency	GROWTH Percentage	VALUE Relative Frequency	VALUE Percentage
−5.00 but less than −2.50	0.0033	0.33%	0.0058	0.58%
−2.50 but less than 0	0.0000	0.00%	0.0058	0.58%
0 but less than 2.50	0.0458	4.58%	0.0462	4.62%
2.50 but less than 5.00	0.0882	8.82%	0.1156	11.56%
5.00 but less than 7.50	0.1961	19.61%	0.3988	39.88%
7.50 but less than 10.00	0.3562	35.62%	0.3873	38.73%
10.00 but less than 12.50	0.2222	22.22%	0.0405	4.05%
12.50 but less than 15.00	0.0850	8.50%	0.0000	0.00%
15.00 but less than 17.50	0.0033	0.33%	0.0000	0.00%
Total	1.0000	100.00%	1.0000	100.00%

restaurant meals cost between $60 and $70 as compared to 4% of the metro area restaurant meals and that 6% of the center city restaurant meals cost between $30 and $40 as compared to 28% of the metro area restaurant meals.

The Cumulative Distribution

The **cumulative percentage distribution** provides a way of presenting information about the percentage of values that are less than a specific amount. You use a percentage distribution as the basis to construct a cumulative percentage distribution.

For example, you might want to know what percentage of the center city restaurant meals cost less than $40 or what percentage cost less than $50. Starting with the Table 2.5 meal cost percentage distribution for center city restaurants on page 49, you combine the percentages of individual class intervals to form the cumulative percentage distribution. Table 2.7 presents the necessary calculations. From this table, you see that none (0%) of the meals cost less than $20, 8% of meals cost less than $30, 14% of meals cost less than $40 (because 6% of the meals cost between $30 and $40), and so on, until all 100% of the meals cost less than $100.

TABLE 2.7

Developing the Cumulative Percentage Distribution for Center City Restaurant Meal Costs

From Table 2.5:		Percentage of Meal Costs That Are Less Than
Class Interval	**Percentage**	**the Class Interval Lower Boundary**
20 but less than 30	8%	0% (there are no meals that cost less than 20)
30 but less than 40	6%	8% = 0 + 8
40 but less than 50	24%	14% = 8 + 6
50 but less than 60	28%	38% = 8 + 6 + 24
60 but less than 70	14%	66% = 8 + 6 + 24 + 28
70 but less than 80	8%	80% = 8 + 6 + 24 + 28 + 14
80 but less than 90	10%	88% = 8 + 6 + 24 + 28 + 14 + 8
90 but less than 100	2%	98% = 8 + 6 + 24 + 28 + 14 + 8 + 10
100 but less than 110	0%	100% = 8 + 6 + 24 + 28 + 14 + 8 + 10 + 2

Table 2.8 is the cumulative percentage distribution for meal costs that uses cumulative calculations for the center city restaurants (shown in Table 2.7) as well as cumulative calculations for the metro area restaurants (which are not shown). The cumulative distribution shows that the cost of metro area restaurant meals is lower than the cost of meals in center city restaurants. This distribution shows that 36% of the metro area restaurant meals cost less than $40 as compared to 14% of the meals at center city restaurants; 68% of the metro area restaurant meals cost less than $50, but only 38% of the center city restaurant meals do; and 92% of the metro area restaurant meals cost less than $60 as compared to 66% of such meals at the center city restaurants.

TABLE 2.8

Cumulative Percentage Distributions of the Meal Costs for Center City and Metro Area Restaurants

Meal Cost ($)	Percentage of Center City Restaurants Meals That Cost Less Than Indicated Amount	Percentage of Metro Area Restaurants Meals That Cost Less Than Indicated Amount
20	0	0
30	8	8
40	14	36
50	38	68
60	66	92
70	80	96
80	88	98
90	98	100
100	100	100

Unlike in other distributions, the rows of a cumulative distribution do not correspond to class intervals. (Recall that class intervals are mutually *exclusive*. The rows of cumulative distributions are not: The next row "down" *includes* all of the rows above it.) To identify a row, you use the lower class boundaries from the class intervals of the percentage distribution as is done in Table 2.8.

EXAMPLE 2.4

Cumulative Percentage Distributions of the Three-Year Return Percentage for Growth and Value Funds

As a member of the company task force in The Choice *Is* Yours scenario (see page 41), you want to continue comparing the three-year return percentages for the growth and value retirement funds. You construct cumulative percentage distributions for the growth and value funds.

SOLUTION The cumulative distribution in Table 2.9 indicates that returns are higher for the growth funds than for the value funds. The table shows that 33.33% of the growth funds and 57.23% of the value funds have returns below 7.5%. The table also reveals that 68.95% of the growth funds have returns below 10 as compared to 95.95% of the value funds.

TABLE 2.9
Cumulative Percentage Distributions of the Three-Year Return Percentages for Growth and Value Funds

Three-Year Return Percentages	Growth Percentage Less Than Indicated Value	Value Percentage Less Than Indicated Value
−5.0	0.00%	0.00%
−2.5	0.33%	0.58%
0.0	0.33%	1.16%
2.5	4.90%	5.78%
5.0	13.73%	17.34%
7.5	33.33%	57.23%
10.0	68.95%	95.95%
12.5	91.18%	100.00%
15.0	99.67%	100.00%
17.5	100.00%	100.00%

PROBLEMS FOR SECTION 2.2

LEARNING THE BASICS

2.11 Construct an ordered array, given the following data from a sample of $n = 7$ midterm exam scores in accounting:

68 94 63 75 71 88 64

2.12 Construct an ordered array, given the following data from a sample of midterm exam scores in marketing:

88 78 78 73 91 78 85

2.13 Planning and preparing for the unexpected, especially in response to a security incident, is one of the greatest challenges faced by information technology professionals today. An incident is described as any violation of policy, law, or unacceptable act that involves information assets. Incident Response (IR) teams should be evaluating themselves on metrics, such as incident detection or dwell time, to determine how quickly they can detect and respond to incidents in the environment. In 2016, the SANS Institute surveyed organizations about internal response capabilities. The frequency distribution that summarizes the average time organizations took to detect incidents is:

Average Dwell Time	Frequency
Less than 1 day	166
Between 1 and less than 2 days	100
Between 2 and less than 8 days	124
Between 8 and less than 31 days	77
Between 31 and less than 90 days	59
90 days or more	65

Source: **bit.ly/2oZGXGx**.

a. What percentage of organizations took fewer than 2 days, on average, to detect incidents?
b. What percentage of organizations took between 2 and 31 days, on average, to detect incidents?
c. What percentage of organizations took 31 or more days, on average, to detect incidents?
d. What conclusions can you reach about average dwell time of incidents?

2.14 Data was collected on salaries of compliance specialists in corporate accounting firms. The salaries ranged from $61,000 to $261,000.
a. If these salaries were grouped into six class intervals, indicate the class boundaries.
b. What class interval width did you choose?
c. What are the six class midpoints?

APPLYING THE CONCEPTS

2.15 The file **NBACost** contains the total cost ($) for four tickets purchased on the secondary market, two beers, two soft drinks, two hot dogs, and one parking space at each of the 30 National Basketball Association arenas during a recent season. These costs were:

222.67 262.50 262.67 276.40 278.00 290.83 292.87 298.00
318.67 324.33 332.93 345.09 346.70 380.67 398.55 418.14
422.45 423.50 429.00 441.00 492.71 505.77 539.68 571.50
585.20 696.33 718.50 726.40 789.20 878.20

Source: Data extracted from **www.nerdwallet.com/blog/which-nba-teams-most-affordable**.

a. Organize these costs as an ordered array.
b. Construct a frequency distribution and a percentage distribution for these costs.
c. Around which class grouping, if any, are the costs of attending a basketball game concentrated? Explain.

SELF TEST **2.16** The file **Utility** contains the following data about the cost of electricity (in $) during July 2017 for a random sample of 50 one-bedroom apartments in a large city.

96	171	202	178	147	102	153	197	127	82
157	185	90	116	172	111	148	213	130	165
141	149	206	175	123	128	144	168	109	167
95	163	150	154	130	143	187	166	139	149
108	119	183	151	114	135	191	137	129	158

a. Construct a frequency distribution and a percentage distribution that have class intervals with the upper class boundaries $99, $119, and so on.
b. Construct a cumulative percentage distribution.
c. Around what amount does the monthly electricity cost seem to be concentrated?

2.17 How much time do commuters living in or near cities spend commuting to work each week? The file **CommutingTime** contains the average weekly commuting time in 30 U.S. cities.

Source: Data extracted from Office of the New York City Comptroller, "NYC Economics Brief," March 2015, p. 3.

For the weekly commuting time data,
a. Construct a frequency distribution and a percentage distribution.
b. Construct a cumulative percentage distribution.
c. What conclusions can you reach concerning the weekly commuting time of Americans living in cities?

2.18 How do the average credit scores of people living in different American cities differ? The data in **Credit Scores** is an ordered array of the average credit scores of 2,570 American cities.

Source: Data extracted from **www.bizjournals.com/sanantonionews/2016/01/11/study-shows-cities-with-highest-and-lowest-credit.htm**.

a. Construct a frequency distribution and a percentage distribution.
b. Construct a cumulative percentage distribution.

c. What conclusions can you reach concerning the average credit scores of people living in different American cities?

2.19 One operation of a mill is to cut pieces of steel into parts that will later be used as the frame for front seats in an automobile. The steel is cut with a diamond saw and requires the resulting parts to be within ±0.005 inch of the length specified by the automobile company. Data are collected from a sample of 100 steel parts and stored in **Steel**. The measurement reported is the difference in inches between the actual length of the steel part, as measured by a laser measurement device, and the specified length of the steel part. For example, the first value, −0.002, represents a steel part that is 0.002 inch shorter than the specified length.
a. Construct a frequency distribution and a percentage distribution.
b. Construct a cumulative percentage distribution.
c. Is the steel mill doing a good job meeting the requirements set by the automobile company? Explain.

2.20 Call centers today play an important role in managing day-to-day business communications with customers. Call centers must be monitored with a comprehensive set of metrics so that businesses can better understand the overall performance of those centers. One key metric for measuring overall call center performance is *service level*, the percentage of calls answered by a human agent within a specified number of seconds. The file **ServiceLevel** contains the following data for time, in seconds, to answer 50 incoming calls to a financial services call center:

16 14 16 19 6 14 15 5 16 18 17 22 6 18 10 15 12 6
19 16 16 15 13 25 9 17 12 10 5 15 23 11 12 14 24 9
10 13 14 26 19 20 13 24 28 15 21 8 16 12

a. Construct a frequency distribution and a percentage distribution.
b. Construct a cumulative percentage distribution.
c. What can you conclude about call center performance if the service level target is set as "80% of calls answered within 20 seconds"?

2.21 The financial services call center in Problem 2.20 also monitors *call duration*, the amount of time spent speaking to customers on the phone. The file **CallDuration** contains the following data for time, in seconds, spent by agents talking to 50 customers:

243 290 199 240 125 151 158 66 350 1141 251 385 239
139 181 111 136 250 313 154 78 264 123 314 135 99
420 112 239 208 65 133 213 229 154 377 69 170 261
230 273 288 180 296 235 243 167 227 384 331

a. Construct a frequency distribution and a percentage distribution.
b. Construct a cumulative percentage distribution.
c. What can you conclude about call center performance if a call duration target of less than 240 seconds is set?

2.22 The file **Bulbs** contains the life (in hours) of a sample of forty 6-watt light emitting diode (LED) light bulbs produced by Manufacturer A and a sample of forty 6-watt light emitting diode (LED) light bulbs produced by Manufacturer B.
a. Construct a frequency distribution and a percentage distribution for each manufacturer, using the class interval widths for each distributionon page 54.

Manufacturer A: 46,500 but less than 47,500; 47,500 but less than 48,500; and so on.

Manufacturer B: 47,500 but less than 48,500; 48,500 but less than 49,500; and so on.

b. Construct cumulative percentage distributions.
c. Which bulbs have a longer life—those from Manufacturer A or Manufacturer B? Explain.

2.23 The file Drink contains the following data for the amount of soft drink (in liters) in a sample of fifty 2-liter bottles:

2.109 2.086 2.066 2.075 2.065 2.057 2.052 2.044 2.036 2.038
2.031 2.029 2.025 2.029 2.023 2.020 2.015 2.014 2.013 2.014
2.012 2.012 2.012 2.010 2.005 2.003 1.999 1.996 1.997 1.992
1.994 1.986 1.984 1.981 1.973 1.975 1.971 1.969 1.966 1.967
1.963 1.957 1.951 1.951 1.947 1.941 1.941 1.938 1.908 1.894

a. Construct a cumulative percentage distribution.
b. On the basis of the results of (a), does the amount of soft drink filled in the bottles concentrate around specific values?

2.3 Visualizing Categorical Variables

Visualizing categorical variables involves making choices about how you seek to present your data. When you visualize a single categorical variable, you must think about what you want to highlight about your data and whether your data are concentrated in only a few of your categories. To highlight how categories directly compare to each other, you use a bar chart. To highlight how categories form parts of a whole, you use a pie or doughnut chart. (Figure 2.4 allows you to compare a bar and pie chart for the same data.) To present data that are concentrated in only a few of your categories, you use a Pareto chart.

You can visualize two categorical variables together, again thinking about what you want to highlight. To highlight direct comparisons, you use a side-by-side chart. To highlight how parts form a whole, you use a doughnut chart.

The Bar Chart

A **bar chart** visualizes a categorical variable as a series of bars, with each bar representing the tallies for a single category. In a bar chart, the length of each bar represents either the frequency or percentage of values for a category and each bar is separated by space, called a gap.

Figure 2.4 includes bar and pie chart visualizations of the Table 2.1 summary table that reports the percentage of the time *millennials*, those born between the years 1983 and 2001, watch movies or television shows on various devices (see page 42). By viewing either of these charts, you can make the same conclusion as reviewing the summary table in the same amount of time: about half of the millennials watch movies and television shows on a television set and half do not. As the complexity of data increases, that equality of time diminishes. With complex data, visualizations will generally allow you to discover relationships among items faster than the equivalent tabular summaries.

FIGURE 2.4
Visualizations of the Table 2.1 summary table: bar chart (left) and pie chart (right)

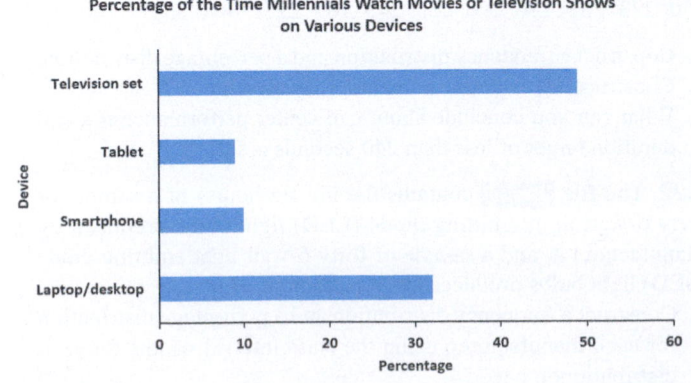

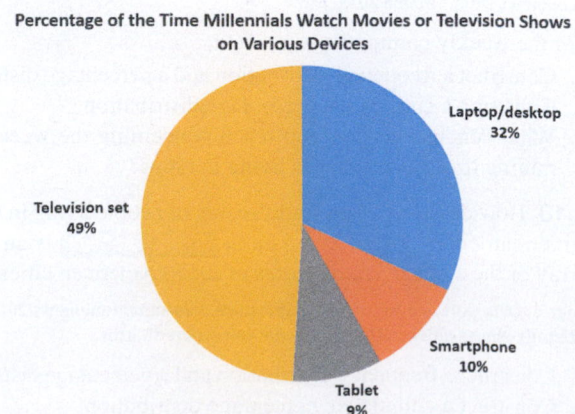

EXAMPLE 2.5

Bar Chart of Levels of Risk of Retirement Funds

As a member of the company task force in The Choice *Is* Yours scenario (see page 41), you want to examine how the Risk Level categories in Figure 2.1 on page 43 compare to each other.

SOLUTION   You construct the bar chart shown in Figure 2.5. You see that average risk is the largest category, followed by low risk followed by high risk.

FIGURE 2.5

Excel and JMP bar chart of the levels of risk of retirement funds

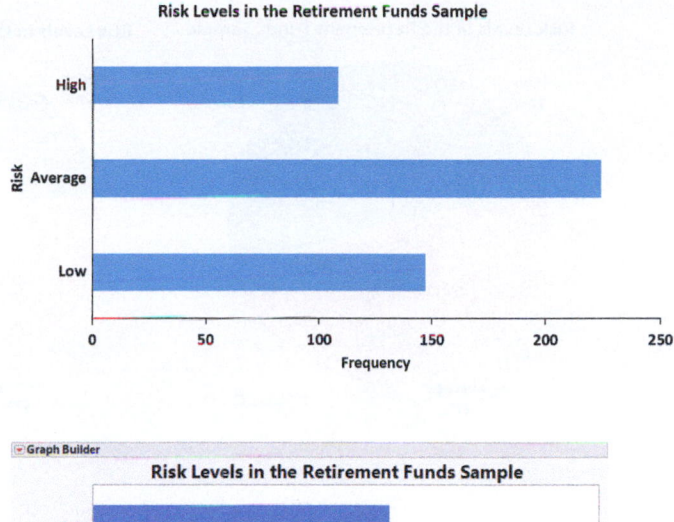

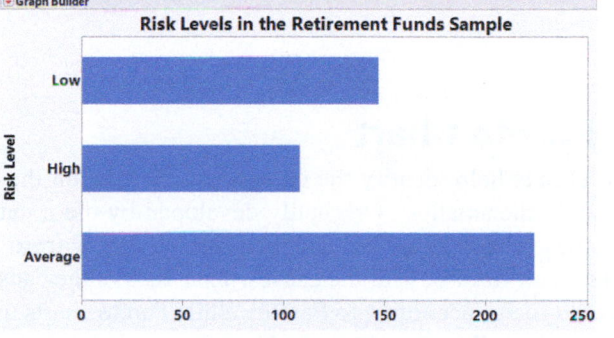

The Pie Chart and the Doughnut Chart

Pie and **doughnut** (or **donut**) charts represent the tallies of each category of a categorical variable as parts of a circle. These parts, or slices, vary by the percentages of the whole for each category. Multiplying category percentages by 360, the number of degrees in a circle, determines the size of each slice, defined as the length of the chord (part of a circle) in degrees. For example, for the Table 2.1 summary table categories, the sizes of the slices would be: desktop/laptop, 115.2 degrees (32% × 360); smartphone, 36 degrees (10% × 360); tablet, 32.4 degrees (9% × 360); and television set, 176.4 degrees (49% × 360). The pie chart in Figure 2.4 displays these slices.

Doughnut charts are pie charts with their centers cut out, creating a hole similar to the holes found in real doughnuts (hence the name). Some believe cutting out centers minimizes a common misperception of pie charts that occurs when people focus on the area of each pie slice and not the length of the chord of each slice. Because most would agree that many pie charts presented together provide an overwhelming visual experience that should be avoided (see reference 2), doughnut charts can be useful when more than one chart is presented together. Doughnut charts can also be used to visualize two variables, as this chapter explains later.

student TIP

While using pie or doughnut charts, avoid all "3D" variations or any "exploded" charts in which one or more slices has been pulled away from the center because these forms introduce known visual distortions that can impede understanding of the data.

EXAMPLE 2.6

Pie Chart and
Doughnut Chart
of the Risk of
Retirement Funds

As a member of the company task force in The Choice *Is* Yours scenario (see page 41), you want to examine how the Risk Level categories in Figure 2.1 on page 43 form parts of a whole.

SOLUTION You construct either the Figure 2.6 pie or doughnut chart. You can immediately see that almost half the funds have an average risk and that of the remaining funds, more have low risk than high risk. (A close reading of the labels reveals the actual percentages.)

FIGURE 2.6

Excel pie chart and
doughnut chart of the risk
of retirement funds

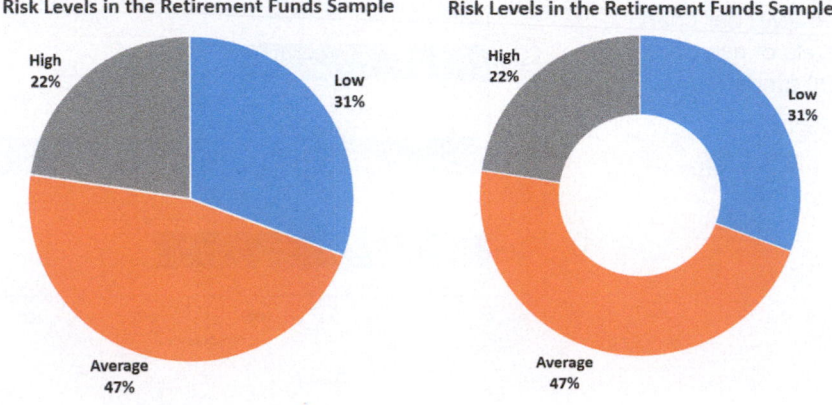

The Pareto Chart

Pareto charts help identify the categories that contain the largest tallies from the categories that contain the smallest. Originally developed by the nineteenth-century economist Vilfredo Pareto, these charts help visualize his principle (the **Pareto principle**) that 80% of the consequences result from 20% of the causes. That 20% of the causes are the "vital few" about which one should focus, according to Pareto. While Pareto charts usually do not demonstrate Pareto's 80/20 rule literally, such charts do identify the vital few from the "trivial many" and can be a useful tool today, especially when looking at the frequencies for a large set of categories. In quality management efforts, Pareto charts are very useful tools for prioritizing improvement efforts, such as when data that identify defective or nonconforming items are collected, as in the example that this section uses.

The vertical scale for each category can be frequency, as Vilfredo Pareto originally used, or percentages of the whole.

Pareto charts combine two different visualizations: a *vertical* bar chart and a **line graph**, a plot of connected points. The vertical bars represent the tallies for each category, arranged in descending order of the tallies. The line graph represents a cumulative percentage of the tallies from the first category through the last category. The line graph uses a percentage vertical scale, while the bars use either Pareto's original vertical frequency scale or a more recent adaptation that uses a percentage vertical scale line to allow both measurements to share the same scale. In cases with too many categories to display clearly in one chart, categories with the fewest tallies can be combined into a Miscellaneous or Other category and shown as the last (rightmost) bar.

studentTIP

Excel Pareto charts use the percentage vertical scale for the bars, while JMP and Minitab Pareto charts use the original frequency scale for the bars.

Using Pareto charts can be an effective way to visualize data for studies that seek causes for an observed phenomenon. For example, consider a bank study team that wants to enhance the user experience of automated teller machines (ATMs). During this study, the team identifies incomplete ATM transactions as a significant issue and decides to collect data about the causes of such transactions. Using the bank's own processing systems as a primary data source, causes of incomplete transactions are collected, stored in ATM Transactions, and then organized in the Table 2.10 summary table.

TABLE 2.10

Summary Table of Causes of Incomplete ATM Transactions

Cause	Frequency	Percentage
ATM malfunctions	32	4.42%
ATM out of cash	28	3.87%
Invalid amount requested	23	3.18%
Lack of funds in account	19	2.62%
Card unreadable	234	32.32%
Warped card jammed	365	50.41%
Wrong keystroke	23	3.18%
Total	724	100.00%

Source: Data extracted from A. Bhalla, "Don't Misuse the Pareto Principle," *Six Sigma Forum Magazine*, May 2009, pp. 15–18.

To separate out the "vital few" causes from the "trivial many" causes, the bank study team creates the Table 2.11 summary table. In this table, causes appear in descending order by frequency, as a Pareto chart requires and the table includes columns for the percentages and cumulative percentages. The team then uses these columns to construct a Figure 2.7 Pareto chart. Note that in Figure 2.7, the left vertical axis represents the percentage due to each cause in the Excel chart, but represents the frequency due to each cause in the Minitab chart. In both charts, the right vertical axis represents the cumulative percentage.

TABLE 2.11

Ordered Summary Table of Causes of Incomplete ATM Transactions

Cause	Frequency	Percentage	Cumulative Percentage
Warped card jammed	365	50.41%	50.41%
Card unreadable	234	32.32%	82.73%
ATM malfunctions	32	4.42%	87.15%
ATM out of cash	28	3.87%	91.02%
Invalid amount requested	23	3.18%	94.20%
Wrong keystroke	23	3.18%	97.38%
Lack of funds in account	19	2.62%	100.00%
Total	724	100.00%	

FIGURE 2.7

Excel and Minitab Pareto charts of incomplete ATM transactions (note the differing left vertical axes)

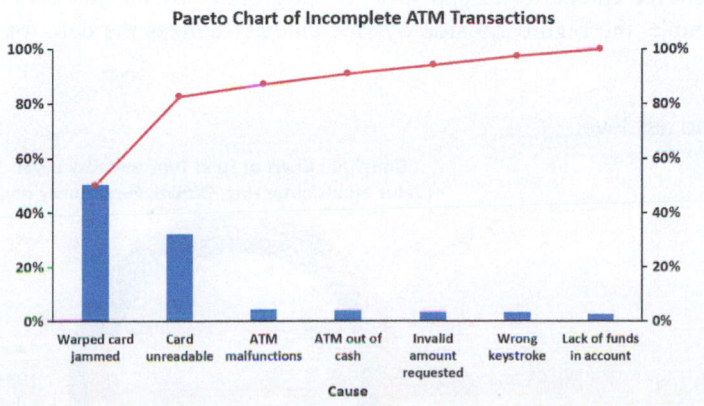
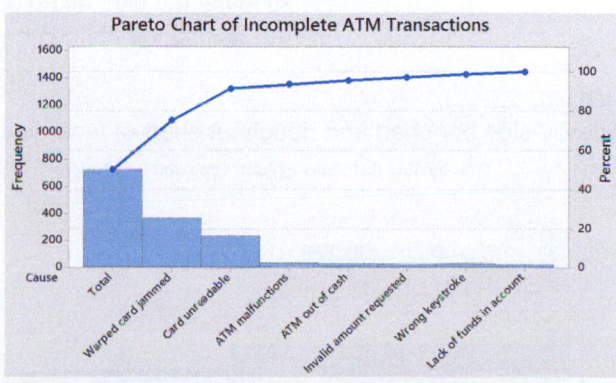

Because the categories in a Pareto chart are ordered by decreasing frequency of occurrence, the team can quickly see which causes contribute the most to the problem of incomplete transactions. (Those causes would be the "vital few," and figuring out ways to avoid such causes would be, presumably, a starting point for improving the user experience of ATMs.) By following the cumulative percentage line in Figure 2.7, you see that the first two causes, warped card jammed (50.41%) and card unreadable (32.3%), account for 82.7% of the incomplete transactions. Attempts to reduce incomplete ATM transactions due to warped or unreadable cards should produce the greatest payoff.

EXAMPLE 2.7

Pareto Chart of the Devices Millennials Use to Watch Movies or Television Shows

Construct a Pareto chart from the Table 2.1 summary table that summarizes the devices that millennials, those born between the years 1983 and 2001, use to watch movies or television shows.

SOLUTION First, create a new table from Table 2.1 in which the categories are ordered by descending frequency and columns for percentages and cumulative percentages for the ordered categories are included (not shown). From that table, create the Pareto chart in Figure 2.8. From Figure 2.8, observe that about half of the millennials watch movies and television shows on a television and half do not. Also observe that televisions and computers together account for over four-fifths of all such viewing by millennials.

FIGURE 2.8

Excel Pareto chart of which devices millennials use to watch movies or television shows

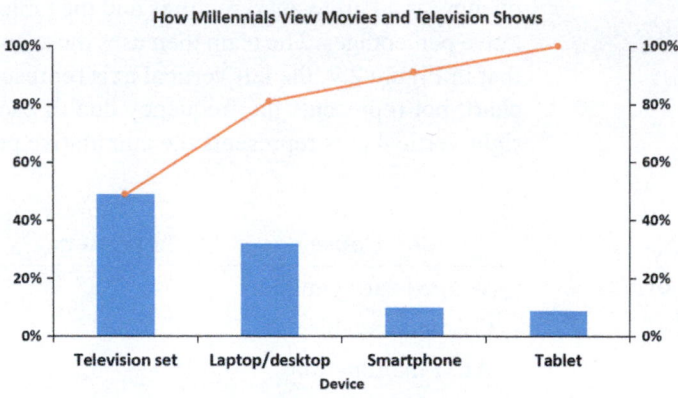

Visualizing Two Categorical Variables

As when you visualize a single variable, visualizing two categorical variables requires making a choice about what you seek to highlight. To highlight how categories directly compare to each other, you use a side-by-side chart. To highlight how categories form parts of a whole, you use a doughnut chart.

The side-by-side chart A **side-by-side chart** visualizes two categorical variables by showing the bars that represent the categories of one variable set grouped by the categories of the second variable. For example, the Figure 2.9 side-by-side chart visualizes the data for the

FIGURE 2.9

Side-by-side bar chart and doughnut chart of fund type and risk level

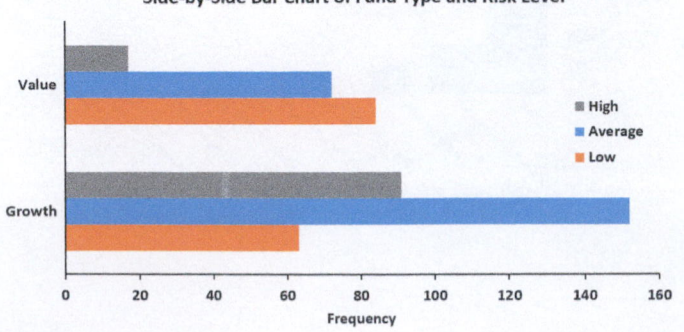

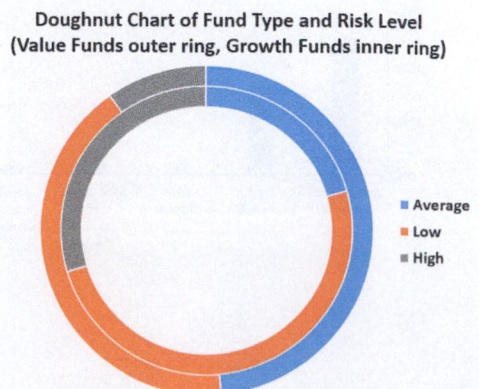

levels of risk for growth and value funds shown in Figure 2.2 on page 43. In Figure 2.9, you see that a substantial portion of the growth funds have average risk. However, more of the value funds have low risk than average or high risk.

The doughnut chart   When visualizing two variables, the doughnut chart appears as two concentric rings, one inside the other, each ring containing the categories of one variable. In Figure 2.9, the doughnut chart of fund type and risk level highlights that the proportion of funds with average risk (darkest color) is different for growth and value.

PROBLEMS FOR SECTION 2.3

APPLYING THE CONCEPTS

2.24 A survey of online shoppers revealed that in 2015 they bought more of their purchases online than in stores. The data in OnlineShopping reveals how their purchases were made.
a. Construct a bar chart, a pie or doughnut chart, and a Pareto chart.
b. Which graphical method do you think is best for portraying these data?
c. What conclusions can you reach concerning how online shoppers make purchases?

2.25 How do college students spend their day? The 2016 American Time Use Survey for college students found the following results:

Activity	Percentage
Eating and Drinking	4%
Educational Activities	14%
Grooming	3%
Leisure and Sports	17%
Sleeping	37%
Traveling	6%
Working and Related Activities	10%
Other	9%

Source: Data extracted from **bit.ly/2qxIjcH**, accessed February 3, 2017.

a. Construct a bar chart, a pie or doughnut chart, and a Pareto chart.
b. Which graphical method do you think is best for portraying these data?
c. What conclusions can you reach concerning how college students spend their day?

2.26 The Energy Information Administration reported the following sources of electricity in the United States in 2016:

Source of Electricity	Percentage
Coal	32%
Hydro and renewables	14%
Natural gas	33%
Nuclear power	19%
Other	2%

Source: Energy Information Administration, 2016.

a. Construct a Pareto chart.
b. What percentage of power is derived from coal, nuclear power, or natural gas?
c. Construct a pie chart.

d. For these data, do you prefer using a Pareto chart or a pie chart? Why?

2.27 The Consumer Financial Protection Bureau reports on consumer financial product and service complaint submissions by state, category, and company. The following table, stored in FinancialComplaints1 , represents complaints received from Louisiana consumers by complaint category for 2016.

Category	Number of Complaints
Bank Account or Service	202
Consumer Loan	132
Credit Card	175
Credit Reporting	581
Debt Collection	486
Mortgage	442
Student Loan	75
Other	72

Source: Data extracted from **bit.ly/2pR7ryO**.

a. Construct a Pareto chart for the categories of complaints.
b. Discuss the "vital few" and "trivial many" reasons for the categories of complaints.

The following table, stored in FinancialComplaints2 , represents complaints received from Louisiana consumers by most-complained-about companies for 2016.

Company	Number of Complaints
Bank of America	42
Capital One	93
Citibank	59
Ditech Financial	31
Equifax	217
Experian	177
JPMorgan	128
Nationstar Mortgage	39
Navient	38
Ocwen	41
Synchrony	43
Trans-Union	168
Wells Fargo	77

c. Construct a bar chart and a pie chart for the complaints by company.

d. What graphical method (Pareto, bar, or pie chart) do you think is best for portraying these data?

2.28 The following table indicates the percentage of residential electricity consumption in the United States, in a recent year organized by type of use.

Type of Use	Percentage
Cooking	2%
Cooling	15%
Electronics	9%
Heating	15%
Lighting	13%
Refrigeration	10%
Water heating	10%
Wet cleaning	3%
Other	23%

Source: Department of Energy.

a. Construct a bar chart, a pie chart, and a Pareto chart.

b. Which graphical method do you think is best for portraying these data?

c. What conclusions can you reach concerning residential electricity consumption in the United States?

2.29 Timetric's 2016 survey of insurance professionals explores the use of technology in the industry. The file Technologies contains the responses to the question that asked what technologies these professionals expected to be most used by the insurance industry in the coming year.

Technology	Frequency
Wearable technology	9
Blockchain technology	9
Artificial Intelligence	17
IoT: retail insurance	23
IoT: commercial insurance	5
Social media	27

Source: Data extracted from **bit.ly/2qxMFRj**.

a. Construct a bar chart and a pie chart.

b. What conclusions can you reach concerning expected technology usage in the insurance industry?

2.30 A survey of 1,520 American adults asked "Do you feel overloaded with too much information?" The results indicate that 23% of females feel information overload compared to 17% of males. The results are:

OVERLOADED	GENDER Male	Female	Total
Yes	134	170	304
No	651	565	1,216
Total	785	735	1,520

Source: Data extracted from **bit.ly/2pR5bHZ**.

a. Construct a side-by-side bar chart of overloaded with too much information and gender.

b. What conclusions can you reach from this chart?

2.31 A study of selected Kickstarter projects showed that overall a majority were successful, achieving their goal and raising, at a minimum, the targeted amounts. In an effort to identify project types that influence success, selected projects were subdivided into project categories (Film & Video, Games, Music, and Technology). The results are as follows:

CATEGORY	OUTCOME Successful	Not Successful	Total
Film & Video	21,759	36,805	58,564
Games	9,329	18,238	27,567
Music	24,285	24,377	48,662
Technology	5,040	20,555	25,595
Total	60,413	99,975	160,388

Source: Kickstarter.com, **kickstarter.com/help/stats**.

a. Construct a side-by-side bar chart and a doughnut chart of project outcome and category.

b. What conclusions concerning the pattern of successful Kickstarter projects can you reach?

2.32 Do social recommendations increase ad effectiveness? A study of online video viewers compared viewers who arrived at an advertising video for a particular brand by following a social media recommendation link to viewers who arrived at the same video by web browsing. Data were collected on whether the viewer could correctly recall the brand being advertised after seeing the video. The results were as follows:

ARRIVAL METHOD	CORRECTLY RECALLED THE BRAND Yes	No
Recommendation	407	150
Browsing	193	91

Source: Data extracted from "Social Ad Effectiveness: An Unruly White Paper," **www.unrulymedia.com**, January 2012, p. 3.

a. Construct a side-by-side bar chart and a doughnut chart of the arrival method and whether the brand was promptly recalled.

b. What do these results tell you about the arrival method and brand recall?

2.4 Visualizing Numerical Variables

You visualize the data for a numerical variable through a variety of techniques that show the distribution of values. These techniques include the stem-and-leaf display, the histogram, the percentage polygon, and the cumulative percentage polygon (ogive), all discussed in this section, as well the boxplot, which requires descriptive summary measures as explained in Section 3.3.

The Stem-and-Leaf Display

A **stem-and-leaf display** visualizes data by presenting the data as one or more row-wise *stems* that represent a range of values. In turn, each stem has one or more *leaves* that branch out to the right of their stem and represent the values found in that stem. For stems with more than one leaf, the leaves are arranged in ascending order.

Stem-and-leaf displays allow you to see how the data are distributed and where concentrations of data exist. Leaves typically present the last significant digit of each value, but sometimes you round values. For example, suppose you collect the following meal costs (in $) for 15 classmates who had lunch at a fast-food restaurant (stored in FastFood):

7.42   6.29   5.83   6.50   8.34   9.51   7.10   6.80   5.90   4.89   6.50   5.52   7.90   8.30   9.60

To construct the stem-and-leaf display, you use whole dollar amounts as the stems and round the cents to one decimal place as the leaves. For the first value, 7.42, the stem is 7 and its leaf is 4. For the second value, 6.29, the stem is 6 and its leaf 3. The completed stem-and-leaf display for these data with the leaves ordered within each stem is:

<table>
<tr><td>4</td><td>9</td></tr>
<tr><td>5</td><td>589</td></tr>
<tr><td>6</td><td>3558</td></tr>
<tr><td>7</td><td>149</td></tr>
<tr><td>8</td><td>33</td></tr>
<tr><td>9</td><td>56</td></tr>
</table>

student TIP

A stem-and-leaf display turned sideways looks like a histogram.

The Histogram

A **histogram** visualizes data as a vertical bar chart in which each bar represents a class interval from a frequency or percentage distribution. In a histogram, you display the numerical variable along the horizontal (X) axis and use the vertical (Y) axis to represent either the frequency or the percentage of values per class interval. There are never any gaps between adjacent bars in a histogram.

Figure 2.11 visualizes the data of Table 2.3 on page 48, meal costs at center city and metro area restaurants, as a pair of frequency histograms. The histogram for center city restaurants shows that the cost of meals is concentrated between approximately $40 and $60. Ten meals at center city restaurants cost $70 or more. The histogram for metro area restaurants shows that the cost of meals is concentrated between $30 and $60. Very few meals at metro area restaurants cost more than $60.

EXAMPLE 2.8

Stem-and-Leaf Display of the Three-Year Return Percentage for the Value Funds

As a member of the company task force in The Choice *Is* Yours scenario (see page 41), you want to study the past performance of the value funds. One measure of past performance is the numerical variable 3YrReturn, the three-year return percentage. Using the data from the 173 value funds, you want to visualize this variable as a stem-and-leaf display.

SOLUTION Figure 2.10 presents JMP and Minitab stem-and-leaf displays of the three-year return percentage for value funds. Note that the Minitab display orders percentages from lowest to highest, while the JMP display orders funds from highest to lowest. You observe:

- the lowest three-year return was −2.6.
- the highest three-year return was 11.9.
- the three-year returns were concentrated between 6 and 9.
- very few of the three-year returns were above 11.
- the distribution of the three-year returns appears to have more high values than low values.

▶(*continued*)

FIGURE 2.10

JMP and Minitab stem-and-leaf display of the three-year return percentage for value funds (JMP orders stems from high to low)

Stem and Leaf

Stem	Leaf	Count
11	90	2
10	00034667	8
9	00133379999	11
8	0001222334444455555566666666667778888999	40
7	000001111222333444455555566888888999	33
6	0001111122234555566666666678888999	31
5	344555566666778999	18
4	1223555566	10
3	118899	6
2	01345566	8
1	3799	4
0		
-0		
-1	0	1
-2	6	1

Stem-and-Leaf Display: 3YrReturn_Value

Stem-and-leaf of 3YrReturn_Value   N = 173

1	-2	6
1	-1	
2	-0	9
2	0	
7	1	36899
14	2	1335556
20	3	017889
30	4	0112455555
50	5	34444555556666789999
81	6	001111112444555555567788888999
(32)	7	00000011222333334455566778889999
60	8	00111122333444444555555566666677777778889
21	9	00033378899999
7	10	33566
2	11	99

Leaf Unit = 0.1

FIGURE 2.11

Minitab frequency histograms for meal costs at center city and metro area restaurants

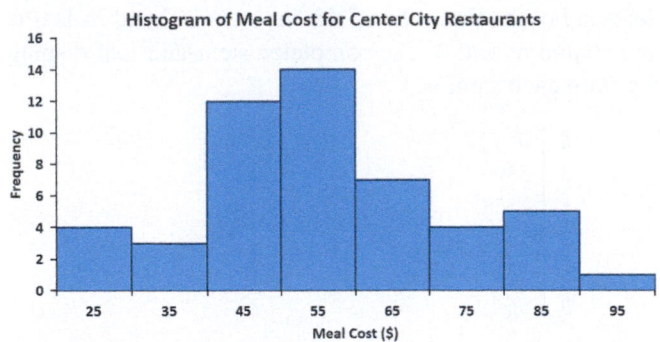

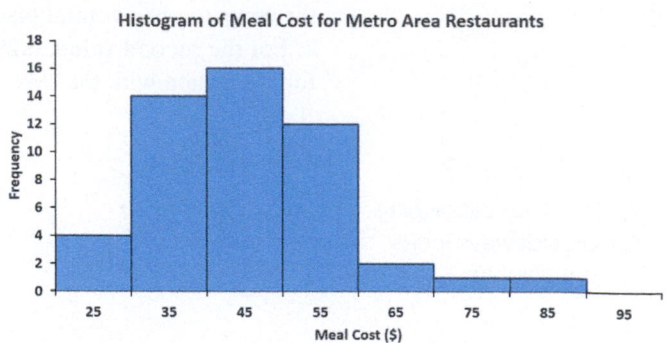

EXAMPLE 2.9

Histograms of the Three-Year Return Percentages for the Growth and Value Funds

As a member of the company task force in The Choice *Is* Yours scenario (see page 41), you seek to compare the past performance of the growth funds and the value funds, using the three-year return percentage variable. Using the data from the sample of 479 funds, you construct histograms for the growth and the value funds to create a visual comparison.

SOLUTION Figure 2.12 displays frequency histograms for the three-year return percentages for the growth and value funds.

FIGURE 2.12

Excel frequency histograms for the three-year return percentages for the growth and value funds

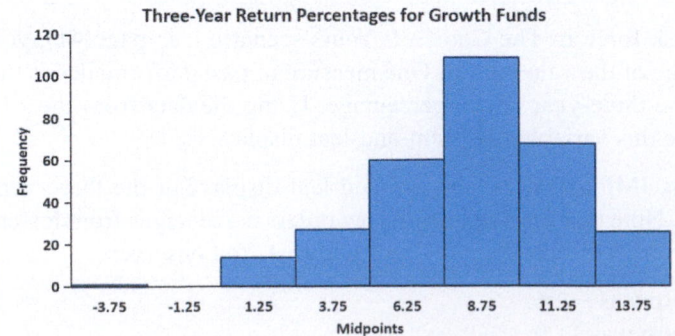

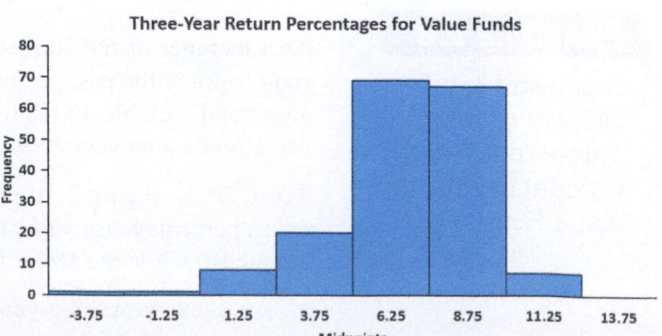

Reviewing the histograms in Figure 2.12 leads you to conclude that the returns were higher for the growth funds than for value funds. The return for the growth funds is more concentrated between 5 and 12.5 while the return for the value funds is more concentrated between 5 and 10.

The Percentage Polygon

When using a categorical variable to divide the data of a numerical variable into two or more groups, you visualize data by constructing a **percentage polygon**. This chart uses the midpoints of each class interval to represent the data of each class and then plots the midpoints, at their respective class percentages, as points on a line along the X axis. While you can construct two or more histograms, as was done in Figures 2.11 and 2.12, a percentage polygon allows you to make a direct comparison that is easier to interpret. (You cannot, of course, combine two histograms into one chart as bars from the two groups would overlap and obscure data.)

Figure 2.13 displays percentage polygons for the cost of meals at center city and metro area restaurants. You can make the same observations from this pair of charts as you made when examining the pair of histograms in Figure 2.11 on page 62. You again note that the center city meal cost is concentrated between $40 and $60 while the metro area meal cost is concentrated between $30 and $60. However, unlike the pair of histograms, the polygons allow you to more easily identify which class intervals have similar percentages for the two groups and which do not.

FIGURE 2.13

Minitab percentage polygons of meal costs for center city and metro area restaurants

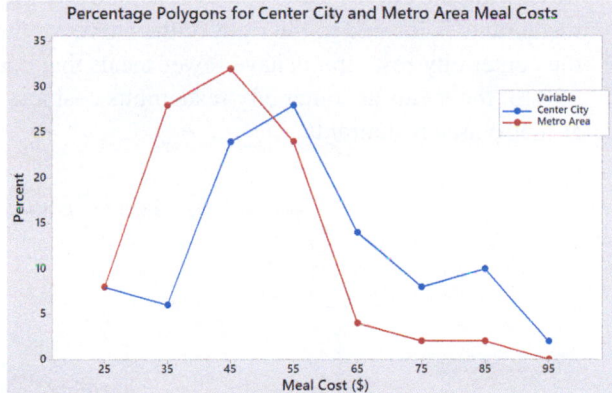

The polygons in Figure 2.13 have points whose values on the X axis represent the midpoint of the class interval. For example, look at the points plotted at X = 35 ($35). The point for meal costs at center city restaurants (the lower one) show that 6% of the meals cost between $30 and $40, while the point for the meal costs at metro area restaurants (the higher one) shows that 28% of meals at these restaurants cost between $30 and $40.

When you construct polygons or histograms, the vertical Y axis should include zero to avoid distorting the character of the data. The horizontal X axis does not need to show the zero point for the numerical variable, but a major portion of the axis should be devoted to the entire range of values for the variable.

EXAMPLE 2.10

Percentage Polygons of the Three-Year Return Percentage for the Growth and Value Funds

As a member of the company task force in The Choice *Is* Yours scenario (see page 41), you seek to compare the past performance of the growth funds and the value funds using the three-year return percentage variable. Using the data from the sample of 479 funds, you construct percentage polygons for the growth and value funds to create a visual comparison.

SOLUTION Figure 2.14 displays percentage polygons of the three-year return percentage for the growth and value funds.

FIGURE 2.14

Excel percentage polygons of the three-year return percentages for the growth and value funds

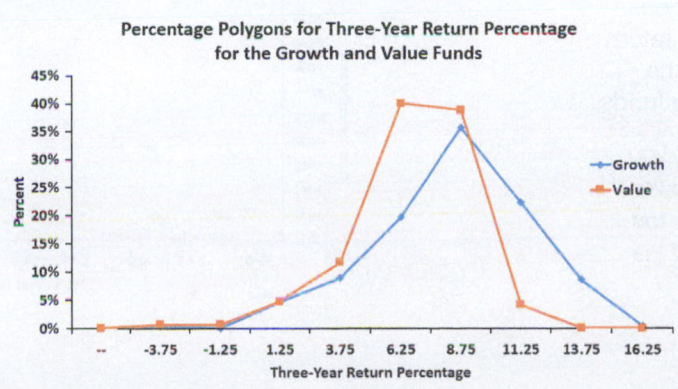

▶(*continued*)

Figure 2.14 shows that the growth funds polygon is to the right of the value funds polygon. This allows you to conclude that the three-year return percentage is higher for growth funds than for value funds. The polygons also show that the return for growth funds is concentrated between 5 and 12.50, and the return for the value funds is concentrated between 5 and 10.

The Cumulative Percentage Polygon (Ogive)

The **cumulative percentage polygon**, or **ogive**, uses the cumulative percentage distribution discussed in Section 2.2 to plot the cumulative percentages along the Y axis. Unlike the percentage polygon, the lower boundaries of the class interval for the numerical variable are plotted, at their respective class percentages as points on a line along the X axis.

Figure 2.15 shows cumulative percentage polygons of meal costs for center city and metro area restaurants. In this chart, the lower boundaries of the class intervals (20, 30, 40, etc.) are approximated by the upper boundaries of the previous bins (19.99, 29.99, 39.99, etc.). Reviewing the curves leads you to conclude that the curve of the cost of meals at the center city restaurants is located to the right of the curve for the metro area restaurants. This indicates that the center city restaurants have fewer meals that cost less than a particular value. For example, 38% of the meals at center city restaurants cost less than $50, as compared to 68% of the meals at metro area restaurants.

FIGURE 2.15

Minitab cumulative percentage polygons of meal costs for center city and metro area restaurants

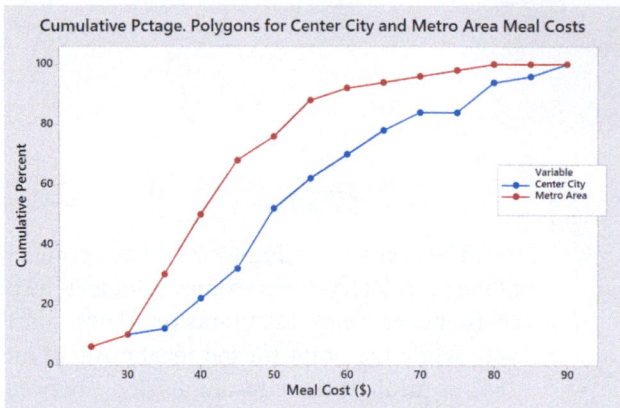

EXAMPLE 2.11

Cumulative Percentage Polygons of the Three-Year Return Percentages for the Growth and Value Funds

As a member of the company task force in The Choice *Is* Yours scenario (see page 41), you seek to compare the past performance of the growth funds and the value funds using the three-year return percentage variable. Using the data from the sample of 479 funds, you construct cumulative percentage polygons for the growth and the value funds.

SOLUTION Figure 2.16 displays cumulative percentage polygons of the three-year return percentages for the growth and value funds.

FIGURE 2.16

Excel cumulative percentage polygons of the three-year return percentages for the growth and value funds

In Microsoft Excel, you approximate the lower boundary by using the upper boundary of the previous bin.

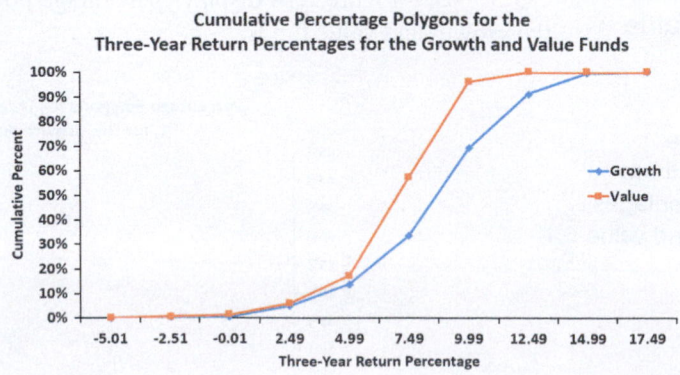

▶(*continued*)

The cumulative percentage polygons in Figure 2.16 show that the curve for the three-year return percentage for the growth funds is located to the right of the curve for the value funds. This allows you to conclude that the growth funds have fewer three-year return percentages that are higher than a particular value. For example, 68.95% of the growth funds had three-year return percentages below 10, as compared to 95.95% of the value funds. You can conclude that, in general, the growth funds outperformed the value funds in their three-year returns.

PROBLEMS FOR SECTION 2.4

LEARNING THE BASICS

2.33 Construct a stem-and-leaf display, given the following data from a sample of midterm exam scores in finance:

54 69 98 93 53 74

2.34 Construct an ordered array, given the following stem-and-leaf display from a sample of $n = 7$ midterm exam scores in information systems:

5	0
6	
7	446
8	19
9	2

APPLYING THE CONCEPTS

2.35 The following is a stem-and-leaf display representing the amount of gasoline purchased, in gallons (with leaves in tenths of gallons), for a sample of 25 cars that use a particular service station on the New Jersey Turnpike:

9	147
10	02238
11	125566777
12	223489
13	02

a. Construct an ordered array.
b. Which of these two displays seems to provide more information? Discuss.
c. What amount of gasoline (in gallons) is most likely to be purchased?
d. Is there a concentration of the purchase amounts in the center of the distribution?

✓ SELF TEST **2.36** The file **NBACost** contains the total cost (in $) for four tickets purchased on the secondary market, two beers, two soft drinks, four hot dogs, and one parking space at each of the 30 National Basketball Association arenas during a recent season.

Source: Data extracted from **www.nerdwallet.com/blog/which-nba-teams-most-affordable**.

a. Construct a stem-and-leaf display.
b. Around what value, if any, are the costs of attending a basketball game concentrated? Explain.

2.37 The file **MobileSpeed** contains the overall download and upload speeds in mbps for nine carriers in the United States.

Source: Data extracted from "Best Mobile Network 2016", **bit.ly/1KGPrMm**, accessed November 10, 2016.

a. Construct an ordered array.
b. Construct a stem-and-leaf display.
c. Does the ordered array or the stem-and-leaf display provide more information? Discuss.
d. Around what value, if any, are the download and upload speeds concentrated? Explain.

2.38 The file **Utility** contains the following data about the cost of electricity during July of a recent year for a random sample of 50 one-bedroom apartments in a large city:

96	171	202	178	147	102	153	197	127	82
157	185	90	116	172	111	148	213	130	165
141	149	206	175	123	128	144	168	109	167
95	163	150	154	130	143	187	166	139	149
108	119	183	151	114	135	191	137	129	158

a. Construct a histogram and a percentage polygon.
b. Construct a cumulative percentage polygon.
c. Around what amount does the monthly electricity cost seem to be concentrated?

2.39 As player salaries have increased, the cost of attending baseball games has increased dramatically. The following histogram visualizes the total cost (in $) for two tickets, two beers, two hot dogs, and parking for one vehicle at each of the 30 Major League Baseball parks during the 2016 season that is stored in **BBCost2016**.

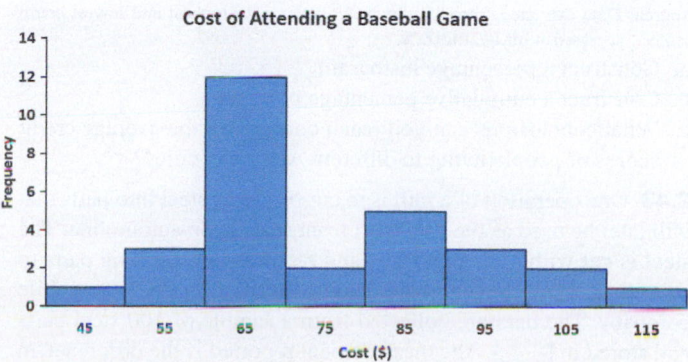

Cost of Attending a Baseball Game

What conclusions can you reach concerning the cost of attending a baseball game at different ballparks?

2.40 The following histogram and cumulative percentage polygon visualize the data about the property taxes on a $176K home for the 50 states and the District of Columbia, stored in Property Taxes .

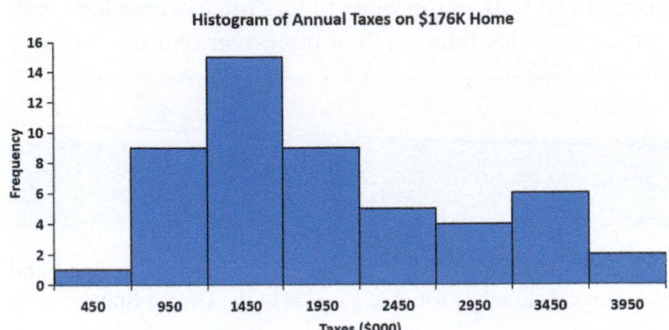

Histogram of Annual Taxes on $176K Home

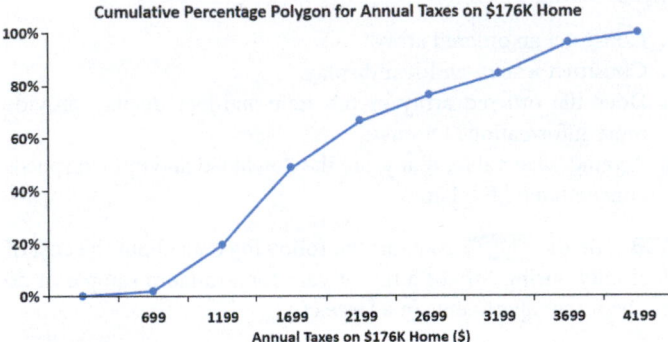

Cumulative Percentage Polygon for Annual Taxes on $176K Home

What conclusions can you reach concerning the property taxes per capita?

2.41 How much time do Americans living in cities spend commuting to work each week? The data in the file CommutingTime include this cost for 30 cities.

Source: Data extracted from "The High Cost of Congestion," NYC Economic Brief, March 2015, p. 3.

For the time Americans living in cities spend commuting to work each week:
a. Construct a percentage histogram.
b. Construct a cumulative percentage polygon.
c. What conclusions can you reach concerning the time Americans living in cities spend commuting to work each week?

2.42 How do the average credit scores of people living in various cities differ? The file Credit Scores contains an ordered array of the average credit scores of 2,570 American cities.

Source: Data extracted from "Study shows cities with highest and lowest credit scores," accessed at **bit.ly/2uubZfX**.

a. Construct a percentage histogram.
b. Construct a cumulative percentage polygon.
c. What conclusions can you reach concerning the average credit scores of people living in different American cities?

2.43 One operation of a mill is to cut pieces of steel into parts that will later be used as the frame for front seats in an automobile. The steel is cut with a diamond saw and requires the resulting parts to be within ± 0.005 inch of the length specified by the automobile company. The data are collected from a sample of 100 steel parts and stored in Steel . The measurement reported is the difference in inches between the actual length of the steel part, as measured by a laser measurement device, and the specified length of the steel part.

For example, the first value, -0.002, represents a steel part that is 0.002 inch shorter than the specified length.
a. Construct a percentage histogram.
b. Is the steel mill doing a good job meeting the requirements set by the automobile company? Explain.

2.44 Call centers today play an important role in managing day-to-day business communications with customers. Call centers must be monitored with a comprehensive set of metrics so that businesses can better understand the overall performance of those centers. One key metric for measuring overall call center performance is *service level*, the percentage of calls answered by a human agent within a specified number of seconds. The file ServiceLevel contains the following data for time, in seconds, to answer 50 incoming calls to a financial services call center:

16 14 16 19 6 14 15 5 16 18 17 22 6 18 10 15 12
 6 19 16 16 15 13 25 9 17 12 10 5 15 23 11 12 14
24 9 10 13 14 26 19 20 13 24 28 15 21 8 16 12

a. Construct a percentage histogram and a percentage polygon.
b. Construct a cumulative percentage polygon.
c. What can you conclude about call center performance if the service level target is set as "80% of calls answered within 20 seconds"?

2.45 The financial services call center in Problem 2.44 also monitors call duration, which is the amount of time spent speaking to customers on the phone. The file CallDuration contains the following data for time, in seconds, spent by agents talking to 50 customers.

243 290 199 240 125 151 158 66 350 1141 251 385 239
139 181 111 136 250 313 154 78 264 123 314 135 99
420 112 239 208 65 133 213 229 154 377 69 170 261
230 273 288 180 296 235 243 167 227 384 331

a. Construct a percentage histogram and a percentage polygon.
b. Construct a cumulative percentage polygon.
c. What can you conclude about call center performance if a call duration target of less than 240 seconds is set?

2.46 The file Bulbs contains the life (in hours) of a sample of forty 6-watt light emitting diode (LED) light bulbs produced by Manufacturer A and a sample of forty 6-watt light emitting diode (LED) light bulbs produced by Manufacturer B.

Use the following class interval widths for each distribution:

Manufacturer A: 46,500 but less than 47,500; 47,500 but less than 48,500; and so on.
Manufacturer B: 47,500 but less than 48,500; 48,500 but less than 49,500; and so on.

a. Construct percentage histograms on separate graphs and plot the percentage polygons on one graph.
b. Plot cumulative percentage polygons on one graph.
c. Which manufacturer has bulbs with a longer life—Manufacturer A or Manufacturer B? Explain.

2.47 The data stored in Drink represents the amount of soft drink in a sample of fifty 2-liter bottles.
a. Construct a histogram and a percentage polygon.
b. Construct a cumulative percentage polygon.
c. On the basis of the results in (a) and (b), does the amount of soft drink filled in the bottles concentrate around specific values?

2.5 Visualizing Two Numerical Variables

Visualizing two numerical variables together can reveal possible relationships between two variables and serve as a basis for applying the methods that Chapters 13 through 16 discuss. To visualize two numerical variables, you use a scatter plot. For the special case in which one of the two variables represents the passage of time, you use a time-series plot.

The Scatter Plot

A **scatter plot** explores the possible relationship between two numerical variables by plotting the values of one numerical variable on the horizontal, or *X*, axis and the values of a second numerical variable on the vertical, or *Y*, axis. For example, a marketing analyst could study the effectiveness of advertising by comparing advertising expenses and sales revenues of 50 stores by using the *X* axis to represent advertising expenses and the *Y* axis to represent sales revenues.

EXAMPLE 2.12

Scatter Plot for NBA Investment Analysis

Suppose that you are an investment analyst who has been asked to review the valuations of the 30 NBA professional basketball teams. You seek to know if the value of a team reflects its revenues. You collect revenue and valuation data (both in $millions) for all 30 NBA teams, organize the data as Table 2.12, and store the data in NBAValues.

TABLE 2.12
Revenues and Values for NBA Teams

Team Code	Revenue ($millions)	Current Value ($millions)	Team Code	Revenue ($millions)	Current Value ($millions)	Team Code	Revenue ($millions)	Current Value ($millions)
ATL	142	825	HOU	237	1500	OKC	157	950
BOS	181	2100	IND	138	840	ORL	143	900
BKN	220	1700	LAC	176	2000	PHI	124	700
CHA	142	750	LAL	304	2700	PHX	154	1000
CHI	228	2300	MEM	147	780	POR	157	975
CLE	191	1100	MIA	180	1300	SAC	141	925
DAL	177	1400	MIL	126	675	SAS	170	1150
DEN	140	855	MIN	146	720	TOR	163	980
DET	154	850	NOH	142	650	UTA	146	875
GSW	201	1900	NYK	307	3000	WAS	146	960

To quickly visualize a possible relationship between team revenues and valuations, you construct the Figure 2.17 scatter plot, in which you plot the revenues on the *X* axis and the value of the team on the *Y* axis.

SOLUTION From Figure 2.17, you see that there appears to be a strong increasing (positive) relationship between revenues and the value of a team. In other words, teams that generate a smaller amount of revenues have a lower value, while teams that generate higher revenues have a higher value. This relationship has been highlighted by the addition of a linear regression prediction line that Chapter 13 explains.

▶*(continued)*

FIGURE 2.17
Scatter plot of revenue
and value for NBA teams

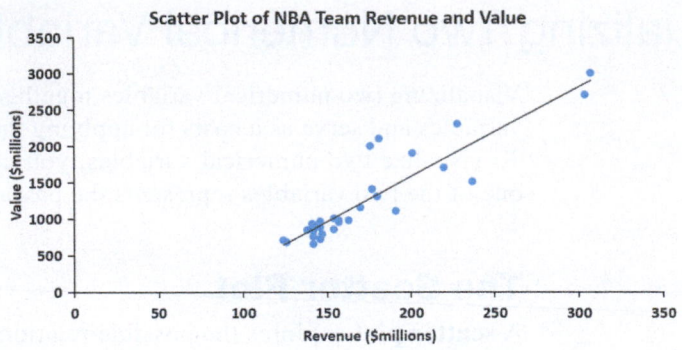

Other pairs of variables may have a decreasing (negative) relationship in which one variable decreases as the other increases. In other situations, there may be a weak or no relationship between the variables.

learnMORE

Read the SHORT TAKES for Chapter 2 for an example that illustrates a negative relationship.

The Time-Series Plot

A **time-series plot** plots the values of a numerical variable on the Y axis and plots the time period associated with each numerical value on the X axis. A time-series plot can help you visualize trends in data that occur over time.

EXAMPLE 2.13

Time-Series Plot
for Movie Revenues

As an investment analyst who specializes in the entertainment industry, you are interested in discovering any long-term trends in movie revenues. You collect the annual revenues (in $billions) for movies released from 1995 to 2016, organize the data as Table 2.13, and store the data in Movie Revenues .

To see if there is a trend over time, you construct the time-series plot shown in Figure 2.18.

TABLE 2.13
Movie Revenues
(in $billions) from
1995 to 2016

Year	Revenue ($billions)	Year	Revenue ($billions)	Year	Revenue ($billions)
1995	5.29	2002	9.19	2009	10.65
1996	5.59	2003	9.35	2010	10.54
1997	6.51	2004	9.11	2011	10.19
1998	6.79	2005	8.93	2012	10.83
1999	7.30	2006	9.25	2013	10.90
2000	7.48	2007	9.63	2014	10.36
2001	8.13	2008	9.95	2015	11.13
				2016	11.38

Source: Data extracted from **www.the-numbers.com/market**

SOLUTION From Figure 2.18, you see that there was a steady increase in the annual movie revenues between 1995 and 2016, followed by an overall upward trend which includes some downturns, reaching new highs in both 2015 and 2016. During that time, the revenues increased from under $6 billion in 1995 to more than $11 billion in 2015 and 2016.

▶*(continued)*

FIGURE 2.18
Time-series plot of
movie revenues per year
from 1995 to 2016

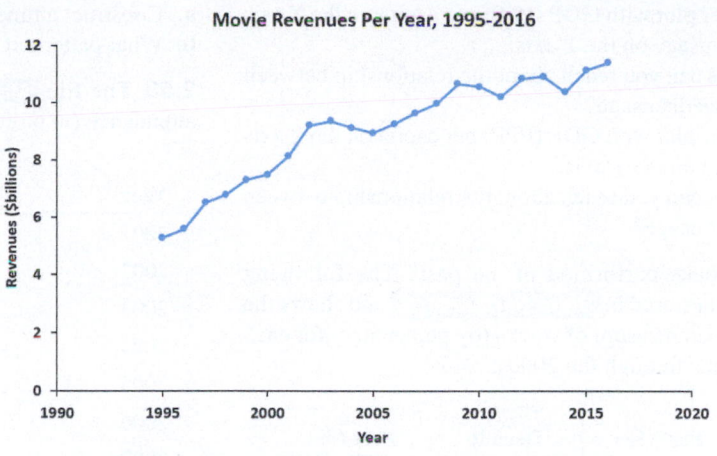

Movie Revenues Per Year, 1995-2016

PROBLEMS FOR SECTION 2.5

LEARNING THE BASICS

2.48 The following is a set of data from a sample of $n = 11$ items:

　　X:　7　5　8　3　6　0　2　4　9　5　8

　　Y:　1　5　4　9　8　0　6　2　7　5　4

a. Construct a scatter plot.
b. Is there a relationship between X and Y? Explain.

2.49 The following is a series of annual sales (in $millions) over an 11-year period (2007 to 2017):

Year:　2007 2008 2009 2010 2011 2012 2013 2014 2015 2016 2017

Sales:　13.0 17.0 19.0 20.0 20.5 20.5 20.5 20.0 19.0 17.0 13.0
a. Construct a time-series plot.
b. Does there appear to be any change in annual sales over time? Explain.

APPLYING THE CONCEPTS

✓ **SELF TEST** **2.50** Movie companies need to predict the gross receipts of individual movies once a movie has debuted. The following results, stored in **PotterMovies**, are the first weekend gross, the U.S. gross, and the worldwide gross (in $millions) of the eight Harry Potter movies:

Title	First Weekend ($millions)	U.S. Gross ($millions)	World-wide Gross ($millions)
Sorcerer's Stone	90.295	317.558	976.458
Chamber of Secrets	88.357	261.988	878.988
Prisoner of Azkaban	93.687	249.539	795.539
Goblet of Fire/	102.335	290.013	896.013
Order of the Phoenix	77.108	292.005	938.469
Half-Blood Prince	77.836	301.460	934.601
Deathly Hallows Part I	125.017	295.001	955.417
Deathly Hallows Part II	169.189	381.011	1,328.111

Source: Data extracted from **www.the-numbers.com/interactive/comp-Harry-Potter.php**

a. Construct a scatter plot with first weekend gross on the X axis and U.S. gross on the Y axis.

b. Construct a scatter plot with first weekend gross on the X axis and worldwide gross on the Y axis.
c. What can you say about the relationship between first weekend gross and U.S. gross and first weekend gross and worldwide gross?

2.51 Data were collected on the typical cost of dining at American-cuisine restaurants within a 1-mile walking distance of a hotel located in a large city. The file **Bundle** contains the typical cost (a per transaction cost in $) as well as a Bundle score, a measure of overall popularity and customer loyalty, for each of 40 selected restaurants.

Source: Data extracted from **www.bundle.com** via the link **on-msn.com/MnlBxo**.

a. Construct a scatter plot with Bundle score on the X axis and typical cost on the Y axis.
b. What conclusions can you reach about the relationship between Bundle score and typical cost?

2.52 The file **MobileSpeed** contains the overall download and upload speeds in mbps for nine carriers in the United States.

Source: Data extracted from "Best Mobile Network 2016", **bit.ly/1KGPrMm**, accessed November 10, 2016.

a. Do you think that carriers with a higher overall download speed also have a higher overall upload speed?
b. Construct a scatter plot with download speed on the X axis and upload speed on the Y axis.
c. Does the scatter plot confirm or contradict your answer in (a)?

2.53 A Pew Research Center survey found a noticeable rise in smartphone ownership and Internet usage in emerging and developing nations. Once online, adults in these nations are hungry for social interaction. The file **GlobalIntenetUsage** contains the level of Internet usage, measured as the percentage of adults polled who use the Internet as least occasionally or report owning a smartphone, and the file **GlobalSocialMedia** contains the level of social media networking, measured as the percentage of Internet users who use social media sites, as well as the GDP at purchasing power parity (PPP, current international $) per capita for each of 28 emerging and developing countries.

Source: Data extracted from Pew Research Center, "Smartphone Ownership and Internet Usage Continues to Climb in Emerging Economies," February 22, 2016, **bit.ly/2oRv0rp**.

a. Construct a scatter plot with GDP (PPP) per capita on the X axis and social media usage on the Y axis.

b. What conclusions can you reach about the relationship between GDP and social media usage?

c. Construct a scatter plot with GDP (PPP) per capita on the X axis and Internet usage on the Y axis.

d. What conclusions can you reach about the relationship between GDP and Internet usage?

2.54 How have stocks performed in the past? The following table presents the data stored in Stock Performance and shows the performance of a broad measure of stocks (by percentage) for each decade from the 1830s through the 2000s:

Decade	Perf (%)	Decade	Perf (%)
1830s	2.8	1920s	13.3
1840s	12.8	1930s	−2.2
1850s	6.6	1940s	9.6
1860s	12.5	1950s	18.2
1870s	7.5	1960s	8.3
1880s	6.0	1970s	6.6
1890s	5.5	1980s	16.6
1900s	10.9	1990s	17.6
1910s	2.2	2000s*	−0.5

*Through December 15, 2009.

Source: Data extracted from T. Lauricella, "Investors Hope the '10s Beat the '00s," *The Wall Street Journal*, December 21, 2009, pp. C1, C2.

a. Construct a time-series plot of the stock performance from the 1830s to the 2000s.

b. Does there appear to be any pattern in the data?

2.55 The file NewHomeSales contains the number of new homes sold (in thousands) and the median sales price of new single-family houses sold in the United States recorded at the end of each month from January 2000 through December 2016.

Source: Data extracted from **bit.ly/2eEcIBR**, accessed March 19, 2017.

a. Construct a times series plot of new home sales prices.

b. What pattern, if any, is present in the data?

2.56 The file Movie Attendance16 contains the yearly movie attendance (in billions) from 2001 through 2016.

Year	Attendance	Year	Attendance
2001	1.44	2009	1.41
2002	1.58	2010	1.34
2003	1.55	2011	1.28
2004	1.47	2012	1.36
2005	1.38	2013	1.34
2006	1.41	2014	1.27
2007	1.40	2015	1.32
2008	1.34	2016	1.32

Source: Data extracted from **boxofficemojo.com/yearly**.

a. Construct a time-series plot for the movie attendance (in billions).

b. What pattern, if any, is present in the data?

2.57 The Super Bowl is a big viewing event watched by close to 200 million Americans that is also a big event for advertisers. The file SuperBowlAds contains the number of ads that ran between the opening kickoff and the final whistle and the total elapsed run time (in minutes) of the commercials for the 2006 to 2015 seasons.

Source: Data extracted from "SuperBowl Viewers Don't Just Watch the Game, *USA Today*, February 5, 2016, p. 3B.

a. Construct a time-series plot.

b. What pattern, if any, is present in the number of ads that ran between the opening kickoff and the final whistle?

c. What pattern, if any, is present in the total elapsed run time (in minutes) of the commercials for the 2006 to 2015 seasons?

2.6 Organizing a Mix of Variables

Earlier sections of this chapter discuss organizing one or two variables of the same type, either categorical or numeric variables. Organizing a mix of many variables into one tabular summary, called a **multidimensional contingency table**, is also possible. Although any number of variables could be theoretically used in multidimensional contingency tables, using many variables together or using a categorical variable that has many categories will produce results that will be hard to comprehend and interpret. As a practical rule, these tables should be limited to no more than three or four variables, which limits their usefulness when exploring sets of data with many variables or analysis that involves big data.[1]

In typical use, these tables either display statistics about each joint response from multiple categorical variables as frequencies or percentages or display statistics about a numerical variable for each joint response from multiple categorical variables. The first form extends contingency tables (see Section 2.1) to two or more row or column variables. The second form replaces the tallies found in a contingency table with summary information about a numeric variable. Figure 2.19 illustrates the first form, adding the variable Market Cap to the Figure 2.2 PivotTable contingency table of Fund Type and Risk Level.

[1]All of the examples in this book follow this rule.

FIGURE 2.19

PivotTables of Fund Type and Risk Level (based on Figure 2.2) and Fund Type, Market Cap, and Risk Level for the sample of the 479 retirement funds

Fund Type ▾	Risk Level ▾ Low	Average	High	Grand Total
Growth	13.15%	31.73%	19.00%	63.88%
Value	17.54%	15.03%	3.55%	36.12%
Grand Total	**30.69%**	**46.76%**	**22.55%**	**100.00%**

Fund Type ▾	Risk Level ▾ Low	Average	High	Grand Total
⊟ Growth	13.2%	31.7%	19.0%	63.88%
Large	9.6%	19.0%	3.5%	32.2%
MidCap	3.3%	9.4%	5.2%	18.0%
Small	0.2%	3.3%	10.2%	13.8%
⊟ Value	17.5%	15.0%	3.5%	36.1%
Large	14.6%	7.9%	0.6%	23.2%
MidCap	2.1%	3.5%	0.8%	6.5%
Small	0.8%	3.5%	2.1%	6.5%
Grand Total	**30.69%**	**46.76%**	**22.55%**	**100.00%**

Entries in this new multidimensional contingency table have been formatted as percentages of the whole with one decimal place to facilitate comparisons. The new table reveals patterns in the sample of retirement funds that a table of just Risk Level and Fund Type would not such as:

- The pattern of risk for Fund Type when Market Cap is considered can be very different than the summary pattern that Figure 2.2 shows.
- A majority of the large and midcap growth funds have average risk, but most small growth funds have high risk.
- Nearly two-thirds of large market cap value funds have low risk, while a majority of midcap and small value funds have average risk.

student TIP

Chapter 3 discusses descriptive statistics for numerical variables, including the mean, also known as the average, that the Figure 2.20 table uses.

Figure 2.20 illustrates the second form of a multidimensional contingency table. To form this table, the numerical variable 10YrReturn has been added to the Figure 2.19 PivotTable of Fund Type, Market Cap, and Risk Level. Note that the numerical variable appears as a statistic that summarizes the variable data, as the mean in these tables. That multidimensional contingency tables can only display a single descriptive statistic for a numerical variable is a limitation of such tables.

Figure 2.20 shows the same PivotTable in two states, with Market Cap *collapsed* into Fund Type (left) and Market Cap *fully expanded* (right). In the collapsed table, funds with high risk have the lowest mean ten-year return percentages. The expanded table discovers that large

FIGURE 2.20

PivotTable (in two states) of Fund Type, Market Cap, and Risk Level, displaying the mean ten-year return percentage for the sample of the 479 retirement funds.

Mean 10YrReturn Fund Type ▾	Risk Level ▾ Low	Average	High	Grand Total
⊞ Growth	8.06	7.78	7.19	7.66
⊞ Value	6.45	6.52	5.97	6.43
Grand Total	**7.14**	**7.38**	**7.00**	**7.22**

Mean 10YrReturn Fund Type ▾	Risk Level ▾⌄ Average	High	Low	Grand Total
⊟ Growth	7.78	7.19	8.06	7.66
Large	7.91	7.88	8.04	7.94
MidCap	7.41	6.60	8.10	7.30
Small	8.14	7.25	8.47	7.49
⊟ Value	6.52	5.97	6.45	6.43
Large	5.87	4.18	6.30	6.10
MidCap	7.69	6.15	6.99	7.27
Small	6.79	6.43	7.61	6.78
Grand Total	**7.38**	**7.00**	**7.14**	**7.22**

growth funds with high risk have one the *highest* mean ten-year return percentages, something not suggested by the collapsed table. The expanded table also reveals that midcap value funds with average risk have the highest mean ten-year return percentage among all value funds.

Drill-down

In addition to their utility to report summaries of variables, multidimensional contingency tables can **drill down** to reveal the data that the table summarizes. When you drill down, you reveal a less summarized form of the data. Expanding a collapsed variable, such as Figure 2.20 demonstrates, is an example of drilling down. In Excel and JMP, you can easily drill down by double-clicking a joint response cell in a multidimensional contingency table. When you double-click a cell, Excel displays the rows of data associated with the joint response in a new worksheet, while JMP highlights those rows in the worksheet data table that is the source for the multidimensional contingency table.

Figure 2.21 shows the drill-down of the small value funds with low risk cell of the Figure 2.20 PivotTables. This drill-down reveals that the ten-year return percentage for this group of four funds ranges from 4.83% to 9.44%, and that the values of some of the other numeric variables also greatly vary.

	Turnover Ratio	SD	Sharpe Ratio	Beta	1YrReturn	3YrReturn	5YrReturn	10YrReturn	Expense Ratio	Star Rating
2	75.00	4.67	0.53	0.20	4.74	2.53	4.82	9.44	1.40	Four
3	23.00	9.61	0.72	0.84	7.74	6.95	8.17	7.30	1.28	Four
4	30.10	10.71	0.70	0.55	5.88	7.60	7.74	4.83	1.70	Two
5	37.00	11.73	0.71	0.79	6.02	8.45	9.29	8.85	0.81	Four

2.7 Visualizing a Mix of Variables

Earlier sections of this chapter discuss visualizing one or two variables of the same type, either categorical or numeric. Visualizing a mix of many variables is also possible and has the following advantages over multidimensional contingency tables:

- More data and more variables can be presented in a form more manageable to review than a table with many row and column variables
- The data, not summary descriptive statistics, can be shown for numerical variables
- Multiple numerical variables can be presented in one summarization
- Visualizations can reveal patterns that can be hard to see in tables

These qualities make visualizations of a mix of variables helpful during initial exploratory data analysis and often a necessity in business analytics applications, especially when such techniques are analyzing big data.

Colored Scatter Plot

Because of the relative newness of these visualizations, Excel, JMP, and Minitab use different ways to visualize a mix of data. Sometimes these programs confusingly use the *same* name to refer to a visual that works *differently* from program to program. For example, JMP and Minitab can create a **colored scatter plot** that can visualize two (and sometimes more than two) numerical variables and at least one categorical variable.

The default JMP color theme may prove problematic for those with certain types of color vision deficiencies ("color blindness"). The color theme can be changed, as the JMP Guide explains.

For example, Figure 2.22 presents a colored scatter plot of the Expense Ratio and 3YrReturn numerical variables and the Market Cap categorical variable for the sample of 479 retirement funds. This visual reveals that for the three-year period, funds with large market capitalizations (red dots) tend to have the best returns and the lowest cost expense ratios (in other words, plot in the lower right quadrant of the chart). However, there are a number of large market cap funds that plot *elsewhere* on the chart, representing funds with relatively high expense ratios or fair to poor three-year returns. For certain types of analyses, the points represented those funds might be drilled down to determine reasons for their different behavior or identify such funds as relative laggards in the set of all large market cap funds.

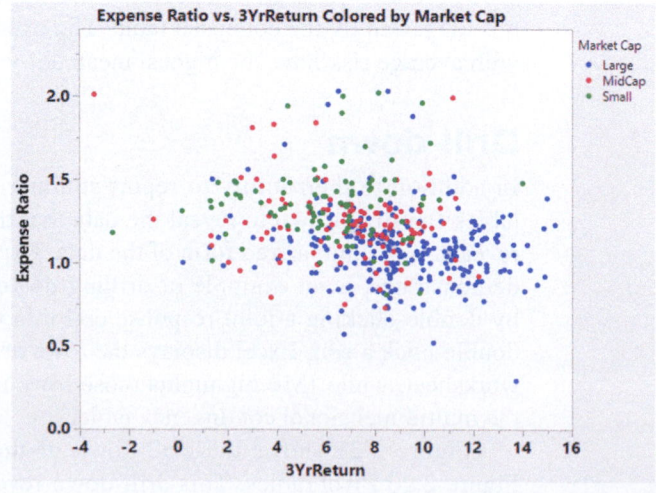

Because they can compare two numerical variables and one categorical variable, colored scatter plots can be considered an "opposite" of multidimensional contingency tables that summarize the two categorical variables and one numerical variable.

Bubble Charts

Bubble charts extend color scatter plots by using the size of the points, now called bubbles, to represent an additional variable. In Excel and Minitab, that additional variable must be numerical, while in JMP the variable can be either numerical or categorical. JMP also permits coloring and sizing of the bubbles as ways of representing additional variables and can handle time series data in a unique way. (Chapter 17 discusses and presents examples of bubble charts.)

PivotChart (Excel)

PivotCharts pull out and visualize specific categories from a PivotTable summary in a way that would otherwise be hard to do in Excel. For example, Figure 2.23 (left) displays a side-by-side PivotChart based on the Figure 2.20 PivotTables of Fund Type, Market Cap, and Risk Level, that displays the mean ten-year return percentage for the sample of the 479 retirement funds. Filtering the chart to display the mean ten-year return percentages for only low risk funds, Figure 2.23 (right), highlights that small market cap growth funds have the highest mean ten-year return percentage.

Treemap (Excel, JMP)

learnMORE

Chapter 17 illustrates an application of the more elaborate version of a treemap.

Treemaps show proportions of the whole of nested categories as colored tiles. In the simplest case (Excel), the size of tiles corresponds to the tallies in a joint response cell in a contingency table. In a more elaborate version (JMP), the tiles can be sized to a numerical variable. Figure 2.24 on page 74 presents Excel and JMP treemaps (simplest case) for Fund Type and Market Cap. Note that Excel can only color the treemap by the categories of first categorical variable (Fund Type), while JMP can color analogous subcategories (the Market Cap categories) while dividing the treemap into parts based on the first categorical variable.

FIGURE 2.23
PivotCharts based on the Figure 2.20 PivotTable of Fund Type, Market Cap, and Risk Level, showing the mean ten-year return percentage

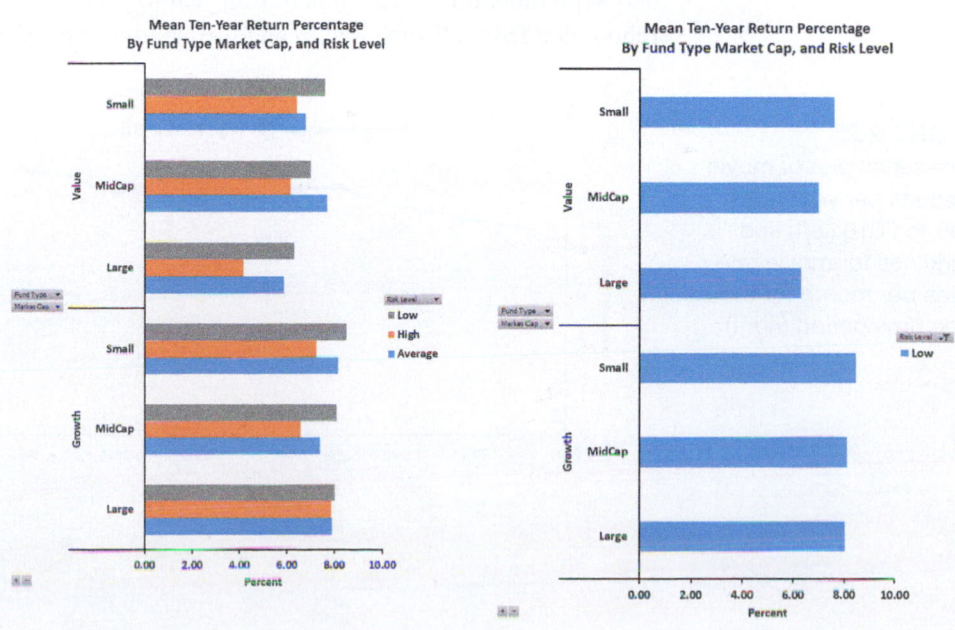

FIGURE 2.24
Excel and JMP treemaps for Fund Type and Market Cap

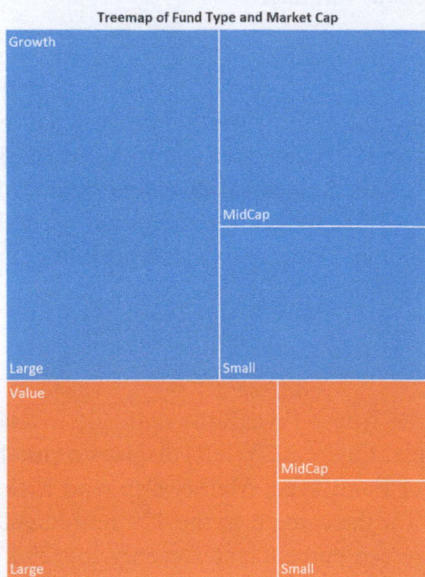
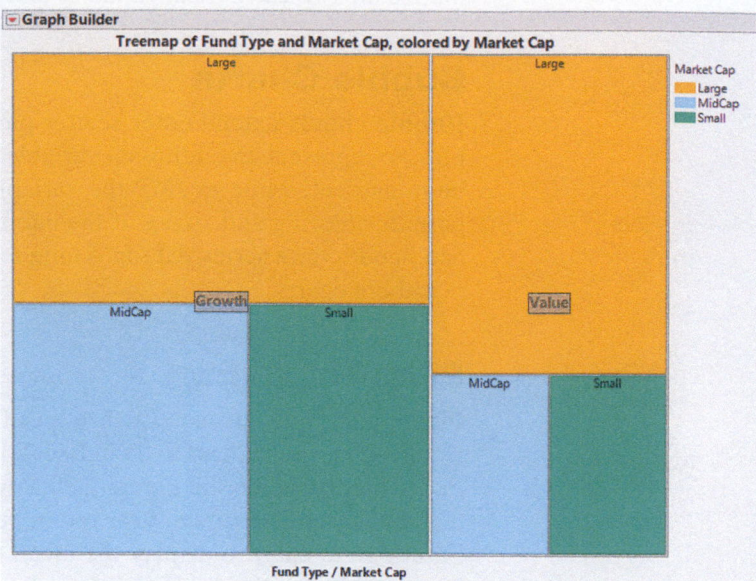

Sparklines (Excel)

Sparklines are compact time-series visualizations of numerical variables. This compact form allows you to view all the visualizations together, which can aid in making comparisons among the variables. Sparklines highlight the trends of the plots over the precise graphing of points found in a time-series plot. Although typically used to plot several independent numerical variables, such as several different business indicators, sparklines can also be used to plot time-series data using smaller time units than a time-series plot to reveal patterns that the time-series plot may not.

For example, Figure 2.25 (left) contains a time-series plot of annual movie revenues (in $billions) from 2005 through 2016, a subset of the data used in Example 2.13 on page 69. Figure 2.25 (right) contains a set of sparklines that plot movie revenues for each month of specific years. The sparklines reveal that movie revenues for the months of February and September do not vary much from year to year, while the monthly revenues for July have rebounded from all-time low to an all-time high for the period 2005–2016.

FIGURE 2.25

Time-series plot of movie revenues per year from 2005 to 2016 (left) and sparklines for movie revenues per month for the same time period (right)

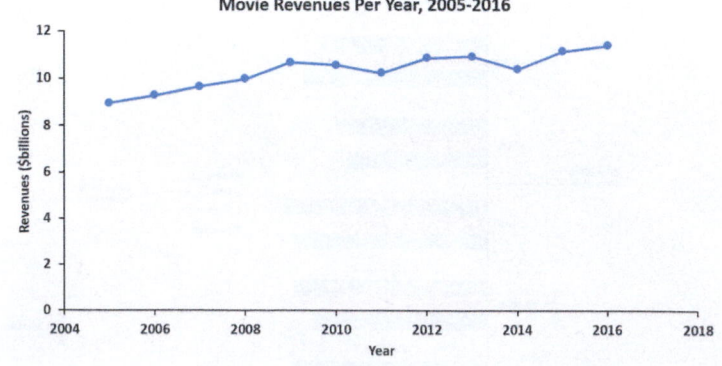

2.8 Filtering and Querying Data

Associated with preparing tabular or visual summaries are two operations that extract subsets of the variables under study. **Data filtering** selects rows of data that match criteria, specified values for specific variables. For example, using the filter that selects all rows in which Fund Type is value, would select 173 rows from the sample of 479 retirement funds that this chapter uses in various examples. In the context of this chapter, **querying** can be a more interactive version of filtering and a method that may not select all of the columns of the matching rows depending how the querying is done.

Chapter 1 discusses the same JMP Select Rows dialog box in the context of data cleaning.

Excel, JMP, and Minitab all have data filtering and query features that vary in their implementation and degree of interactivity and JMP has two complementary ways of filtering a data table). Both JMP and Minitab use row-based filtering that can be expressed as a comparison between a variable and a value or value range. Figure 2.26 shows the JMP Select Rows and the Minitab Subset Worksheet dialog boxes with entries that select all rows in value retirement funds that have ten-year return percentages that are greater than or equal to 9.

FIGURE 2.26
JMP and Minitab subsetting dialog boxes for data filtering

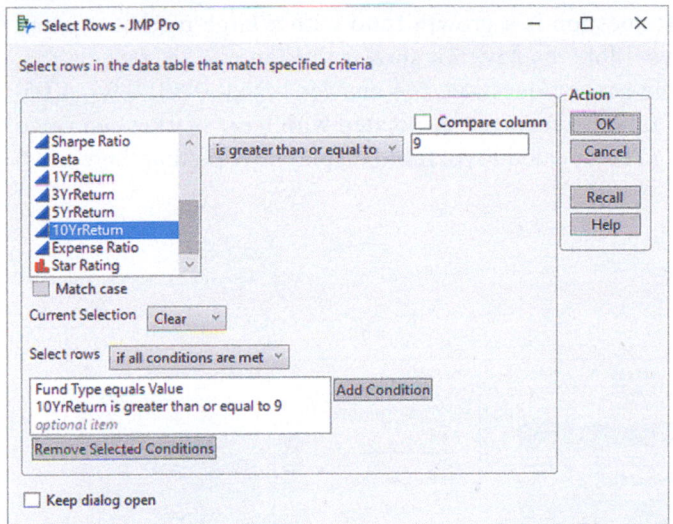
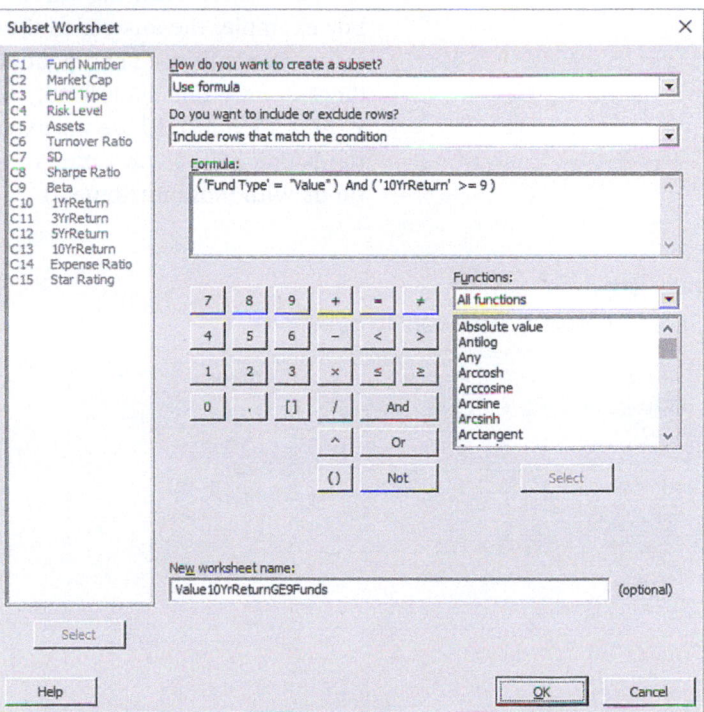

In Excel, selecting **Data ➜ Filter** displays pull-down menus for each column in row 1 cells. In those menus, check boxes for each unique value in the column appear and check boxes can be cleared or checked to select specific values or ranges. Excel also contains *slicers* that filter and query data from a PivotTable.

Excel Slicers

A **slicer** is a panel of clickable buttons that appears superimposed over a worksheet and is unique to a variable in the associated PivotTable. Each button in a slicer represents a unique value of the variable as found in the source data for the PivotTable. You create a slicer for any variable that has been *associated* with a PivotTable, whether or not a variable has been inserted into the PivotTable. This allows you to work with many variables at once in a way that avoids creating an overly complex multidimensional contingency table that would be hard to comprehend and interpret.

By clicking buttons in the slicer panels, you query the data. For example, the Figure 2.27 worksheet contains slicers for the Fund Type, Market Cap, Star Rating, and Expense Ratio variables and a PivotTable that has been associated with the variables stored in the DATA worksheet of the Retirement Funds workbook.

FIGURE 2.27

PivotTable and slicers for the retirement funds sample data

In JMP, selecting
Rows → Data Filter
displays the Data Filter window that contains buttons and sliders analogous to the Excel slider panel.

	A	B	C	D	E	F	G	H	I	J	K	L	M	N
1	PivotTable of Fund Type and Risk Level													
2						**Fund Type**			**Star Rating**			**Expense Ratio**		
3		Risk Level ▼				Growth			Five			0.29		
4	Fund Type ▼	Low	Average	High	Grand Total	Value			Four			0.52		
5	Growth	63	152	91	306				One			0.57		
6	Value	84	72	17	173	**Market Cap**			Three			0.66		
7	Grand Total	147	224	108	479	Large			Two			0.67		
8						MidCap						0.71		
9						Small						0.73		
10												0.74		

With these four slicers, you can ask questions about the data, for example, "What are the attributes of the fund(s) with the lowest expense ratio?" and "What are the expense ratios associated with large market cap value funds that have a star rating of five?" These questions can be answered by clicking the appropriate buttons of the four slicers. For example, Figure 2.28 displays slicers that answer the two questions. Note that Excel dims, or disables, the buttons representing values that the current data filtering excludes to highlight answers. For example, the answer to the first question is a growth fund with a large market cap and a five-star rating. (The updated PivotTable display, not shown in Figure 2.28, reveals that there is only one such fund.) For the second question, the answer is that 0.83, 0.94, 1.05, 1.09, 1.18, and 1.19 are the expense ratio percentages associated with large market cap value funds that have a star rating of five. (The updated PivotTable display reveals that there are 6 funds with those attributes.)

FIGURE 2.28

Slicer displays for answers to questions

PROBLEMS FOR SECTIONS 2.6 THROUGH 2.8

APPLYING THE CONCEPTS

2.58 Using the sample of retirement funds stored in Retirement Funds :

a. Construct a table that tallies Fund Type, Market Cap, and Star Rating.

b. What conclusions can you reach concerning differences among the types of retirement funds (growth and value), based on Market Cap (small, mid-cap, and large) and Star Rating (one, two, three, four, and five)?

c. Construct a table that computes the average three-year return for each fund type, market cap, and star rating.

d. Drill down to examine the large cap growth funds with a rating of three. How many funds are there? What conclusions can you reach about these funds?

2.59 Using the sample of retirement funds stored in Retirement Funds :

a. Construct a table that tallies, Market Cap, Risk Level, and Star Rating.

b. What conclusions can you reach concerning differences among the funds based on Market Cap (small, mid-cap, and large), Risk Level (low, average, and high), and Star Rating (one, two, three, four, and five)?

c. Construct a table that computes the average three-year return for each market cap, risk level, and star rating.

d. Drill down to examine the large cap funds that are high risk with a rating of three. How many funds are there? What conclusions can you reach about these funds?

2.60 Using the sample of retirement funds stored in Retirement Funds :
a. Construct a table that tallies Fund Type, Risk Level and Star Rating.
b. What conclusions can you reach concerning differences among the types of retirement funds, based on the risk levels and star ratings?
c. Construct a table that computes the average three-year return for each fund type, risk level, and star rating.
d. Drill down to examine the growth funds with high risk with a rating of three. How many funds are there? What conclusions can you reach about these funds?

2.61 Using the sample of retirement funds stored in Retirement Funds :
a. Construct a table that tallies type, market cap, risk, and rating.
b. What conclusions can you reach concerning differences among the types of funds based on market cap categories, risk levels, and star ratings?
c. Which do you think is easier to interpret: the table for this problem or the ones for problems 2.58 through 2.60? Explain.
d. Compare the results of this table with those of Figure 2.19 and problems 2.58 through 2.60. What differences can you observe?

2.62 In the sample of 479 retirement funds (Retirement Funds), what are the attributes of the fund with the highest five-year return?

2.63 Using the sample of retirement funds stored in Retirement Funds :
a. Construct a chart that visualizes SD and Assets by Risk Level.
b. Construct a chart that visualizes SD and Assets by Fund Type. Rescale the Assets axis, if necessary, to see more detail.
c. How do the patterns that you can observe in both charts differ? What data relationships, if any, do those patterns suggest?

2.64 In the sample of 479 retirement funds (Retirement Funds), which funds in the sample have the lowest five-year return?

2.65 Using the sample of retirement funds stored in Retirement Funds :
a. Construct one chart that visualizes 10YrReturn and 1YrReturn by Market Cap.
b. Construct one chart that visualizes 5YrReturn and 1YrReturn by Market Cap.
c. How does the patterns to the points of each market cap category change between the two charts?
d. What can you deduce about return percentages in years 6 through 10 included in 10YrReturn but not included in 5YrReturn?

2.66 In the sample of 479 retirement funds (Retirement Funds), what characteristics are associated with the funds that have the lowest five-year return?

2.67 The data in NewHomeSales includes the median sales price of new single-family houses sold in the United States recorded at the end of each month from January 2000 through December 2016.

Source: Data extracted from **bit.ly/2eEcIBR**, March 19, 2017.

a. Construct sparklines of new home sales prices by year.
b. What conclusions can you reach concerning the median sales price of new single-family houses sold in the United States from January 2000 through December 2016?
c. Compare the sparklines in (a) to the time-series plot in Problem 2.55 on p. 70.

2.68 The file Natural Gas includes the monthly average commercial price for natural gas (dollars per thousand cubic feet) in the United States from January 1, 2008, to December 2016.

Source: Data extracted from "U.S. Natural Gas Prices," **bit.ly/2oZIQ5Z**, March 19, 2017.

a. Construct a sparkline of the monthly average commercial price for natural gas (dollars per thousand cubic feet) by year.
b. What conclusions can you reach concerning the monthly average commercial price for natural gas (dollars per thousand cubic feet)?

2.9 Pitfalls in Organizing and Visualizing Variables

The tabular and visual summaries that you create when you organize and visualize your variables of interest can jumpstart the analysis of the variables. However, you must be careful not to produce results that will be hard to comprehend and interpret or to present your data in ways that undercut the usefulness of the methods discussed in this chapter. You can too easily create summaries that obscure the data or create false impressions that would lead to misleading or unproductive analysis. The challenge in organizing and visualizing variables is to avoid these complications.

Obscuring Data

Management specialists have long known that information overload, presenting too many details, can obscure data and hamper decision making (see reference 4). Both tabular summaries and visualizations can suffer from this problem. For example, consider the Figure 2.29 side-by-side bar chart that shows percentages of the overall total for subgroups formed from combinations of fund type, market cap, risk, and star rating. While this chart highlights that there are more large-cap retirement funds with low risk and a three-star rating than any other combination of risk and star rating, other details about the retirement funds

FIGURE 2.29
Side-by-side bar chart for the retirement funds sample showing percentage of overall total for fund type, market cap, risk, and star rating

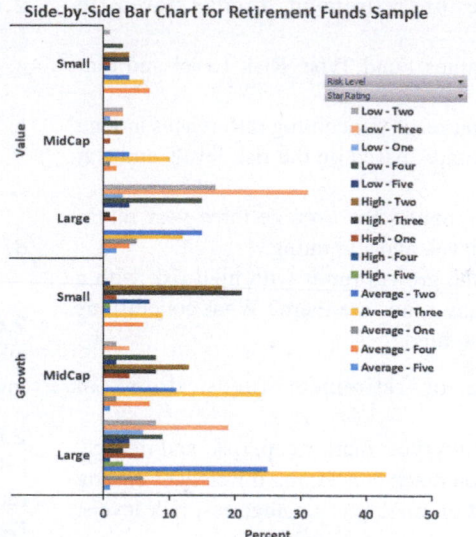

sample are less obvious. The overly complex legend obscures too, and suggests that an equivalent multidimensional contingency table, with 30 joint response cells, would be obscuring, if not overwhelming, for most people.

Creating False Impressions

As you organize and visualize variables, you must be careful not to create false impressions that could affect preliminary conclusions about the data. Selective summarizations and improperly constructed visualizations often create false impressions.

A *selective summarization* is the presentation of only part of the data that have been collected. Frequently, selective summarization occurs when data collected over a long period of time are summarized as percentage changes for a shorter period. For example, Table 2.14 (left) presents the one-year difference in sales of seven auto industry companies for the month of April. The selective summarization tells a different story, particularly for company G, than does Table 2.14 (right) that shows the year-to-year differences for a three-year period that included the 2008 economic downturn.

TABLE 2.14
Left: One-Year Percentage Change in Year-to-Year Sales for the Month of April; Right: Percentage Change for Three Consecutive Years

Company	Change from Prior Year
A	+7.2
B	+24.4
C	+24.9
D	+24.8
E	+12.5
F	+35.1
G	+29.7

Company	Change from Prior Year		
	Year 1	Year 2	Year 3
A	−22.6	−33.2	+7.2
B	−4.5	−41.9	+24.4
C	−18.5	−31.5	+24.9
D	−29.4	−48.1	+24.8
E	−1.9	−25.3	+12.5
F	−1.6	−37.8	+35.1
G	+7.4	−13.6	+29.7

Improperly constructed charts can also create false impressions. Figure 2.30 shows two pie charts that display the market shares of companies in two industries. How quickly did you notice that both pie charts summarize identical data?

FIGURE 2.30
Market shares of companies in "two" industries

If you want to verify that the two pie charts visualize the same data, open the TwoPies worksheet in the Challenging workbook.

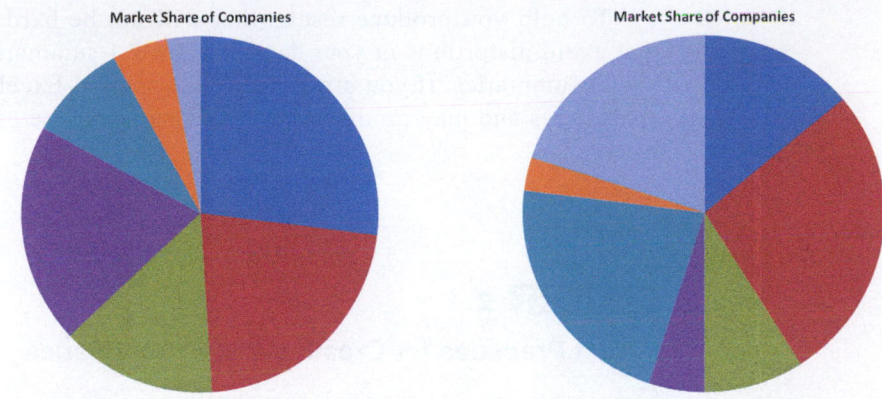

studentTIP

Order pie or doughnut slices from the largest to the smallest slice and color pie and doughnut charts meant for comparison in the same way.

Because of their relative positions and colorings, many people will perceive the dark blue pie slice on the left chart to have a smaller market share than the dark red pie chart on the right chart even though both pie slices represent the company that has 27% market share. In this case, both the ordering of pie slices and the different colorings of the two pie charts contribute to creating the false impression. With other types of charts, improperly scaled axes or a *Y* axis that either does not begin at the origin or is a "broken" axis that is missing intermediate values are other common mistakes that create false impressions.

Chartjunk

Seeking to construct a visualization that can more effectively convey an important point, some people add decorative elements to enhance or replace the simple bar and line shapes of the visualizations discussed in this chapter. While judicious use of such elements may aid in the memorability of a chart (see reference 1), most often such elements either obscure the data or, worse, create a false impression of the data. Such elements are called **chartjunk**.

Figure 2.31 presents a visualization that illustrates mistakes that are common ways of creating chartjunk unintentionally. The grapevine with its leaves and bunch of grapes adds to the clutter of decoration without conveying any useful information. The chart inaccurately shows the 1949–1950 measurement (135,326 acres) at a *higher* point on the *Y* axis than larger values such as the 1969–1970 measurement, 150,300 acres. The inconsistent scale of the *X* axis distorts the time variable. (The last two measurements, eight years apart, are drawn about as far apart as the 30-year gap between 1959 and 1989.) All of these errors create a very wrong impression that obscures the important trend of accelerating growth of land planted in the 1990s.

FIGURE 2.31
Two visualizations of the amount of land planted with grapes for the wine industry

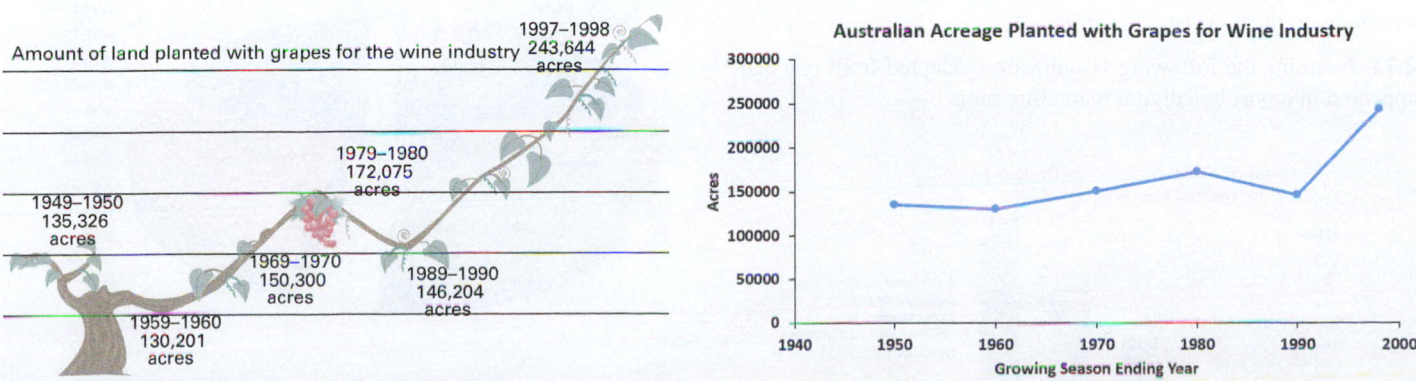

Left illustration adapted from S. Watterson, "Liquid Gold—Australians Are Changing the World of Wine. Even the French Seem Grateful," *Time*, November 22, 1999, p. 68–69.

To help you produce results that will not be hard to comprehend and interpret and that avoid distortions in your data, Exhibit 2.1 summarizes the best practices for creating visual summaries. If you use Excel, be aware that Excel may tempt you to use uncommon chart types and may produce charts that violate some of the best practices that the exhibit lists.

EXHIBIT 2.1

Best Practices for Creating Visual Summaries

- Use the simplest possible visualization
- Include a title and label all axes
- Include a scale for each axis if the chart contains axes
- Begin the scale for a vertical axis at zero and use a constant scale
- Avoid 3D or "exploded" effects and the use of chartjunk
- Use consistent colorings in charts meant to be compared
- Avoid using uncommon chart types including radar, surface, cone, and pyramid charts

PROBLEMS FOR SECTION 2.9

APPLYING THE CONCEPTS

2.69 (Student Project) Bring to class a chart from a website, newspaper, or magazine published recently that you believe to be a poorly drawn representation of a numerical variable. Be prepared to submit the chart to the instructor with comments about why you believe it is inappropriate. Do you believe that the intent of the chart is to purposely mislead the reader? Also, be prepared to present and comment on this in class.

2.70 (Student Project) Bring to class a chart from a website, newspaper, or magazine published this month that you believe to be a poorly drawn representation of a categorical variable. Be prepared to submit the chart to the instructor with comments about why you consider it inappropriate. Do you believe that the intent of the chart is to purposely mislead the reader? Also, be prepared to present and comment on this in class.

2.71 Examine the following visualization, adapted from one that appeared in a post in a digital marketing blog.

a. Describe at least one good feature of this visual display.
b. Describe at least one bad feature of this visual display.
c. Redraw the graph, using the guidelines above.

2.72 Examine the visualization on page 81, adapted from one that appeared in the post "Who Are the Comic Book Fans on Facebook?" on February 2, 2013, as reported by **graphicspolicy.com**.
a. Describe at least one good feature of this visual display.
b. Describe at least one bad feature of this visual display.
c. Redraw the graph, by using best practices given in Exhibit 2.1 above.

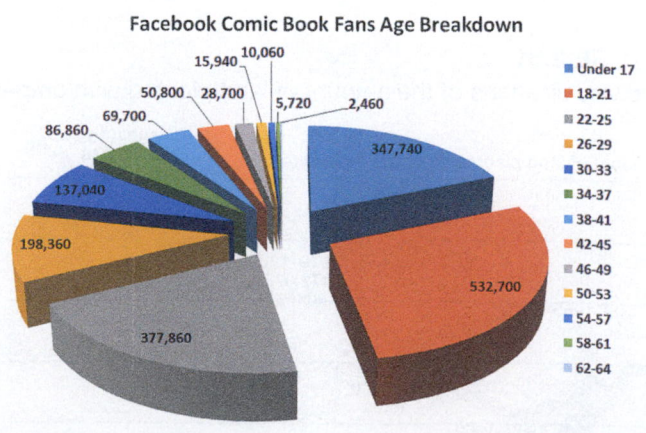

Facebook Comic Book Fans Age Breakdown

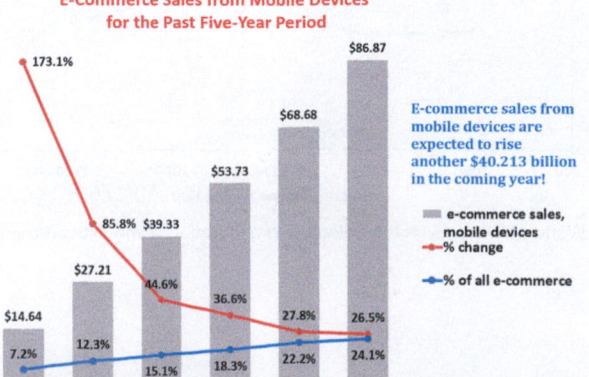

E-Commerce Sales from Mobile Devices for the Past Five-Year Period

2.73 Examine the following visualization, adapted from a management consulting white paper.

When managers believe they will need to make major changes to their IT infrastructure to combat resource scarcity

- 8% — 12 years or more
- 6% — 9-12 Years
- 12% — 4-8 Years
- 25% — 2-4 Years
- 12% — Up to 2 Years
- 23% — Already done!
- 18%

Mid-level managers believe they will not need to make changes for the next **5 years**

a. Describe at least one good feature of this visual display.

b. Describe at least one bad feature of this visual display.

c. Redraw the graph, by using the Exhibit 2.1 guidelines.

2.74 Professor Deanna Oxender Burgess of Florida Gulf Coast University conducted research on annual reports of corporations (see D. Rosato, "Worried About the Numbers? How About the Charts?" *New York Times*, September 15, 2002, p. B7). Burgess found that even slight distortions in a chart changed readers' perception of the information. Using online or library sources, select a corporation and study its most recent annual report. Find at least one chart in the report that you think needs improvement and develop an improved version of the chart. Explain why you believe the improved chart is better than the one included in the annual report.

2.75 Figure 2.4 shows a bar chart and a pie chart for what devices millennials used to watch movies/TV shows (see page 54).

a. Create an exploded pie chart, a cone chart, or a pyramid chart that shows how people paid for purchases and other transactions.

b. Which graphs either seen in Figure 2.4 or created in (a), do you prefer? Explain.

2.76 Figures 2.5 and 2.6 show a bar chart and a pie chart for the risk level for the retirement fund data (see pages 55–56).

a. Create an exploded pie chart, a doughnut chart, a cone chart, and a pyramid chart that show the risk level of retirement funds.

b. Which graphs, either seen in Figures 2.5 and 2.6 or created in (a), do you prefer? Explain.

▼USING **STATISTICS**
"The Choice Is Yours," Revisited

In The Choice *Is* Yours scenario, you were hired to define, collect, organize, and visualize data about a sample of 479 retirement funds in ways that could assist prospective clients to make investment choices. Having verified that each of the 13 variables in the sample were properly defined, you had to consider which tabular and visual summaries were appropriate for each variable and how specific mixes of variables might be used to gain insights about the 479 funds.

From summaries of the risk variable, you learned that nearly half of the funds were of average risk and there are fewer high risk funds than low risk funds. From contingency tables of the fund type and risk level, you observed that high risk funds were proportionally a larger category for growth funds than for value funds. From histograms and percentage polygons of the three-year return percentages, you were able to observe that the three-year returns were higher for the growth funds than for the value funds. Returns for the growth funds were concentrated between 2.5% and 12.5%, with returns for the value funds concentrated between 2.5% and 10%.

From various multi-dimensional contingency tables, you revealed additional relationships. For example, from a table that summarizes fund type, risk level, and market cap, you discovered that nearly two-thirds of large market cap value funds have low risk, while a majority of small and mid-cap value funds have average risk.

You discovered visual summaries that can combine many variables and present data in a more effective and easier-to-explore way than tables. And you also discovered ways to take subsets of the retirement sample for focused analysis. Finally, you learned to avoid the pitfalls that people experience in organizing and visualizing data. You are better prepared to present fund details to prospective clients.

▼SUMMARY

You organize and visualize variables by making tabular and visual summaries. The methods you use vary by the type of variable, as well as the number of variables you seek to organize and visualize at the same time. Table 2.15 summarizes these methods by type of variable and the number of variables being summarized.

Using the appropriate methods to organize and visualize your data allows you to reach preliminary conclusions about the data. In several different chapter examples, tabular and visual summaries helped you reach conclusions about the primary way people pay for purchases and other transactions, the cost of meals at center city and metro area restaurants, and some of the differences among the 479 funds in a retirement fund sample.

Using the appropriate tabular and visual summaries can provide initial insights about your variables and cause you to ask additional questions about your data. Those questions may cause you to use interactive techniques to further explore your data or perform additional analysis at a later time.

Organize and visualize methods can be misused, thereby undermining the usefulness of the tabular and visual summaries those methods create. Following best practices when making visual summaries (see Exhibit 2.1) can minimize common mistakes that lead to displays that obscure data or create a false or misleading impression of data collected.

For numerical variables, there are many additional ways to summarize data that involve computing sample statistics or population parameters. Chapter 3 discusses the most common examples of these *numerical descriptive measures*.

TABLE 2.15
Methods to Organize and Visualize Variables

Categorical variables	
Organize	Summary table, contingency table (Section 2.1)
Visualize one variable	Bar chart, pie chart, doughnut chart, Pareto chart (Section 2.3)
Visualize two variables	Side-by-side chart, doughnut chart, sparklines (Sections 2.3 and 2.6)
Numerical variables	
Organize	Ordered array, frequency distribution, relative frequency distribution, percentage distribution, cumulative percentage distribution (Section 2.2)
Visualize one variable	Stem-and-leaf display, histogram, percentage polygon, cumulative percentage polygon (ogive) (Section 2.4)
Visualize two variables	Scatter plot, time-series plot (Section 2.5)
Mix of variables	
Organize	Multidimensional tables (Section 2.6)
Visualize	Colored scatter plots, bubble charts, PivotChart (Excel), treemap, sparklines (Section 2.7)
Filter and query	Subset tables, slicers (Excel) (Section 2.8)

▼ REFERENCES

1. Batemen, S., R. Mandryk, C. Gutwin, A. Genest, D. McDine, and C. Brooks. "Useful Junk? The Effects of Visual Embellishment on Comprehension and Memorability of Charts," accessed at **bit.ly/1HMDnpc**.
2. Edwardtufte.com. "Edward Tufte forum: Pie Charts." accessed at **bit.ly/1E3l1Pb**.
3. Few, S. *Information Dashbard Design: Displaying Data for At-a-Glance Monitoring*, 2nd ed. Burlingame, CA: Analytics Press, 2013.
4. Gross, B. *The Managing of Organizations: The Administrative Struggle*, Vols. I & II. New York: The Free Press of Glencoe, 1964.
5. Huff, D. *How to Lie with Statistics*. New York: Norton, 1954.
6. Tufte, E. R. *Beautiful Evidence*. Cheshire, CT: Graphics Press, 2006.
7. Tufte, E. R. *The Visual Display of Quantitative Information*, 2nd ed. Cheshire, CT: Graphics Press, 2002.
8. Wainer, H. *Visual Revelations: Graphical Tales of Fate and Deception from Napoleon Bonaparte to Ross Perot*. Mahwah, NJ: Lawrence Erlbaum Associates, 2000.

▼ KEY EQUATIONS

Determining the Class Interval Width

$$\text{Interval width} = \frac{\text{highest value} - \text{lowest value}}{\text{number of classes}} \qquad (2.1)$$

Computing the Proportion or Relative Frequency

$$\text{Proportion} = \text{relative frequency} = \frac{\text{number of values in each class}}{\text{total number of values}} \qquad (2.2)$$

▼ KEY TERMS

bar chart   54
bins   49
bubble chart   73
cell   43
chartjunk   79
class boundaries   47
class interval   47
class interval width   47
class midpoints   47
classes   47
colored scatter plot   73
contingency table   43
cumulative percentage distribution   51
cumulative percentage polygon
   (ogive)   64

data filtering   75
doughnut chart   55
drill down   71
frequency distribution   47
histogram   61
joint response   43
line graph   56
multidimensional contingency table   70
ogive (cumulative percentage polygon)   64
ordered array   46
Pareto chart   56
Pareto principle   56
percentage distribution   49
percentage polygon   63
pie chart   55

PivotChart   73
PivotTable   43
proportion   49
querying   75
relative frequency   49
relative frequency distribution   49
scatter plot   67
side-by-side bar chart   58
slicer   75
sparklines   74
stem-and-leaf display   61
summary table   42
time-series plot   68
treemap   73

▼ CHECKING YOUR UNDERSTANDING

2.77 How do histograms and polygons differ in construction and use?

2.78 Why would you construct a summary table?

2.79 What are the advantages and disadvantages of using a bar chart, a pie chart, a doughnut chart, and a Pareto chart?

2.80 Compare and contrast the bar chart for categorical data with the histogram for numerical data.

2.81 What is the difference between a time-series plot and a scatter plot?

2.82 Why is it said that the main feature of a Pareto chart is its ability to separate the "vital few" from the "trivial many"?

2.83 What are the three different ways to break down the percentages in a contingency table?

2.84 How can a multidimensional table differ from a two-variable contingency table?

2.85 What type of insights can you gain from a contingency table that contains three variables that you cannot gain from a contingency table that contains two variables?

2.86 What is the difference between a drill-down and a slicer?

2.87 What is the difference between a time-series plot and sparklines?

▼ CHAPTER REVIEW PROBLEMS

2.88 The following table shown in the file `TextbookCosts` shows the breakdown of the costs of a typical college textbook.

Revenue Category		Percentage %
Publisher		66.06
	Page, Printing, Ink	4.62
	Editorial production	24.93
	Marketing	11.60
	Freight	0.77
	Misc. Overhead	1.74
	Profit	22.4
Bookstore		22.20
	Store personnel	11.40
	Store operations	5.90
	Store income	4.90
Author		11.74

Source: Data extracted from **bit.ly/2ppEetq**.

a. Using the categories of publisher, bookstore, and author, construct a bar chart, a pie chart, and a Pareto chart.
b. Using the subcategories of publisher and the subcategories of bookstore, along with the author category, construct a Pareto chart.
c. Based on the results of (a) and (b), what conclusions can you reach concerning who gets the revenue from the sales of new college textbooks? Do any of these results surprise you? Explain.

2.89 The following table represents the market share (in number of movies, gross in millions of dollars, and millions of tickets sold) of each type of movie in 2016:

Type	Number	Gross ($millions)	Tickets (millions)
Original screenplay	378	4,726.6	560.7
Based on comic/graphic novel	15	1,907.0	226.2
Based on fiction book/ short story	101	1,852.8	219.8
Spin-off	2	649.1	77.0
Based on real life events	207	460.6	54.6
Based on factual book/ article	26	419.7	49.8
Remake	11	317.7	37.7
Based on game	6	238.7	28.3
Based on TV	3	181.9	21.6
Based on toy	2	154.2	18.3
Based on play	11	126.1	15.0
Based on short film	3	96.2	11.4
Based on folk tale/ legend/fairytale	3	48.2	5.7
Based on religious text	1	36.9	4.4
Based on movie	2	11.7	1.4
Based on web series	2	9.5	1.1
Compilation	2	2.8	0.3
Based on musical group	2	2.8	0.3
Based on musical or opera	3	2.7	0.3

Source: Data Extracted from **www.the-numbers.com/market/2016/ summary**.

a. Construct a bar chart, a pie chart, a doughnut chart, and a Pareto chart for the number of movies, gross (in $millions), and number of tickets sold (in millions).
b. What conclusions can you reach about the market shares of the different types of movies in 2016?

2.90 B2B marketers in North America were surveyed about content marketing usage, organization, and success. Content marketers were asked about how content marketing is structured within their organization and how they would describe their organization's commitment to content marketing. Tables in this problem summarize the survey results.

B2B Content Marketing Organizational Structure	Percentage
Centralized content marketing group	24%
Each brand has own content marketing group	5%
Both: centralized team and individual teams	13%
Small marketing/content marketing team	55%
Other	3%

Source: Data extracted from **bit.ly/2d98EaN**.

a. Construct a bar chart, a pie or doughnut chart, and a Pareto chart for this table.

b. Which graphical method do you think is best for portraying these data?

Commitment to Content Marketing	Percentage
Very/Extremely Committed	63%
Somewhat Committed	30%
Not Very/Not at All Important	7%

Source: Data extracted from **bit.ly/2d98EaN**.

c. Construct a bar chart, a pie or doughnut chart, and a Pareto chart for this table.
d. Which graphical method do you think is best for portraying these data?
e. Based on the two tables, what conclusions can you reach concerning marketer's perspective on content marketing?

2.91 The owner of a restaurant that serves Continental-style entrées has the business objective of learning more about the patterns of patron demand during the Friday-to-Sunday weekend time period. Data were collected from 630 customers on the type of entrée ordered and were organized in the following table (and stored in Entree):

Type of Entrée	Number Ordered
Beef	187
Chicken	103
Mixed	30
Duck	25
Fish	122
Pasta	63
Shellfish	74
Veal	26
Total	630

a. Construct a percentage summary table for the types of entrées ordered.
b. Construct a bar chart, a pie chart, doughnut chart, and a Pareto chart for the types of entrées ordered.
c. Do you prefer using a Pareto chart or a pie chart for these data? Why?
d. What conclusions can the restaurant owner reach concerning demand for different types of entrées?

2.92 Suppose that the owner of the restaurant in Problem 2.91 also wants to study the demand for dessert during the same time period. She decides that in addition to studying whether a dessert was ordered, she will also study the gender of the individual and whether a beef entrée was ordered. Data were collected from 630 customers and organized in the following contingency tables:

DESSERT ORDERED	GENDER		
	Male	Female	Total
Yes	96	50	146
No	234	250	484
Total	330	300	630

DESSERT ORDERED	BEEF ENTRÉE		
	Yes	**No**	**Total**
Yes	74	68	142
No	113	375	488
Total	187	443	630

a. For each of the two contingency tables, construct contingency tables of row percentages, column percentages, and total percentages.

b. Which type of percentage (row, column, or total) do you think is most informative for each gender? For beef entrée? Explain.

c. What conclusions concerning the pattern of dessert ordering can the restaurant owner reach?

2.93 The following data represents the pounds per capita of fresh food and packaged food consumed in the United States, Japan, and Russia in a recent year.

	COUNTRY		
FRESH FOOD	**United States**	**Japan**	**Russia**
Eggs, nuts, and beans	88	94	88
Fruit	124	126	88
Meat and seafood	197	146	125
Vegetables	194	278	335
PACKAGED FOOD			
Bakery goods	108	53	144
Dairy products	298	147	127
Pasta	12	32	16
Processed, frozen, dried, and chilled food, and ready-to-eat meals	183	251	70
Sauces, dressings, and condiments	63	75	49
Snacks and candy	47	19	24
Soup and canned food	77	17	25

Source: Data extracted from H. Fairfield, "Factory Food," *New York Times*, April 4, 2010, p. BU5.

a. For the United States, Japan, and Russia, construct a bar chart, a pie or doughnut chart, and a Pareto chart for different types of fresh foods consumed.

b. For the United States, Japan, and Russia, construct a bar chart, a pie or doughnut chart, and a Pareto chart for different types of packaged foods consumed.

c. What conclusions can you reach concerning differences between the United States, Japan, and Russia in the fresh foods and packaged foods consumed?

2.94 The Air Travel Consumer Report, a monthly product of the Department of Transportation's Office of Aviation Enforcement and Proceedings (OAEP), is designed to assist consumers with information on the quality of services provided by airlines. The report includes a summary of consumer complaints by industry group and by complaint category. A breakdown of 1,303 September

2016 consumer complaints based on industry group is given in the following table:

Industry Group	Number of Consumer Complaints
U.S. Airlines	879
Non-U.S. Airlines	386
Travel agents	26
Miscellaneous	12
Industry total	1,303

Source: Data extracted from "The Travel Consumer Report," Office of Aviation Enforcement and Proceedings, September 2016.

a. Construct a Pareto chart for the number of complaints by industry group. What industry group accounts for most of the complaints?

The 1,303 consumer complaints against airlines are summarized by type in the following table:

Complaint Category	Complaints
Flight problems	432
Oversales	45
Reservation/ticketing/boarding	147
Fares	103
Refunds	96
Baggage	215
Customer service	148
Disability	61
Advertising	11
Discrimination	6
Other	39
Total	1,303

b. Construct pie and doughnut charts to display the percentage of complaints by type. What complaint category accounts for most of the complaints?

2.95 One of the major measures of the quality of service provided by an organization is the speed with which the organization responds to customer complaints. A large family-held department store selling furniture and flooring, including carpet, had undergone a major expansion in the past several years. In particular, the flooring department had expanded from 2 installation crews to an installation supervisor, a measurer, and 15 installation crews. A business objective of the company was to reduce the time between when the complaint is received and when it is resolved. During a recent year, the company received 50 complaints concerning carpet installation. The number of days between the receipt of the complaint and the resolution of the complaint for the 50 complaints, stored in Furniture, are:

54	5	35	137	31	27	152	2	123	81	74	27
11	19	126	110	110	29	61	35	94	31	26	5
12	4	165	32	29	28	29	26	25	1	14	13
13	10	5	27	4	52	30	22	36	26	20	23
33	68										

a. Construct a frequency distribution and a percentage distribution.

b. Construct a histogram and a percentage polygon.

c. Construct a cumulative percentage distribution and plot a cumulative percentage polygon (ogive).

d. On the basis of the results of (a) through (c), if you had to tell the president of the company how long a customer should expect to wait to have a complaint resolved, what would you say? Explain.

2.96 The file DomesticBeer contains the percentage alcohol, number of calories per 12 ounces, and number of carbohydrates (in grams) per 12 ounces for 158 of the best selling domestic beers in the United States.

Source: Data extracted from **www.beer100.com/beercalories.htm,** Dec 1, 2016.

a. Construct a percentage histogram for percentage alcohol, number of calories per 12 ounces, and number of carbohydrates (in grams) per 12 ounces.

b. Construct three scatter plots: percentage alcohol versus calories, percentage alcohol versus carbohydrates, and calories versus carbohydrates.

c. Discuss what you learned from studying the graphs in (a) and (b).

2.97 The file CigaretteTax contains the state cigarette tax ($) for each state and the District of Columbia as of January 1, 2017.

a. Construct an ordered array.

b. Plot a percentage histogram.

c. What conclusions can you reach about the differences in the state cigarette tax among the states?

2.98 The file CDRate contains the yields for one-year certificates of deposit (CDs) and for five-year CDs for 39 banks in the United States, as of January 9, 2017.

Source: Data extracted and compiled from **www.bankrate.com,** January 9, 2017.

a. Construct a stem-and-leaf display for one-year CDs and five-year CDs.

b. Construct a scatter plot of one-year CDs versus five-year CDs.

c. What is the relationship between the one-year CD rate and the five-year CD rate?

2.99 The file CEO2016 includes the total compensation (in $millions) for CEOs of 200 S&P 500 companies and the one-year total shareholder return in 2016.

Source: Data extracted from **bit.ly/1QqpEUZ.**

For total compensation:

a. Construct a frequency distribution and a percentage distribution.

b. Construct a histogram and a percentage polygon.

c. Construct a cumulative percentage distribution and plot a cumulative percentage polygon (ogive).

d. Based on (a) through (c), what conclusions can you reach concerning CEO compensation in 2016?

e. Construct a scatter plot of total compensation and shareholder return in 2016.

f. What is the relationship between the total compensation and shareholder return in 2016?

2.100 Studies conducted by a manufacturer of Boston and Vermont asphalt shingles have shown product weight to be a major factor in customers' perception of quality. Moreover, the weight represents the amount of raw materials being used and is therefore very important to the company from a cost standpoint. The last stage of the assembly line packages the shingles before the packages are placed on wooden pallets. The variable of interest is the weight in pounds of the pallet, which for most brands holds 16 squares of shingles. The company expects pallets of its Boston brand-name shingles to weigh at least 3,050 pounds but less than 3,260 pounds.

For the company's Vermont brand-name shingles, pallets should weigh at least 3,600 pounds but less than 3,800. Data, collected from a sample of 368 pallets of Boston shingles and 330 pallets of Vermont shingles, are stored in Pallet .

a. For the Boston shingles, construct a frequency distribution and a percentage distribution having eight class intervals, using 3,015, 3,050, 3,085, 3,120, 3,155, 3,190, 3,225, 3,260, and 3,295 as the class boundaries.

b. For the Vermont shingles, construct a frequency distribution and a percentage distribution having seven class intervals, using 3,550, 3,600, 3,650, 3,700, 3,750, 3,800, 3,850, and 3,900 as the class boundaries.

c. Construct percentage histograms for the Boston and Vermont shingles.

d. Comment on the distribution of pallet weights for the Boston and Vermont shingles. Be sure to identify the percentages of pallets that are underweight and overweight.

2.101 What was the average price of a room at two-star, three-star, and four-star hotels around the world during 2016? The file Hotel Prices contains the average hotel room prices in Canadian dollars (about U.S. $0.75 as of December 2016) per night paid by Canadian travelers.

Source: Data extracted from Hotels.com Hotel Price Index," **bit.ly/2qmzNAW.**

For each of the three groups of hotels (two-, three-, and four-stars):

a. Construct frequency and percentage distributions.

b. Construct a histogram and a percentage polygon.

c. Construct a cumulative percentage distribution and plot a cumulative percentage polygon (ogive).

d. What conclusions can you reach about the cost of two-star, three-star, and four-star hotels?

e. Construct separate scatter plots of the cost of two-star hotels versus three-star hotels, two-star hotels versus four-star hotels, and three-star hotels versus four-star hotels.

f. What conclusions can you reach about the relationship of the price of two-star, three-star, and four-star hotels?

2.102 The file Protein contains calorie and cholesterol information for popular protein foods (fresh red meats, poultry, and fish).

Source: U.S. Department of Agriculture.

a. Construct frequency and percentage distributions for the number of calories.

b. Construct frequency and percentage distributions for the amount of cholesterol.

c. Construct a percentage histogram for the number of calories.

d. Construct a percentage histogram for the amount of cholesterol.

e. Construct a scatter plot of the number of calories and the amount of cholesterol.

f. What conclusions can you reach from the visualizations?

2.103 The file Natural Gas contains the U.S. monthly average commercial and residential price for natural gas in dollars per thousand cubic feet from January 2008 through December 2016.

Source: Data extracted from "U.S. Natural Gas Prices," **bit.ly/2oZIQ5Z,** accessed March 19, 2017.

For the commercial price and the residential price:

a. Construct a time-series plot.

b. What pattern, if any, is present in the data?

c. Construct a scatter plot of the commercial price and the residential price.

d. What conclusion can you reach about the relationship between the commercial price and the residential price?

2.104 The data stored in `Drink` represent the amount of soft drink in a sample of 50 consecutively filled 2-liter bottles.
a. Construct a time-series plot for the amount of soft drink on the *Y* axis and the bottle number (going consecutively from 1 to 50) on the *X* axis.
b. What pattern, if any, is present in these data?
c. If you had to make a prediction about the amount of soft drink filled in the next bottle, what would you predict?
d. Based on the results of (a) through (c), explain why it is important to construct a time-series plot and not just a histogram, as was done in Problem 2.47 on page 67.

2.105 The file `Currency` contains the exchange rates of the Canadian dollar, the Japanese yen, and the English pound from 1980 to 2016, where the Canadian dollar, the Japanese yen, and the English pound are expressed in units per U.S. dollar.
a. Construct time-series plots for the yearly closing values of the Canadian dollar, the Japanese yen, and the English pound.
b. Explain any patterns present in the plots.
c. Write a short summary of your findings.
d. Construct separate scatter plots of the value of the Canadian dollar versus the Japanese yen, the Canadian dollar versus the English pound, and the Japanese yen versus the English pound.
e. What conclusions can you reach concerning the value of the Canadian dollar, Japanese yen, and English pound in terms of the U.S. dollar?

2.106 A/B testing allows businesses to test a new design or format for a web page to determine if the new web page is more effective than the current one. Web designers decide to create a new call-to-action button for a web page. Every visitor to the web page was randomly shown either the original call-to-action button (the control) or the new variation. The metric used to measure success was the download rate: the number of people who downloaded the file divided by the number of people who saw that particular call-to-action button. Results of the experiment yielded the following:

Variations	Downloads	Visitors
Original call to action button	351	3,642
New call to action button	485	3,556

a. Compute the percentage of downloads for the original call-to-action button and the new call-to-action button.
b. Construct a bar chart of the percentage of downloads for the original call-to-action button and the new call-to-action button.
c. What conclusions can you reach concerning the original call-to-action button and the new call-to-action button?

Web designers then create a new page design for a web page. Every visitor to the web page was randomly shown either the original web design (the control) or the new variation. The metric used to measure success was the download rate: the number of people who downloaded the file divided by the number of people who saw that particular web design. Results of the experiment yielded the following:

Variations	Downloads	Visitors
Original web design	305	3,427
New web design	353	3,751

d. Compute the percentage of downloads for the original web design and the new web design.
e. Construct a bar chart of the percentage of downloads for the original web design and the new web design.
f. What conclusions can you reach concerning the original web design and the new web design?
g. Compare your conclusions in (f) with those in (c).

Web designers next test two factors simultaneously—the call-to-action button and the new page design. Every visitor to the web page was randomly shown one of the following:

Old call-to-action button with original page design
New call-to-action button with original page design
Old call-to-action button with new page design
New call-to-action button with new page design

Again, the metric used to measure success was the download rate: the number of people who downloaded the file divided by the number of people who saw that particular call-to-action button and web design. Results of the experiment yielded the following:

Call-to-Action Button	Page Design	Downloaded	Declined	Total
Original	Original	83	917	1,000
New	Original	137	863	1,000
Original	New	95	905	1,000
New	New	170	830	1,000
Total		485	3,515	4,000

h. Compute the percentage of downloads for each combination of call-to-action button and web design.
i. What conclusions can you reach concerning the original call to action button and the new call to action button and the original web design and the new web design?
j. Compare your conclusions in (i) with those in (c) and (g).

2.107 (Class Project) Have each student in the class respond to the question "Which carbonated soft drink do you most prefer?" so that the instructor can tally the results into a summary table.
a. Convert the data to percentages and construct a Pareto chart.
b. Analyze the findings.

2.108 (Class Project) Cross-classify each student in the class by gender (male, female) and current employment status (yes, no), so that the instructor can tally the results.
a. Construct a table with either row or column percentages, depending on which you think is more informative.
b. What would you conclude from this study?
c. What other variables would you want to know regarding employment in order to enhance your findings?

REPORT WRITING EXERCISES

2.109 Referring to the results from Problem 2.100 on page 86 concerning the weights of Boston and Vermont shingles, write a report that evaluates whether the weights of the pallets of the two types of shingles are what the company expects. Be sure to incorporate tables and charts into the report.

▾CASES

Managing Ashland MultiComm Services

Recently, Ashland MultiComm Services has been criticized for its inadequate customer service in responding to questions and problems about its telephone, cable television, and Internet services. Senior management has established a task force charged with the business objective of improving customer service. In response to this charge, the task force collected data about the types of customer service errors, the cost of customer service errors, and the cost of wrong billing errors. It found the following data:

Types of Customer Service Errors	
Type of Errors	**Frequency**
Incorrect accessory	27
Incorrect address	42
Incorrect contact phone	31
Invalid wiring	9
On-demand programming error	14
Subscription not ordered	8
Suspension error	15
Termination error	22
Website access error	30
Wrong billing	137
Wrong end date	17
Wrong number of connections	19
Wrong price quoted	20
Wrong start date	24
Wrong subscription type	33
Total	448

Cost of Customer Service Errors in the Past Year	
Type of Errors	**Cost ($thousands)**
Incorrect accessory	17.3
Incorrect address	62.4
Incorrect contact phone	21.3
Invalid wiring	40.8
On-demand programming errors	38.8
Subscription not ordered	20.3
Suspension error	46.8
Termination error	50.9
Website access errors	60.7
Wrong billing	121.7
Wrong end date	40.9
Wrong number of connections	28.1
Wrong price quoted	50.3
Wrong start date	40.8
Wrong subscription type	60.1
Total	701.2

Type and Cost of Wrong Billing Errors	
Type of Wrong Billing Errors	**Cost ($thousands)**
Declined or held transactions	7.6
Incorrect account number	104.3
Invalid verification	9.8
Total	121.7

1. Review these data (stored in AMS2-1). Identify the variables that are important in describing the customer service problems. For each variable you identify, construct the graphical representation you think is most appropriate and explain your choice. Also, suggest what other information concerning the different types of errors would be useful to examine. Offer possible courses of action for either the task force or management to take that would support the goal of improving customer service.

2. As a follow-up activity, the task force decides to collect data to study the pattern of calls to the help desk (stored in AMS2-2). Analyze these data and present your conclusions in a report.

Digital Case

In the Using Statistics scenario, you were asked to gather information to help make wise investment choices. Sources for such information include brokerage firms, investment counselors, and other financial services firms. Apply your knowledge about the proper use of tables and charts in this Digital Case about the claims of foresight and excellence by an Ashland-area financial services firm.

Open **EndRunGuide.pdf**, which contains the EndRun Financial Services "Guide to Investing." Review the guide, paying close attention to the company's investment claims and supporting data and then answer the following.

1. How does the presentation of the general information about EndRun in this guide affect your perception of the business?

2. Is EndRun's claim about having more winners than losers a fair and accurate reflection of the quality of its investment service? If you do not think that the claim is a fair and accurate one, provide an alternate presentation that you think is fair and accurate.

3. Review the discussion about EndRun's "Big Eight Difference" and then open and examine the attached sample of mutual funds. Are there any other relevant data from that file that could have been included in the Big Eight table? How would the new data alter your perception of EndRun's claims?

4. EndRun is proud that all Big Eight funds have gained in value over the past five years. Do you agree that EndRun should be proud of its selections? Why or why not?

CardioGood Fitness

The market research team at AdRight is assigned the task to identify the profile of the typical customer for each treadmill product offered by CardioGood Fitness. The market research team decides to investigate whether there are differences across the product lines with respect to customer characteristics. The team decides to collect data on individuals who purchased a treadmill at a CardioGood Fitness retail store during the prior three months. The data are stored in the CardioGood Fitness file. The team identifies the following customer variables to study: product purchased, TM195, TM498, or TM798; gender; age, in years; education, in years; relationship status, single or partnered; annual household income ($); average number of times the customer plans to use the treadmill each week; average number of miles the customer expects to walk/run each week; and self-rated fitness on an 1-to-5 ordinal scale, where 1 is poor shape and 5 is excellent shape.

1. Create a customer profile for each CardioGood Fitness treadmill product line by developing appropriate tables and charts.

2. Write a report to be presented to the management of CardioGood Fitness detailing your findings.

The Choice *Is* Yours Follow-Up

Follow up the Using Statistics Revisited section on page 81 by analyzing the differences in one-year return percentages, five-year return percentages, and ten-year return percentages for the sample of 479 retirement funds stored in Retirement Funds. In your analysis, examine differences between the growth and value funds as well as the differences among the small, mid-cap, and large market cap funds.

Clear Mountain State Student Survey

The student news service at Clear Mountain State University (CMSU) has decided to gather data about the undergraduate students that attend CMSU. They create and distribute a survey of 14 questions (see **CMStudentSurvey.pdf**) and receive responses from 111 undergraduates, stored in StudentSurvey. For each question asked in the survey, construct all the appropriate tables and charts and write a report summarizing your conclusions.

▾EXCEL GUIDE

EG2.1 ORGANIZING CATEGORICAL VARIABLES

The Summary Table

Key Technique Use the PivotTable feature to create a summary table from the set of untallied values for a variable.

Example Create a frequency and percentage summary table similar to Figure 2.1 on page 43.

PHStat Use **One-Way Tables & Charts**.

For the example, open to the **DATA worksheet** of the **Retirement Funds workbook**. Select **PHStat → Descriptive Statistics → One-Way Tables & Charts**. In the procedure's dialog box (shown below):

1. Click **Raw Categorical Data**.
2. Enter **D1:D480** as the **Raw Data Cell Range** and check **First cell contains label**.
3. Enter a **Title**, check **Percentage Column**, and click **OK**.

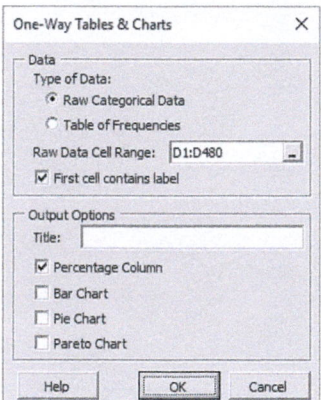

PHStat creates a PivotTable summary table on a new worksheet. For problems with tallied data, click **Table of Frequencies** in step 1. Then, in step 2, enter the cell range of the tabular summary as the **Freq. Table Cell Range** (edit box name changes from Raw Data Cell Range).

In the PivotTable, risk categories appear in alphabetical order and not in the order low, average, and high as would normally be expected. To change to the expected order, use steps 13 and 14 of the *Workbook* instructions but change all references to cell A6 to cell A7 and drop the Low label over cell A5, not cell A4.

Workbook (untallied data) Use the **Summary Table workbook** as a model.

For the example, open to the **DATA worksheet** of the **Retirement Funds workbook** and select **Insert → PivotTable**.

In the Create PivotTable dialog box (shown below):

1. Click **Select a table or range** and enter **D1:D480** as the **Table/Range** cell range.
2. Click **New Worksheet** and then click **OK**.

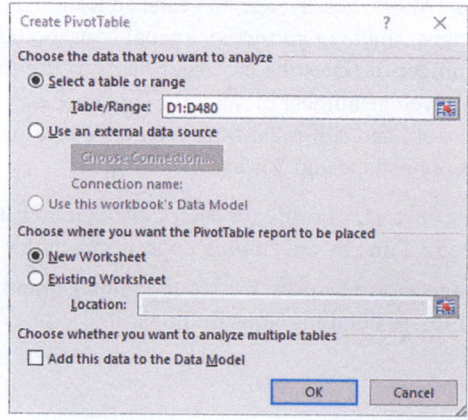

In the PivotTable fields (PivotTable Builder in Excel for Mac PivotTable Field List in older versions) display (shown below):

3. Drag **Risk** in the **Choose fields to add to report** box and drop it in the **Rows** (or **Row Labels**) box.
4. **Drag Risk in the Choose fields to add to report** box a second time and drop it in the **Σ Values** box. This second label changes to **Count of Risk to** indicate that a count, or tally, of the risk categories will be displayed in the PivotTable.

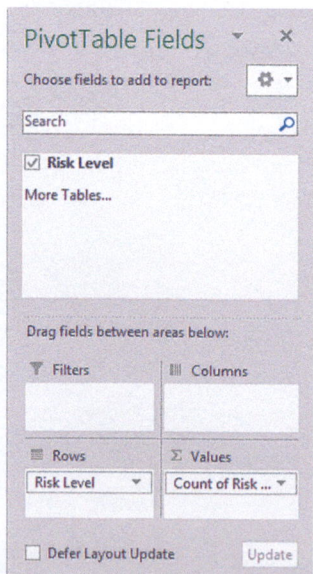

In the PivotTable being created:

5. Enter **Risk** in cell **A3** to replace the heading Row Labels.
6. Right-click cell **A3** and then click **PivotTable Options** in the shortcut menu that appears.

In the PivotTable Options dialog box (Windows version shown below):

7. Click the **Layout & Format** tab. Check **For empty cells show** and enter **0** as its value. Leave all other settings unchanged.
   (Excel for Mac) Click the **Display** tab. Check **Empty cells as** and enter **0** as its value.
8. Click **OK** to complete the PivotTable.

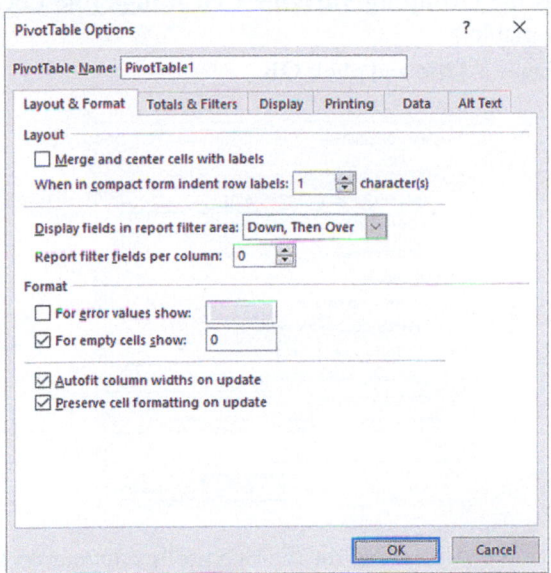

To add a column for the percentage frequency:

9. Enter **Percentage** in cell **C3**. Enter the formula **= B4/B$7** in cell **C4** and copy it down through **row 7**.
10. Select cell range **C4:C7**, right-click, and select **Format Cells** in the shortcut menu.
11. In the **Number** tab of the Format Cells dialog box, select **Percentage** as the **Category** and click **OK**.
12. Adjust the worksheet formatting, if appropriate (see number of Appendix B section to be determined Section B.) and enter a title in cell **A1**.

In the PivotTable, risk categories appear in alphabetical order and not in the order low, average, and high, as would normally be expected. To change to the expected order:

13. Click the **Low** label in cell **A6** to highlight cell A6. Move the mouse pointer to the top edge of the cell until the mouse pointer changes to a four-way arrow (hand icon in OS X).
14. Drag the **Low** label and drop the label over cell **A4**. The risk categories now appear in the order Low, Average, and High in the summary table.

Workbook (tallied data) Use the **SUMMARY_SIMPLE worksheet** of the **Summary Table workbook** as a model for creating a summary table.

The Contingency Table

Key Technique Use the PivotTable feature to create a contingency table from the set of individual values for a variable.

Example Create a contingency table displaying Fund Type and Risk Level similar to Figure 2.2 on page 43.

PHStat (untallied data) Use **Two-Way Tables & Charts**.

For the example, open to the **DATA worksheet** of the **Retirement Funds workbook**. Select **PHStat → Descriptive Statistics → Two-Way Tables & Charts**. In the procedure's dialog box (shown below):

1. Enter **C1:C480** as the **Row Variable Cell Range**.
2. Enter **D1:D480** the **Column Variable Cell Range**.
3. Check **First cell in each range contains label**.
4. Enter a **Title** and click **OK**.

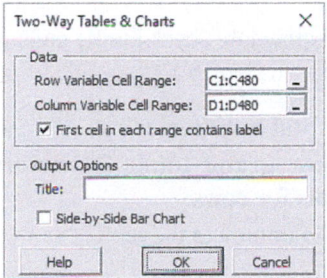

In the PivotTable, risk categories appear in alphabetical order and not in the order low, average, and high as would normally be expected. To change the expected order, use steps 13 and 14 of the *Workbook* instructions in the left column.

Workbook (untallied data) Use the **Contingency Table workbook** as a model.

For the example, open to the **DATA worksheet** of the **Retirement Funds workbook**. Select **Insert → PivotTable**. In the Create PivotTable dialog box:

1. Click **Select a table or range** and enter **A1:N480** as the **Table/Range** cell range.
2. Click **New Worksheet** and then click **OK**.

In the PivotTable Fields (PivotTable Field List in some versions) task pane:

3. Drag **Type** from **Choose fields to add to report** and drop it in the **Rows** (or **Row Labels**) box.
4. Drag **Risk** from **Choose fields to add to report** and drop it in the **Columns** (or **Column Labels**) box.
5. Drag **Type** from **Choose fields to add to report** a second time and drop it in the **Σ Values** box. (**Type** changes to **Count of Type**.)

In the PivotTable being created:

6. Select cell **A3** and enter a **space character** to clear the label **Count of Type**.

7. Enter **Type** in cell **A4** to replace the heading Row Labels.

8. Enter **Risk** in cell **B3** to replace the heading Column Labels.

9. Click the **Low** label in cell **D4** to highlight cell D4. Move the mouse pointer to the left edge of the cell until the mouse pointer changes to a four-way arrow (hand icon in Excel for Mac).

10. Drag the **Low** label to the left and drop the label between columns A and B. The Low label appears in B4 and column B now contains the low risk tallies.

11. Right-click over the PivotTable and then click **Pivot-Table Options** in the shortcut menu that appears.

In the PivotTable Options dialog box:

12. Click the **Layout & Format** tab. Check **For empty cells show** and enter **0** as its value. Leave all other settings unchanged.

    Click the **Display** tab. Check **Empty cells as** and enter **0** as its value. Skip to step 15.

13. Click the **Total & Filters** tab.

14. Check **Show grand totals for columns** and **Show grand totals for rows**.

15. Click **OK** to complete the table.

Workbook (tallied data) Use the **CONTINGENCY_SIMPLE** worksheet of the **Contingency Table workbook** as a model for creating a contingency table.

EG2.2 ORGANIZING NUMERICAL VARIABLES

The Ordered Array

Workbook To create an ordered array, first select the numerical variable to be sorted. Then select **Home → Sort & Filter** (in the Editing group) and in the drop-down menu click **Sort Smallest to Largest**. (You will see **Sort A to Z** as the first drop-down choice if you did not select a cell range of *numerical* data.)

The Frequency Distribution

Key Technique Establish bins (see on page 49) and then use the **FREQUENCY** (untallied data cell range, bins cell range) array function to tally data. (Appendix Section B.2 discusses how array functions differ from other functions.)

Example Create a frequency, percentage, and cumulative percentage distribution for the restaurant meal cost data that contain the information found in Tables 2.3. 2.5 and 2.8 in Section 2.2.

PHStat (untallied data) Use **Frequency Distribution.** If you plan to construct a histogram or polygon and a frequency distribution, use **Histogram & Polygons** (Section EG2.4).

For the example, open to the **DATA worksheet** of the **Restaurants workbook**. This worksheet contains the meal cost data in stacked format in column B and a set of bin numbers appropriate for those data in column I. Select **PHStat → Descriptive Statistics → Frequency Distribution**. In the procedure's dialog box (shown below):

1. Enter **B1:B101** as the **Variable Cell Range**, enter **I1: I10** as the **Bins Cell Range**, and check **First cell in each range contains label**.

2. Click **Multiple Groups - Stacked** and enter **A1:A101** as the **Grouping Variable Cell Range** (the Location variable.)

3. Enter a **Title** and click **OK**.

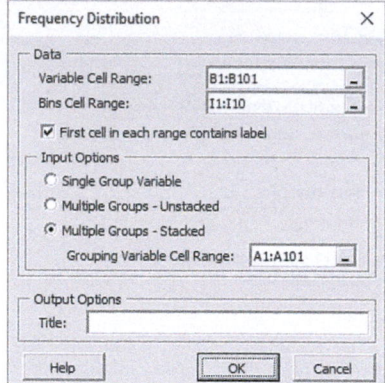

Frequency distributions for the two groups appear on separate worksheets. To display both distributions on the same worksheet, select the cell range **B3:D12** on one of the worksheets. Right-click that range and click **Copy** in the shortcut menu. Open to the other worksheet. In that other worksheet, right-click cell **E3** and click **Paste Special** in the shortcut menu. In the Paste Special dialog box, click **Values and numbers format** and click **OK**. Adjust the worksheet title and headings. (Appendix Section B.3 further explains the Paste Special command.)

Click **Single Group Variable** in step 2 to construct a distribution from a single group. Click **Multiple Groups - Unstacked** in step 2 if the **Variable Cell Range** contains two or more columns of unstacked data.

Workbook (untallied data) Use the **Distributions workbook** as a model.

For the example, open to the **UNSTACKED worksheet** of the **Restaurants workbook**. This worksheet contains the meal cost data unstacked in columns A and B and a set of bin numbers appropriate for those data in column D. Click the **insert worksheet icon** (the plus sign icon to the right of the sheet tabs, below the bottom of the worksheet) to insert a new worksheet.

In the new worksheet:

1. Enter a title in cell **A1**, **Bins** in cell **A3**, and **Frequency** in cell **B3**.

2. Copy the bin number list in the cell range **D2:D10** of the **UNSTACKED worksheet** and paste this list into cell **A4** of the new worksheet.

3. Select the cell range **B4:B12** that will hold the array formula.

4. Type, but do not press the **Enter** or **Tab** key, the formula **=FREQUENCY(UNSTACKED!$A$1:$A$51, $A$4:A$12)**. Then, while holding down the **Ctrl** and **Shift** keys, press the **Enter** key to enter the array formula into the cell range **B4:B12.**

5. Adjust the worksheet formatting as necessary.

Note that in step 4, you enter the cell range as **UNSTACKED! $A$1:$A$51** and not as **$A$1:$A$51** because the untallied data are located on a separate worksheet (UNSTACKED). The cell range takes the form of an absolute cell reference (see in Appendix Section B.3).

Steps 1 through 5 construct a frequency distribution for the meal costs at center city restaurants. To construct a frequency distribution for the meal costs at metro area restaurants, insert another worksheet and repeat steps 1 through 5, entering **=FREQUENCY(UNSTACKED!$B$1:$B$51,A$4:A$12)** as the array formula in step 4.

To display both distributions on the same worksheet, select the cell range **B3:B12** on one of the worksheets. Right-click that range and click **Copy** in the shortcut menu. Open to the other worksheet. In that other worksheet, right-click cell **C3** and click **Paste Special** in the shortcut menu. In the Paste Special dialog box, click **Values and numbers format** and click **OK**. Adjust the worksheet title and headings. (Appendix Section B.3 further explains the Paste Special command.)

Analysis ToolPak (untallied data)   Use **Histogram**.

For the example, open to the **UNSTACKED worksheet** of the **Restaurants workbook**. This worksheet contains the meal cost data unstacked in columns A and B and a set of bin numbers appropriate for those data in column D. Then:

1. Select **Data ➜ Data Analysis**. In the Data Analysis dialog box, select **Histogram** from the **Analysis Tools** list and then click **OK**.

In the Histogram dialog box (shown in right column):

2. Enter **A1:A51** as the **Input Range** and enter **D1:D10** as the **Bin Range**. (If you leave **Bin Range** blank, the procedure creates a set of bins that will not be as well formed as the ones you can specify.)

3. Check **Labels** and click **New Worksheet Ply**.

4. Click **OK** to create the frequency distribution on a new worksheet.

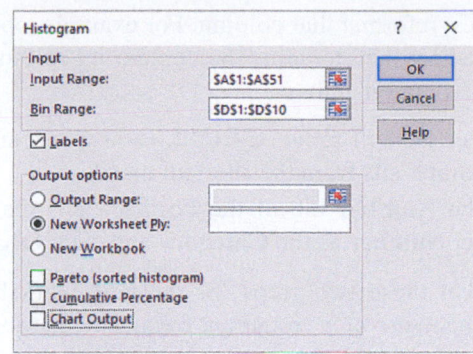

In the new worksheet:

5. Select **row 1**. Right-click this row and click **Insert** in the shortcut menu. Repeat. (This creates two blank rows at the top of the worksheet.)

6. Enter a title in cell **A1**.

The ToolPak creates a frequency distribution that contains an improper bin labeled **More**. Correct this error by using these general instructions:

7. Manually add the frequency count of the **More** row to the frequency count of the preceding row. (For the example, the **More** row contains a zero for the frequency, so the frequency of the preceding row does not change.)

8. Select the worksheet row (for this example, row 14) that contains the More row.

9. Right-click that row and click **Delete** in the shortcut menu.

Steps 1 through 9 construct a frequency distribution for the meal costs at center city restaurants. To construct a frequency distribution for the meal costs at metro area restaurants, repeat these nine steps but in step 2 enter **B1:B51** as the **Input Range**.

The Relative Frequency, Percentage, and Cumulative Distributions

Key Technique   Add columns that contain formulas for the relative frequency or percentage and cumulative percentage to a previously constructed frequency distribution.

Example   Create a distribution that includes the relative frequency or percentage as well as the cumulative percentage information found in Tables 2.5 (relative frequency and percentage) and 2.8 (cumulative percentage) in Section 2.2 for the restaurant meal cost data.

PHStat (untallied data)   Use **Frequency Distribution**.

For the example, use the *PHStat* "The Frequency Distribution" instructions to construct a frequency distribution. PHStat constructs a frequency distribution that also includes columns for the percentages and cumulative percentages. To change the column of percentages to a column of relative frequencies, reformat that column. For example, open to the new worksheet that contains the center city restaurant frequency distribution and:

1. Select the cell range **C4:C12**, right-click, and select **Format Cells** from the shortcut menu.
2. In the **Number** tab of the Format Cells dialog box, select **Number** as the **Category** and click **OK**.

Then repeat these two steps for the new worksheet that contains the metro area restaurant frequency distribution.

Workbook (untallied data) Use the **Distributions workbook** as a model.

For the example, first construct a frequency distribution created using the *Workbook* "The Frequency Distribution" instructions. Open to the new worksheet that contains the frequency distribution for the center city restaurants and:

1. Enter **Percentage** in cell **C3** and **Cumulative Pctage** in cell **D3**.
2. Enter **=B4/SUM($B$4:$B$12)** in cell **C4** and copy this formula down through row **12**.
3. Enter **=C4** in cell **D4**.
4. Enter **=C5+D4** in cell **D5** and copy this formula down through row **12**.
5. Select the cell range **C4:D12**, right-click, and click **Format Cells** in the shortcut menu.
6. In the **Number** tab of the Format Cells dialog box, click **Percentage** in the **Category** list and click **OK**.

Then open to the worksheet that contains the frequency distribution for the metro area restaurants and repeat steps 1 through 6.

If you want column C to display relative frequencies instead of percentages, enter **Rel. Frequencies** in cell **C3**. Select the cell range **C4:C12**, right-click, and click **Format Cells** in the shortcut menu. In the **Number** tab of the Format Cells dialog box, click **Number** in the **Category** list and click **OK**.

Analysis ToolPak Use **Histogram** and then modify the worksheet created.

For the example, first construct the frequency distributions using the *Analysis ToolPak* instructions in "The Frequency Distribution." Then use the *Workbook* instructions to modify those distributions.

EG2 CHARTS GROUP REFERENCE

Certain *Workbook* charting instructions refer to the following labeled Microsoft Windows Excel (left) and Excel for Mac (right) Charts Groups. (There is no #2 icon for the Windows group and no #6 or #7 icons for the Mac group.)

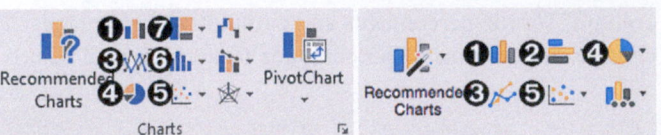

EG2.3 VISUALIZING CATEGORICAL VARIABLES

The Bar Chart and the Pie (or Doughnut) Chart

Key Technique Use the Excel bar, pie, or doughnut chart feature with a tabular summary of the variable. If necessary, use the Section EG2.1 "The Summary Table" to first create that summary.

Example Construct a bar or pie (or doughnut) chart from a summary table similar to Figure 2.1 on page 43.

PHStat Use **One-Way Tables & Charts**.

For the example, use the Section EG1 "The Summary Table" *PHStat* instructions, but in step 3, check either **Bar Chart** or **Pie Chart** (or both) in addition to entering a **Title**, checking **Percentage Column**, and clicking **OK**.

Workbook Use the **Summary Table workbook** as a model.

For the example, open to the **OneWayTable worksheet** of the **Summary Table workbook**. (The PivotTable in this worksheet was constructed using the Section EG2.1 "The Summary Table" instructions.) To construct a bar chart:

1. Select cell range **A4:B6**. (Begin your selection at cell B6 and not at cell A4, as you would normally do.)
2. Select **Insert → Bar** ((#1 in the Windows Charts group, #2 in the Mac Charts group) and select the **Clustered Bar** gallery item.
3. Right-click the **Risk** drop-down button in the chart and click **Hide All Field Buttons** on Chart. (Does not apply to Excel for Mac.)
4. Select **Design** (or **Chart Design**) → **Add Chart Element** → **Axis Titles** → **Primary Horizontal**. In older Excel, select **Layout** → **Axis Titles** → **Primary Horizontal Axis Title** → **Title Below Axis**.
5. Select the words "Axis Title" and enter **Frequency** as the new axis title.
6. Relocate the chart to a chart sheet and turn off the chart legend and gridlines by using the instructions in Appendix Section B.5.

For other problems, the horizontal axis may not begin at 0. If this occurs, right-click the horizontal axis and click **Format Axis** in the shortcut menu. In the Format Axis display, click **Axis Options**. In the Axis Options, enter **0** as the **Minimum** and then close the display. In Excels with two-panel dialog boxes, in the Axis Options right pane, click the first **Fixed** (for **Minimum**), enter **0** as the value, and then click **Close**.

To construct a pie or doughnut chart, replace steps 2, 4, and 6 with these:

2. Select **Insert → Pie** (#4 in the labeled Charts groups) and select the **Pie** gallery item (or the **Doughnut** item).
4. Select **Design** (or **Chart Design**) → **Add Chart Element** → **Data Labels** → **More Data Label Options**.

In the Format Data Labels display, click **Label Options**. In the Label Options, check **Category Name** and **Percentage** and clear the other Label Contains check boxes. Click **Outside End** under Label Position (pie chart only) and close the display.

6. Relocate the chart to a chart sheet and turn off the chart legend and gridlines by using the instructions in Appendix Section B.5.

To see the Label Options in step 4 in the newest versions of Excel, you may need to first click the chart (fourth) icon at the top of the display. In older versions of Excel, select **Layout → Data Labels → More Data Label Options** in step 4. To construct a doughnut chart in those Excels, select **Insert → Other Charts** and then the **Doughnut** item in step 2.

The Pareto Chart

Key Technique Use the Excel chart feature with a modified summary table.

Example Construct a Pareto chart of the incomplete ATM transactions equivalent to Figure 2.7 on page 57.

PHStat Use **One-Way Tables & Charts**.

For the example, open to the **DATA worksheet** of the **ATM Transactions workbook**. Select **PHStat → Descriptive Statistics → One-Way Tables & Charts**. In the procedure's dialog box:

1. Click **Table of Frequencies** (because the worksheet contains tallied data).
2. Enter **A1:B8** as the **Freq. Table Cell Range** and check **First cell contains label**.
3. Enter a **Title**, check **Pareto Chart**, and click **OK**.

Workbook Use the **Pareto workbook** as a model.

Note: The following instructions do not use the new Pareto chart option that Microsoft Windows Excel users can select from the gallery that is displayed when icon #6 is clicked.

For the example, open to the **ATMTable worksheet** of the **ATM Transactions workbook**. Begin by sorting the modified table by decreasing order of frequency:

1. Select row **11** (the Total row), right-click, and click **Hide** in the shortcut menu. (This prevents the total row from getting sorted.)
2. Select cell **B4** (the first frequency), right-click, and select **Sort → Sort Largest to Smallest**.
3. Select rows **10** and **12** (there is no row 11 visible), right-click, and click **Unhide** in the shortcut menu to restore row 11.

Next, add a column for cumulative percentage:

4. Enter **Cumulative Pct.** in cell **D3**. Enter **=C4** in cell **D4**. Enter **=D4+C5** in cell **D5** and copy this formula down through **row 10**.
5. Adjust the formatting of column D as necessary.

Next, create the Pareto chart:

6. Select the cell range **A3:A10** and while holding down the **Ctrl** key also select the cell range **C3:D10**.
7. Select **Insert → Column** (#1 in the labeled Charts groups on page 94), and select the **Clustered Column** gallery item.
8. Select **Format**. In the Current Selection group, select **Series "Cumulative Pct."** from the drop-down list and then click **Format Selection**.
   Select **Series "Cumulative Pct."** from the drop-down list at left and then click **More Formats**.
9. In the Format Data Series display, click **Series Options**. (To see the Series Options, you may have to first click the chart [third] icon near the top of the task pane.) In the Series Options, click **Secondary Axis**, and then close the display.
10. With the "Cumulative Pct." series still selected, select **Design → Change Chart Type.** In the Change Chart Type display, click **Combo** in the **All Charts** tab. In the Cumulative Pct. drop-down list, select the **Line with Markers** gallery item. Check **Secondary Axis** for the Cumulative Pct. and click **OK**.

    With the "Cumulative Pct." series still selected, select **Chart Design → Change Chart Type → Line → Line with Markers**.

In Excel 2010, select the **Line with Markers** gallery item in the Change Chart Type display and click **OK** in step 10.

Next, set the maximum value of the primary and secondary (left and right) *Y* axis scales to 100%. For each *Y* axis:

11. Right-click on the axis and click **Format Axis** in the shortcut menu.
12. In the Format Axis display, click **Axis Options**. In Axis Options, enter **1** as the **Maximum**. (To see the Axis Options, you may have to first click the chart [fourth] icon near the top of the task pane.) Click **Tick Marks**, select **Outside** from the **Major type** dropdown list, and close the display. In Excel versions with two-panel dialog boxes, in the Axis Options right pane, click **Fixed** for **Maximum**, enter **1** as the value, and then click **Close**.
13. Relocate the chart to a chart sheet, turn off the chart legend and gridlines, and add chart and axis titles by using the instructions in Appendix Section B.5.

If you use a PivotTable as a summary table, replace steps 1 through 6 with these steps:

1. Add a percentage column in column C, using steps 9 through 12 of the *Workbook* "The Summary Table" instructions on page 90.
2. Add a cumulative percentage column in column D. Enter **Cumulative Pctage** in cell **D3**.
3. Enter **=C4** in cell **D4**. Enter **=C5+D4** in cell **D5**, and copy the formula down through all the rows in the PivotTable.

4. Select the total row, right-click, and click **Hide** in the shortcut menu. (This prevents the total row from getting sorted.)

5. Right-click the cell that contains the first frequency (cell B4 in the example) and select **Sort→Sort Largest to Smallest**.

6. Select the cell range of only the percentage and cumulative percentage columns (the equivalent of the cell range C3:D10 in the example).

When you construct a Pareto chart from a PivotTable using these steps, the categories will not have proper category labels. To correct the labels:

1. Right-click on the chart and click **Select Data** in the shortcut menu.

2. In the Select Data Source display, click **Edit** that appears under **Horizontal (Category) Axis Labels**. In the Axis Labels display, drag the mouse to select and enter the axis labels cell range (A4:A10 in the example) and then click **OK**.
In the Select Data Source display, click the icon inside the **Horizontal (Category) axis labels** box and drag the mouse to select and enter the axis labels cell range.

3. Click **OK** to close the display.

Do not *type* the axis label cell range in step 2 for the reasons that Appendix Section B.3 explains.

The Side-by-Side Chart

Key Technique Use an Excel bar chart that is based on a contingency table.

Example Construct a side-by-side chart that displays the Fund Type and Risk Level, similar to Figure 2.9 on page 58.

PHStat Use **Two-Way Tables & Charts**.

For the example, use the Section EG2.1 "The Contingency Table" *PHStat* instructions on page 91 but in step 4, check **Side-by-Side Bar Chart** in addition to entering a **Title** and clicking **OK**.

Workbook Use the **Contingency Table workbook** as a model.

For the example, open to the **TwoWayTable worksheet** of the **Contingency Table workbook** and:

1. Select cell **A3** (or any other cell inside the PivotTable).

2. Select **Insert→Bar** and select the **Clustered Bar** gallery item.

3. Right-click the **Risk** drop-down button in the chart and click **Hide All Field Buttons on Chart**. (Does not apply to Excel for Mac.)

4. Relocate the chart to a chart sheet, turn off the gridlines, and add chart and axis titles by using the instructions in Appendix Section B.5.

When creating a chart from a contingency table that is not a PivotTable, select the cell range of the contingency table, including row and column headings, but excluding the total row and total column, as step 1.

To switch the row and column variables in a side-by-side chart, right-click the chart and then click **Select Data** in the shortcut menu. In the Select Data Source dialog box, click **Switch Row/Column** and then click **OK**.

EG2.4 VISUALIZING NUMERICAL VARIABLES

The Stem-and-Leaf Display

Key Technique Enter leaves as a string of digits that begin with the ' (apostrophe) character.

Example Construct a stem-and-leaf display of the three-year return percentage for the value retirement funds, similar to Figure 2.10 on page 62.

PHStat Use **Stem-and-Leaf Display**.

For the example, open to the **UNSTACKED worksheet** of the **Retirement Funds workbook**. Select **PHStat→Descriptive Statistics→Stem-and-Leaf Display**. In the procedure's dialog box (shown below):

1. Enter **B1:B174** as the **Variable Cell Range** and check **First cell contains label**.

2. Click **Set stem unit as** and enter **10** in its box.

3. Enter a **Title** and click **OK**.

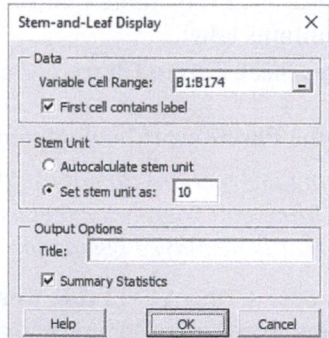

When creating other displays, use the **Set stem unit as** option sparingly and only if Autocalculate stem unit creates a display that has too few or too many stems. (Stem units you specify must be a power of 10.)

Workbook Manually construct the stems and leaves on a new worksheet to create a stem-and-leaf display. Adjust the column width of the column that holds the leaves as necessary.

The Histogram

Key Technique Modify an Excel column chart.

Example Construct histograms for the three-year return percentages for the growth and value retirement funds, similar to Figure 2.12 on page 63.

PHStat Use **Histogram & Polygons**.

For the example, open to the **DATA worksheet** of the **Retirement Funds workbook**. Select **PHStat → Descriptive Statistics → Histogram & Polygons**. In the procedure's dialog box (shown below):

1. Enter **K1:K480** as the **Variable Cell Range**, **Q1:Q11** as the **Bins Cell Range**, **R1:R10** as the **Midpoints Cell Range**, and check **First cell in each range contains label**.

2. Click **Multiple Groups-Stacked** and enter **C1:C480** as the **Grouping Variable Cell Range**. (In the DATA worksheet, the one-year return percentages are stacked. The column C values allow PHStat to unstack the values into growth and value groups.)

3. Enter a **Title**, check **Histogram**, and click **OK**.

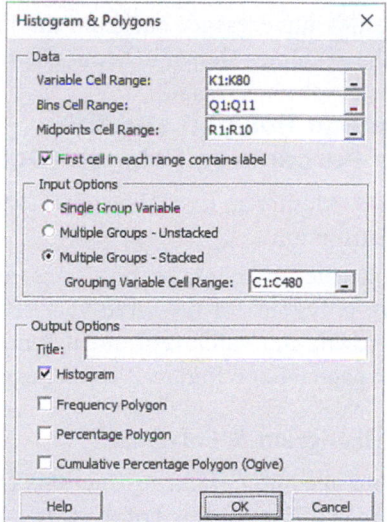

PHStat inserts two new worksheets, each of which contains a frequency distribution and a histogram. To relocate the histograms to their own chart sheets, use the instructions in Appendix Section B.5.

Because you cannot define an explicit lower boundary for the first bin, there can be no midpoint defined for that bin. Therefore, the **Midpoints Cell Range** you enter must have one fewer cell than the **Bins Cell Range**. PHStat uses the first midpoint for the second bin and uses "—" as the label for the first bin.

The example uses the workaround discussed in "Classes and Excel Bins" on page 49 When you use this workaround, the histogram bar labeled—will *always* be a zero bar. Appendix Section B.7 explains how you can delete this unnecessary bar from the histogram, as was done for the examples shown in Section 2.4.

Workbook Use the **Histogram workbook** as a model.

For the example, first construct frequency distributions for the growth and value funds. Open to the **UNSTACKED worksheet** of the **Retirement Funds workbook**. This worksheet

contains the retirement funds data unstacked in columns A and B and a set of bin numbers and midpoints appropriate for those variables in columns D and E. Click the **insert worksheet icon** to insert a new worksheet.

In the new worksheet:

1. Enter a title in cell **A1**, Bins in cell **A3**, **Frequency** in cell **B3**, and **Midpoints** in cell **C3**.

2. Copy the bin number list in the cell range **D2:D11** of the **UNSTACKED worksheet** and paste this list into cell **A4** of the new worksheet.

3. Enter '-- in cell **C4**. Copy the midpoints list in the cell range **E2:E13** of the **UNSTACKED worksheet** and paste this list into cell **C5** of the new worksheet.

4. Select the cell range **B4:B13** that will hold the array formula.

5. Type, but do not press the **Enter** or **Tab** key, the formula **=FREQUENCY(UNSTACKED!$A$2:$A$307, $A$4: $A$13)**. Then, while holding down the **Ctrl** and **Shift** keys, press the **Enter** key to enter the array formula into the cell range **B4:B13**.

6. Adjust the worksheet formatting as necessary.

Steps 1 through 6 construct a frequency distribution for the growth retirement funds. To construct a frequency distribution for the value retirement funds, insert another worksheet and repeat steps 1 through 6, entering **=FREQUENCY (UNSTACKED!$B$1:$B$174, $A$4: $A$13)** as the array formula in step 5.

Having constructed the two frequency distributions, continue by constructing the two histograms. Open to the worksheet that contains the frequency distribution for the growth funds and:

1. Select the cell range **B3:B13** (the cell range of the frequencies).

2. Select **Insert → Column** (#3 in the labeled Charts groups on page 94) and select the **Clustered Column** gallery item.

3. Right-click the chart and click **Select Data** in the shortcut menu.

In the Select Data Source display:

4. Click **Edit** under the **Horizontal (Categories) Axis Labels** heading. In the Axis Labels display, drag the mouse to select and enter the midpoints cell range (C3:C13) and click **OK**.

   In the Select Data Source display, click the icon inside the **Horizontal (Category) axis labels** box and drag the mouse to select and enter the midpoints cell range (C3:C13).

5. Click **OK**.

In the chart:

6. Right-click inside a bar and click **Format Data Series** in the shortcut menu.

7. In the Format Data Series display, click **Series Options**. In the Series Options, click **Series Options**, enter **0** as

the **Gap Width** and then close the display. (To see the second Series Options, you may have to first click the chart [third] icon near the top of the task pane.)

In Excel for Mac, there is only one Series Options label, and the Gap Width setting is displayed without having to click Series Options.

8. Relocate the chart to a chart sheet, turn off the chart legend and gridlines, add axis titles, and modify the chart title by using the instructions in Appendix Section B.5.

Do not *type* the axis label cell range in step 4 for the reasons that Appendix Section B.3 explains. In older versions of Excel, in step 7, click **Series Options** in the left pane, and in the Series Options right pane, change the **Gap Width** slider to **No Gap** and then click **Close**.

This example uses the workaround discussed in "Classes and Excel Bins" on page 49. When you use this workaround, the histogram bar labeled—will *always* be a zero bar. Appendix Section B.7 explains how you can delete this unnecessary bar from the histogram, as was done for the Section 2.4.

Analysis ToolPak   Use **Histogram**.

For the example, open to the **UNSTACKED worksheet** of the **Retirement Funds workbook** and:

1. Select **Data → Data Analysis**. In the Data Analysis dialog box, select **Histogram** from the **Analysis Tools** list and then click **OK**.

In the Histogram dialog box:

2. Enter **A1:A307** as the **Input Range** and enter **D1:D11** as the **Bin Range**.
3. Check **Labels**, click **New Worksheet Ply**, and check **Chart Output**.
4. Click **OK** to create the frequency distribution and histogram on a new worksheet.

In the new worksheet:

5. Follow steps 5 through 9 of the *Analysis ToolPak* instructions in "The Frequency Distribution" on page 93.

These steps construct a frequency distribution and histogram for the growth funds. To construct a frequency distribution and histogram for the value funds, repeat the nine steps but in step 2 enter **B1:B174** as the **Input Range**. You will need to correct several formatting errors to the histograms that Excel constructs. For each histogram, first change the gap widths between bars to 0. Follow steps 6 and 7 of the *Workbook* instructions of this section, noting the special instructions that appear after step 8.

Histogram bars are labeled by bin numbers. To change the labeling to midpoints, open to each of the new worksheets and:

1. Enter **Midpoints** in cell **C3** and '-- in cell **C4**. Copy the cell range **E2:E10** of the **UNSTACKED worksheet** and paste this list into cell **C5** of the new worksheet.
2. Right-click the histogram and click **Select Data**.

In the Select Data Source display:

3. Click **Edit** under the **Horizontal (Categories) Axis Labels** heading. In the Axis Labels display, drag the mouse to select and enter the cell range **C4:C13** and click **OK**.

In the Select Data Source display, click the icon inside the **Horizontal (Category) axis labels** box and drag the mouse to select and enter the cell range C4:C13.

4. Click **OK**.
5. Relocate the chart to a chart sheet, turn off the chart legend, and modify the chart title by using the instructions in Appendix Section B.5.

Do not type the axis label cell range in step 3 as you would otherwise do for the reasons explained in Appendix Section B.3.

This example uses the workaround discussed on page 49 "Classes and Excel Bins." Appendix Section B.7 explains how you can delete this unnecessary bar from the histogram, as was done for the examples shown in Section 2.4.

The Percentage Polygon and the Cumulative Percentage Polygon (Ogive)

Key Technique   Modify an Excel line chart that is based on a frequency distribution.

Example   Construct percentage polygons and cumulative percentage polygons for the three-year return percentages for the growth and value retirement funds, similar to Figure 2.14 on page 64 and Figure 2.16 on page 65.

PHStat   Use **Histogram & Polygons**.

For the example, use the *PHStat* instructions for creating a histogram on page 97 but in step 3 of those instructions, also check **Percentage Polygon** and **Cumulative Percentage Polygon (Ogive)** before clicking **OK**.

Workbook   Use the **Polygons workbook** as a model.

For the example, open to the **UNSTACKED worksheet** of the **Retirement Funds workbook** and follow steps 1 through 6 of the *Workbook* "The Histogram" instructions on page 97 to construct a frequency distribution for the growth funds. Repeat the steps to construct a frequency distribution for the value funds using the instructions that immediately follow step 6. Open to the worksheet that contains the growth funds frequency distribution and:

1. Select column **C**. Right-click and click **Insert** in the shortcut menu. Right-click and click **Insert** in the shortcut menu a second time. (The worksheet contains new, blank columns C and D and the midpoints column is now column E.)
2. Enter **Percentage** in cell **C3** and **Cumulative Pctage**. in cell **D3**.
3. Enter **=B4/SUM($B$4:$B$13)** in cell **C4** and copy this formula down through **row 13**.
4. Enter **=C4** in cell **D4**.

5. Enter **=C5+D4** in cell **D5** and copy this formula down through row **13**.

6. Select the cell range **C4:D13** right-click, and click **Format Cells** in the shortcut menu.

7. In the **Number** tab of the Format Cells dialog box, click **Percentage** in the **Category** list and click **OK**.

Open to the worksheet that contains the value funds frequency distribution and repeat steps 1 through 7. To construct the percentage polygons, open to the worksheet that contains the growth funds distribution and:

1. Select cell range **C4:C13**.

2. Select **Insert → Line** (#4 in the labeled Charts groups on page 94), and select the **Line with Markers** gallery item.

3. Right-click the chart and click **Select Data** in the shortcut menu.

In the Select Data Source display:

4. Click **Edit** under the **Legend Entries (Series)** heading. In the Edit Series dialog box, enter the *formula* **= "Growth Funds"** as the **Series name** and click **OK**. Enter the *formula* = "Growth Funds" as the Name.

5. Click **Edit** under the **Horizontal (Categories) Axis Labels** heading. In the Axis Labels display, drag the mouse to select and enter the cell range **E4:E13** and click **OK**. In the Select Data Source display, click the icon inside the Horizontal (Category) axis labels box and drag the mouse to select and enter the cell range E4:E13.

6. Click **OK**.

7. Relocate the chart to a chart sheet, turn off the chart gridlines, add axis titles, and modify the chart title by using the instructions in Appendix Section B.5.

In the new chart sheet:

8. Right-click the chart and click **Select Data** in the shortcut menu.

In the Select Data Source display:

9. Click **Add** under the **Legend Entries (Series)** heading. In the Edit Series dialog box, enter the *formula* **= "Value Funds"** as the **Series name** and press **Tab**. Click the "**+**" icon below the **Legend entries (Series)** list. Enter the *formula* = "Value Funds" as the **Name**.

10. With the placeholder value in **Series values** highlighted, click the sheet tab for the worksheet that contains the value funds distribution. In that worksheet, drag the mouse to select and enter the cell range **C4:C13** and click **OK**. Click the icon in the **Y** values box. Click the sheet tab for the worksheet that contains the value funds distribution and, in that worksheet, drag the mouse to select and enter the cell range C4:C13.

11. Click **Edit** under the **Horizontal (Categories) Axis Labels** heading. In the Axis Labels display, drag the

mouse to select and enter the cell range **E4:E13** and click **OK**. In the Select Data Source display, click the icon inside the Horizontal (Category) axis labels box and drag the mouse to select and enter the cell range E4:E13. Click **OK**.

Do not *type* the axis label cell range in steps 10 and 11 for the reasons explained in Appendix Section B.3.

To construct the cumulative percentage polygons, open to the worksheet that contains the growth funds distribution and repeat steps 1 through 12, but in step 1, select the cell range **D4:D13;** in step 5, drag the mouse to select and enter the cell range **A4:A13;** and in step 11, drag the mouse to select and enter the cell range **D4:D13**.

If the *Y* axis of the cumulative percentage polygon extends past 100%, right-click the axis and click **Format Axis** in the shortcut menu. In the Format Axis display, click **Axis Options**. In the Axis Options, enter **0** as the **Minimum** and then close the display. In Excels with two-panel dialog boxes, in the Axis Options right pane, click the first **Fixed** (for **Minimum**), enter **0** as the value, and then click **Close**.

EG2.5 VISUALIZING TWO NUMERICAL VARIABLES

The Scatter Plot

Key Technique Use the Excel scatter chart.

Example Construct a scatter plot of revenue and value for NBA teams, similar to Figure 2.17 on page 68.

PHStat Use **Scatter Plot**.

For the example, open to the **DATA worksheet** of the **NBAValues workbook**. Select **PHStat → Descriptive Statistics → Scatter Plot**. In the procedure's dialog box (shown below):

1. Enter **D1:D31** as the **Y Variable Cell Range**.
2. Enter **C1:C31** as the **X Variable Cell Range**.
3. Check **First cells in each range contains label**.
4. Enter a **Title** and click **OK**.

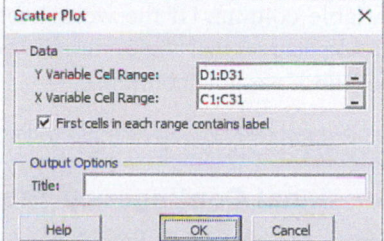

To add a superimposed line like the one shown in Figure 2.17, click the chart and use step 3 of the *Workbook* instructions.

Workbook Use the **Scatter Plot workbook** as a model.

For the example, open to the **DATA worksheet** of the **NBAValues workbook** and:

1. Select the cell range **C1:D31**.
2. Select **Insert → Scatter (X, Y) or Bubble Chart** (#5 in the labeled Charts groups on page 94) and select the **Scatter** gallery item.
   Excel for Mac labels the #5 icon **X Y (Scatter)**.
3. Select **Design** (or **Chart Design**) **→ Add Chart Element → Trendline → Linear**.

In older Excel 2010, select **Scatter** in the Charts group in step 2 and **Layout → Trendline → Linear Trendline** in step 3.

4. Relocate the chart to a chart sheet, turn off the chart legend and gridlines, add axis titles, and modify the chart title by using the instructions in Appendix Section B.5.

When constructing Excel scatter charts with other variables, make sure that the X variable column precedes (is to the left of) the Y variable column. (If the worksheet is arranged Y then X, cut and paste so that the Y variable column appears to the right of the X variable column.)

The Time-Series Plot

Key Technique Use the Excel scatter chart.

Example Construct a time-series plot of movie revenue per year from 1995 to 2016, similar to Figure 2.18 on page 69.

Workbook Use the **Time Series workbook** as a model.

For the example, open to the **DATA worksheet** of the **Movie Revenues workbook** and:

1. Select the cell range **A1:B21**.
2. Select **Insert → Scatter (X, Y) or Bubble Chart** (#5 in the labeled Charts groups on page 94) and select the **Scatter with Straight Lines and Markers** gallery item.
   Excel for Mac labels the #5 icon **X Y (Scatter)**.
3. Relocate the chart to a chart sheet, turn off the chart legend and gridlines, add axis titles, and modify the chart title by using the instructions in Appendix Section B.5.

When constructing time-series charts with other variables, make sure that the X variable column precedes (is to the left of) the Y variable column. (If the worksheet is arranged Y then X, cut and paste so that the Y variable column appears to the right of the X variable column.)

EG2.6 ORGANIZING a MIX of VARIABLES

Multidimensional Contingency Tables

Key Technique Use the Excel PivotTable feature.

Example Construct a PivotTable showing percentage of overall total for Fund Type, Risk Level, and Market Cap for the retirement funds sample, similar to the one shown at the right in Figure 2.19 on page 71.

Workbook Use the **MCT workbook** as a model.

For the example, open to the **DATA worksheet** of the **Retirement Funds workbook** and:

1. Select **Insert → PivotTable**.

In the Create PivotTable display:

2. Click **Select a table or range** and enter **A1: N480** as the **Table/Range**.
3. Click **New Worksheet** and then click **OK**.

In the PivotTable Fields (PivotTable Builder in Excel for Mac, PivotTable Field List in older versions) display (partially shown below):

4. Drag **Fund Type** in the **Choose fields to add to report** box and drop it in the **Rows** (or **Row Labels**) box.
5. Drag **Market Cap** in the **Choose fields to add to report** box and drop it in the **Rows** (or **Row Labels**) box.
6. Drag **Risk Level** in the **Choose fields to add to report** box and drop it in the **Columns** (or **Column Labels**) box.
7. Drag **Fund Type** in the **Choose fields to add to report** box a second time and drop it in the **Σ Values** box. The dropped label changes to **Count of Fun**....

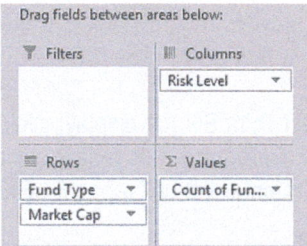

8. Click (not right-click) the dropped label **Count of Type** and then click **Value Field Settings** in the shortcut menu. In the Value Field Settings display, click the **Show Values As** tab and select **% of Grand Total** from the **Show values as** drop-down list (shown below).
   Click the "*i*" icon to the right of the dropped label **Count of Type**. In the PivotTable Field display, click the **Show data as** tab and select **% of total** from the drop-down list.
9. Click **OK**.

In the PivotTable:

10. Enter a title in cell **A1**.
11. Follow steps 6 through 10 of the *Workbook* "The Contingency Table" instructions on page 91 that relabel the rows and columns and rearrange the order of the risk category columns.

Adding a Numerical Variable

Key Technique Alter the contents of the Σ Values box in the PivotTable Field List pane.

Example Construct the Figure 2.20 PivotTable of Fund Type, Risk Level, and Market Cap, showing the mean ten-year return percentage for the retirement funds sample, on page 72.

Workbook Use the **MCT workbook** as a model.

For the example, first construct the PivotTable showing percentage of overall total for Fund Type, Risk Level, and Market Cap for the retirement funds sample using the 11-step instructions of the "Multidimensional Contingency Table" *Workbook* instructions that starts on page 100. Then continue with these steps:

12. If the PivotTable Field List pane is not visible, right-click cell **A3** and click **Show Field List** in the shortcut menu.
    If the PivotTable Builder (or PivotTable Field List) display is not visible, select **PivotTable Analyze → Field List**.

In the display:

13. Drag the blank label (changed from *Count of Fund Type* in a prior step) in the Σ **Values** box and drop it outside the display to delete. In the PivotTable, all of the percentages disappear.
14. Drag **10YrReturn** in the **Choose fields to add to report** box and drop it in the Σ **Values** box. The dropped label changes to *Sum of 10YrReturn*.
15. Click (not right-click) **Sum of 10YrReturn** and then click **Value Field Settings** in the shortcut menu. In the Value Field Settings display, click the **Summarize Values By** tab and select **Average** from the **Summarize value field by** drop-down list.
    Click the "*i*" icon to the right of the label **Sum of 10YrReturn**. In the PivotTable Field display, click the **Summarize by** tab and select **Average** from the list.
16. Click **OK**. The label in the Σ **Values** box changes to *Average of 10YrReturn*.

In the PivotTable:

17. Select cell range **B5:E13**, right-click, and click **Format Cells** in the shortcut menu. In the **Number** tab of the Format Cells dialog box, click Number, set the **Decimal places** to **2**, and click **OK**.

EG2.7 VISUALIZING a MIX of VARIABLES

PivotChart

Key Technique Use the PivotChart feature with a previously constructed PivotTable. (The PivotChart feature is not available in Excel for Mac.)

Example Construct the PivotChart based on the Figure 2.20 PivotTable of type, risk, and market cap showing mean ten-year return percentage, shown in Figure 2.23 on page 74.

Workbook Use the **MCT workbook** as a model.

For the example, open to the **MCT worksheet** of the **MCT workbook** and:

1. Select cell **A3** (or any other cell inside the PivotTable).
2. Select **Insert → PivotChart**.
3. In the Insert Chart display, click **Bar** in the **All Charts** tab and then select the **Clustered Bar** gallery item.
4. Relocate the chart to a chart sheet, turn off the gridlines, and add chart and axis titles by using the instructions in Appendix Section B.5.

In the PivotTable, collapse the **Growth** and **Value** categories, hiding the **Market Cap** categories. Note that contents of PivotChart changes to reflect changes made to the PivotTable.

Treemap

Key Technique Use the Excel treemap feature with a specially prepared tabular summary that includes columns that express hierarchical (tree) relationships. (The treemap feature is available only in some current Excel versions.)

Example Construct the Figure 2.24 treemap on page 74 that summarizes the sample of 479 retirement funds by Fund Type and Market Cap.

Workbook Use **Treemap**.

For the example, open to the **StackedSummary worksheet** of the **Retirement Funds workbook**. This worksheet contains sorted fund type categories in column A, market cap categories in column B, and frequencies in column C. Select the cell range **A1:C7** and:

1. Select **Insert → Insert Hierarchy Chart** (#7 in the Windows Chart Group shown on page 94) and select the **Treemap** gallery item.
2. Click the chart title and enter a new title for the chart.
3. Click one of the tile labels and increase the point size to improve readability. (This will change the point size of all labels.)
4. Right-click in the whitespace near the title and select **Move Chart**.
5. In the Move Chart dialog box, click **New Sheet** and click **OK**.

Sparklines

Key Technique Use the sparklines feature.

Example Construct the sparklines for movie revenues per month for the period 2005 to 2016. shown in Figure 2.25 on page 75.

Workbook Use the **Sparklines workbook** as a model.

For the example, open to the **DATA worksheet** of the **Monthly MovieRevenues workbook** and:

1. Select **Insert→Line** (in the **Sparklines group**).
2. In the Create Sparklines dialog box (shown below), enter **B2:M13** as the **Data Range** and **P2:P13** as the **Location Range**.
3. Click **OK**.

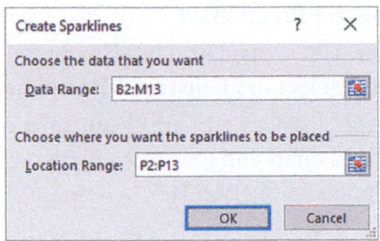

With the sparklines selected:

4. Select **Design→Axis→Same for All Sparklines** (under Vertical Axis Minimum Value Options). Select **Design→Axis→Same for All Sparklines** (under Vertical Axis Maximum Value Options).
5. Select rows 2 through 13. Right-click and click **Row Height** in the shortcut menu. In the Row height dialog box, enter **30** (**0.85** in Excel for Mac) as the **Row Height** and click **OK**.

Optionally, insert one or more rows at the top of the worksheet for a title and copy the month values in column A to column L for easier reference.

EG2.8 FILTERING and QUERYING DATA

Key Technique Use the Excel data filter feature.

Example Filter the DATA worksheet of the Retirement Funds workbook such that only funds with a four or five star ratings are displayed.

Workbook Use **Filter**.

For the example, open to the **DATA worksheet** of the **Retirement Funds workbook**. Select columns A through O (Fund Number through Star Rating) and:

1. Select **Data→Filter**. Each column displays a pull-down list button, similar to the buttons seen in Figure 2.26 on page 76.
2. Click the **pull-down button** for column O (Star Rating).

In the pull-down dialog box (shown below):

3. Clear the **(Select All)** check box to clear all check boxes.
4. Check the **Four** and **Five** check boxes and click **OK**.

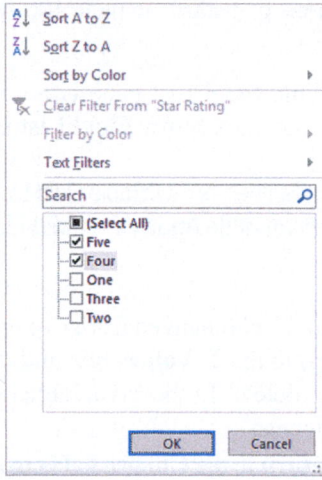

Excel displays the 108 retirement funds that have either a four- or five-star rating. Excel displays the original row number indices of these 108 rows in color and provides visual feedback of the gaps between nonconsecutive row numbers.

To remove this column data filter, click the column O pull-down button and select **Clear Filter from Star Rating**.

CHAPTER

2

▼JMP GUIDE

JG2 JMP CHOICES for CREATING SUMMARIES

JMP offers a choice of using either a menu-driven or interactive approach to create tabular and visual summaries. In the menu-driven approach, you select a procedure from a menu bar, make selections in the procedure's dialog box, click an OK button, and create a summary. If you make a mistake or

want to change your results, you repeat the cycle of procedure selection, dialog box selections, and clicking OK. The type of user interaction can be seen in Minitab, the Excel PHStat and the Data Analysis ToolPak add-ins, and in the open, save, or other file operations of most programs, including JMP.

JMP also offers an interactive approach that displays a window in which you drag-and-drop variable column names from a list onto a template to create summaries. As you drag-and-drop column names, JMP immediately begins to create a summary that you can change at will, allowing you to explore data interactively. To reset a template, you press a Start Over button and to finalize results, you press a Done button. There are no OK buttons in these interactive windows.

The JMP Guides in this book feature the interactive way of using JMP to create summaries. This JMP Guide makes extensive use of the Tabulate and Graph Builder interactive procedures, the windows for which the gallery on page 112 presents. As a one-time exception, this Guide presents both ways of creating a summary table in Section JG2.1. Being familiar with the menu-drive approach will be useful when, in later chapters, you use JMP methods that exclusively use that type of interaction. Using the menu-driven approach for the very first JMP results that you produce is a good, guided way of gaining experience (and confidence) using JMP.

JG2.1 ORGANIZING CATEGORICAL VARIABLES

The Summary Table (classical)

Use **Summary**.

For example, create a frequency and percentage summary table similar to Figure 2.1 on page 43, open to the **Retirement Funds data table**. Select **Tables→Summary**. In that procedure's dialog box (shown here):

1. Click **Risk Level** in the Select Columns list and then click **Group** to add Risk Level to the Group box.
2. Click **Statistics** and select **% of Total** from the pull-down list to add **% of Total (Risk Level)** to the Statistics box.
3. Select **stat of column** from the **statistics column name format**.
4. Click **OK**.

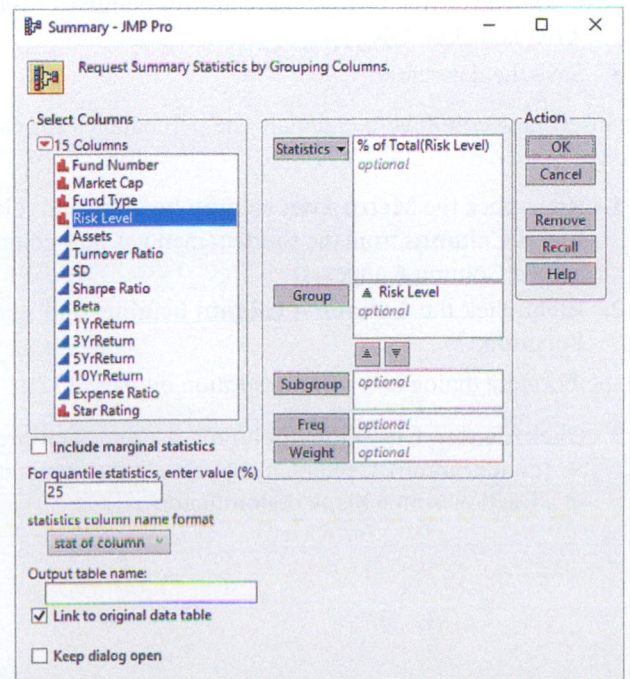

JMP creates the summary table as a new data table in its own window and labels the frequency column N Rows.

The Summary Table (interactive)

Use **Tabulate**.

For example, create a frequency and percentage summary table similar to Figure 2.1 on page 43, open to the **Retirement Funds data table**. Select **Analyze→Tabulate**. In that procedure's window (shown on page 112):

1. Drag **Risk Level** from the columns list and drop it in the **Drop zone for rows** area. A simple summary table in which the frequency column is labeled N appears in place of the template outline (shown below).

Fund Type	N
Growth	306
Value	173

2. Click **N** in the statistics list and while holding down the **Ctrl key**, click **% of Total** from the same list.
3. With the two selections still highlighted, drag then and drop them on the N column heading of the simple summary table. The summary table gains a percentage column. (If you did hold down the **Ctrl key** properly in step 2 the percentage column *replaces* the N column.)
4. Click **Done**.

JMP displays the summary table under the heading Tabulate in a new window (shown below). To save the results as a data table, click the **Tabulate red triangle** and select **Make Into Data Table** from its menu. JMP creates a new data table in its own window. (This data table is equivalent to the one that the "classical" Summary procedure creates.)

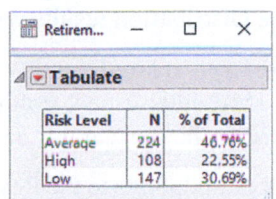

Risk Level	N	% of Total
Average	224	46.76%
High	108	22.55%
Low	147	30.69%

The Contingency Table

Use **Tabulate**.

For example, to create a contingency table displaying Fund Type and Risk Level similar to Figure 2.2 on page 43, open to the **Retirement Funds data table**. Select **Analyze→Tabulate**. In that procedure's window (shown on page 112):

1. Drag **Fund Type** from the columns list and drop it in the **Drop zone for rows** area. A simple summary table in which the frequency column is labeled N appears in place of the template outline.
2. Drag **Risk Level** from the columns list and drop it on the N column heading of the simple summary table.
3. Drag **All** from the statistics list and drop it on the Fund Type column heading.

4. Drag **All** from the statistics list and drop it on the Risk Level column heading.

5. Click **Done**.

JMP displays the summary table under the heading Tabulate in a new window.

JG2.2 ORGANIZING NUMERICAL VARIABLES

The Ordered Array

To create an ordered array, in a data table, right-click the column name of the variable to be sorted and select **Sort → Ascending** or **Sort → Descending** from the shortcut menu. JMP resorts all rows of the data table. If results are linked to the data table, JMP will create a new data table to hold the sorted results rows.

The Frequency, Relative Frequency, Percentage, and Cumulative Percentage Distributions

Use **Distribution** to create a *histogram* from which one or more frequency distributions can be derived.

For example, to create a frequency, percentage, and cumulative percentage distribution for the restaurant meal cost data that contain the information found in Tables 2.3, 2.5, and 2.9 in Section 2.2, open to the **Restaurants data table**. Select **Analyze → Distribution**. In that procedure's dialog box, click **Cost** in the Select Columns list and then click **Y, Columns**, to add Cost to the Y, Columns box. Click **OK**.

JMP opens a new Distribution results window that contains a histogram and various other results. The histogram will serve as the basis for creating the tabular frequency distributions. In the Distribution results window:

1. Click the **Cost red triangle** and select **Save → Level Midpoints**. JMP adds a new column of midpoints, Midpoint Cost, to the Restaurants data table.

JMP adds a column of midpoints to the Restaurants data table that the JMP Summary procedure can use to create a tabular frequency distribution.

2. Select **Tables → Summary**.

In that procedure's dialog box (shown at the top in right column):

3. Click **Midpoint Cost** in the Select Columns list and click **Group** to add Midpoint Cost to the Group box.

4. Click **Location** in the Select Columns list and then click **Subgroup** to add Location to the Subgroup box.

5. Click **OK**.

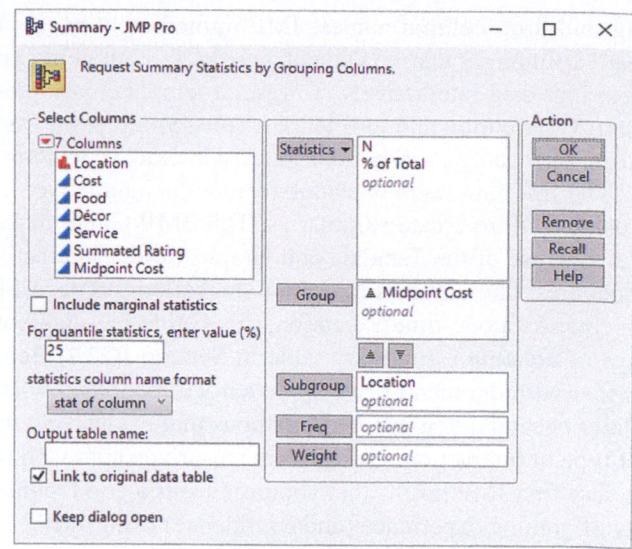

JMP creates a new data table with four columns Midpoint Cost, N Rows, N(Center City), and N(Metro Area) (shown below). Save this data table before continuing.

	Midpoint Cost	N Rows	N(Center City)	N(Metro Area)
1	25	8	4	4
2	35	17	3	14
3	45	28	12	16
4	55	26	14	12
5	65	9	7	2
6	75	5	4	1
7	85	6	5	1
8	95	1	1	0

To better label this data table (and to simplify later entries for adding percentages):

6. Double-click the **N(Center City) column heading** and in the dialog box change the **Column Name** to **Center City** and click **OK**.

7. Double-click the **N(Metro Area) column heading** and in the dialog box change the **Column Name** to **Metro Area** and click **OK**.

8. Save the data table.

To insert new columns to calculate the percentages for each group:

1. Right-click the **Metro Area column heading** and select **Insert Columns** from the shortcut menu. A new column named Column 4 appears.

2. Right-click the **Column 4 column heading** and select **Formula**.

In the Formula dialog box (see illustration on page 112):

3. Click **Center City** in the columns list and then press ÷ (divide button). Center City appears as the numerator in a fraction with a blank denominator.

4. Enter **col sum** in the filter box above the list of formula functions. Click **Col Sum** in the formula function list box to add Col Sum( ) to the denominator.

5. Click **Center City** in the columns list to complete the function as Col Sum(*Center City*).

6. Click **OK**.

Column 4 displays the frequency percentage for the Center City group as decimal fractions. Relabel and reformat Column 4.

7. Double-click the **Column 4 column heading**. In the Column 4 dialog box: enter **Percentage, Center City** as the **Column Name**, select **Percent** from the **Format** pull-down list, enter **2** in the **Dec** box, and click **OK**.

Save the data table before continuing.

8. Double-click the blank, sixth column. JMP names the column Column 6.

9. Right-click the **Column 6 column heading** and select **Formula**.

In the Formula dialog box (see illustration on page 112):

10. Click **Metro Area** in the columns list and then press ÷ (divide button). Metro Area appears as the numerator in a fraction with a blank denominator.

11. Enter **col sum** in the filter box above the list of formula functions. Click **Col Sum** in the formula function list box to add Col Sum( ) to the denominator.

12. Click **Metro Area** in the columns list to complete the function as Col Sum(*Metro Area*).

13. Click **OK**.

Column 6 displays the frequency percentage for the Metro Area group as decimal fractions.

14. Double-click the **Column 6 column heading**. In the Column 6 dialog box, enter **Percentage, Metro Area** as the **Column Name**, select **Percent** from the **Format** pull-down list, enter **2** in the **Dec** box, and click **OK**.

15. Save the data table.

Cumulative Percentages. To insert new columns to calculate the cumulative percentages for each group, first complete the 14-step process to create percentage columns. Then:

1. Right-click the **Metro Area column heading** and select **Insert Columns** from the shortcut menu. A new column named Column 5 appears.

2. Right-click the **Column 5 column heading** and select **Formula**.

In the Formula dialog box (see illustration on page 112):

3. Enter **col cum** in the filter box above the list of formula functions. Click **Col Cumulative Sum** in the formula function list box to add Col Cumulative Sum( ) to the formula workspace area.

4. Click **Percentage, Center City** in the columns list to complete the function as Col Cumulative Sum(*Percentage, Center City*).

5. Click **OK**.

Column 5 displays the cumulative percentage for the Center City group as decimal fractions.

6. Double-click the **Column 5 column heading**. In the Column 5 dialog box, change the Column Name to **Cumulative Pct., Center City**, select **Percent** from the **Format** pull-down list, enter **2** in the **Dec** box, and click **OK**.

7. Double-click the blank, eighth column. JMP names the column Column 8.

8. Right-click the **Column 8 column heading** and select **Formula**.

In the Formula dialog box (see illustration on page 112):

9. Enter **col cum** in the filter box above the list of formula functions. Click **Col Cumulative Sum** in the formula function list box.

10. Click **Percentage, Metro Area** in the columns list to complete the function as Col Cumulative Sum (*Percentage, Metro Area*).

11. Click **OK**.

Column 8 displays the cumulative percentage for the Center City group as decimal fractions.

12. Double-click the **Column 8 column heading**. In the Column 8 dialog box, change the Column Name to **Cumulative Pct., Metro Area**, select **Percent** from the **Format** pull-down list, enter **2** in the **Dec** box, and click **OK**.

The data table contains columns for frequency, percentage, and cumulative percentages for both the Center City and Metro Area restaurants. Save the data table.

Optionally, change the name and contents of the first column to better match the row legends that Tables 2.3, 2.5, and 2.9 use. Select the **N Rows column heading** and select **Delete Columns** from the shortcut menu to delete this unnecessary column for the data table.

Classes

JMP calculates class boundaries for the frequency distribution. In the example that the previous section uses, JMP calculates the same classes that Tables 2.3, 2.5, and 2.9 use. In other cases, either the class interval width or the class boundaries may need to be changed. To adjust either (or both), before following step 4 (saving midpoints) in the first series of instructions, double-click the **X axis** to display the X Axis Settings dialog box, make adjustments in the Tick/Bin Increment group (shown below), and click **OK**.

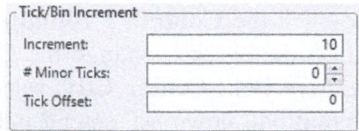

For the example, JMP used a class interval width of 10 and started the first class with a number that ends in 0 (20). To change the class interval width, enter a new value for **Increment**. For example, to change the class interval width to 20, enter **20** as the **Increment**. To change the class boundaries, enter a new value for **Tick Offset**. For example, to start the first class with a number ending in 5, enter **5** as the **Tick Offset**.

JG2.3 VISUALIZING CATEGORICAL VARIABLES

The Bar Chart or the Pie Chart

Use **Graph Builder**.

For example, to construct a bar or pie chart that summarizes Risk Level similar to Figures 2.5 and 2.6 on page 53 open to the **Retirement Funds data table**. Select **Graph → Graph Builder**. In that procedure's window (shown on page 112):

1. Drag **Risk Level** from the columns list and drop it in the **Y** area, for a bar chart, or the **X area**, for a pie chart. A one-variable scatter plot appears as the default chart.
2. Click either the **Bar chart icon** or the **Pie chart icon** (both shown below) to change chart into form sought.

3. Double-click the chart title "Risk Level" and enter a more descriptive title.
4. If creating a bar chart, click the **Graph Builder red triangle** and uncheck **Show Legend**.
5. If creating a pie chart, select **Label by Percent of Total Values** from the **Label** pull-down list.
6. Click **Done**.

JMP displays the chart in a new window. Optionally, use the Appendix Section B.5 instructions to change the font and type characteristics of chart labels.

The Pareto Chart

Use **Pareto Plot**.

For example, to construct a Pareto chart of the incomplete ATM transactions equivalent to Figure 2.7 on page 57, open to the **ATM Transactions data table**. Select **Analyze → Quality and Process → Pareto Plot**. In that procedure's dialog box (shown below):

1. Click **Cause** in the Select Columns list and click **Y, cause** to add Cause to the Y, cause box.
2. Click **Frequency** in the Select Columns list and click **Freq** to add Frequency to the Freq box.
3. Click **OK**.

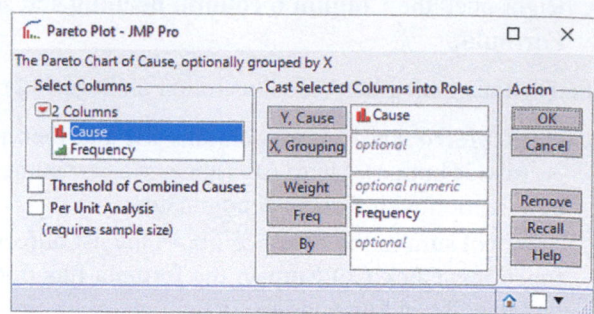

JMP displays the chart in a new window. To see the cumulative percentage points on the line graph, click the **Pareto Chart red triangle** and select **Show Cum Percent Points** from its menu. Optionally, use the Appendix Section B.5 instructions to change the font and type characteristics of chart labels.

Visualizing Two Categorical Variables

Use **Graph Builder**.

Construct a side-by-side chart that displays the Fund Type and Risk Level, similar to Figure 2.9 on page 58, open to the **Retirement Funds data table**. Select **Graph → Graph Builder**. In that procedure's window (shown on page 112):

1. Drag **Fund Type** from the columns list and drop it in the **Y** area.
2. Click either the **Bar chart icon**. A bar chart of the sample of retirement funds sample by Fund Type appears.
3. Drag **Risk Level** from the columns list and drop it on the **Overlay** box.
4. Double-click the chart title and edit title, as necessary.
5. Click **Done**.

JMP displays the chart in a new window. Optionally, use the Appendix Section B.5 instructions to change the font and type characteristics of chart labels. The bars appear in an order (average, high, low) different from the ordering in Figure 2.9 (high, average, low).

To change the order, go back to the Retirement Funds data table, right-click the **Risk Level column heading** and select **Column Info** from the shortcut menu. In the Risk Level dialog box, select **Value Ordering** from the **Column Properties** pull-down list and in the Value Ordering group rearrange the variable categories (shown below, after moving Average to the second position). Click **OK**. The new order of categories will be used by all charts that visualize Risk Level until changed or removed.

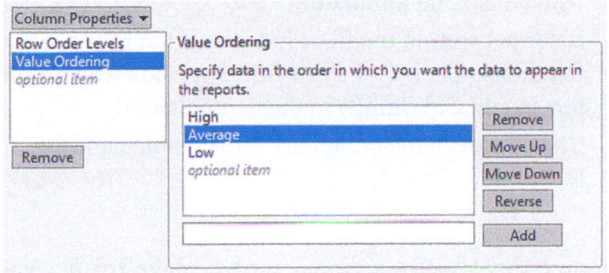

JG2.4 VISUALIZING NUMERICAL VARIABLES

The Stem-and-Leaf Display

Use **Distribution**.

For example, to construct a stem-and-leaf display of the three-year return percentage for the value retirement funds, similar to Figure 2.10 on page 62, open to the **Retirement Funds data table**. Select **Analyze ➝ Distribution**. In the procedure's dialog box:

1. Click **3YrReturn** in the Select Columns list and click **Y, columns** to add 3YrReturn to the Y, columns box.
2. Click **Fund Type** in the Select Columns list and click **By** to add Fund Type to the By box.
3. Click **OK**.

JMP opens a new Distribution results window that contains histograms and various other results.

4. Click the **Distributions Fund Type = Growth red triangle** and select **Stack** from its menu.
5. Click the **3YrReturn red triangle** under the heading Distributions Fund Type = Value and select **Stem and Leaf** from its menu.
6. To obtain a stem and leaf display for the value funds, go to the Distributions Type = Value area, and in the line below, to the left of 3YrReturn, click the red down arrow.

JMP adds a stem-and-leaf display under the heading Distributions Fund Type = Value. To declutter the results window:

1. Click the **3YrReturn red triangle** under the heading Distributions Fund Type = Value and while holding down the **Ctrl key**, select **Display Options ➝ Quantities** (to clear its checkmark).
2. Click the same **3YrReturn red triangle** and while holding down the **Ctrl key**, select **Histogram Options ➝ Histogram** (to clear its checkmark).
3. Click the same **3YrReturn red triangle** and while holding down the **Ctrl key**, select **Outlier Box Plot** (to clear its checkmark).

In these steps, holding down the **Ctrl key** tells JMP to change a setting for both groups. This shortcut avoids having to make the same changes for the **Fund Type = Growth** display separately.

The results window simplifies to a display of two summary statistics tables and the stem-and-leaf-display for the value retirement funds. To hide the summary table for the growth values, click the gray disclosure button for Distribution Fund Type = Growth.

The Histogram

Use **Graph Builder**.

For example, to construct histograms for the three-year return percentages for the growth and value retirement funds, similar to Figure 2.12 on page 63, open to the **Retirement Funds data table**. Select **Graph ➝ Graph Builder**. In that procedure's window (shown on page 112):

1. Drag **3YrReturn** from the columns list and drop it in the **X** area.
2. Click the **histogram icon** (#7) (shown on page 106).
3. Drag **Fund Type** from the columns list and drop it in the **Y** area.
4. Double-click the chart title and edit title, as necessary.
5. Click **Done**.

JMP displays the pair of histograms in a new window. Optionally, use the Appendix Section B.5 instructions to change the font and type characteristics of chart labels.

The Percentage Polygon and the Cumulative Percentage Polygon (Ogive)

Use **Distribution** and **Graph Builder**.

For example, to construct percentage polygons and cumulative percentage polygons for the three-year return percentages for the growth and value retirement funds, similar to Figure 2.14 on page 64 and Figure 2.16 on page 65, open to the **Retirement Funds data table**. Select **Analyze ➝ Distribution**. In that procedure's dialog box, click **3YrReturn** from the Select Columns list and click **Y, Columns** to add 3YrReturn to the Y, Columns box. Click **OK**.

JMP opens a new Distribution results window that contains a histogram and various other results. The histograms will serve as the basis for creating the polygons. In the Distribution results window:

1. Click the **3YrReturn red triangle** and select **Save → Level Midpoints**. JMP adds a new column of midpoints, Midpoint 3YrReturn, to the Retirement Funds data table.

JMP adds a column of midpoints to the Retirement Funds data table that the JMP Summary procedure can use to create a tabular frequency distribution.

2. Select **Tables → Summary**.

In that procedure's dialog box:

3. Click **Midpoint 3YrReturn** from the **Select Columns** list and click **Group** to add Midpoint 3YrReturn the Group box.
4. Click **Fund Type** from the **Select Columns** list and then click **Subgroup** to add Fund Type to the Subgroup box.
5. Click **OK**.

JMP creates a new data table with four columns Midpoint 3YrReturn, N Rows, N(Growth), and N(Value). To better label this data table (and to simplify later entries for adding percentages):

6. Double-click the **N(Growth) column heading** and in the dialog box change the **Column Name** to **Growth** and click **OK**.
7. Double-click the **N(Value) column heading** and in the dialog box change the **Column Name** to **Value** and click **OK**.
8. Save the data table.

Insert new columns to calculate the percentages for each group (necessary for percentage *and* cumulative percentage polygons):

9. Right-click the **Value column heading** and select **Insert Columns** from the shortcut menu. A new column named Column 4 appears.
10. Right-click the **Column 4 column heading** and select **Formula**.

In the Formula dialog box (see illustration on page 00):

11. Click **Growth** in the columns list and then press ÷ (divide button). Growth appears as the numerator in a fraction with a blank denominator.
12. Enter **col sum** in the filter box above the list of formula functions. Click **Col Sum** in the formula function list box to add Col Sum( ) to the denominator.
13. Click **Growth** in the columns list to complete the function as Col Sum(*Growth*).
14. Click **OK**.

Column 4 displays the frequency percentage for the Growth group as decimal fractions. Relabel and reformat Column 4.

15. Double-click the **Column 4 column heading**. In the Column 4 dialog box: enter **Percentage, Growth** as the **Column Name**, select **Percent** from the **Format** pull-down list, enter **2** in the **Dec** box, and click **OK**.

Save the data table before continuing.

16. Double-click the blank, sixth column. JMP names the column Column 6.
17. Right-click the **Column 6 column heading** and select **Formula**.

In the Formula dialog box (see illustration on page 112):

18. Click **Value** in the columns list and then press ÷ (divide button). Value appears as the numerator in a fraction with a blank denominator.
19. Enter **col sum** in the filter box above the list of formula functions. Click **Col Sum** in the formula function list box to add Col Sum( ) to the denominator.
20. Click **Value** in the columns list to complete the function as Col Sum(*Value*).
21. Click **OK**.

Column 6 displays the frequency percentage for the Value group as decimal fractions.

22. Double-click the **Column 6 column heading**. In the Column 6 dialog box, enter **Percentage, Value** as the **Column Name**, select **Percent** from the **Format** pull-down list, enter **2** in the **Dec** box, and click **OK**.
23. Save the data table.

Percentage Polygons. To construct the percentage polygons, select **Graph → Graph Builder**, and in that procedure's window (shown on page 112):

1. Drag **Midpoint 3YrReturn Level** from the columns list and drop it in the **X area**.
2. While holding the **Ctrl key**, click **Percentage, Growth** and **Percentage, Value** to select both columns.
3. Drag these columns and drop them in the **Y area**.
4. Click the **Line icon** (shown on page 106).
5. Right-click anywhere in the whitespace of the chart area and select **Add → Points** from the shortcut menu.
6. Double-click the chart title and edit title, as necessary.
7. Click **Done**.

JMP displays the percentage polygons chart in a new window. Optionally, use the Appendix Section B.5 instructions to change the font and type characteristics of chart labels or axis settings.

Cumulative Percentage Polygons. To construct the cumulative percentage polygons, first insert new columns to calculate the cumulative percentages for each group in the data table saved in step 15 in the earlier instructions.

1. Right-click the **Value column heading** and select **Insert Columns** from the shortcut menu. A new column named Column 5 appears.

2. Right-click the **Column 5 column heading** and select **Formula**.

In the Formula dialog box (see illustration on page 112):

3. Enter **col cum** in the filter box above the list of formula functions. Click **Col Cumulative Sum** in the formula function list box to add Col Cumulative Sum( ) to the formula workspace area.

4. Click **Percentage**, **Growth** in the columns list to complete the function as Col Cumulative Sum(*Percentage, Growth*).

5. Click **OK**.

Column 5 displays the cumulative percentage for the Growth group as decimal fractions.

6. Double-click the **Column 5 column heading**. In the Column 5 dialog box, change the Column Name to **Cumulative Pct., Growth**, select **Percent** from the **Format** pull-down list, enter **2** in the **Dec** box, and click **OK**.

7. Double-click the blank, eighth column. JMP names the column Column 8.

8. Right-click the **Column 8 column heading** and select **Formula.**

In the Formula dialog box (see illustration on page 112):

9. Enter **col cum** in the filter box above the list of formula functions. Click **Col Cumulative Sum** in the formula function list box.

10. Click **Percentage, Value** in the columns list to complete the function as Col Cumulative Sum(*Percentage, Value*).

11. Click **OK**.

Column 8 displays the cumulative percentage for the Value group as decimal fractions.

12. Double-click the **Column 8 column heading**. In the Column 8 dialog box, change the Column Name to **Cumulative Pct., Value**, select **Percent** from the **Format** pull-down list, enter **2** in the **Dec** box, and click **OK**.

13. Save the data table.

The data table contains columns for frequency, percentage, and cumulative percentages for both the growth and value retirement funds. To construct the cumulative percentage polygons, select **Graph ➔ Graph Builder**, and in that procedure's window (shown on page 112):

1. Drag **Midpoint 3YrReturn Level** from the columns list and drop it in the **X area**.

2. While holding the **Ctrl key**, click **Cumulative Pct., Growth** and **Cumulative Pct., Value** to select both columns.

3. Drag these columns and drop them in the **Y area**.

4. Click the **Line icon** (shown on page 112).

5. Right-click anywhere in the whitespace of the chart area and select **Add ➔ Points** from the shortcut menu.

6. Double-click the chart title and edit title, as necessary

7. Click **Done**.

JMP displays the cumulative percentage polygons chart in a new window. Optionally, use the Appendix Section B.5 instructions to change the font and type characteristics of chart labels.

JG2.5 VISUALIZING TWO NUMERICAL VARIABLES

The Scatter Plot

Use **Graph Builder**.

For example, to construct a scatter plot of revenue and value for NBA teams, similar to Figure 2.17 on page 68, open to the **NBAValues** data table. Select **Graph ➔ Graph Builder**. In that procedure's window (shown on page 112):

1. Drag **Revenue** from the columns list and drop it in **X area**.

2. Drag **Current Value** from the columns list and drop it in **Y area**.

3. Click the **Line of Fit chart icon** (#3) (shown on page 106).

4. Double-click the chart title and edit title, as necessary.

5. Click **Done**.

JMP displays the scatter plot in a new window. Optionally, use the Appendix Section B.5 instructions to change the font and type characteristics of chart labels.

The Time-Series Plot

Use **Graph Builder**.

For example, to construct a time-series plot of movie revenue per year from 1995 to 2016, similar to Figure 2.18 on page 69, open to the **Movie Revenues data table**. Select **Graph ➔ Graph Builder**. In that procedure's window (shown on page 00):

1. Drag **Year** from the columns list and drop it in **X area**.

2. Drag **Revenues** from the columns list and drop it in **Y area**.

3. Click the **Line chart icon** (#4) (shown on page 106).

4. Right-click anywhere in the chart and select **Add ➔ Points** from the shortcut menu.

5. Double-click the chart title and edit title, as necessary.

JMP displays a time-series plot in which the Y axis begins at 5 and not 0.

6. Right-click the **Y axis** and select **Axis Settings**.

7. In the Y Axis Setting dialog box, enter **0** as the **Minimum** (in the Scale group) and click **OK**.

8. Back in the Graph Builder window, click **Done**.

JMP displays the time series plot in a new window. Optionally, use the Appendix Section B.5 instructions to change the font and type characteristics of chart labels.

JG2.6 ORGANIZING a MIX of VARIABLES

Multidimensional Contingency Table

Use **Tabulate**.

For example, to construct a table showing percentage of overall total for Fund Type, Risk Level, and Market Cap for the retirement funds sample, similar to the one shown at the right in Figure 2.19 on page 71, open to the **Retirement Funds data table**. Select **Analyze → Tabulate**. In that procedure's window (shown on page 112):

1. Drag **Risk Level** from the columns list and drop it in the **Drop zone for columns**.
2. While holding down the **Ctrl key**, select **Market Cap** and **Fund Type** the columns list.
3. Drag these columns and drop them in gray square to the left of the Risk Level categories.
4. Drag-and-drop the **Fund Type column heading** over the **Market Cap column heading** to reorder table (shown below).

		Risk Level		
Fund Type	Market Cap	High	Average	Low
Growth	Large	17	91	46
	MidCap	25	45	16
	Small	49	16	1
Value	Large	3	38	70
	MidCap	4	17	10
	Small	10	17	4

5. Drag **All** from the statistics list and drop it on the **Market Cap column heading**.
6. Click **All** from the statistics list and drop it on the **Risk Level column heading**.
7. Click **% of Total** from the statistics list and drop it on the joint response cells area of the table.
8. Click **Done**.

JMP displays the summary table under the heading Tabulate in a new window. To change the order of the categories for a variable, go back to the Retirement Funds data table, right-click the variable's **column heading**, and select **Column Info** from the shortcut menu. In the column's dialog box, select **Value Ordering** from the **Column Properties** pull-down list and in the Value Ordering group rearrange the categories as necessary. Then click **OK** and repeat steps 1 through 8.

To construct a PivotTable of Fund Type, Risk Level, and Market Cap that displays the mean ten-year return percentage, similar to the one shown at the right in Figure 2.20 on page 72, repeat steps 1 through 6 and replace steps 7 and 8 with these steps 7 through 9:

7. Click **Mean** from the statistics list and drop it over the numbers in the table. The numbers change to missing values (dots).
8. Drag **10YrReturn** from the columns list and drop it over the missing values.
9. Click **Done**

JG2.7 VISUALIZING a MIX of VARIABLES

Colored Scatter Plots

Use **Graph Builder**.

For example, to create a colored scatter plot of Expense Ratio, 3YrReturn, and Market Cap, similar to Figure 2.22 on page 73, open to the **Retirement Funds data table**. Select **Graph → Graph Builder** and in that procedure's window (shown on page 112):

1. Drag **Expense Ratio** from the columns list and drop it in the **Y area**.
2. Drag **3YrReturn** from the columns list and drop it in the **X area**.
3. Click the **Smoother icon** (shown on page 106) to deselect that icon, leaving **Scatter** selected.
4. Drag **Market Cap** from the columns list and drop it on the **Color area**.
5. Double-click the chart title and edit title, as necessary.
6. Click **Done**.

JMP displays the colored scatter plot in a new window. Optionally, use the Appendix Section B.5 instructions to change the font and type characteristics of chart labels or axis settings.

Note that the chart uses both red and green as category colors. People with color vision deficiency may not be able to fully perceive these colors. To improve the chart, click the **Graph Builder red triangle** and select **Categorical Color Theme** from its menu. In the Categorical Color Themes dialog box, select a more appropriate theme from the **Qualitative** column and click **OK**. (The Figure 2.22 colored scatter plot uses the default color theme that includes the red and green colors. Compare this figure to the Figure 2.24 treemap that uses an alternate color theme.)

Treemap

Use **Graph Builder**.

For example, to construct a treemap for Fund Type and Market Cap, similar to Figure 2.24 on page 74, open to the **Retirement Funds data table**. Select **Graph → Graph Builder** and in that procedure's window (shown on page 112):

1. Click the **Treemap icon** (shown on page 112).
2. Drag **Market Cap** from the columns list and drop it in the **X area**.
3. Drag **Market Cap** from the columns list and drop it on the **Color area**.
4. Drag **Fund Type** from the columns list to under the Market Cap X axis title and drop when the axis title changes to Fund Type/Market Cap and the treemap becomes subdivided.
5. Double-click the chart title and edit title, as necessary.
6. Click **Done**.

JMP displays the treemap in a new window. Optionally, use the Appendix Section B.5 instructions to change the font and type characteristics of chart labels or axis settings.

Note that the chart uses both red and green as category colors. People with color vision deficiency may not be able to fully perceive these colors. To improve the chart, click the **Graph Builder red triangle** and select **Categorical Color Theme** from its menu. In the Categorical Color Themes dialog box, select a more appropriate theme from the **Qualitative** column and click **OK**. (The Figure 2.24 JMP treemap uses the seventh theme in the Qualitative column as its color theme.)

JG2.8 FILTERING and QUERYING DATA

Use **Select Rows** or **Data Filter**.

For example, to filter the Retirement Funds worksheet to select the rows that correspond to value retirement funds that have ten-year return percentages that are greater than or equal to 9, open to the **Retirement Funds data table**. Select **Rows ➔ Row Selection ➔ Select Where**. In the Select Rows dialog box (see Figure 2.26 on page 76):

1. Click **Fund Type** in the columns list.
2. Enter **Value** in the box to the right of the equals pull-down list selection and click **Add Condition** to add Fund Type equals Value to the conditions box.
3. Click **10YrReturn** in the columns list.
4. Select **is greater than or equal to** from the pull-down list.
5. Enter **9** in the box to the right of the equals pull-down list selection and click **Add Condition** to add 10YrReturn is greater than or equal to 9 to the conditions box.
6. Click **OK**.

JMP highlights the (five) rows that contain Value as the value for Fund Type and that have 10YrReturn values that are 9 or more. Using the Select Rows subset is most useful to see a subset of rows highlighted in a visual summary of all the data or to exclude the subset from further analysis through the **Hide** selection in the **Rows red triangle** menu. If one or more columns were selected before step 1, the subset will be

composed of values only from those columns. To take subsets that contain full rows of data, clear the column selections before Step 1. (Clicking an empty area above the diagonal line of the upper left corner data table cell that contains the Columns and Rows red triangle is a shortcut to clear column selections.)

For cases in which you seek to analyze a subset, use Data Filter. For the sample example, with the **Retirement Funds data table** still open, verify that no columns are pre-selected select **Rows ➔ Data Filter**. In the procedure's dialog box:

1. Click **Fund Type** from the columns list and click **Add**.
2. In the changed display (shown below), first click **Value** and then click **AND**.

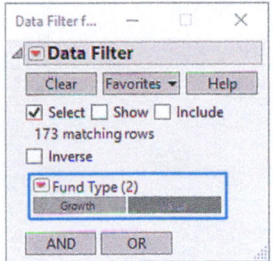

3. Click **10YrReturn** from the columns list and click **Add**.
4. In the changed display, click the minimum value (-1.100), enter **9** and then press **Enter** to form the expression $9.000 \leq 10\,YrReturn \leq 13.000$ (13 is the maximum value for 10YrReturn).
5. Click the **Data Filter red triangle** and select **Show Subset** from its menu.

JMP displays a new data table that contains the selected (five) rows. The open Data Filter window can be closed or used to create other subsets. As with the other method, if one or more columns were selected before step 1, the subset will be composed of values only from those columns. To take subsets that contain full rows of data, clear the column selections before step 1.

JMP GUIDE GALLERY

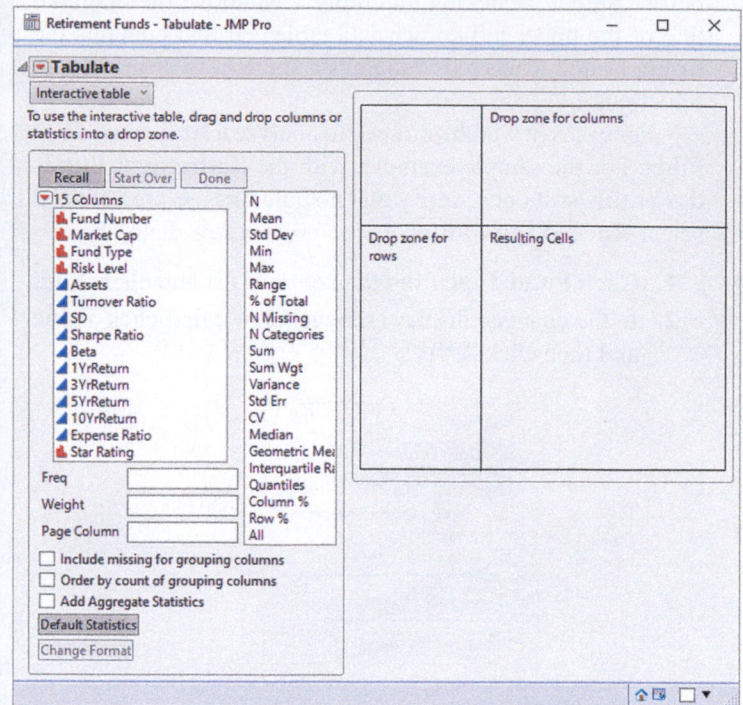

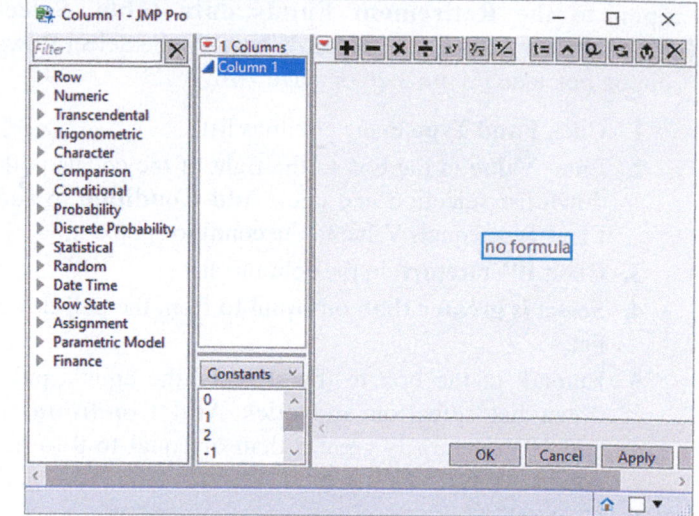

This gallery displays the Tabulate (above) and Graph Builder (below) interactive windows and the Formula dialog box (right) in their initial states. In the enlarged view of the Graph Builder icon bar, the numbered icons are: (1) Points, (2) Smoother, (3) Line of Fit, (4) Line, (5) Bar, (6) Box Plot, (7) Histogram, (8) Pie, and (9) Treemap.

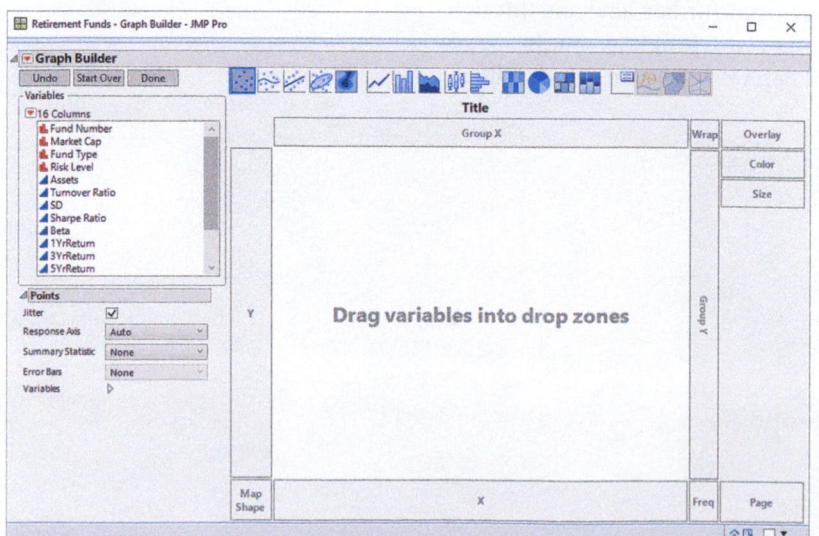

▼MINITAB GUIDE

MG2.1 ORGANIZING CATEGORICAL VARIABLES

The Summary Table

Use **Tally Individual Variables** to create a summary table.

For example, to create a summary table similar to Figure 2.1 on page 43, open to the **Retirement Funds worksheet**. Select **Stat → Tables → Tally Individual Variables**. In the procedure's dialog box (shown at below):

1. Double-click **C4 Risk Level** in the variables list to add **Risk Level** to the **Variables** box.
2. Check **Counts** and **Percents**.
3. Click **OK**.

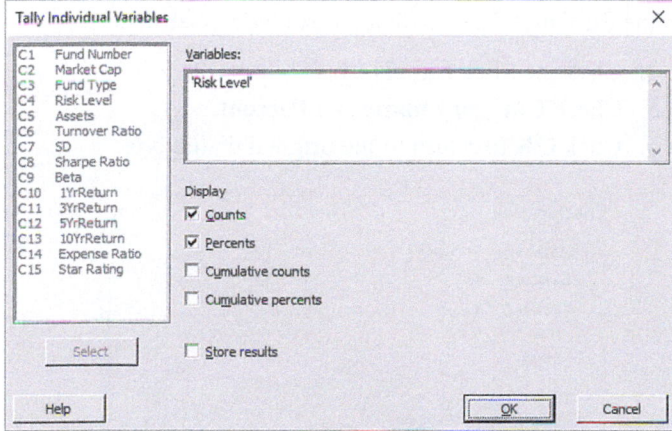

The Contingency Table

Use **Cross Tabulation and Chi-Square** to create a contingency table.

For example, to create a contingency table similar to Figure 2.2 on page 44 open to the **Retirement Funds worksheet**. Select **Stat → Tables → Cross Tabulation and Chi-Square**. In the procedure's dialog box (shown in right column):

1. Select **Raw data (categorical variables)** in the pull-down list.
2. Double-click **C3 Fund Type** in the variables list to add **'Fund Type'** to the **Rows** box.
3. Double-click **C4 Risk Level** in the variables list to add **'Risk Level'** to the **Columns** box.
4. Check **Counts**.
5. Click **OK**.

To create the other types of contingency tables shown in Tables 2.5 through 2.7, check **Row percents**, **Column percents**, or **Total percents**, respectively, in step 3.

MG2.2 ORGANIZING NUMERICAL VARIABLES

The Ordered Array

Use **Sort** to create an ordered array. Select **Data → Sort** and in the Sort dialog box (not shown), double-click a column name in the variables list to add it to the **Sort column(s)** box and then press **Tab**. Double-click the same column name in the variables list to add it to the first **By column** box. Click either **New worksheet**, **Original column(s)**, or **Column(s) of current worksheet**. (If you choose the third option, also enter the name of the column in which to place the ordered data in the box.) Click **OK**.

The Frequency-Distribution

There is no Minitab procedure that directly use classes that you specify to create frequency distributions of the type seen in Tables 2.3, 2.5, and 2.10. However, you can specify classes when using the Histogram procedure (see Section MG2.4).

MG2.3 VISUALIZING CATEGORICAL VARIABLES

The Bar Chart and the Pie Chart

Use **Bar Chart** to create a bar chart and use **Pie Chart** to create a pie chart. Charts can be created from either unsummarized data or summary tables.

For example, to create the Figure 2.5 bar chart on page 55 open to the **Retirement Funds worksheet**. Select **Graph→Bar Chart**. In the procedure's dialog box (shown first in right column):

1. Select **Counts of unique values** from the **Bars represent** drop-down list.
2. In the gallery of choices, click **Simple**.
3. Click **OK**.

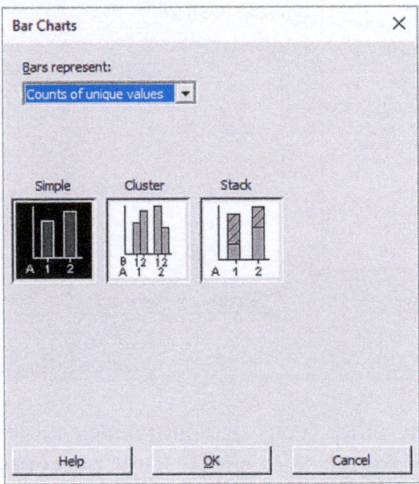

In the Bar Chart: Counts of unique values, Simple dialog box (shown below):

4. Double-click **C4 Risk Level** in the variables list to add **'Risk Level'** to the **Categorical variables** box.
5. Click **OK**.

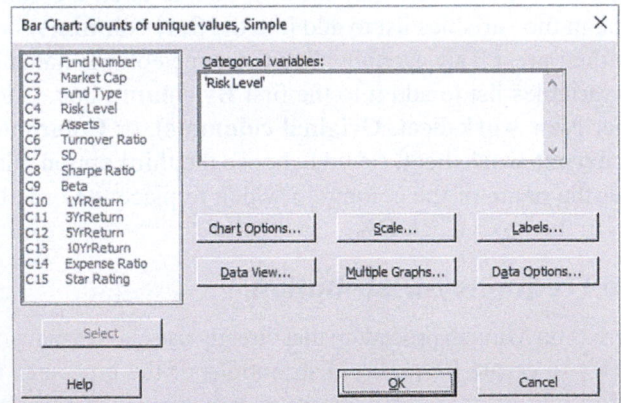

If the data to be visualized already has been summarized by a table of frequencies, select **Values from a table** from the **Bars represent** drop-down list in step 1. With this selection, clicking **OK** in step 3 will display the "Bar Chart: Values from a table, One column of values, Simple" dialog box. In this dialog box, enter the columns to be graphed in the **Graph variables** box and, optionally, enter the column in the worksheet that holds the categories for the table in the **Categorical variable** box.

Use **Pie Chart** to create a pie chart from a summary table. For example, to create the Figure 2.6 pie chart on page 55 open to the **Retirement Funds worksheet**. Select

Graph→Pie Chart. In the Pie Chart dialog box (shown below):

1. Click **Chart counts of unique values** and then press **Tab**.
2. Double-click **C4 Risk Level** in the variables list to add **'Risk Level'** to the **Categorical variables** box.
3. Click **Labels**.

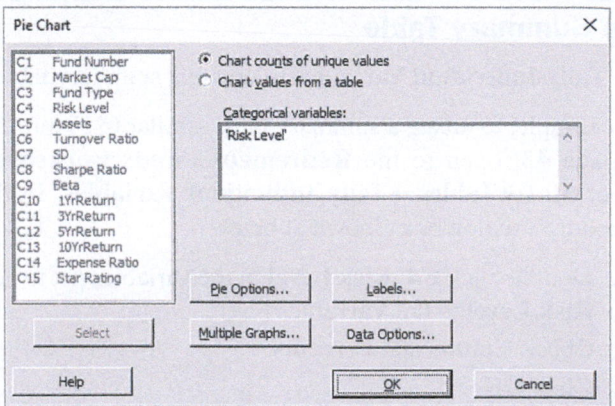

In the Pie Chart: Labels dialog box (shown below):

4. Click the **Slice Labels** tab.
5. Check **Category name** and **Percent**.
6. Click **OK** to return to the original dialog box.

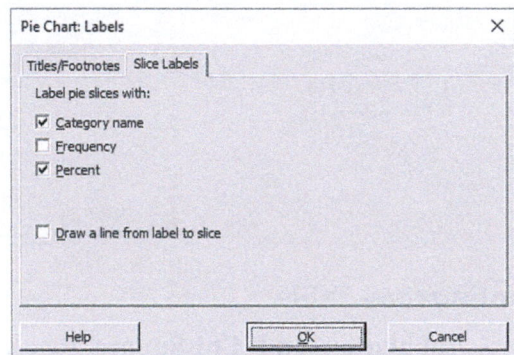

Back in the original Pie Chart dialog box:

7. Click **OK**.

The Pareto Chart

Use **Pareto Chart** to create a Pareto chart.

For example, to create the Figure 2.7 Pareto chart on page 58, open to the **ATM Transactions worksheet**. Select **Stat→Quality Tools→Pareto Chart**. In the procedure's dialog box (shown below):

1. Double-click **C1 Cause** in the variables list to add **Cause** to the **Defects or attribute data in** box.
2. Double-click **C2 Frequency** in the variables list to add **Frequency** to the **Frequencies in** box.
3. Click **Do not combine**.
4. Click **OK**.

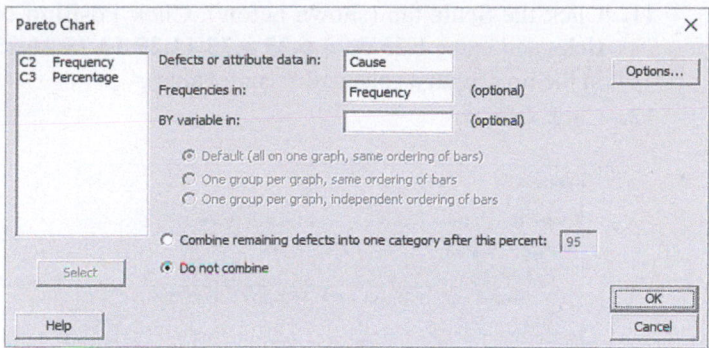

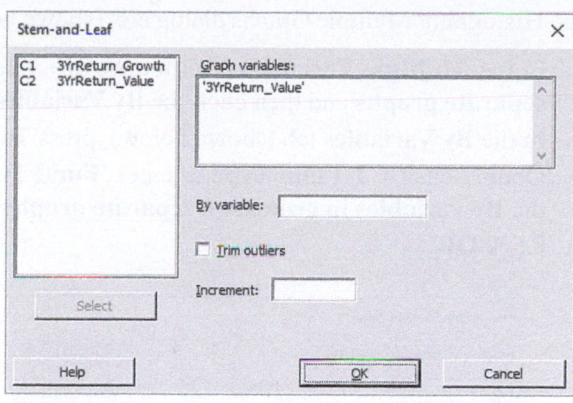

The Side-by-Side Chart

Use **Bar Chart** to create a side-by-side chart.

For example, to create the Figure 2.9 side-by-side chart on page 58, open to the **Retirement Funds worksheet**. Select **Graph→Bar Chart**. In the Bar Charts dialog box:

1. Select **Counts of unique values** from the **Bars represent** drop-down list.
2. In the gallery of choices, click **Cluster**.
3. Click **OK**.

In the "Bar Chart: Counts of unique values, Cluster" dialog box (shown below):

4. Double-click **C3 Fund Type** and **C4 Risk Level** in the variables list to add **'Fund Type'** and **'Risk Level'** to the **Categorical variables (2–4, outermost first)** box.
5. Click **OK**.

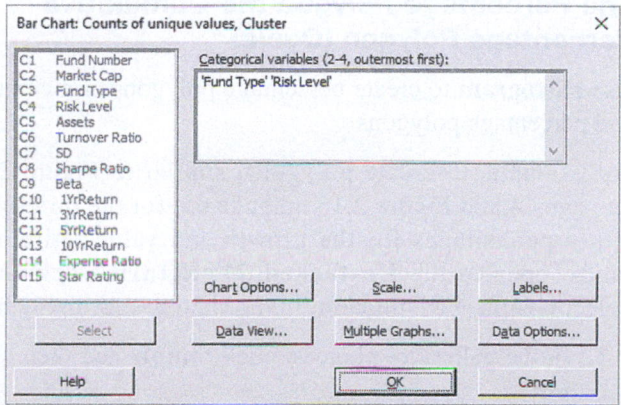

MG2.4 VISUALIZING NUMERICAL VARIABLES

The Stem-and-Leaf Display

Use **Stem-and-Leaf** to create a stem-and-leaf display.

For example, to create the Figure 2.10 stem-and-leaf display on page 62, open to the **Unstacked3YrReturn worksheet**. Select **Graph→Stem-and-Leaf**. In the procedure's dialog box (shown at top in right column):

1. Double-click **C2 3YrReturn_Value** in the variables list to add **'3YrReturn_Value'** in the **Graph variables** box.
2. Click **OK**.

The Histogram

Use **Histogram** to create a histogram.

For example, to create the Figure 2.12 histograms for the three-year return percentages on page 62, open to the **Retirement Funds worksheet**. Select **Graph→Histogram**. In the Histograms dialog box (shown below):

1. Click **Simple** and then click **OK**.

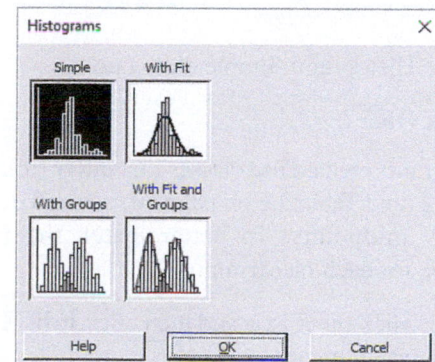

In the Histogram: Simple dialog box (shown below):

2. Double-click **C11 3YrReturn** in the variables list to add **'3YrReturn'** in the **Graph variables** box.
3. Click **Multiple Graphs**.

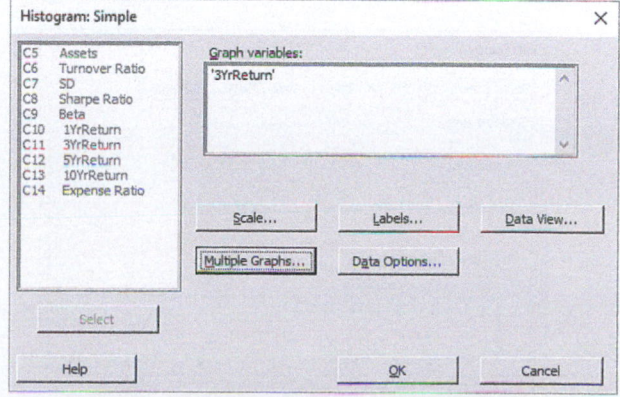

In the Histogram: Multiple Graphs dialog box (shown below):

4. In the **Multiple Variables** tab (not shown), click **On separate graphs** and then click the **By Variables** tab.

5. In the **By Variables** tab (shown below), press **Tab**.

6. Double-click **C3 Fund Type** to enter **'Fund Type'** in the **By variables in groups on separate graphs** box.

7. Click **OK**.

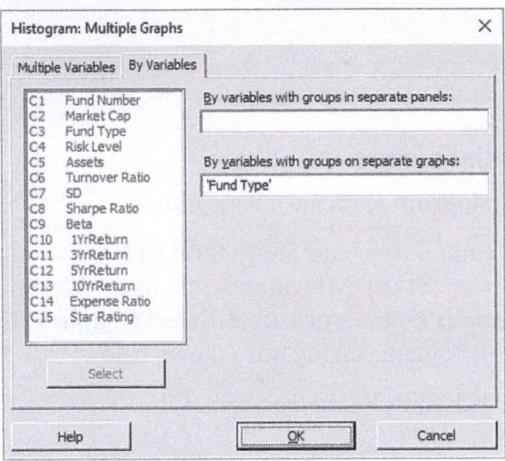

Back in the Histogram: Simple dialog box:

8. Click **OK**.

The histograms created use classes that differ from the classes Figure 2.12 (and Table 2.6 on page 50) use and do not use the Figure 2.9 midpoints. To better match the Figure 2.12 histograms, for each histogram:

9. Right-click the *X* axis and then click **Edit X Scale** from the shortcut menu.

In the Edit Scale dialog box:

10. Click the **Binning** tab (shown below). Click **Cutpoint** (as the **Interval Type**) and **Midpoint/Cutpoint positions** and enter **2.5 5 7.5 10 12.5 15 17.5** in the box (with a space after each value).

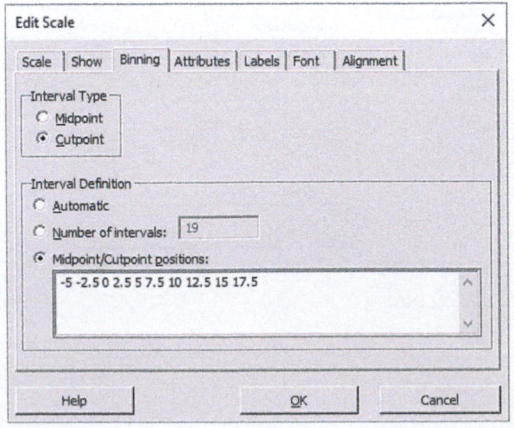

11. Click the **Scale** tab (shown below). Click **Position of ticks** and enter **1.25 3.75 6.25 8.75 11.25 13.75 16.25** in the box (with a space after each value).

12. Click **OK**.

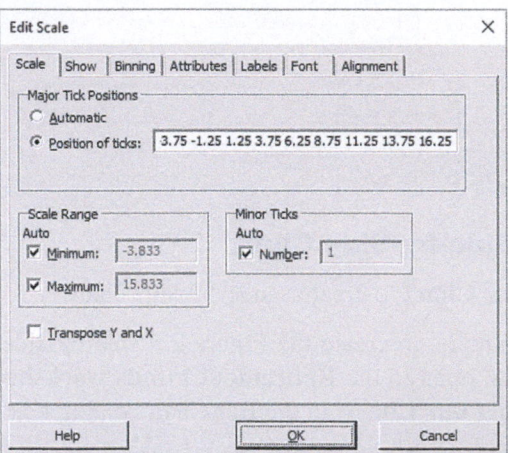

To create the histogram of the one-year return percentage variable for all funds in the retirement fund sample, repeat steps 1 through 11, but in step 5 delete **'Fund Type'** from the **By variables in groups on separate graphs** box.

To modify the histogram bars, double-click over the histogram bars and make the appropriate entries and selections in the Edit Bars dialog box. To modify an axis, double-click the axis and make the appropriate entries and selections in the Edit Scale dialog box.

The Percentage Polygon the Cumulative Percentage Polygon (Ogive)

Use **Histogram** to create percentage polygons or a cumulative percentage polygons.

For example, to create polygons, similar to Figure 2.14 on page 64 and Figure 2.16 on page 65, for the three-year return percentages for the growth and value retirement funds, open to the **Unstacked 3YrReturn worksheet**. Select **Graph→Histogram**. In the Histograms dialog box:

1. In the gallery of choices, click **Simple** and then click **OK**.

In the Histogram: Simple dialog box:

2. Double-click **C1 3YrReturn_Growth** in the variables list to add **'3YrReturn_Growth'** in the **Graph variables** box.

3. Double-click **C2 3YrReturn_Value** in the variables list to add **'3YrReturn%_Value'** in the **Graph variables** box.

4. Click **Scale**.

In the Histogram Scale dialog box:

5. Click the **Y-Scale Type** tab. Click **Percent**, clear **Accumulate values across bins**, and then click **OK**.

Back again in the Histogram: Simple dialog box:

6. Click **Data View**.

In the Histogram: Data View dialog box:

7. Click the **Data Display** tab. Check **Symbols** and clear all of the other check boxes.
8. Click the **Smoother** tab and then click **Lowness** and enter **0** as the **Degree of smoothing** and **1** as the **Number of steps**.
9. Click **OK**.

Back again in the Histogram: Simple dialog box:

10. Click **OK** to create the polygons.

The percentage polygons created do not use the classes and midpoints shown in Figure 2.14. To better match the Figure 2.14 polygons:

11. Right-click the *X* axis and then click **Edit X Scale** from the shortcut menu.

In the Edit Scale dialog box:

12. Click the **Binning** tab. Click **Cutpoint** as the **Interval Type** and **Midpoint/Cutpoint positions** and enter **2.5 5 7.5 10 12.5 15 17.5** in the box (with a space after each value).
13. Click the **Scale** tab. Click **Position of ticks** and enter **1.25 3.75 6.25 8.75 11.25 13.75 16.25** in the box (with a space after each value).
14. Click **OK**.

To create cumulative percentage polygons, replace steps 5 and 12 with the following steps:

5. Click the **Y-Scale Type** tab. Click **Percent**, check **Accumulate values across bins**, and then click **OK**.
12. Click the **Binning** tab. Click **Midpoint** as the **Interval Type** and **Midpoint/Cutpoint positions** and enter **2.5 5 7.5 10 12.5 15 17.5** in the box (with a space after each value).

MG2.5 VISUALIZING TWO NUMERICAL VARIABLES

The Scatter Plot

Use **Scatterplot** to create a scatter plot.

For example, to create a scatter plot similar to the one shown in Figure 2.17 on page 68, open to the **NBAValues**

worksheet. Select **Graph→Scatterplot**. In the Scatterplots dialog box:

1. In the gallery of choices, click **With Regression** and then click **OK**.

In the Scatterplot: With Regression dialog box (shown below):

2. Double-click **C4 Current Value** in the variables list to enter **'Current Value'** in the **row 1 Y variables** cell.
3. Double-click **C3 Revenue** in the variables list to enter **Revenue** in the **row 1 X variables** cell.
4. Click **OK**.

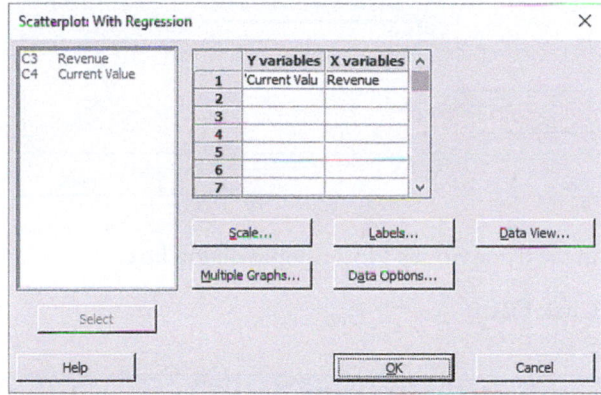

The Time-Series Plot

Use **Time Series Plot** to create a time-series plot.

For example, to create the Figure 2.18 time-series plot on page 69, open to the **Movie Revenues worksheet** and select **Graph→Time Series Plot**. In the Time Series Plots dialog box:

1. In the gallery of choices, click **Simple** and then click **OK**.

In the Time Series Plot: Simple dialog box (shown below):

2. Double-click **C2 Revenues** in the variables list to add **Revenues** in the **Series** box.
3. Click **Time/Scale**.

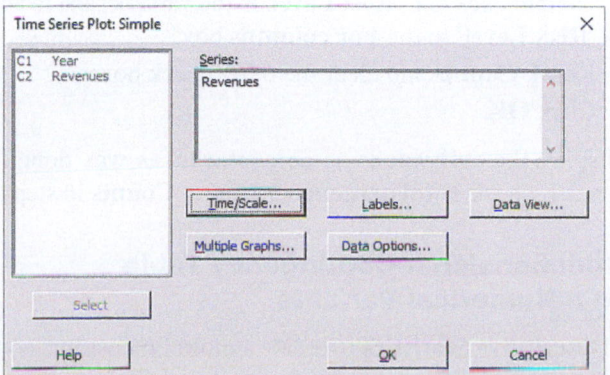

In the Time Series Plot: Time/Scale dialog box (shown below):

4. Click **Stamp** and then press **Tab**.
5. Double-click **C1 Year** in the variables list to add **Year** in the **Stamp columns (1-3, innermost first)** box.
6. Click **OK**.

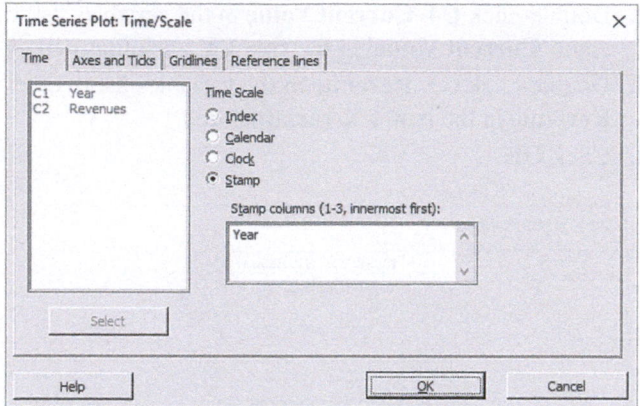

Back in the Time Series Plot: Simple dialog box:

7. Click **OK**.

MG2.6 ORGANIZING a MIX of VARIABLES

Multidimensional Contingency Tables

Use **Cross Tabulation and Chi-Square** to create a multidimensional contingency table.

For example, to create a table similar to the Figure 2.19, Fund Type, Market Cap, and Risk Level, table on page 71, open to the **Retirement Funds worksheet**. Select **Stat → Tables → Cross Tabulation and Chi-Square**. In the procedure's dialog box:

1. Press **Tab** and double-click **C3 Fund Type** in the variables list to add equivalent to Figure 2.20 to the **For rows** box.
2. Double-click **C2 Market Cap** in the variables list to add **'Market Cap'** to the **For rows** box and then press **Tab**.
3. Double-click **C4 Risk Level**, in the variables list to add **'Risk Level'** to the **For columns** box.
4. Check **Counts** and clear the other check boxes.
5. Click **OK**.

To display the cell values as percentages, as was done in Figure 2.1, check **Total percents** instead of **Counts** in step 4.

Multidimensional Contingency Table With a Numerical Variable

Use **Descriptive Statistics** to create a multidimensional contingency table that contains a numerical variable.

For example, to create the table of Fund Type, Risk Level, and Market Cap, showing the mean ten-year return percentage for the retirement funds samples, equivalent to Figure 2.20

on page 72, open to the **Retirement Funds worksheet**. Select **Stat → Tables → Descriptive Statistics**. In the Table of Descriptive Statistics dialog box (shown below):

1. Double-click **C3 'Fund Type'** in the variables list to add **Fund Type** to the **For rows** box and press **Tab**.
2. Double-click **C2 Market Cap** in the variables list to add **'Market Cap'** to the **For rows** box and then press **Tab**.
3. Double-click **C4 Risk Level**, in the variables list to add **'Risk Level'** to the **For columns** box.
4. Click **Associated Variables**.

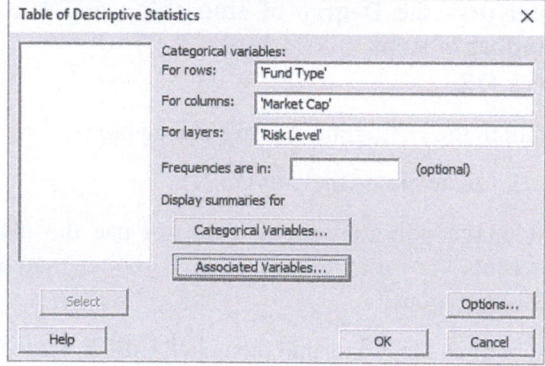

In the Descriptive Statistics: Summaries for Associated Variables dialog box (not shown):

5. Double-click **C13 10YrReturn** in the variables list to add **'10YrReturn'** to the **Associated variables** box.
6. Check **Means**.
7. Click **OK**.

Back in Table of Descriptive Statistics dialog box:

8. Click **OK**.

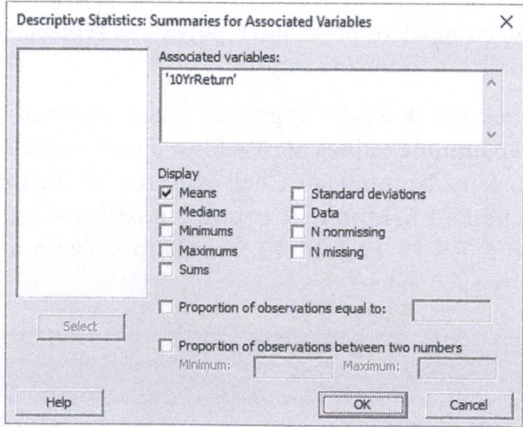

MG2.7 VISUALIZING a MIX of VARIABLES

Colored Scatter Plots

Use **Scatterplot** to create a scatter plot.

For example, to create a colored scatter plot of Expense Ratio, 3YrReturn, and Market Cap, similar to Figure 2.22 on page 73, open to the **Retirement Funds worksheet**. Select **Graph ➔ Scatterplot**. In the Scatterplots dialog box:

1. In the gallery of choices, click **With Groups** and then click **OK**.

In the Scatterplot: With Groups dialog box (shown below):

2. Double-click **C14 Expense Ratio** in the variables list to enter **'Expense Ratio'** in the **row 1 Y variables** cell.

3. Double-click **C11 3YrReturn** in the variables list to enter **'3YrReturn'** in the **row 1 X variables** cell.

4. Click in the **Categorical variables for grouping (0–3)** box.

5. Double-click **C2 Market Cap** in the variables list to enter **'Market Cap'** in that box.

6. Click **OK**.

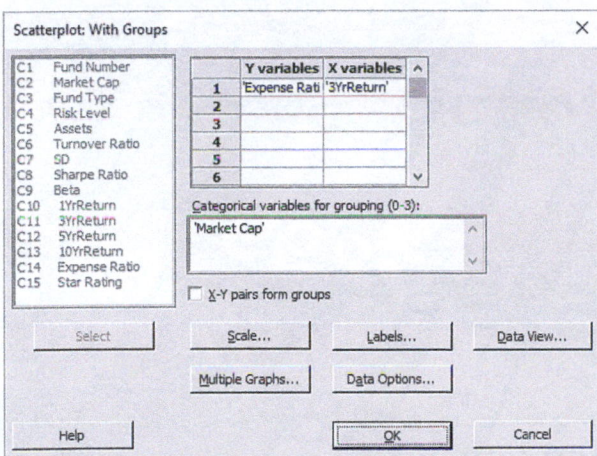

MG2.8 FILTERING and QUERYING DATA

Use **Subset Worksheet** to filter data.

For example, to filter the Retirement Funds worksheet to select the rows that correspond to value retirement funds that have ten-year return percentages that are greater than or equal to 9, open to the **Retirement Funds worksheet**. Select **Data ➔ Subset Worksheet**. In the procedure's dialog box (shown in Figure 2.26 on page 76):

1. Select **Use formula** from the **how do you want to create a subset?** pull-down list.

2. Click in the **Formula** box.

3. Enter **('Fund Type' = 'Value') And ('10YrReturn' > = 9)** in the **Formula** box.

You can key the entire expression or use a mix of clicking calculator-style buttons, double-clicking variable names in the variables list, and keying. You must use a set of the double quotation marks when keying **"Value"**.

4. Enter a new worksheet name in **New worksheet name** box and click **OK**.

Minitab opens a new worksheet windows with that contains the five rows that contain data for value retirement funds that have ten-year return percentages that are greater than or equal to 9.

3

Numerical Descriptive Measures

CONTENTS

OBJECTIVES

- Describe the properties of central tendency, variation, and shape in numerical variables
- Construct and interpret a boxplot
- Compute descriptive summary measures for a population
- Compute the covariance and the coefficient of correlation

▼USING **STATISTICS**
More Descriptive Choices

As a member of a Choice *Is* Yours investment service task force, you helped organize and visualize the variables found in a sample of 479 retirement funds. Now, several weeks later, prospective clients are asking for more information on which they can base their investment decisions. In particular, they would like to compare the results of an individual retirement fund to the results of similar funds.

For example, while the earlier work your team did shows how the three-year return percentages are distributed, prospective clients would like to know how the value for a particular mid-cap growth fund compares to the three-year returns of all mid-cap growth funds. They also seek to understand the variation among the returns. Are all the values relatively similar? And does any variable have outlier values that are either extremely small or extremely large?

While doing a complete search of the retirement funds data could lead to answers to the preceding questions, you wonder if there are better ways than extensive searching to uncover those answers. You also wonder if there are other ways of being more *descriptive* about the sample of funds—providing answers to questions not yet raised by prospective clients. If you can help the Choice *Is* Yours investment service provide such answers, prospective clients will be better able to evaluate the retirement funds that your firm features.

The prospective clients in the More Descriptive Choices scenario have begun asking questions about numerical variables such as how the three-year return percentages vary among the individual funds that comprise the sample of 479 retirement funds. You also need to apply methods that help describe the central tendency, variation, and shape of such variables.

Central tendency is the extent to which the values of a numerical variable group around a typical, or central, value. **Variation** measures the amount of dispersion, or scattering, away from a central value that the values of a numerical variable show. The **shape** of a variable is the pattern of the distribution of values from the lowest value to the highest value.

This chapter describes ways you can compute these numerical descriptive measures as you begin to analyze your data within the DCOVA framework. The chapter also discusses the covariance and the coefficient of correlation, measures that can help show the strength of the association between two numerical variables. Computing the descriptive measures discussed in this chapter would be one way to help prospective clients of the Choice *Is* Yours service find the answers they seek.

3.1 Measures of Central Tendency

Most variables show a distinct tendency to group around a central value. When people talk about an "average value" or the "middle value" or the "most frequent value," they are talking informally about the mean, median, and mode—three measures of central tendency.

The Mean

The **arithmetic mean** (in everyday usage, the **mean**) is the most common measure of central tendency. The mean can suggest a typical or central value and serves as a "balance point" in a set of data, similar to the fulcrum on a seesaw. The mean is the only common measure in which all the values play an equal role. You compute the mean by adding together all the values and then dividing that sum by the number of values in the data set.

The symbol $\overline{X}$, called *X-bar*, is used to represent the mean of a sample. For a sample containing n values, the equation for the mean of a sample is written as

$$\overline{X} = \frac{\text{sum of the values}}{\text{number of values}}$$

Using the series $X_1, X_2, \ldots, X_n$ to represent the set of n values and n to represent the number of values in the sample, the equation becomes

$$\overline{X} = \frac{X_1 + X_2 + \cdots + X_n}{n}$$

By using summation notation (discussed in Appendix A), you replace the numerator $X_1 + X_2 + \cdots + X_n$ with the term $\sum_{i=1}^{n} X_i$, which means sum all the X_i values from the first X value, X_1, to the last X value, X_n, to form Equation (3.1), a formal definition of the sample mean.

SAMPLE MEAN

The **sample mean** is the sum of the values in a sample divided by the number of values in the sample:

$$\overline{X} = \frac{\sum_{i=1}^{n} X_i}{n} \tag{3.1}$$

where

$$\overline{X} = \text{sample mean}$$

$$n = \text{number of values or sample size}$$

$$X_i = i\text{th value of the variable } X$$

$$\sum_{i=1}^{n} X_i = \text{summation of all } X_i \text{ values in the sample}$$

Because all the values play an equal role, a mean is greatly affected by any value that is very different from the others. When you have such extreme values, you should avoid using the mean as a measure of central tendency.

For example, if you knew the typical time it takes you to get ready in the morning, you might be able to arrive at your first destination every day in a more timely manner. Using the DCOVA framework, you first define the time to get ready as the time from when you get out of bed to when you leave your home, rounded to the nearest minute. Then, you collect the times for 10 consecutive workdays and organize and store them in Times .

Using the collected data, you compute the mean to discover the "typical" time it takes for you to get ready. For these data:

Day:	1	2	3	4	5	6	7	8	9	10
Time (minutes):	39	29	43	52	39	44	40	31	44	35

the mean time is 39.6 minutes, computed as follows:

$$\overline{X} = \frac{\text{sum of the values}}{\text{number of values}} = \frac{\sum_{i=1}^{n} X_i}{n}$$

$$\overline{X} = \frac{39 + 29 + 43 + 52 + 39 + 44 + 40 + 31 + 44 + 35}{10}$$

$$= \frac{396}{10} = 39.6$$

Even though no individual day in the sample had a value of 39.6 minutes, allotting this amount of time to get ready in the morning would be a reasonable decision to make. The mean is a good measure of central tendency in this case because the data set does not contain any exceptionally small or large values.

To illustrate how the mean can be greatly affected by any value that is very different from the others, imagine that on Day 3, a set of unusual circumstances delayed you getting ready by an extra hour, so that the time for that day was 103 minutes. This extreme value causes the mean to rise to 45.6 minutes, as follows:

$$\overline{X} = \frac{\text{sum of the values}}{\text{number of values}} = \frac{\sum_{i=1}^{n} X_i}{n}$$

$$\overline{X} = \frac{39 + 29 + 103 + 52 + 39 + 44 + 40 + 31 + 44 + 35}{10}$$

$$\overline{X} = \frac{456}{10} = 45.6$$

The one extreme value has increased the mean by 6 minutes. The extreme value also moved the position of the mean relative to all the values. The original mean, 39.6 minutes, had a middle, or *central*, position among the data values: 5 of the times were less than that mean and 5 were greater than that mean. In contrast, the mean using the extreme value is greater than 9 of the 10 times, making the new mean a poor measure of central tendency.

EXAMPLE 3.1

The Mean Calories in Cereals

Nutritional data about a sample of seven breakfast cereals (stored in [Cereals]) includes the number of calories per serving:

Cereal	Calories
Kellogg's All Bran	80
Kellogg's Corn Flakes	100
Wheaties	100
Nature's Path Organic Multigrain Flakes	110
Kellogg's Rice Krispies	130
Post Shredded Wheat Vanilla Almond	190
Kellogg's Mini Wheats	200

Compute the mean number of calories in these breakfast cereals.

SOLUTION The mean number of calories is 130, computed as follows:

$$\overline{X} = \frac{\text{sum of the values}}{\text{number of values}} = \frac{\sum_{i=1}^{n} X_i}{n} = \frac{910}{7} = 130$$

The Median

The **median** is the middle value in an ordered array of data that has been ranked from smallest to largest. Half the values are smaller than or equal to the median, and half the values are larger than or equal to the median. Extreme values do not affect the median, making the median a good alternative to the mean when such values exist in the data.

     To compute the median for a set of data, you first rank the values from smallest to largest and then use Equation (3.2) to compute the rank of the value that is the median.

MEDIAN

$$\text{Median} = \frac{n + 1}{2} \text{ ranked value} \qquad (3.2)$$

You compute the median by following one of two rules:

- **Rule 1**   If the data set contains an *odd* number of values, the median is the measurement associated with the middle-ranked value.
- **Rule 2**   If the data set contains an *even* number of values, the median is the measurement associated with the average of the two middle-ranked values.

     To further analyze the sample of 10 times to get ready in the morning, you can compute the median. To do so, you rank the daily times as follows:

Ranked values:	29	31	35	39	39	40	43	44	44	52
Ranks:	1	2	3	4	5	6	7	8	9	10

↑

Median = 39.5

student TIP

You must rank the values in order from the smallest to the largest to compute the median.

Because the result of dividing $n + 1$ by 2 for this sample of 10 is $(10 + 1)/2 = 5.5$, you must use Rule 2 and average the measurements associated with the fifth and sixth ranked values, 39 and 40. Therefore, the median is 39.5. The median of 39.5 means that for half the days, the time to get ready is less than or equal to 39.5 minutes, and for half the days, the time to get ready is greater than or equal to 39.5 minutes. In this case, the median time to get ready of 39.5 minutes is very close to the mean time to get ready of 39.6 minutes.

The previous section noted that substituting 103 minutes for the time of 43 minutes increased the mean by 6 minutes. Doing the same substitution does not affect the value of median, which would remain 39.5. This example illustrates that the median is not affected by extreme values.

EXAMPLE 3.2

Computing the Median from an Odd-Sized Sample

Nutritional data about a sample of seven breakfast cereals (stored in `Cereals`) includes the number of calories per serving (see Example 3.1 on page 123). Compute the median number of calories in breakfast cereals.

SOLUTION Because the result of dividing $n + 1$ by 2 for this sample of seven is $(7 + 1)/2 = 4$, using Rule 1, the median is the measurement associated with the fourth-ranked value. The number of calories per serving values are ranked from the smallest to the largest:

Ranked values:	80	100	100	110	130	190	200
Ranks:	1	2	3	4	5	6	7

$$\uparrow$$
$$\text{Median} = 110$$

The median number of calories is 110. Half the breakfast cereals have 110 or less than 110 calories per serving, and half the breakfast cereals have 110 or more than 110 calories per serving.

The Mode

The **mode** is the value that appears most frequently. Like the median and unlike the mean, extreme values do not affect the mode. For a particular variable, there can be several modes or no mode at all. For example, for the sample of 10 times to get ready in the morning:

$$29 \quad 31 \quad 35 \quad 39 \quad 39 \quad 40 \quad 43 \quad 44 \quad 44 \quad 52$$

there are two modes, 39 minutes and 44 minutes, because each of these values occurs twice. However, for this sample of 14 smartphone prices offered by a cellphone provider (stored in `Smartphones`):

$$56 \quad 71 \quad 73 \quad 74 \quad 90 \quad 179 \quad 213 \quad 217 \quad 219 \quad 225 \quad 240 \quad 250 \quad 500 \quad 513$$

there is no mode. None of the values is "most typical" because each value appears the same number of times (once) in the data set.

EXAMPLE 3.3

Determining the Mode

A systems manager in charge of a company's network keeps track of the number of server failures that occur in a day. Determine the mode for the following data, which represent the number of server failures per day for the past two weeks:

$$1 \quad 3 \quad 0 \quad 3 \quad 26 \quad 2 \quad 7 \quad 4 \quad 0 \quad 2 \quad 3 \quad 3 \quad 6 \quad 3$$

SOLUTION The ordered array for these data is

$$0 \quad 0 \quad 1 \quad 2 \quad 2 \quad 3 \quad 3 \quad 3 \quad 3 \quad 3 \quad 4 \quad 6 \quad 7 \quad 26$$

Because 3 occurs five times, more times than any other value, the mode is 3. Thus, the systems manager can say that the most common occurrence is having three server failures in a day. For this data set, the median is also equal to 3, and the mean is equal to 4.5. The value 26 is an extreme value. For these data, the median and the mode are better measures of central tendency than the mean.

The Geometric Mean

To measure the rate of change of a variable over time, you use the geometric mean instead of the arithmetic mean. Equation (3.3) defines the geometric mean.

GEOMETRIC MEAN

The **geometric mean** is the nth root of the product of n values:

$$\overline{X}_G = (X_1 \times X_2 \times \cdots \times X_n)^{1/n} \tag{3.3}$$

The **geometric mean rate of return** measures the mean percentage return of an investment per time period. Equation (3.4) defines the geometric mean rate of return.

GEOMETRIC MEAN RATE OF RETURN

$$\overline{R}_G = [(1 + R_1) \times (1 + R_2) \times \cdots \times (1 + R_n)]^{1/n} - 1 \tag{3.4}$$

where

$$R_i = \text{rate of return in time period } i$$

To illustrate these measures, consider an investment of \$100,000 that declined to a value of \$50,000 at the end of Year 1 and then rebounded back to its original \$100,000 value at the end of Year 2. The rate of return for this investment per year for the two-year period is 0 because the starting and ending value of the investment is unchanged. However, the arithmetic mean of the yearly rates of return of this investment is

$$\overline{X} = \frac{(-0.50) + (1.00)}{2} = 0.25 \text{ or } 25\%$$

because the rate of return for Year 1 is

$$R_1 = \left(\frac{50,000 - 100,000}{100,000}\right) = -0.50 \text{ or } -50\%$$

and the rate of return for Year 2 is

$$R_2 = \left(\frac{100,000 - 50,000}{50,000}\right) = 1.00 \text{ or } 100\%$$

Using equation (3.4), the geometric mean rate of return per year for the two years is

$$\overline{R}_G = [(1 + R_1) \times (1 + R_2)]^{1/n} - 1$$
$$= [(1 + (-0.50)) \times (1 + (1.0))]^{1/2} - 1$$
$$= [(0.50) \times (2.0)]^{1/2} - 1$$
$$= [1.0]^{1/2} - 1 = 1 - 1 = 0$$

Using the geometric mean rate of return more accurately reflects the (zero) change in the value of the investment per year for the two-year period than does the arithmetic mean.

EXAMPLE 3.4

Computing the Geometric Mean Rate of Return

The percentage change in the Russell 2000 Index of the stock prices of 2,000 small companies was −5.7% in 2015 and 18.5% in 2016. Compute the geometric rate of return.

SOLUTION Using equation (3.4), the geometric mean rate of return in the Russell 2000 Index for the two years is

$$\overline{R}_G = [(1 + R_1) \times (1 + R_2)]^{1/n} - 1$$

$$= [(1 + (-0.057)) \times (1 + (0.185))]^{1/2} - 1$$

$$= [(0.943) \times (1.185)]^{1/2} - 1$$

$$= (1.117455)^{1/2} - 1 = 1.0571 - 1 = 0.0571$$

The geometric mean rate of return in the Russell 2000 Index for the two years is 5.71% per year.

3.2 Measures of Variation and Shape

In addition to central tendency, every variable can be characterized by its variation and shape. Variation measures the **spread**, or **dispersion**, of the values. One simple measure of variation is the range, the difference between the largest and smallest values. More commonly used in statistics are the standard deviation and variance, two measures explained later in this section. The shape of a variable represents a pattern of all the values, from the lowest to highest value. As you will learn later in this section, many variables have a pattern that looks approximately like a bell, with a peak of values somewhere in the middle.

The Range

The **range** is the difference between the largest and smallest value and is the simplest descriptive measure of variation for a numerical variable.

> RANGE
>
> The range is equal to the largest value minus the smallest value.
>
> $$\text{Range} = X_{\text{largest}} - X_{\text{smallest}} \tag{3.5}$$

To further analyze the sample of 10 times to get ready in the morning, you can compute the range. To do so, you rank the data from smallest to largest:

$$29 \quad 31 \quad 35 \quad 39 \quad 39 \quad 40 \quad 43 \quad 44 \quad 44 \quad 52$$

Using Equation (3.5), the range is $52 - 29 = 23$ minutes. The range of 23 minutes indicates that the largest difference between any two days in the time to get ready in the morning is 23 minutes.

EXAMPLE 3.5

Computing the Range in the Calories in Cereals

Nutritional data about a sample of seven breakfast cereals (stored in Cereals) includes the number of calories per serving (see Example 3.1 on page 123). Compute the range of the number of calories for the cereals.

SOLUTION Ranked from smallest to largest, the calories for the seven cereals are

$$80 \quad 100 \quad 100 \quad 110 \quad 130 \quad 190 \quad 200$$

Therefore, using Equation (3.5), the range $= 200 - 80 = 120$. The largest difference in the number of calories between any two cereals is 120.

The range measures the *total spread* in the set of data. Although the range is a simple measure of the total variation of the variable, it does not take into account *how* the values are distributed between the smallest and largest values. In other words, the range does not indicate whether the values are evenly distributed, clustered near the middle, or clustered near one or both extremes. Thus, using the range as a measure of variation when at least one value is an extreme value is misleading.

The Variance and the Standard Deviation

Being a simple measure of variation, the range does not consider how the values distribute or cluster between the extremes. Two commonly used measures of variation that account for how all the values are distributed are the **variance** and the **standard deviation**. These statistics measure the "average" scatter around the mean—how larger values fluctuate above it and how smaller values fluctuate below it.

A simple measure of variation around the mean might take the difference between each value and the mean and then sum these differences. However, if you did that, you would find that these differences sum to zero because the mean is the balance point for *every* numerical variable. A measure of variation that *differs* from one data set to another *squares* the difference between each value and the mean and then sums these squared differences. The sum of these squared differences, known as the **sum of squares (SS)**, is then used to compute the sample variance (S^2) and the sample standard deviation (S).

The **sample variance** (S^2) is the sum of squares divided by the sample size minus 1. The **sample standard deviation** (S) is the square root of the sample variance. Because the sum of squares can never be a negative value, the variance and the standard deviation will always be a non-negative value and, in virtually all cases, the variance and standard deviation will be greater than zero. (Both the variance and standard deviation will be zero, meaning no variation, only for the special case in which every value in a sample is the same value.)

For a sample containing n values, $X_1, X_2, X_3, \ldots, X_n$, the sample variance ($S^2$) is

$$S^2 = \frac{(X_1 - \overline{X})^2 + (X_2 - \overline{X})^2 + \cdots + (X_n - \overline{X})^2}{n - 1}$$

Equations (3.6) and (3.7) define the sample variance and sample standard deviation using summation notation. The term $\sum_{i=1}^{n} (X_i - \overline{X})^2$ represents the sum of squares.

SAMPLE VARIANCE

The sample variance is the sum of the squared differences around the mean divided by the sample size minus 1:

$$S^2 = \frac{\sum_{i=1}^{n} (X_i - \overline{X})^2}{n - 1} \tag{3.6}$$

where

$$\overline{X} = \text{sample mean}$$
$$n = \text{sample size}$$
$$X_i = i\text{th value of the variable } X$$

$$\sum_{i=1}^{n}(X_i - \overline{X})^2 = \text{summation of all the squared differences between the } X_i \text{ values and } \overline{X}$$

SAMPLE STANDARD DEVIATION

The sample standard deviation is the square root of the sum of the squared differences around the mean divided by the sample size minus 1:

$$S = \sqrt{S^2} = \sqrt{\frac{\sum_{i=1}^{n} (X_i - \bar{X})^2}{n - 1}} \tag{3.7}$$

Note that in both equations, the sum of squares is divided by the sample size minus 1, $n - 1$. The value is used for reasons related to statistical inference and the properties of sampling distributions, a topic discussed in Section 7.2 on page 253. For now, observe that the difference between dividing by n and by $n - 1$ becomes smaller as the sample size increases.

Because the sample standard deviation will always be a value expressed in the same units as the original sample data, consider using this statistic as your measure of variation. (The sample variance is a squared quantity that may have no real-world meaning.) For almost all samples, the majority of the values in a sample will be within an interval of plus and minus 1 standard deviation above and below the mean. Therefore, computing the sample mean and the sample standard deviation typically helps define where the majority of the values are clustering.

Calculating the variance can be understood as this four-step process:

Step 1 Calculate the difference between each value and the mean.
Step 2 Square each difference.
Step 3 Sum the squared differences.
Step 4 Divide this total by $n - 1$ to compute the sample variance.

student TIP

Neither the variance nor the standard deviation can ever be negative.

The mean ($\bar{X}$) equal to 39.6 was calculated previously using the method that page 122 discusses.

Taking the square root of the sample variance computes the sample standard deviation.

Table 3.1 illustrates these four steps for the sample of 10 get ready times. The middle column performs step 1, the right column performs step 2, the sum of the right column represents step 3, and the division of that sum represents step 4.

TABLE 3.1

Computing the Variance of the Get Ready Times

	Time (X)	Step 1: $(X_i - \bar{X})$	Step 2: $(X_i - \bar{X})^2$
	39	−0.60	0.36
	29	−10.60	112.36
	43	3.40	11.56
	52	12.40	153.76
$n = 10$	39	−0.60	0.36
$\bar{X} = 39.6$	44	4.40	19.36
	40	0.40	0.16
	31	−8.60	73.96
	44	4.40	19.36
	35	−4.60	21.16
		Step 3: **Sum**	412.40
		Step 4: **Divide by ($n - 1$)**	45.82

You can also compute the variance by substituting values for the terms in Equation (3.6):

$$S^2 = \frac{\sum_{i=1}^{n} (X_i - \bar{X})^2}{n - 1} = \frac{(39 - 39.6)^2 + (29 - 39.6)^2 + \cdots + (35 - 39.6)^2}{10 - 1}$$

$$= \frac{412.4}{9} = 45.82$$

Because the variance is in squared units (in squared minutes, for these data), to compute the standard deviation, you take the square root of the variance. Using Equation (3.7) on page 128, the sample standard deviation, S, is

$$S = \sqrt{S^2} = \sqrt{\frac{\sum_{i=1}^{n}(X_i - \overline{X})^2}{n - 1}} = \sqrt{45.82} = 6.77$$

This indicates that the get ready times in this sample are clustering within 6.77 minutes around the mean of 39.6 minutes, between $\overline{X} - 1S = 32.83$ and $\overline{X} + 1S = 46.37$ minutes. In fact, 7 out of 10 get ready times lie within this interval.

While not shown in Table 3.1, the sum of the middle column (that represents differences between each value and the mean) is zero. For any set of data, this sum will always be zero:

$$\sum_{i=1}^{n}(X_i - \overline{X}) = 0 \text{ for all sets of data}$$

This property is one of the reasons that the mean is used as the most common measure of central tendency.

Example 3.6 illustrates that many applications calculate the sample variance and the sample standard deviation, making hand calculations unnecessary.

EXAMPLE 3.6

Computing the Variance and Standard Deviation of the Number of Calories in Cereals

Nutritional data about a sample of seven breakfast cereals (stored in Cereals) includes the number of calories per serving (see Example 3.1 on page 123). Compute the variance and standard deviation of the calories in the cereals.

SOLUTION Figure 3.1 contains the Excel and Minitab results for this example.

FIGURE 3.1

Excel and Minitab results for computing the variance and standard deviation of the calories in the sample of cereals.

▲	A	B	C	D
1	Calories		Calculations	
2	80		Variance directly using VAR.S function	
3	100		in formula =VAR.S(A2:A8)	2200
4	100			
5	110		Standard deviation directly using STDEV.S	
6	130		function in formula =STDEV.S(A2:A8)	46.90
7	190			
8	200			

Descriptive Statistics: Calories

Statistics

Variable	Mean	StDev	Variance
Calories	130.0	46.9	2200.0

Alternatively, using Equation (3.6) on page 127:

$$S^2 = \frac{\sum_{i=1}^{n}(X_i - \overline{X})^2}{n - 1} = \frac{(80 - 130)^2 + (100 - 130)^2 + \cdots + (200 - 130)^2}{7 - 1}$$

$$= \frac{13,200}{6} = 2,200$$

Using Equation (3.7) on page 128, the sample standard deviation, S, is

$$S = \sqrt{S^2} = \sqrt{\frac{\sum_{i=1}^{n}(X_i - \overline{X})^2}{n - 1}} = \sqrt{2,200} = 46.9042$$

The standard deviation of 46.9042 indicates that the calories in the cereals are clustering within ± 46.9042 around the mean of 130 (i.e., clustering between $\overline{X} - 1S = 83.0958$ and $\overline{X} + 1S = 176.9042$). In fact, 57.1% (four out of seven) of the calories lie within this interval.

The Coefficient of Variation

The coefficient of variation is equal to the standard deviation divided by the mean, multiplied by 100%. Unlike the measures of variation presented previously, the **coefficient of variation (CV)** measures the scatter in the data relative to the mean. The coefficient of variation is a *relative measure* of variation that is always expressed as a percentage rather than in terms of the units of the particular data. Equation (3.8) defines the coefficient of variation.

> **COEFFICIENT OF VARIATION**
>
> The coefficient of variation is equal to the standard deviation divided by the mean, multiplied by 100%.
>
> $$CV = \left(\frac{S}{\overline{X}} \right) 100\% \tag{3.8}$$
>
> where
>
> S = sample standard deviation
> $\overline{X}$ = sample mean

For the sample of 10 get ready times, because $\overline{X} = 39.6$ and $S = 6.77$, the coefficient of variation is

$$CV = \left(\frac{S}{\overline{X}} \right) 100\% = \left(\frac{6.77}{39.6} \right) 100\% = 17.10\%$$

For the get ready times, the standard deviation is 17.1% of the size of the mean.

The coefficient of variation is especially useful when comparing two or more sets of data that are measured in different units, as Example 3.7 illustrates.

EXAMPLE 3.7

Comparing Two Coefficients of Variation When the Two Variables Have Different Units of Measurement

Which varies more from cereal to cereal—the number of calories or the amount of sugar (in grams)?

SOLUTION Because calories and the amount of sugar have different units of measurement, you need to compare the relative variability in the two measurements.

For calories, using the mean and variance computed in Examples 3.1 and 3.6 on pages 123 and 129, the coefficient of variation is

$$CV_{\text{Calories}} = \left(\frac{46.9042}{130} \right) 100\% = 36.08\%$$

For the amount of sugar in grams, the values for the seven cereals are

$$6 \quad 2 \quad 4 \quad 4 \quad 4 \quad 11 \quad 10$$

For these data, $\overline{X} = 5.8571$ and $S = 3.3877$. Therefore, the coefficient of variation is

$$CV_{\text{Sugar}} = \left(\frac{3.3877}{5.8571} \right) 100\% = 57.84\%$$

You conclude that relative to the mean, the amount of sugar is much more variable than the calories.

Z Scores

The **Z score** of a value is the difference between that value and the mean, divided by the standard deviation. A Z score of 0 indicates that the value is the same as the mean. If a Z score is a positive or negative number, it indicates whether the value is above or below the mean and by how many standard deviations.

Z scores help identify **outliers**, the values that seem excessively different from most of the rest of the values (see Section 1.4). Values that are very different from the mean will have either very small (negative) Z scores or very large (positive) Z scores. As a general rule, a Z score that is less than -3.0 or greater than $+3.0$ indicates an outlier value.

Z SCORE

The Z score for a value is equal to the difference between the value and the mean, divided by the standard deviation:

$$Z = \frac{X - \overline{X}}{S} \tag{3.9}$$

To further analyze the sample of 10 times to get ready in the morning, you can compute the Z scores. Because the mean is 39.6 minutes, the standard deviation is 6.77 minutes, and the time to get ready on the first day is 39.0 minutes, you compute the Z score for Day 1 by using Equation (3.9):

$$Z = \frac{X - \overline{X}}{S}$$

$$= \frac{39.0 - 39.6}{6.77} = -0.09$$

The Z score of -0.09 for the first day indicates that the time to get ready on that day is very close to the mean. Figure 3.2 presents the Z scores for all 10 days.

FIGURE 3.2

Excel worksheet containing the Z scores for 10 get-ready times

	A	B
1	Get-Ready Time	Z Score
2	39	-0.09
3	29	-1.57
4	43	0.50
5	52	1.83
6	39	-0.09
7	44	0.65
8	40	0.06
9	31	-1.27
10	44	0.65
11	35	-0.68

The largest Z score is 1.83 for Day 4, on which the time to get ready was 52 minutes. The lowest Z score is -1.57 for Day 2, on which the time to get ready was 29 minutes. Because none of the Z scores are less than -3.0 or greater then $+3.0$, you conclude that the get ready times include no apparent outliers.

EXAMPLE 3.8

Computing the Z Scores of the Number of Calories in Cereals

Nutritional data about a sample of seven breakfast cereals (stored in Cereals) includes the number of calories per serving (see Example 3.1 on page 123). Calculate the Z scores of the calories in breakfast cereals.

SOLUTION Figure 3.3 presents the Z scores of the calories for the cereals. The largest Z score is 1.49, for a cereal with 200 calories. The lowest Z score is -1.07, for a cereal with 80 calories. There are no apparent outliers in these data because none of the Z scores are less than -3.0 or greater than $+3.0$.

FIGURE 3.3

JMP worksheet containing the Z scores for 10 cereals

	Calories	Standardize [Calories]
1	80	-1.07
2	100	-0.64
3	100	-0.64
4	110	-0.43
5	130	0.00
6	190	1.28
7	200	1.49

Shape: Skewness

Skewness measures the extent to which the data values are not **symmetrical** around the mean. The three possibilities are:

- **Mean < median:** negative, or **left-skewed distribution**
- **Mean = median:** **symmetrical distribution** (zero skewness)
- **Mean > median:** positive, or **right-skewed distribution**

In a *symmetrical* distribution, the values below the mean are distributed in exactly the same way as the values above the mean, and the skewness is zero. In a **skewed** distribution, there is an imbalance of data values below and above the mean, and the skewness is a nonzero value (less than zero for a left-skewed distribution, greater than zero for a right-skewed distribution). Figure 3.4 visualizes these possibilities.

FIGURE 3.4

The shapes of three data distributions

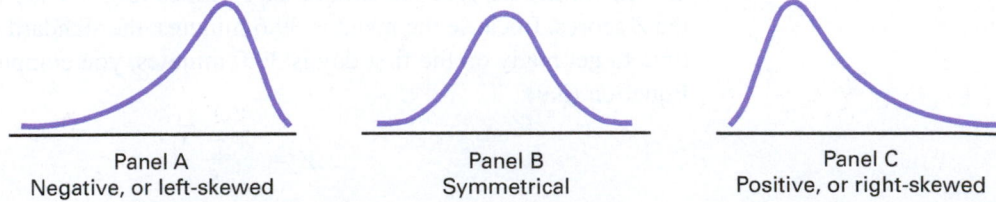

Panel A
Negative, or left-skewed

Panel B
Symmetrical

Panel C
Positive, or right-skewed

Panel A displays a left-skewed distribution. In a left-skewed distribution, most of the values are in the upper portion of the distribution. Some extremely small values cause the long tail and distortion to the left and cause the mean to be less than the median. Because the skewness statistic for such a distribution will be less than zero, some use the term *negative skew* to describe this distribution.

Panel B displays a symmetrical distribution. In a symmetrical distribution, values are equally distributed in the upper and lower portions of the distribution. This equality causes the portion of the curve below the mean to be the mirror image of the portion of the curve above the mean and makes the mean equal to the median.

Panel C displays a right-skewed distribution. In a right-skewed distribution, most of the values are in the lower portion of the distribution. Some extremely large values cause the long tail and distortion to the right and cause the mean to be greater than the median. Because the skewness statistic for such a distribution will be greater than zero, some use the term *positive skew* to describe this distribution.

Shape: Kurtosis

Kurtosis measures the peakedness of the curve of the distribution—that is, how sharply the curve rises approaching the center of the distribution. Kurtosis compares the shape of the peak to the shape of the peak of a bell-shaped normal distribution (see Chapter 6), which, by definition, has a kurtosis of zero.[1] A distribution that has a sharper-rising center peak than the peak of a normal distribution has *positive* kurtosis, a kurtosis value that is greater than zero, and is called **leptokurtic**. A distribution that has a slower-rising (flatter) center peak than the peak of a normal distribution has *negative* kurtosis, a kurtosis value that is less than zero, and is called **platykurtic**. A leptokurtic distribution has a higher concentration of values near the mean of the distribution compared to a normal distribution, while a platykurtic distribution has a lower concentration compared to a normal distribution.

In affecting the shape of the central peak, the relative concentration of values near the mean also affects the ends, or *tails*, of the curve of a distribution. A leptokurtic distribution has *fatter* tails, many more values in the tails, than a normal distribution has. When an analysis mistakenly assumes that a set of data forms a normal distribution, that analysis will underestimate the occurrence of extreme values if the data actually forms a leptokurtic distribution. Some suggest that such a mistake can explain the unanticipated reverses and collapses that financial markets have experienced in the recent past (see reference 3).

[1]Several different operational definitions exist for kurtosis. The definition here, used by Excel, is sometimes called *excess kurtosis* to distinguish it from other definitions. Read the SHORT TAKES for Chapter 3 to learn how Excel calculates kurtosis (and skewness).

EXAMPLE 3.9

Descriptive Statistics for Growth and Value Funds

In the More Descriptive Choices scenario, you are interested in comparing the past performance of the growth and value funds from a sample of 479 funds. One measure of past performance is the three-year return percentage variable. Compute descriptive statistics for the growth and value funds.

SOLUTION Figure 3.5 presents descriptive summary measures for the two types of funds. The results include the mean, median, mode, minimum, maximum, range, variance, standard deviation, coefficient of variation, skewness, kurtosis, count (the sample size), and standard error. The standard error (see Section 7.2) is the standard deviation divided by the square root of the sample size.

FIGURE 3.5

Excel and Minitab descriptive statistics results for the three-year return percentages for the growth and value funds

	A	B	C
1	Descriptive Statistics for the 3YrReturn Variable		
2			
3		Growth	Value	Growth
4	Mean	8.51	6.84	=AVERAGE(UNSTACKED!A:A)
5	Median	8.70	7.07	=MEDIAN(UNSTACKED!A:A)
6	Mode	8.71	8.6	=MODE(UNSTACKED!A:A)
7	Minimum	-3.40	-2.65	=MIN(UNSTACKED!A:A)
8	Maximum	15.32	11.98	=MAX(UNSTACKED!A:A)
9	Range	18.72	14.63	=B8 - B7
10	Variance	10.1983	5.4092	=VAR.S(UNSTACKED!A:A)
11	Standard Deviation	3.1935	2.3258	=STDEV.S(UNSTACKED!A:A)
12	Coeff. of Variation	37.53%	34.00%	=B11/B4
13	Skewness	-0.4883	-0.9260	=SKEW(UNSTACKED!A:A)
14	Kurtosis	0.2327	1.6006	=KURT(UNSTACKED!A:A)
15	Count	306	173	=COUNT(UNSTACKED!A:A)
16	Standard Error	0.1826	0.1768	=B11/SQRT(B15)

Descriptive Statistics: 3YrReturn

Statistics

Variable	Fund Type	Total Count	Mean	StDev	Variance	CoefVar	Minimum	Q1	Median	Q3
3YrReturn	Growth	306	8.509	3.193	10.198	37.53	-3.400	6.660	8.700	10.927
	Value	173	6.841	2.326	5.409	34.00	-2.650	5.670	7.070	8.500

Variable	Fund Type	Maximum	Range	IQR	Mode	N for Mode	Skewness	Kurtosis
3YrReturn	Growth	15.320	18.720	4.267	8.71	4	-0.49	0.23
	Value	11.980	14.630	2.830	4.54, 6.58, 8.6	3	-0.93	1.60

In examining the results, you see that there are some differences in the three-year return for the growth and value funds. The growth funds had a mean three-year return of 8.51 and a median return of 8.70. This compares to a mean of 6.84 and a median of 7.07 for the value funds. The medians indicate that half of the growth funds had three-year returns of 8.70 or better, and half the value funds had three-year returns of 6.84 or better. You conclude that the value funds had a lower return than the growth funds.

The growth funds had a higher standard deviation than the value funds (3.1935, as compared to 2.3258). The growth funds and the value funds each showed left or negative skewness. The skewness of the growth funds was −0.4883 and the skewness of the value funds was −0.9260. The kurtosis of the growth funds was slightly positive, indicating a distribution that was more peaked than a normal distribution. The kurtosis of the value funds was positive indicating a distribution that was much more peaked than a normal distribution.

EXAMPLE 3.10

Descriptive Statistics Using Multidimensional Contingency Tables

Continuing with the More Descriptive Choices scenario, you wish to explore the effects of each combination of Fund Type, Market Cap, and Risk Level on measures of past performance. One measure of past performance is the three-year return percentage. Compute the mean three-year return percentage for each combination of Fund Type, Market Cap, and Risk Level.

SOLUTION A multidimensional contingency table (see Section 2.6) computes the mean three-year return percentage for each combination of the three variables.

▶*(continued)*

FIGURE 3.6
JMP and Excel multidimensional contingency tables for the mean three-year return percentages for each combination of Fund Type, Market Cap, and Risk Level

Mean 3YrReturn	Risk Level ▾			
Fund Type ▾	Low	Average	High	Grand Total
⊟ Growth	9.87	9.06	6.64	8.51
Large	10.22	10.43	9.79	10.30
MidCap	8.93	6.86	5.78	6.93
Small	9.09	7.43	5.99	6.39
⊟ Value	7.76	6.41	4.13	6.84
Large	7.82	6.49	5.02	7.29
MidCap	7.87	7.05	2.22	6.69
Small	6.38	5.60	4.63	5.39
Grand Total	**8.66**	**8.21**	**6.25**	**7.91**

		Risk Level			
		Low	Average	High	All
		3YrReturn	3YrReturn	3YrReturn	3YrReturn
Fund Type	Market Cap	Mean	Mean	Mean	Mean
Growth	Large	10.22	10.43	9.79	10.30
	MidCap	8.93	6.86	5.78	6.93
	Small	9.09	7.43	5.99	6.39
	All	9.87	9.06	6.64	8.51
Value	Large	7.82	6.49	5.02	7.29
	MidCap	7.87	7.05	2.22	6.69
	Small	6.38	5.60	4.63	5.39
	All	7.76	6.41	4.13	6.84

The three-year return is higher for low risk funds than average risk or high risk funds for both the growth funds and value funds. However, this pattern changes when Market Cap categories are considered. For example, the three-year return percentage for growth funds with average risk is much higher for large cap funds than for midcap or small market cap funds. Also, for value funds with average risk, the three-year return for midcap funds is higher than the return for large funds.

PROBLEMS FOR SECTIONS 3.1 AND 3.2

LEARNING THE BASICS

3.1 The following set of data is from a sample of $n = 5$:

$$7\ 4\ 9\ 8\ 2$$

a. Compute the mean, median, and mode.
b. Compute the range, variance, standard deviation, and coefficient of variation.
c. Compute the Z scores. Are there any outliers?
d. Describe the shape of the data set.

3.2 The following set of data is from a sample of $n = 6$:

$$7\ 4\ 9\ 7\ 3\ 12$$

a. Compute the mean, median, and mode.
b. Compute the range, variance, standard deviation, and coefficient of variation.
c. Compute the Z scores. Are there any outliers?
d. Describe the shape of the data set.

3.3 The following set of data is from a sample of $n = 7$:

$$12\ 7\ 4\ 9\ 0\ 7\ 3$$

a. Compute the mean, median, and mode.
b. Compute the range, variance, standard deviation, and coefficient of variation.
c. Compute the Z scores. Are there any outliers?
d. Describe the shape of the data set.

3.4 The following set of data is from a sample of $n = 5$:

$$7\ -5\ -8\ 7\ 9$$

a. Compute the mean, median, and mode.
b. Compute the range, variance, standard deviation, and coefficient of variation.
c. Compute the Z scores. Are there any outliers?
d. Describe the shape of the data set.

3.5 Suppose that the rate of return for a particular stock during the past two years was 10% for the first year and 30% for the second year. Compute the geometric rate of return per year. (*Note:* A rate of return of 10% is recorded as 0.10, and a rate of return of 30% is recorded as 0.30.)

3.6 Suppose that the rate of return for a particular stock during the past two years was 20% for the first year and −30% for the second year. Compute the geometric rate of return per year.

APPLYING THE CONCEPTS

3.7 *Wired*, a magazine that delivers a glimpse into the future of business, culture, innovation, and science, reported the following summary for the household incomes of its two types of subscribers, the print reader and the digital reader.

Audience	Median
Wired reader	$97,661
Wired.com user	87,333

Source: Data extracted from "2017 Media Kit," www.wired.com/wp-content/uploads/2015/03/WMG_Media_Kit_2017_v3.pdf.

Interpret the median household income for the *Wired* readers and the Wired.com users.

3.8 The operations manager of a plant that manufactures tires wants to compare the actual inner diameters of two grades of tires, each of which is expected to be 575 millimeters. A sample of five tires of each grade was selected, and the results representing the inner diameters of the tires, ranked from smallest to largest, are as follows:

Grade X	Grade Y
568 570 575 578 584	573 574 575 577 578

a. For each of the two grades of tires, compute the mean, median, and standard deviation.
b. Which grade of tire is providing better quality? Explain.
c. What would be the effect on your answers in (a) and (b) if the last value for grade Y was 588 instead of 578? Explain.

3.9 According to the U.S. Census Bureau (**census.gov**), in 2016, the median sales price of new houses was $315,500 and the mean sales price was $370,800.

a. Interpret the median sales price.

b. Interpret the mean sales price.

c. Discuss the shape of the distribution of the price of new houses.

✓ SELF TEST **3.10** The file **MobileSpeed** contains the overall download and upload speeds in mbps for nine carriers in the United States.

Carrier	Download Speed	Upload Speed
Verizon	24.0	14.3
T-Mobile	22.7	13.2
AT&T	20.8	9.1
Metro PCS	16.7	11.1
Sprint	11.2	6.4
Virgin Mobile	10.8	6.2
Boost	10.3	6.0
Straight Talk	7.1	3.0
Cricket	4.5	3.8

Source: Data extracted from "Best Mobile Network 2016", **bit.ly/1KGPrMm**, accessed November 10, 2016.

For the download speed and the upload speed separately:

a. Compute the mean and median.

b. Compute the variance, standard deviation, range, and coefficient of variation.

c. Are the data skewed? If so, how?

d. Based on the results of (a) through (c), what conclusions can you reach concerning the download and upload speed of various carriers?

3.11 The file **AirportRating** contains the rating of large and medium size airports in the United States and Canada.

Source: Data extracted from N. Trejos, "Portland, Indianapolis Top Airport Rankings, *USA Today*, December 16, 2016, p. 4B.

For large and medium airports separately:

a. Compute the mean, median, and mode.

b. Compute the variance, standard deviation, range, coefficient of variation, and Z scores.

c. Are the data skewed? If so, how?

d. Based on the results of (a) through (c), what conclusions can you reach about the rating of large and medium size airports?

3.12 The annual NFL Super Bowl is the most widely watched sporting event in the United States each year. In recent years, there has been a great deal of interest in the ads that appear during the game. These ads vary in length with most lasting 30 seconds or 60 seconds. The file **SuperBowlAdScore** contains the ad length and ad scores from a recent Super Bowl.

Source: Data extracted from C. Woodyard, "Funny Bone Wins Out," *USA Today*, February 6, 2016, p. 4B.

For the 30-second ads and the 60-second ads separately:

a. Compute the mean, median, and mode.

b. Compute the variance, standard deviation, range, and coefficient of variation.

c. Are the data skewed? If so, how?

d. Based on the results of (a) through (c), what conclusions can you reach about the scores of 30- and 60-second ads?

3.13 The file **AccountingPartners** contains the number of partners in a cohort of rising accounting firms that have been tagged as "firms to watch." The firms have the following numbers of partners:

```
37 41 26 14 22 29 36 11 16 29 30 20 20 20 26 21
17 21 14 28 24 14 15 19 14 11 18  9 10 13 14 24
25 13  5 13 20 15 17 16 26 18 20 16 11
```

Source: Data extracted from *2017 Top 100 Firms*, Bloomberg BNA, **accounting today.com**.

a. Compute the mean, median, and mode.

b. Compute the variance, standard deviation, range, coefficient of variation, and Z scores. Are there any outliers? Explain.

c. Are the data skewed? If so, how?

d. Based on the results of (a) through (c), what conclusions can you reach concerning the number of partners in rising accounting firms?

3.14 The file **MobileCommerce** contains the following mobile commerce penetration values, the percentage of the country population that bought something online via a mobile phone in the past month, for 28 of the world's economies:

```
23 27 26 25 40 19 26 36 23 33 23 11 38 21
26 23 21 33 40 15 55 30 41 31 47 37 33 28
```

Source: Data extracted from **bit.ly/2jXeS3F**.

a. Compute the mean and median.

b. Compute the variance, standard deviation, range, coefficient of variation, and Z scores. Are there any outliers? Explain.

c. Are the data skewed? If so, how?

d. Based on the results of (a) through (c), what conclusions can you reach concerning mobile commerce population penetration?

3.15 Is there a difference in the variation of the yields of different types of investments? The file **CD Rate** contains the yields for one-year certificates of deposit (CDs) and five-year CDs for 39 banks listed for West Palm Beach, Florida on January 9, 2017.

Source: Data extracted from **www.Bankrate.com**, January 9, 2017.

a. For one-year and five-year CDs, separately compute the variance, standard deviation, range, and coefficient of variation.

b. Based on the results of (a), do one-year CDs or five-year CDs have more variation in the yields offered? Explain.

3.16 The file **HotelAway** contains the average room price (in US$) paid by various nationalities while traveling abroad (away from their home country) in 2016:

```
124 101 115 126 114 112 138 85 138 96 130 116 132
```

Source: Data extracted from **hpi.hotels.com/**.

a. Compute the mean, median, and mode.

b. Compute the range, variance, and standard deviation.

c. Based on the results of (a) and (b), what conclusions can you reach concerning the room price (in USD) paid by international travelers while traveling to various countries in 2016?

d. Suppose that the last value was 175 instead of 132. Repeat (a) through (c), using this value. Comment on the difference in the results.

3.17 A bank branch located in a commercial district of a city has the business objective of developing an improved process for serving customers during the noon-to-1:00 P.M. lunch period. The waiting time, in minutes, is defined as the time the customer enters the line to when he or she reaches the teller window. Data collected from a sample of 15 customers during this hour are stored in **Bank1**:

```
4.21  5.55  3.02  5.13  4.77  2.34  3.54  3.20
4.50  6.10  0.38  5.12  6.46  6.19  3.79
```

a. Compute the mean and median.

b. Compute the variance, standard deviation, range, coefficient of variation, and Z scores. Are there any outliers? Explain.

c. Are the data skewed? If so, how?

d. As a customer walks into the branch office during the lunch hour, she asks the branch manager how long she can expect to wait. The branch manager replies, "Almost certainly less than five minutes." On the basis of the results of (a) through (c), evaluate the accuracy of this statement.

3.18 Suppose that another bank branch, located in a residential area, is also concerned with the noon-to-1:00 P.M. lunch hour. The waiting time, in minutes, collected from a sample of 15 customers during this hour, are stored in Bank2 :

> 9.66 5.90 8.02 5.79 8.73 3.82 8.01 8.35
> 10.49 6.68 5.64 4.08 6.17 9.91 5.47

a. Compute the mean and median.

b. Compute the variance, standard deviation, range, coefficient of variation, and Z scores. Are there any outliers? Explain.

c. Are the data skewed? If so, how?

d. As a customer walks into the branch office during the lunch hour, he asks the branch manager how long he can expect to wait. The branch manager replies, "Almost certainly less than five minutes." On the basis of the results of (a) through (c), evaluate the accuracy of this statement.

3.19 General Electric (GE) is one of the world's largest companies; it develops, manufactures, and markets a wide range of products, including medical diagnostic imaging devices, jet engines, lighting products, and chemicals. In 2015, the stock price rose 23.27%, and in 2016, the stock price rose 1.44%.

Source: Data extracted from **finance.yahoo.com**, January 9, 2017.

a. Compute the geometric mean rate of return per year for the two-year period 2015–2016. (Hint: Denote an increase of 23.27% as $R_2 = 0.2327$.)

b. If you purchased $1,000 of GE stock at the start of 2015 what was its value at the end of 2016?

c. Compare the result of (b) to that of Problem 3.20 (b).

 **3.20** Facebook's stock price in 2015 increased by 34.15%, and in 2016, it increased by 9.93%.

Source: Data extracted from **finance.yahoo.com**, January 9, 2017.

a. Compute the geometric mean rate of return per year for the two-year period 2015–2016. (Hint: Denote an increase of 9.93% as $R_1 = 0.0993$.)

b. If you purchased $1,000 of Facebook stock at the start of 2015, what was its value at the end of 2016?

c. Compare the result of (b) to that of Problem 3.19 (b).

3.21 The file Indices contains the total rate of return percentage for the Dow Jones Industrial Average (DJIA), the Standard & Poor's 500 (S&P 500), and the technology-heavy NASDAQ Composite (NASDAQ) from 2013 through 2016. These data are:

Year	DJIA	S&P 500	NASDAQ
2013	26.5	29.6	38.3
2014	7.5	11.4	13.4
2015	−2.2	−0.7	5.7
2016	13.4	9.5	7.5

a. Compute the geometric mean rate of return per year for the DJIA, S&P 500, and NASDAQ from 2013 through 2016.

b. What conclusions can you reach concerning the geometric mean rates of return per year of the three market indices?

c. Compare the results of (b) to those of Problem 3.22 (b).

3.22 In 2013 through 2016, the value of precious metals fluctuated dramatically. The following data (stored in Metals) represent the total rate of return (in percentage) for platinum, gold, and silver from 2013 through 2016:

Year	Platinum	Gold	Silver
2013	−11.70	6.08	7.13
2014	−0.72	−28.65	−26.65
2015	−26.50	−17.79	−29.43
2016	1.40	8.60	15.80

a. Compute the geometric mean rate of return per year for platinum, gold, and silver from 2013 through 2016.

b. What conclusions can you reach concerning the geometric mean rates of return of the three precious metals?

c. Compare the results of (b) to those of Problem 3.21 (b).

3.23 Using the three-year return percentage variable in Retirement Funds :

a. Construct a table that computes the mean for each combination of type, market cap, and risk.

b. Construct a table that computes the standard deviation for each combination of type, market cap, and risk.

c. What conclusions can you reach concerning differences among the types of retirement funds (growth and value), based on market cap (small, mid-cap, and large) and the risk (low, average, and high)?

3.24 Using the three-year return percentage variable in Retirement Funds :

a. Construct a table that computes the mean for each combination of type, market cap, and rating.

b. Construct a table that computes the standard deviation for each combination of type, market cap, and rating.

c. What conclusions can you reach concerning differences among the types of retirement funds (growth and value), based on market cap (small, mid-cap, and large) and the rating (one, two, three, four, and five)?

3.25 Using the three-year return percentage variable in Retirement Funds :

a. Construct a table that computes the mean for each combination of market cap, risk, and rating.

b. Construct a table that computes the standard deviation for each combination of market cap, risk, and rating.

c. What conclusions can you reach concerning differences based on the market cap (small, mid-cap, and large), risk (low, average, and high), and rating (one, two, three, four, and five)?

3.26 Using the three-year return percentage variable in Retirement Funds :

a. Construct a table that computes the mean for each combination of type, risk, and rating.

b. Construct a table that computes the standard deviation for each combination of type, risk, and rating.

c. What conclusions can you reach concerning differences among the types of retirement funds (growth and value), based on the risk (low, average, and high) and the rating (one, two, three, four, and five)?

3.3 Exploring Numerical Variables

Besides summarizing by calculating the measures of central tendency, variation, and shape, a numerical variable can be explored by examining the distribution of values for the variable. This exploration can include calculating the *quartiles* as well as creating a *boxplot*, a visual summary of the distribution of values.

Quartiles

Quartiles split the values into four equal parts—the **first quartile (Q_1)** divides the smallest 25.0% of the values from the other 75.0% that are larger. The **second quartile (Q_2)** is the median; 50.0% of the values are smaller than or equal to the median, and 50.0% are larger than or equal to the median. The **third quartile (Q_3)** divides the smallest 75.0% of the values from the largest 25.0%. Equations (3.10) and (3.11) define the first and third quartiles.

FIRST QUARTILE, Q_1

25.0% of the values are smaller than or equal to Q_1, the first quartile, and 75.0% are larger than or equal to the first quartile, Q_1:

$$Q_1 = \frac{n + 1}{4} \text{ ranked value} \tag{3.10}$$

THIRD QUARTILE, Q_3

75.0% of the values are smaller than or equal to the third quartile, Q_3, and 25.0% are larger than or equal to the third quartile, Q_3:

$$Q_3 = \frac{3(n + 1)}{4} \text{ ranked value} \tag{3.11}$$

---

student TIP

You must rank the values in order from smallest to largest before computing the quartiles.

Exhibit 3.1 summarizes the rules for calculating the quartiles. These rules require that the values have been first ranked from smallest to largest.

EXHIBIT 3.1

Rules for Calculating the Quartiles from a Set of Ranked Values

Rule 1   If the ranked value is a whole number, the quartile is equal to the measurement that corresponds to that ranked value.

      Example: If the sample size $n = 7$, the first quartile, Q_1, is equal to the measurement associated with the $(7 + 1)/4 =$ second ranked value.

Rule 2   If the ranked value is a fractional half (2.5, 4.5, *etc.*), the quartile is equal to the measurement that corresponds to the average of the measurements corresponding to the two ranked values involved.

      Example: If the sample size $n = 9$, the first quartile, Q_1, is equal to the $(9 + 1)/4 = 2.5$ ranked value, halfway between the second ranked value and the third ranked value.

Rule 3   If the ranked value is neither a whole number nor a fractional half, round the result to the nearest integer and select the measurement corresponding to that ranked value.

      Example: If the sample size $n = 10$, the first quartile, Q_1, is equal to the $(10 + 1)/4 = 2.75$ ranked value. Round 2.75 to 3 and use the third ranked value.

Some sources define different rules for calculating quartiles that may result in slightly different values for the quartiles.

For example, to compute the quartiles for the sample of 10 times to get ready in the morning, you first rank the data from smallest to largest:

Ranked values:	29	31	35	39	39	40	43	44	44	52
Ranks:	1	2	3	4	5	6	7	8	9	10

The first quartile is the $(n + 1)/4 = (10 + 1)/4 = 2.75$ ranked value. Using Rule 3, you round up to the third ranked value. The third ranked value for the get ready times data is 35 minutes. You interpret the first quartile of 35 to mean that on 25% of the days, the time to get ready is less than or equal to 35 minutes, and on 75% of the days, the time to get ready is greater than or equal to 35 minutes.

The third quartile is the $3(n + 1)/4 = 3(10 + 1)/4 = 8.25$ ranked value. Using Rule 3 for quartiles, you round this down to the eighth ranked value. The eighth ranked value is 44 minutes. Thus, on 75% of the days, the time to get ready is less than or equal to 44 minutes, and on 25% of the days, the time to get ready is greater than or equal to 44 minutes.

Percentiles   Related to quartiles are **percentiles** that split a variable into 100 equal parts. By this definition, the first quartile is equivalent to the 25th percentile, the second quartile to the 50th percentile, and the third quartile to the 75th percentile.

EXAMPLE 3.11

Computing the Quartiles

Nutritional data about a sample of seven breakfast cereals (stored in Cereals) includes the number of calories per serving (see Example 3.1 on page 123). Compute the first quartile (Q_1) and third quartile (Q_3) of the number of calories for the cereals.

SOLUTION   Ranked from smallest to largest, the number of calories for the seven cereals are as follows:

Ranked values:	80	100	100	110	130	190	200
Ranks:	1	2	3	4	5	6	7

For these data

$$Q_1 = \frac{(n + 1)}{4} \text{ ranked value}$$

$$= \frac{7 + 1}{4} \text{ ranked value} = \text{2nd ranked value}$$

Therefore, using Rule 1, Q_1 is the second ranked value. Because the second ranked value is 100, the first quartile, Q_1, is 100.

To compute the third quartile, Q_3,

$$Q_3 = \frac{3(n + 1)}{4} \text{ ranked value}$$

$$= \frac{3(7 + 1)}{4} \text{ ranked value} = \text{6th ranked value}$$

Therefore, using Rule 1, Q_3 is the sixth ranked value. Because the sixth ranked value is 190, Q_3 is 190.

The first quartile of 100 indicates that 25% of the cereals contain 100 calories or fewer per serving and 75% contain 100 or more calories. The third quartile of 190 indicates that 75% of the cereals contain 190 calories or fewer per serving and 25% contain 190 or more calories.

The Interquartile Range

The **interquartile range** (also called the **midspread**) measures the difference in the center of a distribution between the third and first quartiles.

> **INTERQUARTILE RANGE**
>
> The interquartile range is the difference between the third quartile and the first quartile:
>
> $$\text{Interquartile range} = Q_3 - Q_1 \qquad (3.12)$$

The interquartile range measures the spread in the middle 50% of the values and is not influenced by extreme values. The interquartile range can be used to determine whether to classify extreme values as outliers. If a value is either more than 1.5 times the interquartile range below the first quartile or more than 1.5 times the interquartile range above the third quartile, that value can be classified as an outlier.

To further analyze the sample of 10 times to get ready in the morning, you can compute the interquartile range. You first order the data as follows:

29   31   35   39   39   40   43   44   44   52

You use Equation (3.12) and the earlier results on page 138, $Q_1 = 35$ and $Q_3 = 44$:

$$\text{Interquartile range} = 44 - 35 = 9 \text{ minutes}$$

Therefore, the interquartile range in the time to get ready is 9 minutes. The interval 35 to 44 is often referred to as the *middle fifty*.

EXAMPLE 3.12

Computing the Interquartile Range for the Number of Calories in Cereals

Nutritional data about a sample of seven breakfast cereals (stored in `Cereals`) includes the number of calories per serving (see Example 3.1 on page 123). Compute the interquartile range of the number of calories in cereals.

SOLUTION Ranked from smallest to largest, the number of calories for the seven cereals are as follows:

80   100   100   110   130   190   200

Using Equation (3.12) and the earlier results from Example 3.11 on page 138 $Q_1 = 100$ and $Q_3 = 190$:

$$\text{Interquartile range} = 190 - 100 = 90$$

Therefore, the interquartile range of the number of calories in cereals is 90 calories.

Because the interquartile range does not consider any value smaller than Q_1 or larger than Q_3, it cannot be affected by extreme values. Descriptive statistics such as the median, Q_1, Q_3, and the interquartile range, which are not influenced by extreme values, are called **resistant measures**.

The Five-Number Summary

The **five-number summary** for a variable consists of the smallest value (X_{smallest}), the first quartile, the median, the third quartile, and the largest value (X_{largest}).

> **FIVE-NUMBER SUMMARY**
>
> $$X_{\text{smallest}} \quad Q_1 \quad \text{Median} \quad Q_3 \quad X_{\text{largest}}$$

The five-number summary provides a way to determine the shape of the distribution for a set of data. Table 3.2 explains how relationships among these five statistics help to identify the shape of the distribution.

TABLE 3.2
Relationships Among the Five-Number Summary and the Type of Distribution

	TYPE OF DISTRIBUTION		
COMPARISON	**Left-Skewed**	**Symmetrical**	**Right-Skewed**
The distance from $X_{smallest}$ to the median versus the distance from the median to $X_{largest}$.	The distance from $X_{smallest}$ to the median is greater than the distance from the median to $X_{largest}$.	The two distances are the same.	The distance from $X_{smallest}$ to the median is less than the distance from the median to $X_{largest}$.
The distance from $X_{smallest}$ to Q_1 versus the distance from Q_3 to $X_{largest}$.	The distance from $X_{smallest}$ to Q_1 is greater than the distance from Q_3 to $X_{largest}$.	The two distances are the same.	The distance from $X_{smallest}$ to Q_1 is less than the distance from Q_3 to $X_{largest}$.
The distance from Q_1 to the median versus the distance from the median to Q_3.	The distance from Q_1 to the median is greater than the distance from the median to Q_3.	The two distances are the same.	The distance from Q_1 to the median is less than the distance from the median to Q_3.

To further analyze the sample of 10 times to get ready in the morning, you can compute the five-number summary. For these data, the smallest value is 29 minutes, and the largest value is 52 minutes (see page 123). Calculations done on pages 123 and 138 show that the median $= 39.5$, $Q_1 = 35$, and $Q_3 = 44$. Therefore, the five-number summary is as follows:

$$29 \quad 35 \quad 39.5 \quad 44 \quad 52$$

The distance from $X_{smallest}$ to the median ($39.5 - 29 = 10.5$) is slightly less than the distance from the median to $X_{largest}$ ($52 - 39.5 = 12.5$). The distance from $X_{smallest}$ to Q_1 ($35 - 29 = 6$) is slightly less than the distance from Q_3 to $X_{largest}$ ($52 - 44 = 8$). The distance from Q_1 to the median ($39.5 - 35 = 4.5$) is the same as the distance from the median to Q_3($44 - 39.5 = 4.5$). Therefore, the get ready times are slightly right-skewed.

EXAMPLE 3.13

Computing the Five-Number Summary of the Number of Calories in Cereals

Nutritional data about a sample of seven breakfast cereals (stored in Cereals) includes the number of calories per serving (see Example 3.1 on page 123). Compute the five-number summary of the number of calories in cereals.

SOLUTION From previous computations for the number of calories in cereals (see pages 124 and 139), you know that the median $= 110$, $Q_1 = 100$, and $Q_3 = 190$.

In addition, the smallest value in the data set is 80, and the largest value is 200. Therefore, the five-number summary is as follows:

$$80 \quad 100 \quad 110 \quad 190 \quad 200$$

The three comparisons listed in Table 3.2 are used to evaluate skewness. The distance from $X_{smallest}$ to the median ($110 - 80 = 30$) is less than the distance ($200 - 110 = 90$) from the median to $X_{largest}$. The distance from $X_{smallest}$ to Q_1 ($100 - 80 = 20$) is greater than the distance from Q_3 to $X_{largest}$ ($200 - 190 = 10$). The distance from Q_1 to the median ($110 - 100 = 10$) is less than the distance from the median to Q_3 ($190 - 110 = 80$). Two comparisons indicate a right-skewed distribution, whereas the other indicates a left-skewed distribution. Therefore, given the small sample size and the conflicting results, the shape cannot be clearly determined.

The Boxplot

The **boxplot** visualizes the shape of the distribution of the values for a variable. Boxplots get their name from the box that defines the range of the middle 50% of the values and the ends of which correspond to Q_1 and Q_3. Inside the box, an additional line marks a median. Extending in either direction away from the box are whiskers, the ends of which may have dashed lines drawn perpendicular to the whiskers.

In one form of the boxplot that JMP can construct, the endpoints of the whiskers represent $X_{smallest}$ and $X_{largest}$, making the boxplot a visual representation of a five-number summary. In a second form, the endpoints of the whiskers define the smallest and largest values that are within the range of 1.5 times the interquartile range from the box. In this second form, values that are beyond this range in either direction are plotted as points or asterisks and can be considered outliers. Both Minitab and JMP can construct this second form, which JMP calls an *outlier box plot*. Only certain Excel versions contain a boxplot feature that constructs boxplots that are similar to, but not identical to, this second form. Five-number summary boxplots can be constructed in any Excel version through the creative use of other Excel charting features as Section EG3.3 *PHStat* and *Workbook* instructions explain. (Such five-number summary boxplots serve as Excel illustrations of boxplots in this book.)

Box plots can be drawn either horizontally or vertically. When drawn horizontally, the lowest values appear to the left and Q_1 is to the left of Q_3. When drawn vertically, the lowest values appear towards the bottom and Q_1 is below Q_3. Figure 3.7 contains a horizontal boxplot that visualizes the five-number summary for the sample of 10 times to get ready in the morning.

JMP can also construct a variation of the five-number summary boxplot called a quantile box plot in which additional lines represent quantiles that further subdivide the distribution of values.

FIGURE 3.7
Boxplot for the get ready times

The Figure 3.7 boxplot for the get ready times shows a slight right-skewness: The distance between the median and the largest value is slightly greater than the distance between the smallest value and the median, and the right tail is slightly longer than the left tail.

EXAMPLE 3.14

Boxplots of the Three-Year Returns for the Growth and Value Funds

In the More Descriptive Choices scenario, you are interested in comparing the past performance of the growth and value funds from a sample of 479 funds. One measure of past performance is the three-year return percentage (the 3YrReturn variable). Construct the boxplots for this variable for the growth and value funds.

SOLUTION Figure 3.8 contains an Excel five-number summary worksheet and boxplot for the three-year return percentages for the growth and value funds. The five-number summary for the growth funds associated with these boxplots is $X_{smallest} = -3.4$, $Q_1 = 6.66$, median $= 8.70$, $Q_3 = 10.92$, and $X_{largest} = 15.32$. The five-number summary for the value funds in this boxplot is $X_{smallest} = -2.65$, $Q_1 = 5.67$, median $= 7.07$, $Q_3 = 8.5$, and $X_{largest} = 11.98$.

FIGURE 3.8
Excel five-number summary and boxplot for the three-year return percentage variable

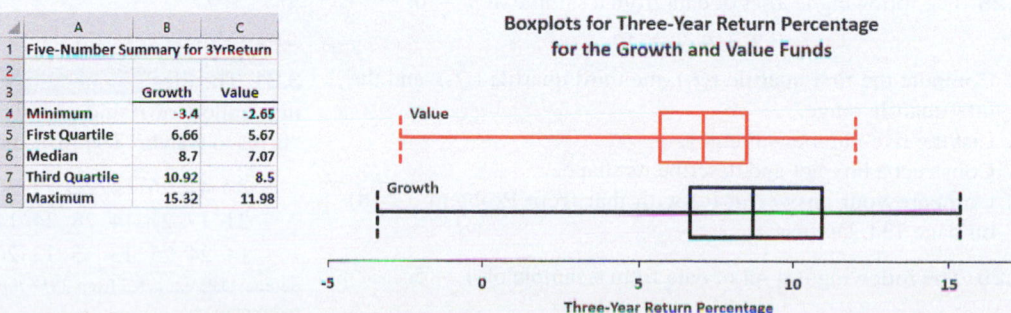

	A	B	C
1	Five-Number Summary for 3YrReturn		
2			
3		Growth	Value
4	Minimum	-3.4	-2.65
5	First Quartile	6.66	5.67
6	Median	8.7	7.07
7	Third Quartile	10.92	8.5
8	Maximum	15.32	11.98

Boxplots for Three-Year Return Percentage for the Growth and Value Funds

The median return, the quartiles, and the maximum returns are higher for the growth funds than for the value funds. Both the growth and value funds are left-skewed. These results are consistent with the Example 3.9 solution on page 133.

Figure 3.9 demonstrates the relationship between the boxplot and the density curve for four different types of distributions. The area under each density curve is split into quartiles corresponding to the five-number summary for the boxplot.

The distributions in Panels A and D of Figure 3.9 are symmetrical. In these distributions, the mean and median are equal. In addition, the length of the left tail is equal to the length of the right tail, and the median line divides the box in half.

FIGURE 3.9
Five-number summary boxplots and corresponding density curves for four distributions

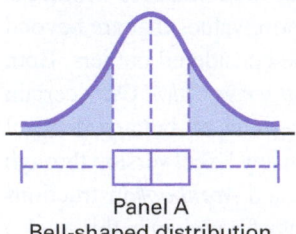

Panel A
Bell-shaped distribution

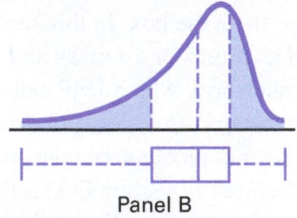

Panel B
Left-skewed distribution

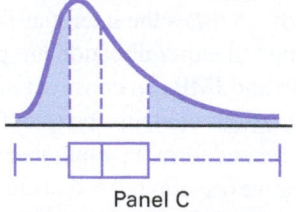

Panel C
Right-skewed distribution

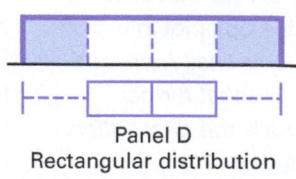

Panel D
Rectangular distribution

studentTIP

A long tail on the left side of the boxplot indicates a left-skewed distribution. A long tail on the right side of the boxplot indicates a right-skewed distribution.

The distribution in Panel B of Figure 3.9 is left-skewed. The few small values distort the mean toward the left tail. For this left-skewed distribution, there is a heavy clustering of values at the high end of the scale (i.e., the right side); 75% of all values are found between the left edge of the box (Q_1) and the end of the right tail ($X_{largest}$). There is a long left tail that contains the smallest 25% of the values, demonstrating the lack of symmetry in this data set.

The distribution in Panel C of Figure 3.9 is right-skewed. The concentration of values is on the low end of the scale (i.e., the left side of the boxplot). Here, 75% of all values are found between the beginning of the left tail and the right edge of the box (Q_3). There is a long right tail that contains the largest 25% of the values, demonstrating the lack of symmetry in this data set.

PROBLEMS FOR SECTION 3.3

LEARNING THE BASICS

3.27 The following is a set of data from a sample of $n = 7$:

12 7 4 9 0 7 3

a. Compute the first quartile (Q_1), the third quartile (Q_3), and the interquartile range.
b. List the five-number summary.
c. Construct a boxplot and describe its shape.
d. Compare your answer in (c) with that from Problem 3.3 (d) on page 134. Discuss.

3.28 The following is a set of data from a sample of $n = 6$:

7 4 9 7 3 12

a. Compute the first quartile (Q_1), the third quartile (Q_3), and the interquartile range.
b. List the five-number summary.
c. Construct a boxplot and describe its shape.
d. Compare your answer in (c) with that from Problem 3.2 (d) on page 134. Discuss.

3.29 The following is a set of data from a sample of $n = 5$:

7 4 9 8 2

a. Compute the first quartile (Q_1), the third quartile (Q_3), and the interquartile range.
b. List the five-number summary.
c. Construct a boxplot and describe its shape.

d. Compare your answer in (c) with that from Problem 3.1 (d) on page 134. Discuss.

3.30 The following is a set of data from a sample of $n = 5$:

7 −5 −8 7 9

a. Compute the first quartile (Q_1), the third quartile (Q_3), and the interquartile range.
b. List the five-number summary.
c. Construct a boxplot and describe its shape.
d. Compare your answer in (c) with that from Problem 3.4 (d) on page 134. Discuss.

APPLYING THE CONCEPTS

3.31 The file **AccountingPartners** contains the number of partners in a cohort of rising accounting firms that have been tagged as "firms to watch." The firms have the following number of partners:

37 41 26 14 22 29 36 11 16 29 30 20 20 20 26
21 17 21 14 28 24 14 15 19 14 11 18 9 10 13
14 24 25 13 5 13 20 15 17 16 26 18 20 16 11

Source: Data extracted from *2017 Top 100 Firms*, Bloomberg BNA, **accounting today.com**.

a. Compute the first quartile (Q_1), the third quartile (Q_3), and the interquartile range.
b. List the five-number summary.
c. Construct a boxplot and describe its shape.

3.32 The file MobileCommerce contains the following mobile commerce penetration values, the percentage of the country population that bought something online via a mobile phone in the past month, for twenty-eight of the world's economies:

23 27 26 25 40 19 26 36 23 33 23 11 38 21
26 23 21 33 40 15 55 30 41 31 47 37 33 28

Source: Data extracted from **www.slideshare.net/wearesocialsg/digital-in-2017-global-overview**.

a. Compute the first quartile (Q_1), the third quartile (Q_3), and the interquartile range.
b. List the five-number summary.
c. Construct a boxplot and describe its shape.

3.33 The file HotelAway contains the average room price (in US$) paid by various nationalities while traveling abroad (away from their home country) in 2016:

124 101 115 126 114 112 138 85 138 96 130 116

Source: Data extracted from **hpi.hotels.com/**.

a. Compute the first quartile (Q_1), the third quartile (Q_3), and the interquartile range.
b. List the five-number summary.
c. Construct a boxplot and describe its shape.

3.34 The annual NFL Super Bowl is the most widely watched sporting event in the United States each year. In recent years, there has been a great deal of interest in the ads that appear during the game. These ads vary in length with most lasting 30 seconds or 60 seconds. The file SuperBowlAdScore contains the ad length and ad scores from a recent SuperBowl.

Source: Data extracted from C. Woodyard, "Funny Bone Wins Out", *USA Today*, February 6, 2016, p. 4B.

For the 30-second ads and the 60-second ads separately:
a. Compute the first quartile (Q_1), the third quartile (Q_3), and the interquartile range.

b. List the five-number summary.
c. Construct a boxplot and describe its shape.

3.35 The file CD Rate contains the yields for one-year CDs and five-year CDs, for 39 banks in the United States, as of January 9, 2017.

Source: Data extracted from **www.Bankrate.com**, January 9, 2017.

For each type of account:
a. Compute the first quartile (Q_1), the third quartile (Q_3), and the interquartile range.
b. List the five-number summary.
c. Construct a boxplot and describe its shape.

✓SELF TEST **3.36** A bank branch located in a commercial district of a city has the business objective of developing an improved process for serving customers during the noon-to-1:00 P.M. lunch period. The waiting time, in minutes, is defined as the time the customer enters the line to when he or she reaches the teller window. Data are collected from a sample of 15 customers during this hour. The file Bank1 contains the results, which are listed below:

4.21 5.55 3.02 5.13 4.77 2.34 3.54 3.20
4.50 6.10 0.38 5.12 6.46 6.19 3.79

Another bank branch, located in a residential area, is also concerned with the noon-to-1:00 P.M. lunch hour. The waiting times, in minutes, collected from a sample of 15 customers during this hour, are contained in the file Bank2 and listed here:

9.66 5.90 8.02 5.79 8.73 3.82 8.01 8.35
10.49 6.68 5.64 4.08 6.17 9.91 5.47

a. List the five-number summaries of the waiting times at the two bank branches.
b. Construct boxplots and describe the shapes of the distributions for the two bank branches.
c. What similarities and differences are there in the distributions of the waiting times at the two bank branches?

3.4 Numerical Descriptive Measures for a Population

Sections 3.1 and 3.2 discuss the statistics that describe the properties of central tendency and variation for a sample. When you collect data from an entire population (see Section 1.2), you compute and analyze population *parameters* for these properties, including the population mean, population variance, and population standard deviation.

To help illustrate these parameters, consider the population of stocks for the 10 companies that comprise the "Dogs of the Dow." "Dogs" are the 10 stocks in the Dow Jones Industrial Average (DJIA) that have the highest dividend yields, or dividend-to-price ratios, as of December 31 of the previous year and form the basis for an investment approach developed by Michael O'Higgins. Table 3.3 presents the "Dogs" for 2016, along with the percentage change in the price of these stocks during 2016. (The file DowDogs contains this population data.)

TABLE 3.3
Percentage Change for the "Dogs of the Dow"

Stock	Percentage Change	Stock	Percentage Change
Caterpillar	36.5	Merck	11.5
Chevron	30.8	Pfizer	0.6
Cisco Systems	11.3	Procter & Gamble	5.9
ExxonMobil	15.8	Verizon	15.5
IBM	20.6	Wal-Mart	12.8

Source: Data extracted from **dogsofthedow.com**.

The Population Mean

The **population mean**, a measure of central tendency, is the sum of the values in the population divided by the population size, N. The Greek lowercase letter mu, μ, represents this parameter, which Equation (3.13) defines.

POPULATION MEAN

The population mean is the sum of the values in the population divided by the population size, N.

$$\mu = \frac{\sum_{i=1}^{N} X_i}{N} \tag{3.13}$$

where

$$\mu = \text{population mean}$$

$$X_i = i\text{th value of the variable } X$$

$$\sum_{i=1}^{N} X_i = \text{summation of all } X_i \text{ values in the population}$$

$$N = \text{number of values in the population}$$

To compute the mean one-year percentage change in stock price for the Table 3.3 population of "Dow Dog" stocks, use Equation (3.13):

$$\mu = \frac{\sum_{i=1}^{N} X_i}{N}$$

$$= \frac{36.5 + 30.8 + 11.3 + 15.8 + 20.6 + 11.5 + 0.6 + 5.9 + 15.5 + 12.8}{10}$$

$$= \frac{161.30}{10} = 16.13$$

The mean one-year percentage change in the stock price for the "Dow Dog" stocks is 16.13 percent.

The Population Variance and Standard Deviation

The population variance and the population standard deviation parameters measure variation in a population. The **population variance** is the sum of the squared differences around the population mean divided by the population size, N, and the **population standard deviation** is the square root of the population variance. In practice, you will most likely use the population standard deviation because, unlike the population variance, the standard deviation will always be a number expressed in the same units as the original population data.

The lowercase Greek letter sigma, σ, represents the population standard deviation, and sigma squared, σ^2, represents the population variance. Equations (3.14) and (3.15) define these parameters. The denominators for the right-side terms in these equations use N and not the $(n - 1)$ term found in Equations (3.6) and (3.7) on pages 127 and 128, which define the sample variance and standard deviation.

POPULATION VARIANCE

$$\sigma^2 = \frac{\sum_{i=1}^{N} (X_i - \mu)^2}{N} \tag{3.14}$$

where

$$\mu = \text{population mean}$$

$$X_i = i\text{th value of the variable } X$$

$$\sum_{i=1}^{N} (X_i - \mu)^2 = \text{summation of all the squared differences between the } X_i \text{ values and } \mu$$

POPULATION STANDARD DEVIATION

$$\sigma = \sqrt{\frac{\sum_{i=1}^{N} (X_i - \mu)^2}{N}} \tag{3.15}$$

To compute the population variance for the data of Table 3.3, you use Equation (3.14) as shown in Figure 3.7:

$$\sigma^2 = \frac{\sum_{i=1}^{N} (X_i - \mu)^2}{N}$$

$$= \frac{1,052.32}{10} = 105.23$$

From Equation (3.15), the population sample standard deviation is

$$\sigma = \sqrt{\sigma^2} = \sqrt{\frac{\sum_{i=1}^{N} (X_i - \mu)^2}{N}} = \sqrt{\frac{1,052.32}{10}} = 10.26$$

Therefore, the typical percentage change in stock price differs from the mean of 16.13 by approximately 10.26 percent. This large amount of variation suggests that the "Dow Dog" stocks produce results that differ greatly.

The Empirical Rule

In most data sets, a large portion of the values tend to cluster somewhere near the mean. In right-skewed data sets, this clustering occurs to the left of the mean—that is, at a value less than the mean. In left-skewed data sets, the values tend to cluster to the right of the mean—that is, greater than the mean. In symmetrical data sets, where the median and mean are the same, the values often tend to cluster around the median and mean, often producing a bell-shaped normal distribution (see Chapter 6).

The **empirical rule** states that for population data from a symmetric mound-shaped distribution such as the normal distribution, the following are true:

- Approximately 68% of the values are within ± 1 standard deviation from the mean.
- Approximately 95% of the values are within ± 2 standard deviations from the mean.
- Approximately 99.7% of the values are within ± 3 standard deviations from the mean.

The empirical rule helps you examine variability in a population as well as identify outliers. The empirical rule implies that in a normal distribution, only about 1 out of 20 values will be beyond 2 standard deviations from the mean in either direction. As a general rule, you can consider values not found in the interval $\mu \pm 2\sigma$ as potential outliers. The rule also implies that only about 3 in 1,000 will be beyond 3 standard deviations from the mean. Therefore, values not found in the interval $\mu \pm 3\sigma$ are almost always considered outliers.

EXAMPLE 3.15

Using the Empirical Rule

A population of 2-liter bottles of cola is known to have a mean fill-weight of 2.06 liters and a standard deviation of 0.02 liter. The population is known to be bell-shaped. Describe the distribution of fill-weights. Is it very likely that a bottle will contain less than 2 liters of cola?

SOLUTION

$$\mu \pm \sigma = 2.06 \pm 0.02 = (2.04, 2.08)$$

$$\mu \pm 2\sigma = 2.06 \pm 2(0.02) = (2.02, 2.10)$$

$$\mu \pm 3\sigma = 2.06 \pm 3(0.02) = (2.00, 2.12)$$

Using the empirical rule, you can see that approximately 68% of the bottles will contain between 2.04 and 2.08 liters, approximately 95% will contain between 2.02 and 2.10 liters, and approximately 99.7% will contain between 2.00 and 2.12 liters. Therefore, it is highly unlikely that a bottle will contain less than 2 liters.

Chebyshev's Theorem

For heavily skewed sets of data and data sets that do not appear to be normally distributed, you should use Chebyshev's theorem instead of the empirical rule. **Chebyshev's theorem** (see reference 2) states that for any data set, regardless of shape, the percentage of values that are found within distances of k standard deviations from the mean must be at least

$$\left(1 - \frac{1}{k^2}\right) \times 100\%$$

You can use this rule for any value of k greater than 1. For example, consider $k = 2$. Chebyshev's theorem states that at least $[1 - (1/2)^2] \times 100\% = 75\%$ of the values must be found within ± 2 standard deviations of the mean.

Chebyshev's theorem is very general and applies to any distribution. The theorem indicates *at least* what percentage of the values fall within a given distance from the mean. However, if the data set is approximately bell-shaped, the empirical rule will more accurately reflect the greater concentration of data close to the mean. Table 3.4 compares Chebyshev's theorem to the empirical rule.

*Section EG3.4 describes the **VE-Variability workbook** that allows you to explore the empirical rule and Chebyshev's theorem.*

TABLE 3.4

How Data Vary Around the Mean

Interval	% of Values Found in Intervals Around the Mean	
	Chebyshev's Theorem (any distribution)	**Empirical Rule** (normal distribution)
$(\mu - \sigma, \mu + \sigma)$	At least 0%	Approximately 68%
$(\mu - 2\sigma, \mu + 2\sigma)$	At least 75%	Approximately 95%
$(\mu - 3\sigma, \mu + 3\sigma)$	At least 88.89%	Approximately 99.7%

You use Chebyshev's theorem and the empirical rules to understand how data are distributed around the mean when you have sample data. With each, you use the value you computed for $\overline{X}$ in place of μ and the value you computed for S in place of σ. The results you compute using the sample statistics are *approximations* because you used sample statistics $(\overline{X}, S)$ and not population parameters (μ, σ).

EXAMPLE 3.16	As in Example 3.15, a population of 2-liter bottles of cola is known to have a mean fill-weight of 2.06 liter and a standard deviation of 0.02 liter. However, the shape of the population is unknown, and you cannot assume that it is bell-shaped. Describe the distribution of fill-weights. Is it very likely that a bottle will contain less than 2 liters of cola?
Using the Chebyshev Rule	

SOLUTION

$$\mu \pm \sigma = 2.06 \pm 0.02 = (2.04, 2.08)$$

$$\mu \pm 2\sigma = 2.06 \pm 2(0.02) = (2.02, 2.10)$$

$$\mu \pm 3\sigma = 2.06 \pm 3(0.02) = (2.00, 2.12)$$

Because the distribution may be skewed, you cannot use the empirical rule. Using Chebyshev's theorem, you cannot say anything about the percentage of bottles containing between 2.04 and 2.08 liters. You can state that at least 75% of the bottles will contain between 2.02 and 2.10 liters and at least 88.89% will contain between 2.00 and 2.12 liters. Therefore, between 0 and 11.11% of the bottles will contain less than 2 liters.

PROBLEMS FOR SECTION 3.4

LEARNING THE BASICS

3.37 The following is a set of data for a population with $N = 10$:

     7   5   11   8   3   6   2   1   9   8

a. Compute the population mean.
b. Compute the population standard deviation.

3.38 The following is a set of data for a population with $N = 10$:

     7   5   6   6   6   4   8   6   9   3

a. Compute the population mean.
b. Compute the population standard deviation.

APPLYING THE CONCEPTS

3.39 The file McDonaldsStores contains the number of McDonald's stores located in each of the 50 U.S. states and the District of Columbia, as of December 31, 2016:

Source: Data extracted from **bit.ly/2qJjFpF**.

a. Compute the mean, variance, and standard deviation for this population.
b. What percentage of the 50 states have a number of McDonald's stores within ±1, ±2, or ±3 standard deviations of the mean?
c. Compare your findings with what would be expected on the basis of the empirical rule. Are you surprised at the results in (b)?

3.40 Consider a population of 1,024 mutual funds that primarily invest in large companies. You have determined that μ, the mean one-year total percentage return achieved by all the funds, is 8.20 and that σ, the standard deviation, is 2.75.

a. According to the empirical rule, what percentage of these funds is expected to be within ±1 standard deviation of the mean?
b. According to the empirical rule, what percentage of these funds is expected to be within ±2 standard deviations of the mean?
c. According to Chebyshev's theorem, what percentage of these funds is expected to be within ±1, ±2, or ±3 standard deviations of the mean?

d. According to Chebyshev's theorem, at least 93.75% of these funds are expected to have one-year total returns between what two amounts?

3.41 The file CigaretteTax contains the state cigarette tax (in $) for each of the 50 states and the District of Columbia as of January 1, 2017.

a. Compute the population mean and population standard deviation for the state cigarette tax.
b. Interpret the parameters in (a).

✓**SELF TEST**   **3.42** The file Energy contains the average residential price for electricity in cents per kilowatt hour in each of the 50 states and the District of Columbia during a recent year.

a. Compute the mean, variance, and standard deviation for the population.
b. What proportion of these states has an average residential price for electricity within ±1 standard deviation of the mean, within ±2 standard deviations of the mean, and within ±3 standard deviations of the mean?
c. Compare your findings with what would be expected based on the empirical rule. Are you surprised at the results in (b)?

3.43 Thirty companies comprise the DJIA. Just how big are these companies? One common method for measuring the size of a company is to use its market capitalization, which is computed by multiplying the number of stock shares by the price of a share of stock. On January 10, 2017, the market capitalization of these companies ranged from Traveler's $33.3 billion to Apple's $625.6 billion. The entire population of market capitalization values is stored in DowMarketCap.

Source: Data extracted from **money.cnn.com**, January 10, 2017.

a. Compute the mean and standard deviation of the market capitalization for this population of 30 companies.
b. Interpret the parameters computed in (a).

3.5 The Covariance and the Coefficient of Correlation

This section presents two measures of the relationship between two numerical variables: the covariance and the coefficient of correlation.

The Covariance

The **covariance** measures the strength of the linear relationship between two numerical variables (X and Y). Equation (3.16) defines the **sample covariance**, and Example 3.17 illustrates its use.

SAMPLE COVARIANCE

$$\text{cov}(X, Y) = \frac{\sum_{i=1}^{n} (X_i - \overline{X})(Y_i - \overline{Y})}{n - 1} \tag{3.16}$$

EXAMPLE 3.17

Computing the Sample Covariance

Section 2.5 uses NBA team revenue and NBA current values stored in NBAValues to construct a scatter plot that showed the relationship between those two variables. Now, measure the association between the team revenue and the current value of a team by determining the sample covariance.

SOLUTION Figure 3.10 contains the data and results worksheets that compute the covariance of revenue and value of 30 NBA teams. From the result in cell B9 of the covariance worksheet, or by using Equation (3.16) directly, you determine that the covariance is 26,323.2184:

$$\text{cov}(X, Y) = \frac{763,373.3333}{30 - 1} = 26,323.2184$$

FIGURE 3.10

Excel data and covariance worksheets for the revenue and value for the 30 NBA teams

	A	B	C	D
1	Revenue	Value	(X-XBar)	(Y-YBar)
2	142	825	-30.67	-420.33
3	181	2100	8.33	854.67
4	220	1700	47.33	454.67
5	142	750	-30.67	-495.33
6	228	2300	55.33	1054.67
7	191	1100	18.33	-145.33
8	177	1400	4.33	154.67
9	140	855	-32.67	-390.33
10	154	850	-18.67	-395.33
11	201	1900	28.33	654.67
12	237	1500	64.33	254.67
13	138	840	-34.67	-405.33
14	176	2000	3.33	754.67
15	304	2700	131.33	1454.67
16	147	780	-25.67	-465.33

	A	B	C	D
1	Revenue	Value	(X-XBar)	(Y-YBar)
17	180	1300	7.33	54.67
18	126	675	-46.67	-570.33
19	146	720	-26.67	-525.33
20	142	650	-30.67	-595.33
21	307	3000	134.33	1754.67
22	157	950	-15.67	-295.33
23	143	900	-29.67	-345.33
24	124	700	-48.67	-545.33
25	154	1000	-18.67	-245.33
26	157	975	-15.67	-270.33
27	141	925	-31.67	-320.33
28	170	1150	-2.67	-95.33
29	163	980	-9.67	-265.33
30	146	875	-26.67	-370.33
31	146	960	-26.67	-285.33

	A	B
1	Covariance Analysis of Revenue and Value	
2		
3	Intermediate Calculations	
4	XBar	172.6667 =AVERAGE(DATA!A:A)
5	YBar	1245.3333 =AVERAGE(DATA!B:B)
6	Σ(X-XBar)(Y-YBar)	763373.3333 =SUMPRODUCT(DATA!C:C, DATA!D:D)
7	n-1	29 =COUNT(DATA!A:A) - 1
8		
9	Covariance	26323.2184 =COVARIANCE.S(DATA!A:A, DATA!B:B)

The covariance has a major flaw as a measure of the linear relationship between two numerical variables. Because the covariance can have any value, you cannot use it to determine the relative strength of the relationship. In Example 3.17, you cannot tell whether the value 26,323.2184 indicates a strong relationship or a weak relationship between revenue and value. To better determine the relative strength of the relationship, you need to compute the coefficient of correlation.

The Coefficient of Correlation

The **coefficient of correlation** measures the relative strength of a linear relationship between two numerical variables. The values of the coefficient of correlation range from -1 for a perfect negative correlation to +1 for a perfect positive correlation. *Perfect* in this case means that if the points were plotted on a scatter plot, all the points could be connected with a straight line.

When dealing with population data for two numerical variables, the Greek letter ρ (*rho*) is used as the symbol for the coefficient of correlation. Figure 3.11 illustrates three different types of association between two variables.

In Panel A of Figure 3.11, there is a perfect negative linear relationship between X and Y. Thus, the coefficient of correlation, ρ, equals -1, and when X increases, Y decreases in a perfectly predictable manner. Panel B shows a situation in which there is no relationship between X and Y. In this case, the coefficient of correlation, ρ, equals 0, and as X increases, there is no tendency for Y to increase or decrease. Panel C illustrates a perfect positive relationship where ρ equals $+1$. In this case, Y increases in a perfectly predictable manner when X increases.

FIGURE 3.11

Types of association between variables

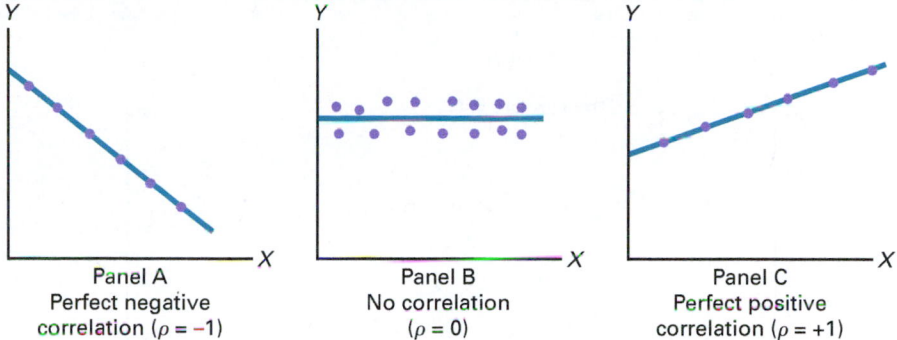

Panel A	Panel B	Panel C
Perfect negative correlation ($\rho = -1$)	No correlation ($\rho = 0$)	Perfect positive correlation ($\rho = +1$)

Correlation alone cannot prove that there is a causation effect—that is, that the change in the value of one variable caused the change in the other variable. A strong correlation can be produced by chance; by the effect of a **lurking variable**, a third variable not considered in the calculation of the correlation; or by a cause-and-effect relationship. You would need to perform additional analysis to determine which of these three situations actually produced the correlation. Therefore, you can say that *causation implies correlation, but correlation alone does not imply causation.*

Equation (3.17) defines the **sample coefficient of correlation (*r*)**.

SAMPLE COEFFICIENT OF CORRELATION

$$r = \frac{\text{cov}(X, Y)}{S_X S_Y} \tag{3.17}$$

where

$$\text{cov}(X, Y) = \frac{\sum_{i=1}^{n} (X_i - \overline{X})(Y_i - \overline{Y})}{n - 1}$$

$$S_X = \sqrt{\frac{\sum_{i=1}^{n} (X_i - \overline{X})^2}{n - 1}}$$

$$S_Y = \sqrt{\frac{\sum_{i=1}^{n} (Y_i - \overline{Y})^2}{n - 1}}$$

When you have sample data, you can compute the sample coefficient of correlation, r. When using sample data, you are unlikely to have a sample coefficient of correlation of exactly $+1$, 0, or -1. Figure 3.12 on page 150 presents scatter plots along with their respective sample coefficients of correlation, r, for six data sets, each of which contains 100 X and Y values.

FIGURE 3.12

Six scatter plots and their sample coefficients of correlation, r

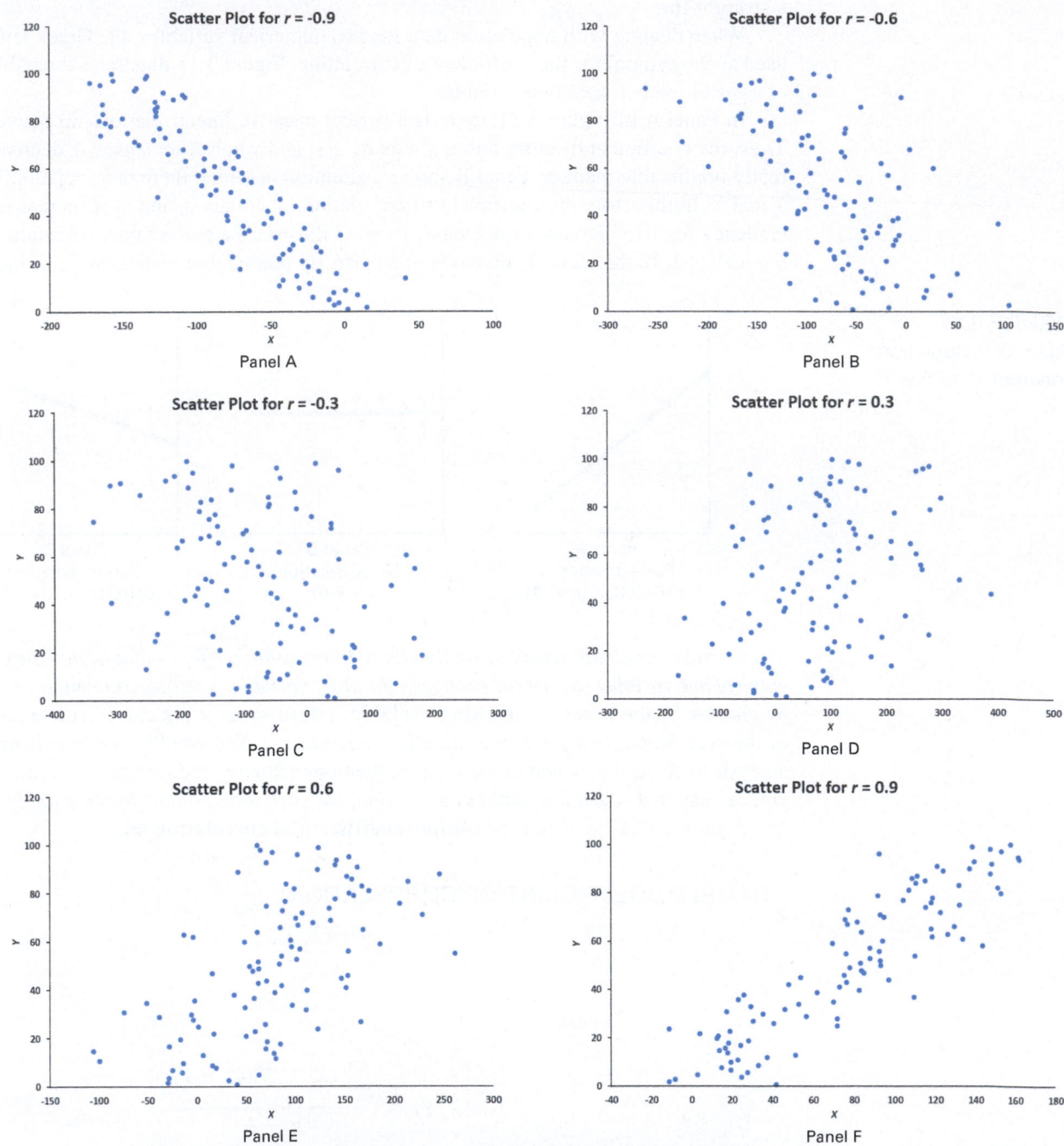

In Panel A, the coefficient of correlation, r, is -0.9. You can see that for small values of X, there is a very strong tendency for Y to be large. Likewise, the large values of X tend to be paired with small values of Y. The data do not all fall on a straight line, so the association between X and Y cannot be described as perfect.

In Panel B, the coefficient of correlation is -0.6, and the small values of X tend to be paired with large values of Y. The linear relationship between X and Y in Panel B is not as strong as that in Panel A. Thus, the coefficient of correlation in Panel B is not as negative as that in Panel A.

In Panel C, the linear relationship between X and Y is very weak, $r = -0.3$, and there is only a slight tendency for the small values of X to be paired with the large values of Y.

Panels D through F depict data sets that have positive coefficients of correlation because small values of X tend to be paired with small values of Y, and large values of X tend to be associated with large values of Y. Panel D shows weak positive correlation, with $r = 0.3$. Panel E shows stronger positive correlation, with $r = 0.6$. Panel F shows very strong positive correlation, with $r = 0.9$.

EXAMPLE 3.18

Computing the
Sample Coefficient
of Correlation

In Example 3.17 on page 148 you computed the covariance of the Revenue and Current Value for the 30 NBA teams. Now, you want to measure the relative strength of a linear relationship between the revenue and value by determining the sample coefficient of correlation.

SOLUTION By using Equation (3.17) directly (shown below) or from cell B14 in the coefficient of correlation worksheet (shown in Figure 3.13), you determine that the sample coefficient of correlation is 0.9083:

$$r = \frac{\text{cov}(X, Y)}{S_X S_Y} = \frac{26{,}323.2184}{(46.0983)(628.6383)} = 0.9083$$

FIGURE 3.13
Excel worksheet to
compute the sample
coefficient of correlation
between Revenue and
Current Value

*This worksheet uses
the Figure 3.10 data
worksheet shown
on page 148.*

	A	B	
1	Coefficient of Correlation Analysis		
2			
3	Intermediate Calculations		
4	XBar	172.6667	=AVERAGE(DATA!A:A)
5	YBar	1245.3333	=AVERAGE(DATA!B:B)
6	Σ(X-XBar)²	61626.6667	=DEVSQ(DATA!A:A)
7	Σ(Y-YBar)²	11460396.6667	=DEVSQ(DATA!B:B)
8	Σ(X-XBar)(Y-YBar)	763373.3333	=SUMPRODUCT(DATA!C:C, DATA!D:D)
9	n-1	29	=COUNT(DATA!A:A) - 1
10	Covariance	26323.2184	=COVARIANCE.S(DATA!A:A, DATA!B:B)
11	S_X	46.0983	=SQRT(B6/B9)
12	S_Y	628.6383	=SQRT(B7/B9)
13			
14	r	0.9083	=CORREL(DATA!A:A, DATA!B:B)

The current value and revenue of the NBA teams are very highly correlated. The teams with the lowest revenues have the lowest values. The teams with the highest revenues have the highest values. This relationship is very strong, as indicated by the coefficient of correlation, $r = 0.9083$.

In general, do not assume that just because two variables are correlated, changes in one variable caused changes in the other variable. However, for this example, it makes sense to conclude that changes in revenue would tend to cause changes in the value of a team.

In summary, the coefficient of correlation indicates the linear relationship, or association, between two numerical variables. When the coefficient of correlation gets closer to +1 or −1, the linear relationship between the two variables is stronger. When the coefficient of correlation is near 0, little or no linear relationship exists. The sign of the coefficient of correlation indicates whether the data are positively correlated (i.e., the larger values of X are typically paired with the larger values of Y) or negatively correlated (i.e., the larger values of X are typically paired with the smaller values of Y). The existence of a strong correlation does not imply a causation effect. It only indicates the tendencies present in the data.

PROBLEMS FOR SECTION 3.5

LEARNING THE BASICS

3.44 The following is a set of data from a sample of $n = 11$ items:

| X | 7 | 5 | 8 | 3 | 6 | 10 | 12 | 4 | 9 | 15 | 18 |
| Y | 21 | 15 | 24 | 9 | 18 | 30 | 36 | 12 | 27 | 45 | 54 |

a. Compute the covariance.
b. Compute the coefficient of correlation.
c. How strong is the relationship between X and Y? Explain.

APPLYING THE CONCEPTS

3.45 A study of 267 college students investigated the impact of smartphones on student connectedness and out-of-class involvement.

Source: Liu X, *et al.*, "The Impact of Smartphone Educational Use on Student Connectedness and Out-of-Class Involvement," *The Electronic Journal of Communication* (2016).

One finding showed that students reporting a higher perceived usefulness of smartphones in educational settings used their smartphone a higher number of times to send or read email for class purposes than students reporting a lower perceived usefulness of smartphones in educational settings.

a. Does the study suggest that perceived usefulness of smartphones in educational settings and use of smartphones for class purposes are positively correlated or negatively correlated?
b. Do you think that there might be a cause-and-effect relationship between perceived usefulness of smartphones in educational settings and use of smartphones for class purposes? Explain.

3.46 The file Cereals lists the calories and sugar, in grams, in one serving of seven breakfast cereals:

Cereal	Calories	Sugar
Kellogg's All Bran	80	6
Kellogg's Corn Flakes	100	2
Wheaties	100	4
Nature's Path Organic Multigrain Flakes	110	4
Kellogg's Rice Krispies	130	4
Post Shredded Wheat Vanilla Almond	190	11
Kellogg's Mini Wheats	200	10

a. Compute the covariance.
b. Compute the coefficient of correlation.
c. Which do you think is more valuable in expressing the relationship between calories and sugar—the covariance or the coefficient of correlation? Explain.
d. Based on (a) and (b), what conclusions can you reach about the relationship between calories and sugar?

3.47 Movie companies need to predict the gross receipts of individual movies once a movie has debuted. The data, shown below and stored in PotterMovies, are the first weekend gross, the U.S. gross, and the worldwide gross (in $ millions) of the eight Harry Potter movies:

Title	First Weekend	U.S. Gross	Worldwide Gross
Sorcerer's Stone	90.295	317.558	976.458
Chamber of Secrets	88.357	261.988	878.988
Prisoner of Azkaban	93.687	249.539	795.539
Goblet of Fire	102.335	290.013	896.013
Order of the Phoenix	77.108	292.005	938.469
Half-Blood Prince	77.836	301.460	934.601
Deathly Hallows Part 1	125.017	295.001	955.417
Deathly Hallows Part 2	169.189	381.011	1,328.111

Source: Data extracted from **www.the-numbers.com/interactive/comp-Harry-Potter.php**.

a. Compute the covariance between first weekend gross and U.S. gross, first weekend gross and worldwide gross, and U.S. gross and worldwide gross.
b. Compute the coefficient of correlation between first weekend gross and U.S. gross, first weekend gross and worldwide gross, and U.S. gross and worldwide gross.
c. Which do you think is more valuable in expressing the relationship between first weekend gross, U.S. gross, and worldwide gross—the covariance or the coefficient of correlation? Explain.
d. Based on (a) and (b), what conclusions can you reach about the relationship between first weekend gross, U.S. gross, and worldwide gross?

3.48 The file MobileSpeed contains the overall download and upload speeds in mbps for nine carriers in the U.S.

Source: Data extracted from "Best Mobile Network 2016," **bit.ly/1KGPrMm**, accessed November 10, 2016.

a. Compute the covariance between download speed and upload speed.
b. Compute the coefficient of correlation between download speed and upload speed.
c. Based on (a) and (b), what conclusions can you reach about the relationship between download speed and upload speed?

3.49 A Pew Research Center survey found a noticeable rise in smartphone ownership and internet usage in emerging and developing nations, and once online, adults in these nations are hungry for social interaction. The file GlobalInternetUsage contains the level of Internet usage, measured as the percentage of adults polled who use the Internet at least occasionally or who report owning a smartphone, and the GDP. The file GlobalSocialMedia contains the level of social media networking, measured as the percentage of Internet users who use social media sites, and the GDP at purchasing power parity (PPP, current international $) per capita for each of 28 emerging and developing countries.

Source: Data extracted from Pew Research Center, "Smartphone Ownership and Internet Usage Continues to Climb in Emerging Economies," February 22, 2016, **pewrsr.ch/1RX3Iqq**.

For the relationship between percentage of Internet users polled who use social networking sites, and GDP and the relationship between the percentage of adults polled who use the Internet at least occasionally and GDP:
a. Compute the covariance.
b. Compute the coefficient of correlation.
c. Based on (a) and (b), what conclusions can you reach about the relationship between the GDP and social media use and the relationship between the percentage of adults polled who use the Internet at least occasionally and GDP?

3.6 Descriptive Statistics: Pitfalls and Ethical Issues

This chapter describes how a set of numerical data can be characterized by the statistics that measure the properties of central tendency, variation, and shape. In business, descriptive statistics such as the ones discussed in this chapter are frequently included in summary reports that are prepared periodically.

The volume of information available from online, broadcast, or print media has produced much skepticism in the minds of many about the objectivity of data. When you are reading information that contains descriptive statistics, you should keep in mind the quip often attributed to the famous nineteenth-century British statesman Benjamin Disraeli: "There are three kinds of lies: lies, damned lies, and statistics."

For example, in examining statistics, you need to compare the mean and the median. Are they similar, or are they very different? Or is only the mean provided? The answers to these questions will help you determine whether the data are skewed or symmetrical and whether the median might be a better measure of central tendency than the mean. In addition, you should look to see whether the standard deviation or interquartile range for a very skewed set of data has been included in the statistics provided. Without this, it is impossible to determine the amount of variation that exists in the data.

Ethical considerations arise when you are deciding what results to include in a report. You should document both good and bad results. In addition, in all presentations, you need to report results in a fair, objective, and neutral manner. Unethical behavior occurs when you selectively fail to report pertinent findings that are detrimental to the support of a particular position.

▼USING **STATISTICS**
More Descriptive Choices, Revisited

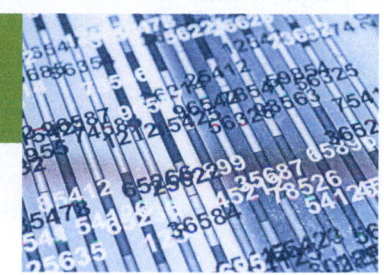

In the More Descriptive Choices scenario, you were hired by the Choice *Is* Yours investment company to assist investors interested in stock mutual funds. A sample of 479 stock mutual funds included 306 growth funds and 173 value funds. By comparing these two categories, you were able to provide investors with valuable insights.

The three-year returns for both the growth funds and the value funds were left-skewed, as the Figure 3.8 boxplot on page 141 reveals. The descriptive statistics (see Figure 3.5 on page 133) allowed you to compare the central tendency, variability, and shape of the returns of the growth funds and the value funds.

The mean indicated that the growth funds returned a mean of 8.51, and the median indicated that half of the growth funds had returns of 8.70 or more. The value funds' central tendencies were lower than those of the growth funds—they had a mean of 6.84, and half the funds had three-year returns above 7.07.

The growth funds showed more variability than the value funds, with a standard deviation of 3.1935 as compared to 2.3258. The kurtosis of value funds was very positive, indicating a distribution that was much more peaked than a normal distribution.

Although the three-year returns were greater for growth funds than value funds, that relationship may not hold when the one-year, five-year, or ten-year returns for the growth and value fund groups are examined. (Analyze the other return percentage variables in Retirement Funds to see if the relationship holds for these other periods of time.)

▼ SUMMARY

In this chapter, you learned how descriptive statistics such as the mean, median, quartiles, range, and standard deviation describe the characteristics of central tendency, variability, and shape. You also learned these concepts about variation in data:

- The greater the spread or dispersion of the data, the larger the range, variance, and standard deviation.
- The smaller the spread or dispersion of the data, the smaller the range, variance, and standard deviation.

- If the values are all the same (no variation in the data), the range, variance, and standard deviation will all equal zero.
- Measures of variation (the range, variance, and standard deviation) are never negative.

In addition, you constructed boxplots to visualize the distribution of the data. You also learned how the coefficient of correlation describes the relationship between two numerical variables. Table 3.5 summarizes the methods discussed in this chapter.

TABLE 3.5
Chapter 3 Descriptive Statistics Methods

Type of Analysis	Methods
Central tendency	Mean, median, mode (Section 3.1)
Variation and shape	Quartiles, range, interquartile range, variance, standard deviation, coefficient of variation, Z scores, skewness, kurtosis, boxplot (Sections 3.2 through 3.4)
Describing the relationship between two numerical variables	Covariance, coefficient of correlation (Section 3.5)

▼REFERENCES

1. Booker, J., and L. Ticknor. "A Brief Overview of Kurtosis." **www.osti.gov/scitech/servlets/purl/677174**.
2. Kendall, M. G., A. Stuart, and J. K. Ord. *Kendall's Advanced Theory of Statistics, Volume 1: Distribution Theory*, 6th ed. New York: Oxford University Press, 1994.
3. Taleb, N. *The Black Swan*, 2nd ed. New York: Random House, 2010.

▼KEY EQUATIONS

Sample Mean

$$\overline{X} = \frac{\sum_{i=1}^{n} X_i}{n} \tag{3.1}$$

Median

$$\text{Median} = \frac{n+1}{2} \text{ ranked value} \tag{3.2}$$

Geometric Mean

$$\overline{X}_G = (X_1 \times X_2 \times \cdots \times X_n)^{1/n} \tag{3.3}$$

Geometric Mean Rate of Return

$$\overline{R}_G = [(1 + R_1) \times (1 + R_2) \times \cdots \times (1 + R_n)]^{1/n} - 1 \tag{3.4}$$

Range

$$\text{Range} = X_{\text{largest}} - X_{\text{smallest}} \tag{3.5}$$

Sample Variance

$$S^2 = \frac{\sum_{i=1}^{n} (X_i - \overline{X})^2}{n-1} \tag{3.6}$$

Sample Standard Deviation

$$S = \sqrt{S^2} = \sqrt{\frac{\sum_{i=1}^{n} (X_i - \overline{X})^2}{n-1}} \tag{3.7}$$

Coefficient of Variation

$$CV = \left(\frac{S}{\overline{X}}\right)100\% \tag{3.8}$$

Z Score

$$Z = \frac{X - \overline{X}}{S} \tag{3.9}$$

First Quartile, Q_1

$$Q_1 = \frac{n+1}{4} \text{ ranked value} \tag{3.10}$$

Third Quartile, Q_3

$$Q_3 = \frac{3(n+1)}{4} \text{ ranked value} \tag{3.11}$$

Interquartile Range

$$\text{Interquartile range} = Q_3 - Q_1 \tag{3.12}$$

Population Mean

$$\mu = \frac{\sum_{i=1}^{N} X_i}{N} \tag{3.13}$$

Population Variance

$$\sigma^2 = \frac{\sum_{i=1}^{N} (X_i - \mu)^2}{N} \tag{3.14}$$

Population Standard Deviation

$$\sigma = \sqrt{\frac{\sum_{i=1}^{N} (X_i - \mu)^2}{N}} \tag{3.15}$$

Sample Covariance

$$\text{cov}(X, Y) = \frac{\sum_{i=1}^{n} (X_i - \overline{X})(Y_i - \overline{Y})}{n-1} \tag{3.16}$$

Sample Coefficient of Correlation

$$r = \frac{\text{cov}(X, Y)}{S_X S_Y} \tag{3.17}$$

▼KEY TERMS

▼ CHECKING YOUR UNDERSTANDING

3.50 What are the properties of a set of numerical data?

3.51 What is meant by the property of central tendency?

3.52 What are the differences among the mean, median, and mode, and what are the advantages and disadvantages of each?

3.53 How do you interpret the first quartile, median, and third quartile?

3.54 What is meant by the property of variation?

3.55 What does the Z score measure?

3.56 What are the differences among the various measures of variation, such as the range, interquartile range, variance, standard

deviation, and coefficient of variation, and what are the advantages and disadvantages of each?

3.57 How does the empirical rule help explain the ways in which the values in a set of numerical data cluster and distribute?

3.58 How do the empirical rule and the Chebyshev rule differ?

3.59 What is meant by the property of shape?

3.60 What is the difference between skewness and kurtosis?

3.61 What is the difference between the arithmetic mean and the geometric mean?

3.62 How do the covariance and the coefficient of correlation differ?

▼ CHAPTER REVIEW PROBLEMS

3.63 The American Society for Quality (ASQ) conducted a salary survey of all its members. ASQ members work in all areas of manufacturing and service-related institutions, with a common theme of an interest in quality. Manager and quality engineer were the most frequently reported job titles among the valid responses. Master Black Belt, a person who takes a leadership role as the keeper of the Six Sigma process (see Section 19.6) and Green Belt, someone who works on Six Sigma projects part time, were among the other job titles cited. Descriptive statistics concerning salaries for these four titles are given in the following table:

Job Title	Sample Size	Minimum	Maximum	Standard Deviation	Mean	Median
Green Belt	39	20,000	127,000	28,086	79,749	76,500
Manager	1,523	28,080	572,000	31,193	96,609	93,500
Quality Engineer	914	36,000	314,000	25,523	83,991	80,000
Master Black Belt	57	62,620	200,000	23,879	125,093	123,000

Source: Data extracted from "Salary Survey 2016: The Complete Report," bit.ly/2pdFPjr.

Compare the salaries of Green Belts, managers, quality engineers, and Master Black Belts.

3.64 An insurance company has the business objective of reducing the amount of time it takes to approve applications for life insurance. The approval process consists of underwriting, which includes a review of the application, a medical information bureau check, possible requests for additional medical information and medical exams, and a policy compilation stage, in which the policy pages are generated and sent for delivery. The ability to deliver approved policies to customers in a timely manner is critical to the profitability of this service. Using the DCOVA framework you define the variable of interest as the total processing time in days. You collect the data by selecting a random sample of 27 approved policies during a period of one month. You organize the data collected in a worksheet and store them in **Insurance** :

a. Compute the mean, median, first quartile, and third quartile.
b. Compute the range, interquartile range, variance, standard deviation, and coefficient of variation.
c. Construct a boxplot. Are the data skewed? If so, how?
d. What would you tell a customer who wishes to purchase this type of insurance policy and asks how long the approval process takes?

3.65 One of the major measures of the quality of service provided by an organization is the speed with which it responds to customer complaints. A large family-held department store selling furniture and flooring, including carpet, had undergone a major expansion in the past several years. In particular, the flooring department had expanded from 2 installation crews to an installation supervisor, a measurer, and 15 installation crews. The business objective of the company was to reduce the time between when a complaint is received and when it is resolved. During a recent year, the company received 50 complaints concerning carpet installation. The data from the 50 complaints, organized in Furniture , represent the number of days between the receipt of a complaint and the resolution of the complaint:

54	5	35	137	31	27	152	2	123	81	74	27	11
19	126	110	110	29	61	35	94	31	26	5	12	4
165	32	29	28	29	26	25	1	14	13	13	10	5
27	4	52	30	22	36	26	20	23	33	68		

a. Compute the mean, median, first quartile, and third quartile.
b. Compute the range, interquartile range, variance, standard deviation, and coefficient of variation.
c. Construct a boxplot. Are the data skewed? If so, how?
d. On the basis of the results of (a) through (c), if you had to tell the president of the company how long a customer should expect to wait to have a complaint resolved, what would you say? Explain.

3.66 Call centers today play an important role in managing day-to-day business communications with customers. It's important, therefore, to monitor a comprehensive set of metrics, which can help businesses understand the overall performance of a call center. One key metric for measuring overall call center performance is service level which is defined as the percentage of calls answered by a human agent within a specified number of seconds. The file ServiceLevel contains the following data for time, in seconds, to answer 50 incoming calls to a financial services call center:

16	14	16	19	6	14	15	5	16	18	17	22	6	18	10
15	12	6	19	16	16	15	13	25	9	17	12	10	5	15
23	11	12	14	24	9	10	13	14	26	19	20	13	24	28
15	21	8	16	12										

a. Compute the mean, median, range, and standard deviation for the speed of answer, which is the time to answer incoming calls.
b. List the five-number summary.
c. Construct a boxplot and describe its shape.
d. What can you conclude about call center performance if the service level target is set as "75% of calls answered in under 20 seconds?"

3.67 The financial services call center in Problem 3.66 also monitors call duration, which is the amount of time spent speaking to customers on the phone. The file CallDuration contains the following data for time, in seconds, spent by agents talking to 50 customers:

243	290	199	240	125	151	158	66	350	1141	251	385	239
139	181	111	136	250	313	154	78	264	123	314	135	99
420	112	239	208	65	133	213	229	154	377	69	170	261
230	273	288	180	296	235	243	167	227	384	331		

a. Compute the mean, median, range, and standard deviation for the call duration, which is the amount of time spent speaking

to customers on the phone. Interpret these measures of central tendency and variability.
b. List the five-number summary.
c. Construct a boxplot and describe its shape.
d. What can you conclude about call center performance if a call duration target of less than 240 seconds is set?

3.68 Data were collected on the typical cost of dining at American-cuisine restaurants within a 1-mile walking distance of a hotel located in a large city. The file Bundle contains the typical cost (a per transaction cost in $) as well as a Bundle score, a measure of overall popularity and customer loyalty, for each of 40 selected restaurants.

Source: Data extracted from **www.bundle.com** via the link **on-msn.com/MnlBxo**.

a. For each variable, compute the mean, median, first quartile, and third quartile.
b. For each variable, compute the range, interquartile range, variance, standard deviation, and coefficient of variation.
c. For each variable, construct a boxplot. Are the data skewed? If so, how?
d. Compute the coefficient of correlation between Bundle score and typical cost.
e. What conclusions can you reach concerning Bundle score and typical cost?

3.69 A quality characteristic of interest for a tea-bag-filling process is the weight of the tea in the individual bags. If the bags are underfilled, two problems arise. First, customers may not be able to brew the tea to be as strong as they wish. Second, the company may be in violation of the truth-in-labeling laws. For this product, the label weight on the package indicates that, on average, there are 5.5 grams of tea in a bag. If the mean amount of tea in a bag exceeds the label weight, the company is giving away product. Getting an exact amount of tea in a bag is problematic because of variation in the temperature and humidity inside the factory, differences in the density of the tea, and the extremely fast filling operation of the machine (approximately 170 bags per minute). The file Teabags contains these weights, in grams, of a sample of 50 tea bags produced in one hour by a single machine:

5.65	5.44	5.42	5.40	5.53	5.34	5.54	5.45	5.52	5.41
5.57	5.40	5.53	5.54	5.55	5.62	5.56	5.46	5.44	5.51
5.47	5.40	5.47	5.61	5.53	5.32	5.67	5.29	5.49	5.55
5.77	5.57	5.42	5.58	5.58	5.50	5.32	5.50	5.53	5.58
5.61	5.45	5.44	5.25	5.56	5.63	5.50	5.57	5.67	5.36

a. Compute the mean, median, first quartile, and third quartile.
b. Compute the range, interquartile range, variance, standard deviation, and coefficient of variation.
c. Interpret the measures of central tendency and variation within the context of this problem. Why should the company producing the tea bags be concerned about the central tendency and variation?
d. Construct a boxplot. Are the data skewed? If so, how?
e. Is the company meeting the requirement set forth on the label that, on average, there are 5.5 grams of tea in a bag? If you were in charge of this process, what changes, if any, would you try to make concerning the distribution of weights in the individual bags?

3.70 The manufacturer of Boston and Vermont asphalt shingles provides its customers with a 20-year warranty on most of its products. To determine whether a shingle will last as long as the warranty period, accelerated-life testing is conducted at the manufacturing plant. Accelerated-life testing exposes a shingle to the stresses it would be subject to in a lifetime of normal use via an experiment in a laboratory setting that takes only a few minutes to conduct. In this test, a shingle is repeatedly scraped with a brush for a short period of time, and the shingle granules removed by the brushing are weighed (in grams). Shingles that experience low amounts of granule loss are expected to last longer in normal use than shingles that experience high amounts of granule loss. In this situation, a shingle should experience no more than 0.8 gram of granule loss if it is expected to last the length of the warranty period. The file Granule contains a sample of 170 measurements made on the company's Boston shingles and 140 measurements made on Vermont shingles.

a. List the five-number summaries for the Boston shingles and for the Vermont shingles.

b. Construct side-by-side boxplots for the two brands of shingles and describe the shapes of the distributions.

c. Comment on the ability of each type of shingle to achieve a granule loss of 0.8 gram or less.

3.71 The file Restaurants contains the cost per meal and the ratings of 50 center city and 50 metro area restaurants on their food, décor, and service (and their summated ratings).

Source: Data extracted from *Zagat Survey 2016 New York City Restaurants*.

Complete the following for the center city and metro area restaurants:

a. Construct the five-number summary of the cost of a meal.

b. Construct a boxplot of the cost of a meal. What is the shape of the distribution?

c. Compute and interpret the correlation coefficient of the summated rating and the cost of a meal.

d. What conclusions can you reach about the cost of a meal at center city and metro area restaurants?

3.72 The file Protein contains calories, protein, and cholesterol of popular protein foods (fresh red meats, poultry, and fish).

Source: U.S. Department of Agriculture.

a. Compute the correlation coefficient between calories and protein.

b. Compute the correlation coefficient between calories and cholesterol.

c. Compute the correlation coefficient between protein and cholesterol.

d. Based on the results of (a) through (c), what conclusions can you reach concerning calories, protein, and cholesterol?

3.73 What was the mean price of a room at two-star, three-star, and four-star hotels in the major cities of the world during 2016? The file HotelPrices contains the prices in Canadian dollars (about US $0.75 as of December 2016).

Source: Data extracted from "**Hotels.com** Hotel Price Index," **bit.ly/2qmzNAW**.

For each of the three groups of hotels (two-, three-, and four-stars):

a. Compute the mean, median, first quartile, and third quartile.

b. Compute the range, interquartile range, variance, standard deviation, and coefficient of variation.

c. Interpret the measures of central tendency and variation within the context of this problem.

d. Construct a boxplot. Are the data skewed? If so, how?

e. Compute the covariance between the mean price at two-star and three-star hotels, between two-star and four-star hotels, and between three-star and four-star hotels.

f. Compute the coefficient of correlation between the mean price at two-star and three-star hotels, between two-star and four-star hotels, and between three-star and four-star hotels.

g. Which do you think is more valuable in expressing the relationship between the mean price of a room at two-star, three-star, and four-star hotels—the covariance or the coefficient of correlation? Explain.

h. Based on (f), what conclusions can you reach about the relationship between the mean price of a room at two-star, three-star, and four-star hotels?

3.74 The file Property Taxes contains the property taxes on a $176K home and the median home value ($000) for the 50 states and the District of Columbia. For each of these two variables:

a. Compute the mean, median, first quartile, and third quartile.

b. Compute the range, interquartile range, variance, standard deviation, and coefficient of variation.

c. Construct a boxplot. Are the data skewed? If so, how?

d. Compute the coefficient of correlation between the property taxes on a $176K home and the median home value.

e. Based on the results of (a) through (c), what conclusions can you reach concerning property taxes on a $176K home and the median home value ($000) for each state and the District of Columbia?

3.75 Have you wondered how Internet connection speed varies around the globe? The file ConnectionSpeed contains the mean connection speed, the mean peak connection speed, the % of the time the speed is above 4 Mbs, and the % of the time the connection speed is above 10 Mbps for various countries.

Source: Data extracted from **bit.ly/1hHaHVD**.

Answer (a) through (c) for each variable.

a. Compute the mean, median, first quartile, and third quartile.

b. Compute the range, interquartile range, variance, standard deviation, and coefficient of variation.

c. Construct a boxplot. Are the data skewed? If so, how?

d. Compute the coefficient of correlation between mean connection speed, mean peak connection speed, percent of the time the speed is above 4 Mbps, and the percent of the time the connection speed is above 10 Mbps.

e. Based on the results of (a) through (c), what conclusions can you reach concerning the connection speed around the globe?

f. Based on (d), what conclusions can your reach about the relationship between mean connection speed, mean peak connection speed, percent of the time the speed is above 4 Mbps, and the percent of the time the connection speed is above 10 Mbps?

3.76 311 is Chicago's web and phone portal for government information and nonemergency services. 311 serves as a comprehensive one-stop shop for residents, visitors, and business owners; therefore, it is critical that 311 representatives answer calls and respond to requests in a timely and accurate fashion. The target response time for answering 311 calls is 45 seconds. Agent abandonment rate is one of several call center metrics tracked by 311 officials. This metric tracks the percentage of callers who hang up after the target response time of 45 seconds has elapsed. The file 311CallCenter contains the agent abandonment rate for 22 weeks of call center operation during the 7:00 A.M.–3:00 P.M. shift.

a. Compute the mean, median, first quartile, and third quartile.

b. Compute the range, interquartile range, variance, standard deviation, and coefficient of variation.

c. Construct a boxplot. Are the data skewed? If so, how?

d. Compute the correlation coefficient between day and agent abandonment rate.

e. Based on the results of (a) through (c), what conclusions might you reach concerning 311 call center performance operation?

3.77 How much time do commuters living in or near cities spend commuting to work each week? The file CommutingTime contains the average weekly commuting time in 30 U.S. cities.

Source: Data extracted from *New York City Economics Brief*, March 2015, p. 3.

For the weekly commuting time data:

a. Compute the mean, median, first quartile, and third quartile.

b. Compute the range, interquartile range, variance, standard deviation, and coefficient of variation.

c. Construct a boxplot. Are the data skewed? If so, how?

d. Based on the results of (a) through (c), what conclusions might you reach concerning the commuting time.

3.78 How do the mean credit scores of people living in various American cities differ? The file Credit Scores is an ordered array of the average credit scores of people living in 2,570 American cities.

Source: Data extracted from "Study shows cities with highest and lowest credit scores," accessed at **bit.ly/2uubZfX**.

a. Compute the mean, median, first quartile, and third quartile.

b. Compute the range, interquartile range, variance, standard deviation, and coefficient of variation.

c. Construct a boxplot. Are the data skewed? If so, how?

d. Based on the results of (a) through (c), what conclusions might you reach concerning the average credit scores of people living in various American cities?

3.79 You are planning to study for your statistics examination with a group of classmates, one of whom you particularly want to impress. This individual has volunteered to use Microsoft Excel to generate the needed summary information, tables, and charts for a data set that contains several numerical and categorical variables assigned by the instructor for study purposes. This person comes over to you with the printout and exclaims, "I've got it all—the means, the medians, the standard deviations, the boxplots, the pie charts—for all our variables. The problem is, some of the output looks weird—like the boxplots for gender and for major and the pie charts for grade point average and for height. Also, I can't understand why Professor Szabat said we can't get the descriptive stats for some of the variables; I got them for everything! See, the mean for height is 68.23, the mean for grade point average is 2.76, the mean for gender is 1.50, the mean for major is 4.33." What is your reply?

REPORT WRITING EXERCISES

3.80 The file DomesticBeer contains the percentage alcohol, number of calories per 12 ounces, and number of carbohydrates (in grams) per 12 ounces for 158 of the best-selling domestic beers in the United States.

Source: Data extracted from **bit.ly/1A4E6AF**, December 1, 2016.

Write a report that includes a complete descriptive evaluation of each of the numerical variables—percentage of alcohol, number of calories per 12 ounces, and number of carbohydrates (in grams) per 12 ounces. Append to your report all appropriate tables, charts, and numerical descriptive measures.

CHAPTER 3

▼CASES

Managing Ashland MultiComm Services

For what variable in the Chapter 2 "Managing Ashland Multi-Comm Services" case (see page 88) are numerical descriptive measures needed?

1. For the variable you identify, compute the appropriate numerical descriptive measures and construct a boxplot.

2. For the variable you identify, construct a graphical display. What conclusions can you reach from this other plot that cannot be made from the boxplot?

3. Summarize your findings in a report that can be included with the task force's study.

Digital Case

Apply your knowledge about the proper use of numerical descriptive measures in this continuing Digital Case.

Open **EndRunGuide.pdf**, the EndRun Financial Services "Guide to Investing." Re-examine EndRun's supporting data for the "More Winners Than Losers" and "The Big Eight Difference" and then answer the following:

1. Can descriptive measures be computed for any variables? How would such summary statistics support EndRun's claims? How would those summary statistics affect your perception of EndRun's record?

2. Evaluate the methods EndRun used to summarize the results presented on the "Customer Survey Results" page. Is there anything you would do differently to summarize these results?

3. Note that the last question of the survey has fewer responses than the other questions. What factors may have limited the number of responses to that question?

CardioGood Fitness

Return to the CardioGood Fitness case first presented on page 33. Using the data stored in CardioGood Fitness:

1. Compute descriptive statistics to create a customer profile for each CardioGood Fitness treadmill product line.

2. Write a report to be presented to the management of CardioGood Fitness, detailing your findings.

More Descriptive Choices Follow-up

Follow up the Using Statistics Revisited section on page 153 by computing descriptive statistics to analyze the differences in 1-year return percentages, 5-year return percentages, and 10-year return percentages for the sample of 479 retirement funds stored in Retirement Funds . In your analysis, examine differences between the growth and value funds as well as the differences among the small, mid-cap, and large market cap funds.

Clear Mountain State Student Survey

The student news service at Clear Mountain State University (CMSU) has decided to gather data about the undergraduate students who attend CMSU. They create and distribute a survey of 14 questions (see **CMStudentSurvey.pdf**) and receive responses from 111 undergraduates (stored in StudentSurvey). For each numerical variable included in the survey, compute all the appropriate descriptive statistics and write a report summarizing your conclusions.

▼EXCEL GUIDE

EG3.1 MEASURES of CENTRAL TENDENCY

The Mean, Median, and Mode

Key Technique Use the **AVERAGE(*variable cell range*)**, **MEDIAN(*variable cell range*)**, and **MODE(*variable cell range*)** functions to compute these measures.

Example Compute the mean, median, and mode for the sample of get ready times that Section 3.1 introduces.

PHStat Use **Descriptive Summary**.

For the example, open to the **DATA worksheet** of the **Times workbook**. Select **PHStat → Descriptive Statistics → Descriptive Summary**. In the procedure's dialog box (shown below):

1. Enter **A1:A11** as the **Raw Data Cell Range** and check **First cell contains label**.
2. Click **Single Group Variable**.
3. Enter a **Title** and click **OK**.

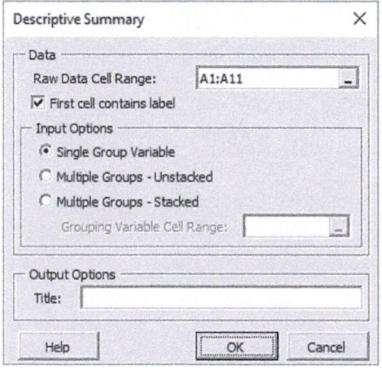

PHStat inserts a new worksheet that contains various measures of central tendency, variation, and shape discussed in Sections 3.1 and 3.2. This worksheet is similar to the CompleteStatistics worksheet of the Descriptive workbook.

Workbook Use the **CentralTendency worksheet** of the **Descriptive workbook** as a model.

For the example, open the **Times workbook**, insert a new worksheet (see Section EG.4), and:

1. Enter a title in cell **A1**.
2. Enter **Get-Ready Times** in cell **B3**, **Mean** in cell **A4**, **Median** in cell **A5**, and **Mode** in cell **A6**.
3. Enter the formula **=AVERAGE(DATA!A:A)** in cell **B4**, the formula **=MEDIAN(DATA!A:A)** in cell **B5**, and the formula **=MODE(DATA!A:A)** in cell **B6**.

For these functions, the *variable cell range* includes the name of the DATA worksheet because the data being summarized appears on the separate DATA worksheet. For another problem, paste the data for the problem into column A of the DATA worksheet, overwriting the existing get ready times.

Analysis ToolPak Use **Descriptive Statistics**.

For the example, open to the **DATA worksheet** of the **Times workbook** and:

1. Select **Data → Data Analysis**.
2. In the Data Analysis dialog box, select **Descriptive Statistics** from the **Analysis Tools** list and then click **OK**.

In the Descriptive Statistics dialog box (shown below):

1. Enter **A1:A11** as the **Input Range**. Click **Columns** and check **Labels in first row**.
2. Click **New Worksheet Ply** and check **Summary statistics**, **Kth Largest**, and **Kth Smallest**.
3. Click **OK**.

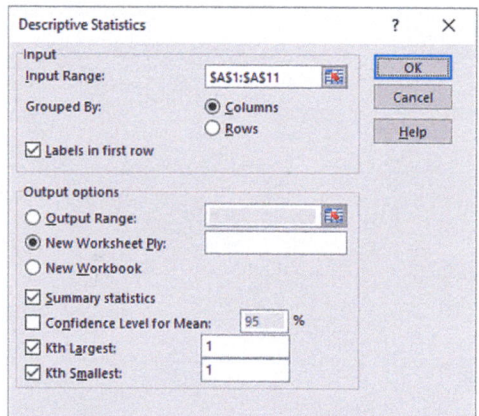

The ToolPak inserts a new worksheet that contains various measures of central tendency, variation, and shape discussed in Sections 3.1 and 3.2.

The Geometric Mean

Key Technique Use the **GEOMEAN((1 + R1), (1 + R2), ...(1 + Rn)) − 1** function to compute the geometric mean rate of return.

Example Compute the geometric mean rate of return in the Russell 2000 Index for the two years as shown in Example 3.4 on page 160.

Workbook Enter the formula **=GEOMEAN((1 + (−0.057)), (1 + 0.185)) − 1** in any cell.

EG3.2   MEASURES of VARIATION and SHAPE

The Range

Key Technique   Use the **MIN(***variable cell range***)** and **MAX (***variable cell range***)** functions to help compute the range.

Example   Compute the range for the sample of get ready times first introduced in Section 3.1.

PHStat   Use **Descriptive Summary** (see Section EG3.1).

Workbook   Use the **Range worksheet** of the **Descriptive workbook** as a model.

For the example, open the worksheet constructed in the *Workbook* "The Mean, Median, and Mode" instructions. Enter **Minimum** in cell **A7**, **Maximum** in cell **A8**, and **Range** in cell **A9**. Enter the formula **=MIN(DATA!A:A)** in cell **B7**, the formula **=MAX(DATA!A:A)** in cell **B8**, and the formula **=B8−B7** in cell **B9**.

The Variance, Standard Deviation, Coefficient of Variation, and Z Scores

Key Technique   Use the **VAR.S(***variable cell range***)** and **STDEV.S(***variable cell range***)** functions to compute the sample variance and the sample standard deviation, respectively.

Use the AVERAGE and STDEV.S functions for the coefficient of variation. Use the **STANDARDIZE(***value, mean, standard deviation***)** function to compute Z scores.

Example   Compute the variance, standard deviation, coefficient of variation, and Z scores for the sample of get ready times first introduced in Section 3.1.

PHStat   Use **Descriptive Summary** (see Section EG3.1).

Workbook   Use the **Variation** and **ZScores worksheets** of the **Descriptive workbook** as models.

For the example, the Variation and ZScores worksheets already compute these statistics using the get ready times in the DATA worksheet. To compute the variance, standard deviation, and coefficient of variation for another problem, paste the data for the problem into column A of the DATA worksheet, overwriting the existing get ready times.

To compute the Z scores for another problem, copy the updated DATA worksheet. In the new, copied worksheet:

1. Enter **Z Score** in cell **B1**.
2. Enter **=STANDARDIZE(A2, Variation!$B$4, Variation!$B$11)** in cell **B2**.
3. Copy the formula down through row 11.

Analysis ToolPak   Use **Descriptive Statistics** (see Section EG3.1). This procedure does not compute Z scores.

Shape: Skewness and Kurtosis

Key Technique   Use the **SKEW(***variable cell range***)** and the **KURT(***variable cell range***)** functions to compute these measures.

Example   Compute the skewness and kurtosis for the sample of get ready times first introduced in Section 3.1.

PHStat   Use **Descriptive Summary** (see Section EG3.1).

Workbook   Use the **Shape worksheet** of the **Descriptive workbook** as a model.

For the example, the Shape worksheet already computes the skewness and kurtosis using the get ready times in the DATA worksheet. To compute these statistics for another problem, paste the data for the problem into column A of the DATA worksheet, overwriting the existing get ready times.

Analysis ToolPak   Use **Descriptive Statistics** (see Section EG3.1).

EG3.3   EXPLORING NUMERICAL VARIABLES

Quartiles

Key Technique   Use the MEDIAN and COUNT, and SMALL, INT, FLOOR, CEILING, and IF functions (see Appendix F) to compute the quartiles. Avoid using any of the Excel quartile functions because they do not use the Section 3.3 rules to calculate quartiles.

Example   Compute the quartiles for the sample of get ready times first introduced in Section 3.1.

PHStat   Use **Boxplot** (discussed on page 162).

Workbook   Use the **COMPUTE worksheet** of the **Quartiles workbook** as a model.

For the example, the COMPUTE worksheet already computes the quartiles for the get ready times. To compute the quartiles for another problem, paste the data into column A of the DATA worksheet, overwriting the existing get ready times.

The COMPUTE worksheet uses a number of arithmetic and logical formulas that use the IF function to produce results consistent to the Section 3.3 rules. Open to the **COMPUTE_FORMULAS worksheet** to review these formulas and read the Short Takes for Chapter 3 for a detailed explanation of those formulas.

The **COMPUTE** worksheet avoids using any of the current Excel **QUARTILE** functions because none of them calculate quartiles using the Section 3.3 rules. The COMPARE worksheet compares the **COMPUTE** worksheet results to the quartiles calculated by the Excel QUARTILE.EXC and QUARTILE.INC functions.

The Interquartile Range

Key Technique Use a formula to subtract the first quartile from the third quartile.

Example Compute the interquartile range for the sample of get ready times first introduced in Section 3.1.

Workbook Use the **COMPUTE worksheet** of the **Quartiles workbook** (see previous section) as a model.

For the example, the interquartile range is already computed in cell B19 using the formula $= \mathbf{B18H} - \mathbf{B16}$.

The Five-Number Summary and the Boxplot

Key Technique Plot a series of line segments on the same chart to construct a five-number summary boxplot.

Example Compute the five-number summary and construct the boxplots of the three-year return percentage variable for the growth and value funds used in Example 3.14 on page 141.

PHStat Use **Boxplot**.

For the example, open to the **DATA worksheet** of the **Retirement Funds workbook**. Select **PHStat → Descriptive Statistics → Boxplot**. In the procedure's dialog box (shown below):

1. Enter **K1:K480** as the **Raw Data Cell Range** and check **First cell contains label**.
2. Click **Multiple Groups - Stacked** and enter **C1:C480** as the **Grouping Variable Cell Range**.
3. Enter a **Title**, check **Five-Number Summary**, and click **OK**.

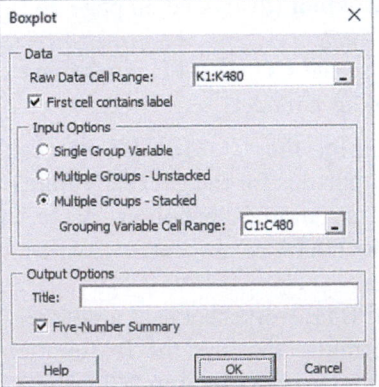

The boxplot appears on its own chart sheet, separate from the worksheet that contains the five-number summary.

Workbook Use the worksheets of the **Boxplot workbook** as templates for five-number summary boxplots.

For the example, use the **PLOT_DATA worksheet** which already shows the five-number summary and boxplot for the value funds. To compute the five-number summary and construct a boxplot for the growth funds, copy the growth funds from **column A** of the **UNSTACKED worksheet** of

the **Retirement Funds workbook** and paste into **column A** of the **DATA worksheet** of the **Boxplot workbook**.

For other problems, use the **PLOT_SUMMARY worksheet** as the template if the five-number summary has already been determined; otherwise, paste your unsummarized data into column A of the DATA worksheet and use the PLOT_DATA worksheet as was done for the example.

The worksheets creatively use charting features to construct a boxplot as the SHORT TAKES for Chapter 3 explains.

EG3.4 NUMERICAL DESCRIPTIVE MEASURES for a POPULATION

The Population Mean, Population Variance, and Population Standard Deviation

Key Technique Use **AVERAGE(***variable cell range***)**, **VAR.P(***variable cell range***)**, and **STDEV.P(***variable cell range***)** to compute these measures.

Example Compute the population mean, population variance, and population standard deviation for the "Dow Dogs" population data of Table 3.3 on page 143.

Workbook Use the **Parameters workbook** as a model.

For the example, the **COMPUTE worksheet** of the **Parameters workbook** already computes the three population parameters for the "Dow Dogs."

The Empirical Rule and Chebyshev's Theorem

Use the **COMPUTE worksheet** of the **VE-Variability workbook** to explore the effects of changing the mean and standard deviation on the ranges associated with ± 1 standard deviation, ± 2 standard deviations, and ± 3 standard deviations from the mean. Change the mean in cell **B4** and the standard deviation in cell **B5** and then note the updated results in rows 9 through 11.

EG3.5 THE COVARIANCE and the COEFFICIENT of CORRELATION

The Covariance

Key Technique Use the **COVARIANCE.S(***variable 1 cell range, variable 2 cell range***)** function to compute this measure.

Example Compute the sample covariance for the NBA team revenue and value shown in Figure 3.10 on page 148.

Workbook Use the **Covariance workbook** as a model.

For the example, the revenue and value have already been placed in columns A and B of the DATA worksheet and the COMPUTE worksheet displays the computed covariance in cell B9. For other problems, paste the data for two variables into columns A and B of the DATA worksheet, overwriting the revenue and value data.

Read the SHORT TAKES for Chapter 3 for an explanation of the formulas found in the DATA and COMPUTE worksheets.

The Coefficient of Correlation

Key Technique Use the **CORREL**(*variable 1 cell range, variable 2 cell range*) function to compute this measure.

Example Compute the coefficient of correlation for the NBA team revenue and value data of Example 3.18 on page 151.

Workbook Use the **Correlation workbook** as a model.

For the example, the revenue and value have already been placed in columns A and B of the DATA worksheet and the COMPUTE worksheet displays the coefficient of correlation in cell B14. For other problems, paste the data for two variables into columns A and B of the DATA worksheet, overwriting the revenue and value data.

The COMPUTE worksheet that uses the COVARIANCE.S function to compute the covariance (see the previous section) and also uses the DEVSQ, COUNT, and SUMPRODUCT functions discussed in Appendix F. Open to the **COMPUTE_FORMULAS worksheet** to examine the use of all these functions.

CHAPTER

3

▼JMP GUIDE

JG3.1 MEASURES of CENTRAL TENDENCY

The Mean, Median, and Mode

Use **Distribution**.

For example, to compute the mean, median, and mode for the sample of get ready times that Section 3.1 introduces, open to the **Times data table**. Select **Analyze➔ Distribution**. In that procedure's dialog box:

1. Click **Get-Ready Time** in the Select Columns list and then click **Y, Columns** to add Get-Ready Time to the Y, Columns box.
2. Click **OK**.

In the Distribution results window:

3. Click the **Get-Ready Time red triangle** and select **Display Options➔ Customize Summary Statistics** from its menu.
4. In the Customize Summary Statistics dialog box, first click **Deselect All Summary Statistics** and then click **Mean, Median**, and **Mode**.
5. Click **OK**.

JMP displays a revised table of summary statistics in the new Distribution window. For the get-ready times, there are two modes and JMP notes that "The mode shown is the smallest of 2 modes with a count of 2." To show the other mode, click the **Summary Statistics red triangle** and select **Show All Modes** from its menu. JMP appends an All Modes table to summary statistics table.

The Geometric Mean

Use **Tabulate**.

For example, to compute the geometric mean rate of return in the Russell 2000 Index for the two years as shown in Example 3.4 on page 126, open to the **Geometric Mean data table**. This data table serves as a partial template for computing the geometric mean and already contains the rates of return for Example 3.4 in the first column and $1 + R$ values in the second column. Select **Analyze➔Tabulate**. In that procedure's window (shown on page 112):

1. Drag **Geometric Mean** from the statistics list and drop it in the **Drop zone for columns** area.
2. Drag **OnePlusR** from the columns list and drop it on the blank gray cell of the blank first column in the table.
3. Click **Done**.

JMP displays the geometric mean in new Tabulate window. Subtract 1 from the geometric mean to calculate the geometric rate of return for the example. To calculate the geometric rate of return for more than two time periods, click the **Rows red triangle** and select **Add Rows** from its menu. Enter the number of additional time periods in the **How many rows to add** box and click **OK**. Then enter the rates of return in the first column and follow steps 1 through 3.

JG3.2 MEASURES OF VARIATION AND SHAPE

The Range, Variance, Standard Deviation, Coefficient of Variation, Skewness, and Kurtosis

Use the Section JG3.1 instructions, but in step 4 check **N, Range, Variance, Std Dev, CV, Skewness**, and **Kurtosis** in the Customize Summary Statistics dialog box. For a report that looks similar to Figure 3.5 on page 133, additionally check **Minimum** and **Maximum** and the Section JG3.1 choices, **Mean, Median**, and **Mode**.

Z Scores

Use **Standardize**.

To compute the Z scores for the sample of get ready times that Section 3.1 introduces, open to the **Times data table**. Right-click the **Get-Ready Time column heading** and select **New Formula Column → Distributional → Standardize**. JMP inserts a new column in the data table Standardize[Get-Ready Time] that contains the Z scores.

JG3.3 EXPLORING NUMERICAL VARIABLES

Quartiles, the Interquartile Range, the Five-Number Summary, and the Boxplot

Use **Distribution**.

For example, to compute the quartiles for the sample of get ready times that Section 3.1 introduces, open to the **Times data table**. Select **Analyze → Distribution**. In that procedure's dialog box:

1. Click **Get-Ready Time** in the Select Columns list and then click **Y, Columns** to add Get-Ready Time to the Y, Columns box.
2. Click **OK**.

The quartiles and the five-number summary appear as part of the Quantiles report in the new Distribution window that JMP displays. In the Distribution results window:

1. Click the **Get-Ready Time red triangle** and select **Display Options → Customize Summary Statistics** from its menu.
2. In the Customize Summary Statistics dialog box, click **Interquartile Range**.
3. Click **OK**.

JMP revises the Summary Statistics report to include the Interquartile Range:

4. Click the **Get-Ready Time red triangle** and select **Histogram Options** and click **Histogram** to clear its checkmark and remove chart from the Distribution window.
5. Click **Done**.

The five-number summary boxplot remains in the decluttered Distribution window. Optionally, use the Appendix Section B.5 instructions to change the font and type characteristics of chart labels or axis settings.

The Boxplot (second form)

Use **Graph Builder**. Use this method to construct boxplots in which the endpoints of the whiskers define the smallest and largest values that are within the range of 1.5 times the interquartile range from the box.

For example, to construct the five-number summary boxplots of the three-year return percentage variable for the growth and value funds used in Example 3.14 on page 141, open to the **Retirement Funds data table**. Select **Graph → Graph Builder**. In that procedure's window (shown on page 112):

1. Drag **3YrReturn** from the columns list and drop it in the **Y** area for a vertical boxplot or in the **X** area for a horizontal boxplot.
2. Click the **Box Plot chart icon**.
3. Drag **Fund Type** from the columns list and drop it in the **Overlay** area.
4. Click **Done**.

JMP displays the pair of boxplots in a new window. Optionally, use the Appendix Section B.5 instructions to change the font and type characteristics of chart labels.

JG3.4 NUMERICAL DESCRIPTIVE MEASURES for a POPULATION

The Population Mean, Population Variance, and Population Standard Deviation

JMP does not contain commands that compute these population parameters directly.

The Empirical Rule and the Chebyshev Rule

Manually compute the values needed to apply these rules using the statistics that the Section JG3.1 instructions compute.

JG3.5 THE COVARIANCE and the COEFFICIENT of CORRELATION

The Covariance and the Coefficient of Correlation

Use **Multivariate**.

For example, to compute the coefficient of correlation for Example 3.18 on page 151, open to the **NBAValues data table**. Select **Analyze → Multivariate Methods → Multivariate**. In that procedure's dialog box (shown below):

1. Click **Revenue** in the Select Columns list and then click **Y, Columns** to add Revenue to the Y, Columns box.
2. Click **Current Value** in the Select Columns list and then click **Y, Columns** to add Current Value to the Y, Columns box.
3. Click **OK**.

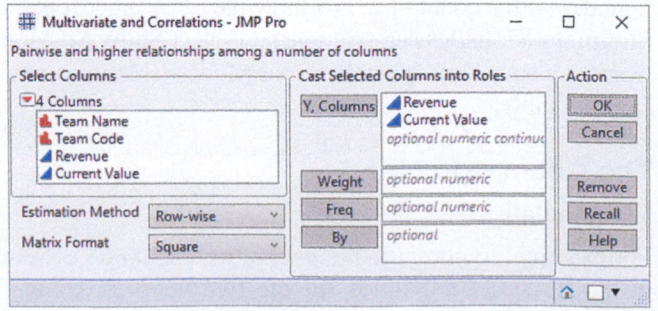

JMP displays a new Multivariate results window. The coefficient of correlation appears in the Correlations report in the Revenue-Current Value cells. In that window, click the **Multivariate red triangle** and check **Covariance Matrix**. The covariance appears in the Covariance matrix report in the Revenue-Current Value cells.

▼MINITAB GUIDE

MG3.1 MEASURES of CENTRAL TENDENCY

The Mean, Median, and Mode

Use **Descriptive Statistics** to compute the mean, the median, the mode, and selected measures of variation and shape.

For example, to create results similar to Figure 3.5 on page 133 that presents descriptive statistics of the three-year return percentage variable for the growth and value funds, open to the **Retirement Funds worksheet**. Select **Stat → Basic Statistics → Display Descriptive Statistics**. In the Display Descriptive Statistics dialog box (shown below):

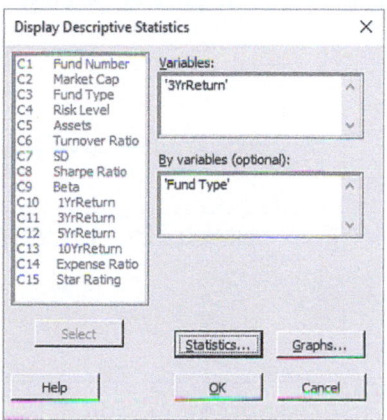

1. Double-click **C11 3YrReturn** in the variables list to add **'3YrReturn'** to the **Variables** box and then press **Tab**.
2. Double-click **C3 Fund Type** in the variables list to add **'Fund Type'** to the **By variables (optional)** box.
3. Click **Statistics**.

In the Display Descriptive Statistics: Statistics dialog box (shown below):

4. Check **Mean, Standard deviation, Variance, Coefficient of variation, First quartile, Median, Third quartile, Interquartile range, Mode, Minimum, Maximum, Range, Skewness, Kurtosis**, and **N total**.
5. Click **OK**.
6. Back in the Display Descriptive Statistics dialog box, click **OK**.

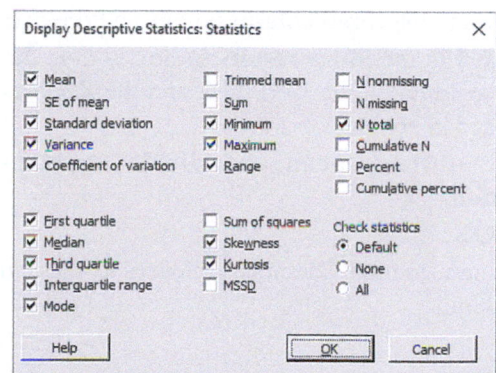

The Geometric Mean

Use **Calculator** to compute the geometric mean.

For example, to compute the geometric mean rate of return in the Russell 2000 Index for the two years as shown in Example 3.4 on page 126, open to the **Geometric Mean worksheet**. This worksheet serves as a partial template for computing the geometric mean and already contains the rates of return for Example 3.4 in column C1 and $1 + R$ values in column C2. Select **Calc → Calculator**. In the Calculator dialog box:

1. Enter **C3** in the **Store result in variable** box and press **Tab**.
2. Enter **GMEAN(C2) − 1** in the **Expression** box.
3. Click **OK**.

Minitab places the result, 0.0570974, in the first cell of the second column, C3. To calculate the geometric rate of return for more than two time periods, enter the rates of return in the first column for all time periods and then follow steps 1 through 3.

MG3.2 MEASURES of VARIATION and SHAPE

The Range, Variance, Standard Deviation, Coefficient of Variation, Skewness, and Kurtosis

Use **Descriptive Statistics** to compute these measures of variation and shape. The Section MG3.1 instruction for computing the mean, median, and mode also compute these measures.

Z Scores

Use **Standardize** to compute Z scores.

For example, to compute the Figure 3.3 Z scores on page 131, open to the **CEREALS worksheet**. Select **Calc ➔ Standardize**. In the Standardize dialog box (shown below):

1. Double-click **C2 Calories** in the variables list to add **Calories** to the **Input column(s)** box and press **Tab**.
2. Enter **C5** in the **Store results in** box. (C5 is the first empty column on the worksheet and the Z scores will be placed in column C5.)
3. Click **Subtract mean and divide by standard deviation**.
4. Click **OK**.
5. In the new column C5, enter **Z Scores** as the name of the column.

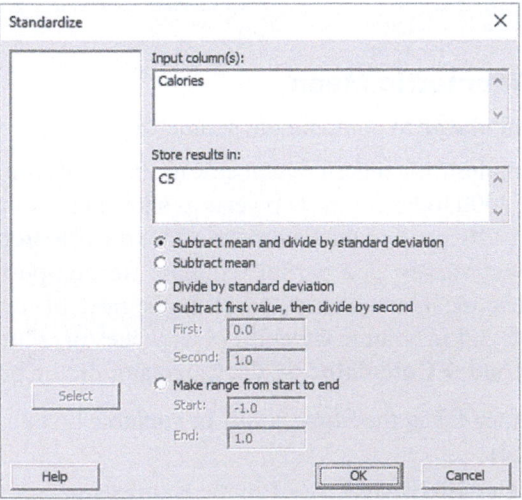

MG3.3 EXPLORING NUMERICAL VARIABLES

Quartiles, the Interquartile Range, and the Five-Number Summary

Use **Descriptive Statistics** to compute these measures. The instructions in Section MG3.1 for computing the mean, median, and mode also compute these measures.

The Boxplot

Use **Boxplot**.

For example, to create the Figure 3.8 boxplots on page 141, open to the **Retirement Funds worksheet**. Select **Graph ➔ Boxplot**.

In the Boxplots dialog box:

1. Click **With Groups** in the **One Y gallery** and then click **OK**.

In the Boxplot: One Y, With Groups dialog box (shown below):

2. Double-click **C11 3YrReturn** in the variables list to add **'3YrReturn'** to the **Graph variables** box and then press **Tab**.
3. Double-click **C3 Fund Type** in the variables list to add **'Fund Type'** in the **Categorical variables** box.
4. Click **OK**.

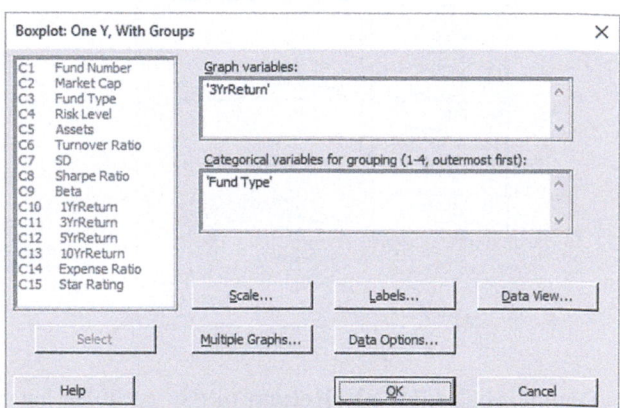

In the boxplot created, pausing the mouse pointer over the boxplot reveals a number of measures, including the quartiles. For problems that involve single-group data, click **Simple** in the **One Y gallery** in step 1.

To rotate the boxplots 90 degrees (as was done in Figure 3.4), replace step 4 with these steps 4 through 6:

4. Click **Scale**.
5. In the **Axes and Ticks** tab of the Boxplot-Scale dialog box, check **Transpose value and category scales** and click **OK**.
6. Back in the Boxplot: One Y, With Groups dialog box, click **OK**.

MG3.4   NUMERICAL DESCRIPTIVE MEASURES for a POPULATION

The Population Mean, Population Variance, and Population Standard Deviation

Minitab does not contain commands that compute these population parameters directly.

The Empirical Rule and the Chebyshev Rule

Manually compute the values needed to apply these rules using the statistics computed in the Section MG3.1 instructions.

MG3.5   THE COVARIANCE and the COEFFICIENT of CORRELATION

The Covariance

Use **Covariance**.

For example, to compute the covariance for Example 3.17 on page 148, open to the **NBAValues worksheet**. Select **Stat → Basic Statistics → Covariance**. In the Covariance dialog box (shown below):

1. Double-click **C3 Revenue** in the variables list to add **Revenue** to the **Variables** box.
2. Double-click **C4 Current Value** in the variables list to add **'Current Value'** to the **Variables** box.
3. Click **OK**.

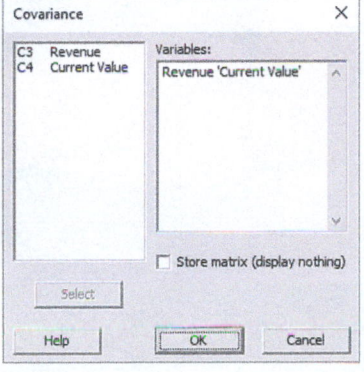

In the table of numbers produced, the covariance is the number that appears in the cell position that is the intersection of the two variables (the lower-left cell).

The Coefficient of Correlation

Use **Correlation**.

For example, to compute the coefficient of correlation for Example 3.18 on page 151, open to the **NBAValues worksheet**. Select **Stat → Basic Statistics → Correlation**. In the Correlation dialog box (shown below):

1. Double-click **C3 Revenue** in the variables list to add **Revenue** to the **Variables** box.
2. Double-click **C4 Current Value** in the variables list to add **'Current Value'** to the **Variables** box.
3. Select **Pearson correlation** from the **Method** pull-down list.
4. Check **Display p-values**.
5. Click **OK**.

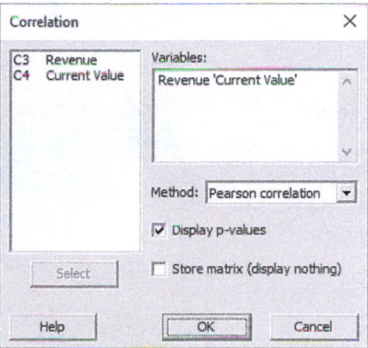

4

Basic Probability

CONTENTS

OBJECTIVES

- Understand basic probability concepts
- Understand conditional probability
- Use Bayes' theorem to revise probabilities
- Apply counting rules

▼USING **STATISTICS**
Possibilities at M&R Electronics World

As the marketing manager for M&R Electronics World, you are analyzing the results of an intent-to-purchase study. The heads of 1,000 households were asked about their intentions to purchase a large TV (screen size of at least 60 inches, measured diagonally) sometime during the next 12 months. As a follow-up, you plan to survey the same people 12 months later to see whether they purchased a large TV. For households that did purchase a large TV, you would like to know whether the television they purchased had a faster refresh rate (120 Hz or higher) or a standard refresh rate (60 Hz), whether they also purchased a streaming media player in the past 12 months, and whether they were satisfied with their purchase of the large TV.

You plan to use the results of this survey to form a new marketing strategy that will enhance sales and better target those households likely to purchase multiple or more expensive products. What questions can you ask in this survey? How can you express the relationships among the various intent-to-purchase responses of individual households?

The principles of probability help bridge the worlds of descriptive statistics and inferential statistics. Probability principles are the foundation for the probability distribution, the concept of mathematical expectation, and the binomial and Poisson distributions. In this chapter, you will learn to apply probability to intent-to-purchase survey responses to answer purchase behavior questions such as:

- What is the probability that a household is planning to purchase a large TV in the next year?
- What is the probability that a household will actually purchase a large TV?
- What is the probability that a household is planning to purchase a large TV and actually purchases the television?
- Given that the household is planning to purchase a large TV, what is the probability that the purchase is made?
- Does knowledge of whether a household *plans* to purchase a large TV change the likelihood of predicting whether the household *will* purchase a large TV?
- What is the probability that a household that purchases a large TV will purchase a television with a faster refresh rate?
- What is the probability that a household that purchases a large TV with a faster refresh rate will also purchase a streaming media player?
- What is the probability that a household that purchases a large TV will be satisfied with the purchase?

With answers to questions such as these, you can begin to form a marketing strategy. You can consider whether to target households that have indicated an intent to purchase or to focus on selling televisions that have faster refresh rates or both. You can also explore whether households that purchase large TVs with faster refresh rates can be easily persuaded to also purchase streaming media players.

4.1 Basic Probability Concepts

In everyday usage, *probability*, according to the Oxford English Dictionary, indicates the extent to which something is likely to occur or exist but can also mean the most likely cause of something. If you observe storm clouds forming, wind shifts, and drops in the barometric pressure, the probability of rain coming soon increases (first meaning). If you observe people entering an office building with wet clothes or otherwise drenched, there is a strong probability that it is currently raining outside (second meaning).

In statistics, **probability** is a numerical value that expresses the ratio between the value sought and the set of all possible values that could occur. A six-sided die has faces for 1, 2, 3, 4, 5, and 6. Therefore, for one roll of a *fair* six-sided die, the set of all possible values are the values 1 through 6. If the value sought is "a value greater than 4," then the values 5 or 6 would be sought. One would say the probability of this *event* is 2 outcomes divided by 6 outcomes or 1/3.

Consider tossing a fair coin heads or tails two times. What is the probability of tossing two tails? The set of possible values for tossing two coins are HH, TT, HT, TH. Therefore, the probability of tossing two tails is 1/4 because there is only one value (TT) that matches what is being sought and there are 4 values in the set of all possible values.

Events and Sample Spaces

When discussing probability, one formally uses **outcomes** in place of *values* and calls the set of all possible outcomes the **sample space**. **Events** are subsets of the sample space, the set of all outcomes that produce a specific result. For tossing a fair coin twice, the event "toss at least 1 head" is the subset of outcomes HH, HT, and TH and the event "toss two tails" is the subset TT. Both of these events are also examples of a **joint event**, an event that has two or more characteristics. In contrast, a **simple event** has only one characteristic, an outcome that cannot be further subdivided. The event "rolling a value greater 4" in the first example results in the subset of outcomes 5 and 6 and is an example of a simple event because "5" and "6" represent one characteristic and cannot be further divided.

student TIP

Events are represented by letters of the alphabet.

student TIP

By definition, *an event and its complement* are always both mutually exclusive and collectively exhaustive.

student TIP

A probability cannot be negative or greater than 1.

The **complement** of an event *A*, noted by the symbol *A'*, is the subset of outcomes that are not part of the event. For tossing a fair coin twice, the complement of the event "toss at least 1 head" is the subset TT, while the complement of the event "toss two tails" is HH, HT, and TH.

A set of events are **mutually exclusive** if they cannot occur at the same. The events "roll a value greater than 4" and "roll a value less than 3" are mutually exclusive when rolling one fair die. However, the events "roll a value greater than 4" and "roll a value greater than 5" are not because both share the outcome of rolling a 6.

A set of events are **collectively exhaustive** if one of the events must occur. For rolling a fair six-sided die, the events "roll a value 3 or less" and "roll a value 4 or more" are collectively exhaustive because these two subsets include all possible outcomes in the sample space. However, the set of events "roll a value 3 or less" and "roll a value greater than 4" is not because this set does not include the outcome of rolling a 4.

Not all sets of collectively exhaustive events are mutually exclusive. For rolling a fair six-sided die, the set of events "roll a value 3 or less," "roll an even numbered value," and "roll a value greater than 4" is collectively exhaustive but is not mutually exclusive as, for example, "a value 3 or less" and "an even numbered value" could *both* occur if a 2 is rolled.

Certain and *impossible* events represent special cases. A **certain event** is an event that is sure to occur such as "roll a value greater than 0" for rolling one fair die. Because the subset of outcomes for a certain event is the entire set of outcomes in the sample, a certain event has a probability of 1. An **impossible event** is an event that has no chance of occurring, such as "roll a value greater than 6" for rolling one fair die. Because the subset of outcomes for an impossible event is empty—there are no outcomes in the sample space that represent that event—an impossible event has a probability of 0.

Types of Probability

The concepts and vocabulary related to events and sample spaces are helpful to understanding how to calculate probabilities. Also affecting such calculations are the type of probability being used: *a priori*, empirical, or subjective.

In *a priori* **probability**, the probability of an occurrence is based on having prior knowledge of the outcomes that can occur. Consider a standard deck of cards that has 26 red cards and 26 black cards. The probability of selecting a black card is $26/52 = 0.50$ because there are 26 black cards and 52 total cards. What does this probability mean? If each card is replaced after it is selected, does it mean that 1 out of the next 2 cards selected will be black? No, because you cannot say for certain what will happen on the next several selections. However, you can say that in the long run, if this selection process is continually repeated, the proportion of black cards selected will approach 0.50. Example 4.1 shows another example of computing an *a priori* probability.

EXAMPLE 4.1

Finding *A Priori* Probabilities

A standard six-sided die has six faces. Each face of the die contains either one, two, three, four, five, or six dots. If you roll a die, what is the probability that you will get a face with five dots?

SOLUTION Each face is equally likely to occur. Because there are six faces, the probability of getting a face with five dots is 1/6.

The preceding examples use the *a priori* probability approach because the number of ways the event occurs and the total number of possible outcomes are known from the composition of the deck of cards or the faces of the die.

In the **empirical probability** approach, the probabilities are based on observed data, not on prior knowledge of how the outcomes can occur. Surveys are often used to generate empirical probabilities. Examples of this type of probability are the proportion of individuals in the M&R World Electronics scenario who actually purchase a large TV, the proportion of registered voters who prefer a certain political candidate, and the proportion of students who have part-time jobs. For example, if you take a survey of students, and 60% state that they have part-time jobs, then there is a 0.60 probability that an individual student has a part-time job.

The third approach to probability, **subjective probability**, differs from the other two approaches because subjective probability differs from person to person. For example, the development team for a new product may assign a probability of 0.60 to the chance of success for the product, while the president of the company may be less optimistic and assign a probability of 0.30. The assignment of subjective probabilities to various outcomes is usually based on a combination of an individual's past experience, personal opinion, and analysis of a particular situation. Subjective probability is especially useful in making decisions in situations in which you cannot use *a priori* probability or empirical probability.

Summarizing Sample Spaces

Sample spaces can be presented as in tabular form using contingency tables (see Section 2.1) or visualized using Venn diagrams. Table 4.1 in Example 4.2 summarizes a sample space as a contingency table. When used for probability, each cell in a contingency table represents one joint *event*, analogous to the one joint *response* when these tables are used to summarize categorical variables. For example, 200 of the respondents correspond to the joint event "planned to purchase a large TV and subsequently did purchase the large TV".

EXAMPLE 4.2

Events and Sample Spaces

The M&R Electronics World scenario on page 168 concerns analyzing the results of an intent-to-purchase study. Table 4.1 presents the results of the sample of 1,000 households surveyed in terms of purchase behavior for large TVs.

TABLE 4.1

Purchase Behavior for Large TVs

PLANNED TO PURCHASE	ACTUALLY PURCHASED		
	Yes	No	Total
Yes	200	50	250
No	100	650	750
Total	300	700	1,000

What is the sample space? Give examples of simple events and joint events.

SOLUTION The sample space consists of the 1,000 respondents. Simple events are "planned to purchase," "did not plan to purchase," "purchased," and "did not purchase." The complement of the event "planned to purchase" is "did not plan to purchase." The event "planned to purchase and actually purchased" is a joint event because in this joint event, the respondent must plan to purchase the television *and* actually purchase it.

Venn diagrams visualize a sample space. This diagram represents the various events as "unions" and "intersections" of circles. Figure 4.1 presents a typical Venn diagram for a two-variable situation, with each variable having only two events (*A* and *A'*, *B* and *B'*). The circle on the left (the red one) represents all events that are part of *A*.

FIGURE 4.1
Venn diagram for events
A and *B*

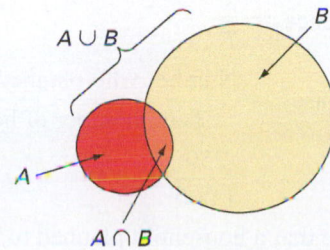

FIGURE 4.2
Venn diagram for the M&R
Electronics World example

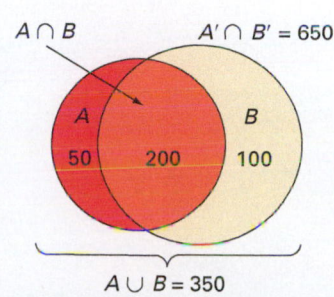

The circle on the right (the yellow one) represents all events that are part of B. The area contained within circle A and circle B (center area) is the intersection of A and B (written as $A \cap B$), because it is part of A and also part of B. The total area of the two circles is the union of A and B (written as $A \cup B$) and contains all outcomes that are just part of event A, just part of event B, or part of both A and B. The area in the diagram outside of $A \cup B$ contains outcomes that are neither part of A nor part of B.

You must define A and B in order to develop a Venn diagram. You can define either event as A or B, as long as you are consistent in evaluating the various events. For the Example 4.2 large-screen HDTV example, you define the events as follows:

$$A = \text{planned to purchase} \qquad B = \text{actually purchased}$$

$$A' = \text{did not plan to purchase} \quad B' = \text{did not actually purchase}$$

In drawing the Venn diagram for this problem (see Figure 4.2 on page 171), you determine the value of the intersection of A and B so that the sample space can be divided into its parts. $A \cap B$ consists of all 200 households who planned to purchase and actually purchased a large-screen HDTV. The remainder of event A (planned to purchase) consists of the 50 households who planned to purchase a large-screen HDTV but did not actually purchase one. The remainder of event B (actually purchased) consists of the 100 households who did not plan to purchase a large-screen HDTV but actually purchased one. The remaining 650 households represent those who neither planned to purchase nor actually purchased a large-screen HDTV.

Simple Probability

Simple probability is the probability of occurrence of a simple event A, $P(A)$ in which each outcome is *equally likely* to occur. Equation (4.1) defines the probability of occurrence for simple probability.

PROBABILITY OF OCCURRENCE

$$\text{Probability of occurrence} = \frac{X}{T} \qquad \textbf{(4.1)}$$

where

$$X = \text{number of outcomes in which the event occurs}$$
$$T = \text{total number of possible outcomes}$$

Equation 4.1 represents what some people wrongly think *is* the probability of occurrence for *all* probability problems. (Not all probability problems can be solved by Equation 4.1 as later examples in this chapter illustrate.) In the M&R Electronics scenario, the survey data collected represent an example of empirical probability and you can use Equation (4.1) to determine answers to questions that can be expressed as a simple probability. For example, one question asked respondents if they planned to purchase a large TV posed in the Using Statistics scenario.

How can you determine the probability of selecting a household that planned to purchase a large TV? Using the Table 4.1 summary table, you determine the value of X as 250, the total of the Planned-to-Purchase Yes row and determine the value of T as 1,000, the overall total of respondents located in the lower right corner cell of the table. Using Equation (4.1) and Table 4.1 or Figure 4.2:

$$\text{Probability of occurrence} = \frac{X}{T}$$

$$P(\text{Planned to purchase}) = \frac{\text{Number who planned to purchase}}{\text{Total number of households}}$$

$$= \frac{250}{1,000} = 0.25$$

Thus, there is a 0.25 (or 25%) chance that a household planned to purchase a large TV.

Example 4.3 illustrates another application of simple probability.

EXAMPLE 4.3	In a M&R World Electronics follow-up survey, additional questions were asked of the 300 households that actually purchased large TVs. Table 4.2 indicates the consumers' responses to whether the television purchased had a faster refresh rate and whether they also purchased a streaming media player in the past 12 months.

Computing the Probability That the Large TV Purchased Had a Faster Refresh Rate

Find the probability that if a household that purchased a large TV is randomly selected, the television purchased had a faster refresh rate.

TABLE 4.2

Purchase Behavior About Purchasing a Faster Refresh Rate Television and a Streaming Media Player

REFRESH RATE OF TELEVISION PURCHASED	STREAMING MEDIA PLAYER		
	Yes	No	Total
Faster	38	42	80
Standard	70	150	220
Total	108	192	300

SOLUTION Using the following definitions:

$$A = \text{purchased a television with a faster refresh rate}$$

$$A' = \text{purchased a television with a standard refresh rate}$$

$$B = \text{purchased a streaming media player}$$

$$B' = \text{did not purchase a streaming media player}$$

$$P(\text{Faster refresh rate}) = \frac{\text{Number of faster refresh rate televisions purchased}}{\text{Total number of televisions}}$$

$$= \frac{80}{300} = 0.267$$

There is a 26.7% chance that a randomly selected large TV purchased has a faster refresh rate.

Joint Probability

Whereas simple probability refers to the probability of occurrence of simple events, **joint probability** refers to the probability of an occurrence involving two or more events. An example of joint probability is the probability that you will get heads on the first toss of a coin and heads on the second toss of a coin.

In Table 4.1 on page 171, the count of the group of individuals who planned to purchase and actually purchased a large TV corresponds to the cell that represents Planned to Purchase Yes and Actually Purchased Yes, the upper left numerical cell. (In the Figure 4.2 Venn diagram, the intersection of A and B represents the count of this group.) Because this group consists of 200 households, the probability of picking a household that planned to purchase *and* actually purchased a large TV is

$$P(\text{Planned to purchase } and \text{ actually purchased}) = \frac{\text{Planned to purchase } and \text{ actually purchased}}{\text{Total number of respondents}}$$

$$= \frac{200}{1,000} = 0.20$$

Example 4.4 also demonstrates how to determine joint probability.

EXAMPLE 4.4

Determining the Joint Probability That a Household Purchased a Large TV with a Faster Refresh Rate and Purchased a Streaming Media Box

In Table 4.2 on page 173, the purchases are cross-classified as having a faster refresh rate or having a standard refresh rate and whether the household purchased a streaming media player. Find the probability that a randomly selected household that purchased a large TV also purchased a television that had a faster refresh rate and purchased a streaming media player.

SOLUTION Using Equation (4.1) on page 172 and Table 4.2 on page 173,

$$P(\text{TV with a faster refresh rate } and \text{ streaming media player}) = \frac{\text{Number that purchased a TV with a faster refresh rate } and \text{ purchased a streaming media player}}{\text{Total number of large TV purchasers}}$$

$$= \frac{38}{300} = 0.127$$

Therefore, there is a 12.7% chance that a randomly selected household that purchased a large TV purchased a television that had a faster refresh rate and purchased a streaming media player.

Marginal Probability

The **marginal probability** of an event consists of a set of joint probabilities. You can determine the marginal probability of a particular event by using the concept of joint probability just discussed. For example, if B consists of two events, B_1 and B_2, then $P(A)$, the probability of event A, consists of the joint probability of event A occurring with event B_1 and the joint probability of event A occurring with event B_2. You use Equation (4.2) to compute marginal probabilities.

MARGINAL PROBABILITY

$$P(A) = P(A \text{ and } B_1) + P(A \text{ and } B_2) + \cdots + P(A \text{ and } B_k) \qquad (4.2)$$

where $B_1, B_2, \ldots, B_k$ are k mutually exclusive and collectively exhaustive events, defined as follows:

You can use Equation (4.2) to compute the marginal probability of "planned to purchase" a large TV:

$$P(\text{Planned to purchase}) = P(\text{Planned to purchase } and \text{ purchased})$$

$$+ P(\text{Planned to purchase } and \text{ did not purchase})$$

$$= \frac{200}{1,000} + \frac{50}{1,000} = \frac{250}{1,000} = 0.25$$

You get the same result if you add the number of outcomes that make up the simple event "planned to purchase."

General Addition Rule

student TIP

The key word when using the addition rule is *or*.

How do you find the probability of event "*A or B*"? You need to consider the occurrence of either event A or event B or both A and B. For example, how can you determine the probability that a household planned to purchase *or* actually purchased a large TV?

The event "planned to purchase *or* actually purchased" includes all households that planned to purchase and all households that actually purchased a large TV. You examine each cell of the contingency table (Table 4.1 on page 171) to determine whether it is part of this event. From Table 4.1, the cell "planned to purchase *and* did not actually purchase" is part of the event because it includes respondents who planned to purchase. The cell "did not plan to purchase *and* actually purchased" is included because it contains respondents who actually purchased. Finally, the cell "planned to purchase *and* actually purchased" has both characteristics of interest. Therefore, one way to calculate the probability of "planned to purchase *or* actually purchased" is

$$
\begin{aligned}
P(\text{Planned to purchase } or \text{ actually purchased}) = {} & P(\text{Planned to purchase } and \text{ did not actually} \\
& \text{purchase}) + P(\text{Did not plan to} \\
& \text{purchase } and \text{ actually purchased}) + \\
& P(\text{Planned to purchase } and \\
& \text{actually purchased})
\end{aligned}
$$

$$
= \frac{50}{1,000} + \frac{100}{1,000} + \frac{200}{1,000}
$$

$$
= \frac{350}{1,000} = 0.35
$$

Often, it is easier to determine $P(A \ or \ B)$, the probability of the event $A \ or \ B$, by using the **general addition rule**, defined in Equation (4.3).

GENERAL ADDITION RULE

The probability of *A or B* is equal to the probability of *A* plus the probability of *B* minus the probability of *A and B*.

$$
P(A \ or \ B) = P(A) + P(B) - P(A \ and \ B) \tag{4.3}
$$

Applying Equation (4.3) to the previous example produces the following result:

$$
\begin{aligned}
P(\text{Planned to purchase } or \text{ actually purchased}) = {} & P(\text{Planned to purchase}) \\
& + P(\text{Actually purchased}) - P(\text{Planned to} \\
& \text{purchase } and \text{ actually purchased})
\end{aligned}
$$

$$
= \frac{250}{1,000} + \frac{300}{1,000} - \frac{200}{1,000}
$$

$$
= \frac{350}{1,000} = 0.35
$$

The general addition rule consists of taking the probability of *A* and adding it to the probability of *B* and then subtracting the probability of the joint event *A and B* from this total because the joint event has already been included in computing both the probability of *A* and the probability of *B*. For example, in Table 4.1 on page 171, if the outcomes of the event "planned to purchase" are added to those of the event "actually purchased," the joint event "planned to purchase *and* actually purchased" has been included in each of these simple events. Therefore, because this joint event has been included twice, you must subtract it to compute the correct result. Example 4.5 illustrates another application of the general addition rule.

EXAMPLE 4.5

Using the General Addition Rule for the Households That Purchased Large TVs

▶(*continued*)

In Example 4.3 on page 173, the purchases were cross-classified in Table 4.2 as televisions that had a faster refresh rate or televisions that had a standard refresh rate and whether the household purchased a streaming media player. Find the probability that among households that purchased a large TV, they purchased a television that had a faster refresh rate or purchased a streaming media player.

SOLUTION Using Equation (4.3),

$$P(\text{Television had a faster refresh rate}) = P(\text{Television had a faster refresh rate})$$
$$or \text{ purchased a streaming media player}) \quad + P(\text{purchased a streaming media player})$$
$$- P(\text{Television had a faster refresh rate } and$$
$$\text{purchased a streaming media player})$$

$$= \frac{80}{300} + \frac{108}{300} - \frac{38}{300}$$

$$= \frac{150}{300} = 0.50$$

Therefore, of households that purchased a large TV, there is a 50% chance that a randomly selected household purchased a television that had a faster refresh rate or purchased a streaming media player.

PROBLEMS FOR SECTION 4.1

LEARNING THE BASICS

4.1 Three coins are tossed.
a. Give an example of a simple event.
b. Give an example of a joint event.
c. What is the complement of a head on the first toss?
d. What does the sample space consist of?

4.2 An urn contains 12 red balls and 8 white balls. One ball is to be selected from the urn.
a. Give an example of a simple event.
b. What is the complement of a red ball?
c. What does the sample space consist of?

4.3 Consider the following contingency table:

	B	*B'*
A	10	20
A'	20	40

What is the probability of event
a. *A*?
b. *A'*?
c. *A and B*?
d. *A or B*?

4.4 Consider the following contingency table:

	B	*B'*
A	10	30
A'	25	35

What is the probability of event
a. *A'*?
b. *A and B*?
c. *A' and B'*?
d. *A' or B'*?

APPLYING THE CONCEPTS

4.5 For each of the following, indicate whether the type of probability involved is an example of *a priori* probability, empirical probability, or subjective probability.

a. The next toss of a fair coin will land on heads.
b. Italy will win soccer's World Cup the next time the competition is held.
c. The sum of the faces of two dice will be seven.
d. The train taking a commuter to work will be more than 10 minutes late.

4.6 For each of the following, state whether the events created are mutually exclusive and whether they are collectively exhaustive.
a. Undergraduate business students were asked whether they were sophomores or juniors.
b. Each respondent was classified by the type of car he or she drives: sedan, SUV, American, European, Asian, or none.
c. People were asked, "Do you currently live in (i) an apartment or (ii) a house?"
d. A product was classified as defective or not defective.

4.7 Which of the following events occur with a probability of zero? For each, state why or why not.
a. A company is listed on the New York Stock Exchange and NASDAQ.
b. A consumer owns a smartphone and a tablet.
c. A cellphone is an Apple and a Samsung.
d. An automobile is a Toyota and was manufactured in the United States.

4.8 Do Millennials or Gen-Xers feel more tense or stressed out at work? A survey of employed adults conducted online by Harris Interactive on behalf of the American Psychological Association revealed the following:

	FELT TENSE OR STRESSED OUT AT WORK	
AGE GROUP	Yes	No
Millennials	175	206
Gen-Xers	183	390

Source: Data extracted from "The 2016 Work and Well-Being Survey," American Psychological Association and Harris Interactive, March 2016, p. 45.

a. Give an example of a simple event.
b. Give an example of a joint event.

c. What is the complement of "Felt tense or stressed out at work"?

d. Why is "Male and felt tense or stressed out at work" a joint event?

4.9 Referring to the contingency table in Problem 4.8, if an employed adult is selected at random, what is the probability that

a. the employed adult felt tense or stressed out at work?

b. the employed adult was a millennial who felt tense or stressed out at work?

c. the employed adult was a millennial *or* felt tense or stressed out at work?

d. Explain the difference in the results in (b) and (c).

4.10 How will marketers change their social media use in the near future? A survey by Social Media Examiner reported that 76% of B2B marketers (marketers that focus primarily on attracting businesses) plan to increase their use of LinkedIn, as compared to 52% of B2C marketers (marketers that primarily target consumers). The survey was based on 1,780 B2B marketers and 3,306 B2C marketers. The following table summarizes the results:

INCREASE USE OF LINKEDIN?	BUSINESS FOCUS		
	B2B	**B2C**	**Total**
Yes	1,353	1,719	3,072
No	427	1,587	2,014
Total	1,780	3,306	5,086

Source: Data extracted from "2016 Social Media Marketing Industry Report," **socialmediaexaminer.com**.

a. Give an example of a simple event.

b. Give an example of a joint event.

c. What is the complement of a marketer who plans to increase use of LinkedIn?

d. Why is a marketer who plans to increase use of LinkedIn and is a B2C marketer a joint event?

4.11 Referring to the contingency table in Problem 4.10, if a marketer is selected at random, what is the probability that

a. he or she plans to increase use of LinkedIn?

b. he or she is a B2C marketer?

c. he or she plans to increase use of LinkedIn *or* is a B2C marketer?

d. Explain the difference in the results in (b) and (c).

✓ SELF TEST **4.12** Have the gains in student learning attributed to education technology justified colleges' spending in this area? As part of Inside Higher Ed's 2016 Survey of Faculty Attitudes on Technology, academic professionals, professors and technology leaders, were asked this question. The following table summarizes the responses:

JUSTIFIED?	ACADEMIC PROFESSIONAL		
	Professor	**Technology Leader**	**Total**
Yes	952	58	1,010
No	719	11	730
Total	1,671	69	1,740

Source: Data extracted from "The 2016 Insider Higher Ed Survey of Faculty Attitudes on Technology," **bit.ly/2pxRc65**

If an academic professional is selected at random, what is the probability that he or she

a. indicates gains in students' learning attributable to education technology have justified colleges' spending in this area?

b. is a technology leader?

c. indicates gains in students' learning attributable to education technology have justified colleges' spending in this area *or* is a technology leader?

d. Explain the difference in the results in (b) and (c).

4.13 Do Generation X and Boomers differ in how they use credit cards? A sample of 1,000 Generation X and 1,000 Boomers revealed the following results:

PAY FULL AMOUNT EACH MONTH	GENERATION		
	Generation X	**Boomers**	**Total**
Yes	440	630	1,070
No	560	370	930
Total	1,000	1,000	2,000

Source: Data extracted from "C. Jones, "Gen X, Boomers see Credit Cards as a Lifeline," *USA Today*, July 7, 2015, p. 1A.

If a respondent is selected at random, what is the probability that he or she

a. pays the full amount each month?

b. is a Generation X *and* pays the full amount each month?

c. is a Generation X *or* pays the full amount each month?

d. Explain the difference in the results of (b) and (c).

4.14 A survey of 1,520 Americans adults asked, "Do you feel overloaded with too much information?" The results indicated that of 785 males, 134 answered yes. Of 735 females, 170 answered yes.

Source: Data extracted from "Information Overload," **pewrsr.ch/2h2OSQP**.

Construct a contingency table to evaluate the probabilities. What is the probability that a respondent chosen at random

a. indicates that he/she feels overloaded with too much information?

b. is a female *and* indicates that he/she feels overloaded with too much information?

c. is a female *or* is a person who feels overloaded with too much information?

d. is a male *or* a female?

4.15 Each year, ratings are compiled concerning the performance of new cars during the first 90 days of use. Suppose that the cars have been categorized according to whether a car needs a warranty-related repair (yes or no) and the country in which the company manufacturing a car is based (United States or not United States). Based on the data collected, the probability that the new car needs a warranty repair is 0.04, the probability that the car was manufactured by a U.S.-based company is 0.60, and the probability that the new car needs a warranty repair *and* was manufactured by a U.S.-based company is 0.025.

Construct a contingency table to evaluate the probabilities of a warranty-related repair. What is the probability that a new car selected at random

a. needs a warranty repair?

b. needs a warranty repair *and* was manufactured by a U.S.-based company?

c. needs a warranty repair *or* was manufactured by a U.S.-based company?

d. needs a warranty repair *or* was not manufactured by a U.S.-based company?

4.2 Conditional Probability

Each example in Section 4.1 involves finding the probability of an event when sampling from the entire sample space. How do you determine the probability of an event if you know certain information about the events involved?

Computing Conditional Probabilities

Conditional probability refers to the probability of event A, given information about the occurrence of another event, B.

CONDITIONAL PROBABILITY

The probability of A given B is equal to the probability of A *and* B divided by the probability of B.

$$P(A|B) = \frac{P(A \text{ and } B)}{P(B)} \qquad (4.4a)$$

The probability of B given A is equal to the probability of A *and* B divided by the probability of A.

$$P(B|A) = \frac{P(A \text{ and } B)}{P(A)} \qquad (4.4b)$$

where

$$P(A \text{ and } B) = \text{joint probability of } A \text{ and } B$$
$$P(A) = \text{marginal probability of } A$$
$$P(B) = \text{marginal probability of } B$$

---

student TIP

The variable that is *given* goes in the denominator of Equation (4.4). Because you were given planned to purchase, planned to purchase is in the denominator.

Referring to the M&R Electronics World scenario involving the purchase of large TVs, suppose you were told that a household planned to purchase a large TV. Now, what is the probability that the household actually purchased the television?

In this example, the objective is to find $P(\text{Actually purchased}|\text{Planned to purchase})$. Here you are given the information that the household planned to purchase the large TV. Therefore, the sample space does not consist of all 1,000 households in the survey. It consists of only those households that planned to purchase the large TV. Of 250 such households, 200 actually purchased the large TV. Therefore, based on Table 4.1 on page 171, the probability that a household actually purchased the large TV given that they planned to purchase is

$$P(\text{Actually purchased}|\text{Planned to purchase}) = \frac{\text{Planned to purchase } and \text{ actually purchased}}{\text{Planned to purchase}}$$

$$= \frac{200}{250} = 0.80$$

You can also use Equation (4.4b) to compute this result:

$$P(B|A) = \frac{P(A \text{ and } B)}{P(A)}$$

where

$$A = \text{planned to purchase}$$
$$B = \text{actually purchased}$$

then

$$P(\text{Actually purchased}|\text{Planned to purchase}) = \frac{200/1,000}{250/1,000} = \frac{200}{250} = 0.80$$

Example 4.6 further illustrates conditional probability.

EXAMPLE 4.6

Finding the Conditional Probability of Purchasing a Streaming Media Player

Table 4.2 on page 173 is a contingency table for whether a household purchased a television with a faster refresh rate and whether the household purchased a streaming media player. If a household purchased a television with a faster refresh rate, what is the probability that it also purchased a streaming media player?

SOLUTION Because you know that the household purchased a television with a faster refresh rate, the sample space is reduced to 80 households. Of these 80 households, 38 also purchased a streaming media player. Therefore, the probability that a household purchased a streaming media player, given that the household purchased a television with a faster refresh rate, is

$$P(\text{Purchased streaming media player}\,|\,\text{Purchased television with faster refresh rate}) = \frac{\text{Number purchasing television with faster refresh rate } and \text{ streaming media player}}{\text{Number purchasing television with faster refresh rate}}$$

$$= \frac{38}{80} = 0.475$$

Using Equation (4.4b) on page 178 and the following definitions:

A = purchased a television with a faster refresh rate

B = purchased a streaming media player

then

$$P(B\,|\,A) = \frac{P(A \text{ and } B)}{P(A)} = \frac{38/300}{80/300} = 0.475$$

Therefore, given that the household purchased a television with a faster refresh rate, there is a 47.5% chance that the household also purchased a streaming media player. You can compare this conditional probability to the marginal probability of purchasing a streaming media player, which is $108/300 = 0.36$, or 36%. These results tell you that households that purchased televisions with a faster refresh rate are more likely to purchase a streaming media player than are households that purchased large TVs that have a standard refresh rate.

Decision Trees

In Table 4.1 on page 171, households are classified according to whether they planned to purchase and whether they actually purchased large TVs. A **decision tree** is an alternative to the contingency table. Figure 4.3 represents the decision tree for this example.

FIGURE 4.3
Decision tree for planned to purchase and actually purchased

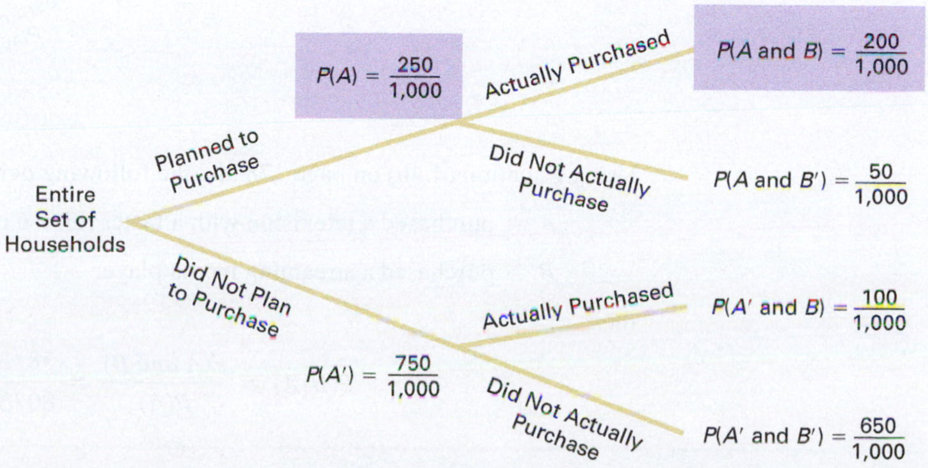

In Figure 4.3, beginning at the left with the entire set of households, there are two "branches" for whether or not the household planned to purchase a large TV. Each of these branches has two subbranches, corresponding to whether the household actually purchased or did not actually purchase the large TV. The probabilities at the end of the initial branches represent the marginal probabilities of A and A'. The probabilities at the end of each of the four subbranches represent the joint probability for each combination of events A and B. You compute the conditional probability by dividing the joint probability by the appropriate marginal probability.

For example, to compute the probability that the household actually purchased, given that the household planned to purchase the large TV, you take P(Planned to purchase *and* actually purchased) and divide by P(Planned to purchase). From Figure 4.3,

$$P(\text{Actually purchased} \mid \text{Planned to purchase}) = \frac{200/1,000}{250/1,000}$$

$$= \frac{200}{250} = 0.80$$

Example 4.7 illustrates how to construct a decision tree.

EXAMPLE 4.7

Constructing the Decision Tree for the Households That Purchased Large TVs

Using the cross-classified data in Table 4.2 on page 173, construct the decision tree. Use the decision tree to find the probability that a household purchased a streaming media player, given that the household purchased a television with a faster refresh rate.

SOLUTION The decision tree for purchased a streaming media player and a television with a faster refresh rate is displayed in Figure 4.4.

FIGURE 4.4
Decision tree for purchased a television with a faster refresh rate and a streaming media player

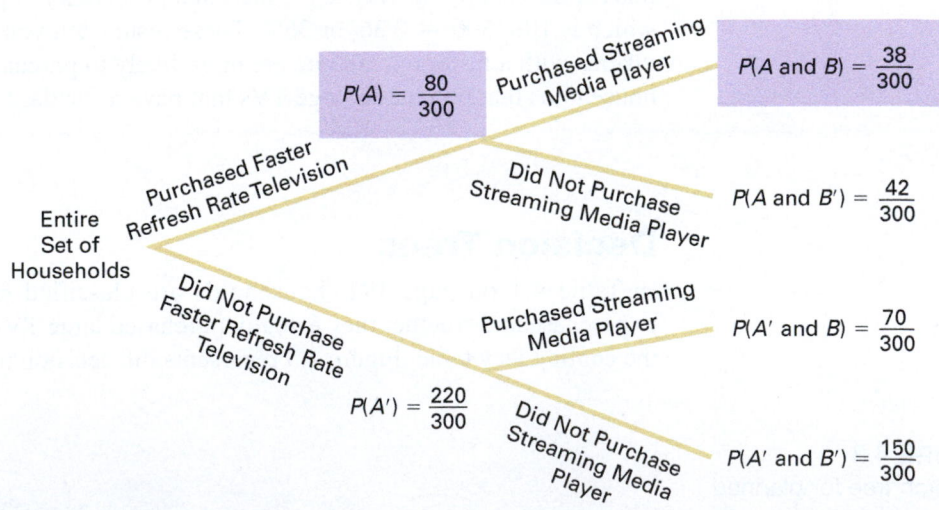

Using Equation (4.4b) on page 178 and the following definitions:

A = purchased a television with a faster refresh rate

B = purchased a streaming media player

then

$$P(B \mid A) = \frac{P(A \text{ and } B)}{P(A)} = \frac{38/300}{80/300} = 0.475$$

Independence

In the example concerning the purchase of large TVs, the conditional probability is $200/250 = 0.80$ that the selected household actually purchased the large TV, given that the household planned to purchase. The simple probability of selecting a household that actually purchased is $300/1,000 = 0.30$. This result shows that the prior knowledge that the household planned to purchase affected the probability that the household actually purchased the television. In other words, the outcome of one event is *dependent* on the outcome of a second event.

When the outcome of one event does *not* affect the probability of occurrence of another event, the events are said to be independent. **Independence** can be determined by using Equation (4.5).

INDEPENDENCE

Two events, A and B, are independent if and only if

$$P(A|B) = P(A) \qquad\qquad (4.5)$$

where

$$P(A|B) = \text{conditional probability of } A \text{ given } B$$
$$P(A) = \text{marginal probability of } A$$

Example 4.8 demonstrates the use of Equation (4.5).

EXAMPLE 4.8

Determining Independence

In the follow-up survey of the 300 households that actually purchased large TVs, the households were asked if they were satisfied with their purchases. Table 4.3 cross-classifies the responses to the satisfaction question with the responses to whether the television had a faster refresh rate.

TABLE 4.3
Satisfaction with Purchase of Large TVs

TELEVISION REFRESH RATE	SATISFIED WITH PURCHASE?		
	Yes	**No**	**Total**
Faster	64	16	80
Standard	176	44	220
Total	240	60	300

Determine whether being satisfied with the purchase and the refresh rate of the television purchased are independent.

SOLUTION For these data,

$$P(\text{Satisfied}\,|\,\text{Faster refresh rate}) = \frac{64/300}{80/300} = \frac{64}{80} = 0.80$$

which is equal to

$$P(\text{Satisfied}) = \frac{240}{300} = 0.80$$

Thus, being satisfied with the purchase and the refresh rate of the television purchased are independent. Knowledge of one event does not affect the probability of the other event.

Multiplication Rules

The **general multiplication rule** is derived using Equation (4.4a) on page 178:

$$P(A \mid B) = \frac{P(A \text{ and } B)}{P(B)}$$

and solving for the joint probability $P(A \text{ and } B)$.

GENERAL MULTIPLICATION RULE

The probability of A and B is equal to the probability of A given B times the probability of B.

$$P(A \text{ and } B) = P(A \mid B)P(B) \tag{4.6}$$

Example 4.9 demonstrates the use of the general multiplication rule.

EXAMPLE 4.9

Using the General Multiplication Rule

Consider the 80 households that purchased televisions that had a faster refresh rate. In Table 4.3 on page 181, you see that 64 households are satisfied with their purchase, and 16 households are dissatisfied. Suppose 2 households are randomly selected from the 80 households. Find the probability that both households are satisfied with their purchase.

SOLUTION Here you can use the multiplication rule in the following way. If

$$A = \text{second household selected is satisfied}$$

$$B = \text{first household selected is satisfied}$$

then, using Equation (4.6),

$$P(A \text{ and } B) = P(A \mid B)P(B)$$

The probability that the first household is satisfied with the purchase is 64/80. However, the probability that the second household is also satisfied with the purchase depends on the result of the first selection. If the first household is not returned to the sample after the satisfaction level is determined (i.e., sampling without replacement), the number of households remaining is 79. If the first household is satisfied, the probability that the second is also satisfied is 63/79 because 63 satisfied households remain in the sample. Therefore,

$$P(A \text{ and } B) = \left(\frac{63}{79}\right)\left(\frac{64}{80}\right) = 0.6380$$

There is a 63.80% chance that both of the households sampled will be satisfied with their purchase.

The **multiplication rule for independent events** is derived by substituting $P(A)$ for $P(A \mid B)$ in Equation (4.6).

MULTIPLICATION RULE FOR INDEPENDENT EVENTS

If A and B are independent, the probability of A and B is equal to the probability of A times the probability of B.

$$P(A \text{ and } B) = P(A)P(B) \tag{4.7}$$

If this rule holds for two events, A and B, then A and B are independent. Therefore, there are two ways to determine independence:

1. Events A and B are independent if, and only if, $P(A|B) = P(A)$.
2. Events A and B are independent if, and only if, $P(A \text{ and } B) = P(A)P(B)$.

Marginal Probability Using the General Multiplication Rule

In Section 4.1, marginal probability was defined using Equation (4.2) on page 174. You can state the equation for marginal probability by using the general multiplication rule. If

$$P(A) = P(A \text{ and } B_1) + P(A \text{ and } B_2) + \cdots + P(A \text{ and } B_k)$$

then, using the general multiplication rule, Equation (4.8) defines the marginal probability.

> MARGINAL PROBABILITY USING THE GENERAL MULTIPLICATION RULE
>
> $$P(A) = P(A|B_1)P(B_1) + P(A|B_2)P(B_2) + \cdots + P(A|B_k)P(B_k) \qquad (4.8)$$
>
> where $B_1, B_2, \ldots, B_k$ are k mutually exclusive and collectively exhaustive events.

To illustrate Equation (4.8), refer to Table 4.1 on page 171. Let

$$P(A) = \text{probability of planned to purchase}$$

$$P(B_1) = \text{probability of actually purchased}$$

$$P(B_2) = \text{probability of did not actually purchase}$$

Then, using Equation (4.8), the probability of planned to purchase is

$$P(A) = P(A|B_1)P(B_1) + P(A|B_2)P(B_2)$$

$$= \left(\frac{200}{300}\right)\left(\frac{300}{1,000}\right) + \left(\frac{50}{700}\right)\left(\frac{700}{1,000}\right)$$

$$= \frac{200}{1,000} + \frac{50}{1,000} = \frac{250}{1,000} = 0.25$$

PROBLEMS FOR SECTION 4.2

LEARNING THE BASICS

4.16 Consider the following contingency table:

	B	B'
A	10	20
A'	20	40

What is the probability of
a. $A|B$?
b. $A|B'$?
c. $A'|B'$?
d. Are events A and B independent?

4.17 Consider the following contingency table:

	B	B'
A	10	30
A'	25	35

What is the probability of
a. $A|B$?
b. $A'|B'$?
c. $A|B'$?
d. Are events A and B independent?

4.18 If $P(A \text{ and } B) = 0.4$ and $P(B) = 0.8$, find $P(A|B)$.

4.19 If $P(A) = 0.7$, $P(B) = 0.6$, and A and B are independent, find $P(A \text{ and } B)$.

4.20 If $P(A) = 0.3$, $P(B) = 0.4$, and $P(A \text{ and } B) = 0.2$, are A and B independent?

APPLYING THE CONCEPTS

4.21 Do Millennials or Gen-Xers feel more tense or stressed out at work? A survey of employed adults conducted online by Harris Interactive on behalf of the American Psychological Association revealed the following:

	FELT TENSE OR STRESSED OUT AT WORK	
AGE GROUP	**Yes**	**No**
Millennials	175	206
Gen-Xers	183	390

Source: Data extracted from "The 2016 Work and Well-Being Survey," American Psychological Association and Harris Interactive, March 2016, p. 45.

a. Given that the employed adult felt tense or stressed out at work, what is the probability that the employed adult was a millennial?
b. Given that the employed adult is a millennial, what is the probability that the person felt tense or stressed out at work?
c. Explain the difference in the results in (a) and (b).
d. Is feeling tense or stressed out at work and age group independent?

4.22 How will marketers change their social media use in the near future? A survey by Social Media Examiner of B2B marketers (marketers that focus primarily on attracting businesses) and B2C marketers (marketers that primarily target consumers) was based on 1,780 B2B marketers and 3,306 B2C marketers. The following table summarizes the results:

	BUSINESS FOCUS		
INCREASE USE OF LINKEDIN?	**B2B**	**B2C**	**Total**
Yes	1,353	1,719	3,072
No	427	1,587	2,014
Total	1,780	3,306	5,086

Source: Data extracted from "2016 Social Media Marketing Industry Report," **socialmediaexaminer.com**.

a. Suppose you know that the marketer is a B2B marketer. What is the probability that he or she plans to increase use of LinkedIn?
b. Suppose you know that the marketer is a B2C marketer. What is the probability that he or she plans to increase use of LinkedIn?
c. Are the two events, increase use of LinkedIn and business focus, independent? Explain.

4.23 Do Generation X and Boomers differ in how they use credit cards? A sample of 1,000 Generation X and 1,000 Boomers revealed the following results:

PAY FULL AMOUNT EACH MONTH	GENERATION		
	Generation X	**Boomers**	**Total**
Yes	440	630	1,070
No	560	370	930
Total	1,000	1,000	2,000

Source: Data extracted from C. Jones, "Gen X, Boomers see Credit Cards as a Lifeline," *USA Today*, July 7, 2015, p. 1A.

a. If a respondent selected is a member of Generation X, what is the probability that he or she pays the full amount each month?
b. If a respondent selected is a Boomer, what is the probability that he or she pays the full amount each month?
c. Is payment each month independent of generation?

SELF TEST **4.24** Have the gains in student learning attributed to education technology justified colleges' spending in this area? As part of Inside Higher Ed's 2016 Survey of Faculty Attitudes on Technology, professors, and technology leaders, were asked this question. The following table summarizes the responses:

	ACADEMIC PROFESSIONAL		
JUSTIFIED?	**Professor**	**Technology Leader**	**Total**
Yes	952	58	1,010
No	719	11	730
Total	1,671	69	1,740

Source: Data extracted from "The 2016 Insider Higher Ed Survey of Faculty Attitudes on Technology," **bit.ly/2pxRc65**.

a. Given that an academic professional is a professor, what is the probability that the professional indicates gains in students' learning attributable to education technology have justified colleges' spending in this area?
b. Given that an academic professional is a professor, what is the probability that the professor does not indicate gains in students' learning attributable to education technology have justified colleges' spending in this area?
c. Given that an academic professional is a technology leader, what is the probability that the professor indicates gains in students' learning attributable to education technology have justified colleges' spending in this area?
d. Given that an academic professional is a technology leader, what is the probability that the professional does not indicate gains in students' learning attributable to education technology have justified colleges' spending in this area?

4.25 A survey of 1,520 Americans adults asked "Do you feel overloaded with too much information?" The results indicated that of 785 males, 134 answered yes. Of 735 females, 170 answered yes.

Source: Data extracted from "Information Overload," **pewrsr.ch/2h2OSQP**.

a. Suppose that the respondent chosen is a female. What is the probability that she felt overloaded with too much information?

b. Suppose that the respondent chosen does indicate that he/she feels overloaded with too much information. What is the probability that the individual is a male?

c. Are overload with too much information and the gender of the individual independent? Explain.

4.26 Each year, ratings are compiled concerning the performance of new cars during the first 90 days of use. Suppose that the cars have been categorized according to whether a car needs warranty-related repair (yes or no) and the country in which the company manufacturing a car is based (United States or not United States). Based on the data collected, the probability that the new car needs a warranty repair is 0.04, the probability that the car is manufactured by a U.S.-based company is 0.60, and the probability that the new car needs a warranty repair *and* was manufactured by a U.S.-based company is 0.025.

a. Suppose you know that a company based in the United States manufactured a particular car. What is the probability that the car needs a warranty repair?

b. Suppose you know that a company based in the United States did not manufacture a particular car. What is the probability that the car needs a warranty repair?

c. Are need for a warranty repair and location of the company manufacturing the car independent?

4.27 In 42 of the 66 years from 1950 through 2016 (in 2011 there was virtually no change), the S&P 500 finished higher after the first five days of trading. In 37 out of 42 years, the S&P 500 finished higher for the year. Is a good first week a good omen for the upcoming year? The following table gives the first-week and annual performance over this 66-year period:

FIRST WEEK	S&P 500'S ANNUAL PERFORMANCE	
	Higher	Lower
Higher	37	5
Lower	12	12

a. If a year is selected at random, what is the probability that the S&P 500 finished higher for the year?

b. Given that the S&P 500 finished higher after the first five days of trading, what is the probability that it finished higher for the year?

c. Are the two events "first-week performance" and "annual performance" independent? Explain.

d. Look up the performance after the first five days of 2017 and the 2017 annual performance of the S&P 500 at **finance.yahoo.com**. Comment on the results.

4.28 A standard deck of cards is being used to play a game. There are four suits (hearts, diamonds, clubs, and spades), each having 13 faces (ace, 2, 3, 4, 5, 6, 7, 8, 9, 10, jack, queen, and king), making a total of 52 cards. This complete deck is thoroughly mixed, and you will receive the first 2 cards from the deck, without replacement (the first card is not returned to the deck after it is selected).

a. What is the probability that both cards are queens?

b. What is the probability that the first card is a 10 and the second card is a 5 or 6?

c. If you were sampling with replacement (the first card is returned to the deck after it is selected), what would be the answer in (a)?

d. In the game of blackjack, the face cards (jack, queen, king) count as 10 points, and the ace counts as either 1 or 11 points. All other cards are counted at their face value. Blackjack is achieved if 2 cards total 21 points. What is the probability of getting blackjack in this problem?

4.29 A box of nine iPhone 7 cellphones contains two red cellphones and seven black cellphones.

a. If two cellphones are randomly selected from the box, without replacement (the first cellphone is not returned to the box after it is selected), what is the probability that both cellphones selected will be red?

b. If two cellphones are randomly selected from the box, without replacement (the first cellphone is not returned to the box after it is selected), what is the probability that there will be one red cellphone and one black cellphone selected?

c. If three cellphones are selected, with replacement (the cellphones are returned to the box after they are selected), what is the probability that all three will be red?

d. If you were sampling with replacement (the first cellphone is returned to the box after it is selected), what would be the answers to (a) and (b)?

4.3 Ethical Issues and Probability

Ethical issues can arise when any statements related to probability are presented to the public, particularly when these statements are part of an advertising campaign for a product or service. Unfortunately, many people are not comfortable with numerical concepts (see reference 5) and tend to misinterpret the meaning of the probability. In some instances, the misinterpretation is not intentional, but in other cases, advertisements may unethically try to mislead potential customers.

One example of a potentially unethical application of probability relates to advertisements for state lotteries. When purchasing a lottery ticket, the customer selects a set of numbers (such as 6) from a larger list of numbers (such as 54). Although virtually all participants know that they are unlikely to win the lottery, they also have very little idea of how unlikely it is for them to select all 6 winning numbers from the list of 54 numbers. They have even less of an idea of the probability of not selecting any winning numbers.

Given this background, you might consider a recent commercial for a state lottery that stated, "We won't stop until we have made everyone a millionaire" to be deceptive and possibly unethical. Do you think the state has any intention of ever stopping the lottery, given the fact that the state relies on it to bring millions of dollars into its treasury? Is it possible that the lottery can make everyone a millionaire? Is it ethical to suggest that the purpose of the lottery is to make everyone a millionaire?

Another example of a potentially unethical application of probability relates to an investment newsletter promising a 90% probability of a 20% annual return on investment. To make the claim in the newsletter an ethical one, the investment service needs to (a) explain the basis on which this probability estimate rests, (b) provide the probability statement in another format, such as 9 chances in 10, and (c) explain what happens to the investment in the 10% of the cases in which a 20% return is not achieved (e.g., is the entire investment lost?).

These are serious ethical issues. If you were going to write an advertisement for the state lottery that ethically describes the probability of winning a certain prize, what would you say? If you were going to write an advertisement for the investment newsletter that ethically states the probability of a 20% return on an investment, what would you say?

4.4 Bayes' Theorem

Developed by Thomas Bayes in the eighteenth century (see references 1, 2, 3, and 6), **Bayes' theorem** is an extension of what you previously learned about conditional probability. Bayes' theorem revises previously calculated probabilities using additional information and forms the basis for Bayesian analysis.

In recent years, Bayesian analysis has gained new prominence for its application to and in analyzing big data using predictive analytics that Chapter 17 discusses. However, Bayesian analysis does not require big data and can be used in a variety of problems to better determine the *revised probability* of certain events. The *Consider This* feature in this section explores an application of Bayes' theorem that many use every day.

Certain types of marketing decisions represent one type of example in which Bayes' theorem can be applied. Consider a scenario in which an electronics manufacturer is considering marketing a new model of television. In the past, 40% of the new-model televisions have been successful, and 60% have been unsuccessful. Before introducing the new-model television, the marketing research department conducts an extensive study and releases a report, either favorable or unfavorable. In the past, 80% of the successful new-model television(s) had received favorable market research reports, and 30% of the unsuccessful new-model television(s) had received favorable reports. For the new model of television under consideration, the marketing research department has issued a favorable report. What is the probability that the television will be successful?

Bayes' theorem is developed from the definition of conditional probability. To find the conditional probability of B given A, consider Equation (4.4b):

$$P(B|A) = \frac{P(A \text{ and } B)}{P(A)} = \frac{P(A|B)P(B)}{P(A)}$$

Bayes' theorem is derived by substituting Equation (4.8) on page 183 for $P(A)$ in the denominator of Equation (4.4b).

BAYES' THEOREM

$$P(B_i|A) = \frac{P(A|B_i)P(B_i)}{P(A|B_1)P(B_1) + P(A|B_2)P(B_2) + \cdots + P(A|B_k)P(B_k)} \tag{4.9}$$

where B_i is the ith event out of k mutually exclusive and collectively exhaustive events.

To use Equation (4.9) for the television-marketing example, let

event S = successful television   event F = favorable report

event S' = unsuccessful television   event F' = unfavorable report and

$$P(S) = 0.40 \quad P(F|S) = 0.80$$
$$P(S') = 0.60 \quad P(F|S') = 0.30$$

Then, using Equation (4.9),

$$
\begin{aligned}
P(S|F) &= \frac{P(F|S)P(S)}{P(F|S)P(S) + P(F|S')P(S')} \\[2mm]
&= \frac{(0.80)(0.40)}{(0.80)(0.40) + (0.30)(0.60)} \\[2mm]
&= \frac{0.32}{0.32 + 0.18} = \frac{0.32}{0.50} \\[2mm]
&= 0.64
\end{aligned}
$$

The probability of a successful television, given that a favorable report was received, is 0.64. Thus, the probability of an unsuccessful television, given that a favorable report was received, is $1 - 0.64 = 0.36$.

Table 4.4 summarizes the computation of the probabilities, and Figure 4.5 presents the decision tree.

TABLE 4.4

Bayes' Theorem Computations for the Television-Marketing Example

Event S_i		Prior Probability $P(S_i)$	Conditional Probability $P(F|S_i)$	Joint Probability $P(F|S_i)P(S_i)$	Revised Probability $P(S_i|F)$
S =	successful television	0.40	0.80	0.32	$P(S|F) = 0.32/0.50$ = 0.64
S' =	unsuccessful television	0.60	0.30	0.18 0.50	$P(S'F) = 0.18/0.50$ = 0.36

FIGURE 4.5

Decision tree for marketing a new television

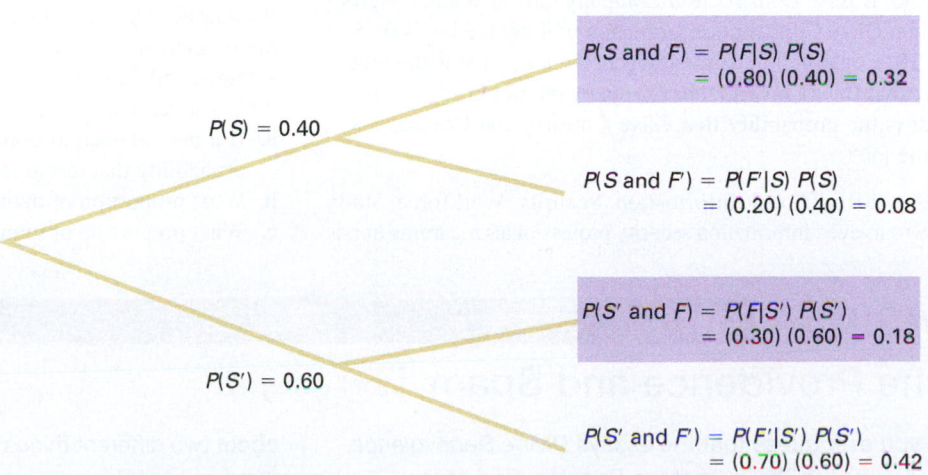

$P(S \text{ and } F) = P(F|S)\,P(S)$
$= (0.80)\,(0.40) = 0.32$

$P(S) = 0.40$

$P(S \text{ and } F') = P(F'|S)\,P(S)$
$= (0.20)\,(0.40) = 0.08$

$P(S' \text{ and } F) = P(F|S')\,P(S')$
$= (0.30)\,(0.60) = 0.18$

$P(S') = 0.60$

$P(S' \text{ and } F') = P(F'|S')\,P(S')$
$= (0.70)\,(0.60) = 0.42$

The SHORT TAKES for Chapter 4 includes Example 4.10 that applies Bayes' theorem to a medical diagnosis problem.

PROBLEMS FOR SECTION 4.4

LEARNING THE BASICS

4.30 If $P(B) = 0.05$, $P(A|B) = 0.80$, $P(B') = 0.95$, and $P(A|B') = 0.40$, find $P(B|A)$.

4.31 If $P(B) = 0.30$, $P(A|B) = 0.60$, $P(B') = 0.70$, and $P(A|B') = 0.50$, find $P(B|A)$.

APPLYING THE CONCEPTS

4.32 In Example 4.10, suppose that the probability that a medical diagnostic test will give a positive result if the disease is not present is reduced from 0.02 to 0.01.
a. If the medical diagnostic test has given a positive result (indicating that the disease is present), what is the probability that the disease is actually present?
b. If the medical diagnostic test has given a negative result (indicating that the disease is not present), what is the probability that the disease is not present?

4.33 Big Commerce launched a study to analyze modern, omni-channel consumer behavior. The data uncovers the details on how, when, where, and why Americans buy, educating the entire commerce industry on today's consumer shopping preferences. Findings indicate that 23% of online shoppers shop online while in the office. Of those who shop online while in the office, 57% are male. Of those who do not shop online while in the office, 48% are male.
a. Find the probability that if the online shopper is a male, the online shopper shops while in the office.
b. Find the probability that the online shopper is a male.

4.34 Olive Construction Company is determining whether it should submit a bid for a new shopping center. In the past, Olive's main competitor, Base Construction Company, has submitted bids 70% of the time. If Base Construction Company does not bid on a job, the probability that Olive Construction Company will get the job is 0.50. If Base Construction Company bids on a job, the probability that Olive Construction Company will get the job is 0.25.
a. If Olive Construction Company gets the job, what is the probability that Base Construction Company did not bid?
b. What is the probability that Olive Construction Company will get the job?

4.35 The 2016 Global Information Security Workforce Study (GISWS) surveyed information security professionals regarding trends and issues affecting their profession and careers. In the study, women were asked about their impact on the security posture of their organization. Twenty-eight percent of women indicated that their opinions are not valued. When comparing women who did not feel valued and women who did feel valued, the most substantial difference concerned training and leadership programs. Forty-seven percent of women that feel undervalued say their organization does not provide adequate training and leadership development resources, whereas 61% of women who do feel valued in their position indicate that their organization does provide adequate training and leadership development resources.

If a woman is selected at random and that woman indicates that her organization does not provide adequate training and leadership development resources, what is the probability that this woman feels undervalued?

4.36 The editor of a textbook publishing company is trying to decide whether to publish a proposed business statistics textbook. Information on previous textbooks published indicates that 10% are huge successes, 20% are modest successes, 40% break-even, and 30% are losers. However, before a publishing decision is made, the book will be reviewed. In the past, 99% of the huge successes received favorable reviews, 70% of the moderate successes received favorable reviews, 40% of the break-even books received favorable reviews, and 20% of the losers received favorable reviews.
a. If the proposed textbook receives a favorable review, how should the editor revise the probabilities of the various outcomes to take this information into account?
b. What proportion of textbooks receive favorable reviews?

4.37 A municipal bond service has three rating categories (A, B, and C). Suppose that in the past year, of the municipal bonds issued throughout the United States, 70% were rated A, 20% were rated B, and 10% were rated C. Of the municipal bonds rated A, 50% were issued by cities, 40% by suburbs, and 10% by rural areas. Of the municipal bonds rated B, 60% were issued by cities, 20% by suburbs, and 20% by rural areas. Of the municipal bonds rated C, 90% were issued by cities, 5% by suburbs, and 5% by rural areas.
a. If a new municipal bond is to be issued by a city, what is the probability that it will receive an A rating?
b. What proportion of municipal bonds are issued by cities?
c. What proportion of municipal bonds are issued by suburbs?

CONSIDER THIS

Divine Providence and Spam

Would you ever guess that the essays *Divine Benevolence: Or, An Attempt to Prove That the Principal End of the Divine Providence and Government Is the Happiness of His Creatures* and *An Essay Towards Solving a Problem in the Doctrine of Chances* were written by the same person? Probably not, and in doing so, you illustrate a modern-day application of Bayesian statistics: spam, or junk mail filters.

In not guessing correctly, you probably looked at the words in the titles of the essays and concluded that they were talking about two different things. An implicit rule you used was that word frequencies vary by subject matter. A statistics essay would very likely contain the word *statistics* as well as words such as *chance*, *problem*, and *solving*. An eighteenth-century essay about theology and religion would be more likely to contain the uppercase forms of *Divine* and *Providence*.

Likewise, there are words you would guess to be very unlikely to appear in either book, such as technical terms from finance, and words that are most likely to appear in both—common words such as *a*, *and*, and *the*. That words would be either likely or unlikely suggests an application of probability theory. Of course, likely and unlikely are fuzzy concepts, and we might occasionally misclassify an essay if we kept things too simple, such as relying solely on the occurrence of the words *Divine* and *Providence*.

For example, a profile of the late Harris Milstead, better known as *Divine*, the star of *Hairspray* and other films, visiting Providence (Rhode Island), would most certainly not be an essay about theology. But if we widened the number of words we examined and found such words as movie or the name John Waters (Divine's director in many films), we probably would quickly realize the essay had something to do with twentieth-century cinema and little to do with theology and religion.

We can use a similar process to try to classify a new email message in your in-box as either spam or a legitimate message (called "ham," in this context). We would first need to add to your email program a "spam filter" that has the ability to track word frequencies associated with spam and ham messages as you identify them on a day-to-day basis. This would allow the filter to constantly update the prior probabilities necessary to use Bayes' theorem. With these probabilities, the filter can ask, "What is the probability that an email is spam, given the presence of a certain word?"

Applying the terms of Equation (4.9), such a Bayesian spam filter would multiply the probability of finding the word in a spam email, $P(A|B)$, by the probability that the email is spam, $P(B)$, and then divide by the probability of finding the word in an email, the denominator in Equation (4.9). Bayesian spam filters also use shortcuts by focusing on a small set of words that have a high probability of being found in a spam message as well as on a small set of other words that have a low probability of being found in a spam message.

As spammers (people who send junk email) learned of such new filters, they tried to outfox them. Having learned that Bayesian filters might be assigning a high $P(A|B)$ value to words commonly found in spam, such as Viagra, spammers thought they could fool the filter by misspelling the word as Vi@gr@ or V1agra. What they overlooked was that the misspelled variants were even more likely to be found in a spam message than the original word. Thus, the misspelled variants made the job of spotting spam easier for the Bayesian filters.

Other spammers tried to fool the filters by adding "good" words, words that would have a low probability of being found in a spam message, or "rare" words, words not frequently encountered in any message. But these spammers overlooked the fact that the conditional probabilities are constantly updated and that words once considered "good" would be soon discarded from the good list by the filter as their $P(A|B)$, value increased. Likewise, as "rare" words grew more common in spam and yet stayed rare in ham, such words acted like the misspelled variants that others had tried earlier.

Even then, and perhaps after reading about Bayesian statistics, spammers thought that they could "break" Bayesian filters by inserting random words in their messages. Those random words would affect the filter by causing it to see many words whose $P(A|B)$, value would be low. The Bayesian filter would begin to label many spam messages as ham and end up being of no practical use. Spammers again overlooked that conditional probabilities are constantly updated.

Other spammers decided to eliminate all or most of the words in their messages and replace them with graphics so that Bayesian filters would have very few words with which to form conditional probabilities. But this approach failed, too, as Bayesian filters were rewritten to consider things other than words in a message. After all, Bayes' theorem concerns events, and "graphics present with no text" is as valid an event as "some word, *X*, present in a message." Other future tricks will ultimately fail for the same reason. (By the way, spam filters use non-Bayesian techniques as well, which makes spammers' lives even more difficult.)

Bayesian spam filters are an example of the unexpected way that applications of statistics can show up in your daily life. You will discover more examples as you read the rest of this book. By the way, the author of the two essays mentioned earlier was Thomas Bayes, who is a lot more famous for the second essay than the first essay, a failed attempt to use mathematics and logic to prove the existence of God.

4.5 Counting Rules

In many cases, there are a large number of possible outcomes and determining the exact number of outcomes can be difficult. In these situations, rules have been developed for counting the exact number of possible outcomes. This section presents five such **counting rules**.

Counting Rule 1   Counting rule 1 determines the number of possible outcomes for a set of mutually exclusive and collectively exhaustive events.

COUNTING RULE 1

If any one of k different mutually exclusive and collectively exhaustive events can occur on each of n trials, the number of possible outcomes is equal to

$$k^n \tag{4.10}$$

For example, using Equation (4.10), the number of different possible outcomes from tossing a two-sided coin five times is $2^5 = 2 \times 2 \times 2 \times 2 \times 2 = 32$.

EXAMPLE 4.11

Rolling a Die Twice

Suppose you roll a die twice. How many different possible outcomes can occur?

SOLUTION If a six-sided die is rolled twice, using Equation (4.10), the number of different outcomes is $6^2 = 36$.

Counting Rule 2   The second counting rule is a more general version of the first counting rule and allows the number of possible events to differ from trial to trial.

COUNTING RULE 2

If there are k_1 events on the first trial, k_2 events on the second trial, . . . , and k_n events on the nth trial, then the number of possible outcomes is

$$(k_1)(k_2)\ldots(k_n) \tag{4.11}$$

For example, a state motor vehicle department would like to know how many license plate numbers are available if a license plate number consists of three letters followed by three numbers (0 through 9). Using Equation (4.11), if a license plate number consists of three letters followed by three numbers, the total number of possible outcomes is $(26)(26)(26)(10)(10)(10) = 17,576,000$.

EXAMPLE 4.12

Determining the Number of Different Dinners

A restaurant menu has a price-fixed complete dinner that consists of an appetizer, an entrée, a beverage, and a dessert. You have a choice of 5 appetizers, 10 entrées, 3 beverages, and 6 desserts. Determine the total number of possible dinners.

SOLUTION Using Equation (4.11), the total number of possible dinners is $(5)(10)(3)(6) = 900$.

Counting Rule 3   The third counting rule involves computing the number of ways that a set of items can be arranged in order.

COUNTING RULE 3

The number of ways that all n items can be arranged in order is

$$n! = (n)(n - 1)\ldots(1) \tag{4.12}$$

where $n!$ is called n factorial, and $0!$ is defined as 1.

EXAMPLE 4.13

Using Counting Rule 3

If a set of six books is to be placed on a shelf, in how many ways can the six books be arranged?

SOLUTION To begin, you must realize that any of the six books could occupy the first position on the shelf. Once the first position is filled, there are five books to choose from in filling the second position. You continue this assignment procedure until all the positions are occupied. The number of ways that you can arrange six books is

$$n! = 6! = (6)(5)(4)(3)(2)(1) = 720$$

Counting Rule 4 In many instances you need to know the number of ways in which a subset of an entire group of items can be arranged in *order*. Each possible arrangement is called a **permutation**.

student TIP

Both permutations and combinations assume that you are sampling without replacement.

[1]On many scientific calculators, there is a button labeled nPr that allows you to compute permutations. The symbol *r* is used instead of *x*.

COUNTING RULE 4: PERMUTATIONS

The number of ways of arranging x objects selected from n objects in order is

$$_nP_x = \frac{n!}{(n-x)!} \qquad (4.13)$$

where

n = total number of objects

x = number of objects to be arranged

$n!$ = n factorial = $n(n) - 1) \ldots (1)$

P = symbol for permutations[1]

EXAMPLE 4.14

Using Counting Rule 4

Modifying Example 4.13, if you have six books, but there is room for only four books on the shelf, in how many ways can you arrange these books on the shelf?

SOLUTION Using Equation (4.13), the number of ordered arrangements of four books selected from six books is equal to

$$_nP_x = \frac{n!}{(n-x)!} = \frac{6!}{(6-4)!} = \frac{(6)(5)(4)(3)(2)(1)}{(2)(1)} = 360$$

Counting Rule 5 In many situations, you are not interested in the *order* of the outcomes but only in the number of ways that x items can be selected from n items, *irrespective of order*. Each possible selection is called a **combination**.

COUNTING RULE 5: COMBINATIONS

The number of ways of selecting x objects from n objects, irrespective of order, is equal to

$$_nC_x = \frac{n!}{x!(n-x)!} \qquad (4.14)$$

where

n = total number of objects

x = number of objects to be arranged

$n!$ = n factorial = $n(n-1) \ldots (1)$

C = symbol for combinations[2]

[2]On many scientific calculators, there is a button labeled nCr that allows you to compute combinations. The symbol *r* is used instead of *x*.

If you compare this rule to counting rule 4, you see that it differs only in the inclusion of a term $x!$ in the denominator. When permutations were used, all of the arrangements of the x objects are distinguishable. With combinations, the $x!$ possible arrangements of objects are irrelevant.

EXAMPLE 4.15

Using Counting Rule 5

Modifying Example 4.14, if the order of the books on the shelf is irrelevant, in how many ways can you arrange these books on the shelf?

SOLUTION Using Equation (4.14), the number of combinations of four books selected from six books is equal to

$$_nC_x = \frac{n!}{x!(n-x)!} = \frac{6!}{4!(6-4)!} = \frac{(6)(5)(4)(3)(2)(1)}{(4)(3)(2)(1)(2)(1)} = 15$$

PROBLEMS FOR SECTION 4.5

APPLYING THE CONCEPTS

4.38 If there are 10 multiple-choice questions on an exam, each having three possible answers, how many different sequences of answers are there?

4.39 A lock on a bank vault consists of three dials, each with 30 positions. In order for the vault to open, each of the three dials must be in the correct position.
a. How many different possible dial combinations are there for this lock?
b. What is the probability that if you randomly select a position on each dial, you will be able to open the bank vault?
c. Explain why "dial combinations" are not mathematical combinations expressed by Equation (4.14).

4.40 a. If a coin is tossed seven times, how many different outcomes are possible?
b. If a die is tossed seven times, how many different outcomes are possible?
c. Discuss the differences in your answers to (a) and (b).

4.41 A particular brand of women's jeans is available in seven different sizes, three different colors, and three different styles. How many different women's jeans does the store manager need to order to have one pair of each type?

4.42 You would like to "build-your-own-burger" at a fast-food restaurant. There are five different breads, seven different cheeses, four different cold toppings, and five different sauces on the menu. If you want to include one choice from each of these ingredient categories, how many different burgers can you build?

4.43 A team is being formed that includes four different people. There are four different positions on the teams. How many different ways are there to assign the four people to the four positions?

4.44 In the National Basketball League there are five teams in the Pacific Division: Golden State, Los Angeles Clippers, Los Angeles Lakers, Phoenix, and Sacramento. How many different orders of finish are there for these five teams? (Assume that there are no ties in the standings.) Do you believe that all these orders are equally likely? Discuss.

4.45 Referring to Problem 4.44 how many different orders of finish are possible for the first four positions?

4.46 A gardener has six rows available in his vegetable garden to place tomatoes, eggplant, peppers, cucumbers, beans, and lettuce. Each vegetable will be allowed one and only one row. How many ways are there to position these vegetables in this garden?

4.47 How many different ways can a senior project manager and an associate project manager be selected for an analytics project if there are eight data scientists available?

4.48 Four members of a group of 10 people are to be selected to a team. How many ways are there to select these four members?

4.49 A student has seven books that she would like to place in her backpack. However, there is room for only four books. Regardless of the arrangement, how many ways are there of placing four books into the backpack?

4.50 A daily lottery is conducted in which 2 winning numbers are selected out of 100 numbers. How many different combinations of winning numbers are possible?

4.51 There are 15 exercise bikes in a fitness store showroom. The fitness store owner wishes to select three of them to display at a fitness expo. How many ways can a group of three be selected?

▼USING **STATISTICS**
Possibilities at M&R Electronics World, Revisited

As the marketing manager for M&R Electronics World, you analyzed the survey results of an intent-to-purchase study. This study asked the heads of 1,000 households about their intentions to purchase a large TV sometime during the next 12 months, and as a follow-up, M&R surveyed the same people 12 months later to see whether such a television was purchased. In addition, for households purchasing large TVs, the survey asked whether the television they purchased had a faster refresh rate, whether they also purchased a streaming media player in the past 12 months, and whether they were satisfied with their purchase of the large TV.

By analyzing the results of these surveys, you were able to uncover many pieces of valuable information that will help you plan a marketing strategy to enhance sales and better target those households likely to purchase multiple or more expensive products. Whereas only 30% of the households actually purchased a large TV, if a household indicated that it planned to purchase a large TV in the next 12 months, there was an 80% chance that the household actually made the purchase. Thus the marketing strategy should target those households that have indicated an intention to purchase.

You determined that for households that purchased a television that had a faster refresh rate, there was a 47.5% chance that the household also purchased a streaming media player. You then compared this conditional probability to the marginal probability of purchasing a streaming media player, which was 36%. Thus, households that purchased televisions that had a faster refresh rate are more likely to purchase a streaming media player than are households that purchased large TVs that have a standard refresh rate.

▼ SUMMARY

This chapter began by developing the basic concepts of probability. You learned that probability is a numeric value from 0 to 1 that represents the chance, likelihood, or possibility that a particular event will occur. In addition to simple probability, you learned about conditional probabilities and independent events. Throughout the chapter, you gained experience using contingency tables and decision trees to summarize and present probability information. You also learned about several counting rules helpful to determine the total number of possible outcomes for problems with many outcomes.

▼ REFERENCES

1. Anderson-Cook, C. M. "Unraveling Bayes' Theorem." *Quality Progress*, March 2014, p. 52–54.
2. Bellhouse, D. R. "The Reverend Thomas Bayes, FRS: A Biography to Celebrate the Tercentenary of His Birth." *Statistical Science*, 19 (2004), 3–43.
3. Hooper, W. "Probing Probabilities." *Quality Progress*, March 2014, pp. 18–22.
4. Lowd, D., and C. Meek. "Good Word Attacks on Statistical Spam Filters." Presented at the Second Conference on Email and Anti-Spam, 2005.
5. Paulos, J. A. *Innumeracy*. New York: Hill and Wang, 1988.
6. Silberman, S. "The Quest for Meaning," *Wired 8.02*, February 2000.
7. Zeller, T. "The Fight Against V1@gra (and Other Spam)." *The New York Times*, May 21, 2006, pp. B1, B6.

▼ KEY EQUATIONS

Probability of Occurrence

$$\text{Probability of occurrence} = \frac{X}{T} \tag{4.1}$$

Marginal Probability

$$P(A) = P(A \text{ and } B_1) + P(A \text{ and } B_2)$$
$$+ \cdots + P(A \text{ and } B_k) \tag{4.2}$$

General Addition Rule

$$P(A \text{ or } B) = P(A) + P(B) - P(A \text{ and } B) \tag{4.3}$$

Conditional Probability

$$P(A|B) = \frac{P(A \text{ and } B)}{P(B)} \tag{4.4a}$$

$$P(B|A) = \frac{P(A \text{ and } B)}{P(A)} \tag{4.4b}$$

Independence

$$P(A|B) = P(A) \tag{4.5}$$

General Multiplication Rule

$$P(A \text{ and } B) = P(A|B)P(B) \tag{4.6}$$

Multiplication Rule for Independent Events

$$P(A \text{ and } B) = P(A)P(B) \tag{4.7}$$

Marginal Probability Using the General Multiplication Rule

$$P(A) = P(A|B_1)P(B_1) + P(A|B_2)P(B_2)$$
$$+ \cdots + P(A|B_k)P(B_k) \tag{4.8}$$

Bayes' Theorem

$$P(B_i|A) =$$
$$\frac{P(A|B_i)P(B_i)}{P(A|B_1)P(B_1) + P(A|B_2)P(B_2) + \cdots + P(A|B_k)P(B_k)} \tag{4.9}$$

Counting Rule 1

$$k^n \tag{4.10}$$

Counting Rule 2

$$(k_1)(k_2)\ldots(k_n) \tag{4.11}$$

Counting Rule 3

$$n! = (n)(n-1)\ldots(1) \tag{4.12}$$

Counting Rule 4: Permutations

$$_nP_x = \frac{n!}{(n-x)!} \tag{4.13}$$

Counting Rule 5: Combinations

$$_nC_x = \frac{n!}{x!(n-x)!} \tag{4.14}$$

▼ KEY TERMS

a priori probability   170
Bayes' theorem   186
certain event   170
collectively exhaustive   170
combination   191
complement   170
conditional probability   171
counting rules   189
decision tree   179
empirical probability   170

event   169
general addition rule   175
general multiplication rule   182
impossible event   170
independence   181
joint event   169
joint probability   173
marginal probability   174
multiplication rule for independent
   events   182

mutually exclusive   170
outcomes   169
permutation   191
probability   169
sample space   169
simple event   169
simple probability   172
subjective probability   171
Venn diagram   171

▼ CHECKING YOUR UNDERSTANDING

4.52 What are the differences between *a priori* probability, empirical probability, and subjective probability?

4.53 What is the difference between a simple event and a joint event?

4.54 How can you use the general addition rule to find the probability of occurrence of event *A* or *B*?

4.55 What is the difference between mutually exclusive events and collectively exhaustive events?

4.56 How does conditional probability relate to the concept of independence?

4.57 How does the multiplication rule differ for events that are and are not independent?

4.58 How can you use Bayes' theorem in light of new information?

4.59 In Bayes' theorem, how does the prior probability differ from the revised probability?

4.60 What is the difference between Counting Rule 1 and Counting Rule 2?

4.61 What is the difference between a permutation and a combination?

▼ CHAPTER REVIEW PROBLEMS

4.62 A survey by Accenture indicated that 64% of millennials as compared to 28% of baby boomers prefer "hybrid" investment advice—a combination of traditional advisory services and low-cost digital tools—over either a dedicated human advisor or conventional robo-advisory services (computer-generated advice and services without human advisors) alone.

Source: Data extracted from Business Wire, "Majority of Wealthy Investors Prefer a Mix of Human and Robo-Advice, According to Accenture Research," **/bit.ly/2qZY9Ou**.

Suppose that the survey was based on 500 respondents from each of the two generation groups.
a. Construct a contingency table.
b. Give an example of a simple event and a joint event.
c. What is the probability that a randomly selected respondent prefers hybrid investment advice?
d. What is the probability that a randomly selected respondent prefers hybrid investment advice *and* is a baby boomer?
e. Are the events "generation group" and "prefers hybrid investment advice" independent? Explain.

4.63 Chartered Institute of Personnel and Development (CIPD) provides commentary and insight about the trends and challenges facing the HR profession in its HR Outlook Report. The report represents the results of an online survey conducted in 2016 with HR professionals at all levels of seniority, with responsibilities in

the United Kingdom who are employed by an organization. CIPD was interested in examining differences between respondents in the private sector and those in the public sector. One area of focus was on HR professionals' response to future organization priorities. The findings are summarized here.

Source: Data extracted from "HR Outlook Report," *CIPD*, Winter 2016–17, p. 8.

	COST MANAGEMENT IS A PRIORITY		
SECTOR	**Yes**	**No**	**Total**
Private	128	219	347
Public	117	72	189
Total	245	291	536

	TALENT MANAGEMENT IS A PRIORITY		
SECTOR	**Yes**	**No**	**Total**
Private	156	191	347
Public	66	123	189
Total	222	314	536

What is the probability that a randomly chosen HR professional

a. is in the private sector?

b. is in the private sector *or* indicates that talent management is a future priority in his/her organization?

c. does not indicate that cost management is a future priority in his/her organization" *and* is in the public sector?

d. does not indicate that cost management is a future priority in his/her organization" *or* is in the public sector?

e. Suppose the randomly chosen HR professional does indicate that cost management is a future priority in his/her organization. What is the probability that the HR professional is in the public sector?

f. Are "cost management is a priority" and "sector" independent?

g. Is "talent management is a priority" independent of "sector"?

4.64 To better understand the website builder market, Clutch surveyed individuals who created a website using a do-it-yourself (DIY) website builder. Respondents, categorized by the type of website they built—business or personal, were asked to indicate the primary purpose for building their website. The following table summarizes the findings:

PRIMARY PURPOSE	TYPE OF WEBSITE		
	Business	Personal	Total
Online Business Presence	52	4	56
Online Sales	32	13	45
Creative Display	28	54	82
Informational Resources	9	24	33
Blog	8	52	60
Total	129	147	276

Source: Data extracted from "How Business Use DIY Web Builders: Clutch 2017 Survey," **bit.ly/2qQjXiq**.

If a website builder is selected at random, what is the probability that he or she

a. indicated creative display as the primary purpose for building his/her website?

b. indicated creative display *or* informational resources as the primary purpose for building his/her website?

c. is a business website builder *or* indicated online sales as the primary purpose for building his/her website?

d. is a business website builder *and* indicated online sales as the primary purpose for building his/her website?

e. Given that the website builder selected is a personal website builder, what is the probability that he/she indicated online business presence as the primary purpose for building his/her website?

4.65 Content Marketing Institute provides insights on the content marketing habits of nonprofit professionals representing a broad range of nonprofit agencies and organizations. A survey of nonprofit marketers conducted by the Content Marketing Institute indicated that 26% of nonprofit marketers rated their organization as *effective* in terms of use of content marketing. Furthermore, of the nonprofit marketers who rated their organization as *effective* in terms of use of content marketing, 42% reported having a documented content marketing strategy in their organization. Of the nonprofit marketers

who did not rate their organization as *effective* in terms of use of content marketing, 19% reported having a documented content marketing strategy.

Source: Data extracted from "2016 Nonprofit Content Marketing," **bit.ly/2qQdLXy**.

If a nonprofit marketer is known to have a documented content strategy in their organization, what is the probability that the nonprofit marketer rates his/her organization as *effective* in terms of use of content marketing?

4.66 The CMO Survey collects and disseminates the opinions of top marketers in order to predict the future of markets, track marketing excellence, and improve the value of marketing in firms and in society. Part of the survey is devoted to the topic of marketing analytics and the understanding of what factors prevent companies from using more marketing analytics. The following findings are based on responses from 272 senior marketers within B2B firms and 114 senior marketers within B2C firms.

Source: Data extracted from "Results by Firm & Industry Characteristics," *The CMO Survey,* February 2017, p. 148. **bit.ly/2qY3Qvk**.

FIRM	LACK OF PROCESS/TOOLS TO MEASURE SUCCESS		
	Yes	No	Total
B2B	90	182	272
B2C	35	79	114
Total	125	261	386

FIRM	LACK OF PEOPLE WHO CAN LINK TO PRACTICE		
	Yes	No	Total
B2B	75	197	272
B2C	36	78	114
Total	111	275	386

a. What is the probability that a randomly selected senior marketer indicates that lack of process/tools to measure success through analytics is a factor that prevents his/her company from using more marketing analytics?

b. Given that a randomly selected senior marketer is within a B2B firm, what is the probability that the senior marketer indicates that lack of process/tools to measure success through analytics is a factor that prevents his/her company from using more marketing analytics?

c. Given that a randomly selected senior marketer is within a B2C firm, what is the probability that the senior marketer indicates that lack of process/tools to measure success through analytics is a factor that prevents his/her company from using more marketing analytics?

d. What is the probability that a randomly selected senior marketer indicates that lack of people who can link to marketing practice is a factor that prevents his/her company from using more marketing analytics?

e. Given that a randomly selected senior marketer is within a B2B firm, what is the probability that the senior marketer indicates that lack of people who can link to marketing practice is a factor that prevents his/her company from using more marketing analytics?

f. Given that a randomly selected senior marketer is within a B2C firm, what is the probability that the senior marketer indicates that lack of people who can link to marketing practice is a factor that prevents his/her company from using more marketing analytics?

g. Comment on the results in (a) through (f).

▾CASES

Digital Case

Apply your knowledge about contingency tables and the proper application of simple and joint probabilities in this continuing Digital Case from Chapter 3.

Open **EndRunGuide.pdf**, the EndRun Financial Services "Guide to Investing," and read the information about the Guaranteed Investment Package (GIP). Read the claims and examine the supporting data. Then answer the following questions:
How accurate is the claim of the probability of success for EndRun's GIP? In what ways is the claim misleading? How would you calculate and state the probability of having an annual rate of return not less than 15%?

1. Using the table found under the "Show Me the Winning Probabilities" subhead, compute the proper probabilities for the group of investors. What mistake was made in reporting the 7% probability claim?

2. Are there any probability calculations that would be appropriate for rating an investment service? Why or why not?

CardioGood Fitness

1. For each CardioGood Fitness treadmill product line (see CardioGood Fitness), construct two-way contingency tables of gender, education in years, relationship status, and self-rated fitness. (There will be a total of six tables for each treadmill product.)

2. For each table you construct, compute all conditional and marginal probabilities.

3. Write a report detailing your findings to be presented to the management of CardioGood Fitness.

The Choice *Is* Yours Follow-Up

1. Follow up the "Using Statistics: The Choice *Is* Yours, Revisited" on page 81 by constructing contingency tables of market cap and type, market cap and risk, market cap and rating, type and risk, type and rating, and risk and rating for the sample of 479 retirement funds stored in Retirement Funds .

2. For each table you construct, compute all conditional and marginal probabilities.

3. Write a report summarizing your conclusions.

Clear Mountain State Student Survey

The Student News Service at Clear Mountain State University (CMSU) has decided to gather data about the undergraduate students that attend CMSU. CMSU creates and distributes a survey of 14 questions and receive responses from 111 undergraduates (stored in StudentSurvey).

For these data, construct contingency tables of gender and major, gender and graduate school intention, gender and employment status, gender and computer preference, class and graduate school intention, class and employment status, major and graduate school intention, major and employment status, and major and computer preference.

1. For each of these contingency tables, compute all the conditional and marginal probabilities.

2. Write a report summarizing your conclusions.

▾EXCEL GUIDE

EG4.1 BASIC PROBABILITY CONCEPTS

Simple Probability, Joint Probability, and the General Addition Rule

Key Technique Use Excel arithmetic formulas.

Example Compute simple and joint probabilities for the Table 4.1 on page 171 purchase behavior data.

PHStat Use **Simple & Joint Probabilities**.

For the example, select **PHStat → Probability & Prob. Distributions → Simple & Joint Probabilities**. In the new template, similar to the worksheet shown below, fill in the **Sample Space** area with the data.

Workbook Use the **COMPUTE worksheet** of the **Probabilities workbook** as a template.

The worksheet (shown below) already contains the Table 4.1 purchase behavior data. For other problems, change the sample space table entries in the cell ranges **C3:D4** and **A5:D6**.

As you change the event names in cells, B5, B6, C5, and C5, the column A row labels for simple and joint probabilities and the addition rule change as well. These column A labels are *formulas* that use the concatenation operator (&) to form row labels from the event names you enter. For example, the cell A10 formula **="P ("& B5 & ")"** combines the two characters **P(** with the **Yes** B5 cell value and the character **)** to form the label **P(Yes)**. To examine all of the COMPUTE worksheet formulas below, open to the COMPUTE_FORMULAS worksheet.

	A	B	C	D	E
1	Probabilities				
2					
3	Sample Space		ACTUALLY PURCHASED		
4			Yes	No	Totals
5	PLANNED TO PURCHASE	Yes	200	50	250
6		No	100	650	750
7		Totals	300	700	1000
8					
9	Simple Probabilities				
10	P(Yes)	0.25	=E5/E7		
11	P(No)	0.75	=E6/E7		
12	P(Yes)	0.30	=C7/E7		
13	P(No)	0.70	=D7/E7		
14					
15	Joint Probabilities				
16	P(Yes and Yes)	0.20	=C5/E7		
17	P(Yes and No)	0.05	=D5/E7		
18	P(No and Yes)	0.10	=C6/E7		
19	P(No and No)	0.65	=D6/E7		
20					
21	Addition Rule				
22	P(Yes or Yes)	0.35	=B10 + B12 - B16		
23	P(Yes or No)	0.90	=B10 + B13 - B17		
24	P(No or Yes)	0.95	=B11 + B12 - B18		
25	P(No or No)	0.80	=B11 + B13 - B19		

EG4.4 BAYES' THEOREM

Key Technique Use Excel arithmetic formulas.

Example Apply Bayes' theorem to the television marketing example on page 187.

Workbook Use the **COMPUTE worksheet** of the **Bayes workbook** as a template.

The worksheet (shown below) already contains the probabilities for the online section example. For other problems, change those probabilities in the cell range **B5:C6**.

	A	B	C	D	E
1	Bayes' Theorem Computations				
2					
3			Probabilities		
4	Event	Prior	Conditional	Joint	Revised
5	S	0.4	0.8	0.32	0.64
6	S'	0.6	0.3	0.18	0.36
7			Total:	0.5	

Joint	Revised
=B5 * C5	=D5/$D$7
=B6 * C6	=D6/$D$7
=D5 + D6	

Open to the **COMPUTE_FORMULAS worksheet** to examine the arithmetic formulas that compute the probabilities, which are also shown as an inset to the worksheet.

EG4.5 COUNTING RULES

Counting Rule 1

Workbook Use the **POWER(k, n)** worksheet function in a cell formula to compute the number of outcomes given k events and n trials.

For example, the formula **=POWER(6, 2)** computes the answer for Example 4.11.

Counting Rule 2

Workbook Use a formula that takes the product of successive **POWER(k, n)** functions to solve problems related to counting rule 2.

For example, **=POWER(26, 3) * POWER(10, 3)** computes the answer for the state motor vehicle department example.

Counting Rule 3

Workbook Use the **FACT(n)** worksheet function in a cell formula to compute how many ways n items can be arranged.

For example, the formula **=FACT(6)** computes 6!.

Counting Rule 4

Workbook Use the **PERMUT(n, x)** worksheet function in a cell formula to compute the number of ways of arranging x objects selected from n objects in order.

For example, the formula **=PERMUT(6, 4)** computes the answer for Example 4.14.

Counting Rule 5

Workbook Use the **COMBIN(n, x)** worksheet function in a cell formula to compute the number of ways of arranging *x* objects selected from *n* objects, irrespective of order. For example, the formula = **COMBIN(6, 4)** computes the answer for Example 4.15.

▼ JMP GUIDE

CHAPTER 4

JG4.4 BAYES' THEOREM

Use **arithmetic formulas**.

For example, to apply Bayes' theorem to the television marketing on page 187, open to the **Bayes data table**. The data table, similar to the Section EG4.4 Bayes Excel template, already contains the probabilities for the online section example. For other problems, change the probabilities in the Prior and Conditional columns.

▼ MINITAB GUIDE

CHAPTER 4

MG4.5   COUNTING RULES

Use **Calculator** to apply the counting rules. Select **Calc → Calculator**. In the Calculator dialog box (shown below):

1. Enter the column name of an empty column in the **Store result in variable** box and then press **Tab**.
2. Build the appropriate expression (as discussed later in this section) in the **Expression** box. To apply counting rules 3 through 5, select **Arithmetic** from the **Functions** drop-down list to facilitate the function selection.
3. Click **OK**.

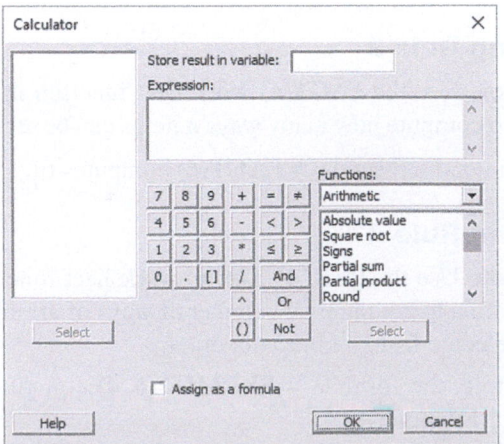

If you have previously used the Calculator during your Minitab session, you may have to clear the contents of the Expression box by selecting the contents and pressing **Del** before you begin step 2.

Counting Rule 1

Enter an expression that uses the exponential operator **. For example, the expression **6 ** 2** computes the answer for Example 4.11 on page 190.

Counting Rule 2

Enter an expression that uses the exponential operator **. For example, the expression **26 ** 3 * 10 ** 3** computes the answer for the state motor vehicle department example on page 190.

Counting Rule 3

Enter an expression that uses the **FACTORIAL(n)** function to compute how many ways *n* items can be arranged. For example, the expression **FACTORIAL(6)** computes 6!

Counting Rule 4

Enter an expression that uses the **PERMUTATIONS(n, x)** function to compute the number of ways of arranging *x* objects selected from *n* objects in order. For example, the expression **PERMUTATIONS(6, 4)** computes the answer for Example 4.14 on page 191.

Counting Rule 5

Enter an expression that uses the **COMBINATIONS(n, x)** function to compute the number of ways of arranging *x* objects selected from *n* objects, irrespective of order. For example, the expression **COMBINATIONS(6, 4)** computes the answer for Example 4.15 on page 191.

Discrete Probability Distributions

CONTENTS

OBJECTIVES

- Learn the properties of a probability distribution
- Compute the expected value and variance of a probability distribution
- Compute probabilities from the binomial and Poisson distributions
- Use the binomial and Poisson distributions to solve business problems

▼USING **STATISTICS**
Events of Interest at Ricknel Home Centers

Like most other large businesses, Ricknel Home Centers, LLC, a regional home improvement chain, uses an accounting information system (AIS) to manage its accounting and financial data. The Ricknel AIS collects, organizes, stores, analyzes, and distributes financial information to decision makers both inside and outside the firm.

One important function of the Ricknel AIS is to continuously audit accounting information, looking for errors or incomplete or improbable information. For example, when customers submit orders online, the Ricknel AIS scans orders looking to see which orders have possible mistakes. The system tags those orders and includes them in a daily *exceptions report*. Recent data collected by the company show that the likelihood is 0.10 that an order form will be tagged.

As a member of the AIS team, you have been asked by Ricknel management to determine the likelihood of finding a certain number of tagged forms in a sample of a specific size. For example, what would be the likelihood that none of the order forms are tagged in a sample of four forms? That one of the order forms is tagged?

How could you determine the solution to this type of probability problem?

T his chapter introduces you to the concept and characteristics of probability distributions. You will learn how the binomial and Poisson distributions can be applied to help solve business problems. In the Rickel Home Centers scenario, you could use a *probability distribution* as a mathematical model, or small-scale representation, that approximates the process. By using such an approximation, you could make inferences about the actual order process including the likelihood of finding a certain number of tagged forms in a sample.

5.1 The Probability Distribution for a Discrete Variable

Section 1.1 identifies numerical variables as either having *discrete*, integer values that represent a count of something, or *continuous*, values that arise from a measuring process. This chapter deals with probability distributions that represent a discrete numerical variable, such as the number of social media sites to which a person belongs or, in the Ricknel Home Centers scenario, the number of orders that the system has tagged for possible errors.

> **PROBABILITY DISTRIBUTION FOR A DISCRETE VARIABLE**
>
> A **probability distribution for a discrete variable** is a mutually exclusive list of all the possible numerical outcomes along with the probability of occurrence of each outcome.

For example, Table 5.1 gives the distribution of the number of interruptions per day in a large computer network. The list in Table 5.1 is collectively exhaustive because all possible outcomes are included. Thus, the probabilities sum to 1. Figure 5.1 is a graphical representation of Table 5.1.

TABLE 5.1
Probability Distribution of the Number of Interruptions per Day

Interruptions per Day	Probability
0	0.35
1	0.25
2	0.20
3	0.10
4	0.05
5	0.05

FIGURE 5.1
Probability distribution of the number of interruptions per day

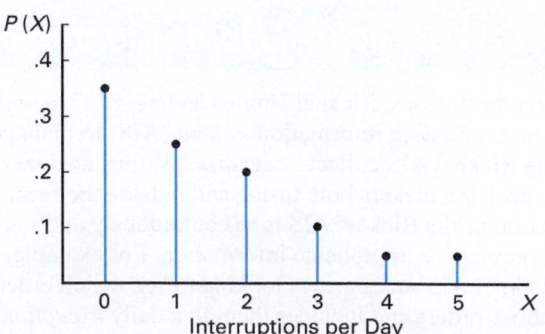

Expected Value of a Discrete Variable

The **expected value** of a discrete variable is the population mean, μ, of its probability distribution. To calculate the expected value, you multiply each possible outcome, x_i, by its corresponding probability, $P(X = x_i)$, and then sum these products.

EXPECTED VALUE, μ, OF A DISCRETE VARIABLE

$$\mu = E(X) = \sum_{i=1}^{N} x_i P(X = x_i) \tag{5.1}$$

where

$$x_i = \text{the } i\text{th value of the discrete variable } X$$
$$P(X = x_i) = \text{probability of occurrence of the ith value of } X$$
$$N = \text{number of values of the discrete variable } X$$

For the Table 5.1 probability distribution of the number of interruptions per day in a large computer network, Table 5.2 shows all intermediate steps for calculating the expected value using Equation (5.1).

$$\mu = E(X) = \sum_{i=1}^{N} x_i P(X = x_i)$$

$$= 0 + 0.25 + 0.40 + 0.30 + 0.20 + 0.25$$

$$= 1.40$$

TABLE 5.2

Computing the Expected Value of the Number of Interruptions per Day

Interruptions per Day (x_i)	$P(X = x_i)$	$x_i P(X = x_i)$
0	0.35	$(0)(0.35) = 0.00$
1	0.25	$(1)(0.25) = 0.25$
2	0.20	$(2)(0.20) = 0.40$
3	0.10	$(3)(0.10) = 0.30$
4	0.05	$(4)(0.05) = 0.20$
5	0.05	$(5)(0.05) = 0.25$
	1.00	$\mu = E(X) = 1.40$

The expected value is 1.40. The expected value of 1.40 interruptions per day represents the *mean* number of interruptions per day even though you cannot get 1.4 interruptions on any given day.

Variance and Standard Deviation of a Discrete Variable

You compute the variance of a probability distribution by multiplying each possible squared difference $[x_i - E(X)]^2$ by its corresponding probability, $P(X = x_i)$, and then summing the resulting products. Equation (5.2) defines the **variance of a discrete variable**, and Equation (5.3) defines the **standard deviation of a discrete variable**.

VARIANCE OF A DISCRETE VARIABLE

$$\sigma^2 = \sum_{i=1}^{N} [x_i - E(X)]^2 P(X = x_i) \tag{5.2}$$

where

$$x_i = \text{the ith value of the discrete variable } X$$
$$P(X = x_i) = \text{probability of occurrence of the ith value of } X$$
$$N = \text{number of values of the discrete variable } X$$

STANDARD DEVIATION OF A DISCRETE VARIABLE

$$\sigma = \sqrt{\sigma^2} = \sqrt{\sum_{i=1}^{N} [x_i - E(X)]^2 P(X = x_i)} \tag{5.3}$$

Table 5.3 shows all intermediate steps for calculating the variance and the standard deviation of the number of interruptions per day using Equations (5.2) and (5.3).

$$\sigma^2 = \sum_{i=1}^{N} [x_i - E(X)]^2 P(X = x_i)$$
$$= 0.686 + 0.040 + 0.072 + 0.256 + 0.338 + 0.648$$
$$= 2.04$$

and

$$\sigma = \sqrt{\sigma^2} = \sqrt{2.04} = 1.4283$$

TABLE 5.3

Computing the Variance and Standard Deviation of the Number of Interruptions per Day

Interruptions per Day (x_i)	$P(X = x_i)$	$x_i P(X = x_i)$	$[x_i - E(X)]^2$	$[x_i - E(X)]^2 P(X = x_i)$
0	0.35	0.00	$(0 - 1.4)^2 =$ 1.96	$(1.96)(0.35) = 0.686$
1	0.25	0.25	$(1 - 1.4)^2 =$ 0.16	$(0.16)(0.25) = 0.040$
2	0.20	0.40	$(2 - 1.4)^2 =$ 0.36	$(0.36)(0.20) = 0.072$
3	0.10	0.30	$(3 - 1.4)^2 =$ 2.56	$(2.56)(0.10) = 0.256$
4	0.05	0.20	$(4 - 1.4)^2 =$ 6.76	$(6.76)(0.05) = 0.338$
5	0.05	0.25	$(5 - 1.4)^2 =$ 12.96	$(12.96)(0.05) = 0.648$
	1.00	$\mu = E(X) = 1.40$		$\sigma^2 = 2.04$
				$\sigma = \sqrt{\sigma^2} = 1.4283$

Thus, the mean number of interruptions per day is 1.4, the variance is 2.04, and the standard deviation is approximately 1.43 interruptions per day.

PROBLEMS FOR SECTION 5.1

LEARNING THE BASICS

5.1 Given the following probability distributions:

Distribution A		Distribution B	
x_i	$P(X = x_i)$	x_i	$P(X = x_i)$
0	0.50	0	0.05
1	0.20	1	0.10
2	0.15	2	0.15
3	0.10	3	0.20
4	0.05	4	0.50

a. Compute the expected value for each distribution.
b. Compute the standard deviation for each distribution.
c. What is the probability that x will be at least 3 in Distribution A and Distribution B?
d. Compare the results of distributions A and B.

APPLYING THE CONCEPTS

✓**SELF TEST** **5.2** The following table contains the probability distribution for the number of traffic accidents daily in a small town:

Number of Accidents Daily (X)	$P(X = x_i)$
0	0.10
1	0.20
2	0.45
3	0.15
4	0.05
5	0.05

a. Compute the mean number of accidents per day.
b. Compute the standard deviation.
c. What is the probability that there will be at least 2 accidents on a given day?

5.3 Recently, a regional automobile dealership sent out fliers to perspective customers indicating that they had already won one of three different prizes: an automobile valued at $25,000, a $100 gas card, or a $5 Walmart shopping card. To claim his or her prize, a prospective customer needed to present the flier at the dealership's showroom. The fine print on the back of the flier listed the probabilities of winning. The chance of winning the car was 1 out of 31,478, the chance of winning the gas card was 1 out of 31,478, and the chance of winning the shopping card was 31,476 out of 31,478.

a. How many fliers do you think the automobile dealership sent out?

b. Using your answer to (a) and the probabilities listed on the flier, what is the expected value of the prize won by a prospective customer receiving a flier?

c. Using your answer to (a) and the probabilities listed on the flier, what is the standard deviation of the value of the prize won by a prospective customer receiving a flier?

d. Do you think this is an effective promotion? Why or why not?

5.4 In the carnival game Under-or-Over-Seven, a pair of fair dice is rolled once, and the resulting sum determines whether the player wins or loses his or her bet. For example, the player can bet $1 that the sum will be under 7—that is, 2, 3, 4, 5, or 6. For this bet, the player wins $1 if the result is under 7 and loses $1 if the outcome equals or is greater than 7. Similarly, the player can bet $1 that the sum will be over 7—that is, 8, 9, 10, 11, or 12. Here, the player wins $1 if the result is over 7 but loses $1 if the result is 7 or under. A third method of play is to bet $1 on the outcome 7. For this bet, the player wins $4 if the result of the roll is 7 and loses $1 otherwise.

a. Construct the probability distribution representing the different outcomes that are possible for a $1 bet on under 7.

b. Construct the probability distribution representing the different outcomes that are possible for a $1 bet on over 7.

c. Construct the probability distribution representing the different outcomes that are possible for a $1 bet on 7.

d. Show that the expected long-run profit (or loss) to the player is the same, no matter which method of play is used.

5.5 The number of arrivals per minute at a bank located in the central business district of a large city was recorded over a period of 200 minutes, with the following results:

Arrivals	Frequency
0	14
1	31
2	47
3	41
4	29
5	21
6	10
7	5
8	2

a. Compute the expected number of arrivals per minute.

b. Compute the standard deviation.

c. What is the probability that there will be fewer than 2 arrivals in a given minute?

5.6 The manager of the commercial mortgage department of a large bank has collected data during the past two years concerning the number of commercial mortgages approved per week. The results from these two years (104 weeks) are as follows:

Number of Commercial Mortgages Approved	Frequency
0	13
1	25
2	32
3	17
4	9
5	6
6	1
7	1

a. Compute the expected number of mortgages approved per week.

b. Compute the standard deviation.

c. What is the probability that there will be more than one commercial mortgage approved in a given week?

5.7 You are trying to develop a strategy for investing in two different stocks. The anticipated annual return for a $1,000 investment in each stock under four different economic conditions has the following probability distribution:

		Returns	
Probability	Economic Condition	Stock X	Stock Y
0.1	Recession	−50	−100
0.3	Slow growth	20	50
0.4	Moderate growth	100	130
0.2	Fast growth	150	200

Compute the

a. expected return for stock X and for stock Y.

b. standard deviation for stock X and for stock Y.

c. Would you invest in stock X or stock Y? Explain.

5.8 You plan to invest $1,000 in a corporate bond fund or in a common stock fund. The following table presents the annual return (per $1,000) of each of these investments under various economic conditions and the probability that each of those economic conditions will occur.

Probability	Economic Condition	Corporate Bond Fund	Common Stock Fund
0.01	Extreme recession	−300	−999
0.09	Recession	−70	−300
0.15	Stagnation	30	−100
0.35	Slow growth	60	100
0.30	Moderate growth	100	150
0.10	High growth	120	350

Compute the

a. expected return for the corporate bond fund and for the common stock fund.

b. standard deviation for the corporate bond fund and for the common stock fund.

c. Would you invest in the corporate bond fund or the common stock fund? Explain.

d. If you chose to invest in the common stock fund in (c), what do you think about the possibility of losing $999 of every $1,000 invested if there is an extreme recession?

5.2 Binomial Distribution

In some cases, a mathematical expression or **model** can be used to calculate the probability of a value, or outcome, for a variable of interest. For discrete variables, such mathematical models are also known as **probability distribution functions**. One such function that can be used in many business situations is the **binomial distribution**. Exhibit 5.1 presents the important properties of this distribution.

studentTIP

Do not confuse this use of the Greek letter pi, π, to represent the probability of an event of interest with the constant that is the ratio of the circumference to a diameter of a circle— approximately 3.14159.

> **EXHIBIT 5.1**
>
> **Properties of the Binomial Distribution**
>
> - The sample consists of a fixed number of observations, n.
> - Each observation is classified into one of two mutually exclusive and collectively exhaustive categories.
> - The probability of an observation being classified as the event of interest, π, is constant from observation to observation. Thus, the probability of an observation being classified as not being the event of interest, $1 - \pi$, is constant over all observations.
> - The value of any observation is independent of the value of any other observation.

You use the binomial distribution when the discrete variable is the number of events of interest in a sample of n observations. For example, in the Ricknel Home Improvement scenario suppose the event of interest is a tagged order form and you want to determine the number of tagged order forms in a given sample of orders.

What results can occur? If the sample contains four orders, there could be none, one, two, three, or four tagged order forms. No other value can occur because the number of tagged order forms cannot be more than the sample size, n, and cannot be less than zero. Therefore, the range of the binomial variable is from 0 to n.

Suppose that you observe the following result in a sample of four orders:

First Order	Second Order	Third Order	Fourth Order
Tagged	Tagged	Not tagged	Tagged

What is the probability of having three tagged order forms in a sample of four orders in this particular sequence? Because the historical probability of a tagged order is 0.10, the probability that each order occurs in the sequence is

First Order	Second Order	Third Order	Fourth Order
$\pi = 0.10$	$\pi = 0.10$	$1 - \pi = 0.90$	$\pi = 0.10$

Each outcome is independent of the others because the order forms were selected from an extremely large or practically infinite population and each order form could only be selected once. Therefore, the probability of having this particular sequence is

$$\pi\pi(1 - \pi)\pi = \pi^3(1 - \pi)^1$$

$$= (0.10)^3(0.90)^1 = (0.10)(0.10)(0.10)(0.90)$$

$$= 0.0009$$

This result indicates only the probability of three tagged order forms (events of interest) from a sample of four order forms in a *specific sequence*. To find the number of ways of selecting x objects from n objects, *irrespective of sequence*, you use the **rule of combinations** given in Equation (5.4).

[1]On many scientific calculators, there is a button labeled $_nC_r$ that allows you to compute the number of combinations. On these calculators, the symbol r is used instead of x.

COMBINATIONS

The number of combinations of selecting x objects[1] out of n objects is given by

$$_nC_x = \frac{n!}{x!(n-x)!} \tag{5.4}$$

where

$n! = (n)(n-1)\cdots(1)$ is called n factorial. By definition, $0! = 1$.

With $n = 4$ and $x = 3$, there are

$$_nC_x = \frac{n!}{x!(n-x)!} = \frac{4!}{3!(4-3)!} = \frac{4 \times 3 \times 2 \times 1}{(3 \times 2 \times 1)(1)} = 4$$

such sequences. The four possible sequences are

Sequence 1 = (*tagged, tagged, tagged, not tagged*), with probability
$$\pi\pi\pi(1-\pi) = \pi^3(1-\pi)^1 = 0.0009$$

Sequence 2 = (*tagged, tagged, not tagged, tagged*), with probability
$$\pi\pi(1-\pi)\pi = \pi^3(1-\pi)^1 = 0.0009$$

Sequence 3 = (*tagged, not tagged, tagged, tagged*), with probability
$$\pi(1-\pi)\pi\pi = \pi^3(1-\pi)^1 = 0.0009$$

Sequence 4 = (*not tagged, tagged, tagged, tagged*), with probability
$$(1-\pi)\pi\pi\pi = \pi^3(1-\pi)^1 = 0.0009$$

Therefore, the probability of three tagged order forms is equal to

(number of possible sequences) $\times$ (probability of a particular sequence)
$$= (4) \times (0.0009) = 0.0036$$

You can make a similar, intuitive derivation for the other possible values of the variable—zero, one, two, and four tagged order forms. However, as n, the sample size, gets large, the computations involved in using this intuitive approach become time-consuming. Equation (5.5) is the mathematical model that provides a general formula for computing any probability from the binomial distribution with the number of events of interest, x, given n and π.

BINOMIAL DISTRIBUTION

$$P(X = x \mid n, \pi) = \frac{n!}{x!(n-x)!}\pi^x(1-\pi)^{n-x} \tag{5.5}$$

where

$P(X = x \mid n, \pi)$ = probability that $X = x$ events of interest, given n and π

n = number of observations

π = probability of an event of interest

$1 - \pi$ = probability of not having an event of interest

x = number of events of interest in the sample ($X = 0, 1, 2, \ldots, n$)

$\dfrac{n!}{x!(n-x)!}$ = number of combinations of x events of interest out of n observations

Equation (5.5) restates what was intuitively derived previously. The binomial variable X can have any integer value x from 0 through n. In Equation (5.5), the product

$$\pi^x(1-\pi)^{n-x}$$

represents the probability of exactly x events of interest from n observations in a *particular sequence*.

The term

$$\frac{n!}{x!(n-x)!}$$

learnMORE

The **Binomial Table online topic** contains binomial probabilities and cumulative binomial probabilities tables and explains how to use the tables to compute binomial and cumulative binomial probabilities.

is the number of *combinations* of the x events of interest from the n observations possible. Hence, given the number of observations, n, and the probability of an event of interest, π, the probability of x events of interest is

$$P(X = x \mid n, \pi) = \text{(number of combinations)} \times \text{(probability of a particular combination)}$$

$$= \frac{n!}{x!(n-x)!} \pi^x (1-\pi)^{n-x}$$

Example 5.1 illustrates the use of Equation (5.5). Examples 5.2 and 5.3 show the computations for other values of X.

EXAMPLE 5.1

Determining
$P(X = 3)$, Given
$n = 4$ and $\pi = 0.1$

If the likelihood of a tagged order form is 0.1, what is the probability that there are three tagged order forms in the sample of four?

SOLUTION Using Equation (5.5), the probability of three tagged orders from a sample of four is

$$P(X = 3 \mid n = 4, \pi = 0.1) = \frac{4!}{3!(4-3)!}(0.1)^3(1-0.1)^{4-3}$$

$$= \frac{4!}{3!(1)!}(0.1)^3(0.9)^1$$

$$= 4(0.1)(0.1)(0.1)(0.9) = 0.0036$$

EXAMPLE 5.2

Determining
$P(X \geq 3)$, Given
$n = 4$ and $\pi = 0.1$

If the likelihood of a tagged order form is 0.1, what is the probability that there are three or more (i.e., at least three) tagged order forms in the sample of four?

SOLUTION In Example 5.1, you found that the probability of *exactly* three tagged order forms from a sample of four is 0.0036. To compute the probability of *at least* three tagged order forms, you need to add the probability of three tagged order forms to the probability of four tagged order forms. The probability of four tagged order forms is

studentTIP

Another way of saying "three or more" is "at least three."

$$P(X = 4 \mid n = 4, \pi = 0.1) = \frac{4!}{4!(4-4)!}(0.1)^4(1-0.1)^{4-4}$$

$$= 1(0.1)(0.1)(0.1)(0.1)(1) = 0.0001$$

Thus, the probability of at least three tagged order forms is

$$P(X \geq 3) = P(X = 3) + P(X = 4)$$

$$= 0.0036 + 0.0001 = 0.0037$$

There is a 0.37% chance that there will be at least three tagged order forms in a sample of four.

EXAMPLE 5.3

Determining
$P(X < 3)$, Given
$n = 4$ and $\pi = 0.1$

▶(continued)

If the likelihood of a tagged order form is 0.1, what is the probability that there are less than three tagged order forms in the sample of four?

SOLUTION The probability that there are less than three tagged order forms is

$$P(X < 3) = P(X = 0) + P(X = 1) + P(X = 2)$$

Using Equation (5.5) on page 205, these probabilities are

$$P(X = 0 \mid n = 4, \pi = 0.1) = \frac{4!}{0!(4-0)!}(0.1)^0(1-0.1)^{4-0} = 0.6561$$

$$P(X = 1 \mid n = 4, \pi = 0.1) = \frac{4!}{1!(4-1)!}(0.1)^1(1-0.1)^{4-1} = 0.2916$$

$$P(X = 2 \mid n = 4, \pi = 0.1) = \frac{4!}{2!(4-2)!}(0.1)^2(1-0.1)^{4-2} = 0.0486$$

Therefore, $P(X < 3) = 0.6561 + 0.2916 + 0.0486 = 0.9963$. $P(X < 3)$ could also be calculated from its complement, $P(X \geq 3)$, as follows:

$$P(X < 3) = 1 - P(X \geq 3)$$
$$= 1 - 0.0037 = 0.9963$$

Excel, JMP, and Minitab can automate binomial probability calculations, which become tedious as n gets large. Figure 5.2 contains the computed binomial probabilities for $n = 4$ and $\pi = 0.1$.

FIGURE 5.2

Excel, JMP, and Minitab results for computing binomial probabilities with $n = 4$ and $\pi = 0.1$

	A	B
1	Binomial Probabilities	
2		
3	Data	
4	Sample size	4
5	Probability of an event of interest	0.1
6		
7	Parameters	
8	Mean	0.4
9	Variance	0.36
10	Standard deviation	0.6
11		
12	Binomial Probabilities Table	
13	X	P(X)
14	0	0.6561
15	1	0.2916
16	2	0.0486
17	3	0.0036
18	4	0.0001

2/1 Cols		
5/0 Rows	X	P(X)
1	0	0.6561
2	1	0.2916
3	2	0.0486
4	3	0.0036
5	4	0.0001

	C1	C2
	X	P(X)
1	0	0.6561
2	1	0.2916
3	2	0.0486
4	3	0.0036
5	4	0.0001

Histograms for Discrete Variables

Discrete histograms visualize binomial distributions. Figure 5.3 visualizes the binomial probabilities for Example 5.3. Unlike histograms for continuous variables that Section 2.4 discusses, the bars for the values in a discrete histogram are very thin and there is a large gap between each pair of bars. Ideally, discrete histogram bars would have no width and some programs, such as JMP, can suggest that lack of width by graphing vertical lines ("needles") in lieu of solid bars.

FIGURE 5.3

Histogram of the binomial probability with $n = 4$ and $\pi = 0.1$

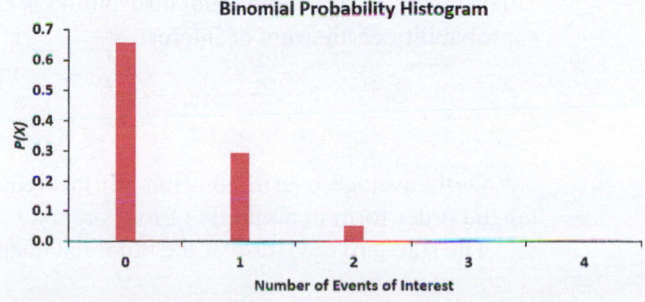

Binomial Probability Histogram

For a binomial probability distribution, the shape depends on the values of π and n. Whenever $\pi = 0.5$, the binomial distribution is symmetrical, regardless of how large or small the value of n. When $\pi \neq 0.5$, both π and n affect the skewness of the distribution.

Figure 5.4 illustrates the effect of π on a binomial distribution. Holding the sample size constant, low values for π, such as 0.2, cause the binomial distribution to be right-skewed (left histogram), while high values, such as 0.8, cause the distribution to be left-skewed (right histogram). Figure 5.5 illustrates that increasing n makes a binomial distribution more symmetrical when π does not equal 0.5. Generally, the closer π is to 0.5 or the larger the number of observations, n, the less skewed the binomial distribution will be.

FIGURE 5.4

Effect of π on the binomial distribution, holding n constant

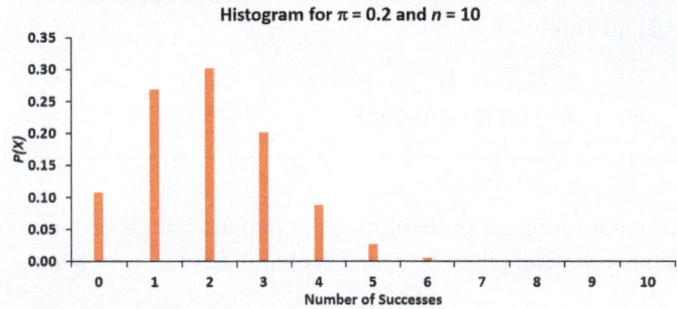
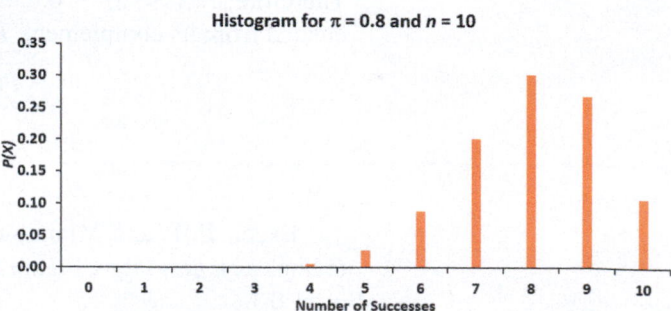

FIGURE 5.5

Effect of n on the binomial distribution, holding π constant

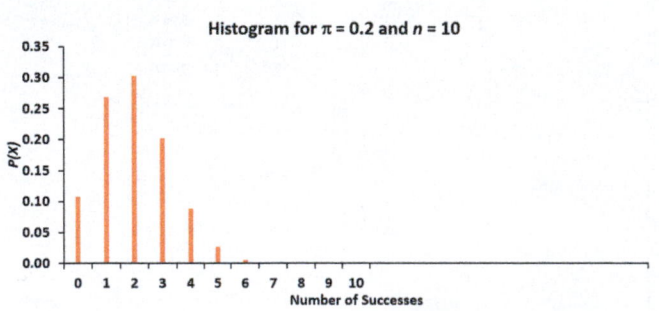
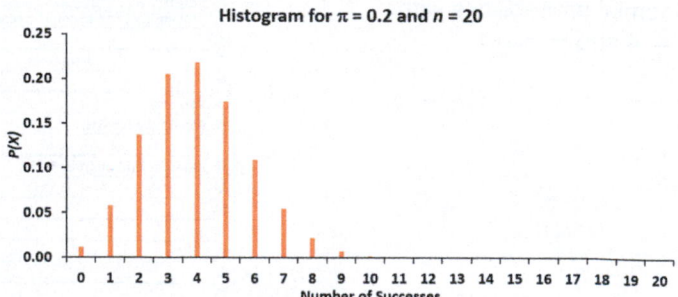

Summary Measures for the Binomial Distribution

The mean (or expected value) of the binomial distribution is equal to the product of n and π. Instead of using Equation (5.1) on page 201 to compute the mean of the probability distribution, you can use Equation (5.6) to compute the mean for variables that follow the binomial distribution.

MEAN OF THE BINOMIAL DISTRIBUTION

The mean, μ, of the binomial distribution is equal to the sample size, n, multiplied by the probability of an event of interest, π.

$$\mu = E(X) = n\pi \tag{5.6}$$

On the average, over the long run, you theoretically expect $\mu = E(X) = n\pi = (4)(0.1) = 0.4$ tagged order form in a sample of four orders.

The standard deviation of the binomial distribution can be calculated using Equation (5.7).

STANDARD DEVIATION OF THE BINOMIAL DISTRIBUTION

$$\sigma = \sqrt{\sigma^2} = \sqrt{Var(X)} = \sqrt{n\pi(1 - \pi)} \tag{5.7}$$

The standard deviation of the number of tagged order forms is

$$\sigma = \sqrt{4(0.1)(0.9)} = 0.60$$

You get the same result if you use Equation (5.3) on page 202.

Example 5.4 applies the binomial distribution to service at a fast-food restaurant.

EXAMPLE 5.4	
Computing Binomial Probabilities for Service at a Fast-Food Restaurant	Accuracy in taking orders at a drive-through window is important for fast-food chains. Periodically, *QSR Magazine* publishes "The Drive-Thru Performance Study: Order Accuracy" that measures the percentage of orders that are filled correctly. In a recent month, the percentage of orders filled correctly at Wendy's was approximately 86.9%.

Suppose that you go to the drive-through window at Wendy's and place an order. Two friends of yours independently place orders at the drive-through window at the same Wendy's. What are the probabilities that all three, that none of the three, and that at least two of the three orders will be filled correctly? What are the mean and standard deviation of the binomial distribution for the number of orders filled correctly?

SOLUTION Because there are three orders and the probability of a correct order is 0.869, $n = 3$, and $\pi = 0.869$, using Equation (5.5) on page 205,

$$P(X = 3 | n = 3, \pi = 0.869) = \frac{3!}{3!(3 - 3)!}(0.869)^3(1 - 0.869)^{3-3}$$

$$= 1(0.869)(0.869)(0.869)(1) = 0.6562$$

$$P(X = 0 | n = 3, \pi = 0.869) = \frac{3!}{0!(3 - 0)!}(0.869)^0(1 - 869)^{3-0}$$

$$= 1(1)(0.131)(0.131)(0.131) = 0.0022$$

$$P(X = 2 | n = 3, \pi = 0.869) = \frac{3!}{2!(3 - 2)!}(0.869)^2(1 - 0.869)^{3-2}$$

$$= 3(0.869)(0.869)(0.131) = 0.2968$$

$$P(X \geq 2) = P(X = 2) + P(X = 3)$$

$$= 0.2968 + 0.6562$$

$$= 0.9530$$

Using Equations (5.6) and (5.7),

$$\mu = E(X) = n\pi = 3(0.869) = 2.607$$

$$\sigma = \sqrt{\sigma^2} = \sqrt{Var(X)} = \sqrt{n\pi(1 - \pi)}$$

$$= \sqrt{3(0.869)(0.131)}$$

$$= \sqrt{0.3415} = 0.5844$$

The mean number of orders filled correctly in a sample of three orders is 2.607, and the standard deviation is 0.5844. The probability that all three orders are filled correctly is 0.6562, or 65.62%. The probability that none of the orders are filled correctly is 0.0022 (0.22%). The probability that at least two orders are filled correctly is 0.9530 (95.30%).

Figure 5.6 shows the Example 5.4 Excel results. The answer to the third question can be found in the last column of the "Binomial Probabilities Table" in the $X = 2$ row.

▶(*continued*)

FIGURE 5.6
Excel results for computing the binomial probability for Example 5.4

	A	B	C	D	E	F
1	Probability of Correct Order at Wendy's					
2						
3	Data					
4	Sample size	3				
5	Probability of an event of interest	0.869				
6						
7	Parameters					
8	Mean	2.607				
9	Variance	0.3415				
10	Standard deviation	0.5844				
11						
12	Binomial Probabilities Table					
13		X	P(X)	P(<=X)	P(<X)	P(>X)	P(>=X)
14		0	0.0022	0.0022	0.0000	0.9978	1.0000
15		1	0.0447	0.0470	0.0022	0.9530	0.9978
16		2	0.2968	0.3438	0.0470	0.6562	0.9530
17		3	0.6562	1.0000	0.3438	0.0000	0.6562

PROBLEMS FOR SECTION 5.2

LEARNING THE BASICS

5.9 Determine the following:
a. For $n = 4$ and $\pi = 0.12$, what is $P(X = 0)$?
b. For $n = 10$ and $\pi = 0.40$, what is $P(X = 9)$?
c. For $n = 10$ and $\pi = 0.50$, what is $P(X = 8)$?
d. For $n = 6$ and $\pi = 0.83$, what is $P(X = 5)$?

5.10 Determine the mean and standard deviation of the variable X in each of the following binomial distributions:
a. $n = 4$ and $\pi = 0.10$
b. $n = 4$ and $\pi = 0.40$
c. $n = 5$ and $\pi = 0.80$
d. $n = 3$ and $\pi = 0.50$

APPLYING THE CONCEPTS

5.11 The increase or decrease in the price of a stock between the beginning and the end of a trading day is assumed to be an equally likely random event. What is the probability that a stock will show an increase in its closing price on five consecutive days?

5.12 According to the Pew Research Center, 51% of American adults own tablets.

Source: Data extracted from **pewrsr.ch/2riDGV6**.

Using the binomial distribution, what is the probability that in the next six American adults surveyed,
a. four will own a tablet?
b. all six will own a tablet?
c. at least four will own a tablet?
d. What are the mean and standard deviation of the number of American adults who will own a tablet in a survey of six?
e. What assumptions do you need to make in (a) through (c)?

5.13 A student is taking a multiple-choice exam in which each question has four choices. Assume that the student has no knowledge of the correct answers to any of the questions. She has decided on a strategy in which she will place four balls (marked A, B, C, and D) into a box. She randomly selects one ball for each question and replaces the ball in the box. The marking on the ball will determine her answer to the question. There are five multiple-choice questions on the exam. What is the probability that she will get

a. five questions correct?
b. at least four questions correct?
c. no questions correct?
d. no more than two questions correct?

5.14 A manufacturing company regularly conducts quality control checks at specified periods on the products it manufactures. Historically, the failure rate for LED light bulbs that the company manufactures is 3%. Suppose a random sample of 10 LED light bulbs is selected. What is the probability that
a. none of the LED light bulbs are defective?
b. exactly one of the LED light bulbs is defective?
c. two or fewer of the LED light bulbs are defective?
d. three or more of the LED light bulbs are defective?

5.15 Past records indicate that the probability of online retail orders that turn out to be fraudulent is 0.08. Suppose that, on a given day, 20 online retail orders are placed. Assume that the number of online retail orders that turn out to be fraudulent is distributed as a binomial random variable.
a. What are the mean and standard deviation of the number of online retail orders that turn out to be fraudulent?
b. What is the probability that zero online retail orders will turn out to be fraudulent?
c. What is the probability that one online retail order will turn out to be fraudulent?
d. What is the probability that two or more online retail orders will turn out to be fraudulent?

SELF TEST **5.16** In Example 5.4 on page 209, you and two friends decided to go to Wendy's. Now, suppose that instead you go to Burger King, which recently filled approximately 90.5% of orders correctly. What is the probability that
a. all three orders will be filled correctly?
b. none of the three will be filled correctly?
c. at least two of the three will be filled correctly?
d. What are the mean and standard deviation of the binomial distribution used in (a) through (c)? Interpret these values.
e. Compare the result of (a) through (d) with those of Wendy's in Example 5.4 on page 209 and McDonald's in Problem 5.17.

5.17 In Example 5.4 on page 209, you and two friends decided to go to Wendy's. Now, suppose that instead you go to McDonald's, which recently filled approximately 92.2% of the orders correctly. What is the probability that

a. all three orders will be filled correctly?

b. none of the three will be filled correctly?

c. at least two of the three will be filled correctly?

d. What are the mean and standard deviation of the binomial distribution used in (a) through (c)? Interpret these values.

e. Compare the result of (a) through (d) with those of Burger King in Problem 5.16 and Wendy's in Example 5.4 on page 209.

5.3 Poisson Distribution

Many studies are based on counts of the occurrences of a particular event in a fixed interval of time or space (often referred to as an *area of opportunity*). In such an **area of opportunity** there can be more than one occurrence of an event. The Poisson distribution can be used to compute probabilities in such situations (see Reference 3). Examples of variables that follow the Poisson distribution are the surface defects on a new refrigerator, the number of network failures in a day, the number of people arriving at a bank, and the number of fleas on the body of a dog. You can use the **Poisson distribution** to calculate probabilities in situations such as these if the following properties hold:

- You are interested in counting the number of times a particular event occurs in a given area of opportunity. The area of opportunity is defined by time, length, surface area, and so forth.
- The probability that an event occurs in a given area of opportunity is the same for all the areas of opportunity.
- The number of events that occur in one area of opportunity is independent of the number of events that occur in any other area of opportunity.
- The probability that two or more events will occur in an area of opportunity approaches zero as the area of opportunity becomes smaller.

Consider the number of customers arriving during the lunch hour at a bank located in the central business district in a large city. You are interested in the number of customers who arrive each minute. Does this situation match the four properties of the Poisson distribution given earlier?

First, the *event* of interest is a customer arriving, and the *given area of opportunity* is defined as a one-minute interval. Will zero customers arrive, one customer arrive, two customers arrive, and so on? Second, it is reasonable to assume that the probability that a customer arrives during a particular one-minute interval is the same as the probability for all the other one-minute intervals. Third, the arrival of one customer in any one-minute interval has no effect on (i.e., is independent of) the arrival of any other customer in any other one-minute interval. Finally, the probability that two or more customers will arrive in a given time period approaches zero as the time interval becomes small. For example, the probability is virtually zero that two customers will arrive in a time interval of 0.01 second. Thus, you can use the Poisson distribution to determine probabilities involving the number of customers arriving at the bank in a one-minute time interval during the lunch hour.

The Poisson distribution has one parameter, called λ (the Greek lowercase letter *lambda*), which is the mean or expected number of events per unit. The variance of a Poisson distribution is also equal to λ, and the standard deviation is equal to $\sqrt{\lambda}$. The number of events, X, of the Poisson variable ranges from 0 to infinity (∞).

Equation (5.8) is the mathematical expression for the Poisson distribution for computing the probability of $X = x$ events, given that λ events are expected.

POISSON DISTRIBUTION

$$P(X = x \mid \lambda) = \frac{e^{-\lambda}\lambda^x}{x!} \tag{5.8}$$

where

$P(X = x \mid \lambda)$ = probability that $X = x$ events in an area of opportunity given λ

λ = expected number of events per unit

e = mathematical constant approximated by 2.71828

x = number of events ($x = 0, 1, 2, \ldots$)

To illustrate an application of the Poisson distribution, suppose that the mean number of customers who arrive per minute at the bank during the noon-to-1 P.M. hour is equal to 3.0. What is the probability that in a given minute, exactly two customers will arrive? And what is the probability that more than two customers will arrive in a given minute?

Using Equation (5.8) and $\lambda = 3$, the probability that in a given minute exactly two customers will arrive is

$$P(X = 2 \mid \lambda = 3) = \frac{e^{-3.0}(3.0)^2}{2!} = \frac{9}{(2.71828)^3(2)} = 0.2240$$

To determine the probability that in any given minute more than two customers will arrive,

$$P(X > 2) = P(X = 3) + P(X = 4) + \cdots$$

Because in a probability distribution, all the probabilities must sum to 1, the terms on the right side of the equation $P(X > 2)$ also represent the complement of the probability that X is less than or equal to 2 [i.e., $1 - P(X \leq 2)$]. Thus,

$$P(X > 2) = 1 - P(X \leq 2) = 1 - [P(X = 0) + P(X = 1) + P(X = 2)]$$

Now, using Equation (5.8),

$$P(X > 2) = 1 - \left[\frac{e^{-3.0}(3.0)^0}{0!} + \frac{e^{-3.0}(3.0)^1}{1!} + \frac{e^{-3.0}(3.0)^2}{2!} \right]$$

$$= 1 - [0.0498 + 0.1494 + 0.2240]$$

$$= 1 - 0.4232 = 0.5768$$

learnMORE

The **Poisson Table** online topic contains a table of Poisson probabilities and explains how to use the table to compute Poisson probabilities.

Thus, there is a 57.68% chance that more than two customers will arrive in the same minute.

Excel, JMP, and Minitab can automate Poisson probability calculations, which can be tedious. Figure 5.7 contains the computed Poisson probabilities for the bank customer arrival example.

FIGURE 5.7

Excel and Minitab results for computing Poisson probabilities with $\lambda = 3$

⊿	A	B	C	D	E
1	Poisson Probabilities				
2					
3			Data		
4	Mean/Expected number of events of interest:				3
5					
6	Poisson Probabilities Table				
7	**X**	**P(X)**			
8	0	0.0498	=POISSON.DIST(A8, $E$4, FALSE)		
9	1	0.1494	=POISSON.DIST(A9, $E$4, FALSE)		
10	2	0.2240	=POISSON.DIST(A10, $E$4, FALSE)		
11	3	0.2240	=POISSON.DIST(A11, $E$4, FALSE)		
12	4	0.1680	=POISSON.DIST(A12, $E$4, FALSE)		
13	5	0.1008	=POISSON.DIST(A13, $E$4, FALSE)		
14	6	0.0504	=POISSON.DIST(A14, $E$4, FALSE)		
15	7	0.0216	=POISSON.DIST(A15, $E$4, FALSE)		
16	8	0.0081	=POISSON.DIST(A16, $E$4, FALSE)		
17	9	0.0027	=POISSON.DIST(A17, $E$4, FALSE)		
18	10	0.0008	=POISSON.DIST(A18, $E$4, FALSE)		
19	11	0.0002	=POISSON.DIST(A19, $E$4, FALSE)		
20	12	0.0001	=POISSON.DIST(A20, $E$4, FALSE)		
21	13	0.0000	=POISSON.DIST(A21, $E$4, FALSE)		
22	14	0.0000	=POISSON.DIST(A22, $E$4, FALSE)		
23	15	0.0000	=POISSON.DIST(A23, $E$4, FALSE)		

Probability Density Function

Poisson with mean = 3

x	P(X = x)
0	0.049787
1	0.149361
2	0.224042
3	0.224042
4	0.168031
5	0.100819
6	0.050409
7	0.021604
8	0.008102
9	0.002701
10	0.000810
11	0.000221
12	0.000055
13	0.000013
14	0.000003
15	0.000001

EXAMPLE 5.5

Computing Poisson Probabilities

Assume that the number of new visitors to a website in one minute follows a Poisson distribution with a mean of 2.5. What is the probability that in a given minute, there are no new visitors to the website? That there is at least one new visitor to the website?

SOLUTION Using Equation (5.8) on page 211 with $\lambda = 2.5$ (or Excel, JMP, or Minitab or a Poisson table lookup), the probability that there are no new visitors to the website is

$$P(X = 0 \mid \lambda = 2.5) = \frac{e^{-2.5}(2.5)^0}{0!} = \frac{1}{(2.71828)^{2.5}(1)} = 0.0821$$

▶*(continued)*

The probability that there will be no new visitors to the website in a given minute is 0.0821, or 8.21%. Thus,

$$P(X \geq 1) = 1 - P(X = 0)$$

$$= 1 - 0.0821 = 0.9179$$

The probability that there will be at least one new visitor to the website in a given minute is 0.9179, or 91.79%. Figure 5.8 shows the Example 5.5 Excel results. The answer to the questions can be found in the boldface cells in the "Poisson Probabilities Table."

FIGURE 5.8
Excel results for computing the Poisson probability for Example 5.5

	A	B	C	D	E
1	Poisson Probabilities for Website Visitors				
2					
3		Data			
4	Mean/Expected number of events of interest:				2.5
5					
6	Poisson Probabilities Table				
7	X	P(X)	P(<=X)	P(<X)	P(>X)
8	0	0.0821	0.0821	0.0000	0.9179

PROBLEMS FOR SECTION 5.3

LEARNING THE BASICS

5.18 Assume a Poisson distribution.
a. If $\lambda = 2.5$, find $P(X = 2)$.
b. If $\lambda = 8.0$, find $P(X = 8)$.
c. If $\lambda = 0.5$, find $P(X = 1)$.
d. If $\lambda = 3.7$, find $P(X = 0)$.

5.19 Assume a Poisson distribution.
a. If $\lambda = 2.0$, find $P(X \geq 2)$.
b. If $\lambda = 8.0$, find $P(X \geq 3)$.
c. If $\lambda = 0.5$, find $P(X \leq 1)$.
d. If $\lambda = 4.0$, find $P(X \geq 1)$.
e. If $\lambda = 5.0$, find $P(X \leq 3)$.

5.20 Assume a Poisson distribution with $\lambda = 5.0$. What is the probability that
a. $X = 1$?
b. $X < 1$?
c. $X > 1$?
d. $X \leq 1$?

APPLYING THE CONCEPTS

5.21 Assume that the number of airline customer service complaints filed with the Department of Transportation's Office of Aviation Enforcement and Proceedings (OAEP) in one day is distributed as a Poisson variable. The mean number of airline customer service complaints filed is 5.0 per day.
Source: Data extracted from **bit.ly/2pCTdBZ**.

What is the probability that in any given day
a. zero airline customer service complaints will be filed?
b. exactly one airline customer service complaint will be filed?
c. two or more airline customer service complaints will be filed?
d. fewer than three airline customer service complaints will be filed?

5.22 The quality control manager of Marilyn's Cookies is inspecting a batch of chocolate-chip cookies that has just been baked. If the production process is in control, the mean number of chocolate-chip parts per cookie is 6.0. What is the probability that in any particular cookie being inspected
a. fewer than five chocolate-chip parts will be found?
b. exactly five chocolate-chip parts will be found?
c. five or more chocolate-chip parts will be found?
d. either four or five chocolate-chip parts will be found?

5.23 Refer to Problem 5.22. How many cookies in a batch of 100 should the manager expect to discard if company policy requires that all chocolate-chip cookies sold have at least four chocolate-chip parts?

5.24 The U.S. Department of Transportation maintains statistics for mishandled bags per 1,000 airline passengers. In September 2016, Delta mishandled 1.35 bags per 1,000 passengers. What is the probability that in the next 1,000 passengers, Delta will have
a. no mishandled bags?
b. at least one mishandled bag?
c. at least two mishandled bags?

5.25 The U.S. Department of Transportation maintains statistics for mishandled bags. In September 2016, the American Airlines rate of mishandled bags was 0.68 per 1,000 passengers. What is the probability that in the next 1,000 passengers, there will be
a. no mishandled bags?
b. at least one mishandled bag?
c. at least two mishandled bags?

5.26 The Consumer Financial Protection Bureau's Consumer Response team hears directly from consumers about the challenges they face in the marketplace, brings their concerns to the attention of financial institutions, and assists in addressing their complaints. An analysis of complaints registered in March 2017 indicates that the mean number of vehicle lease complaints registered by consumers is 3.5 per day.
Sorce: Data extracted from **bit.ly/2nGDsc7**.

Assume that the number of vehicle lease complaints registered by consumers is distributed as a Poisson random variable. What is the probability that in a given day

a. no vehicle lease complaint will be registered by consumers?

b. exactly one vehicle lease complaint will be registered by consumers?

c. more than one vehicle lease complaint will be registered by consumers?

d. fewer than two vehicle lease complaints will be registered by consumers?

5.27 J.D. Power and Associates calculates and publishes various statistics concerning car quality. The dependability score measures problems experienced during the past 12 months by owners of vehicles (2016). For these models of cars, Ford had 1.02 problems per car and Toyota had 0.93 problems per car.

Source: Data extracted from **www.jdpower.com/press-release/2016-us-initial-qwuality-study**.

Let X be equal to the number of problems with a Ford.

a. What assumptions must be made in order for X to be distributed as a Poisson random variable? Are these assumptions reasonable?

Making the assumptions as in (a), if you purchased a Ford in the 2016 model year, what is the probability that in the past 12 months, the car had

b. zero problems?

c. two or fewer problems?

d. Give an operational definition for *problem*. Why is the operational definition important in interpreting the initial quality score?

5.28 Refer to Problem 5.27. If you purchased a Toyota in the 2016 model year, what is the probability that in the past 12 months the car had

a. zero problems?

b. two or fewer problems?

c. Compare your answers in (a) and (b) to those for the Ford in Problem 5.27 (b) and (c).

5.29 A toll-free phone number is available from 9 A.M. to 9 P.M. for your customers to register complaints about a product purchased from your company. Past history indicates that a mean of 0.8 calls is received per minute.

a. What properties must be true about the situation described here in order to use the Poisson distribution to calculate probabilities concerning the number of phone calls received in a one-minute period?

Assuming that this situation matches the properties discussed in (a), what is the probability that during a one-minute period

b. zero phone calls will be received?

c. three or more phone calls will be received?

d. What is the maximum number of phone calls that will be received in a one-minute period 99.99% of the time?

5.4 Covariance of a Probability Distribution and Its Application in Finance

Section 5.1 defines the expected value, variance, and standard deviation for the probability distribution of a *single* variable. The **Section 5.4 online topic** discusses covariance between *two* variables and explores how financial analysts apply this method as a tool for modern portfolio management.

5.5 Hypergeometric Distribution

The hypergeometric distribution determines the probability of x events of interest when sample data *without* replacement from a *finite* population has been collected. The **Section 5.5 online topic** discusses the hypergeometric distribution and illustrates its use.

5.6 Using the Poisson Distribution to Approximate the Binomial Distribution

The Poisson distribution approximates the binomial distribution when n is large and π is very small. The approximation gets better as n gets larger and π gets smaller. The **Section 5.6 online topic** explains how to use this approximation.

▼ USING **STATISTICS**
Events of Interest ... , Revisited

In the Ricknel Home Centers scenario at the beginning of this chapter, you were an accountant for the Ricknel Home Centers, LLC. The company's accounting information system automatically reviews order forms from online customers for possible mistakes. Any questionable invoices are tagged and included in a daily exceptions report. Knowing that the probability that an order will be tagged is 0.10, you were able to use the binomial distribution to determine the chance of finding a certain number of tagged forms in a sample of size four. There was a 65.6% chance that none of the forms would be tagged, a 29.2% chance that one would be tagged, and a 5.2% chance that two or more would be tagged. You were also able to determine that, on average, you would expect 0.4 form to be tagged, and the standard deviation of the number of tagged order forms would be 0.6. Now that you have learned the mechanics of using the binomial distribution for a known probability of 0.10 and a sample size of four, you will be able to apply the same approach to any given probability and sample size. Thus, you will be able to make inferences about the online ordering process and, more importantly, evaluate any changes or proposed changes to the process.

▼ SUMMARY

In this chapter, you have studied the probability distribution for a discrete variable and two important discrete probability distributions: the binomial and Poisson distributions. In the next chapter, you will study the normal and uniform distributions.

Use the following rules to select which discrete distribution to use for a particular situation:

- If there is a fixed number of observations, n, each of which is classified as an event of interest or not an event of interest, use the binomial distribution.
- If there is an area of opportunity, use the Poisson distribution.

▼ REFERENCES

1. Hogg, R. V., J. T. McKean, and A. V. Craig. *Introduction to Mathematical Statistics*, 7th ed. New York: Pearson Education, 2013.
2. Levine, D. M., P. Ramsey, and R. Smidt. *Applied Statistics for Engineers and Scientists Using Microsoft Excel and Minitab*. Upper Saddle River, NJ: Prentice Hall, 2001.
3. McGinty, J. "The Science Behind Your Long Wait in Line." *Wall Street Journal*, October 8, 2016, p. A2.

▼ KEY EQUATIONS

Expected Value, μ, of a Discrete Variable

$$\mu = E(X) = \sum_{i=1}^{N} x_i P(X = x_i) \tag{5.1}$$

Variance of a Discrete Variable

$$\sigma^2 = \sum_{i=1}^{N} [x_i - E(X)]^2 P(X = x_i) \tag{5.2}$$

Standard Deviation of a Discrete Variable

$$\sigma = \sqrt{\sigma^2} = \sqrt{\sum_{i=1}^{N} [x_i - E(X)]^2 P(X = x_i)} \tag{5.3}$$

Combinations

$$_nC_x = \frac{n!}{x!(n-x)!} \tag{5.4}$$

Binomial Distribution

$$P(X = x \mid n, \pi) = \frac{n!}{x!(n-x)!} \pi^x (1 - \pi)^{n-x} \tag{5.5}$$

Mean of the Binomial Distribution

$$\mu = E(X) = n\pi \tag{5.6}$$

Standard Deviation of the Binomial Distribution

$$\sigma = \sqrt{\sigma^2} = \sqrt{\text{Var}(X)} = \sqrt{n\pi(1 - \pi)} \tag{5.7}$$

Poisson Distribution

$$P(X = x \mid \lambda) = \frac{e^{-\lambda}\lambda^x}{x!} \tag{5.8}$$

▼ KEY TERMS

area of opportunity   211
binomial distribution   204
expected value   200
mathematical model   204

Poisson distribution   211
probability distribution for a discrete
    variable   200
probability distribution function   204

rule of combinations   204
standard deviation of a discrete
    variable   201
variance of a discrete variable   201

▼ CHECKING YOUR UNDERSTANDING

5.30 What is the meaning of the expected value of a variable?

5.31 What are the four properties that must be present in order to use the binomial distribution?

5.32 What are the four properties that must be present in order to use the Poisson distribution?

▼ CHAPTER REVIEW PROBLEMS

5.33 Darwin Head, a 35-year-old sawmill worker, won $1 million and a Chevrolet Malibu Hybrid by scoring 15 goals within 24 seconds at the Vancouver Canucks National Hockey League game (B. Ziemer, "Darwin Evolves into an Instant Millionaire," *Vancouver Sun*, February 28, 2008, p. 1). Head said he would use the money to pay off his mortgage and provide for his children, and he had no plans to quit his job. The contest was part of the Chevrolet Malibu Million Dollar Shootout, sponsored by General Motors Canadian Division. Did GM-Canada risk the $1 million? No! GM-Canada purchased event insurance from a company specializing in promotions at sporting events such as a half-court basketball shot or a hole-in-one giveaway at the local charity golf outing. The event insurance company estimates the probability of a contestant winning the contest, and for a modest charge, insures the event. The promoters pay the insurance premium but take on no added risk as the insurance company will make the large payout in the unlikely event that a contestant wins. To see how it works, suppose that the insurance company estimates that the probability a contestant would win a million-dollar shootout is 0.001 and that the insurance company charges $4,000.
a. Calculate the expected value of the profit made by the insurance company.
b. Many call this kind of situation a win–win opportunity for the insurance company and the promoter. Do you agree? Explain.

5.34 Between 1896—when the Dow Jones index was created—and 2016, the index rose in 67% of the years.
Sources: M. Hulbert, "What the Past Can't Tell Investors," *The New York Times*, January 3, 2010, p. BU2 and **bit.ly/100zwvT**.
Based on this information, and assuming a binomial distribution, what do you think is the probability that the stock market will rise
a. next year?
b. the year after next?
c. in four of the next five years?
d. in none of the next five years?
e. For this situation, what assumption of the binomial distribution might not be valid?

5.35 Smartphone adoption among American younger adults has increased substantially and mobile access to the Internet is pervasive. Seventeen percent of young adults, ages 18–29, who own a smartphone are "smartphone-dependent," meaning that they do not

have home broadband service and have limited options for going online other than their mobile device.
Source: Data extracted from **www.pewinternet.org/fact-sheet/mobile/**.
If a sample of 10 American young adults is selected, what is the probability that
a. 3 are smartphone-dependent?
b. at least 3 are smartphone-dependent?
c. at most 6 are smartphone-dependent?
d. If you selected the sample in a particular geographical area and found that none of the 10 respondents are smartphone-dependent, what conclusions might you reach about whether the percentage of smartphone-dependent young adults in this area was 17%?

5.36 One theory concerning the Dow Jones Industrial Average is that it is likely to increase during U.S. presidential election years. From 1964 through 2016, the Dow Jones Industrial Average increased in 11 of the 14 U.S. presidential election years. Assuming that this indicator is a random event with no predictive value, you would expect that the indicator would be correct 50% of the time.
a. What is the probability of the Dow Jones Industrial Average increasing in 11 or more of the 14 U.S. presidential election years if the probability of an increase in the Dow Jones Industrial Average is 0.50?
b. What is the probability that the Dow Jones Industrial Average will increase in 11 or more of the 14 U.S. presidential election years if the probability of an increase in the Dow Jones Industrial Average in any year is 0.75?

5.37 Medical billing errors and fraud are on the rise. According to Medical Billing Advocates of America, three out of four times, the medical bills that they review contain errors.
Source: Kelly Gooch, "Medical billing errors growing, says Medical Billing Advocates of America," *Becker's Hospital Review*, **bit.ly/2qkA8mR**.
If a sample of 10 medical bills is selected, what is the probability that
a. 0 medical bills will contain errors?
b. exactly 5 medical bills will contain errors?
c. more than 5 medical bills will contain errors?
d. What are the mean and standard deviation of the probability distribution?

5.38 Refer to Problem 5.37. Suppose that a quality improvement initiative has reduced the percentage of medical bills containing errors to 40%. If a sample of 10 medical bills is selected, what is the probability that

a. 0 medical bills will contain errors?

b. exactly 5 medical bills will contain errors?

c. more than 5 medical bills contain errors?

d. What are the mean and standard deviation of the probability distribution?

e. Compare the results of (a) through (c) to those of Problem 5.37 (a) through (c).

5.39 Social log-ins involve recommending or sharing an article that you read online. According to Janrain, in the first quarter of 2017, 45% signed in via Facebook compared with 26% for Google.

Source: Jainrain.com blog, "Identity and social login trends across the web," **www.janrain.com/blog/identity-trends-across-web/**.

If a sample of 10 social log-ins is selected, what is the probability that

a. more than 5 signed in using Facebook?

b. more than 5 signed in using Google?

c. none signed in using Facebook?

d. What assumptions did you have to make to answer (a) through (c)?

5.40 The Consumer Financial Protection Bureau's Consumer Response Team hears directly from consumers about the challenges they face in the marketplace, brings their concerns to the attention of financial institutions, and assists in addressing their complaints. Of the consumers who registered a bank account and service complaint, 46% cited "account management," complaints related to the marketing or management of an account, as their complaint.

Source: *Consumer Response Annual Report,* **bit.ly/2x4CN5w**.

Consider a sample of 20 consumers who registered bank account and service complaints. Use the binomial model to answer the following questions:

a. What is the expected value, or mean, of the binomial distribution?

b. What is the standard deviation of the binomial distribution?

c. What is the probability that 10 of the 20 consumers cited "account management" as the type of complaint?

d. What is the probability that no more than 5 of the consumers cited "account management" as the type of complaint?

e. What is the probability that 5 or more of the consumers cited "account management" as the type of complaint?

5.41 Refer to Problem 5.40. In the same time period, 24% of the consumers registering a bank account and service compliant cited "deposit and withdrawal" as the type of complaint; these are issues such as transaction holds and unauthorized transactions.

a. What is the expected value, or mean, of the binomial distribution?

b. What is the standard deviation of the binomial distribution?

c. What is the probability that none of the 20 consumers cited "deposit and withdrawal" as the type of complaint?

d. What is the probability that no more than 2 of the consumers cited "deposit and withdrawal" as the type of complaint?

e. What is the probability that 3 or more of the consumers cited "deposit and withdrawal" as the type of complaint?

5.42 One theory concerning the S&P 500 Index is that if it increases during the first five trading days of the year, it is likely to increase during the entire year. From 1950 through 2016, the S&P 500 Index had these early gains in 42 years (in 2011 there was virtually no change). In 37 of these 42 years, the S&P 500 Index increased for the entire year. Assuming that this indicator is a random event with no predictive value, you would expect that the indicator would be correct 50% of the time. What is the probability of the S&P 500 Index increasing in 37 or more years if the true probability of an increase in the S&P 500 Index is

a. 0.50?

b. 0.70?

c. 0.90?

d. Based on the results of (a) through (c), what do you think is the probability that the S&P 500 Index will increase if there is an early gain in the first five trading days of the year? Explain.

5.43 *Spurious correlation* refers to the apparent relationship between variables that either have no true relationship or are related to other variables that have not been measured. One widely publicized stock market indicator in the United States that is an example of spurious correlation is the relationship between the winner of the National Football League Super Bowl and the performance of the Dow Jones Industrial Average in that year. The "indicator" states that when a team that existed before the National Football League merged with the American Football League wins the Super Bowl, the Dow Jones Industrial Average will increase in that year. (Of course, any correlation between these is spurious as one thing has absolutely nothing to do with the other!) Since the first Super Bowl was held in 1967 through 2016, the indicator has been correct 38 out of 50 times. Assuming that this indicator is a random event with no predictive value, you would expect that the indicator would be correct 50% of the time.

a. What is the probability that the indicator would be correct 38 or more times in 50 years?

b. What does this tell you about the usefulness of this indicator?

5.44 The United Auto Courts Reports blog notes that the National Insurance Crime Bureau says that Miami-Dade, Broward, and Palm Beach counties account for a substantial number of questionable insurance claims referred to investigators. Assume that the number of questionable insurance claims referred to investigators by Miami-Dade, Broward, and Palm Beach counties is distributed as a Poisson random variable with a mean of 7 per day.

a. What assumptions need to be made so that the number of questionable insurance claims referred to investigators by Miami-Dade, Broward, and Palm Beach counties is distributed as a Poisson random variable?

Making the assumptions given in (a), what is the probability that

b. 5 questionable insurance claims will be referred to investigators by Miami-Dade, Broward, and Palm Beach counties in a day?

c. 10 or fewer questionable insurance claims will be referred to investigators by Miami-Dade, Broward, and Palm Beach counties in a day?

d. 11 or more questionable insurance claims will be referred to investigators by Miami-Dade, Broward, and Palm Beach counties in a day?

▾CASES

Managing Ashland MultiComm Services

The Ashland MultiComm Services (AMS) marketing department wants to increase subscriptions for its *3-For-All* telephone, cable, and Internet combined service. AMS marketing has been conducting an aggressive direct-marketing campaign that includes postal and electronic mailings and telephone solicitations. Feedback from these efforts indicates that including premium channels in this combined service is a very important factor for both current and prospective subscribers. After several brainstorming sessions, the marketing department has decided to add premium cable channels as a no-cost benefit of subscribing to the *3-For-All* service.

The research director, Mona Fields, is planning to conduct a survey among prospective customers to determine how many premium channels need to be added to the *3-For-All* service in order to generate a subscription to the service. Based on past campaigns and on industry-wide data, she estimates the following:

Number of Free Premium Channels	Probability of Subscriptions
0	0.02
1	0.04
2	0.06
3	0.07
4	0.08
5	0.085

1. If a sample of 50 prospective customers is selected and no free premium channels are included in the *3-For-All* service offer, given past results, what is the probability that
   a. fewer than 3 customers will subscribe to the *3-For-All* service offer?
   b. 0 customers or 1 customer will subscribe to the *3-For-All* service offer?
   c. more than 4 customers will subscribe to the *3-For-All* service offer?
   d. Suppose that in the actual survey of 50 prospective customers, 4 customers subscribe to the *3-For-All* service offer. What does this tell you about the previous estimate of the proportion of customers who would subscribe to the *3-For-All* service offer?

2. Instead of offering no premium free channels as in Problem 1, suppose that two free premium channels are included in the *3-For-All* service offer. Given past results, what is the probability that

a. fewer than 3 customers will subscribe to the *3-For-All* service offer?
b. 0 customers or 1 customer will subscribe to the *3-For-All* service offer?
c. more than 4 customers will subscribe to the *3-For-All* service offer?
d. Compare the results of (a) through (c) to those of Problem 1.
e. Suppose that in the actual survey of 50 prospective customers, 6 customers subscribe to the *3-For-All* service offer. What does this tell you about the previous estimate of the proportion of customers who would subscribe to the *3-For-All* service offer?
f. What do the results in (e) tell you about the effect of offering free premium channels on the likelihood of obtaining subscriptions to the *3-For-All* service?

3. Suppose that additional surveys of 50 prospective customers were conducted in which the number of free premium channels was varied. The results were as follows:

Number of Free Premium Channels	Number of Subscriptions
1	5
3	6
4	6
5	7

How many free premium channels should the research director recommend for inclusion in the *3-For-All* service? Explain.

Digital Case

Apply your knowledge about expected value in this continuing Digital Case from Chapters 3 and 4.

Open **BullsAndBears.pdf**, a marketing brochure from EndRun Financial Services. Read the claims and examine the supporting data. Then answer the following:

1. Are there any "catches" about the claims the brochure makes for the rate of return of Happy Bull and Worried Bear funds?

2. What subjective data influence the rate-of-return analyses of these funds? Could EndRun be accused of making false and misleading statements? Why or why not?

3. The expected-return analysis seems to show that the Worried Bear fund has a greater expected return than the Happy Bull fund. Should a rational investor never invest in the Happy Bull fund? Why or why not?

▼EXCEL GUIDE

EG5.1 The PROBABILITY DISTRIBUTION for a DISCRETE VARIABLE

Key Technique Use **SUMPRODUCT(***X cell range, P(X) cell range***)** to compute the expected value. Use **SUMPRODUCT(***squared differences cell range, P(X) cell range***)** to compute the variance.

Example Compute the expected value, variance, and standard deviation for the number of interruptions per day data of Table 5.1 on page 200.

Workbook Use the **Discrete Variable workbook** as a model.

For the example, open to the **DATA worksheet** of the **Discrete Variable workbook**. The worksheet contains the column A and B entries needed to compute the expected value, variance, and standard deviation for the example. Unusual for a DATA worksheet in this book, column C contains formulas. These formulas use the expected value that cell B4 in the COMPUTE worksheet of the same workbook computes (first three rows shown below) and are equivalent to the fourth column calculations in Table 5.3.

	A	B	C
1	x	P(X)	[X-E(X)]^2
2	0	0.35	=(A2 - COMPUTE!$B$4)^2
3	1	0.25	=(A3 - COMPUTE!$B$4)^2
4	2	0.20	=(A4 - COMPUTE!$B$4)^2

For other problems, modify the DATA worksheet. Enter the probability distribution data into columns A and B and, if necessary, extend column C, by first selecting cell C7 and then copying that cell down as many rows as necessary. If the probability distribution has fewer than six outcomes, select the rows that contain the extra, unwanted outcomes, right-click, and then click Delete in the shortcut menu.

Appendix F further explains the SUMPRODUCT function that the COMPUTE worksheet uses to compute the expected value and variance.

EG5.2 BINOMIAL DISTRIBUTION

Key Technique Use the **BINOM.DIST(***number of events of interest, sample size, probability of an event of interest, FALSE***)** function.

Example Compute the binomial probabilities for $n = 4$ and $\pi = 0.1$, and construct a histogram of that probability distribution, similar to Figures 5.2 and 5.3 on page 207.

PHStat Use **Binomial**.

For the example, select **PHStat → Probability & Prob. Distributions → Binomial**. In the procedure's dialog box (shown below):

1. Enter **4** as the **Sample Size**.
2. Enter **0.1** as the **Prob. of an Event of Interest**.
3. Enter **0** as the **Outcomes From** value and enter **4** as the (Outcomes) **To** value.
4. Enter a **Title**, check **Histogram**, and click **OK**.

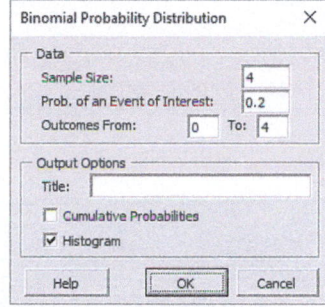

Check **Cumulative Probabilities** before clicking **OK** in step 4 to have the procedure include columns for $P(\leq X)$, $P(<X)$, $P(>X)$, and $P(\geq X)$ in the binomial probabilities table.

Workbook Use the **Binomial workbook** as a template and model.

For the example, open to the **COMPUTE worksheet** of the **Binomial workbook**, shown in Figure 5.2 on page 207. The worksheet already contains the entries needed for the example. For other problems, change the sample size in cell B4 and the probability of an event of interest in cell B5. If necessary, extend the binomial probabilities table by first selecting cell range A18:B18 and then copying that cell range down as many rows as necessary. To construct a histogram of the probability distribution, use the Appendix Section B.6 instructions.

For problems that require cumulative probabilities, use the CUMULATIVE worksheet in the Binomial workbook. The SHORT TAKES for Chapter 5 explains and documents this worksheet.

EG5.3 POISSON DISTRIBUTION

Key Technique Use the **POISSON.DIST(***number of events of interest, the average or expected number of events of interest, FALSE***)** function.

Example Compute the Poisson probabilities for the Figure 5.7 customer arrival problem on page 212.

PHStat Use **Poisson**.

For the example, select **PHStat→Probability & Prob. Distributions→Poisson**. In this procedure's dialog box (shown below):

1. Enter **3** as the **Mean/Expected No. of Events of Interest**.
2. Enter a **Title** and click **OK**.

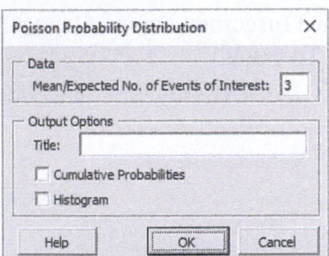

Check **Cumulative Probabilities** before clicking **OK** in step 2 to have the procedure include columns for $P(\leq X)$, $P(<X)$, $P(>X)$, and $P(\geq X)$ in the Poisson probabilities table. Check **Histogram** to construct a histogram of the Poisson probability distribution.

Workbook Use the **Poisson workbook** as a template.

For the example, open to the **COMPUTE worksheet** of the **Poisson workbook**, shown in Figure 5.7 on page 212. The worksheet already contains the entries for the example. For other problems, change the mean or expected number of events of interest in cell E4. To construct a histogram of the probability distribution, use the Appendix Section B.6 instructions.

For problems that require cumulative probabilities, use the CUMULATIVE worksheet in the Binomial workbook. The SHORT TAKES for Chapter 5 explains and documents this worksheet.

CHAPTER 5

▼ JMP GUIDE

JG5.1   The PROBABILITY DISTRIBUTION for a DISCRETE VARIABLE

Expected Value of a Discrete Variable

Use **Formula**.

For example, to compute the expected value for the number of interruptions per day of Table 5.1 on page 200, open to the **Table 5.1 data table** that contains X and $P(X)$ values in the first two columns and:

1. Double-click the blank third column. JMP labels column as **Column 3** (and fills it with missing values).
2. Right-click the **Column 3 column heading** and select **Formula**.

In the Formula dialog box (see the Chapter 2 JMP Gallery on page 112).

3. Enter **col sum** in the filter box above the list of formula functions. Click **Col Sum** in the formula function list box to add Col Sum( ) to the formula workspace.
4. Click **X** in the columns list to add **X** to the formula.
5. Click the **multiply icon (x)** to add a multiply symbol to the formula.
6. Click **P(X)** in the columns list to complete the function as Col Sum($X \cdot P(X)$).
7. Click **OK**.

The cells of Column 3 each display the expected value $E(X)$.

JG5.2   BINOMIAL DISTRIBUTION

Use **Formula**.

For example, to compute the binomial probabilities for $n = 4$ and $\pi = 0.1$, select **File→New→Data Table** and:

1. Double-click the **Column 1 column heading**.

In the Column 1 dialog box

2. Enter **X** as the **Column name**.
3. Select **Ordinal** as the **Modeling Type**.
4. Click **OK**.

Back in the data table:

5. Enter the values **0** through **4** in the first column, starting with the first row.
6. Double-click the blank second column. JMP labels column as **Column 2** (and fills it with missing values).
7. Right-click the **Column 2 column heading** and select **Formula**.

In the Formula dialog box (see the Chapter 2 JMP Gallery on page 112):

8. Enter **binom** in the filter box above the list of formula functions. Click **Binomial Probability** in the formula function list box to add Binomial Distribution (p, n, k) to the formula workspace.
9. Enter **0.1** and press **Enter** to replace p with 0.1 in the workspace.

10. Click **n** (in formula), enter **4**, and press **Enter** to replace n with 4.

11. Click **k** (in formula) and then click **X** in the columns list to replace k to complete the function as Binomial Probability (0.1, 4, *X*).

12. Click **OK**.

13. Double-click the **Column 2 column heading** and in the Column 2 dialog box, enter **P(X)** as the **Column Name** and then click **OK**.

JMP inserts a column of binomial probabilities in Column 2. To construct a histogram of this distribution, use the Appendix Section B.6 instructions. To create a column of cumulative probabilities, click **Binomial Distribution** in step 3.

JG5.3   POISSON DISTRIBUTION

Use **Formula**.

For example, to compute the Poisson probabilities for the Figure 5.7 bank customer arrival problem on page 212, select **File ➔ New ➔ Data Table** and:

1. Double-click the **Column 1 column heading**.

In the Column 1 dialog box:

2. Enter **X** as the **Column name**.
3. Select **Ordinal** as the **Modeling Type**.
4. Click **OK**.

Back in the data table:

5. Enter **0** in the **row 1 cell** of the first column and enter **1** in **row 2 cell**.
6. Select the rows 1 and 2 cell, right-click and select **Fill ➔ Continue sequence to**.
7. In the Please Enter a Number dialog box (shown in next column), enter **16** in the **Continue to row** box and click **OK**.

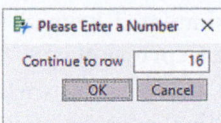

JMP enters integers through 15 into the first column:

8. Double-click the blank second column. JMP labels the column as **Column 2** (and fills it with missing values).
9. Right-click the **Column 2 column heading** and select **Formula**.

In the Formula dialog box (see the Chapter 2 JMP Gallery on page 112):

10. Enter **poi** in the filter box above the list of formula functions. Click **Poisson Probability** in the formula function list box to add Poisson Distribution (lambda, 3) to the formula workspace.
11. Enter **3** and press **Enter** to replace lambda in the workspace.
12. Click **k** (in formula) and then click **X** in the columns list to replace k to complete the function as Poisson Probability (3, *X*).
13. Click **OK**.
14. Double-click the **Column 2 column heading** and

In the Column 2 dialog box:

15. Enter **P(X)** in the **Column Name**, select **Fixed Dec** from the **Format** pull-down list, and enter **6** in the **Dec** box.
16. Click **OK**.

JMP inserts a column of Poisson probabilities in Column 2. To construct a histogram of this distribution, use the Appendix Section B.6 instructions. To create a column of cumulative probabilities, click **Poisson Distribution** in step 3.

CHAPTER 5

▼MINITAB GUIDE

MG5.1   The PROBABILITY DISTRIBUTION for a DISCRETE VARIABLE

Expected Value of a Discrete Variable

Use **Assign Formula to Column** to compute the expected value of a discrete variable.

For example, to compute the expected value for the number of interruptions per day of Table 5.1 on page 200, open to the **Table_5.1 worksheet** that contains *X* and *P(X)* values in columns C1 and C2 and:

1. Select **column C3** and enter **E(X)** as its name.
2. Right-click and select **Formulas ➔ Assign Formula to Column** from the shortcut menu.

In the Assign Formula to C3 box (shown on page 222):

3. Double-click **Sum** in the **Functions** list box to add SUM(number) to the Expression box.
4. Double-click **C1 X** in the variables list to form SUM(X') in the **Expression** box.

5. Click ***** on the simulated keypad to add ***** to form SUM('X' *) in the **Expression** box.
6. Double-click **C2 P(X)** in the variables list to form SUM('X' * 'P(X)') in the **Expression** box.
7. Click **OK**.

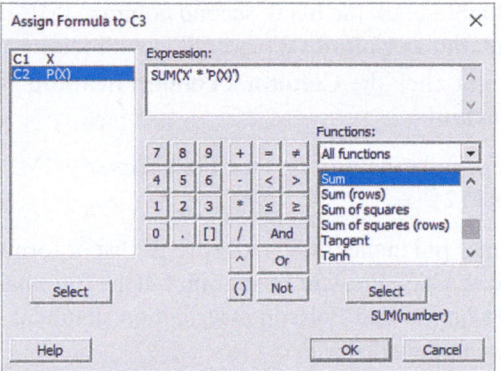

The expected value $E(X)$ appears in the first row of column C3.

MG5.2   BINOMIAL DISTRIBUTION

Use **Binomial**.

For example, to compute binomial probabilities for $n = 4$ and $\pi = 0.1$, open to a new, blank worksheet and:

1. Enter **X** as the name of **column C1**.
2. Enter the values **0** through **4** in **column C1**, starting with row 1.
3. Enter **P(X)** as the name of **column C2**.
4. Select **Calc → Probability Distributions → Binomial**.

In the Binomial Distribution dialog box (shown below):

5. Click **Probability** (to compute the probabilities of exactly X events of interest for all values of X).

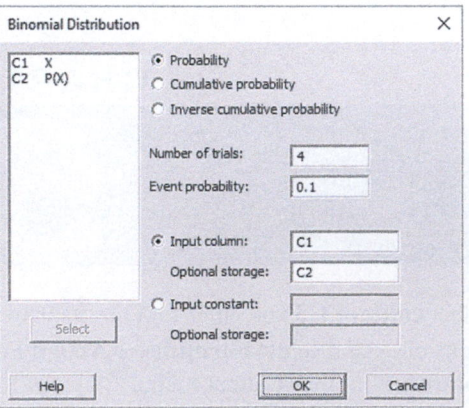

6. Enter **4** (the sample size) in the **Number of trials** box.
7. Enter **0.1** in the **Event probability** box.
8. Click **Input column**, enter **C1** in its box, and press **Tab**.
9. Enter **C2** in the first **Optional storage** box.
10. Click **OK**.

Minitab inserts a column of binomial probabilities in column C2. To create the Figure 5.2 tabular results, skip step 9.

MG5.3   POISSON DISTRIBUTION

Use **Poisson**.

For example, to compute these probabilities for the Figure 5.7 customer arrival problem on page 212 open to a new, blank worksheet and:

1. Enter **X** as the name of **column C1**.
2. Enter the values **0** through **15** in **column C1**, starting with row 1.
3. Enter **P(X)** as the name of **column C2**.
4. Select **Calc → Probability Distributions → Poisson**.

In the Poisson Distribution dialog box (shown below):

5. Click **Probability** (to compute the probabilities of exactly X events of interest for all values of X).
6. Enter **3** in the **Mean** box.
7. Click **Input column**, enter **C1** in its box, and press **Tab**.
8. Enter **C2** in the first **Optional storage** box.
9. Click **OK**.

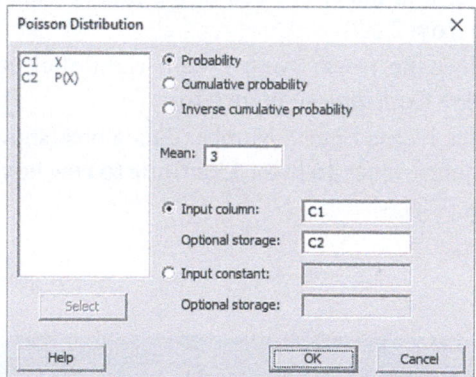

Minitab inserts a column of Poisson probabilities in column C2. To create the Figure 5.7 tabular results, skip step 8. To obtain cumulative probabilities, click **Cumulative probability** in step 5.

The Normal Distribution and Other Continuous Distributions

6

CONTENTS

OBJECTIVES

- Compute probabilities from the normal distribution
- Use the normal distribution to solve business problems
- Use the normal probability plot to determine whether a set of data is approximately normally distributed
- Compute probabilities from the uniform distribution

▼ USING **STATISTICS**
Normal Load Times at MyTVLab

You are the vice president in charge of sales and marketing for MyTVLab, a web-based business that has evolved into a full-fledged, subscription-based streaming video service. To differentiate MyTVLab from the other companies that sell similar services, you decide to create a "Why Choose Us" web page to help educate new and prospective subscribers about all that MyTVLab offers.

As part of that page, you have produced a new video that samples the content MyTVLab streams as well as demonstrates the relative ease of setting up MyTVLab on many types of devices. You want this video to download with the page so that a visitor can jump to different segments immediately or view the video later, when offline.

You know from research (see reference 3) and past observations, Internet visitors will not tolerate waiting too long for a web page to load. One wait time measure is load time, the time in seconds that passes from first pointing a browser to a web page until the web page is fully loaded and content such as video is ready to be viewed. You have set a goal that the load time for the new sales page should rarely exceed 10 seconds (too long for visitors to wait) and, ideally, should rarely be less than 1 second (a waste of company Internet resources).

To measure this time, you point a web browser at the MyTVLab corporate test center to the new sales web page and record the load time. In your first test, you record a time of 6.67 seconds. You repeat the test and record a time of 7.52 seconds. Though consistent to your goal, you realize that two load times do not constitute strong proof of anything, especially as your assistant has performed his own test and recorded a load time of 8.83 seconds.

Could you use a method based on probability theory to ensure that most load times will be within the range you seek? MyTVLab has recorded past load times of a similar page with a similar video and determined the mean load time of that page is 7 seconds, the standard deviation of those times is 2 seconds, that approximately two-thirds of the load times are between 5 and 9 seconds, and about 95% of the load times are between 3 and 11 seconds.

Could you use these facts to assure yourself that the load time goal you have set for the new sales page is likely to be met?

223

n Chapter 5 you learned how to use probability distributions for a *discrete* numerical variable. In the MyTVLab scenario, you are examining the load time, a *continuous* numerical variable. You are no longer considering a table of discrete (specific) values, but a continuous range of values. For example, the phrase "load times are between 5 and 9 seconds" includes *any* value between 5 and 9 and not just the values 5, 6, 7, 8, and 9. If you plotted the phrase on a graph, you would draw a *continuous* line from 5 to 9 and not just plot five specific points.

When you add information about the shape of the range of values, such as two-thirds of the load times are between 5 and 9 seconds or about 95% of the load times are between 3 and 11 seconds, you can visualize the plot of all values as an area under a curve. If that area under the curve follows the well-known pattern of certain continuous distributions, you can use the continuous probability distribution for that pattern to estimate the likelihood that a load time is within a range of values. In the MyTVLab scenario, the past load times of a similar page describes a pattern that conforms to the pattern associated with the normal distribution, the subject of Section 6.2. That would allow you, as the vice president for sales and marketing, to use the normal distribution with the statistics given to determine if your load time goal is likely to be met.

6.1 Continuous Probability Distributions

Continuous probability distributions vary by the shape of the area under the curve. Figure 6.1 visualizes the normal, uniform, and exponential probability distributions.

FIGURE 6.1
Three continuous
probability distributions

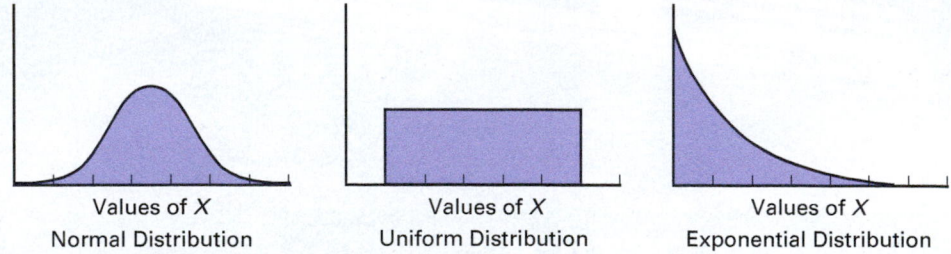

Values of *X*	Values of *X*	Values of *X*
Normal Distribution	Uniform Distribution	Exponential Distribution

Some distributions, including the normal and uniform distributions in Figure 6.1, show a symmetrical shape. Distributions such as the right-skewed exponential distribution do not. In symmetrical distributions the mean equals the median, whereas in a right-skewed distribution the mean is greater than the median. Each of the three distributions also has unique properties.

The **normal distribution** is not only symmetrical, but bell-shaped, a shape that (loosely) suggests the profile of a bell. Being bell-shaped means that most values of the continuous variable will cluster around the mean. Although the values in a normal distribution can range from negative infinity to positive infinity, the shape of the normal distribution makes it very unlikely that extremely large or extremely small values will occur.

The **uniform distribution**, also known as the rectangular distribution, contains values that are equally distributed in the range between the smallest value and the largest value. In a uniform distribution, every value is equally likely.

The **exponential distribution** contains values from zero to positive infinity and is right-skewed, making the mean greater than the median. Its shape makes it unlikely that extremely large values will occur.

Besides visualizations such as those in Figure 6.1, a continuous probability distribution can be expressed mathematically as a *probability density function*. A **probability density function** for a specific continuous probability distribution, represented by the symbol $f(X)$, defines the distribution of the values for a continuous variable and can be used as the basis for calculations that determine the likelihood or probability that a value will be within a certain range.

6.2 The Normal Distribution

The most commonly used continuous probability distribution, the normal distribution, plays an important role in statistics and business. Because of its relationship to the Central Limit Theorem (see Section 7.2), the distribution provides the basis for classical statistical inference and can be used to approximate various discrete probability distributions. For business, many continuous variables used in decision making have distributions that closely resemble the normal distribution. The normal distribution can be used to estimate values for such variables, specifically, the probability that values occur within a specific range or interval. This probability corresponds to an area under a curve that the normal distribution defines. Because a single point on a curve, representing a specific value, cannot define an area, the area under any single point/specific value will be 0. Therefore, when using the normal distribution to estimate values of a continuous variable, the probability that the variable will be exactly a specified value is always zero.

For the MyTVLab scenario, the load time for the new sales page would be an example of a continuous variable whose distribution approximated the normal distribution. This would allow you to estimate probabilities such as the probability that the load time would be between 7 and 10 seconds, the probability that the load time would be between 8 and 9 seconds, or the probability that the load time would be between 7.99 and 8.01 seconds. You would also say properly that the probability that the load time is *exactly* 7 seconds (or any other specific value) is zero.

Exhibit 6.1 presents four important theoretical properties of the normal distribution. The distributions of many business decision-making continuous variables share all but the last of these properties which is sufficient to allow the use of the normal distribution to *estimate* the probability for specific ranges or intervals of values.

EXHIBIT 6.1

Normal Distribution Important Theoretical Properties

Symmetrical distribution. Its mean and median are equal.

Bell-shaped. Values cluster around the mean.

Interquartile range is roughly 1.33 standard deviations. Therefore, the middle 50% of the values are contained within an interval that is approximately two-thirds of a standard deviation below and two-thirds of a standard deviation above the mean.

The distribution has an infinite range ($-\infty < X < \infty$). Six standard deviations approximate this range (see page 230).

Table 6.1 presents the fill amounts, the volume of liquid placed inside a bottle, for a production run of 10,000 one-liter water bottles. Due to minor irregularities in the machinery and the water pressure, the fill amounts will vary slightly from the desired target amount, which is a bit more than 1.0 liters to prevent underfilling of bottles and the subsequent consumer unhappiness that such underfilling would cause.

TABLE 6.1

Fill Amounts for 10,000 One-liter Water Bottles

Fill Amount (liters)	Relative Frequency
< 1.025	48/10,000 = 0.0048
1.025 < 1.030	122/10,000 = 0.0122
1.030 < 1.035	325/10,000 = 0.0325
1.035 < 1.040	695/10,000 = 0.0695
1.040 < 1.045	1,198/10,000 = 0.1198
1.045 < 1.050	1,664/10,000 = 0.1664
1.050 < 1.055	1,896/10,000 = 0.1896
1.055 < 1.060	1,664/10,000 = 0.1664
1.060 < 1.065	1,198/10,000 = 0.1198
1.065 < 1.070	695/10,000 = 0.0695
1.070 < 1.075	325/10,000 = 0.0325
1.075 < 1.080	122/10,000 = 0.0122
1.080 or above	48/10,000 = 0.0048
Total	1.0000

The fill amounts for the 10,000-bottle run cluster in the interval 1.05 to 1.055 liters. The fill amounts distribute symmetrically around that grouping, forming a bell-shaped pattern which the relative frequency polygon that has been superimposed over the Figure 6.2 histogram highlights. These properties of the fill amount permit the normal distribution to be used to estimate values. Note that the distribution of fill amounts does not have an infinite range as fill amounts can never be less than 0 or more than the entire, fixed volume of a bottle. Therefore, the normal distribution can only be an approximation of the fill amount distribution, a distribution that fails to have that fourth important property of a true normal distribution.

studentTIP

Section 2.4 discusses histograms and relative frequency polygons.

FIGURE 6.2
Relative frequency histogram and polygon of the amount filled in 10,000 water bottles

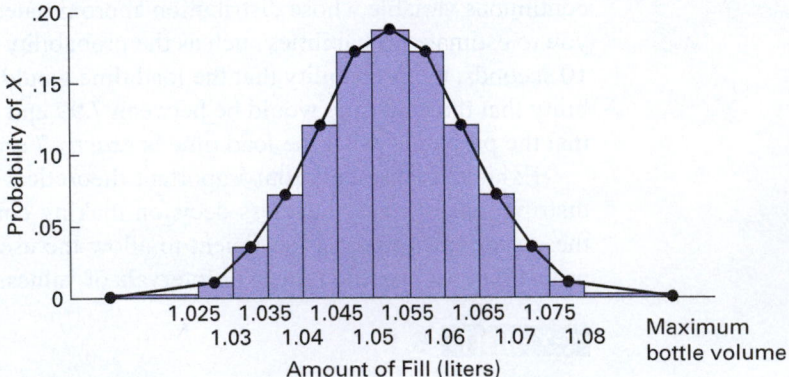

Role of the Mean and the Standard Deviation

Each combination of a mean μ and a standard deviation σ defines a separate normal distribution. Figure 6.3 shows the normal distribution for three such combinations. Distributions A and B have the same mean but have different standard deviations. Distributions A and C have the same standard deviation but have different means. Distributions B and C have different values for both the mean and standard deviation.

FIGURE 6.3
Three normal distributions

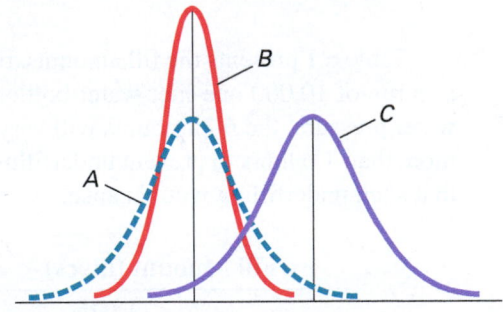

Not surprisingly, both the mean, μ, and the standard deviation, σ, appear in Equation (6.1) that defines the probability density function for the normal distribution.

NORMAL PROBABILITY DENSITY FUNCTION

$$f(X) = \frac{1}{\sqrt{2\pi\sigma}}e^{-(1/2)[(X-\mu)/\sigma]^2}$$ **(6.1)**

where

e = mathematical constant approximated by 2.71828
π = mathematical constant approximated by 3.14159
μ = mean
σ = standard deviation
X = any value of the continuous variable, where $-\infty < X < \infty$

Calculating Normal Probabilities

Examining Equation (6.1) reveals that the only terms that are not numerical constants are the mean, μ, and the standard deviation, σ. This insight allows normal probabilities to be calculated using an alternative method based in part on using the **transformation formula** that Equation (6.2) defines. Using this second method avoids the calculational complexities that the direct use of Equation (6.1) would create.

Z TRANSFORMATION FORMULA

The Z value is equal to the difference between X and the mean, μ, divided by the standard deviation, σ.

$$Z = \frac{X - \mu}{\sigma}$$

(6.2)

The transformation formula converts a normally distributed variable, X, to a corresponding **standardized normal variable, Z**. The formula calculates a Z value that expresses the difference of the X value from the mean, μ, in standard deviation units called *standardized units*. While a variable, X, has mean, μ, and standard deviation, σ, the standardized variable, Z, always has mean $\mu = 0$ and standard deviation $\sigma = 1$.

With a calculated Z value, you can use Table E.2, the **cumulative standardized normal distribution**, to determine the probability. For example, recall from the MyTVLab scenario on page 223 that past data indicate that the sales page load time is normally distributed, with a mean $\mu = 7$ seconds and a standard deviation $\sigma = 2$ seconds. From Figure 6.4, you see that every measurement X has a corresponding standardized measurement Z, computed from Equation (6.2), the transformation formula.

FIGURE 6.4

Transformation of scales

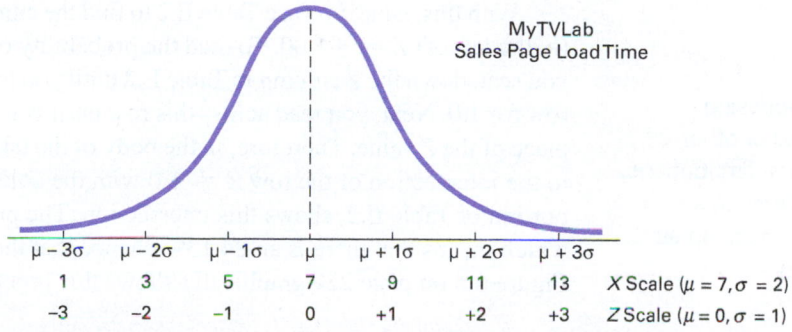

Therefore, a load time of 9 seconds is equivalent to 1 standardized unit (1 standard deviation) above the mean because

$$Z = \frac{9 - 7}{2} = +1$$

A load time of 1 second is equivalent to -3 standardized units (3 standard deviations) below the mean because

$$Z = \frac{1 - 7}{2} = -3$$

In Figure 6.4, the standard deviation is the unit of measurement. In other words, a time of 9 seconds is 2 seconds (1 standard deviation) higher, or *slower*, than the mean time of 7 seconds. Similarly, a time of 1 second is 6 seconds (3 standard deviations) lower, or *faster*, than the mean time.

To further illustrate the transformation formula, suppose that the technical support web page has a load time that is normally distributed, with a mean $\mu = 4$ seconds and a standard deviation $\sigma = 1$ second. Figure 6.5 shows this distribution.

FIGURE 6.5

A different transformation of scales

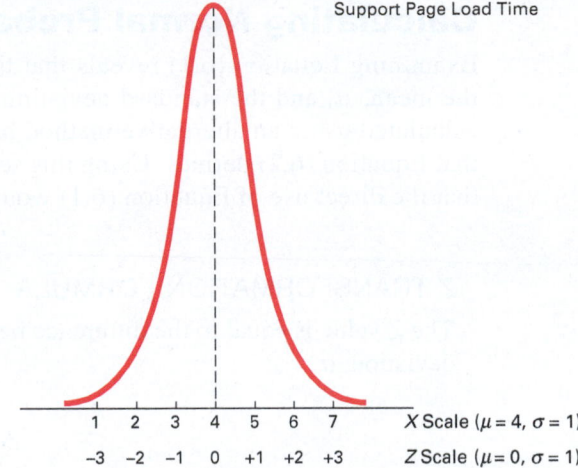

| X Scale ($\mu = 4$, $\sigma = 1$) |
| Z Scale ($\mu = 0$, $\sigma = 1$) |

Comparing these results with those of the sales page, you see that a load time of 5 seconds is 1 standard deviation above the mean download time because

$$Z = \frac{5 - 4}{1} = +1$$

A time of 1 second is 3 standard deviations below the mean load time because

$$Z = \frac{1 - 4}{1} = -3$$

Having determined the Z value, you use a table of values from the cumulative standardized normal distribution to look up the normal probability. Suppose you wanted to find the probability that the load time for the MyTVLab sales page is less than 9 seconds. Recall from page 227 that transforming $X = 9$ to standardized Z units, given a mean $\mu = 7$ seconds and a standard deviation $\sigma = 2$ seconds, leads to a Z value of $+1.00$.

With this value, you use Table E.2 to find the cumulative area under the normal curve less than (to the left of) $Z = +1.00$. To read the probability or area under the curve less than $Z = +1.00$, you scan down the Z column in Table E.2 until you locate the Z value of interest (in 10ths) in the Z row for 1.0. Next, you read across this row until you intersect the column that contains the 100ths place of the Z value. Therefore, in the body of the table, the probability for $Z = 1.00$ corresponds to the intersection of the row $Z = 1.0$ with the column $Z = .00$. Table 6.2, which reproduces a portion of Table E.2, shows this intersection. The probability listed at the intersection is 0.8413, which means that there is an 84.13% chance that the download time will be less than 9 seconds. Figure 6.6 on page 229 graphically shows this probability.

student TIP

When discussing the normal or other continuous distributions, the word *area* has the same meaning as *probability*.

TABLE 6.2

Finding a Cumulative Area under the Normal Curve

Source: Extracted from Table E.2.

					Cumulative Probabilities					
Z	**.00**	**.01**	**.02**	**.03**	**.04**	**.05**	**.06**	**.07**	**.08**	**.09**
0.0	.5000	.5040	.5080	.5120	.5160	.5199	.5239	.5279	.5319	.5359
0.1	.5398	.5438	.5478	.5517	.5557	.5596	.5636	.5675	.5714	.5753
0.2	.5793	.5832	.5871	.5910	.5948	.5987	.6026	.6064	.6103	.6141
0.3	.6179	.6217	.6255	.6293	.6331	.6368	.6406	.6443	.6480	.6517
0.4	.6554	.6591	.6628	.6664	.6700	.6736	.6772	.6808	.6844	.6879
0.5	.6915	.6950	.6985	.7019	.7054	.7088	.7123	.7157	.7190	.7224
0.6	.7257	.7291	.7324	.7357	.7389	.7422	.7454	.7486	.7518	.7549
0.7	.7580	.7612	.7642	.7673	.7704	.7734	.7764	.7794	.7823	.7852
0.8	.7881	.7910	.7939	.7967	.7995	.8023	.8051	.8078	.8106	.8133
0.9	.8159	.8186	.8212	.8238	.8264	.8289	.8315	.8340	.8365	.8389
1.0	.8413	.8438	.8461	.8485	.8508	.8531	.8554	.8577	.8599	.8621

FIGURE 6.6

Determining the area less than *Z* from a cumulative standardized normal distribution

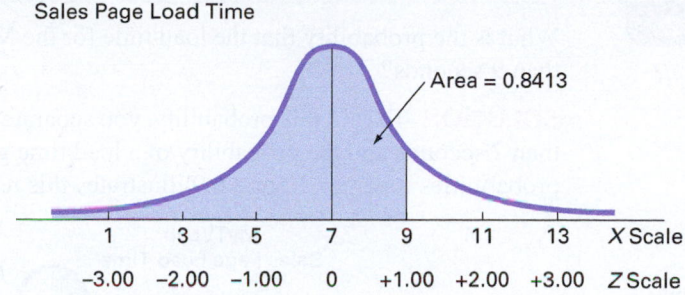

Sales Page Load Time

Area = 0.8413

However, for the other website, you see that a time of 5 seconds is 1 standardized unit above the mean time of 4 seconds. Thus, the probability that the load time will be less than 5 seconds is also 0.8413. Figure 6.7 shows that regardless of the value of the mean, μ, and standard deviation, σ, of a normally distributed variable, Equation (6.2) can transform the *X* value to a *Z* value.

Now that you have learned to use Table E.2 with Equation (6.2), you can answer many questions related to the sales page load time, including whether achieving the load time goal is likely, using the normal distribution.

FIGURE 6.7

Demonstrating a transformation of scales for corresponding cumulative portions under two normal curves

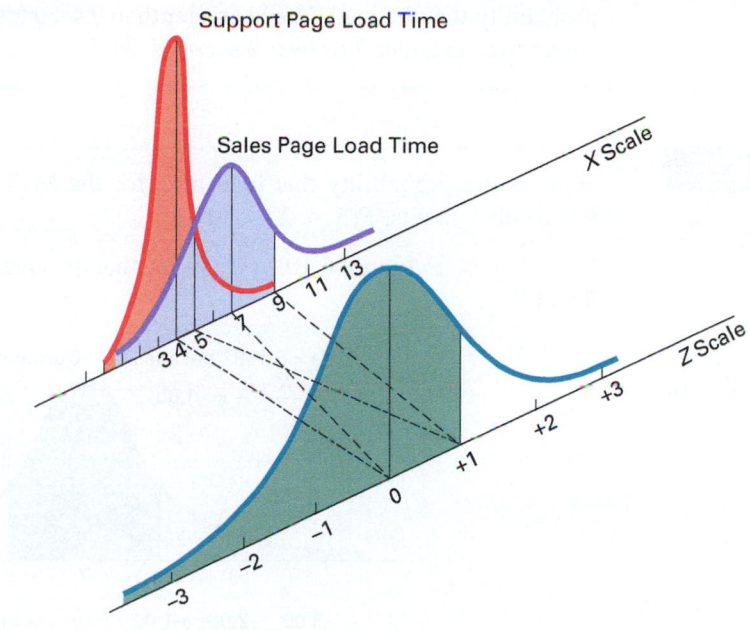

Support Page Load Time

Sales Page Load Time

X Scale

Z Scale

student TIP

You will find it very helpful when computing probabilities under the normal curve if you draw a normal curve and then enter the values for the mean and *X* below the curve and shade the desired area to be determined under the curve.

EXAMPLE 6.1

Finding $P(X > 9)$

What is the probability that the load time for the MyTVLab sales page will be more than 9 seconds?

SOLUTION The probability that the load time will be less than 9 seconds is 0.8413 (see Figure 6.6). Thus, the probability that the load time will be more than 9 seconds is the *complement* of less than 9 seconds, $1 - 0.8413 = 0.1587$. Figure 6.8 illustrates this result.

FIGURE 6.8

Finding $P(X > 9)$

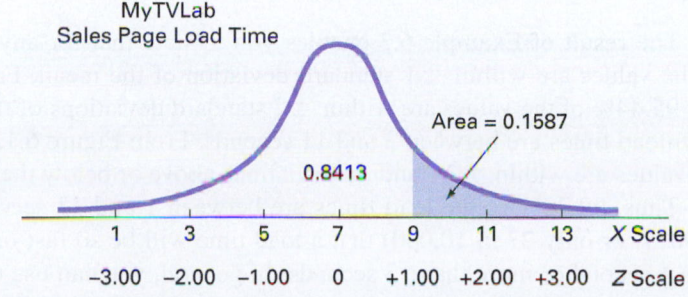

MyTVLab Sales Page Load Time

Area = 0.1587

0.8413

EXAMPLE 6.2

Finding $P(X < 7$ or $X > 9)$

What is the probability that the load time for the MyTVLab will be less than 7 seconds or more than 9 seconds?

SOLUTION To find this probability, you separately calculate the probability of a load time less than 7 seconds and the probability of a load time greater than 9 seconds and then add these two probabilities together. Figure 6.9 illustrates this result.

FIGURE 6.9

Finding
$P(X < 7$ or $X > 9)$

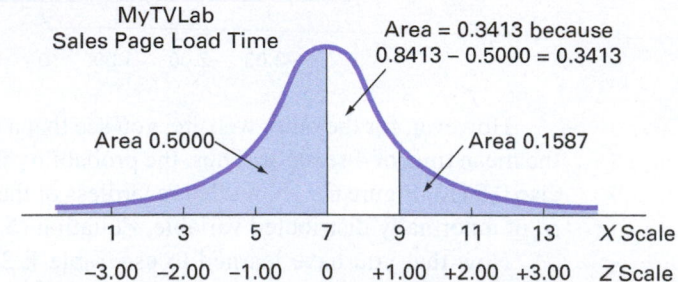

Because the mean is 7 seconds, and because the mean is equal to the median in a normal distribution, 50% of load times are under 7 seconds. From Example 6.1, you know that the probability that the load time is greater than 9 seconds is 0.1587. Therefore, the probability that a load time is under 7 or over 9 seconds, $P(X < 7$ or $X > 9)$, is $0.5000 + 0.1587 = 0.6587$.

EXAMPLE 6.3

Finding
$P(5 < X < 9)$

What is the probability that load time for the MyTVLab sales page will be between 5 and 9 seconds—that is, $P(5 < X < 9)$?

SOLUTION In Figure 6.10, you can see that the area of interest is located between two values, 5 and 9.

FIGURE 6.10

Finding $P(5 < X < 9)$

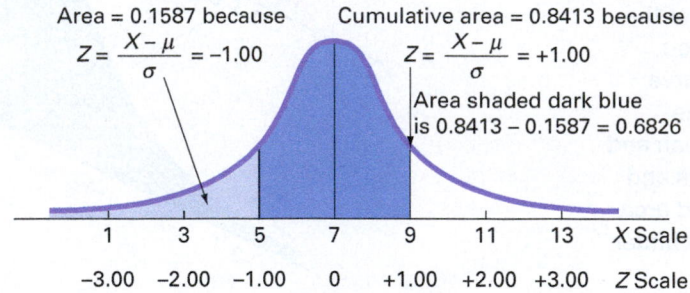

In Example 6.1 on page 229, you already found that the area under the normal curve less than 9 seconds is 0.8413. To find the area under the normal curve less than 5 seconds,

$$Z = \frac{5 - 7}{2} = -1.00$$

Using Table E.2, you look up $Z = -1.00$ and find 0.1587. Therefore, the probability that the load time will be between 5 and 9 seconds is $0.8413 - 0.1587 = 0.6826$, as displayed in Figure 6.10.

The result of Example 6.3 enables you to state that for any normal distribution, 68.26% of the values are within ± 1 standard deviation of the mean. From Figure 6.11, you can see that 95.44% of the values are within ± 2 standard deviations of the mean. Thus, 95.44% of the download times are between 3 and 11 seconds. From Figure 6.12, you can see that 99.73% of the values are within ± 3 standard deviations above or below the mean.

Thus, 99.73% of the load times are between 1 and 13 seconds. Therefore, it is unlikely (0.0027, or only 27 in 10,000) that a load time will be so fast or so slow that it will take less than 1 second or more than 13 seconds. In general, you can use 6σ (i.e., 3 standard deviations below the mean to 3 standard deviations above the mean) as a practical approximation of the range for normally distributed data.

FIGURE 6.11
Finding $P(3 < X < 11)$

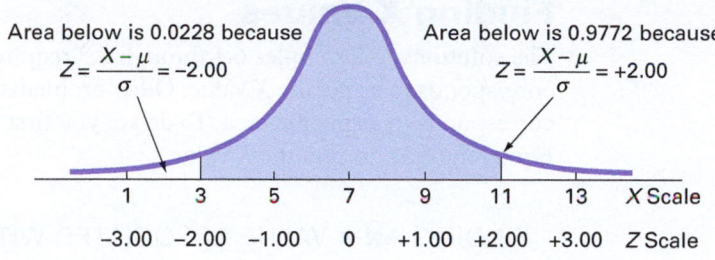

FIGURE 6.12
Finding $P(1 < X < 13)$

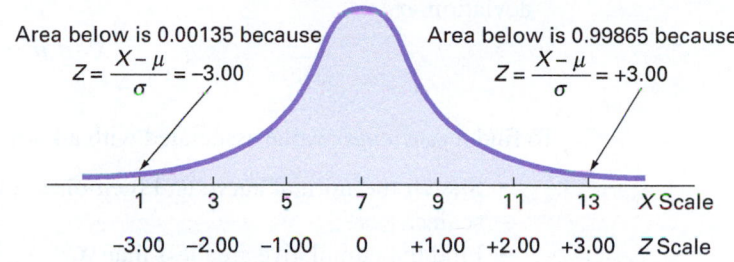

Figures 6.10, 6.11, and 6.12 illustrate that for any normal distribution,

- Approximately 68.26% of the values fall within ± 1 standard deviation of the mean
- Approximately 95.44% of the values fall within ± 2 standard deviations of the mean
- Approximately 99.73% of the values fall within ± 3 standard deviations of the mean

This result is the justification for the empirical rule presented on page 145. The accuracy of the empirical rule increases the closer the variable follows the normal distribution.

VISUAL EXPLORATIONS

Exploring the Normal Distribution

Open the **VE-Normal Distribution add-in workbook** to explore the normal distribution. (For Excel technical requirements, see Appendix D.) When this workbook opens properly, it adds a Normal Distribution menu in the Add-ins tab (Apple menu in Excel for Mac).

To explore the effects of changing the mean and standard deviation on the area under a normal distribution curve, select **Normal Distribution → Probability Density Function**. The add-in displays a normal curve for the MyTVLab website download example and a floating control panel (top right). Use the control panel spinner buttons to change the values for the mean, standard deviation, and X value and then note the effects of these changes on the probability of $X <$ value and the corresponding shaded area under the curve. To see the normal curve labeled with Z values, click **Z Values**. Click **Reset** to reset the control panel values. Click **Finish** to finish exploring.

To create shaded areas under the curve for problems similar to Examples 6.2 and 6.3, select **Normal Distribution → Areas**. In the Areas dialog box (bottom right), enter values, select an Area Option, and click **OK**. The add-in creates a normal distribution curve with areas that are shaded according to the values you entered.

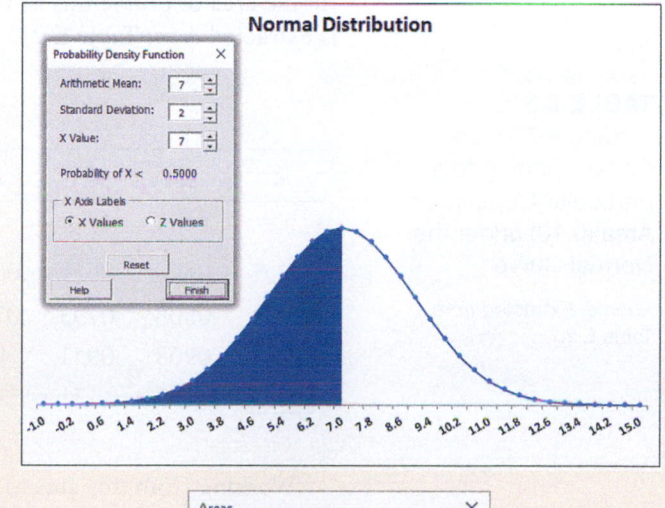

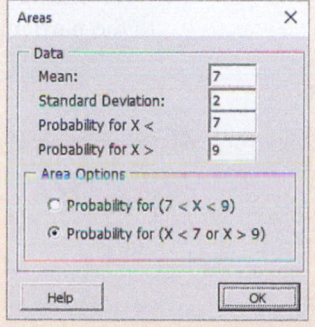

Finding X Values

The solutions to Examples 6.1 through 6.3 require finding the area under the normal curve that corresponds to a specific X value. Other problems require the opposite: Finding the X value that corresponds to a specific area. To do so, you first solve Equation (6.2) for X and use that result, Equation (6.3), to find the X value.

FINDING AN X VALUE ASSOCIATED WITH A KNOWN PROBABILITY

The X value is equal to the mean, μ, plus the product of the Z value and the standard deviation, σ.

$$X = \mu + Z\sigma \tag{6.3}$$

To find a *particular* value associated with a known probability, follow these steps:

- Sketch the normal curve and then place the values for the mean and X on the X and Z scales.
- Find the cumulative area less than X.
- Shade the area of interest.
- Using Table E.2, determine the Z value corresponding to the area under the normal curve less than X.
- Using Equation (6.3), solve for X: $X = \mu + Z\sigma$

Examples 6.4 and 6.5 demonstrate this technique using the five-step procedure to find a particular value associated with a known probability.

EXAMPLE 6.4

Finding the X Value for a Cumulative Probability of 0.10

How much time (in seconds) will elapse before the fastest 10% of the MyTVLab sales pages load time occur?

SOLUTION Because 10% of the load times are expected to occur in under X seconds, the area under the normal curve less than this value is 0.1000. Using the body of Table E.2, you search for the area or probability of 0.1000. The closest result is 0.1003, as shown in Table 6.3 (which is extracted from Table E.2).

TABLE 6.3
Finding a Z Value Corresponding to a Particular Cumulative Area (0.10) under the Normal Curve

Source: Extracted from Table E.2.

					Cumulative Probabilities					
Z	.00	.01	.02	.03	.04	.05	.06	.07	.08	.09
⋮	⋮	⋮	⋮	⋮	⋮	⋮	⋮	⋮	⋮	⋮
−1.5	.0668	.0655	.0643	.0630	.0618	.0606	.0594	.0582	.0571	.0559
−1.4	.0808	.0793	.0778	.0764	.0749	.0735	.0721	.0708	.0694	.0681
−1.3	.0968	.0951	.0934	.0918	.0901	.0885	.0869	.0853	.0838	.0823
−1.2	.1151	.1131	.1112	.1093	.1075	.1056	.1038	.1020	.1003	.0985

Working from this area to the margins of the table, you find that the Z value corresponding to the particular Z row (−1.2) and Z column (.08) is −1.28 (see Figure 6.13).

FIGURE 6.13
Finding Z to determine X

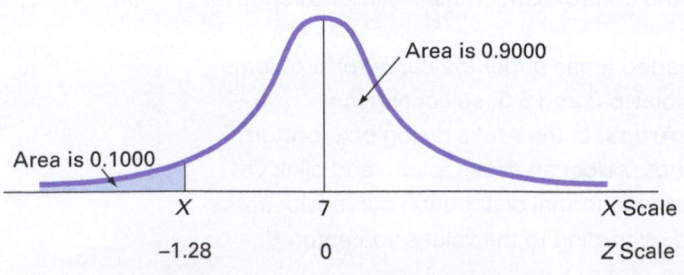

▶ *(continued)*

Once you find Z, you use Equation (6.3) on page 232 to determine the X value. Substituting $\mu = 7$, $\sigma = 2$, and $Z = -1.28$,

$$X = \mu + Z\sigma$$
$$X = 7 + (-1.28)(2) = 4.44 \text{ seconds}$$

Thus, 10% of the load times are 4.44 seconds or less.

EXAMPLE 6.5

Finding the X Values That Include 95% of the Download Times

What are the lower and upper values of X, symmetrically distributed around the mean, that include 95% of the load times for the MyTVLab sales page?

You need to find the lower value of X (called X_L). Then, you find the upper value of X (called X_U). Because 95% of the values are between X_L and X_U, and because X_L and X_U are equally distant from the mean, 2.5% of the values are below X_L (see Figure 6.14).

FIGURE 6.14

Finding Z to determine X_L

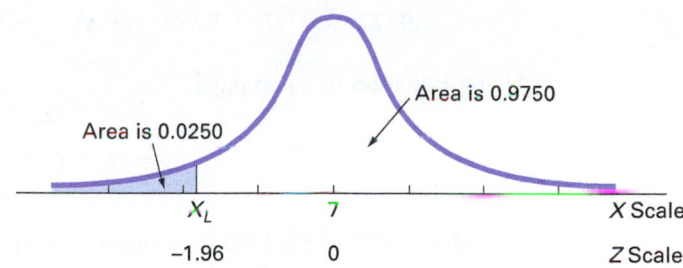

Although X_L is not known, you can find the corresponding Z value because the area under the normal curve less than this Z is 0.0250. Using the body of Table 6.4, you search for the probability 0.0250.

TABLE 6.4

Finding a Z Value Corresponding to a Cumulative Area of 0.025 Under the Normal Curve

Source: Extracted from Table E.2.

					Cumulative Area					
Z	.00	.01	.02	.03	.04	.05	.06	.07	.08	.09
⋮	⋮	⋮	⋮	⋮	⋮	⋮	⋮	⋮	⋮	⋮
−2.0	.0228	.0222	.0217	.0212	.0207	.0202	.0197	.0192	.0188	.0183
−1.9	.0287	.0281	.0274	.0268	.0262	.0256	.0250	.0244	.0239	.0233
−1.8	.0359	.0351	.0344	.0336	.0329	.0322	.0314	.0307	.0301	.0294

Working from the body of the table to the margins of the table, you see that the Z value corresponding to the particular Z row (−1.9) and Z column (.06) is −1.96.

Once you find Z, the final step is to use Equation (6.3) on page 232 as follows:

$$X = \mu + Z\sigma$$
$$= 7 + (-1.96)(2)$$
$$= 7 - 3.92 = 3.08 \text{ seconds}$$

You use a similar process to find X_U. Because only 2.5% of the load times take longer than X_U seconds, 97.5% of the load times take less than X_U seconds. From the symmetry of the normal distribution, you find that the desired Z value, as shown in Figure 6.15 on page 234, is +1.96 (because Z lies to the right of the standardized mean of 0). You can also extract this Z value from Table 6.5. You can see that 0.975 is the area under the normal curve less than the Z value of +1.96.

▶(continued)

FIGURE 6.15
Finding Z to
determine X_U

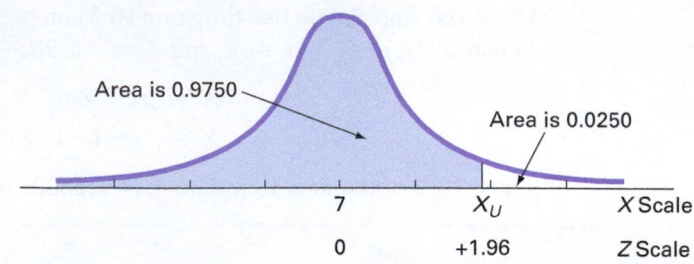

TABLE 6.5
Finding a Z Value
Corresponding to
a Cumulative Area
of 0.975 Under the
Normal Curve

Source: Extracted from
Table E.2.

					Cumulative Area				
Z	.00	.01	.02	.03	.04	.05	.06	.07	.08	.09
⋮	⋮	⋮	⋮	⋮	⋮	⋮	⋮	⋮	⋮	⋮
+1.8	.9641	.9649	.9656	.9664	.9671	.9678	.9686	.9693	.9699	.9706
+1.9	.9713	.9719	.9726	.9732	.9738	.9744	.9750	.9756	.9761	.9767
+2.0	.9772	.9778	.9783	.9788	.9793	.9798	.9803	.9808	.9812	.9817

Using Equation (6.3) on page 232,

$$X = \mu + Z\sigma$$
$$= 7 + (+1.96)(2)$$
$$= 7 + 3.92 = 10.92 \text{ seconds}$$

Therefore, 95% of the load times are between 3.08 and 10.92 seconds.

Excel, JMP, and Minitab can automate normal probability calculations. The Normal Excel Guide Workbook and the Normal JMP and Minitab projects present this functionality as a worksheet or data table template designed to help solve the various types of normal probability problems that Examples 6.1 through 6.5 illustrate. Figure 6.16 displays these templates. For Excel, the entire template consists of the COMPUTE worksheet of the Normal workbook (shown in two parts). For JMP and Minitab, the template consists of two data tables (or worksheets) named Normal Probabilities1 and Normal Probabilities2 in the Normal project.

FIGURE 6.16
Excel (left), JMP (right), and Minitab (bottom) templates for computing normal probabilities and finding X values

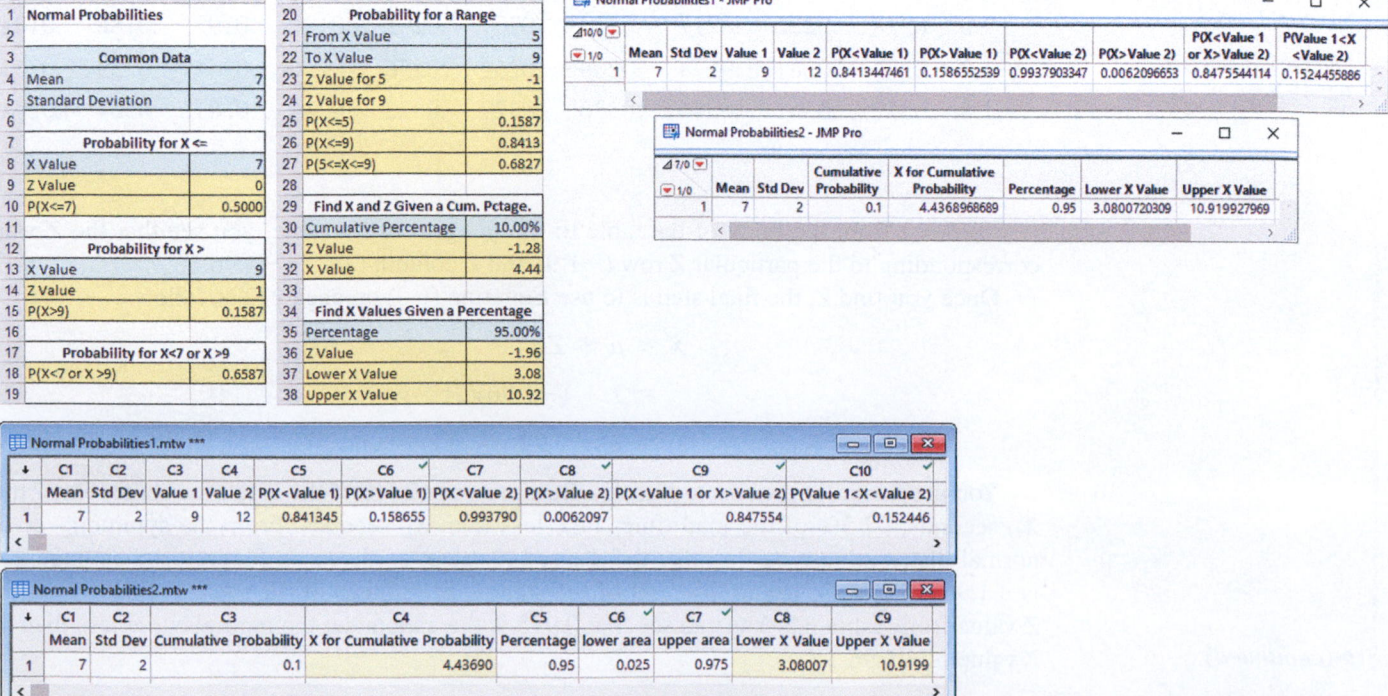

All three templates use formulas to compute cell values and two, the Excel and JMP templates, automatically recalculate when you enter new values for the mean, standard deviation, and, if applicable, the X value(s) and percentages. (The Minitab template is semi-automatic and the values in the tinted cells require using menu commands as the Minitab Guide for this chapter explains.) The Excel, JMP, and Minitab Guides for this chapter explain how to use the templates to solve specific Example (6.1 through 6.5) problems. The SHORT TAKES for Chapter 6 discuss the formulas that each template uses, explaining all statistical functions that those formulas use.

CONSIDER THIS

What Is Normal?

Ironically, the statistician who popularized the use of "normal" to describe the distribution discussed in Section 6.2 was someone who saw the distribution as anything but the everyday, anticipated occurrence that the adjective *normal* usually suggests.

Starting with an 1894 paper, Karl Pearson argued that measurements of phenomena do not naturally, or "normally," conform to the classic bell shape. While this principle underlies much of statistics today, Pearson's point of view was radical to contemporaries who saw the world as standardized and normal. Pearson changed minds by showing that some populations are naturally *skewed* (coining that term in passing), and he helped put to rest the notion that the normal distribution underlies all phenomena.

Today, people still make the type of mistake that Pearson refuted. As a student, you are probably familiar with discussions about grade inflation, a real phenomenon at many schools. But have you ever realized that a "proof" of this inflation—that there are "too few" low grades because grades are skewed toward A's and B's—wrongly implies that grades should be "normally" distributed? Because college students represent small *nonrandom* samples, there are plenty of reasons to suspect that the distribution of grades would not be "normal."

Misunderstandings about the normal distribution have occurred both in business and in the public sector through the years. These misunderstandings have caused a number of business blunders and have sparked several public policy debates, including the causes of the collapse of large financial institutions in 2008. According to one theory, the investment banking industry's application of the normal distribution to assess risk may have contributed to the global collapse (see "A Finer Formula for Assessing Risks," *New York Times*, May 11, 2010, p. B2 and reference 8). Using the normal distribution led these banks to overestimate the probability of having stable market conditions and underestimate the chance of unusually large market losses.

According to this theory, the use of other distributions that have less area in the middle of their curves, and, therefore, more in the "tails" that represent unusual market outcomes, may have led to less serious losses.

As you study this chapter, make sure you understand the assumptions that must hold for the proper use of the "normal" distribution, assumptions that were not explicitly verified by the investment bankers. And, most importantly, always remember that the name *normal distribution* does not mean normal in the everyday sense of the word.

PROBLEMS FOR SECTION 6.2

LEARNING THE BASICS

6.1 Given a standardized normal distribution (with a mean of 0 and a standard deviation of 1, as in Table E.2), what is the probability that
a. Z is less than 1.57?
b. Z is greater than 1.84?
c. Z is between 1.57 and 1.84?
d. Z is less than 1.57 or greater than 1.84?

6.2 Given a standardized normal distribution (with a mean of 0 and a standard deviation of 1, as in Table E.2), what is the probability that
a. Z is between -1.57 and 1.84?
b. Z is less than -1.57 or greater than 1.84?
c. What is the value of Z if only 2.5 percent of all possible Z values are larger?
d. Between what two values of Z (symmetrically distributed around the mean) will 68.26 percent of all possible Z values be contained?

6.3 Given a standardized normal distribution (with a mean of 0 and a standard deviation of 1, as in Table E.2), what is the probability that
a. Z is less than 1.08?
b. Z is greater than -0.21?
c. Z is less than -0.21 or greater than the mean?
d. Z is less than -0.21 or greater than 1.08?

6.4 Given a standardized normal distribution (with a mean of 0 and a standard deviation of 1, as in Table E.2), determine the following probabilities:
a. $P(Z > 1.08)$
b. $P(Z < -0.21)$
c. $P(-1.96 < Z < -0.21)$
d. What is the value of Z if only 15.87 percent of all possible Z values are larger?

6.5 Given a normal distribution with $\mu = 100$ and $\sigma = 10$, what is the probability that

a. $X > 75$?

b. $X < 70$?

c. $X < 80$ or $X > 110$?

d. Between what two X values (symmetrically distributed around the mean) are 80 percent of the values?

6.6 Given a normal distribution with $\mu = 50$ and $\sigma = 4$, what is the probability that

a. $X > 43$?

b. $X < 42$?

c. Five percent of the values are less than what X value?

d. Between what two X values (symmetrically distributed around the mean) are 60 percent of the values?

APPLYING THE CONCEPTS

6.7 In 2015, the per capita consumption of bottled water in the United States was reported to be 36.2 gallons.

Source: Data extracted from **bottledwater.org/economics/bottled-water-market**.

Assume that the per capita consumption of bottled water in the United States is approximately normally distributed with a mean of 36.2 gallons and a standard deviation of 10 gallons.

a. What is the probability that someone in the United States consumed more than 33 gallons of bottled water in 2015?

b. What is the probability that someone in the United States consumed between 10 and 20 gallons of bottled water in 2015?

c. What is the probability that someone in the United States consumed less than 10 gallons of bottled water in 2015?

d. Ninety-nine percent of the people in the United States consumed less than how many gallons of bottled water?

✓ SELF TEST **6.8** Toby's Trucking Company determined that the distance traveled per truck per year is normally distributed, with a mean of 50 thousand miles and a standard deviation of 12 thousand miles.

a. What proportion of trucks can be expected to travel between 34 and 50 thousand miles in a year?

b. What percentage of trucks can be expected to travel either less than 30 or more than 60 thousand miles in a year?

c. How many miles will be traveled by at least 80 percent of the trucks?

d. What are your answers to (a) through (c) if the standard deviation is 10 thousand miles?

6.9 Millennials spent an average of $103 on monthly dining in 2016.

Source: Data extracted from *Consumer Response Annual Report,* available at **bit.ly/2x4CN5w**.

Assume that the amount spent on a monthly dining is normally distributed and that the standard deviation is $12.

a. What is the probability that a randomly selected millennial spent more than $110?

b. What is the probability that a randomly selected millennial spent between $70 and $124?

c. Between what two values will the middle 95 percent of the amounts spent fall?

6.10 A set of final examination grades in an introductory statistics course is normally distributed, with a mean of 73 and a standard deviation of 8.

a. What is the probability that a student scored below 91 on this exam?

b. What is the probability that a student scored between 65 and 89?

c. The probability is 5 percent that a student taking the test scores higher than what grade?

d. If the professor grades on a curve (i.e., gives As to the top ten percent of the class, regardless of the score), are you better off with a grade of 81 on this exam or a grade of 68 on a different exam, where the mean is 62 and the standard deviation is 3? Show your answer statistically and explain.

6.11 A Nielsen study indicates that 18- to 34-year olds spend a mean of 93 minutes watching video on their smartphones per week.

Source: Data extracted from **bit.ly/2rj8GHm**.

Assume that the amount of time watching video on a smartphone per week is normally distributed and that the standard deviation is 15 minutes.

a. What is the probability that an 18- to 34-year-old spends less than 77 minutes watching video on his or her smartphone per week?

b. What is the probability that an 18- to 34-year-old spends between 77 minutes and 109 minutes watching video on his or her smartphone per week?

c. What is the probability that an 18- to 34-year-old spends more than 109 minutes watching video on his or her smartphone per week?

d. One percent of all 18- to 34-year-olds will spend less than how many minutes watching video on his or her smartphone per week?

6.12 In 2015, the per capita consumption of soft drinks in the United States was reported to be 650 eight-ounce servings.

Source: Data extracted from **fortune.com/2016/03/29/soda-sales-drop-11th-year**.

Assume that the per capita consumption of soft drinks in the United States is approximately normally distributed with a mean of 650 eight-ounce servings and a standard deviation of 100 eight-ounce servings.

a. What is the probability that someone in the United States consumed more than 750 eight-ounce servings in 2015?

b. What is the probability that someone in the United States consumed between 450 and 500 eight-ounce servings in 2015?

c. What is the probability that someone in the United States consumed less than 450 eight-ounce servings in 2015?

d. Ninety-nine percent of the people in the United States consumed less than how many servings of eight-ounce soft drinks in 2015?

6.13 Many manufacturing problems involve the matching of machine parts, such as shafts that fit into a valve hole. A particular design requires a shaft with a diameter of 22.000 mm, but shafts with diameters between 21.990 mm and 22.010 mm are acceptable. Suppose that the manufacturing process yields shafts with diameters normally distributed, with a mean of 22.002 mm and a standard deviation of 0.005 mm. For this process, what is

a. the proportion of shafts with a diameter between 21.99 mm and 22.00 mm?

b. the probability that a shaft is acceptable?

c. the diameter that will be exceeded by only two percent of the shafts?

d. What would be your answers in (a) through (c) if the standard deviation of the shaft diameters were 0.004 mm?

6.3 Evaluating Normality

Recall the important theoretical properties of the normal distribution that Exhibit 6.1 lists on page 225. As Section 6.2 notes, many continuous variables used in business closely follow a normal distribution. To determine whether a set of data can be approximated by the normal distribution, you either compare the characteristics of the data with the theoretical properties of the normal distribution or construct a normal probability plot.

Comparing Data Characteristics to Theoretical Properties

Many continuous variables have characteristics that approximate theoretical properties. However, other continuous variables are often neither normally distributed nor approximately normally distributed. For such variables, the descriptive characteristics of the data are inconsistent with the properties of a normal distribution. For such a variable, you can compare the observed characteristics of the variable with what you would expect to occur if the variable follows a normal distribution. To use this method:

- Construct charts and observe their appearance. For small- or moderate-sized data sets, create a stem-and-leaf display or a boxplot. For large data sets, in addition, plot a histogram or polygon.
- Compute descriptive statistics and compare these statistics with the theoretical properties of the normal distribution. Compare the mean and median. Is the interquartile range approximately 1.33 times the standard deviation? Is the range approximately 6 times the standard deviation?
- Evaluate how the values are distributed. Determine whether approximately two-thirds of the values lie between the mean and ± 1 standard deviation. Determine whether approximately four-fifths of the values lie between the mean and ± 1.28 standard deviations. Determine whether approximately 19 out of every 20 values lie between the mean and ± 2 standard deviations.

For example, you can use these techniques to determine whether the three-year return percentages in the sample of retirement funds that Chapters 2 and 3 discuss follow a normal distribution. Table 6.6 presents the descriptive statistics and the five-number summary for the 3YrReturn variable found in Retirement Funds that contains those return percentages and Figure 6.17 uses boxplots to visualize the 3YrReturn variable.

TABLE 6.6

Descriptive Statistics and Five-Number Summary for the Three-Year Return Percentages

Descriptive Statistics		Five-Number Summary	
Mean	7.91	Minimum	−3.40
Median	8.09	First quartile	6.14
Mode	11.93	Median	8.09
Minimum	−3.40	Third quartile	9.86
Maximum	15.32	Maximum	15.32
Range	18.72		
Variance	9.10		
Standard deviation	3.02		
Coeff. of variation	38.15%		
Skewness	−0.33		
Kurtosis	0.42		
Count	479		
Standard error	0.14		

FIGURE 6.17
Excel (top), JMP (bottom left), and Minitab (bottom right) boxplots for the three-year return percentages

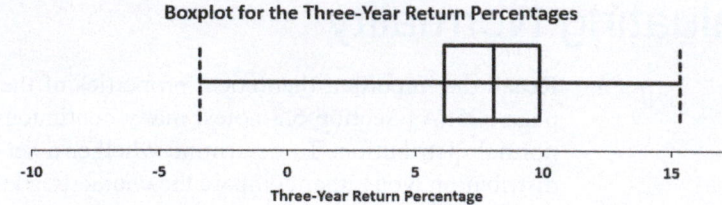

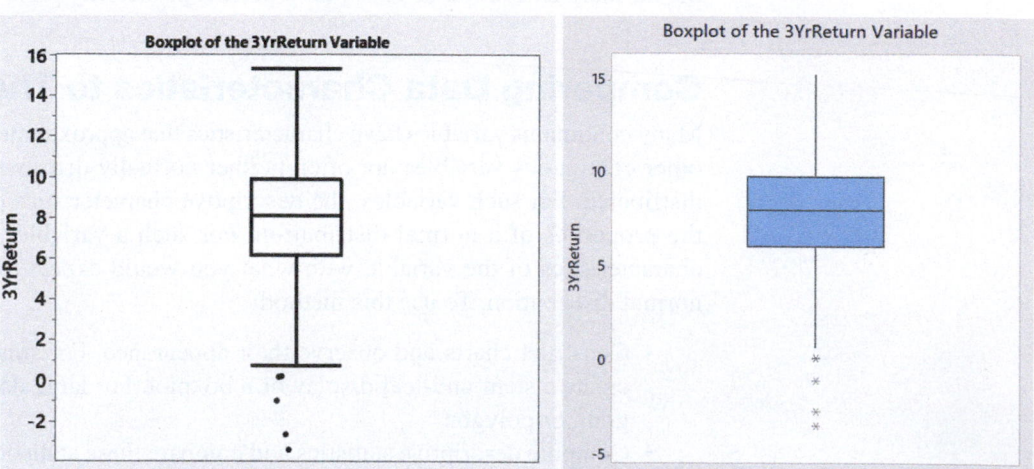

From Table 6.6, Figure 6.17, and from an ordered array of the returns (not shown), you can make the following statements about the three-year returns:

- The mean of 7.91 is slightly less than the median of 8.09. (In a normal distribution, the mean and median are equal.)
- The boxplot is slightly left-skewed. (The normal distribution is symmetrical.)
- The interquartile range of 3.72 is approximately 1.23 standard deviations. (In a normal distribution, the interquartile range is 1.33 standard deviations.)
- The range of 18.72 is equal to 6.21 standard deviations. (In a normal distribution, the range is approximately 6 standard deviations.)
- 68.75% of the returns are within ±1 standard deviation of the mean. (In a normal distribution, 68.26% of the values lie within ±1 standard deviation of the mean.)
- 79.38% of the returns are within ±1.28 standard deviations of the mean. (In a normal distribution, 80% of the values lie within ±1.28 standard deviations of the mean.)
- 94.58% of the returns are within ±2 standard deviations of the mean. (In a normal distribution, 95.44% of the values lie within ±2 standard deviations of the mean.)
- The skewness statistic is −0.3288 and the kurtosis statistic is 0.4189. (In a normal distribution, each of these statistics equals zero.)

Based on these statements and the criteria given on page 237, you can conclude that the three-year returns are approximately normally distributed or, at most, slightly left-skewed. The skewness is slightly negative, and the kurtosis indicates a distribution that is slightly more peaked than a normal distribution.

Constructing the Normal Probability Plot

A **normal probability plot** is a visual display that helps you evaluate whether the data are normally distributed. One common plot is called the **quantile–quantile plot**. To create this plot, you first transform each ordered value to a Z value. For example, if you have a sample of $n = 19$, the Z value for the smallest value corresponds to a cumulative area of

$$\frac{1}{n + 1} = \frac{1}{19 + 1} = \frac{1}{20} = 0.05$$

The Z value for a cumulative area of 0.05 (from Table E.2) is −1.65. Table 6.7 illustrates the entire set of Z values for a sample of $n = 19$.

TABLE 6.7

Ordered Values and Corresponding Z Values for a Sample of $n = 19$

Ordered Value	Z Value	Ordered Value	Z Value	Ordered Value	Z Value
1	−1.65	8	−0.25	14	0.52
2	−1.28	9	−0.13	15	0.67
3	−1.04	10	−0.00	16	0.84
4	−0.84	11	0.13	17	1.04
5	−0.67	12	0.25	18	1.28
6	−0.52	13	0.39	19	1.65
7	−0.39				

In a quantile–quantile plot, the Z values are plotted on the X axis, and the corresponding values of the variable are plotted on the Y axis. If the data are normally distributed, the values will plot along an approximately straight line. Figure 6.18 illustrates the typical shape of the quantile–quantile normal probability plot for a left-skewed distribution (Panel A), a normal distribution (Panel B), and a right-skewed distribution (Panel C). If the data are left-skewed, the curve will rise more rapidly at first and then level off. If the data are normally distributed, the points will plot along an approximately straight line. If the data are right-skewed, the data will rise more slowly at first and then rise at a faster rate for higher values of the variable being plotted.

FIGURE 6.18

Normal probability plots for a left-skewed distribution, a normal distribution, and a right-skewed distribution

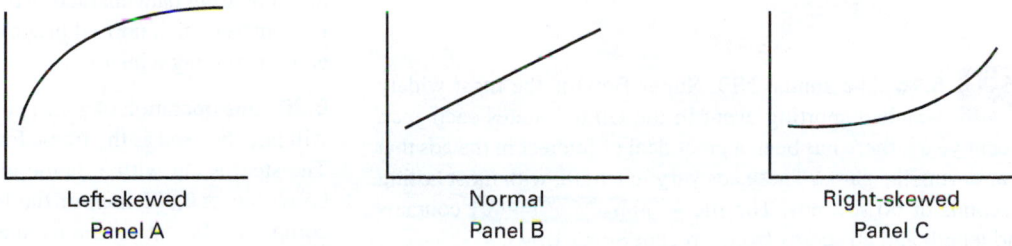

Left-skewed
Panel A

Normal
Panel B

Right-skewed
Panel C

Figure 6.19 shows Excel and JMP (quantile–quantile) normal probability plot and a Minitab normal probability plot for the three-year returns. The Excel and JMP, quantile–quantile plots show several low values followed by the bulk of the points that approximately follow a straight line except for a few low values.

FIGURE 6.19

Excel and JMP (quantile–quantile) normal probability plots and a Minitab normal probability plot for the three-year returns

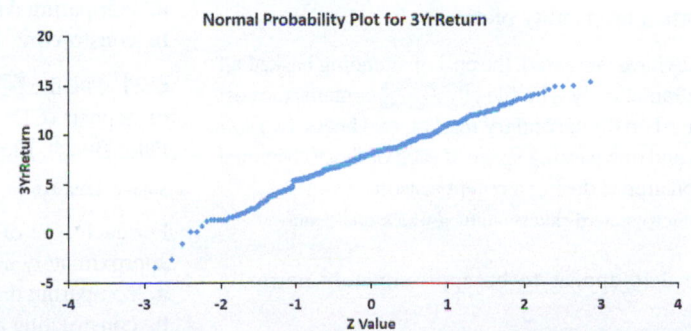

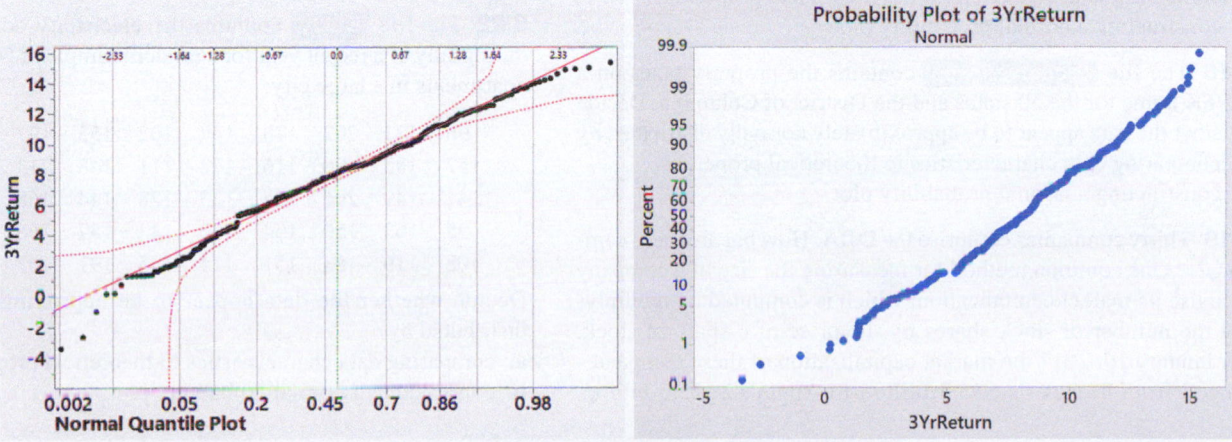

The Minitab normal probability plot has the 3YrReturn variable on the X axis and the cumulative percentage for a normal distribution on the Y axis. In this plot, if the data are normally distributed, the points will plot along an approximately straight line. In Figure 6.19, most points, other than several extreme values, approximately follow a straight line, indicating an approximately normal distribution. Had the data been right-skewed, the curve would have risen more rapidly at first and then leveled off. Had the data been left-skewed, the data would have risen more slowly at first and then risen at a faster rate for larger values of the variable.

PROBLEMS FOR SECTION 6.3

LEARNING THE BASICS

6.14 Show that for a sample of $n = 39$, the smallest and largest Z values are -1.96 and $+1.96$, and the middle (i.e., 20th) Z value is 0.00.

6.15 For a sample of $n = 6$, list the six Z values.

APPLYING THE CONCEPTS

✓SELF TEST **6.16** The annual NFL Super Bowl is the most widely watched sporting event in the United States each year. In recent years, there has been a great deal of interest in the ads that appear during the game. These ads vary in length, with most lasting 30 seconds or 60 seconds. The file `SuperBowlAdScore` contains the ad length and ad scores from a recent Super Bowl.

Source: Data extracted from C. Woodyard, "Funny Bone Wins Out," *USA Today*, February 6, 2016, p. 4B.

Decide whether the data appear to be approximately normally distributed by
a. comparing data characteristics to theoretical properties.
b. constructing a normal probability plot.

6.17 As player salaries have increased, the cost of attending basketball games has increased dramatically. The file `NBACost` contains the cost of four tickets purchased on the secondary market, two beers, two soft drinks, four hot dogs, and one parking space at each of the 30 National Basketball Association arenas during a recent season.

Source: Data extracted from **www.nerdwallet.com/blog/which-nba-teams-most-affordable**.

Decide whether the data appear to be approximately normally distributed by
a. comparing data characteristics to theoretical properties.
b. constructing a normal probability plot.

6.18 The file `Property Taxes` contains the property taxes on a $176K home for the 50 states and the District of Columbia. Decide whether the data appear to be approximately normally distributed by
a. comparing data characteristics to theoretical properties.
b. constructing a normal probability plot.

6.19 Thirty companies comprise the DJIA. How big are these companies? One common method for measuring the size of a company is to use its market capitalization, which is computed by multiplying the number of stock shares by the price of a share of stock. On January 10, 2017 the market capitalization of these companies ranged from Traveler's $33.3 billion to Apple's $625.6 billion.

The entire population of market capitalization values is stored in `DowMarketCap`.

Source: Data extracted from **money.cnn.com**, January 10, 2017.

Decide whether the market capitalization of companies in the DJIA appears to be approximately normally distributed by
a. comparing data characteristics to theoretical properties.
b. constructing a normal probability plot.
c. constructing a histogram.

6.20 One operation of a mill is to cut pieces of steel into parts that will later be used as the frame for front seats in an automotive plant. The steel is cut with a diamond saw, and the resulting parts must be within ± 0.005 inch of the length specified by the automobile company. The data come from a sample of 100 steel parts and are stored in `Steel`. The measurement reported is the difference, in inches, between the actual length of the steel part, as measured by a laser measurement device, and the specified length of the steel part. Determine whether the data appear to be approximately normally distributed by
a. comparing data characteristics to theoretical properties.
b. constructing a normal probability plot.

6.21 The file `CD Rate` contains the yields for a one-year certificate of deposit (CD) and a five-year CD for 39 banks listed for West Palm Beach, Florida on January 9, 2017.

Source: Data extracted from **www.Bankrate.com**, January 9, 2017.

For each type of investment, decide whether the data appear to be approximately normally distributed by
a. comparing data characteristics to theoretical properties.
b. constructing a normal probability plot.

6.22 The file `Utility` contains the electricity costs, in dollars, during July of a recent year for a random sample of 50 one-bedroom apartments in a large city:

96	171	202	178	147	102	153	197	127	82
157	185	90	116	172	111	148	213	130	165
141	149	206	175	123	128	144	168	109	167
95	163	150	154	130	143	187	166	139	149
108	119	183	151	114	135	191	137	129	158

Decide whether the data appear to be approximately normally distributed by
a. comparing data characteristics to theoretical properties.
b. constructing a normal probability plot.

6.4 The Uniform Distribution

In the **uniform distribution**, the values are evenly distributed in the range between the smallest value, a, and the largest value, b. Selecting random numbers is one of the most common uses of the uniform distribution. When you use simple random sampling (see Section 1.3), you assume that each random digit comes from a uniform distribution that has a minimum value of 0 and a maximum value of 9.

Equation (6.4) defines the probability density function for the uniform distribution.

UNIFORM PROBABILITY DENSITY FUNCTION

$$f(X) = \frac{1}{b-a} \text{ if } a \leq X \leq b \text{ and } 0 \text{ elsewhere} \tag{6.4}$$

where

$$a = \text{minimum value of } X$$
$$b = \text{maximum value of } X$$

Equation (6.5) defines the mean of the uniform distribution, and Equation (6.6) defines the variance and standard deviation of the uniform distribution.

MEAN OF THE UNIFORM DISTRIBUTION

$$\mu = \frac{a+b}{2} \tag{6.5}$$

VARIANCE AND STANDARD DEVIATION OF THE UNIFORM DISTRIBUTION

$$\sigma^2 = \frac{(b-a)^2}{12} \tag{6.6a}$$

$$\sigma = \sqrt{\frac{(b-a)^2}{12}} \tag{6.6b}$$

Because of its shape, the uniform distribution is sometimes called the **rectangular distribution** (see Figure 6.1 Panel B on page 224). Figure 6.20 illustrates the uniform distribution with $a = 0$ and $b = 1$. The total area inside the rectangle is 1.0, equal to the base (1.0) times the height (1.0). Having an area of 1.0 satisfies the requirement that the area under any probability density function equals 1.0.

FIGURE 6.20
Probability density function for a uniform distribution with $a = 0$ and $b = 1$

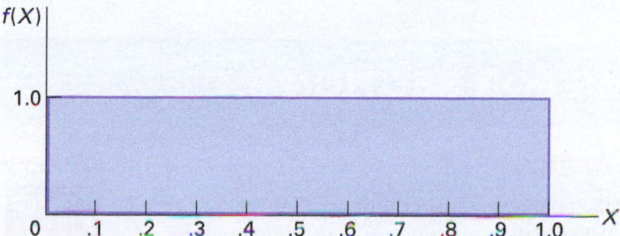

In this uniform distribution, what is the probability of getting a random number between 0.10 and 0.30? The area between 0.10 and 0.30, depicted in Figure 6.21, is equal to the base (which is $0.30 - 0.10 = 0.20$) times the height (1.0). Therefore,

$$P(0.10 < X < 0.30) = (\text{Base})(\text{Height}) = (0.20)(1.0) = 0.20$$

FIGURE 6.21

Finding $P(0.10 < X < 0.30)$ for a uniform distribution with $a = 0$ and $b = 1$

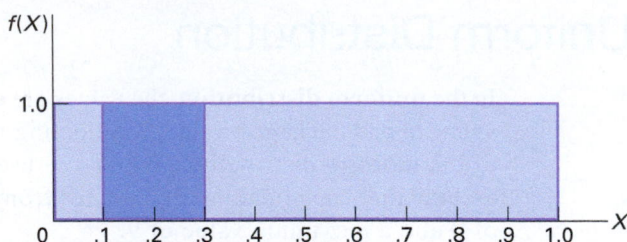

From Equations (6.5) and (6.6), the mean and standard deviation of the uniform distribution for $a = 0$ and $b = 1$ are computed as follows:

$$\mu = \frac{a + b}{2}$$

$$= \frac{0 + 1}{2} = 0.5$$

and

$$\sigma^2 = \frac{(b - a)^2}{12}$$

$$= \frac{(1 - 0)^2}{12}$$

$$= \frac{1}{12} = 0.0833$$

$$\sigma = \sqrt{0.0833} = 0.2887.$$

Thus, the mean is 0.5, and the standard deviation is 0.2887.

Example 6.6 provides another application of the uniform distribution.

EXAMPLE 6.6

Computing Uniform Probabilities

In the MyTVLab scenario on page 223, the load time of the new sales page was assumed to be normally distributed with a mean of 7 seconds. Suppose that the load time follows a uniform (instead of a normal) distribution between 4.5 and 9.5 seconds. What is the probability that a load time will take more than 9 seconds?

SOLUTION The load time is uniformly distributed from 4.5 to 9.5 seconds. The area between 9 and 9.5 seconds is equal to 0.5 seconds, and the total area in the distribution is $9.5 - 4.5 = 5$ seconds. Therefore, the probability of a load time between 9 and 9.5 seconds is the portion of the area greater than 9, which is equal to $0.5/5.0 = 0.10$. Because 9.5 is the maximum value in this distribution, the probability of a load time above 9 seconds is 0.10. In comparison, if the load time is normally distributed with a mean of 7 seconds and a standard deviation of 2 seconds (see Example 6.1 on page 229), the probability of a load time above 9 seconds is 0.1587.

PROBLEMS FOR SECTION 6.4

LEARNING THE BASICS

6.23 Suppose you select one value from a uniform distribution with $a = 0$ and $b = 10$. What is the probability that the value will be
a. between 5 and 7?
b. between 2 and 3?
c. What is the mean?
d. What is the standard deviation?

APPLYING THE CONCEPTS

✓ **SELF TEST** **6.24** The time between arrivals of customers at a bank during the noon-to-1 P.M. hour has a uniform distribution between 0 to 120 seconds. What is the probability that the time between the arrival of two customers will be
a. less than 20 seconds?
b. between 10 and 30 seconds?
c. more than 35 seconds?
d. What are the mean and standard deviation of the time between arrivals?

6.25 A study of the time spent shopping in a supermarket for a market basket of 20 specific items showed an approximately uniform distribution between 20 minutes and 40 minutes. What is the probability that the shopping time will be

a. between 25 and 30 minutes?

b. less than 35 minutes?

c. What are the mean and standard deviation of the shopping time?

6.26 How long does it take to download a two-hour HD movie from the iTunes store? According to Apple's technical support site, **support.apple.com/en-us/HT201587**, downloading such a movie using a 15 Mbit/s broadband connection should take 29–43 minutes. Assume that the download times are uniformly distributed between 29 and 43 minutes. If you download a two-hour movie, what is the probability that the download time will be

a. less than 30 minutes?

b. more than 36 minutes?

c. between 30 and 40 minutes?

d. What are the mean and standard deviation of the download times?

6.27 The scheduled commuting time on the Long Island Railroad from Glen Cove to New York City is 65 minutes. Suppose that the actual commuting time is uniformly distributed between 64 and 74 minutes. What is the probability that the commuting time will be

a. less than 70 minutes?

b. between 65 and 70 minutes?

c. greater than 65 minutes?

d. What are the mean and standard deviation of the commuting time?

6.5 The Exponential Distribution

The **exponential distribution** is a continuous distribution that is right-skewed and ranges from 0 to positive infinity (see Figure 6.1 on page 224). The **Section 6.5 online topic** discusses this distribution and illustrates its application.

6.6 The Normal Approximation to the Binomial Distribution

In many circumstances, the normal distribution can be used to approximate the binomial distribution, discussed in Section 5.2. The **Section 6.6 online topic** discusses this technique and illustrates its use.

▼ USING **STATISTICS**
Normal Load Times . . . , Revisited

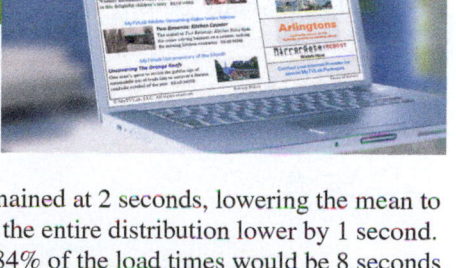

In the Normal Downloading at MyTVLab scenario, you were the sales and marketing vice president for a web-based business. You sought to ensure that the load time for a new sales web page would be within a certain range. By running experiments in the corporate offices, you determined that the amount of time, in seconds, that passes from first pointing a browser to a web page until the web page is fully loaded is a bell-shaped distribution with a mean load time of 7 seconds and standard deviation of 2 seconds. Using the normal distribution, you were able to calculate that approximately 84% of the load times are 9 seconds or less, and 95% of the load times are between 3.08 and 10.92 seconds.

Now that you understand how to compute probabilities from the normal distribution, you can evaluate load times of similar sales web pages that use other designs. For example, if the standard deviation remained at 2 seconds, lowering the mean to 6 seconds would shift the entire distribution lower by 1 second. Thus, approximately 84% of the load times would be 8 seconds or less, and 95% of the load times would be between 2.08 and 9.92 seconds. Another change that could reduce long load times would be reducing the variation. For example, consider the case where the mean remained at the original 7 seconds but the standard deviation was reduced to 1 second. Again, approximately 84% of the load times would be 8 seconds or less, and 95% of the load times would be between 5.04 and 8.96 seconds.

▼ SUMMARY

In this and the previous chapter, you have learned about mathematical models called probability distributions and how they can be used to solve business problems. In Chapter 5, you used discrete probability distributions in situations where the values come from a counting process such as the number of social media sites to which you belong or the number of tagged order forms in a report generated by an accounting information system. In this chapter, you learned about continuous probability distributions where the values come from a measuring process such as your height or the download time of a video.

Continuous probability distributions come in various shapes, but the most common and most important in business is the normal distribution. The normal distribution is symmetrical; thus, its mean and median are equal. It is also bell-shaped, and approximately 68.26% of its values are within ± 1 standard deviation of the mean, approximately 95.44% of its values are within ± 2 standard deviations of the mean, and approximately 99.73% of its values are within ± 3 standard deviations of the mean. Although many variables in business are closely approximated by the normal distribution, do not think that all variables can be approximated by the normal distribution.

In Section 6.3, you learned about various methods for evaluating normality in order to determine whether the normal distribution is a reasonable mathematical model to use in specific situations. In Section 6.4, you learned about another continuous distribution, the uniform distribution, that was not normal. Chapter 7 uses the normal distribution to develop the subject of statistical inference.

▼ REFERENCES

1. Gunter, B. "Q-Q Plots." *Quality Progress* (February 1994): 81–86.
2. Hogg, R. V., J. T. McKean, and A. V. Craig. *Introduction to Mathematical Statistics*, 7th ed. New York: Pearson Education, 2013.
3. Kishnan, S. and R. Sitaraman. "Video stream quality impacts viewer behavior: inferring causality using quasi-experimental designs," in *Proceedings of the 2012 ACM conference on Internet measurement conference*: 211–224. New York: ACM.
4. Levine, D. M., P. Ramsey, and R. Smidt. *Applied Statistics for Engineers and Scientists Using Microsoft Excel and Minitab*. Upper Saddle River, NJ: Prentice Hall, 2001.
5. Miller, J. "Earliest Known Uses of Some of the Words of Mathematics." **jeff560.tripod.com/mathword.html**.
6. Pearl, R. "Karl Pearson, 1857–1936." *Journal of the American Statistical Association*, 31 (1936): 653–664.
7. Pearson, E. S. "Some Incidents in the Early History of Biometry and Statistics, 1890–94." *Biometrika* 52 (1965): 3–18.
8. Taleb, N. *The Black Swan*, 2nd ed. New York: Random House, 2010.
9. Walker, H. "The Contributions of Karl Pearson." *Journal of the American Statistical Association* 53 (1958): 11–22.

▼ KEY EQUATIONS

Normal Probability Density Function

$$f(X) = \frac{1}{\sqrt{2\pi}\sigma}e^{-(1/2)[(X-\mu)/\sigma]^2} \qquad \textbf{(6.1)}$$

Z Transformation Formula

$$Z = \frac{X - \mu}{\sigma} \qquad \textbf{(6.2)}$$

Finding an *X* Value Associated with a Known Probability

$$X = \mu + Z\sigma \qquad \textbf{(6.3)}$$

Uniform Probability Density Function

$$f(X) = \frac{1}{b - a} \qquad \textbf{(6.4)}$$

Mean of the Uniform Distribution

$$\mu = \frac{a + b}{2} \qquad \textbf{(6.5)}$$

Variance and Standard Deviation of the Uniform Distribution

$$\sigma^2 = \frac{(b - a)^2}{12} \qquad \textbf{(6.6a)}$$

$$\sigma = \sqrt{\frac{(b - a)^2}{12}} \qquad \textbf{(6.6b)}$$

KEY TERMS

cumulative standardized normal distribution   227
exponential distribution   224
normal distribution   224
normal probability plot   238

probability density function   224
probability density function for the normal distribution   226
quantile–quantile plot   238
rectangular distribution   241

standardized normal variable   227
transformation formula   227
uniform distribution   224

CHECKING YOUR UNDERSTANDING

6.28 How do you find the area between two values under the normal curve?

6.29 How do you find the X value that corresponds to a given percentile of the normal distribution?

6.30 What are some of the distinguishing properties of a normal distribution?

6.31 How does the shape of the normal distribution differ from the shapes of the uniform and exponential distributions?

6.32 How can you use the normal probability plot to evaluate whether a set of data is normally distributed?

▼ CHAPTER REVIEW PROBLEMS

6.33 An industrial sewing machine uses ball bearings that are targeted to have a diameter of 0.75 inch. The lower and upper specification limits under which the ball bearings can operate are 0.74 inch and 0.76 inch, respectively. Past experience has indicated that the actual diameter of the ball bearings is approximately normally distributed, with a mean of 0.753 inch and a standard deviation of 0.004 inch. What is the probability that a ball bearing is
a. between the target and the actual mean?
b. between the lower specification limit and the target?
c. above the upper specification limit?
d. below the lower specification limit?
e. Of all the ball bearings, 93% of the diameters are greater than what value?

6.34 The fill amount in 2-liter soft drink bottles is normally distributed, with a mean of 2.0 liters and a standard deviation of 0.05 liter. If bottles contain less than 95% of the listed net content (1.90 liters, in this case), the manufacturer may be subject to penalty by the state office of consumer affairs. Bottles that have a net content above 2.10 liters may cause excess spillage upon opening. What proportion of the bottles will contain
a. between 1.90 and 2.0 liters?
b. between 1.90 and 2.10 liters?
c. below 1.90 liters or above 2.10 liters?
d. At least how much soft drink is contained in 99% of the bottles?
e. Ninety-nine percent of the bottles contain an amount that is between which two values (symmetrically distributed) around the mean?

6.35 In an effort to reduce the number of bottles that contain less than 1.90 liters, the bottler in Problem 6.34 sets the filling machine so that the mean is 2.02 liters. Under these circumstances, what are your answers in Problem 6.34 (a) through (e)?

6.36 *Webrooming*, researching products online before buying them in store, has become the new norm for some consumers and contrasts with *showrooming*, researching products in a physical store before purchasing online. A recent study by Interactions reported that most shoppers have a specific spending limit in place while shopping online. Findings indicate that men spend an average of $250 online before they decide to visit a store.

Source: Data extracted from **bit.ly/1JEcmqh**.

Assume that the spending limit is normally distributed and that the standard deviation is $20.
a. What is the probability that a male spent less than $210 online before deciding to visit a store?

b. What is the probability that a male spent between $270 and $300 online before deciding to visit a store?
c. Ninety percent of the amounts spent online by a male before deciding to visit a store are less than what value?
d. Eighty percent of the amounts spent online by a male before deciding to visit a store are between what two values symmetrically distributed around the mean?

Suppose that the spending limit follows a uniform distribution between $200 and $300.

e. What is the probability that a male spent less than $210 online before deciding to visit a store?
f. What is the probability that a male spent between $270 and $300 online before deciding to visit a store?
g. Compare the results of (a) and (b) to those of (e) and (f).

6.37 The file **DomesticBeer** contains the percentage alcohol, number of calories per 12 ounces, and number of carbohydrates (in grams) per 12 ounces for 158 of the best-selling domestic beers in the United States. Determine whether each of these variables appears to be approximately normally distributed. Support your decision through the use of appropriate statistics and graphs.

Source: Data extracted from **www.Beer100.com**, December 1, 2016.

6.38 The evening manager of a restaurant was very concerned about the length of time some customers were waiting in line to be seated. She also had some concern about the seating times—that is, the length of time between when a customer is seated and the time he or she leaves the restaurant. Over the course of one week, 100 customers (no more than 1 per party) were randomly selected, and their waiting and seating times (in minutes) were recorded in **Wait**.
a. Think about your favorite restaurant. Do you think waiting times more closely resemble a uniform, an exponential, or a normal distribution?
b. Again, think about your favorite restaurant. Do you think seating times more closely resemble a uniform, an exponential, or a normal distribution?
c. Construct a histogram and a normal probability plot of the waiting times. Do you think these waiting times more closely resemble a uniform, an exponential, or a normal distribution?
d. Construct a histogram and a normal probability plot of the seating times. Do you think these seating times more closely resemble a uniform, an exponential, or a normal distribution?

6.39 The major stock market indexes had strong results in 2016. The mean one-year return for stocks in the S&P 500, a group of 500 very large companies, was +9.54%. The mean one-year return for the NASDAQ, a group of 3,200 small and medium-sized companies, was +7.50%. Historically, the one-year returns are approximately normally distributed, the standard deviation in the S&P 500 is approximately 20%, and the standard deviation in the NASDAQ is approximately 30%.

a. What is the probability that a stock in the S&P 500 gained value in 2016?
b. What is the probability that a stock in the S&P 500 gained 10% or more in 2016?
c. What is the probability that a stock in the S&P 500 lost 20% or more in 2016?
d. What is the probability that a stock in the S&P 500 lost 30% or more in 2016?
e. Repeat (a) through (d) for a stock in the NASDAQ.
f. Write a short summary on your findings. Be sure to include a discussion of the risks associated with a large standard deviation.

6.40 Interns report that when deciding on where to work, career growth, salary and compensation, location and commute, and company culture and values are important factors to them. According to reports by interns to Glassdoor, the mean monthly pay of interns at Intel is $5,940.

Source: Data extracted from **www.glassdoor.com/index.htm**.

Suppose that the intern monthly pay is normally distributed, with a standard deviation of $400. What is the probability that the monthly pay of an intern at Intel is

a. less than $5,900?
b. between $5,700 and $6,100?
c. above $6,500?
d. Ninety-nine percent of the intern monthly pays are higher than what value?
e. Ninety-five percent of the intern monthly pays are between what two values, symmetrically distributed around the mean?

6.41 According to the same Glassdoor source mentioned in Problem 6.40, the mean monthly pay for interns at Facebook is $6,589. Suppose that the intern monthly pay is normally distributed, with a standard deviation of $500. What is the probability that the monthly pay of an intern at Facebook is

a. less than $5,900?
b. between $5,700 and $6,100?
c. above $6,500?
d. Ninety-nine percent of the intern monthly pays are higher than what value?
e. Ninety-five percent of the intern monthly pays are between what two values, symmetrically distributed around the mean?
f. Compare the results for the Intel interns computed in Problem 6.40 to those of the Facebook interns.

6.42 **(Class Project)** One theory about the daily changes in the closing price of a stock is that these changes follow a *random walk*—that is, these daily events are independent of each other and move upward or downward in a random manner—and can be approximated by a normal distribution. To test this theory, use either a newspaper or the Internet to select one company traded on the NYSE, one company traded on the American Stock Exchange, and one company traded on the NASDAQ and then do the following:

1. Record the daily closing stock price of each of these companies for six consecutive weeks (so that you have 30 values per company).
2. Compute the daily changes in the closing stock price of each of these companies for six consecutive weeks (so that you have 30 values per company).

Note: The random-walk theory pertains to the daily changes in the closing stock price, not the daily closing stock price.

For each of your six data sets, decide whether the data are approximately normally distributed by

a. constructing the stem-and-leaf display, histogram or polygon, and boxplot.
b. comparing data characteristics to theoretical properties.
c. constructing a normal probability plot.
d. Discuss the results of (a) through (c). What can you say about your three stocks with respect to daily closing prices and daily changes in closing prices? Which, if any, of the data sets are approximately normally distributed?

CHAPTER 6

▼CASES

Managing Ashland MultiComm Services

The AMS technical services department has embarked on a quality improvement effort. Its first project relates to maintaining the target upload speed for its Internet service subscribers. Upload speeds are measured on a standard scale in which the target value is 1.0. Data collected over the past year indicate that the upload speed is approximately normally distributed, with a mean of 1.005 and a standard deviation of 0.10. Each day, one upload speed is measured. The upload speed is considered acceptable if the measurement on the standard scale is between 0.95 and 1.05.

1. Assuming that the distribution of upload speed has not changed from what it was in the past year, what is the probability that the upload speed is
   a. less than 1.0?
   b. between 0.95 and 1.0?
   c. between 1.0 and 1.05?
   d. less than 0.95 or greater than 1.05?

2. The objective of the operations team is to reduce the probability that the upload speed is below 1.0. Should the team focus on process improvement that increases the mean upload speed to 1.05 or on process improvement that reduces the standard deviation of the upload speed to 0.075? Explain.

CardioGood Fitness

Return to the CardioGood Fitness case (stored in CardioGood Fitness) first presented on page 33.

1. For each CardioGood Fitness treadmill product line, determine whether the age, income, usage, and the number of miles the customer expects to walk/run each week can be approximated by the normal distribution.

2. Write a report to be presented to the management of CardioGood Fitness detailing your findings.

More Descriptive Choices Follow-up

Follow up the More Descriptive Choices Revisited Using Statistics scenario on page 159 by constructing normal probability plots for the 1-year return percentages, 5-year return percentages, and 10-year return percentages for the sample of 479 retirement funds stored in Retirement Funds . In your analysis, examine differences between the growth and value funds as well as the differences among the small, mid-cap, and large market cap funds.

Clear Mountain State Student Survey

The Student News Service at Clear Mountain State University (CMSU) has decided to gather data about the undergraduate students who attend CMSU. They create and distribute a survey of 14 questions and receive responses from 111 undergraduates (stored in StudentSurvey). For each numerical variable in the survey, decide whether the variable is approximately normally distributed by

a. comparing data characteristics to theoretical properties.
b. constructing a normal probability plot.
c. writing a report summarizing your conclusions.

Digital Case

Apply your knowledge about the normal distribution in this Digital Case, which extends the Using Statistics scenario from this chapter.

To satisfy concerns of potential customers, the management of MyTVLab has undertaken a research project to learn how much time it takes users to load a complex video features page. The research team has collected data and has made some claims based on the assertion that the data follow a normal distribution.

Open **MTL_QRTStudy.pdf**, which documents the work of a quality response team at MyTVLab. Read the internal report that documents the work of the team and their conclusions. Then answer the following:

1. Can the collected data be approximated by the normal distribution?

2. Review and evaluate the conclusions made by the MyTVLab research team. Which conclusions are correct? Which ones are incorrect?

3. If MyTVLab could improve the mean time by 5 seconds, how would the probabilities change?

▼ EXCEL GUIDE

EG6.2   The NORMAL DISTRIBUTION

Key Technique   Use the **NORM.DIST(***X value, mean, standard deviation***, True)** function to compute normal probabilities and use the **NORM.S.INV(***percentage***)** function and the STANDARDIZE function (see Section EG3.2) to compute the *Z* value.

Example   Compute the normal probabilities for Examples 6.1 through 6.3 on pages 229 and 230 and the *X* and *Z* values for Examples 6.4 and 6.5 on pages 232 and 233.

PHStat   Use **Normal**.

For the example, select **PHStat → Probability & Prob. Distributions → Normal**. In this procedure's dialog box (shown below):

1. Enter **7** as the **Mean** and **2** as the **Standard Deviation**.
2. Check **Probability for: X <=** and enter **7** in its box.
3. Check **Probability for: X >** and enter **9** in its box.
4. Check **Probability for range** and enter **5** in the first box and **9** in the second box.
5. Check **X for Cumulative Percentage** and enter **10** in its box.
6. Check **X Values for Percentage** and enter **95** in its box.
7. Enter a **Title** and click **OK**.

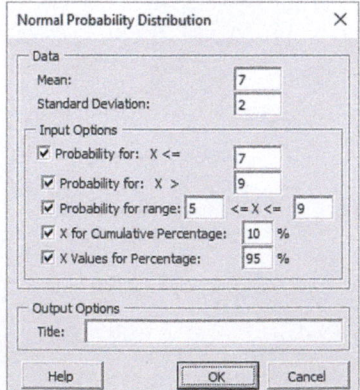

Workbook   Use the **COMPUTE worksheet** of the **Normal workbook** as a template.

The worksheet already contains the data for solving the problems in Examples 6.1 through 6.5. For other problems, change the values for the **Mean**, **Standard Deviation**, **X Value**, **From X Value**, **To X Value**, **Cumulative Percentage**, and/or **Percentage**.

Unlike most other Excel Guide COMPUTE worksheets, this worksheet uses formulas in column A to dynamically create labels based on the data values you enter. These formulas

make extensive use of the ampersand operator (&) to construct the actual label. For example, the cell A10 formula **="P(X<="&B8&")"** results in the display of P(X<=7) because the initial contents of cell B8, 7, is combined with "*P(X<=*" and ")". Changing the value in cell B8 to 9, changes the label in cell A10 to P(X<=9).

EG6.3   EVALUATING NORMALITY

Comparing Data Characteristics to Theoretical Properties

Use the Section EG3.1 through EG3.3 instructions to compare data characteristics to theoretical properties.

Constructing the Normal Probability Plot

Key Technique   Use an Excel Scatter (X, Y) chart with *Z* values computed using the NORM.S.INV function.

Example   Construct the Figure 6.19 normal probability plot for three-year return percentages for the sample of 479 retirement funds that is shown on page 239.

PHStat   Use **Normal Probability Plot**.

For the example, open to the **DATA worksheet** of the **Retirement Funds workbook**. Select **PHStat → Probability & Prob. Distributions → Normal Probability Plot**. In the procedure's dialog box (shown below):

1. Enter **K1:K480** as the **Variable Cell Range**.
2. Check **First cell contains label**.
3. Enter a **Title** and click **OK**.

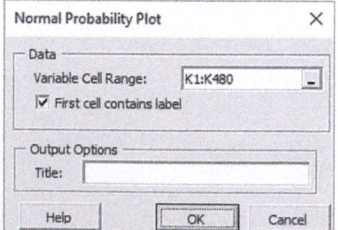

In addition to the chart sheet containing the normal probability plot, the procedure creates a plot data worksheet identical to the PlotData worksheet discussed in the *Worksheet Excel* instructions.

Workbook   Use the worksheets of the **NPP workbook** as templates.

The **NormalPlot chart sheet** displays a normal probability plot using the rank, the proportion, the *Z* value, and the variable found in the **PLOT_DATA worksheet**. The

PLOT_DATA worksheet already contains the three-year return percentages for the example.

To construct a plot for a different variable, paste the *sorted* values for that variable in **column D** of the **PLOT_DATA worksheet**. Adjust the number of ranks in **column A** and the divisor in the formulas in **column B** to compute cumulative percentages to reflect the quantity $n + 1$ (480 for the example). (Column C formulas use the NORM.S.INV function to compute the Z values for those cumulative percentages.)

If you have fewer than 479 values, delete rows from the bottom up. If you have more than 479 values, select row 480, right-click, click **Insert** in the shortcut menu, and copy down the formulas in columns B and C to the new rows. To create your own normal probability plot for the 3YrReturn variable, open to the PLOT_DATA worksheet and select the cell range **C1:D480**. Then select **Insert → Scatter (X, Y) or Bubble Chart icon** and select the **Scatter** gallery item. Excel for Mac labels the same icon as **X Y (Scatter)**. (The icon to select is labeled as #5 in the Charts Group Reference on page 94.)

Relocate the chart to a chart sheet, turn off the chart legend and gridlines, add axis titles, and modify the chart title.

CHAPTER 6

▾JMP GUIDE

JG6.2 The NORMAL DISTRIBUTION

Use the **Normal project worksheet templates**.

For example, to compute the normal probability for Example 6.1 on page 229, open to the **Normal Probabilities1 data table**:

1. Enter **7** in the row 1 cell of the **Mean column**.
2. Enter **2** in the row 1 cell of the **Std Dev column**.
3. Enter **9** in the row 1 cell of the **Value 1 column**.

JMP computes the probability for $P(X > 9)$ in the row 1 cell of the P(X>Value 1) column. The Normal Probabilities1 worksheet can also solve problems that are similar to Examples 6.2 and 6.3. For problems of that type, enter the second comparison value in the Value 2 column and note the computed probabilities that appear in the P(X<Value 1 or X>Value 2) column or the P(Value 1<X <Value 2) column.

Finding X Values

To solve problems of the type that Examples 6.4 and 6.5 on pages 232 and 233 represent, requires using the Normal Probabilities2 data table in the Normal project. For example, to find the X value for a cumulative probability of 0.10 (Example 6.4), open to the **Normal Probabilities2 data table** and:

1. Enter **7** in the row 1 cell of the **Mean column**.
2. Enter **2** in the row 1 cell of the **Std Dev column**.
3. Enter **0.1** in the row 1 cell of the **Cumulative Probability column**.

JMP computes the X value for the cumulative probability in the row 1 cell of the X for Cumulative Probability column. For problems similar to Example 6.5, enter the mean and standard deviation and then enter the percentage value in the Percentage column. Note the values that JMP computes in the Lower X Value and Upper X Value columns.

JG6.3 EVALUATING NORMALITY

Comparing Data Characteristics to Theoretical Properties

Use the Section JG3.1 through JG3.3 instructions to compare data characteristics to theoretical properties.

Constructing the Normal Probability Plot

Use **Distribution**.

For example, to construct the Figure 6.19 normal probability plot for the three-year return percentages for the sample of 479 retirement funds that is shown on page 239, open to the **Retirement Funds data table**. Select **Analyze → Distribution**. In that procedure's dialog box:

1. Click **3YrReturn** in the Select Columns list and then click **Y, Columns** to add 3YrReturn to the Y, Columns box.
2. Click **OK**.

The quartiles and the five-number summary appear as part of the Quantiles report in the new Distribution window that JMP displays. In the Distribution results window:

3. Click the **3YrReturn red triangle** and select **Normal Quantile Plot** from its menu.

JMP revises the Summary Statistics report to include the normal probability plot. Optionally, use the Section B.5 instructions to change the font and type characteristics of chart labels or axis settings.

▼MINITAB GUIDE

MG6.2 The NORMAL DISTRIBUTION

Use the **Normal project worksheet templates** *and* **Normal**.

For example, to compute the normal probability for Example 6.1 on page 229, open to the **Normal Probabilities1 worksheet**.

1. Enter **7** in the row 1 cell of the **Mean column** (C1).
2. Enter **2** in the row 1 cell of the **Std Dev column** (C2).
3. Enter **9** in the row 1 cell of the **Value 1 column** (C3).
4. Select **Calc → Probability Distributions → Normal**.

In the Normal Distribution dialog box (shown below):

5. Click **Cumulative probability**.
6. Enter **7** in the **Mean** box.
7. Enter **2** in the **Standard deviation** box.
8. Click **Input column** and enter **C3** in its box and press **Tab**.
9. Enter **C5** in the first **Optional storage** box.
10. Click **OK**.

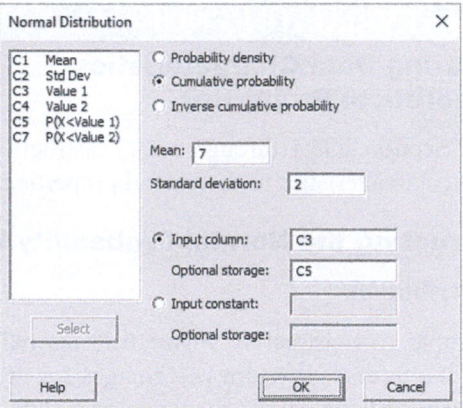

Minitab places the value 0.841345 in the row 1 cell of the P(X<Value 1) column (C5). With that value inserted, the formula in the P(>Value 1) column (C6) computes the $P(X> 9)$ solution. The Normal Probabilities1 worksheet can also solve problems that are similar to Examples 6.2 and 6.3 on page 230. For problems of that type, enter the second comparison value in the Value 2 column (C4), follow steps 1 through 10, changing the values for the mean, standard deviation, and Value 1 as necessary. Then select **Calc → Probability Distributions → Normal** and in the Normal Distribution dialog box:

1. Click **Cumulative probability**.
2. Enter the proper values in the **Mean** and **Standard deviation** boxes.
3. Click **Input column** and enter **C4** in its box and press **Tab**.

4. Enter **C7** in the first **Optional storage** box.
5. Click **OK**.

Finding X Values

To solve problems of the type that Examples 6.4 and 6.5 on pages 232 and 233 represent, requires using the Normal Probabilities2 worksheet in the Normal project. For example, to find the X value for a cumulative probability of 0.10 (Example 6.4), open to the **Normal Probabilities2 worksheet** and:

1. Enter **7** as the **Mean**, **2** as the **Std Dev**, and **0.1** as the **Cumulative Probability** in the row 1 cells of columns C1 through C3.
2. Select **Calc → Probability Distributions → Normal**.

In the Normal Distribution dialog box:

3. Click **Inverse cumulative probability**.
4. Enter **7** in the **Mean** box and **2** in the **Standard deviation** box.
5. Click **Input column** and enter **C3** in its box and press **Tab**.
6. Enter **C4** in the first **Optional storage** box.
7. Click **OK**.

Minitab places the X value 4.43690 in the row 1 cell of the X for Cumulative Probability column (C4). That value is the solution to the problem.

For problems similar to Example 6.5, enter the percentage value in the Percentage column (C5) and use steps 2 through 7, but enter **C6** as the **Input column** in step 5 and enter **C8** as the **Optional storage** in step 6 (to compute the Lower X Value). Then repeat steps 2 through 7, entering **C7** as the **Input column** and **C9** as the **Optional storage** column (to compute the Upper X Value).

MG6.3 EVALUATING NORMALITY

Comparing Data Characteristics to Theoretical Properties

Use instructions in Sections MG3.1 through MG3.3 to compare data characteristics to theoretical properties.

Constructing the Normal Probability Plot

Use **Probability Plot**.

For example, to construct the normal probability plot for the three-year return percentage for the sample of 479 retirement funds shown in Figure 6.19 on page 239, open to the

Retirement Funds worksheet. Select **Graph➜Probability Plot** and:

1. In the Probability Plots dialog box, click **Single** and then click **OK**.

In the Probability Plot: Single dialog box (shown below):

2. Double-click **C11 3YrReturn** in the variables list to add **'3YrReturn'** to the **Graph variables** box.

3. Click **Distribution**.

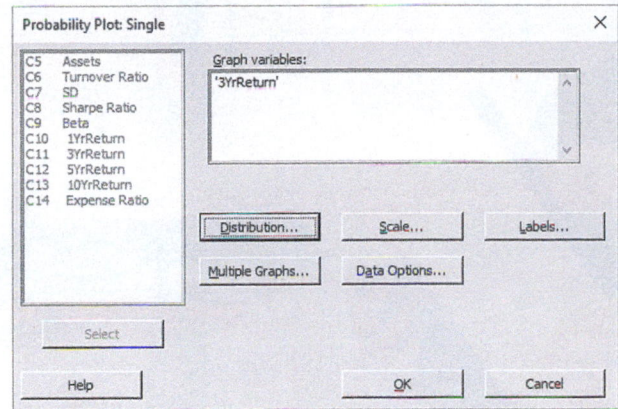

In the Probability Plot: Distribution dialog box (shown below):

4. Click the **Distribution** tab and select **Normal** from the **Distribution** drop-down list.

5. Click the **Data Display** tab. Click **Symbols only**. If the **Show confidence interval** check box is not disabled (as shown below), clear this check box.

6. Click **OK**.

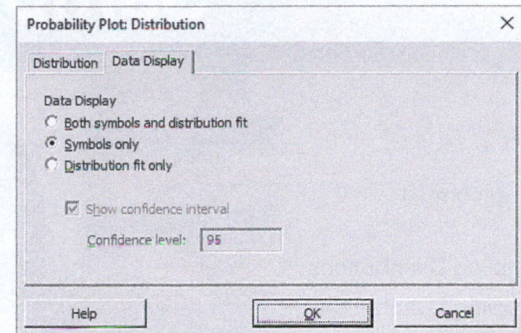

7. Back in the Probability Plot: Single dialog box, click **Scale**.

8. Click the **Gridlines** tab. Clear all check boxes and then click **OK**.

9. Back in the Probability Plot: Single dialog box, click **OK**.

7

Sampling Distributions

OBJECTIVES

- Learn about the concept of the sampling distribution
- Compute probabilities related to the sample mean and the sample proportion
- Understand the importance of the Central Limit Theorem

▼USING **STATISTICS**
Sampling Oxford Cereals

As the cereal lines manager for Oxford Cereals Plant #3, you are part of the project team overseeing the installation of three new fill production lines. By automating the bag formation, fill, bag sealing, and weighing operations, three identical lines running at Plant #1 have increased the production of boxes of flaked cereals at that plant by 20% and similar gains are expected at Plant #3. In the future, these lines will give Oxford Cereals management greater production flexibility by allowing the option to use packaging other than the standard pillow bags long used.

For now, you must verify the calibration of the Plant #3 fill production machines. Proper calibration should ensure that filled boxes will contain a mean of 368 grams of cereal, among other attributes. If the calibration is imperfect, the mean weight of the boxes could vary too much from the 368 grams claimed on the preprinted boxes used in the lines. You decide to take samples of the cereal boxes being produced in the initial runs of the new lines. For each sample of cereal boxes you select, you plan to weigh each box in the sample and then calculate a sample mean. You need to determine the probability that such a sample mean could have been randomly selected from a population whose mean is 368 grams. Based on your analysis, you will have to decide whether to maintain, alter, or shut down the cereal-filling process.

n Chapter 6, you used the normal distribution to study the distribution of load times for a MyTVLab web page. In this chapter, you need to make a decision about a cereal-filling process, based on the weights of a sample of cereal boxes packaged at Oxford Cereals. You will learn about sampling distributions and how to use them to solve business problems.

7.1 Sampling Distributions

In many applications, you want to make inferences that are based on statistics calculated from samples to estimate the values of population parameters. In the next two sections, you will learn about how the sample mean (a statistic) is used to estimate the population mean (a parameter) and how the sample proportion (a statistic) is used to estimate the population proportion (a parameter). Your main concern when making a statistical inference is reaching conclusions about a population, *not* about a sample. For example, a political pollster is interested in the sample results only as a way of estimating the actual proportion of the votes that each candidate will receive from the population of voters. Likewise, as plant operations manager for Oxford Cereals, you are only interested in using the mean weight calculated from a sample of cereal boxes to estimate the mean weight of a population of boxes.

In practice, you select a single random sample of a predetermined size from the population. Hypothetically, to use the sample statistic to estimate the population parameter, you could examine *every* possible sample of a given size that could occur. A **sampling distribution** is the distribution of the results if you actually selected all possible samples. The single result you obtain in practice is just one of the results in the sampling distribution.

7.2 Sampling Distribution of the Mean

In Chapter 3, several measures of central tendency, including the mean, median, and mode, were discussed. For several reasons, the mean is the most widely used measure of central tendency, and the sample mean is often used to estimate the population mean. The **sampling distribution of the mean** is the distribution of all possible sample means if you select all possible samples of a given size.

The Unbiased Property of the Sample Mean

The sample mean is **unbiased** because the mean of all the possible sample means (of a given sample size, n) is equal to the population mean, μ. A simple example concerning a population of four administrative assistants demonstrates this property. Each assistant is asked to apply the same set of updates to a human resources database. Table 7.1 presents the number of errors made by each of the administrative assistants. This population distribution is shown in Figure 7.1.

TABLE 7.1
Number of Errors Made by Each of Four Administrative Assistants

Administrative Assistant	Number of Errors
Ann	$X_1 = 3$
Bob	$X_2 = 2$
Carla	$X_3 = 1$
Dave	$X_4 = 4$

FIGURE 7.1
Number of errors made by a population of four administrative assistants

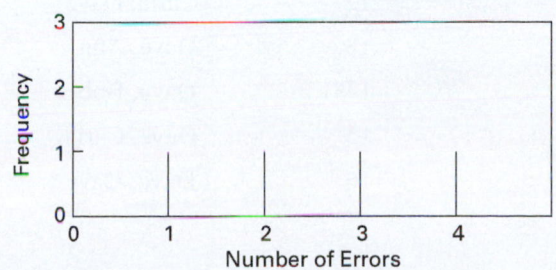

When you have data from a population, you compute the population mean by using Equation (7.1), and you compute the population standard deviation, σ, by using Equation (7.2).

student TIP

Recall from Section 3.4 that the population mean is the sum of the values in the population divided by the population size, *N*.

POPULATION MEAN

$$\mu = \frac{\sum_{i=1}^{N} X_i}{N} \tag{7.1}$$

POPULATION STANDARD DEVIATION

$$\sigma = \sqrt{\frac{\sum_{i=1}^{N}(X_i - \mu)^2}{N}} \tag{7.2}$$

For the data of Table 7.1,

$$\mu = \frac{3 + 2 + 1 + 4}{4} = 2.5 \text{ errors}$$

and

$$\sigma = \sqrt{\frac{(3 - 2.5)^2 + (2 - 2.5)^2 + (1 - 2.5)^2 + (4 - 2.5)^2}{4}} = 1.12 \text{ errors}$$

If you select samples of two administrative assistants *with* replacement from this population, there are 16 possible samples ($N^n = 4^2 = 16$). Table 7.2 lists the 16 possible sample outcomes. If you average all 16 of these sample means, the mean of these values is equal to 2.5, which is also the mean of the population, μ.

TABLE 7.2

All 16 Samples of $n = 2$ Administrative Assistants from a Population of $N = 4$ Administrative Assistants When Sampling with Replacement

Sample	Administrative Assistants	Sample Outcomes	Sample Mean
1	Ann, Ann	3, 3	$\bar{X}_1 = 3$
2	Ann, Bob	3, 2	$\bar{X}_2 = 2.5$
3	Ann, Carla	3, 1	$\bar{X}_3 = 2$
4	Ann, Dave	3, 4	$\bar{X}_4 = 3.5$
5	Bob, Ann	2, 3	$\bar{X}_5 = 2.5$
6	Bob, Bob	2, 2	$\bar{X}_6 = 2$
7	Bob, Carla	2, 1	$\bar{X}_7 = 1.5$
8	Bob, Dave	2, 4	$\bar{X}_8 = 3$
9	Carla, Ann	1, 3	$\bar{X}_9 = 2$
10	Carla, Bob	1, 2	$\bar{X}_{10} = 1.5$
11	Carla, Carla	1, 1	$\bar{X}_{11} = 1$
12	Carla, Dave	1, 4	$\bar{X}_{12} = 2.5$
13	Dave, Ann	4, 3	$\bar{X}_{13} = 3.5$
14	Dave, Bob	4, 2	$\bar{X}_{14} = 3$
15	Dave, Carla	4, 1	$\bar{X}_{15} = 2.5$
16	Dave, Dave	4, 4	$\bar{X}_{16} = 4$
			$\mu_{\bar{X}} = 2.5$

Because the mean of the 16 sample means is equal to the population mean, the sample mean is an unbiased estimator of the population mean. Therefore, although you do not know how close the sample mean of any particular sample selected is to the population mean, you are assured that the mean of all the possible sample means that could have been selected is equal to the population mean.

Standard Error of the Mean

Figure 7.2 illustrates the variation in the sample means when selecting all 16 possible samples.

FIGURE 7.2

Sampling distribution of the mean, based on all possible samples containing two administrative assistants

Source: Data are from Table 7.2.

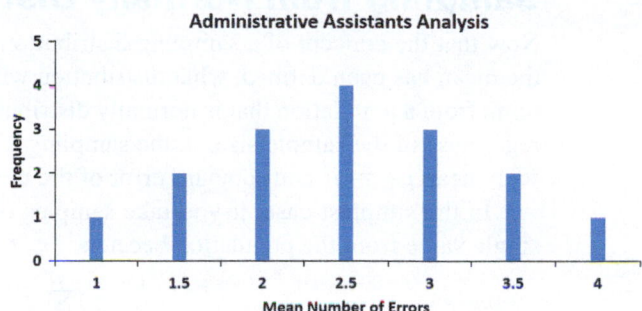

In this small example, although the sample means vary from sample to sample, depending on which two administrative assistants are selected, the sample means do not vary as much as the individual values in the population. That the sample means are less variable than the individual values in the population follows directly from the fact that each sample mean averages together all the values in the sample. A population consists of individual outcomes that can take on a wide range of values, from extremely small to extremely large. However, if a sample contains an extreme value, although this value will have an effect on the sample mean, the effect is reduced because the value is averaged with all the other values in the sample. As the sample size increases, the effect of a single extreme value becomes smaller because it is averaged with more values.

The value of the standard deviation of all possible sample means, called the **standard error of the mean**, expresses how the sample means vary from sample to sample. As the sample size increases, the standard error of the mean decreases by a factor equal to the square root of the sample size. Equation (7.3) defines the standard error of the mean when sampling *with* replacement or sampling *without* replacement from large or infinite populations.

student TIP

Remember, the standard error of the mean measures variation among the means not the individual values.

STANDARD ERROR OF THE MEAN

The standard error of the mean, $\sigma_{\bar{X}}$, is equal to the standard deviation in the population, σ, divided by the square root of the sample size, n.

$$\sigma_{\bar{X}} = \frac{\sigma}{\sqrt{n}} \tag{7.3}$$

Example 7.1 computes the standard error of the mean when the sample selected without replacement contains less than 5% of the entire population.

EXAMPLE 7.1

Computing the Standard Error of the Mean

▶(*continued*)

Returning to the cereal-filling process described in the Using Statistics scenario on page 252, if you randomly select a sample of 25 boxes without replacement from the thousands of boxes filled during a shift, the sample contains a very small portion of the population. Given that the standard deviation of the cereal-filling process is 15 grams, compute the standard error of the mean.

SOLUTION Using Equation (7.3) with $n = 25$ and $\sigma = 15$ the standard error of the mean is

$$\sigma_{\overline{X}} = \frac{\sigma}{\sqrt{n}} = \frac{15}{\sqrt{25}} = \frac{15}{5} = 3$$

The variation in the sample means for samples of $n = 25$ is much less than the variation in the individual boxes of cereal (i.e., $\sigma_{\overline{X}} = 3$, while $\sigma = 15$).

Sampling from Normally Distributed Populations

Now that the concept of a sampling distribution has been introduced and the standard error of the mean has been defined, what distribution will the sample mean, $\overline{X}$, follow? If you are sampling from a population that is normally distributed with mean μ and standard deviation σ, then regardless of the sample size, n, the sampling distribution of the mean is normally distributed, with mean $\mu_{\overline{X}} = \mu$ and standard error of the mean $\sigma_{\overline{X}} = \sigma/\sqrt{n}$.

In the simplest case, if you take samples of size $n = 1$, each possible sample mean is a single value from the population because

$$\overline{X} = \frac{\sum\limits_{i=1}^{n} X_i}{n} = \frac{X_1}{1} = X_1$$

Therefore, if the population is normally distributed, with mean μ and standard deviation σ, the sampling distribution $\overline{X}$ for samples of $n = 1$ must also follow the normal distribution, with mean $\mu_{\overline{X}} = \mu$ and standard error of the mean $\sigma_{\overline{X}} = \sigma/\sqrt{1} = \sigma$. In addition, as the sample size increases, the sampling distribution of the mean still follows a normal distribution, with $\mu_{\overline{X}} = \mu$, but the standard error of the mean decreases so that a larger proportion of sample means are closer to the population mean. Figure 7.3 illustrates this reduction in variability. Note that 500 samples of size 1, 2, 4, 8, 16, and 32 were randomly selected from a normally distributed population. From the polygons in Figure 7.3, you can see that, although the sampling distribution of the mean is approximately[1] normal for each sample size, the sample means are distributed more tightly around the population mean as the sample size increases.

[1] Remember that "only" 500 samples out of an infinite number of samples have been selected, so that the sampling distributions shown are only approximations of the population distribution.

FIGURE 7.3
Sampling distributions of the mean from 500 samples of sizes $n = 1, 2, 4, 8, 16,$ and 32 selected from a normal population

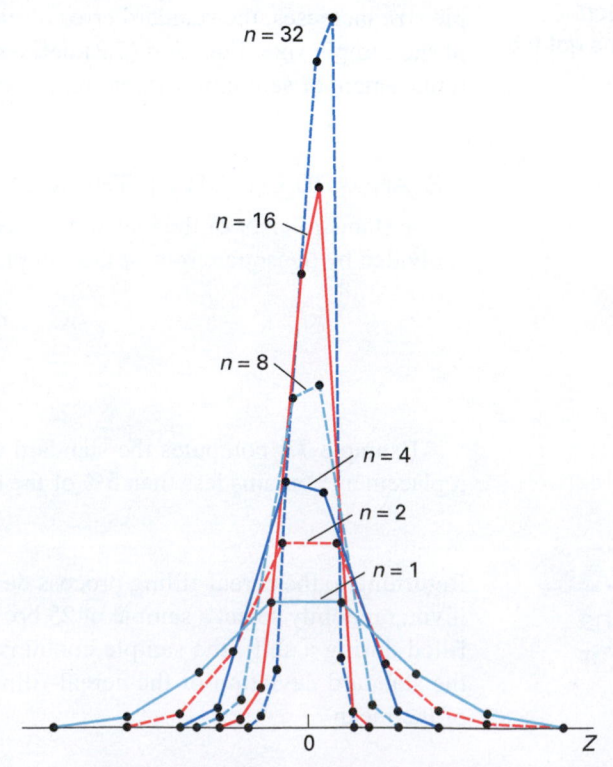

To further examine the concept of the sampling distribution of the mean, consider the Using Statistics scenario described on page 252. The packaging equipment that is filling 368-gram boxes of cereal is set so that the amount of cereal in a box is normally distributed, with a mean of 368 grams. From past experience, you know the population standard deviation for this filling process is 15 grams.

If you randomly select a sample of 25 boxes from the many thousands that are filled in a day and the mean weight is computed for this sample, what type of result could you expect? For example, do you think that the sample mean could be 368 grams? 200 grams? 365 grams?

The sample acts as a miniature representation of the population, so if the values in the population are normally distributed, the values in the sample should be approximately normally distributed. Thus, if the population mean is 368 grams, the sample mean has a good chance of being close to 368 grams.

How can you determine the probability that the sample of 25 boxes will have a mean below 365 grams? From the normal distribution (Section 6.2), you know that you can find the area below any value X by converting to standardized Z values:

$$Z = \frac{X - \mu}{\sigma}$$

In the examples in Section 6.2, you studied how any single value, X, differs from the population mean. Now, in this example, you want to study how a sample mean, $\overline{X}$, differs from the population mean. Substituting $\overline{X}$ for X, $\mu_{\overline{X}}$ for μ, and $\sigma_{\overline{X}}$ for σ in the equation above results in Equation (7.4).

FINDING Z FOR THE SAMPLING DISTRIBUTION OF THE MEAN

The Z value is equal to the difference between the sample mean, $\overline{X}$, and the population mean, μ, divided by the standard error of the mean, $\sigma_{\overline{X}}$.

$$Z = \frac{\overline{X} - \mu_{\overline{X}}}{\sigma_{\overline{X}}} = \frac{\overline{X} - \mu}{\dfrac{\sigma}{\sqrt{n}}} \tag{7.4}$$

To find the area below 365 grams, from Equation (7.4),

$$Z = \frac{\overline{X} - \mu_{\overline{X}}}{\sigma_{\overline{X}}} = \frac{365 - 368}{\dfrac{15}{\sqrt{25}}} = \frac{-3}{3} = -1.00$$

The area corresponding to $Z = -1.00$ in Table E.2 is 0.1587. Therefore, 15.87% of all the possible samples of 25 boxes have a sample mean below 365 grams.

The preceding statement is not the same as saying that a certain percentage of *individual* boxes will contain less than 365 grams of cereal. You compute that percentage as follows:

$$Z = \frac{X - \mu}{\sigma} = \frac{365 - 368}{15} = \frac{-3}{15} = -0.20$$

The area corresponding to $Z = -0.20$ in Table E.2 is 0.4207. Therefore, 42.07% of the *individual* boxes are expected to contain less than 365 grams. Comparing these results, you see that many more *individual boxes* than *sample means* are below 365 grams. This result is explained by the fact that each sample consists of 25 different values, some small and some large. The averaging process dilutes the importance of any individual value, particularly when the sample size is large. Therefore, the chance that the sample mean of 25 boxes is very different from the population mean is less than the chance that a *single* box is very different from the population mean.

Examples 7.2 and 7.3 show how these results are affected by using different sample sizes.

EXAMPLE 7.2

The Effect of Sample Size, *n*, on the Computation of $\sigma_{\bar{X}}$

How is the standard error of the mean affected by increasing the sample size from 25 to 100 boxes?

SOLUTION If $n = 100$ boxes, then using Equation (7.3) on page 255,

$$\sigma_{\bar{X}} = \frac{\sigma}{\sqrt{n}} = \frac{15}{\sqrt{100}} = \frac{15}{10} = 1.5$$

The fourfold increase in the sample size from 25 to 100 reduces the standard error of the mean by half—from 3 grams to 1.5 grams. This demonstrates that taking a larger sample results in less variability in the sample means from sample to sample.

EXAMPLE 7.3

The Effect of Sample Size, *n*, on the Clustering of Means in the Sampling Distribution

If you select a sample of 100 boxes, what is the probability that the sample mean is below 365 grams?

SOLUTION Using Equation (7.4) on page 257,

$$Z = \frac{\bar{X} - \mu_{\bar{X}}}{\sigma_{\bar{X}}} = \frac{365 - 368}{\frac{15}{\sqrt{100}}} = \frac{-3}{1.5} = -2.00$$

From Table E.2, the area less than $Z = -2.00$ is 0.0228. Therefore, 2.28% of the samples of 100 boxes have means below 365 grams, as compared with 15.87% for samples of 25 boxes.

Sometimes you need to find the interval that contains a specific proportion of the sample means. To do so, you determine a distance below and above the population mean containing a specific area of the normal curve. From Equation (7.4) on page 257,

$$Z = \frac{\bar{X} - \mu}{\frac{\sigma}{\sqrt{n}}}$$

Solving for $\bar{X}$ results in Equation (7.5).

> **FINDING $\bar{X}$ FOR THE SAMPLING DISTRIBUTION OF THE MEAN**
>
> $$\bar{X} = \mu + Z\frac{\sigma}{\sqrt{n}} \qquad (7.5)$$

Example 7.4 illustrates the use of Equation (7.5).

EXAMPLE 7.4

Determining the Interval That Includes a Fixed Proportion of the Sample Means

In the cereal-filling example, find an interval symmetrically distributed around the population mean that will include 95% of the sample means, based on samples of 25 boxes.

SOLUTION If 95% of the sample means are in the interval, then 5% are outside the interval. Divide the 5% into two equal parts of 2.5%. The value of Z in Table E.2 corresponding to an area of 0.0250 in the lower tail of the normal curve is -1.96, and the value of Z corresponding to a cumulative area of 0.9750 (i.e., 0.0250 in the upper tail of the normal curve) is $+1.96$.

The lower value of $\overline{X}$ (called $\overline{X}_L$) and the upper value of $\overline{X}$ (called $\overline{X}_U$) are found by using Equation (7.5):

$$\overline{X}_L = 368 + (-1.96)\frac{15}{\sqrt{25}} = 368 - 5.88 = 362.12$$

$$\overline{X}_U = 368 + (1.96)\frac{15}{\sqrt{25}} = 368 + 5.88 = 373.88$$

Therefore, 95% of all sample means, based on samples of 25 boxes, are between 362.12 and 373.88 grams.

Sampling from Non-normally Distributed Populations— The Central Limit Theorem

So far in this section, only the sampling distribution of the mean for a normally distributed population has been considered. However, for many analyses, you will either be able to know that the population is not normally distributed or conclude that it would be unrealistic to assume that the population is normally distributed. An important theorem in statistics, the **Central Limit Theorem**, deals with these situations.

THE CENTRAL LIMIT THEOREM

As the sample size (the number of values in each sample) gets *large enough*, the sampling distribution of the mean is approximately normally distributed. This is true regardless of the shape of the distribution of the individual values in the population.

What sample size is *large enough*? As a general rule, statisticians have found that for many population distributions, when the sample size is at least 30, the sampling distribution of the mean is approximately normal. However, you can apply the Central Limit Theorem for even smaller sample sizes if the population distribution is approximately bell-shaped. In the case in which the distribution of a variable is extremely skewed or has more than one mode, you may need sample sizes larger than 30 to ensure normality in the sampling distribution of the mean.

Figure 7.4 illustrates that the Central Limit Theorem applies to all types of populations, regardless of their shape. In the figure, the effects of increasing sample size are shown for

- a normally distributed population in the left column.
- a uniformly distributed population, in which the values are evenly distributed between the smallest and largest values, in the center column.
- an exponentially distributed population, in which the values are heavily right-skewed, in the right column.

For each population, as the sample size increases, the variation in the sample means decreases, resulting in a narrowing of the width of the graph as the sample size increases from 2 to 30.

FIGURE 7.4

Sampling distribution of the mean for samples of $n = 2$, 5, and 30, for three different populations

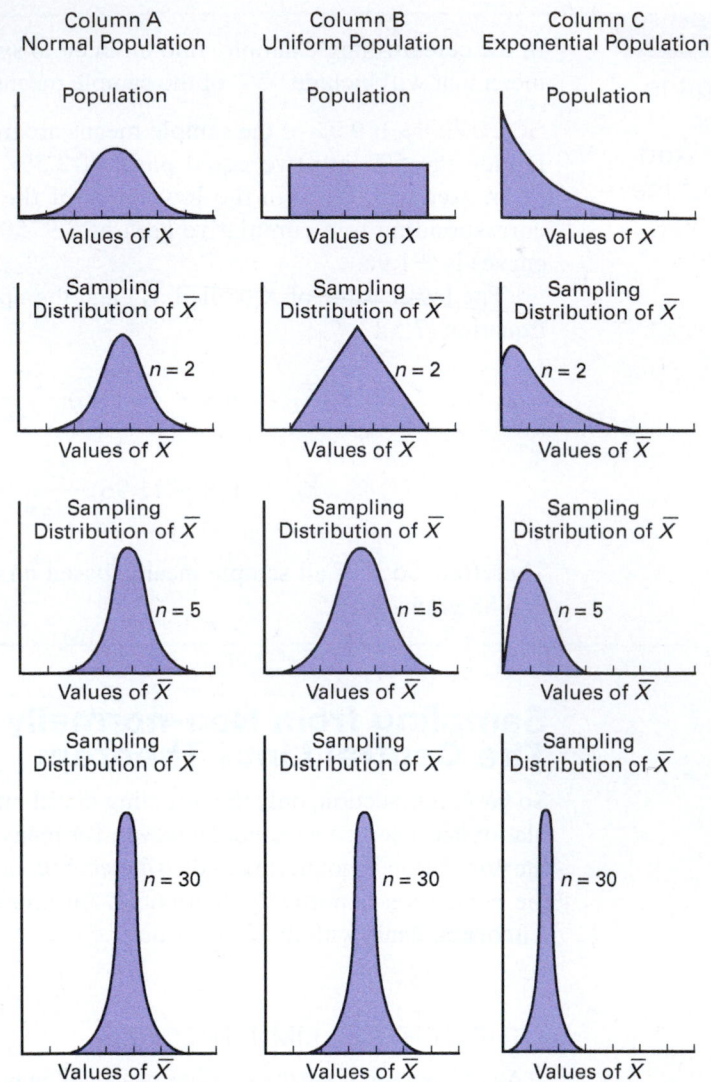

Because the sample mean is an unbiased estimator of the population mean, the mean of any sampling distribution in a column will be equal to the mean of the population that the column represents. Because the sampling distribution of the mean is always normally distributed for a normally distributed population, the Column A sampling distribution is always normally distributed.

For the other two populations, a *central limiting* effect causes the sample means to become more similar and the shape of the graphs to become more like a normal distribution. This effect happens initially more slowly for the heavily skewed exponential distribution than for the uniform distribution, but when the sample size is increased to 30, the sampling distributions of these two populations converge to the shape of the sampling distribution of the normal population. Using the results from all three distributions, you can reach the conclusions regarding the Central Limit Theorem that Exhibit 7.1 presents.

EXHIBIT   7.1

Normality and the Sampling Distribution of the Mean

For most distributions, regardless of shape of the population, the sampling distribution of the mean is approximately normally distributed if samples of at least size 30 are selected.

If the distribution of the population is fairly symmetrical, the sampling distribution of the mean is approximately normal for samples as small as size 5.

If the population is normally distributed, the sampling distribution of the mean is normally distributed, regardless of the sample size.

The Central Limit Theorem is of crucial importance in using statistical inference to reach conclusions about a population. It allows you to make inferences about the population mean without having to know the specific shape of the population distribution. Example 7.5 illustrates a sampling distribution for a skewed population.

EXAMPLE 7.5

Constructing a Sampling Distribution for a Skewed Population

Figure 7.5 shows the distribution of the time it takes to fill orders at a fast-food chain drive-through lane. Note that the probability distribution table is unlike Table 7.1 (page 253), which presents a population in which each value is equally likely to occur.

FIGURE 7.5

Probability distribution and histogram of the service time (in minutes) at a fast-food chain drive-through lane

Service Time (minutes)	Probability
1	0.10
2	0.40
3	0.20
4	0.15
5	0.10
6	0.05

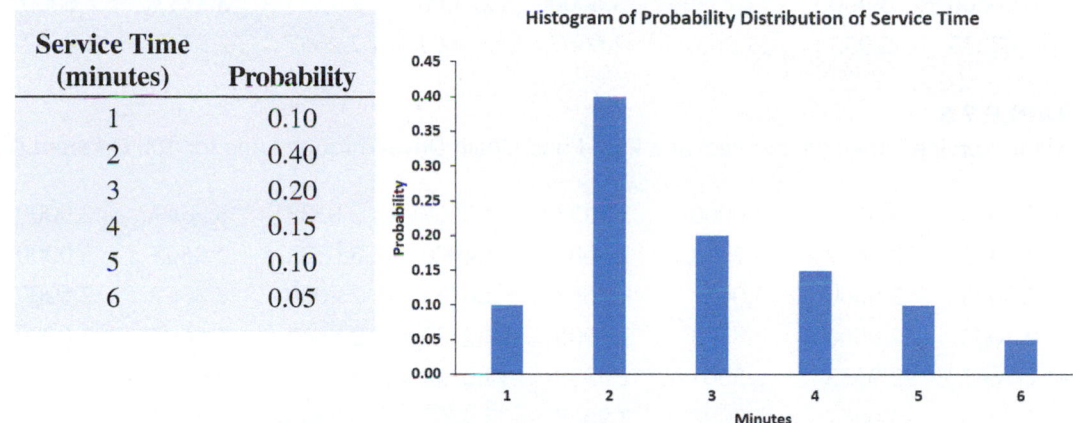

Histogram of Probability Distribution of Service Time

Using Equation (5.1) on page 201, the population mean is computed as 2.9 minutes. Using Equation (5.3) on page 202, the population standard deviation is computed as 1.34. Select 100 samples of $n = 2$, $n = 15$, and $n = 30$. What conclusions can you reach about the sampling distribution of the service time (in minutes) at the fast-food chain drive-through lane?

SOLUTION Table 7.3 represents the mean service time (in minutes) at the fast-food chain drive-through lane for 100 different random samples of $n = 2$. The mean of these 100 sample means is 2.825 minutes, and the standard error of the mean is 0.883.

TABLE 7.3

Mean Service Times (in minutes) at a Fast-Food Chain Drive-Through Lane for 100 Different Random Samples of $n = 2$

3.5	2.5	3	3.5	4	3	2.5	2	2	2.5
3	3	2.5	2.5	2	2.5	2.5	2	3.5	1.5
2	3	2.5	3	3	2	3.5	3.5	2.5	2
4.5	3.5	4	2	2	4	3.5	2.5	2.5	3.5
3.5	3.5	2	1.5	2.5	2	3.5	3.5	2.5	2.5
2.5	3	3	3.5	2	3.5	2	1.5	5.5	2.5
3.5	3	3	2	1.5	3	2.5	2.5	2.5	2.5
3.5	1.5	6	2	1.5	2.5	3.5	2	3.5	5
2.5	3.5	4.5	3.5	3.5	2	4	2	3	3
4.5	1.5	2.5	2	2.5	2.5	2	2	2	4

Table 7.4 represents the mean service time (in minutes) at the fast-food chain drive-through lane for 100 different random samples of $n = 15$. The mean of these 100 sample means is 2.9313 minutes, and the standard error of the mean is 0.3458.

Table 7.5 represents the mean service time (in minutes) at the fast-food chain drive-through lane for 100 different random samples of $n = 30$. The mean of these 100 sample means is 2.9527 minutes, and the standard error of the mean is 0.2701.

▶(continued)

TABLE 7.4
Mean Service Times (in minutes) at a Fast-Food Chain Drive-Through Lane for 100 Different Random Samples of $n = 15$

3.5333	2.8667	3.1333	3.6000	2.5333	2.8000	2.8667	3.1333	3.2667	3.3333
3.0000	3.3333	2.7333	2.6000	2.8667	3.0667	2.1333	2.5333	2.8000	3.1333
2.8000	2.7333	2.6000	3.1333	2.8667	3.4667	2.9333	2.8000	2.2000	3.0000
2.9333	2.6000	2.6000	3.1333	3.1333	3.1333	2.5333	3.0667	3.9333	2.8000
3.0000	2.7333	2.6000	2.4667	3.2000	2.4667	3.2000	2.9333	2.8667	3.4667
2.6667	3.0000	3.1333	3.1333	2.7333	2.7333	3.3333	3.4000	3.2000	3.0000
3.2000	3.0000	2.6000	2.9333	3.0667	2.8667	2.2667	2.5333	2.7333	2.2667
2.8000	2.8000	2.6000	3.1333	2.9333	3.0667	3.6667	2.6667	2.8667	2.6667
3.0000	3.4000	2.7333	3.6000	2.6000	2.7333	3.3333	2.6000	2.8667	2.8000
3.7333	2.9333	3.0667	2.6667	2.8667	2.2667	2.7333	2.8667	3.5333	3.2000

TABLE 7.5
Mean Service Times (in minutes) at a Fast-Food Chain Drive-Through Lane for 100 Different Random Samples of $n = 30$

3.0000	3.3667	3.0000	3.1333	2.8667	2.8333	3.2667	2.9000	2.7000	3.2000
3.2333	2.7667	3.2333	2.8000	3.4000	3.0333	2.8667	3.0000	3.1333	3.4000
2.3000	3.0000	3.0667	2.9667	3.0333	2.4000	2.8667	2.8000	2.5000	2.7000
2.7000	2.9000	2.8333	3.3000	3.1333	2.8667	2.6667	2.6000	3.2333	2.8667
2.7667	2.9333	2.5667	2.5333	3.0333	3.2333	3.0667	2.9667	2.4000	3.3000
2.8000	3.0667	3.2000	2.9667	2.9667	3.2333	3.3667	2.9000	3.0333	3.1333
3.3333	2.8667	2.8333	3.0667	3.3667	3.0667	3.0667	3.2000	3.1667	3.3667
3.0333	3.1667	2.4667	3.0000	2.6333	2.6667	2.9667	3.1333	2.8000	2.8333
2.9333	2.7000	3.0333	2.7333	2.6667	2.6333	3.1333	3.0667	2.5333	3.3333
3.1000	2.5667	2.9000	2.9333	2.9000	2.7000	2.7333	2.8000	2.6667	2.8333

Figure 7.6 Panels A through C show histograms of the mean service time (in minutes) at the fast-food chain drive-through lane for the three sets of 100 different random samples shown in Tables 7.3 through 7.5. Panel A, the histogram for the mean service time for 100 different random samples of $n = 2$, shows a skewed distribution, but a distribution that is not as skewed as the population distribution of service times shown in Figure 7.5.

FIGURE 7.6
Histograms of the mean service time (in minutes) at the fast-food chain drive-through lane of 100 different random samples of $n = 2$ (Panel A, left), 100 different random samples of $n = 15$ (Panel B, right), and 100 different random samples of $n = 30$ (Panel C, next page)

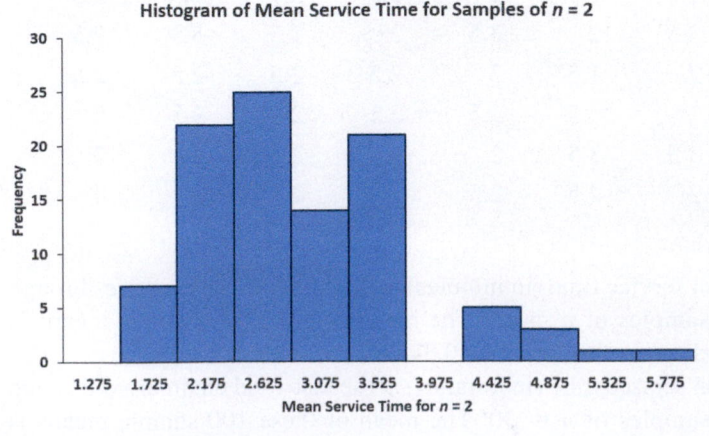
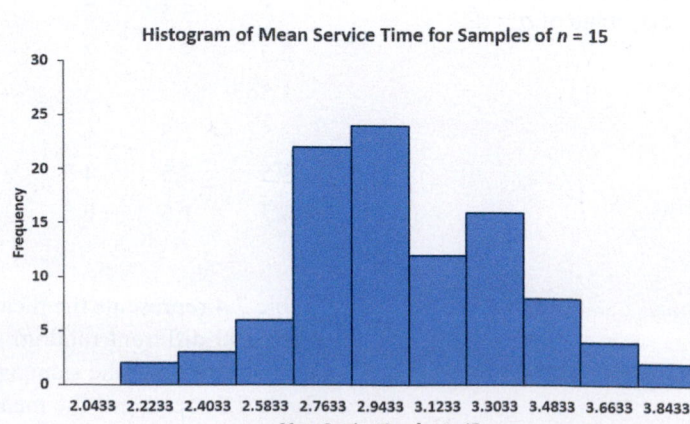

▶(*continued*)

FIGURE 7.6
(*continued*)

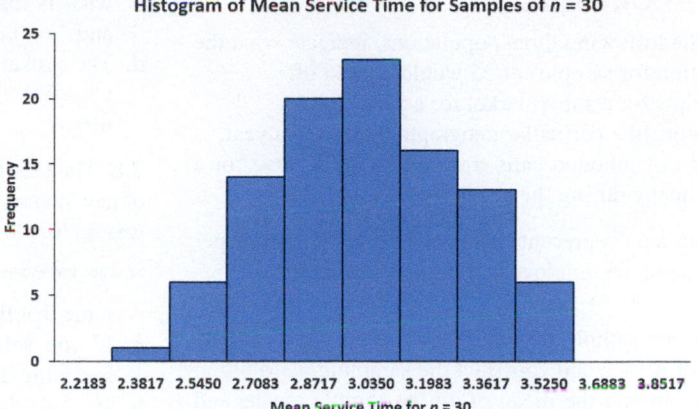

Panel B, the histogram for the mean service time for 100 different random samples of $n = 15$, shows a somewhat symmetrical distribution that contains a concentration of values in the center of the distribution. Panel C, the histogram for the mean service time for 100 different random samples of $n = 30$, shows a distribution that appears to be approximately bell-shaped with a concentration of values in the center of the distribution. The progression of the histograms from a skewed population toward a bell-shaped distribution as the sample size increases is consistent with the Central Limit Theorem.

VISUAL EXPLORATIONS

Exploring Sampling Distributions

Open the **VE-Sampling Distribution add-in workbook** to observe the effects of simulated rolls on the frequency distribution of the sum of two dice. (For Excel technical requirements, see Appendix D.) When this workbook opens properly, it adds a Sampling Distribution menu to the Add-ins tab (Apple menu in Excel for Mac).

To observe the effects of simulated throws on the frequency distribution of the sum of the two dice, select **Sampling Distribution → Two Dice Simulation**. In the Sampling Distribution dialog box, enter the **Number of rolls per tally** and click **Tally**. Click **Finish** when done.

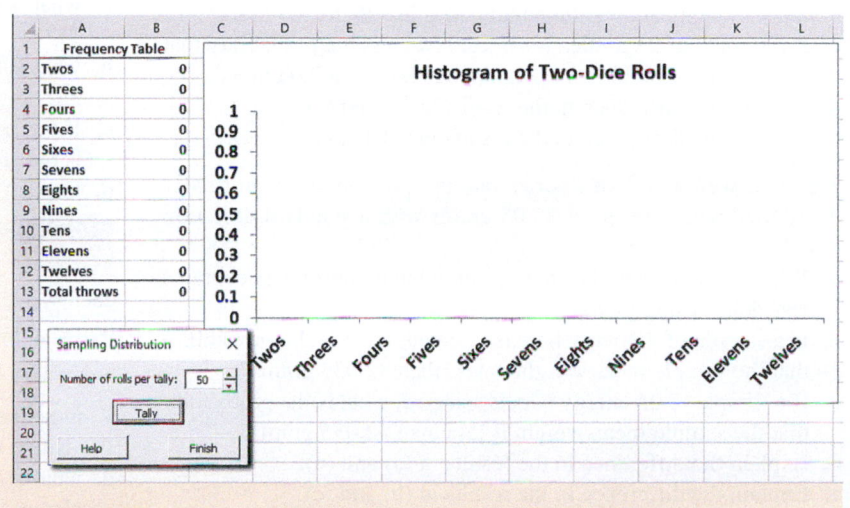

PROBLEMS FOR SECTION 7.2

LEARNING THE BASICS

7.1 Given a normal distribution with $\mu = 100$ and $\sigma = 10$, if you select a sample of $n = 25$, what is the probability that $\overline{X}$ is
a. less than 95?
b. between 95 and 97.5?
c. above 102.2?
d. There is a 65% chance that $\overline{X}$ is above what value?

7.2 Given a normal distribution with $\mu = 50$ and $\sigma = 5$, if you select a sample of $n = 100$, what is the probability that $\overline{X}$ is
a. less than 47?
b. between 47 and 49.5?
c. above 51.1?
d. There is a 35% chance that $\overline{X}$ is above what value?

APPLYING THE CONCEPTS

7.3 For each of the following three populations, indicate what the sampling distribution for samples of 25 would consist of:

a. Customer receipts for a supermarket for a year.

b. Insurance payouts in a particular geographical area in a year.

c. Call center logs of inbound calls tracking handling time for a credit card company during the year.

7.4 The following data represent the number of days absent per year in a population of six employees of a small company:

$$1 \quad 3 \quad 6 \quad 7 \quad 9 \quad 10$$

a. Assuming that you sample without replacement, select all possible samples of $n = 2$ and construct the sampling distribution of the mean. Compute the mean of all the sample means and also compute the population mean. Are they equal? What is this property called?

b. Repeat (a) for all possible samples of $n = 3$.

c. Compare the shape of the sampling distribution of the mean in (a) and (b). Which sampling distribution has less variability? Why?

d. Assuming that you sample with replacement, repeat (a) through (c) and compare the results. Which sampling distributions have the least variability—those in (a) or (b)? Why?

7.5 The amount of water in a two-liter bottle is approximately normally distributed with a mean of 2.05 liters with a standard deviation of 0.025 liter.

a. What is the probability that an individual bottle contains less than 2.03 liters?

b. If a sample of 4 bottles is selected, what is the probability that the sample mean amount contained is less than 2.03 liters?

c. If a sample of 25 bottles is selected, what is the probability that the sample mean amount contained is less than 2.03 liters?

d. Explain the difference in the results in (a) and (c).

e. Explain the difference in the results in (b) and (c).

7.6 The weight of an energy bar is approximately normally distributed with a mean of 42.05 grams with a standard deviation of 0.025 gram.

a. What is the probability that an individual energy bar contains less than 42.035 grams?

b. If a sample of 4 energy bars is selected, what is the probability that the sample mean weight is less than 42.035 grams?

c. If a sample of 25 energy bars is selected, what is the probability that the sample mean weight is less than 42.035 grams?

d. Explain the difference in the results in (a) and (c).

e. Explain the difference in the results in (b) and (c).

7.7 The diameter of a brand of tennis balls is approximately normally distributed, with a mean of 2.63 inches and a standard deviation of 0.03 inch. If you select a random sample of nine tennis balls,

a. what is the sampling distribution of the mean?

b. what is the probability that the sample mean is less than 2.61 inches?

c. what is the probability that the sample mean is between 2.62 and 2.64 inches?

d. The probability is 60% that the sample mean will be between what two values symmetrically distributed around the population mean?

7.8 The U.S. Census Bureau announced that the median sales price of new houses sold in 2016 was $316,500, and the mean sales price was $370,800

Source: **www.census.gov/newhomesales**, April 1, 2017.

Assume that the standard deviation of the prices is $90,000.

a. If you select samples of $n = 4$, describe the shape of the sampling distribution of $\overline{X}$.

b. If you select samples of $n = 100$, describe the shape of the sampling distribution of $\overline{X}$.

c. If you select a random sample of $n = 100$, what is the probability that the sample mean will be less than $370,000?

d. If you select a random sample of $n = 100$, what is the probability that the sample mean will be between 350,000 and 365,000?

7.9 According to a report by App Annie, a business intelligence company that produces tools and reports for the apps and digital goods industry, smartphone owners are using an average of 30 apps per month.

Source: "Report: Smartphone owners are using 9 apps per day, 30 per month," 2017, **tcrn.ch/2qK4iRr**.

Assume that number of apps used per month by smartphone owners is normally distributed and that the standard deviation is 5. If you select a random sample of 25 smartphone owners,

a. what is the probability that the sample mean is between 29 and 31?

b. what is the probability that the sample mean is between 28 and 32?

c. If you select a random sample of 100 smartphone owners, what is the probability that the sample mean is between 29 and 31?

d. Explain the difference in the results of (a) and (c).

✓SELF TEST **7.10** According to the National Survey of Student Engagement, the average student spends about 15 hours each week preparing for classes; preparation for classes includes homework, reading and any other assignments.

Source: Data extracted from **bit.ly/2qSNwNo**.

Assume the standard deviation of time spent preparing for classes is 4 hours. If you select a random sample of 16 students,

a. what is the probability that the mean time spent preparing for classes is at least 14 hours per week?

b. there is an 85% chance that the sample mean is less than how many hours per week?

c. What assumption must you make in order to solve (a) and (b)?

d. If you select a random sample of 64 students, there is an 85% chance that the sample mean is less than how many hours per week?

7.3 Sampling Distribution of the Proportion

When analyzing a categorical variable, you often want to know what proportion of the data consists of one specific categorical value, or *characteristic of interest*. In the simplest case, a categorical variable that has only two categories such as yes and no, you calculate

student TIP

Do not confuse this use of the Greek letter pi, π, to represent the population proportion with the mathematical constant that represents the ratio of the circumference to a diameter of a circle.

the sample proportion, p, that Equation (7.6) defines, as part of process to estimate the population proportion, π, the proportion of items in the entire population with the characteristic of interest.

SAMPLE PROPORTION

$$p = \frac{X}{n} = \frac{\text{Number of items having the characteristic of interest}}{\text{Sample size}} \tag{7.6}$$

The sample proportion calculation is a simple fraction. For example, for a yes-no variable in a sample size of 5 responses, if there are 3 responses with the characteristic of interest yes, the sample proportion would be 0.6 (three fifths, or 3 divided by 5).

The sample proportion, p, will be between 0 and 1. If all items have the characteristic, p is equal to 1. If half the items have the characteristic, p is equal to 0.5. If none of the items have the characteristic, p is equal to 0.

In Section 7.2, you learned that the sample mean, $\overline{X}$, is an unbiased estimator of the population mean, μ. Similarly, the statistic p is an unbiased estimator of the population proportion, π. By analogy to the sampling distribution of the mean, whose standard error is $\sigma_{\overline{X}} = \dfrac{\sigma}{\sqrt{n}}$, the **standard error of the proportion**, σ_p, is given in Equation (7.7).

student TIP

Remember that the sample proportion cannot be negative and also cannot be greater than 1.0.

STANDARD ERROR OF THE PROPORTION

$$\sigma_p = \sqrt{\frac{\pi(1-\pi)}{n}} \tag{7.7}$$

The **sampling distribution of the proportion** follows the binomial distribution, as discussed in Section 5.2, when sampling with replacement (or without replacement from extremely large populations). However, you can use the normal distribution to approximate the binomial distribution when $n\pi$ and $n(1-\pi)$ are each at least 5. In most cases in which inferences are made about the population proportion, the sample size is substantial enough to meet the conditions for using the normal approximation (see reference 1).

Substituting p for $\overline{X}$, π for μ, and $\sqrt{\dfrac{\pi(1-\pi)}{n}}$ for $\dfrac{\sigma}{\sqrt{n}}$ in Equation (7.4) on page 257 results in Equation (7.8).

FINDING Z FOR THE SAMPLING DISTRIBUTION OF THE PROPORTION

$$Z = \frac{p - \pi}{\sqrt{\dfrac{\pi(1-\pi)}{n}}} \tag{7.8}$$

To illustrate the sampling distribution of the proportion, a recent survey (L. Petrecca, "Always On: How You Can Disconnect From Work" *USA Today*, January 16, 2017, p. 5B) reported that 46% of American workers said that they work during nonbusiness hours. Suppose that you select a random sample of 200 American workers and you want to determine the probability that more than 50% of them stated that they worked during nonbusiness hours. Because $n\pi = 200(0.46) = 92 > 5$ and $n(1 - \pi) = 200(1 - 0.46) = 108 > 5$, the sample size is large enough to assume that the sampling distribution of the proportion is approximately normally distributed. Then, using the survey percentage of 46% as the population proportion, you can calculate the probability that more than 50% of American workers say that they work during nonbusiness hours using Equation (7.8):

$$Z = \frac{p - \pi}{\sqrt{\dfrac{\pi(1 - \pi)}{n}}}$$

$$= \frac{0.50 - 0.46}{\sqrt{\dfrac{(0.46)(0.54)}{200}}} = \frac{0.04}{\sqrt{\dfrac{0.2484}{200}}} = \frac{0.04}{0.0352}$$

$$= 1.14$$

Using Table E.2, the area under the normal curve greater than 1.14 is $1 - 0.8729 = 0.1271$. Therefore, if the population proportion is 0.46, the probability is 12.71% that more than 50% of the 200 American workers in the sample will say that they work during non-business hours.

PROBLEMS FOR SECTION 7.3

LEARNING THE BASICS

7.11 In a random sample of 64 people, 48 are classified as "successful."
a. Determine the sample proportion, p, of "successful" people.
b. If the population proportion is 0.70, determine the standard error of the proportion.

7.12 A random sample of 50 households was selected for a phone (landline and cellphone) survey. The key question asked was, "Do you or any member of your household own an Apple product (iPhone, iPod, iPad, or Mac computer)?" Of the 50 respondents, 20 said yes and 30 said no.
a. Determine the sample proportion, p, of households that own an Apple product.
b. If the population proportion is 0.45, determine the standard error of the proportion.

7.13 The following data represent the responses (Y for yes and N for no) from a sample of 40 college students to the question "Do you currently own shares in any stocks?"

N N Y N N Y N Y N Y N N Y N Y Y Y N N N Y

N Y N N N N Y N N Y Y N N N Y N N Y N N

a. Determine the sample proportion, p, of college students who own shares of stock.
b. If the population proportion is 0.30, determine the standard error of the proportion.

APPLYING THE CONCEPTS

✓SELF TEST **7.14** A political pollster is conducting an analysis of sample results in order to make predictions on election night. Assuming a two-candidate election, if a specific candidate receives at least 55% of the vote in the sample, that candidate will be forecast as the winner of the election. If you select a random sample of 100 voters, what is the probability that a candidate will be forecast as the winner when
a. the population percentage of her vote is 50.1%?
b. the population percentage of her vote is 60%?
c. the population percentage of her vote is 49% (and she will actually lose the election)?
d. If the sample size is increased to 400, what are your answers to (a) through (c)? Discuss.

7.15 You plan to conduct a marketing experiment in which students are to taste one of two different brands of soft drink. Their task is to correctly identify the brand tasted. You select a random sample of 200 students and assume that the students have no ability to distinguish between the two brands. (Hint: If an individual has no ability to distinguish between the two soft drinks, then the two brands are equally likely to be selected.)
a. What is the probability that the sample will have between 50% and 60% of the identifications correct?
b. The probability is 90% that the sample percentage is contained within what symmetrical limits of the population percentage?
c. What is the probability that the sample percentage of correct identifications is greater than 65%?
d. Which is more likely to occur—more than 60% correct identifications in the sample of 200 or more than 55% correct identifications in a sample of 1,000? Explain.

7.16 What do millennials around the world want in a job? A Deloitte survey of millennials on work-life challenges found that millennials are looking for stability in an uncertain world, with 65% of millennials preferring a permanent, full-time job rather than working freelance or as a consultant on a flexible or short-term basis.

Source: Data extracted from "Freelance flexibility with full-time stability," **bit.ly/2pr6h9r**.

Suppose you select a sample of 100 millennials.
a. What is the probability that in the sample fewer than 70% prefer a permanent, full-time job?
b. What is the probability that in the sample between 60% and 70% prefer a permanent, full-time job?
c. What is the probability that in the sample more than 70% prefer a permanent, full-time job?
d. If a sample of 400 is taken, how does this change your answers to (a) through (c)?

7.17 The goal of corporate sustainability is to manage the environmental, economic, and social effects of a corporation's operations so it is profitable over the long-term while acting in a responsible manner to society. An international study by Unilever reveals that 33% of consumers are choosing to buy from brands they believe are doing social or environmental good.

Source: Data extracted from "Report shows a third of consumers prefer sustainable brands," **bit.ly/2pTyEzO**.

Suppose you select a sample of 100 consumers.

a. What is the probability that in the sample fewer than 30% are choosing to buy from brands they believe are doing social or environmental good?

b. What is the probability that in the sample between 28% and 38% are choosing to buy from brands they believe are doing social or environmental good?

c. What is the probability that in the sample more than 38% are choosing to buy from brands they believe are doing social or environmental good?

d. If a sample of 400 is taken, how does this change your answers to (a) through (c)?

7.18 According to the MSCI 2016 Survey of Women on Boards, women hold 20% of director seats on U.S. corporate boards. This study also reports that 34% of U.S. companies have three or more female board directors.

Source: Data extracted from "The Tipping Point: Women on Boards and Financial Performance," **bit.ly/2pYDt9A**.

If you select a random sample of 200 U.S. companies,

a. what is the probability that the sample will have between 30% and 38% U.S. companies that have three or more female board directors?

b. the probability is 90% that the sample percentage of U.S. companies that have three or more female board directors will be contained within what symmetrical limits of the population percentage?

c. the probability is 95% that the sample percentage of U.S. companies that have three or more female board directors will be contained within what symmetrical limits of the population percentage?

7.19 The topic of global warming increasingly appears in the news. It has the potential to impact companies' operations through changes in governmental regulations, new reporting requirements, necessary operational changes, and so on. The Institute of Management Accountants (IMA) conducted a survey of senior finance professionals to gauge members' thoughts on global warming and its impact on their companies. The survey found that 65% of senior finance professionals believe that global warming is having a significant impact on the environment.

Source: Data extracted from "Global Warming: How Has It Affected Your Company?" **bit.ly/2pd341h**.

Suppose that you select a sample of 100 senior finance professionals.

a. What is the probability that the sample percentage indicating global warming is having a significant impact on the environment will be between 64% and 69%?

b. The probability is 90% that the sample percentage will be contained within what symmetrical limits of the population percentage?

c. The probability is 95% that the sample percentage will be contained within what symmetrical limits of the population percentage?

d. Suppose you selected a sample of 400 senior finance professionals. How does this change your answers in (a) through (c)?

7.20 An IAB study on the state of original digital video showed that original data video is becoming increasingly popular. Original digital video is defined as professionally produced video only for ad-supported online distribution and viewing (not TV). According to IAB data, 26% of American adults 18+ watch original digital videos each month.

Source: Data extracted from "IAB Original Digital Video Consumer Study," May 2016, **bit.ly/2aUPkzk**.

a. Suppose that you take a sample of 100 U.S. adults. If the population proportion of U.S. adults who watch original digital videos is 0.26, what is the probability that fewer than 21% in your sample will watch digital videos?

b. Suppose that you take a sample of 500 U.S. adults. If the population proportion of U.S. adults who watch original digital videos is 0.26, what is the probability that fewer than 21% in your sample will watch digital videos?

c. Discuss the effect of sample size on the sampling distribution of the proportion in general and the effect on the probabilities in (a) and (b).

7.4 Sampling from Finite Populations

The Central Limit Theorem and the standard errors of the mean and of the proportion are based on samples selected with replacement. However, in nearly all survey research, you sample *without* replacement from populations that are of a finite size, *N*. The **Section 7.4 online Topic** explains how you use a **finite population correction factor** to compute the standard error of the mean and the standard error of the proportion for such samples.

▼USING **STATISTICS**
Sampling Oxford Cereals, Revisited

As the plant operations manager for Oxford Cereals, you were responsible for monitoring the amount of cereal placed in each box. To be consistent with package labeling, boxes should contain a mean of 368 grams of cereal. Because weighing each of the thousands of boxes produced each shift would be too time-consuming, costly, and inefficient, you selected a sample of boxes. Based on your analysis of this sample, you had to decide whether to maintain, alter, or shut down the process.

Using the concept of the sampling distribution of the mean, you were able to determine probabilities that such a sample mean could have been randomly selected from a population with a mean of 368 grams. Specifically, if a sample of size $n = 25$ is selected from a population with a mean of 368 and standard deviation of 15, you calculated the probability of selecting a sample with a mean of 365 grams or less to be 15.87%. If a larger sample size is selected, the sample mean should be closer to the population mean. This result was illustrated when you calculated the probability if the sample size were increased to $n = 100$. Using the larger sample size, you determined the probability of selecting a sample with a mean of 365 grams or less to be 2.28%.

▼ SUMMARY

You studied the sampling distribution of the sample mean and the sampling distribution of the sample proportion and their relationship to the Central Limit Theorem. You learned that the sample mean is an unbiased estimator of the population mean, and the sample proportion is an unbiased estimator of the population proportion. In the next five chapters, the techniques of confidence intervals and tests of hypotheses commonly used for statistical inference are discussed.

▼ REFERENCES

1. Cochran, W. G. *Sampling Techniques*, 3rd ed. New York: Wiley, 1977.

▼ KEY EQUATIONS

Population Mean

$$\mu = \frac{\sum_{i=1}^{N} X_i}{N} \tag{7.1}$$

Population Standard Deviation

$$\sigma = \sqrt{\frac{\sum_{i=1}^{N} (X_i - \mu)^2}{N}} \tag{7.2}$$

Standard Error of the Mean

$$\sigma_{\bar{X}} = \frac{\sigma}{\sqrt{n}} \tag{7.3}$$

Finding Z for the Sampling Distribution of the Mean

$$Z = \frac{\bar{X} - \mu_{\bar{X}}}{\sigma_{\bar{X}}} = \frac{\bar{X} - \mu}{\frac{\sigma}{\sqrt{n}}} \tag{7.4}$$

Finding $\bar{X}$ for the Sampling Distribution of the Mean

$$\bar{X} = \mu + Z \frac{\sigma}{\sqrt{n}} \tag{7.5}$$

Sample Proportion

$$p = \frac{X}{n} \tag{7.6}$$

Standard Error of the Proportion

$$\sigma_p = \sqrt{\frac{\pi(1 - \pi)}{n}} \tag{7.7}$$

Finding Z for the Sampling Distribution of the Proportion

$$Z = \frac{p - \pi}{\sqrt{\frac{\pi(1 - \pi)}{n}}} \tag{7.8}$$

▼ KEY TERMS

▼ CHECKING YOUR UNDERSTANDING

7.21 Why is the sample mean an unbiased estimator of the population mean?

7.22 Why does the standard error of the mean decrease as the sample size, n, increases?

7.23 Why does the sampling distribution of the mean follow a normal distribution for a large enough sample size, even though the population may not be normally distributed?

7.24 What is the difference between a population distribution and a sampling distribution?

7.25 Under what circumstances does the sampling distribution of the proportion approximately follow the normal distribution?

▼ CHAPTER REVIEW PROBLEMS

7.26 An industrial sewing machine uses ball bearings that are targeted to have a diameter of 0.75 inch. The lower and upper specification limits under which the ball bearing can operate are 0.74 inch (lower) and 0.76 inch (upper). Past experience has indicated that the actual diameter of the ball bearings is approximately normally distributed, with a mean of 0.753 inch and a standard deviation of 0.004 inch. If you select a random sample of 25 ball bearings, what is the probability that the sample mean is
a. between the target and the population mean of 0.753?
b. between the lower specification limit and the target?
c. greater than the upper specification limit?
d. less than the lower specification limit?
e. The probability is 93% that the sample mean diameter will be greater than what value?

7.27 The fill amount of bottles of a soft drink is normally distributed, with a mean of 2.0 liters and a standard deviation of 0.05 liter. If you select a random sample of 25 bottles, what is the probability that the sample mean will be
a. between 1.99 and 2.0 liters?
b. below 1.98 liters?
c. greater than 2.01 liters?
d. The probability is 99% that the sample mean amount of soft drink will be at least how much?
e. The probability is 99% that the sample mean amount of soft drink will be between which two values (symmetrically distributed around the mean)?

7.28 An orange juice producer buys oranges from a large orange grove that has one variety of orange. The amount of juice squeezed from these oranges is approximately normally distributed, with a mean of 4.70 ounces and a standard deviation of 0.40 ounce. Suppose that you select a sample of 25 oranges.
a. What is the probability that the sample mean amount of juice will be at least 4.60 ounces?
b. The probability is 70% that the sample mean amount of juice will be contained between what two values symmetrically distributed around the population mean?
c. The probability is 77% that the sample mean amount of juice will be greater than what value?

7.29 In Problem 7.28, suppose that the mean amount of juice squeezed is 5.0 ounces.
a. What is the probability that the sample mean amount of juice will be at least 4.60 ounces?
b. The probability is 70% that the sample mean amount of juice will be contained between what two values symmetrically distributed around the population mean?
c. The probability is 77% that the sample mean amount of juice will be greater than what value?
d. Compare the results of (a) through (c) with the results of Problem 7.28 (a) through (c).

7.30 The stock market in Canada reported strong returns in 2016. The population of stocks earned a mean return of 17.5% in 2016.
Source: Data extracted from *The Wall Street Journal*, December 31, 2016–Janaury 1, 2017, p. B6.

Assume that the returns for stocks on the Canadian stock market were distributed as a normal variable, with a mean of 17.5 and a standard deviation of 20. If you selected a random sample of 16 stocks from this population, what is the probability that the sample would have a mean return
a. less than 0 (i.e., a loss)?
b. between 0 and 10?
c. greater than 10?

7.31 The article mentioned in Problem 7.30 reported that the stock market in Germany had a mean return of 6.9% in 2016. Assume that the returns for stocks on the German stock market were distributed normally, with a mean of 6.9 and a standard deviation of 10. If you select an individual stock from this population, what is the probability that it would have a return
a. less than 0 (i.e., a loss)?
b. between -10 and -20?
c. greater than -5?

If you selected a random sample of four stocks from this population, what is the probability that the sample would have a mean return
d. less than 0 (a loss)?
e. between -10 and -20?
f. greater than -5?
g. Compare your results in parts (d) through (f) to those in (a) through (c).

7.32 (Class Project) The table of random numbers is an example of a uniform distribution because each digit is equally likely to occur. Starting in the row corresponding to the day of the month in which you were born, use a table of random numbers (Table E.1) to take one digit at a time.

Select five different samples each of $n = 2$, $n = 5$, and $n = 10$. Compute the sample mean of each sample. Develop a frequency distribution of the sample means for the results of the entire class, based on samples of sizes $n = 2$, $n = 5$, and $n = 10$.

What can be said about the shape of the sampling distribution for each of these sample sizes?

7.33 (Class Project) Toss a coin 10 times and record the number of heads. If each student performs this experiment five times, a frequency distribution of the number of heads can be developed from the results of the entire class. Does this distribution seem to approximate the normal distribution?

7.34 (Class Project) The number of cars waiting in line at a car wash is distributed as follows:

Number of Cars	Probability
0	0.25
1	0.40
2	0.20
3	0.10
4	0.04
5	0.01

You can use a table of random numbers (Table E.1) to select samples from this distribution by assigning numbers as follows:

1. Start in the row corresponding to the day of the month in which you were born.

2. Select a two-digit random number.
3. If you select a random number from 00 to 24, record a length of 0; if from 25 to 64, record a length of 1; if from 65 to 84, record a length of 2; if from 85 to 94, record a length of 3; if from 95 to 98, record a length of 4; if 99, record a length of 5.

Select samples of $n = 2$, $n = 15$, and $n = 30$. Compute the mean for each sample. For example, if a sample of size 2 results in the random numbers 18 and 46, these would correspond to lengths 0 and 1, respectively, producing a sample mean of 0.5. If each student selects five different samples for each sample size, a frequency distribution of the sample means (for each sample size) can be developed from the results of the entire class. What conclusions can you reach concerning the sampling distribution of the mean as the sample size is increased?

7.35 (Class Project) The file `Credit Scores` contains the average credit scores of people living in 2,750 American cities.

Source: Data extracted from **bit.ly/2oCgnbi**.

a. Select five different samples of $n = 2$, $n = 5$, $n = 15$, and $n = 30$.
b. Compute the sample mean of each sample. Develop a frequency distribution of the sample means for the results of the entire class, based on samples of sizes $n = 2$, $n = 5$, and $n = 15$, and $n = 30$.
c. What can be said about the shape of the sampling distribution for each of these sample sizes?

CHAPTER 7

▾ CASES

Managing Ashland MultiComm Services

Continuing the quality improvement effort first described in the Chapter 6 Managing Ashland MultiComm Services case, the target upload speed for AMS Internet service subscribers has been monitored. As before, upload speeds are measured on a standard scale in which the target value is 1.0. Data collected over the past year indicate that the upload speeds are approximately normally distributed, with a mean of 1.005 and a standard deviation of 0.10.

1. Each day, at 25 random times, the upload speed is measured. Assuming that the distribution has not changed from what it was in the past year, what is the probability that the mean upload speed is

a. less than 1.0?
b. between 0.95 and 1.0?
c. between 1.0 and 1.05?
d. less than 0.95 or greater than 1.05?
e. Suppose that the mean upload speed of today's sample of 25 is 0.952. What conclusion can you reach about the mean upload speed today based on this result? Explain.

2. Compare the results of AMS Problem 1 (a) through (d) to those of AMS Problem 1 in Chapter 6 on page 246. What conclusions can you reach concerning the differences?

Digital Case

Apply your knowledge about sampling distributions in this Digital Case, which reconsiders the Oxford Cereals Using Statistics scenario.

The advocacy group Consumers Concerned About Cereal Cheaters (CCACC) suspects that cereal companies, including Oxford Cereals, are cheating consumers by packaging cereals at less than labeled weights. Recently, the group investigated the package weights of two popular Oxford brand cereals. Open **CCACC.pdf** to examine the group's claims and supporting data, and then answer the following questions:

1. Are the data collection procedures that the CCACC uses to form its conclusions flawed? What procedures could the group follow to make its analysis more rigorous?

2. Assume that the two samples of five cereal boxes (one sample for each of two cereal varieties) listed on the CCACC website were collected randomly by organization members. For each sample,

   a. calculate the sample mean.

   b. assuming that the standard deviation of the process is 15 grams and the population mean is 368 grams, calculate the percentage of all samples for each process that have a sample mean less than the value you calculated in (a).

   c. assuming that the standard deviation is 15 grams, calculate the percentage of individual boxes of cereal that have a weight less than the value you calculated in (a).

3. What, if any, conclusions can you form by using your calculations about the filling processes for the two different cereals?

4. A representative from Oxford Cereals has asked that the CCACC take down its page discussing shortages in Oxford Cereals boxes. Is this request reasonable? Why or why not?

5. Can the techniques discussed in this chapter be used to prove cheating in the manner alleged by the CCACC? Why or why not?

▾EXCEL GUIDE

EG7.2 SAMPLING DISTRIBUTION of the MEAN

Key Technique Use an add-in procedure to create a simulated sampling distribution and use the **RAND()** function to create lists of random numbers.

Example Create a simulated sampling distribution that consists of 100 samples of $n = 30$ from a uniformly distributed population.

PHStat Use **Sampling Distributions Simulation**.

For the example, select **PHStat→Sampling→Sampling Distributions Simulation**. In the procedure's dialog box (shown below):

1. Enter **100** as the **Number of Samples**.
2. Enter **30** as the **Sample Size**.
3. Click **Uniform**.
4. Enter a **Title** and click **OK**.

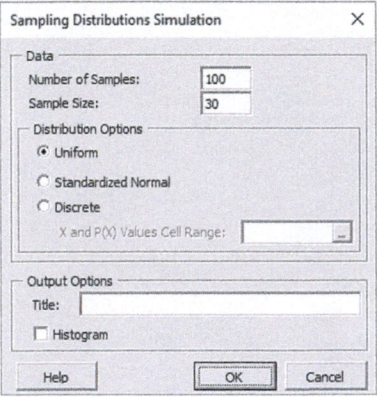

The procedure inserts a new worksheet in which the sample means, overall mean, and standard error of the mean can be found starting in row 34.

Workbook Use the **SDS worksheet** of the **SDS workbook** as a model.

For the example, in a new worksheet, first enter a title in cell A1. Then enter the formula **=RAND()** in cell **A2** and then copy the formula down 30 rows and across 100 columns (through

column CV). Then select this cell range (**A2:CV31**) and use **copy and paste values** as discussed in Appendix Section B.4.

Use the formulas that appear in rows 33 through 37 in the **SDS_FORMULAS worksheet** as models if you want to compute sample means, the overall mean, and the standard error of the mean.

Analysis ToolPak Use **Random Number Generation**.

For the example, select **Data→Data Analysis**. In the Data Analysis dialog box, select **Random Number Generation** from the **Analysis Tools** list and then click **OK**.

In the procedure's dialog box (shown below):

1. Enter **100** as the **Number of Variables**.
2. Enter **30** as the **Number of Random Numbers**.
3. Select **Uniform** from the **Distribution** drop-down list.
4. Keep the **Parameters** values as is.
5. Click **New Worksheet Ply** and then click **OK**.

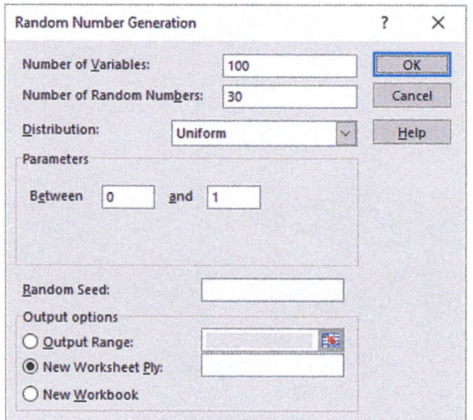

If, for other problems, you select **Discrete** in step 3, you must be open to a worksheet that contains a cell range of X and $P(X)$ values. Enter this cell range as the **Value and Probability Input Range** (not shown when **Uniform** has been selected) in the **Parameters** section of the dialog box.

Use the formulas that appear in rows 33 through 37 in the **SDS_FORMULAS worksheet** of the **SDS workbook** as models if you want to compute sample means, the overall mean, and the standard error of the mean.

▾**JMP** GUIDE

JG7.2 SAMPLING DISTRIBUTION of the MEAN

Use **New Columns**, **Tabulate**, and **Distribution**.

To create a simulated sampling distribution, use JMP random data generation features to create random samples of a sample size, then use Tabulate to create a table of sample means, and then use Distribution to construct a histogram and display tabular summaries about the set of sample means.

For example, to create 100 samples of $n = 30$ from a uniformly distributed population, open to a new data table and:

1. Click the **Columns red triangle** and select **New Columns** from its menu.

In the New Columns dialog box (partially shown below):

2. Enter **Column** as the **Column Name**.
3. Select **Random** from the **Initialize Data** pull-down list.
4. Enter **30** as the **Number of rows**.
5. Click **Random Uniform** and verify that the **Range** is from 0 to 1.
6. Enter **100** as the **Number of columns to add**.
7. Click **OK**.

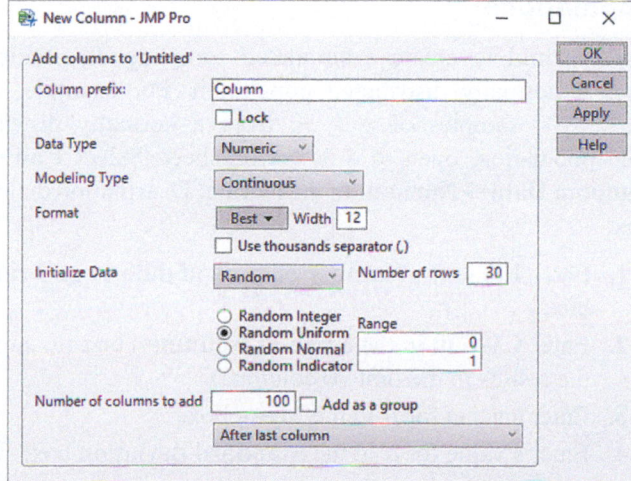

JMP inserts 100 columns of random data from an uniform distribution into the data table. With the data table still open:

8. Select **Analyze➔Tabulate**.

In the Tabulate window (shown on page 112):

9. Drag **Mean** from the statistics list and drop it in the **Drop zone for columns** area.

10. Click the **first column** in the columns list and then press **Ctrl+A** to select all 100 columns.
11. Drag the **selected 100 columns** from the columns list and drop it on the blank gray cell of the blank first column in the table. JMP displays a table of sample means in the Tabulate window.
12. Click the **Tabulate red triangle** and select **Make Into Data Table** from its menu.

JMP creates a new two-column data table of column names and means. With this new data table still open:

13. Select **Analyze➔Distribution**.

In the Distribution dialog box (shown below):

14. Click **Mean** in the Select Columns list and then click **Y, Columns** to add Mean to the Y, Columns box.
15. Click **OK**.

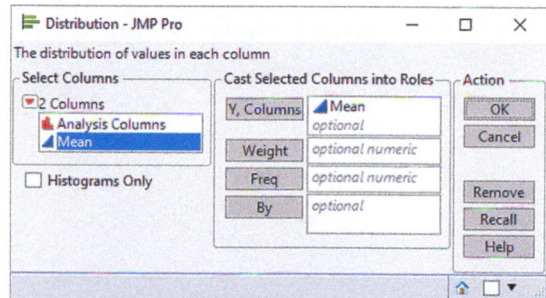

JMP displays a histogram and tables of summary information in the new Distribution window. Adjust contents of this window as necessary. Close the Tabulate window that remains on screen to declutter the screen.

Sampling from Normally Distributed Populations

Adapt the previous 15-step instructions to create samples from a normally distributed population.

For example, to create 100 samples of $n = 30$ from a normally distributed population, repeat steps 1 through 15 but in step 5, click **Random Normal** and enter the mean and standard deviation (in that order) in the **Mean/StdDev** boxes.

▾MINITAB GUIDE

MG7.2 SAMPLING DISTRIBUTION of the MEAN

Use **Uniform** to create a simulated sampling distribution from a uniformly distributed population. For example, to create 100 samples of $n = 30$ from a uniformly distributed population, open to a new worksheet. Select **Calc➔ Random Data➔Uniform**. In the Uniform Distribution dialog box (shown below):

1. Enter **100** in the **Number of rows of data to generate** box.
2. Enter **C1-C30** in the **Store in column(s)** box (to store the results in the first 30 columns).
3. Enter **0.0** in the **Lower endpoint** box.
4. Enter **1.0** in the **Upper endpoint** box.
5. Click **OK**.

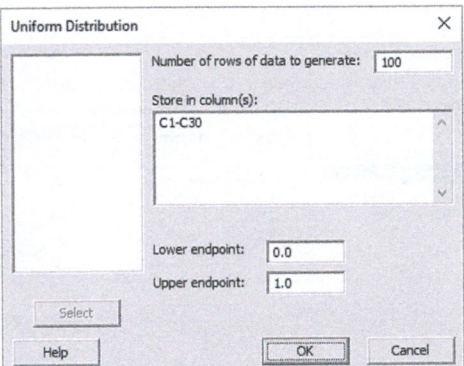

The 100 samples of $n = 30$ are entered *row-wise* in columns C1 through C30, an exception to the rule used in this book to enter data column-wise. (Row-wise data facilitates the computation of means.) While still opened to the worksheet with the 100 samples, enter **Sample Means** as the name of column **C31**. Select **Calc➔Row Statistics**. In the Row Statistics dialog box (shown below):

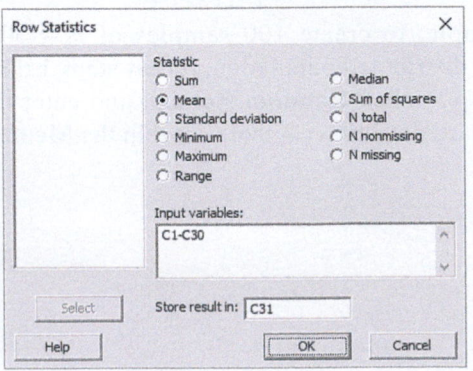

6. Click **Mean**.
7. Enter **C1-C30** in the **Input variables** box.
8. Enter **C31** in the **Store result in** box.
9. Click **OK**.
10. With the mean for each of the 100 row-wise samples in column C31, select **Stat➔Basic Statistics➔Display Descriptive Statistics**.
11. In the Display Descriptive Statistics dialog box, enter **C31** in the **Variables** box and click **Statistics**.
12. In the Display Descriptive Statistics: Statistics dialog box, select **Mean** and **Standard deviation** and then click **OK**.
13. Back in the Display Descriptive Statistics dialog box, click **OK**.

While still open to the worksheet created in steps 1 through 13, select **Graph➔Histogram** and in the Histograms dialog box, click **Simple** and then click **OK**. In the Histogram: Simple dialog box:

1. Enter **C31** in the **Graph variables** box.
2. Click **OK**.

Sampling from Normally Distributed Populations

Use **Normal** to create a simulated sampling distribution from a normally distributed population. For example, to create 100 samples of $n = 30$ from a normally distributed population, open to a new worksheet. Select **Calc➔ Random Data➔Normal**. In the Normal Distribution dialog box:

1. Enter **100** in the **Number of rows of data to generate** box.
2. Enter **C1-C30** in the **Store in column(s)** box (to store the results in the first 30 columns).
3. Enter a value for μ in the **Mean** box.
4. Enter a value for σ in the **Standard deviation** box.
5. Click **OK**.

The 100 samples of $n = 30$ are entered row-wise in columns C1 through C30. To compute statistics, select **Calc➔Row Statistics** and follow steps 6 through 13 from the set of instructions for a uniformly distributed population.

Confidence Interval Estimation

8

▼ USING **STATISTICS**
Getting Estimates at Ricknel Home Centers

As a member of the AIS team at Ricknel Home Centers, you have already examined the probability of discovering questionable, or *tagged*, invoices. Now you have been assigned the task of auditing the accuracy of the integrated inventory management and point of sale component of the firm's retail management system.

You could review the contents of *every* inventory and sales transaction to check the accuracy of the information system, but such a detailed review would be time-consuming and costly. Could you use statistical inference techniques to reach conclusions about the population of all records from a relatively small sample collected during an audit? At the end of each month, could you select a sample of the sales invoices to estimate population parameters such as

- The mean dollar amount listed on the sales invoices for the month
- The proportion of invoices that contain errors that violate the internal control policy of the company

If you used a sampling technique, how accurate would the results from the sample be? How would you use the results you generate? How could you be certain that the sample size is large enough to give you the information you need?

OBJECTIVES

- Construct and interpret confidence interval estimates for the mean and the proportion
- Determine the sample size necessary to develop a confidence interval estimate for the mean or proportion

Section 7.2 explains how the Central Limit Theorem and insight about a population distribution can be used to determine the percentage of sample means that are within certain distances of the population mean. In the Oxford Cereals scenario that Chapter 7 features, Example 7.4 on page 259 uses this knowledge to conclude that 95% of all sample means are between 362.12 and 373.88 grams. That conclusion is an example of *deductive* reasoning, a conclusion based on taking something that is true in general (for the population) and applying it to something specific (the sample means).

Getting the results that Ricknel Home Centers needs requires *inductive* reasoning. Inductive reasoning uses some specifics to make broader generalizations. You cannot guarantee that the broader generalizations are absolutely correct, but with a careful choice of the specifics and a rigorous methodology, you can reach useful conclusions. As a Ricknel AIS team member, you need to use inferential statistics, which uses sample results (the "some specifics") to *estimate* unknown population parameters such as a population mean or a population proportion (the "broader generalizations"). Note that statisticians use the word *estimate* in the same sense of the everyday usage: something about which you are reasonably certain but cannot say is absolutely correct.

You estimate population parameters by using either point estimates or interval estimates. A **point estimate** is the value of a single sample statistic, such as a sample mean. A **confidence interval estimate** is a range of numbers, called an *interval*, constructed around the point estimate. The confidence interval is constructed such that the probability that the interval includes the population parameter is known.

Suppose you want to estimate the mean GPA of all the students at your university. The mean GPA for all the students is an unknown population mean, denoted by μ. You select a sample of students and compute the sample mean, denoted by $\overline{X}$, to be 3.20. As a *point estimate* of the population mean, μ, you ask how accurate is the 3.20 value as an estimate of the population mean, μ? By taking into account the variability from sample to sample (see Section 7.2, concerning the sampling distribution of the mean), you can construct a confidence interval estimate for the population mean to answer this question.

When you construct a confidence interval estimate, you indicate the confidence of correctly estimating the value of the population parameter, μ. This allows you to say that there is a specified confidence that μ is somewhere in the range of numbers defined by the interval.

After studying this chapter, you might find that a 95% confidence interval for the mean GPA at your university is $3.15 \leq \mu \leq 3.25$. You can interpret this interval estimate by stating that you are 95% confident that the interval that states that the mean GPA at your university is between 3.15 and 3.25 is an interval that includes the population mean.

In this chapter, you learn to construct a confidence interval for the population mean and the population proportion. You also learn how to determine the sample size that is necessary to construct a confidence interval of a desired width.

8.1 Confidence Interval Estimate for the Mean (σ Known)

For the Chapter 7 Oxford Cereals scenario, suppose you seek to estimate the population mean, using the information from a single sample. Instead of using $\mu \pm (1.96)(\sigma/\sqrt{n})$ to find the upper and lower limits around μ, as Section 7.2 does, you substitute the sample mean, $\overline{X}$, for the unknown μ and use $\overline{X} \pm (1.96)(\sigma/\sqrt{n})$ as the interval to estimate the unknown μ.

Examining a set of all possible samples of the same sample size helps explain the insight that allows the sample mean to be used in this way.

Suppose that a sample of $n = 25$ cereal boxes has a mean of 362.3 grams and a standard deviation of 15 grams. Using the Section 7.2 method, you can estimate the interval that includes μ to be $362.3 \pm (1.96)(15)/(\sqrt{25})$, or 362.3 ± 5.88. Therefore, the estimate of μ is $356.42 \leq \mu \leq 368.18$. This sample results in a correct statement about μ because the population mean, μ, known to be 368 grams, is included within the interval.

Figure 8.1 shows the interval around the population mean from 362.12 through 373.88 grams, that, by the results of Example 7.4, you can conclude will hold 95% of all sample means. Under the graph of the normal distribution, the estimate of μ made using the sample of $n = 25$ with the mean 362.3 grams is shown. Four other samples of $n = 25$ are also shown. Note that a second sample of $n = 25$, with a mean of 369.5 grams, estimates an interval that includes the population mean, but that a third sample of $n = 25$, with a mean of 360 grams, does not estimate an interval that includes the population mean (shown in red) and therefore the estimate of $354.12 \leq \mu \leq 365.88$ is an incorrect statement.

FIGURE 8.1
Confidence interval estimates for five different samples of $n = 25$ taken from a population where $\mu = 368$ and $\sigma = 15$

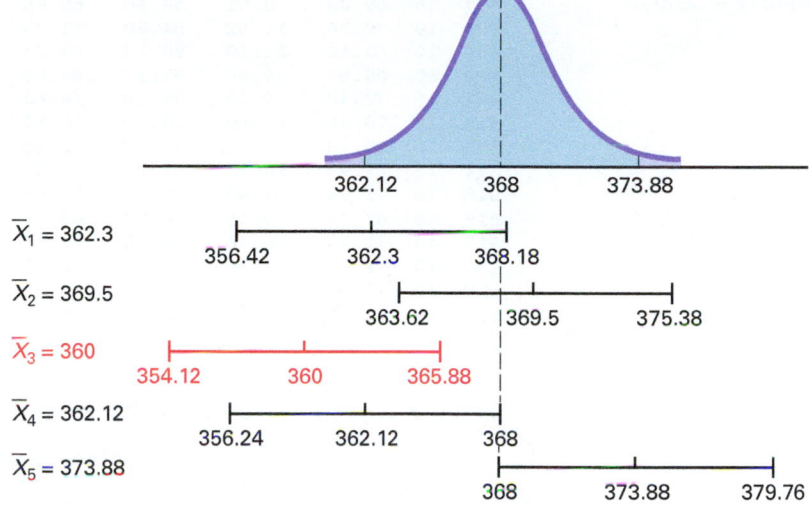

The fourth and fifth samples of $n = 25$ shown in Figure 8.1 contain the lowest (362.12) and highest (373.88) means for samples of $n = 25$ that can be used to correctly estimate the population mean. Should a subsequent sample of $n = 25$ be taken that has a sample mean less than 362.12 or greater than 373.88, that sample mean will not lead to a correct estimate of the population mean. By the results of Example 7.4, you can conclude that 95% of the sample means for samples of $n = 25$ will be between the same range of 362.12 through 373.88 grams. Therefore, you can further conclude that 95% of all samples of $n = 25$ will have sample means that can be used to estimate an interval for the population mean.

student TIP

These observations and conclusions are the cornerstones of confidence interval estimation of the population mean.

Unfortunately, in real-world situations, the population mean, μ, will be unknown for most cases, unlike the example that Figure 8.1 illustrates. Therefore, you will not be able to judge whether the estimate of the population mean developed from a single sample mean is a correct statement. However, by the principles that Chapters 6 and 7 discuss, and by using the conclusions of the previous paragraph, you *can* conclude that if you were to take all possible samples of a specific sample size n and use their sample means to estimate their 95% confidence intervals for the population mean that 95% of those intervals will include the population mean (and 5% will not). In other words, you have 95% confidence that the population mean is somewhere in an interval estimated by a sample mean.

learnMORE

See reference 4 for a technical discussion of the different ways to interpret confidence intervals.

The intervals shown in Figure 8.1 are properly called 95% confidence intervals. Saying that something is a 95% confidence interval is a shorthand way of saying the following:

"I am 95% confident that the interval that states that the mean amount of cereal in the population of filled boxes is somewhere between 356.42 and 368.18 grams is correct."

Sampling Error

To further understand confidence intervals, consider the order-filling process for an online retailer. Filling orders consists of several steps, including receiving an order, picking the parts of the order, checking the order, packing, and shipping the order. The file **Order** contains the time, in minutes, to fill orders for a population of $N = 200$ orders on a recent day. Although in practice the population characteristics are rarely known, for this population of orders, the mean, μ, is known to be equal to 69.637 minutes; the standard deviation, σ, is known to be equal to 10.411 minutes; and the population is normally distributed.

student TIP

The confidence interval estimates the population mean not the sample mean.

To illustrate how the sample mean and sample standard deviation can vary from one sample to another, 20 different samples of $n = 10$ were selected from the population of 200 orders, and the sample mean and sample standard deviation (and other statistics) were calculated for each sample. Figure 8.2 shows these results.

FIGURE 8.2

Sample statistics and 95% confidence intervals for 20 samples of $n = 10$ randomly selected from the population of $N = 200$ orders

```
Sample  n   Mean  Std Dev Minimum  Median Maximum  Range  95% Conf. Int.
 S01   10  74.15   13.39   56.10    76.85   97.70   41.60  (67.70, 80.60)
 S02   10  61.10   10.60   46.80    61.35   79.50   32.70  (54.65, 67.55)
 S03   10  74.36    6.50   62.50    74.50   84.00   21.50  (67.91, 80.81)
 S04   10  70.40   12.80   47.20    70.95   84.00   36.80  (63.95, 76.85)
 S05   10  62.18   10.85   47.10    59.70   84.00   36.90  (55.73, 68.63)
 S06   10  67.03    9.68   51.10    69.60   83.30   32.20  (60.58, 73.48)
 S07   10  69.03    8.81   56.60    68.85   83.70   27.10  (62.58, 75.48)
 S08   10  72.30   11.52   54.20    71.35   87.00   32.80  (65.85, 78.75)
 S09   10  68.18   14.10   50.10    69.95   86.20   36.10  (61.73, 74.63)
 S10   10  66.67    9.08   57.10    64.65   86.10   29.00  (60.22, 73.12)
 S11   10  72.42    9.76   59.60    74.65   86.10   26.50  (65.97, 78.87)
 S12   10  76.26   11.69   50.10    80.60   87.00   36.90  (69.81, 82.71)
 S13   10  65.74   12.11   47.10    62.15   86.10   39.00  (59.29, 72.19)
 S14   10  69.99   10.97   51.00    73.40   84.60   33.60  (63.54, 76.44)
 S15   10  75.76    8.60   61.10    75.05   87.80   26.70  (69.31, 82.21)
 S16   10  67.94    9.19   56.70    67.70   87.80   31.10  (61.49, 74.39)
 S17   10  71.05   10.48   50.10    71.15   86.20   36.10  (64.60, 77.50)
 S18   10  71.68    7.96   55.60    72.35   82.60   27.00  (65.23, 78.13)
 S19   10  70.97    9.83   54.40    70.05   84.00   30.20  (64.52, 77.42)
 S20   10  74.48    8.80   62.00    76.25   85.70   23.70  (68.03, 80.93)
```

From Figure 8.2, you can see the following:

- The sample statistics differ from sample to sample. The sample means vary from 61.10 to 76.26 minutes, the sample standard deviations vary from 6.50 to 14.10 minutes, the sample medians vary from 59.70 to 80.60 minutes, and the sample ranges vary from 21.50 to 41.60 minutes.
- Some of the sample means are greater than the population mean of 69.637 minutes, and some of the sample means are less than the population mean.
- Some of the sample standard deviations are greater than the population standard deviation of 10.411 minutes, and some of the sample standard deviations are less than the population standard deviation.
- The variation in the sample ranges is much more than the variation in the sample standard deviations.

The variation of sample statistics from sample to sample is called *sampling error*. **Sampling error** is the variation that occurs due to selecting a single sample from the population. The size of the sampling error is primarily based on the amount of variation in the population and on the sample size. Large samples have less sampling error than small samples, but large samples cost more to select.

The last column of Figure 8.2 contains 95% confidence interval estimates of the population mean order-filling time, based on the results of those 20 samples of $n = 10$. Begin by examining the first sample selected. The sample mean is 74.15 minutes, and the interval estimate for the population mean is 67.70 to 80.60 minutes. In a typical study, you would not know for sure whether this interval estimate is correct because you rarely know the value of the population mean. However, for this population of orders, the population mean is known to be 69.637 minutes. If you examine the interval 67.70 to 80.60 minutes, you see that the population mean of 69.637 minutes is located *between* these lower and upper limits. Thus, the first sample provides a correct estimate of the population mean in the form of an interval estimate. Looking over the other 19 samples, you see that similar results occur for all the other samples *except* for samples 2, 5, and 12. For each of the intervals generated (other than samples 2, 5, and 12), the population mean of 69.637 minutes is located *somewhere* within the interval.

For sample 2, the sample mean is 61.10 minutes, and the interval is 54.65 to 67.55 minutes; for sample 5, the sample mean is 62.18, and the interval is between 55.73 and 68.63; for sample 12, the sample mean is 76.26, and the interval is between 69.81 and 82.71 minutes. The population mean of 69.637 minutes is *not* located within any of these intervals, and the estimate of the population mean made using these intervals is incorrect. Although 3 of the 20 intervals did not include the population mean, if you had selected all the possible samples of $n = 10$ from a population of $N = 200$, 95% of the intervals would include the population mean.

In some situations, you might want a higher degree of confidence of including the population mean within the interval (such as 99%). In other cases, you might accept less confidence (such as 90%) of correctly estimating the population mean. In general, the **level of confidence** is symbolized by $(1 - \alpha) \times 100\%$, where α is the proportion in the tails of the distribution that is outside the confidence interval. The proportion in the upper tail of the distribution is $\alpha/2$, and the proportion in the lower tail of the distribution is $\alpha/2$. You use Equation (8.1) to construct a $(1 - \alpha) \times 100\%$ confidence interval estimate for the mean with σ known.

CONFIDENCE INTERVAL FOR THE MEAN (σ KNOWN)

$$\overline{X} \pm Z_{\alpha/2}\frac{\sigma}{\sqrt{n}}$$

or

$$\overline{X} - Z_{\alpha/2}\frac{\sigma}{\sqrt{n}} \le \mu \le \overline{X} + Z_{\alpha/2}\frac{\sigma}{\sqrt{n}} \qquad (8.1)$$

where

$Z_{\alpha/2}$ is the value for an upper-tail probability of $\alpha/2$ from the standardized normal distribution (i.e., a cumulative area of $1 - \alpha/2$)

$Z_{\alpha/2}\dfrac{\sigma}{\sqrt{n}}$ is the sampling error

The value of $Z_{\alpha/2}$ needed for constructing a confidence interval is called the **critical value** for the distribution. 95% confidence corresponds to an α value of 0.05. The critical Z value corresponding to a cumulative area of 0.975 is 1.96 because there is 0.025 in the upper tail of the distribution, and the cumulative area less than $Z = 1.96$ is 0.975.

There is a different critical value for each level of confidence, $1 - \alpha$. A level of confidence of 95% leads to a Z value of 1.96 (see Figure 8.3). 99% confidence corresponds to an α value of 0.01. The Z value is approximately 2.58 because the upper-tail area is 0.005 and the cumulative area less than $Z = 2.58$ is 0.995 (see Figure 8.4).

FIGURE 8.3
Normal curve for determining the Z value needed for 95% confidence

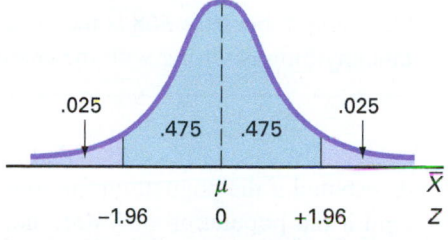

FIGURE 8.4
Normal curve for determining the Z value needed for 99% confidence

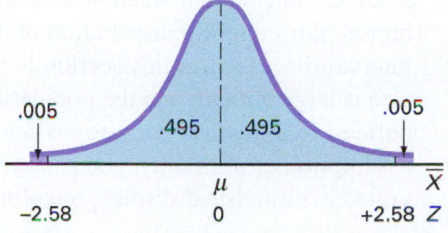

student TIP

If you want more confidence you will get a wider interval unless you select a larger sample size.

Now that various levels of confidence have been considered, why not make the confidence level as close to 100% as possible? Before doing so, you need to realize that any increase in the level of confidence is achieved only by widening (and making less precise) the confidence interval. There is no "free lunch" here. You would have more confidence that the population mean is within a broader range of values; however, this might make the interpretation of the confidence interval less useful. The trade-off between the width of the confidence interval and the level of confidence is discussed in greater depth in the context of determining the sample size in Section 8.4. Example 8.1 illustrates the application of the confidence interval estimate.

EXAMPLE 8.1

Estimating the Mean Cereal Fill Amount with 95% Confidence

Returning to the Chapter 7 Oxford Cereals scenario, managers must ensure that the mean weight of filled boxes is 368 grams to be consistent with the labeling on those boxes. To determine whether the mean weight is consistent with the expected amount of 368 grams, managers periodically select a random sample of 100 filled boxes from the large number of boxes filled. Past experience states that the standard deviation of the fill amount is 15 grams. One random sample of 100 filled boxes they selected has a sample mean of 369.27 grams. Construct a 95% confidence interval estimate of the mean fill amount.

SOLUTION Using Equation (8.1) on page 279, with $Z_{\alpha/2} = 1.96$ for 95% confidence,

$$\overline{X} \pm Z_{\alpha/2}\frac{\sigma}{\sqrt{n}} = 369.27 \pm (1.96)\frac{15}{\sqrt{100}}$$

$$= 369.27 \pm 2.94$$

$$366.33 \le \mu \le 372.21$$

Thus, with 95% confidence, the population mean is between 366.33 and 372.21 grams. Because the interval includes 368, the value indicating that the cereal filling process is working properly, there is no evidence to suggest that anything is wrong with the cereal filling process.

Example 8.2 illustrates the effect of using a 99% confidence interval.

EXAMPLE 8.2

Estimating the Mean Cereal Fill Amount with 99% Confidence

Construct a 99% confidence interval estimate for the population mean fill amount.

SOLUTION Using Equation (8.1) on page 279, with $Z_{\alpha/2} = 2.58$ for 99% confidence,

$$\overline{X} \pm Z_{\alpha/2}\frac{\sigma}{\sqrt{n}} = 369.27 \pm (2.58)\frac{15}{\sqrt{100}}$$

$$= 369.27 \pm 3.87$$

$$365.40 \le \mu \le 373.14$$

Once again, because 368 is included within this wider interval, there is no evidence to suggest that anything is wrong with the cereal filling process.

As discussed in Section 7.2, the sampling distribution of the sample mean, $\overline{X}$, is normally distributed if the population for your characteristic of interest, X, follows a normal distribution. And if the population of X does not follow a normal distribution, the Central Limit Theorem almost always ensures that $\overline{X}$ is approximately normally distributed when n is large. However, when dealing with a small sample size and a population that does not follow a normal distribution, the sampling distribution of $\overline{X}$ is not normally distributed, and therefore the confidence interval discussed in this section is inappropriate. In practice, however, as long as the sample size is large enough and the population is not very skewed, you can use the confidence interval defined in Equation (8.1) to estimate the population mean when σ is known. To assess the assumption of normality, you can evaluate the shape of the sample data by constructing a histogram, stem-and-leaf display, boxplot, or normal probability plot.

student TIP

Understanding the confidence interval concept is very important when reading the rest of this book. Review Section 8.1 carefully to understand its foundational concepts—even if you have no practical reason to use the confidence interval estimate of the mean (σ known) method.

Can You Ever Know the Population Standard Deviation?

To use Equation (8.1), you must know the value for σ, the population standard deviation. To know σ implies that you know all the values in the entire population. (How else would you know the value of this population parameter?) If you knew all the values in the entire population, you could directly compute the population mean. There would be no need to use the *inductive* reasoning of inferential statistics to *estimate* the population mean. In other words, if you know σ, you really do not have a need to use Equation (8.1) to construct a confidence interval estimate of the mean (σ known).

More significantly, in virtually all real-world business situations, you would never know the standard deviation of the population. In business situations, populations are often too large to examine all the values. So why study the confidence interval estimate of the mean (σ known) at all? This method serves as an important introduction to the concept of a confidence interval because it uses the normal distribution, that Chapters 6 and 7 fully discusses. The next section explains that constructing a confidence interval estimate when σ is not known requires another distribution (the t distribution) not previously mentioned in this book.

PROBLEMS FOR SECTION 8.1

LEARNING THE BASICS

8.1 If $\overline{X} = 85$, $\sigma = 8$, and $n = 64$, construct a 95% confidence interval estimate for the population mean, μ.

8.2 If $\overline{X} = 125$, $\sigma = 24$, and $n = 36$, construct a 99% confidence interval estimate for the population mean, μ.

8.3 Why is it not possible in Example 8.1 on page 280 to have 100% confidence? Explain.

8.4 Is it true in Example 8.1 on page 280 that you do not know for sure whether the population mean is between 366.33 and 372.21 grams? Explain.

APPLYING THE CONCEPTS

8.5 A market researcher selects a simple random sample of $n = 100$ Twitter users from a population of over 100 million Twitter registered users. After analyzing the sample, she states that she has 95% confidence that the mean time spent on the site per day is between 15 and 57 minutes. Explain the meaning of this statement.

8.6 Suppose that you are going to collect a set of data, either from an entire population or from a random sample taken from that population.
a. Which statistical measure would you compute first: the mean or the standard deviation? Explain.
b. What does your answer to (a) tell you about the "practicality" of using the confidence interval estimate formula given in Equation (8.1)?

8.7 Consider the confidence interval estimate discussed in Problem 8.5. Suppose the population mean time spent on the site is 36 minutes a day. Is the confidence interval estimate stated in Problem 8.5 correct? Explain.

8.8 You are working as an assistant to the dean of institutional research at your university. The dean wants to survey members of the alumni association who obtained their baccalaureate degrees five years ago to learn what their starting salaries were in their first full-time job after receiving their degrees. A sample of 100 alumni is to be randomly selected from the list of 2,500 graduates in that class. If the dean's goal is to construct a 95% confidence interval estimate for the population mean starting salary, why is it not possible that you will be able to use Equation (8.1) on page 279 for this purpose? Explain.

8.9 A bottled water distributor wants to estimate the amount of water contained in 1-gallon bottles purchased from a nationally known water bottling company. The water bottling company's specifications state that the standard deviation of the amount of water is equal to 0.02 gallon. A random sample of 50 bottles is selected, and the sample mean amount of water per 1-gallon bottle is 0.995 gallon.
a. Construct a 99% confidence interval estimate for the population mean amount of water included in a 1-gallon bottle.
b. On the basis of these results, do you think that the distributor has a right to complain to the water bottling company about the amount of water that the bottles contain? Why?
c. Must you assume that the population amount of water per bottle is normally distributed here? Explain.
d. Construct a 95% confidence interval estimate. How does this change your answer to (b)?

SELF TEST **8.10** The operations manager at a light emitting diode (LED) light bulb factory needs to estimate the mean life of a large shipment of LEDs. The manufacturer's specifications are that the standard deviation is 1,500 hours. A random sample of 64 LEDs indicated a sample mean life of 49,875 hours.
a. Construct a 95% confidence interval estimate for the population mean life of LED light bulbs in this shipment.
b. Do you think that the manufacturer has the right to state that the LED light bulbs have a mean life of 50,000 hours? Explain.
c. Must you assume that the population LED light bulb life is normally distributed? Explain.
d. Suppose that the standard deviation changes to 500 hours. What are your answers in (a) and (b)?

8.2 Confidence Interval Estimate for the Mean (σ Unknown)

Section 8.1 explains that, in most business situations, you do not know σ, the population standard deviation. This section discusses a method of constructing a confidence interval estimate of μ that uses the sample statistic S as an estimate of the population parameter σ.

Student's *t* Distribution

At the start of the twentieth century, William S. Gosset was working at Guinness in Ireland, trying to help brew better beer less expensively (see reference 5). As he had only small samples to study, he needed to find a way to make inferences about means without having to know σ. Writing under the pen name "Student,"[1] Gosset solved this problem by developing what today is known as the **Student's *t* distribution**, or the *t* distribution.

[1]Guinness considered all research conducted to be proprietary and a trade secret. The firm prohibited its employees from publishing their results. Gosset circumvented this ban by using the pen name "Student" to publish his findings.

If the variable *X* is normally distributed, then the following statistic:

$$t = \frac{\overline{X} - \mu}{\dfrac{S}{\sqrt{n}}}$$

has a *t* distribution with $n - 1$ **degrees of freedom**. This expression has the same form as the *Z* statistic in Equation (7.4) on page 257, except that *S* is used to estimate the unknown σ.

The Concept of Degrees of Freedom

Equation 3.6 (see page 103) defines the sample variance, S^2, as a fraction, the numerator of which is the sum of squares around the sample mean:

$$\sum_{i=1}^{n}(X_i - \overline{X})^2$$

In order to calculate S^2, you first need to know $\overline{X}$. If you know $\overline{X}$, then once you know $n - 1$ of the values, the last value is not "free to vary" because the sum of the values is known from the calculation of $\overline{X}$. This observation is what is meant by saying "having $n - 1$ degrees of freedom." For example, suppose a sample of five values has a mean of 20. How many values do you need to know before you can determine the remainder of the values? The fact that $n = 5$ and $\overline{X} = 20$ also tells you that

$$\sum_{i=1}^{n}X_i = 100$$

because

$$\frac{\sum_{i=1}^{n}X_i}{n} = \overline{X}$$

Therefore, when you know four of the values, the fifth one is *not* free to vary because the sum must be 100. For example, if four of the values are 18, 24, 19, and 16, the fifth value must be 23, so that the sum is 100.

Properties of the *t* Distribution

The *t* distribution is very similar in appearance to the standardized normal distribution. Both distributions are symmetrical and bell-shaped, with the mean and the median equal to zero. However, because *S* is used to estimate the unknown σ, the values of *t* are more variable than those for *Z*. Therefore, the *t* distribution has more area in the tails and less in the center than does the standardized normal distribution (see Figure 8.5).

FIGURE 8.5

Standardized normal distribution and *t* distribution for 5 degrees of freedom

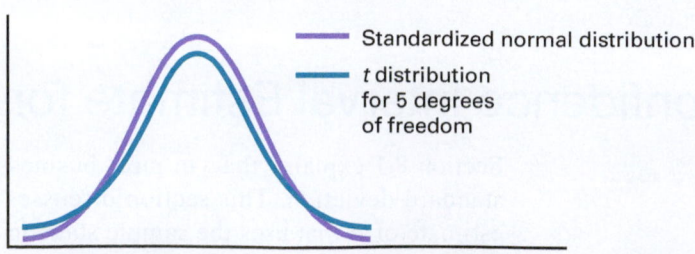

— Standardized normal distribution

— *t* distribution for 5 degrees of freedom

As the sample size and degrees of freedom increase, S becomes a better estimate of σ, and the t distribution gradually approaches the standardized normal distribution, until the two are virtually identical. With a sample size of about 120 or more, S estimates σ closely enough so that there is little difference between the t and Z distributions.

As stated earlier, the t distribution assumes that the variable X is normally distributed. In practice, however, when the sample size is large enough and the population is not very skewed, in most cases use the t distribution to estimate the population mean when σ is unknown. When dealing with a small sample size and a skewed population distribution, the confidence interval estimate may not provide a valid estimate of the population mean. To assess the assumption of normality, evaluate the shape of the sample data by constructing a histogram, stem-and-leaf display, boxplot, or normal probability plot. However, the ability of any of these graphs to help evaluate normality is limited when you have a small sample size.

Find the critical values of t for the appropriate degrees of freedom from the table of the t distribution (see Table E.3). The columns of the table present the most commonly used cumulative probabilities and corresponding upper-tail areas. The rows of the table represent the degrees of freedom. The critical t values are found in the cells of the table. For example, with 99 degrees of freedom, if you want 95% confidence, you find the appropriate value of t, as shown in Table 8.1. The 95% confidence level means that 2.5% of the values (an area of 0.025) are in each tail of the distribution.

TABLE 8.1

Determining the Critical Value from the t Table for an Area of 0.025 in Each Tail with 99 Degrees of Freedom

	Cumulative Probabilities					
	.75	.90	.95	.975	.99	.995
	Upper-Tail Areas					
Degrees of Freedom	.25	.10	.05	.025	.01	.005
1	1.0000	3.0777	6.3138	12.7062	31.8207	63.6574
2	0.8165	1.8856	2.9200	4.3027	6.9646	9.9248
3	0.7649	1.6377	2.3534	3.1824	4.5407	5.8409
4	0.7407	1.5332	2.1318	2.7764	3.7469	4.6041
5	0.7267	1.4759	2.0150	2.5706	3.3649	4.0322
⋮	⋮	⋮	⋮	⋮	⋮	⋮
96	0.6771	1.2904	1.6609	1.9850	2.3658	2.6280
97	0.6770	1.2903	1.6607	1.9847	2.3654	2.6275
98	0.6770	1.2902	1.6606	1.9845	2.3650	2.6269
99	0.6770	1.2902	1.6604	1.9842	2.3646	2.6264
100	0.6770	1.2901	1.6602	1.9840	2.3642	2.6259

Source: Extracted from Table E.3.

Looking in the column for a cumulative probability of 0.975 and an upper-tail area of 0.025 in the row corresponding to 99 degrees of freedom gives you a critical value for t of 1.9842 (see Figure 8.6). Because t is a symmetrical distribution with a mean of 0, if the upper-tail value is $+1.9842$, the value for the lower-tail area (lower 0.025) is -1.9842. A t value of -1.9842 means that the probability that t is less than -1.9842 is 0.025, or 2.5%.

FIGURE 8.6

t distribution with 99 degrees of freedom

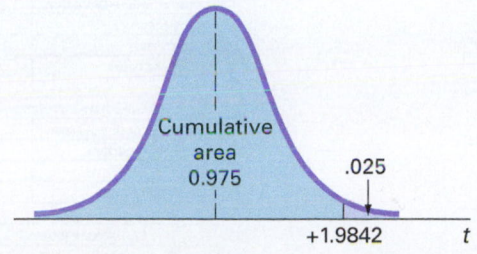

Note that for a 95% confidence interval, you will always have a cumulative probability of 0.975 and an upper-tail area of 0.025. Similarly, for a 99% confidence interval, you will have 0.995 and 0.005, and for a 90% confidence interval you will have 0.95 and 0.05.

The Confidence Interval Statement

Equation (8.2) defines the $(1 - \alpha) \times 100$ confidence interval estimate for the mean with σ unknown.

CONFIDENCE INTERVAL FOR THE MEAN (σ UNKNOWN)

$$\overline{X} \pm t_{\alpha/2}\frac{S}{\sqrt{n}}$$

or

$$\overline{X} - t_{\alpha/2}\frac{S}{\sqrt{n}} \le \mu \le \overline{X} + t_{\alpha/2}\frac{S}{\sqrt{n}} \tag{8.2}$$

where

$t_{\alpha/2}$ is the critical value for an upper-tail probability of $\alpha/2$ (i.e., a cumulative area of $1 - \alpha/2$) from the t distribution with $n - 1$ degrees of freedom.

$t_{\alpha/2}\dfrac{S}{\sqrt{n}}$ is the sampling error

To illustrate the application of the confidence interval estimate for the mean when the standard deviation is unknown, recall the Ricknel Home Centers scenario on page 275. In that scenario, the mean dollar amount listed on the sales invoices for the month was one of the population parameters you sought to estimate.

To calculate this estimate, apply the DCOVA framework (see First Things First Chapter) and define the variable of interest as the dollar amount listed on the sales invoices for the month. You then collect data by selecting a sample of 100 sales invoices from the population of sales invoices during the month and organize the data as a worksheet or data table.

Construct various graphs (not shown here) to better visualize the distribution of the dollar amounts. Using the data, calculate the sample mean of the 100 sales invoices as $110.27 and the sample standard deviation as $28.95. For 95% confidence, the critical value from the t distribution (as shown in Table 8.1 on page 283) is 1.9842. Using Equation (8.2),

$$\overline{X} \pm t_{\alpha/2}\frac{S}{\sqrt{n}} = 110.27 \pm (1.9842)\frac{28.95}{\sqrt{100}}$$

$$= 110.27 \pm 5.74$$

$$104.53 \le \mu \le 116.01$$

Figure 8.7 shows the Excel and Minitab confidence interval estimate of the mean dollar amount results. (See Section JG8.2 for the JMP results.)

FIGURE 8.7
Excel and Minitab results for the confidence interval estimate for the mean sales invoice amount worksheet results for the Ricknel Home Centers example

	A	B
1	Confidence Interval Estimate for the Mean	
2		
3	Data	
4	Sample Standard Deviation	28.95
5	Sample Mean	110.27
6	Sample Size	100
7	Confidence Level	95%
8		
9	Intermediate Calculations	
10	Standard Error of the Mean	2.895
11	Degrees of Freedom	99
12	t Value	1.9842
13	Interval Half Width	5.7443
14		
15	Confidence Interval	
16	Interval Lower Limit	104.53
17	Interval Upper Limit	116.01

One-Sample T
Descriptive Statistics

N	Mean	StDev	SE Mean	95% CI for μ
100	110.27	28.95	2.90	(104.53, 116.01)

μ: mean of Sample

Thus, with 95% confidence, you conclude that the mean amount of all the sales invoices is between $104.53 and $116.01. The 95% confidence level indicates that if you selected all possible samples of 100 (something that is never done in practice), 95% of the intervals developed would include the population mean somewhere within the interval. The validity of this confidence interval estimate depends on the assumption of normality for the distribution of the amount of the sales invoices. With a sample of 100, the normality assumption is valid, and the use of the *t* distribution is likely appropriate. Example 8.3 further illustrates how to construct the confidence interval for a mean when the population standard deviation is unknown.

EXAMPLE 8.3

Estimating the Mean Processing Time of Life Insurance Applications

An insurance company has the business objective of reducing the amount of time it takes to approve applications for life insurance. The approval process consists of underwriting, which includes a review of the application, a medical information bureau check, possible requests for additional medical information and medical exams, and a policy compilation stage in which the policy pages are generated and sent for delivery. Using the DCOVA steps first discussed on page 3, you define the variable of interest as the total processing time in days. You collect the data by selecting a random sample of 27 approved policies during a period of one month. You organize the data collected in a worksheet. Table 8.2, stored as Insurance , lists the total processing time, in days. To analyze the data, you need to construct a 95% confidence interval estimate for the population mean processing time.

TABLE 8.2

Processing Time for Life Insurance Applications

8	11	15	17	19	22	25	27	32	35	38	41	41	45
48	50	51	56	56	60	63	64	69	73	80	84	91	

SOLUTION To visualize the data, you construct a boxplot of the processing time, shown in Figure 8.8, and a normal probability plot, shown in Figure 8.9. To analyze the data, you construct the confidence interval estimate, shown in Figure 8.10 on page 286.

FIGURE 8.8

Excel and Minitab boxplots for the processing time for life insurance applications

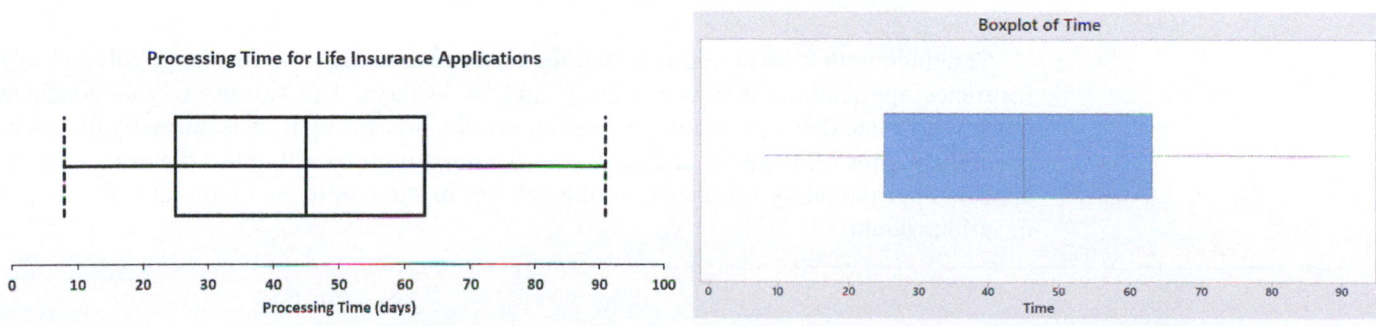

FIGURE 8.9

Excel and JMP (with boxplot) normal probability plots for the processing time for life insurance applications

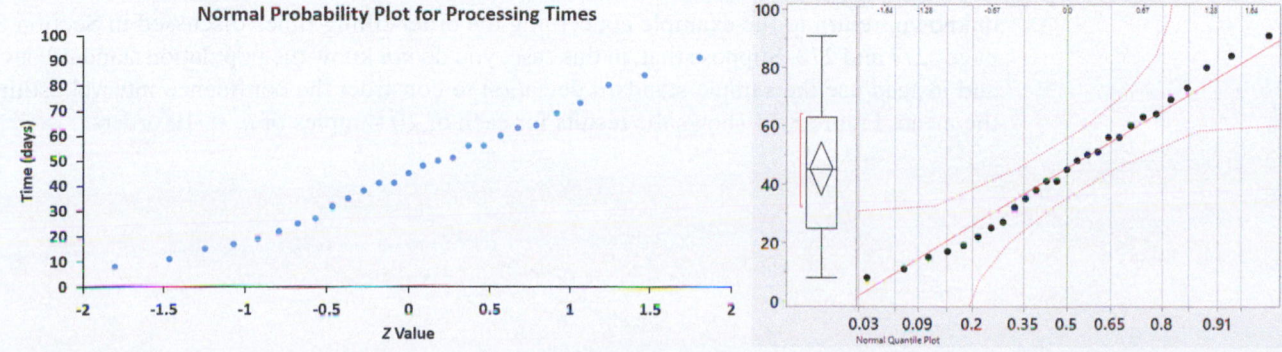

▶(continued)

FIGURE 8.10

Excel, JMP, and Minitab confidence interval estimates for the mean processing time results for life insurance applications

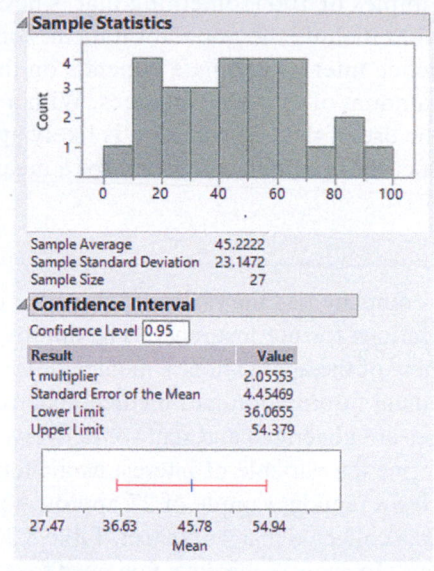

	A	B
1	Processing Time for Life Insurance Applications	
2		
3	Data	
4	Sample Standard Deviation	23.1472
5	Sample Mean	45.2222
6	Sample Size	27
7	Confidence Level	95%
8		
9	Intermediate Calculations	
10	Standard Error of the Mean	4.4547
11	Degrees of Freedom	26
12	t Value	2.0555
13	Interval Half Width	9.1567
14		
15	Confidence Interval	
16	Interval Lower Limit	36.07
17	Interval Upper Limit	54.38

Sample Statistics

Sample Average   45.2222
Sample Standard Deviation   23.1472
Sample Size   27

Confidence Interval

Confidence Level 0.95

Result	Value
t multiplier	2.05553
Standard Error of the Mean	4.45469
Lower Limit	36.0655
Upper Limit	54.379

27.47   36.63   45.78   54.94
Mean

One-Sample T: Time
Descriptive Statistics

N	Mean	StDev	SE Mean	95% CI for μ
27	45.22	23.15	4.45	(36.07, 54.38)

μ: mean of Time

Figure 8.10 shows that the sample mean is $\overline{X} = 45.2222$ days and the sample standard deviation is $S = 23.1472$ days. To use Equation (8.2) on page 284 to construct the confidence interval, first determine the critical value from the t table, using the row for 26 degrees of freedom. For 95% confidence, use the column corresponding to an upper-tail area of 0.025 and a cumulative probability of 0.975. From Table E.3, you see that $t_{\alpha/2} = 2.0555$. Thus, using $\overline{X} = 45.2222$, $S = 23.1472$, $n = 27$, and $t_{\alpha/2} = 2.0555$,

$$\overline{X} \pm t_{\alpha/2}\frac{S}{\sqrt{n}} = 45.2222 \pm (2.0555)\frac{23.1472}{\sqrt{27}}$$

$$= 45.2222 \pm 9.1567$$

$$36.07 \leq \mu \leq 54.38$$

Conclude with 95% confidence that the mean processing time for the population of life insurance applications is between 36.07 and 54.38 days. The validity of this confidence interval estimate depends on the assumption that the processing time is normally distributed. From the Figure 8.8 boxplots and the Figure 8.9 normal probability plots the processing time appears approximately symmetric so the validity of the confidence interval estimate is not in serious doubt.

The interpretation of the confidence interval when σ is unknown is the same as when σ is known. To illustrate the fact that the confidence interval for the mean varies more when σ is unknown, return to the example concerning the order-filling times discussed in Section 8.1 on pages 277 and 278. Suppose that, in this case, you do *not* know the population standard deviation and instead use the sample standard deviation to construct the confidence interval estimate of the mean. Figure 8.11 shows the results for each of 20 samples of $n = 10$ orders.

FIGURE 8.11

Confidence interval estimates of the mean for 20 samples of $n = 10$ randomly selected from the population of $N = 200$ orders with σ unknown

Sample	N	Mean	Std Dev	SE Mean	95% Conf. Int.
S01	10	71.64	7.58	2.40	(66.22, 77.06)
S02	10	67.22	10.95	3.46	(59.39, 75.05)
S03	10	67.97	14.83	4.69	(57.36, 78.58)
S04	10	73.90	10.59	3.35	(66.33, 81.47)
S05	10	67.11	11.12	3.52	(59.15, 75.07)
S06	10	68.12	10.83	3.43	(60.37, 75.87)
S07	10	65.80	10.85	3.43	(58.03, 73.57)
S08	10	77.58	11.04	3.49	(69.68, 85.48)
S09	10	66.69	11.45	3.62	(58.50, 74.88)
S10	10	62.55	8.58	2.71	(56.41, 68.69)
S11	10	71.12	12.82	4.05	(61.95, 80.29)
S12	10	70.55	10.52	3.33	(63.02, 78.08)
S13	10	65.51	8.16	2.58	(59.67, 71.35)
S14	10	64.90	7.55	2.39	(59.50, 70.30)
S15	10	66.22	11.21	3.54	(58.20, 74.24)
S16	10	70.43	10.21	3.23	(63.12, 77.74)
S17	10	72.04	6.25	1.96	(67.57, 76.51)
S18	10	73.91	11.29	3.57	(65.83, 81.99)
S19	10	71.49	9.76	3.09	(64.51, 78.47)
S20	10	70.15	10.84	3.43	(62.39, 77.91)

In Figure 8.11, observe that the standard deviation of the samples varies from 6.25 (sample 17) to 14.83 (sample 3). Thus, the width of the confidence interval developed varies from 8.94 in sample 17 to 21.22 in sample 3. Because you know that the population mean order time $\mu = 69.637$ minutes, you can see that the interval for sample 8 (69.68 − 85.48) and the interval for sample 10 (56.41 − 68.69) do not correctly estimate the population mean. All the other intervals correctly estimate the population mean. Once again, remember that in practice you select only one sample, and you are unable to know for sure whether your one sample provides a confidence interval that includes the population mean.

PROBLEMS FOR SECTION 8.2

LEARNING THE BASICS

8.11 If $\overline{X} = 75$, $S = 24$, and $n = 36$, and assuming that the population is normally distributed, construct a 95% confidence interval estimate for the population mean, μ.

8.12 Determine the critical value of t in each of the following circumstances:
a. $1 - \alpha = 0.95$, $n = 10$
b. $1 - \alpha = 0.99$, $n = 10$
c. $1 - \alpha = 0.95$, $n = 32$
d. $1 - \alpha = 0.95$, $n = 65$
e. $1 - \alpha = 0.90$, $n = 16$

8.13 Assuming that the population is normally distributed, construct a 95% confidence interval estimate for the population mean for each of the following samples:

Sample A: 1 1 1 1 8 8 8 8
Sample B: 1 2 3 4 5 6 7 8

Explain why these two samples produce different confidence intervals even though they have the same mean and range.

8.14 Assuming that the population is normally distributed, construct a 95% confidence interval for the population mean, based on the following sample of size $n = 7$:

1 2 3 4 5 6 20

Change the value of 20 to 7 and recalculate the confidence interval. Using these results, describe the effect of an outlier (i.e., an extreme value) on the confidence interval.

APPLYING THE CONCEPTS

8.15 A marketing researcher wants to estimate the mean amount spent ($) on Amazon.com by Amazon Prime member shoppers. Suppose a random sample of 100 Amazon Prime member shoppers who recently made a purchase on Amazon.com yielded a mean of $1,500 and a standard deviation of $200.
a. Construct a 95% confidence interval estimate for the mean spending for all Amazon Prime member shoppers.
b. Interpret the interval constructed in (a).

SELF TEST **8.16** A survey of nonprofit organizations showed that online fundraising has increased in the past year. Based on a random sample of 133 nonprofits, the mean one-time gift donation resulting from email outreach in the past year was $87. Assume that the sample standard deviation is $9.
a. Construct a 95% confidence interval estimate for the population mean one-time gift donation.
b. Interpret the interval constructed in (a).

8.17 The U.S. Department of Transportation requires tire manufacturers to provide tire performance information on the sidewall of a tire to better inform prospective customers as they make purchasing decisions. One very important measure of tire performance is the tread wear index, which indicates the tire's resistance to tread wear compared with a tire graded with a base of 100. A tire with a grade of 200 should last twice as long, on average, as a tire graded with a base of 100. A consumer organization wants to estimate the actual tread wear index of a brand name of tires that claims "graded 200" on the sidewall of the tire. A random sample of $n = 18$ indicates a sample mean tread wear index of 195.3 and a sample standard deviation of 21.4.

a. Assuming that the population of tread wear indexes is normally distributed, construct a 95% confidence interval estimate for the population mean tread wear index for tires produced by this manufacturer under this brand name.

b. Do you think that the consumer organization should accuse the manufacturer of producing tires that do not meet the performance information provided on the sidewall of the tire? Explain.

c. Explain why an observed tread wear index of 210 for a particular tire is not unusual, even though it is outside the confidence interval developed in (a).

8.18 The file **FastFood** contains the amount that a sample of 15 customers spent for lunch ($) at a fast-food restaurant:

   7.42 6.29 5.83 6.50 8.34 9.51 7.10 6.80 5.90

   4.89 6.50 5.52 7.90 8.30 9.60

a. Construct a 95% confidence interval estimate for the population mean amount spent for lunch ($) at a fast-food restaurant.

b. Interpret the interval constructed in (a).

c. What assumption must you make about the population distribution in order to construct the confidence interval estimate in (a)?

d. Do you think that the assumption needed in order to construct the confidence interval estimate in (a) is valid? Explain.

8.19 The file **AirportRating** contains the rating of large and medium size airports in the United States and Canada.

Source: Data extracted from N. Trejos, "Portland, Indianapolis Top Airport Rankings, *USA Today*, December 16, 2016, p. 4B.

For large and medium airports separately:

a. Construct a 95% confidence interval estimate for the population mean rating.

b. Interpret the interval constructed in (a).

c. What assumption must you make about the population distribution in order to construct the confidence interval estimate in (a)?

d. Do you think that the assumption needed in order to construct the confidence interval estimate in (a) is valid? Explain.

8.20 The annual NFL Super Bowl is the most widely watched sporting event in the United States each year. In recent years, there has been a great deal of interest in the ads that appear during the game. These ads vary in length with most lasting 30 seconds or 60 seconds. The file **SuperBowlAdScore** contains the ad length and ad scores from a recent SuperBowl.

Source: Data extracted from C. Woodyard, "Funny Bone Wins Out," *USA Today*, February 6, 2016, p. 4B.

For the 30-second ads and the 60-second ads separately:

a. Construct a 95% confidence interval estimate for the population mean ad score.

b. Interpret the interval constructed in (a).

c. What conclusions can you reach about the ad scores of 30-second and 60-second ads?

d. What assumption must you make about the population distribution in order to construct the confidence interval estimate in (a)?

e. Do you think that the assumption needed in order to construct the confidence interval estimate in (a) is valid? Explain.

8.21 Is there a difference in the yields of different types of investments? The file **CDRate** contains the yields for a one-year certificate of deposit (CD) and a five-year CD for 39 banks listed for West Palm Beach, Florida on January 9, 2017.

Source: Data extracted from **www.Bankrate.com**, January 9, 2017.

a. Construct a 95% confidence interval estimate for the mean yield of one-year CDs.

b. Construct a 95% confidence interval estimate for the mean yield of five-year CDs.

c. Compare the results of (a) and (b).

8.22 One of the major measures of the quality of service provided by any organization is the speed with which the organization responds to customer complaints. A large family-held department store selling furniture and flooring, including carpet, had undergone a major expansion in the past several years. In particular, the flooring department had expanded from 2 installation crews to an installation supervisor, a measurer, and 15 installation crews. The store had the business objective of improving its response to complaints. The variable of interest was defined as the number of days between when the complaint was made and when it was resolved. Data were collected from 50 complaints that were made in the past year. The data, stored in **Furniture**, are as follows:

54	5	35	137	31	27	152	2	123	81	74	27	11
19	126	110	110	29	61		35	94	31	26	5	12	4
165	32	29	28	29	26	25	1	14	13	13	10
5	27	4	52	30	22	36	26	20	23	33	68

a. Construct a 95% confidence interval estimate for the population mean number of days between the receipt of a complaint and the resolution of the complaint.

b. What assumption must you make about the population distribution in order to construct the confidence interval estimate in (a)?

c. Do you think that the assumption needed in order to construct the confidence interval estimate in (a) is valid? Explain.

d. What effect might your conclusion in (c) have on the validity of the results in (a)?

8.23 A manufacturing company produces electric insulators. You define the variable of interest as the strength of the insulators. If the insulators break when in use, a short circuit is likely. To test the strength of the insulators, you carry out destructive testing to determine how much force is required to break the insulators. You measure force by observing how many pounds are applied to the insulator before it breaks. You collect the force data for 30 insulators selected for the experiment and organize and store these data in **Force**:

1,870	1,728	1,656	1,610	1,634	1,784	1,552	1,696
1,592	1,662	1,866	1,764	1,734	1,662	1,734	1,774
1,550	1,756	1,762	1,886	1,820	1,744	1,788	1,688
1,810	1,752	1,680	1,810	1,652	1,736		

a. Construct a 95% confidence interval estimate for the population mean force.

b. What assumption must you make about the population distribution in order to construct the confidence interval estimate in (a)?

c. Do you think that the assumption needed in order to construct the confidence interval estimate in (a) is valid? Explain.

8.24 The file **MobileCommerce** contains mobile commerce penetration values (the percentage of the country population that bought something online via a mobile phone in the past month) for twenty-eight of the world's economies:

23	27	26	25	40	19	26	36	23	33	23
11	38	21	26	23	21	33	40	15	55	30
41	31	47	37	33	28					

Source: Data extracted from **bit.ly/2jXeS3F**.

a. Construct a 95% confidence interval estimate for the population mean mobile commerce penetration.
b. What assumption do you need to make about the population to construct the interval in (a)?
c. Given the data presented, do you think the assumption needed in (a) is valid? Explain.

8.25 One operation of a mill is to cut pieces of steel into parts that are used in the frame for front seats in an automobile. The steel is cut with a diamond saw, and the resulting parts must be cut to be within ±0.005 inch of the length specified by the automobile company. The measurement reported from a sample of 100 steel parts (stored in **Steel**) is the difference, in inches, between the actual length of the steel part, as measured by a laser measurement device, and the specified length of the steel part. For example, the first observation, −0.002, represents a steel part that is 0.002 inch shorter than the specified length.

a. Construct a 95% confidence interval estimate for the population mean difference between the actual length of the steel part and the specified length of the steel part.
b. What assumption must you make about the population distribution in order to construct the confidence interval estimate in (a)?
c. Do you think that the assumption needed in order to construct the confidence interval estimate in (a) is valid? Explain.
d. Compare the conclusions reached in (a) with those of Problem 2.43 on page 66.

8.3 Confidence Interval Estimate for the Proportion

The concept of a confidence interval also applies to categorical data. With categorical data, you want to estimate the proportion of items in a population having a certain characteristic of interest. The unknown population proportion is represented by the Greek letter π. The point estimate for π is the sample proportion, $p = X/n$, where n is the sample size and X is the number of items in the sample having the characteristic of interest. Equation (8.3) defines the confidence interval estimate for the population proportion.

CONFIDENCE INTERVAL ESTIMATE FOR THE PROPORTION

$$p \pm Z_{\alpha/2}\sqrt{\frac{p(1-p)}{n}}$$

or

$$p - Z_{\alpha/2}\sqrt{\frac{p(1-p)}{n}} \le \pi \le p + Z_{\alpha/2}\sqrt{\frac{p(1-p)}{n}} \tag{8.3}$$

where

$p = $ sample proportion $= \dfrac{X}{n} = \dfrac{\text{Number of items having the characteristic}}{\text{sample size}}$

$\pi = $ population proportion

$Z_{\alpha/2} = $ critical value from the standardized normal distribution

$n = $ sample size

Note: To use this equation for the confidence interval, the sample size n must be large enough to ensure that both X and $n - X$ are greater than 5.

Use the confidence interval estimate for the proportion defined in Equation (8.3) to estimate the proportion of sales invoices that contain errors (see the Ricknel Home Centers scenario on page 275). Using the DCOVA steps, first define the variable of interest as whether the invoice contains errors (yes or no). Then, collect the data from a sample of 100 sales invoices and organize and store the results that show 10 invoices contain errors. To analyze the data, compute $p = X/n = 10/100 = 0.10$. Because both $X = 10$ and $n - X = 100 - 10 = 90$ are > 5, using Equation (8.3) and $Z_{\alpha/2} = 1.96$, for 95% confidence,

$$p \pm Z_{\alpha/2}\sqrt{\frac{p(1-p)}{n}}$$

$$= 0.10 \pm (1.96)\sqrt{\frac{(0.10)(0.90)}{100}}$$

$$= 0.10 \pm (1.96)(0.03)$$

$$= 0.10 \pm 0.0588$$

$$0.0412 \leq \pi \leq 0.1588$$

Therefore, with 95% confidence, the population proportion of all sales invoices containing errors is between 0.0412 and 0.1588. The estimate is that between 4.12% and 15.88% of all the sales invoices contain errors. Figure 8.12 shows Excel, JMP, and Minitab confidence interval estimates for this example.

FIGURE 8.12
Excel, JMP, and Minitab confidence interval estimate results for the proportion of sales invoices that contain errors

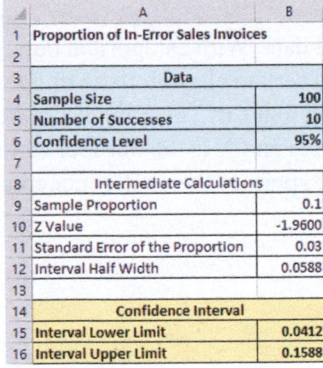
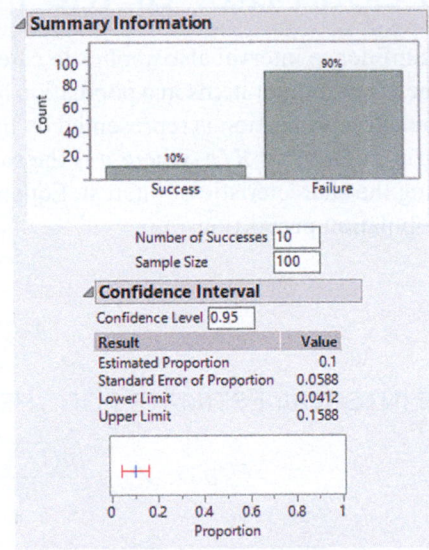
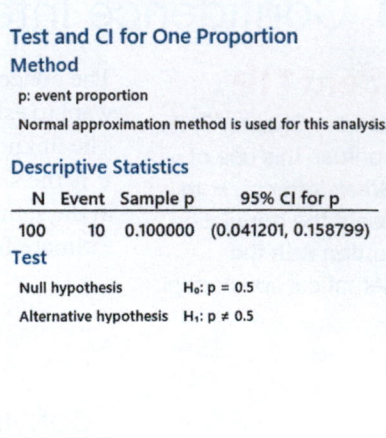

Example 8.4 illustrates another application of a confidence interval estimates for the proportion.

EXAMPLE 8.4

Estimating the Proportion of Nonconforming Newspapers Printed

The operations manager at a large newspaper wants to estimate the proportion of newspapers printed that have a nonconforming attribute. Using the DCOVA steps, you define the variable of interest as whether the newspaper has excessive rub-off, improper page setup, missing pages, or duplicate pages. You collect the data by selecting a random sample of $n = 200$ newspapers from all the newspapers printed during a single day. You organize the results in a worksheet, which shows that 35 newspapers contain some type of nonconformance. To analyze the data, you need to construct and interpret a 90% confidence interval estimate for the proportion of newspapers printed during the day that have a nonconforming attribute.

SOLUTION Using Equation (8.3),

$$p = \frac{X}{n} = \frac{35}{200} = 0.175, \text{ and with a 90\% level of confidence } Z_{\alpha/2} = 1.645$$

$$p \pm Z_{\alpha/2}\sqrt{\frac{p(1-p)}{n}}$$

$$= 0.175 \pm (1.645)\sqrt{\frac{(0.175)(0.825)}{200}}$$

$$= 0.175 \pm (1.645)(0.0269)$$

$$= 0.175 \pm 0.0442$$

$$0.1308 \leq \pi \leq 0.2192$$

▶(*continued*)

You conclude with 90% confidence that the population proportion of all newspapers printed that day with nonconformities is between 0.1308 and 0.2192. This means you estimate that between 13.08% and 21.92% of the newspapers printed on that day have some type of nonconformance.

Equation (8.3) contains a Z statistic because you can use the normal distribution to approximate the binomial distribution when the sample size is sufficiently large. In Example 8.4, the confidence interval using Z provides an excellent approximation for the population proportion because both X and $n - X$ are greater than 5. However, if you do not have a sufficiently large sample size, you should use the binomial distribution rather than Equation (8.3) (see references 1, 3, and 7). The exact confidence intervals for various sample sizes and proportions of items of interest have been tabulated by Fisher and Yates (reference 3).

PROBLEMS FOR SECTION 8.3

LEARNING THE BASICS

8.26 If $n = 200$ and $X = 50$, construct a 95% confidence interval estimate for the population proportion.

8.27 If $n = 400$ and $X = 25$, construct a 99% confidence interval estimate for the population proportion.

APPLYING THE CONCEPTS

✓ SELF TEST   **8.28** A cellphone provider has the business objective of wanting to estimate the proportion of subscribers who would upgrade to a new cellphone with improved features if it were made available at a substantially reduced cost. Data are collected from a random sample of 500 subscribers. The results indicate that 135 of the subscribers would upgrade to a new cellphone at a reduced cost.

a. Construct a 99% confidence interval estimate for the population proportion of subscribers that would upgrade to a new cellphone at a reduced cost.
b. How would the manager in charge of promotional programs use the results in (a)?

8.29 In a survey of 1,003 adults concerning complaints about restaurants, 732 complained about dirty or ill-equipped bathrooms and 381 complained about loud or distracting diners at other tables.

Source: Data extracted from "The Gripe-O-Meter Restaurants," *Consumer Reports*, August 2014, p. 11.

a. Construct a 95% confidence interval estimate of the population proportion of adults who complained about dirty or ill-equipped bathrooms.
b. Construct a 95% confidence interval estimate of the population proportion of adults who complained about loud or distracting diners at other tables.
c. How would the manager of a chain of restaurants use the results of (a) and (b)?

8.30 What do you value most when shopping in a retail store? According to a TimeTrade survey, 26% of consumers value *personalized experience* most.

Source: Data extracted from "The State of Retail, 2017," TimeTrade, **bit.ly/2rFGf7o**.

a. Suppose that the survey had a sample size of $n = 1,000$. Construct a 95% confidence interval estimate for the population proportion of consumers that value *personalized experience* most when shopping in a retail store?
b. Based on (a), can you claim that more than a quarter of all consumers value *personalized experience* most when shopping in a retail store?

c. Repeat parts (a) and (b), assuming that the survey had a sample size of $n = 10,000$.
d. Discuss the effect of sample size on confidence interval estimation.

8.31 In a survey of 823 human resource professionals concerning challenges they faced in the workplace, 329 said that employee retention/turnover was an important challenge and 181 said that employee satisfaction was an important challenge.

Source: Data extracted from R. King, "Companies Want to Know How Do Workers Feel," *Wall Street Journal*, October 14, 2015, p. R3.

a. Construct a 95% confidence interval estimate of the population proportion of human resource professionals who believe that employee retention/turnover was an important challenge.
b. Construct a 95% confidence interval estimate of the population proportion of human resource professionals who believe that employee satisfaction was an important challenge.
c. How would a human resource professional use the results of (a) and (b)?

8.32 A Pew Research Center survey of 4,787 adults found that 4,178 had bought something online. Of these online shoppers, 789 are weekly online shoppers.

a. Construct a 95% confidence interval estimate of the population proportion of adults who had bought something online.
b. Construct a 95% confidence interval estimate of the population proportion of online shoppers who are weekly online shoppers.
c. How would the director of e-commerce sales for a company use the results of (a) and (b)?

8.33 What business, economic, policy, and environmental threats to organization growth are CEOs extremely concerned about? In a survey by PricewaterhouseCoopers (PwC), 57 of 114 U.S. CEOs are extremely concerned about cyber threats, and 22 are extremely concerned about lack of trust in business.

Source: Data extracted from PWC, "US business leadership in the world in 2017," **pwc.to/2kHRGnE**.

a. Construct a 95% confidence interval estimate for the population proportion of U.S. CEOs who are extremely concerned about cyber threats.
b. Construct a 95% confidence interval estimate for the population proportion of U.S. CEOs who are extremely concerned about lack of trust in business.
c. Interpret the intervals in (a) and (b).

8.4 Determining Sample Size

In each confidence interval developed so far in this chapter, the sample size was reported along with the results, with little discussion of the width of the resulting confidence interval. In the business world, sample sizes are determined prior to data collection to ensure that the confidence interval is narrow enough to be useful in making decisions. Determining the proper sample size is a complicated procedure, subject to the constraints of budget, time, and the amount of acceptable sampling error. In the Ricknel Home Centers scenario, if you want to estimate the mean dollar amount of the sales invoices, you must determine in advance how large a sampling error to allow in estimating the population mean. You must also determine, in advance, the level of confidence (i.e., 90%, 95%, or 99%) to use in estimating the population parameter.

Sample Size Determination for the Mean

To develop an equation for determining the appropriate sample size needed when constructing a confidence interval estimate for the mean, recall Equation (8.1) on page 279:

$$\overline{X} \pm Z_{\alpha/2}\frac{\sigma}{\sqrt{n}}$$

[2]In this context, Minitab and some statisticians refer to e as the **margin of error**.

The amount added to or subtracted from $\overline{X}$ is equal to half the width of the interval. This quantity represents the amount of imprecision in the estimate that results from sampling error.[2] The sampling error, e, is defined as

$$e = Z_{\alpha/2}\frac{\sigma}{\sqrt{n}}$$

Solving for n gives the sample size needed to construct the appropriate confidence interval estimate for the mean. "Appropriate" means that the resulting interval will have an acceptable amount of sampling error.

SAMPLE SIZE DETERMINATION FOR THE MEAN

The sample size, n, is equal to the product of the $Z_{\alpha/2}$ value squared and the standard deviation, σ, squared, divided by the square of the sampling error, e.

$$n = \frac{Z_{\alpha/2}^2 \sigma^2}{e^2} \tag{8.4}$$

To compute the sample size, you must know three quantities:

[3]You use Z instead of t because, to determine the critical value of t, you need to know the sample size, but you do not know it yet. For most studies, the sample size needed is large enough that the standardized normal distribution is a good approximation of the t distribution.

- The desired confidence level, which determines the value of $Z_{\alpha/2}$, the critical value from the standardized normal distribution[3]
- The acceptable sampling error, e
- The standard deviation, σ

In some business-to-business relationships that require estimation of important parameters, legal contracts specify acceptable levels of sampling error and the confidence level required. For companies in the food and drug sectors, government regulations often specify sampling errors and confidence levels. In general, however, it is usually not easy to specify the three quantities needed to determine the sample size. How can you determine the level of confidence and sampling error? Typically, these questions are answered only by a subject matter expert (i.e., an individual very familiar with the variables under study). Although 95% is the most common confidence level used, if more confidence is desired, then 99% might be more appropriate; if less confidence is deemed acceptable, then 90% might be used. For the sampling error, you should think not of how much sampling error you would like to have (you really do not want any error) but of how much you can tolerate when reaching conclusions from the confidence interval.

In addition to specifying the confidence level and the sampling error, you need to estimate the standard deviation. Unfortunately, you rarely know the population standard deviation, σ. In some instances, you can estimate the standard deviation from past data. In other situations, you can make an educated guess by taking into account the range and distribution of the variable. For example, if you assume a normal distribution, the range is approximately equal to 6σ (i.e., $\pm 3\sigma$ around the mean) so that you estimate σ as the range divided by 6. If you cannot estimate σ in this way, you can conduct a small-scale study and estimate the standard deviation from the resulting data.

To explore how to determine the sample size needed for estimating the population mean, consider again the audit at Ricknel Home Centers. In Section 8.2, you selected a sample of 100 sales invoices and constructed a 95% confidence interval estimate for the population mean sales invoice amount. How was this sample size determined? Should you have selected a different sample size?

Suppose that, after consulting with company officials, you determine that a sampling error of no more than $\pm \$5$ desired, along with 95% confidence. Past data indicate that the standard deviation of the sales amount is approximately \$25. Thus, $e = \$5$, $\sigma = \$25$, and $Z_{\alpha/2} = 1.96$ (for 95% confidence). Using Equation (8.4),

$$n = \frac{Z_{\alpha/2}^2 \, \sigma^2}{e^2} = \frac{(1.96)^2 (25)^2}{(5)^2}$$

$$= 96.04$$

Because the general rule is to slightly oversatisfy the criteria by rounding the sample size up to the next whole integer, a sample size of 97 is needed. The Section 8.2 example on page 284 uses a sample size $n = 100$, slightly more than what is necessary to satisfy the needs of the company, based on the estimated standard deviation, desired confidence level, and sampling error. Because the calculated sample standard deviation is slightly higher than expected, \$28.95 compared to \$25.00, the confidence interval is slightly wider than desired. Figure 8.13 presents Excel and Minitab results for determining the sample size. (See Section JG8.4 for the JMP results.)

FIGURE 8.13

Excel and Minitab results for determining the sample size for estimating the mean sales invoice amount for the Ricknel Home Centers example

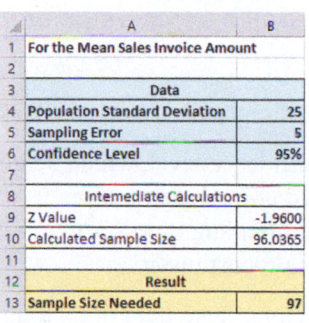

Example 8.5 illustrates another application of determining the sample size needed to develop a confidence interval estimate for the mean.

EXAMPLE 8.5	Returning to Example 8.3 on page 285, suppose you want to estimate, with 95% confidence, the population mean processing time to within ± 4 days. On the basis of a study conducted the previous year, you believe that the standard deviation is 25 days. Determine the sample size needed.

Determining the Sample Size for the Mean

SOLUTION Using Equation (8.4) on page 292 and $e = 4$, $\sigma = 25$, and $Z_{\alpha/2} = 1.96$ for 95% confidence,

$$n = \frac{Z_{\alpha/2}^2 \, \sigma^2}{e^2} = \frac{(1.96)^2 (25)^2}{(4)^2}$$

$$= 150.06$$

Therefore, you should select a sample of 151 applications because the general rule for determining sample size is to always round up to the next integer value in order to slightly oversatisfy the criteria desired. An actual sampling error larger than 4 will result if the sample standard deviation calculated in this sample of 151 is greater than 25 and smaller if the sample standard deviation is less than 25.

Sample Size Determination for the Proportion

So far in this section, you have learned how to determine the sample size needed for estimating the population mean. Now suppose that you want to determine the sample size necessary for estimating a population proportion.

To determine the sample size needed to estimate a population proportion, π, you use a method similar to the method for a population mean. Recall that in developing the sample size for a confidence interval for the mean, the sampling error is defined by

$$e = Z_{\alpha/2}\frac{\sigma}{\sqrt{n}}$$

When estimating a proportion, you replace σ with $\sqrt{\pi(1-\pi)}$. Thus, the sampling error is

$$e = Z_{\alpha/2}\sqrt{\frac{\pi(1-\pi)}{n}}$$

Solving for n, you have the sample size necessary to develop a confidence interval estimate for a proportion.

SAMPLE SIZE DETERMINATION FOR THE PROPORTION

The sample size n is equal to the product of $Z_{\alpha/2}$ squared, the population proportion, π, and 1 minus the population proportion, π, divided by the square of the sampling error, e.

$$n = \frac{Z_{\alpha/2}^2\pi(1-\pi)}{e^2} \tag{8.5}$$

To determine the sample size, you must know three quantities:

- The desired confidence level, which determines the value of $Z_{\alpha/2}$, the critical value from the standardized normal distribution
- The acceptable sampling error (or margin of error), e
- The population proportion, π

In practice, selecting these quantities requires some planning. Once you determine the desired level of confidence, you can find the appropriate $Z_{\alpha/2}$ value from the standardized normal distribution. The sampling error, e, indicates the amount of error that you are willing to tolerate in estimating the population proportion. The third quantity, π, is actually the population parameter that you want to estimate! Thus, how do you state a value for what you are trying to determine?

Here you have two alternatives. In many situations, you may have past information or relevant experience that provides an educated estimate of π. If you do not have past information or relevant experience, you can try to provide a value for π that would never *underestimate* the sample size needed. Referring to Equation (8.5), you can see that the quantity $\pi(1-\pi)$ appears in the numerator. Thus, you need to determine the value of π that will make the quantity $\pi(1-\pi)$ as large as possible. When $\pi = 0.5$, the product $\pi(1-\pi)$ achieves its maximum value. To show this result, consider the following values of π, along with the accompanying products of $\pi(1-\pi)$:

When $\pi = 0.9$, then $\pi(1-\pi) = (0.9)(0.1) = 0.09$.

When $\pi = 0.7$, then $\pi(1-\pi) = (0.7)(0.3) = 0.21$.

When $\pi = 0.5$, then $\pi(1-\pi) = (0.5)(0.5) = 0.25$.

When $\pi = 0.3$, then $\pi(1-\pi) = (0.3)(0.7) = 0.21$.

When $\pi = 0.1$, then $\pi(1-\pi) = (0.1)(0.9) = 0.09$.

Therefore, when you have no prior knowledge or estimate for the population proportion, π, you should use $\pi = 0.5$ for determining the sample size. Using $\pi = 0.5$ produces the largest possible sample size and results in the narrowest and most precise confidence interval. This increased precision comes at the cost of spending more time and money for an increased sample size. Also, note that if you use $\pi = 0.5$ and the proportion is different from 0.5, you will overestimate the sample size needed, because you will get a confidence interval narrower than originally intended.

In the Ricknel Home Centers scenario, suppose that the auditing procedures require you to have 95% confidence in estimating the population proportion of sales invoices with errors to within ± 0.07. The results from past months indicate that the largest proportion has been no more than 0.15. Thus, using Equation (8.5) with $e = 0.07$, $\pi = 0.15$, and $Z_{\alpha/2} = 1.96$ for 95% confidence,

$$ n = \frac{Z_{\alpha/2}^2 \pi(1 - \pi)}{e^2} = \frac{(1.96)^2(0.15)(0.85)}{(0.07)^2} $$

$$ = 99.96 $$

Because the general rule rounds up the sample size to the next whole integer to slightly oversatisfy the criteria, a sample size of 100 is needed. The sample size needed to satisfy the requirements of the company, based on the estimated proportion, desired confidence level, and sampling error, is the same as the sample size that the Section 8.3 example on page 290 uses. The actual confidence interval is narrower than required because the sample proportion is 0.10, whereas 0.15 was used for π in Equation (8.5). Figure 8.14 presents Excel and Minitab results for determining the sample size. Because Minitab uses the binomial distribution, Minitab computes a much larger sample size than either Excel or JMP. (See Section JG8.4 for the JMP results.)

FIGURE 8.14

Excel and Minitab for determining the sample size for estimating the proportion of in-error sales invoices for Ricknel Home Centers

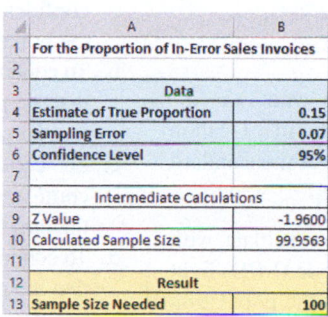

	A	B
1	For the Proportion of In-Error Sales Invoices	
2		
3	Data	
4	Estimate of True Proportion	0.15
5	Sampling Error	0.07
6	Confidence Level	95%
7		
8	Intermediate Calculations	
9	Z Value	-1.9600
10	Calculated Sample Size	99.9563
11		
12	Result	
13	Sample Size Needed	100

Sample Size for Estimation

Method

Parameter	Proportion
Distribution	Binomial
Proportion	0.15
Confidence level	95%
Confidence interval	Two-sided

Results

Margin of Error	Sample Size
0.07	141

Example 8.6 provides another application of determining the sample size for estimating the population proportion.

EXAMPLE 8.6

Determining the Sample Size for the Population Proportion

You want to have 90% confidence of estimating the proportion of office workers who respond to email within an hour to within ± 0.05. Because you have not previously undertaken such a study, there is no information available from past data. Determine the sample size needed.

SOLUTION Because no information is available from past data, assume that $\pi = 0.50$. Using Equation (8.5) on page 294 and $e = 0.05$, $\pi = 0.50$, and $Z_{\alpha/2} = 1.645$ for 90% confidence,

$$ n = \frac{Z_{\alpha/2}^2 \pi(1 - \pi)}{e^2} = \frac{(1.645)^2(0.50)(0.50)}{(0.05)^2} $$

$$ = 270.6 $$

Therefore, you need a sample of 271 office workers to estimate the population proportion to within ± 0.05 with 90% confidence.

PROBLEMS FOR SECTION 8.4

LEARNING THE BASICS

8.34 If you want to be 95% confident of estimating the population mean to within a sampling error of ± 5 and the standard deviation is assumed to be 15, what sample size is required?

8.35 If you want to be 99% confident of estimating the population mean to within a sampling error of ± 20 and the standard deviation is assumed to be 100, what sample size is required?

8.36 If you want to be 99% confident of estimating the population proportion to within a sampling error of ± 0.04, what sample size is needed?

8.37 If you want to be 95% confident of estimating the population proportion to within a sampling error of ± 0.02 and there is historical evidence that the population proportion is approximately 0.40, what sample size is needed?

APPLYING THE CONCEPTS

✓**SELF TEST** **8.38** A survey is planned to determine the mean annual family medical expenses of employees of a large company. The management of the company wishes to be 95% confident that the sample mean is correct to within $\pm \$50$ of the population mean annual family medical expenses. A previous study indicates that the standard deviation is approximately $400.
a. How large a sample is necessary?
b. If management wants to be correct to within $\pm \$25$, how many employees need to be selected?

8.39 If the manager of a bottled water distributor wants to estimate, with 95% confidence, the mean amount of water in a 1-gallon bottle to within ± 0.004 gallon and also assumes that the standard deviation is 0.02 gallon, what sample size is needed?

8.40 If a light bulb manufacturing company wants to estimate, with 95% confidence, the mean life of light emitting diode (LED) light bulbs to within ± 400 hours and also assumes that the population standard deviation is 1,500 hours, how many LED light bulbs need to be selected?

8.41 If the inspection division of a county weights and measures department wants to estimate the mean amount of soft-drink fill in 2-liter bottles to within ± 0.01 liter with 95% confidence and also assumes that the standard deviation is 0.05 liter, what sample size is needed?

8.42 An advertising media analyst wants to estimate the mean weekly amount of time consumers spend watching television daily. Based on previous studies, the standard deviation is assumed to be 20 minutes. The media analyst wants to estimate, with 99% confidence, the mean weekly amount of time to within ± 5 minutes.
a. What sample size is needed?
b. If 95% confidence is desired, how many consumers need to be selected?

8.43 An advertising media analyst wants to estimate the mean amount of time that consumers spend with digital media daily. From past studies, the standard deviation is estimated as 45 minutes.

a. What sample size is needed if the media analyst wants to be 90% confident of being correct to within ± 5 minutes?
b. If 99% confidence is desired, how many consumers need to be selected?

8.44 A growing niche in the restaurant business is gourmet-casual breakfast, lunch, and brunch. Chains in this group include Panera Bread. Suppose that the mean per-person check for breakfast at Panera Bread is approximately $9.50.
a. Assuming a standard deviation of $2.00, what sample size is needed to estimate, with 95% confidence, the mean per-person check for Panera Bread to within $\pm \$0.25$?
b. Assuming a standard deviation of $2.50, what sample size is needed to estimate, with 95% confidence, the mean per-person check for Panera Bread to within $\pm \$0.25$?
c. Assuming a standard deviation of $3.00, what sample size is needed to estimate, with 95% confidence, the mean per-person check for Panera Bread to within $\pm \$0.25$?
d. Discuss the effect of variation on the sample size needed.

8.45 What does brand loyalty mean to consumers? According to a Rare research report, 20% of consumers associate *trust* with brand loyalty.

Source: Data extracted from "Redefining Loyalty," Rare, 2016, **bit.ly/2solA40**.

a. To conduct a follow-up study that would provide 95% confidence that the point estimate is correct to within ± 0.04 of the population proportion, how large a sample size is required?
b. To conduct a follow-up study that would provide 99% confidence that the point estimate is correct to within ± 0.04 of the population proportion, how many consumers need to be sampled?
c. To conduct a follow-up study that would provide 95% confidence that the point estimate is correct to within ± 0.02 of the population proportion, how large a sample size is required?
d. To conduct a follow-up study that would provide 99% confidence that the point estimate is correct to within ± 0.02 of the population proportion, how many consumers need to be sampled?
e. Discuss the effects on sample size requirements of changing the desired confidence level and the acceptable sampling error.

8.46 A Federal Reserve Bank of Atlanta report looks at what strategies and measures financial institutions are pursuing to provide mobile financial services to their customers. In response to a survey question about barriers hindering greater consumer adoption of mobile banking, in a survey of 115 financial institutions, 81 said security concerns is a barrier, 68 said lack of trust in the technology is a barrier, and 16 said difficulty of use was a barrier.

Source: Data extracted from "2016 Mobile Banking and Payments Survey of Financial Institutions in the Sixth District," Federal Reserve Bank of Atlanta **bit.ly/2sfe0co**.

Construct a 95% confidence interval estimate of the population proportion of financial institution who said:
a. security concerns are a barrier hindering greater consumer adoption of mobile banking.
b. lack of trust is a barrier hindering greater consumer adoption of mobile banking.

c. difficulty of use is a barrier hindering greater consumer adoption of mobile banking.

d. You have been asked to update the results of this study. Determine the sample size necessary to estimate, with 95% confidence, the population proportions in (a) through (c) to within ± 0.02.

8.47 In a study of 443 nonprofits nationwide, 130 indicated that the greatest diversity staffing challenge they face is retaining younger staff (those under 30).

Source: Data extracted from "2016 Nonprofit Employment Practices Survey," Nonprofit HR, 2016, **bit.ly/23ZHwhb**.

a. Construct a 95% confidence interval for the population proportion of nonprofits that indicate retaining younger staff is the greatest diversity staffing challenge for their organization.

b. Interpret the interval constructed in (a).

c. If you wanted to conduct a follow-up study to estimate the population proportion of nonprofits that indicate retaining younger staff is the greatest diversity staffing challenge for their organization to within ± 0.01 with 95% confidence, how many nonprofits would you survey?

8.48 Cybersecurity is a critical business issue that demands the attention of business and IT executives. According to a study released by PwC, 38% of surveyed business and IT executives reported phishing scams at their institutions.

Source: Data extracted from "Toward new possibilities in threat management," PwC, 2017 **pwc.to/2kwhP.Jv**.

a. If you conduct a follow-up study to estimate the population proportion of business and IT executives reporting phishing scams at their institutions, would you use a π of 0.38 or 0.50 in the sample size formula?

b. Using your answer in part (a), find the sample size necessary to estimate, with 95% confidence, the population proportion to within ± 0.03.

8.49 Personal data is the new currency of the digital economy. How do consumers feel about sharing personal data with their communication service providers (CSPs)? A recent IBM report highlights that 40% of 18- to 25-year-old consumers are comfortable sharing personal data with their CSPs.

Source: Data extracted from "The trust factor in the cognitive era," IBM Institute for Business Value, 2017 **ibm.co/2rq48Pd**.

a. To conduct a follow-up study that would provide 99% confidence that the point estimate is correct to within ± 0.03 of the population proportion, how many 18- to 25-year-old consumers need to be sampled?

b. To conduct a follow-up study that would provide 99% confidence that the point estimate is correct to within ± 0.05 of the population proportion, how many 18- to 25-year-old consumers need to be sampled?

c. Compare the results of (a) and (b).

8.5 Confidence Interval Estimation and Ethical Issues

The selection of samples and the inferences that accompany them raise several ethical issues. The major ethical issue concerns whether confidence interval estimates accompany point estimates. Failure to include a confidence interval estimate might mislead the user of the results into thinking that the point estimate is all that is needed to predict the population characteristic with certainty. Confidence interval limits (typically set at 95%), the sample size used, and an interpretation of the meaning of the confidence interval in terms that a person untrained in statistics can understand should always accompany point estimates.

When media outlets publicize the results of a political poll, they often overlook this type of information. Sometimes, the results of a poll include the sampling error, but the sampling error is often presented in fine print or as an afterthought to the story being reported. A fully ethical presentation of poll results would give equal prominence to the confidence levels, sample size, sampling error, and confidence limits of the poll.

When you prepare your own point estimates, always state the interval estimate in a *prominent* place and include a brief explanation of the meaning of the confidence interval. In addition, make sure you highlight the sample size and sampling error.

8.6 Application of Confidence Interval Estimation in Auditing

Auditing is the collection and evaluation of evidence about information related to an economic entity in order to determine and report on how well the information corresponds to established criteria. Auditing uses probability sampling methods to develop confidence interval estimates. The **Section 8.6 online topic** reviews three common applications of confidence interval estimation in auditing.

8.7 Estimation and Sample Size Estimation for Finite Populations

To develop confidence interval estimates for population parameters or determine sample sizes when estimating population parameters, you use the finite population correction factor when samples are selected without replacement from a finite population. The **Section 8.7 online topic** explains how to use the finite population correction factor for these purposes.

8.8 Bootstrapping

The confidence interval estimation procedures discussed in this chapter make assumptions that are often not valid, especially for small samples. Bootstrapping, the selection of an initial sample and repeated sampling from that initial sample, provides an alternative approach that does not rely on those assumptions. The **Section 8.8 online topic** explains this alternative technique.

▼USING **STATISTICS**
Getting Estimates..., Revisited

In the Ricknel Home Centers scenario, you were an accountant for a distributor of home improvement supplies in the northeastern United States. You were responsible for the accuracy of the integrated inventory management and sales information system. You used confidence interval estimation techniques to draw conclusions about the population of all records from a relatively small sample collected during an audit.

At the end of the month, you collected a random sample of 100 sales invoices and made the following inferences:

- With 95% confidence, you concluded that the mean amount of all the sales invoices is between $104.53 and $116.01.

- With 95% confidence, you concluded that between 4.12% and 15.88% of all the sales invoices contain errors.

These estimates provide an interval of values that you believe contain the true population parameters. If these intervals are too wide (i.e., the sampling error is too large) for the types of decisions Ricknel Home Centers needs to make, you will need to take a larger sample. You can use the sample size formulas in Section 8.4 to determine the number of sales invoices to sample to ensure that the size of the sampling error is acceptable.

▼SUMMARY

This chapter discusses confidence intervals for estimating the characteristics of a population, along with how you can determine the necessary sample size. You learned how to apply these methods to numerical and categorical data. Table 8.3 provides a list of topics covered in this chapter.

To determine what equation to use for a particular situation, you need to answer these questions:

- Are you constructing a confidence interval, or are you determining sample size?
- Do you have a numerical variable, or do you have a categorical variable?

TABLE 8.3
Summary of Topics
in Chapter 8

	TYPE OF DATA	
TYPE OF ANALYSIS	**Numerical**	**Categorical**
Confidence interval for a population parameter	Confidence interval estimate for the mean (Sections 8.1 and 8.2)	Confidence interval estimate for the proportion (Section 8.3)
Determining sample size	Sample size determination for the mean (Section 8.4)	Sample size determination for the proportion (Section 8.4)

▼ REFERENCES

1. Cochran, W. G. *Sampling Techniques*, 3rd ed. New York: Wiley, 1977.
2. Daniel, W. W. *Applied Nonparametric Statistics*, 2nd ed. Boston: PWS Kent, 1990.
3. Fisher, R. A., and F. Yates. *Statistical Tables for Biological, Agricultural and Medical Research*, 5th ed. Edinburgh: Oliver & Boyd, 1957.
4. Hahn, G., and W. Meeker. *Statistical Intervals: A Guide for Practitioners*. New York: John Wiley and Sons, Inc., 1991.
5. Kirk, R. E., Ed. *Statistical Issues: A Reader for the Behavioral Sciences*. Belmont, CA: Wadsworth, 1972.
6. Larsen, R. L., and M. L. Marx. *An Introduction to Mathematical Statistics and Its Applications*, 5th ed. Upper Saddle River, NJ: Prentice Hall, 2012.
7. Snedecor, G. W., and W. G. Cochran. *Statistical Methods*, 7th ed. Ames, IA: Iowa State University Press, 1980.

▼ KEY EQUATIONS

Confidence Interval for the Mean (σ Known)

$$\overline{X} \pm Z_{\alpha/2} \frac{\sigma}{\sqrt{n}}$$

or

$$\overline{X} - Z_{\alpha/2} \frac{\sigma}{\sqrt{n}} \leq \mu \leq \overline{X} + Z_{\alpha/2} \frac{\sigma}{\sqrt{n}} \qquad (8.1)$$

Confidence Interval for the Mean (σ Unknown)

$$\overline{X} \pm t_{\alpha/2} \frac{S}{\sqrt{n}}$$

or

$$\overline{X} - t_{\alpha/2} \frac{S}{\sqrt{n}} \leq \mu \leq \overline{X} + t_{\alpha/2} \frac{S}{\sqrt{n}} \qquad (8.2)$$

Confidence Interval Estimate for the Proportion

$$p \pm Z_{\alpha/2} \sqrt{\frac{p(1-p)}{n}}$$

or

$$p - Z_{\alpha/2} \sqrt{\frac{p(1-p)}{n}} \leq \pi \leq p + Z_{\alpha/2} \sqrt{\frac{p(1-p)}{n}} \qquad (8.3)$$

Sample Size Determination for the Mean

$$n = \frac{Z_{\alpha/2}^2 \sigma^2}{e^2} \qquad (8.4)$$

Sample Size Determination for the Proportion

$$n = \frac{Z_{\alpha/2}^2 \pi(1-\pi)}{e^2} \qquad (8.5)$$

▼ KEY TERMS

confidence interval estimate 276	level of confidence 278	sampling error 278
critical value 279	margin of error 292	Student's *t* distribution 282
degrees of freedom 282	point estimate 276	

▼ CHECKING YOUR UNDERSTANDING

8.50 Why can you never really have 100% confidence of correctly estimating the population characteristic of interest?

8.51 When should you use the *t* distribution to develop the confidence interval estimate for the mean?

8.52 Why is it true that for a given sample size, *n*, an increase in confidence is achieved by widening (and making less precise) the confidence interval?

8.53 Why is the sample size needed to determine the proportion smaller when the population proportion is 0.20 than when the population proportion is 0.50?

▼ CHAPTER REVIEW PROBLEMS

8.54 A GlobalWebIndex study noted the percentage of Internet users that owned various devices. Suppose that a survey of 1,000 Internet users found that 840 own a PC/laptop, 910 own a smartphone, 500 own a tablet, and 100 own a smart watch.

Source: Data extracted from "GWI Device," GlobalWebIndex Quarterly Report, Q1 2017 **bit.ly/2qBks0x**.

a. Construct 95% confidence interval estimates for the population proportion of the devices Internet users own.
b. What conclusions can you reach concerning what devices Internet users own?

8.55 How do smartphone owners use their smartphones when shopping in a grocery store? A sample of 731 smartphone owners in the United States revealed that 358 use their smartphone to access digital coupons, 355 look up recipes, 234 read reviews of products and brands, and 154 locate in-store items.

Source: Data extracted from "U.S. Grocery Shopping Trends, 2016," FMI, **bit.ly/2h9Q4Sl**.

a. For each smartphone user grocery shopping online activity, construct a 95% confidence interval estimate of the population proportion.
b. What conclusions can you reach concerning how smartphone owners use their smartphones when shopping in a grocery store?

8.56 A market researcher for a consumer electronics company wants to study the media viewing behavior of residents of a particular area. A random sample of 40 respondents is selected, and each respondent is instructed to keep a detailed record of time spent engaged viewing content across all screens (traditional TV, DVD/Blu-ray, game console, Internet on a computer, video on a computer, video on a smartphone) in a particular week. The results are as follows:

Content viewing time per week: $\overline{X} = 51$ hours, $S = 3.5$ hours. 32 respondents have high definition (HD) on at least one television set.

a. Construct a 95% confidence interval estimate for the mean content viewing time per week in this area.
b. Construct a 95% confidence interval estimate for the population proportion of residents who have HD on at least one television set.

Suppose that the market researcher wants to take another survey in a different location. Answer these questions:
c. What sample size is required to be 95% confident of estimating the population mean content viewing time to within ±2 hours assuming that the population standard deviation is equal to 5 hours?
d. How many respondents need to be selected to be 95% confident of being within ±0.06 of the population proportion who have HD on at least one television set if no previous estimate is available?
e. Based on (c) and (d), how many respondents should the market researcher select if a single survey is being conducted?

8.57 An information technology (IT) provider of cloud backup and restore solutions for small to midsize businesses wants to study the consequences of ransomware attacks. A random sample of 50 small to midsized companies in the United States that have experienced a ransomware attack reveals the following:

Time spent dealing with and containing a ransomware incident: $\overline{X} = 42$ hours, $S = 8$ hours
Thirteen small to midsize companies lost customers as a result of a ransomware incident

a. Construct a 99% confidence interval estimate for the population mean time spent dealing with and containing a ransomware incident.
b. Construct a 95% confidence interval estimate for the population proportion of small to midsized companies who have lost customers as a result of a ransomware incident.

8.58 The human resource (HR) director of a large corporation wishes to study absenteeism among its mid-level managers at its central office during the year. A random sample of 25 mid-level managers reveals the following:

Absenteeism: $\overline{X} = 6.2$ days, $S = 7.3$ days.
13 mid-level managers cite stress as a cause of absence.

a. Construct a 95% confidence interval estimate for the mean number of absences for mid-level managers during the year.
b. Construct a 95% confidence interval estimate for the population proportion of mid-level managers who cite stress as a cause of absence.

Suppose that the HR director wishes to administer a survey in one of its regional offices. Answer these questions:
c. What sample size is needed to have 95% confidence in estimating the population mean absenteeism to within ±1.5 days if the population standard deviation is estimated to be 8 days?
d. How many mid-level managers need to be selected to have 90% confidence in estimating the population proportion of mid-level managers who cite stress as a cause of absence to within ±0.075 if no previous estimate is available?
e. Based on (c) and (d), what sample size is needed if a single survey is being conducted?

8.59 A national association devoted to HR and workplace programs, practices, and training wants to study HR department practices and employee turnover of its member organizations. HR professionals and organization executives focus on turnover not only because it has significant cost implications but also because it affects overall business performance. A survey is designed to estimate the proportion of member organizations that have both talent and development programs in place to drive human-capital management as well as the member organizations' mean annual employee turnover cost (cost to fill a frontline employee position left vacant due to turnover). A random sample of 100 member organizations reveals the following:

Frontline employee turnover cost: $\overline{X} = \$12,500$, $S = \$1,000$.
Thirty member organizations have both talent and development programs in place to drive human-capital management.

a. Construct a 95% confidence interval estimate for the population mean frontline employee turnover cost of member organizations.
b. Construct a 95% confidence interval estimate for the population proportion of member organizations that have both talent and development programs in place to drive human-capital management.
c. What sample size is needed to have 99% confidence of estimating the population mean frontline employee turnover cost to within ±$250?

d. How many member organizations need to be selected to have 90% confidence of estimating the population proportion of organizations that have both talent and development programs in place to drive human-capital management to within ±0.045?

8.60 The financial impact of IT systems downtime is a concern of plant operations management today. A survey of manufacturers examined the satisfaction level with the reliability and availability of their manufacturing IT applications. The variables of focus are whether the manufacturer experienced downtime in the past year that affected one or more manufacturing IT applications, the number of downtime incidents that occurred in the past year, and the approximate cost of a typical downtime incident. The results from a sample of 200 manufacturers are as follows:

Sixty-two experienced downtime this year that affected one or more manufacturing applications.
Number of downtime incidents: $\overline{X} = 3.5, S = 2.0$
Cost of downtime incidents: $\overline{X} = \$18,000, S = \$3,000$.

a. Construct a 90% confidence interval estimate for the population proportion of manufacturers who experienced downtime in the past year that affected one or more manufacturing IT applications.
b. Construct a 95% confidence interval estimate for the population mean number of downtime incidents experienced by manufacturers in the past year.
c. Construct a 95% confidence interval estimate for the population mean cost of downtime incidents.

8.61 The branch manager of an outlet (Store 1) of a nationwide chain of pet supply stores wants to study characteristics of her customers. In particular, she decides to focus on two variables: the amount of money spent by customers and whether the customers own only one dog, only one cat, or more than one dog and/or cat. The results from a sample of 70 customers are as follows:

- Amount of money spent: $\overline{X} = \$21.34, S = \$9.22$.
- Thirty-seven customers own only a dog.
- Twenty-six customers own only a cat.
- Seven customers own more than one dog and/or cat.

a. Construct a 95% confidence interval estimate for the population mean amount spent in the pet supply store.
b. Construct a 90% confidence interval estimate for the population proportion of customers who own only a cat.

The branch manager of another outlet (Store 2) wishes to conduct a similar survey in his store. The manager does not have access to the information generated by the manager of Store 1. Answer the following questions:

c. What sample size is needed to have 95% confidence of estimating the population mean amount spent in this store to within ±$1.50 if the standard deviation is estimated to be $10?
d. How many customers need to be selected to have 90% confidence of estimating the population proportion of customers who own only a cat to within ±0.045?
e. Based on your answers to (c) and (d), how large a sample should the manager take?

8.62 Scarlett and Heather, the owners of an upscale restaurant in Dayton, Ohio, want to study the dining characteristics of their customers. They decide to focus on two variables: the amount of money spent by customers and whether customers order dessert. The results from a sample of 60 customers are as follows:

Amount spent: $\overline{X} = \$38.54, S = \$7.26$.
Eighteen customers purchased dessert.

a. Construct a 95% confidence interval estimate for the population mean amount spent per customer in the restaurant.
b. Construct a 90% confidence interval estimate for the population proportion of customers who purchase dessert.

Jeanine, the owner of a competing restaurant, wants to conduct a similar survey in her restaurant. Jeanine does not have access to the information that Scarlett and Heather have obtained from the survey they conducted. Answer the following questions:

c. What sample size is needed to have 95% confidence of estimating the population mean amount spent in her restaurant to within ±$1.50, assuming that the standard deviation is estimated to be $8?
d. How many customers need to be selected to have 90% confidence of estimating the population proportion of customers who purchase dessert to within ±0.04?
e. Based on your answers to (c) and (d), how large a sample should Jeanine take?

8.63 The manufacturer of Ice Melt claims that its product will melt snow and ice at temperatures as low as 0° Fahrenheit. A representative for a large chain of hardware stores is interested in testing this claim. The chain purchases a large shipment of 5-pound bags for distribution. The representative wants to know, with 95% confidence and within ±0.05, what proportion of bags of Ice Melt perform the job as claimed by the manufacturer.

a. How many bags does the representative need to test? What assumption should be made concerning the population proportion? (This is called *destructive testing*; i.e., the product being tested is destroyed by the test and is then unavailable to be sold.)
b. Suppose that the representative tests 50 bags, and 42 of them do the job as claimed. Construct a 95% confidence interval estimate for the population proportion that will do the job as claimed.
c. How can the representative use the results of (b) to determine whether to sell the Ice Melt product?

8.64 Claims fraud (illegitimate claims) and buildup (exaggerated loss amounts) continue to be major issues of concern among automobile insurance companies. Fraud is defined as specific material misrepresentation of the facts of a loss; buildup is defined as the inflation of an otherwise legitimate claim. A recent study examined auto injury claims closed with payment under private passenger coverages. Detailed data on injury, medical treatment, claimed losses, and total payments, as well as claim-handling techniques, were collected. In addition, auditors were asked to review the claim files to indicate whether specific elements of fraud or buildup appeared in the claim and, in the case of buildup, to specify the amount of excess payment. The file InsuranceClaims contains data for 90 randomly selected auto injury claims. The following variables are included: CLAIM—Claim ID; BUILDUP—1 if buildup indicated, 0 if not; and EXCESSPAYMENT—excess payment amount, in dollars.

a. Construct a 95% confidence interval for the population proportion of all auto injury files that have exaggerated loss amounts.
b. Construct a 95% confidence interval for the population mean dollar excess payment amount.

8.65 A quality characteristic of interest for a tea-bag-filling process is the weight of the tea in the individual bags. In this example, the label weight on the package indicates that the mean amount is 5.5 grams of tea in a bag. If the bags are underfilled, two problems arise. First, customers may not be able to brew the tea to be as strong as they wish. Second, the company may be in violation of the truth-in-labeling laws. On the other hand, if the mean amount of tea in a bag exceeds the label weight, the company is giving away product. Getting an exact amount of tea in a bag is problematic because of variation in the temperature and humidity inside the factory, differences in the density of the tea, and the extremely fast filling operation of the machine (approximately 170 bags per minute). The following data (stored in Teabags) are the weights, in grams, of a sample of 50 tea bags produced in one hour by a single machine:

5.65	5.44	5.42	5.40	5.53	5.34	5.54	5.45	5.52	5.41
5.57	5.40	5.53	5.54	5.55	5.62	5.56	5.46	5.44	5.51
5.47	5.40	5.47	5.61	5.53	5.32	5.67	5.29	5.49	5.55
5.77	5.57	5.42	5.58	5.58	5.50	5.32	5.50	5.53	5.58
5.61	5.45	5.44	5.25	5.56	5.63	5.50	5.57	5.67	5.36

a. Construct a 99% confidence interval estimate for the population mean weight of the tea bags.
b. Is the company meeting the requirement set forth on the label that the mean amount of tea in a bag is 5.5 grams?
c. Do you think the assumption needed to construct the confidence interval estimate in (a) is valid?

8.66 Call centers today play an important role in managing day-to-day business communications with customers. It's important, therefore, to monitor a comprehensive set of metrics, which can help businesses understand the overall performance of a call center. One key metric for measuring overall call center performance is service level which is defined as the percentage of calls answered by a human agent within a specified number of seconds. The file ServiceLevel contains the following data for time, in seconds, to answer 50 incoming calls to a financial services call center:

16	14	16	19	6	14	15	5	16	18	17	22	6	18	10	15	12
6	19	16	16	15	13	25	9	17	12	10	5	15	23	11	12	14
24	9	10	13	14	26	19	20	13	24	28	15	21	8	16	12

a. Construct a 95% confidence interval estimate for the population mean time, in seconds, to answer incoming calls.
b. What assumption do you need to make about the population to construct the interval in (a)?
c. Given the data presented, do you think the assumption needed in (a) is valid? Explain.

8.67 The manufacturer of Boston and Vermont asphalt shingles knows that product weight is a major factor in a customer's perception of quality. The last stage of the assembly line packages the shingles before they are placed on wooden pallets. Once a pallet is full (a pallet for most brands holds 16 squares of shingles), it is weighed, and the measurement is recorded. The file Pallet contains the weight (in pounds) from a sample of 368 pallets of Boston shingles and 330 pallets of Vermont shingles.

a. For the Boston shingles, construct a 95% confidence interval estimate for the mean weight.
b. For the Vermont shingles, construct a 95% confidence interval estimate for the mean weight.
c. Do you think the assumption needed to construct the confidence interval estimates in (a) and (b) is valid?
d. Based on the results of (a) and (b), what conclusions can you reach concerning the mean weight of the Boston and Vermont shingles?

8.68 The manufacturer of Boston and Vermont asphalt shingles provides its customers with a 20-year warranty on most of its products. To determine whether a shingle will last the entire warranty period, accelerated-life testing is conducted at the manufacturing plant. Accelerated-life testing exposes the shingle to the stresses it would be subject to in a lifetime of normal use via a laboratory experiment that takes only a few minutes to conduct. In this test, a shingle is repeatedly scraped with a brush for a short period of time, and the shingle granules removed by the brushing are weighed (in grams). Shingles that experience low amounts of granule loss are expected to last longer in normal use than shingles that experience high amounts of granule loss. In this situation, a shingle should experience no more than 0.8 grams of granule loss if it is expected to last the length of the warranty period. The file Granule contains a sample of 170 measurements made on the company's Boston shingles and 140 measurements made on Vermont shingles.

a. For the Boston shingles, construct a 95% confidence interval estimate for the mean granule loss.
b. For the Vermont shingles, construct a 95% confidence interval estimate for the mean granule loss.
c. Do you think the assumption needed to construct the confidence interval estimates in (a) and (b) is valid?
d. Based on the results of (a) and (b), what conclusions can you reach concerning the mean granule loss of the Boston and Vermont shingles?

REPORT WRITING EXERCISE

8.69 Referring to the results in Problem 8.66 concerning the answer time of calls, write a report that summarizes your conclusions.

CASES

CHAPTER 8

Managing Ashland MultiComm Services

Marketing Manager Lauren Adler seeks to increase the number of subscribers to the AMS *3-For-All* cable TV & Internet and smartphone service. Her staff has designed the following 10-question survey to help determine various characteristics of households who subscribe to AMS cable or cellphone services.

1. Does your household subscribe to smartphone service from Ashland?
  (1) Yes
  (2) No
2. Does your household subscribe to Internet service from Ashland?
  (1) Yes
  (2) No

3. How often do you watch streaming video on any device?
   (1) Every day   (2) Most days
   (3) Occasionally or never

4. What type of cable television service do you have?
   (1) Basic or none   (2) Enhanced

5. How often do you watch premium content that requires an extra fee?
   (1) Almost every day   (2) Several times a week
   (3) Rarely   (4) Never

6. Which method did you use to obtain your current AMS subscription?
   (1) AMS email/text offer   (4) In-store signup
   (2) AMS toll-free number   (5) MyTVLab promotion
   (3) AMS website

7. Would you consider subscribing to the *3-For-All* service for a trial period if a discount were offered?
   (1) Yes   (2) No
   (If no, skip to question 9.)

8. If purchased separately, cable TV and Internet and smartphone service would currently cost $160 per month. How much would you be willing to pay per month for the *3-For-All* service?

9. Does your household use another provider of cellphone services?
   (1) Yes   (2) No

10. AMS may distribute vouchers good for one free smartphone for subscribers who agree to a two-year subscription contract to the *3-For-All* service. Would being eligible to receive a voucher cause you to agree to the two-year term?
    (1) Yes   (2) No

Of the 500 households selected that subscribe to cable television service from Ashland, 82 households either refused to participate, could not be contacted after repeated attempts, or had telephone numbers that were not in service. The summary results for the 418 households that were contacted are as follows:

Household Has AMS Smartphone Service	Frequency
Yes	83
No	335
Household Has AMS Internet Service	**Frequency**
Yes	262
No	156
Streams Video	**Frequency**
Every day	170
Most days	166
Occasionally or never	82
Type of Cable Service	**Frequency**
Basic or none	164
Enhanced	254
Watches Premium Content	**Frequency**
Almost every day	16
Several times a week	40
Rarely	179
Never	183

Method Used to Obtain Subscription	Frequency
AMS email/text offer	70
AMS toll-free number	64
AMS website	236
In-store signup	36
MyTVLab promotion	12
Would Consider Discounted Trial Offer	**Frequency**
Yes	40
No	378

Trial Monthly Rate ($) Willing to Pay (stored in AMS8)
100 79 114 50   91 106 67 110 70 113 90 115 98 75 119
100 90   60 89 105   65 91   86 91   84 92   95 85 80 108
90 97   79 91 125   99 98   50 77   85

Uses Another Cellphone Provider	Frequency
Yes	369
No	49
Voucher for Two-Year Agreement	**Frequency**
Yes	38
No	380

Analyze the results of the survey of Ashland households that receive AMS cable television service. Write a report that discusses the marketing implications of the survey results for Ashland MultiComm Services.

Digital Case

Apply your knowledge about confidence interval estimation in this Digital Case, which extends the MyTVLab Digital Case from Chapter 6.

Among its other features, the MyTVLab website allows customers to purchase MyTVLab LifeStyles merchandise online. To handle payment processing, the management of MyTVLab has contracted with the following firms:

- **PayAFriend (PAF)**—This is an online payment system with which customers and businesses such as MyTVLab register in order to exchange payments in a secure and convenient manner, without the need for a credit card.
- **Continental Banking Company (Conbanco)**—This processing services provider allows MyTVLab customers to pay for merchandise using nationally recognized credit cards issued by a financial institution.

To reduce costs, management is considering eliminating one of these two payment systems. However, Lorraine Hildick of the sales department suspects that customers use the two forms of payment in unequal numbers and that customers display different buying behaviors when using the two forms of payment. Therefore, she would like to first determine the following:

- The proportion of customers using PAF and the proportion of customers using a credit card to pay for their purchases.
- The mean purchase amount when using PAF and the mean purchase amount when using a credit card.

Assist Ms. Hildick by preparing an appropriate analysis. Open **PaymentsSample.pdf**, read Ms. Hildick's comments, and use her random sample of 50 transactions as the basis for your analysis. Summarize your findings to determine whether Ms. Hildick's conjectures about MyTVLab LifeStyle customer purchasing behaviors are correct. If you want the sampling error to be no more than $3 when estimating the mean purchase amount, is Ms. Hildick's sample large enough to perform a valid analysis?

Sure Value Convenience Stores

You work in the corporate office for a nationwide convenience store franchise that operates nearly 10,000 stores. The per-store daily customer count has been steady, at 900, for some time (i.e., the mean number of customers in a store in one day is 900). To increase the customer count, the franchise is considering cutting coffee prices. The 12-ounce size will now be $0.59 instead of $0.99, and the 16-ounce size will be $0.69 instead of $1.19. Even with this reduction in price, the franchise will have a 40% gross margin on coffee. To test the new initiative, the franchise has reduced coffee prices in a sample of 34 stores, where customer counts have been running almost exactly at the national average of 900. After four weeks, the sample stores stabilize at a mean customer count of 974 and a standard deviation of 96. This increase seems like a substantial amount to you, but it also seems like a pretty small sample. Is there some way to get a feel for what the mean per-store count in all the stores will be if you cut coffee prices nationwide? Do you think reducing coffee prices is a good strategy for increasing the mean number of customers?

CardioGood Fitness

Return to the CardioGood Fitness case first presented on page 33. Using the data stored in CardioGood Fitness :

1. Construct 95% confidence interval estimates to create a customer profile for each CardioGood Fitness treadmill product line.

2. Write a report to be presented to the management of CardioGood Fitness detailing your findings.

More Descriptive Choices Follow-Up

Follow up the More Descriptive Choices Revisited, Using Statistics scenario on page 159 by constructing 95% confidence intervals estimates of the one-year return percentages, five-year return percentages, and ten-year return percentages for the sample of growth and value funds and for the small, mid-cap, and large market cap funds (stored in Retirement Funds). In your analysis, examine differences between the growth and value funds as well as the differences among the small, mid-cap, and large market cap funds.

Clear Mountain State Student Survey

The Student News Service at Clear Mountain State University (CMSU) has decided to gather data about the undergraduate students that attend CMSU. They create and distribute a survey of 14 questions and receive responses from 111 undergraduates (stored in StudentSurvey). For each variable included in the survey, construct a 95% confidence interval estimate for the population characteristic and write a report summarizing your conclusions.

▾EXCEL GUIDE

EG8.1 CONFIDENCE INTERVAL ESTIMATE for the MEAN (σ KNOWN)

Key Technique Use the **NORM.S.INV**(*cumulative percentage*) to compute the Z value for one-half of the $(1 - \alpha)$ value and use the **CONFIDENCE(1–***confidence level, population standard deviation***,** *sample size*) function to compute the half-width of a confidence interval.

Example Compute the confidence interval estimate for the mean for the Example 8.1 mean fill amount problem on page 280.

PHStat Use **Estimate for the Mean, sigma known**.

For the example, select **PHStat➔Confidence Intervals➔ Estimate for the Mean, sigma known**. In the procedure's dialog box (shown below):

1. Enter **15** as the **Population Standard Deviation**.
2. Enter **95** as the **Confidence Level** percentage.
3. Click **Sample Statistics Known** and enter **100** as the **Sample Size** and **369.27** as the **Sample Mean**.
4. Enter a **Title** and click **OK**.

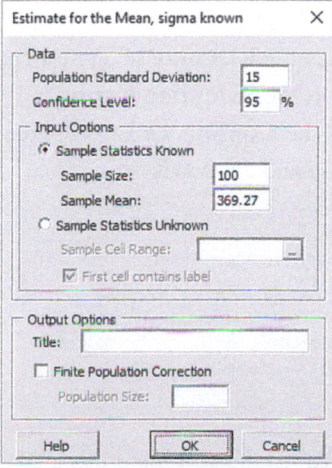

When using unsummarized data, click **Sample Statistics Unknown** and enter the **Sample Cell Range** in step 3.

Workbook Use the **COMPUTE worksheet** of the **CIE sigma known workbook** as a template.
The worksheet already contains the data for the example.

For other problems, change the **Population Standard Deviation, Sample Mean, Sample Size**, and **Confidence Level** values in cells B4 through B7.

EG8.2 CONFIDENCE INTERVAL ESTIMATE for the MEAN (σ UNKNOWN)

Key Technique Use the **T.INV.2T(1–***confidence level, degrees of freedom*) function to determine the critical value from the t distribution.

Example Compute the Figure 8.7 confidence interval estimate for the mean sales invoice amount show on page 284.

PHStat Use **Estimate for the Mean, sigma unknown**.

For the example, select **PHStat➔Confidence Intervals➔ Estimate for the Mean, sigma unknown**. In the procedure's dialog box (shown below):

1. Enter **95** as the **Confidence Level** percentage.
2. Click **Sample Statistics Known** and enter **100** as the **Sample Size**, **110.27** as the **Sample Mean**, and **28.95** as the **Sample Std. Deviation**.
3. Enter a **Title** and click **OK**.

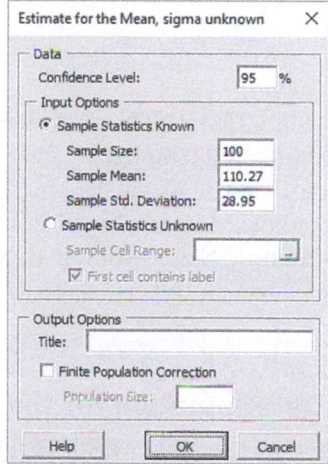

When using unsummarized data, click **Sample Statistics Unknown** and enter the **Sample Cell Range** in step 2.

Workbook Use the **COMPUTE worksheet** of the **CIE sigma unknown workbook** as a template.
The worksheet already contains the data for the example.

For other problems, change the **Sample Standard Deviation, Sample Mean, Sample Size**, and **Confidence Level** values in cells B4 through B7.

EG8.3 CONFIDENCE INTERVAL ESTIMATE for the PROPORTION

Key Technique Use the **NORM.S.INV((1–***confidence level***)/2)** function to compute the Z value.

Example Compute the Figure 8.12 confidence interval estimate for the proportion of in-error sales invoices on page 290.

PHStat Use **Estimate for the Proportion**.

For the example, select **PHStat→Confidence Intervals→ Estimate for the Proportion**. In the procedure's dialog box (shown below):

1. Enter **100** as the **Sample Size**.
2. Enter **10** as the **Number of Successes**.
3. Enter **95** as the **Confidence Level** percentage.
4. Enter a **Title** and click **OK**.

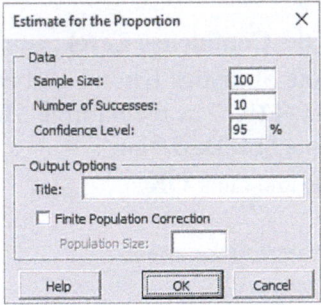

Workbook Use the **COMPUTE worksheet** of the **CIE Proportion workbook** as a template.
The worksheet already contains the data for the example.

To compute confidence interval estimates for other problems, change the **Sample Size**, **Number of Successes**, and **Confidence Level** values in cells B4 through B6.

EG8.4 DETERMINING SAMPLE SIZE

Sample Size Determination for the Mean

Key Technique Use the **NORM.S.INV((1–***confidence level***)/2)** function to compute the Z value and use the **ROUNDUP(***calculated sample size***, 0)** function to round up the computed sample size to the next higher integer.

Example Determine the sample size for the Figure 8.13 mean sales invoice amount example on page 293.

PHStat Use **Determination for the Mean**.

For the example, select **PHStat→Sample Size→ Determination for the Mean**. In the procedure's dialog box (shown at the top right):

1. Enter **25** as the **Population Standard Deviation**.
2. Enter **5** as the **Sampling Error**.
3. Enter **95** as the **Confidence Level** percentage.
4. Enter a **Title** and click **OK**.

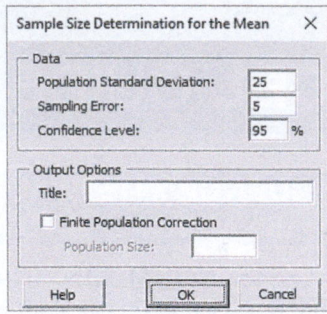

Workbook Use the **COMPUTE worksheet** of the **Sample Size Mean workbook** as a template.
The worksheet already contains the data for the example.

For other problems, change the **Population Standard Deviation**, **Sampling Error**, and **Confidence Level** values in cells B4 through B6.

Sample Size Determination for the Proportion

Key Technique Use the **NORM.S.INV** and **ROUNDUP** functions discussed previously to help determine the sample size needed for estimating the proportion.

Example Determine the sample size for the Figure 8.14 proportion of in-error sales invoices example on page 295.

PHStat Use **Determination for the Proportion**.

For the example, select **PHStat→Sample Size→ Determination for the Proportion**. In the procedure's dialog box (shown below):

1. Enter **0.15** as the **Estimate of True Proportion**.
2. Enter **0.07** as the **Sampling Error**.
3. Enter **95** as the **Confidence Level** percentage.
4. Enter a **Title** and click **OK**.

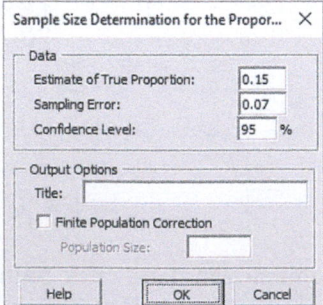

Workbook Use the **COMPUTE worksheet** of the **Sample Size Proportion workbook** as a template.
The worksheet already contains the data for the example.

To compute confidence interval estimates for other problems, change the **Estimate of True Proportion**, **Sampling Error**, and **Confidence Level** in cells B4 through B6.

▾JMP GUIDE

JG8.1 CONFIDENCE INTERVAL ESTIMATE for the MEAN (σ KNOWN)

Use the **Confidence Interval for One Mean calculator**.

For example, to compute the confidence interval estimate for the mean for the Example 8.1 mean fill amount problem on page 280, select **Help → Sample Data** and:

1. In the Sample Data Index window, click the **Calculators disclosure button** (gray triangle).
2. Click **Confidence Interval for One Mean** in the revealed list.
3. In the Choose Input dialog box, click **Summary Statistics** and then click **OK**.

In the CI for Mean from Summary Statistics dialog box (shown below):

4. Select the **z** option.
5. Enter **369.27** as the **Sample Average**.
6. Enter **15** as the **Population Standard Deviation**.
7. Enter **100** as the **Sample Size**.
8. Enter **0.95** as the **Confidence Level**.
9. Click **OK**.

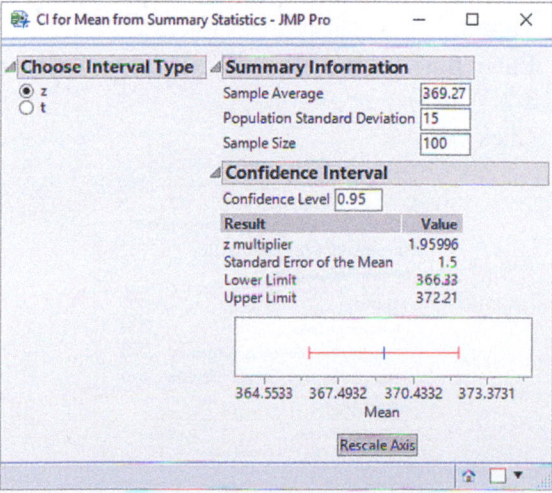

JMP displays results in the calculator window as shown. Because of the nature of JMP calculators, to save results, save window as a JMP journal (*.jrn) file. For unsummarized data, open to the data table that contains the data and follow steps 1 through 2, and modify step 3 to click **Raw Data**. In the next (Select Columns) dialog box, select a column and click **Pick a Numeric Column** and then press **OK**. JMP displays a new window of results. In this window, the known sigma value can be entered.

JG8.2 CONFIDENCE INTERVAL ESTIMATE for the MEAN (σ UNKNOWN)

Use the **Confidence Interval for One Mean calculator**.

For example, to compute the confidence interval estimate for the mean for the Section 8.2 invoice amount problem on page 284, select **Help → Sample Data** and:

1. In the Sample Data Index window, click the **Calculators disclosure button** (gray triangle).
2. Click **Confidence Interval for One Mean** in the revealed list.
3. In the Choose Input dialog box, click **Summary Statistics** and then click **OK**.

In the CI for Mean from Summary Statistics dialog box (shown below):

4. Select the **t** option.
5. Enter **110.27** as the **Sample Average**.
6. Enter **28.95** as the **Sample Standard Deviation**.
7. Enter **100** as the **Sample Size**.
8. Enter **0.95** as the **Confidence Level**.
9. Click **OK**.

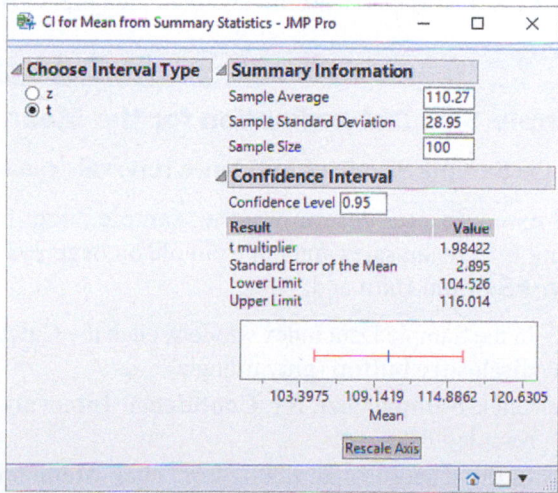

JMP displays results in the calculator window as shown above. Because of the nature of JMP calculators, to save results, save window as a JMP journal (*.jrn) file. For unsummarized data, open to the data table that contains the data and follow steps 1 through 2, and modify step 3 to click **Raw Data**. In the next (Select Columns) dialog box, select a column and click **Pick a Numeric Column** and then press **OK**. JMP displays a new window of results. In this window, select the **t** option.

JG8.3 CONFIDENCE INTERVAL ESTIMATE for the PROPORTION

Use the **Confidence Interval for One Proportion calculator**.

For example, to compute the Figure 8.12 confidence interval estimate for the proportion of in-error sales invoices on page 290, select **Help ➔ Sample Data** and:

1. In the Sample Data Index window, click the **Calculators disclosure button** (gray triangle).
2. Click **Confidence Interval for One Proportion** in the revealed list.
3. In the Choose Input dialog box, click **Summary Statistics** and then click **OK**.

In the CI for Proportion from Summary Statistics dialog box:

4. Select the **Normal Approximation** option.
5. Enter **10** as the **Number of Successes**.
6. Enter **100** as the **Sample Size**.
7. Enter **0.95** as the **Confidence Level**.
8. Click **OK**.

JMP displays the calculator window results shown in Figure 8.12. Because of the nature of JMP calculators, to save results, save window as a JMP journal (*.jrn) file. For unsummarized data, open to the data table that contains the data and follow steps 1 through 2, and modify step 3 to click **Raw Data**. In the next (Select Columns) dialog box, select a column and click **Pick a Numeric Column** and then then press **OK**.

JG8.4 DETERMINING SAMPLE SIZE

Sample Size Determination for the Mean

Use the **Sample Size for Confidence Intervals calculator**.

For example, to determine the sample size for the Figure 8.13 mean sales amount example on page 293, select **Help ➔ Sample Data** and:

1. In the Sample Data Index window, click the **Calculators disclosure button** (gray triangle).
2. Click **Sample Size for Confidence Intervals** in the revealed list.
3. In the Choose Input dialog box, click **Mean** and then click **OK**.

In the Sample Size Determination dialog box (shown at the top right):

4. Enter **0.95** as the **Confidence Level**.
5. Enter **25** as the **Population Std. Dev. (Planning Value)**.
6. Enter **5** as the **Desired Margin of Error (C.I. 1/2-Width)**.
7. Click **OK**.

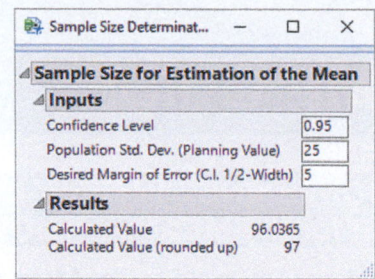

JMP displays results in the calculator window as shown. Because of the nature of JMP calculators, to save results, save window as a JMP journal (*.jrn) file.

Sample Size Determination for the Proportion

Use the **Sample Size for Confidence Intervals calculator**.

For example, to determine the sample size for the Figure 8.14 proportion of in-error sales invoices example on page 295, select **Help ➔ Sample Data** and:

1. In the Sample Data Index window, click the **Calculators disclosure button** (gray triangle).
2. Click **Sample Size for Confidence Intervals** in the revealed list.
3. In the Choose Input dialog box, click **Proportion** and then click **OK**.

In the Sample Size Determination dialog box:

1. Enter **0.95** as the **Confidence Level**.
2. Enter **0.15** as the **Expected Proportion (Planning Value)**.
3. Enter **0.07** as the **Desired Margin of Error (C.I. 1/2-Width)**.
4. Click **OK**.

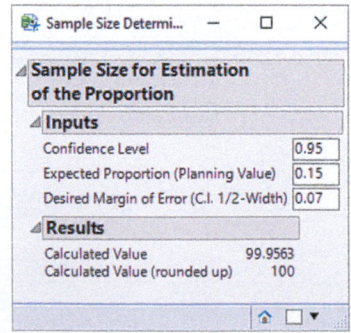

JMP displays results in the calculator window as shown. Because of the nature of JMP calculators, to save results, save window as a JMP journal (*.jrn) file.

▼MINITAB GUIDE

MG8.1 CONFIDENCE INTERVAL ESTIMATE for the MEAN (σ KNOWN)

Use **1-Sample Z**.

For example, to compute the estimate for the Example 8.1 mean fill amount problem on page 280, select **Stat → Basic Statistics → 1-Sample Z**. In the One-Sample Z for the Mean dialog box (shown below):

1. Select **Summarized data** from the pull-down list.

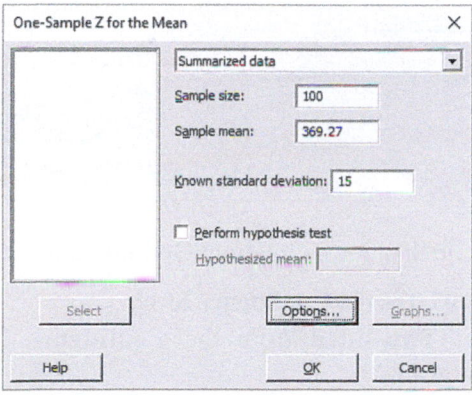

2. Enter **100** in the **Sample size** box and **369.27** in the **Mean** box.
3. Enter **15** in the **Known Standard deviation** box.
4. Click **Options**.

In the One-Sample Z: Options dialog box (shown below):

5. Enter **95.0** in the **Confidence level** box.
6. Select **Mean ≠ hypothesized mean** from the **Alternative hypothesis** drop-down list.
7. Click **OK**.

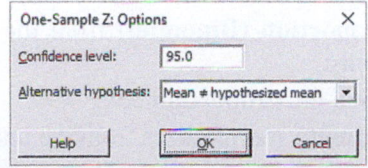

8. Back in the original dialog box, click **OK**.

When using unsummarized data, select **One or more samples, each in a column** in step 1 and, in step 2, enter the name of the column that contains the data in the unlabeled box below the pull-down list.

MG8.2 CONFIDENCE INTERVAL ESTIMATE for the MEAN (σ UNKNOWN)

Use **1-Sample t**.

For example, to compute the Figure 8.7 estimate for the mean sales invoice amount on page 284, select **Stat → Basic Statistics → 1-Sample t**. In the One-Sample t for the Mean dialog box (shown below):

1. Select **Summarized data** from the pull-down list.
2. Enter **100** in the **Sample size** box, **110.27** in the **Mean** box, and **28.95** in the **Standard deviation** box.
3. Click **Options**.

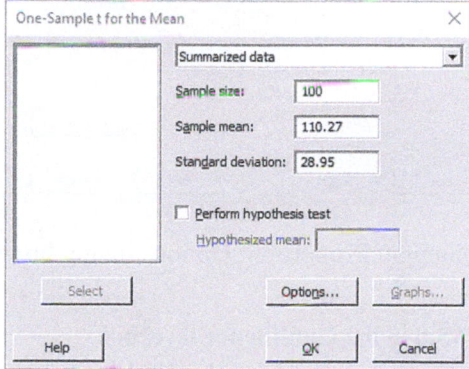

In the One-Sample t: Options dialog box (similar to the One-Sample Z: Options dialog box):

4. Enter **95.0** in the **Confidence level** box.
5. Select **Mean ≠ hypothesized mean** from the **Alternative hypothesis** drop-down list.
6. Click **OK**.
7. Back in the original dialog box, click **OK**.

When using unsummarized data, select **One or more Samples, each in a column** in step 1 and, in step 2, enter the name of the column that contains the data in the unlabeled box below the pull-down list. To create the Figure 8.9 boxplot on page 285, replace step 7 with these steps 7 through 9:

7. Back in the original dialog box, click **Graphs**.
8. In the 1-Sample t: Graphs dialog box, check **Boxplot of data** and then click **OK**.
9. Back in the original dialog box, click **OK**.

MG8.3 CONFIDENCE INTERVAL ESTIMATE for the PROPORTION

Use **1 Proportion**.

For example, to compute the Figure 8.12 estimate for the proportion of in-error sales invoices on page 290, select **Stat → Basic Statistics → 1 Proportion**. In the One-Sample Proportion dialog box (shown below):

1. Select **Summarized data** from the pull-down list.
2. Enter **10** in the **Number of events** box and **100** in the **Number of trials** box.
3. Click **Options**.

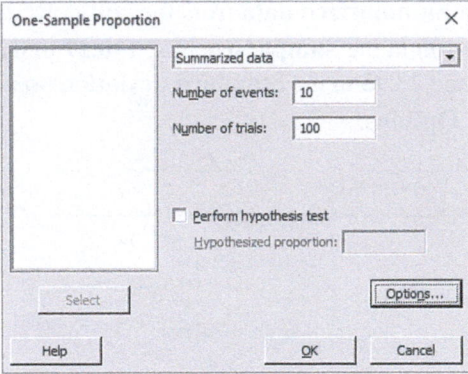

In the One-Sample Proportion: Options dialog box (shown below):

4. Enter **95.0** in the **Confidence level** box.
5. Select **Proportion ≠ hypothesized proportion** from the **Alternative hypothesis** drop-down list.
6. Select **Normal approximation** from the **Method** pull-down list.
7. Click **OK**.

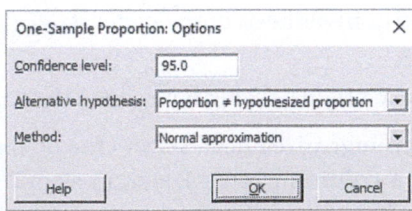

8. Back in the original dialog box, click **OK**.

When using unsummarized data, select **One or more samples, each in a column** in step 1 and enter the name of the column that contains the data in the unlabeled box below the pull-down list in step 2.

MG8.4 DETERMINING SAMPLE SIZE

Sample Size Determination for the Mean

Use **Sample Size for Estimation**.

For example, to determine the sample size for the Figure 8.13 mean sales amount example on page 293, select **Stat → Power**

and **Sample Size → Sample Size for Estimation**. In the procedure's dialog box (shown below):

1. Select **Mean (Normal)** from the **Parameter** pull-down list.
2. Enter **25** in the **Standard deviation** box.
3. Select **Estimate sample sizes** from the unlabeled pull-down list.
4. Enter **5** in the **Margins of error for confidence intervals**.
5. Click **Options**.

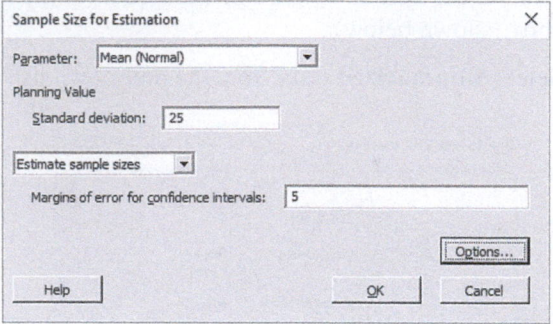

In the Sample Size for Estimation: Options dialog box:

6. Enter **95.0** as the **Confidence level**.
7. Select **Two-sided** from the **Confidence interval** pull-down list.
8. Check **Assume population standard deviation is known**.
9. Click **OK**.
10. Back in the original dialog box, click **OK**.

Sample Size Determination for the Proportion

Use **Sample Size for Estimation**.

For example, to determine the sample size for the Figure 8.14 proportion of in-error sales invoices example on page 295, select **Stat → Power and Sample Size → Sample Size for Estimation**. In the procedure's dialog box:

1. Select **Proportion (Binomial)** from the **Parameter** pull-down list.
2. Enter **0.15** in the **Proportion** box.
3. Select **Estimate sample sizes** from the unlabeled pull-down list.
4. Enter **0.07** in the **Margins of error for confidence intervals**.
5. Click **Options**.

In the Sample Size for Estimation: Options dialog box:

6. Enter **95.0** as the **Confidence level**.
7. Select **Two-sided** from the **Confidence interval** pull-down list.
8. Click **OK**.
9. Back in the original dialog box, click **OK**.

Fundamentals of Hypothesis Testing: One-Sample Tests

9

CONTENTS

"Significant Testing at Oxford Cereals"

OBJECTIVES

- Learn the basic principles of hypothesis testing
- How to use hypothesis testing to test a mean or proportion
- Identify the assumptions of each hypothesis-testing procedure, how to evaluate them, and the consequences if they are seriously violated
- Become aware of the pitfalls and ethical issues involved in hypothesis testing
- How to avoid the pitfalls involved in hypothesis testing

▼USING **STATISTICS**
Significant Testing at Oxford Cereals

As in Chapter 7, you again find yourself as plant operations manager for Oxford Cereals. Among other responsibilities, you are responsible for monitoring the amount in each cereal box filled. Company specifications require a mean weight of 368 grams per box. You must adjust the cereal-filling process when the mean fill-weight in the population of boxes differs from 368 grams. Adjusting the process requires shutting down the cereal production line temporarily, so you do not want to make unnecessary adjustments.

What decision-making method can you use to decide if the cereal-filling process needs to be adjusted? You decide to begin by selecting a random sample of 25 filled boxes and weighing each box. From the weights collected, you compute a sample mean. How could that sample mean be used to help decide whether adjustment is necessary?

Chapter 7 discusses methods to determine whether the value of a sample mean is consistent with a known population mean. In this second Oxford Cereals scenario, you seek to use a sample mean to validate a claim about the population mean, a somewhat different analysis. For such analyses, you use the inferential method called *hypothesis testing*. In hypothesis testing, you state a claim, or *null hypothesis*, unambiguously. You examine a sample statistic to see if it better supports the null hypothesis or a mutually exclusive *alternative hypothesis*. For the Oxford Cereals scenario, hypothesis testing would permit you to infer either

- the mean weight of the cereal boxes in a sample is a value consistent with what you would expect if the mean of the entire population of cereal boxes were 368 grams, *or*
- the population mean is not equal to 368 grams because the sample mean is significantly different from 368 grams.

9.1 Fundamentals of Hypothesis Testing

Hypothesis testing analyzes *differences* between a sample statistic and the results you would expect if a null hypothesis was true. In doing so, hypothesis testing gives you a method to make inferences about a population parameter that is based on the sample statistic a hypothesis test examines. For the Oxford Cereals scenario, a hypothesis test would examine the sample mean fill amount of the random sample of 25 filled boxes in order to make inferences of the population mean fill amount.

The **null hypothesis**, represented by the symbol H_0, often states a status quo case. For the Oxford Cereals scenario, the status quo case would be the cereal filling process is working as intended and, therefore, the population mean fill amount is 368 grams, stated as:

$$H_0: \mu = 368$$

The **alternative hypothesis**, represented by the symbol H_1, states a claim that is contrary to the null hypothesis. For the Oxford Cereals scenario, the contrary claim would be stated as:

$$H_1: \mu \neq 368$$

studentTIP

Hypothesis testing reaches conclusions about parameters, not statistics.

A pair of null and alternative hypotheses are always mutually exclusive—only one of them can be true. To use the hypothesis test methods that this book discusses, a pair of null and alternative hypotheses must also be collectively exhaustive, as the pair for the Oxford Cereals scenario is. Note that the null and alternative hypotheses are always stated in terms of the population parameter because a hypothesis test always examines a sample statistic.

You reject the null hypothesis in favor of the alternative hypothesis when a hypothesis test provides sufficient evidence from the sample data to show that the null hypothesis is false. The alternative hypothesis is often the focus of underlying research. For example, in new product research sponsored by the developer of that product, the null hypothesis would be that the new product is as equally effective as existing products, even as focus of the research would be proving evidence that suggests the product is different. In the Oxford Cereals scenario, discovering sufficient evidence that would cause you to reject the null hypothesis would lead to corrective action: stopping production and taking corrective action. In a sense, hypothesis testing for this case is focused on whether these special actions are required.

Finding insufficient evidence causes you not to reject the null hypothesis. This does not mean that hypothesis testing can "prove" that the null hypothesis is true; hypothesis testing can only show that the results have failed to prove that the null hypothesis is false—an important distinction. For the Oxford Cereals scenario, if you do not reject the null hypothesis, you cannot claim that the hypothesis test "proves" that the population mean fill amount is 368 grams. You can only say that insufficient evidence exists to challenge your assertion that the population mean is 368 grams.

Understanding precisely what hypothesis testing does and avoiding misstatements about hypothesis testing such as that a test has *proved* a null (or alternative) hypothesis claim to be true forms the basis for using hypothesis testing correctly. Exhibit 9.1 summarizes the fundamental hypothesis testing concepts that you need to know to use hypothesis testing knowingly.

EXHIBIT 9.1

Fundamental Hypothesis Testing Concepts

The null hypothesis, H_0, states a status quo claim.

The alternative hypothesis, H_1, states a claim that is contrary to the null hypothesis and often represents a research claim or specific inference that an analyst seeks to prove.

A null and alternative pair of hypotheses are always collectively exhaustive.

If you reject the null hypothesis, you have strong statistical evidence that the alternative hypothesis is correct.

If you do not reject the null hypothesis, you have not proven the null hypothesis. (Rather, you have only failed to prove the alternative hypothesis.)

The null hypothesis always refers to a population parameter such as μ and not a sample statistic such as $\overline{X}$.

The null hypothesis always includes an equals sign when stating a claim about the population parameter, for example, H_0: $\mu = 368$ grams.

The alternative hypothesis never includes an equals sign when stating a claim about the population parameter.

EXAMPLE 9.1

The Null and Alternative Hypotheses

You are the manager of a fast-food restaurant. You want to determine whether the waiting time to place an order has changed in the past month from its previous population mean value of 4.5 minutes. State the null and alternative hypotheses.

SOLUTION The null hypothesis is that the population mean has not changed from its previous value of 4.5 minutes. This is stated as

$$H_0: \mu = 4.5$$

The alternative hypothesis is the opposite of the null hypothesis. Because the null hypothesis is that the population mean is 4.5 minutes, the alternative hypothesis is that the population mean is not 4.5 minutes. This is stated as

$$H_1: \mu \neq 4.5$$

The Critical Value of the Test Statistic

Hypothesis testing uses sample data to determine how likely it is that the null hypothesis is true. In the Oxford Cereal Company scenario, the null hypothesis is that the mean amount of cereal per box in the entire filling process is 368 grams (the population parameter specified by the company). You select a sample of boxes from the filling process, weigh each box, and compute the sample mean $\overline{X}$. This sample statistic is an estimate of the corresponding parameter, the population mean, μ. Even if the null hypothesis is true, the sample statistic $\overline{X}$ is likely to differ from the value of the parameter (the population mean, μ) because of variation due to sampling.

You do expect the sample statistic to be close to the population parameter if the null hypothesis is true. If the sample statistic is close to the population parameter, you have insufficient evidence to reject the null hypothesis. For example, if the sample mean is 367.9 grams, you might conclude that the population mean has not changed (i.e., $\mu = 368$) because a sample mean of 367.9 grams is very close to the hypothesized value of 368 grams. Intuitively, you think that it is likely that you could get a sample mean of 367.9 grams from a population whose mean is 368.

However, if there is a large difference between the value of the sample statistic and the hypothesized value of the population parameter, you might conclude that the null hypothesis is false. For example, if the sample mean is 320 grams, you might conclude that the population mean is not 368 grams (i.e., $\mu \neq 368$) because the sample mean is very far from the hypothesized value of 368 grams. In such a case, you might conclude that it is very unlikely to get a sample mean of 320 grams if the population mean is really 368 grams. Therefore, it is more logical to conclude that the population mean is not equal to 368 grams. Here you reject the null hypothesis.

However, the decision-making process is not always so clear-cut. Determining what is "very close" and what is "very different" is arbitrary without clear definitions. Hypothesis-testing methodology provides clear definitions for evaluating differences. Furthermore, it enables you to quantify the decision-making process by computing the probability of getting a certain sample result if the null hypothesis is true. You calculate this probability by determining the sampling distribution for the sample statistic of interest (e.g., the sample mean) and then computing the particular **test statistic** based on the given sample result. Because the sampling distribution for the test statistic often follows a well-known statistical distribution, such as the standardized normal distribution or *t* distribution, you can use these distributions to help determine whether the null hypothesis is true.

Regions of Rejection and Nonrejection

The sampling distribution of the test statistic is divided into two regions, a **region of rejection** (sometimes called the critical region) and a **region of nonrejection** (see Figure 9.1). If the test statistic falls into the region of nonrejection, you do not reject the null hypothesis. In the Oxford Cereals scenario, you conclude that there is insufficient evidence that the population mean fill is different from 368 grams. If the test statistic falls into the rejection region, you reject the null hypothesis. In this case, you conclude that the population mean is not 368 grams.

FIGURE 9.1

Regions of rejection and nonrejection in hypothesis testing

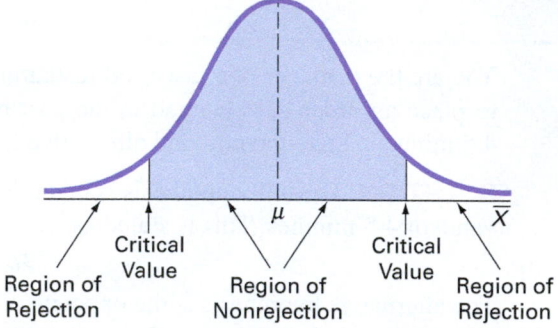

The region of rejection consists of the values of the test statistic that are unlikely to occur if the null hypothesis is true. These values are much more likely to occur if the null hypothesis is false. Therefore, if a value of the test statistic falls into this rejection region, you reject the null hypothesis because that value is unlikely if the null hypothesis is true.

To make a decision concerning the null hypothesis, you first determine the **critical value** of the test statistic. The critical value divides the nonrejection region from the rejection region. Determining the critical value depends on the size of the rejection region. The size of the rejection region is directly related to the risks involved in using only sample evidence to make decisions about a population parameter.

Risks in Decision Making Using Hypothesis Testing

Using hypothesis testing involves the risk of reaching an incorrect conclusion. You might wrongly reject a true null hypothesis, H_0, or, conversely, you might wrongly *not* reject a false null hypothesis, H_0. These types of risk are called Type I and Type II errors.

TYPE I AND TYPE II ERRORS

A **Type I error** occurs if you reject the null hypothesis, H_0, when it is true and should not be rejected. A Type I error is a "false alarm." The probability of a Type I error occurring is α.

A **Type II error** occurs if you do not reject the null hypothesis, H_0, when it is false and should be rejected. A Type II error represents a "missed opportunity" to take some corrective action. The probability of a Type II error occurring is β.

In the Oxford Cereals scenario, you would make a Type I error if you concluded that the population mean fill is *not* 368 grams when it *is* 368 grams. This error causes you to needlessly adjust the filling process (the "false alarm") even though the process is working properly. In the same scenario, you would make a Type II error if you concluded that the population mean fill *is* 368 grams when it is *not* 368 grams. In this case, you would allow the process to continue without adjustment, even though an adjustment is needed (the "missed opportunity").

Traditionally, you control the Type I error by determining the risk level, α (the lowercase Greek letter *alpha*), that you are willing to have of rejecting the null hypothesis when it is true. This risk, or probability, of committing a Type I error is called the *level of significance* (α). Because you specify the level of significance before you perform the hypothesis test, you directly control the risk of committing a Type I error. Traditionally, you select a level of 0.01, 0.05, or 0.10. The choice of a particular risk level for making a Type I error depends on the cost of making a Type I error. After you specify the value for α, you can then determine the critical values that divide the rejection and nonrejection regions. You know the size of the rejection region because α is the probability of rejection when the null hypothesis is true. From this, you can then determine the critical value or values that divide the rejection and nonrejection regions.

The probability of committing a Type II error is called the β *risk*. Unlike the Type I error, which you control through the selection of α, the probability of making a Type II error depends on the difference between the hypothesized and actual values of the population parameter. Because large differences are easier to find than small ones, if the difference between the hypothesized and actual values of the population parameter is large, β is small. For example, if the population mean is 330 grams, there is a small chance (β) that you will conclude that the mean has not changed from 368 grams. However, if the difference between the hypothesized and actual values of the parameter is small, β is large. For example, if the population mean is actually 367 grams, there is a large chance (β) that you will conclude that the mean is still 368 grams.

PROBABILITY OF TYPE I AND TYPE II ERRORS

The **level of significance (α)** of a statistical test is the probability of committing a Type I error.

The $\boldsymbol{\beta}$ **risk** is the probability of committing a Type II error.

The complement of the probability of a Type I error, $(1 - \alpha)$, is called the *confidence coefficient*. The confidence coefficient is the probability that you will not reject the null hypothesis, H_0, when it is true and should not be rejected. In the Oxford Cereals scenario, the confidence coefficient measures the probability of concluding that the population mean fill is 368 grams when it is actually 368 grams.

The complement of the probability of a Type II error, $(1 - \beta)$, is called the *power of a statistical test*. The power of a statistical test is the probability that you will reject the null hypothesis when it is false and should be rejected (see online Section 9.6 for a detailed discussion of the power of the test). In the Oxford Cereals scenario, the power of the test is the probability that you will correctly conclude that the mean fill amount is not 368 grams when it actually is not 368 grams.

COMPLEMENTS OF TYPE I AND TYPE II ERRORS

The **confidence coefficient**, $(1 - \alpha)$, is the probability that you will not reject the null hypothesis, H_0, when it is true and should not be rejected.

The **power of a statistical test**, $(1 - \beta)$, is the probability that you will reject the null hypothesis when it is false and should be rejected.

Table 9.1 illustrates the results of the two possible decisions (do not reject H_0 or reject H_0) that you can make in any hypothesis test. You can make a correct decision or make one of two types of errors.

TABLE 9.1
Hypothesis Testing and Decision Making

	ACTUAL SITUATION	
STATISTICAL DECISION	H_0 **True**	H_0 **False**
Do not reject H_0	Correct decision Confidence coefficient $= (1 - \alpha)$	Type II error $P(\text{Type II error}) = \beta$
Reject H_0	Type I error $P(\text{Type I error}) = \alpha$	Correct decision Power $= (1 - \beta)$

One way to reduce the probability of making a Type II error is by increasing the sample size. Large samples generally permit you to detect even very small differences between the hypothesized values and the actual population parameters. For a given level of α, increasing the sample size decreases β and therefore increases the power of the statistical test to detect that the null hypothesis, H_0, is false.

However, there is always a limit to your resources, and this affects the decision of how large a sample you can select. For any given sample size, you must consider the trade-offs between the two possible types of errors. Because you can directly control the risk of a Type I error, you can reduce this risk by selecting a smaller value for α. For example, if the negative consequences associated with making a Type I error are substantial, you could select $\alpha = 0.01$ instead of 0.05. However, when you decrease α, you increase β, so reducing the risk of a Type I error results in an increased risk of a Type II error. However, to reduce β, you could select a larger value for α. Therefore, if it is important to try to avoid a Type II error, you can select an α of 0.05 or 0.10 instead of 0.01.

In the Oxford Cereals scenario, the risk of a Type I error occurring involves concluding that the mean fill amount has changed from the hypothesized 368 grams when it actually has not changed. The risk of a Type II error occurring involves concluding that the mean fill amount has not changed from the hypothesized 368 grams when it actually has changed. The choice of reasonable values for α and β depends on the costs inherent in each type of error. For example, if it is very costly to change the cereal-filling process, you would want to be very confident that a change is needed before making any changes. In this case, the risk of a Type I error occurring is more important, and you would choose a small α. However, if you want to be very certain of detecting changes from a mean of 368 grams, the risk of a Type II error occurring is more important, and you would choose a higher level of α.

Now that you have been introduced to hypothesis testing, recall that in the Oxford Cereals scenario on page 311, the business problem facing Oxford Cereals is to determine if the mean fill-weight in the population of boxes in the cereal-filling process differs from 368 grams. To make this determination, you select a random sample of 25 boxes, weigh each box, compute the sample mean, $\overline{X}$, and then evaluate the difference between this sample statistic and the hypothesized population parameter by comparing the sample mean weight (in grams) to the expected population mean of 368 grams specified by the company. The null and alternative hypotheses are:

$$H_0: \mu = 368$$
$$H_1: \mu \neq 368$$

Z Test for the Mean (σ Known)

When the standard deviation, σ, is known (which rarely occurs), you use the **Z test for the mean** if the population is normally distributed. If the population is not normally distributed, you can still use the Z test if the sample size is large enough for the Central Limit Theorem to take effect (see Section 7.2). Equation (9.1) defines the Z_{STAT} test statistic for determining the difference between the sample mean, $\overline{X}$, and the population mean, μ, when the standard deviation, σ, is known.

Z TEST FOR THE MEAN (σ KNOWN)

$$Z_{STAT} = \frac{\overline{X} - \mu}{\dfrac{\sigma}{\sqrt{n}}} \qquad (9.1)$$

In Equation (9.1), the numerator measures the difference between the observed sample mean, $\overline{X}$, and the hypothesized mean, μ. The denominator is the standard error of the mean, so Z_{STAT} represents the difference between $\overline{X}$ and μ in standard error units.

Hypothesis Testing Using the Critical Value Approach

The critical value approach compares the value of the computed Z_{STAT} test statistic from Equation (9.1) to critical values that divide the normal distribution into regions of rejection and nonrejection. The critical values are expressed as standardized Z values that are determined by the level of significance.

For example, if you use a level of significance of 0.05, the size of the rejection region is 0.05. Because the null hypothesis contains an equal sign and the alternative hypothesis contains a not equal sign, you have a **two-tail test** in which the rejection region is divided into the two tails of the distribution, with two equal parts of 0.025 in each tail. For this two-tail test, a rejection region of 0.025 in each tail of the normal distribution results in a cumulative area of 0.025 below the lower critical value and a cumulative area of 0.975 ($1 - 0.025$) below the upper critical value (which leaves an area of 0.025 in the upper tail). According to the cumulative standardized normal distribution table (Table E.2), the critical values that divide the rejection and nonrejection regions are -1.96 and $+1.96$. Figure 9.2 illustrates that if the mean is actually 368 grams, as H_0 claims, the values of the Z_{STAT} test statistic have a standardized normal distribution centered at $Z = 0$ (which corresponds to an $\overline{X}$ value of 368 grams). Values of Z_{STAT} greater than $+1.96$ and less than -1.96 indicate that $\overline{X}$ is sufficiently different from the hypothesized $\mu = 368$ that such an $\overline{X}$ value would be unlikely to occur if H_0 were true.

student TIP

Remember, first you determine the level of significance. This enables you to then determine the critical value. A different level of significance leads to a different critical value.

FIGURE 9.2
Testing a hypothesis about the mean (σ known) at the 0.05 level of significance

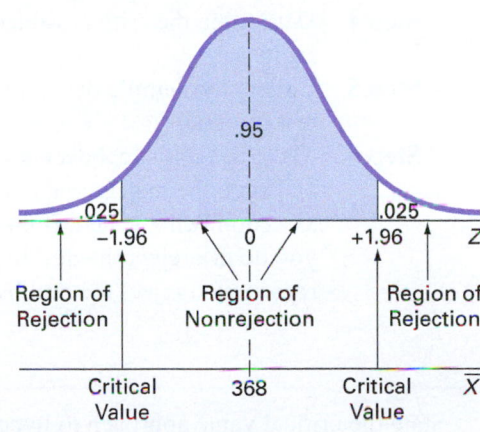

student TIP

In a two-tail test, there is a rejection region in each tail of the distribution.

Therefore, the decision rule is

reject H_0 if $Z_{STAT} > +1.96$
or if $Z_{STAT} < -1.96$;
otherwise, do not reject H_0.

student TIP

Remember, the decision rule always concerns H_0. Either you reject H_0 or you do not reject H_0.

Suppose that the sample of 25 cereal boxes indicates a sample mean, $\overline{X}$, of 372.5 grams, and the population standard deviation, σ, is 15 grams. Using Equation (9.1),

$$Z_{STAT} = \frac{\overline{X} - \mu}{\dfrac{\sigma}{\sqrt{n}}} = \frac{372.5 - 368}{\dfrac{15}{\sqrt{25}}} = +1.50$$

Because $Z_{STAT} = +1.50$ is greater than -1.96 and less than $+1.96$, you do not reject H_0 (see Figure 9.3).

You continue to believe that the mean fill amount is 368 grams. To take into account the possibility of a Type II error, you state the conclusion as "there is insufficient evidence that the mean fill is different from 368 grams."

FIGURE 9.3
Testing a hypothesis about the mean cereal weight (σ known) at the 0.05 level of significance

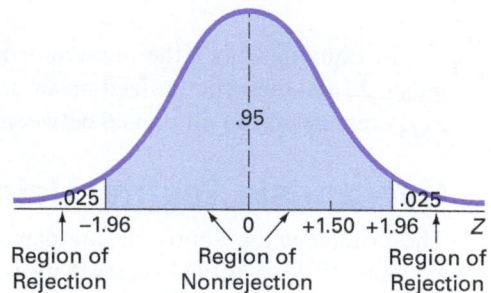

Exhibit 9.2 summarizes the critical value approach to hypothesis testing. Steps 1 and 2 are part of the Define task, step 5 combines the Collect and Organize tasks, and steps 3, 4, and 6 involve the Visualize and Analyze tasks of the DCOVA framework first introduced on page 3. Examples 9.2 and 9.3 apply the critical value approach to hypothesis testing to Oxford Cereals and to a fast-food restaurant.

EXHIBIT 9.2

The Critical Value Approach to Hypothesis Testing

Step 1 State the null hypothesis, H_0, and the alternative hypothesis, H_1.

Step 2 Choose the level of significance, α, and the sample size, n. The level of significance is based on the relative importance of the risks of committing Type I and Type II errors in the problem.

Step 3 Determine the appropriate test statistic and sampling distribution.

Step 4 Determine the critical values that divide the rejection and nonrejection regions.

Step 5 Collect the sample data, organize the results, and compute the value of the test statistic.

Step 6 Make the statistical decision, determine whether the assumptions are valid, and state the managerial conclusion in the context of the theory, claim, or assertion being tested. If the test statistic falls into the nonrejection region, you do not reject the null hypothesis. If the test statistic falls into the rejection region, you reject the null hypothesis.

EXAMPLE 9.2

Applying the Critical Value Approach to Hypothesis Testing at Oxford Cereals

State the critical value approach to hypothesis testing at Oxford Cereals.

SOLUTION

Step 1 State the null and alternative hypotheses. The null hypothesis, H_0, is always stated as a mathematical expression, using population parameters. In testing whether the mean fill is 368 grams, the null hypothesis states that μ equals 368. The alternative hypothesis, H_1, is also stated as a mathematical expression, using population parameters. Therefore, the alternative hypothesis states that μ is not equal to 368 grams.

Step 2 Choose the level of significance and the sample size. Choose the level of significance, α, according to the relative importance of the risks of committing Type I and Type II errors in the problem. The smaller the value of α, the less risk there is of making a

▶(*continued*)

Type I error. In this example, making a Type I error means that you conclude that the population mean is not 368 grams when it is 368 grams. You would take corrective action on the filling process even though the process is working properly. In the example, $\alpha = 0.05$ and the sample size, n, is 25.

Step 3 Select the appropriate test statistic. Because σ is known from information about the filling process, you use the Z_{STAT} test statistic because, by the central limit theorem, the sample size is large enough that the sampling distribution is approximately normally distributed.

Step 4 Determine the rejection region. Critical values for the appropriate test statistic are selected so that the rejection region contains a total area of α when H_0 is true and the nonrejection region contains a total area of $1 - \alpha$ when H_0 is true. Because $\alpha = 0.05$ in the cereal example, the critical values of the Z_{STAT} test statistic are -1.96 and $+1.96$. The rejection region is therefore $Z_{STAT} < -1.96$ or $Z_{STAT} > +1.96$. The nonrejection region is $-1.96 \leq Z_{STAT} \leq +1.96$.

Step 5 Collect the sample data and compute the value of the test statistic. In the cereal example, $\overline{X} = 372.5$, and the value of the test statistic is $Z_{STAT} = +1.50$.

Step 6 State the statistical decision and the managerial conclusion. First, determine whether the test statistic has fallen into the rejection region or the nonrejection region. For the cereal example, $Z_{STAT} = +1.50$ is in the region of nonrejection because $-1.96 \leq Z_{STAT} = +1.50 \leq +1.96$. Because the test statistic falls into the nonrejection region, the statistical decision is to not reject the null hypothesis, H_0. The managerial conclusion is that insufficient evidence exists to prove that the mean fill is different from 368 grams. No corrective action on the filling process is needed.

EXAMPLE 9.3

Testing and Rejecting a Null Hypothesis

You are the manager of a fast-food restaurant. The business problem is to determine whether the population mean waiting time to place an order has changed in the past month from its previous population mean value of 4.5 minutes. From past experience, you can assume that the population is normally distributed, with a population standard deviation of 1.2 minutes. You select a sample of 36 orders during a one-hour period. The sample mean is 5.1 minutes. Use the Exhibit 9.2 six-step approach on page 318 to determine whether there is evidence at the 0.05 level of significance that the population mean waiting time to place an order has changed in the past month from its previous population mean value of 4.5 minutes.

SOLUTION

Step 1 The null hypothesis is that the population mean has not changed from its previous value of 4.5 minutes:

$$H_0: \mu = 4.5$$

Because the null hypothesis is that the population mean is 4.5 minutes, the alternative hypothesis is that the population mean is not 4.5 minutes:

$$H_1: \mu \neq 4.5$$

Step 2 You have selected a sample of $n = 36$. The level of significance is 0.05 ($\alpha = 0.05$).

Step 3 Because σ is assumed to be known, you use the Z_{STAT} test statistic because the sample size is large enough so that the central limit theorem tells you that the sampling distribution is approximately normally distributed.

Step 4 Because $\alpha = 0.05$, the critical values of the Z_{STAT} test statistic are -1.96 and $+1.96$. The rejection region is $Z_{STAT} < -1.96$ or $Z_{STAT} > +1.96$. The nonrejection region is $-1.96 \leq Z_{STAT} \leq +1.96$.

▶(continued)

Step 5   You collect the sample data and compute $\bar{X} = 5.1$. Using Equation (9.1) on page 317, you compute the test statistic:

$$Z_{STAT} = \frac{\bar{X} - \mu}{\dfrac{\sigma}{\sqrt{n}}} = \frac{5.1 - 4.5}{\dfrac{1.2}{\sqrt{36}}} = +3.00$$

Step 6   Because $Z_{STAT} = +3.00 > +1.96$, you reject the null hypothesis. You conclude that there is evidence that the population mean waiting time to place an order has changed from its previous value of 4.5 minutes. The mean waiting time for customers is longer now than it was last month. As the manager, you would now want to determine how waiting time could be reduced to improve service.

Hypothesis Testing Using the *p*-Value Approach

The ***p*-value** is the probability of getting a test statistic equal to or more extreme than the sample result, given that the null hypothesis, H_0, is true. The *p*-value is also known as the *observed level of significance*. Using the *p*-value to determine rejection and nonrejection is another approach to hypothesis testing.

The decision rules for rejecting H_0 in the *p*-value approach are

- If the *p*-value is greater than or equal to α, do not reject the null hypothesis.
- If the *p*-value is less than α, reject the null hypothesis.

studentTIP

A small (low) *p*-value indicates a small probability that H_0 is true. A large (high) *p*-value indicates a large probability that H_0 is true.

Many people confuse these rules, mistakenly believing that a high *p*-value is reason for rejection. Avoid this confusion by remembering the following:

If the *p*-value is low, then H_0 must go.

To understand the *p*-value approach, consider the Oxford Cereals scenario. You tested whether the mean fill was equal to 368 grams. The test statistic resulted in a Z_{STAT} value of $+1.50$ and you did not reject the null hypothesis because $+1.50$ was less than the upper critical value of $+1.96$ and greater than the lower critical value of -1.96.

To use the *p*-value approach for the *two-tail test*, you find the probability that the test statistic Z_{STAT} is equal to or *more extreme than* 1.50 standard error units from the center of a standardized normal distribution. In other words, you need to compute the probability that the Z_{STAT} value is greater than $+1.50$ along with the probability that the Z_{STAT} value is less than -1.50. Table E.2 shows that the probability of a Z_{STAT} value below -1.50 is 0.0668. The probability of a value below $+1.50$ is 0.9332, and the probability of a value above $+1.50$ is $1 - 0.9332 = 0.0668$. Therefore, the *p*-value for this two-tail test is $0.0668 + 0.0668 = 0.1336$ (see Figure 9.4). Thus, the probability of a test statistic equal to or more extreme than the sample result is 0.1336. Because 0.1336 is greater than $\alpha = 0.05$, you do not reject the null hypothesis.

FIGURE 9.4

Finding a *p*-value for a two-tail test

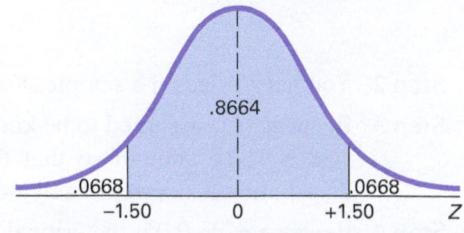

In this example, the observed sample mean is 372.5 grams, 4.5 grams above the hypothesized value, and the *p*-value is 0.1336. If the population mean is 368 grams, there is a 13.36% chance that the sample mean differs from 368 grams by at least 4.5 grams and, therefore, is ≥ 372.5 grams or ≤ 363.5 grams. Therefore, even though 372.5 grams is above the hypothesized value of 368 grams, a result as extreme as or more extreme than 372.5 grams is not highly unlikely when the population mean is 368 grams.

    Unless you are dealing with a test statistic that follows the normal distribution, you will only be able to approximate the p-value from the tables of the distribution. However, Excel, JMP, and Minitab can compute the p-value for any hypothesis test, and this allows you to substitute the p-value approach for the critical value approach when you conduct hypothesis testing.

    Figure 9.5 presents the Z test for the mean results for the cereal-filling example that this section uses.

FIGURE 9.5

Excel, JMP, and Minitab Z test for the mean (σ known) results for the cereal-filling example

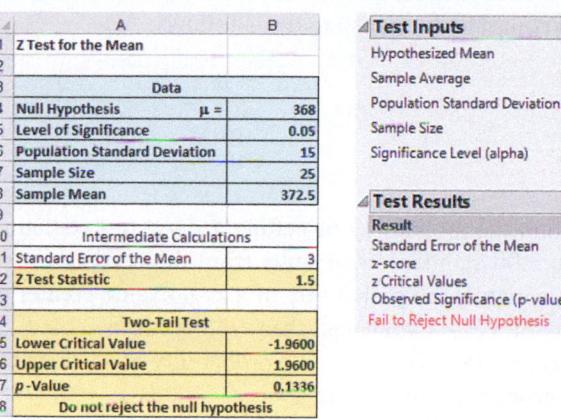

Exhibit 9.3 summarizes the p-value approach to hypothesis testing. Example 9.4 applies the p-value approach to the fast-food restaurant example.

EXHIBIT 9.3

The p-Value Approach to Hypothesis Testing

Step 1   State the null hypothesis, H_0, and the alternative hypothesis, H_1.

Step 2   Choose the level of significance, α, and the sample size, n. The level of significance is based on the relative importance of the risks of committing Type I and Type II errors in the problem.

Step 3   Determine the appropriate test statistic and the sampling distribution.

Step 4   Collect the sample data, compute the value of the test statistic, and compute the p-value.

Step 5   Make the statistical decision and state the managerial conclusion in the context of the theory, claim, or assertion being tested. If the p-value is greater than or equal to α, do not reject the null hypothesis. If the p-value is less than α, reject the null hypothesis.

EXAMPLE 9.4

Testing and Rejecting a Null Hypothesis Using the p-Value Approach

You are the manager of a fast-food restaurant. The business problem is to determine whether the population mean waiting time to place an order has changed in the past month from its previous value of 4.5 minutes. From past experience, you can assume that the population standard deviation is 1.2 minutes and the population waiting time is normally distributed. You select a sample of 36 orders during a one-hour period. The sample mean is 5.1 minutes. Use the Exhibit 9.3 five-step p-value approach to determine whether there is evidence that the population mean waiting time to place an order has changed in the past month from its previous population mean value of 4.5 minutes.

SOLUTION

Step 1   The null hypothesis is that the population mean has not changed from its previous value of 4.5 minutes:

$$H_0: \mu = 4.5$$

▶*(continued)*

Because the null hypothesis is that the population mean is 4.5 minutes, the alternative hypothesis is that the population mean is not 4.5 minutes:

$$H_1: \mu \neq 4.5$$

Step 2   You have selected a sample of $n = 36$ and you have chosen a 0.05 level of significance (i.e., $\alpha = 0.05$).

Step 3   Select the appropriate test statistic. Because σ is assumed known, you use the normal distribution and the Z_{STAT} test statistic.

Step 4   You collect the sample data and compute $\overline{X} = 5.1$. Using Equation (9.1) on page 317, you compute the test statistic as follows:

$$Z_{STAT} = \frac{\overline{X} - \mu}{\dfrac{\sigma}{\sqrt{n}}} = \frac{5.1 - 4.5}{\dfrac{1.2}{\sqrt{36}}} = +3.00$$

To find the probability of getting a Z_{STAT} test statistic that is equal to or more extreme than 3.00 standard error units from the center of a standardized normal distribution, you compute the probability of a Z_{STAT} value greater than +3.00 along with the probability of a Z_{STAT} value less than −3.00. From Table E.2, the probability of a Z_{STAT} value below −3.00 is 0.00135. The probability of a value below +3.00 is 0.99865. Therefore, the probability of a value above +3.00 is 1 − 0.99865 = 0.00135. Thus, the *p*-value for this two-tail test is 0.00135 + 0.00135 = 0.0027.

Step 5   Because the *p*-value = 0.0027 < α = 0.05, you reject the null hypothesis. You conclude that there is evidence that the population mean waiting time to place an order has changed from its previous population mean value of 4.5 minutes. The mean waiting time for customers is longer now than it was last month.

A Connection Between Confidence Interval Estimation and Hypothesis Testing

This chapter and Chapter 8 discuss confidence interval estimation and hypothesis testing, the two major elements of statistical inference. Although confidence interval estimation and hypothesis testing share the same conceptual foundation, they are used for different purposes. In Chapter 8, confidence intervals estimated parameters. In this chapter, hypothesis testing makes decisions about specified values of population parameters. Hypothesis tests are used when trying to determine whether a parameter is less than, more than, or not equal to a specified value. Proper interpretation of a confidence interval, however, can also indicate whether a parameter is less than, more than, or not equal to a specified value. For example, in this section, you tested whether the population mean fill amount was different from 368 grams by using Equation (9.1) on page 317:

$$Z_{STAT} = \frac{\overline{X} - \mu}{\dfrac{\sigma}{\sqrt{n}}}$$

Instead of testing the null hypothesis that $\mu = 368$ grams, you can reach the same conclusion by constructing a confidence interval estimate of μ. If the hypothesized value of $\mu = 368$ is contained within the interval, you do not reject the null hypothesis because 368 would not be considered an unusual value. However, if the hypothesized value does not fall into the interval, you reject the null hypothesis because $\mu = 368$ grams is then considered an unusual value. Using Equation (8.1) on page 279 and the following results:

$$\overline{X} \pm Z_{\alpha/2} \frac{\sigma}{\sqrt{n}}$$

$$n = 25, \overline{X} = 372.5 \text{ grams}, \sigma = 15 \text{ grams}$$

for a confidence level of 95% (i.e., $\alpha = 0.05$),

$$\overline{X} \pm Z_{\alpha/2} \frac{\sigma}{\sqrt{n}}$$

$$372.5 \pm (1.96) \frac{15}{\sqrt{25}}$$

$$372.5 \pm 5.88$$

so that

$$366.62 \le \mu \le 378.38$$

Because the interval includes the hypothesized value of 368 grams, you do not reject the null hypothesis. There is insufficient evidence that the mean fill amount for the entire filling process is not 368 grams. You reached the same decision by using a two-tail hypothesis test.

Can You Ever Know the Population Standard Deviation?

Section 8.1 concludes with the thought that you would be unlikely to use a confidence interval estimation method that required knowing σ, the population standard deviation, because if you knew the population standard deviation you could directly compute the population mean—you would not need to use a method to estimate that statistic!

Likewise, for most practical applications, you are unlikely to use a hypothesis-testing method that requires knowing σ. If you knew the population standard deviation, you would also know the population mean and therefore have no need to form and then test. **Then why study a hypothesis test of the mean which requires that σ is known?** Explaining the fundamentals of hypothesis testing is simpler when using such a test. With a known population standard deviation, you can use the normal distribution and compute p-values using the tables of the normal distribution.

Because it is important that you understand the concept of hypothesis testing when reading the rest of this book, review this section carefully—even if you have no practical reason to use the test that Equation (9.1) defines.

PROBLEMS FOR SECTION 9.1

LEARNING THE BASICS

9.1 If you use a 0.05 level of significance in a two-tail hypothesis test, what decision will you make if $Z_{STAT} = -0.76$?

9.2 If you use a 0.05 level of significance in a two-tail hypothesis test, what decision will you make if $Z_{STAT} = +2.21$?

9.3 If you use a 0.10 level of significance in a two-tail hypothesis test, what is your decision rule for rejecting a null hypothesis that the population mean equals 500 if you use the Z test?

9.4 If you use a 0.01 level of significance in a two-tail hypothesis test, what is your decision rule for rejecting $H_0 : \mu = 12.5$ if you use the Z test?

9.5 What is your decision in Problem 9.4 if $Z_{STAT} = -2.61$?

9.6 What is the p-value if, in a two-tail hypothesis test, $Z_{STAT} = +2.00$?

9.7 In Problem 9.6, what is your statistical decision if you test the null hypothesis at the 0.10 level of significance?

9.8 What is the p-value if, in a two-tail hypothesis test, $Z_{STAT} = -1.38$?

APPLYING THE CONCEPTS

9.9 In the U.S. legal system, a defendant is presumed innocent until proven guilty. Consider a null hypothesis, H_0, that a defendant is innocent, and an alternative hypothesis, H_1, that the defendant is guilty. A jury has two possible decisions: Convict the defendant (i.e., reject the null hypothesis) or do not convict the defendant (i.e., do not reject the null hypothesis). Explain the meaning of the risks of committing either a Type I or Type II error in this example.

9.10 Suppose the defendant in Problem 9.9 is presumed guilty until proven innocent. How do the null and alternative hypotheses differ from those in Problem 9.9? What are the meanings of the risks of committing either a Type I or Type II error here?

9.11 Many consumer groups feel that the U.S. Food and Drug Administration (FDA) drug approval process is too easy and, as a result, too many drugs are approved that are later found to be unsafe. On the other hand, a number of industry lobbyists have pushed for a more lenient approval process so that pharmaceutical companies can get new drugs approved more easily and quickly. Consider a null hypothesis that a new, unapproved drug is unsafe and an alternative hypothesis that a new, unapproved drug is safe.

a. Explain the risks of committing a Type I or Type II error.
b. Which type of error are the consumer groups trying to avoid? Explain.
c. Which type of error are the industry lobbyists trying to avoid? Explain.
d. How would it be possible to lower the chances of both Type I and Type II errors?

9.12 As a result of complaints from both students and faculty about lateness, the registrar at a large university is ready to undertake a study to determine whether the scheduled break between classes should be changed. Until now, the registrar has believed that there should be 20 minutes between scheduled classes. State the null hypothesis, H_0, and the alternative hypothesis, H_1.

9.13 Do business seniors at your school prepare for class more than, less than, or about the same as business seniors at other schools? The National Survey of Student Engagement (NSSE) annual results, available at **bit.ly/1j3Ob7N**, found that business seniors spent a mean of 13 hours per week preparing for class.

a. State the null and alternative hypotheses to try to prove that the mean number of hours preparing for class by business seniors at your school is different from the 13-hour-per-week benchmark reported by the NSSE.
b. What is a Type I error for your test?
c. What is a Type II error for your test?

✓SELF TEST **9.14** The quality-control manager at a light emitting diode (LED) factory needs to determine whether the mean life of a large shipment of LEDs is equal to 50,000 hours.

The population standard deviation is 1,500 hours. A random sample of 64 LEDs indicates a sample mean life of 49,875 hours.

a. At the 0.05 level of significance, is there evidence that the mean life is different from 50,000 hours?
b. Compute the p-value and interpret its meaning.
c. Construct a 95% confidence interval estimate of the population mean life of the LEDs.
d. Compare the results of (a) and (c). What conclusions do you reach?

9.15 Suppose that in Problem 9.14, the standard deviation is 500 hours.

a. Repeat (a) through (d) of Problem 9.14, assuming a standard deviation of 500 hours.
b. Compare the results of (a) to those of Problem 9.14.

9.16 A bottled water distributor wants to determine whether the mean amount of water contained in 1-gallon bottles purchased from a nationally known water bottling company is actually 1 gallon. You know from the water bottling company specifications that the standard deviation of the amount of water per bottle is 0.02 gallon. You select a random sample of 50 bottles, and the mean amount of water per 1-gallon bottle is 0.995 gallon.

a. Is there evidence that the mean amount is different from 1.0 gallon? (Use $\alpha = 0.01$.)
b. Compute the p-value and interpret its meaning.
c. Construct a 99% confidence interval estimate of the population mean amount of water per bottle.
d. Compare the results of (a) and (c). What conclusions do you reach?

9.17 Suppose that in Problem 9.16, the standard deviation is 0.012 gallon.

a. Repeat (a) through (d) of Problem 9.16, assuming a standard deviation of 0.012 gallon.
b. Compare the results of (a) to those of Problem 9.16.

9.2 *t* Test of Hypothesis for the Mean (σ Unknown)

In virtually all hypothesis-testing situations concerning the population mean, μ, you do not know the population standard deviation, σ. However, you will always be able to know the sample standard deviation, S. If you assume that the population is normally distributed, then the sampling distribution of the mean will follow a t distribution with $n - 1$ degrees of freedom and you can use the **t test for the mean**. If the population is not normally distributed, you can still use the t test if the population is not too skewed and the sample size is not too small. Equation (9.2) defines the test statistic for determining the difference between the sample mean, $\overline{X}$, and the population mean, μ, when using the sample standard deviation, S.

t TEST FOR THE MEAN (σ UNKNOWN)

$$t_{STAT} = \frac{\overline{X} - \mu}{\dfrac{S}{\sqrt{n}}} \tag{9.2}$$

where the t_{STAT} test statistic follows a t distribution having $n - 1$ degrees of freedom.

To illustrate the use of the t test for the mean, return to the Chapter 8 Ricknel Home Centers scenario on page 275. The business objective is to determine whether the mean amount per sales invoice is unchanged from the $120 of the past five years. As an accountant for the company, you need to determine whether this amount has changed. In other words, the hypothesis test is used to try to determine whether the mean amount per sales invoice is increasing or decreasing.

studentTIP

Remember, the null hypothesis uses an equals sign and the alternative hypothesis *never* uses an equals sign.

The Critical Value Approach

To perform this two-tail hypothesis test, use the Exhibit 9.2 six-step method on page 318.

Step 1 Define the following hypotheses:

$$H_0: \mu = 120$$

$$H_1: \mu \neq 120$$

The alternative hypothesis contains the statement you are trying to prove. If the null hypothesis is rejected, then there is statistical evidence that the population mean amount per sales invoice is no longer $120. If the statistical conclusion is "do not reject H_0," then you will conclude that there is insufficient evidence to prove that the mean amount differs from the long-term mean of $120.

Step 2 Collect the data from a sample of $n = 12$ sales invoices. You decide to use $\alpha = 0.05$.

Step 3 Because σ is unknown, you use the t distribution and the t_{STAT} test statistic. You must assume that the population of sales invoices is approximately normally distributed in order to use the t distribution because the sample size is only 12. (See "Checking the Normality Assumption" on page 327.)

studentTIP

Because this is a two-tail test, the level of significance, $\alpha = 0.05$, is divided into two equal 0.025 parts, in each of the two tails of the distribution.

Step 4 For a given sample size, n, the test statistic t_{STAT} follows a t distribution with $n - 1$ degrees of freedom. The critical values of the t distribution with $12 - 1 = 11$ degrees of freedom are found in Table E.3, as illustrated in Table 9.2 and Figure 9.6. The alternative hypothesis, $H_1: \mu \neq 120$, has two tails. The area in the rejection region of the t distribution's left (lower) tail is 0.025, and the area in the rejection region of the t distribution's right (upper) tail is also 0.025.

From the t table as given in Table E.3, a portion of which is shown in Table 9.2, the critical values are ± 2.2010. The decision rule is

$$\text{reject } H_0 \text{ if } t_{STAT} < -2.2010$$

$$\text{or if } t_{STAT} > +2.2010;$$

$$\text{otherwise, do not reject } H_0.$$

TABLE 9.2

Determining the Critical Value from the *t* Table for an Area of 0.025 in Each Tail, with 11 Degrees of Freedom

			Cumulative Probabilities			
	.75	.90	.95	.975	.99	.995
			Upper-Tail Areas			
Degrees of Freedom	.25	.10	.05	.025	.01	.005
1	1.0000	3.0777	6.3138	12.7062	31.8207	63.6574
2	0.8165	1.8856	2.9200	4.3027	6.9646	9.9248
3	0.7649	1.6377	2.3534	3.1824	4.5407	5.8409
4	0.7407	1.5332	2.1318	2.7764	3.7469	4.6041
5	0.7267	1.4759	2.0150	2.5706	3.3649	4.0322
6	0.7176	1.4398	1.9432	2.4469	3.1427	3.7074
7	0.7111	1.4149	1.8946	2.3646	2.9980	3.4995
8	0.7064	1.3968	1.8595	2.3060	2.8965	3.3554
9	0.7027	1.3830	1.8331	2.2622	2.8214	3.2498
10	0.6998	1.3722	1.8125	2.2281	2.7638	3.1693
11	0.6974	1.3634	1.7959	2.2010	2.7181	3.1058

Source: Extracted from Table E.3.

FIGURE 9.6

Testing a hypothesis about the mean (σ unknown) at the 0.05 level of significance with 11 degrees of freedom

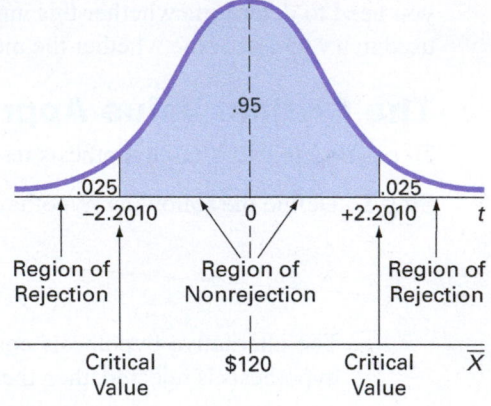

.95

.025   .025

−2.2010   0   +2.2010 t

| Region of Rejection | Region of Nonrejection | Region of Rejection |

Critical Value $120   Critical Value $\overline{X}$

Step 5 You organize and store the data from a random sample of 12 sales invoices in Invoices :

| 108.98 | 152.22 | 111.45 | 110.59 | 127.46 | 107.26 |
| 93.32 | 91.97 | 111.56 | 75.71 | 128.58 | 135.11 |

Using Equations (3.1) and (3.7) on pages 121 and 128,

$$\overline{X} = \$112.85 \text{ and } S = \$20.80$$

From Equation (9.2) on page 324,

$$t_{STAT} = \frac{\overline{X} - \mu}{\dfrac{S}{\sqrt{n}}} = \frac{112.85 - 120}{\dfrac{20.80}{\sqrt{12}}} = -1.1908$$

Step 6 Because $-2.2010 < t_{STAT} = -1.1908 < 2.2010$, you do not reject H_0. You have insufficient evidence to conclude that the mean amount per sales invoice differs from $120. The audit suggests that the mean amount per invoice has not changed.

Figure 9.7 displays the Excel, JMP, and Minitab results for this test of hypothesis for the mean amount per sales invoice.

FIGURE 9.7

Excel, JMP, and Minitab results for the sales invoices example t test

	A	B
1	t Test for the Hypothesis of the Mean	
2		
3	Data	
4	Null Hypothesis μ=	120
5	Level of Significance	0.05
6	Sample Size	12
7	Sample Mean	112.85
8	Sample Standard Deviation	20.8
9		
10	Intermediate Calculations	
11	Standard Error of the Mean	6.0044
12	Degrees of Freedom	11
13	t Test Statistic	-1.1908
14		
15	Two-Tail Test	
16	Lower Critical Value	-2.2010
17	Upper Critical Value	2.2010
18	p-Value	0.2588
19	Do not reject the null hypothesis	

Test Inputs

Hypothesized Mean	120
Sample Average	112.85
Sample Standard Deviation	20.8
Sample Size	12
Significance Level (alpha)	0.05

Test Results

Result	Value
Standard Error of the Mean	6.0044
t-score	-1.1908
t Critical Values	+/- 2.201
Observed Significance (p-value)	0.2588

Fail to Reject Null Hypothesis

One-Sample T

Descriptive Statistics

N	Mean	StDev	SE Mean	95% CI for μ
12	112.85	20.80	6.00	(99.63, 126.07)

μ: mean of Sample

Test

Null hypothesis	H₀: μ = 120
Alternative hypothesis	H₁: μ ≠ 120

T-Value	P-Value
-1.19	0.259

p-Value Approach

To perform this two-tail hypothesis test, you use the Exhibit 9.3 five-step method on page 321.

Step 1–3 These steps are the same as the critical value approach steps on page 325.

Step 4 From the Figure 9.7 results, $t_{STAT} = -1.19$ and the *p*-value = 0.2588.

Step 5 Because the *p*-value of 0.2588 is greater than $\alpha = 0.05$, you do not reject H_0. The data provide insufficient evidence to conclude that the mean amount per sales invoice differs from $120. The audit suggests that the mean amount per invoice has not changed. The *p*-value indicates that if the null hypothesis is true, the probability that a sample of 12 invoices could have a sample mean that differs by $7.15 or more from the stated $120 is 0.2588. In other words, if the mean amount per sales invoice is truly $120, then there is a 25.88% chance of observing a sample mean below $112.85 or above $127.15.

In the preceding example, it is incorrect to state that there is a 25.88% chance that the null hypothesis is true. Remember that the *p*-value is a conditional probability, calculated by *assuming* that the null hypothesis is true. In general, it is proper to state the following:

If the null hypothesis is true, there is a (*p*-value) × 100% chance of observing a test statistic at least as contradictory to the null hypothesis as the sample result.

Checking the Normality Assumption

You use the *t* test when the population standard deviation, σ, is not known and is estimated using the sample standard deviation, *S*. To use the *t* test, you assume that the data represent a random sample from a population that is normally distributed. In practice, as long as the sample size is not very small and the population is not very skewed, the *t* distribution provides a good approximation of the sampling distribution of the mean when σ is unknown.

There are several ways to evaluate the normality assumption necessary for using the *t* test. You can examine how closely the sample statistics match the normal distribution's theoretical properties. You can also construct a histogram, stem-and-leaf display, boxplot, or normal probability plot to visualize the distribution of the sales invoice amounts. For details on evaluating normality, see Section 6.3.

Figure 9.8 presents descriptive statistics and a boxplot and Figure 9.9 presents normal probability plots for the sales invoice data.

FIGURE 9.8

Excel descriptive statistics and boxplot for the sales invoice data

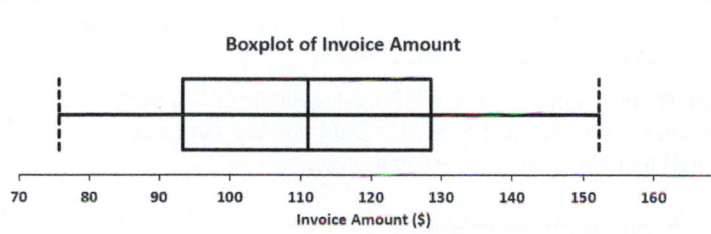

Invoice Amount	
Mean	112.8508
Median	111.02
Mode	#N/A
Minimum	75.71
Maximum	152.22
Range	76.51
Variance	432.5565
Standard Deviation	20.7980
Coeff. of Variation	18.43%
Skewness	0.1336
Kurtosis	0.1727
Count	12
Standard Error	6.0039

FIGURE 9.9

JMP and Minitab normal probability plots for the sales invoice data

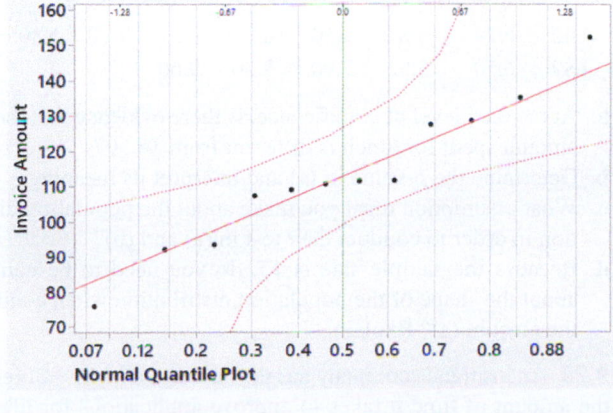

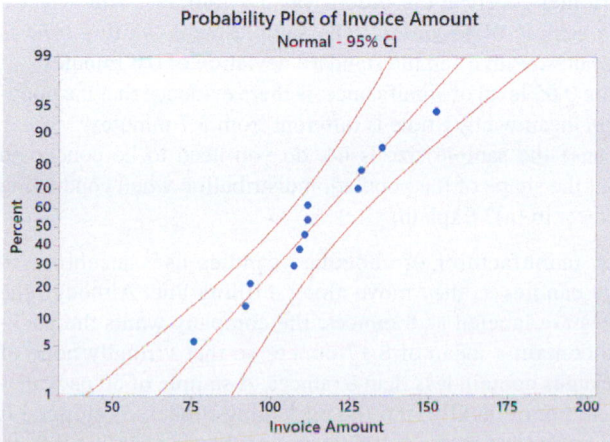

The mean is very close to the median, and the points on the normal probability plot appear to be increasing approximately in a straight line. The boxplot appears to be approximately symmetrical. Thus, you can assume that the population of sales invoices is approximately normally distributed. The normality assumption is valid, and therefore the auditor's results are valid.

The t test is a **robust** test. A robust test does not lose power if the shape of the population departs somewhat from a normal distribution, particularly when the sample size is large enough to enable the test statistic t to follow the t distribution. However, you can reach erroneous conclusions and can lose statistical power if you use the t test incorrectly. If the sample size, n, is small (i.e., less than 30) and you cannot easily make the assumption that the underlying population is at least approximately normally distributed, then *nonparametric* testing procedures are more appropriate (see references 2 and 3).

PROBLEMS FOR SECTION 9.2

LEARNING THE BASICS

9.18 If, in a sample of $n = 16$ selected from a normal population, $\overline{X} = 56$ and $S = 12$, what is the value of t_{STAT} if you are testing the null hypothesis $H_0: \mu = 50$?

9.19 In Problem 9.18, how many degrees of freedom does the t test have?

9.20 In Problems 9.18 and 9.19, what are the critical values of t if the level of significance, α, is 0.05 and the alternative hypothesis, H_1, is $\mu \neq 50$?

9.21 In Problems 9.18, 9.19, and 9.20, what is your statistical decision if the alternative hypothesis, H_1, is $\mu \neq 50$?

9.22 If, in a sample of $n = 16$ selected from a left-skewed population, $\overline{X} = 65$, and $S = 21$, would you use the t test to test the null hypothesis $H_0: \mu = 60$? Discuss.

9.23 If, in a sample of $n = 160$ selected from a left-skewed population, $\overline{X} = 65$, and $S = 21$, would you use the t test to test the null hypothesis $H_0: \mu = 60$? Discuss.

APPLYING THE CONCEPTS

✓SELF TEST **9.24** You are the manager of a restaurant for a fast-food franchise. Last month, the mean waiting time at the drive-through window for branches in your geographic region, as measured from the time a customer places an order until the time the customer receives the order, was 3.7 minutes. You select a random sample of 64 orders. The sample mean waiting time is 3.57 minutes, with a sample standard deviation of 0.8 minute.
a. At the 0.05 level of significance, is there evidence that the population mean waiting time is different from 3.7 minutes?
b. Because the sample size is 64, do you need to be concerned about the shape of the population distribution when conducting the t test in (a)? Explain.

9.25 A manufacturer of chocolate candies uses machines to package candies as they move along a filling line. Although the packages are labeled as 8 ounces, the company wants the packages to contain a mean of 8.17 ounces so that virtually none of the packages contain less than 8 ounces. A sample of 50 packages is selected periodically, and the packaging process is stopped if there is evidence that the mean amount packaged is different from 8.17 ounces. Suppose that in a particular sample of 50 packages, the mean amount dispensed is 8.159 ounces, with a sample standard deviation of 0.051 ounce.
a. Is there evidence that the population mean amount is different from 8.17 ounces? (Use a 0.05 level of significance.)
b. Determine the p-value and interpret its meaning.

9.26 A marketing researcher wants to estimate the mean amount spent per year (\$) on Amazon.com by Amazon Prime member shoppers. Suppose a random sample of 100 Amazon Prime member shoppers who recently made a purchase on Amazon.com yielded a mean amount spent of \$1,500 and a standard deviation of \$200.
a. Is there evidence that the population mean amount spent per year on Amazon.com by Amazon Prime member shoppers is different from \$1,475? (Use a 0.05 level of significance.)
b. Determine the p-value and interpret its meaning.

9.27 The U.S. Department of Transportation requires tire manufacturers to provide performance information on tire sidewalls to help prospective buyers make their purchasing decisions. One very important piece of information is the tread wear index, which indicates the tire's resistance to tread wear. A tire with a grade of 200 should last twice as long, on average, as a tire with a grade of 100.

A consumer organization wants to test the actual tread wear index of a brand name of tires that claims "graded 200" on the sidewall of the tire. A random sample of $n = 18$ indicates a sample mean tread wear index of 195.3 and a sample standard deviation of 21.4.
a. Is there evidence that the population mean tread wear index is different from 200? (Use a 0.05 level of significance.)
b. Determine the p-value and interpret its meaning.

9.28 The file **FastFood** contains the amount that a sample of fifteen customers spent for lunch (\$) at a fast-food restaurant:

7.42	6.29	5.83	6.50	8.34	9.51	7.10	6.80	5.90
4.89	6.50	5.52	7.90	8.30	9.60			

a. At the 0.05 level of significance, is there evidence that the mean amount spent for lunch is different from \$6.50?
b. Determine the p-value in (a) and interpret its meaning.
c. What assumption must you make about the population distribution in order to conduct the t test in (a) and (b)?
d. Because the sample size is 15, do you need to be concerned about the shape of the population distribution when conducting the t test in (a)? Explain.

9.29 An insurance company has the business objective of reducing the amount of time it takes to approve applications for life insurance. The approval process consists of underwriting, which includes a review of the application, a medical information bureau check, possible requests for additional medical information and medical exams, and a policy compilation stage in which the policy pages are generated and sent for delivery. The ability to deliver approved policies to customers in a timely manner is critical to the profitability of this service. During a period of one month, you collect a random sample of 27 approved policies and store their total processing times, in days, in Insurance .

a. In the past, the mean processing time was 45 days. At the 0.05 level of significance, is there evidence that the mean processing time has changed from 45 days?
b. What assumption about the population distribution is needed in order to conduct the *t* test in (a)?
c. Construct a boxplot or a normal probability plot to evaluate the assumption made in (b).
d. Do you think that the assumption needed in order to conduct the *t* test in (a) is valid? Explain.

9.30 The following data (in Drink) represent the amount of soft drink filled in a sample of 50 consecutive 2-liter bottles. The results, listed horizontally in the order of being filled, were:

2.109	2.086	2.066	2.075	2.065	2.057	2.052	2.044
2.036	2.038	2.031	2.029	2.025	2.029	2.023	2.020
2.015	2.014	2.013	2.014	2.012	2.012	2.012	2.010
2.005	2.003	1.999	1.996	1.997	1.992	1.994	1.986
1.984	1.981	1.973	1.975	1.971	1.969	1.966	1.967
1.963	1.957	1.951	1.951	1.947	1.941	1.941	1.938
1.908	1.894						

a. At the 0.05 level of significance, is there evidence that the mean amount of soft drink filled is different from 2.0 liters?
b. Determine the *p*-value in (a) and interpret its meaning.
c. In (a), you assumed that the distribution of the amount of soft drink filled was normally distributed. Evaluate this assumption by constructing a boxplot or a normal probability plot.
d. Do you think that the assumption needed in order to conduct the *t* test in (a) is valid? Explain.
e. Examine the values of the 50 bottles in their sequential order, as given in the problem. Does there appear to be a pattern to the results? If so, what impact might this pattern have on the validity of the results in (a)?

9.31 One of the major measures of the quality of service provided by any organization is the speed with which it responds to customer complaints. A large family-held department store selling furniture and flooring, including carpet, had undergone a major expansion in the past several years. In particular, the flooring department had expanded from 2 installation crews to an installation supervisor, a measurer, and 15 installation crews. The store had the business objective of improving its response to complaints. The variable of interest was defined as the number of days between when the complaint was made and when it was resolved. Data were collected from 50 complaints that were made in the past year. These data, stored in Furniture , are:

54	5	35	137	31	27	152	2	123	81	74	27
11	19	126	110	110	29	61	35	94	31	26	5
12	4	165	32	29	28	29	26	25	1	14	13
13	10	5	27	4	52	30	22	36	26	20	23
33	68										

a. The installation supervisor claims that the mean number of days between the receipt of a complaint and the resolution of the complaint is 20 days. At the 0.05 level of significance, is there evidence that the claim is not true (i.e., the mean number of days is different from 20)?
b. What assumption about the population distribution is needed in order to conduct the *t* test in (a)?
c. Construct a boxplot or a normal probability plot to evaluate the assumption made in (b).

d. Do you think that the assumption needed in order to conduct the *t* test in (a) is valid? Explain.

9.32 A manufacturing company produces steel housings for electrical equipment. The main component part of the housing is a steel trough that is made out of a 14-gauge steel coil. It is produced using a 250-ton progressive punch press with a wipe-down operation that puts two 90-degree forms in the flat steel to make the trough. The distance from one side of the form to the other is critical because of weatherproofing in outdoor applications. The company requires that the width of the trough be between 8.31 inches and 8.61 inches. The file Trough contains the widths of the troughs, in inches, for a sample of $n = 49$:

8.312	8.343	8.317	8.383	8.348	8.410	8.351	8.373	8.481	8.422
8.476	8.382	8.484	8.403	8.414	8.419	8.385	8.465	8.498	8.447
8.436	8.413	8.489	8.414	8.481	8.415	8.479	8.429	8.458	8.462
8.460	8.444	8.429	8.460	8.412	8.420	8.410	8.405	8.323	8.420
8.396	8.447	8.405	8.439	8.411	8.427	8.420	8.498	8.409	

a. At the 0.05 level of significance, is there evidence that the mean width of the troughs is different from 8.46 inches?
b. What assumption about the population distribution is needed in order to conduct the *t* test in (a)?
c. Evaluate the assumption made in (b).
d. Do you think that the assumption needed in order to conduct the *t* test in (a) is valid? Explain.

9.33 One operation of a steel mill is to cut pieces of steel into parts that are used in the frame for front seats in an automobile. The steel is cut with a diamond saw and requires the resulting parts must be cut to be within ± 0.005 inch of the length specified by the automobile company. The file Steel contains a sample of 100 steel parts. The measurement reported is the difference, in inches, between the actual length of the steel part, as measured by a laser measurement device, and the specified length of the steel part. For example, a value of -0.002 represents a steel part that is 0.002 inch shorter than the specified length.

a. At the 0.05 level of significance, is there evidence that the mean difference is different from 0.0 inches?
b. Construct a 95% confidence interval estimate of the population mean. Interpret this interval.
c. Compare the conclusions reached in (a) and (b).
d. Because $n = 100$, do you have to be concerned about the normality assumption needed for the *t* test and *t* interval?

9.34 In Problem 3.69 on page 156, you were introduced to a teabag-filling operation. An important quality characteristic of interest for this process is the weight of the tea in the individual bags. The file Teabags contains an ordered array of the weight, in grams, of a sample of 50 tea bags produced during an 8-hour shift.

a. Is there evidence that the mean amount of tea per bag is different from 5.5 grams? (Use $\alpha = 0.01$.)
b. Construct a 99% confidence interval estimate of the population mean amount of tea per bag. Interpret this interval.
c. Compare the conclusions reached in (a) and (b).

9.35 We Are Social and Hootsuite reported that the typical American spends 2.02 hours (121 minutes) per day accessing the Internet via mobile devices.

Source: *Digital in 2017 Global Overview*, available at **bit.ly/2jXeS3F**.

In order to test the validity of this statement, you select a sample of 30 friends and family. The results for the time spent per day accessing the Internet via mobile devices (in minutes) are stored in InternetMobileTime .

a. Is there evidence that the population mean time spent per day accessing the Internet via mobile devices is different from 121 minutes? Use the *p*-value approach and a level of significance of 0.05.

b. What assumption about the population distribution is needed in order to conduct the *t* test in (a)?

c. Make a list of the various ways you could evaluate the assumption noted in (b).

d. Evaluate the assumption noted in (b) and determine whether the test in (a) is valid.

9.3 One-Tail Tests

The examples of hypothesis testing in Sections 9.1 and 9.2 are called two-tail tests because the rejection region is divided into the two tails of the sampling distribution of the mean. In contrast, some hypothesis tests are one-tail tests because they require an alternative hypothesis that focuses on a *particular direction*.

One example of a one-tail hypothesis test would test whether the population mean is *less than* a specified value. One such situation involves the business problem concerning the service time at the drive-through window of a fast-food restaurant. According to a *QSR* magazine report (**www.qsrmagazine.com/content/drive-thru-2016-speed-service**), the speed with which customers are served is of critical importance to the success of the service. In that study, an audit of McDonald's drive-throughs had a mean service time of 208.16 seconds, which was slower than the drive-throughs of several other fast-food chains. Suppose that McDonald's began a quality improvement effort to reduce the service time by deploying an improved drive-through service process in a sample of 25 stores. Because McDonald's would want to institute the new process in all of its stores only if the test sample saw a *decreased* drive-through time, the entire rejection region is located in the lower tail of the distribution.

The Critical Value Approach

You wish to determine whether the new drive-through process has a mean that is less than 208.16 seconds. To perform this one-tail hypothesis test, you use the Exhibit 9.2 six-step method on page 318:

Step 1 You define the null and alternative hypotheses:

$$H_0: \mu \geq 208.16$$
$$H_1: \mu < 208.16$$

The alternative hypothesis contains the statement for which you are trying to find evidence. If the conclusion of the test is "reject H_0," there is statistical evidence that the mean drive-through time is less than the drive-through time in the old process. This would be reason to change the drive-through process for the entire population of stores. If the conclusion of the test is "do not reject H_0," then there is insufficient evidence that the mean drive-through time in the new process is significantly less than the drive-through time in the old process. If this occurs, there would be insufficient reason to institute the new drive-through process in the population of stores.

Step 2 You collect the data by selecting a sample of $n = 25$ stores. You decide to use $\alpha = 0.05$.

Step 3 Because σ is unknown, you use the *t* distribution and the t_{STAT} test statistic. You need to assume that the drive-through time is normally distributed because a sample of only 25 drive-through times is selected.

Step 4 The rejection region is entirely contained in the lower tail of the sampling distribution of the mean because you want to reject H_0 only when the sample mean is significantly less than 208.16 seconds. When the entire rejection region is contained in one tail of the sampling distribution of the test statistic, the test is called a **one-tail test**, or **directional test**. If the alternative hypothesis includes the *less than* sign, the critical value of *t* is negative.

studentTIP

The rejection region matches the direction of the alternative hypothesis. If the alternative hypothesis contains a < sign, the rejection region is in the lower tail. If the alternative hypothesis contains a > sign, the rejection region is in the upper tail.

As shown in Table 9.3 and Figure 9.10, because the entire rejection region is in the lower tail of the t distribution and contains an area of 0.05, due to the symmetry of the t distribution, the critical value of the t test statistic with $25 - 1 = 24$ degrees of freedom is -1.7109. The decision rule is

$$\text{reject } H_0 \text{ if } t_{STAT} < -1.7109;$$

$$\text{otherwise, do not reject } H_0.$$

TABLE 9.3

Determining the Critical Value from the t Table for an Area of 0.05 in the Lower Tail, with 24 Degrees of Freedom

	Cumulative Probabilities					
	.75	.90	.95	.975	.99	.995
	Upper-Tail Areas					
Degrees of Freedom	.25	.10	.05	.025	.01	.005
1	1.0000	3.0777	6.3138	12.7062	31.8207	63.6574
2	0.8165	1.8856	2.9200	4.3027	6.9646	9.9248
3	0.7649	1.6377	2.3534	3.1824	4.5407	5.8409
⋮	⋮	⋮	⋮	⋮	⋮	⋮
23	0.6853	1.3195	1.7139	2.0687	2.4999	2.8073
24	0.6848	1.3178	1.7109	2.0639	2.4922	2.7969
25	0.6844	1.3163	1.7081	2.0595	2.4851	2.7874

Source: Extracted from Table E.3.

FIGURE 9.10

One-tail test of hypothesis for a mean (σ unknown) at the 0.05 level of significance

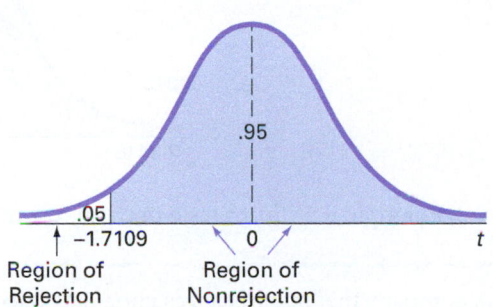

Step 5 From the sample of 25 stores you selected, you find that the sample mean service time at the drive-through equals 195.6 seconds and the sample standard deviation equals 22.1 seconds. Using $n = 25$, $\overline{X} = 195.6$, $S = 22.1$ and Equation (9.2) on page 324,

$$t_{STAT} = \frac{\overline{X} - \mu}{\dfrac{S}{\sqrt{n}}} = \frac{195.6 - 208.16}{\dfrac{22.1}{\sqrt{25}}} = -2.8416$$

Step 6 Because $t_{STAT} = -2.8416 < -1.7109$, you reject the null hypothesis (see Figure 9.10). You conclude that the mean service time at the drive-through is less than 208.16 seconds. There is sufficient evidence to change the drive-through process for the entire population of stores.

The p-Value Approach

Use the five steps listed in Exhibit 9.3 on page 321 to illustrate the t test for the drive-through time study using the p-value approach:

Step 1–3 These steps are the same as was used in the critical value approach on page 330.

Step 4 $t_{STAT} = -2.8416$ (see step 5 of the critical value approach). Because the alternative hypothesis indicates a rejection region entirely in the lower tail of the sampling distribution, to compute the *p*-value, you need to find the probability that the t_{STAT} test statistic will be less than -2.8416. Figure 9.11 shows that the *p*-value is 0.0045.

Step 5   The *p*-value of 0.0045 is less than $\alpha = 0.05$ (see Figure 9.12). You reject H_0 and conclude that the mean service time at the drive-through is less than 208.16 seconds. There is sufficient evidence to change the drive-through process for the entire population of stores.

FIGURE 9.11

Excel, JMP, and Minitab *t* test worksheet results for the drive-through time study

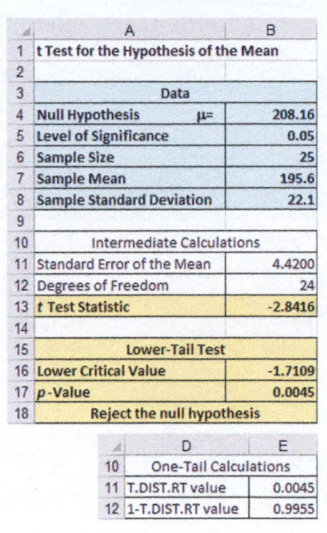

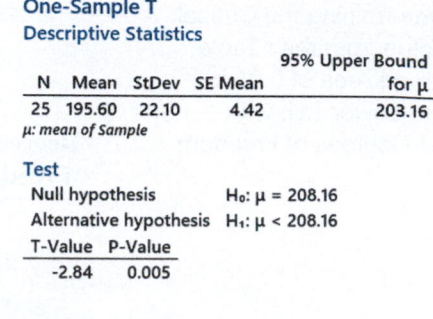

FIGURE 9.12

Determining the *p*-value for a one-tail test

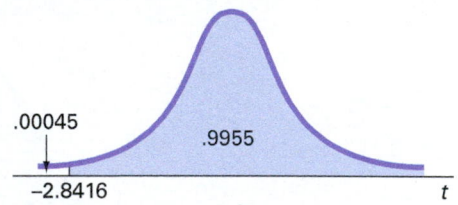

Example 9.5 illustrates a one-tail test in which the rejection region is in the upper tail.

EXAMPLE 9.5

A One-Tail Test for the Mean

A company that manufactures chocolate bars is particularly concerned that the mean weight of a chocolate bar is not greater than 6.03 ounces. A sample of 50 chocolate bars is selected; the sample mean is 6.034 ounces, and the sample standard deviation is 0.02 ounce. Using the $\alpha = 0.01$ level of significance, is there evidence that the population mean weight of the chocolate bars is greater than 6.03 ounces?

SOLUTION   Using the Exhibit 9.2 critical value approach on page 318,

Step 1   First, define the null and alternative hypotheses:

$$H_0: \mu \leq 6.03$$
$$H_1: \mu > 6.03$$

Step 2   Collect the data from a sample of $n = 50$. You decide to use $\alpha = 0.01$.

Step 3   Because σ is unknown, you use the *t* distribution and the t_{STAT} test statistic.

Step 4   The rejection region is entirely contained in the upper tail of the sampling distribution of the mean because you want to reject H_0 only when the sample mean is significantly greater than 6.03 ounces. Because the entire rejection region is in the upper tail of the *t* distribution and contains an area of 0.01, the critical value of the *t* distribution with $50 - 1 = 49$ degrees of freedom is 2.4049 (see Table E.3).

The decision rule is

$$\text{reject } H_0 \text{ if } t_{STAT} > 2.4049;$$

$$\text{otherwise, do not reject } H_0.$$

▶(continued)

Step 5 From your sample of 50 chocolate bars, you find that the sample mean weight is 6.034 ounces, and the sample standard deviation is 0.02 ounces. Using $n = 50$, $\overline{X} = 6.034$, $S = 0.02$, and Equation (9.2) on page 324,

$$t_{STAT} = \frac{\overline{X} - \mu}{\dfrac{S}{\sqrt{n}}} = \frac{6.034 - 6.03}{\dfrac{0.02}{\sqrt{50}}} = 1.414$$

Step 6 Because $t_{STAT} = 1.414 < 2.4049$ or the p-value (from Excel, JMP, or Minitab) is $0.0818 > 0.01$, you do not reject the null hypothesis. There is insufficient evidence to conclude that the population mean weight is greater than 6.03 ounces.

To perform one-tail tests of hypotheses, you must properly formulate H_0 and H_1. Exhibit 9.4 summarizes the key points about the null and alternative hypotheses for one-tail tests.

EXHIBIT 9.4

The Null and Alternative Hypotheses in One-Tail Tests

The null hypothesis, H_0, states a status quo claim.

The alternative hypothesis, H_1, states a claim that is contrary to the null hypothesis and often represents a research claim or specific inference that an analyst seeks to prove.

A null and alternative pair of hypotheses are always collectively exhaustive.

If you reject the null hypothesis, you have strong statistical evidence that the alternative hypothesis is correct.

If you do not reject the null hypothesis, you have not proven the null hypothesis. (Rather, you have only failed to prove the alternative hypothesis.)

The null hypothesis always refers to a population parameter such as μ and not a sample statistic such as $\overline{X}$.

The null hypothesis always includes an equals sign when stating a claim about the population parameter, for example, H_0: $\mu \geq 208.16$ grams.

The alternative hypothesis never includes an equals sign when stating a claim about the population parameter, for example, H_1: $\mu < 208.16$ grams.

PROBLEMS FOR SECTION 9.3

LEARNING THE BASICS

9.36 In a one-tail hypothesis test where you reject H_0 only in the *upper* tail, what is the p-value if $Z_{STAT} = +2.00$?

9.37 In Problem 9.36, what is your statistical decision if you test the null hypothesis at the 0.05 level of significance?

9.38 In a one-tail hypothesis test where you reject H_0 only in the *lower* tail, what is the p-value if $Z_{STAT} = -1.38$?

9.39 In Problem 9.38, what is your statistical decision if you test the null hypothesis at the 0.01 level of significance?

9.40 In a one-tail hypothesis test where you reject H_0 only in the *lower* tail, what is the p-value if $Z_{STAT} = +1.38$?

9.41 In Problem 9.40, what is the statistical decision if you test the null hypothesis at the 0.01 level of significance?

9.42 In a one-tail hypothesis test where you reject H_0 only in the *upper* tail, what is the critical value of the t-test statistic with 10 degrees of freedom at the 0.01 level of significance?

9.43 In Problem 9.42, what is your statistical decision if $t_{STAT} = +2.39$?

9.44 In a one-tail hypothesis test where you reject H_0 only in the *lower* tail, what is the critical value of the t_{STAT} test statistic with 20 degrees of freedom at the 0.01 level of significance?

9.45 In Problem 9.44, what is your statistical decision if $t_{STAT} = -1.15$?

APPLYING THE CONCEPTS

9.46 The Washington Metropolitan Area Transit Authority has set a bus fleet reliability goal of 8,000 bus miles. Bus reliability is measured specifically as the number of bus miles traveled before a mechanical breakdown that requires the bus to be removed from service or deviate from the schedule. Suppose a sample of 64 buses resulted in a sample mean of 8,210 bus miles and a sample standard deviation of 625 bus miles.

a. Is there evidence that the population mean bus miles is greater than 8,000 bus miles? (Use a 0.05 level of significance.)
b. Determine the *p*-value and interpret its meaning.

9.47 *CarMD* reports that after two years of flat U.S. car repair costs, 2016 saw an increase. One of the most common problems that trigger the "check engine" light is the catalytic converter. Repairing the catalytic converter had a mean repair cost of $1,190 in 2016.

Source: *Digital in 2017 Global Overview*, available at **bit.ly/2qL9KVc**.

Suppose a sample of 100 catalytic converter repairs completed in the last month was selected. The sample mean repair cost was $1,125 with the sample standard deviation of $250.

a. Is there evidence that the population mean repair cost is less than $1,190? (Use a 0.05 level of significance.)
b. Determine the *p*-value and interpret its meaning.

✓**SELF**
TEST **9.48** Patient waiting is a common phenomenon in the doctor's waiting room. One acceptable standard of practice states that waiting time for patients to be seen by the first provider in hospital outpatient and public health clinics should be less than 30 minutes. A study was conducted to assess patient waiting at a primary healthcare clinic. Data were collected on a sample of 860 patients. In this sample, the mean wait time was 24.05 minutes, with a standard deviation of 16.5 minutes.

Source: Data extracted from BA Ahmad, K. Khairatul, and A. Farnazza, "An assessment of patient waiting and consultation time in a primary healthcare clinic," *Malaysian Family Practice*, 2017, 12(1), pp. 14–21.

a. If you test the null hypothesis at the 0.01 level of significance, is there evidence that the population mean wait time is less than 30 minutes?
b. Interpret the meaning of the *p*-value in this problem.

9.49 You are the manager of a restaurant that delivers pizza to college dormitory rooms. You have just changed your delivery process in an effort to reduce the mean time between the order and completion of delivery from the current 25 minutes. A sample of 36 orders using the new delivery process yields a sample mean of 22.4 minutes and a sample standard deviation of 6 minutes.

a. Using the six-step critical value approach, at the 0.05 level of significance, is there evidence that the population mean delivery time has been reduced below the previous population mean value of 25 minutes?
b. At the 0.05 level of significance, use the five-step *p*-value approach.
c. Interpret the meaning of the *p*-value in (b).
d. Compare your conclusions in (a) and (b).

9.50 A survey of nonprofit organizations showed that online fundraising has increased in the past year. Based on a random sample of 133 nonprofits, the mean one-time gift donation resulting from email outreach in the past year was $87. Assume that the sample standard deviation is $9.

a. If you test the null hypothesis at the 0.01 level of significance, is there evidence that the mean one-time gift donation is greater than $85.50?
b. Interpret the meaning of the *p*-value in this problem.

9.51 The population mean waiting time to check out of a supermarket has been 4 minutes. Recently, in an effort to reduce the waiting time, the supermarket has experimented with a system in which infrared cameras use body heat and in-store software to determine how many lanes should be opened. A sample of 100 customers was selected, and their mean waiting time to check out was 3.10 minutes, with a sample standard deviation of 2.5 minutes.

a. At the 0.05 level of significance, using the critical value approach to hypothesis testing, is there evidence that the population mean waiting time to check out is less than 4 minutes?
b. At the 0.05 level of significance, using the *p*-value approach to hypothesis testing, is there evidence that the population mean waiting time to check out is less than 4 minutes?
c. Interpret the meaning of the *p*-value in this problem.
d. Compare your conclusions in (a) and (b).

9.4 *Z* Test of Hypothesis for the Proportion

studentTIP

Do not confuse this use of the Greek letter pi, π, to represent the population proportion with the mathematical constant that uses the same letter to represent the ratio of the circumference to a diameter of a circle—approximately 3.14159.

In some situations, you want to test a hypothesis about the proportion of events of interest in the population, π, rather than test the population mean. To begin, you select a random sample and compute the **sample proportion**, $p = X/n$. You then compare the value of this statistic to the hypothesized value of the parameter, π, in order to decide whether to reject the null hypothesis.

If the number of events of interest (X) and the number of events that are not of interest ($n - X$) are each at least five, the sampling distribution of a proportion approximately follows a normal distribution, and you can use the **Z test for the proportion**. Equation (9.3) defines this hypothesis test for the difference between the sample proportion, p, and the hypothesized population proportion, π.

Z TEST FOR THE PROPORTION

$$Z_{STAT} = \frac{p - \pi}{\sqrt{\dfrac{\pi(1 - \pi)}{n}}}$$

(9.3)

where

$$p = \text{sample proportion} = \frac{X}{n} = \frac{\text{number of events of interest in the sample}}{\text{sample size}}$$

$$\pi = \text{hypothesized proportion of events of interest in the population}$$

The Z_{STAT} test statistic approximately follows a standardized normal distribution when X and $(n - X)$ are each at least 5.

Alternatively, by multiplying the numerator and denominator by n, you can write the Z_{STAT} test statistic in terms of the number of events of interest, X, as shown in Equation (9.4).

Z TEST FOR THE PROPORTION IN TERMS OF THE NUMBER OF EVENTS OF INTEREST

$$Z_{STAT} = \frac{X - n\pi}{\sqrt{n\pi(1 - \pi)}} \tag{9.4}$$

The Critical Value Approach

[1]as reported by L. Petrecca in "Always 'on': How you can disconnect from work," *USA Today*, January 16, 2017.

According to a 2016 survey conducted by CareerBuilder,[1] 45% of American workers reported that they work during nonbusiness hours. Suppose you have decided to take a new survey to determine whether the proportion has changed from what it was in 2016. In the new survey, 208 of 400 American workers reported that they work during nonbusiness hours. To investigate this question, the null and alternative hypotheses are as follows:

$H_1: \pi = 0.45$ (the proportion of American workers who reported that they work during nonbusiness hours has not changed from the previous year)

$H_1: \pi \neq 0.45$ (the proportion of American workers who reported that they work during nonbusiness hours has changed from the previous year)

Because you are interested in determining whether the population proportion of American workers who reported that they work during nonbusiness hours has changed from 0.45 in the previous year, you use a two-tail test. If you select the $\alpha = 0.05$ level of significance, the rejection and nonrejection regions are set up as in Figure 9.13, and the decision rule is

reject H_0 if $Z_{STAT} < -1.96$ or if $Z_{STAT} > +1.96$;

otherwise, do not reject H_0.

FIGURE 9.13
Two-tail test of hypothesis for the proportion at the 0.05 level of significance

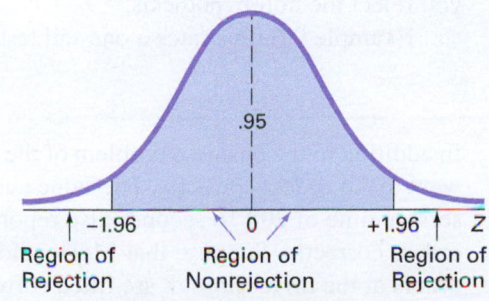

Because 208 of 400 American workers reported that they work during nonbusiness hours.

$$p = \frac{208}{400} = 0.52$$

Because $X = 208$ and $n - X = 192$, each > 5, using Equation (9.3),

$$Z_{STAT} = \frac{p - \pi}{\sqrt{\dfrac{\pi(1 - \pi)}{n}}} = \frac{0.52 - 0.45}{\sqrt{\dfrac{0.45(1 - 0.45)}{400}}} = \frac{0.0700}{0.0249} = 2.8141$$

or, using Equation (9.4),

$$Z_{STAT} = \frac{X - n\pi}{\sqrt{n\pi(1 - \pi)}} = \frac{208 - (400)(0.45)}{\sqrt{(400)(0.45)(0.55)}} = \frac{28}{9.9499} = 2.8141$$

Because $Z_{STAT} = 2.8141 > 1.96$, you reject H_0. There is evidence that the population proportion of American workers who reported that they work during nonbusiness hours has changed from 0.46 in the previous year. Figure 9.14 presents the Excel, JMP, and Mintab results for these data.

FIGURE 9.14

Excel, JMP, and Minitab Z test results for whether the proportion of American workers who reported that they work during nonbusiness hours has changed from 0.45 in the previous year

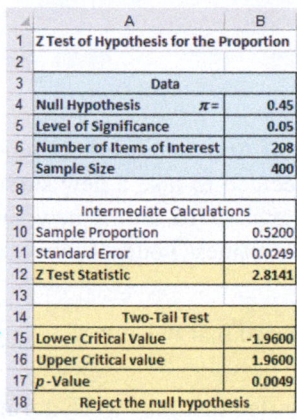

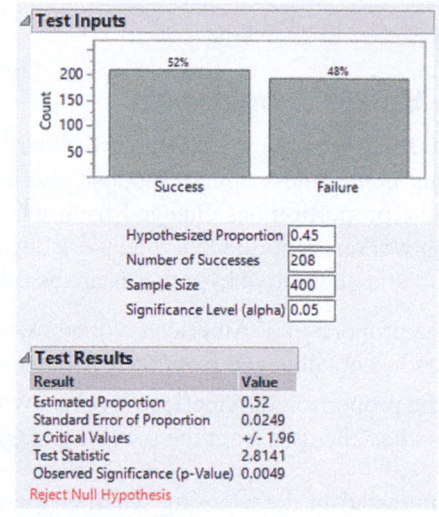

Test and CI for One Proportion

Method

p: event proportion
Normal approximation method is used for this analysis.

Descriptive Statistics

N	Event	Sample p	95% CI for p
400	208	0.520000	(0.471040, 0.568960)

Test

Null hypothesis	H_0: p = 0.45
Alternative hypothesis	H_1: p ≠ 0.45

Z-Value	P-Value
2.81	0.005

The *p*-Value Approach

As an alternative to the critical value approach, you can compute the *p*-value. For this two-tail test in which the rejection region is located in the lower tail and the upper tail, you need to find the area below a Z value of -2.8141 and above a Z value of $+2.8141$. Figure 9.14 reports a *p*-value of 0.0049. Because this value is less than the selected level of significance ($\alpha = 0.05$), you reject the null hypothesis.

Example 9.6 illustrates a one-tail test for a proportion.

EXAMPLE 9.6

Testing a Hypothesis for a Proportion

▶(continued)

In addition to the business problem of the speed of service at the drive-through, fast-food chains want to fill orders correctly. The same audit that reported that McDonald's had a drive-through service time of 208.16 seconds also reported that McDonald's filled 92.2% of its drive-through orders correctly. Suppose that McDonald's begins a quality improvement effort to ensure that orders at the drive-through are filled correctly. The business problem is defined as determining whether the new process can increase the percentage of orders filled correctly. Data are collected from a sample of 500 orders using the new process. The results indicate that 476 orders were filled correctly. At the 0.01 level of significance, can you conclude that the new process has increased the proportion of orders filled correctly?

SOLUTION The null and alternative hypotheses are

H_0: $\pi \leq 0.922$ (the population proportion of orders filled correctly using the new process is less than or equal to 0.922)

H_1: $\pi > 0.922$ (the population proportion of orders filled correctly using the new process is greater than 0.922)

Because $X = 476$ and $n - X = 24$, both > 5, using Equation (9.3) on page 334,

$$p = \frac{X}{n} = \frac{476}{500} = 0.952$$

$$Z_{STAT} = \frac{p - \pi}{\sqrt{\dfrac{\pi(1 - \pi)}{n}}} = \frac{0.952 - 0.922}{\sqrt{\dfrac{0.922(1 - 0.922)}{500}}} = \frac{0.0300}{0.0120} = 2.5015$$

The p-value (computed by Excel) for $Z_{STAT} > 2.5015$ is 0.0062.

Using the critical value approach, you reject H_0 if $Z_{STAT} > 2.33$. Using the p-value approach, you reject H_0 if the p-value < 0.01. Because $Z_{STAT} = 2.5015 > 2.33$ or the p-value $= 0.0062 < 0.01$, you reject H_0. You have evidence that the new process has increased the proportion of correct orders above 0.922 or 92.2%. Therefore, McDonald's should institute the new process at all of its stores.

PROBLEMS FOR SECTION 9.4

LEARNING THE BASICS

9.52 If, in a random sample of 400 items, 88 are defective, what is the sample proportion of defective items?

9.53 In Problem 9.52, if the null hypothesis is that 20% of the items in the population are defective, what is the value of Z_{STAT}?

9.54 In Problems 9.52 and 9.53, suppose you are testing the null hypothesis H_0: $\pi = 0.20$ against the two-tail alternative hypothesis H_1: $\pi \neq 0.20$ and you choose the level of significance $\alpha = 0.05$. What is your statistical decision?

APPLYING THE CONCEPTS

9.55 According to a recent National Association of Colleges and Employers (NACE) report, 44% of college students who had unpaid internships received full-time job offers post-graduation compared to 72% of college students who had paid internships.

Source: Data extracted from "Here's Why You May Want to Rethink That Unpaid Internship," available at **for.tn/29CAnU9**.

A recent survey of 60 college unpaid interns at a local university found that 30 received full-time job offers post-graduation.
a. Use the five-step p-value approach to hypothesis testing and a 0.05 level of significance to determine whether the proportion of college unpaid interns that received full-time job offers post-graduation is different from 0.44.
b. Assume that the study found that 35 of the 60 college unpaid interns had received full-time job offers post-graduation and repeat (a). Are the conclusions the same?

9.56 The worldwide market share for the Chrome web browser was 56.43% in a recent month.

Source: Data extracted from **netmarketshare.com**.

Suppose that you decide to select a sample of 100 students at your university and you find that 60 use the Chrome web browser.
a. Use the five-step p-value approach to determine whether there is evidence that the market share for the Chrome web browser at your university is greater than the worldwide market share of 56.43%. (Use the 0.05 level of significance.)
b. Suppose that the sample size is $n = 600$, and you find that 60% of the sample of students at your university (360 out of 600) use the Chrome web browser. Use the five-step p-value approach to try to determine whether there is evidence that the market share for the Chrome web browser at your university is greater than the worldwide market share of 56.43%. (Use the 0.05 level of significance.)
c. Discuss the effect that sample size has on hypothesis testing.
d. What do you think are your chances of rejecting any null hypothesis concerning a population proportion if a sample size of $n = 20$ is used?

9.57 One of the issues facing organizations is increasing diversity throughout an organization. One of the ways to evaluate an organization's success at increasing diversity is to compare the percentage of employees in the organization in a particular position with a specific background to the percentage in a particular position with that specific background in the general workforce. Recently, a large academic medical center determined that 9 of 17 employees in a particular position were female, whereas 55% of the employees for this position in the general workforce were female. At the 0.05 level of significance, is there evidence that the proportion of females in this position at this medical center is different from would be expected in the general workforce?

 **9.58** What are companies' biggest obstacles to attracting the best talent? Of 703 surveyed U.S. and Canadian

talent acquisition professionals, 464 reported that competition for talent is the biggest obstacle at their company.

Source: *U.S. and Canadian Recruiting Trends 2017*, LinkedIn Talent Solutions, **bit.ly/2s2S6Mc**.

At the 0.05 level of significance, is there evidence that the proportion of all talent acquisition professionals who report competition is the biggest obstacle to attracting the best talent at their company is different from 60%?

9.59 A cellphone provider has the business objective of wanting to determine the proportion of subscribers who would upgrade to a new cellphone with improved features if it were made available at a substantially reduced cost. Data are collected from a random sample of 500 subscribers. The results indicate that 135 of the subscribers would upgrade to a new cellphone at a reduced cost.

a. At the 0.05 level of significance, is there evidence that more than 20% of the customers would upgrade to a new cellphone at a reduced cost?

b. How would the manager in charge of promotional programs concerning residential customers use the results in (a)?

9.60 Actuation Consulting conducted a global survey of product teams with the goal of better understanding the dynamics of product team performance and uncovering the practices that make these teams successful. Having a clear definition of "done" is a basic element of successful product management process. One of the survey findings was that 29.4% of organizations indicated that a collective decision by the product team established this important definition of "done."

Source: *The Study of Product Team Performance, 2016*, available at **bit.ly/2rAGhMT**.

Suppose another study is conducted to check the validity of this result, with the goal of proving that the percentage is less than 29.4%.

a. State the null and research hypotheses.

b. A sample of 100 organizations is selected, and results show that 27 indicated that a collective decision by the product team established this important definition of "done." Use either the six-step critical value hypothesis testing approach or the five-step p-value approach to determine at the 0.05 level of significance whether there is evidence that the percentage is less than 29.4%.

9.5 Potential Hypothesis-Testing Pitfalls and Ethical Issues

To this point, you have studied the fundamental concepts of hypothesis testing. You have used hypothesis testing to analyze differences between sample statistics and hypothesized population parameters in order to make business decisions concerning the underlying population characteristics. You have also learned how to evaluate the risks involved in making these decisions.

When planning to carry out a hypothesis test based on a survey, research study, or designed experiment, you must ask and answer the questions presented in Exhibit 9.5.

EXHIBIT 9.5

Questions for the Planning Stage of Hypothesis Testing

1. What is the goal of the survey, study, or experiment? How can you translate the goal into a null hypothesis and an alternative hypothesis?
2. Is the hypothesis test a two-tail test or one-tail test?
3. Can you select a random sample from the underlying population of interest?
4. What types of data will you collect in the sample? Are the variables numerical or categorical?
5. At what level of significance should you conduct the hypothesis test?
6. Is the intended sample size large enough to achieve the desired power of the test for the level of significance chosen?
7. Which statistical test procedure should you use and why?
8. What conclusions and interpretations can you reach from the results of the hypothesis test?

Failing to consider these questions early in the planning process can lead to biased or incomplete results. Proper planning can help ensure that the statistical study will provide objective information needed to make good business decisions.

Statistical Significance Versus Practical Significance

You need to make a distinction between the existence of a statistically significant result and its practical significance in a field of application. Sometimes, due to a very large sample size, you may get a result that is statistically significant but has little practical significance.

For example, suppose that prior to a national marketing campaign focusing on a series of expensive television commercials, you believe that the proportion of people who recognize your brand is 0.30. At the completion of the campaign, a survey of 20,000 people indicates that 6,168 recognized your brand. A one-tail test trying to prove that the proportion is now greater than 0.30 results in a p-value of 0.0048, and the correct statistical conclusion is that the proportion of consumers recognizing your brand name has now increased. Was the campaign successful? The result of the hypothesis test indicates a statistically significant increase in brand awareness, but is this increase practically important? The population proportion is now estimated at $6,168/20,000 = 0.3084 = 0.3084$ or 30.84%. This increase is less than 1% more than the hypothesized value of 30%. Did the large expenses associated with the marketing campaign produce a result with a meaningful increase in brand awareness? Because of the minimal real-world impact that an increase of less than 1% has on the overall marketing strategy and the huge expenses associated with the marketing campaign, you should conclude that the campaign was not successful. On the other hand, if the campaign increased brand awareness from 30% to 50%, you would be inclined to conclude that the campaign was successful.

Statistical *Insignificance* Versus Importance

In contrast to the issue of the practical significance of a statistically significant result is the situation in which an important result may not be statistically significant. In a recent case (see reference 1), the U.S. Supreme Court ruled that companies cannot rely solely on whether the result of a study is significant when determining what they communicate to investors.

In some situations (see reference 4), the lack of a large enough sample size may result in a nonsignificant result when in fact an important difference does exist. A study that compared male and female entrepreneurship rates globally and within Massachusetts found a significant difference globally but not within Massachusetts, even though the entrepreneurship rates for females and for males in the two geographic areas were similar (8.8% for males in Massachusetts as compared to 8.4% globally; 5% for females in both geographic areas). The difference was due to the fact that the global sample size was 20 times larger than the Massachusetts sample size.

Reporting of Findings

In conducting research, you should document both good and bad results. You should not just report the results of hypothesis tests that show statistical significance but omit those for which there is insufficient evidence in the findings. In instances in which there is insufficient evidence to reject H_0, you must make it clear that this does not prove that the null hypothesis is true. What the result indicates is that with the sample size used, there is not enough information to *disprove* the null hypothesis.

Ethical Issues

You need to distinguish between poor research methodology and unethical behavior. Ethical considerations arise when the hypothesis-testing process is manipulated. Some of the areas where ethical issues can arise include the use of human subjects in experiments, the data collection method, the type of test (one-tail or two-tail test), the choice of the level of significance, the cleansing and discarding of data, and the failure to report pertinent findings.

9.6 Power of the Test

The power of a hypothesis test is the probability that you correctly reject a false null hypothesis. The power of the test is affected by the level of significance, the sample size, and whether the test is one-tail or two-tail. The **Section 9.6 online topic** further explains the power of the test and illustrates its use.

▼USING **STATISTICS**
Significant Testing... Revisited

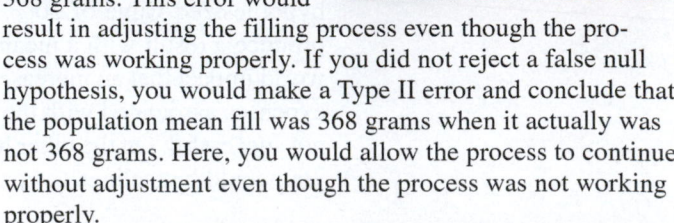

As the plant operations manager for Oxford Cereals, you were responsible for the cereal-filling process. It was your responsibility to adjust the process when the mean fill-weight in the population of boxes deviated from the company specification of 368 grams. You chose to conduct a hypothesis test.

You determined that the null hypothesis should be that the population mean fill was 368 grams. If the mean weight of the sampled boxes was sufficiently above or below the expected 368-gram mean specified by Oxford Cereals, you would reject the null hypothesis in favor of the alternative hypothesis that the mean fill was different from 368 grams. If this happened, you would stop production and take whatever action was necessary to correct the problem. If the null hypothesis was not rejected, you would continue to believe in the status quo—that the process was working correctly—and therefore take no corrective action.

Before proceeding, you considered the risks involved with hypothesis tests. If you rejected a true null hypothesis, you would make a Type I error and conclude that the population mean fill was not 368 when it actually was 368 grams. This error would result in adjusting the filling process even though the process was working properly. If you did not reject a false null hypothesis, you would make a Type II error and conclude that the population mean fill was 368 grams when it actually was not 368 grams. Here, you would allow the process to continue without adjustment even though the process was not working properly.

After collecting a random sample of 25 cereal boxes, you used either the six-step critical value approach or the five-step *p*-value approach to hypothesis testing. Because the test statistic fell into the nonrejection region, you did not reject the null hypothesis. You concluded that there was insufficient evidence to prove that the mean fill differed from 368 grams. No corrective action on the filling process was needed.

▼SUMMARY

This chapter presented the foundation of hypothesis testing. You learned how to perform tests on the population mean and on the population proportion. The chapter developed both the critical value approach and the *p*-value approach to hypothesis testing.

In deciding which test to use, you should ask the following question: Does the test involve a numerical variable or a categorical variable? If the test involves a numerical variable, you use the *t* test for the mean. If the test involves a categorical variable, you use the *Z* test for the proportion. Table 9.4 lists the hypothesis tests covered in the chapter.

TABLE 9.4
Summary of Topics

TYPE OF ANALYSIS	TYPE OF DATA	
	Numerical	Categorical
Hypothesis test concerning a single parameter	Z test of hypothesis for the mean (Section 9.1) t test of hypothesis for the mean (Section 9.2)	Z test of hypothesis for the proportion (Section 9.4)

▼REFERENCES

1. Bialik, C. "Making a Stat Less Significant." *The Wall Street Journal*, April 2, 2011, A5.
2. Bradley, J. V. *Distribution-Free Statistical Tests*. Upper Saddle River, NJ: Prentice Hall, 1968.
3. Daniel, W. *Applied Nonparametric Statistics*, 2nd ed. Boston: Houghton Mifflin, 1990.
4. Seaman, J., and E. Allen. "Not Significant, But Important?" *Quality Progress*, August 2011, 57–59.
5. Seaman, J., and E. Allen. "The Significance of Power." *Quality Progress*, July 2015, 51–53.

▼ KEY EQUATIONS

Z Test for the Mean (σ Known)

$$Z_{STAT} = \frac{\overline{X} - \mu}{\dfrac{\sigma}{\sqrt{n}}} \qquad (9.1)$$

t Test for the Mean (σ Unknown)

$$t_{STAT} = \frac{\overline{X} - \mu}{\dfrac{S}{\sqrt{n}}} \qquad (9.2)$$

Z Test for the Proportion

$$Z_{STAT} = \frac{p - \pi}{\sqrt{\dfrac{\pi(1 - \pi)}{n}}} \qquad (9.3)$$

Z Test for the Proportion in Terms of the Number of Events of Interest

$$Z_{STAT} = \frac{X - n\pi}{\sqrt{n\pi(1 - \pi)}} \qquad (9.4)$$

▼ KEY TERMS

▼ CHECKING YOUR UNDERSTANDING

9.61 What is the difference between a null hypothesis, H_0, and an alternative hypothesis, H_1?

9.62 What is the difference between a Type I error and a Type II error?

9.63 What is meant by the power of a test?

9.64 What is the difference between a one-tail test and a two-tail test?

9.65 What is meant by a p-value?

9.66 How can a confidence interval estimate for the population mean provide conclusions for the corresponding two-tail hypothesis test for the population mean?

9.67 What is the six-step critical value approach to hypothesis testing?

9.68 What is the five-step p-value approach to hypothesis testing?

▼ CHAPTER REVIEW PROBLEMS

9.69 In hypothesis testing, the common level of significance is $\alpha = 0.05$. Some might argue for a level of significance greater than 0.05. Suppose that web designers tested the proportion of potential web page visitors with a preference for a new web design over the existing web design. The null hypothesis was that the population proportion of web page visitors preferring the new design was 0.50, and the alternative hypothesis was that it was not equal to 0.50. The p-value for the test was 0.20.

a. State, in statistical terms, the null and alternative hypotheses for this example.

b. Explain the risks associated with Type I and Type II errors in this case.

c. What would be the consequences if you rejected the null hypothesis for a p-value of 0.20?

d. What might be an argument for raising the value of α?

e. What would you do in this situation?

f. What is your answer in (e) if the p-value equals 0.12? What if it equals 0.06?

9.70 Financial institutions utilize prediction models to predict bankruptcy. One such model is the Altman Z-score model, which uses multiple corporate income and balance sheet values to measure the financial health of a company. If the model predicts a low Z-score value, the firm is in financial stress and is predicted to go bankrupt within the next two years. If the model predicts a moderate or high Z-score value, the firm is financially healthy and is predicted to be a nonbankrupt firm. This decision-making procedure can be expressed in the hypothesis-testing framework. The null hypothesis is that a firm is predicted to be a nonbankrupt firm. The alternative hypothesis is that the firm is predicted to be a bankrupt firm.

a. Explain the risks associated with committing a Type I error in this case.

b. Explain the risks associated with committing a Type II error in this case.

c. Which type of error do you think executives want to avoid? Explain.

d. How would changes in the model affect the probabilities of committing Type I and Type II errors?

9.71 IAB conducted a study of 821 U.S. adults to understand the behavioral shift of consumers' TV viewing experience. The study found that 460 of U.S. adults own streaming enabled TVs, including smart TVs and video streaming devices.

Source: *The Changing TV Experience: 2017*, available at **bit.ly/2sz4Mal**.

The authors of the report imply that the survey proves that more than half of all U.S. adults own streaming enabled TVs, including smart TVs and video streaming devices.

a. Use the five-step *p*-value approach to hypothesis testing and a 0.05 level of significance to try to prove that more than half of all U.S. adults own streaming enabled TVs, including smart TVs and video streaming devices.

b. Based on your result in (a), is the claim implied by the authors valid?

c. Suppose the study found that 428 of U.S. adults own streaming enabled TVs, including smart TVs and video streaming devices. Repeat parts (a) and (b).

d. Compare the results of (b) and (c).

9.72 The owner of a specialty coffee shop wants to study coffee purchasing habits of customers at her shop. She selects a random sample of 60 customers during a certain week, with the following results:

- The amount spent was $\overline{X} = \$7.25$, $S = \$1.75$.
- Thirty-one customers say they "definitely will" recommend the specialty coffee shop to family and friends.

a. At the 0.05 level of significance, is there evidence that the population mean amount spent was different from $6.50?

b. Determine the *p*-value in (a).

c. At the 0.05 level of significance, is there evidence that more than 50% of all the customers say they "definitely will" recommend the specialty coffee shop to family and friends?

d. What is your answer to (a) if the sample mean equals $6.25?

e. What is your answer to (c) if 39 customers say they "definitely will" recommend the specialty coffee shop to family and friends?

9.73 An auditor for a government agency was assigned the task of evaluating reimbursement for office visits to physicians paid by Medicare. The audit was conducted on a sample of 75 reimbursements, with the following results:

- In 12 of the office visits, there was an incorrect amount of reimbursement.
- The amount of reimbursement was $\overline{X} = \$93.70$, $S = \$34.55$.

a. At the 0.05 level of significance, is there evidence that the population mean reimbursement was less than $100?

b. At the 0.05 level of significance, is there evidence that the proportion of incorrect reimbursements in the population was greater than 0.10?

c. Discuss the underlying assumptions of the test used in (a).

d. What is your answer to (a) if the sample mean equals $90?

e. What is your answer to (b) if 15 office visits had incorrect reimbursements?

9.74 A bank branch located in a commercial district of a city has the business objective of improving the process for serving customers during the noon-to-1:00 p.m. lunch period. The waiting time (defined as the time the customer enters the line until he or she reaches the teller window) of a random sample of 15 customers is collected, and the results are organized and stored in Bank1. These data are:

4.21	5.55	3.02	5.13	4.77	2.34	3.54	3.20
4.50	6.10	0.38	5.12	6.46	6.19	3.79	

a. At the 0.05 level of significance, is there evidence that the population mean waiting time is less than 5 minutes?

b. What assumption about the population distribution is needed in order to conduct the *t* test in (a)?

c. Construct a boxplot or a normal probability plot to evaluate the assumption made in (b).

d. Do you think that the assumption needed in order to conduct the *t* test in (a) is valid? Explain.

e. As a customer walks into the branch office during the lunch hour, she asks the branch manager how long she can expect to wait. The branch manager replies, "Almost certainly not longer than 5 minutes." On the basis of the results of (a), evaluate this statement.

9.75 Call centers today play an important role in managing day-to-day business communications with customers. It's important, therefore, to monitor a comprehensive set of metrics, which can help businesses understand the overall performance of a call center. One key metric for measuring overall call center performance is service level which is defined as the percentage of calls answered by a human agent within a specified number of seconds. The file ServiceLevel contains the following data for time, in seconds, to answer 50 incoming calls to a financial services call center:

16	14	16	19	6	14	15	5	16	18	17	22	6	18	10
15	12	6	19	16	16	15	13	25	9	17	12	10	5	15
23	11	12	14	24	9	10	13	14	26	19	20	13	24	28
15	21	8	16	12										

a. At the 0.05 level of significance, is there evidence that the population mean time to answer calls is less than 20 seconds?

b. What assumption about the population distribution is needed in order to conduct the *t* test in (a)?

c. Construct a histogram, boxplot, or normal probability plot to evaluate the assumption made in (b).

d. Do you think that the assumption needed in order to conduct the *t* test in (a) is valid? Explain.

9.76 An important quality characteristic used by the manufacturer of Boston and Vermont asphalt shingles is the amount of moisture the shingles contain when they are packaged. Customers may feel that they have purchased a product lacking in quality if they find moisture and wet shingles inside the packaging. In some cases, excessive moisture can cause the granules attached to the shingles for texture and coloring purposes to fall off the shingles, resulting in appearance problems. To monitor the amount of moisture present, the company conducts moisture tests. A shingle is weighed and then dried. The shingle is then reweighed, and, based on the amount of moisture taken out of the product, the pounds of moisture per 100 square feet are calculated. The company would like to show that the mean moisture content is less than 0.35 pound per 100 square feet. The file Moisture includes 36 measurements (in pounds per 100 square feet) for Boston shingles and 31 for Vermont shingles.

a. For the Boston shingles, is there evidence at the 0.05 level of significance that the population mean moisture content is less than 0.35 pound per 100 square feet?

b. Interpret the meaning of the *p*-value in (a).

c. For the Vermont shingles, is there evidence at the 0.05 level of significance that the population mean moisture content is less than 0.35 pound per 100 square feet?

d. Interpret the meaning of the *p*-value in (c).

e. What assumption about the population distribution is needed in order to conduct the *t* tests in (a) and (c)?

f. Construct histograms, boxplots, or normal probability plots to evaluate the assumption made in (a) and (c).

g. Do you think that the assumption needed in order to conduct the *t* tests in (a) and (c) is valid? Explain.

9.77 Studies conducted by the manufacturer of Boston and Vermont asphalt shingles have shown product weight to be a major factor in the customer's perception of quality. Moreover, the weight represents the amount of raw materials being used and is therefore very important to the company from a cost standpoint. The last stage of the assembly line packages the shingles before the packages are placed on wooden pallets. Once a pallet is full (a pallet for most brands holds 16 squares of shingles), it is weighed, and the measurement is recorded. The file Pallet contains the weight (in pounds) from a sample of 368 pallets of Boston shingles and 330 pallets of Vermont shingles.

a. For the Boston shingles, is there evidence at the 0.05 level of significance that the population mean weight is different from 3,150 pounds?

b. Interpret the meaning of the *p*-value in (a).

c. For the Vermont shingles, is there evidence at the 0.05 level of significance that the population mean weight is different from 3,700 pounds?

d. Interpret the meaning of the *p*-value in (c).

e. In (a) through (d), do you have to be concerned with the normality assumption? Explain.

9.78 The manufacturer of Boston and Vermont asphalt shingles provides its customers with a 20-year warranty on most of its products. To determine whether a shingle will last through the warranty period, accelerated-life testing is conducted at the manufacturing plant. Accelerated-life testing exposes the shingle to the stresses it would be subject to in a lifetime of normal use in a laboratory setting via an experiment that takes only a few minutes to conduct. In this test, a shingle is repeatedly scraped with a brush for a short period of time, and the shingle granules removed by the brushing are weighed (in grams). Shingles that experience low amounts of granule loss are expected to last longer in normal use than shingles that experience high amounts of granule loss. The file Granule contains a sample of 170 measurements made on the company's Boston shingles and 140 measurements made on Vermont shingles.

a. For the Boston shingles, is there evidence at the 0.05 level of significance that the population mean granule loss is different from 0.30 grams?

b. Interpret the meaning of the *p*-value in (a).

c. For the Vermont shingles, is there evidence at the 0.05 level of significance that the population mean granule loss is different from 0.30 grams?

d. Interpret the meaning of the *p*-value in (c).

e. In (a) through (d), do you have to be concerned with the normality assumption? Explain.

REPORT WRITING EXERCISE

9.79 Referring to the results of Problems 9.76 through 9.78 concerning Boston and Vermont shingles, write a report that evaluates the moisture level, weight, and granule loss of the two types of shingles.

CHAPTER

▾CASES

9

Managing Ashland MultiComm Services

Continuing its monitoring of the upload speed first described in the Chapter 6 Managing Ashland MultiComm Services case on page 246, the technical operations department wants to ensure that the mean target upload speed for all Internet service subscribers is at least 0.97 on a standard scale in which the target value is 1.0. Each day, upload speed was measured 50 times, with the following results (stored in AMS9).

```
0.854 1.023 1.005 1.030 1.219 0.977 1.044 0.778 1.122 1.114
1.091 1.086 1.141 0.931 0.723 0.934 1.060 1.047 0.800 0.889
1.012 0.695 0.869 0.734 1.131 0.993 0.762 0.814 1.108 0.805
1.223 1.024 0.884 0.799 0.870 0.898 0.621 0.818 1.113 1.286
1.052 0.678 1.162 0.808 1.012 0.859 0.951 1.112 1.003 0.972
```

1. Compute the sample statistics and determine whether there is evidence that the population mean upload speed is less than 0.97.

2. Write a memo to management that summarizes your conclusions.

Digital Case

Apply your knowledge about hypothesis testing in this Digital Case, which continues the cereal-fill-packaging dispute first discussed in the Digital Case from Chapter 7.

In response to the negative statements made by the Concerned Consumers About Cereal Cheaters (CCACC) in the Chapter 7 Digital Case, Oxford Cereals recently conducted an experiment concerning cereal packaging. The company claims that the results of the experiment refute the CCACC allegations that Oxford Cereals has been cheating consumers by packaging cereals at less than labeled weights.

Open **OxfordCurrentNews.pdf**, a portfolio of current news releases from Oxford Cereals. Review the relevant press releases and supporting documents. Then answer the following questions:

1. Are the results of the experiment valid? Why or why not? If you were conducting the experiment, is there anything you would change?

2. Do the results support the claim that Oxford Cereals is not cheating its customers?

3. Is the claim of the Oxford Cereals CEO that many cereal boxes contain *more* than 368 grams surprising? Is it true?

4. Could there ever be a circumstance in which the results of the Oxford Cereals experiment *and* the CCACC's results are both correct? Explain.

Sure Value Convenience Stores

You work in the corporate office for a nationwide convenience store franchise that operates nearly 10,000 stores. The per-store daily customer count (i.e., the mean number of customers in a store in one day) has been steady, at 900, for some time. To increase the customer count, the chain is considering cutting prices for coffee beverages. The small size will now be $0.59 instead of $0.99, and the medium size will be $0.69 instead of $1.19. Even with this reduction in price, the chain will have a 40% gross margin on coffee.

To test the new initiative, the chain has reduced coffee prices in a sample of 34 stores, where customer counts have been running almost exactly at the national average of 900. After four weeks, the stores sampled stabilize at a mean customer count of 974 and a standard deviation of 96. This increase seems like a substantial amount to you, but it also seems like a pretty small sample. Is there statistical evidence that reducing coffee prices is a good strategy for increasing the mean customer count? Be prepared to explain your conclusion.

▾EXCEL GUIDE

EG9.1 FUNDAMENTALS of HYPOTHESIS TESTING

Key Technique Use the **NORM.S.INV(***level of significance/2***)** and **NORM.S.INV(1 –** *level of significance/2***)** functions to compute the lower and upper critical values. Use **NORM.S.DIST (***absolute value of the Z test statistic***, True)** as part of a formula to compute the *p*-value.

Example Perform the Figure 9.5 two-tail Z test for the mean for the cereal-filling example on page 321.

PHStat Use **Z Test for the Mean, sigma known**.

For the example, select **PHStat → One-Sample Tests → Z Test for the Mean, sigma known**. In the procedure's dialog box (shown below):

1. Enter **368** as the **Null Hypothesis**.
2. Enter **0.05** as the **Level of Significance**.
3. Enter **15** as the **Population Standard Deviation**.
4. Click **Sample Statistics Known** and enter **25** as the **Sample Size** and **372.5** as the **Sample Mean**.
5. Click **Two-Tail Test**.
6. Enter a **Title** and click **OK**.

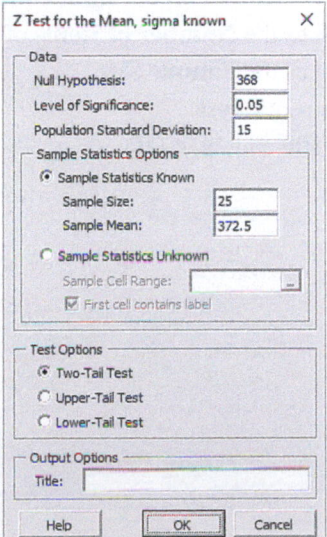

When using unsummarized data, click **Sample Statistics Unknown** in step 4 and enter the cell range of the unsummarized data as the **Sample Cell Range**.

Workbook Use the **COMPUTE worksheet** of the **Z Mean workbook** as a template.

The worksheet already contains the data for the example. For other problems, change the null hypothesis, level of significance, population standard deviation, sample size, and sample mean values in cells B4 through B8 as necessary.

EG9.2 *t* TEST of HYPOTHESIS for the MEAN (σ UNKNOWN)

Key Technique Use the **T.INV.2T(***level of significance, degrees of freedom***)** function to compute the lower and upper critical values.

Use **T.DIST.2T(***absolute value of the t test statistic, degrees of freedom***)** to compute the *p*-value.

Example Perform the Figure 9.7 two-tail *t* test for the mean for the sales invoices example on page 326.

PHStat Use **t Test for the Mean, sigma unknown**.

For the example, select **PHStat → One-Sample Tests → t Test for the Mean, sigma unknown**. In the procedure's dialog box (shown below):

1. Enter **120** as the **Null Hypothesis**.
2. Enter **0.05** as the **Level of Significance**.
3. Click **Sample Statistics Known** and enter **12** as the **Sample Size**, **112.85** as the **Sample Mean**, and **20.8** as the **Sample Standard Deviation**.
4. Click **Two-Tail Test**.
5. Enter a **Title** and click **OK**.

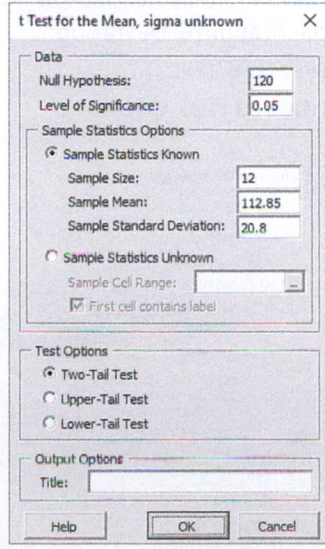

When using unsummarized data, click **Sample Statistics Unknown** in step 3 and enter the cell range of the unsummarized data as the **Sample Cell Range**.

Workbook Use the **COMPUTE worksheet** of the **T mean workbook**, as a template.

The worksheet already contains the data for the example. For other problems, change the values in cells B4 through B8 as necessary.

EG9.3 ONE-TAIL TESTS

Key Technique (Z test for the mean) Use the **NORM.S.INV** with (*level of significance*) and (*1 – level of significance*) to compute the lower and upper critical values.

Use **NORM.S.DIST**(*Z test statistic*, **True**) and **1 – NORM.S.DIST**(*Z test statistic*, **True**) to compute the lower-tail and upper-tail *p*-values.

Key Technique (t test for the mean) Use the **–T.INV.2T** and **T.INV.2T** functions with (*2 * level of significance*, *degrees of freedom*) to compute the lower and upper critical values.

Use an IF function that tests the *t* test statistic to determine whether **T.DIST.RT**(*absolute value of the t test statistic, degrees of freedom*) or **1 – T.DIST.RT**(*absolute value of the t test statistic, degrees of freedom*) computes the *p*-value.

Example Perform the Figure 9.11 lower-tail *t* test for the mean for the drive-through time study example on page 332.

PHStat Click either **Lower-Tail Test** or **Upper-Tail Test** in the procedure dialog boxes discussed in Sections EG9.1 and EG9.2 to perform a one-tail test.

For the example, select **PHStat → One-Sample Tests → t Test for the Mean, sigma unknown**. In the procedure's dialog box (shown below):

1. Enter **208.16** as the **Null Hypothesis**.
2. Enter **0.05** as the **Level of Significance**.
3. Click **Sample Statistics Known** and enter **25** as the **Sample Size**, **195.6** as the **Sample Mean**, and **22.1** as the **Sample Standard Deviation**.
4. Click **Lower-Tail Test**.
5. Enter a **Title** and click **OK**.

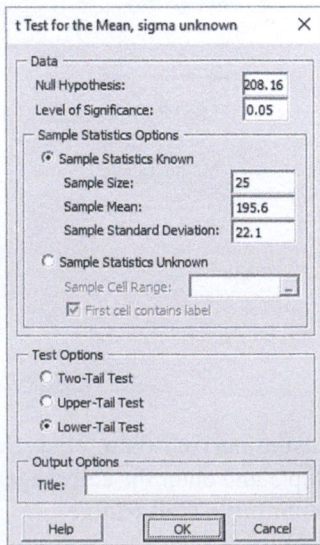

Workbook Use the **COMPUTE_LOWER worksheet** or the **COMPUTE_UPPER worksheet** of the **Z Mean and T mean workbooks** as templates.

For the example, open to the **COMPUTE_LOWER worksheet** of the **T mean workbook**. For other problems that require a *t* test, open to the appropriate worksheet and

change the **Null Hypothesis, Level of Significance, Sample Size, Sample Mean**, and **Sample Standard Deviation** in the cell range B4:B8.

For other problems that require a *Z* test, open to the appropriate worksheet and change the **Null Hypothesis, Level of Significance, Population Standard Deviation, Sample Size**, and **Sample Mean** in the cell range B4:B8.

To see the all of the formulas used in the one-tail test worksheets, open to the COMPUTE_ALL_FORMULAS worksheet.

EG9.4 *Z* TEST of HYPOTHESIS for the PROPORTION

Key Technique Use the **NORM.S.INV**(*level of significance/2*) and **NORM.S.INV**(*1 – level of significance/2*) functions to compute the lower and upper critical values.

Use **NORM.S.DIST**(*absolute value of the Z test statistic*, **True**) as part of a formula to compute the *p*-value.

Example Perform the Figure 9.14 two-tail *Z* test for the proportion for whether the proportion of American workers who reported that they work during nonbusiness hours has changed on page 336.

PHStat Use **Z Test for the Proportion**.

For the example, select **PHStat → One-Sample Tests → Z Test for the Proportion**. In the procedure's dialog box (shown below):

1. Enter **0.45** as the **Null Hypothesis**.
2. Enter **0.05** as the **Level of Significance**.
3. Enter **208** as the **Number of Items of Interest**.
4. Enter **400** as the **Sample Size**.
5. Click **Two-Tail Test**.
6. Enter a **Title** and click **OK**.

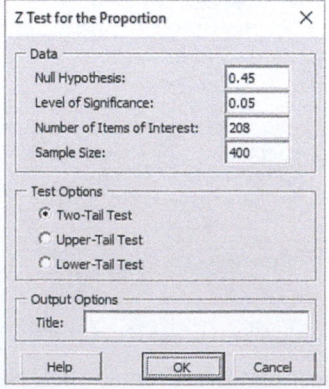

Workbook Use the **COMPUTE worksheet** of the **Z Proportion workbook** as a template.

The worksheet already contains the data for the example. For other problems, change the null hypothesis, level of significance, population standard deviation, sample size, and sample mean values in cells B4 through B7 as necessary.

Use the COMPUTE_LOWER or COMPUTE_UPPER worksheets as templates for performing one-tail tests.

▾ JMP GUIDE

JG9.1 FUNDAMENTALS of HYPOTHESIS TESTING

Use the **Hypothesis Test for One Mean calculator**.

For example, to perform the Figure 9.5 Z test for the mean for the cereal-filling example on page 321, select **Help ➔ Sample Data** and:

1. In the Sample Data Index window, click the **Calculators disclosure button** (gray triangle).
2. Click **Hypothesis Test for One Mean** in the revealed list.
3. In the Choose Input dialog box, click **Summary Statistics** and then click **OK**.

In the left side of the Hypothesis Test on Mean dialog box (partially shown below):

4. Select the **z-test** option.
5. Select **Population mean is not equal to hypothesized mean (two-tailed)**.
6. Check **Reveal Decision**.

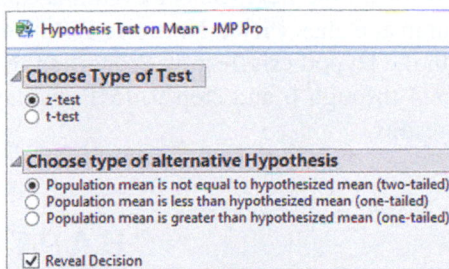

In the right side of the Hypothesis Test on Mean dialog box (partially shown below):

7. Enter **368** as the **Hypothesized Mean**.
8. Enter **372.5** as the **Sample Average**.
9. Enter **15** as the **Population Standard Deviation**.
10. Enter **25** as the **Sample Size**.
11. Enter **0.05** as the **Significance Level (alpha)**.

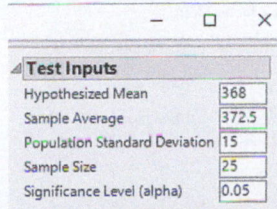

JMP displays results in the calculator window as shown in Figure 9.5. Because of the nature of JMP calculators, to save results, save window as a JMP journal (*.jrn) file. For unsummarized data, open to the data table that contains the data and

follow Steps 1 through 2, and modify step 3 to click **Raw Data**. In the next (Select Columns) dialog box, select a column and click **Pick a Numeric Column** and then press **OK**. In the Hypothesis Test on Mean dialog box, follow steps 4 through 6 and then enter values for the **Hypothesized Mean**, **Population Standard Deviation**, and **Significance Level (alpha)**. JMP displays a new window of results. In this window, the known sigma value can be entered.

JG9.2 t TEST of HYPOTHESIS for the MEAN (σ UNKNOWN)

Use the **Hypothesis Test for One Mean calculator**.

For example, to perform the Figure 9.7 two-tail t test for the mean for the sales invoice example on page 326, select **Help ➔ Sample Data** and:

1. In the Sample Data Index window, click the **Calculators disclosure button** (gray triangle).
2. Click **Hypothesis Test for One Mean** in the revealed list.
3. In the Choose Input dialog box, click **Summary Statistics** and then click **OK**.

In the left side of the Hypothesis Test on Mean dialog box:

4. Select the **t-test** option.
5. Select **Population mean is not equal to hypothesized mean (two-tailed)**.
6. Check **Reveal Decision**.

In the right side of the Hypothesis Test on Mean dialog box (partially shown below):

7. Enter **120** as the **Null Hypothesis**.
8. Enter **112.85** as the **Sample Average**.
9. Enter **20.8** as the **Sample Standard Deviation**.
10. Enter **12** as the **Sample Size**.
11. Enter **0.05** as the **Significance Level (alpha)**.

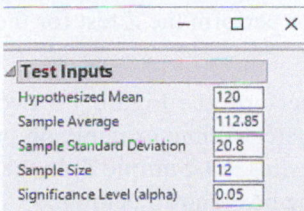

JMP displays results in the calculator window as shown in Figure 9.7. Because of the nature of JMP calculators, to save results, save window as a JMP journal (*.jrn) file. For unsummarized data, open to the data table that contains the data and follow steps 1 through 2, and modify step 3 to click **Raw Data**. In the next (Select Columns) dialog box, select a column and click **Pick a Numeric Column** and then press **OK**. In the Hypothesis Test on Mean dialog box, follow steps 4 through 6 and then enter values for the **Hypothesized Mean** and **Significance Level (alpha)**. JMP displays a new window of results.

JG9.3   ONE-TAIL TESTS

Use the **Hypothesis Test for One Mean calculator**.

To perform a one-tail test, select **Population mean is less than hypothesized mean (one-tailed)** or **Population mean is greater than hypothesized mean (one-tailed)** in step 5 in the Section JG8.1 instructions (Z test for the mean) or in the Section JG8.2 instructions (*t* test for the mean, σ unknown).

JG9.4   Z TEST of HYPOTHESIS for the PROPORTION

Use the **Hypothesis Test for One Proportion calculator**.

For example, to perform the Figure 9.14 Z test for the proportion for whether the proportion of American workers who reported that they work during nonbusiness hours has changed on page 336, select **Help → Sample Data** and:

1. In the Sample Data Index window, click the **Calculators disclosure button** (gray triangle).
2. Click **Hypothesis Test for One Proportion** in the revealed list.
3. In the Choose Input dialog box, click **Summary Statistics** and then click **OK**.

In the left side of the Hypothesis Test on Proportion dialog box:

4. Select **Population proportion is not equal to hypothesized proportion (two-tailed)**.
5. Check **Reveal Decision**.

In the right side of the Hypothesis Test on Proportion dialog box (partially shown below):

6. Enter **0.45** as the **Hypothesized Proportion**.
7. Enter **208** as the **Number of Successes**.
8. Enter **400** as the **Sample Size**.
9. Enter **0.05** as the **Significance Level (alpha)**.

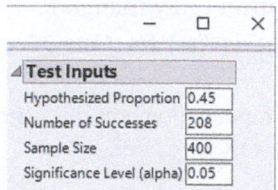

JMP displays results in the calculator window as shown in Figure 9.14. Because of the nature of JMP calculators, to save results, save window as a JMP journal (*.jrn) file.

For unsummarized data, open to the data table that contains the data and follow steps 1 through 2, and modify step 3 to click **Raw Data**. In the next (Select Columns) dialog box, select a column and click **Pick a Numeric Column** and then press **OK**. In the Hypothesis Test on Proportion dialog box, follow steps 4 through 6 and step 9. JMP displays a new window of results.

CHAPTER 9

▼MINITAB GUIDE

MG9.1   FUNDAMENTALS of HYPOTHESIS TESTING

Use **1-Sample Z** to perform the Z test for the mean when σ is known.

For example, to perform the Figure 9.5 two-tail Z test for the mean for the cereal-filling example on page 321, select **Stat → Basic Statistics → 1-Sample Z**. In the One-Sample Z for the Mean dialog box (shown below):

1. Select **Summarized data** from the unlabeled pull-down list.
2. Enter **25** in the **Sample size** box and **372.5** in the **Mean** box.
3. Enter **15** in the **Known Standard deviation** box.

4. Check **Perform hypothesis test** and enter **368** in the **Hypothesized mean** box.
5. Click **Options**.

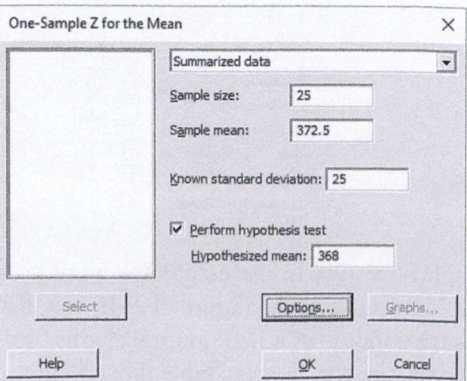
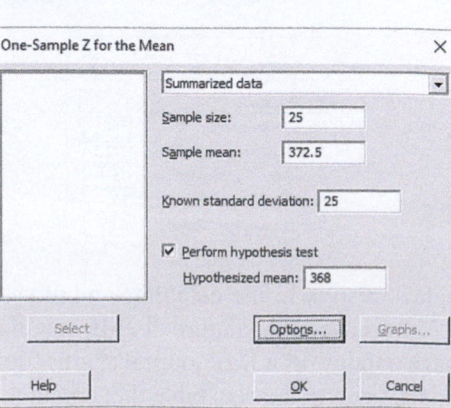

In the One-Sample Z dialog box:

6. Enter **95.0** in the **Confidence level** box.
7. Select **Mean ≠ hypothesized mean** from the **Alternative hypothesis** drop-down list.
8. Click **OK**.
9. Back in the original dialog box, click **OK**.

When using unsummarized data, open the worksheet that contains the data and replace steps 1 and 2 with these steps:

1. Select **One or more samples, each in a column** from the unlabeled pull-down list.
2. Enter the name of the column containing the unsummarized data in the unlabeled box below the pull-down list.

MG9.2 *t* TEST of HYPOTHESIS for the MEAN (σ UNKNOWN)

Use **1-Sample t** to perform the *t* test for the mean when σ is unknown.

For example, to perform the Figure 9.7 two-tail *t* test for the example on page 326, select **Stat → Basic Statistics → 1-Sample t**.

In the One-Sample t for the Mean dialog box (shown below):

1. Select **Summarized data** from the unlabeled pull-down list.
2. Enter **12** in the **Sample size** box, **112.85** in the **Mean** box, and **20.8** in the **Standard deviation** box.
3. Check **Perform hypothesis test** and enter **120** in the **Hypothesized mean** box.
4. Click **Options**.

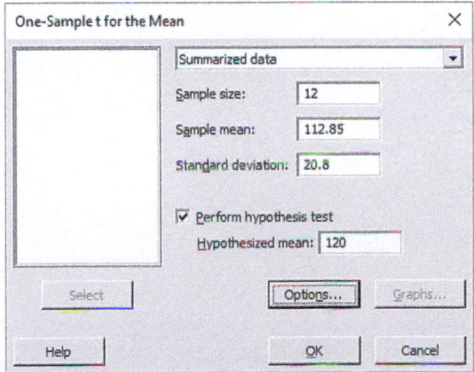

In the One-Sample t: Options dialog box:

5. Enter **95.0** in the **Confidence level** box.
6. Select **Mean ≠ hypothesized mean** from the **Alternative hypothesis** drop-down list.
7. Click **OK**.
8. Back in the original dialog box, click **OK**.

When using unsummarized data, open the worksheet that contains the data and replace steps 1 and 2 with these steps:

1. Select **One or more samples, each in a column** from the unlabeled pull-down list.
2. Enter the name of the column containing the unsummarized data in unlabeled box below the pull-down list.

To create a boxplot of the unsummarized data, replace step 8 with the following steps 8 through 10:

8. Back in the original dialog box, click **Graphs**.
9. In the One-Sample t: Graphs dialog box, check **Boxplot** and then click **OK**.
10. Back in the original dialog box, click **OK**.

MG9.3   ONE-TAIL TESTS

To perform a one-tail test for **1-Sample Z**, select **Mean > hypothesized mean** or **Mean < hypothesized mean** from the drop-down list in step 7 of the Section MG9.1 instructions.

To perform a one-tail test for **1-Sample t**, select **Mean > hypothesized mean** or **Mean < hypothesized mean** from the drop-down list in step 6 of the Section MG9.2 instructions.

MG9.4   *Z* TEST of HYPOTHESIS for the PROPORTION

Use **1 Proportion**.

For example, to perform the Figure 9.14 *Z* test for the proportion for whether the proportion of American workers who reported that they work during nonbusiness hours has changed on page 336, select **Stat → Basic Statistics → 1 Proportion**. In the One-Sample Proportion dialog box (shown below):

1. Select **Summarized data** from the unlabeled pull-down list.
2. Enter **208** in the **Number of events** box and **400** in the **Number of trials** box.
3. Check **Perform hypothesis test** and enter **0.45** in the **Hypothesized proportion** box.
4. Click **Options**.

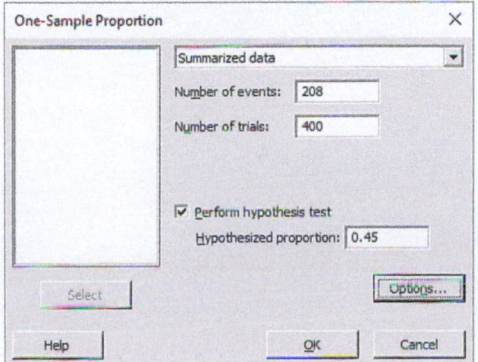

In the One-Sample Proportion: Options dialog box (shown below):

5. Enter **95.0** in the **Confidence level** box.

6. Select **Proportion ≠ hypothesized proportion** from the **Alternative hypothesis** drop-down list.

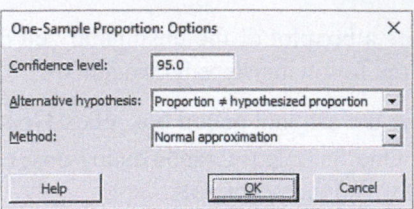

7. Select **Normal approximation** from the **Method** pull-down list.

8. Click **OK**.

9. Back in the original dialog box, click **OK**.

When using unsummarized data, open the worksheet that contains the data and replace steps 1 and 2 with these steps:

1. Select **One or more samples, each in a column** from the unlabeled pull-down list.

2. Enter the name of the column containing the unsummarized data in the unlabeled box below the pull-down list.

To perform a one-tail test, select **Proportion > hypothesized proportion** or **Proportion < hypothesized proportion** from the drop-down list in step 6.

Two-Sample Tests

▼ USING **STATISTICS**
Differing Means for Selling Streaming Media Players at Arlingtons?

To what extent does the location of products in a store affect sales? At Arlingtons, a general merchandiser that competes with discount and wholesale club retailers, management has been considering this question as part of a general review. Seeking to enhance revenues, managers have decided to create a new sales area at the front of the each Arlingtons store, near the checkout lanes. Management plans to charge product manufacturers a placement fee for placing specific products in this front area, but first need to demonstrate that the area would boost sales.

While some manufacturers refuse to pay such placement fees, Arlingtons has found a willing partner in Pierrsöhn Technologies. Pierrsöhn wants to introduce VLABGo, their new mobile streaming player, and is willing to pay a placement fee to be featured at the front of each Arlingtons store. However, Pierrsöhn management wants reassurance that the front of the store will be worth the placement fee. As the retail operations chief at Arlingtons, you have been asked to negotiate with Pierrsöhn. You propose a test that will involve 20 Arlingtons locations, all with similar storewide sales volumes and shopper demographics. You explain that you will randomly select 10 stores to sell the VLABGo player among other, similar items in the mobile electronics aisle in those Arlingtons stores. For the other 10 stores, you will place the VLABGo players in a special area at the front of the store.

At the end of the one-month test period, the sales of VLABGo players from the two store samples will be recorded and compared. You wonder how you could determine whether the sales in the in-aisle stores are different from the sales in the stores where the VLABGo players appear in the special front area. You also would like to decide if the variability in sales from store to store is different for the two types of sales location. If you can demonstrate a difference in sales, you will have a stronger case for asking for a special front of the store placement fee from Pierrsöhn. What should you do?

OBJECTIVES

- Compare the means of two independent populations
- Compare the means of two related populations
- Compare the proportions of two independent populations
- Compare the variances of two independent populations

C hapter 9 discusses several hypothesis-testing procedures commonly used to test a single sample of data selected from a single population. Hypothesis testing can be extended to **two-sample tests** that compare statistics from samples selected from *two* populations. In the Arlingtons scenario one such test would be "Are the mean VLABGo player monthly sales at the special front location (one population) different from the mean VLABGo player monthly sales at the in-aisle location (a second population)?"

10.1 Comparing the Means of Two Independent Populations

Using the correct two-sample test to compare the means of samples selected from each of two independent populations requires first establishing whether the assumption that the variances in the two populations are equal holds. If the assumption holds, you use a *pooled-variance t test*, otherwise you use a *separate variance t test*. Determining whether the assumption that the two variances are equal can be complicated because when you sample from two independent populations, you almost always do not know the standard deviation of either population, as Sections 8.1 and 9.1 note. However, using the sample variances, you can test whether the two population variances are equal using the method that Section 10.4 discusses.

student TIP

Whichever population is defined as population 1 in the null and alternative hypotheses must be defined as population 1 in Equation (10.1). Whichever population is defined as population 2 in the null and alternative hypotheses must be defined as population 2 in Equation (10.1).

Pooled-Variance t Test for the Difference Between Two Means Assuming Equal Variances

If you assume that the random samples are independently selected from two populations and that the populations are normally distributed and have equal variances, you can use a **pooled-variance t test** to determine whether there is a significant difference between the means. If the populations do not differ greatly from a normal distribution, you can still use the pooled-variance t test, especially if the sample sizes are large enough (typically ≥ 30 for each sample).

Using subscripts to distinguish between the population mean of the first population, μ_1, and the population mean of the second population, μ_2, the null hypothesis of no difference in the means of two independent populations can be stated as

$$H_0: \mu_1 = \mu_2 \quad \text{or} \quad \mu_1 - \mu_2 = 0$$

and the alternative hypothesis, that the means are different, can be stated as

$$H_1: \mu_1 \neq \mu_2 \quad \text{or} \quad \mu_1 - \mu_2 \neq 0$$

[1]When the two sample sizes are equal (i.e., $n_1 = n_2$), the equation for the pooled variance can be simplified to

$$S_p^2 = \frac{S_1^2 + S_2^2}{2}$$

To test the null hypothesis, you use the pooled-variance t test statistic t_{STAT} shown in Equation (10.1). The pooled-variance t test gets its name from the fact that the test statistic pools, or combines, the two sample variances S_1^2 and S_2^2 to compute S_p^2, the best estimate of the variance common to both populations, under the assumption that the two population variances are equal.[1]

POOLED-VARIANCE t TEST FOR THE DIFFERENCE BETWEEN TWO MEANS

$$t_{STAT} = \frac{(\overline{X}_1 - \overline{X}_2) - (\mu_1 - \mu_2)}{\sqrt{S_p^2\left(\frac{1}{n_1} + \frac{1}{n_2}\right)}} \tag{10.1}$$

where

$$S_p^2 = \frac{(n_1 - 1)S_1^2 + (n_2 - 1)S_2^2}{(n_1 - 1) + (n_2 - 1)}$$

and $S_p^2 =$ pooled variance

$\overline{X}_1 =$ mean of the sample taken from population 1

$S_1^2 =$ variance of the sample taken from population 1

$n_1 =$ size of the sample taken from population 1

$\overline{X}_2 =$ mean of the sample taken from population 2

$S_2^2 =$ variance of the sample taken from population 2

$n_2 =$ size of the sample taken from population 2

The t_{STAT} test statistic follows a t distribution with $n_1 + n_2 - 2$ degrees of freedom.

For a given level of significance, α, in a two-tail test, you reject the null hypothesis if the computed t_{STAT} test statistic is greater than the upper-tail critical value from the t distribution or if the computed t_{STAT} test statistic is less than the lower-tail critical value from the t distribution. Figure 10.1 displays the regions of rejection.

FIGURE 10.1

Regions of rejection and nonrejection for the pooled-variance t test for the difference between the means (two-tail test)

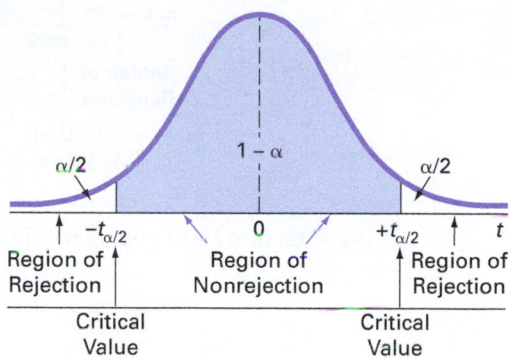

When *lower* or *less than* is used in an example, you have a lower-tail test. When *upper* or *more than* is used in an example, you have an upper-tail test. When *different* or *the same as* is used in an example, you have a two-tail test.

In a one-tail test in which the rejection region is in the lower tail, you reject the null hypothesis if the computed t_{STAT} test statistic is less than the lower-tail critical value from the t distribution. In a one-tail test in which the rejection region is in the upper tail, you reject the null hypothesis if the computed t_{STAT} test statistic is greater than the upper-tail critical value from the t distribution.

To demonstrate the pooled-variance t test, return to the Arlingtons scenario on page 351. Using the DCOVA problem-solving approach, you define the business objective as determining whether there is a difference in the mean VLABGo player monthly sales at the special front and in-aisle locations. There are two populations of interest. The first population is the set of all possible VLABGo player monthly sales at the special front location. The second population is the set of all possible VLABGo player monthly sales at the in-aisle location. You collect the data from a sample of 10 Arlingtons stores that have been assigned the special front location and another sample of 10 Arlingtons stores that have been assigned the in-aisle location. You organize the data as Table 10.1 and store the data in VLABGo.

TABLE 10.1

Comparing VLABGo player Sales from Two Different Locations

SALES LOCATION									
Special Front					**In-Aisle**				
224	189	248	285	273	192	236	164	154	189
190	243	215	280	317	220	261	186	219	202

The null and alternative hypotheses are

$$H_0: \mu_1 = \mu_2 \quad \text{or} \quad \mu_1 - \mu_2 = 0$$

$$H_1: \mu_1 \neq \mu_2 \quad \text{or} \quad \mu_1 - \mu_2 \neq 0$$

Assuming that the samples are from normal populations having equal variances, you can use the pooled-variance t test. The t_{STAT} test statistic follows a t distribution with $10 + 10 - 2 = 18$ degrees of freedom. Using an $\alpha = 0.05$ level of significance, you divide the rejection region into the two tails for this two-tail test (i.e., two equal parts of 0.025 each). Table E.3 shows that the critical values for this two-tail test are $+2.1009$ and -2.1009. As shown in Figure 10.2 on page 354, the decision rule is

Reject H_0 if $t_{STAT} > +2.1009$

or if $t_{STAT} < -2.1009$;

otherwise, do not reject H_0.

FIGURE 10.2

Two-tail test of hypothesis for the difference between the means at the 0.05 level of significance with 18 degrees of freedom

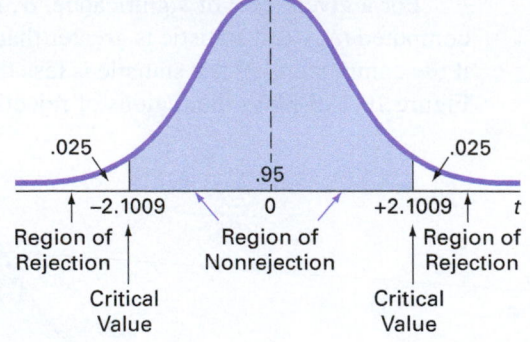

Using Equation (10.1) on page 352 and the Figure 10.3 descriptive statistics,

$$t_{STAT} = \frac{(\overline{X}_1 - \overline{X}_2) - (\mu_1 - \mu_2)}{\sqrt{S_p^2 \left(\dfrac{1}{n_1} + \dfrac{1}{n_2} \right)}}$$

where

$$S_p^2 = \frac{(n_1 - 1)S_1^2 + (n_2 - 1)S_2^2}{(n_1 - 1) + (n_2 - 1)} = \frac{9(42.5420)^2 + 9(32.5271)^2}{9 + 9} = 1,433.9167$$

resulting in

$$t_{STAT} = \frac{(246.4 - 202.3) - 0.0}{\sqrt{1,433.9167 \left(\dfrac{1}{10} + \dfrac{1}{10} \right)}} = \frac{44.1}{\sqrt{286.7833}} = 2.6041$$

Figure 10.3 shows the Excel, JMP, and Minitab results for the two different sales locations data.

FIGURE 10.3

Excel, JMP, and Minitab pooled-variance *t* test results with confidence interval estimate for the two different sales locations data

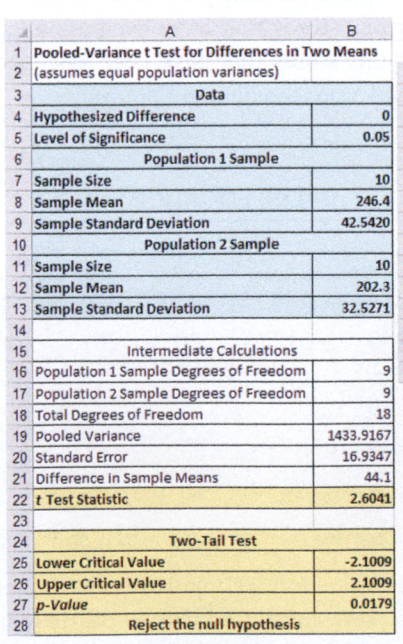

	A	B
1	Pooled-Variance t Test for Differences in Two Means	
2	(assumes equal population variances)	
3	Data	
4	Hypothesized Difference	0
5	Level of Significance	0.05
6	Population 1 Sample	
7	Sample Size	10
8	Sample Mean	246.4
9	Sample Standard Deviation	42.5420
10	Population 2 Sample	
11	Sample Size	10
12	Sample Mean	202.3
13	Sample Standard Deviation	32.5271
14		
15	Intermediate Calculations	
16	Population 1 Sample Degrees of Freedom	9
17	Population 2 Sample Degrees of Freedom	9
18	Total Degrees of Freedom	18
19	Pooled Variance	1433.9167
20	Standard Error	16.9347
21	Difference in Sample Means	44.1
22	t Test Statistic	2.6041
23		
24	Two-Tail Test	
25	Lower Critical Value	-2.1009
26	Upper Critical Value	2.1009
27	p-Value	0.0179
28	Reject the null hypothesis	

	D	E
3	Confidence Interval Estimate	
4	for the Difference Between Two Means	
5		
6	Data	
7	Confidence Level	95%
8		
9	Intermediate Calculations	
10	Degrees of Freedom	18
11	t Value	2.1009
12	Interval Half Width	35.5784
13		
14	Confidence Interval	
15	Interval Lower Limit	8.5216
16	Interval Upper Limit	79.6784

Summary Statistics

Sample 1 Mean	202.3
Sample 1 Standard Deviation	32.5271
Sample 1 Size	10
Sample 2 Mean	246.4
Sample 2 Standard Deviation	42.542
Sample 2 Size	10
Pooled Estimate of Standard Deviation	30.3509
Difference in Sample Means (Mean 2 - Mean 1)	44.1

Test Results

Result	Value
Standard Error of the Difference (Mean 2 - Mean 1)	16.9347
t-score	2.6041
t Critical Value(s)	+/- 2.1009
Observed Significance (p-value)	0.0179
Reject Null Hypothesis	

Two-Sample T-Test and CI: Special Front, In-Aisle

Method

μ₁: mean of Special Front
μ₂: mean of In-Aisle
Difference: μ₁ - μ₂
Equal variances are assumed for this analysis.

Descriptive Statistics

Sample	N	Mean	StDev	SE Mean
Special Front	10	246.4	42.5	13
In-Aisle	10	202.3	32.5	10

Estimation for Difference

Difference	Pooled StDev	95% CI for Difference
44.1	37.9	(8.5, 79.7)

Test

Null hypothesis	H₀: μ₁ - μ₂ = 0
Alternative hypothesis	H₁: μ₁ - μ₂ ≠ 0

T-Value	DF	P-Value
2.60	18	0.018

Table 10.2 summarizes the results of the pooled-variance t test for the difference between the two sales locations using the calculations on page 354 and the Figure 10.3 results. Based on the conclusions, the special front location generates significantly higher sales. Therefore, as part of the last step of the DCOVA framework, you can offer a justification for charging a placement fee for the special front location.

TABLE 10.2

Pooled-variance t test summary for the two sales locations.

Result	Conclusions
The $t_{STAT} = 2.6041$ is greater than 2.1009.	1. Reject the null hypothesis H_0.
	2. Conclude that evidence exists that the mean sales are different for the two sales locations.
The t test p-value $= 0.0179$ is less than the level of significance, $\alpha = 0.05$.	3. The probability of observing a difference in the two sample means this large or larger is 0.0179.
The t_{STAT} is positive.	4. Conclude that the mean sales are higher for the special front location.

Evaluating the Normality Assumption

In testing for the difference between the means, you assume that the populations are normally distributed, with equal variances. For situations in which the two populations have equal variances, the pooled-variance t test is **robust** (i.e., not sensitive) to moderate departures from the assumption of normality, provided that the sample sizes are large. In such situations, you can use the pooled-variance t test without serious effects on its power. However, if you cannot assume that both populations are normally distributed, you have two choices. You can use a nonparametric procedure, such as the Wilcoxon rank sum test (see Section 12.4), that does not depend on the assumption of normality for the two populations, or you can use a normalizing transformation (see reference 4) on each of the values and then use the pooled-variance t test.

To check the assumption of normality in each of the two populations, you can construct a boxplot of the sales for the two display locations shown in Figure 10.4. For these two small samples, there appears to be only slight departure from normality, so the assumption of normality needed for the t test is not seriously violated.

FIGURE 10.4

Excel and Minitab boxplots for sales at the special front and in-aisle locations

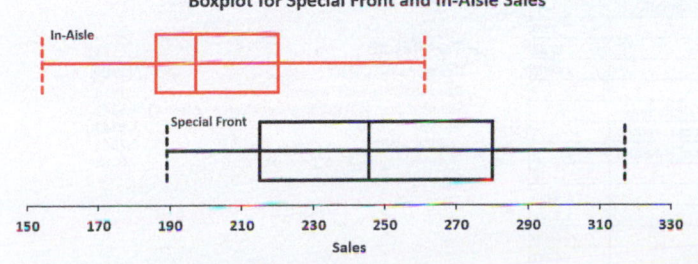
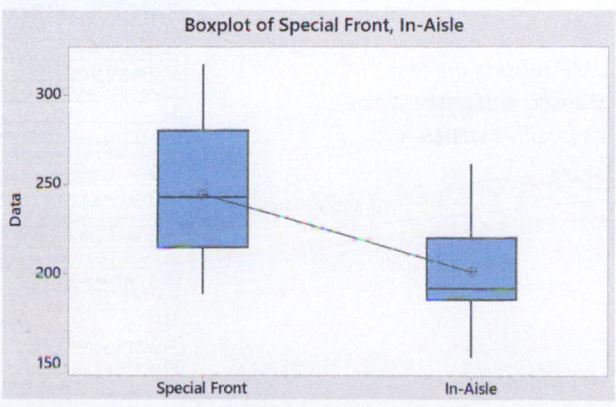

Example 10.1 provides another application of the pooled-variance *t* test.

EXAMPLE 10.1

Testing for the Difference in the Mean Delivery Times

You and some friends have decided to test the validity of an advertisement by a local pizza restaurant, which says it delivers to the dormitories faster than a local branch of a national chain. Both the local pizza restaurant and national chain are located across the street from your college campus. You define the variable of interest as the delivery time, in minutes, from the time the pizza is ordered to when it is delivered. You collect the data by ordering 10 pizzas from the local pizza restaurant and 10 pizzas from the national chain at different times. You organize and store the data in **PizzaTime**. Table 10.3 shows the delivery times.

TABLE 10.3

Delivery Times (in minutes) for a Local Pizza Restaurant and a National Pizza Chain

Local		Chain	
16.8	18.1	22.0	19.5
11.7	14.1	15.2	17.0
15.6	21.8	18.7	19.5
16.7	13.9	15.6	16.5
17.5	20.8	20.8	24.0

At the 0.05 level of significance, is there evidence that the mean delivery time for the local pizza restaurant is less than the mean delivery time for the national pizza chain?

SOLUTION Because you want to know whether the mean is *lower* for the local pizza restaurant than for the national pizza chain, you have a one-tail test with the following null and alternative hypotheses:

$H_0: \mu_1 \geq \mu_2$ (The mean delivery time for the local pizza restaurant is equal to or greater than the mean delivery time for the national pizza chain.)

$H_1: \mu_1 < \mu_2$ (The mean delivery time for the local pizza restaurant is less than the mean delivery time for the national pizza chain.)

Figure 10.5 displays the results for the pooled-variance *t* test for these data.

FIGURE 10.5

Excel and JMP pooled-variance *t* test results for the pizza delivery time data

JMP reports the test statistic and critical value as positive values.

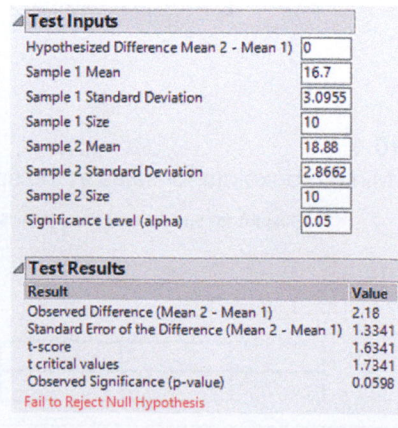

▶(*continued*)

To illustrate the computations, using Equation (10.1) on page 352,

$$t_{STAT} = \frac{(\bar{X}_1 - \bar{X}_2) - (\mu_1 - \mu_2)}{\sqrt{S_p^2 \left(\dfrac{1}{n_1} + \dfrac{1}{n_2} \right)}}$$

where

$$S_p^2 = \frac{(n_1 - 1)S_1^2 + (n_2 - 1)S_2^2}{(n_1 - 1) + (n_2 - 1)}$$

$$= \frac{9(3.0955)^2 + 9(2.8662)^2}{9 + 9} = 8.8986$$

Therefore,

$$t_{STAT} = \frac{(16.7 - 18.88) - 0.0}{\sqrt{8.8986 \left(\dfrac{1}{10} + \dfrac{1}{10} \right)}} = \frac{-2.18}{\sqrt{1.7797}} = -1.6341$$

Table 10.4 summarizes the results of the pooled-variance t test for the pizza delivery data using the calculations above and Figure 10.5 results. Based on the conclusions, the local branch of the national chain and a local pizza restaurant have similar delivery times. Therefore, as part of the last step of the DCOVA framework, you and your friends exclude delivery time as a decision criteria when choosing from which store to order pizza.

TABLE 10.4

Pooled-variance t test summary for the delivery times for the two pizza restaurants

Result	Conclusions
The $t_{STAT} = -1.6341$ is greater than -1.7341.	1. Do not reject the null hypothesis H_0.
The t test p-value $= 0.0598$ is greater than the level of significance, $\alpha = 0.05$.	2. Conclude that insufficient evidence exists that the mean delivery time is lower for the local restaurant than for the branch of the national chain.
	3. There is a probability of 0.0598 that $t_{STAT} < -1.6341$.

Confidence Interval Estimate for the Difference Between Two Means

Instead of, or in addition to, testing for the difference between the means of two independent populations, you can use Equation (10.2) to develop a confidence interval estimate of the difference in the means.

CONFIDENCE INTERVAL ESTIMATE FOR THE DIFFERENCE BETWEEN THE MEANS OF TWO INDEPENDENT POPULATIONS

$$(\bar{X}_1 - \bar{X}_2) \pm t_{\alpha/2} \sqrt{S_p^2 \left(\frac{1}{n_1} + \frac{1}{n_2} \right)} \tag{10.2}$$

or

$$(\bar{X}_1 - \bar{X}_2) - t_{\alpha/2} \sqrt{S_p^2 \left(\frac{1}{n_1} + \frac{1}{n_2} \right)} \le \mu_1 - \mu_2 \le (\bar{X}_1 - \bar{X}_2) + t_{\alpha/2} \sqrt{S_p^2 \left(\frac{1}{n_1} + \frac{1}{n_2} \right)}$$

where $t_{\alpha/2}$ is the critical value of the t distribution, with $n_1 + n_2 - 2$ degrees of freedom, for an area of $\alpha/2$ in the upper tail.

For the sample statistics pertaining to the two locations reported in Figure 10.3 on page 354, using 95% confidence, and Equation (10.2),

$$\overline{X}_1 = 246.4, \; n_1 = 10, \overline{X}_2 = 202.3, \; n_2 = 10, \; S_p^2 = 1{,}433.9167, \text{ and with } 10 + 10 - 2$$

$$= 18 \text{ degrees of freedom}, \; t_{0.025} = 2.1009$$

$$(246.4 - 202.3) \pm (2.1009)\sqrt{1{,}433.9167\left(\frac{1}{10} + \frac{1}{10}\right)}$$

$$44.10 \pm (2.1009)(16.9347)$$

$$44.10 \pm 35.5784$$

$$8.5216 \leq \mu_1 - \mu_2 \leq 79.6784$$

Therefore, you are 95% confident that the difference in mean sales between the special front and in-aisle locations is between 8.5216 and 79.6784 VLABGo players sold. In other words, you can estimate, with 95% confidence, that the special front location has mean sales of between 8.5216 and 79.6784 more VLABGo players than the in-aisle location. From a hypothesis-testing perspective, using a two-tail test at the 0.05 level of significance, because the interval does not include zero, you reject the null hypothesis of no difference between the means of the two populations.

Separate-Variance *t* Test for the Difference Between Two Means, Assuming Unequal Variances

If you can assume that the two independent populations are normally distributed but cannot assume that they have equal variances, you cannot pool the two sample variances into the common estimate S_p^2 and therefore cannot use the pooled-variance *t* test. Instead, you use the **separate-variance *t* test** developed by Satterthwaite that uses the two separate sample variances (see reference 3 and the online topic **Separate-Variance *t* Test Calculations**).

Figure 10.6 displays the separate-variance *t* test results for the two different sales locations data. Observe that the test statistic $t_{STAT} = 2.6041$ and the *p*-value is $0.019 < 0.05$. The results for the separate-variance *t* test are nearly the same as those of the pooled-variance *t* test. The assumption of equality of population variances had no appreciable effect on the results.

Sometimes, the results from the pooled-variance and separate-variance *t* tests conflict because the assumption of equal variances is violated. Therefore, you must evaluate the assumptions and use those results as a guide in selecting a test procedure. In Section 10.4, the

FIGURE 10.6

Excel, JMP, and Minitab separate-variance *t* test results for the two different sales locations data

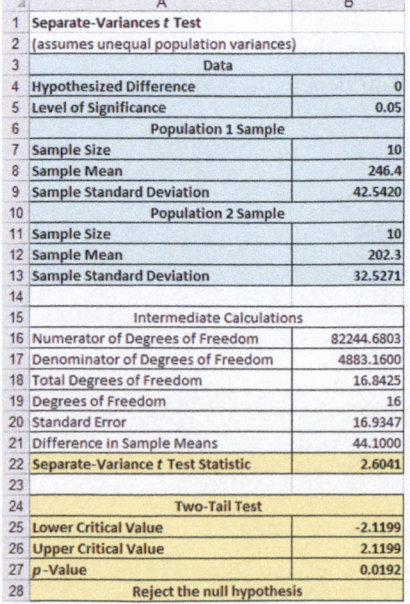

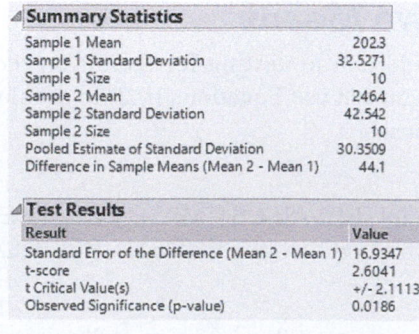

Two-Sample T-Test and CI: Special Front, In-Aisle

Method

μ_1: mean of Special Front
μ_2: mean of In-Aisle
Difference: $\mu_1 - \mu_2$
Equal variances are not assumed for this analysis.

Descriptive Statistics

Sample	N	Mean	StDev	SE Mean
Special Front	10	246.4	42.5	13
In-Aisle	10	202.3	32.5	10

Estimation for Difference

	95% CI for
Difference	Difference
44.1	(8.2, 80.0)

Test

Null hypothesis H_0: $\mu_1 - \mu_2 = 0$
Alternative hypothesis H_1: $\mu_1 - \mu_2 \neq 0$

T-Value	DF	P-Value
2.60	16	0.019

F test for the ratio of two variances is used to determine whether there is evidence of a difference in the two population variances. The results of that test can help you decide which of the *t* tests—pooled-variance or separate-variance—is more appropriate.

CONSIDER THIS

Do People Really Do This?

Some question whether decision makers really use confirmatory methods, such as hypothesis testing, in this emerging era of big data. The following real case study, contributed by a former student of a colleague of the authors, reveals a role that confirmatory methods still play in business as well as answering another question: "Do businesses really monitor their customer service calls for quality assurance purposes as they sometime claim?"

In her first full-time job at a financial services company, a student was asked to improve a training program for new hires at a call center that handled customer questions about outstanding loans. For feedback and evaluation, she planned to randomly select phone calls received by each new employee and rate the employee on 10 aspects of the call, including whether the employee maintained a pleasant tone with the customer. When she presented her plan to her boss for approval, her boss wanted proof that her new training program would improve customer service. The boss, quoting a famous statistician, said "In God we trust; all others must bring data." Faced with this request, she called her business statistics professor. "Hello, Professor, you'll never believe why I called. I work for a large company, and in the project I am currently working on, I have to put some of the statistics you taught us to work! Can you help?" Together they formulated this test:

- Randomly assign the 60 most recent hires to two training programs. Assign half to the preexisting training program and the other half to the new training program.
- At the end of the first month, compare the mean score for the 30 employees in the new training program against the mean score for the 30 employees in the preexisting training program.

She listened as her professor explained, "What you are trying to show is that the mean score from the new training program is higher than the mean score from the current program. You can make the null hypothesis that the means are equal and see if you can reject it in favor of the alternative that the mean score from the new program is higher."

"Or, as you used to say, 'if the *p*-value is low, H_o must go!'—yes, I do remember!" she replied. Her professor chuckled and added, "If you can reject H_o you will have the evidence to present to your boss." She thanked him for his help and got back to work, with the newfound confidence that she would be able to successfully apply the *t* test that compares the means of two independent populations.

PROBLEMS FOR SECTION 10.1

LEARNING THE BASICS

10.1 If you have samples of $n_1 = 12$ and $n_2 = 15$, in performing the pooled-variance *t* test, how many degrees of freedom do you have?

10.2 Assume that you have a sample of $n_1 = 8$, with the sample mean $\overline{X}_1 = 42$, and a sample standard deviation $S_1 = 4$, and you have an independent sample of $n_2 = 15$ from another population with a sample mean of $\overline{X}_2 = 34$ and a sample standard deviation $S_2 = 5$.
a. What is the value of the pooled-variance t_{STAT} test statistic for testing $H_0: \mu_1 = \mu_2$?
b. In finding the critical value, how many degrees of freedom are there?
c. Using the level of significance $\alpha = 0.01$, what is the critical value for a one-tail test of the hypothesis $H_0: \mu_1 \leq \mu_2$ against the alternative, $H_1: \mu_1 > \mu_2$?
d. What is your statistical decision?

10.3 What assumptions about the two populations are necessary in Problem 10.2?

10.4 Referring to Problem 10.2, construct a 95% confidence interval estimate of the population mean difference between μ_1 and μ_2.

10.5 Referring to Problem 10.2, if $n_1 = 5$ and $n_2 = 4$, how many degrees of freedom do you have?

10.6 Referring to Problem 10.2, if $n_1 = 5$ and $n_2 = 4$, at the 0.01 level of significance, is there evidence that $\mu_1 > \mu_2$?

APPLYING THE CONCEPTS

10.7 When people make estimates, they are influenced by anchors to their estimates. A study was conducted in which students were asked to estimate the number of calories in a cheeseburger. One group was asked to do this after thinking about a calorie-laden cheesecake. A second group was asked to do this after thinking about an organic fruit salad. The mean number of calories estimated in a cheeseburger was

780 for the group that thought about the cheesecake and 1,041 for the group that thought about the organic fruit salad.

Source: Data extracted from "Drilling Down, Sizing Up a Cheeseburger's Caloric Heft," *New York Times*, October 4, 2010, p. B2.

Suppose that the study was based on a sample of 20 people who thought about the cheesecake first and 20 people who thought about the organic fruit salad first, and the standard deviation of the number of calories in the cheeseburger was 128 for the people who thought about the cheesecake first and 140 for the people who thought about the organic fruit salad first.

a. State the null and alternative hypotheses if you want to determine whether the mean estimated number of calories in the cheeseburger is lower for the people who thought about the cheesecake first than for the people who thought about the organic fruit salad first.
b. In the context of this study, what is the meaning of the Type I error?
c. In the context of this study, what is the meaning of the Type II error?
d. At the 0.01 level of significance, is there evidence that the mean estimated number of calories in the cheeseburger is lower for the people who thought about the cheesecake first than for the people who thought about the organic fruit salad first?
e. If you were developing a commercial for a cheeseburger, based on the results of (d), what other foods might you show in the commercial?

10.8 A recent study found that 51 children who watched a commercial for Walker Crisps (potato chips) featuring a long-standing sports celebrity endorser ate a mean of 36 grams of Walker Crisps as compared to a mean of 25 grams of Walker Crisps for 41 children who watched a commercial for an alternative food snack.

Source: Data extracted from E. J. Boyland et al., "Food Choice and Overconsumption: Effect of a Premium Sports Celebrity Endorser," *Journal of Pediatrics*, March 13, 2013, **bit.ly/16NR4Bi**.

Suppose that the sample standard deviation for the children who watched the sports celebrity–endorsed Walker Crisps commercial was 21.4 grams and the sample standard deviation for the children who watched the alternative food snack commercial was 12.8 grams.

a. Assuming that the population variances are equal and $\alpha = 0.05$, is there evidence that the mean amount of Walker Crisps eaten was significantly higher for the children who watched the sports celebrity–endorsed Walker Crisps commercial?
b. Assuming that the population variances are equal, construct a 95% confidence interval estimate of the difference between the mean amount of Walker Crisps eaten by children who watched the sports celebrity–endorsed Walker Crisps commercial and children who watched the alternative food snack commercial.
c. Compare and discuss the results of (a) and (b).
d. Based on the results of (a) and (b), if you wanted to increase the consumption of Walker Crisps, which commercial would you choose?

10.9 Is there a difference in the satisfaction rating of traditional cellphone providers who bill for service at the end of a month often under a contract and prepaid cellphone service providers who bill in advance without a contract? The file CellphoneProviders contains the satisfaction rating for 10 traditional cellphone providers and 13 prepaid cellphone service providers.

Source: Data extracted from "Carrier Ratings: Why It Pays to Think Small," *Consumer Reports*, February 2016, p. 51.

a. Assuming that the population variances from both types of cellphone providers are equal, is there evidence of a difference in the mean ratings between the two types of cellphone providers? (Use $\alpha = 0.05$.)
b. Find the *p*-value in (a) and interpret its meaning.
c. What other assumption is necessary in (a)?
d. Assuming that the population variances from both cellphone providers are equal, construct and interpret a 95% confidence interval estimate of the difference between the population means of the two cellphone providers.
e. What conclusions can you reach about the satisfaction rating of traditional cellphone providers who bill for service at the end of a month often under a contract and prepaid cellphone service providers who bill in advance without a contract?

✓SELF TEST **10.10** *Accounting Today* identified the top accounting firms in 10 geographic regions across the United States. All 10 regions reported growth in 2016. The Southeast and Gulf Coast regions reported growth of 12.03% and 9.47%, respectively. A characteristic description of the accounting firms in the Southeast and Gulf Coast regions included the number of partners in the firm. The file AccountingPartners2 contains the number of partners.

Source: Data extracted from *2017 Top 100 Firms*, Accounting Today, available at **www.accountingtoday.com/the-2017-top-100-firms-and-regional-leaders**.

a. At the 0.05 level of significance, is there evidence of a difference between Southeast region accounting firms and Gulf Coast accounting firms with respect to the mean number of partners?
b. Determine the *p*-value and interpret its meaning.
c. What assumptions do you have to make about the two populations in order to justify the use of the *t* test?

10.11 The annual NFL Super Bowl is the most widely watched sporting event in the United States each year. In recent years, there has been a great deal of interest in the ads that appear during the game. These ads vary in length with most lasting 30 seconds or 60 seconds. The file SuperBowlAdScore represent the ad length and ad scores from a recent Super Bowl.

Source: Data extracted from C. Woodyard, "Funny Bone Wins Out," *USA Today*, February 6, 2016, p. 4B.

a. Assuming that the population variances from the 30-second ads and the 60-second ads are equal, is there evidence of a difference in the mean score between the two types of ads? (Use $\alpha = 0.05$.)
b. Determine the *p*-value in (a) and interpret its meaning.
c. Assuming that the population variances from both types of ads are equal, construct and interpret a 95% confidence interval estimate of the difference between the population mean score of the two types of ads.

10.12 A bank with a branch located in a commercial district of a city has the business objective of developing an improved process for serving customers during the noon-to-1 P.M. lunch period. Management decides to first study the waiting time in the current process. The waiting time is defined as the number of minutes that elapses from when the customer enters the line until he or she reaches the teller window. Data are collected from a random sample of 15 customers and stored in Bank1 . These data are:

4.21	5.55	3.02	5.13	4.77	2.34	3.54	3.20
4.50	6.10	0.38	5.12	6.46	6.19	3.79	

Suppose that another branch, located in a residential area, is also concerned with improving the process of serving customers in the noon-to-1 P.M. lunch period. Data are collected from a random sample of 15 customers and stored in Bank2. These data are:

9.66	5.90	8.02	5.79	8.73	3.82	8.01	8.35
10.49	6.68	5.64	4.08	6.17	9.91	5.47	

a. Assuming that the population variances from both banks are equal, is there evidence of a difference in the mean waiting time between the two branches? (Use $\alpha = 0.05$.)
b. Determine the p-value in (a) and interpret its meaning.
c. In addition to equal variances, what other assumption is necessary in (a)?
d. Construct and interpret a 95% confidence interval estimate of the difference between the population means in the two branches.

10.13 Repeat Problem 10.12 (a), assuming that the population variances in the two branches are not equal. Compare these results with those of Problem 10.12 (a).

10.14 As a member of the international strategic management team in your company, you are assigned the task of exploring potential foreign market entry. As part of your initial investigation, you want to know if there is a difference between developed markets and emerging markets with respect to the time required to start a business. You select 15 developed countries and 15 emerging countries. The time required to start a business, defined as the number of days needed to complete the procedures to legally operate a business in these countries, is stored in ForeignMarket.

Source: Data extracted from **data.worldbank.org**.

a. Assuming that the population variances for developed countries and emerging countries are equal, is there evidence of a difference in the mean time required to start a business between developed countries and emerging countries? (Use $\alpha = 0.05$.)
b. Determine the p-value in (a) and interpret its meaning.
c. In addition to equal variances, what other assumption is necessary in (a)?
d. Construct a 95% confidence interval estimate of the difference between the population means of developed countries and emerging countries.

10.15 Repeat Problem 10.14 (a), assuming that the population variances from developed and emerging countries are not equal. Compare these results with those of Problem 10.14 (a).

10.16 We Are Social and Hootsuite reported that the typical American spends 2.02 hours (121 minutes) per day accessing the Internet through a mobile device.

Source: *Digital in 2017 Global Overview*, available at **bit.ly/2jXeS3F**.

You wonder if males and females spend differing amounts of time per day accessing the Internet through a mobile device.

You select a sample of 60 friends and family (30 males and 30 females), collect times spent per day accessing the Internet through a mobile device (in minutes), and store the data collected in InternetMobileTime2.

a. Assuming that the variances in the population of times spent per day accessing the Internet via a mobile device are equal, is there evidence of a difference between males and females in the mean time spent per day accessing the Internet via a mobile device? (Use a 0.05 level of significance.)
b. In addition to equal variances, what other assumption is necessary in (a)?

10.17 Brand valuations are critical to CEOs, financial and marketing executives, security analysts, institutional investors, and others who depend on well-researched, reliable information needed for assessments, and comparisons in decision making. Millward Brown Optimor has developed the BrandZ Top 100 Most Valuable Global Brands for WPP, the world's largest communications services group. Unlike other studies, the BrandZ Top 100 Most Valuable Global Brands fuses consumer measures of brand equity with financial measures to place a financial value on brands. The file BrandZ-TechFin contains the brand values for the technology sector and the financial institution sector in the BrandZ Top 100 Most Valuable Global Brands for 2016.

Source: Data extracted from *BrandZ Top100 Most Valuable Global Brands 2016*, available at **wppbaz.com/admin/uploads/files/BZ_Global_2016_Report.pdf**.

a. Assuming that the population variances are equal, is there evidence of a difference between the technology sector and the financial institutions sector with respect to mean brand value? (Use $\alpha = .05$.)
b. Repeat (a), assuming that the population variances are not equal.
c. Compare the results of (a) and (b).

10.2 Comparing the Means of Two Related Populations

The hypothesis-testing procedures presented in Section 10.1 enable you to examine differences between the means of two *independent* populations. In this section, you will learn about a procedure for examining the mean difference between two populations when you collect sample data from populations that are related—that is, when results of the first population are *not* independent of the results of the second population.

There are two situations that involve related data: when you take repeated measurements from the same set of items or individuals or when you match items or individuals according to some characteristic. In either situation, you are interested in the *difference between the two related values* rather than the *individual values* themselves.

When you take **repeated measurements** on the same items or individuals, you assume that the same items or individuals will behave alike if treated alike. Your objective is to show that any differences between two measurements of the same items or individuals are due to different treatments that have been applied to the items or individuals. For example, to conduct an experiment that compares the prices of items from two retailers, you would collect the prices of equivalent items that the retailers sell. For each item, those two prices are the "repeated measurements" of the item.

Using repeated measurements enables you to answer questions such as "Do prices for the same items differ between two retailers?" By collecting the prices of the *same* items from both sellers, you create two related samples and can use a test that is more powerful than the tests Section 10.1 discusses. Those tests use two *independent* samples that most likely will not contain the same sample of items. That means that differences observed might be due to one sample having products that are inherently costlier than the other.

Matched samples represent another type of related data between populations. In matched samples, items or individuals are paired together according to some characteristic of interest. For example, in test marketing a product in two different advertising campaigns, a sample of test markets can be *matched* on the basis of the test-market population size and/or demographic variables. By accounting for the differences in test-market population size and/or demographic variables, you are better able to measure the effects of the two different advertising campaigns.

Regardless of whether you have matched samples or repeated measurements, the objective is to study the difference between two measurements by reducing the effect of the variability that is due to the items or individuals themselves. Table 10.5 shows the differences between the individual values for two related populations. To read this table, let $X_{11}, X_{12}, \ldots, X_{1n}$ represent the n values from the first sample. And let $X_{21}, X_{22}, \ldots, X_{2n}$ represent either the corresponding n matched values from a second sample or the corresponding n repeated measurements from the initial sample. Then $D_1, D_2, \ldots, D_n$ will represent the corresponding set of n *difference scores* such that

$$D_1 = X_{11} - X_{21}, D_2 = X_{12} - X_{22}, \ldots, \text{ and } D_n = X_{1n} - X_{2n}.$$

To test for the mean difference between two related populations, you treat the difference scores, each D_i, as values from a single sample.

TABLE 10.5
Determining the Difference Between Two Related Samples

Value	Sample 1	Sample 2	Difference
1	X_{11}	X_{21}	$D_1 = X_{11} - X_{21}$
2	X_{12}	X_{22}	$D_2 = X_{12} - X_{22}$
$\vdots$	$\vdots$	$\vdots$	$\vdots$
i	X_{1i}	X_{2i}	$D_i = X_{1i} - X_{2i}$
$\vdots$	$\vdots$	$\vdots$	$\vdots$
n	X_{1n}	X_{2n}	$D_n = X_{1n} - X_{2n}$

student TIP

Which sample you define as sample 1 determines the type of one-tail test that would be appropriate to perform, if a one-tail test is needed.

Paired *t* Test

If you assume that the difference scores are randomly and independently selected from a population that is normally distributed, you can use the **paired *t* test for the mean difference** in related populations to determine whether there is a significant population mean difference. As with the one-sample *t* test developed in Section 9.2 [see Equation (9.2) on page 324], the paired *t* test statistic follows the *t* distribution with $n - 1$ degrees of freedom. Although the paired *t* test assumes that the population is normally distributed, since this test is robust, you can use this test as long as the sample size is not very small and the population is not highly skewed.

To test the null hypothesis that there is no difference in the means of two related populations:

$$H_0: \mu_D = 0 \text{ (where } \mu_D = \mu_1 - \mu_2)$$

against the alternative that the means are not the same:

$$H_1: \mu_D \neq 0$$

you compute the t_{STAT} test statistic using Equation (10.3).

PAIRED t TEST FOR THE MEAN DIFFERENCE

$$t_{STAT} = \frac{\overline{D} - \mu_D}{\dfrac{S_D}{\sqrt{n}}} \tag{10.3}$$

where

$$\mu_D = \text{hypothesized mean difference}$$

$$\overline{D} = \frac{\sum\limits_{i=1}^{n} D_i}{n}$$

$$S_D = \sqrt{\frac{\sum\limits_{i=1}^{n}(D_i - \overline{D})^2}{n-1}}$$

The t_{STAT} test statistic follows a t distribution with $n - 1$ degrees of freedom.

For a two-tail test with a given level of significance, α, you reject the null hypothesis if the computed t_{STAT} test statistic is greater than the upper-tail critical value $t_{\alpha/2}$ from the t distribution, or, if the computed t_{STAT} test statistic is less than the lower-tail critical value $-t_{\alpha/2}$, from the t distribution. The decision rule is

$$\text{Reject } H_0 \text{ if } t_{STAT} > t_{\alpha/2}$$

$$\text{or if } t_{STAT} < -t_{\alpha/2};$$

$$\text{otherwise, do not reject } H_0.$$

You can use the paired t test for the mean difference to investigate if the prices of the same or equivalent grocery items differ between Costco, a warehouse club that sells only to members who pay an annual fee, and Walmart, a large general retailer that sells groceries. In this repeated measures experiment, you use one market basket (set) of products. For each product, you determine the price of the item at Costco and the price of the same or equivalent item at Walmart. By using the same market basket, you reduce the variability in the prices that would occur if you used two different market baskets that contained different sets of items. A shared market basket enables you to focus on the differences between the prices of the equivalent products offered by the two retailers.

Table 10.6, stored in MarketBasket , contains market basket prices for the $n = 7$ selected items at both Costco and Walmart.

TABLE 10.6
Prices (in dollars) of Equivalent Items at Costco and Walmart

Product	Costco	Walmart
Chicken broth per 32 oz.	1.92	1.89
Vanilla ice cream per 48 oz.	4.13	3.45
Dishwasher detergent per load	0.09	0.17
Laundry detergent per 100 loads	11.00	12.00
Paper towels per 100 square feet	1.47	2.09
Toilet paper per 100 sheets	0.12	0.27
Tissues per 100 tissues	1.23	1.12

Source: "The Best Everyday Products," *Consumer Reports*, January 2015, p. 29.

Your objective is to determine whether there is any difference between the mean price at Costco and Walmart. In other words, is there evidence that the mean price is different between the two retailers? Thus, the null and alternative hypotheses are

$H_0: \mu_D = 0$ (There is no difference in the mean price between Costco and Walmart.)

$H_1: \mu_D \neq 0$ (There is a difference in the mean price between Costco and Walmart.)

Choosing the level of significance $\alpha = 0.05$ and assuming that the differences are normally distributed, you use the paired t test [Equation (10.3)]. For a sample of $n = 7$ items there are $n - 1 = 6$ degrees of freedom. Using Table E.3, the decision rule is

$$\text{Reject } H_0 \text{ if } t_{STAT} > 2.4469$$

$$\text{or if } t_{STAT} < -2.4469;$$

$$\text{otherwise, do not reject } H_0.$$

FIGURE 10.7
Two-tail paired t test at the 0.05 level of significance with 6 degrees of freedom

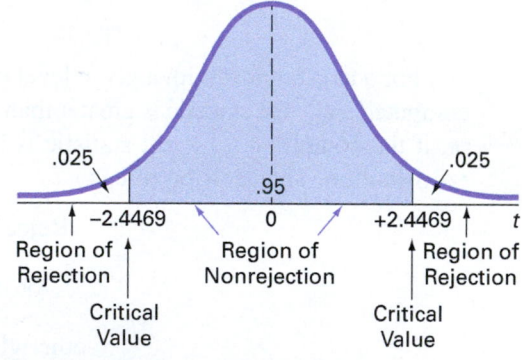

For the $n = 7$ differences (calculated from the Table 10.6 data), the sample mean difference is

$$\overline{D} = \frac{\sum\limits_{i=1}^{n} D_i}{n} = \frac{-1.03}{7} = -0.1471$$

and

$$S_D = \sqrt{\frac{\sum\limits_{i=1}^{n} (D_i - \overline{D})^2}{n - 1}} = 0.5381$$

From Equation (10.3) on page 363,

$$t_{STAT} = \frac{\overline{D} - \mu_D}{\dfrac{S_D}{\sqrt{n}}} = \frac{-0.1471 - 0}{\dfrac{0.5381}{\sqrt{7}}} = -0.7235$$

Table 10.7 summarizes the results of the paired t test for the difference between the two sales locations using the calculation on page 364 and Figure 10.8 results. Based on the conclusions, Costco and Walmart sell equivalent items at similar prices. Therefore, as part of the last step of the DCOVA framework, you state that a price-sensitive shopper would do equally well shopping for the market basket of items at either retailer.

TABLE 10.7

Paired t test summary for the prices of equivalent items at Costco and Walmart

Result	Conclusions
The $t_{STAT} = -0.7235$ is greater than -2.4469 and less than 2.4469.	1. Do not reject the null hypothesis H_0.
The t test p-value $= 0.4966$ is greater than the level of significance, $\alpha = 0.05$.	2. Conclude that no evidence exists that there is a difference in the mean price of equivalent items purchased at Costco and Walmart.

FIGURE 10.8

Excel, JMP, and Minitab paired t test results for the equivalent products price data

To evaluate the validity of the assumption of normality, if you have a sufficient sample size which this data set lacks, you can construct a boxplot, histogram, or normal probability plot. If these plots reveal that the assumption of underlying normality in the population is severely violated, then the t test may be inappropriate, especially if the sample size is small. If you believe that the t test is inappropriate, you can use either a *nonparametric* procedure that does not make the assumption of underlying normality (see online Section 12.8) or make a data transformation (see reference 4) and then check the assumptions again to determine whether you should use the t test.

EXAMPLE 10.2

Paired t Test of Pizza Delivery Times

Recall from Example 10.1 on page 356 that a local pizza restaurant situated across the street from your college campus advertises that it delivers to the dormitories faster than the local branch of a national pizza chain. In order to determine whether this advertisement is valid, you and some friends decided to order 10 pizzas from the local pizza restaurant and 10 pizzas from the national chain. In fact, each time you ordered a pizza from the local pizza restaurant, at the same time, your friends ordered a pizza from the national pizza chain. Therefore, you have matched samples (because each pair of pizzas was ordered at the same time). For each of the 10 times that pizzas were ordered, you have one measurement from the local pizza restaurant and one from the national chain. At the 0.05 level of significance, is the mean delivery time for the local pizza restaurant less than the mean delivery time for the national pizza chain?

SOLUTION Use the paired t test to analyze the Table 10.8 data (stored in PizzaTime). Figure 10.9 on page 366 shows the paired t test results for the pizza delivery data.

▶(continued)

TABLE 10.8
Delivery Times for Local
Pizza Restaurant and
National Pizza Chain

Time	Local	Chain	Difference
1	16.8	22.0	−5.2
2	11.7	15.2	−3.5
3	15.6	18.7	−3.1
4	16.7	15.6	1.1
5	17.5	20.8	−3.3
6	18.1	19.5	−1.4
7	14.1	17.0	−2.9
8	21.8	19.5	2.3
9	13.9	16.5	−2.6
10	20.8	24.0	−3.2
			−21.8

FIGURE 10.9
Excel and Minitab paired
t test results for the
pizza delivery data

	A	B	C	D	E
1	Paired *t* Test				
2					
3	Data				
4	Hypothesized Mean Diff.	0			
5	Level of significance	0.05			
6					
7	Intermediate Calculations				
8	Sample Size	10			
9	DBar	-2.1800			
10	degrees of freedom	9			
11	S_D	2.2641			
12	Standard Error	0.7160			
13	*t* Test Statistic	-3.0448			
14					
15	Lower-Tail Test		One-Tail Calculations		
16	Lower Critical Value	-1.8331	T.DIST.RT	0.0070	
17	*p*-Value	0.0070	1 - T.DIST.RT	0.9930	
18	Reject the null hypothesis				

Paired T-Test and CI: Local, Chain

Descriptive Statistics

Sample	N	Mean	StDev	SE Mean
Local	10	16.700	3.096	0.979
Chain	10	18.880	2.866	0.906

Estimation for Paired Difference

Mean	StDev	SE Mean	95% Upper Bound for μ_difference
-2.180	2.264	0.716	-0.868

μ_difference: mean of (Local - Chain)

Test

Null hypothesis	H_0: μ_difference = 0
Alternative hypothesis	H_1: μ_difference < 0

T-Value	P-Value
-3.04	0.007

The null and alternative hypotheses are:

H_0: $\mu_D \geq 0$ (Mean difference in the delivery time between the local pizza restaurant and the national pizza chain is greater than or equal to 0.)

H_1: $\mu_D < 0$ (Mean difference in the delivery time between the local pizza restaurant and the national pizza chain is less than 0.)

Choosing the level of significance $\alpha = 0.05$ and assuming that the differences are normally distributed, you use the paired t test [Equation (10.3) on page 363]. For a sample of $n = 10$ delivery times, there are $n - 1 = 9$ degrees of freedom. Using Table E.3, the decision rule is

$$\text{Reject } H_0 \text{ if } t_{STAT} < -t_{0.05} = -1.8331;$$

otherwise, do not reject H_0.

To illustrate the computations, for $n = 10$ differences (see Table 10.8), the sample mean difference is

$$\overline{D} = \frac{\sum_{i=1}^{n} D_i}{n} = \frac{-21.8}{10} = -2.18$$

and the sample standard deviation of the difference is

$$S_D = \sqrt{\frac{\sum_{i=1}^{n}(D_i - \overline{D})^2}{n - 1}} = 2.2641$$

▶(continued)

From Equation (10.3) on page 363,

$$t_{STAT} = \frac{\overline{D} - \mu_D}{\frac{S_D}{\sqrt{n}}} = \frac{-2.18 - 0}{\frac{2.2641}{\sqrt{10}}} = -3.0448$$

Table 10.9 summarizes the results of the paired t test for the pizza delivery data using the calculation above and Figure 10.9 results. Based on the conclusions, the local pizza restaurant has a faster (lower) delivery time than the branch of the national chain. Therefore, as part of the last step of the DCOVA framework, you and your friends should order from the local pizza restaurant if delivery time is an important decision-making criterion for choosing a restaurant.

TABLE 10.9

Paired t test summary for the delivery times for the two pizza restaurants

Result	Conclusions
The $t_{STAT} = -3.0447$ is less than -1.8331. The t test p-value $= 0.0070$ is less than the level of significance, $\alpha = 0.05$.	1. Reject the null hypothesis H_0. 2. Conclude that evidence exists that the mean delivery time is lower for the local restaurant than for the branch of the national chain. 3. There is a probability of 0.0070 that $t_{STAT} < -1.8331$.

This conclusion differs from the conclusion reached when using the pooled-variance t test for these data (see Example 10.1 on page 356). By pairing the delivery times, you are able to focus on the differences between the two pizza delivery services and not the variability created by ordering pizzas at different times of day. The paired t test is a more powerful statistical procedure that reduces the variability in the delivery time because you are controlling for the time of day the pizza was ordered.

Confidence Interval Estimate for the Mean Difference

When you are conducting a two-tail test for the mean difference between two related populations, you can use Equation (10.4) to construct a confidence interval estimate for the population mean difference.

CONFIDENCE INTERVAL ESTIMATE FOR THE MEAN DIFFERENCE

$$\overline{D} \pm t_{\alpha/2}\frac{S_D}{\sqrt{n}} \tag{10.4}$$

or

$$\overline{D} - t_{\alpha/2}\frac{S_D}{\sqrt{n}} \le \mu_D \le \overline{D} + t_{\alpha/2}\frac{S_D}{\sqrt{n}}$$

where $t_{\alpha/2}$ is the critical value of the t distribution, with $n - 1$ degrees of freedom, for an area of $\alpha/2$ in the upper tail.

Recall the example comparing equivalent item prices at Costco and Walmart on page 364. Using Equation (10.4), $\overline{D} = -0.1471$, $S_D = 0.5381$, $n = 7$, and $t_{\alpha/2} = 2.4469$ (for 95% confidence and $n - 1 = 7$ degrees of freedom),

$$-0.1471 \pm (2.4469)\frac{0.5381}{\sqrt{7}}$$

$$-0.1471 \pm 0.4977$$

$$-0.6448 \le \mu_D \le 0.3506$$

Thus, with 95% confidence, you estimate that the population mean difference in equivalent item prices between Costco and Walmart is between −$0.6448 and $0.3506. Because the interval estimate contains zero, using the 0.05 level of significance and a two-tail test, you can conclude that there is no evidence of a difference in the mean item prices between Costco and Walmart.

PROBLEMS FOR SECTION 10.2

LEARNING THE BASICS

10.18 An experimental design for a paired t test has 20 pairs of identical twins. How many degrees of freedom are there in this t test?

10.19 Fifteen volunteers are recruited to participate in an experiment. A measurement is made (such as blood pressure) before each volunteer is asked to read a particularly upsetting passage from a book and after each volunteer reads the passage from the book. In the analysis of the data collected from this experiment, how many degrees of freedom are there in the test?

APPLYING THE CONCEPTS

✓ SELF TEST **10.20** Nine experts rated two brands of coffee in a taste-testing experiment. A rating on a 7-point scale (1 = extremely unpleasing, 7 = extremely pleasing) is given for each of four characteristics: taste, aroma, richness, and acidity. The following data stored in **Coffee** contain the ratings accumulated over all four characteristics:

	BRAND	
EXPERT	**A**	**B**
C.C.	24	26
S.E.	27	27
E.G.	19	22
B.L.	24	27
C.M.	22	25
C.N.	26	27
G.N.	27	26
R.M.	25	27
P.V.	22	23

a. At the 0.05 level of significance, is there evidence of a difference in the mean ratings between the two brands?
b. What assumption is necessary in order to perform this test?
c. Determine the p-value in (a) and interpret its meaning.
d. Construct and interpret a 95% confidence interval estimate of the difference in the mean ratings between the two brands.

10.21 How do the ratings of TV and Internet services compare? The file **Telecom** contains the rating of 10 different providers.

Source: Data extracted from *ACSI Telecommunication Report 2017*, available at **bit.ly/2syfcbA**.

a. At the 0.05 level of significance, is there evidence of a difference in the mean service rating between TV and Internet services?
b. What assumption is necessary in order to perform this test?
c. Use a graphical method to evaluate the validity of the assumption in (a).
d. Construct and interpret a 95% confidence interval estimate of the difference in the mean service rating between TV and Internet services.

10.22 Does LTE network performance vary between providers? The file **LTE** contains the download speed (in Mbps) on LTE connections of AT&T and Verizon providers in 31 U.S. large metro markets.

Source: Data extracted from *State of Mobile Networks: USA*, August 2016, available at **bit.ly/2aYXxox**.

a. At the 0.05 level of significance, is there evidence of a difference in the mean download speed between AT&T and Verizon?
b. What assumption is necessary to perform this test?
c. Use a graphical method to evaluate the assumption made in (a).
d. Construct and interpret a 95% confidence interval estimate of the difference in the mean download speed between AT&T and Verizon.

10.23 How do the fares for airlines that directly compete compare? The file **Airlines** contains roundtrip fares for nonstop travel from Philadelphia to 10 different U.S. destinations on Southwest Airlines and American Airlines that a frequent flyer collected.

Source: Data extracted from **www.southwest.com/** and **www.aa.com/**.

a. At the 0.05 level of significance, is there evidence of a difference in mean roundtrip fare between Southwest Airlines and American Airlines?
b. What assumption is necessary in order to perform this test?
c. Use a graphical method to evaluate the validity of the assumption in (b).

10.24 Multiple myeloma, or blood plasma cancer, is characterized by increased blood vessel formulation (angiogenesis) in the bone marrow that is a predictive factor in survival. One treatment approach used for multiple myeloma is stem cell transplantation with the patient's own stem cells. The data stored in **Myeloma**, and shown on page 369 represent the bone marrow microvessel density for patients who had a complete response to the stem cell transplant (as measured by blood and urine tests). The measurements were taken immediately prior to the stem cell transplant and at the time the complete response was determined.

Patient	Before	After
1	158	284
2	189	214
3	202	101
4	353	227
5	416	290
6	426	176
7	441	290

Data extracted from S. V. Rajkumar, R. Fonseca, T. E. Witzig, M. A. Gertz, and P. R. Greipp, "Bone Marrow Angiogenesis in Patients Achieving Complete Response After Stem Cell Transplantation for Multiple Myeloma," *Leukemia* 13 (1999): 469–472.

a. At the 0.05 level of significance, is there evidence that the mean bone marrow microvessel density is higher before the stem cell transplant than after the stem cell transplant?

b. Interpret the meaning of the *p*-value in (a).

c. Construct and interpret a 95% confidence interval estimate of the mean difference in bone marrow microvessel density before and after the stem cell transplant.

d. What assumption is necessary in order to perform the test in (a)?

10.25 To assess the effectiveness of a cola video ad, a random sample of 38 individuals from a target audience was selected to participate in a copy test. Participants viewed two ads, one of which was the ad being tested. Participants then answered a series of questions about how much they liked the ads. An adindex measure was created and stored in Adindex ; the higher the adindex value, the more likeable the ad. Compute descriptive statistics and perform a paired *t* test. State your findings and conclusions in a report. (Use the 0.05 level of significance.)

10.26 The file Concrete1 contains the compressive strength, in thousands of pounds per square inch (psi), of 40 samples of concrete taken two and seven days after pouring.

Source: Data extracted from O. Carrillo-Gamboa and R. F. Gunst, "Measurement-Error-Model Collinearities," *Technometrics*, 34 (1992): 454–464.

a. At the 0.01 level of significance, is there evidence that the mean strength is lower at two days than at seven days?

b. What assumption is necessary in order to perform this test?

c. Find the *p*-value in (a) and interpret its meaning.

10.3 Comparing the Proportions of Two Independent Populations

Often, you need to make comparisons and analyze differences between two population proportions. You can perform a test for the difference between two proportions selected from independent populations by using two different methods. This section presents a procedure whose test statistic, Z_{STAT}, is approximated by a standardized normal distribution. In Section 12.1, a procedure whose test statistic, χ^2_{STAT}, is approximated by a chi-square distribution is used. As explained in the latter section, the results from these two tests are equivalent.

Z Test for the Difference Between Two Proportions

In evaluating differences between two population proportions, you can use a **Z test for the difference between two proportions**. The Z_{STAT} test statistic is based on the difference between two sample proportions $(p_1 - p_2)$. This test statistic, given in Equation (10.5), approximately follows a standardized normal distribution for large enough sample sizes.

Z TEST FOR THE DIFFERENCE BETWEEN TWO PROPORTIONS

$$Z_{STAT} = \frac{(p_1 - p_2) - (\pi_1 - \pi_2)}{\sqrt{\bar{p}(1 - \bar{p})\left(\frac{1}{n_1} + \frac{1}{n_2}\right)}} \tag{10.5}$$

where

$$\bar{p} = \frac{X_1 + X_2}{n_1 + n_2} \qquad p_1 = \frac{X_1}{n_1} \qquad p_2 = \frac{X_2}{n_2}$$

and

p_1 = proportion of items of interest in sample 1

X_1 = number of items of interest in sample 1

n_1 = sample size of sample 1

π_1 = proportion of items of interest in population 1

p_2 = proportion of items of interest in sample 2

X_2 = number of items of interest in sample 2

n_2 = sample size of sample 2

π_2 = proportion of items of interest in population 2

$\bar{p}$ = pooled estimate of the population proportion of items of interest

The Z_{STAT} test statistic approximately follows a standardized normal distribution.

student TIP

Do not confuse this use of the Greek letter pi, π, to represent the population proportion with the mathematical constant that uses the same letter and is approximately 3.14159.

The null hypothesis in the Z test for the difference between two proportions states that the two population proportions are equal ($\pi_1 = \pi_2$). Because the pooled estimate for the population proportion is based on the null hypothesis, you combine, or pool, the two sample proportions to compute $\bar{p}$, an overall estimate of the common population proportion. This estimate is equal to the number of items of interest in the two samples ($X_1 + X_2$) divided by the total sample size from the two samples ($n_1 + n_2$).

As shown in the following table, you can use this Z test for the difference between population proportions to determine whether there is a difference in the proportion of items of interest in the two populations (two-tail test) or whether one population has a higher proportion of items of interest than the other population (one-tail test):

Two-Tail Test	One-Tail Test	One-Tail Test
$H_0: \pi_1 = \pi_2$	$H_0: \pi_1 \geq \pi_2$	$H_0: \pi_1 \leq \pi_2$
$H_1: \pi_1 \neq \pi_2$	$H_1: \pi_1 < \pi_2$	$H_1: \pi_1 > \pi_2$

where

π_1 = proportion of items of interest in population 1

π_2 = proportion of items of interest in population 2

To test the null hypothesis that there is no difference between the proportions of two independent populations:

$$H_0: \pi_1 = \pi_2$$

against the alternative that the two population proportions are not the same:

$$H_1: \pi_1 \neq \pi_2$$

you use the Z_{STAT} test statistic, given by Equation (10.5). For a given level of significance, α, you reject the null hypothesis if the computed Z_{STAT} test statistic is greater than the upper-tail critical value from the standardized normal distribution or if the computed Z_{STAT} test statistic is less than the lower-tail critical value from the standardized normal distribution.

To illustrate the use of the Z test for the equality of the two proportions, recall the Chapter 6 Using Statistics MyTVLab scenario concerning a new "Why Choose Us" web page. MyTVLab web designers now look to revise the signup page for the website. The designers ponder whether this page should ask for many personal details or just a few. They decide to design both types of signup pages and devise an experiment. Every visitor going to the signup page will be randomly shown one of the two new designs. Effectiveness will be measured by whether the visitor clicks the signup button that appears on the page displayed.

Using the DCOVA problem-solving approach, you define the business objective as determining if there is evidence of a significant difference in signups generated by the two pages. The results of the experiment showed that of 4,325 visitors to the signup page that asks only a few personal details, 387 clicked the signup button while of 4,639 visitors to the signup page that asks for many personal details, 283 clicked the signup button. At the 0.05 level of significance, is there evidence of a significant difference in signup between a signup page that asks only a few personal details and a signup page that asks for many personal details?

The null and alternative hypotheses are

$$H_0: \pi_1 = \pi_2 \quad \text{or} \quad \pi_1 - \pi_2 = 0$$
$$H_1: \pi_1 \neq \pi_2 \quad \text{or} \quad \pi_1 - \pi_2 \neq 0$$

Using the 0.05 level of significance, the critical values are -1.96 and $+1.96$ (see Figure 10.10), and the decision rule is

$$\text{Reject } H_0 \text{ if } Z_{STAT} < -1.96$$

$$\text{or if } Z_{STAT} > +1.96;$$

$$\text{otherwise, do not reject } H_0.$$

FIGURE 10.10

Regions of rejection and nonrejection when testing a hypothesis for the difference between two proportions at the 0.05 level of significance

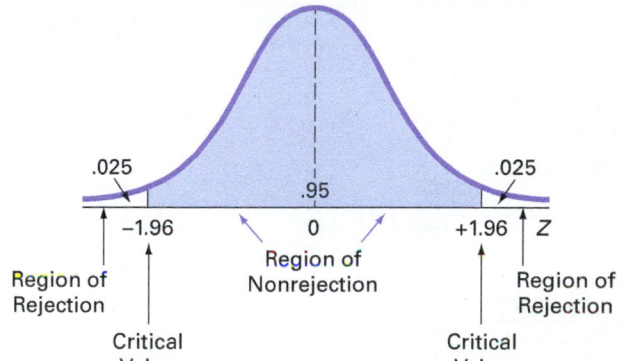

Using Equation (10.5) on page 369,

$$Z_{STAT} = \frac{(p_1 - p_2) - (\pi_1 - \pi_2)}{\sqrt{\bar{p}(1 - \bar{p})\left(\dfrac{1}{n_1} + \dfrac{1}{n_2}\right)}}$$

given $\quad p_1 = \dfrac{X_1}{n_1} = \dfrac{387}{4,325} = 0.0895, \quad p_2 = \dfrac{X_2}{n_2} = \dfrac{283}{4,639} = 0.0610,$ and

$$\bar{p} = \frac{X_1 + X_2}{n_1 + n_2} = \frac{387 + 283}{4,325 + 4,639} = 0.0747$$

the calculation is

$$Z_{STAT} = \frac{(0.0895 - 0.0610) - (0)}{\sqrt{0.0747(1 - 0.0747)\left(\dfrac{1}{4,325} + \dfrac{1}{4,639}\right)}}$$

$$= \frac{0.0285}{\sqrt{(0.06912)(0.0004467)}} = \frac{0.0285}{\sqrt{0.000308}}$$

$$= \frac{0.0285}{0.00555} = +5.1228$$

Table 10.10 summarizes the results of the Z test for the difference between the two signup proportions using the calculation above and Figure 10.11 results. Based on the conclusions, the signup page that asks fewer personal details generates a significantly greater proportion of visitors who sign up. Therefore, as part of the last step of the DCOVA framework, you would recommend that MyTVLab use the signup page that asks the fewer number of personal questions.

TABLE 10.10

Z test summary for the two signup pages problem

Result	Conclusions
The $Z_{STAT} = +5.1228$ is greater than $+1.96$. (JMP reverses the samples and therefore reports Z_{STAT} as -5.1228.)	1. Reject the null hypothesis H_0. 2. Conclude that evidence exists that the signup pages are significantly different with respect to signups.
The *Z* test *p*-value $= 0.0000$ is less than the level of significance, $\alpha = 0.05$.	3. There is a probability of 0.0000 that $Z_{STAT} > 5.1228$ or < -5.1228.

FIGURE 10.11

Excel, JMP, and Minitab *Z* test results for the difference between two proportions for the two signup pages problem (JMP shows a negative test statistic.)

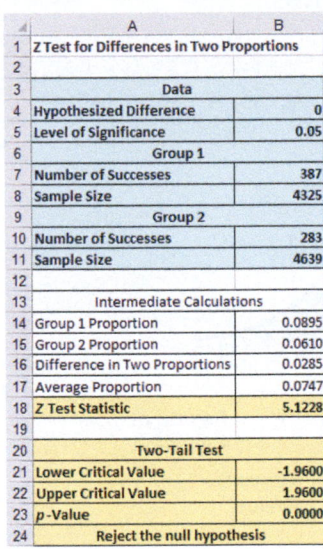

Test Results

Result	Value
Sample 1 Proportion	0.0895
Sample 2 Proportion	0.061
Difference in Proportions (p2-p1)	-0.0285
Standard Error of the Difference (p2-p1)	0.0056
z-score	-5.1228
z Critical Value(s)	+/- 1.96
Observed Significance (p-value)	<.0001
Reject Null Hypothesis	

Test and CI for Two Proportions

Method

p_1: proportion where Sample 1 = Event
p_2: proportion where Sample 2 = Event
Difference: $p_1 - p_2$

Descriptive Statistics

Sample	N	Event	Sample p
Sample 1	4325	387	0.089480
Sample 2	4639	283	0.061005

Estimation for Difference

Difference	95% CI for Difference
0.0284752	(0.017530, 0.039421)

CI based on normal approximation

Test

Null hypothesis	$H_0: p_1 - p_2 = 0$
Alternative hypothesis	$H_1: p_1 - p_2 \neq 0$

Method	Z-Value	P-Value
Normal approximation	5.12	0.000
Fisher's exact		0.000

The pooled estimate of the proportion (0.0747434) is used for the tests.

EXAMPLE 10.3

Testing for the Difference Between Two Proportions

Are men less likely than women to say that a major reason they use Facebook is to share with many people at once? A survey reported that 42% of men (193 out of 459 sampled) and 50% of women (250 out of 501 sampled) said that a major reason they use Facebook is to share with many people at once. (Source: "6 new facts about Facebook," **bit.ly/1kENZcA**.)

SOLUTION   Because you want to know whether there is evidence that the proportion of men who say that a major reason they use Facebook is to share with many people at once is *less* than the proportion of women who say that a major reason they use Facebook is to share with many people at once, you have a one-tail test. The null and alternative hypotheses are

$H_0: \pi_1 \geq \pi_2$ (The proportion of men who say that a major reason they use Facebook is to share with many people at once is greater than or equal to the proportion of women who say that a major reason they use Facebook is to share with many people at once.)

$H_1: \pi_1 < \pi_2$ (The proportion of men who say that a major reason they use Facebook is to share with many people at once is less than the proportion of women who say that a major reason they use Facebook is to share with many people at once.)

Using the 0.05 level of significance, for the one-tail test in the lower tail, the critical value is $+1.645$. The decision rule is

$$\text{Reject } H_0 \text{ if } Z_{STAT} < -1.645;$$

$$\text{otherwise, do not reject } H_0.$$

▶(continued)

Using Equation (10.5) on page 369,

$$Z_{STAT} = \frac{(p_1 - p_2) - (\pi_1 - \pi_2)}{\sqrt{\bar{p}(1 - \bar{p})\left(\dfrac{1}{n_1} + \dfrac{1}{n_2}\right)}}$$

given $\quad p_1 = \dfrac{X_1}{n_1} = \dfrac{193}{459} = 0.4205, \quad p_2 = \dfrac{X_2}{n_2} = \dfrac{250}{501} = 0.4990,$ and

$$\bar{p} = \frac{X_1 + X_2}{n_1 + n_2} = \frac{193 + 250}{459 + 501} = 0.4615$$

the calculation is

$$Z_{STAT} = \frac{(0.4205 - 0.4990) - (0)}{\sqrt{0.4615(1 - 0.4615)\left(\dfrac{1}{459} + \dfrac{1}{501}\right)}}$$

$$= \frac{-0.0785}{\sqrt{(0.2485)(0.0042)}} = \frac{-0.0785}{\sqrt{0.0010437}}$$

$$= \frac{-0.0785}{0.0322} = -2.4379$$

Table 10.11 summarizes the results of the Z test for the difference between the gender proportions using the calculation above and Figure 10.12 results. Based on the conclusions, the proportion of men who say that sharing with many people at once is a major reason they use Facebook is less than the proportion of women who say that. Therefore, as part of the last step of the DCOVA framework, you might recommend that Facebook explore other ways in which the two genders differently view the usefulness of Facebook.

TABLE 10.11

Z test summary for the difference in the proportion of men and women who say sharing with many people at once is a major reason they use Facebook

Result	Conclusions
The $Z_{STAT} = -2.4379$ is less than -1.96. The Z test p-value $= 0.0074$ is less than the level of significance, $\alpha = 0.05$.	1. Reject the null hypothesis H_0. 2. Conclude that evidence exists that men are significantly less likely than women to say that sharing with many people at once is a major reason they use Facebook. 3. There is a probability of 0.0074 that $Z_{STAT} < -2.4379$.

FIGURE 10.12

Excel and JMP Z test results for the major reason men and women use Facebook

JMP shows a positive test statistic.

	A	B
1	Z Test for Differences in Two Proportions	
2		
3	Data	
4	Hypothesized Difference	0
5	Level of Significance	0.05
6	Group 1	
7	Number of Items of Interest	193
8	Sample Size	459
9	Group 2	
10	Number of Items of Interest	250
11	Sample Size	501
12		
13	Intermediate Calculations	
14	Group 1 Proportion	0.4205
15	Group 2 Proportion	0.4990
16	Difference in Two Proportions	-0.0785
17	Average Proportion	0.4615
18	Z Test Statistic	-2.4379
19		
20	Lower-Tail Test	
21	Lower Critical Value	-1.6449
22	p-Value	0.0074
23	Reject the null hypothesis	

Test Inputs

Hypothesized Difference (p2-p1)	0
Sample 1 Count (x1)	193
Sample 1 Size (n1)	459
Sample 2 Count (x2)	250
Sample 2 Size (n2)	501
Significance Level (alpha)	0.05

Test Results

Result	Value
Sample 1 Proportion	0.4205
Sample 2 Proportion	0.499
Difference in Proportions (p2-p1)	0.0785
Standard Error of the Difference (p2-p1)	0.0322
z-score	2.4379
z Critical Value(s)	1.6449
Observed Significance (p-value)	0.0074
Reject Null Hypothesis	

Confidence Interval Estimate for the Difference Between Two Proportions

Instead of, or in addition to, testing for the difference between the proportions of two independent populations, you can construct a confidence interval estimate for the difference between the two proportions using Equation (10.6).

CONFIDENCE INTERVAL ESTIMATE FOR THE DIFFERENCE
BETWEEN TWO PROPORTIONS

$$(p_1 - p_2) \pm Z_{\alpha/2}\sqrt{\frac{p_1(1 - p_1)}{n_1} + \frac{p_2(1 - p_2)}{n_2}} \qquad (10.6)$$

or

$$(p_1 - p_2) - Z_{\alpha/2}\sqrt{\frac{p_1(1 - p_1)}{n_1} + \frac{p_2(1 - p_2)}{n_2}} \leq (\pi_1 - \pi_2)$$

$$\leq (p_1 - p_2) + Z_{\alpha/2}\sqrt{\frac{p_1(1 - p_1)}{n_1} + \frac{p_2(1 - p_2)}{n_2}}$$

To construct a 95% confidence interval estimate for the population difference between the proportion of visitors to the few personal details page who signed up and the proportion of visitors to the many personal details page who signed signed up, you use the results on page 371 or from Figure 10.11 on page 372:

$$p_1 = \frac{X_1}{n_1} = \frac{387}{4{,}325} = 0.0895 \quad p_2 = \frac{X_2}{n_2} = \frac{283}{4{,}639} = 0.0610$$

Using Equation (10.6),

$$(0.0895 - 0.0610) \pm (1.96)\sqrt{\frac{0.0895(1 - 0.0895)}{4{,}325} + \frac{0.0610(1 - 0.0610)}{4{,}639}}$$

$$0.0285 \pm (1.96)(0.0056)$$

$$0.0285 \pm 0.0109$$

$$0.0175 \leq (\pi_1 - \pi_2) \leq 0.0394$$

You have 95% confidence that the difference between the population proportion of visitors to the few personal details page who signed up and the population proportion of visitors to the many personal details page who signed up is between 0.0175 and 0.0394. In percentages, the difference is between 1.75% and 3.94%. Visitors are more likely to sign up if they are presented with a signup page that asks for fewer personal details.

PROBLEMS FOR SECTION 10.3

LEARNING THE BASICS

10.27 Let $n_1 = 100$, $X_1 = 50$, $n_2 = 100$, and $X_2 = 30$.
a. At the 0.05 level of significance, is there evidence of a significant difference between the two population proportions?
b. Construct a 95% confidence interval estimate for the difference between the two population proportions.

10.28 Let $n_1 = 100$, $X_1 = 45$, $n_2 = 50$, and $X_2 = 25$.
a. At the 0.01 level of significance, is there evidence of a significant difference between the two population proportions?
b. Construct a 99% confidence interval estimate for the difference between the two population proportions.

APPLYING THE CONCEPTS

10.29 An online survey asked 1,004 adults "If purchasing a used car made certain upgrades or features more affordable, what would be your preferred luxury upgrade?" The results indicated that 9% of the males and 14% of the females answered window tinting.

Source: Data extracted from Ipsos, "Safety Technology Tops the List of Most Desired Features Should They Be More Affordable When Purchasing a Used Car—Particularly Collision Avoidance," **bit.ly/1RCcc1L**.

The sample sizes of males and females were not provided. Suppose that both sample sizes were 502 and that 46 of 502 males and 71 of 502 females reported window tinting as their preferred luxury upgrade of choice.

a. Is there evidence of a difference between males and females in the proportion who said they prefer window tinting as a luxury upgrade at the 0.01 level of significance?

b. Find the *p*-value in (a) and interpret its meaning.

c. Construct and interpret a 99% confidence interval estimate for the difference between the proportion of males and females who said they prefer window tinting as a luxury upgrade.

d. What are your answers to (a) through (c) if 60 males said they prefer window tinting as a luxury upgrade?

10.30 Does Cable Video on Demand (VOD D4+) increase ad effectiveness? A 2015 VOD study compared general TV and VOD D4+ audiences after viewing a brand ad. Data were collected on whether the viewer indicated that the ad made them want to visit the brand website. The results were:

VIEWING AUDIENCE	MADE ME WANT TO VISIT THE BRAND WEBSITE	
	Yes	No
VOD D4+	147	103
General TV	35	166

Source: Data extracted from Canoe Ventures, *Understanding VOD Advertising Effectiveness*, **bit.ly/1JnmMup**.

a. Set up the null and alternative hypotheses to try to determine whether ad impact is stronger following VOD D4+ viewing than following general TV viewing.

b. Conduct the hypothesis test defined in (a), using the 0.05 level of significance.

c. Does the result of your test in (b) make it appropriate to claim that ad impact is stronger following VOD D4+ than following general TV viewing?

10.31 Are you an impulse shopper? A survey of 500 grocery shoppers indicated that 29% of males and 40% of females make an impulse purchase every time they shop. Assume that the survey consisted of 250 males and 250 females.

Soruce: Data extracted from *Women shoppers are impulsive while men snap up bargains*, available at **bit.ly/2sLYmVx**.

a. At the 0.05 level of significance, is there evidence of a difference in the proportion of males and females who make an impulse purchase every time they shop?

b. Find the *p*-values and interpret its meaning.

10.32 The Society for Human Resource Management (SHRM) collaborated with Globoforce on a series of organizational surveys with the goal of identifying challenges that HR leaders face and what strategies help them conquer those challenges. A 2016 survey indicates that employee retention/turnover (46%) and employee engagement (36%) were cited as the most important organizational challenges currently faced by HR professionals. One strategy that may have an impact on employee retention, turnover and engagement is a successful employee recognition program. Surveying small organizations, those with 500 to 2,499 employees, and large organizations, those with 10,000 or more employees, SHRM and Globoforce showed that 326 (77%) of the 423 small organizations have employee retention programs as compared to 167 (87%) of the 192 large organizations.

Source: Data extracted from *SHRM Survey Finding: Influencing Workplace Culture Through Employee Retention and Other Efforts*, **bit.ly/2rFvE9w**.

a. At the 0.01 level of significance, is there evidence of a significant difference between organizations with 500 to 2,499 employees and organizations with 10,000+ employees with respect to the proportion that have employee recognition programs?

b. Find the *p*-value in (a) and interpret its meaning.

c. Construct and interpret a 99% confidence interval estimate for the difference between organizations with 500 to 2,499 employees and organizations with 10,000 or more employees with respect to the proportion that have employee recognition programs.

10.33 What social media tools do marketers commonly use? A survey by Social Media Examiner of B2B marketers (marketers that focus primarily on attracting businesses) and B2C marketers (marketers that primarily target consumers) reported that 267 (81%) of B2B marketers and 295 (44%) of B2C marketers commonly use LinkedIn as a social media tool. The study also revealed that 149 (45%) of B2B marketers and 308 (46%) of B2C marketers commonly use YouTube as a social media tool.

Data extracted from *2017 Social Media Marketing Industry Report*, **www.social mediaexaminer.com/wp-content/uploads/2017/05/Industry-Report-2017.pdf**.

Suppose the survey was based on 330 B2B marketers and 670 B2C marketers.

a. At the 0.05 level of significance, is there evidence of a difference between B2B marketers and B2C marketers in the proportion that commonly use LinkedIn as a social media tool?

b. Find the *p*-value in (a) and interpret its value.

c. At the 0.05 level of significance, is there evidence of a difference between B2B marketers and B2C marketers in the proportion that commonly use YouTube as a social media tool?

10.34 Does co-browsing have positive effects on the customer experience? Co-browsing refers to the ability to have a contact center agent and customer jointly navigate an online document or mobile application on a real-time basis through the web. A study of businesses indicates that 81 of 129 co-browsing organizations use skills-based routing to match the caller with the *right* agent, whereas 65 of 176 non-co-browsing organizations use skills-based routing to match the caller with the *right* agent.

Source: *Cobrowsing Presents a 'Lucrative' Customer Service Opportunity*, available at **bit.ly/1wwALWr**.

a. At the 0.05 level of significance, is there evidence of a difference between co-browsing organizations and non-co-browsing organizations in the proportion that use skills-based routing to match the caller with the *right* agent?

b. Find the *p*-value in (a) and interpret its meaning.

10.35 One of the most innovative advances in online fundraising during the past decade has been the rise of crowd-funding websites. While features differ from site to site, crowd-funding websites give people an opportunity to set up an online fundraising web page and to accept money directly from that page through an online payments system. Kickstarter, one such crowd-funding website, reported that 72 of 415 *technology* crowd-funding projects in Canada were successfully funded in the past year and 88 of 300 *film and video* crowd-funding projects were successfully funded in Canada in the past year.

Source: Data extracted from **bit.ly/2rSCPtp**.

a. Is there evidence of a significant difference in the proportion of *technology* crowd-funding projects and *film and video* crowd-funding projects that were successful? (Use $\alpha = 0.05$.)

b. Determine the *p*-value in (a) and interpret its meaning.

c. Construct and interpret a 95% confidence interval estimate for the difference between the proportion of *technology* crowd-funding projects and *film and video* crowd-funding projects that are successful.

10.4 *F* Test for the Ratio of Two Variances

Often you need to determine whether two independent populations have the same variability. By testing variances, you can detect differences in the variability in two independent populations. One important reason to test for the difference between the variances of two populations is to determine whether to use the pooled-variance *t* test (which assumes equal variances) or the separate-variance *t* test (which does not assume equal variances) when comparing the means of two independent populations.

The test for the difference between the variances of two independent populations is based on the ratio of the two sample variances. If you assume that each population is normally distributed, then the sampling distribution of the ratio S_1^2/S_2^2 is distributed as an *F* distribution (see Table E.5). Unlike the normal and *t* distributions which are symmetric, the *F* distribution is right-skewed. The critical values of the **F distribution** in Table E.5 depend on the degrees of freedom in the two samples. In addition, the degrees of freedom in the numerator of the ratio are for the first sample, and the degrees of freedom in the denominator are for the second sample. The first sample taken from the first population is defined as the sample that has the *larger* sample variance. The second sample taken from the second population is the sample with the *smaller* sample variance. Equation (10.7) defines the **F test for the ratio of two variances**.

F TEST STATISTIC FOR TESTING THE RATIO OF TWO VARIANCES

studentTIP

Since the numerator of Equation (10.7) contains the larger variance, the F_{STAT} statistic is always greater than or equal to 1.0.

The F_{STAT} test statistic is equal to the variance of sample 1 (the larger sample variance) divided by the variance of sample 2 (the smaller sample variance).

$$F_{STAT} = \frac{S_1^2}{S_2^2} \tag{10.7}$$

where

S_1^2 = variance of sample 1 (the larger sample variance)
S_2^2 = variance of sample 2 (the smaller sample variance)
n_1 = sample size selected from population 1
n_2 = sample size selected from population 2
$n_1 - 1$ = degrees of freedom from sample 1 (the numerator degrees of freedom)
$n_2 - 1$ = degrees of freedom from sample 2 (the denominator degrees of freedom)

The F_{STAT} test statistic follows an *F* distribution with $n_1 - 1$ and $n_2 - 1$ degrees of freedom.

For a given level of significance, α, to test the null hypothesis of equality of population variances:

$$H_0: \sigma_1^2 = \sigma_2^2$$

against the alternative hypothesis that the two population variances are not equal:

$$H_1: \sigma_1^2 \neq \sigma_2^2$$

you reject the null hypothesis if the computed F_{STAT} test statistic is greater than the upper-tail critical value, $F_{\alpha/2}$, from the *F* distribution, with $n_1 - 1$ degrees of freedom in the numerator and $n_2 - 1$ degrees of freedom in the denominator. Thus, the decision rule is

$$\text{Reject } H_0 \text{ if } F_{STAT} > F_{\alpha/2};$$

otherwise, do not reject H_0.

To illustrate how to use the F test to determine whether the two variances are equal, return to the Arlingtons scenario on page 351 concerning the sales of VLABGo players in two different sales locations. To determine whether to use the pooled-variance t test or the separate-variance t test in Section 10.1, you can test the equality of the two population variances. The null and alternative hypotheses are

$$H_0: \sigma_1^2 = \sigma_2^2$$

$$H_1: \sigma_1^2 \neq \sigma_2^2$$

Because you are defining sample 1 as the group with the larger sample variance, the rejection region in the upper tail of the F distribution contains $\alpha/2$. Using the level of significance $\alpha = 0.05$, the rejection region in the upper tail contains 0.025 of the distribution.

Because there are samples of 10 stores for each of the two sales locations, there are $10 - 1 = 9$ degrees of freedom in the numerator (the sample with the larger variance) and also in the denominator (the sample with the smaller variance). $F_{\alpha/2}$, the upper-tail critical value of the F distribution, is found directly from Table E.5, a portion of which is presented in Table 10.12. Because there are 9 degrees of freedom in the numerator and 9 degrees of freedom in the denominator, you find the upper-tail critical value, $F_{\alpha/2}$, by looking in the column labeled 9 and the row labeled 9. Thus, the upper-tail critical value of this F distribution is 4.03. Therefore, the decision rule is

$$\text{Reject } H_0 \text{ if } F_{STAT} > F_{0.025} = 4.03;$$

otherwise, do not reject H_0.

TABLE 10.12

Finding the Upper-Tail Critical Value of F with 9 Degrees of Freedom for an Upper-Tail Area of 0.025

	Cumulative Probabilities = 0.975 Upper-Tail Area = 0.025 Numerator df_1						
Denominator df_2	**1**	**2**	**3**	...	**7**	**8**	**9**
1	647.80	799.50	864.20	...	948.20	956.70	963.30
2	38.51	39.00	39.17	...	39.36	39.37	39.39
3	17.44	16.04	15.44	...	14.62	14.54	14.47
⋮	⋮	⋮	⋮	⋮	⋮	⋮	⋮
7	8.07	6.54	5.89	...	4.99	4.90	4.82
8	7.57	6.06	5.42	...	4.53	4.43	4.36
9	7.21	5.71	5.08	...	4.20	4.10	4.03

Source: Extracted from Table E.5.

Using Equation (10.7) on page 376 and the VLABGo sales data (see Table 10.1 on page 353),

$$S_1^2 = (42.5420)^2 = 1{,}809.8222 \quad S_2^2 = (32.5271)^2 = 1{,}058.0111$$

so that

$$F_{STAT} = \frac{S_1^2}{S_2^2}$$

$$= \frac{1{,}809.8222}{1{,}058.0111} = 1.7106$$

Because $F_{STAT} = 1.7106 < 4.03$, you do not reject H_0. Figure 10.13 shows the results for this test, including the p-value, 0.4361. Because $0.4361 > 0.05$, you conclude that there is no evidence of a significant difference in the variability of the sales of the VLABGo players for the two sales locations.

FIGURE 10.13

Excel, JMP, and Minitab F test results for the two different sales locations data

	A	B
1	F Test for Differences in Two Variances	
2		
3	Data	
4	Level of Significance	0.05
5	Larger-Variance Sample	
6	Sample Size	10
7	Sample Variance	1809.822
8	Smaller-Variance Sample	
9	Sample Size	10
10	Sample Variance	1058.011
11		
12	Intermediate Calculations	
13	F Test Statistic	1.7106
14	Population 1 Sample Degrees of Freedom	9
15	Population 2 Sample Degrees of Freedom	9
16		
17	Two-Tail Test	
18	Upper Critical Value	4.0260
19	p-Value	0.4361
20	Do not reject the null hypothesis	

Level	Count	Std Dev	MeanAbsDif to Mean	MeanAbsDif to Median
In-Aisle	10	32.52708	25.36000	25.30000
Special Front	10	42.54201	34.20000	34.20000

Test	F Ratio	DFNum	DFDen	p-Value
O'Brien[.5]	1.0004	1	18	0.3305
Brown-Forsythe	0.8909	1	18	0.3577
Levene	0.9154	1	18	0.3514
Bartlett	0.6071	1	.	0.4359
F Test 2-sided	1.7106	9	9	0.4361

Test and CI for Two Variances: Special Front, In-Aisle

Method

σ_1: standard deviation of Special Front
σ_2: standard deviation of In-Aisle
Ratio: σ_1/σ_2
F method was used. This method is accurate for normal data only.

Descriptive Statistics

Variable	N	StDev	Variance	95% CI for σ
Special Front	10	42.542	1809.822	(29.262, 77.665)
In-Aisle	10	32.527	1058.011	(22.373, 59.382)

Ratio of Standard Deviations

Estimated Ratio	95% CI for Ratio using F
1.30789	(0.652, 2.624)

Test

Null hypothesis	$H_0: \sigma_1 / \sigma_2 = 1$
Alternative hypothesis	$H_1: \sigma_1 / \sigma_2 \neq 1$
Significance level	$\alpha = 0.05$

Method	Test Statistic	DF1	DF2	P-Value
F	1.71	9	9	0.436

In testing for a difference between two variances using the F test, you assume that each of the two populations is normally distributed. The F test is very sensitive to the normality assumption. If boxplots or normal probability plots suggest even a mild departure from normality for either of the two populations, you should not use the F test. If this happens, you should use the Levene test (see Section 11.1) or a nonparametric approach (see references 1 and 2).

In testing for the equality of variances as part of assessing the appropriateness of the pooled-variance t test procedure, the F test is a two-tail test with $\alpha/2$ in the upper tail. However, when you are interested in examining the variability in situations other than the pooled-variance t test, the F test is often a one-tail test. Example 10.4 illustrates a one-tail test.

EXAMPLE 10.4

A One-Tail Test for the Difference Between Two Variances

Waiting time is a critical issue at fast-food chains, which not only want to minimize the mean service time but also want to minimize the variation in the service time from customer to customer. One fast-food chain carried out a study to measure the variability in the waiting time (defined as the time in minutes from when an order was completed to when it was delivered to the customer) at lunch and breakfast at one of the chain's stores. The results were as follows:

$$\text{Lunch: } n_1 = 25 \quad S_1^2 = 4.4$$

$$\text{Breakfast: } n_2 = 21 \quad S_2^2 = 1.9$$

At the 0.05 level of significance, is there evidence that there is more variability in the service time at lunch than at breakfast? Assume that the population service times are normally distributed.

SOLUTION The null and alternative hypotheses are

$$H_0: \sigma_L^2 \leq \sigma_B^2$$

$$H_1: \sigma_L^2 > \sigma_B^2$$

The F_{STAT} test statistic is given by Equation (10.7) on page 376:

$$F_{STAT} = \frac{S_1^2}{S_2^2}$$

You use Table E.5 to find the upper critical value of the F distribution. With $n_1 - 1 = 25 - 1 = 24$ degrees of freedom in the numerator, $n_2 - 1 = 21 - 1 = 20$ degrees of freedom in the denominator, and $\alpha = 0.05$, the upper-tail critical value, $F_{0.05}$, is 2.08. The decision rule is

$$\text{Reject } H_0 \text{ if } F_{STAT} > 2.08;$$

►(continued) otherwise, do not reject H_0.

From Equation (10.7) on page 376,

$$F_{STAT} = \frac{S_1^2}{S_2^2}$$

$$= \frac{4.4}{1.9} = 2.3158$$

Because $F_{STAT} = 2.3158 > 2.08$, you reject H_0. Using a 0.05 level of significance, you conclude that there is evidence that there is more variability in the service time at lunch than at breakfast.

PROBLEMS FOR SECTION 10.4

LEARNING THE BASICS

10.36 Determine the upper-tail critical values of *F* in each of the following two-tail tests.
a. $\alpha = 0.10$, $n_1 = 16$, $n_2 = 21$
b. $\alpha = 0.05$, $n_1 = 16$, $n_2 = 21$
c. $\alpha = 0.01$, $n_1 = 16$, $n_2 = 21$

10.37 Determine the upper-tail critical value of *F* in each of the following one-tail tests.
a. $\alpha = 0.05$, $n_1 = 16$, $n_2 = 21$
b. $\alpha = 0.01$, $n_1 = 16$, $n_2 = 21$

10.38 The following information is available for two samples selected from independent normally distributed populations:

Population A: $n_1 = 25$ $S_1^2 = 16$

Population B: $n_2 = 25$ $S_2^2 = 25$

a. Which sample variance do you place in the numerator of F_{STAT}?
b. What is the value of F_{STAT}?

10.39 The following information is available for two samples selected from independent normally distributed populations:

Population A: $n_1 = 25$ $S_1^2 = 161.9$

Population B: $n_2 = 25$ $S_2^2 = 133.7$

What is the value of F_{STAT} if you are testing the null hypothesis $H_0: \sigma_1^2 = \sigma_2^2$?

10.40 In Problem 10.39, how many degrees of freedom are there in the numerator and denominator of the *F* test?

10.41 In Problems 10.38 and 10.39, what is the upper-tail critical value for *F* if the level of significance, α, is 0.05 and the alternative hypothesis is $H_1: \sigma_1^2 \neq \sigma_2^2$?

10.42 In Problem 10.39, what is your statistical decision?

10.43 The following information is available for two samples selected from independent but very right-skewed populations:

Population A: $n_1 = 16$ $S_1^2 = 47.3$

Population B: $n_2 = 13$ $S_2^2 = 36.4$

Should you use the *F* test to test the null hypothesis of equality of variances? Discuss.

10.44 In Problem 10.43, assume that two samples are selected from independent normally distributed populations.
a. At the 0.05 level of significance, is there evidence of a difference between σ_1^2 and σ_2^2?
b. Suppose that you want to perform a one-tail test. At the 0.05 level of significance, what is the upper-tail critical value of *F* to determine whether there is evidence that $\sigma_1^2 > \sigma_2^2$? What is your statistical decision?

APPLYING THE CONCEPTS

10.45 Is there a difference in the variance of the satisfaction rating of traditional cellphone providers who bill for service at the end of a month (often under a contract) and prepaid cellphone service providers who bill in advance without a contract? The file **CellphoneProviders** contains the satisfaction rating for 10 traditional cellphone providers and 13 prepaid cellphone service providers.

Source: Data extracted from "Carrier Ratings: Why It Pays to Think Small," *Consumer Reports*, February 2016, p. 51.

a. At the 0.05 level of significance, is there evidence of a difference in the variability of the satisfaction rating between the types of cellphone providers?
b. Determine the *p*-value in (a) and interpret its meaning.
c. What assumption do you need to make in (a) about the two populations in order to justify your use of the *F* test?
d. Based on the results of (a) and (b), which *t* test defined in Section 10.1 should you use to compare the mean satisfaction rating of the two types of cellphone providers?

✓ SELF TEST **10.46** *Accounting Today* identified top accounting firms in 10 geographic regions across the United States. All 10 regions reported growth in 2016. The Southeast and Gulf Coast regions reported growths of 12.03% and 9.47%, respectively. A characteristic description of the accounting firms in the Southeast and Gulf Coast regions included the number of partners in the firm. The file **AccountingPartners2** contains the number of partners.

Source: Data extracted from *Accounting Today*, "Special Report: The 2017 Top 100 Firms and Regional Leaders," **bit.ly/2sNGVqH**.

a. At the 0.05 level of significance, is there evidence of a difference in the variability in numbers of partners for Southeast region accounting firms and Gulf Coast accounting firms?
b. Determine the *p*-value in (a) and interpret its meaning.

c. What assumption do you have to make about the two populations in order to justify the use of the F test?

d. Based on (a) and (b), which t test defined in Section 10.1 should you use to test whether there is a significant difference in the mean number of partners for Southeast region accounting firms and Gulf Coast accounting firms?

10.47 A bank with a branch located in a commercial district of a city has the business objective of improving the process for serving customers during the noon-to-1 P.M. lunch period. To do so, the waiting time (defined as the number of minutes that elapses from when the customer enters the line until he or she reaches the teller window) needs to be shortened to increase customer satisfaction. A random sample of 15 customers is selected and the waiting times are collected and stored in Bank1 . These data are:

4.21	5.55	3.02	5.13	4.77	2.34	3.54	3.20
4.50	6.10	0.38	5.12	6.46	6.19	3.79	

Suppose that another branch, located in a residential area, is also concerned with the noon-to-1 P.M. lunch period. A random sample of 15 customers is selected and the waiting times are collected and stored in Bank2 . These data are:

9.66	5.90	8.02	5.79	8.73	3.82	8.01	8.35
10.49	6.68	5.64	4.08	6.17	9.91	5.47	

a. Is there evidence of a difference in the variability of the waiting time between the two branches? (Use $\alpha = 0.05$.)

b. Determine the p-value in (a) and interpret its meaning.

c. What assumption about the population distribution of each bank is necessary in (a)? Is the assumption valid for these data?

d. Based on the results of (a), is it appropriate to use the pooled-variance t test to compare the means of the two branches?

10.48 The annual NFL Super Bowl is the most widely watched sporting event in the United States each year. In recent years, there has been a great deal of interest in the ads that appear during the game. These ads vary in length with most lasting 30 seconds or 60 seconds. The file SuperBowlAdScore contains the ad length and ad scores from a recent Super Bowl.

Source: Data extracted from C. Woodyard, "Funny Bone Wins Out," *USA Today*, February 6, 2016, p. 4B.

a. Is there evidence of a difference in the variability of the scores between the two types of ads? (Use $\alpha = 0.05$.)

b. Determine the p-value in (a) and interpret its meaning.

c. What assumption about the population distribution of the two types of ads is necessary in (a)? Is the assumption valid for these data?

d. Based on the results of (a), which t test defined in Section 10.1 should you use to compare the mean scores of the two types of ads?

10.49 We Are Social and Hootsuite reported that the typical American spends 2.02 hours (121 minutes) per day accessing the Internet through a mobile device.

Source: *Digital in 2017 Global Overview*, available at **bit.ly/2jXeS3F**.

You wonder if males and females spend differing amounts of time per day accessing the Internet through a mobile device.

You select a sample of 60 friends and family (30 males and 30 females), collect times spent per day accessing the Internet through a mobile device (in minutes), and store the data collected in InternetMobileTime2 .

a. Using a 0.05 level of significance, is there evidence of a difference in the variances of time spent per day accessing the Internet via mobile device between males and females?

b. On the basis of the results in (a), which t test that Section 10.1 defines should you use to compare the means of males and females? Discuss.

10.50 A taxicab company has been receiving an increasing number of complaints concerning the delay time between when a call for a taxicab is received and when the passenger is picked up. The file TaxiDelays contains the delay times (in minutes) for two drivers on the same route for a period of 35 days.

Source: Data extracted from M. Sharma, "Above and Beyond," *Six Sigma Forum Magazine*, May 2015, p. 21–25.

a. At the 0.05 level of significance, is there evidence of a difference in the variance of the delay times between the two drivers?

b. What assumption do you need to make in order to do (a)?

c. Evaluate the validity of the assumption in (a).

d. Based on the results of (a), which t-test for the difference between the means from Section 10.1 should you use to determine whether there is evidence of a difference in the mean delay time between the two drivers?

10.5 Effect Size

Section 9.5 discusses the issue of the practical significance of a statistically significant test and explains that when a very large sample is selected, a statistically significant result can be of limited importance. The **Section 10.5 online topic** shows how to measure the effect size of a statistical test.

▼ USING **STATISTICS**
Differing Means for Selling…, Revisited

I n the Arlingtons scenario, you sought to show that the sales location in a store could affect sales of a product. If you could show such an effect, you would have an argument for charging a placement fee for the better location. You designed an experiment that would sell the new VLABGo mobile streaming media player in one of two sales locations, at a special front of store location or in the mobile electronics aisle. You conducted an experiment in which 10 stores used the special front location to sell VLABGo players and 10 stores used the mobile electronics aisle.

Using a *t* test for the difference between two means, you were able to conclude that the mean sales using the special front location are higher than the mean sales for the in-aisle location. A confidence interval allowed you to infer with 95% confidence that population mean amount sold at the special front location was between 8.52 and 79.68 more than the in-aisle location. You also performed the *F* test for the difference between two variances to see if the store-to-store variability in sales in stores using the special front location differed from the store-to-store variability in sales in stores using the in-aisle location. You concluded that there was no significant difference in the variability of the sales of VLABGo players for the sales locations. That you now have evidence that sales are higher in the special front location gives you one argument for charging manufacturers a placement fee for that location.

▼ SUMMARY

In this chapter, you were introduced to a variety of tests for two populations. For situations in which the samples are independent, you learned statistical test procedures for analyzing possible differences between means, proportions, and variances. In addition, you learned a test procedure that is frequently used when analyzing differences between the means of two related samples. Remember that you need to select the test that is most appropriate for a given set of conditions and to critically investigate the validity of the assumptions underlying each of the hypothesis-testing procedures.

Table 10.13 provides a list of topics covered in this chapter. The roadmap in Figure 10.14 illustrates the steps needed in determining which two-sample test of hypothesis to use. The following are the questions you need to consider:

1. What type of variables do you have? If you are dealing with categorical variables, use the *Z* test for the difference between two proportions. (This test assumes independent samples.)
2. If you have a numerical variable, determine whether you have independent samples or related samples. If you have related samples, and you can assume approximate normality, use the paired *t* test.
3. If you have independent samples, is your focus on variability or central tendency? If the focus is on variability, and you can assume approximate normality, use the *F* test.
4. If your focus is central tendency and you can assume approximate normality, determine whether you can assume that the variances of the two populations are equal. (This assumption can be tested using the *F* test.)
5. If you can assume that the two populations have equal variances, use the pooled-variance *t* test. If you cannot assume that the two populations have equal variances, use the separate-variance *t* test.

TABLE 10.13
Summary of Topics in Chapter 10

TYPE OF ANALYSIS	TYPES OF DATA	
	Numerical	**Categorical**
Compare two populations	*t* tests for the difference in the means of two independent populations (Section 10.1)	*Z* test for the difference between two proportions (Section 10.3)
	Paired *t* test (Section 10.2)	
	F test for the difference between two variances (Section 10.4)	

FIGURE 10.14
Roadmap for selecting a
test of hypothesis for two
populations

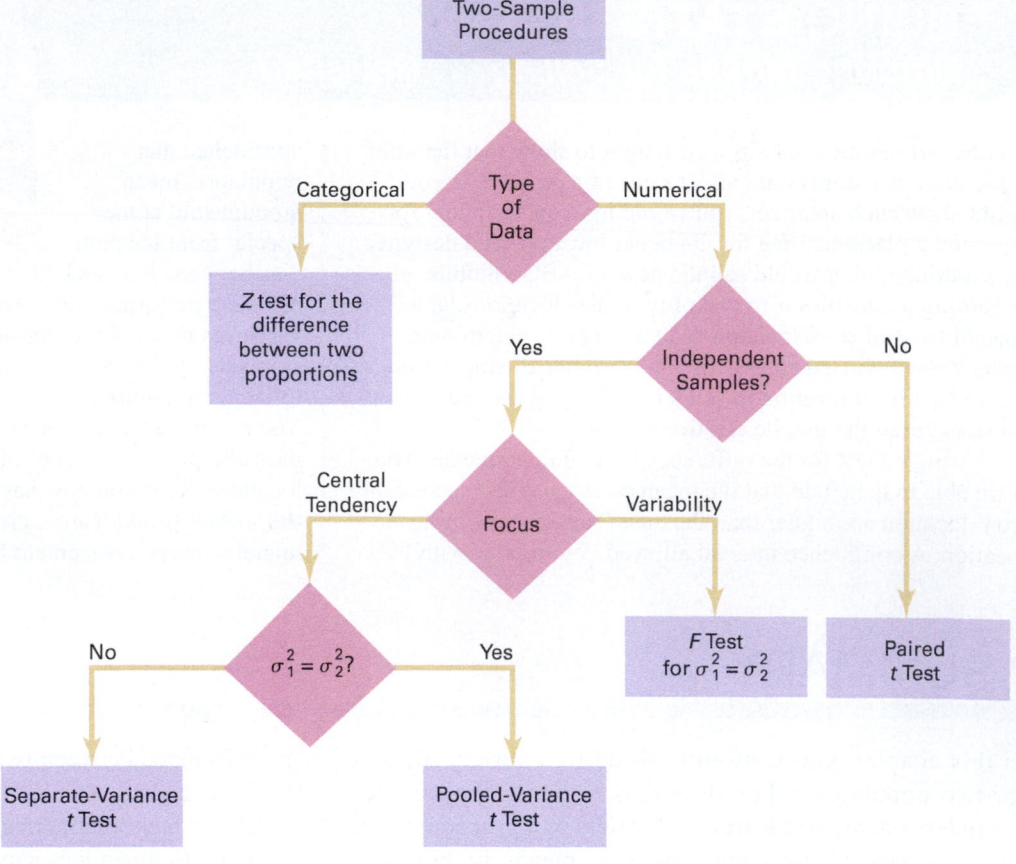

▼REFERENCES

1. Corder, G. W., and D. I. Foreman, *Nonparametric Statistics: A Step-by-Step Approach*. New York: Wiley, 2014.
2. Daniel, W. *Applied Nonparametric Statistics*, 2nd ed. Boston: Houghton Mifflin, 1990.
3. Satterthwaite, F. E. "An Approximate Distribution of Estimates of Variance Components." *Biometrics Bulletin*, 2(1946): 110–114.
4. Snedecor, G. W., and W. G. Cochran. *Statistical Methods*, 8th ed. Ames, IA: Iowa State University Press, 1989.

▼KEY EQUATIONS

Pooled-Variance t Test for the Difference Between Two Means

$$t_{STAT} = \frac{\left(\overline{X}_1 - \overline{X}_2\right) - (\mu_1 - \mu_2)}{\sqrt{S_p^2\left(\frac{1}{n_1} + \frac{1}{n_2}\right)}} \qquad (10.1)$$

Confidence Interval Estimate for the Difference Between the Means of Two Independent Populations

$$\left(\overline{X}_1 - \overline{X}_2\right) \pm t_{\alpha/2}\sqrt{S_p^2\left(\frac{1}{n_1} + \frac{1}{n_2}\right)} \qquad (10.2)$$

or

$$\left(\overline{X}_1 - \overline{X}_2\right) - t_{\alpha/2}\sqrt{S_p^2\left(\frac{1}{n_1} + \frac{1}{n_2}\right)} \leq \mu_1 - \mu_2$$

$$\leq \left(\overline{X}_1 - \overline{X}_2\right) + t_{\alpha/2}\sqrt{S_p^2\left(\frac{1}{n_1} + \frac{1}{n_2}\right)}$$

Paired t Test for the Mean Difference

$$t_{STAT} = \frac{\overline{D} - \mu_D}{\frac{S_D}{\sqrt{n}}} \qquad (10.3)$$

Confidence Interval Estimate for the Mean Difference

$$\overline{D} \pm t_{\alpha/2} \frac{S_D}{\sqrt{n}} \qquad (10.4)$$

or

$$\overline{D} - t_{\alpha/2} \frac{S_D}{\sqrt{n}} \leq \mu_D \leq \overline{D} + t_{\alpha/2} \frac{S_D}{\sqrt{n}}$$

Z Test for the Difference Between Two Proportions

$$Z_{STAT} = \frac{(p_1 - p_2) - (\pi_1 - \pi_2)}{\sqrt{\overline{p}(1 - \overline{p})\left(\frac{1}{n_1} + \frac{1}{n_2}\right)}} \qquad (10.5)$$

Confidence Interval Estimate for the Difference Between Two Proportions

$$(p_1 - p_2) \pm Z_{\alpha/2}\sqrt{\left(\frac{p_1(1 - p_1)}{n_1} + \frac{p_2(1 - p_2)}{n_2}\right)} \qquad (10.6)$$

or

$$(p_1 - p_2) - Z_{\alpha/2}\sqrt{\frac{p_1(1 - p_1)}{n_1} + \frac{p_2(1 - p_2)}{n_2}} \leq (\pi_1 - \pi_2)$$

$$\leq (p_1 - p_2) + Z_{\alpha/2}\sqrt{\frac{p_1(1 - p_1)}{n_1} + \frac{p_2(1 - p_2)}{n_2}}$$

F Test Statistic for Testing the Ratio of Two Variances

$$F_{STAT} = \frac{S_1^2}{S_2^2} \qquad (10.7)$$

▼ KEY TERMS

F distribution   376
F test for the ratio of two variances   376
matched samples   362
paired t test for the mean difference   362

pooled-variance t test   352
repeated measurements   361
robust   355
separate-variance t test   358

two-sample tests   352
Z test for the difference between
    two proportions   369

▼ CHECKING YOUR UNDERSTANDING

10.51 What are some of the criteria used in the selection of a particular hypothesis-testing procedure?

10.52 Under what conditions should you use the pooled-variance t test to examine possible differences in the means of two independent populations?

10.53 Under what conditions should you use the F test to examine possible differences in the variances of two independent populations?

10.54 What is the distinction between two independent populations and two related populations?

10.55 What is the distinction between repeated measurements and matched items?

10.56 When you have two independent populations, explain the similarities and differences between the test of hypothesis for the difference between the means and the confidence interval estimate for the difference between the means.

10.57 Under what conditions should you use the paired t test for the mean difference between two related populations?

▼ CHAPTER REVIEW PROBLEMS

10.58 The American Society for Quality (ASQ) conducted a salary survey of all its members. ASQ members work in all areas of manufacturing and service-related institutions, with a common theme of an interest in quality. Two job titles are black belt and green belt. (See Section 19.6 for a description of these titles in a Six Sigma quality improvement initiative.) Descriptive statistics concerning salaries for these two job titles are given in the following table:

Job Title	Sample Size	Mean	Standard Deviation
Black belt	109	98,445	24,120
Green belt	39	79,749	28,086

Source: Data extracted from "QP Salary Survey," *Quality Progress*, December 2016, p. 11.

a. Using a 0.05 level of significance, is there a difference in the variability of salaries between black belts and green belts?
b. Based on the result of (a), which t test defined in Section 10.1 is appropriate for comparing mean salaries?
c. Using a 0.05 level of significance, is the mean salary of black belts greater than the mean salary of green belts?

10.59 How do private universities and public colleges compare with respect to debt at graduation incurred by students? The file CollegeDebt contains the average debt at graduation incurred by students for 100 private universities and 100 public colleges, as reported by Kiplinger.

Source: Data extracted from "Kiplinger's Best College Values," available at bit.ly/1z39qsT.

a. At the 0.05 level of significance, is there a difference in the variance of average graduation debt incurred by students for private universities and public colleges?

b. Using the results of (a), which *t* test is appropriate for comparing mean debt at graduation incurred by students at private universities and public colleges.

c. At the 0.05 level of significance, conduct the test selected in (b).

d. Write a short summary of your findings.

10.60 Do males and females differ in the amount of time they spend online and the amount of time they spend playing games while online? A study reported that women spent a mean of 1,254 minutes per week online as compared to 1,344 minutes per week for men. Suppose that the sample sizes were 100 each for women and men and that the standard deviation for women was 60 minutes per week as compared to 70 minutes per week for men.

Source: Data extracted from Ofcom, *Adults' Media Use and Attitudes, Report 2016*, **bit.ly/2emgWRk**.

a. Using a 0.01 level of significance, is there evidence of a difference in the variances of the amount of time spent online between women and men?

b. To test for a difference in the mean online time of women and men, is it most appropriate to use the pooled-variance *t* test or the separate-variance *t* test? Using a 0.01 level of significance, use the most appropriate test to determine if there is a difference in the mean amount of time spent online between women and men.

The report found that women spent a mean of 294 minutes per week playing games while online compared to a mean of 360 minutes per week for men. Suppose that the standard deviation for women was 15 minutes per week compared to 20 minutes per week for men.

c. Using a 0.01 level of significance, is there evidence of a difference in the variances of the amount of time spent playing games while online per week by women and men?

d. Based on the results of (c), use the most appropriate test to determine, at the 0.01 level of significance, whether there is evidence of a difference in the mean amount of time spent playing games online per week by women and men.

10.61 The file Restaurants contains the ratings for food, décor, service, and the price per person for a sample of 50 restaurants located in a center city and 50 restaurants located in an outlying area. Completely analyze the differences between center city and outlying area restaurants for the variables food rating, décor rating, service rating, and cost per person, using $\alpha = 0.05$.

Source: Data extracted from *Zagat Survey 2016 New York City Restaurants*.

10.62 A computer information systems professor is interested in studying the amount of time it takes students enrolled in the Introduction to Computers course to write a program in VB.NET. The professor hires you to analyze the following results (in minutes), stored in VB , from a random sample of nine students:

$$10 \quad 13 \quad 9 \quad 15 \quad 12 \quad 13 \quad 11 \quad 13 \quad 12$$

a. At the 0.05 level of significance, is there evidence that the population mean time is greater than 10 minutes? What will you tell the professor?

b. Suppose that the professor, when checking her results, realizes that the fourth student needed 51 minutes rather than the recorded 15 minutes to write the VB.NET program. At the 0.05 level of significance, reanalyze the question posed in (a), using the revised data. What will you tell the professor now?

c. The professor is perplexed by these paradoxical results and requests an explanation from you regarding the justification for the difference in your findings in (a) and (b). Discuss.

d. A few days later, the professor calls to tell you that the dilemma is completely resolved. The original number 15 (the fourth data value) was correct, and therefore your findings in (a) are being used in the article she is writing for a computer journal. Now she wants to hire you to compare the results from that group of Introduction to Computers students against those from a sample of 11 computer majors in order to determine whether there is evidence that computer majors can write a VB.NET program in less time than introductory students. For the computer majors, the sample mean is 8.5 minutes, and the sample standard deviation is 2.0 minutes. At the 0.05 level of significance, completely analyze these data. What will you tell the professor?

e. A few days later, the professor calls again to tell you that a reviewer of her article wants her to include the *p*-value for the "correct" result in (a). In addition, the professor inquires about an unequal-variances problem, which the reviewer wants her to discuss in her article. In your own words, discuss the concept of *p*-value and also describe the unequal-variances problem. Then, determine the *p*-value in (a) and discuss whether the unequal-variances problem had any meaning in the professor's study.

10.63 Do social shoppers differ from other online consumers with respect to spending behavior? A study of browser-based shopping sessions reported that social shoppers, consumers who click away from social networks to retail sites or share an item on a social network, spent a mean of $126.12 on a retail site in a 30-day period compared to other online shoppers who spent a mean of $115.55.

Source: Data extracted from "Social shoppers spend 8% more than other online consumers," **bit.ly/1FyyXP5**.

Suppose that the study consisted of 500 social shoppers and 500 other online shoppers and the standard deviation of the order value was $40 for social shoppers and $10 for other online shoppers. Assume a level of significance of 0.05.

a. Is there evidence of a difference in the variances of the order values between social shoppers and other online shoppers?

b. Is there evidence of a difference in the mean order value between social shoppers and other online shoppers?

c. Construct a 95% confidence interval estimate for the difference in mean order value between social shoppers and other online shoppers.

10.64 The lengths of life (in hours) of a sample of 40 6-watt light emitting diode (LED) light bulbs produced by manufacturer A and a sample of 40 6-watt light emitting diode (LED) light bulbs produced by manufacturer B are stored in Bulbs . Completely analyze the differences between the lengths of life of the light emitting diode (LED) light bulbs produced by the two manufacturers. (Use $\alpha = 0.05$.)

10.65 A hotel manager looks to enhance the initial impressions that hotel guests have when they check in. Contributing to initial impressions is the time it takes to deliver a guest's luggage to the room after check-in. A random sample of 20 deliveries on a particular day were selected in Wing A of the hotel, and a random sample of 20 deliveries were selected in Wing B. The results are stored in Luggage . Analyze the data and determine whether there is a difference between the mean delivery times in the two wings of the hotel. (Use $\alpha = 0.05$.)

10.66 The owner of a restaurant that serves Continental-style entrées has the business objective of learning more about the patterns of patron demand during the Friday-to-Sunday weekend time period. She decided to study the demand for dessert during this time period. In addition to studying whether a dessert was ordered, she will study the gender of the individual and whether a beef entrée was ordered. Data were collected from 630 customers and organized in the following contingency tables:

DESSERT ORDERED	GENDER		
	Male	Female	Total
Yes	96	50	146
No	234	250	484
Total	330	300	630

DESSERT ORDERED	BEEF ENTRÉE		
	Yes	No	Total
Yes	74	68	142
No	123	365	488
Total	197	433	630

a. At the 0.05 level of significance, is there evidence of a difference between males and females in the proportion who order dessert?
b. At the 0.05 level of significance, is there evidence of a difference in the proportion who order dessert based on whether a beef entrée has been ordered?

10.67 The manufacturer of Boston and Vermont asphalt shingles knows that product weight is a major factor in the customer's perception of quality. Moreover, the weight represents the amount of raw materials being used and is therefore very important to the company from a cost standpoint. The last stage of the assembly line packages the shingles before they are placed on wooden pallets. Once a pallet is full (a pallet for most brands holds 16 squares of shingles), it is weighed, and the measurement is recorded. The file Pallet contains the weight (in pounds) from a sample of 368 pallets of Boston shingles and 330 pallets of Vermont shingles. Completely analyze the differences in the weights of the Boston and Vermont shingles, using $\alpha = 0.05$.

10.68 The manufacturer of Boston and Vermont asphalt shingles provides its customers with a 20-year warranty on most of its products. To determine whether a shingle will last as long as the warranty period, the manufacturer conducts accelerated-life testing. Accelerated-life testing exposes the shingle to the stresses it would be subject to in a lifetime of normal use in a laboratory setting via an experiment that takes only a few minutes to conduct. In this test, a shingle is repeatedly scraped with a brush for a short period of time, and the shingle granules removed by the brushing are weighed (in grams). Shingles that experience low amounts of granule loss are expected to last longer in normal use than shingles that experience high amounts of granule loss. In this situation, a shingle should experience no more than 0.8 grams of granule loss if it is expected to last the length of the warranty period. The file Granule contains a sample of 170 measurements made on the company's Boston shingles and 140 measurements made on Vermont shingles. Completely analyze the differences in the granule loss of the Boston and Vermont shingles, using $\alpha = 0.05$.

10.69 Market data indicates that smartphone users are very concerned about the battery life of their smartphones. An experiment is conducted in which the battery life of a newly designed smartphone battery is compared to the battery life of an existing smartphone battery. The following table summarizes the results of the experiment.

Design	Sample Size	Mean (hours)	Standard Deviation (hours)
Existing	30	18.45	0.35
New	30	16.10	0.15

Source: Data extracted from L. Ferryanto, "Are These The Same?," *Quality Progress*, May 2017, 29–36.

Completely analyze these data and indicate which battery design you prefer.

REPORT WRITING EXERCISE

10.70 Referring to the results of Problems 10.67 and 10.68 concerning the weight and granule loss of Boston and Vermont shingles, write a report that summarizes your conclusions.

CHAPTER

10

▼CASES

Managing Ashland MultiComm Services

Part 1 AMS communicates with customers who subscribe to telecommunications services through a special secured email system that sends messages about service changes, new features, and billing information to in-home digital set-top boxes for later display. To enhance customer service, the operations department established the business objective of reducing the amount of time to fully update each subscriber's set of messages. The department selected two candidate messaging systems and conducted an experiment in which 30 randomly chosen cable subscribers were assigned one of the two systems (15 assigned to each system). Update times were measured, and the results are organized in Table AMS 10.1 and stored in AMS10.

TABLE AMS 10.1
Update Times (in seconds) for Two Different Email Interfaces

Email Interface 1	Email Interface 2
4.13	3.71
3.75	3.89
3.93	4.22
3.74	4.57
3.36	4.24
3.85	3.90
3.26	4.09
3.73	4.05
4.06	4.07
3.33	3.80
3.96	4.36
3.57	4.38
3.13	3.49
3.68	3.57
3.63	4.74

1. Analyze the data in Table AMS 10.1 and write a report to the computer operations department that indicates your findings. Include an appendix in which you discuss the reason you selected a particular statistical test to compare the two independent groups of callers.

2. Suppose that instead of the research design described in the case, there were only 15 subscribers sampled, and the update process for each subscriber email was measured for each of the two messaging systems. Suppose that the results were organized in Table AMS 10.1—making each row in the table a pair of values for an individual subscriber. Using these suppositions, reanalyze the Table AMS 10.1 data and write a report for presentation to the team that indicates your findings.

Digital Case

Apply your knowledge about hypothesis testing in this Digital Case, which continues the cereal-fill packaging dispute Digital Case from Chapters 7 and 9.

Even after the recent public experiment about cereal box weights, Consumers Concerned About Cereal Cheaters (CCACC) remains convinced that Oxford Cereals has misled the public. The group has created and circulated **MoreCheating .pdf**, a document in which it claims that cereal boxes produced at Plant Number 2 in Springville weigh less than the claimed mean of 368 grams. Review this document and then answer the following questions:

1. Do the CCACC's results prove that there is a statistically significant difference in the mean weights of cereal boxes produced at Plant Numbers 1 and 2?

2. Perform the appropriate analysis to test the CCACC's hypothesis. What conclusions can you reach based on the data?

Sure Value Convenience Stores

You continue to work in the corporate office for a nationwide convenience store franchise that operates nearly 10,000 stores. The per-store daily customer count (i.e., the mean number of customers in a store in one day) has been steady, at 900, for some time. To increase the customer count, the chain is considering cutting prices for coffee beverages. The small size will now be either $0.59 or $0.79 instead of $0.99. Even with this reduction in price, the chain will have a 40% gross margin on coffee.

The question to be determined is how much to cut prices to increase the daily customer count without reducing the gross margin on coffee sales too much. The chain decides to carry out an experiment in a sample of 30 stores where customer counts have been running almost exactly at the national average of 900. In 15 of the stores, the price of a small coffee will now be $0.59 instead of $0.99, and in 15 other stores, the price of a small coffee will now be $0.79. After four weeks, the 15 stores that priced the small coffee at $0.59 had a mean daily customer count of 964 and a standard deviation of 88, and the 15 stores that priced the small coffee at $0.79 had a mean daily customer count of 941 and a standard deviation of 76. Analyze these data (using the 0.05 level of significance) and answer the following questions.

1. Does reducing the price of a small coffee to either $0.59 or $0.79 increase the mean per-store daily customer count?

2. If reducing the price of a small coffee to either $0.59 or $0.79 increases the mean per-store daily customer count, is there any difference in the mean per-store daily customer count between stores in which a small coffee was priced at $0.59 and stores in which a small coffee was priced at $0.79?

3. What price do you recommend for a small coffee?

CardioGood Fitness

Return to the CardioGood Fitness case first presented on page 33. Using the data stored in CardioGood Fitness :

1. Determine whether differences exist between males and females in their age in years, education in years, annual household income ($), mean number of times the customer plans to use the treadmill each week, and mean number of miles the customer expects to walk or run each week.

2. Write a report to be presented to the management of CardioGood Fitness detailing your findings.

More Descriptive Choices Follow-Up

Follow up the Using Statistics scenario "More Descriptive Choices, Revisited" on page 159.

Determine whether there is a difference in the one-year return percentage, five-year return percentages, and ten-year return percentages of the growth and value funds (stored in Retirement Funds).

Clear Mountain State Student Survey

The Student News Service at Clear Mountain State University (CMSU) has decided to gather data about the undergraduate students that attend CMSU. It creates and distributes a survey of 14 questions and receives responses from 111 undergraduates (stored in StudentSurvey).

1. At the 0.05 level of significance, is there evidence of a difference between males and females in grade point average, expected starting salary, number of social networking sites registered for, age, spending on textbooks and supplies, text messages sent in a week, and the wealth needed to feel rich?

2. At the 0.05 level of significance, is there evidence of a difference between students who plan to go to graduate school and those who do not plan to go to graduate school in grade point average, expected starting salary, number of social networking sites registered for, age, spending on textbooks and supplies, text messages sent in a week, and the wealth needed to feel rich?

EXCEL GUIDE

EG10.1 COMPARING the MEANS of TWO INDEPENDENT POPULATIONS

Pooled-Variance *t* Test for the Difference Between Two Means

Key Technique Use the **T.INV.2T**(*level of significance, total degrees of freedom*) function to compute the lower and upper critical values.

Use the **T.DIST.2T**(*absolute value of the t test statistic, total degrees of freedom*) to compute the *p*-value.

Example Perform the Figure 10.3 pooled-variance *t* test for the Table 10.1 Arlingtons sales data for the two in-store sales locations.

PHStat Use **Pooled-Variance t Test**.

For the example, open to the **DATA worksheet** of the **VLABGo workbook**. Select **PHStat → Two-Sample Tests (Unsummarized Data) → Pooled-Variance t Test**. In the procedure's dialog box (shown below):

1. Enter **0** as the **Hypothesized Difference**.
2. Enter **0.05** as the **Level of Significance**.
3. Enter **A1:A11** as the **Population 1 Sample Cell Range**.
4. Enter **B1:B11** as the **Population 2 Sample Cell Range**.
5. Check **First cells in both ranges contain label**.
6. Click **Two-Tail Test**.
7. Check **Confidence Interval Estimate** and enter **95** as the **Confidence level**.
8. Enter a **Title** and click **OK.**

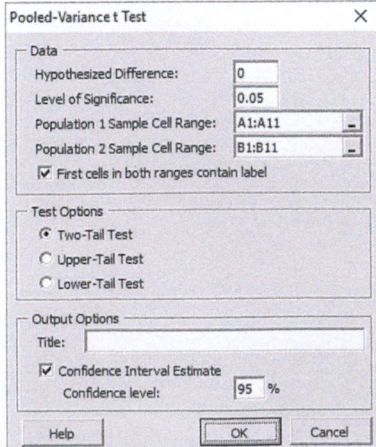

When using summarized data, select **PHStat → Two-Sample Tests (Summarized Data) → Pooled-Variance t Test**. In that procedure's dialog box, enter the hypothesized difference and

level of significance, as well as the sample size, sample mean, and sample standard deviation for each sample.

Workbook Use the **COMPUTE worksheet** of the **Pooled-Variance T workbook** as a template.

The worksheet already contains the data and formulas to use the unsummarized data for the example. For other problems, use this worksheet with either unsummarized or summarized data.

For unsummarized data, paste the data in columns A and B in the **DataCopy** worksheet and keep the COMPUTE worksheet formulas that compute the sample size, sample mean, and sample standard deviation in the cell range B7:B13. For summarized data, replace the formulas in the cell range B7:B13 with the sample statistics and ignore the DataCopy worksheet.

Use the **COMPUTE_LOWER** or **COMPUTE_UPPER** worksheets in the same workbook as templates for performing one-tail pooled-variance *t* tests with either unsummarized or summarized data. For unsummarized data, paste the new data into the DataCopy worksheet. For summarized data, replace COMPUTE worksheet formulas with sample statistics.

Analysis ToolPak Use **t-Test: Two-Sample Assuming Equal Variances**.

For the example, open to the **DATA worksheet** of the **VLABGo workbook** and:

1. Select **Data → Data Analysis**.
2. In the Data Analysis dialog box, select **t-Test: Two-Sample Assuming Equal Variances** from the **Analysis Tools** list and then click **OK**.

In the procedure's dialog box (shown below):

3. Enter **A1:A11** as the **Variable 1 Range**.
4. Enter **B1:B11** as the **Variable 2 Range**.
5. Enter **0** as the **Hypothesized Mean Difference**.
6. Check **Labels** and enter **0.05** as **Alpha**.
7. Click **New Worksheet Ply**.
8. Click **OK**.

Results (shown below) appear in a new worksheet that contains both two-tail and one-tail test critical values and *p*-values. Unlike the results shown in Figure 10.3, only the positive (upper) critical value is listed for the two-tail test.

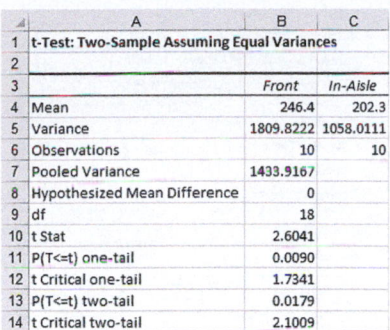

	A	B	C
1	t-Test: Two-Sample Assuming Equal Variances		
2			
3		Front	In-Aisle
4	Mean	246.4	202.3
5	Variance	1809.8222	1058.0111
6	Observations	10	10
7	Pooled Variance	1433.9167	
8	Hypothesized Mean Difference	0	
9	df	18	
10	t Stat	2.6041	
11	P(T<=t) one-tail	0.0090	
12	t Critical one-tail	1.7341	
13	P(T<=t) two-tail	0.0179	
14	t Critical two-tail	2.1009	

Confidence Interval Estimate for the Difference Between Two Means

PHStat The *PHStat* instructions for the pooled-variance *t* test includes a step to create a confidence interval estimate.

Workbook Use the *Workbook* instructions for the pooled-variance *t* test. The COMPUTE worksheet of the Pooled-Variance T workbook includes confidence interval estimate calculations in columns D and E.

Separate-Variance *t* Test for the Difference Between Two Means, Assuming Unequal Variances

Key Technique Use the **T.INV.2T**(*level of significance, degrees of freedom*) function to compute the lower and upper critical values.

Use the **T.DIST.2T**(*absolute value of the t test statistic, degrees of freedom*) to compute the *p*-value.

Example Perform the Figure 10.6 separate-variance *t* test for the two in-store sales locations data on page 358.

PHStat Use **Separate-Variance t Test**.

For the example, open to the **DATA worksheet** of the **VLABGo workbook**. Select **PHStat → Two-Sample Tests (Unsummarized Data) → Separate-Variance t Test**. In the procedure's dialog box (shown in the right column):

1. Enter **0** as the **Hypothesized Difference**.
2. Enter **0.05** as the **Level of Significance**.
3. Enter **A1:A11** as the **Population 1 Sample Cell Range**.
4. Enter **B1:B11** as the **Population 2 Sample Cell Range**.
5. Check **First cells in both ranges contain label**.
6. Click **Two-Tail Test**.
7. Enter a **Title** and click **OK**.

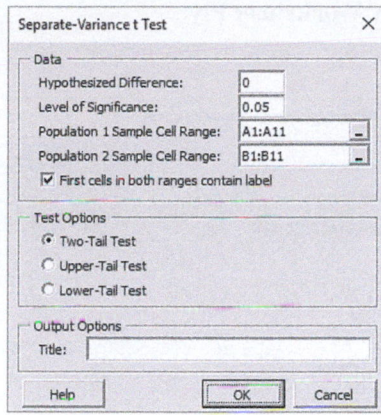

When using summarized data, select **PHStat → Two-Sample Tests (Summarized Data) → Separate-Variance t Test**. In that procedure's dialog box, enter the hypothesized difference and the level of significance, as well as the sample size, sample mean, and sample standard deviation for each group.

Workbook Use the **COMPUTE worksheet** of the **Separate-Variance T workbook** as a template.

The worksheet already contains the data and formulas to use the unsummarized data for the example. For other problems, use this worksheet with either unsummarized or summarized data.

For unsummarized data, paste the data in columns A and B in the **DataCopy worksheet** and keep the COMPUTE worksheet formulas that compute the sample size, sample mean, and sample standard deviation in the cell range B7:B13. For summarized data, replace those formulas in the cell range B7:B13 with the sample statistics and ignore the DataCopy worksheet.

Use the **COMPUTE_LOWER** or **COMPUTE_UPPER worksheets** in the same workbook as templates for performing one-tail pooled-variance *t* tests with either unsummarized or summarized data. For unsummarized data, paste the new data into the DataCopy worksheet. For summarized data, replace the COMPUTE worksheet formulas with sample statistics.

Analysis ToolPak Use **t-Test: Two-Sample Assuming Unequal Variances**.

For the example, open to the **DATA worksheet** of the **VLabGo workbook** and:

1. Select **Data → Data Analysis**.
2. In the Data Analysis dialog box, select **t-Test: Two-Sample Assuming Unequal Variances** from the **Analysis Tools** list and then click **OK**.

In the procedure's dialog box (shown on page 390):

3. Enter **A1:A11** as the **Variable 1 Range**.
4. Enter **B1:B11** as the **Variable 2 Range**.
5. Enter **0** as the **Hypothesized Mean Difference**.
6. Check **Labels** and enter **0.05** as **Alpha**.

7. Click **New Worksheet Ply**.

8. Click **OK**.

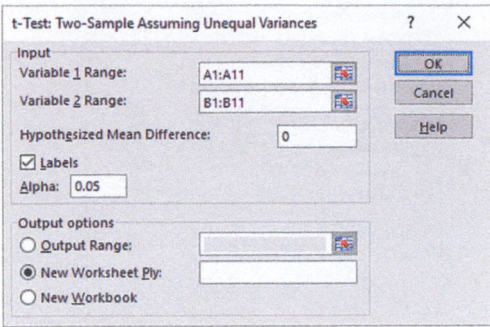

Results (shown below) appear in a new worksheet that contains both two-tail and one-tail test critical values and *p*-values. Unlike the results shown in Figure 10.6, only the positive (upper) critical value is listed for the two-tail test. Because the Analysis ToolPak uses table lookups to approximate the critical values and the *p*-value, the results will differ slightly from the values shown in Figure 10.6.

	A	B	C
1	t-Test: Two-Sample Assuming Unequal Variances		
2			
3		Special Front	In-Aisle
4	Mean	246.4	202.3
5	Variance	1809.8222	1058.0111
6	Observations	10	10
7	Hypothesized Mean Difference	0	
8	df	17	
9	t Stat	2.6041	
10	P(T<=t) one-tail	0.0093	
11	t Critical one-tail	1.7396	
12	P(T<=t) two-tail	0.0185	
13	t Critical two-tail	2.1098	

EG10.2 COMPARING the MEANS of TWO RELATED POPULATIONS

Paired *t* Test

Key Technique Use the **T.INV.2T**(*level of significance, degrees of freedom*) function to compute the lower and upper critical values.

Use the **T.DIST.2T**(*absolute value of the t test statistic, degrees of freedom*) to compute the *p*-value.

Example Perform the Figure 10.8 paired *t* test for the equivalent products price data on page 365.

PHStat Use **Paired t Test**.

For the example, open to the **DATA worksheet** of the **Market Basket workbook**. Select **PHStat ➔ Two-Sample Tests (Unsummarized Data) ➔ Paired t Test**. In the procedure's dialog box (shown in the right column):

1. Enter **0** as the **Hypothesized Mean Difference**.

2. Enter **0.05** as the **Level of Significance**.

3. Enter **B1:B8** as the **Population 1 Sample Cell Range**.

4. Enter **C1:C8** as the **Population 2 Sample Cell Range**.

5. Check **First cells in both ranges contain label**.

6. Click **Two-Tail Test**.

7. Enter a **Title** and click **OK**.

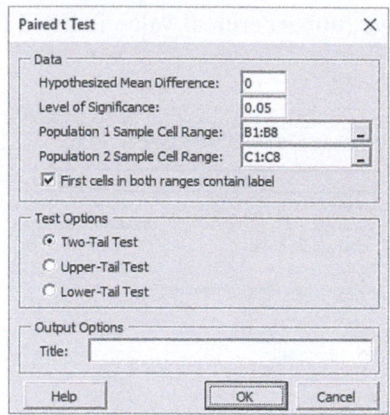

The procedure creates two worksheets, one of which is similar to the PtCalcs worksheet discussed in the following Workbook section. When using summarized data, select **PHStat ➔ Two-Sample Tests (Summarized Data) ➔ Paired t Test**. In that procedure's dialog box, enter the hypothesized mean difference, the level of significance, and the differences cell range.

Workbook Use the **COMPUTE** and **PtCalcs worksheets** of the **Paired T workbook** as a template.

The COMPUTE and supporting PtCalcs worksheets already contain the equivalent products price data for the example. The PtCalcs worksheet also computes the differences that allow the COMPUTE worksheet to compute the S_D in cell B11.

For other problems, paste the unsummarized data into columns A and B of the PtCalcs worksheet. For sample sizes greater than 7, select cell C8 and copy the formula in that cell down through the last data row. For sample sizes less than 7, delete the column C formulas for which there are no column A and B values.

If you know the sample size, $\overline{D}$, and S_D values, you can ignore the PtCalcs worksheet and enter the values in cells B8, B9, and B11 of the COMPUTE worksheet, overwriting the formulas that those cells contain.

Use the similar **COMPUTE_LOWER** and **COMPUTE_UPPER worksheets** in the same workbook as templates for performing one-tail tests. For unsummarized data, paste the new data into the DataCopy worksheet. For summarized data, replace COMPUTE worksheet formulas with sample statistics.

Analysis ToolPak Use **t-Test: Paired Two Sample for Means**.

For the example, open to the **DATA worksheet** of the **MarketBasket workbook** and:

1. Select **Data ➔ Data Analysis**.

2. In the Data Analysis dialog box, select **t-Test: Paired Two Sample for Means** from the **Analysis Tools** list and then click **OK**.

In the procedure's dialog box (shown below):

3. Enter **B1:B8** as the **Variable 1 Range**.
4. Enter **C1:C8** as the **Variable 2 Range**.
5. Enter **0** as the **Hypothesized Mean Difference**.
6. Check **Labels** and enter **0.05** as **Alpha**.
7. Click **New Worksheet Ply**.
8. Click **OK**.

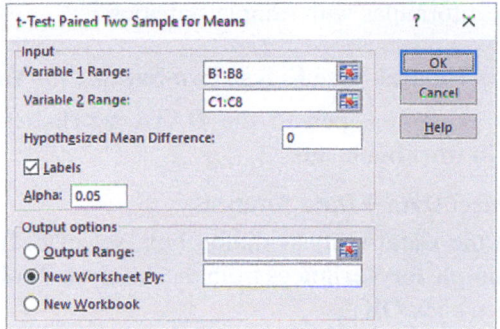

Results (shown below) appear in a new worksheet that contains both two-tail and one-tail test critical values and *p*-values. Unlike in Figure 10.8, only the positive (upper) critical value is listed for the two-tail test.

⊿	A	B	C
1	t-Test: Paired Two Sample for Means		
2			
3		Costco	Walmart
4	Mean	2.8514	2.9986
5	Variance	14.7542	17.0431
6	Observations	7	7
7	Pearson Correlation	0.9935	
8	Hypothesized Mean Difference	0	
9	df	6	
10	t Stat	-0.7235	
11	P(T<=t) one-tail	0.2483	
12	t Critical one-tail	1.9432	
13	P(T<=t) two-tail	0.4966	
14	t Critical two-tail	2.4469	

EG10.3 COMPARING the PROPORTIONS of TWO INDEPENDENT POPULATIONS

Z Test for the Difference Between Two Proportions

Key Technique Use the **NORM.S.INV** (*percentage*) function to compute the critical values.

Use the **NORM.S.DIST** (*absolute value of the Z test statistic, True*) function to compute the *p*-value.

Example Perform the Figure 10.11 Z test for the web signup page experiment.

PHStat Use **Z Test for Differences in Two Proportions**.

For the example, select **PHStat → Two-Sample Tests (Summarized Data) → Z Test for Differences in Two Proportions**. In the procedure's dialog box (shown in the right column):

1. Enter **0** as the **Hypothesized Difference**.
2. Enter **0.05** as the **Level of Significance**.

3. For the Population 1 Sample, enter **387** as the **Number of Items of Interest** and **4325** as the **Sample Size**.
4. For the Population 2 Sample, enter **283** as the **Number of Items of Interest** and **4639** as the **Sample Size**.
5. Click **Two-Tail Test.**
6. Enter a **Title** and click **OK**.

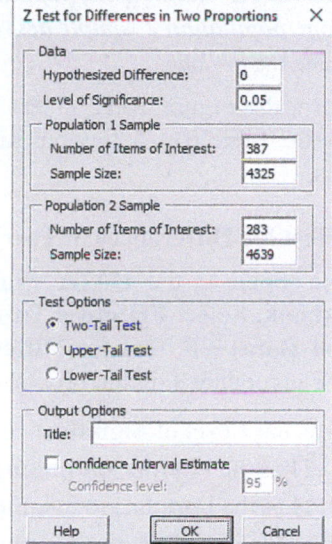

Workbook Use the **COMPUTE worksheet** of the **Z Two Proportions workbook** as a template.

The worksheet already contains data for the website signup survey. For other problems, change the hypothesized difference, the level of significance, and the number of items of interest and sample size for each group in the cell range B4:B11.

Use the similar **COMPUTE_LOWER** and **COMPUTE_UPPER worksheets** in the same workbook as templates for performing one-tail Z tests for the difference between two proportions. For unsummarized data, paste the new data into the DataCopy worksheet. For summarized data, replace COMPUTE worksheet formulas with sample statistics.

Confidence Interval Estimate for the Difference Between Two Proportions

PHStat Modify the *PHStat* instructions for the Z test for the difference between two proportions. In step 6, also check **Confidence Interval Estimate** and enter a **Confidence Level** in its box, in addition to entering a **Title** and clicking **OK**.

Workbook Use the "Z Test for the Difference Between Two Proportions" *Workbook* instructions in this section. The Z Two Proportions workbook worksheets include a confidence interval estimate for the difference between two means in the cell range D3:E16.

EG10.4 *F* TEST for the RATIO of TWO VARIANCES

Key Technique Use the **F.INV.RT**(*level of significance/2, population 1 sample degrees of freedom, population 2 sample degrees of freedom*) function to compute the upper critical value.

Use the **F.DIST.RT**(*F test statistic, population 1 sample degrees of freedom, population 2 sample degrees of freedom*) function to compute the *p*-values.

Example Perform the Figure 10.13 *F* test for the ratio of two variances for the Table 10.1 Arlingtons sales data for two in-store locations.

PHStat Use **F Test for Differences in Two Variances**.

For the example, open to the **DATA worksheet** of the **VLABGo workbook**. Select **PHStat → Two-Sample Tests (Unsummarized Data) → F Test for Differences in Two Variances**. In the procedure's dialog box (shown below):

1. Enter **0.05** as the **Level of Significance**.
2. Enter **A1:A11** as the **Population 1 Sample Cell Range**.
3. Enter **B1:B11** as the **Population 2 Sample Cell Range**.
4. Check **First cells in both ranges contain label**.
5. Click **Two-Tail Test**.
6. Enter a **Title** and click **OK**.

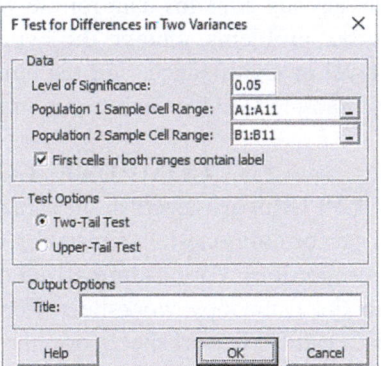

When using summarized data, select **PHStat → Two-Sample Tests (Summarized Data) → F Test for Differences in Two Variances**. In that procedure's dialog box, enter the level of significance and the sample size and sample variance for each sample.

Workbook Use the **COMPUTE worksheet** of the **F Two Variances workbook** as a template.

The worksheet already contains the data and formulas for using the unsummarized data for the example. For unsummarized data, paste the data in columns A and B in the **DataCopy worksheet** and keep the COMPUTE worksheet

formulas that compute the sample size and sample variance for the two samples in cell range B4:B10. For summarized data, replace the COMPUTE worksheet formulas in cell ranges B4:B10 with the sample statistics and ignore the Data-Copy worksheet.

Use the similar **COMPUTE_UPPER** worksheet in the same workbook as a template for performing the upper-tail test. For unsummarized data, paste the new data into the Data-Copy worksheet. For summarized data, replace COMPUTE worksheet formulas with sample statistics.

Analysis ToolPak Use **F-Test Two-Sample for Variances**.

For the example, open to the **DATA worksheet** of the **VALBGo workbook** and:

1. Select **Data → Data Analysis**.
2. In the Data Analysis dialog box, select **F-Test Two-Sample for Variances** from the **Analysis Tools** list and then click **OK**.

In the procedure's dialog box (shown below):

3. Enter **A1:A11** as the **Variable 1 Range** and enter **B1:B11** as the **Variable 2 Range**.
4. Check **Labels** and enter **0.05** as **Alpha**.
5. Click **New Worksheet Ply**.
6. Click **OK**.

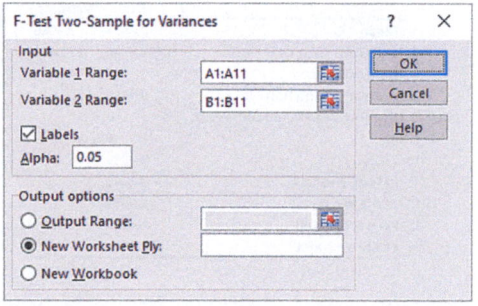

Results (shown below) appear in a new worksheet and include only the one-tail test *p*-value (0.2181), which must be doubled for the two-tail test shown in Figure 10.13 on page 378.

	A	B	C
1	F-Test Two-Sample for Variances		
2			
3		*Special Front*	*In-Aisle*
4	Mean	246.4	202.3
5	Variance	1809.8222	1058.0111
6	Observations	10	10
7	df	9.0000	9
8	F	1.7106	
9	P(F<=f) one-tail	0.2181	
10	F Critical one-tail	3.1789	

▾ **JMP** GUIDE

JG10.1   COMPARING the MEANS of TWO INDEPENDENT POPULATIONS

Pooled-Variance *t* Test for the Difference Between Two Means

Use the **Hypothesis Test for Two Means calculator** or **Fit Y by X**.

For example, to perform the Figure 10.3 pooled-variance *t* test for the Table 10.1 Arlingtons sales data for the two in-store sales locations, open to the **VLABGo data table**. Select **Help➔Sample Data** and:

1. In the Sample Data Index window, click the **Calculators disclosure button** (gray triangle).
2. Click **Hypothesis Test for Two Means** in the revealed list.
3. In the Choose Input dialog box, click **Raw Data** and then click **OK**.

In the Select Columns dialog box,

4. Click **Location** in the Select Columns list and then click **Pick a Column Containing the Names of the 2 Groups** to add Location to the first box.
5. Click **Sales** in the Select Columns list and then click **Pick a Column Containing the Sample Values** to add Sales to the second box.
6. Click **OK**.

In the left side of the Hypothesis Test on Means of Two Independent Samples dialog box (partially shown below):

7. Select **t-test**.
8. Select **Assume Equal Variances (Pooled)**.
9. Select **(Mean 2 – Mean 1) is unequal to hypothesized value (two-tailed)**.

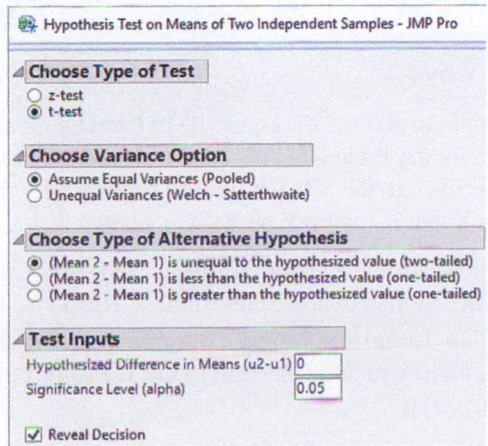

10. Enter **0** as the **Hypothesized Difference in Means (u2 –u1)**.
11. Enter **0.05** as the **Significance Level (alpha)**.
12. Check **Reveal Decision**.

JMP displays results in the right side of the calculator window as shown in Figure 10.3. Because of the nature of JMP calculators, to save results, save the window as a JMP journal (*.jrn) file. For summarized data, open to the data table that contains the data and follow steps 1 through 2, modify step 3 to click **Summary Statistics**, skip steps 4 through 6, and follow steps 7 through 12. Then, enter the sample size, mean, and standard deviation for both samples in the calculator window.

(**Fit Y and X** instructions appear in the next section.)

Confidence Interval Estimate for the Difference Between Two Means

Use **Fit Y by X**.

For example, to compute the confidence interval estimate for the Table 10.1 Arlingtons sales data for the two in-store sales locations, open to the **VLABGo data table**. Select **Analyze➔ Fit Y by X** and in the Fit Y by X – Contextual dialog box:

1. Click **Sales** in the columns list and then click **Y, Response** to add Sales to the Y, Response box.
2. Click **Location** in the columns list and then click **X, Factor** to add Location to the Y, Factor box.
3. Click **OK**.

JMP displays a plot of the sales for the two locations in a new window.

4. Click the **Oneway Analysis of Sales by Location red triangle** and select **Means/Anova/Pooled t** from its menu.
5. To create a boxplot, click the **Oneway Analysis of Sales by Location red triangle** a second time and select **Quantiles** from the menu.

JMP adds tabular summaries to the new window. The confidence interval estimate appears as part of the *t* test summary.

Separate-Variance *t* Test for the Difference Between Two Means, Assuming Unequal Variances

Modify either of the previous two sets of instructions. If using the **Hypothesis Test for Two Means calculator** instructions, in step 8, select **Unequal Variances (Welch – Satterthwaite)**. If using the **Fit Y by X** instructions, in step 4, select **t Test** from the red triangle menu.

JG10.2 COMPARING the MEANS of TWO RELATED POPULATIONS

Paired *t* Test

Use **Matched Pairs**.

For example, to perform the Figure 10.8 paired *t* test for the equivalent products price data, open to the **MarketBasket data table**. Select **Analyze → Specialized Modeling → Matched Pairs** and in the Matched Pairs dialog box:

1. Click **Walmart** in the columns list and then click **Y, Response** to add Walmart to the Y, Response box
2. Click **Costco** in the columns list and then click **Y, Response** to add Costco to the Y, Response box.
3. Click **OK**.

JMP displays a plot and a table of results in a new window. To declutter the results window, click the **Matched Pairs red triangle** and uncheck **Plot Dif by Mean**.

JG10.3 COMPARING the PROPORTIONS of TWO INDEPENDENT POPULATIONS

Z Test for the Difference Between Two Proportions

Use the **Hypothesis Test for Two Proportions calculator**.

For example, to perform the Figure 10.11 Z test for the web signup page experiment, select **Help → Sample Data** and:

1. In the Sample Data Index window, click the **Calculators disclosure button** (gray triangle).
2. Click **Hypothesis Test for Two Proportions** in the revealed list.
3. In the Choose Input dialog box, click **Summary Statistics** and then click **OK**.

In the left side of the Z-Test on Proportions of Two Independent Samples dialog box (shown below):

4. Select **(p2-p1) is not equal to hypothesized proportion (two-tailed)**.
5. Select **Used Pooled Estimate of Variances**.
6. Check **Reveal Decision**.

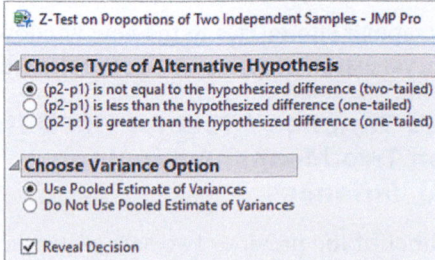

In the right side of the dialog box (partially shown below):

7. Enter **0** as the **Hypothesized Difference (p2-p1)**.
8. Enter **387** as the **Sample 1 Count (x1)**.
9. Enter **4325** as the **Sample 1 Size (n1)**.
10. Enter **283** as the **Sample 2 Count (x2)**.
11. Enter **4639** as the **Sample 2 Size (n2)**.
12. Enter **0.05** as the **Significance Level (alpha)**.

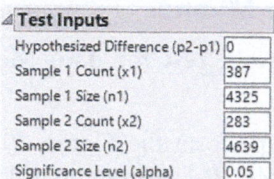

JMP displays results in the calculator window as shown in Figure 10.11. Because of the nature of JMP calculators, to save results, save window as a JMP journal (*.jrn) file. For unsummarized data, open to the data table that contains the data and follow steps 1 through 2 and in the Choose Input dialog box, click **Raw Data** and then click **OK**. In the next (Select Columns) dialog box, select a column and click **Pick a Numeric Column** and then press **OK**. In the Select Columns dialog box:

1. Click **Location** in the Select Columns list and then click **Pick a Column Containing the Names of the 2 Groups** to add Location to the first box.
2. Click **Sales** in the Select Columns list and then click **Pick a Column Containing the Result of Each Individual Trial** to add Sales to the second box.
3. Click **OK**.

In the left side of the Z-Test on Proportions of Two Independent Samples dialog box (not shown):

4. Enter **0** as the **Hypothesized Difference (p2-p1)**.
5. Enter **0.05** as the **Significance Level (alpha)**.
6. Check **Reveal Decision**.

JG10.4 F TEST for the RATIO of TWO VARIANCES

Use **Fit Y by X**.

For example, to perform the Figure 10.13 *F* test for the ratio of two variances for the Table 10.1 Arlingtons sales data for two in-store locations, open to the **VLABGo data table**. Select **Analyze → Fit Y by X** and in the Fit Y by X – Contextual dialog box:

1. Click **Sales** in the columns list and then click **Y, Response** to add Sales to the Y, Response box.
2. Click **Location** in the columns list and then click **X, Factor** to add Location to the Y, Factor box.
3. Click **OK**.

JMP displays a plot of the sales for the two locations in a new window.

4. Click the **Oneway Analysis of Sales by Location red triangle** and select **Means/Anova/Pooled t** from its menu.

5. To test for the ratio of two variances, click the **Oneway Analysis of Sales by Location red triangle** a second time and select **Unequal Variance** from the menu.

JMP adds tabular summaries to the new window. The *F* test results appear in the F Test 2-sided row of the second table in the window.

CHAPTER 10

▼MINITAB GUIDE

MG10.1 COMPARING the MEANS of TWO INDEPENDENT POPULATIONS

Pooled-Variance *t* Test for the Difference Between Two Means

Use **2-Sample t**.

For example, to perform the Figure 10.3 pooled-variance *t* test for the Table 10.1 Arlingtons sales data for the two in-store sales locations, open to the **VLABGo worksheet**. Select **Stat → Basic Statistics → 2-Sample t**. In the Two-Sample t for the Mean dialog box (shown below):

1. Select **Each sample is in its own column** from the unlabeled pull-down list and press **Tab**.
2. Double-click **C1 Special Front** in the variables list to add **'Special Front'** to the **Sample 1** box.
3. Double-click **C2 In-Aisle** in the variables list to add **'In-Aisle'** to the **Sample 2** box.
4. Click **Options**.

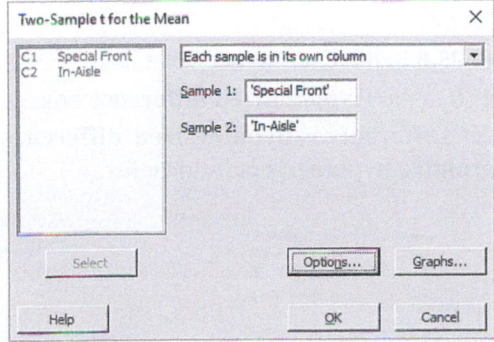

In the Two-Sample t: Options dialog box (shown in the right column):

5. Enter **95.0** in the **Confidence level** box.
6. Enter **0** in the **Hypothesized difference** box.
7. Select **Difference ≠ hypothesized difference** in the **Alternative hypothesis** pull-down list.

8. Check **Assume equal variances**.
9. Click **OK**.

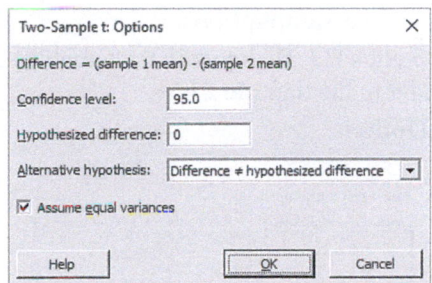

10. Back in the original dialog box, click **OK**.

For stacked data, use these replacement steps 1 through 3:

1. Select **Both samples are in one column** from the unlabeled pull-down list and press **Tab**.
2. Enter the name of the column that contains the measurement in the **Samples** box.
3. Enter the name of the column that contains the sample names in the **Sample IDs** box.

To create a boxplot for the analysis, replace step 10 with the following steps 10 through 12:

10. Back in the original dialog box, click **Graphs**.
11. In the Two-Sample t: Graphs dialog box (not shown), check **Boxplot** and then click **OK**.
12. Back in the original dialog box, click **OK**.

For a one-tail test, select **Difference > hypothesized difference** or **Difference < hypothesized difference** in step 7.

Confidence Interval Estimate for the Difference Between Two Means

Use the instructions for the pooled-variance *t* test, which computes a confidence interval estimate as part of the analysis.

Separate-Variance *t* Test for the Difference Between Two Means, Assuming Unequal Variances

Use the pooled-variance *t* test instructions but in step 8 *clear* **Assume equal variances**.

MG10.2   COMPARING the MEANS of TWO RELATED POPULATIONS

Paired *t* Test

Use **Paired t**.

For example, to perform the Figure 10.8 paired *t* test for the equivalent items price data, open to the **MarketBasket worksheet**. Select **Stat → Basic Statistics → Paired t**. In the Paired t from the Mean dialog box (shown below):

1. Select **Each sample is in a column** from the unlabeled pull-down list and press **Tab**.
2. Double-click **C2 Costco** in the variables list to enter **Costco** in the **Sample 1** box.
3. Double-click **C3 Walmart** in the variables list to enter **Walmart** in the **Sample 2** box.
4. Click **Options**.

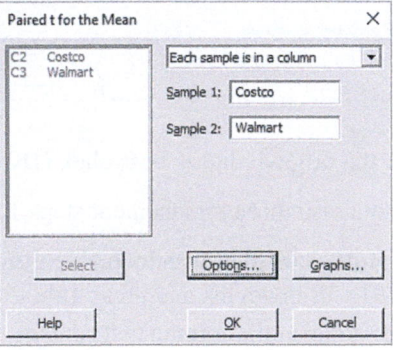

In the Paired t: Options dialog box (not shown):

5. Enter **95.0** in the **Confidence level** box.
6. Enter **0** in the **Hypothesized difference** box.
7. Select **Difference ≠ hypothesized difference** in the **Alternative hypothesis** pull-down list.
8. Click **OK**.
9. Back in the original dialog box, click **OK**.

To create a boxplot, replace step 9 with the following steps 9 through 11:

9. Back in the original dialog box, click **Graphs**.
10. In the Paired t-Graphs dialog box (not shown), check **Boxplots of data** and then click **OK**.
11. Back in the original dialog box, click **OK**.

For a one-tail test, select **Difference > hypothesized difference** or **Difference < hypothesized difference** in step 7.

Confidence Interval Estimate for the Mean Difference

Use the instructions for the paired *t* test, which computes a confidence interval estimate as part of the analysis.

MG10.3   COMPARING the PROPORTIONS of TWO INDEPENDENT POPULATIONS

Z Test for the Difference Between Two Proportions

Use **2 Proportions**.

For example, to perform the Figure 10.11 *Z* test for the web signup page experiment, select **Stat → Basic Statistics → 2 Proportions**. In the Two-Sample Proportions dialog box (shown below):

1. Select **Summarized data** from the unlabeled pull-down list and press **Tab**.
2. In the **Sample 1** column, enter **387** in the **Number of Events** box and **4325** in the **Number of Trials** box.
3. In the **Sample 2** column, enter **283** in the **Number of Events** box and **4639** in the **Number of Trials** box.
4. Click **Options**.

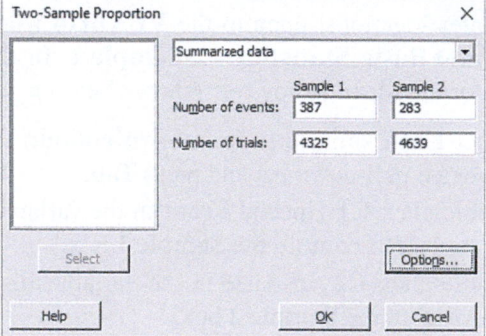

In the Two-Sample Proportions: Options dialog box (shown below):

5. Enter **95.0** in the **Confidence level** box.
6. Enter **0** in the **Hypothesized difference** box.
7. Select **Difference ≠ hypothesized difference** in the **Alternative hypothesis** pull-down list.

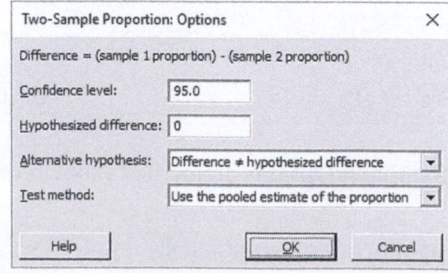

8. Select **Use the pooled estimate of the proportion** in the **Test Method** pull-down list.
9. Click **OK**.
10. Back in the Two-Sample Proportion dialog box, click **OK**.

Confidence Interval Estimate for the Difference Between Two Proportions

Use the instructions for the Z test for the difference between two proportions, which computes a confidence interval estimate as part of the analysis.

MG10.4   *F* TEST for the RATIO of TWO VARIANCES

Use **2 Variances**.

For example, to perform the Figure 10.13 F test for the ratio of two variances for the Table 10.1 Arlingtons sales data for two in-store locations, open to the **VLABGo worksheet**. Select **Stat → Basic Statistics → 2 Variances**. In the Two-Sample Variance dialog box (shown below):

1. Select **Each sample is in its own column** from the unlabeled pull-down list and press **Tab**.
2. Double-click **C1 Special Front** in the variables list to add **'Special Front'** to the **Sample 1** box.
3. Double-click **C2 In-Aisle** in the variables list to add **'In-Aisle'** to the **Sample 2** box.
4. Click **Options**.

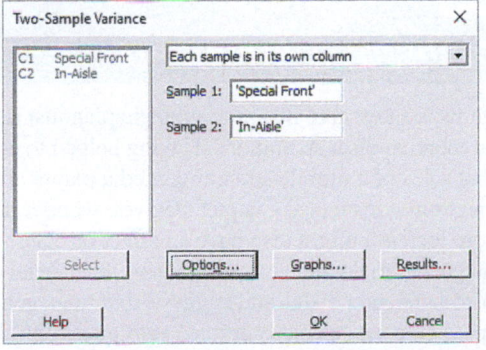

5. In the Options dialog box (not shown), check **Use test and confidence intervals based on normal distribution** and then click **OK**.
6. Back in the Two-Sample Variances dialog box, click **Graphs**.

In the Two-Sample Variance: Graphs dialog box (not shown):

7. Clear all check boxes.
8. Click **OK**.
9. Back in the Two-Sample Variances dialog box, click **OK**.

For summarized data, select **Sample standard deviations** or **Sample variances** in step 1 and enter the sample size and the sample statistics for the two variables in lieu of steps 2 and 3.

For stacked data, use these replacement steps 1 through 3:

1. Select **Both samples are in one column** from the unlabeled pull-down list and press **Tab**.
2. Enter the name of the column that contains the measurement in the **Samples** box.
3. Enter the name of the column that contains the sample names in the **Sample IDs** box.

11

Analysis of Variance

CONTENTS

OBJECTIVES

- Introduce the basic concepts of experimental design
- Learn to use the one-way analysis of variance to test for differences among the means of several groups
- Learn to use the two-way analysis of variance and interpret the interaction effect
- Learn to perform multiple comparisons in a one-way analysis of variance and a two-way analysis of variance

▼ USING **STATISTICS**
The Means to Find Differences at Arlingtons

Boosting sales of mobile electronics items is a key goal in a new strategic plan just issued by the senior management at the general merchandiser Arlingtons. Having helped to conduct an experiment that provided evidence that sales of a mobile streaming media player are higher in a special front location than in the mobile electronics aisle (see Chapter 10), you wonder if moving all mobile electronics items to another in-store location might also have an effect on sales.

The strategic plan also encourages managers to make better use of kiosks, the special end-of-aisle endcap areas that face customers as customers enter aisles and suggests that managers create *expert counters*, positions that customers can visit to ask specially-trained staff questions about items for sale in a particular department, such as mobile electronics, or to see live demonstrations of particular items. Might these two in-store locations be combined with the two locations of the previous experiment (the special front location and the regular in-aisle location) into one larger experiment?

You suggest an experiment in which mobile electronics in selected Arlingtons stores will be sold at one of four in-store locations: the current in-aisle location, the special front of the store location, in a special endcap kiosk, or at the expert counter position for mobile electronics. You propose to select 20 Arlingtons stores that have similar annual sales and divide the stores into four groups of five stores each. To each group, you assign a different in-store sales location for mobile electronics: current in-aisle, special front, kiosk, or expert counter.

How would you determine if varying the locations had an effect on mobile electronics sales? As you consider this, another manager suggests that customers who use mobile payment methods might be more likely to buy mobile electronics items. If you also wanted to later explore the effects of permitting customers to use mobile payment methods to purchase mobile electronics items, could you design an experiment that examined this second factor while it was examining the effects of in-store location?

Comparing possible differences has been the subject of the statistical methods discussed in the previous two chapters. In the one-sample tests of Chapter 9, the comparison is to a standard, such as a certain mean weight for a cereal box being filled by a production line. In Chapter 10, the comparison is between samples taken from two populations. **Analysis of variance**, known by the acronym **ANOVA**, allows statistical comparison among samples taken from many populations.

In ANOVA, the comparison is typically the result of an experiment. For example, the management of a general merchandiser might be brainstorming ways of improving sales of mobile electronics items. At Arlingtons, the management decided to try selling those items in four different in-store locations and then observe what the sales would be in each of those locations. The basis for an ANOVA experiment is called the **factor**, which in the Arlingtons scenario is in-store location. The statistical use of the word "factor" complements the everyday usage, illustrated by a question such as "How much of a *factor* is in-store location in determining mobile electronics sales?"

The actual different locations (in-aisle, special front, kiosk, and expert counter) are the **levels** of the factor. Levels of a factor are analogous to the categories of a categorical variable, but you call in-store location a *factor* and not a categorical variable because the variable under study is mobile electronics sales. Levels provide the basis of comparison by dividing the variable under study into **groups**. In the Arlingtons scenario, the groups are the stores selling the mobile electronics items in the mobile electronics aisle, the stores selling those items at the special front location, the stores selling those items at the kiosk location, and the stores selling those items at the expert counter.

When performing ANOVA analysis, among the types of experiments that can be conducted are:

- Completely randomized design: An experiment with only one factor.
- Factorial design: An experiment in which more than one factor is considered. This chapter discusses two-way ANOVA that involves two factors as an example of this type of design. (Arlingtons considering the effects of allowing mobile payments while also experimenting with in-store location would be an example of a factorial design.)
- Randomized block design: An experiment in which the members of each group have been placed in blocks either by being matched or subjected to repeated measurements as was done with the two populations of a paired *t* test (see online Section 11.3).

student TIP

ANOVA is also related to regression, a topic discussed later in this book. Because of ANOVA's special relationship with both hypothesis testing and regression, understanding the foundational concepts of ANOVA will prove very helpful in understanding the analyses that Chapters 13 through 17 present.

Determining the type of design and the factor or factors the design uses becomes an additional step in the Define task of the DCOVA framework when performing ANOVA analysis.

While ANOVA literally does analyze variation, the purpose of ANOVA is to reach conclusions about possible differences among the *means* of each group, analogous to the hypothesis tests of the previous chapter. Every ANOVA design uses samples that represent each group and subdivides the total variation observed across all samples (all groups) toward the goal of analyzing possible differences among the means of each group. How this subdivision, called *partitioning*, works is a function of the design being used, but total variation, represented by the quantity **sum of squares total** (*SST*), will always be the starting point. As with other statistical methods, ANOVA requires making assumptions about the populations that the groups represent. While these assumptions are discussed on page 407 as part of Section 11.1, the assumptions apply for all of the ANOVA methods discussed in this chapter.

11.1 The Completely Randomized Design: One-Way ANOVA

The **completely randomized design** is the ANOVA method that analyzes a single factor. You execute this design using the statistical method **one-way ANOVA**. One-way ANOVA is a two-part process. You first determine if there is a significant difference among the group means. If you reject the null hypothesis that there is no difference among the means, you continue with a second method that seeks to identify the groups whose means are significantly different from the other group means.

Analyzing Variation in One-Way ANOVA

In one-way ANOVA, to analyze variation towards the goal of determining possible differences among the group means, you partition the total variation into variation that is due to differences among the groups and variation that is due to differences within the groups (see Figure 11.1). The **within-group variation (SSW)** measures random variation. The **among-group variation (SSA)** measures differences from group to group. The symbol n represents the number of values in all groups and the symbol c represents the number of groups.

FIGURE 11.1
Partitioning the total variation in a completely randomized design

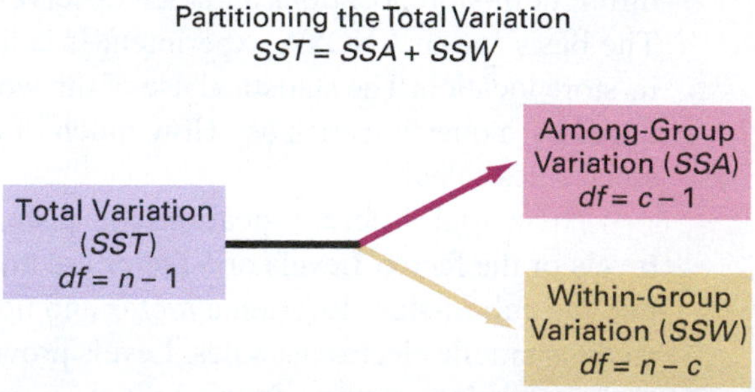

Partitioning the Total Variation
$SST = SSA + SSW$

Total Variation (SST)
$df = n - 1$

Among-Group Variation (SSA)
$df = c - 1$

Within-Group Variation (SSW)
$df = n - c$

When using Excel, always organize multiple-sample data as unstacked data, one column per group. (See Section 1.4 for more information about unstacked data.)

Assuming that the c groups represent populations whose values are randomly and independently selected, follow a normal distribution, and have equal variances, the null hypothesis of no differences in the population means:

$$H_0: \mu_1 = \mu_2 = \cdots = \mu_c$$

is tested against the alternative that not all the c population means are equal:

$$H_1: \text{Not all } \mu_j \text{ are equal (where } j = 1, 2, \ldots, c).$$

student TIP

Another way of stating the alternative hypothesis, H_1, is that at least one population mean is different from the others.

To perform an ANOVA test of equality of population means, you subdivide the total variation in the values into two parts—that which is due to variation among the groups and that which is due to variation within the groups. The **total variation** is represented by the **sum of squares total (SST)**. Because the population means of the c groups are assumed to be equal under the null hypothesis, you compute the total variation among all the values by summing the squared differences between each individual value and the **grand mean**, $\bar{\bar{X}}$. The grand mean is the mean of all the values in all the groups combined. Equation (11.1) shows the computation of the total variation.

TOTAL VARIATION IN ONE-WAY ANOVA

$$SST = \sum_{j=1}^{c} \sum_{i=1}^{n_j} (X_{ij} - \bar{\bar{X}})^2 \qquad (11.1)$$

where

$$\bar{\bar{X}} = \frac{\sum_{j=1}^{c} \sum_{i=1}^{n_j} X_{ij}}{n} = \text{grand mean}$$

$X_{ij} = i$th value in group j

$n_j = $ number of values in group j

$n = $ total number of values in all groups combined

(that is, $n = n_1 + n_2 + \ldots + n_c$)

$c = $ number of groups

studentTIP

Remember that a sum of squares (SS) cannot be negative.

You compute the among-group variation, usually called the **sum of squares among groups (SSA)**, by summing the squared differences between the sample mean of each group, $\overline{X}_j$, and the grand mean, $\overline{\overline{X}}$, weighted by the sample size, n_j, in each group. Equation (11.2) shows the computation of the among-group variation.

AMONG-GROUP VARIATION IN ONE-WAY ANOVA

$$SSA = \sum_{j=1}^{c} n_j \left(\overline{X}_j - \overline{\overline{X}} \right)^2 \tag{11.2}$$

where

c = number of groups

n_j = number of values in group j

$\overline{X}_j$ = sample mean of group j

$\overline{\overline{X}}$ = grand mean

The within-group variation, usually called the **sum of squares within groups (SSW)**, measures the difference between each value and the mean of its own group and sums the squares of these differences over all groups. Equation (11.3) shows the computation of the within-group variation.

WITHIN-GROUP VARIATION IN ONE-WAY ANOVA

$$SSW = \sum_{j=1}^{c} \sum_{i=1}^{n_j} \left(X_{ij} - \overline{X}_j \right)^2 \tag{11.3}$$

where

X_{ij} = ith value in group j

$\overline{X}_j$ = sample mean of group j

Because you are comparing c groups, there are $c - 1$ degrees of freedom associated with the sum of squares among groups. Because each of the c groups contributes $n_j - 1$ degrees of freedom, there are $n - c$ degrees of freedom associated with the sum of squares within groups. In addition, there are $n - 1$ degrees of freedom associated with the sum of squares total because you are comparing each value, X_{ij}, to the grand mean, $\overline{\overline{X}}$, based on all n values.

If you divide each of these sums of squares by its respective degrees of freedom, you have three variances, which in ANOVA are known as **mean squares**: *MSA* (mean square among), and *MSW* (mean square within).

studentTIP

Remember, *mean square* is just another term for *variance* that is used in the analysis of variance. Also, because the mean square is equal to the sum of squares divided by the degrees of freedom, a mean square can never be negative.

MEAN SQUARES IN ONE-WAY ANOVA

$$MSA = \frac{SSA}{c - 1} \tag{11.4a}$$

$$MSW = \frac{SSW}{n - c} \tag{11.4b}$$

[1] As Section 10.4 discusses, the F distribution is right-skewed with a minimum value of 0.

F Test for Differences Among More Than Two Means

To determine if there is a significant difference among the group means, you use the F test for differences among more than two means.[1] If the null hypothesis is true and there are no differences among the c group means, MSA, MSW, and MST, will provide estimates of the overall variance in the population. Thus, to test the null hypothesis:

$$H_0: \mu_1 = \mu_2 = \cdots = \mu_c$$

against the alternative:

$$H_1: \text{Not all } \mu_j \text{ are equal (where } j = 1, 2, \ldots, c)$$

you compute the one-way ANOVA F_{STAT} test statistic as the ratio of MSA to MSW, as in Equation (11.5).

student TIP

The test statistic compares mean squares (the variances) because one-way ANOVA reaches conclusions about possible differences among the *means* of c groups by examining variances.

ONE-WAY ANOVA F_{STAT} TEST STATISTIC

$$F_{STAT} = \frac{MSA}{MSW} \tag{11.5}$$

The F_{STAT} test statistic follows an **F distribution**, with $c - 1$ degrees of freedom in the numerator and $n - c$ degrees of freedom in the denominator.

For a given level of significance, α, you reject the null hypothesis if the F_{STAT} test statistic computed in Equation (11.5) is greater than the upper-tail critical value, F_α, from the F distribution with $c - 1$ degrees of freedom in the numerator and $n - c$ in the denominator (see Table E.5). Thus, as shown in Figure 11.2, the decision rule is

$$\text{Reject } H_0 \text{ if } F_{STAT} > F_\alpha;$$

otherwise, do not reject H_0.

FIGURE 11.2

Regions of rejection and nonrejection when using ANOVA

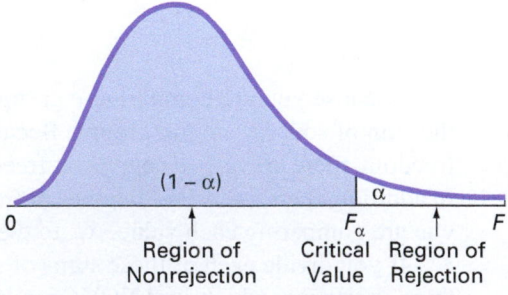

If the null hypothesis is true, the computed F_{STAT} test statistic is expected to be approximately equal to 1 because both the numerator and denominator mean square terms are estimating the overall variance in the population. If H_0 is false (and there are differences in the group means), the computed F_{STAT} test statistic is expected to be larger than 1 because the numerator, MSA, is estimating the differences among groups in addition to the overall variability in the values, while the denominator, MSW, is measuring only the overall variability in the values. Therefore, you reject the null hypothesis at a selected level of significance, α, only if the computed F_{STAT} test statistic is *greater than* F_α, the upper-tail critical value of the F distribution having $c - 1$ and $n - c$ degrees of freedom.

Table 11.1 presents the **ANOVA summary table** that is typically used to summarize the results of a one-way ANOVA. The table includes entries for the sources of variation (among groups, within groups, and total), the degrees of freedom, the sums of squares, the mean squares (the variances), and the computed F_{STAT} test statistic. The table may also include the p-value, the probability of having an F_{STAT} value as large as or larger than the one computed, given that the null hypothesis is true. The p-value allows you to reach conclusions about the null hypothesis without needing to refer to a table of critical values of the F distribution. If the p-value is less than the chosen level of significance, α, you reject the null hypothesis.

TABLE 11.1

ANOVA Summary Table

Source	Degrees of Freedom	Sum of Squares	Mean Square (Variance)	F
Among groups	$c - 1$	SSA	$MSA = \dfrac{SSA}{c - 1}$	$F_{STAT} = \dfrac{MSA}{MSW}$
Within groups	$n - c$	SSW	$MSW = \dfrac{SSW}{n - c}$	
Total	$n - 1$	SST		

To illustrate the one-way ANOVA F test, return to the Arlington's scenario (see page 398). You define the business problem as whether significant differences exist in the mobile electronics sales for the four different in-store locations, the four groups for the ANOVA analysis.

To test the comparative effectiveness of the four in-store locations, you conduct a 60-day experiment at 20 same-sized stores that have similar storewide net sales. You randomly assign five stores to use the current mobile electronics aisle (in-aisle), five stores to use the special front location (front), five stores to use the kiosk location (kiosk), and five stores to use the expert counter (expert). At the end of the experiment, you organize the mobile electronics sales data by group and store the data in unstacked format in Mobile Electronics . Figure 11.3 presents that unstacked data, along with the sample mean and the sample standard deviation for each group.

FIGURE 11.3

Mobile electronic sales ($000), sample means, and sample standard deviations for four different in-store locations

In-aisle	Front	Kiosk	Expert
30.06	32.22	30.78	30.33
29.96	31.47	30.91	30.29
30.19	32.13	30.79	30.25
29.96	31.86	30.95	30.25
27.74	32.29	31.13	30.55
Sample Mean 29.582	31.994	30.912	30.334
Sample Standard Deviation 1.034	0.335	0.143	0.125

Figure 11.3 shows differences among the sample means for the mobile electronics sales for the four in-store locations. For the original in-aisle location, mean sales were $29.582 thousands, whereas mean sales at the three new locations varied from $30.334 thousands ("expert" location) to $30.912 thousands ("kiosk" location) to $31.994 thousands ("front" location).

Differences in the mobile electronic sales for the four in-store locations can also be presented visually. The Figure 11.4 scatter plots present the mobile electronics sales at each store in each group that visualize differences *within* each location as well as among the four locations. The Figure 11.4 main effects plot (Minitab) displays the mean of each group.

FIGURE 11.4

Excel and JMP scatter plots and a Minitab main effects plot of mobile electronics sales for four in-store locations

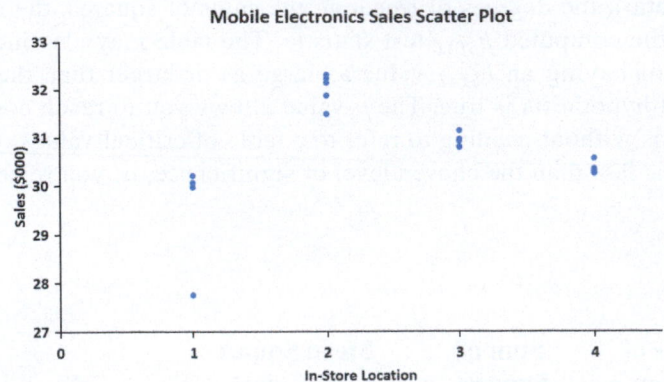

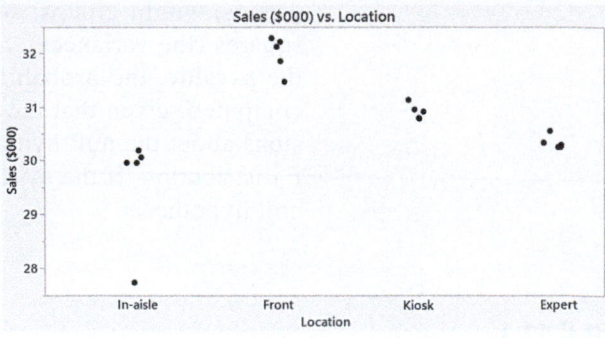

For the Excel chart, the locations have been relabeled 1, 2, 3, and 4 in order to use the scatter plot chart type. Also, the Y axis minimum value has been set to 27 to match the JMP chart.

The JMP chart includes jitter to minimize overlap of same or similar values.

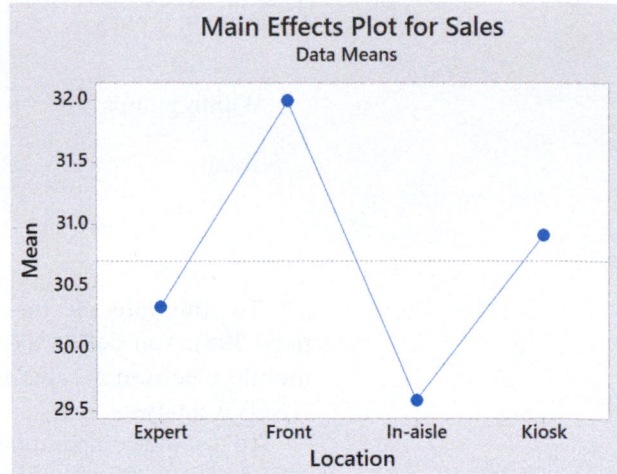

Having observed that the four sample means appear to be different, you use the F test for differences among more than two means to determine if these sample means are sufficiently different to conclude that the *population* means are not all equal. The null hypothesis states that there is no difference in the mean sales among the four in-store locations:

$$H_0: \mu_1 = \mu_2 = \mu_3 = \mu_4$$

The alternative hypothesis states that at least one of the in-store location mean sales differs from the other means:

$$H_1: \text{Not all the means are equal.}$$

To construct the ANOVA summary table, you first compute the sample means in each group (see Figure 11.3 on page 403). Then you compute the grand mean by summing all 20 values and dividing by the total number of values:

$$\overline{\overline{X}} = \frac{\sum_{j=1}^{c}\sum_{j=1}^{n_j} X_{ij}}{n} = \frac{614.12}{20} = 30.706$$

Then, using Equations (11.1) through (11.3) on pages 400–401, you compute the sum of squares:

$$SSA = \sum_{j=1}^{c} n_j (\overline{X}_j - \overline{\overline{X}})^2 = (5)(29.582 - 30.706)^2 + (5)(31.994 - 30.706)^2$$
$$+ (5)(30.912 - 30.706)^2 + (5)(30.334 - 30.706)^2$$
$$= 15.5157$$

$$SSW = \sum_{j=1}^{c} \sum_{i=1}^{n_j} (X_{ij} - \bar{X}_j)^2$$

$$= (30.06 - 29.582)^2 + (29.96 - 29.582)^2 + (30.19 - 29.582)^2$$

$$+ (29.96 - 29.582)^2 + (27.74 - 29.582)^2 + \cdots + (30.55 - 30.334)^2$$

$$= 4.8706$$

$$SST = \sum_{j=1}^{c} \sum_{i=1}^{n_j} (X_{ij} - \bar{\bar{X}})^2$$

$$= (30.06 - 30.706)^2 + (29.96 - 30.706)^2 + \cdots + (30.55 - 30.706)^2$$

$$= 20.3863$$

You compute the mean squares by dividing the sum of squares by the corresponding degrees of freedom [see Equation (11.4) on page 401]. Because $c = 4$ and $n = 20$,

$$MSA = \frac{SSA}{c-1} = \frac{15.5157}{4-1} = 5.1719$$

$$MSW = \frac{SSW}{n-c} = \frac{4.8706}{20-4} = 0.3044$$

so that using Equation (11.5) on page 402,

$$F_{STAT} = \frac{MSA}{MSW} = \frac{5.1719}{0.3044} = 16.9898$$

Because you are trying to determine whether MSA is greater than MSW, you only reject H_0 if F_{STAT} is greater than the upper critical value of F. For a selected level of significance, α, you find the upper-tail critical value, F_α, from the F distribution using Table E.5. A portion of Table E.5 is presented in Table 11.2. In the in-store location sales experiment, there are 3 degrees of freedom in the numerator and 16 degrees of freedom in the denominator. F_α, the upper-tail critical value at the 0.05 level of significance, is 3.24.

TABLE 11.2

Finding the Critical Value of F with 3 and 16 Degrees of Freedom at the 0.05 Level of Significance

		Cumulative Probabilities $= 0.95$							
		Upper-Tail Area $= 0.05$							
				Numerator df_1					
Denominator df_2	**1**	**2**	**3**	**4**	**5**	**6**	**7**	**8**	**9**
⋮	⋮	⋮	⋮	⋮	⋮	⋮	⋮	⋮	⋮
11	4.84	3.98	3.59	3.36	3.20	3.09	3.01	2.95	2.90
12	4.75	3.89	3.49	3.26	3.11	3.00	2.91	2.85	2.80
13	4.67	3.81	3.41	3.18	3.03	2.92	2.83	2.77	2.71
14	4.60	3.74	3.34	3.11	2.96	2.85	2.76	2.70	2.65
15	4.54	3.68	3.29	3.06	2.90	2.79	2.71	2.64	2.59
16	4.49	3.63	3.24	3.01	2.85	2.74	2.66	2.59	2.54

Source: Extracted from Table E.5.

Because $F_{STAT} = 16.9898$ is greater than $F_\alpha = 3.24$, you reject the null hypothesis (see Figure 11.5). You conclude that there is a significant difference in the mean sales for the four in-store locations.

FIGURE 11.5

Regions of rejection and nonrejection for the one-way ANOVA at the 0.05 level of significance, with 3 and 16 degrees of freedom

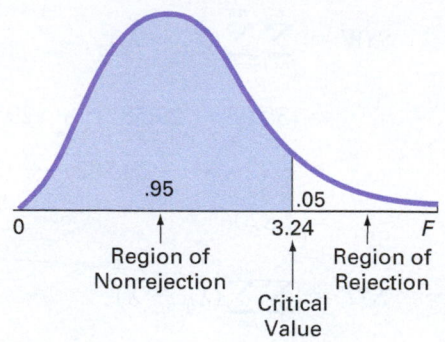

Figure 11.6 shows the ANOVA results for the in-store location sales experiment, including the p-value. In Figure 11.6, what Table 11.1 (see page 403) labels Among Groups is labeled Between Groups in the Excel worksheet.

FIGURE 11.6

Excel, JMP, and Minitab ANOVA results for the in-store location sales experiment

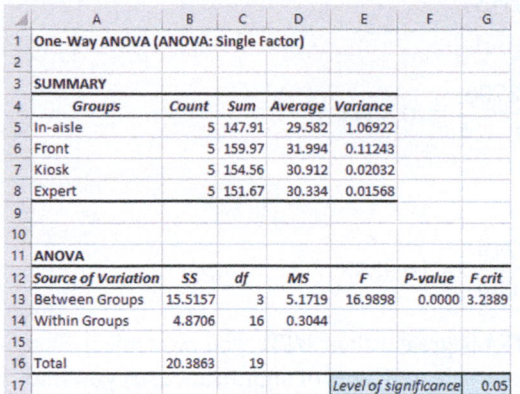

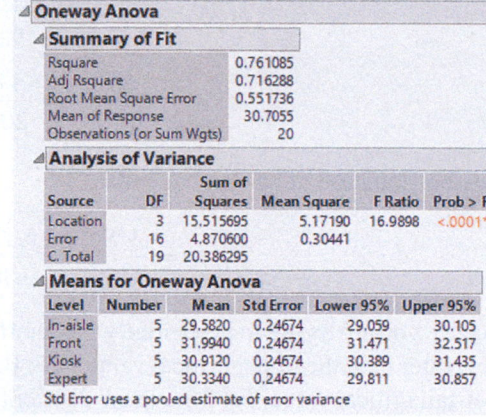

One-way ANOVA: In-aisle, Front, Kiosk, Expert

Method

Null hypothesis	All means are equal
Alternative hypothesis	Not all means are equal
Significance level	α = 0.05

Equal variances were assumed for the analysis.

Factor Information

Factor	Levels	Values
Factor	4	In-aisle, Front, Kiosk, Expert

Analysis of Variance

Source	DF	Adj SS	Adj MS	F-Value	P-Value
Factor	3	15.516	5.1719	16.99	0.000
Error	16	4.871	0.3044		
Total	19	20.386			

Model Summary

S	R-sq	R-sq(adj)	R-sq(pred)
0.551736	76.11%	71.63%	62.67%

Means

Factor	N	Mean	StDev	95% Upper Bound
In-aisle	5	29.582	1.034	30.013
Front	5	31.994	0.335	32.425
Kiosk	5	30.9120	0.1425	31.3428
Expert	5	30.3340	0.1252	30.7648

Pooled StDev = 0.551736

Table 11.3 summarizes the results of the one-way ANOVA for the mobile electronics data using the calculations on page 405 and Figure 11.6 results. Based on the conclusions, there is a difference in sales among the in-store locations. However, you still do not know *which* in-store locations differ. All you know is that there is sufficient evidence to state that the population means are not all the same. In other words, one or more population means are significantly different. To determine which in-store locations differ, you can use a multiple comparisons procedure such as the Tukey-Kramer procedure discussed on page 409.

TABLE 11.3

One-Way ANOVA Summary for the Mobile Electronics Data

Result	Conclusions
The $F_{STAT} = 16.9898$ is greater than 3.24.	1. Reject the null hypothesis H_0.
The F test p-value = 0.0000 is less than the level of significance, $\alpha = 0.05$.	2. Conclude that evidence exists that the mean sales are different at the in-store locations.
	3. There is a probability of 0.0000 that $F_{STAT} > 3.24$.

One-Way ANOVA *F* Test Assumptions

To use the one-way ANOVA *F* test, you must make three assumptions about your data:

- **Randomness and independence** of the samples selected
- **Normality** of the *c* groups from which the samples are selected
- **Homogeneity of variance** (the variances of the *c* groups are equal)

Most critical of all is the first assumption. The validity of any experiment depends on random sampling and/or the randomization process. To avoid biases in the outcomes, you need to select random samples from the *c* groups or use the randomization process to randomly assign the items to the *c* levels of the factor. Selecting a random sample or randomly assigning the levels ensures that a value from one group is independent of any other value in the experiment. Departures from this assumption can seriously affect inferences from the ANOVA. These problems are discussed more thoroughly in references 5 and 8.

As for the second assumption, **normality**, the one-way ANOVA *F* test is fairly robust against departures from the normal distribution. As long as the distributions are not extremely different from a normal distribution, the level of significance of the ANOVA *F* test is usually not greatly affected, particularly for large samples. You can assess the normality of each of the *c* samples by constructing a normal probability plot or a boxplot.

As for the third assumption, **homogeneity of variance**, if you have equal sample sizes in each group, inferences based on the *F* distribution are not seriously affected by unequal variances. However, if you have unequal sample sizes, unequal variances can have a serious effect on inferences from the ANOVA procedure. Thus, when possible, you should have equal sample sizes in all groups. You can use the Levene test for homogeneity of variance discussed below, to test whether the variances of the *c* groups are equal.

When only the normality assumption is violated, you can use the Kruskal-Wallis rank test, a nonparametric procedure (see Section 12.5). When only the homogeneity-of-variance assumption is violated, you can use procedures similar to those used in the separate-variance test of Section 10.1 (see references 1 and 2). When both the normality and homogeneity-of variance assumptions have been violated, you need to use an appropriate data transformation that both normalizes the data and reduces the differences in variances (see reference 6) or use a more general nonparametric procedure (see references 2 and 3).

Levene Test for Homogeneity of Variance

Although the one-way ANOVA *F* test is relatively robust with respect to the assumption of equal group variances, large differences in the group variances can seriously affect the level of significance and the power of the *F* test. One powerful yet simple procedure for testing the equality of the variances is the modified **Levene test** (see references 1 and 7). To test for the homogeneity of variance, you use the following null hypothesis:

$$H_0: \sigma_1^2 = \sigma_2^2 = \cdots = \sigma_c^2$$

against the alternative hypothesis:

$$H_1: \text{Not all } \sigma_j^2 \text{ are equal } (j = 1, 2, 3, \ldots, c)$$

To test the null hypothesis of equal variances, you first compute the absolute value of the difference between each value and the median of the group. Then you perform a one-way ANOVA on these *absolute differences*, typically using a level of significance of $\alpha = 0.05$.

To illustrate the modified Levene test, return to the Figure 11.6 data and summary statistics on page 406 for the in-store location sales experiment. Table 11.4 calculates the absolute differences from the median of each location.

TABLE 11.4
Absolute Differences from the Median Sales for Four Locations

In-Aisle (Median = 29.96)	Front (Median = 32.13)	Kiosk (Median = 30.91)	Expert (Median = 30.29)
$\lvert 30.06 - 29.96 \rvert = 0.10$	$\lvert 32.22 - 32.13 \rvert = 0.09$	$\lvert 30.78 - 30.91 \rvert = 0.13$	$\lvert 30.33 - 30.29 \rvert = 0.04$
$\lvert 29.96 - 29.96 \rvert = 0.00$	$\lvert 31.47 - 32.13 \rvert = 0.66$	$\lvert 30.91 - 30.91 \rvert = 0.00$	$\lvert 30.29 - 30.29 \rvert = 0.00$
$\lvert 30.19 - 29.96 \rvert = 0.23$	$\lvert 32.13 - 32.13 \rvert = 0.00$	$\lvert 30.79 - 30.91 \rvert = 0.12$	$\lvert 30.25 - 30.29 \rvert = 0.04$
$\lvert 29.96 - 29.96 \rvert = 0.00$	$\lvert 31.86 - 32.13 \rvert = 0.27$	$\lvert 30.95 - 30.91 \rvert = 0.04$	$\lvert 30.25 - 30.29 \rvert = 0.04$
$\lvert 27.74 - 29.96 \rvert = 2.22$	$\lvert 32.29 - 32.13 \rvert = 0.16$	$\lvert 31.13 - 30.91 \rvert = 0.22$	$\lvert 30.55 - 30.29 \rvert = 0.26$

Figure 11.7 presents the results of performing a one-way ANOVA using the Table 11.4 absolute differences. JMP labels the Levene test that this section describes as Brown-Forsythe, *not* Levene. From those results, observe that $F_{STAT} = 0.7849$. (Excel labels this value F and JMP labels this value F Ratio.) Because $F_{STAT} = 0.7849 < 3.2389$ (or because the p-value = 0.5197 > 0.05), you do not reject H_0. You conclude that insufficient evidence of a significant difference among the four variances exists. You can claim that because the four in-store locations have an equal amount of variability in sales, the homogeneity-of-variance assumption has not been violated.

FIGURE 11.7
Excel, JMP, and Minitab Levene test results for the absolute differences for the in-store location sales experiment

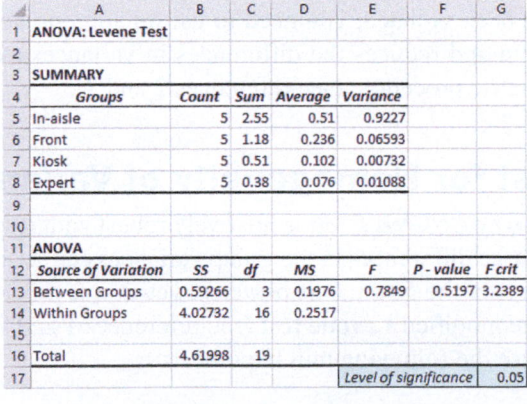

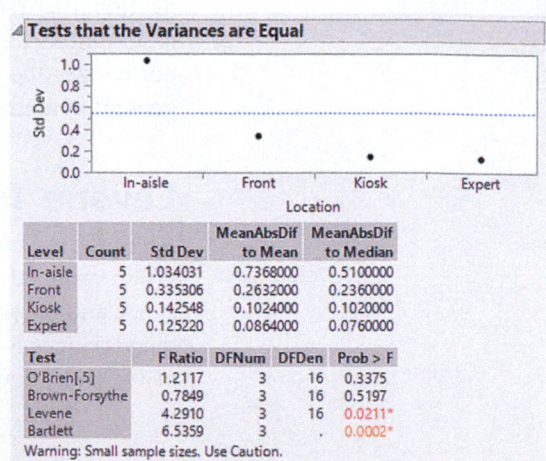

Test for Equal Variances: In-aisle, Front, Kiosk, Expert
Method

Null hypothesis	All variances are equal
Alternative hypothesis	At least one variance is different
Significance level	α = 0.05

95% Bonferroni Confidence Intervals for Standard Deviations

Sample	N	StDev	CI
In-aisle	5	1.03403	(0.180537, 11.8340)
Front	5	0.33531	(0.091643, 2.4514)
Kiosk	5	0.14255	(0.039448, 1.0293)
Expert	5	0.12522	(0.024634, 1.2719)

Individual confidence level = 98.75%

Tests

Method	Test Statistic	P-Value
Multiple comparisons	—	0.054
Levene	0.78	0.520

Multiple Comparisons: The Tukey-Kramer Procedure

In the Arlingtons scenario on page 398, you used the one-way ANOVA F test to determine that there was a difference among the in-store locations. The next step is to construct **multiple comparisons** to test the null hypothesis that the differences in the means of all pairs of in-store locations are equal to 0.

Although many procedures are available (see references 5, 6, and 8), this book uses the **Tukey-Kramer multiple comparisons procedure for one-way ANOVA** to determine which of the c means are significantly different. This procedure enables you to simultaneously make comparisons between *all* pairs of groups. The procedure consists of the following four steps:

1. Compute the absolute mean differences, $|\bar{X}_j - \bar{X}_{j'}|$ (where j refers to group j, j' refers to group j', and $j \neq j'$), among all pairs of sample means [$c(c - 1)/2$ pairs].
2. Compute the **critical range** for the Tukey-Kramer procedure, using Equation (11.6). If the sample sizes differ, compute a critical range for each pairwise comparison of sample means.

CRITICAL RANGE FOR THE TUKEY-KRAMER PROCEDURE

$$\text{Critical range} = Q_\alpha \sqrt{\frac{MSW}{2}\left(\frac{1}{n_j} + \frac{1}{n_{j'}}\right)} \tag{11.6}$$

where

n_j = the sample size in group j

$n_{j'}$ = the sample size in group j'

Q_α = the upper-tail critical value from a **Studentized range distribution** having c degrees of freedom in the numerator and $n - c$ degrees of freedom in the denominator.

---

3. Compare each of the $c(c - 1)/2$ pairs of means against its corresponding critical range. Declare a specific pair significantly different if the absolute difference in the sample means, $|\bar{X}_j - \bar{X}_{j'}|$, is greater than the critical range.
4. Interpret the results.

In the mobile electronics sales example, there are four in-store locations. Thus, there are $4(4 - 1)/2 = 6$ pairwise comparisons. To apply the Tukey-Kramer multiple comparisons procedure, you first compute the absolute mean differences for all six pairwise comparisons:

1. $|\bar{X}_1 - \bar{X}_2| = |29.582 - 31.994| = 2.412$
2. $|\bar{X}_1 - \bar{X}_3| = |29.582 - 30.912| = 1.330$
3. $|\bar{X}_1 - \bar{X}_4| = |29.582 - 30.334| = 0.752$
4. $|\bar{X}_2 - \bar{X}_3| = |31.994 - 30.912| = 1.082$
5. $|\bar{X}_2 - \bar{X}_4| = |31.994 - 30.334| = 1.660$
6. $|\bar{X}_3 - \bar{X}_4| = |30.912 - 30.334| = 0.578$

You then compute only one critical range because the sample sizes in the four groups are equal. (Had the sample sizes in some of the groups been different, you would compute several critical ranges.) From the Figure 11.6 ANOVA summary table (on page 406), $MSW = 0.3044$ and $n_j = n_{j'} = 5$. From Table E.7, for $\alpha = 0.05$, $c = 4$, and $n - c = 20 - 4 = 16$, Q_α, the upper-tail critical value of the test statistic, is 4.05 (see Table 11.5).

TABLE 11.5

Finding the Studentized Range, Q_α, Statistic for $\alpha = 0.05$, with 4 and 16 Degrees of Freedom

Cumulative Probabilities = 0.95
Upper Tail Area = 0.05
Numerator df_1

Denominator df_2	2	3	4	5	6	7	8	9
⋮	⋮	⋮	⋮	⋮	⋮	⋮	⋮	⋮
11	3.11	3.82	4.26	4.57	4.82	5.03	5.20	5.35
12	3.08	3.77	4.20	4.51	4.75	4.95	5.12	5.27
13	3.06	3.73	4.15	4.45	4.69	4.88	5.05	5.19
14	3.03	3.70	4.11	4.41	4.64	4.83	4.99	5.13
15	3.01	3.67	4.08	4.37	4.60	4.78	4.94	5.08
16	3.00	3.65	4.05	4.33	4.56	4.74	4.90	5.03

Source: Extracted from Table E.7.

From Equation (11.6),

$$\text{Critical range} = 4.05\sqrt{\left(\frac{0.3044}{2}\right)\left(\frac{1}{5} + \frac{1}{5}\right)} = 0.9993$$

Because the absolute mean difference for four pairs (1, 2, 4, and 5) is greater than 0.9993, you can conclude that there is a significant difference between the mobile electronic sales means of those pairs. Because the absolute mean difference for pair 3 (in-aisle and expert locations) is 0.752, which is less than 0.9993, you conclude that there is no evidence of a difference in the means of those two locations. Also, because the absolute mean difference for pair 6 (kiosk and expert) 0.578 which is less than 0.9993, you conclude that there is no evidence of a difference in the means of these two locations.

These results allow you to estimate that the population mean sales for mobile electronics items will be higher at the front location than any other location *and* that the population mean sales for mobile electronics items at kiosk locations will be higher when compared to the in-aisle location. As a member of Arlingtons management team, you conclude that selling mobile electronics items at the special front location would increase sales the most, but that selling those items at the kiosk location would also improve sales. (These results also present additional evidence for charging a placement fee for the special front location, the subject of the Chapter 10 Using Statistics scenario.)

Figure 11.8 presents the Tukey-Kramer procedure results for the mobile electronics sales in-store location experiment. By using $\alpha = 0.05$, all six of the comparisons can be made with an overall error rate of only 5%. JMP and Minitab report results by vertically listing connections between groups.

FIGURE 11.8

Excel, JMP, and Minitab Tukey-Kramer procedure results for the in-store location sales experiment

	A	B	C	D	E	F	G	H	I
1	Tukey Kramer Multiple Comparisons								
2									
3		Sample	Sample			Absolute	Std. Error	Critical	
4	Group	Mean	Size		Comparison	Difference	of Difference	Range	Results
5	1: In-aisle	29.582	5		Group 1 to Group 2	2.412	0.2467	0.9993	Means are different
6	2: Front	31.994	5		Group 1 to Group 3	1.33	0.2467	0.9993	Means are different
7	3: Kiosk	30.912	5		Group 1 to Group 4	0.752	0.2467	0.9993	Means are not different
8	4: Expert	30.334	5		Group 2 to Group 3	1.082	0.2467	0.9993	Means are different
9					Group 2 to Group 4	1.66	0.2467	0.9993	Means are different
10	Other Data				Group 3 to Group 4	0.578	0.2467	0.9993	Means are not different
11	Level of significance	0.05							
12	Numerator d.f.	4							
13	Denominator d.f.	16							
14	MSW	0.3044							
15	Q Statistic	4.05							

Connecting Letters Report

Level		Mean
Front	A	31.994000
Kiosk	B	30.912000
Expert	B C	30.334000
In-aisle	C	29.582000

Levels not connected by same letter are significantly different.

Tukey Pairwise Comparisons

Grouping Information Using the Tukey Method and 95% Confidence

Location	N	Mean	Grouping	
Front	5	31.994	A	
Kiosk	5	30.9120	B	
Expert	5	30.3340	B	C
In-aisle	5	29.582		C

Means that do not share a letter are significantly different.

Example 11.1 illustrates another example of the one-way ANOVA.

EXAMPLE 11.1

ANOVA of the Speed of Drive-Through Service at Fast-Food Chains

For fast-food restaurants, the drive-through window is an important revenue source. The chain that offers the fastest service is likely to attract additional customers. Each year *QSR Magazine*, **www.qsrmagazine.com**, publishes its results of a survey of drive-through service times (from menu board to departure) at fast-food chains. In a recent year, the mean time was 169.11 seconds for Wendy's, 220.11 seconds for Taco Bell, 201.18 seconds for Burger King, 208.16 seconds for McDonald's, and 257.54 seconds for Chick-fil-A. Suppose the study was based on 20 customers for each fast-food chain. At the 0.05 level of significance, is there evidence of a difference in the mean drive-through service times of the five chains?

Table 11.6 contains the ANOVA table for this problem.

TABLE 11.6

ANOVA Summary Table of Drive-Through Service Times at Fast-Food Chains

Source	Degrees of Freedom	Sum of Squares	Mean Squares	F	p-value
Among chains	4	96,507.118	24,126.7795	184.7380	0.0000
Within chains	95	12,407.00	130.60		

SOLUTION

$H_0: \mu_1 = \mu_2 = \mu_3 = \mu_4 = \mu_5$ where 1 = Wendy's, 2 = Taco Bell, 3 = Burger King,

   4 = McDonald's, 5 = Chick-fil-A

H_1: Not all μ_j are equal   where j = 1, 2, 3, 4, 5

Decision rule: If the *p*-value < 0.05, reject H_0. Because the *p*-value is 0.0000, which is less than $\alpha = 0.05$, reject H_0. You have sufficient evidence to conclude that the mean drive-through times of the five chains are not all equal.

To determine which of the means are significantly different from one another, use the Tukey-Kramer procedure [Equation (11.6) on page 409] to establish the critical range:

Critical value of Q with 5 and 95 degrees of freedom ≈ 3.92

$$\text{Critical range} = Q_\alpha \sqrt{\left(\frac{MSW}{2}\right)\left(\frac{1}{n_j} + \frac{1}{n_{j'}}\right)} = (3.92)\sqrt{\left(\frac{130.6}{2}\right)\left(\frac{1}{20} + \frac{1}{20}\right)}$$

$$= 10.02$$

Any observed difference greater than 10.02 is considered significant. The mean drive-through service times are different between Wendy's (mean of 169.11 seconds) and Taco Bell, Burger King, McDonald's, and Chick-fil-A and also between Taco Bell (mean of 220.11) and Burger King, McDonald's, and Chick-fil-A. In addition, the mean drive-through service time is different between McDonald's and Chick-fil-A. Thus, with 95% confidence, you can conclude that the estimated population mean drive-through service time is faster for Wendy's than for Taco Bell. In addition, the population mean service time for Wendy's and for Taco Bell is faster than those of Burger King, McDonald's, and Chick-fil-A. Also, the population mean drive-through service time for McDonald's is faster than for Chick-Fil-A.

The Analysis of Means (ANOM)

The **analysis of means (ANOM)** provides an alternative approach that allows you to determine which, if any, of the *c* groups has a mean significantly different from the overall mean of all the group means combined. The **ANOM online topic** explains this alternative approach and illustrates its use.

PROBLEMS FOR SECTION 11.1

LEARNING THE BASICS

11.1 An experiment has a single factor with five groups and seven values in each group.
a. How many degrees of freedom are there in determining the among-group variation?
b. How many degrees of freedom are there in determining the within-group variation?
c. How many degrees of freedom are there in determining the total variation?

11.2 You are working with the same experiment as in Problem 11.1.
a. If $SSA = 60$ and $SST = 210$, what is SSW?
b. What is MSA?
c. What is MSW?
d. What is the value of F_{STAT}?

11.3 You are working with the same experiment as in Problems 11.1 and 11.2.
a. Construct the ANOVA summary table and fill in all values in the table.
b. At the 0.05 level of significance, what is the upper-tail critical value from the F distribution?
c. State the decision rule for testing the null hypothesis that all five groups have equal population means.
d. What is your statistical decision?

11.4 Consider an experiment with three groups, with seven values in each.
a. How many degrees of freedom are there in determining the among-group variation?
b. How many degrees of freedom are there in determining the within-group variation?
c. How many degrees of freedom are there in determining the total variation?

11.5 Consider an experiment with four groups, with eight values in each. For the ANOVA summary table below, fill in all the missing results:

Source	Degrees of Freedom	Sum of Squares	Mean Square (Variance)	F
Among groups	$c - 1 = ?$	$SSA = ?$	$MSA = 80$	$F_{STAT} = ?$
Within groups	$n - c = ?$	$SSW = 560$	$MSW = ?$	
Total	$n - 1 = ?$	$SST = ?$		

11.6 You are working with the same experiment as in Problem 11.5.
a. At the 0.05 level of significance, state the decision rule for testing the null hypothesis that all four groups have equal population means.
b. What is your statistical decision?
c. At the 0.05 level of significance, what is the upper-tail critical value from the Studentized range distribution?
d. To perform the Tukey-Kramer procedure, what is the critical range?

APPLYING THE CONCEPTS

11.7 One of the steps involved in the processing of corn flakes for cereals involves toasting the flakes. The file CornFlakes contains the following data for corn flakes thickness (mm) for four different toasting times (seconds).

20sec	40sec	60sec	80sec
1.6	1.7	2.0	1.0
0.6	1.6	1.2	0.7
0.7	0.8	0.7	0.3

Source: Data extracted from C. Borror, "Blocking benefits," *Quality Progress*, November 2015, pp. 60–62.

a. At the 0.05 level of significance, is there evidence of a difference in the mean thickness of the corn flakes for the different toasting times?
b. If appropriate, determine which toasting times differ in mean thickness.
c. At the 0.05 level of significance, is there evidence of a difference in the variation in the mean thickness of the corn flakes?
d. Which toasting times differ in thickness of the corn flakes? Explain.

✓ SELF TEST **11.8** The more costly and time-consuming it is to export and import, the more difficult it is for local companies to be competitive and to reach international markets. As part of an initial investigation exploring foreign market entry, 10 countries were selected from each of four global regions. The cost associated with compliance of the economy's customs regulations to import a shipment in these countries (in US$), is stored in ForeignMarket2.
Source: Data extracted from **doingbusiness.org/data**.

a. At the 0.05 level of significance, is there evidence of a difference in the mean cost of importing across the four global regions?
b. If appropriate, determine which global regions differ in mean cost of importing?
c. At the 0.05 level of significance, is there evidence of a difference in the variation in cost of importing among the four global regions?
d. Which global region(s) should you consider for foreign market entry? Explain.

11.9 A hospital conducted a study of the waiting time in its emergency room. The hospital has a main campus and three affiliated locations. Management had a business objective of reducing waiting time for emergency room cases that did not require immediate attention. To study this, a random sample of 15 emergency room cases that did not require immediate attention at each location were selected on a particular day, and the waiting times (measured from check-in to when the patient was called into the clinic area) were collected and stored in ERWaiting.
a. At the 0.05 level of significance, is there evidence of a difference in the mean waiting times in the four locations?
b. If appropriate, determine which locations differ in mean waiting time.
c. At the 0.05 level of significance, is there evidence of a difference in the variation in waiting time among the four locations?

11.10 A manufacturer of pens has hired an advertising agency to develop an advertising campaign for the upcoming holiday season. To prepare for this project, the research director decides to initiate a study of the effect of advertising on product perception. An experiment is designed to compare five different advertisements. Advertisement *A* greatly undersells the pen's characteristics. Advertisement *B* slightly undersells the pen's characteristics. Advertisement *C* slightly oversells the pen's characteristics. Advertisement *D* greatly oversells the pen's characteristics. Advertisement *E* attempts to correctly state the pen's characteristics. A sample of 30 adult respondents, taken from a larger focus group, is randomly assigned to the five advertisements (so that there are 6 respondents to each advertisement). After reading the advertisement and developing a sense of "product expectation," all respondents unknowingly receive the same pen to evaluate. The respondents are permitted to test the pen and the plausibility of the advertising copy. The respondents are then asked to rate the pen from 1 to 7 (lowest to highest) on the product characteristic scales of appearance, durability, and writing performance. The *combined* scores of three ratings (appearance, durability, and writing performance) for the 30 respondents, stored in Pen , are as follows:

A	B	C	D	E
15	16	8	5	12
18	17	7	6	19
17	21	10	13	18
19	16	15	11	12
19	19	14	9	17
20	17	14	10	14

a. At the 0.05 level of significance, is there evidence of a difference in the mean rating of the pens following exposure to five advertisements?
b. If appropriate, determine which advertisements differ in mean ratings.
c. At the 0.05 level of significance, is there evidence of a difference in the variation in ratings among the five advertisements?
d. Which advertisement(s) should you use, and which advertisement(s) should you avoid? Explain.

11.11 *QSR* reports on the largest quick-serve and fast-casual brands in the United States. The file FastFoodChain contains the food segment (burger, chicken, sandwich or pizza/pasta) and U.S. mean sales per unit ($ thousands) for each of 37 quick-service brands.

Source: Data extracted from **qsrmagazine.com/reports/top-50-break-down-market-segments**.

a. At the 0.05 level of significance, is there evidence of a difference in the mean U.S. mean sales per unit ($ thousands) among the food segments?
b. At the 0.05 level of significance, is there a difference in the variation in U.S. average sales per unit ($ thousands) among the food segments?
c. What effect does your result in (b) have on the validity of the results in (a)?
d. If appropriate, determine which food segments differ in mean sales.

11.12 Brand valuations are critical to CEOs, financial and marketing executives, security analysts, institutional investors, and others who depend on well-researched, reliable information needed for assessments and comparisons in decision making. Millward Brown Optimor has developed the BrandZ Top 100 Most Valuable Global Brands for WPP, the world's largest communications services group. Unlike other studies, the BrandZ Top 100 Most Valuable Global Brands fuses consumer measures of brand equity with financial measures to place a financial value on brands. A research assistant compared brand values for three sectors in the BrandZ Top 100 Most Valuable Global Brands for 2016: the financial institution sector, the technology sector, and the telecom sector. The research assistant findings were as follows:

Source	Degrees of Freedom	Sums of Squares	Mean Squares	F
Among groups	2	12,463,043,330		
Within groups	46	102,945,347,500		
Total	48	115,408,390,800		

Group	N	Mean
Financial Institution	20	24,906.95
Technology	18	61,092.17
Telecom	11	39,428.91

Source: Data extracted from *BrandZ Top100 Most Valuable Global Brands 2016*, available at **bit.ly/1Y8gPqK**.

a. Complete the ANOVA summary table.
b. At the 0.05 level of significance, is there evidence of a difference in mean brand value among the sectors?
c. If the results in (b) indicate that it is appropriate, use the Tukey-Kramer procedure to determine which sectors differ in mean rating. Discuss your findings.

11.13 A pet food company has a business objective of expanding its product line beyond its current kidney and shrimp-based cat foods. The company developed two new products, one based on chicken liver and the other based on salmon. The company conducted an experiment to compare the two new products with its two existing ones, as well as a generic beef-based product sold at a supermarket chain.

For the experiment, a sample of 50 cats from the population at a local animal shelter was selected. Ten cats were randomly assigned to each of the five products being tested. Each of the cats was then presented with 3 ounces of the selected food in a dish at feeding time. The researchers defined the variable to be measured as the number of ounces of food that the cat consumed within a 10-minute time interval that began when the filled dish was presented. The results for this experiment are summarized in the table on page 414 and stored in CatFood .

a. At the 0.05 level of significance, is there evidence of a difference in the mean amount of food eaten among the various products?
b. If appropriate, determine which products appear to differ significantly in the mean amount of food eaten.
c. At the 0.05 level of significance, is there evidence of a difference in the variation in the amount of food eaten among the various products?
d. What should the pet food company conclude? Fully describe the pet food company's options with respect to the products.

Kidney	Shrimp	Chicken Liver	Salmon	Beef
2.37	2.26	2.29	1.79	2.09
2.62	2.69	2.23	2.33	1.87
2.31	2.25	2.41	1.96	1.67
2.47	2.45	2.68	2.05	1.64
2.59	2.34	2.25	2.26	2.16
2.62	2.37	2.17	2.24	1.75
2.34	2.22	2.37	1.96	1.18
2.47	2.56	2.26	1.58	1.92
2.45	2.36	2.45	2.18	1.32
2.32	2.59	2.57	1.93	1.94

11.14 A transportation strategist wanted to compare the traffic congestion levels across four continents: Asia, Europe, North America, and South America. The file CongestionLevel contains congestion level, defined as the increase (%) in overall travel time when compared to a free flow situation (an uncongested situation) for 10 cities in each continent.

Source: Data extracted from **ciorporate.tomtom.com/releasedetail .cfm?releaseiid=1012517**

a. At the 0.05 level of significance, is there evidence of a difference in the mean congestion level across continents?
b. If the results in (a) indicate that it is appropriate to do so, use the Tukey-Kramer procedure to determine which continents differ in congestion level
c. What assumptions are necessary in (a)?
d. At the 0.05 level of significance, is there evidence of a difference in the variation of the congestion level across continents?

11.2 The Factorial Design: Two-Way ANOVA

In Section 11.1, you learned about the completely randomized design. In this section, the single-factor completely randomized design is extended to the **two-factor factorial design**, in which two factors are simultaneously evaluated. Each factor is evaluated at two or more levels. For example, in the Arlingtons scenario on page 398, the company faces the business problem of simultaneously evaluating four locations and the effectiveness of providing mobile payment to determine which location should be used and whether mobile payment should be made available. Although this section uses only two factors, you can extend factorial designs to three or more factors (see references 4, 5, 7, and 8).

To analyze data from a two-factor factorial design, you use **two-way ANOVA**. The following definitions are needed to develop the two-way ANOVA procedure:

r = number of levels of factor A

c = number of levels of factor B

n' = number of values (replicates) for each cell (combination of a particular level of factor A and a particular level of factor B)

n = number of values in the entire experiment (where $n = rcn'$)

X_{ijk} = value of the kth observation for level i of factor A and level j of factor B

$$\overline{\overline{X}} = \frac{\sum_{i=1}^{r}\sum_{j=1}^{c}\sum_{k=1}^{n'} X_{ijk}}{rcn'} = \text{grand mean}$$

$$\overline{X}_{i..} = \frac{\sum_{j=1}^{c}\sum_{k=1}^{n'} X_{ijk}}{cn'} = \text{mean of the } i\text{th level of factor } A \text{ (where } i = 1, 2, \ldots, r)$$

$$\overline{X}_{.j.} = \frac{\sum_{i=1}^{r}\sum_{k=1}^{n'} X_{ijk}}{rn'} = \text{mean of the } j\text{th level of factor } B \text{ (where } i = 1, 2, \ldots, c)$$

$$\overline{X}_{ij.} = \frac{\sum_{k=1}^{n'} X_{ijk}}{n'} = \text{mean of the cell } ij, \text{ the combination of the } i\text{th level of factor } A \text{ and the } j\text{th level of factor } B$$

Because of the complexity of these computations, you should only use computerized methods when performing this analysis. However, to help explain the two-way ANOVA, the decomposition of the total variation is illustrated. In this discussion, only cases in which there are an equal number of values (also called **replicates**) (sample sizes n') for each combination of the levels of factor A with those of factor B are considered. (See references 1, 6, and 8 for a discussion of two-factor factorial designs with unequal sample sizes.)

Factor and Interaction Effects

There is an **interaction** between factors A and B if the effect of factor A is different for various levels of factor B. Thus, when dividing the total variation into different sources of variation, you need to account for a possible interaction effect, as well as for factor A, factor B, and random variation. To accomplish this, the total variation (SST) is subdivided into sum of squares due to factor A (or SSA), sum of squares due to factor B (or SSB), sum of squares due to the interaction effect of A and B (or $SSAB$), and sum of squares due to random variation (or SSE). This decomposition of the total variation (SST) is displayed in Figure 11.9.

FIGURE 11.9
Partitioning the total variation in a two-factor factorial design

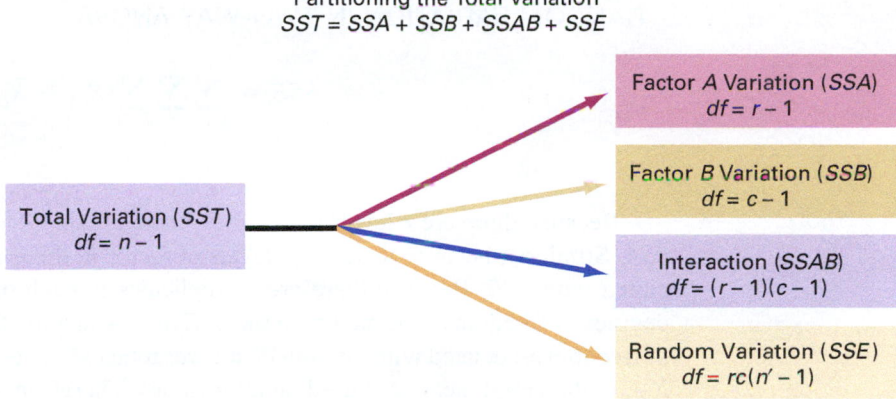

Partitioning the Total Variation
$SST = SSA + SSB + SSAB + SSE$

Total Variation (SST)
$df = n - 1$

Factor A Variation (SSA)
$df = r - 1$

Factor B Variation (SSB)
$df = c - 1$

Interaction (SSAB)
$df = (r - 1)(c - 1)$

Random Variation (SSE)
$df = rc(n' - 1)$

The sum of squares total (SST) represents the total variation among all the values around the grand mean. Equation (11.7) shows the computation for total variation.

TOTAL VARIATION IN TWO-WAY ANOVA

$$SST = \sum_{i=1}^{r} \sum_{j=1}^{c} \sum_{k=1}^{n'} (X_{ijk} - \bar{\bar{X}})^2 \tag{11.7}$$

The **sum of squares due to factor A (SSA)** represents the differences among the various levels of factor A and the grand mean. Equation (11.8) shows the computation for factor A variation.

FACTOR A VARIATION

$$SSA = cn' \sum_{i=1}^{r} (\bar{X}_{i..} - \bar{\bar{X}})^2 \tag{11.8}$$

The **sum of squares due to factor B (SSB)** represents the differences among the various levels of factor B and the grand mean. Equation (11.9) shows the computation for factor B variation.

FACTOR B VARIATION

$$SSB = rn' \sum_{j=1}^{c} (\bar{X}_{.j.} - \bar{\bar{X}})^2 \tag{11.9}$$

The **sum of squares due to interaction (*SSAB*)** represents the interacting effect of specific combinations of factor A and factor B. Equation (11.10) shows the computation for interaction variation.

INTERACTION VARIATION

$$SSAB = n' \sum_{i=1}^{r} \sum_{j=1}^{c} (\overline{X}_{ij.} - \overline{X}_{i..} - \overline{X}_{.j.} + \overline{\overline{X}})^2 \tag{11.10}$$

The **sum of squares error (*SSE*)** represents random variation—that is, the differences among the values within each cell and the corresponding cell mean. Equation (11.11) shows the computation for random variation.

RANDOM VARIATION IN TWO-WAY ANOVA

$$SSE = \sum_{i=1}^{r} \sum_{j=1}^{c} \sum_{k=1}^{n'} (X_{ijk} - \overline{X}_{ij.})^2 \tag{11.11}$$

Because there are r levels of factor A, there are $r - 1$ degrees of freedom associated with *SSA*. Similarly, because there are c levels of factor B, there are $c - 1$ degrees of freedom associated with *SSB*. Because there are n' replicates in each of the rc cells, there are $rc(n' - 1)$ degrees of freedom associated with the *SSE* term. Carrying this further, there are $n - 1$ degrees of freedom associated with the sum of squares total (*SST*) because you are comparing each value, X_{ijk}, to the grand mean, $\overline{\overline{X}}$, based on all n values. Therefore, because the degrees of freedom for each of the sources of variation must add to the degrees of freedom for the total variation (*SST*), you can calculate the degrees of freedom for the interaction component (*SSAB*) by subtraction. The degrees of freedom for interaction are $(r - 1)(c - 1)$.

If you divide each sum of squares by its associated degrees of freedom, you have the four variances or mean square terms (*MSA*, *MSB*, *MSAB*, and *MSE*). Equations (11.12a–d) give the mean square terms needed for the two-way ANOVA table.

student TIP

Remember, *mean square* is another term for *variance*.

MEAN SQUARES IN TWO-WAY ANOVA

$$MSA = \frac{SSA}{r - 1} \tag{11.12a}$$

$$MSB = \frac{SSB}{c - 1} \tag{11.12b}$$

$$MSAB = \frac{SSAB}{(r - 1)(c - 1)} \tag{11.12c}$$

$$MSE = \frac{SSE}{rc(n' - 1)} \tag{11.12d}$$

Testing for Factor and Interaction Effects

There are three different tests to perform in a two-way ANOVA:

- A test of the hypothesis of no difference due to factor A
- A test of the hypothesis of no difference due to factor B
- A test of the hypothesis of no interaction of factors A and B

To test the hypothesis of no difference due to factor A:

$$H_0: \mu_{1..} = \mu_{2..} = \cdots = \mu_{r..}$$

against the alternative:

$$H_1: \text{Not all } \mu_{i..} \text{ are equal}$$

you use the F_{STAT} test statistic in Equation (11.13).

F TEST FOR FACTOR A EFFECT

$$F_{STAT} = \frac{MSA}{MSE} \qquad\qquad (11.13)$$

You reject the null hypothesis at the α level of significance if

$$F_{STAT} = \frac{MSA}{MSE} > F_\alpha$$

where F_α is the upper-tail critical value from an F distribution with $r - 1$ and $rc(n' - 1)$ degrees of freedom.

To test the hypothesis of no difference due to factor B:

$$H_0: \mu_{.1.} = \mu_{.2.} = \cdots = \mu_{.c.}$$

against the alternative:

$$H_1: \text{Not all } \mu_{.j.} \text{ are equal}$$

you use the F_{STAT} test statistic in Equation (11.14).

F TEST FOR FACTOR B EFFECT

$$F_{STAT} = \frac{MSB}{MSE} \qquad\qquad (11.14)$$

You reject the null hypothesis at the α level of significance if

$$F_{STAT} = \frac{MSB}{MSE} > F_\alpha$$

where F_α is the upper-tail critical value from an F distribution with $c - 1$ and $rc(n' - 1)$ degrees of freedom.

To test the hypothesis of no interaction of factors A and B:

$$H_0: \text{The interaction of } A \text{ and } B \text{ is equal to zero}$$

against the alternative:

$$H_1: \text{The interaction of } A \text{ and } B \text{ is not equal to zero}$$

you use the F_{STAT} test statistic in Equation (11.15).

F TEST FOR INTERACTION EFFECT

$$F_{STAT} = \frac{MSAB}{MSE} \qquad\qquad (11.15)$$

---

student TIP

In each of these F tests, the denominator of the F_{STAT} statistic is MSE.

You reject the null hypothesis at the α level of significance if

$$F_{STAT} = \frac{MSAB}{MSE} > F_\alpha$$

where F_α is the upper-tail critical value from an F distribution with $(r - 1)(c - 1)$ and $rc(n' - 1)$ degrees of freedom.

Table 11.7 presents the entire two-way ANOVA table.

TABLE 11.7

Analysis of Variance Table for the Two-Factor Factorial Design

Source	Degrees of Freedom	Sum of Squares	Mean Square (Variance)	F
A	$r - 1$	SSA	$MSA = \dfrac{SSA}{r - 1}$	$F_{STAT} = \dfrac{MSA}{MSE}$
B	$c - 1$	SSB	$MSB = \dfrac{SSB}{c - 1}$	$F_{STAT} = \dfrac{MSB}{MSE}$
AB	$(r - 1)(c - 1)$	SSAB	$MSAB = \dfrac{SSAB}{(r - 1)(c - 1)}$	$F_{STAT} = \dfrac{MSAB}{MSE}$
Error	$rc(n' - 1)$	SSE	$MSE = \dfrac{SSE}{rc(n' - 1)}$	
Total	$n - 1$	SST		

To illustrate two-way ANOVA, return to the Arlingtons scenario on page 398. As a member of the sales team, you first explored how different in-store locations might affect the sales of mobile electronics items using one-way ANOVA. Now, to explore the effects of permitting mobile payment methods to buy mobile electronics items, you design an experiment that examines this second (B) factor as it studies the effects of in-store location (factor A) using two-way ANOVA. Two-way ANOVA will allow you to determine if there is a significant difference in mobile electronics sales among the four in-store locations *and* whether permitting mobile payment methods makes a difference.

To test the effects of the two factors, you conduct a 60-day experiment at 40 same-sized stores that have similar storewide net sales. You randomly assign ten stores to use the current in-aisle location, ten stores to use the special front location, ten stores to use the kiosk location, and ten stores to use the expert counter. In five stores in each of the four groups, you permit mobile payment methods (for the other five in each group, mobile payment methods are not permitted). At the end of the experiment, you organize the mobile electronics sales data by group and store the data in Mobile Electronics2 . Table 11.8 presents the data of the experiment.

TABLE 11.8

Mobile Electronics Sales ($000) at Four In-Store Locations with Mobile Payments Permitted and Not Permitted

MOBILE PAYMENTS	IN-STORE LOCATION			
	In-Aisle	Front	Kiosk	Expert
No	30.06	32.22	30.78	30.33
No	29.96	31.47	30.91	30.29
No	30.19	32.13	30.79	30.25
No	29.96	31.86	30.95	30.25
No	27.74	32.29	31.13	30.55
Yes	30.66	32.81	31.34	31.03
Yes	29.99	32.65	31.80	31.77
Yes	30.73	32.81	32.00	30.97
Yes	30.72	32.42	31.07	31.43
Yes	30.73	33.12	31.69	30.72

Figure 11.10 presents the results for this example. In the Excel worksheet, the *A*, *B*, and Error sources of variation in Table 11.7 on page 418 are labeled Sample, Columns, and Within, respectively.

FIGURE 11.10

Excel, JMP, and Minitab two-way ANOVA results for the in-store location sales and mobile payment experiment

	A	B	C	D	E	F	G
1	ANOVA: Two-Factor With Replication						
2							
3	SUMMARY	In-aisle	Front	Kiosk	Expert	Total	
4	No						
5	Count	5	5	5	5	20	
6	Sum	147.91	159.97	154.56	151.67	614.11	
7	Average	29.582	31.994	30.912	30.334	30.7055	
8	Variance	1.0692	0.1124	0.0203	0.0157	1.0730	
9							
10	Yes						
11	Count	5	5	5	5	20	
12	Sum	152.83	163.81	157.9	155.92	630.46	
13	Average	30.566	32.762	31.58	31.184	31.5230	
14	Variance	0.1045	0.0656	0.1387	0.1722	0.7773	
15							
16	Total						
17	Count	10	10	10	10		
18	Sum	300.74	323.78	312.46	307.59		
19	Average	30.074	32.378	31.246	30.759		
20	Variance	0.7906	0.2430	0.1946	0.2842		
21							
22							
23	ANOVA						
24	Source of Variation	SS	df	MS	F	P-value	F crit
25	Sample	6.6831	1	6.6831	31.4760	0.0000	4.1491
26	Columns	28.2274	3	9.4091	44.3154	0.0000	2.9011
27	Interaction	0.1339	3	0.0446	0.2103	0.8885	2.9011
28	Within	6.7943	32	0.2123			
29							
30	Total	41.8388	39				
31						Level of significance	0.05

Effect Tests

Source	Nparm	DF	Sum of Squares	F Ratio	Prob > F
Mobile Payments	1	1	6.683063	31.4760	<.0001*
Location	3	3	28.227448	44.3154	<.0001*
Mobile Payments*Location	3	3	0.133947	0.2103	0.8885

General Linear Model: Sales versus Mobile Payments, Location

Method

Factor coding   (-1, 0, +1)

Factor Information

Factor	Type	Levels	Values
Mobile Payments	Fixed	2	No, Yes
Location	Fixed	4	Expert, Front, In-aisle, Kiosk

Analysis of Variance

Source	DF	Adj SS	Adj MS	F-Value	P-Value
Mobile Payments	1	6.6831	6.68306	31.48	0.000
Location	3	28.2274	9.40915	44.32	0.000
Mobile Payments*Location	3	0.1339	0.04465	0.21	0.889
Error	32	6.7943	0.21232		
Total	39	41.8388			

[2]Table E.5 does not provide the upper-tail critical values from the *F* distribution with 32 degrees of freedom in the denominator. When the desired degrees of freedom are not provided in the table, use the *p*-value computed by Excel, JMP, or Minitab.

To interpret the results, you start by testing whether there is an interaction effect between factor *A* (mobile payments) and factor *B* (in-store locations). If the interaction effect is significant, further analysis will focus on this interaction. If the interaction effect is not significant, you can focus on the **main effects**—the potential effect of permitting mobile payment (factor *A*) and the potential differences in in-store locations (factor *B*).

Using the 0.05 level of significance, to determine whether there is evidence of an interaction effect, you reject the null hypothesis of no interaction between mobile payments and in-store locations if the computed F_{STAT} statistic is greater than 2.9011, the upper-tail critical value from the *F* distribution, with 3 and 32 degrees of freedom (see Figures 11.10 and 11.11).[2]

FIGURE 11.11

Regions of rejection and nonrejection at the 0.05 level of significance, with 3 and 32 degrees of freedom

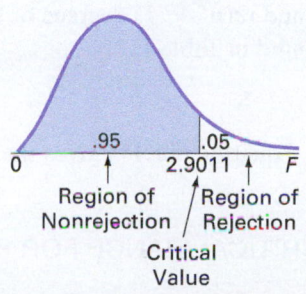

Because $F_{STAT} = 0.2103 < 2.9011$ or the *p*-value $= 0.8885 > 0.05$, you do not reject H_0. You conclude that there is insufficient evidence of an interaction effect between mobile payment and in-store location. You can now focus on the main effects.

Using the 0.05 level of significance and testing whether there is an effect due to mobile payment options (yes or no) (factor A), you reject the null hypothesis if the computed F_{STAT} test statistic is greater than 4.1491, the upper-tail critical value from the F distribution with 1 and 32 degrees of freedom (see Figures 11.10 and 11.12). Because $F_{STAT} = 31.4760 > 4.1491$ or the p-value $= 0.0000 < 0.05$, you reject H_0. You conclude that there is evidence of a difference in the mean sales when mobile payment methods are permitted as compared to when they are not. Because the mean sales when mobile payment methods are permitted is 31.523 and is 30.7055 when they are not, you can conclude that permitting mobile payment methods has led to an increase in mean sales.

FIGURE 11.12

Regions of rejection and nonrejection at the 0.05 level of significance, with 1 and 32 degrees of freedom

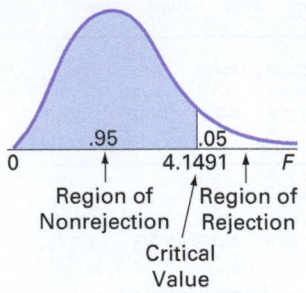

Using the 0.05 level of significance and testing for a difference among the in-store locations (factor B), you reject the null hypothesis of no difference if the computed F_{STAT} test statistic is greater than 2.9011, the upper-tail critical value from the F distribution with 3 degrees of freedom in the numerator and 32 degrees of freedom in the denominator (see Figures 11.10 and 11.11). Because $F_{STAT} = 44.3154 > 2.9011$ or the p-value $= 0.0000 < 0.05$, you reject H_0. You conclude that there is evidence of a difference in the mean sales among the four in-store locations.

Multiple Comparisons: The Tukey Procedure

If one or both of the factor effects are significant and there is no significant interaction effect, when there are more than two levels of a factor, you can determine the particular levels that are significantly different by using the **Tukey multiple comparisons procedure for two-way ANOVA** (see references 6 and 8). Equation (11.16) gives the critical range for factor A.

CRITICAL RANGE FOR FACTOR A

$$\text{Critical range} = Q_\alpha \sqrt{\frac{MSE}{cn'}} \qquad (11.16)$$

where Q_α is the upper-tail critical value from a Studentized range distribution having r and $rc(n' - 1)$ degrees of freedom. (Values for the Studentized range distribution are found in Table E.7.)

Equation (11.17) gives the critical range for factor B.

CRITICAL RANGE FOR FACTOR B

$$\text{Critical range} = Q_\alpha \sqrt{\frac{MSE}{rn'}} \qquad (11.17)$$

where Q_α is the upper-tail critical value from a Studentized range distribution having c and $rc(n' - 1)$ degrees of freedom. (Values for the Studentized range distribution are found in Table E.7.)

To use the Tukey procedure, return to the Table 11.8 mobile electronics sales data on page 418. In the ANOVA summary table in Figure 11.10 on page 419, the interaction effect is not significant. Because there are only two categories for mobile payment (yes and no), there are no multiple comparisons to be constructed. Using $\alpha = 0.05$, there is evidence of a significant difference among the four in-store locations that comprise factor B. Thus, you can use the Tukey multiple comparisons procedure to determine which of the four in-store locations differ.

Because there are four in-store locations, there are $4(4 - 1)/2 = 6$ pairwise comparisons. Using the calculations presented in Figure 11.10, the absolute mean differences are as follows:

1. $|\overline{X}_{.1.} - \overline{X}_{.2.}| = |30.074 - 32.378| = 2.124$
2. $|\overline{X}_{.1.} - \overline{X}_{.3.}| = |30.074 - 31.246| = 1.172$
3. $|\overline{X}_{.1.} - \overline{X}_{.4.}| = |30.074 - 30.759| = 0.685$
4. $|\overline{X}_{.2.} - \overline{X}_{.3.}| = |32.378 - 31.246| = 1.132$
5. $|\overline{X}_{.2.} - \overline{X}_{.4.}| = |32.378 - 30.759| = 1.619$
6. $|\overline{X}_{.3.} - \overline{X}_{.4.}| = |31.246 - 30.759| = 0.487$

To determine the critical range, refer to Figure 11.10 to find $MSE = 0.2123$, $r = 2$, $c = 4$, and $n' = 5$. From Table E.7 [for $\alpha = 0.05$, $c = 4$, and $rc(n' - 1) = 32$], Q_α, the upper-tail critical value of the Studentized range distribution with 4 and 32 degrees of freedom is approximately 3.84. Using Equation (11.17),

$$\text{Critical range} = 3.84 \sqrt{\frac{0.2123}{10}} = 0.5595$$

Because five of the six comparisons are greater than the critical range of 0.5595, you can conclude that the population mean sales is different for the in-store locations except for the kiosk and expert locations. The front location is estimated to have higher mean sales than the other three in-store locations. The kiosk location is estimated to have higher mean sales than the in-aisle location. The expert location is estimated to have higher mean sales than the in-aisle location. Note that by using $\alpha = 0.05$, you are able to make all six comparisons with an overall error rate of only 5%. Consistent with the results of the one-factor experiment, you have additional evidence that selling mobile electronics items at the front location will increase sales the most. In addition, you now have evidence that enabling mobile payment will also lead to increased sales.

Visualizing Interaction Effects: The Cell Means Plot

You can get a better understanding of the interaction effect by plotting the **cell means**, the means of all possible factor-level combinations. Figure 11.13 presents a cell means plot that uses the cell means for the mobile payments permitted/in-store location combinations shown

FIGURE 11.13

Excel and Minitab cell means plots for mobile electronic sales based on mobile payments permitted and in-store location

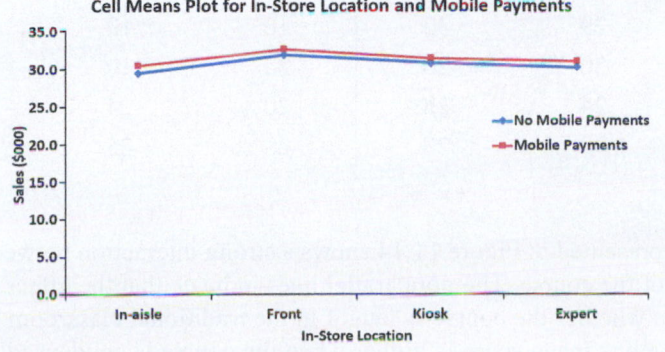
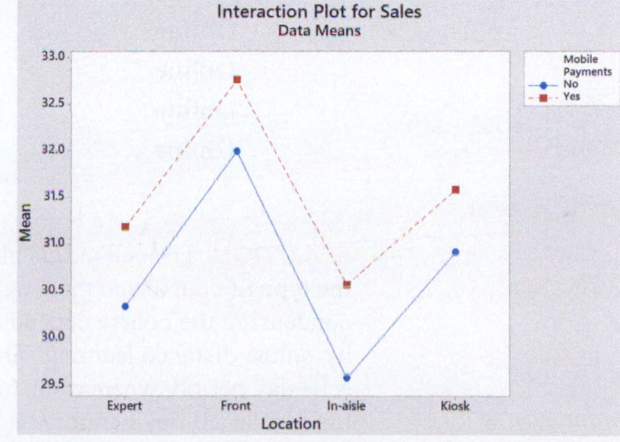

in Figure 11.10 on page 419. From the plot of the mean sales for each combination of mobile payments permitted and in-store location, observe that the two lines (representing the two levels of mobile payments, yes and no,) are roughly parallel. This indicates that the *difference* between the mean sales for stores that permit mobile payment methods and those that do not is virtually the same for the four in-store locations. In other words, there is no *interaction* between these two factors, as was indicated by the *F* test.

Interpreting Interaction Effects

How do you interpret an interaction? When there is an interaction, some levels of factor *A* respond better with certain levels of factor *B*. For example, with respect to mobile electronics sales, suppose that some in-store locations were better when mobile payment methods were permitted and other in-store locations were better when mobile payment methods were not permitted. If this were true, the lines of Figure 11.13 would not be nearly as parallel, and the interaction effect might be statistically significant. In such a situation, the difference between whether mobile payment methods were permitted is no longer the same for all in-store locations. Such an outcome would also complicate the interpretation of the *main effects* because differences in one factor (whether mobile payment methods were permitted) would not be consistent across the other factor (the in-store locations).

Example 11.2 illustrates a situation with a significant interaction effect.

EXAMPLE 11.2

Interpreting Significant Interaction Effects

A nationwide company specializing in preparing students for college and graduate school entrance exams, such as the SAT, ACT, GRE, and LSAT, had the business objective of improving its ACT preparatory course. Two factors of interest to the company are the length of the course (a condensed 10-day period or a regular 30-day period) and the type of course (traditional classroom or online distance learning). The company collected data by randomly assigning 10 clients to each of the four cells that represent a combination of length of the course and type of course. The results are organized in the file ACT and presented in Table 11.9.

What are the effects of the type of course and the length of the course on ACT scores?

TABLE 11.9
ACT Scores for Different Types and Lengths of Courses

	LENGTH OF COURSE			
TYPE OF COURSE	**Condensed**		**Regular**	
Traditional	26	18	34	28
Traditional	27	24	24	21
Traditional	25	19	35	23
Traditional	21	20	31	29
Traditional	21	18	28	26
Online	27	21	24	21
Online	29	32	16	19
Online	30	20	22	19
Online	24	28	20	24
Online	30	29	23	25

SOLUTION The cell means plot presented in Figure 11.14 shows a strong interaction between the type of course and the length of the course. The nonparallel lines indicate that the effect of condensing the course depends on whether the course is taught in the traditional classroom or by online distance learning. The online mean score is higher when the course is condensed to a 10-day period, whereas the traditional mean score is higher when the course takes place over the regular 30-day period.

▶*(continued)*

FIGURE 11.14

Excel and Minitab cell means plot of mean ACT scores

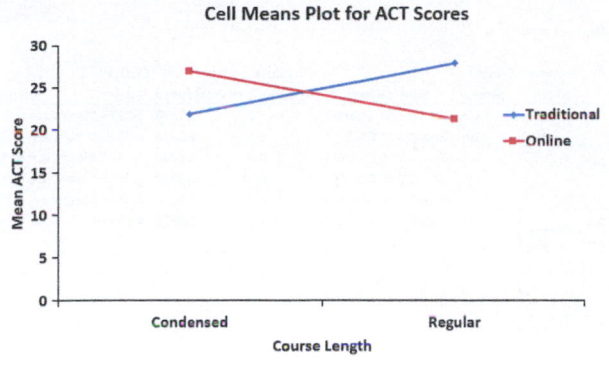
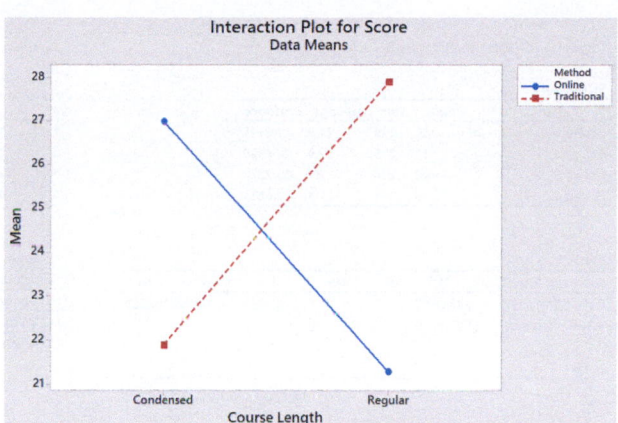

To verify the visual analysis provided by interpreting the cell means plot, you begin by testing whether there is a statistically significant interaction between factor A (length of course) and factor B (type of course). Using a 0.05 level of significance, you reject the null hypothesis because $F_{STAT} = 24.2569 > 4.1132$ or the p-value equals $0.0000 < 0.05$ (see Figure 11.15 shown below). Thus, the hypothesis test confirms the interaction evident in the cell means plot.

FIGURE 11.15

Excel, JMP, and Minitab two-way ANOVA results for the ACT scores

	A	B	C	D	E	F	G
1	ANOVA: Two-Factor With Replication						
2							
3	SUMMARY	Condensed	Regular	Total			
4	*traditional*						
5	Count	10	10	20			
6	Sum	219	279	498			
7	Average	21.9	27.9	24.9			
8	Variance	11.2111	20.9889	24.7263			
9							
10	*online*						
11	Count	10	10	20			
12	Sum	270	213	483			
13	Average	27	21.3	24.15			
14	Variance	16.2222	8.0111	20.0289			
15							
16	*Total*						
17	Count	20	20				
18	Sum	489	492				
19	Average	24.45	24.6				
20	Variance	19.8395	25.2000				
21							
22							
23	ANOVA						
24	*Source of Variation*	*SS*	*df*	*MS*	*F*	*P-value*	*F crit*
25	Sample	5.6250	1	5.6250	0.3987	0.5318	4.1132
26	Columns	0.2250	1	0.2250	0.0159	0.9002	4.1132
27	Interaction	342.2250	1	342.2250	24.2569	0.0000	4.1132
28	Within	507.9000	36	14.1083			
29							
30	Total	855.9750	39				
31						*Level of significance*	0.05

Effect Tests

Source	Nparm	DF	Sum of Squares	F Ratio	Prob > F
Method	1	1	5.62500	0.3987	0.5318
Length of Course	1	1	0.22500	0.0159	0.9002
Method*Length of Course	1	1	342.22500	24.2569	<.0001*

General Linear Model: Score versus Method, Course Length

Method

Factor coding   (-1, 0, +1)

Factor Information

Factor	Type	Levels	Values
Method	Fixed	2	Online, Traditional
Course Length	Fixed	2	Condensed, Regular

Analysis of Variance

Source	DF	Adj SS	Adj MS	F-Value	P-Value
Method	1	5.625	5.625	0.40	0.532
Course Length	1	0.225	0.225	0.02	0.900
Method*Course Length	1	342.225	342.225	24.26	0.000
Error	36	507.900	14.108		
Total	39	855.975			

The existence of this significant interaction effect complicates the interpretation of the hypothesis tests concerning the two main effects. You cannot directly conclude that there is no effect with respect to length of course and type of course, even though both have p-values > 0.05.

Given that the interaction is significant, you can reanalyze the data with the two factors collapsed into four groups of a single factor rather than a two-way ANOVA with two levels of each of the two factors. You reorganize the data as follows: Group 1 is traditional condensed, Group 2 is traditional regular, Group 3 is online condensed, and Group 4 is online regular. Figure 11.16 shows the results for these data, that are stored in ACT-OneWay.

▶(*continued*)

FIGURE 11.16
Excel one-way ANOVA and Tukey-Kramer results for the ACT scores

	A	B	C	D	E	F	G
1	One-Way ANOVA (ANOVA: Single Factor)						
2							
3	SUMMARY						
4	Groups	Count	Sum	Average	Variance		
5	Group 1	10	219	21.9	11.2111		
6	Group 2	10	279	27.9	20.9889		
7	Group 3	10	270	27	16.2222		
8	Group 4	10	213	21.3	8.0111		
9							
10							
11	ANOVA						
12	Source of Variation	SS	df	MS	F	P-value	F crit
13	Between Groups	348.0750	3	116.0250	8.2239	0.0003	2.8663
14	Within Groups	507.9000	36	14.1083			
15							
16	Total	855.9750	39				
17						Level of significance	0.05

	A	B	C	D	E	F	G	H	I
1	Tukey Kramer Multiple Comparisons								
2									
3		Sample	Sample			Absolute	Std. Error	Critical	
4	Group	Mean	Size		Comparison	Difference	of Difference	Range	Results
5	1: Group 1	21.9	10		Group 1 to Group 2	6	1.1878	4.5373	Means are different
6	2: Group 2	27.9	10		Group 1 to Group 3	5.1	1.1878	4.5373	Means are different
7	3: Group 3	27	10		Group 1 to Group 4	0.6	1.1878	4.5373	Means are not different
8	4: Group 4	21.3	10		Group 2 to Group 3	0.9	1.1878	4.5373	Means are not different
9					Group 2 to Group 4	6.6	1.1878	4.5373	Means are different
10	Other Data				Group 3 to Group 4	5.7	1.1878	4.5373	Means are different
11	Level of significance	0.05							
12	Numerator d.f.	4							
13	Denominator d.f.	36							
14	MSW	14.10833							
15	Q Statistic	3.82							

From Figure 11.16, because $F_{STAT} = 8.2239 > 2.8663$ or p-value $= 0.0003 < 0.05$, there is evidence of a significant difference in the four groups (traditional condensed, traditional regular, online condensed, and online regular). Using the Tukey-Kramer multiple comparisons procedure, traditional condensed is different from traditional regular and from online condensed. Traditional regular is also different from online regular, and online condensed is also different from online regular.

Therefore, whether condensing a course is a good idea depends on whether the course is offered in a traditional classroom or as an online distance learning course. To ensure the highest mean ACT scores, the company should use the traditional approach for courses that are given over a 30-day period but use the online approach for courses that are condensed into a 10-day period.

PROBLEMS FOR SECTION 11.2

LEARNING THE BASICS

11.15 Consider a two-factor factorial design with three levels for factor A, three levels for factor B, and four replicates in each of the nine cells.
a. How many degrees of freedom are there in determining the factor A variation and the factor B variation?
b. How many degrees of freedom are there in determining the interaction variation?
c. How many degrees of freedom are there in determining the random variation?
d. How many degrees of freedom are there in determining the total variation?

11.16 Assume that you are working with the results from Problem 11.15, and $SSA = 120$, $SSB = 110$, $SSE = 270$, and $SST = 540$.
a. What is $SSAB$?
b. What are MSA and MSB?
c. What is $MSAB$?
d. What is MSE?

11.17 Assume that you are working with the results from Problems 11.15 and 11.16.
a. What is the value of the F_{STAT} test statistic for the interaction effect?

b. What is the value of the F_{STAT} test statistic for the factor A effect?
c. What is the value of the F_{STAT} test statistic for the factor B effect?
d. Form the ANOVA summary table and fill in all values in the body of the table.

11.18 Given the results from Problems 11.15 through 11.17,
a. at the 0.05 level of significance, is there an effect due to factor A?
b. at the 0.05 level of significance, is there an effect due to factor B?
c. at the 0.05 level of significance, is there an interaction effect?

11.19 Given a two-way ANOVA with two levels for factor A, five levels for factor B, and four replicates in each of the 10 cells, with $SSA = 18$, $SSB = 64$, $SSE = 60$, and $SST = 150$,
a. form the ANOVA summary table and fill in all values in the body of the table.
b. at the 0.05 level of significance, is there an effect due to factor A?
c. at the 0.05 level of significance, is there an effect due to factor B?
d. at the 0.05 level of significance, is there an interaction effect?

11.20 Given a two-factor factorial experiment and the ANOVA summary table that follows, fill in all the missing results:

Source	Degrees of Freedom	Sum of Squares	Mean Square (Variance)	F
A	$r - 1 = 2$	$SSA = ?$	$MSA = 80$	$F_{STAT} = ?$
B	$c - 1 = ?$	$SSB = 220$	$MSB = ?$	$F_{STAT} = 11.0$
AB	$(r - 1)(c - 1) = 8$	$SSAB = ?$	$MSAB = 10$	$F_{STAT} = ?$
Error	$rc(n' - 1) = 30$	$SSE = ?$	$MSE = ?$	
Total	$n - 1 = ?$	$SST = ?$		

11.21 Given the results from Problem 11.20,
a. at the 0.05 level of significance, is there an effect due to factor A?
b. at the 0.05 level of significance, is there an effect due to factor B?
c. at the 0.05 level of significance, is there an interaction effect?

APPLYING THE CONCEPTS

11.22 An experiment was conducted to study the extrusion process of biodegradable packaging foam. Two of the factors considered for their effect on the unit density (mg/ml) were the die temperature (145°C vs. 155°C) and the die diameter (3 mm vs. 4 mm). The results are stored in PackagingFoam1 .

Source: Data extracted from W. Y. Koh, K. M. Eskridge, and M. A. Hanna, "Supersaturated Split-Plot Designs," *Journal of Quality Technology*, 45, January 2013, pp. 61–72.

At the 0.05 level of significance,
a. is there an interaction between die temperature and die diameter?
b. is there an effect due to die temperature?
c. is there an effect due to die diameter?
d. Plot the mean unit density for each die temperature for each die diameter.
e. What can you conclude about the effect of die temperature and die diameter on mean unit density?

11.23 Referring to Problem 11.22, the effect of die temperature and die diameter on the foam diameter was also measured and the results stored in PackagaingFoam2 .

At the 0.05 level of significance,
a. is there an interaction between die temperature and die diameter?
b. is there an effect due to die temperature?
c. is there an effect due to die diameter?
d. Plot the mean foam diameter for each die temperature and die diameter.
e. What conclusions can you reach concerning the importance of each of these two factors on the foam diameter?

✓SELF TEST **11.24** A plastic injection molding process is often used in manufacturing because of its ability to mold complicated shapes. An experiment was conducted on the manufacture of a television remote part, and the warpage (mm) of the part was measured and stored in TVRemote .

Source: Data extracted from M. A. Barghash and F. A. Alkaabneh, "Shrinkage and Warpage Detailed Analysis and Optimization for the Injection Molding Process Using Multistage Experimental Design," *Quality Engineering*, 26, 2014, pp. 319–334.

Two factors were to be considered, the filling time (1, 2, or 3 sec) and the mold temperature (60, 72.5, or 85°C).

At the 0.05 level of significance,
a. is there an interaction between filling time and mold temperature?
b. is there an effect due to filling time?

c. is there an effect due to mold temperature?
d. Plot the mean warpage for each filling time for each mold temperature.
e. If appropriate, use the Tukey multiple comparison procedure to determine which of the filling times and mold temperatures differ.
f. Discuss the results of (a) through (e).

11.25 A glass manufacturing company wanted to investigate the effect of breakoff pressure and stopper height on the percentage of breaking off chips. The results, stored in Glass1 , were as follows:

BREAK OFF PRESSURE	STOPPER HEIGHT Twenty	STOPPER HEIGHT Twenty-Five
Two	1.75	0.75
Two	1.00	0.50
Two	0.00	0.00
Two	1.00	0.25
Three	2.25	1.50
Three	1.50	1.25
Three	0.25	0.25
Three	0.75	0.75

Source: K. Kumar and S. Yadav, "Breakthrough Solution," *Six Sigma Forum Magazine*, November 2016, pp. 7–22.

At the 0.05 level of significance,
a. is there an interaction between the breakoff pressure and the stopper height?
b. is there an effect due to the breakoff pressure?
c. is there an effect due to the stopper height?
d. Plot the percentage breakoff for each breakoff pressure for each stopper height.
e. Discuss the results of (a) through (d).

11.26 A glass manufacturing company wanted to investigate the effect of zone 1 lower temperature (630 vs. 650) and zone 3 upper temperature (695 vs. 715) on the roller imprint of glass. The results stored in Glass2 were as follows:

ZONE 1 LOWER	ZONE 3 UPPER 695	ZONE 3 UPPER 715
630	50	100
630	25	0
630	50	25
630	125	75
650	25	75
650	25	25
650	50	0
650	20	125

Source: K. Kumar and S. Yadav, "Breakthrough Solution," *Six Sigma Forum Magazine*, November 2016, pp. 7–22.

At the 0.05 level of significance,
a. is there an interaction between zone 1 lower and zone 3 upper?
b. is there an effect due to zone 1 lower?
c. is there an effect due to zone 3 upper?
d. Plot the roller imprint for each level of zone 1 lower for level of zone 3 upper.
e. Discuss the results of (a) through (d).

11.3 The Randomized Block Design

Section 10.2 discusses how to use the paired t test to evaluate the difference between the means of two groups when you have repeated measurements or matched samples. The **randomized block design** evaluates differences among more than two groups that contain matched samples or repeated measures that have been placed in blocks. The **Section 11.3 online topic** discusses this method and illustrates its use.

11.4 Fixed Effects, Random Effects, and Mixed Effects Models

Sections 11.1 through 11.3 do not consider the distinction between how the levels of a factor were selected. The equation for the F test depends on whether the levels of a factor were specifically selected or randomly selected from a population. The **Section 11.4** online topic presents the appropriate F tests to use when the levels of a factor are either specifically selected or randomly selected from a population of levels.

▼USING **STATISTICS**
The Means to Find Differences at Arlingtons Revisited

In the Arlingtons scenario, you needed to determine whether there were differences in mobile electronics sales among four in-store locations as well as determine whether permitting mobile payments had an effect on those sales.

Using the one-way ANOVA, you determined that there was a difference in the mean sales for the four in-store locations. You then were able to conclude that the mean sales for the front location was higher than the current in-aisle or experimental end-cap or expert locations, that the kiosk location mean sales were higher than the in-aisle location, and that there was no evidence of a difference between the mean sales for the in-aisle and expert locations and the kiosk and expert locations. Using the two-way ANOVA, you determined that there was no interaction between in-store location and permitting mobile payment methods and that mean sales were higher when mobile payment methods were permitted than when such methods were not. In addition, you concluded that the population mean sales is different for the four in-store locations and reached these other conclusions:

- The front location is estimated to have higher mean sales than the other three locations.
- The kiosk location is estimated to have higher mean sales than the current in-aisle location.
- The expert location is estimated to have higher mean sales than the current in-aisle location.

Your next step as a member of the sales team might be to further investigate the differences among the sales locations as well as examine other factors that could influence mobile electronics sale.

▼SUMMARY

In this chapter, various statistical procedures were used to analyze the effect of one or two factors of interest. The assumptions required for using these procedures were discussed in detail. Remember that you need to critically investigate the validity of the assumptions underlying the hypothesis-testing procedures. Table 11.10 summarizes the topics covered in this chapter.

TABLE 11.10
Summary of Chapter 11

Type of Analysis (numerical variables)	Type of Design
Comparing more than two groups	One-way analysis of variance (Section 11.1)
	Two-way analysis of variance (Section 11.2)
	Randomized block design (online Section 11.3)

▼ REFERENCES

1. Berenson, M. L., D. M. Levine, and M. Goldstein. *Intermediate Statistical Methods and Applications: A Computer Package Approach*. Upper Saddle River, NJ: Prentice Hall, 1983.

2. Corder, G. W., and D. I. Foreman, *Nonparametric Statistics: A Step-by-Step Approach*. New York: Wiley, 2014.

3. Daniel, W. W. *Applied Nonparametric Statistics*, 2nd ed. Boston: PWS Kent, 1990.

4. Gitlow, H. S., R. Melnyck, and D. Levine. *A Guide to Six Sigma and Process Improvement for Practitioners and Students*, 2nd ed. Old Tappan, NJ: Pearson Education, 2015.

5. Hicks, C. R., and K. Turner. *Fundamental Concepts in the Design of Experiments*, 5th ed. New York: Oxford University Press, 1999.

6. Kutner, M., J. Neter, C. Nachtsheim, and W. Li. *Applied Linear Statistical Models*, 5th ed. New York: McGraw-Hill-Irwin, 2005.

7. Levine, D. *Statistics for Six Sigma Green Belts*. Upper Saddle River, NJ: Financial Times/Prentice Hall, 2006.

8. Montgomery, D. M. *Design and Analysis of Experiments*, 8th ed. New York: Wiley, 2013.

▼ KEY EQUATIONS

Total Variation in One-Way ANOVA

$$SST = \sum_{j=1}^{c} \sum_{i=1}^{n_j} \left(X_{ij} - \overline{\overline{X}} \right)^2 \tag{11.1}$$

Among-Group Variation in One-Way ANOVA

$$SSA = \sum_{j=1}^{c} n_j \left(\overline{X}_j - \overline{\overline{X}} \right)^2 \tag{11.2}$$

Within-Group Variation in One-Way ANOVA

$$SSW = \sum_{j=1}^{c} \sum_{i=1}^{n_j} \left(X_{ij} - \overline{X}_j \right)^2 \tag{11.3}$$

Mean Squares in One-Way ANOVA

$$MSA = \frac{SSA}{c - 1} \tag{11.4a}$$

$$MSW = \frac{SSW}{n - c} \tag{11.4b}$$

One-Way ANOVA F_{STAT} Test Statistic

$$F_{STAT} = \frac{MSA}{MSW} \tag{11.5}$$

Critical Range for the Tukey-Kramer Procedure

$$\text{Critical range} = Q_\alpha \sqrt{\frac{MSW}{2} \left(\frac{1}{n_j} + \frac{1}{n_{j'}} \right)} \tag{11.6}$$

Total Variation in Two-Way ANOVA

$$SST = \sum_{i=1}^{r} \sum_{j=1}^{c} \sum_{k=1}^{n'} \left(X_{ijk} - \overline{\overline{X}} \right)^2 \tag{11.7}$$

Factor A Variation in Two-Way ANOVA

$$SSA = cn' \sum_{i=1}^{r} \left(\overline{X}_{i..} - \overline{\overline{X}} \right)^2 \tag{11.8}$$

Factor B Variation in Two-Way ANOVA

$$SSB = rn' \sum_{j=1}^{c} \left(\overline{X}_{.j.} - \overline{\overline{X}} \right)^2 \tag{11.9}$$

Interaction Variation in Two-Way ANOVA

$$SSAB = n' \sum_{i=1}^{r} \sum_{j=1}^{c} \left(\overline{X}_{ij.} - \overline{X}_{i..} - \overline{X}_{.j.} + \overline{\overline{X}} \right)^2 \tag{11.10}$$

Random Variation in Two-Way ANOVA

$$SSE = \sum_{i=1}^{r} \sum_{j=1}^{c} \sum_{k=1}^{n'} (X_{ijk} - \overline{X}_{ij.})^2 \tag{11.11}$$

Mean Squares in Two-Way ANOVA

$$MSA = \frac{SSA}{r - 1} \tag{11.12a}$$

$$MSB = \frac{SSB}{c - 1} \tag{11.12b}$$

$$MSAB = \frac{SSAB}{(r - 1)(c - 1)} \tag{11.12c}$$

$$MSE = \frac{SSE}{rc(n' - 1)} \tag{11.12d}$$

F Test for Factor A Effect

$$F_{STAT} = \frac{MSA}{MSE} \tag{11.13}$$

F Test for Factor B Effect

$$F_{STAT} = \frac{MSB}{MSE} \tag{11.14}$$

F Test for Interaction Effect

$$F_{STAT} = \frac{MSAB}{MSE} \tag{11.15}$$

Critical Range for Factor A

$$\text{Critical range} = Q_\alpha \sqrt{\frac{MSE}{cn'}} \tag{11.16}$$

Critical Range for Factor B

$$\text{Critical range} = Q_\alpha \sqrt{\frac{MSE}{rn'}} \tag{11.17}$$

▼KEY TERMS

▼CHECKING YOUR UNDERSTANDING

11.27 In a one-way ANOVA, what is the difference between the among-groups variance MSA and the within-groups variance MSW?

11.28 What are the distinguishing features of the completely randomized design and two-factor factorial designs?

11.29 What are the assumptions of ANOVA?

11.30 Under what conditions should you use the one-way ANOVA F test to examine possible differences among the means of c independent populations?

11.31 When and how should you use multiple comparison procedures for evaluating pairwise combinations of the group means?

11.32 What is the difference between the one-way ANOVA F test and the Levene test?

11.33 Under what conditions should you use the two-way ANOVA F test to examine possible differences among the means of each factor in a factorial design?

11.34 What is meant by the concept of interaction in a two-factor factorial design?

11.35 How can you determine whether there is an interaction in the two-factor factorial design?

▼CHAPTER REVIEW PROBLEMS

11.36 You are the production manager at a parachute manufacturing company. Parachutes are woven in your factory using a synthetic fiber purchased from one of four different suppliers. The strength of these fibers is an important characteristic that ensures quality parachutes. You need to decide whether the synthetic fibers from each of your four suppliers result in parachutes of equal strength. Furthermore, to produce parachutes your factory uses two types of looms, the Jetta and the Turk. You need to determine if the parachutes woven on each type of loom are equally strong. You also want to know if any differences in the strength of the parachute can be attributed to the four suppliers are dependent on the type of loom used. You conduct an experiment in which five different parachutes from each supplier are manufactured on each of the two different looms and collect and store the data in ParachuteTwoWay .

At the 0.05 level of significance,
a. is there an interaction between supplier and loom?
b. is there an effect due to loom?
c. is there an effect due to supplier?
d. Plot the mean strength for each supplier for each loom.
e. If appropriate, use the Tukey procedure to determine differences between suppliers.
f. Repeat the analysis, using the Parachuteoneway file with suppliers as the only factor. Compare your results to those of (e).

11.37 Medical wires are used in the manufacture of cardiovascular devices. A study was conducted to determine the effect of several factors on the ratio of the load on a test specimen (YS) to the ultimate tensile strength (UTS). The file MedicalWires1 contains the study results, which examined factors including the machine (W95 vs. W96) and the reduction angle (narrow vs. wide).

Source: Data extracted from B. Nepal, S. Mohanty, and L. Kay, "Quality Improvement of Medical Wire Manufacturing Process," *Quality Engineering* 25, 2013, pp. 151–163.

At the 0.05 level of significance,
a. is there an interaction between machine type and reduction angle?
b. is there an effect due to machine type?
c. is there an effect due to reduction angle?
d. Plot the mean ratio of the load on a test specimen (YS) to the ultimate tensile strength (UTS) for each machine type for each reduction angle.
e. What can you conclude about the effects of machine type and reduction angle on the ratio of the load on a test specimen (YS) to the ultimate tensile strength (UTS)? Explain.
f. Repeat the analysis, using reduction angle as the only factor (see the MedicalWires2 file. Compare your results to those of (c) and (e).

11.38 An operations manager wants to examine the effect of air-jet pressure (in pounds per square inch [psi]) on the breaking strength of yarn. Three different levels of air-jet pressure are to be considered: 30 psi, 40 psi, and 50 psi. A random sample of 18 yarns are selected from the same batch, and the yarns are randomly assigned, 6 each, to the 3 levels of air-jet pressure. The breaking strength scores are stored in Yarn .

a. Is there evidence of a significant difference in the variances of the breaking strengths for the three air-jet pressures? (Use $\alpha = 0.05$.)
b. At the 0.05 level of significance, is there evidence of a difference among mean breaking strengths for the three air-jet pressures?
c. If appropriate, use the Tukey-Kramer procedure to determine which air-jet pressures significantly differ with respect to mean breaking strength. (Use $\alpha = 0.05$.)
d. What should the operations manager conclude?

11.39 Suppose that, when setting up the experiment in Problem 11.38, the operations manager is able to study the effect of side-to-side aspect in addition to air-jet pressure. Thus, instead of the one-factor completely randomized design in Problem 11.38, a two-factor factorial design was used, with the first factor, side-to-side aspect, having two levels (nozzle and opposite) and the second factor, air-jet pressure, having three levels (30 psi, 40 psi, and 50 psi). A sample of 18 yarns is randomly assigned, 3 to each of the 6 side-to-side aspect and pressure level combinations. The breaking-strength scores, stored in Yarn , are as follows:

SIDE-TO-SIDE ASPECT	AIR-JET PRESSURE		
	30 psi	40 psi	50 psi
Nozzle	25.5	24.8	23.2
Nozzle	24.9	23.7	23.7
Nozzle	26.1	24.4	22.7
Opposite	24.7	23.6	22.6
Opposite	24.2	23.3	22.8
Opposite	23.6	21.4	24.9

At the 0.05 level of significance,
a. is there an interaction between side-to-side aspect and air-jet pressure?
b. is there an effect due to side-to-side aspect?
c. is there an effect due to air-jet pressure?
d. Plot the mean yarn breaking strength for each level of side-to-side aspect for each level of air-jet pressure.
e. If appropriate, use the Tukey procedure to study differences among the air-jet pressures.
f. On the basis of the results of (a) through (e), what conclusions can you reach concerning yarn breaking strength? Discuss.
g. Compare your results in (a) through (f) with those from the completely randomized design in Problem 11.38. Discuss fully.

11.40 A hotel wanted to develop a new system for delivering room service breakfasts. In the current system, an order form is left on the bed in each room. If the customer wishes to receive a room service breakfast, he or she places the order form on the doorknob before 11 P.M. The current system requires customers to select a 15-minute interval for desired delivery time (6:30–6:45 A.M., 6:45–7:00 A.M., etc.). The new system is designed to allow the customer to request a specific delivery time. The hotel wants to measure the difference (in minutes) between the actual delivery time and the requested delivery time of room service orders for breakfast. (A negative time means that the order was delivered before the requested time. A positive time means that the order was delivered after the requested time.) The factors included were the menu choice (American or Continental) and the desired time period in which the order was to be delivered (Early Time Period [6:30–8:00 A.M.] or Late Time Period [8:00–9:30 A.M.]). Ten orders for each combination of menu choice and desired time period were studied on a particular day. The data, stored in Breakfast , are as follows:

TYPE OF BREAKFAST	DESIRED TIME	
	Early Time Period	Late Time Period
Continental	1.2	-2.5
Continental	2.1	3.0
Continental	3.3	-0.2
Continental	4.4	1.2
Continental	3.4	1.2
Continental	5.3	0.7
Continental	2.2	-1.3
Continental	1.0	0.2
Continental	5.4	-0.5
Continental	1.4	3.8
American	4.4	6.0
American	1.1	2.3
American	4.8	4.2
American	7.1	3.8
American	6.7	5.5
American	5.6	1.8
American	9.5	5.1
American	4.1	4.2
American	7.9	4.9
American	9.4	4.0

At the 0.05 level of significance,
a. is there an interaction between type of breakfast and desired time?
b. is there an effect due to type of breakfast?
c. is there an effect due to desired time?
d. Plot the mean delivery time difference for each desired time for each type of breakfast.
e. On the basis of the results of (a) through (d), what conclusions can you reach concerning delivery time difference? Discuss.

11.41 Refer to the room service experiment in Problem 11.40. Now suppose that the results are as shown below and stored in Breakfast2 . Repeat (a) through (e), using these data, and compare the results to those of (a) through (e) of Problem 11.40.

TYPE OF BREAKFAST	DESIRED TIME	
	Early	Late
Continental	1.2	-0.5
Continental	2.1	5.0
Continental	3.3	1.8
Continental	4.4	3.2
Continental	3.4	3.2

TYPE OF BREAKFAST	DESIRED TIME	
	Early	Late
Continental	5.3	2.7
Continental	2.2	0.7
Continental	1.0	2.2
Continental	5.4	1.5
Continental	1.4	5.8
American	4.4	6.0
American	1.1	2.3
American	4.8	4.2
American	7.1	3.8
American	6.7	5.5
American	5.6	1.8
American	9.5	5.1
American	4.1	4.2
American	7.9	4.9
American	9.4	4.0

11.42 A pet food company has the business objective of having the weight of a can of cat food come as close to the specified weight as possible. Realizing that the size of the pieces of meat contained in a can and the can fill height could impact the weight of a can, a team studying the weight of canned cat food wondered whether the current larger chunk size produced higher can weight and more variability. The team decided to study the effect on weight of a cutting size that was finer than the current size. In addition, the team slightly lowered the target for the sensing mechanism that determines the fill height in order to determine the effect of the fill height on can weight.

Twenty cans were filled for each of the four combinations of piece size (fine and current) and fill height (low and current). The contents of each can were weighed, and the amount above or below the label weight of 3 ounces was recorded as the variable coded weight. For example, a can containing 2.90 ounces was given a coded weight of -0.10. Results were stored in CatFood2 .

Analyze these data and write a report for presentation to the team. Indicate the importance of the piece size and the fill height on the weight of the canned cat food. Be sure to include a recommendation for the level of each factor that will come closest to meeting the target weight and the limitations of this experiment, along with recommendations for future experiments that might be undertaken.

CASES

CHAPTER 11

Managing Ashland MultiComm Services
PHASE 1

The computer operations department had a business objective of reducing the amount of time to fully update each subscriber's set of messages in a special secured email system. An experiment was conducted in which 24 subscribers were selected and three different messaging systems were used. Eight subscribers were assigned to each system, and the update times were measured. The results, stored in AMS11-1 , are presented in Table AMS11.1.

TABLE AMS11.1
Update Times (in seconds) for Three Different Systems

System 1	System 2	System 3
38.8	41.8	32.9
42.1	36.4	36.1
45.2	39.1	39.2
34.8	28.7	29.3
48.3	36.4	41.9
37.8	36.1	31.7
41.1	35.8	35.2
43.6	33.7	38.1

1. Analyze the data in Table AMS11.1 and write a report to the computer operations department that indicates your findings. Include an appendix in which you discuss the reason you selected a particular statistical test to compare the three email interfaces.

DO NOT CONTINUE UNTIL THE PHASE 1 EXERCISE HAS BEEN COMPLETED.

PHASE 2

After analyzing the data in Table AMS11.1, the computer operations department team decided to also study the effect of the connection media used (cable or fiber).

The team designed a study in which a total of 30 subscribers were chosen. The subscribers were randomly assigned to one of the three messaging systems so that there were five subscribers in each of the six combinations of the two factors—messaging system and media used. Measurements were taken on the updated time. Table AMS11.2 summarizes the results that are stored in AMS11-2 .

TABLE AMS11.2
Update Times (in seconds), Based on Messaging System and Media Used

MEDIA	INTERFACE		
	System 1	System 2	System 3
Cable	45.6	41.7	35.3
	49.0	42.8	37.7
	41.8	40.0	41.0
	35.6	39.6	28.7
	43.4	36.0	31.8
Fiber	44.1	37.9	43.3
	40.8	41.1	40.0
	46.9	35.8	43.1
	51.8	45.3	39.6
	48.5	40.2	33.2

2. Completely analyze these data and write a report to the team that indicates the importance of each of the two factors and/or the interaction between them on the update time. Include recommendations for future experiments to perform.

Digital Case

Apply your knowledge about ANOVA in this Digital Case, which continues the cereal-fill packaging dispute Digital Case from Chapters 7, 9, and 10.

After reviewing CCACC's latest document (see the Digital Case for Chapter 10 on page 386), Oxford Cereals has released **Second Analysis.pdf**, a press kit that Oxford Cereals has assembled to refute the claim that it is guilty of using selective data. Review the Oxford Cereals press kit and then answer the following questions.

1. Does Oxford Cereals have a legitimate argument? Why or why not?
2. Assuming that the samples Oxford Cereals has posted were randomly selected, perform the appropriate analysis to resolve the ongoing weight dispute.
3. What conclusions can you reach from your results? If you were called as an expert witness, would you support the claims of the CCACC or the claims of Oxford Cereals? Explain.

Sure Value Convenience Stores

You work in the corporate office for a nationwide convenience store franchise that operates nearly 10,000 stores. The per-store daily customer count (i.e., the mean number of customers in a store in one day) has been steady, at 900, for some time. To increase the customer count, the chain is considering cutting prices for coffee beverages. The question to be determined is how much to cut prices to increase the daily customer count without reducing the gross margin on coffee sales too much.

You decide to carry out an experiment in a sample of 24 stores where customer counts have been running almost exactly at the national average of 900. In 6 of the stores, the price of a small coffee will now be $0.59, in 6 stores the price of a small coffee will now be $0.69, in 6 stores, the price of a small coffee will now be $0.79, and in 6 stores, the price of a small coffee will now be $0.89. After four weeks of selling the coffee at the new price, the daily customer counts in the stores were recorded and stored in CoffeeSales .

1. Analyze the data and determine whether there is evidence of a difference in the daily customer count, based on the price of a small coffee.
2. If appropriate, determine which mean prices differ in daily customer counts.
3. What price do you recommend for a small coffee?

CardioGood Fitness

Return to the CardioGood Fitness case (stored in CardioGood Fitness) first presented on page 33.

1. Determine whether differences exist between customers based on the product purchased (TM195, TM498, TM798) in their age in years, education in years, annual household income ($), mean number of times the customer plans to use the treadmill each week, and mean number of miles the customer expects to walk or run each week.
2. Write a report to be presented to the management of Cardio-Good Fitness detailing your findings.

More Descriptive Choices Follow-Up

Follow up the Using Statistics scenario "More Descriptive Choices, Revisited" on page 159 by determining whether there is a difference between the small, mid-cap, and large market cap funds in the one-year return percentages, five-year return percentages, and ten-year return percentages (stored in Retirement Funds).

Clear Mountain State Student Survey

The Student News Service at Clear Mountain State University (CMSU) has decided to gather data about the undergraduate students who attend CMSU. They create and distribute a survey of 14 questions and receive responses from 111 undergraduates (stored in StudentSurvey).

1. At the 0.05 level of significance, is there evidence of a difference based on academic major in expected starting salary, number of social networking sites registered for, age, spending on textbooks and supplies, text messages sent in a week, and the wealth needed to feel rich?
2. At the 0.05 level of significance, is there evidence of a difference based on graduate school intention in grade point average, expected starting salary, number of social networking sites registered for, age, spending on textbooks and supplies, text messages sent in a week, and the wealth needed to feel rich?

▾ **EXCEL** GUIDE

EG11.1 The COMPLETELY RANDOMIZED DESIGN: ONE-WAY ANOVA

Analyzing Variation in One-Way ANOVA

Key Technique Use the Section EG2.5 instructions to construct scatter plots using stacked data. If necessary, change the levels of the factor to consecutive integers beginning with 1, as was done for the Figure 11.4 in-store location sales experiment data on page 404.

F Test for Differences Among More Than Two Means

Key Technique Use the **DEVSQ** (*cell range of data of all groups*) function to compute *SST*.

Use an expression in the form **SST – DEVSQ** (*group 1 data cell range*) – **DEVSQ** (*group 2 data cell range*)... – **DEVSQ** (*group n data cell range*) to compute *SSA*.

Example Perform the Figure 11.6 one-way ANOVA for the in-store location sales experiment on page 406.

PHStat Use One-Way ANOVA.

For the example, open to the **DATA worksheet** of the **Mobile Electronics workbook**. Select **PHStat → Multiple-Sample Tests → One-Way ANOVA**. In the procedure's dialog box (shown below):

1. Enter **0.05** as the **Level of Significance**.
2. Enter **A1:D6** as the **Group Data Cell Range**.
3. Check **First cells contain label**.
4. Enter a **Title**, clear the **Tukey-Kramer Procedure** check box, and click **OK**.

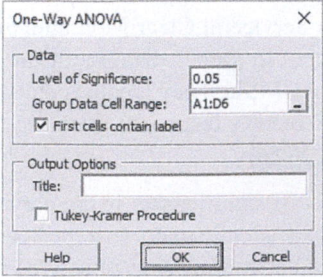

In addition to the worksheet shown in Figure 11.6, this procedure creates an **ASFData worksheet** to hold the data used for the test. See the following *Workbook* section for a complete description of this worksheet.

Workbook Use the **COMPUTE worksheet** of the **One-Way ANOVA workbook** as a template.

The COMPUTE worksheet uses the ASFDATA worksheet that already contains the data for the example. Modifying the COMPUTE worksheet for other problems involves multiple steps and is more complex than template modifications discussed in earlier chapters.

To modify the One-Way ANOVA workbook for other problems, first paste the data for the new problem into the ASF-Data worksheet, overwriting the in-store locations sales data. Then, in the COMPUTE worksheet (shown in Figure 11.6):

1. Edit the *SST* formula **=DEVSQ(ASFData!A1:D6)** in cell B16 to use the cell range of the new data just pasted into the ASFData worksheet.
2. Edit the cell B13 *SSA* formula so there are as many **DEVSQ**(*group column cell range*) terms as there are groups.
3. Change the level of significance in cell G17, if necessary.
4. If the problem contains three groups, select **row 8**, right-click, and select **Delete** from the shortcut menu.

   If the problem contains more than four groups, select **row 8**, right-click, and click **Insert** from the shortcut menu. Repeat this step as many times as necessary.
5. If you inserted new rows, enter (not copy) the formulas for those rows, using the formulas in row 7 as models.
6. Adjust table formatting as necessary.

To see the arithmetic formulas that the COMPUTE worksheet uses, not shown in Figure 11.6, open to the COMPUTE_FORMULAS worksheet.

Analysis ToolPak Use **Anova: Single Factor**.

For the example, open to the **DATA worksheet** of the **Mobile Electronics workbook** and:

1. Select **Data → Data Analysis**.
2. In the Data Analysis dialog box, select **Anova: Single Factor** from the **Analysis Tools** list and then click **OK**.

In the procedure's dialog box (shown on page 433):

3. Enter **A1:D6** as the **Input Range**.
4. Click **Columns**, check **Labels in First Row**, and enter **0.05** as **Alpha**.
5. Click **New Worksheet Ply**.
6. Click **OK**.

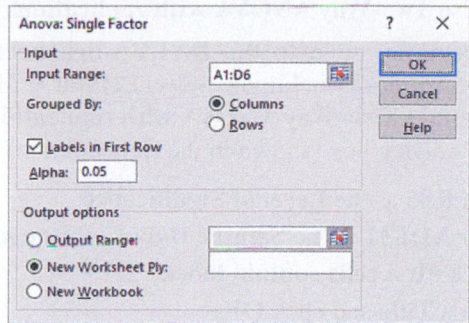

The Analysis ToolPak creates a worksheet that does not use formulas but is similar in layout to the Figure 11.6 worksheet on page 406.

Levene Test for Homogeneity of Variance

Key Technique Use the techniques for performing a one-way ANOVA.

Example Perform the Figure 11.7 Levene test for the in-store location sales experiment on page 408.

PHStat Use **Levene Test**.

For the example, open to the **DATA worksheet** of the **Mobile Electronics workbook**. Select **PHStat → Multiple-Sample Tests → Levene Test**. In the procedure's dialog box (shown below):

1. Enter **0.05** as the **Level of Significance**.
2. Enter **A1:D6** as the **Sample Data Cell Range**.
3. Check **First cells contain label**.
4. Enter a **Title** and click **OK**.

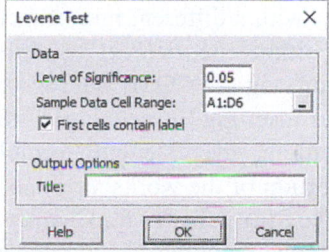

The procedure creates a worksheet that performs the Table 11.4 absolute differences computations (see page 408) as well as the Figure 11.7 worksheet. See the following *Workbook* section for a description of these worksheets.

Workbook Use the **COMPUTE worksheet** of the **Levene workbook** as a template.

The COMPUTE worksheet and the supporting AbsDiffs and DATA worksheets already contain the data for the example.

For other problems in which the absolute differences are already known, paste the absolute differences into the AbsDiffs worksheet. Otherwise, paste the problem data into the DATA worksheet, add formulas to compute the median for each group, and adjust the AbsDiffs worksheet as necessary. For example, for the in-store location sales experiment,

the following steps 1 through 7 were done with the workbook open to the DATA worksheet:

1. Enter the label **Medians** in **cellA7**, the first empty cell in column A.
2. Enter the formula **=MEDIAN(A2:A6)** in **cellA8**. (Cell range A2:A6 contains the data for the first group, in-aisle.)
3. Copy the cell A8 formula across through column D.
4. Open to the **AbsDiffs worksheet**.

In the AbsDiffs worksheet:

5. Enter row 1 column headings **AbsDiff1**, **AbsDiff2**, **AbsDiff3**, and **AbsDiff4** in columns A through D.
6. Enter the formula **=ABS(DATA!A2 − DATA!A8)** in cell A2. Copy this formula down through row 6.
7. Copy the formulas now in cell range A2:A6 across through column D. Absolute differences now appear in the cell range A2:D6.

Analysis ToolPak Use **Anova: Single Factor** with absolute difference data to perform the Levene test. If the absolute differences have not already been calculated, first use the preceding *Workbook* instructions to compute those values.

Multiple Comparisons: The Tukey-Kramer Procedure

Key Technique Use arithmetic formulas to compute the absolute mean differences and use the **IF** function to compare pairs of means.

Example Perform the Figure 11.8 Tukey-Kramer procedure for the in-store location sales experiment shown on page 408.

PHStat Use **One-Way ANOVA** with the **Tukey-Kramer procedure** option.

For the example, use the Section EG11.1 "*F* Test…" PHStat instructions, checking, not clearing, the **Tukey-Kramer Procedure** check box in step 4.

With this option, the procedure creates a second worksheet that is identical to the Figure 11.8 worksheet on page 410, other than missing a proper *Q* statistic value. Use Table E.7 to look up and enter the missing Studentized range *Q* statistic (4.05, for the example) for the level of significance and the numerator and denominator degrees of freedom that are given in the worksheet. (The second worksheet that the option creates will be identical to one of the "TK" worksheets discussed in the following *Workbook* instructions.)

Workbook Use the appropriate **"TK" worksheet** in the **One-Way ANOVA workbook** and manually look up and enter the appropriate Studentized range *Q* statistic value.

For the example, the **TK4 worksheet**, shown in Figure 11.8 on page 410, already has the appropriate *Q* statistic value (4.05) entered in cell B15. To see the arithmetic formulas that the TK4 worksheet uses, not shown in Figure 11.8, open to the TK4_FORMULAS worksheet.

For other problems, first modify the COMPUTE worksheet using the Section EG11.1 *Workbook* "*F* Test ..." instructions. Then, open to the appropriate "TK" worksheet: TK3 (three groups), TK4 (four groups), TK5 (five groups), TK6 (six groups), or TK7 (seven groups). Use Table E.7 to look up the proper value of the Studentized range *Q* statistic for the level of significance and the numerator and denominator degrees of freedom for the problem.

When using the TK5, TK6, or TK7 worksheets, you must also enter the name, sample mean, and sample size for the fifth and subsequent, if applicable, groups.

Analysis ToolPak Modify the previous instructions to perform the Tukey-Kramer procedure in conjunction with using the **Anova: Single Factor** procedure. Transfer selected values from the Analysis ToolPak results worksheet to one of the TK worksheets in the **One-Way ANOVA workbook**.

For the example:

1. Use the Analysis ToolPak "*F* Test ..." instructions on page 432 to create a worksheet that contains ANOVA results for the in-store locations experiment.
2. Record the name, **sample size** (in the **Count** column), and **sample mean** (in the **Average** column) of each group. Also record the *MSW* value, found in the cell that is the intersection of the **MS** column and **Within Groups** row, and the **denominator degrees of freedom**, found in the cell that is the intersection of the **df** column and **Within Groups** row.
3. Open to the **TK4 worksheet** of the **One-Way ANOVA workbook**.

In the TK4 worksheet:

4. Overwrite the formulas in cell range **A5:C8** by entering the name, sample mean, and sample size of each group into that range.
5. Enter **0.05** as the **Level of significance** in cell **B11**.
6. Enter **4** as the **Numerator d.f.** (equal to the number of groups) in cell **B12**.
7. Enter **16** as the **Denominator d.f** in cell **B13**.
8. Enter **0.3044** as the **MSW** in cell **B14**.
9. Enter **4.05** as the **Q Statistic** in cell **B15**. (Use Table E.7 to look up the Studentized range *Q* statistic.)

EG11.2 The FACTORIAL DESIGN: TWO-WAY ANOVA

Key Technique Use the **DEVSQ** function to compute *SSA*, *SSB*, *SSAB*, *SSE*, and *SST*.

Example Perform the Figure 11.10 two-way ANOVA for the in-store location sales and mobile payment experiment on page 419.

PHStat Use **Two-Way ANOVA with replication**.

For the example, open to the **DATA worksheet** of the **Mobile Electronics2 workbook**. Select **PHStat → Multiple-Sample Tests → Two-Way ANOVA with replication**. In the procedure's dialog box (shown in the right column):

1. Enter **0.05** as the **Level of Significance**.
2. Enter **A1:E11** as the **Sample Data Cell Range**.
3. Check **First cells contain label**.
4. Enter a **Title** and click **OK**.

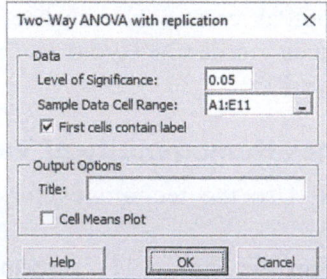

This procedure requires that the labels that identify factor *A* appear stacked in column A, followed by columns for factor *B*.

Workbook Use the **COMPUTE worksheet** of the **Two-Way ANOVA workbook** as a model.

For the example, the COMPUTE worksheet uses the ATFDATA worksheet that already contains the data to perform the test for the example.

For other problems in which *r* = 2 and *c* = 4, paste the data for the problem into the ATFData worksheet, overwriting the in-store location and mobile payments data and then adjust the factor level headings in the COMPUTE worksheet.

For problems with a different mix of factors and levels, consider using either the *PHStat* or *Analysis ToolPak* instructions. Modifying the COMPUTE worksheet for such problems requires inserting (or deleting) both rows and columns as well as editing several lengthy formulas found in the ANOVA table portion of the worksheet, operations that can be error-prone. The SHORT TAKES for Chapter 11 includes the instructions for these operations, should you choose to make such manual modifications.

To see the arithmetic formulas that the COMPUTE worksheet uses, not shown in Figure 11.10, open to the COMPUTE_FORMULAS worksheet.

Analysis ToolPak Use **Anova: Two-Factor With Replication**.

For the example, open to the **DATA worksheet** of the **Mobile Electronics2 workbook** and:

1. Select **Data → Data Analysis**.
2. In the Data Analysis dialog box, select **Anova: Two-Factor With Replication** from the **Analysis Tools** list and then click **OK**.

In the procedure's dialog box (shown below):

3. Enter **A1:E11** as the **Input Range**.
4. Enter **5** as the **Rows per sample**.
5. Enter **0.05** as **Alpha**.
6. Click **New Worksheet Ply**.
7. Click **OK**.

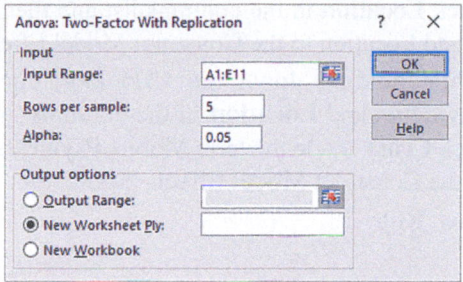

This procedure requires that the labels that identify factor *A* appear stacked in column A, followed by columns for factor *B*. The Analysis ToolPak creates a worksheet that does not use formulas but is similar in layout to the Figure 11.10 worksheet.

Visualizing Interaction Effects: The Cell Means Plot

Key Technique Create a worksheet that contains the means for each factor *B* level, by factor *A* level.

Example Construct the Figure 11.13 cell means plot for mobile electronics sales based on mobile payments permitted and in-store location on page 421.

PHStat Modify the *PHStat* instructions for the two-way ANOVA. In step 4, check **Cell Means Plot** before clicking **OK**.

Analysis ToolPak Use the *Workbook* instructions.

Workbook Create a cell means plot from a two-way ANOVA COMPUTE worksheet.

For the example, open to the **COMPUTE worksheet** of the **Two-Way ANOVA** workbook and:

1. Insert a new worksheet.
2. Copy cell range **B3:E3** of the COMPUTE worksheet (the factor *B* level names) to cell **B1** of the new worksheet, using the Paste Special **Values** option.
3. Copy the cell range **B7:E7** of the COMPUTE worksheet (the AVERAGE row for the factor *A* No level) and paste to cell **B2** of the new worksheet, using the Paste Special **Values** option.
4. Copy the cell range **B13:E13** of the COMPUTE worksheet (the AVERAGE row for the factor *A* Yes level) and paste to cell **B3** of a new worksheet, using the Paste Special **Values** option.
5. Enter **No** in cell **B3** and **Yes** in cell **A3** of the new worksheet as labels for the factor *A* levels.
6. Select the cell range **A1:E3**.
7. Select **Insert → Line** and select the **Line with Markers** gallery item.
8. Relocate the chart to a chart sheet, add axis titles, and modify the chart title by using the instructions in Appendix Section B.5.

For other problems, insert a new worksheet and first copy and paste the factor *B* level names to row 1 of the new worksheet and then copy and use Paste Special to transfer the values in the **Average** rows data for each factor *B* level to the new worksheet. (See Appendix B to learn more about the Paste Special command.)

CHAPTER 11

▾JMP GUIDE

JG11.1 The COMPLETELY RANDOMIZED DESIGN: ONE-WAY ANOVA

Analyzing Variation in One-Way ANOVA

Use the Section JG2.5 instructions to construct a scatter plot using stacked data.

For example, to construct the Figure 11.4 plot on page 404, open to the **Mobile Electronics Stacked data table**. Select **Graph → Graph Builder**. In that procedure's window (shown on page 112):

1. Drag **Location** from the columns list and drop it in **X area**.
2. Drag **Sales** from the columns list and drop it in **Y area**.
3. Double-click the chart title and edit the title, as necessary.
4. Click **Done**.

JMP displays the scatter plot in a new window. JMP uses jitter (small horizontal displacements) to minimize the overlap of points for each location. Optionally, use the Section B.5 instructions to change the font and type characteristics of chart labels.

F Test for Differences Among More Than Two Means

Use **Fit Y by X**.

For example, to perform the Figure 11.6 one-way ANOVA for the in-store location sales experiment on page 406, open to the **Mobile Electronics Stacked data table**. Select **Analyze→Fit Y by X** and in the Fit Y by X - Contextual dialog box:

1. Click **Sales** in the columns list and then click **Y, Response** to add Sales to the Y, Response box.
2. Click **Location** in the columns list and then click **X, Factor** to add Location to the Y, Factor box.
3. Click **OK**.

JMP displays a plot of the sales for the four locations in a new window:

4. Click the **Oneway Analysis of Sales by Location red triangle** and select **Means/Anova** from its menu.

JMP adds tabular ANOVA summaries to the new window. The *F* test results appear in the Analysis of Variance (second) table in the window.

Levene Test for Homogeneity of Variance

Use the previous *F* test instructions, but also select **Unequal Variances** from the Oneway Analysis of Sales by Location red triangle menu. Results appear under the heading Tests that the Variances are Equal, in the second row of the second table, labeled BrownForsythe. Note that the row labeled Levene is an alternate form of the Levene test that uses absolute differences from the means and not absolute differences from the medians.

Multiple Comparisons: The Tukey-Kramer Procedure

Use the previous *F* test instructions, but also select **Compare Means→All Pairs, Tukey HSD** from the Oneway Analysis of Sales by Location red triangle menu. Results appear under the heading Means Comparisons and Comparisons for all pairs using Tukey-Kramer HSD in the Connecting Letters Report.

JG11.2   The FACTORIAL DESIGN: TWO-WAY ANOVA

Use **Fit Model**.

For example, to perform the Figure 11.10 two-way ANOVA for the in-store location sales and mobile payment experiment on page 419, open to the **Mobile Electronics2 data**

table. Select **Analyze → Fit Model** and in the Fit Model dialog box (shown below):

1. Click **Sales** in the columns list and then click **Y** to add Sales to the Y box.
2. Click **Mobile Payments** in the columns list and then click **Add** to add Mobile Payments to the Construct Model Effects box.
3. Click **Location** in the columns list and then click **Add** to add Location to the Construct Model Effects box.
4. While holding down the **Ctrl key**, click **Mobile Payments** and **Location** in the columns list and then click **Cross** to add the term Mobile Payments*Location to the Construct Model Effects box.
5. Click **Run**.

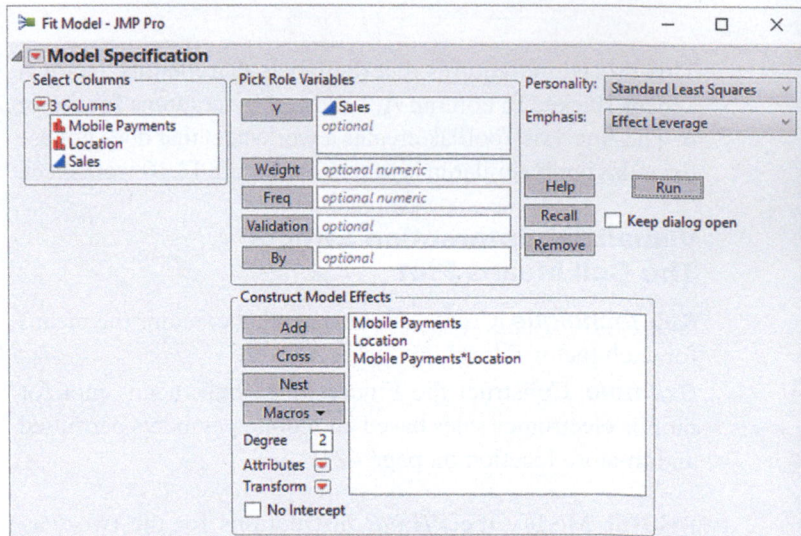

JMP displays results in a new window. ANOVA results appear under the heading Response Sales and Whole Model in the Effect Tests table.

Visualizing Interaction Effects: The Cell Means Plot

Use the previous instructions to construct a plot equivalent to the cell means plot. Equivalent plots appear under the heading Mobile Payments and Leverage Plot (and, also, Location and Leverage Plot).

▼ **MINITAB** GUIDE

MG11.1 The COMPLETELY RANDOMIZED DESIGN: ONE-WAY ANOVA

Analyzing Variation in One-Way ANOVA

Use **Main Effects Plot** (requires stacked data).

For example, to construct the Figure 11.4 main effects plot for the in-store location sales experiment on page 404, open to the **Mobile Electronics Stacked** worksheet. Select **Stat → ANOVA → Main Effects Plot**. In the Main Effects Plot dialog box (shown below):

1. Double-click **C2 Sales** in the variables list to add **Sales** to the **Responses** box and press **Tab**.
2. Double-click **C1 Location** in the variables list to add **Location** to the **Factors** box.
3. Click **OK**.

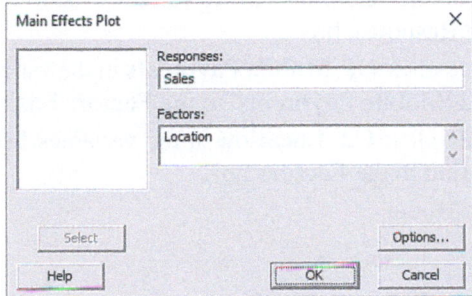

When the Factors box contains a text variable such as Location in the example, Minitab sorts the factor levels alphabetically.

F Test for Differences Among More Than Two Means

Use **One-Way**.

For example, to perform the Figure 11.6 one-way ANOVA for the in-store location sales experiment on page 406, open to the **Mobile Electronics worksheet**. Select **Stat → ANOVA → One-Way**. In the One-Way Analysis of Variance dialog box (shown in the right column):

1. Select **Response data are in a separate column for each factor level** from the pull-down list and press **Tab**.
2. Enter **C1-C4** in the **Responses** box.
3. Click **Options**.

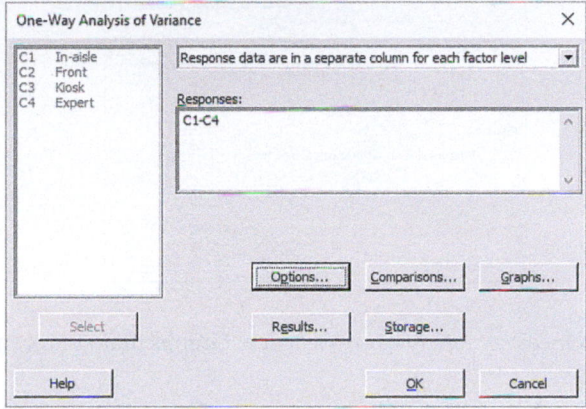

In the One-Way Analysis of Variance: Options dialog box (shown below):

4. Check **Assume equal variances**.
5. Enter 95 in the **Confidence level** box.
6. Select **Upper bound** from the **Type of confidence interval** pull-down list.
7. Click **OK**.

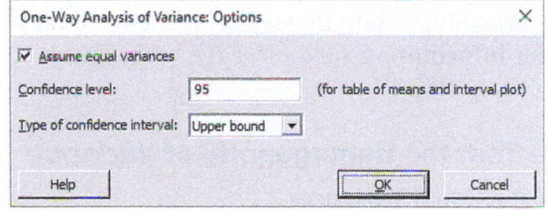

8. Back in the original dialog box, click **Comparisons**.

In the One-Way Analysis of Variance: Comparisons dialog box (shown on page 438):

9. Enter **5** in the **Error rate for comparisons** box. (An error rate of 5 produces comparisons with an overall confidence level of 95%.)
10. Clear all check boxes and then click **OK**.
11. Back in the original dialog box, click **Graphs**.

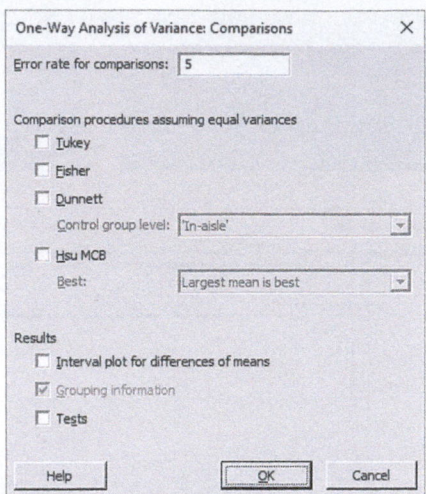

In the One-Way Analysis of Variance: Graphs dialog box (not shown):

12. Check **Boxplot of data**.
13. Click **OK**.
14. Back in the original dialog box, click **OK**.

When using stacked data, select **Response data are in one column for all factor levels** in step 1.

Multiple Comparisons: The Tukey-Kramer Procedure

Use the previous set of instructions to perform the Tukey-Kramer procedure, but in step 10, check **Tukey** and **Grouping information** (and clear the other check boxes) before clicking **OK**.

Levene Test for Homogeneity of Variance

Use **Test for Equal Variances**.

For example, to perform the Figure 11.7 Levene test for the in-store location sales experiment on page 408, open to the **Mobile Electronics Stacked** worksheet, which contains the data of the Mobile Electronics worksheet in stacked order. Select **Stat → ANOVA → Test for Equal Variances**. In the Test for Equal Variances dialog box (shown below):

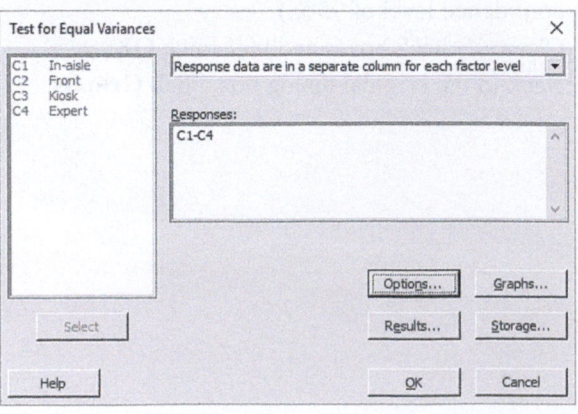

1. Select **Response data are in a separate column for each factor level** from the pull-down list and press **Tab**.
2. Enter **C1-C4** in the **Responses** box.
3. Click **Options**.
4. In the Test for Equal Variables: Options dilaog box (not shown), enter **95.0** in the **Confidence level** box and click **OK**.
5. Back in the original dialog box, click **OK**.

The Levene test results shown in Figure 11.7 on page 408 appear last in the results this procedure creates.

MG11.2 The FACTORIAL DESIGN: TWO-WAY ANOVA

Use **Two-Way**.

For example, to perform the Figure 11.10 two-way ANOVA for the in-store location sales and mobile payment experiment on page 419, open to the **Mobile Electronics2 worksheet**. Select **Stat → ANOVA → General Linear Model → Fit General Linear Model**. In the General Linear Model dialog box (shown below):

1. Double-click **C3 Sales** in the variables list to add **Sales** to the **Response** box.
2. Double-click **C1 Mobile Payments** in the variables list to add **'Mobile Payments'** to the **Factors** box.
3. Double-click **C2 Location** in the variables list to add **Location** to the **Factors** box.
4. Click **Model**.

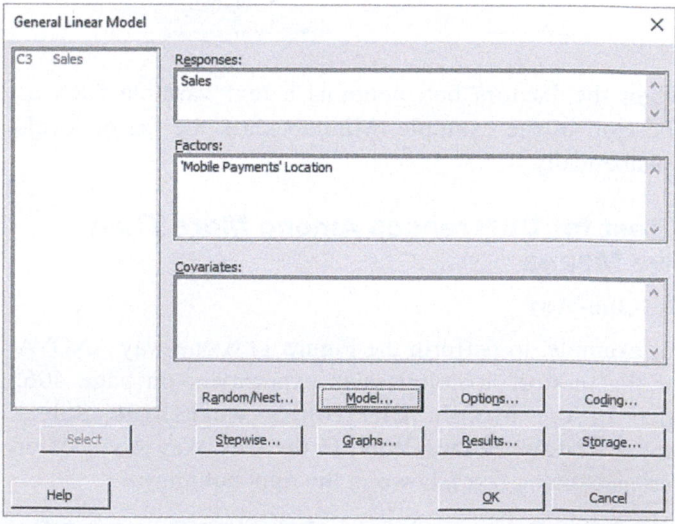

In the General Linear Model: Model dialog box (not shown):

5. Select **'Mobile Payments'** and **Location** in the **Factors and covariates** box and then click **Add**. (Minitab adds the term 'Mobile Payments'*Location to the **Terms in the model** box.)
6. Click **OK**.

7. Back in the original dialog box, click **Options**.

8. In the General Linear Model: Options dialog box (not shown), enter **95** in the **Confidence level for all intervals** box and then click **OK**.

9. Back in the original dialog box, click **OK**.

Visualizing Interaction Effects: The Cell Means Plot

Use **Interactions Plot**. This procedure requires stacked data.

For example, to construct the Figure 11.13 cell means plot for mobile electronic sales based on mobile payments permitted and in-store location shown on page 421, open to the **Mobile Electronics2 worksheet**. Select **Stat → ANOVA → Interaction Plot**. In the Interaction Plot dialog box (shown in the right column):

1. Double-click **C3 Sales** in the variables list to add **Sales** to the **Responses** box and press **Tab**.

2. Enter **C1-C2** to the **Factors** box.

3. Clear **Display full interaction plot matrix**.

4. Click **OK**.

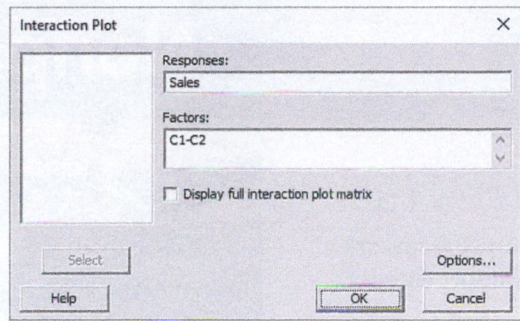

12

Chi-Square and Nonparametric Tests

OBJECTIVES

- Understand the chi-square test for contingency tables
- Understand application of the Marascuilo procedure
- Use nonparametric tests

▼USING **STATISTICS**
Avoiding Guesswork About Resort Guests

You are the manager of T.C. Resort Properties, a collection of five upscale hotels located on two tropical islands. Guests who are satisfied with the quality of services during their stay are more likely to return on a future vacation and to recommend the hotel to friends and relatives. You have defined the business objective as improving the percentage of guests who choose to return to the hotels later. To assess the quality of services being provided by your hotels, your staff encourages guests to complete a satisfaction survey when they check out or via email after they check out.

You need to analyze the data from these surveys to determine the overall satisfaction with the services provided, the likelihood that the guests will return to the hotel, and the reasons some guests indicate that they will not return. For example, on one island, T.C. Resort Properties operates the Beachcomber and Windsurfer hotels. Is the perceived quality at the Beachcomber Hotel the same as at the Windsurfer Hotel? If there is a difference, how can you use this information to improve the overall quality of service at T.C. Resort Properties? Furthermore, if guests indicate that they are not planning to return, what are the most common reasons cited for this decision? Are the reasons cited unique to a certain hotel or common to all hotels operated by T.C. Resort Properties?

Τhe preceding three chapters discuss hypothesis-testing procedures to analyze both numerical and categorical data. This chapter extends hypothesis testing to analyze differences between population *proportions* based on two or more samples and to test the hypothesis of independence in the joint responses to two categorical variables. The chapter concludes with nonparametric tests as alternatives to several Chapter 10 and 11 hypothesis tests.

12.1 Chi-Square Test for the Difference Between Two Proportions

Section 10.3 describes the Z test for the difference between two proportions. Differences between two proportions can also be examined using a different hypothesis test. This second test uses a test statistic whose sampling distribution is approximated by a chi-square (χ^2) distribution, a right-skewed distribution whose shape depends solely on the number of degrees of freedom. The results of this χ^2 test are equivalent to those of the Z test that Section 10.3 describes.

To compare the counts of categorical responses between two independent groups, you develop a **two-way contingency table** to display the frequency of occurrence of items of interest and items not of interest for each group. (Contingency tables were first discussed in Section 2.1, and, in Chapter 4, contingency tables were used to define and study probability.)

To illustrate a contingency table, return to the T.C. Resort Properties scenario. On one of the islands, T.C. Resort Properties has two hotels (the Beachcomber and the Windsurfer). You collect data from customer satisfaction surveys and focus on the responses to the single question "Are you likely to choose this hotel again?" You organize the results of the survey and determine that 163 of 227 guests at the Beachcomber responded yes to "Are you likely to choose this hotel again?" and 154 of 262 guests at the Windsurfer responded yes to "Are you likely to choose this hotel again?" You want to analyze the results to determine whether, at the 0.05 level of significance, there is evidence of a significant difference in guest satisfaction (as measured by likelihood to return to the hotel) between the two hotels.

The Table 12.1 contingency table, which has two rows and two columns, is called a **2 × 2 contingency table**. Table cells contain the frequency for each row-and-column combination.

TABLE 12.1

Layout of a 2 × 2 Contingency Table

	COLUMN VARIABLE		
ROW VARIABLE	**Group 1**	**Group 2**	**Totals**
Items of interest	X_1	X_2	X
Items not of interest	$n_1 - X_1$	$n_2 - X_2$	$n - X$
Totals	n_1	n_2	n

where

X_1 = number of items of interest in group 1

X_2 = number of items of interest in group 2

$n_1 - X_1$ = number of items that are not of interest in group 1

$n_2 - X_2$ = number of items that are not of interest in group 2

$X = X_1 + X_2$, the total number of items of interest

$n - X = (n_1 - X_1) + (n_2 - X_2)$, the total number of items that are not of interest

n_1 = sample size in group 1

n_2 = sample size in group 2

$n = n_1 + n_2$ = total sample size

Table 12.2 is the contingency table for the hotel guest satisfaction study. The contingency table has two rows, indicating whether the guests would return to the hotel or would not return to the hotel, and two columns, one for each hotel. The cells in the table indicate the frequency of each row-and-column combination. The row totals indicate the number of guests who would return and would not return to the hotels. The column totals are the sample sizes for each hotel location.

TABLE 12.2

2 × 2 Contingency Table for the Hotel Guest Satisfaction Survey

| | **HOTEL** | | |
CHOOSE HOTEL AGAIN?	**Beachcomber**	**Windsurfer**	**Total**
Yes	163	154	317
No	64	108	172
Total	227	262	489

student TIP

Do not confuse this use of the Greek letter pi, π, to represent the population proportion with the constant that uses the same letter to represent the ratio of the circumference to a diameter of a circle— approximately 3.14159.

To test whether the population proportion of guests who would return to the Beachcomber, π_1, is equal to the population proportion of guests who would return to the Windsurfer, π_2, you can use the **chi-square (χ^2) test for the difference between two proportions**. To test the null hypothesis that there is no difference between the two population proportions:

$$H_0: \pi_1 = \pi_2$$

against the alternative that the two population proportions are not the same:

$$H_1: \pi_1 \neq \pi_2$$

you use the χ^2_{STAT} test statistic, shown in Equation (12.1). The sampling distribution of this test statistic follows the **chi-square (χ^2) distribution**, which is right-skewed and whose lowest value is 0, unlike the normal and t distributions discussed in earlier chapters. (Table E.4 contains the cumulative probabilities for the chi-square distribution.)

student TIP

You are computing the squared difference between f_o and f_e. Therefore, unlike the Z_{STAT} and t_{STAT} test statistics, the χ^2_{STAT} test statistic can never be negative.

χ^2 TEST FOR THE DIFFERENCE BETWEEN TWO PROPORTIONS

The χ^2_{STAT} test statistic is equal to the squared difference between the observed and expected frequencies, divided by the expected frequency in each cell of the table, summed over all cells of the table.

$$\chi^2_{STAT} = \sum_{\text{all cells}} \frac{(f_o - f_e)^2}{f_e} \tag{12.1}$$

where

f_o = **observed frequency** in a particular cell of a contingency table

f_e = **expected frequency** in a particular cell if the null hypothesis is true

The χ^2_{STAT} test statistic approximately follows a chi-square distribution with 1 degree of freedom.[1]

[1] In general, the degrees of freedom in a contingency table are equal to (number of rows −1) multiplied by (number of columns −1).

To compute the expected frequency, f_e, in any cell, you need to know that if the null hypothesis is true, the proportion of items of interest in the two populations will be equal. In such situations, the sample proportions you compute from each of the two groups would differ from each other only by chance. Each would provide an estimate of the common population parameter, π. A statistic that combines these two separate estimates together into one overall estimate of the population parameter provides more information than either of the two separate estimates could provide by itself. This statistic, given by the symbol $\bar{p}$, represents the estimated overall proportion of items of interest for the two groups combined (i.e., the total number of items of

student TIP

Remember, the sample proportion, p, must be between 0 and 1.

interest divided by the total sample size). The complement of $\bar{p}$, $1 - \bar{p}$, represents the estimated overall proportion of items that are not of interest in the two groups. Using the notation presented in Table 12.1 on page 441, Equation (12.2) defines $\bar{p}$.

COMPUTING THE ESTIMATED OVERALL PROPORTION FOR TWO GROUPS

$$\bar{p} = \frac{X_1 + X_2}{n_1 + n_2} = \frac{X}{n} \tag{12.2}$$

To compute the expected frequency, f_e, for cells that involve items of interest (i.e., the cells in the first row in the contingency table), you multiply the sample size (or column total) for a group by $\bar{p}$. To compute the expected frequency, f_e, for cells that involve items that are not of interest (i.e., the cells in the second row in the contingency table), you multiply the sample size (or column total) for a group by $1 - \bar{p}$.

The sampling distribution of the χ^2_{STAT} test statistic shown in Equation (12.1) on page 442 approximately follows a chi-square (χ^2) distribution with 1 degree of freedom. Using a level of significance α, you reject the null hypothesis if the computed χ^2_{STAT} test statistic is greater than χ^2_α, the upper-tail critical value from the χ^2 distribution with 1 degree of freedom. Thus, the decision rule is

$$\text{Reject } H_0 \text{ if } \chi^2_{STAT} > \chi^2_\alpha;$$

otherwise, do not reject H_0.

Figure 12.1 illustrates the decision rule.

FIGURE 12.1
Regions of rejection and nonrejection when using the chi-square test for the difference between two proportions, with level of significance α

If the null hypothesis is true, the computed χ^2_{STAT} test statistic should be close to zero because the squared difference between what is actually observed in each cell, f_o, and what is theoretically expected, f_e, should be very small. If H_0 is false, then there are differences in the population proportions, and the computed χ^2_{STAT} test statistic is expected to be large. However, what is a large difference in a cell is relative. Because you are dividing by the expected frequencies, the same actual difference between f_o and f_e from a cell with a small number of expected frequencies contributes more to the χ^2_{STAT} test statistic than a cell with a large number of expected frequencies.

To illustrate the use of the chi-square test for the difference between two proportions, return to the T.C. Resort Properties scenario on page 440 and the Table 12.2 contingency table on page 442. The null hypothesis ($H_0: \pi_1 = \pi_2$) states that there is no difference between the proportion of guests who are likely to choose either of these hotels again. To begin,

$$\bar{p} = \frac{X_1 + X_2}{n_1 + n_2} = \frac{163 + 154}{227 + 262} = \frac{317}{489} = 0.6483$$

$\bar{p}$ is the estimate of the common parameter π, the population proportion of guests who are likely to choose either of these hotels again if the null hypothesis is true. The estimated proportion of guests who are *not* likely to choose these hotels again is the complement of $\bar{p}$, $1 - 0.6483 = 0.3517$. Multiplying these two proportions by the sample size for the Beachcomber Hotel gives the number of guests expected to choose the Beachcomber again and the number not expected to choose this hotel again. In a similar manner, multiplying the two proportions by the Windsurfer Hotel's sample size yields the corresponding expected frequencies for that group.

EXAMPLE 12.1

Computing the Expected Frequencies

Compute the expected frequencies for each of the four cells of Table 12.2 on page 442.

SOLUTION

Yes—Beachcomber: $\bar{p} = 0.6483$ and $n_1 = 227$, so $f_e = 147.16$
Yes—Windsurfer: $\bar{p} = 0.6483$ and $n_2 = 262$, so $f_e = 169.84$
No —Beachcomber: $1 - \bar{p} = 0.3517$ and $n_1 = 227$, so $f_e = 79.84$
No —Windsurfer: $1 - \bar{p} = 0.3517$ and $n_2 = 262$, so $f_e = 92.16$

Table 12.3 presents these expected frequencies next to the corresponding observed frequencies.

TABLE 12.3
Comparing the Observed (f_o) and Expected (f_e) Frequencies

| | HOTEL | | | | |
| | Beachcomber | | Windsurfer | | |
CHOOSE HOTEL AGAIN?	Observed	Expected	Observed	Expected	Total
Yes	163	147.16	154	169.84	317
No	64	79.84	108	92.16	172
Total	227	227.00	262	262.00	489

To test the null hypothesis that the population proportions are equal:

$$H_0: \pi_1 = \pi_2$$

against the alternative that the population proportions are not equal:

$$H_1: \pi_1 \neq \pi_2$$

you use the observed and expected frequencies from Table 12.3 to compute the χ^2_{STAT} test statistic given by Equation (12.1) on page 442. Table 12.4 presents these calculations.

TABLE 12.4
Computing the χ^2_{STAT} Test Statistic for the Hotel Guest Satisfaction Survey

f_o	f_e	$(f_o - f_e)$	$(f_o - f_e)^2$	$(f_o - f_e)^2/f_e$
163	147.16	15.84	250.91	1.71
154	169.84	−15.84	250.91	1.48
64	79.84	−15.84	250.91	3.14
108	92.16	15.84	250.91	2.72
				9.05

You find the critical value for the χ^2 test from Table E.4, a portion of which is presented in Table 12.5.

TABLE 12.5
Finding the Critical Value from the Chi-Square Distribution with 1 Degree of Freedom, Using the 0.05 Level of Significance

	Cumulative Probabilities						
	.005	.01	. . .	.95	.975	.99	.995
	Upper-Tail Area						
Degrees of Freedom	.995	.99	. . .	.05	.025	.01	.005
1			. . .	3.841	5.024	6.635	7.879
2	0.010	0.020	. . .	5.991	7.378	9.210	10.597
3	0.072	0.115	. . .	7.815	9.348	11.345	12.838
4	0.207	0.297	. . .	9.488	11.143	13.277	14.860
5	0.412	0.554	. . .	11.071	12.833	15.086	16.750

The values in Table 12.5 refer to selected upper-tail areas of the χ^2 distribution. A 2×2 contingency table has 1 degree of freedom because there are two rows and two columns. [The degrees of freedom are equal to the (number of rows -1)(number of columns -1).] Using $\alpha = 0.05$, with 1 degree of freedom, the critical value of χ^2 from Table 12.5 is 3.841. You reject H_0 if the computed χ^2_{STAT} test statistic is greater than 3.841 (see Figure 12.2). Because $\chi^2_{STAT} = 9.05 > 3.841$, you reject H_0. You conclude that the proportion of guests who would return to the Beachcomber is different from the proportion of guests who would return to the Windsurfer.

FIGURE 12.2

Regions of rejection and nonrejection when finding the χ^2 critical value with 1 degree of freedom, at the 0.05 level of significance

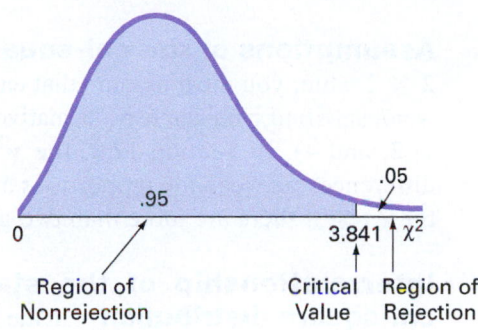

Figure 12.3 shows the Excel, JMP, and Minitab results for the Table 12.2 guest satisfaction contingency table on page 442. Note the JMP and Minitab label the test result as Pearson.

FIGURE 12.3

Excel, JMP, and Minitab chi-square test results for the two-hotel guest satisfaction survey

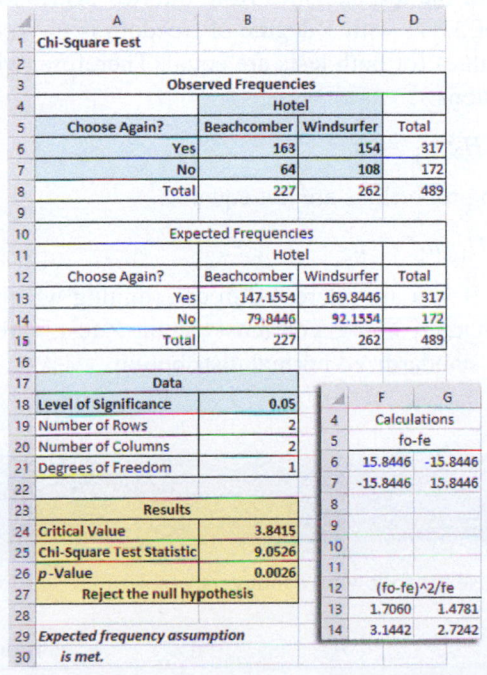

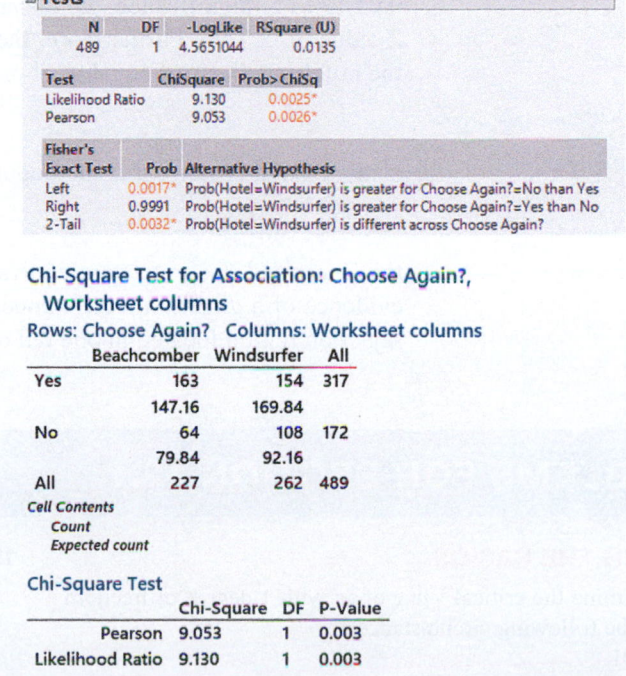

Table 12.6 summarizes the results of the chi-square test for the guest satisfaction survey for the Beachcomber and Windsurfer hotels using the calculations on page 444 and the Figure 12.3 results. Based on the results, there is strong evidence to conclude that the two hotels are significantly different with respect to guest satisfaction, as measured by whether a guest is likely to return to the hotel again. Therefore, as part of the DCOVA framework, you can conclude that a greater proportion of guests are likely to return to the Beachcomber than to the Windsurfer.

TABLE 12.6
Chi-square test summary for the guest satisfaction survey for two hotels

Results	Conclusions
$\chi^2_{Stat} = 9.0526$ is greater than 3.8416. The p-value $= 0.0026$ is less than the level of significance, $\alpha = 0.05$.	1. Reject the null hypothesis H_0. 2. Conclude that evidence exists that the two hotels are significantly different with respect to guest satisfaction. 3. The probability is 0.0026 that $\chi^2_{Stat} > 9.0526$.

Assumptions of the chi-square test   For the χ^2 test to give accurate results for a 2×2 table, you must assume that each expected frequency is at least 5. If this assumption is not satisfied, you can use alternative procedures, such as Fisher's exact test (see references 1, 2, and 4). In Section 12.2, the χ^2 test is extended to make comparisons and evaluate differences between the proportions among more than two groups. However, you cannot use the Z test if there are more than two groups.

Interrelationship of the standardized normal distribution and the chi-square distribution   In the hotel guest satisfaction survey, both the Z test for the difference between two proportions (see Section 10.3) and the χ^2 test lead to the same conclusion. You explain this result by the interrelationship between the standardized normal distribution and a chi-square distribution with 1 degree of freedom. For such situations, the χ^2_{STAT} test statistic is the square of the Z_{STAT} test statistic.

For example, in the guest satisfaction study, using Equation (10.5) on page 369, the calculated Z_{STAT} test statistic is $+3.0088$, and the calculated χ^2_{STAT} test statistic is 9.0526. Except for rounding differences, this 9.0526 value is the square of $+3.0088$ [i.e., $(+3.0088)^2 \cong 9.0526$]. Also, if you compare the critical values of the test statistics from the two distributions, at the 0.05 level of significance, the χ^2 value of 3.841 with 1 degree of freedom is the square of the Z value of ±1.96. Furthermore, the p-values for both tests are equal. Therefore, when testing the null hypothesis of equality of proportions:

$$H_0: \pi_1 = \pi_2$$

against the alternative that the population proportions are not equal:

$$H_1: \pi_1 \neq \pi_2$$

the Z test and the χ^2 test are equivalent. If you are interested in determining whether there is evidence of a *directional* difference, such as $\pi_1 > \pi_2$, you must use the Z test, with the entire rejection region located in one tail of the standardized normal distribution.

PROBLEMS FOR SECTION 12.1

LEARNING THE BASICS

12.1 Determine the critical value of χ^2 with 1 degree of freedom in each of the following circumstances:
a. $\alpha = 0.01$
b. $\alpha = 0.005$
c. $\alpha = 0.10$

12.2 Determine the critical value of χ^2 with 1 degree of freedom in each of the following circumstances:
a. $\alpha = 0.05$
b. $\alpha = 0.025$
c. $\alpha = 0.01$

12.3 Use the following contingency table:

	A	B	Total
1	20	30	50
2	30	45	75
Total	50	75	125

a. Compute the expected frequency for each cell.
b. Compare the observed and expected frequencies for each cell.
c. Compute χ^2_{STAT}. Is it significant at $\alpha = 0.05$?

12.4 Use the following contingency table:

	A	B	Total
1	20	30	50
2	30	20	50
Total	50	50	100

a. Compute the expected frequency for each cell.
b. Compute χ^2_{STAT}. Is it significant at $\alpha = 0.05$?

APPLYING THE CONCEPTS

12.5 An Ipsos poll asked 1,004 adults "If purchasing a used car made certain upgrades or features more affordable, what would be your preferred luxury upgrade?" The results indicated that 9% of the males and 14% of the females answered window tinting.

Source: Ipsos, "Safety Technology Tops the List of Most Desired Features Should They Be More Affordable When Purchasing a Used Car—Particularly Collision Avoidance," available at **bit.ly/2ufbS8Z**.

The poll description did not state the sample sizes of males and females. Suppose that both sample sizes were 502 and that 46 of 502 males and 71 of 502 females reported window tinting as their preferred luxury upgrade of choice.

a. Is there evidence of a difference between males and females in the proportion who said they prefer window tinting as a luxury upgrade at the 0.01 level of significance?
b. Find the p-value in (a) and interpret its meaning.
c. What are your answers to (a) and (b) if 60 males said they prefer window tinting as a luxury upgrade and 442 did not?
d. Compare the results of (a) through (c) to those of Problem 10.29 (a), (b), and (d) on page 374.

12.6 Does Cable Video on Demand (VOD D4+) increase ad effectiveness? A 2015 VOD study compared general TV and VOD D4+ audiences after viewing a brand ad. Whether the viewer indicated that the ad made them want to visit the brand website was collected and organized in the following table.

VIEWING AUDIENCE	MADE ME WANT TO VISIT THE BRAND WEBSITE	
	Yes	No
General TV	35	166
VOD D4+	147	103

Source: Data extracted from *Understanding VOD Advertising Effectiveness*, **bit.ly/1JnmMup**.

a. Set up the null and alternative hypotheses to try to determine whether there is a difference in ad impact between general TV viewing and VOD D4+ viewing.
b. Conduct the hypothesis test defined in (a), using the 0.05 level of significance.
c. Compare the results of (a) and (b) to those of Problem 10.30 (a) and (b) on page 375.

12.7 Are you an impulse shopper? A survey of 500 grocery shoppers indicated that 29% of males and 40% of females make an impulse purchase every time they shop.

Source: Data extracted from *Women shoppers are impulsive while men snap up bargains*, available at **bit.ly/2sLYmVx**.

Assume that the survey consisted of 250 males and 250 females.
a. At the 0.05 level of significance, is there evidence of a difference in the proportion of males and females who make an impulse purchase every time they shop?
b. Find the p-values and interpret its meaning.

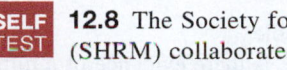 **12.8** The Society for Human Resource Management (SHRM) collaborated with Globoforce on a series of organizational surveys with the goal of identifying challenges that HR leaders face and what strategies help them conquer those challenges. A 2016 survey indicates that employee retention/turnover (46%) and employee engagement (36%) were cited as the most important organizational challenges currently faced by HR professionals. One strategy that may have an impact on employee retention, turnover, and engagement is a successful employee recognition program. Surveying small organizations, those with 500 to 2,499 employees, and large organizations, those with 10,000 or more employees, SHRM and Globoforce showed that 326 (77%) of the 423 small organizations have employee retention programs as compared to 167 (87%) of the 192 large organizations.

Source: Data extracted from *SHRM Survey Finding: Influencing Workplace Culture Through Employee Retention and Other Efforts*, available at **bit.ly/2rFvE9w**.

a. At the 0.01 level of significance, is there evidence of a significant difference between organizations with 500 to 2,499 employees and organizations with 10,000 or more employees with respect to the proportion that have employee recognition programs?
b. Find the p-value in (a) and interpret its meaning.
c. Compare the results of (a) and (b) to those of Problem 10.32 on page 375.

12.9 What social media tools do marketers commonly use? A survey by Social Media Examiner of B2B marketers (marketers that focus primarily on attracting businesses) and B2C marketers (marketers that primarily target consumers) reported that 267 (81%) of B2B marketers and 295 (44%) of B2C marketers commonly use LinkedIn as a social media tool. The study also revealed that 149 (45%) of B2B marketers and 308 (46%) of B2C marketers commonly use YouTube as a social media tool.

Source: Data extracted from *2017 Social Media Marketing Industry Report*, available at **bit.ly/2rFmLzh**.

Suppose the survey was based on 330 B2B marketers and 670 B2C marketers.
a. At the 0.05 level of significance, is there evidence of a difference between B2B marketers and B2C marketers in the proportion that commonly use LinkedIn as a social media tool?
b. Find the p-value in (a) and interpret its value.
c. At the 0.05 level of significance, is there evidence of a difference between B2B marketers and B2C marketers in the proportion that commonly use YouTube as a social media tool?
d. Find the p-value in (c) and interpret its value.

12.10 Does co-browsing have positive effects on the customer experience? Co-browsing refers to the ability to have a contact center agent and customer jointly navigate an application (e.g., web page, digital document, or mobile application) on a real time basis through the web. A study of businesses indicates that 81 of 129 co-browsing organizations use skills-based routing to match the caller with the *right* agent, whereas 65 of 176 non-co-browsing organizations use skills-based routing to match the caller with the *right* agent.

Source: Data extracted from *Cobrowsing Presents a "Lucrative" Customer Service Opportunity*, **bit.ly/1wwALWr.**

a. Construct a 2 × 2 contingency table.
b. At the 0.05 level of significance, is there evidence of a difference between co-browsing organizations and non-co-browsing

organizations in the proportion that use skills-based routing to match the caller with the *right* agent?
c. Find the *p*-value in (a) and interpret its meaning.
d. Compare the results of (a) and (b) to those of Problem 10.34 on page 375.

12.2 Chi-Square Test for Differences Among More Than Two Proportions

In this section, the χ^2 test is extended to compare more than two independent populations. The letter c is used to represent the number of independent populations under consideration. Thus, the contingency table now has two rows and c columns. To test the null hypothesis that there are no differences among the c population proportions:

$$H_0: \pi_1 = \pi_2 = \cdots = \pi_c$$

against the alternative that not all the c population proportions are equal:

$$H_1: \text{Not all } \pi_j \text{ are equal (where } j = 1, 2, \ldots, c)$$

you use Equation (12.1) on page 442:

$$\chi^2_{STAT} = \sum_{\text{all cells}} \frac{(f_o - f_e)^2}{f_e}$$

where

f_o = observed frequency in a particular cell of a 2 × c contingency table

f_e = expected frequency in a particular cell if the null hypothesis is true

If the null hypothesis is true and the proportions are equal across all c populations, the c sample proportions should differ only by chance. In such a situation, a statistic that combines these c separate estimates into one overall estimate of the population proportion, π, provides more information than any one of the c separate estimates alone. To expand on Equation (12.2) on page 443, the statistic $\bar{p}$ in Equation (12.3) represents the estimated overall proportion for all c groups combined.

> ### COMPUTING THE ESTIMATED OVERALL PROPORTION FOR c GROUPS
>
> $$\bar{p} = \frac{X_1 + X_2 + \ldots + X_c}{n_1 + n_2 + \ldots + n_c} = \frac{X}{n} \qquad (12.3)$$

To compute the expected frequency, f_e, for each cell in the first row in the contingency table, multiply each sample size (or column total) by $\bar{p}$. To compute the expected frequency, f_e, for each cell in the second row in the contingency table, multiply each sample size (or column total) by $(1 - \bar{p})$. The sampling distribution of the test statistic shown in Equation (12.1) on page 442 approximately follows a chi-square distribution, with degrees of freedom equal to the number of rows in the contingency table minus 1, multiplied by the number of columns in the table minus 1. For a **2 × c contingency table**, there are $c - 1$ degrees of freedom:

$$\text{Degrees of freedom} = (2 - 1)(c - 1) = c - 1$$

Using the level of significance α, you reject the null hypothesis if the computed χ_{STAT}^2 test statistic is greater than χ_α^2, the upper-tail critical value from a chi-square distribution with $c - 1$ degrees of freedom. Therefore, the decision rule is

$$\text{Reject } H_0 \text{ if } \chi_{STAT}^2 > \chi_\alpha^2;$$
$$\text{otherwise, do not reject } H_0.$$

Figure 12.4 illustrates this decision rule.

FIGURE 12.4
Regions of rejection and nonrejection when testing for differences among c proportions using the χ^2 test

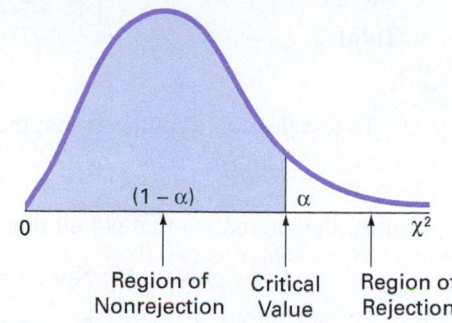

To illustrate the χ^2 test for equality of proportions when there are more than two groups, return to the T.C. Resort Properties scenario on page 440. Once again, you define the business objective as improving the quality of service, but this time, you are comparing three hotels located on a different island. Data are collected from customer satisfaction surveys at these three hotels. You organize the responses into the Table 12.7 contingency table.

TABLE 12.7
2×3 Contingency Table for Guest Satisfaction Survey

CHOOSE HOTEL AGAIN?	Golden Palm	Palm Royale	Palm Princess	Total
	HOTEL			
Yes	128	199	186	513
No	88	33	66	187
Total	216	232	252	700

Because the null hypothesis states that there are no differences among the three hotels in the proportion of guests who would likely return again, you use Equation (12.3) to calculate an estimate of π, the population proportion of guests who would likely return again:

$$\bar{p} = \frac{X_1 + X_2 + \ldots + X_c}{n_1 + n_2 + \ldots + n_c} = \frac{X}{n}$$

$$= \frac{(128 + 199 + 186)}{(216 + 232 + 252)} = \frac{513}{700}$$

$$= 0.733$$

The estimated overall proportion of guests who would *not* be likely to return again is the complement, $(1 - \bar{p})$, or 0.267. Multiplying these two proportions by the sample size for each hotel yields the expected number of guests who would and would not likely return.

EXAMPLE 12.2

Computing the Expected Frequencies

Compute the expected frequencies for each of the six cells in Table 12.7.

SOLUTION

Yes—Golden Palm: $\bar{p} = 0.733$ and $n_1 = 216$, so $f_e = 158.30$
Yes—Palm Royale: $\bar{p} = 0.733$ and $n_2 = 232$, so $f_e = 170.02$
Yes—Palm Princess: $\bar{p} = 0.733$ and $n_3 = 252$, so $f_e = 184.68$
No —Golden Palm: $1 - \bar{p} = 0.267$ and $n_1 = 216$, so $f_e = 57.70$
No —Palm Royale: $1 - \bar{p} = 0.267$ and $n_2 = 232$, so $f_e = 61.98$
No —Palm Princess: $1 - \bar{p} = 0.267$ and $n_3 = 252$, so $f_e = 67.32$

Table 12.8 presents these expected frequencies.

TABLE 12.8

Contingency Table of Expected Frequencies from a Guest Satisfaction Survey of Three Hotels

	HOTEL			
CHOOSE HOTEL AGAIN?	**Golden Palm**	**Palm Royale**	**Palm Princess**	**Total**
Yes	158.30	170.02	184.68	513
No	57.70	61.98	67.32	187
Total	216.00	232.00	252.00	700

To test the null hypothesis that the proportions are equal:

$$H_0: \pi_1 = \pi_2 = \pi_3$$

against the alternative that not all three proportions are equal:

$$H_1: \text{Not all } \pi_j \text{ are equal (where } j = 1, 2, 3)$$

use the observed frequencies from Table 12.7 and the expected frequencies from Table 12.8 to compute the χ^2_{STAT} test statistic [given by Equation (12.1) on page 442]. Table 12.9 presents the calculations.

TABLE 12.9

Computing the χ^2_{STAT} Test Statistic for the Three-Hotel Guest Satisfaction Survey

f_o	f_e	$(f_o - f_e)$	$(f_o - f_e)^2$	$(f_o - f_e)^2/f_e$
128	158.30	−30.30	918.09	5.80
199	170.02	28.98	839.84	4.94
186	184.68	1.32	1.74	0.01
88	57.70	30.30	918.09	15.91
33	61.98	−28.98	839.84	13.55
66	67.32	−1.32	1.74	0.02
				40.23

Use Table E.4 to find the critical value of the χ^2 test statistic. In the guest satisfaction survey, because there are three hotels, there are $(2 - 1)(3 - 1) = 2$ degrees of freedom. Using $\alpha = 0.05$, the χ^2 critical value with 2 degrees of freedom is 5.991 (see Figure 12.5).

FIGURE 12.5

Regions of rejection and nonrejection when testing for differences in three proportions at the 0.05 level of significance, with 2 degrees of freedom

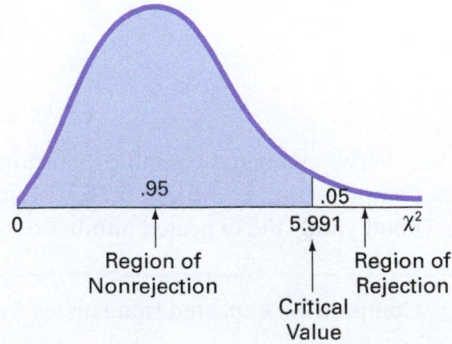

Table 12.10 summarizes the results of the chi-square test for the guest satisfaction survey for the Golden Palm, Palm Royale, and Palm Princess hotels using the Table 12.9 calculations and the Figure 12.6 results. Based on the results, there is strong evidence to conclude that the three hotels are significantly different with respect to guest satisfaction, as measured by whether a guest is likely to return to the hotel again. Therefore, as part of the DCOVA framework, you can conclude that the hotels are different in terms of the proportion of guests who are likely to return.

TABLE 12.10

Chi-square test summary for the guest satisfaction survey for the three hotels

Results	Conclusions
$\chi^2_{STAT} = 40.23$ is greater than 5.9915. The p-value $= 0.0000$ is less than the level of significance, $\alpha = 0.05$.	1. Reject the null hypothesis H_0. 2. Conclude that evidence exists that the three hotels are significantly different with respect to guest satisfaction. 3. The probability is 0.0000 that $\chi^2_{STAT} > 40.23$.

FIGURE 12.6

Excel, JMP, and Minitab chi-square test results for the three-hotel guest satisfaction survey (JMP and Minitab label the test result as Pearson)

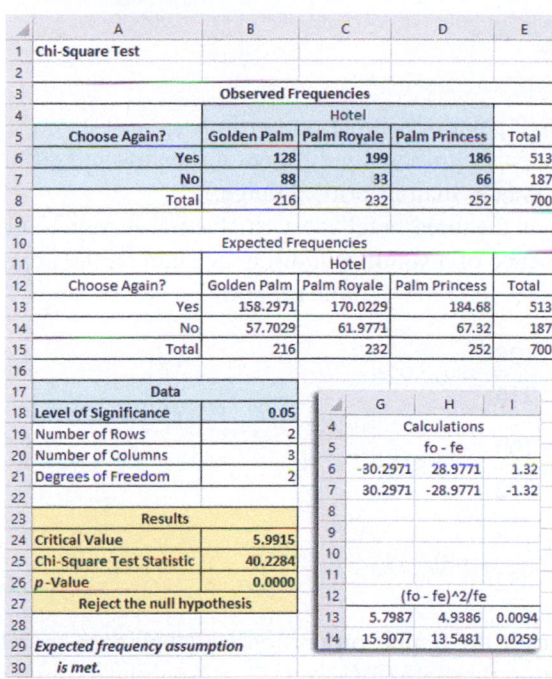

Assumptions of the chi-square test for the 2 × c contingency table

For the χ^2 test to give accurate results when dealing with $2 \times c$ contingency tables, all expected frequencies must be large. The definition of "large" has led to research among statisticians. Some statisticians (see reference 5) have found that the test gives accurate results as long as all expected frequencies are at least 0.5. Other statisticians believe that no more than 20% of the cells should contain expected frequencies less than 5, and no cells should have expected frequencies less than 1 (see reference 3). As a reasonable compromise between these points of view, to ensure the validity of the test, you should make sure that each expected frequency is at least 1. To do this, you may need to collapse two or more low-expected-frequency categories into one category in the contingency table before performing the test. If combining categories is undesirable, you can use one of the available alternative procedures (see references 1, 2, and 7).

The Marascuilo Procedure

Rejecting the null hypothesis in a χ^2 test of equality of proportions in a $2 \times c$ table allows you to only reach the conclusion that not all c population proportions are equal. To determine which proportions differ, you use a multiple-comparisons procedure such as the Marascuilo procedure.

The **Marascuilo procedure** enables you to make comparisons between all pairs of groups. First, you compute the sample proportions. Then, you use Equation (12.4) to compute the critical ranges for the Marascuilo procedure. You compute a different critical range for each pairwise comparison of sample proportions.

CRITICAL RANGE FOR THE MARASCUILO PROCEDURE

$$\text{Critical range} = \sqrt{\chi_\alpha^2}\sqrt{\frac{p_j(1-p_j)}{n_j} + \frac{p_{j'}(1-p_{j'})}{n_{j'}}} \qquad (12.4)$$

where

p_j = proportion of items of interest in group j

$p_{j'}$ = proportion of items of interest in group j'

n_j = sample size in group j

$n_{j'}$ = sample size in group j'

studentTIP

You have an α level of risk in the entire set of comparisons not just a single comparison.

Then, you compare each of the $c(c-1)/2$ pairs of sample proportions against its corresponding critical range. You declare a specific pair significantly different if the absolute difference in the sample proportions, $|p_j - p_{j'}|$, is greater than its critical range.

To apply the Marascuilo procedure, return to the three-hotel guest satisfaction survey. Using the χ^2 test, you concluded that there was evidence of a significant difference among the population proportions. From Table 12.7 on page 449, the three sample proportions are

$$p_1 = \frac{X_1}{n_1} = \frac{128}{216} = 0.5926$$

$$p_2 = \frac{X_2}{n_2} = \frac{199}{232} = 0.8578$$

$$p_3 = \frac{X_3}{n_3} = \frac{186}{252} = 0.7381$$

Next, you compute the absolute differences in the sample proportions and their corresponding critical ranges. Because there are three hotels, there are $(3)(3-1)/2 = 3$ pairwise comparisons. Using Table E.4 and an overall level of significance of 0.05, the upper-tail critical value for a chi-square distribution having $(c-1) = 2$ degrees of freedom is 5.991. Thus,

$$\sqrt{\chi_\alpha^2} = \sqrt{5.991} = 2.4477$$

The following displays the absolute differences and the critical ranges for each comparison.

Absolute Difference in Proportions	**Critical Range**
$\|p_j - p_{j'}\|$	$2.4477\sqrt{\dfrac{p_j(1-p_j)}{n_j} + \dfrac{p_{j'}(1-p_{j'})}{n_{j'}}}$
$\|p_1 - p_2\| = \|0.5926 - 0.8578\| = 0.2652$	$2.4477\sqrt{\dfrac{(0.5926)(0.4074)}{216} + \dfrac{(0.8578)(0.1422)}{232}} = 0.0992$
$\|p_1 - p_3\| = \|0.5926 - 0.7381\| = 0.1455$	$2.4477\sqrt{\dfrac{(0.5926)(0.4074)}{216} + \dfrac{(0.7381)(0.2619)}{252}} = 0.1063$
$\|p_2 - p_3\| = \|0.8578 - 0.7381\| = 0.1197$	$2.4477\sqrt{\dfrac{(0.8578)(0.1422)}{232} + \dfrac{(0.7381)(0.2619)}{252}} = 0.0880$

Figure 12.7 shows Excel results for this example.

FIGURE 12.7

Excel Marascuilo procedure results for the three-hotel guest satisfaction survey

	A	B	C	D
1	Marascuilo Procedure for Guest Satisfaction Analysis			
2				
3	Level of Significance	0.05		
4	Square Root of Critical Value	2.4477		
5				
6	Group Sample Proportions			
7	1: Golden Palm	0.5926		
8	2: Palm Royale	0.8578		
9	3: Palm Princess	0.7381		
10				
11	MARASCUILO TABLE			
12	Proportions	Absolute Differences	Critical Range	
13	| Group 1 - Group 2 |	0.2652	0.0992	Significant
14	| Group 1 - Group 3 |	0.1455	0.1063	Significant
15				
16	| Group 2 - Group 3 |	0.1197	0.0880	Significant

As the final step, you compare the absolute differences to the critical ranges. If the absolute difference is greater than the critical range, the proportions are significantly different. At the 0.05 level of significance, you can conclude that guest satisfaction is higher at the Palm Royale ($p_2 = 0.858$) than at either the Golden Palm ($p_1 = 0.593$) or the Palm Princess ($p_3 = 0.738$) and that guest satisfaction is also higher at the Palm Princess than at the Golden Palm. These results clearly suggest that you should investigate possible reasons for these differences. In particular, you should try to determine why satisfaction is significantly lower at the Golden Palm than at the other two hotels.

The Analysis of Proportions (ANOP)

The analysis of proportions (ANOP) method provides a confidence interval approach that allows you to determine which, if any, of the c groups has a proportion significantly different from the overall mean of all the group proportions combined. The **ANOP online topic** discusses this method and illustrates its use.

PROBLEMS FOR SECTION 12.2

LEARNING THE BASICS

12.11 Consider a contingency table with two rows and five columns.
a. How many degrees of freedom are there in the contingency table?
b. Determine the critical value for $\alpha = 0.05$.
c. Determine the critical value for $\alpha = 0.01$.

12.12 Use the following contingency table:

	A	B	C	Total
1	10	30	50	90
2	40	45	50	135
Total	50	75	100	225

a. Compute the expected frequency for each cell.
b. Compute χ^2_{STAT}. Is it significant at $\alpha = 0.05$?

12.13 Use the following contingency table:

	A	B	C	Total
1	20	30	25	75
2	30	20	25	75
Total	50	50	50	150

a. Compute the expected frequency for each cell.
b. Compute χ^2_{STAT}. Is it significant at $\alpha = 0.05$?

APPLYING THE CONCEPTS

12.14 How common are financial cost or contractual constraints associated with smartphone ownership? A survey of smartphone owners found that 48% of the 18- to 29-year-olds, 38% of the 30- to 49-year-olds, 25% of the 50- to 64-year-olds, and 19% of those age 65 or older have reached the maximum amount of data they are allowed to use as part of their plan, at least on occasion.

Source: Data extracted from *U.S. Smartphone Use 2015*, **bit.ly/1KL2WcW**.

Suppose the survey was based on 200 smartphone owners in each of the four age groups: 18 to 29, 30 to 49, 50 to 64, and 65+.
a. At the 0.05 level of significance, is there evidence of a difference among the age groups in the proportion of smartphone owners who have reached the maximum amount of data they are allowed to use as part of their plan, at least on occasion?
b. Determine the p-value in (a) and interpret its meaning.
c. If appropriate, use the Marascuilo procedure and $\alpha = 0.05$ to determine which age groups differ.

12.15 Business sensor technology provides a way for companies to learn about their customers, employees, and operations; data captured from sensors can be used to improve engagement, sales, productivity, safety, and much more. A PwC survey of global business and IT executives found that 25% of automotive executives; 27% of energy, utilities, and mining executives; 30% of hospitality and leisure executives; 33% of industrial products executives; and 52% of retail and consumer executives say their companies are currently investing in business sensor technology.

Source: Data extracted from *Three surprising digital bets for 2015*, **pwc.to/1H8jcOY**.

Suppose these results were based on 500 business and IT executives in each of the five industries: Automotive; Energy, Utilities, and Mining; Hospitality and Leisure; Industrial Products; and Retail and Consumer.

a. At the 0.05 level of significance, is there evidence of a difference among the industries with respect to the proportion of executives that say their companies are currently investing in business sensor technology?

b. Compute the p-value and interpret its meaning.

c. If appropriate, use the Marascuilo procedure and $a = 0.05$ to determine which companies differ in their current investing in business sensor technology.

✓SELF TEST **12.16** An Employee Value Proposition (EVP) is about defining the essence of a company. The EVP is the value an employee receives from the employer; it defines the commitment the company will make to develop the employee in exchange for the effort the employee puts in to benefit the company. But do all agree on what makes a unique and compelling EVP? A study showed that 14% of business executives, 38% of HR leaders, and 33% of employees say that compensation (pay and rewards) makes for a unique and compelling EVP.

Source: Data extracted from "Mercer Talent Trends 2017 Global Study," available at **bit.ly/2sbrUzh**.

Assume that 200 individuals within each business group were surveyed.

a. Is there evidence of a difference among business groups with respect to the proportion that say compensation (pay and rewards) makes for a unique and compelling EVP?

b. Determine the p-value in (a) and interpret its meaning.

c. If appropriate, use the Marascuilo procedure and $\alpha = 0.05$ to determine which business groups differ in the proportion that say compensation (pay and rewards) makes for a unique and compelling EVP.

12.17 Repeat (a) and (b) of Problem 12.16, assuming that only 100 individuals from each business group were surveyed. Discuss the implications of sample size on the χ^2 test for differences among more than two populations.

12.18 What kinds of activities do you engage in when using a device while viewing video content on a TV screen? An IAB and MARU Matchbox study captured multitasking activities of adults who use different devices while watching TV. The study reported that 320 of 444 (72%) smartphone users sampled, 194 of 347 (56%) of computer users sampled, and 141 of 261 (54%) of tablet users sampled used their device to check social media unrelated to the video while watching TV.

Source: Data extracted from "The Changing TV Experience: 2017," available at **bit.ly/2sz4Mal**.

a. Is there evidence of a significant difference among the smartphone, computer, and tablet users with respect to the proportion who use their device to check social media unrelated to the video while watching TV? (Use $\alpha = 0.05$).

b. Determine the p-value and interpret its meaning.

c. If appropriate, use the Marascuilo procedure and $\alpha = 0.05$ to determine which groups differ.

12.19 The MSCI 2016 Survey of Women on Boards Survey showed that there continues to be a slow increase in the overall percentage of women on boards globally. The study reported that 69 of 70 (99%) French companies sampled, 39 of 53 (74%) German companies sampled, 8 of 22 (36%) Irish companies, 15 of 24 (63%) Spanish companies, and 12 of 42 (29%) Swiss companies sampled have at least three female directors on their boards.

Source: Data extracted from "The Tipping Point: Women on Boards and Financial Performance," **bit.ly/2pYDt9A**.

a. Is there evidence of a significant difference among the countries with respect to the proportion of companies who have at least three female directors on their boards? (Use $\alpha = 0.05$).

b. Determine the p-value and interpret its meaning.

c. If appropriate, use the Marascuilo procedure and $\alpha = 0.05$ to determine which groups differ.

12.3 Chi-Square Test of Independence

In Sections 12.1 and 12.2, you used the χ^2 test to evaluate potential differences among population proportions. For a contingency table that has r rows and c columns, you can generalize the χ^2 test as a *test of independence* for two categorical variables.

For a test of independence, the null and alternative hypotheses follow:

H_0:The two categorical variables are independent (i.e., there is no relationship between them).

H_1:The two categorical variables are dependent (i.e., there is a relationship between them).

Once again, you use Equation (12.1) on page 442 to compute the test statistic:

$$\chi^2_{STAT} = \sum_{\text{all cells}} \frac{(f_o - f_e)^2}{f_e}$$

You reject the null hypothesis at the α level of significance if the computed value of the χ^2_{STAT} test statistic is greater than χ^2_α, the upper-tail critical value from a chi-square distribution with $(r - 1)(c - 1)$ degrees of freedom (see Figure 12.8).

FIGURE 12.8
Regions of rejection and nonrejection when testing for independence in an $r \times c$ contingency table, using the χ^2 test

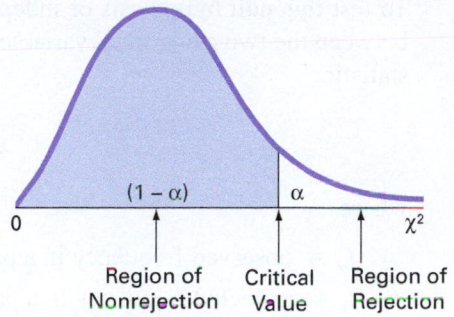

$(1 - \alpha)$ α

0

Region of Nonrejection   Critical Value   Region of Rejection

Thus, the decision rule is

$$\text{Reject } H_0 \text{ if } \chi^2_{STAT} > \chi^2_\alpha;$$
$$\text{otherwise, do not reject } H_0.$$

The **chi-square (χ^2) test of independence** is similar to the χ^2 test for equality of proportions. The test statistics and the decision rules are the same, but the null and alternative hypotheses and conclusions are different. For example, in the guest satisfaction survey of Sections 12.1 and 12.2, there is evidence of a significant difference between the hotels with respect to the proportion of guests who would return. From a different viewpoint, you could conclude that there is a significant relationship between the hotels and the likelihood that a guest would return. However, the two types of tests differ in how the samples are selected.

In a test for equality of proportions, there is one factor of interest, with two or more levels. These levels represent samples selected from independent populations. The categorical responses in each group or level are classified into two categories, such as *an item of interest* and *not an item of interest*. The objective is to make comparisons and evaluate differences between the proportions of the *items of interest* among the various levels. However, in a test for independence, there are two factors of interest, each of which has two or more levels. You select one sample and tally the joint responses to the two categorical variables into the cells of a contingency table.

To illustrate the χ^2 test for independence, suppose that, in the three-hotel guest satisfaction survey, respondents who stated that they were not likely to return also indicated the primary reason for their unwillingness to return. Table 12.11 presents the resulting 4×3 contingency table.

TABLE 12.11
Contingency Table of Primary Reason for Not Returning and Hotel

PRIMARY REASON FOR NOT RETURNING	HOTEL			
	Golden Palm	Palm Royale	Palm Princess	Total
Amenities	23	7	37	67
Dining Options	13	5	13	31
Quality of Room	39	13	8	60
Staff/Service Issues	13	8	8	29
Total	88	33	66	187

In Table 12.11, observe that of the primary reasons for not planning to return to the hotel, 67 were due to amenities, 60 were due to quality of room, 31 were due to room dining options, and 29 were due to staff/service issues. In Table 12.7 on page 449, there were 88 guests at the Golden Palm, 33 guests at the Palm Royale, and 66 guests at the Palm Princess who were not planning to return. The observed frequencies in the cells of the 4×3 contingency table represent the joint tallies of the sampled guests with respect to primary reason for not returning and the hotel where they stayed. The null and alternative hypotheses are

H_0: There is no relationship between the primary reason for not returning and the hotel.
H_1: There is a relationship between the primary reason for not returning and the hotel.

To test this null hypothesis of independence against the alternative that there is a relationship between the two categorical variables, you use Equation (12.1) on page 442 to compute the test statistic:

$$\chi^2_{STAT} = \sum_{\text{all cells}} \frac{(f_o - f_e)^2}{f_e}$$

where

f_o = observed frequency in a particular cell of the $r \times c$ contingency table

f_e = expected frequency in a particular cell if the null hypothesis of independence is true

To compute the expected frequency, f_e, in any cell, you use the multiplication rule for independent events discussed on page 182 [see Equation (4.7)]. For example, under the null hypothesis of independence, the probability of responses expected in the upper-left-corner cell representing primary reason of amenities for the Golden Palm is the product of the two separate probabilities $P(\text{Amenities})$ and $P(\text{Golden Palm})$. For this example, the proportion for the primary reason Amenities, $P(\text{Amenities})$, is $67/187 = 0.3583$, and the proportion of all Golden Palm responses, $P(\text{Golden Palm})$, is $88/187 = 0.4706$. If the null hypothesis is true, then the primary reason for not returning and the hotel are independent:

$$P(\text{Amenities } and \text{ Golden Palm}) = P(\text{Amenities}) \times P(\text{Golden Palm})$$

$$= (0.3583) \times (0.4706)$$

$$= 0.1686$$

The expected frequency is the product of the overall sample size, n, and this probability, $187 \times 0.1686 = 31.53$. Table 12.12 shows the f_e values for the remaining cells.

TABLE 12.12

Contingency Table of Expected Frequencies of Primary Reason for Not Returning with Hotel

PRIMARY REASON FOR NOT RETURNING	HOTEL			
	Golden Palm	**Palm Royale**	**Palm Princess**	**Total**
Amenities	31.53	11.82	23.65	67
Dining Options	14.59	5.47	10.94	31
Quality of Room	28.24	10.59	21.18	60
Staff/Service Issues	13.65	5.12	10.24	29
Total	88.00	33.00	66.00	187

You can also compute the expected frequency by taking the product of the row total and column total for a cell and dividing this product by the overall sample size, as Equation (12.5) shows.

COMPUTING THE EXPECTED FREQUENCY

The expected frequency in a cell is the product of its row total and column total, divided by the overall sample size.

$$f_e = \frac{\text{Row total} \times \text{Column total}}{n} \tag{12.5}$$

where

Row total = sum of the frequencies in the row
Column total = sum of the frequencies in the column
n = overall sample size

This alternate method results in simpler computations. For example, using Equation (12.5) for the upper-left-corner cell (amenities for the Golden Palm),

$$f_e = \frac{\text{Row total} \times \text{Column total}}{n} = \frac{(67)(88)}{187} = 31.53$$

and for the lower-right-corner cell (staff/service issues for the Palm Princess),

$$f_e = \frac{\text{Row total} \times \text{Column total}}{n} = \frac{(29)(66)}{187} = 10.24$$

To perform the test of independence, you use the χ^2_{STAT} test statistic shown in Equation (12.1) on page 442. The sampling distribution of the χ^2_{STAT} test statistic approximately follows a chi-square distribution, with degrees of freedom equal to the number of rows in the contingency table minus 1, multiplied by the number of columns in the table minus 1:

$$\text{Degrees of freedom} = (r - 1)(c - 1)$$
$$= (4 - 1)(3 - 1) = 6$$

Table 12.13 presents the computations for the χ^2_{STAT} test statistic.

TABLE 12.13

Computing the χ^2_{STAT} Test Statistic for the Test of Independence

Cell	f_o	f_e	$(f_o - f_e)$	$(f_o - f_e)^2$	$(f_o - f_e)^2/f_e$
Amenities/Golden Palm	23	31.53	−8.53	72.76	2.31
Amenities/Palm Royale	7	11.82	−4.82	23.23	1.97
Amenities/Palm Princess	37	23.65	13.35	178.22	7.54
Dining Options/Golden Palm	13	14.59	−1.59	2.53	0.17
Dining Options/Palm Royale	5	5.47	−0.47	0.22	0.04
Dining Options/Palm Princess	13	10.94	2.06	4.24	0.39
Quality of Room/Golden Palm	39	28.24	10.76	115.78	4.10
Quality of Room/Palm Royale	13	10.59	2.41	5.81	0.55
Quality of Room/Palm Princess	8	21.18	−13.18	173.71	8.20
Staff/Service Issues/Golden Palm	13	13.65	−0.65	0.42	0.03
Staff/Service Issues/Palm Royale	8	5.12	2.88	8.29	1.62
Staff/Service Issues/Palm Princess	8	10.24	−2.24	5.02	0.49
					27.41

Using the $\alpha = 0.05$ level of significance, the upper-tail critical value from the chi-square distribution with 6 degrees of freedom is 12.592 (see Table E.4). Because $\chi^2_{STAT} = 27.41 > 12.592$, you reject the null hypothesis of independence (see Figure 12.9).

FIGURE 12.9

Regions of rejection and nonrejection when testing for independence in the three hotel guest satisfaction survey example at the 0.05 level of significance, with 6 degrees of freedom

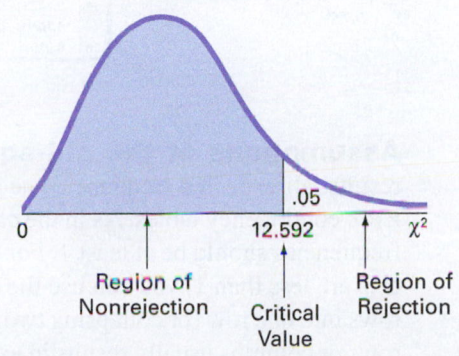

Table 12.14 summarizes the results of the chi-square test for the primary reason for not returning survey using the Table 12.13 calculations and the Figure 12.10 results. Based on the results, there is strong evidence to conclude that there is a relationship between the reason for not returning to the hotel again and the hotel that the guest stayed at. Therefore, as part of the DCOVA framework, you can conclude that the hotels are different in terms of why guests are not likely to return. Amenities are underrepresented as a reason for not returning to the Golden Palm, but are overrepresented at the Palm Princess. Guests are more satisfied with amenities at the Golden Palm than at the Palm Princess. Quality of room is overrepresented as a reason for not returning to the Golden Palm, but greatly underrepresented at the Palm Princess. Guests are much more satisfied with the quality of rooms of the Palm Princess than at the Golden Palm.

TABLE 12.14
Chi-square test summary for the primary reason for not returning survey

Results	Conclusions
$\chi^2_{STAT} = 27.41$ is greater than 12.592. The p-value $= 0.0000$ is less than the level of significance, $\alpha = 0.05$.	1. Reject the null hypothesis H_0. 2. Conclude that there is a relationship between the reason for not returning to the hotel again and the hotel that the guest stayed at. 3. The probability is 0.0000 that $\chi^2_{STAT} > 27.41$.

FIGURE 12.10
Excel, JMP, and Minitab chi-square test results for the Table 12.11 primary reason for not returning to hotel data

JMP and Minitab label the chi-square test result as Pearson.

	A	B	C	D	E
1	Chi-Square Test of Independence				
2					
3	Observed Frequencies				
4		Hotel			
5	Reason for Not Returning	Golden Palm	Palm Royale	Palm Princess	Total
6	Amenities	23	7	37	67
7	Dining Options	13	5	13	31
8	Quality of Room	39	13	8	60
9	Staff/service Issues	13	8	8	29
10	Total	88	33	66	187
11					
12	Expected Frequencies				
13		Hotel			
14	Reason for Not Returning	Golden Palm	Palm Royale	Palm Princess	Total
15	Amenities	31.5294	11.8235	23.6471	67
16	Dining Options	14.5882	5.4706	10.9412	31
17	Quality of Room	28.2353	10.5882	21.1765	60
18	Staff/service Issues	13.6471	5.1176	10.2353	29
19	Total	88	33	66	187
20					
21	Data				
22	Level of Significance	0.05			
23	Number of Rows	4			
24	Number of Columns	3			
25	Degrees of Freedom	6			
26					
27	Results				
28	Critical Value	12.5916			
29	Chi-Square Test Statistic	27.4104			
30	*p*-Value	0.0001			
31	Reject the null hypothesis				
32					
33	*Expected frequency assumption*				
34	*is met.*				

	G	H	I
4	Calculations		
5	fo - fe		
6	-8.5294	-4.8235	13.3529
7	-1.5882	-0.4706	2.0588
8	10.7647	2.4118	-13.1765
9	-0.6471	2.8824	-2.2353
10			
11			
12			
13			
14	(fo - fe)^2/fe		
15	2.3074	1.9678	7.5401
16	0.1729	0.0405	0.3874
17	4.1040	0.5493	8.1987
18	0.0307	1.6234	0.4882

Tests

N	DF	-LogLike	RSquare (U)
187	6	14.381206	0.0748

Test	ChiSquare	Prob>ChiSq
Likelihood Ratio	28.762	<.0001*
Pearson	27.410	0.0001*

Chi-Square Test for Association: Reason for Not ... Worksheet columns

Rows: Reason for Not Returning Columns: Worksheet columns

	Golden Palm	Palm Royale	Palm Princess	All
Amenities	23	7	37	67
	31.53	11.82	23.65	
Dining Options	13	5	13	31
	14.59	5.47	10.94	
Quality of Room	39	13	8	60
	28.24	10.59	21.18	
Staff/service Issues	13	8	8	29
	13.65	5.12	10.24	
All	88	33	66	187

Cell Contents
Count
Expected count

Chi-Square Test

	Chi-Square	DF	P-Value
Pearson	27.410	6	0.000
Likelihood Ratio	28.762	6	0.000

Assumptions of the chi-square test of independence To ensure accurate results, all expected frequencies need to be large in order to use the χ^2 test when dealing with $r \times c$ contingency tables. As in the case of $2 \times c$ contingency tables in Section 12.2, all expected frequencies should be at least 1. For contingency tables in which one or more expected frequencies are less than 1, you can use the chi-square test after collapsing two or more low-frequency rows into one row (or collapsing two or more low-frequency columns into one column). Merging rows or columns usually results in expected frequencies sufficiently large to ensure the accuracy of the χ^2 test.

PROBLEMS FOR SECTION 12.3

LEARNING THE BASICS

12.20 If a contingency table has three rows and four columns, how many degrees of freedom are there for the χ^2 test of independence?

12.21 When performing a χ^2 test of independence in a contingency table with r rows and c columns, determine the upper-tail critical value of the test statistic in each of the following circumstances:

a. $\alpha = 0.05$, $r = 4$ rows, $c = 5$ columns
b. $\alpha = 0.01$, $r = 4$ rows, $c = 5$ columns
c. $\alpha = 0.01$, $r = 4$ rows, $c = 6$ columns
d. $\alpha = 0.01$, $r = 3$ rows, $c = 6$ columns
e. $\alpha = 0.01$, $r = 6$ rows, $c = 3$ columns

APPLYING THE CONCEPTS

12.22 The owner of a restaurant serving Continental-style entrées has the business objective of learning more about the patterns of patron demand during the Friday-to-Sunday weekend time period. Data were collected from 630 customers on the type of entrée and dessert ordered and organized into the following table:

TYPE OF DESSERT	TYPE OF ENTRÉE				
	Beef	Poultry	Fish	Pasta	Total
Ice cream	13	8	12	14	47
Cake	98	12	29	6	145
Fruit	8	10	6	2	26
None	124	98	149	41	412
Total	243	128	196	63	630

At the 0.05 level of significance, is there evidence of a relationship between type of dessert and type of entrée?

12.23 A Gallup survey across generations of workers gathered data on engagement at work. The results for a sample of 1,000 workers are as follows:

LEVEL OF ENGAGEMENT	GENERATION				
	Millennials	Gen Xers	Baby Boomers	Traditionalists	Total
Engaged	102	109	93	14	318
Not Engaged	193	170	134	12	509
Actively Disengaged	55	61	53	4	173
Total	350	340	280	30	1,000

Source: Gallup, "How Millennials Want to Work and Live," available at **bit.ly/1T9dl7p**.

At the 0.05 level of significance, is there evidence of a significant relationship between generation and level of engagement in the workplace?

 12.24 How often do Facebook users post? A study by the Pew Research Center revealed the following results:

FREQUENCY	AGE GROUP					
	16–17	18–29	30–49	50–64	65+	Total
Several times a day	36	322	353	147	64	922
About once a day	4	69	135	100	48	356
A few times a week	20	55	90	74	27	266
Every few weeks	4	11	8	25	7	55
Less often	4	14	21	25	11	75
Total	68	471	607	371	157	1,674

Source: Data extracted from Pew Research Center, "Datasets 2016," available at **pewrsr.ch/2qSa3th**.

At the 0.01 level of significance, is there evidence of a significant relationship between frequency of posting on Facebook and age?

12.25 What makes sales leaders tick? Mercuri International conducted a study to explore sales strategies, processes, and support systems within businesses. Organizations were categorized by sales performance level (top performers vs. middle performers vs. bottom performers) and extent to which the organization invests in customer satisfaction. Results were organized into the following table.

LEVEL OF INVESTMENT	SALES PERFORMANCE LEVEL			
	Top	Middle	Bottom	Total
Annually	53	318	44	104
Every 2–4 years	40	245	23	721
Never	11	158	34	101
Total	104	721	101	926

Source: "Sales Excellence Survey 2017," available at **bit.ly/2qRYna2**.

At the 0.05 level of significance, is there evidence of a significant relationship between sales performance level and level of investment in customer satisfaction?

12.26 PwC takes a closer look at what CEOs are looking for and are finding as new sources of value in their businesses and industries. Based on a 2017 Global CEO survey, CEOs are categorized by the main activity they identified that would strengthen their company in order to capitalize on new opportunities as well as the geographic region in which they are located. The results are as follows:

IDENTIFIED MAIN ACTIVITY	GEOGRAPHIC REGION				
	Asia Pacific	Latin America	North America	Western Europe	Total
Innovation	117	41	27	66	251
Human capital	73	28	24	40	165
Competitive advantage	68	16	14	12	110
Digital and tech capabilities	54	19	21	60	154
Customer experience	39	14	14	42	109
M & A and partnerships	39	4	16	15	74
Trust and transparency	25	8	9	17	59
Funding growth	25	2	5	4	36
Big data and analytics	20	4	10	12	46
Cost containment	16	11	2	8	37
Navigating risk and regulation	6	7	5	4	22
Cybersecurity	6	2	2	2	12
Total	488	156	149	282	1,075

Source: "20th Annual Global CEO Survey," available at **pwc.to/2sbopsz**.

At the 0.05 level of significance, is there evidence of a significant relationship between identified main activity and geographic region?

12.4 Wilcoxon Rank Sum Test for Two Independent Populations

Section 10.1 uses the t test for the difference between the means of two independent populations. If sample sizes are small and you cannot assume that the data in each sample are from normally distributed populations, you can choose to use the pooled-variance t test, following a *normalizing transformation* on the data (see reference 8), or use a nonparametric method that does not depend on the assumption of normality for the two populations.

Nonparametric methods require few or no assumptions about the populations from which data are obtained (see reference 4). The **Wilcoxon rank sum test** for whether there is a difference between two medians is one such method. You use this method when you cannot meet the assumptions that the pooled-variance and separate-variance t tests discussed in Section 10.1 require. In such conditions, the Wilcoxon rank sum test is likely to have more statistical power (see Section 9.6) than those t tests. (When assumptions can be met, the test has almost as much power as the t tests.) You can also use the Wilcoxon rank sum test when you have only ordinal data, as often happens in consumer behavior and marketing research.

student TIP

Remember that you combine the two groups before you rank the values.

To perform the Wilcoxon rank sum test, you replace the values in the two samples of sizes n_1 and n_2 with their combined ranks (unless the data contained the ranks initially). You begin by defining $n = n_1 + n_2$ as the total sample size. Next, you assign the ranks so that rank 1 is given to the smallest of the n combined values, rank 2 is given to the second smallest, and so on, until rank n is given to the largest. If several values are tied, you assign each value the average of the ranks that otherwise would have been assigned had there been no ties.

Whenever the two sample sizes are unequal, n_1 represents the smaller sample and n_2 the larger sample. The Wilcoxon rank sum test statistic, T_1, is defined as the sum of the ranks assigned to the n_1 values in the smaller sample. (For equal-sized samples, either sample may be used for determining T_1.) For any integer value n, the sum of the first n consecutive integers is $n(n + 1)/2$. Therefore, T_1 plus T_2, the sum of the ranks assigned to the n_2 items in the second sample, must equal $n(n + 1)/2$. You can use Equation (12.6) to check the accuracy of your rankings.

CHECKING THE RANKINGS

$$T_1 + T_2 = \frac{n(n + 1)}{2} \tag{12.6}$$

For the Figure 12.11 two-tail test, you reject the null hypothesis if the computed value of T_1 is greater than or equal to the upper critical value, or if T_1 is less than or equal to the lower critical value. Figure 12.11 also illustrates the two one-tail tests. For lower-tail tests which have the alternative hypothesis $H_1: M_1 < M_2$ that the median of population 1 (M_1) is less than the median of population 2 (M_2), you reject the null hypothesis if the observed value of T_1 is less than or equal to the lower critical value. For upper-tail tests which have the alternative hypothesis $H_1: M_1 > M_2$, you reject the null hypothesis if the observed value of T_1 equals or is greater than the upper critical value.

FIGURE 12.11

Regions of rejection and nonrejection using the Wilcoxon rank sum test

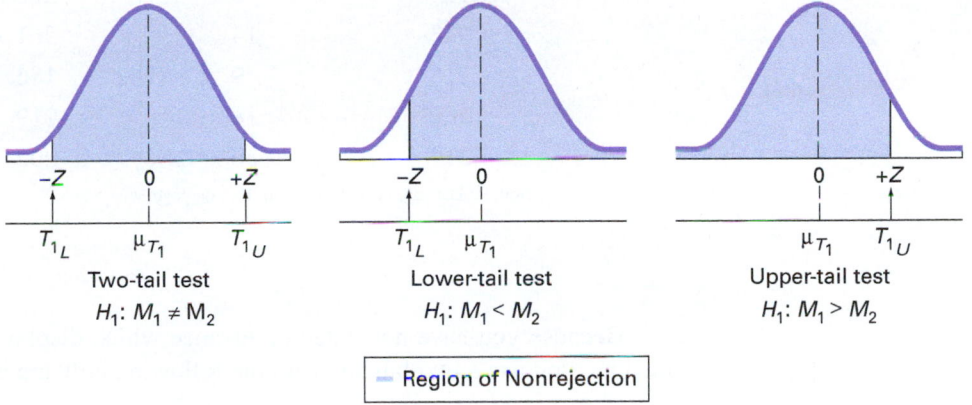

Two-tail test
$H_1: M_1 \neq M_2$

Lower-tail test
$H_1: M_1 < M_2$

Upper-tail test
$H_1: M_1 > M_2$

─ Region of Nonrejection

When n_1 and n_2 are each ≤ 10, use Table E.6 to find the critical values of the test statistic T_1. For large sample sizes, the test statistic T_1 is approximately normally distributed, with the mean, μ_{T_1}, equal to

$$\mu_{T_1} = \frac{n_1(n + 1)}{2}$$

and the standard deviation, σ_{T_1}, equal to

$$\sigma_{T_1} = \sqrt{\frac{n_1 n_2(n + 1)}{12}}$$

Therefore, Equation (12.7) defines the standardized Z test statistic for the Wilcoxon rank sum test.

LARGE-SAMPLE WILCOXON RANK SUM TEST

$$Z_{STAT} = \frac{T_1 - \dfrac{n_1(n + 1)}{2}}{\sqrt{\dfrac{n_1 n_2(n + 1)}{12}}} \tag{12.7}$$

where the test statistic Z_{STAT} approximately follows a standardized normal distribution.

Use Equation (12.7) when the sample sizes are outside the range of Table E.6. Based on α, the level of significance selected, you reject the null hypothesis if the Z_{STAT} test statistic falls in the rejection region.

To study an application of the Wilcoxon rank sum test, recall the Chapter 10 Arlingtons scenario about VLABGo player monthly sales at the special front location and at the in-aisle location (stored in VLABGo). If you cannot assume that the populations are normally distributed,

[2]To test for differences in the median sales between the two locations, you must assume that the distributions of sales in both populations are identical except for differences in central tendency (i.e., the medians).

you can use the Wilcoxon rank sum test to evaluate possible differences in the median sales for the two display locations.[2] The VLABGo sales data and the combined ranks are shown in Table 12.15.

TABLE 12.15

Forming the Combined Rankings

Special Front $(n_1 = 10)$	Combined Ranking	In-Aisle $(n_2 = 10)$	Combined Ranking
224	12	192	7
189	4.5	236	13
248	15	164	2
285	19	154	1
273	17	189	4.5
190	6	220	11
243	14	261	16
215	9	186	3
280	18	219	10
317	20	202	8

Source: Data are taken from Table 10.1 on page 353.

Because you have not stated in advance which display location is likely to have a higher median, you use a two-tail test with the following null and alternative hypotheses:

$$H_0: M_1 = M_2 \text{ (the median sales are equal)}$$

$$H_1: M_1 \neq M_2 \text{ (the median sales are not equal)}$$

Next, you compute T_1, the sum of the ranks assigned to the *smaller* sample. When the sample sizes are equal, as in this example, you can define either sample as the group from which to compute T_1. Choosing the special front location as the first group,

$$T_1 = 12 + 4.5 + 15 + 19 + 17 + 6 + 14 + 9 + 18 + 20 = 134.5$$

As a check on the ranking procedure, you compute T_2 from

$$T_2 = 7 + 13 + 2 + 1 + 4.5 + 11 + 16 + 3 + 10 + 8 = 75.5$$

and then use Equation (12.6) on page 461 to show that the sum of the first $n = 20$ integers in the combined ranking is equal to $T_1 + T_2$:

$$T_1 + T_2 = \frac{n(n + 1)}{2}$$

$$134.5 + 75.5 = \frac{20(21)}{2} = 210$$

$$210 = 210$$

Next, you use Table E.6 to determine the lower- and upper-tail critical values for the test statistic T_1. From Table 12.16, a portion of Table E.6, observe that for a level of significance of 0.05, the critical values are 78 and 132. The decision rule is

Reject H_0 if $T_1 \leq 78$ or if $T_1 \geq 132$;

otherwise, do not reject H_0.

TABLE 12.16

Finding the Lower- and Upper-Tail Critical Values for the Wilcoxon Rank Sum Test Statistic, T_1, Where $n_1 = 10$, $n_2 = 10$, and $\alpha = 0.05$

n_2	α One-tail	α Two-tail	n_1 4	5	6	7	8	9	10
						(Lower, Upper)			
	.05	.10	16,40	24,51	33,63	43,76	54,90	66,105	
9	.025	.05	14,42	22,53	31,65	40,79	51,93	62,109	
	.01	.02	13,43	20,55	28,68	37,82	47,97	59,112	
	.005	.01	11,45	18,57	26,70	35,84	45,99	56,115	
	.05	.10	17,43	26,54	35,67	45,81	56,96	69,111	82,128
10	.025	.05	15,45	23,57	32,70	42,84	53,99	65,115	78,132
	.01	.02	13,47	21,59	29,73	39,87	49,103	61,119	74,136
	.005	.01	12,48	19,61	27,75	37,89	47,105	58,122	71,139

Source: Extracted from Table E.6.

Table 12.17 summarizes the results of the Wilcoxon rank sum test for VLABGo player monthly sales at the special front location and at the in-aisle location using the calculations on page 462 and the Figure 12.12 results. Based on the results, there is strong evidence to conclude that the two locations are significantly different in sales. Therefore, as part of the DCOVA framework, you can conclude that sales will be higher at the front location than the in-aisle location.

TABLE 12.17

Wilcoxon test summary for the monthly sales at two different locations

Results	Conclusions
$T_1 = 134.5$ is greater than 132.	1. Reject the null hypothesis H_0.
The p-value $= 0.028$ is less than the level of significance, $\alpha = 0.05$. (The Excel result uses an approximation and therefore reports a p-value $= 0.026$.)	2. Conclude that evidence exists that the two locations are significantly different with respect to sales.
	3. The probability is 0.028 that $T_1 > 134.5$.

FIGURE 12.12

Excel, JMP, and Minitab Wilcoxon rank sum test results for VLABGo player monthly sales for two in-store locations

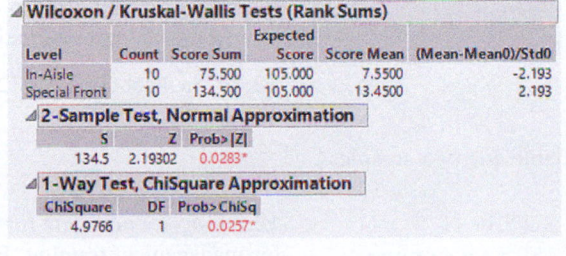

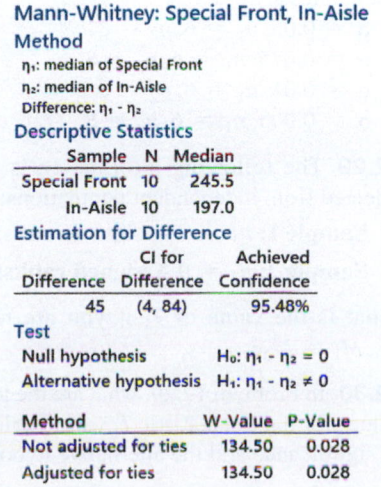

Table E.6 shows the lower and upper critical values of the Wilcoxon rank sum test statistic, T_1, but only for situations in which both n_1 and n_2 are less than or equal to 10. If either one or both of the sample sizes are greater than 10, you *must* use the large-sample Z approximation formula [Equation (12.7) on page 461]. To demonstrate the large-sample Z approximation formula, consider the VLABGo player monthly sales data. Using Equation (12.7),

$$Z_{STAT} = \frac{T_1 - \frac{n_1(n + 1)}{2}}{\sqrt{\frac{n_1 n_2 (n + 1)}{12}}}$$

$$= \frac{134.5 - \frac{(10)(21)}{2}}{\sqrt{\frac{(10)(10)(21)}{12}}}$$

$$= \frac{134.5 - 105}{13.2288} = 2.2300$$

student TIP

If the assumption of normality is met, use the pooled-variance or separate-variance test as these tests are more powerful. Use the Wilcoxon rank sum test when you doubt the normality of the populations.

Because $Z_{STAT} = 2.2300 > 1.96$, the critical value of Z at the 0.05 level of significance (or p-value $= 0.0257 < 0.05$), you reject H_0.

PROBLEMS FOR SECTION 12.4

LEARNING THE BASICS

12.27 Using Table E.6, determine the lower- and upper-tail critical values for the Wilcoxon rank sum test statistic, T_1, in each of the following two-tail tests:
a. $\alpha = 0.10$, $n_1 = 6$, $n_2 = 8$
b. $\alpha = 0.05$, $n_1 = 6$, $n_2 = 8$
c. $\alpha = 0.01$, $n_1 = 6$, $n_2 = 8$
d. Given the results in (a) through (c), what do you conclude regarding the width of the region of nonrejection as the selected level of significance, α, gets smaller?

12.28 Using Table E.6, determine the lower-tail critical value for the Wilcoxon rank sum test statistic, T_1, in each of the following one-tail tests:
a. $\alpha = 0.05$, $n_1 = 6$, $n_2 = 8$
b. $\alpha = 0.025$, $n_1 = 6$, $n_2 = 8$
c. $\alpha = 0.01$, $n_1 = 6$, $n_2 = 8$
d. $\alpha = 0.005$, $n_1 = 6$, $n_2 = 8$

12.29 The following information is available for two samples selected from independent populations:

Sample 1: $n_1 = 7$ **Assigned ranks:** 4 1 8 2 5 10 11

Sample 2: $n_2 = 9$ **Assigned ranks:** 7 16 12 9 3 14 13 6 15

What is the value of T_1 if you are testing the null hypothesis $H_0: M_1 = M_2$?

12.30 In Problem 12.29, what are the lower- and upper-tail critical values for the test statistic T_1 from Table E.6 if you use a 0.05 level of significance and the alternative hypothesis is $H_1: M_1 \neq M_2$?

12.31 In Problems 12.29 and 12.30, what is your statistical decision?

12.32 The following information is available for two samples selected from independent and similarly shaped right-skewed populations:

Sample 1: $n_1 = 5$ 1.1 2.3 2.9 3.6 14.7

Sample 2: $n_2 = 6$ 2.8 4.4 4.4 5.2 6.0 18.5

a. Replace the observed values with the corresponding ranks (where $1 =$ smallest value; $n = n_1 + n_2 = 13 =$ largest value) in the combined samples.
b. What is the value of the test statistic T_1?
c. Compute the value of T_2, the sum of the ranks in the larger sample.
d. To check the accuracy of your rankings, use Equation (12.6) on page 461 to demonstrate that $T_1 + T_2 = \frac{n(n + 1)}{2}$

12.33 From Problem 12.32, at the 0.05 level of significance, determine the lower-tail critical value for the Wilcoxon rank sum test statistic, T_1, if you want to test the null hypothesis, $H_0: M_1 \geq M_2$, against the one-tail alternative, $H_1: M_1 < M_2$.

12.34 In Problems 12.32 and 12.33, what is your statistical decision?

APPLYING THE CONCEPTS

12.35 A vice president for marketing recruits 20 college graduates for management training. Each of the 20 individuals is randomly assigned to one of two groups (10 in each group). A "traditional" method of training (T) is used in one group, and an "experimental" method (E) is used in the other. After the graduates spend six months on the job, the vice president ranks them on the basis of their performance, from 1 (worst) to 20 (best), with the following results (stored in the file TestRank):

T: 1 2 3 5 9 10 12 13 14 15

E: 4 6 7 8 11 16 17 18 19 20

Is there evidence of a difference in the median performance between the two methods? (Use $\alpha = 0.05$.)

12.36 Wine experts Gaiter and Brecher use a six-category scale when rating wines: Yech, OK, Good, Very Good, Delicious, and Delicious! Suppose Gaiter and Brecher tested wines from a random sample of eight inexpensive California Cabernets and a random sample of eight inexpensive Washington Cabernets, where *inexpensive* means wines with a U.S. suggested retail price of less than $20, and assigned the following ratings:

California—Good, Delicious, Yech, OK, OK, Very Good, Yech, OK

Washington—Very Good, OK, Delicious!, Very Good, Delicious, Good, Delicious, Delicious!

The ratings were then ranked and the ratings and the rankings stored in Cabernet .

Soruce: Data extracted from D. Gaiter and J. Brecher, "A Good U.S. Cabernet Is Hard to Find," *The Wall Street Journal*, May 19, 2006, p. W7.

a. Are the data collected by rating wines using this scale nominal, ordinal, interval, or ratio?
b. Why is the two-sample *t* test defined in Section 10.1 inappropriate to test the mean rating of California Cabernets versus Washington Cabernets?
c. Is there evidence of a significant difference in the median rating of California Cabernets and Washington Cabernets? (Use $\alpha = 0.05$.)

12.37 Is there a difference in the satisfaction rating of traditional cellphone providers who bill for service at the end of a month often under a contract and prepaid cellphone service providers who bill in advance without a contract? The file CellphoneProviders contains the satisfaction rating for 10 traditional cellphone providers and 13 prepaid cellphone service providers.

Source: Data extracted from "Carrier Ratings: Why It Pays to Think Small," *Consumer Reports*, February 2016, p. 51.

a. Is there evidence of a difference in the median satisfaction rating for traditional and prepaid providers? (Use $\alpha = 0.05$.)
b. What assumptions must you make in (a)?
c. Compare the results of (a) with those of Problem 10.9(a) on page 360.

✓SELF TEST **12.38** The management of a hotel has the business objective of increasing the return rate for hotel guests. One aspect of first impressions by guests relates to the time it takes to deliver a guest's luggage to the room after check-in to the hotel. A random sample of 20 deliveries on a particular day were selected in Wing A of the hotel, and a random sample of 20 deliveries were selected in Wing B. Delivery times were collected and stored in Luggage .
a. Is there evidence of a difference in the median delivery times in the two wings of the hotel? (Use $\alpha = 0.05$.)
b. Compare the results of (a) with those of Problem 10.65 on page 384.

12.39 The lengths of life (in hours) of a sample of 40 6-watt light emitting diode (LED) light bulbs produced by Manufacturer A and a sample of 40 6-watt LED light bulbs produced by Manufacturer B are stored in Bulbs .
a. Using a 0.05 level of significance, is there evidence of a difference in the median life of bulbs produced by the two manufacturers?
b. What assumptions must you make in (a)?
c. Compare the results of (a) with those of Problem 10.64 on page 384. Discuss.

12.40 Brand valuations are critical to CEOs, financial and marketing executives, security analysts, institutional investors, and others who depend on well-researched, reliable information for assessments and comparisons in decision making. WPP and Millward Brown annually publish the BrandZ Top 100 Most Valuable Global Brands. The BrandZ rankings combines consumer measures of brand equity with financial measures to establish a *brand value* for each brand. The file BrandZTechFin contains the 2016 brand values for the technology sector and the financial institutions sector.

Source: Data extracted from BrandZ Top 1000 Most Valuable Global Brands 2016, **bit.ly/1Y8gPqK**.

a. Using a 0.05 level of significance, is there evidence of a difference in the median brand value between the two sectors?
b. What assumptions must you make in (a)?
c. Compare the results of (a) with those of Problem 10.17 on page 361. Discuss.

12.41 A bank with a branch located in a commercial district of a city has developed an improved process for serving customers during the noon-to-1 P.M. lunch period. The bank has the business objective of reducing the waiting time (defined as the number of minutes that elapse from when the customer enters the line until he or she reaches the teller window) to increase customer satisfaction. A random sample of 15 customers is selected and waiting times are collected and stored in Bank1 . These waiting times (in minutes) are:

4.21 5.55 3.02 5.13 4.77 2.34 3.54 3.20

4.50 6.10 0.38 5.12 6.46 6.19 3.79

Another branch, located in a residential area, is also concerned with the noon-to-1 P.M. lunch period. A random sample of 15 customers is selected and waiting times are collected and stored in Bank2 . These waiting times (in minutes) are:

9.66 5.90 8.02 5.79 8.73 3.82 8.01 8.35

10.49 6.68 5.64 4.08 6.17 9.91 5.47

a. Is there evidence of a difference in the median waiting time between the two branches? (Use $\alpha = 0.05$.)
b. What assumptions must you make in (a)?
c. Compare the results (a) with those of Problem 10.12 (a) on page 360. Discuss.

12.42 The annual NFL Super Bowl is the most widely watched sporting event in the United States each year. In recent years, there has been a great deal of interest in the ads that appear during the game. These ads vary in length with most lasting 30 seconds or 60 seconds. The file SuperBowlAdScore contains the ad length and ad scores from a recent Super Bowl.

Source: Data extracted from C. Woodyard, "Funny Bone Wins Out," *USA Today*, February 6, 2016, p. 4B.

a. Is there evidence of a difference in the median rating between 30-second ads and 60-second ads? (Use $\alpha = 0.05$.)
b. What assumptions must you make in (a)?
c. Compare the results of (a) with those of Problem 10.11 (a) on page 360. Discuss.

12.5 Kruskal-Wallis Rank Test for the One-Way ANOVA

If the normality assumption of the one-way ANOVA F test is violated, you can use the Kruskal-Wallis rank test. The **Kruskal-Wallis rank test** for differences among more than two medians is an extension of the Wilcoxon rank sum test for two independent populations, that Section 12.4 discusses. The Kruskal-Wallis test has the same power relative to the one-way ANOVA F test that the Wilcoxon rank sum test has relative to the t test.

You use the Kruskal-Wallis rank test to test whether c independent groups have equal medians. The null hypothesis is

$$H_0: M_1 = M_2 = \cdots = M_c$$

and the alternative hypothesis is

$$H_1: \text{Not all } M_j \text{ are equal (where } j = 1, 2, \ldots, c).$$

student TIP

Remember that you combine the groups before you rank the values.

To use the Kruskal-Wallis rank test, you first replace the values in the c samples with their combined ranks (if necessary). Rank 1 is given to the smallest of the combined values and rank n to the largest of the combined values (where $n = n_1 + n_2 + \cdots + n_c$). If any values are tied, you assign each of them the mean of the ranks they would have otherwise been assigned if ties had not been present in the data.

The Kruskal-Wallis test is an alternative to the one-way ANOVA F test. Instead of comparing each of the c group means against the grand mean, the Kruskal-Wallis test compares the mean rank in each of the c groups against the overall mean rank, based on all n combined values. Equation (12.8) defines the Kruskal-Wallis test statistic, H.

KRUSKAL-WALLIS RANK TEST FOR DIFFERENCES AMONG c MEDIANS

$$H = \left[\frac{12}{n(n+1)} \sum_{j=1}^{c} \frac{T_j^2}{n_j} \right] - 3(n+1) \qquad (12.8)$$

where

n = total number of values over the combined samples

n_j = number of values in the jth sample ($j = 1, 2, \ldots, c$)

T_j = sum of the ranks assigned to the jth sample

T_j^2 = square of the sum of the ranks assigned to the jth sample

c = number of groups

If there is a significant difference among the c groups, the mean rank differs considerably from group to group. In the process of squaring these differences, the test statistic H becomes large. If there are no differences present, the test statistic H is small because the mean of the ranks assigned in each group should be very similar from group to group.

As the sample sizes in each group get large (i.e., at least 5), the sampling distribution of the test statistic, H, approximately follows the chi-square distribution with $c - 1$ degrees of freedom. Thus, you reject the null hypothesis if the computed value of H is greater than the upper-tail critical value (see Figure 12.13). Therefore, the decision rule is

$$\text{Reject } H_0 \text{ if } H > \chi_\alpha^2;$$

otherwise, do not reject H_0.

FIGURE 12.13
Determining the rejection region for the Kruskal-Wallis test

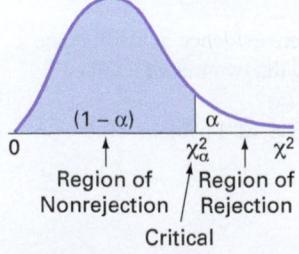

To illustrate the Kruskal-Wallis rank test for differences among c medians, return to the Arlingtons scenario on page 398 that concerns the in-store sales location experiment. If you cannot assume that the mobile electronics sales are normally distributed in all c groups, you can use the Kruskal-Wallis rank test.

The null hypothesis is that the median mobile electronics sales from each of the four in-store locations are equal. The alternative hypothesis is that at least one of these medians differs from the others:

$$H_0\text{: } M_1 = M_2 = M_3 = M_4$$

$$H_1\text{: Not all } M_j \text{ are equal (where } j = 1, 2, 3, 4).$$

Table 12.18 presents the data (stored in MobileElectronics), along with the corresponding ranks of the in-store location sales experiment at Arlingtons.

TABLE 12.18

Mobile Electronics Sales and Rank for Four In-Store Locations

IN-AISLE		FRONT		KIOSK		EXPERT	
Sales	**Rank**	**Sales**	**Rank**	**Sales**	**Rank**	**Sales**	**Rank**
27.74	1	31.47	16	30.78	11	30.25	6.5
29.96	2.5	31.86	17	30.79	12	30.25	6.5
29.96	2.5	32.13	18	30.91	13	30.29	8
30.06	4	32.22	19	30.95	14	30.33	9
30.19	5	32.29	20	31.13	15	30.55	10

In assigning ranks to the sales, the lowest sales, the first in-aisle sales in Table 12.18, is assigned the rank of 1 and the highest sales, the fifth front sales, is assigned the rank of 20. Because the second and third in-aisle sales are tied for ranks 2 and 3, each is assigned the rank 2.5.

After all the ranks are assigned, you compute the sum of the ranks for each group:

Rank sums: $T_1 = 15$ $T_2 = 90$ $T_3 = 65$ $T_4 = 40$

As a check on the rankings, recall from Equation (12.6) on page 461 that for any integer n, the sum of the first n consecutive integers is $n(n + 1)/2$. Therefore,

$$T_1 + T_2 + T_3 + T_4 = \frac{n(n + 1)}{2}$$

$$15 + 90 + 65 + 40 = \frac{(20)(21)}{2}$$

$$210 = 210$$

To test the null hypothesis of equal population medians, you calculate the test statistic H using Equation (12.8) on page 466:

$$H = \left[\frac{12}{n(n + 1)} \sum_{j=1}^{c} \frac{T_j^2}{n_j} \right] - 3(n + 1)$$

$$= \left\{ \frac{12}{(20)(21)} \left[\frac{(15)^2}{5} + \frac{(90)^2}{5} + \frac{(65)^2}{5} + \frac{(40)^2}{5} \right] \right\} - 3(21)$$

$$= \left(\frac{12}{420} \right)(2{,}830) - 63 = 17.8571$$

Table 12.20 summarizes the results of the Kruskal-Wallis rank test test for the differences among the median mobile electronics sales for four in-store locations using the Table 12.19 calculations and the Figure 12.14 results. Based on the results, there is strong evidence that the four locations are significantly different in sales. Therefore, as part of the DCOVA framework, you can conclude that sales appear to be higher at the front location and the endcap location.

TABLE 12.19

Finding χ_α^2, the Upper-Tail Critical Value for the Kruskal-Wallis Rank Test, at the 0.05 Level of Significance with 3 Degrees of Freedom

					Cumulative Area					
	.005	.01	.025	.05	.10	.25	.75	.90	.95	.975
					Upper-Tail Area					
Degrees of Freedom	.995	.99	.975	.95	.90	.75	.25	.10	.05	.025
1	—	—	0.001	0.004	0.016	0.102	1.323	2.706	3.841	5.024
2	0.010	0.020	0.051	0.103	0.211	0.575	2.773	4.605	5.991	7.378
3	0.072	0.115	0.216	0.352	0.584	1.213	4.108	6.251	7.815	9.348
4	0.207	0.297	0.484	0.711	1.064	1.923	5.385	7.779	9.488	11.143
5	0.412	0.554	0.831	1.145	1.610	2.675	6.626	9.236	11.071	12.833

Source: Extracted from Table E.4.

TABLE 12.20

Kruskal-Wallis rank test summary for median mobile electronics sales for four in-store locations

Results

$\chi_{STAT}^2 = 17.88$ is greater than 7.815. (The Excel result, 17.8571, does not adjust for ties.)

The p-value $= 0.0005$ is less than the level of significance, $\alpha = 0.05$.

Conclusions

1. Reject the null hypothesis H_0.
2. Conclude that evidence exists that the four in-store locations are significantly different with respect to sales. (See Reference 2 to simultaneously compare all four locations.)
3. The probability is 0.0005 that $\chi_{STAT}^2 > 17.8571$.

FIGURE 12.14

Excel, JMP, and Minitab Kruskal-Wallis rank test results for the differences among the median mobile electronics sales for four in-store locations (JMP and Minitab show an adjustment for ties)

JMP and Minitab results contain an adjustment for ties.

	A	B
1	Kruskal-Wallis Rank Test	
2		
3	Data	
4	Level of Significance	0.05
5		
6	Intermediate Calculations	
7	Sum of Squared Ranks/Sample Size	2830
8	Sum of Sample Sizes	20
9	Number of Groups	4
10		
11	Test Result	
12	H Test Statistic	17.8571
13	Critical Value	7.8147
14	p-Value	0.0005
15	Reject the null hypothesis	

	D	E	F	G
3		Calculations		
4	Group	Sample Size	Sum of Ranks	Mean Rank
5	In-aisle	5	15	3
6	Front	5	90	18
7	Kiosk	5	65	13
8	Expert	5	40	8

Wilcoxon / Kruskal-Wallis Tests (Rank Sums)

Level	Count	Score Sum	Expected Score	Score Mean	(Mean-Mean0)/Std0
In-aisle	5	15.000	52.500	3.0000	-3.232
Front	5	90.000	52.500	18.0000	3.232
Kiosk	5	65.000	52.500	13.0000	1.048
Expert	5	40.000	52.500	8.0000	-1.048

1-Way Test, ChiSquare Approximation

ChiSquare	DF	Prob>ChiSq
17.8840	3	0.0005*

Small sample sizes. Refer to statistical tables for tests, rather than large-sample approximations.

Kruskal-Wallis Test: Sales versus Location

Descriptive Statistics

Location	N	Median	Mean Rank	Z-Value
Expert	5	30.29	8.0	-1.09
Front	5	32.13	18.0	3.27
In-aisle	5	29.96	3.0	-3.27
Kiosk	5	30.91	13.0	1.09
Overall	20		10.5	

Test

Null hypothesis	H_0: All medians are equal
Alternative hypothesis	H_1: At least one median is different

Method	DF	H-Value	P-Value
Not adjusted for ties	3	17.86	0.000
Adjusted for ties	3	17.88	0.000

Assumptions of the Kruskal-Wallis Rank Test

To use the Kruskal-Wallis rank test, you make the following assumptions:

- The c samples are randomly and independently selected from their respective populations.
- The underlying variable is continuous.
- The data provide at least a set of ranks, both within and among the c samples.
- The c populations have the same variability.
- The c populations have the same shape.

The Kruskal-Wallis procedure makes less stringent assumptions than does the F test. If you ignore the last two assumptions (variability and shape), you can still use the Kruskal-Wallis rank test to determine whether at least one of the populations differs from the other populations in some characteristic—such as central tendency, variation, or shape.

To use the F test, you must assume that the c samples are from normal populations that have equal variances. When the more stringent assumptions of the F test hold, you should use the F test instead of the Kruskal-Wallis test because it has slightly more power to detect significant differences among groups. However, if the assumptions of the F test do not hold, you should use the Kruskal-Wallis test.

PROBLEMS FOR SECTION 12.5

LEARNING THE BASICS

12.43 What is the upper-tail critical value from the chi-square distribution if you use the Kruskal-Wallis rank test for comparing the medians in six populations at the 0.01 level of significance?

12.44 For this problem, use the results of Problem 12.43.
a. State the decision rule for testing the null hypothesis that all six groups have equal population medians.
b. What is your statistical decision if the computed value of the test statistic H is 13.77?

APPLYING THE CONCEPTS

12.45 A pet food company has the business objective of expanding its product line beyond its current kidney and shrimp-based cat foods. The company developed two new products—one based on chicken livers and the other based on salmon. The company conducted an experiment to compare the two new products with its two existing ones, as well as a generic beef-based product sold at a supermarket chain.

For the experiment, a sample of 50 cats from the population at a local animal shelter was selected. Ten cats were randomly assigned to each of the five products being tested. Each of the cats was then presented with 3 ounces of the selected food in a dish at feeding time. The researchers defined the variable to be measured as the number of ounces of food that the cat consumed within a 10-minute time interval that began when the filled dish was presented. The results for this experiment are summarized in the table in the next column and stored in CatFood .
a. At the 0.05 level of significance, is there evidence of a significant difference in the median amount of food eaten among the various products?
b. Compare the results of (a) with those of Problem 11.13 (a) on page 413.
c. Which test is more appropriate for these data: the Kruskal-Wallis rank test or the one-way ANOVA F test? Explain.

Kidney	Shrimp	Chicken Liver	Salmon	Beef
2.37	2.26	2.29	1.79	2.09
2.62	2.69	2.23	2.33	1.87
2.31	2.25	2.41	1.96	1.67
2.47	2.45	2.68	2.05	1.64
2.59	2.34	2.25	2.26	2.16
2.62	2.37	2.17	2.24	1.75
2.34	2.22	2.37	1.96	1.18
2.47	2.56	2.26	1.58	1.92
2.45	2.36	2.45	2.18	1.32
2.32	2.59	2.57	1.93	1.94

✓ SELF TEST **12.46** A hospital conducted a study of the waiting time in its emergency room. The hospital has a main campus, along with three affiliated locations. Management had a business objective of reducing waiting time for emergency room cases that did not require immediate attention. To study this, a random sample of 15 emergency room cases at each location were selected on a particular day, and the waiting time (recorded from check-in to when the patient was called into the clinic area) was measured. The results are stored in ERWaiting .
a. At the 0.05 level of significance, is there evidence of a difference in the median waiting times in the four locations?
b. Compare the results of (a) with those of Problem 11.9 (a) on page 412.

12.47 *QSR* magazine reports on the largest quick-serve and fast-casual brands in the United States. The file FastFoodChain contains the food segment (burger, chicken, sandwich, or pizza/pasta) and U.S. mean sales per unit ($thousands) for each of 37 quick-service brands.

Source: Data extracted from "The QSR 50," **bit.ly/2rYVYP3**.

a. At the 0.05 level of significance, is there evidence of a difference in the median U.S. average sales per unit ($thousands) among the food segments?

b. Compare the results of (a) with those of Problem 11.11 (a) on page 413.

12.48 An advertising agency has been hired by a manufacturer of pens to develop an advertising campaign for the upcoming holiday season. To prepare for this project, the research director decides to initiate a study of the effect of advertising on product perception. An experiment is designed to compare five different advertisements. Advertisement A greatly undersells the pen's characteristics. Advertisement B slightly undersells the pen's characteristics. Advertisement C slightly oversells the pen's characteristics. Advertisement D greatly oversells the pen's characteristics. Advertisement E attempts to correctly state the pen's characteristics.

A sample of 30 adult respondents, taken from a larger focus group, is randomly assigned to the five advertisements (so that there are six respondents to each). After reading the advertisement and developing a sense of product expectation, all respondents unknowingly receive the same pen to evaluate. The respondents are permitted to test the pen and the plausibility of the advertising copy. The respondents are then asked to rate the pen from 1 to 7 on the product characteristic scales of appearance, durability, and writing performance. The *combined* scores of three ratings (appearance, durability, and writing performance) for the 30 respondents are stored in Pen . These data are:

A	B	C	D	E
15	16	8	5	12
18	17	7	6	19
17	21	10	13	18
19	16	15	11	12
19	19	14	9	17
20	17	14	10	14

a. At the 0.05 level of significance, is there evidence of a difference in the median ratings of the five advertisements?

b. Compare the results of (a) with those of Problem 11.10 (a) on page 413.

c. Which test is more appropriate for these data: the Kruskal-Wallis rank test or the one-way ANOVA F test? Explain.

12.49 A transportation strategist wanted to compare the traffic congestion levels across four continents: Asia, Europe, North America, and South America. The file CongestionLevel contains congestion level, defined as the increase (%) in overall travel time when compared to a free flow situation (an uncongested situation) for 10 cities in each continent.

Source: Data extracted from "TomTom Traffic Index," **bit.ly/1RxyKAl**.

a. At the 0.05 level of significance, is there evidence of a difference in the median congestion levels across continents?

b. Compare the results of (a) with those of Problem 11.14 (a) on page 414.

12.50 The more costly and time consuming it is to export and import, the more difficult it is for local companies to be competitive and to reach international markets. As part of an initial investigation exploring foreign market entry, 10 countries were selected from each of four global regions. The cost associated with importing a standardized cargo of goods by sea transport in these countries (in US$ per container) is stored in ForeignMarket2 .

Source: Data extracted from **doingbusiness.org/data**.

a. At the 0.05 level of significance, is there evidence of a difference in the median cost across the four global regions associated with importing a standardized cargo of goods by sea transport?

b. Compare the results in (a) to those in Problem 11.8 (a) on page 412.

12.6 McNemar Test for the Difference Between Two Proportions (Related Samples)

Tests such as chi-square test for the difference between two proportions discussed in Section 12.1 require independent samples from each population. However, sometimes when you are testing differences between the proportion of items of interest, the data are collected from repeated measurements or matched samples.

To test whether there is evidence of a difference between the proportions when the data have been collected from two related samples, you can use the McNemar test. The **Section 12.6 online topic** discusses this test and illustrates its use.

12.7 Chi-Square Test for the Variance or Standard Deviation

When analyzing numerical data, sometimes you need to test a hypothesis about the population variance or standard deviation. Assuming that the data are normally distributed, you use the χ^2 test for the variance or standard deviation to test whether the population variance or standard deviation is equal to a specified value. The **Section 12.7 online topic** discusses this test and illustrates its use.

12.8 Wilcoxon Signed Ranks Test for Two Related Populations

Section 10.2 discusses using the paired t test to compare the means of two related populations. The paired t test assumes that the data are measured on an interval or a ratio scale and are normally distributed. When these assumptions cannot be made, the nonparametric **Wilcoxon signed ranks test** can be used to test for the median difference. The **Section 12.8 online topic** discusses this test and illustrates its use.

12.9 Friedman Rank Test for the Randomized Block Design

When analyzing a randomized block design, sometimes the data consists only of ranks within each block. When the data from each of the c groups cannot be assumed to be from normally distributed populations, the nonparametric **Friedman rank test** can be used. The **Section 12.9 online topic** discusses this test and illustrates its use.

▼USING **STATISTICS**
Avoiding Guesswork ... , Revisited

In the Using Statistics scenario, you were the manager of T.C. Resort Properties, a collection of five upscale hotels located on two tropical islands. To assess the quality of services being provided by your hotels, guests are encouraged to complete a satisfaction survey at check-out time or later, via email. You analyzed the data from these surveys to determine the overall satisfaction with the services provided, the likelihood that the guests will return to the hotel, and the reasons given by some guests for not wanting to return.

On one island, T.C. Resort Properties operates the Beachcomber and Windsurfer hotels. You performed a chi-square test for the difference in two proportions and concluded that a greater proportion of guests are willing to return to the Beachcomber Hotel than to the Windsurfer. On the other island, T.C. Resort Properties operates the Golden Palm, Palm Royale, and Palm Princess hotels. To see if guest satisfaction was the same among the three hotels, you performed a chi-square test for the differences among more than two proportions. The test confirmed that the three proportions are not equal, and guests seem to be most likely to return to the Palm Royale and least likely to return to the Golden Palm.

In addition, you investigated whether the reasons given for not returning to the Golden Palm, Palm Royale, and Palm Princess were unique to a certain hotel or common to all three hotels. By performing a chi-square test of independence, you determined that the reasons given for wanting to return or not depended on the hotel where the guests had been staying. By examining the observed and expected frequencies, you concluded that guests were more satisfied with the amenities at the Golden Palm and were much more satisfied with the quality of the Palm Princess rooms. Guest satisfaction with dining options was not significantly different among the three hotels.

▼SUMMARY

Figure 12.15 on page 472 presents a roadmap for this chapter. First, you used hypothesis testing for analyzing categorical data from two independent samples and from more than two independent samples. In addition, the rules of probability from Section 4.2 were extended to the hypothesis of independence in the joint responses to two categorical variables. You also studied two nonparametric tests. You used the Wilcoxon rank sum test when the assumptions of the t test for two independent samples were violated and the Kruskal-Wallis test when the assumptions of the one-way ANOVA F test were violated.

FIGURE 12.15
Roadmap of Chapter 12

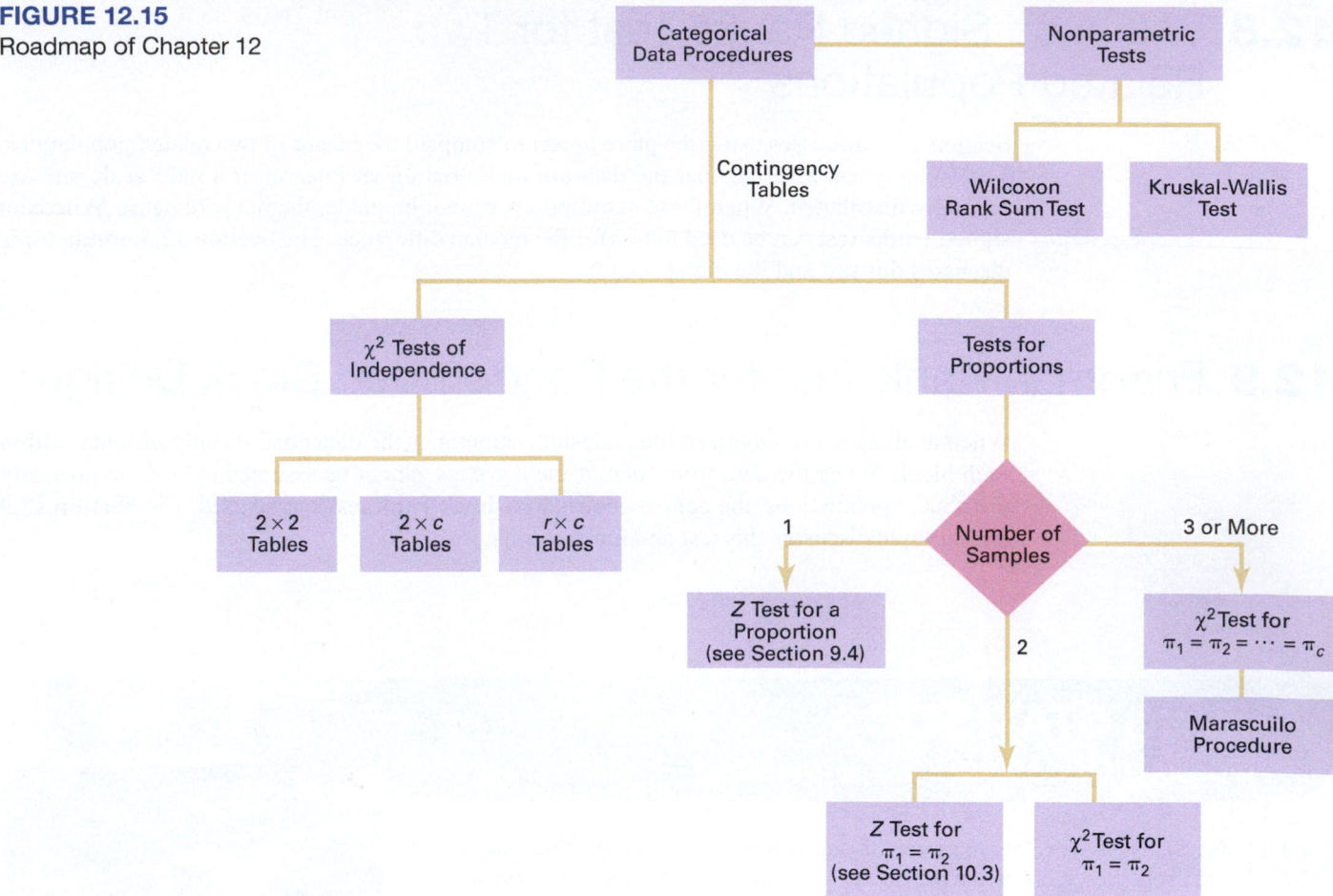

▼REFERENCES

1. Corder, G. W., and D. I. Foreman, *Nonparametric Statistics: A Step-by-Step Approach*. New York: Wiley, 2014.
2. Daniel, W. W. *Applied Nonparametric Statistics*, 2nd ed. Boston: PWS Kent, 1990.
3. Dixon, W. J., and F. J. Massey, Jr. *Introduction to Statistical Analysis*, 4th ed. New York: McGraw-Hill, 1983.
4. Hollander, M., D. A. Wolfe, and E. Chicken, *Nonparametric Statistical Methods*, 3rd ed. New York: Wiley, 2014.
5. Lewontin, R. C., and J. Felsenstein. "Robustness of Homogeneity Tests in 2 × n Tables," *Biometrics*, 21(March 1965): 19–33.
6. Marascuilo, L. A. "Large-Sample Multiple Comparisons," *Psychological Bulletin*, 65(1966): 280–290.
7. Marascuilo, L. A., and M. McSweeney. *Nonparametric and Distribution-Free Methods for the Social Sciences*. Monterey, CA: Brooks/Cole, 1977.
8. Winer, B. J., D. R. Brown, and K. M. Michels. *Statistical Principles in Experimental Design*, 3rd ed. New York: McGraw-Hill, 1989.

▼KEY EQUATIONS

χ^2 Test for the Difference Between Two Proportions

$$\chi^2_{STAT} = \sum_{\text{all cells}} \frac{(f_o - f_e)^2}{f_e} \tag{12.1}$$

Computing the Estimated Overall Proportion for Two Groups

$$\bar{p} = \frac{X_1 + X_2}{n_1 + n_2} = \frac{X}{n} \tag{12.2}$$

Computing the Estimated Overall Proportion for c Groups

$$\bar{p} = \frac{X_1 + X_2 + \ldots + X_c}{n_1 + n_2 + \ldots + n_c} = \frac{X}{n} \tag{12.3}$$

Critical Range for the Marascuilo Procedure

$$\text{Critical range} = \sqrt{\chi_\alpha^2} \sqrt{\frac{p_j(1 - p_j)}{n_j} + \frac{p_{j'}(1 - p_{j'})}{n_{j'}}} \tag{12.4}$$

Computing the Expected Frequency

$$f_e = \frac{\text{Row total} \times \text{Column total}}{n} \tag{12.5}$$

Checking the Rankings

$$T_1 + T_2 = \frac{n(n + 1)}{2} \tag{12.6}$$

Large-Sample Wilcoxon Rank Sum Test

$$Z_{STAT} = \frac{T_1 - \frac{n_1(n + 1)}{2}}{\sqrt{\frac{n_1 n_2(n + 1)}{12}}} \tag{12.7}$$

Kruskal-Wallis Rank Test for Differences Among c Medians

$$H = \left[\frac{12}{n(n + 1)} \sum_{j=1}^{c} \frac{T_j^2}{n_j} \right] - 3(n + 1) \tag{12.8}$$

▼ KEY TERMS

chi-square (χ^2) distribution   442
chi-square (χ^2) test for the difference between two proportions   442
chi-square (χ^2) test of independence   455
expected frequency (f_e)   442

Kruskal-Wallis rank test   466
Marascuilo procedure   451
nonparametric methods   460
observed frequency (f_o)   442

$2 \times c$ contingency table   448
2×2 contingency table   441
two-way contingency table   441
Wilcoxon rank sum test   460

▼ CHECKING YOUR UNDERSTANDING

12.51 Under what conditions should you use the χ^2 test to determine whether there is a difference between the proportions of two independent populations?

12.52 Under what conditions should you use the χ^2 test to determine whether there is a difference among the proportions of more than two independent populations?

12.53 Under what conditions should you use the χ^2 test of independence?

12.54 Under what conditions should you use the Wilcoxon rank sum test instead of the t test for the difference between the means?

12.55 Under what conditions should you use the Kruskal-Wallis rank test instead of the one-way ANOVA?

▼ CHAPTER REVIEW PROBLEMS

12.56 Undergraduate students at Miami University in Oxford, Ohio, were surveyed in order to evaluate the effect of gender and price on purchasing a pizza from Pizza Hut. Students were told to suppose that they were planning to have a large two-topping pizza delivered to their residence that evening. The students had to decide between ordering from Pizza Hut at a reduced price of $8.49 (the regular price for a large two-topping pizza from the Oxford Pizza Hut at the time was $11.49) and ordering a pizza from a different pizzeria. The results from this question are summarized in the following contingency table:

| | PIZZERIA | | |
GENDER	Pizza Hut	Other	Total
Female	4	13	17
Male	6	12	18
Total	10	25	35

a. Using a 0.05 level of significance, is there evidence of a difference between males and females in their pizzeria selection?
b. What is your answer to (a) if nine of the male students selected Pizza Hut and nine selected another pizzeria?

A subsequent survey evaluated purchase decisions at other prices. These results are summarized in the following contingency table:

	PRICE			
PIZZERIA	**$8.49**	**$11.49**	**$14.49**	**Total**
Pizza Hut	10	5	2	17
Other	25	23	27	75
Total	35	28	29	92

c. Using a 0.05 level of significance and using the data in the second contingency table, is there evidence of a difference in pizzeria selection based on price?
d. Determine the p-value in (c) and interpret its meaning.

12.57 What social media tools do marketers commonly use? The Social Media Examiner surveyed marketers who commonly use an indicated social media tool. Surveyed were both B2B marketers, marketers that focus primarily on attracting businesses, and B2C marketers, marketers that primarily target consumers. Suppose the survey was based on 500 B2B marketers and 500 B2C marketers and yielded the results in the following table.

Data extracted from *2017 Social Media Marketing Industry Report*, available at **bit.ly/2rFmLzh**.

	BUSINESS FOCUS	
SOCIAL MEDIA TOOL	**B2B**	**B2C**
Facebook	89%	97%
Twitter	75%	65%
LinkedIn	81%	44%
Pinterest	26%	32%

For *each social media tool*, at the 0.05 level of significance, determine whether there is a difference between B2B marketers and B2C marketers in the proportion who used each social media tool.

12.58 Business leaders around the world are becoming aware of the huge potential of digital transformation. Fujitsu conducted as global survey to find out more about how business leaders are responding to the digital transformation revolution. To assess the extent of business embarkment on digital transformation, a sample of 745 managers and key decision makers in mid- and large-sized companies was selected and asked whether their organization has embarked on digital transformation specific to their industry sector. The results are summarized as follows:

	INDUSTRY SECTOR					
EMBARKED?	**Finance, Insurance**	**Healthcare**	**Manufacturing**	**Transport (Logistic)**	**Wholesale, Retail Trade**	**Total**
Yes	70	51	149	26	50	346
No	68	49	165	30	87	399
Total	138	100	314	56	137	745

Source: "Global Digit Transformation Survey Report," available at **bit.ly/2qRXlLb**.

a. At the 0.05 level of significance, is there evidence of a difference in the proportion of organizations that have embarked on digital transformation on the basis of industry sector?

Respondents associated with organizations that have embarked on digital transformation were asked to describe the progress of the digital transformation. The results, cross-classified by industry sector, are as follows:

	INDUSTRY SECTOR					
PROGRESS	**Finance, Insurance**	**Healthcare**	**Manufacturing**	**Transport (Logistic)**	**Wholesale, Retail Trade**	**Total**
Planning	7	15	15	5	10	52
Testing	31	12	24	5	11	83
Implementing	12	12	54	9	15	102
Outcomes delivered	20	12	56	7	14	109
Total	70	51	149	26	50	346

b. At the 0.05 level of significance, is there evidence of a relationship between digital transformation progress and industry sector?

12.59 Do Americans trust advertisements? A survey by YouGov asked Americans who view advertisements at least once a month how honest the advertisements that they see, read, and hear are. The results were:

	GEOGRAPHIC REGION				
HONEST?	**Northeast**	**Midwest**	**South**	**West**	**Total**
Yes	102	118	220	115	555
No	74	93	135	130	432
Total	176	211	355	245	987

Source: "Truth in advertising: 50% don't trust what they see, read and hear," **bit.ly/1ivIllLX**.

a. At the 0.05 level of significance, is there evidence of a difference in the proportion of Americans who say advertisements are honest on the basis of geographic region?

YouGov also asked Americans who view advertisements at least once a month how much they trust the advertisements that they see, read, and hear. The results were:

TRUST?	GEOGRAPHIC REGION				
	Northeast	Midwest	South	West	Total
Yes	88	108	202	93	491
No	88	103	153	152	496
Total	176	211	355	245	987

Source: "Truth in advertising: 50% don't trust what they see, read and hear," **bit.ly/1ivIlLX**.

b. At the 0.05 level of significance, is there evidence of a difference in the proportion of Americans who say they trust advertisements on the basis of geographic region?

CHAPTER 12

▾CASES

Managing Ashland MultiComm Services
PHASE 1

Reviewing the results of its research, the marketing department team concluded that a segment of Ashland households might be interested in a discounted trial subscription to the AMS *3-For-All* service. The team decided to test various discounts before determining the type of discount to offer during the trial period. It decided to conduct an experiment using three types of discounts plus a plan that offered no discount during the trial period:

1. No discount for the *3-For-All* service. Subscribers would pay $99.99 per month for the *3-For-All* service during the trial period.

2. Moderate discount for the *3-For-All* service. Subscribers would pay $79.99 per month for the *3-For-All* service during the trial period.

3. Substantial discount for the *3-For-All* service. Subscribers would pay $59.99 per month for the *3-For-All* service during the trial period.

4. Discount restaurant card. Subscribers would be given a special card providing a discount of 15% at selected restaurants in Ashland during the trial period.

Each participant in the experiment was randomly assigned to a discount plan. A random sample of 100 subscribers to each plan during the trial period was tracked to determine how many would continue to subscribe to the *3-For-All* service after the trial period. Table AMS 12.1 summarizes the results.

TABLE AMS12.1
Number of Subscribers Who Continue Subscriptions after Trial Period with Four Discount Plans

CONTINUE SUBSCRIPTIONS AFTER TRIAL PERIOD	DISCOUNT PLANS				
	No Discount	Moderate Discount	Substantial Discount	Restaurant Card	Total
Yes	24	30	38	51	143
No	76	70	62	49	257
Total	100	100	100	100	400

1. Analyze the results of the experiment. Write a report to the team that includes your recommendation for which discount plan to use. Be prepared to discuss the limitations and assumptions of the experiment.

PHASE 2

The marketing department team discussed the results of the survey presented in Chapter 8, on pages 302–303. The team realized that the evaluation of individual questions was providing only limited information. In order to further understand the market for the *3-For-All* service, the data were organized in the following contingency tables:

HAS AMS SMARTPHONE	HAS AMS INTERNET SERVICE		
	Yes	No	Total
Yes	55	28	83
No	207	128	335
Total	262	156	418

DISCOUNT TRIAL			
TYPE OF SERVICE	Yes	No	Total
Basic or none	8	156	164
Enhanced	32	222	254
Total	40	378	418

	WATCHES PREMIUM CONTENT				
SERVICE	Almost Every Day	Several Times a Week	Almost Never	Never	Total
Basic or none	2	5	30	127	164
Enhanced	14	35	149	56	254
Total	16	40	179	183	418

	WATCHES PREMIUM CONTENT				
DISCOUNT	Almost Every Day	Several Times a Week	Almost Never	Never	Total
Yes	5	6	16	13	40
No	11	34	163	170	378
Total	16	40	179	183	418

	METHOD FOR CURRENT SUBSCRIPTION					
DISCOUNT	Email/ Text	Toll-Free Number	AMS Website	In-store Signup	MyTVLab Promo	Total
Yes	5	14	12	4	5	40
No	65	50	224	32	7	378
Total	70	64	236	36	12	418

	METHOD FOR CURRENT SUBSCRIPTION					
GOLD CARD	Email/ Text	Toll-Free Number	AMS Website	In-store Signup	MyTVLab Promo	Total
Yes	4	12	12	4	6	38
No	66	52	224	32	6	380
Total	70	64	236	36	12	418

2. Analyze the results of the contingency tables. Write a report for the marketing department team, discussing the marketing implications of the results for Ashland MultiComm Services.

Digital Case

Apply your knowledge of testing for the difference between two proportions in this Digital Case, which extends the T.C. Resort Properties Using Statistics scenario of this chapter.

As T.C. Resort Properties seeks to improve its customer service, the company faces new competition from SunLow Resorts. SunLow has recently opened resort hotels on the islands where T.C. Resort Properties has its five hotels. SunLow is currently

advertising that a random survey of 300 customers revealed that about 60% of the customers preferred its "Concierge Class" travel reward program over the T.C. Resorts "TCRewards Plus" program.

Open and review **ConciergeClass.pdf**, an electronic brochure that describes the Concierge Class program and compares it to the T.C. Resorts program. Then answer the following questions:

1. Are the claims made by SunLow valid?
2. What analyses of the survey data would lead to a more favorable impression about T.C. Resort Properties?
3. Perform one of the analyses identified in your answer to step 2.
4. Review the data about the T.C. Resort Properties customers presented in this chapter. Are there any other questions that you might include in a future survey of travel reward programs? Explain.

Sure Value Convenience Stores

You work in the corporate office for a nationwide convenience store franchise that operates nearly 10,000 stores. The per-store daily customer count (i.e., the mean number of customers in a store in one day) has been steady, at 900, for some time. To increase the customer count, the chain is considering cutting prices for coffee beverages. Management needs to determine how much prices can be cut in order to increase the daily customer count without reducing the gross margin on coffee sales too much. You decide to carry out an experiment in a sample of 24 stores where customer counts have been running almost exactly at the national average of 900. In 6 of the stores, a small coffee will be $0.59, in another 6 stores the price will be $0.69, in a third group of 6 stores, the price will be $0.79, and in a fourth group of 6 stores, the price will now be $0.89. After four weeks, the daily customer count in the stores is stored in CoffeeSales .

At the 0.05 level of significance, is there evidence of a difference in the median daily customer count based on the price of a small coffee? What price should the stores sell the coffee for?

CardioGood Fitness

Return to the CardioGood Fitness case first presented on page 33. The data for this case are stored in CardioGood Fitness .

1. Determine whether differences exist in the median age in years, education in years, annual household income ($), number of times the customer plans to use the treadmill each week, and the number of miles the customer expects to walk or run each week based on the product purchased (TM195, TM498, TM798).
2. Determine whether differences exist in the relationship status (single or partnered), and the self-rated fitness based on the product purchased (TM195, TM498, TM798).
3. Write a report to be presented to the management of CardioGood Fitness, detailing your findings.

More Descriptive Choices Follow-Up

Follow up the "Using Statistics: More Descriptive Choices, Revisited" on page 159 by using the data that are stored in Retirement Funds to:

1. Determine whether there is a difference between the growth and value funds in the median one-year return percentages, five-year return percentages, and ten-year return percentages.

2. Determine whether there is a difference between the small, mid-cap, and large market cap funds in the median one-year return percentages, five-year return percentages, and ten-year return percentages.

3. Determine whether there is a difference in risk based on market cap, a difference in rating based on market cap, a difference in risk based on type of fund, and a difference in rating based on type of fund.

4. Write a report summarizing your findings.

Clear Mountain State Student Survey

The Student News Service at Clear Mountain State University (CMSU) has decided to gather data about the undergraduate students that attend CMSU. It creates and distributes a survey of 14 questions and receives responses from 111 undergraduates, which it stores in StudentSurvey .

1. Construct contingency tables using gender, major, plans to go to graduate school, and employment status. (You need to construct six tables, taking two variables at a time.) Analyze the data at the 0.05 level of significance to determine whether any significant relationships exist among these variables.

2. At the 0.05 level of significance, is there evidence of a difference between males and females in median grade point average, expected starting salary, number of social networking sites registered for, age, spending on textbooks and supplies, text messages sent in a week, and the wealth needed to feel rich?

3. At the 0.05 level of significance, is there evidence of a difference between students who plan to go to graduate school and those who do not plan to go to graduate school in median grade point average, expected starting salary, number of social networking sites registered for, age, spending on textbooks and supplies.

▾EXCEL GUIDE

EG12.1 CHI-SQUARE TEST for the DIFFERENCE BETWEEN TWO PROPORTIONS

Key Technique Use the **CHISQ.INV.RT**(*level of significance, degrees of freedom*) function to compute the critical value.

Use the **CHISQ.DIST.RT**(*chi-square test statistic, degrees of freedom*) function to compute the *p*-value.

Example Perform the Figure 12.3 chi-square test for the two-hotel guest satisfaction data on page 445.

PHStat Use **Chi-Square Test for Differences in Two Proportions**.

For the example, select **PHStat→Two-Sample Tests (Summarized Data)→Chi-Square Test for Differences in Two Proportions**. In the procedure's dialog box, enter **0.05** as the **Level of Significance**, enter a **Title**, and click **OK**. In the new worksheet:

1. Read the yellow note about entering values and then press the **Delete** key to delete the note.
2. Enter **Hotel** in cell **B4** and **Choose Again?** in cell **A5**.
3. Enter **Beachcomber** in cell **B5** and **Windsurfer** in cell **C5**.
4. Enter **Yes** in cell **A6** and **No** in cell **A7**.
5. Enter **163**, **64**, **154**, and **108** in cells **B6**, **B7**, **C6**, and **C7**, respectively.

Workbook Use the **COMPUTE worksheet** of the **Chi-Square workbook** as a template.

The worksheet already contains the Table 12.2 two-hotel guest satisfaction data. For other problems, change the **Observed Frequencies** cell counts and row and column labels in rows 4 through 7.

EG12.2 CHI-SQUARE TEST for DIFFERENCES AMONG MORE THAN TWO PROPORTIONS

Key Technique Use the **CHISQ.INV.RT** and **CHISQ.DIST.RT** functions to compute the critical value and the *p*-value, respectively.

Example Perform the Figure 12.6 chi-square test for the three-hotel guest satisfaction data on page 451.

PHStat Use **Chi-Square Test**.

For the example, select **PHStat→Multiple-Sample Tests→Chi-Square Test**. In the procedure's dialog box (shown in right column):

1. Enter **0.05** as the **Level of Significance**.
2. Enter **2** as the **Number of Rows**.
3. Enter **3** as the **Number of Columns**.
4. Enter a **Title** and click **OK**.

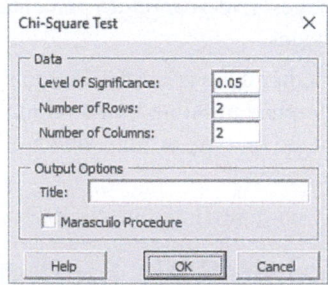

In the new worksheet:

5. Read the yellow note instructions about entering values and then press the **Delete key** to delete the note.
6. Enter the Table 12.7 data (on page 449), including row and column labels, in rows 4 through 7. The **#DIV/0!** error messages will disappear when you finish entering all the table data.

Workbook Use the **ChiSquare2×3 worksheet** of the **Chi-Square Worksheets workbook** as a model.

The worksheet already contains the page 449 Table 12.7 guest satisfaction data. For other 2 × 3 problems, change the **Observed Frequencies** cell counts and row and column labels in rows 4 through 7.

For 2 × 4 problems, use the **ChiSquare2×4 worksheet** and change the **Observed Frequencies** cell counts and row and column labels in that worksheet. For 2 × 5 problems, use the **ChiSquare2×5 worksheet** and change the **Observed Frequencies** cell counts and row and column labels in that worksheet.

The Marascuilo Procedure

Key Technique Use formulas to compute the absolute differences and the critical range.

Example Perform the Figure 12.7 Marascuilo procedure for the guest satisfaction survey on page 453.

PHStat Modify the *PHStat* instructions of the previous section. In step 4, check **Marascuilo Procedure** in addition to entering a **Title** and clicking **OK**.

Workbook Use the **Marascuilo2×3** of the **Chi-Square Worksheets workbook** as a template.

The worksheet requires no entries or changes to use. For 2 × 4 problems, use the **Marascuilo2×4 worksheet** and for 2 × 5 problems, use the **Marascuilo2×5 worksheet**.

Every Marascuilo worksheet uses values from the observed frequencies table in the companion ChiSquare worksheet to compute critical range values in the Marascuilo table area (rows 11 through 16 in Figure 12.7). In column D, the worksheet uses an IF function to compare the absolute difference to the critical range for each pair of groups and then displays either "Significant" or "Not Significant".

EG12.3 CHI-SQUARE TEST of INDEPENDENCE

Key Technique Use the **CHISQ.INV.RT** and **CHISQ.DIST.RT** functions to compute the critical value and the *p*-value, respectively.

Example Perform the Figure 12.10 chi-square test for the primary reason for not returning to hotel data on page 458.

PHStat Use **Chi-Square Test**.

For the example, select **PHStat → Multiple-Sample Tests → Chi-Square Test**. In the procedure's dialog box (shown below):

1. Enter **0.05** as the **Level of Significance**.
2. Enter **4** as the **Number of Rows**.
3. Enter **3** as the **Number of Columns**.
4. Enter a **Title** and click **OK**.

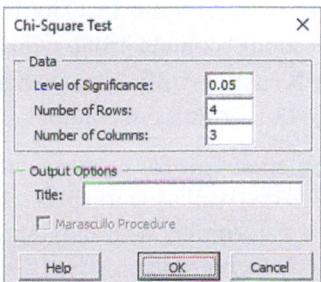

In the new worksheet:

5. Read the yellow note about entering values and then press the **Delete key** to delete the note.
6. Enter the Table 12.11 data on page 455, including row and column labels, in rows 4 through 9. The **#DIV/0!** error messages will disappear when you finish entering all of the table data.

Workbook Use the **ChiSquare4×3 worksheet** of the **Chi-Square Worksheets workbook** as a model.

The worksheet already contains the page 455 Table 12.11 primary reason for not returning to hotel data. For other 4 × 3 problems, change the **Observed Frequencies** cell counts and row and column labels in rows 4 through 9.

For problems that use an *r* × *c* contingency table of a different size, use the appropriate ChiSquare worksheets. For example, for 3 × 4 problems, use the **ChiSquare3×4 worksheet** and for 4 × 3 problems, use the **ChiSquare4×3 worksheet**. For each of these other worksheets, enter the contingency table data for the problem in the Observed Frequencies area.

EG12.4 WILCOXON RANK SUM TEST: A NONPARAMETRIC METHOD for TWO INDEPENDENT POPULATIONS

Key Technique Use the **NORM.S.INV**(*level of significance*) function to compute the upper and lower critical values and use **NORM.S.DIST**(*absolute value of the Z test statistic*) as part of a formula to compute the *p*-value.

For unsummarized data, use the **COUNTIF** and **SUMIF** functions (see Appendix Section F.2) to compute the sample size and the sum of ranks for each sample.

Example Perform the Figure 12.12 Wilcoxon rank sum test for the VLABGo player monthly sales for two in-store locations.

PHStat Use **Wilcoxon Rank Sum Test**.

For the example, open to the **DATA worksheet** of the **VLABGo workbook**. Select **PHStat → Two-Sample Tests (Unsummarized Data) → Wilcoxon Rank Sum Test**. In the procedure's dialog box (shown below):

1. Enter **0.05** as the **Level of Significance**.
2. Enter **A1:A11** as the **Population 1 Sample Cell Range**.
3. Enter **B1:B11** as the **Population 2 Sample Cell Range**.
4. Check **First cells in both ranges contain label**.
5. Click **Two-Tail Test**.
6. Enter a **Title** and click **OK**.

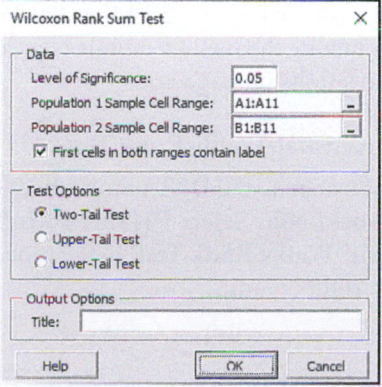

The procedure creates a SortedRanks worksheet that contains the sorted ranks in addition to the worksheet shown in Figure 12.12. Both of these worksheets are discussed in the following *Workbook* instructions.

Workbook Use the **COMPUTE worksheet** of the **Wilcoxon workbook** as a template.

The worksheet already contains data and formulas to use the unsummarized data for the example. For other problems that use unsummarized data:

1. Open to the **SortedRanks worksheet**.
2. Enter the sorted values for both groups in stacked format, entering sample names in column A and sorted values in column B.
3. Assign a rank for each value and enter the ranks in column C.
4. If performing a two-tail test, open to the **COMPUTE worksheet**, otherwise open to the similar **COMPUTE_ALL worksheet** that includes the one-tail tests.
5. Edit the cell ranges in the formulas in cells **B7**, **B8**, **B10**, and **B11** to match the cell range of the new data.

For problems with summarized data, overwrite the formulas that compute the **Sample Size** and **Sum of Ranks** in the cell range **B7:B11**, with the values for these statistics.

EG12.5 KRUSKAL-WALLIS RANK TEST: A NONPARAMETRIC METHOD for the ONE-WAY ANOVA

Key Technique Use the **CHISQ.INV.RT(*level of significance, number of groups - 1*)** function to compute the critical value and use the **CHISQ.DIST.RT(*H test statistic, number of groups - 1*)** function to compute the *p*-value.

For unsummarized data, use the **COUNTIF** and **SUMIF** functions (see Appendix Section F.2) to compute the sample size and the sum of ranks for each sample.

Example Perform the Figure 12.14 Kruskal-Wallis rank test for differences among the median mobile electronics sales for four in-store locations on page 468.

PHStat Use **Kruskal-Wallis Rank Test**.

For the example, open to the **DATA worksheet** of the **Mobile Electronics workbook**. Select **PHStat → Multiple-Sample Tests → Kruskal-Wallis Rank Test**. In the procedure's dialog box (shown in right column):

1. Enter **0.05** as the **Level of Significance**.
2. Enter **A1:D6** as the **Sample Data Cell Range**.
3. Check **First cells contain label**.
4. Enter a **Title** and click **OK**.

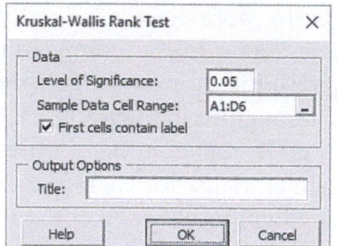

The procedure creates a SortedRanks worksheet that contains sorted ranks in addition to the worksheet shown in Figure 12.14 on page 468. Both of these worksheets are discussed in the following *Workbook* instructions.

Workbook Use the **KruskalWallis4 worksheet** of the **Kruskal-Wallis Worksheets workbook** as a template.

The worksheet already contains the data and formulas to use the unsummarized data for the example. For other problems with four groups and unsummarized data:

1. Open to the **SortedRanks worksheet**.
2. Enter the sorted values for both groups in stacked format, entering sample names in column A and sorted values in column B.
3. Assign a rank for each value and enter the ranks in column C.
4. Paste the unsummarized stacked data into this worksheet starting with Column E. (The first row of this pasted range should contain group names.)
5. Open to the **KruskalWallis4 worksheet** and edit the cell ranges in the formulas in columns **E** and **F**.

For other problems with four groups and summarized data, open to the KruskalWallis4 worksheet and overwrite the columns D, E, and F formulas with the name, sample size, and sum of ranks for each group.

For other problems with three groups, use the similar **KruskalWallis3 worksheet** and use the previous instructions for either unsummarized or summarized data, as appropriate.

▼ JMP GUIDE

JG12.1 CHI-SQUARE TEST for the DIFFERENCE BETWEEN TWO PROPORTIONS

Use **Fit Y by X**.

For example, to perform the Figure 12.3 chi-square test for the two-hotel guest satisfaction data on page 445, open to the **Two-Hotel Survey Stacked data table**. Select **Analyze→Fit Y by X** and in the Fit Y by X - Contextual dialog box (shown below):

1. Click **Hotel** in the columns list and then click **Y, Response** to add Hotel to the Y, Response box.
2. Click **Choose Again?** in the columns list and then click **X, Factor** to add Choose Again? to the X, Factor box.
3. Click **Frequency** in the columns list and then click **Freq** to add Frequency to the Freq box.
4. Click **OK**.

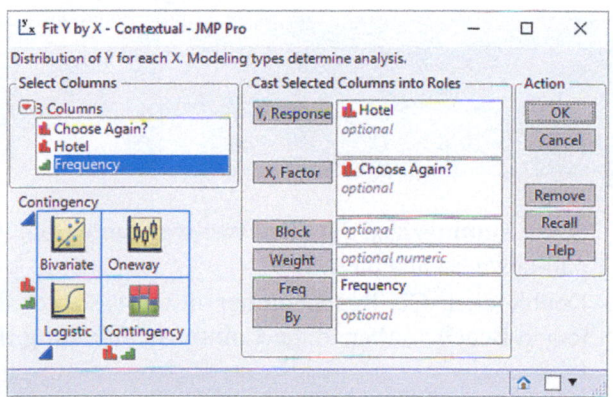

JMP displays results in a new window. The test results of interest appear in the row labeled Pearson under the subheading Tests. To declutter the results window, click the **Contingency Analysis of Hotel By Choose Again? Red triangle** and select **Mosaic Plot** from its menu to clear the check mark by that entry. When redoing the analysis, JMP will change the **Y, Response** to **Y, Response Category** and change **X, Factor** to **X, Grouping Category** in the dialog box to better match the data type of the Hotel and Choose Again? variables.

JG12.2 CHI-SQUARE TEST for DIFFERENCE AMONG MORE THAN TWO PROPORTIONS

Use **Fit Y by X**.

For example, to perform the Figure 12.6 chi-square test for the three-hotel guest satisfaction data on page 451, open to the **Three-Hotel Survey Stacked data table**. Select **Analyze→Fit Y by X** and follow steps 1 through 4 of the Section JG12.1 instructions.

JMP displays results in a new window. The test results of interest appear in the row labeled Pearson under the subheading Tests.

The Marascuilo Procedure

There are no JMP instructions for this procedure.

JG12.3 CHI-SQUARE TEST of INDEPENDENCE

Use **Fit Y by X**.

For example, to perform the Figure 12.10 chi-square test for the primary reason for not returning to hotel data on page 458, open to the **Three-Hotel Reasons Stacked data table**. Select **Analyze→Fit Y by X** and in the Fit Y by X - Contextual dialog box:

1. Click **Hotel** in the columns list and then click **Y, Response** to add Hotel to the Y, Response box.
2. Click **Reason** in the columns list and then click **X, Factor** to add Choose Again? to the X, Factor box.
3. Click **Frequency** in the columns list and then click **Freq** to add Frequency to the Freq box.
4. Click **OK**.

JMP displays results in a new window. The test results of interest appear in the row labeled Pearson under the subheading Tests. To declutter the results window, click the **Contingency Analysis of Hotel By Choose Again? Red triangle** and select **Mosaic Plot** from its menu to clear the check mark by that entry. When redoing the analysis, JMP will change the **Y, Response** to **Y, Response Category** and change **X, Factor** to **X, Grouping Category** in the dialog box to better match the data type of the Hotel and Reason variables.

JG12.4 WILCOXON RANK SUM TEST for TWO INDEPENDENT POPULATIONS

Use **Fit Y by X**.

For example, to perform the Figure 12.12 Wilcoxon rank sum test for the primary reason for VLABGo player monthly sales for two in-store locations on page 463, open to the **VLABGo Stacked data table**. Select **Analyze→Fit Y by X** and in the Fit Y by X - Contextual dialog box:

1. Click **Sales** in the columns list and then click **Y, Response** to add Sales to the Y, Response box.
2. Click **Location** in the columns list and then click **X, Factor** to add Location to the X, Factor box.
3. Click **OK**.

JMP displays results in a new window. In that window:

4. Click the **Oneway Analysis of Sales By Location Red triangle** and select **Nonparametric→ Wilcoxon Test** from its menu.

The test results of interest appear under the subheading Tests 2-Sample Means, Normal Approximation. When redoing the analysis, JMP will change **X, Factor** to **X, Grouping Category** in the dialog box to better match the data type of the Location variable.

JG12.5 KRUSKAL-WALLIS RANK TEST for the ONE-WAY ANOVA

Use **Fit Y by X**.

For example, to perform the Figure 12.14 Kruskal-Wallis rank test for differences among the median mobile electronics sales for four in-store locations on page 468, open to the **Mobile Electronics Stacked data table**. Select **Analyze→ Fit Y by X** and in the Fit Y by X - Contextual dialog box:

1. Click **Sales** in the columns list and then click **Y, Response** to add Sales to the Y, Response box.
2. Click **Location** in the columns list and then click **X, Factor** to add Location to the X, Factor box.
3. Click **OK**.

JMP displays results in a new window. In that window:

4. Click the **Oneway Analysis of Sales By Location Red triangle** and select **Nonparametric→ Wilcoxon Test** from its menu.

(Selecting Wilcoxon Test will cause JMP to perform a Kruskal-Wallis test when JMP detects more than two levels. There is no Kruskal-Wallis test choice on the menu.) The test results of interest appear under the subheading Tests 1-Way Test, ChiSquare Approximation. When redoing the analysis, JMP will change **X, Factor** to **X, Grouping Category** in the dialog box to better match the data type of the Location variable.

CHAPTER 12

▾MINITAB GUIDE

MG12.1 CHI-SQUARE TEST for the DIFFERENCE BETWEEN TWO PROPORTIONS

Use **Chi-Square Test for Association**.

For example, to perform the Figure 12.3 chi-square test for the two-hotel guest satisfaction data on page 445, open to the **Two-Hotel Survey worksheet**. Select **Stat→Tables→Chi-Square Test for Association**. In the procedure's dialog box (shown below):

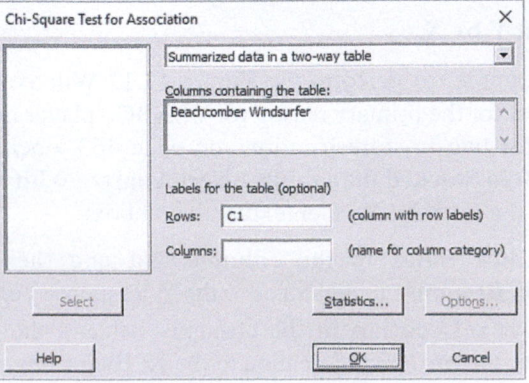

1. Select **Summarized data in a two-way table** from the pull-down list and press **Tab**.
2. Double-click **C2 Beachcomber** in the variables list to add **Beachcomber** to the **Columns containing the table** box.
3. Double-click **C3 Windsurfer** in the variables list to add **Windsurfer** to the **Columns containing the table** box.
4. Enter **C1** in the **Rows** box.
5. Click **OK**.

The test results of interest appear in the row labeled Pearson in the Chi-Square Test table.

For unsummarized data, open to a worksheet that contains two column variables, one variable that defines the categories of the rows and the other variable that defines the categories for the columns. Select **Stat→ Tables→ Chi-Square Test for Association** and:

1. Select **Raw data (categorical variables)** from the pull-down list and press **Tab**.
2. Enter the variable that contains the row categories in the **Rows** box.
3. Enter the variable that contains the column categories in the **Columns** box.
4. Click **OK**.

MG12.2 CHI-SQUARE TEST for DIFFERENCES AMONG MORE THAN TWO PROPORTIONS

Use **Chi-Square Test for Association**.

For example, to perform the Figure 12.6 chi-square test for the three-hotel guest satisfaction data on page 451, open to the **Three-Hotel Survey worksheet**, select **Stat → Tables → Chi-Square Test for Association**. In the procedure's dialog box:

1. Select **Summarized data in a two-way table** from the pull-down list and press **Tab**.
2. Enter **C2-C4** in the **Columns containing the table** box.
3. Enter **C1** in the **Rows** box.
4. Click **OK**.

For unsummarized data, use the Section MG12.1 instructions for unsummarized data.

The Marascuilo Procedure

There are no Minitab Guide instructions for this procedure.

MG12.3 CHI-SQUARE TEST of INDEPENDENCE

Use the Section MG12.2 instructions.

For example, to perform the Figure 12.10 chi-square test, open to the **Three-Hotel Reasons worksheet** and follow steps 1 through 4 of those instructions.

MG12.4 WILCOXON RANK SUM TEST: A NONPARAMETRIC METHOD for TWO INDEPENDENT POPULATIONS

Use **Mann-Whitney** to perform a test equivalent to the Wilcoxon rank sum test.

For example, to perform the Figure 12.12 VLABGo player monthly sales for two in-store locations on page 463, open to the **VLABGo worksheet**. Select **Stat → Nonparametrics → Mann-Whitney**. In the Mann-Whitney dialog box (shown in the right column):

1. Double-click **C1 Special Front** in the variables list to add **'Special Front'** in the **First Sample** box.
2. Double-click **C2 In-Aisle** in the variables list to add **'In-Aisle'** in the **Second Sample** box.

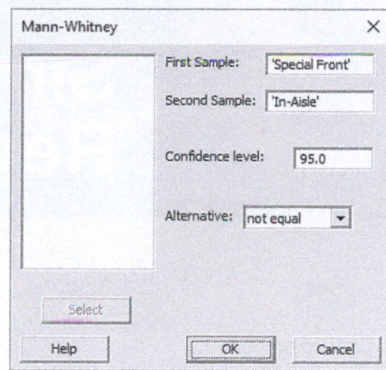

3. Enter **95.0** in the **Confidence level** box.
4. Select **not equal** in the **Alternative** drop-down list.
5. Click **OK**.

MG12.5 KRUSKAL-WALLIS RANK TEST: A NONPARAMETRIC METHOD for the ONE-WAY ANOVA

Use **Kruskal-Wallis** (requires stacked data).

For example, to perform the Figure 12.14 Kruskal-Wallis rank test for differences among the median mobile electronics sales for four in-store locations on page 468, open to the **Mobile Electronics Stacked worksheet**. Select **Stat → Nonparametrics → Kruskal-Wallis**. In the Kruskal-Wallis dialog box (shown below):

1. Double-click **C2 Sales** in the variables list to add **Sales** in the **Response** box.
2. Double-click **C1 Location** in the variables list to add **Location** in the **Factor** box.
3. Click **OK**.

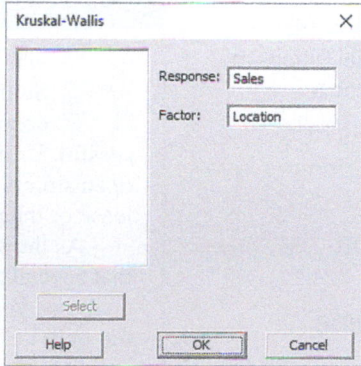

13

Simple Linear Regression

CONTENTS

OBJECTIVES

- Understand the meaning of the regression coefficients b_0 and b_1
- Understand the usefulness of regression analysis.

▼USING **STATISTICS**
Knowing Customers at Sunflowers Apparel

Having survived recent economic slowdowns that have diminished their competitors, Sunflowers Apparel, a chain of upscale fashion stores for women, is in the midst of a companywide review that includes researching the factors that make their stores successful. Until recently, Sunflowers managers did not use data analysis to help select where to open stores, relying instead on subjective factors, such as the availability of an inexpensive lease or the perception that a particular location seemed ideal for one of their stores.

As the new director of planning, you have already consulted with marketing analytics firms that specialize in identifying and classifying groups of consumers. Based on such preliminary analyses, you have already tentatively discovered that the profile of Sunflowers shoppers may not only be the upper middle class long suspected of being the chain's clientele but may also include younger, aspirational families with young children, and, surprisingly, urban hipsters who set trends and are mostly single.

You seek to develop a systematic approach that will lead to making better decisions during the site-selection process. As a starting point, you have asked one marketing analytics firm to collect and organize data for the number of people in the identified groups of interest who live within a fixed radius of each store. You believe that the greater numbers of profiled customers contribute to store sales, and you want to explore the possible use of this relationship in the decision-making process. How can you use statistics so that you can forecast the annual sales of a proposed store based on the number of profiled customers who reside within a fixed radius of a Sunflowers store?

- Understand how to properly perform regression analysis.

The preceding four chapters focus on hypothesis testing methods. Chapter 9 discusses methods that allow you to make inferences about a population parameter. Chapters 10, 11, and 12 present methods that look for differences among two or more populations. Beginning with this chapter, and continuing through Chapter 16, the focus shifts from examining differences among groups to predicting values of variables of interest.

Consider the data that a business generates as a by-product of ongoing operations, such as the Sunflowers Apparel sales data. How would you go about examining such data? You must go looking for possible relationships. **Regression analysis** techniques help uncover relationships between variables.

[1] Independent variables are also known as **predictor** or **explanatory variables** and dependent variables are also known as **response variables**.

Regression methods seek to discover how one or more X variables can predict the value of a Y variable. The Y variable is known as the **dependent variable** because its values depend on the X values in a regression model. X variables are also known as predictor variables or **independent variables**, in contrast to the dependent Y variable.[1]

Regression methods first fit a **model** that describes the relationship between the X and Y variables and then evaluate the *goodness of fit*, how well the model describes the relationship. Decision makers then evaluate whether the mathematical assumptions that a model requires are valid for the data being analyzed. Should the assumptions hold, the regression model can then be used to make predictions about the Y variable for a given range of X values. Decision makers also use regression methods to help define or refine other models or to estimate values to be used in a model. Models also help you identify unusual values that may be outliers (see references 2, 3, and 4).

Simple regression explores the relationship between one independent X variable and the dependent Y variable. *Multiple* regression, the subject of Chapters 14 and 15, explores the relationship between two or more independent X variables and the dependent Y variable. As the least complicated regression method to study, **simple linear regression** provides a good starting point for exploring and understanding regression, an important statistical technique that one often uses to understand data better and to help explore results of business analytics models.

Preliminary Analysis

Using a **scatter plot** (also known as **scatter diagram**) to visualize the X and Y variables, a technique that Section 2.5 discusses, can help suggest a starting point for regression analysis. The Figure 13.1 scatter plots illustrate six possible relationships between an X variable and a Y variable.

FIGURE 13.1
Six types of relationships found in scatter plots

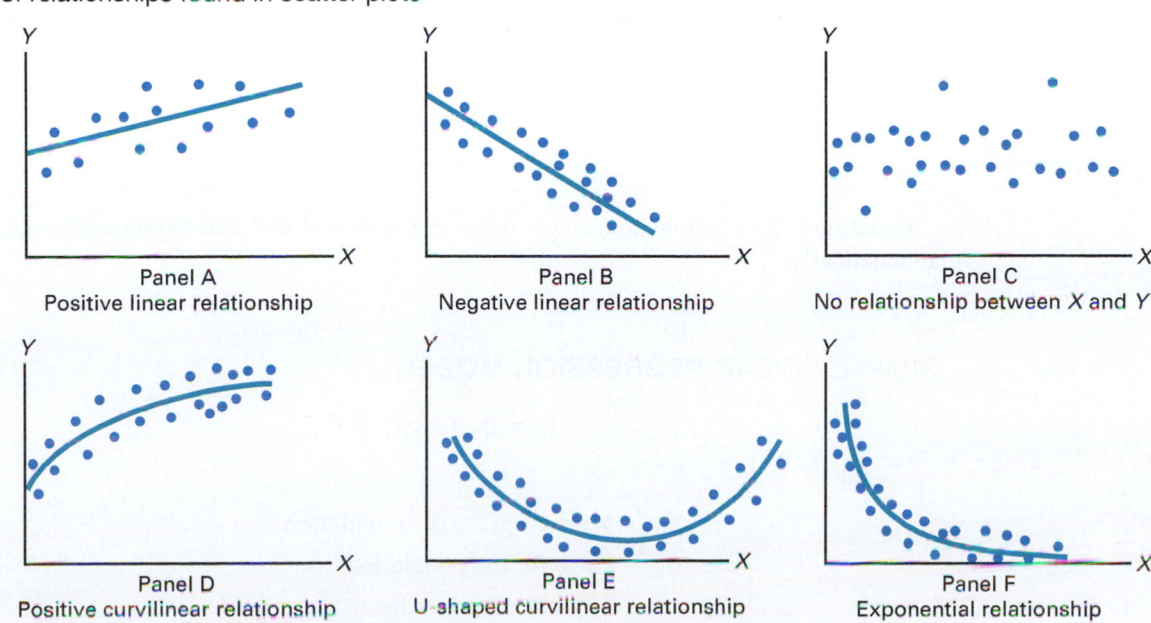

Panel A
Positive linear relationship

Panel B
Negative linear relationship

Panel C
No relationship between X and Y

Panel D
Positive curvilinear relationship

Panel E
U-shaped curvilinear relationship

Panel F
Exponential relationship

In Panel A, values of Y are generally increasing linearly as X increases. Figure 13.3 on page 487 shows another positive linear relationship, between the number of profiled customers of the store and the store's annual sales for the Sunflowers Apparel women's clothing store chain.

Panel B illustrates a negative linear relationship. As X increases, the values of Y are generally decreasing. An example of this type of relationship might be the price of a particular product and the amount of sales. As the price charged for the product increases, the amount of sales may tend to decrease.

Panel C shows a set of data in which there is very little or no relationship between X and Y. High and low values of Y appear at each value of X.

Panel D illustrates a positive curvilinear relationship between X and Y. The values of Y increase as X increases, but this increase tapers off beyond certain values of X. An example of a positive curvilinear relationship might be the age and maintenance cost of an automobile. As an automobile gets older, the maintenance cost may rise rapidly at first but then level off beyond a certain number of years.

Panel E illustrates a U-shaped relationship between X and Y. As X increases, at first Y generally decreases; but as X continues to increase, Y then increases above its minimum value. An example of this type of relationship might be entrepreneurial activity and levels of economic development as measured by GDP per capita. Entrepreneurial activity occurs more in the least and most developed countries.

Panel F illustrates an exponential relationship between X and Y. In this case, Y decreases very rapidly as X first increases, but then it decreases much less rapidly as X continues to increase. An example of an exponential relationship could be the value of an automobile and its age. The value drops drastically from its original price in the first year, but it decreases much less rapidly in subsequent years.

13.1 Simple Linear Regression Models

Simple linear regression models examine the straight line (*linear*) relationship between a dependent Y variable and a single independent X variable. Figure 13.2 presents a generalized **positive linear relationship** that contains a positive slope.

FIGURE 13.2
Generalized positive
linear relationship

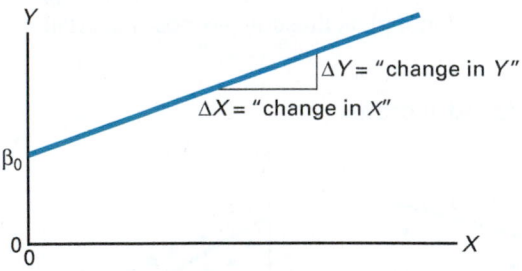

Equation (13.1) defines the simple linear regression model that expresses the relationship mathematically.

SIMPLE LINEAR REGRESSION MODEL

$$Y_i = \beta_0 + \beta_1 X_i + \varepsilon_i \tag{13.1}$$

where

$\beta_0 = Y$ intercept for the population

$\beta_1 = $ slope for the population

$\varepsilon_i = $ random error in Y for observation i

$Y_i = $ dependent variable for observation i

$X_i = $ independent variable for observation i

The $Y_i = \beta_0 + \beta_1 X_i$ portion of the simple linear regression model expressed in Equation (13.1) is a straight line. The **slope** of the line, β_1, represents the expected change in Y per unit change in X. It represents the mean amount that Y changes (either positively or negatively) for a one-unit change in X. The **Y intercept**, β_0, represents the mean value of Y when X equals 0. The last component of the model, ε_i, represents the random error in Y for each observation, i. In other words, ε_i is the vertical distance of the actual value of Y_i above or below the expected value of Y_i on the line.

13.2 Determining the Simple Linear Regression Equation

As the new director of planning in the Sunflowers Apparel scenario, you suspect that the greater the number of profiled customers who reside within a fixed radius of a store, the greater the store sales will be. You wonder if a linear relationship between the number of profiled customers, as the numerical independent X variable, and annual store sales, as the dependent Y variable, exists. To examine this relationship, you collect data from a sample of 14 stores. Table 13.1, stored in Site Selection , presents these data.

TABLE 13.1

Number of Profiled Customers (in millions) and Annual Sales (in $millions) for a Sample of 14 Sunflowers Apparel Stores

Store	Profiled Customers (millions)	Annual Sales ($millions)	Store	Profiled Customers (millions)	Annual Sales ($millions)
1	3.7	5.7	8	3.1	4.7
2	3.6	5.9	9	3.2	6.1
3	2.8	6.7	10	3.5	4.9
4	5.6	9.5	11	5.2	10.7
5	3.3	5.4	12	4.6	7.6
6	2.2	3.5	13	5.8	11.8
7	3.3	6.2	14	3.0	4.1

Figure 13.3 displays the scatter plot for the data in Table 13.1. Observe the increasing relationship between profiled customers (X) and annual sales (Y). As the number of profiled customers increases, annual sales increase approximately as a straight line. Thus, you can assume that a straight line provides a useful mathematical model of this relationship. Now you need to determine the specific straight line that is the *best* fit to these data.

FIGURE 13.3

Scatter plot for the Sunflowers Apparel data

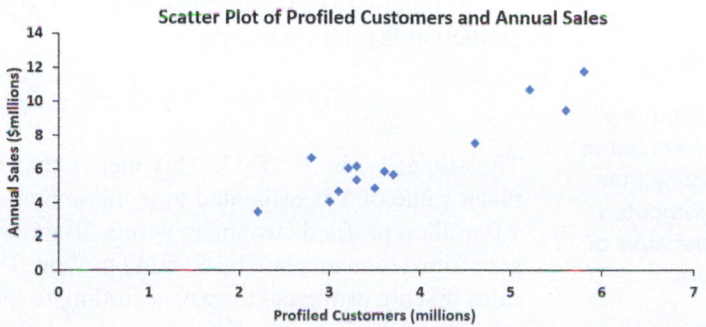

The Least-Squares Method

As the Sunflowers director of planning, you have hypothesized a statistical model to represent the relationship between two variables—number of profiled customers and sales—in the entire population of Sunflowers Apparel stores. However, as Table 13.1 shows, the data are collected from a *random sample* of stores. If certain assumptions are valid (see Section 13.4), you can use the sample Y intercept, b_0, and the sample slope, b_1, as estimates of the respective population parameters, β_0 and β_1. Equation (13.2) uses these estimates to form the **simple linear regression equation**. This straight line is often referred to as the **prediction line**.

SIMPLE LINEAR REGRESSION EQUATION: THE PREDICTION LINE

The predicted value of Y equals the Y intercept plus the slope multiplied by the value of X.

$$\hat{Y}_i = b_0 + b_1X_i \qquad (13.2)$$

where

$$\hat{Y}_i = \text{predicted value of } Y \text{ for observation } i$$
$$X_i = \text{value of } X \text{ for observation } i$$
$$b_0 = \text{sample } Y \text{ intercept}$$
$$b_1 = \text{sample slope}$$

Equation (13.2) requires you to determine two **regression coefficients**—b_0 (the sample Y intercept) and b_1 (the sample slope). The most common approach to finding b_0 and b_1 is using the least-squares method. This method minimizes the sum of the squared differences between the actual values (Y_i) and the predicted values ($\hat{Y}_i$), using the simple linear regression equation [i.e., the prediction line; see Equation (13.2)]. This sum of squared differences is equal to

$$\sum_{i=1}^{n}(Y_i - \hat{Y}_i)^2$$

Because $\hat{Y}_i = b_0 + b_1X_i$,

$$\sum_{i=1}^{n}(Y_i - \hat{Y}_i)^2 = \sum_{i=1}^{n}[Y_i - (b_0 + b_1X_i)]^2$$

Because this equation has two unknowns, b_0 and b_1, the sum of squared differences depends on the sample Y intercept, b_0, and the sample slope, b_1. The **least-squares method** determines the values of b_0 and b_1 that minimize the sum of squared differences around the prediction line. Any values for b_0 and b_1 other than those determined by the least-squares method result in a greater sum of squared differences between the actual values (Y_i) and the predicted values ($\hat{Y}_i$).

Figure 13.4 presents results for the simple linear regression model for the Sunflowers Apparel data. Excel and JMP label b_0 as Intercept, while Minitab labels this coefficient as Constant. All three label b_1 as Profiled Customers.

In Figure 13.4, observe that $b_0 = -1.2088$ and $b_1 = 2.0742$. Using Equation (13.2), the prediction line for these data is

$$\hat{Y}_i = -1.2088 + 2.0742X_i$$

The slope, b_1, is $+2.0742$. This means that for each increase of 1 unit in X, the predicted mean value of Y is estimated to increase by 2.0742 units. In other words, for each increase of 1.0 million profiled customers within 30 minutes of the store, the predicted mean annual sales are estimated to increase by \$2.0742 million. Thus, the slope represents the portion of the annual sales that are estimated to vary according to the number of profiled customers.

FIGURE 13.4

Excel, JMP, and Minitab simple linear regression model results for the Sunflowers Apparel data

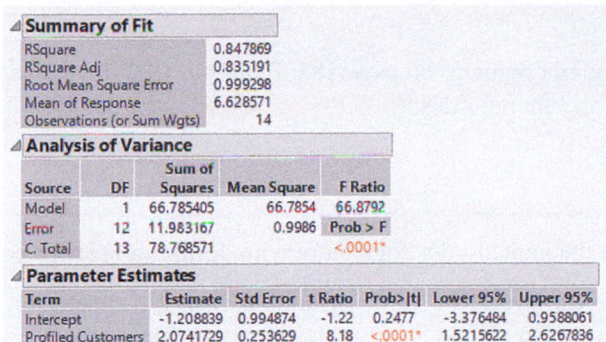

▲	A	B	C	D	E	F	G
1	Simple Linear Regression						
2							
3	*Regression Statistics*						
4	Multiple R	0.9208					
5	R Square	0.8479					
6	Adjusted R Square	0.8352					
7	Standard Error	0.9993					
8	Observations	14					
9							
10	ANOVA						
11		df	SS	MS	F	Significance F	
12	Regression	1	66.7854	66.7854	66.8792	0.0000	
13	Residual	12	11.9832	0.9986			
14	Total	13	78.7686				
15							
16		Coefficients	Standard Error	t Stat	P-value	Lower 95%	Upper 95%
17	Intercept	-1.2088	0.9949	-1.2151	0.2477	-3.3765	0.9588
18	Profiled Customers	2.0742	0.2536	8.1780	0.0000	1.5216	2.6268

▲	K	L	M
1	Intermediate Calculations		
2	b1, b0 Coefficients	2.0742	-1.2088
3	b1, b0 Standard Error	0.2536	0.9949
4	R Square, Standard Error	0.8479	0.9993
5	F, Residual df	66.8792	12.0000
6	Regression SS, Residual SS	66.7854	11.9832
7			
8	Confidence level	95%	
9	t Critical Value	2.1788	
10	Half Width b0	2.1676	
11	Half Width b1	0.5526	

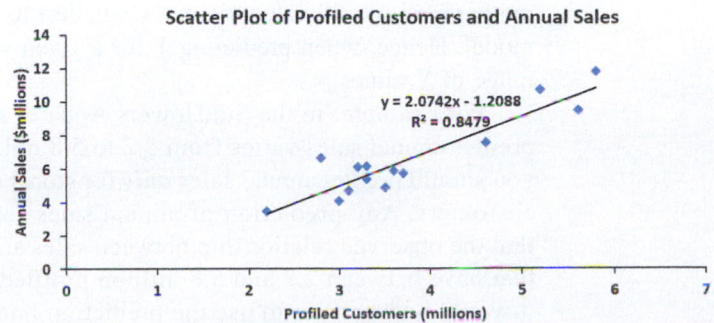

Summary of Fit

RSquare	0.847869
RSquare Adj	0.835191
Root Mean Square Error	0.999298
Mean of Response	6.628571
Observations (or Sum Wgts)	14

Analysis of Variance

Source	DF	Sum of Squares	Mean Square	F Ratio
Model	1	66.785405	66.7854	66.8792
Error	12	11.983167	0.9986	Prob > F
C. Total	13	78.768571		<.0001*

Parameter Estimates

Term	Estimate	Std Error	t Ratio	Prob>|t|	Lower 95%	Upper 95%
Intercept	-1.208839	0.994874	-1.22	0.2477	-3.376484	0.9588061
Profiled Customers	2.0741729	0.253629	8.18	<.0001*	1.5215622	2.6267836

Regression Analysis: Annual Sales versus Profiled Customers

Analysis of Variance

Source	DF	Adj SS	Adj MS	F-Value	P-Value
Regression	1	66.7854	66.7854	66.88	0.000
Profiled Customers	1	66.7854	66.7854	66.88	0.000
Error	12	11.9832	0.9986		
Lack-of-Fit	11	11.6632	1.0603	3.31	0.406
Pure Error	1	0.3200	0.3200		
Total	13	78.7686			

Model Summary

S	R-sq	R-sq(adj)	R-sq(pred)
0.999298	84.79%	83.52%	78.27%

Coefficients

Term	Coef	SE Coef	T-Value	P-Value	VIF
Constant	-1.209	0.995	-1.22	0.248	
Profiled Customers	2.074	0.254	8.18	0.000	1.00

Regression Equation

Annual Sales = -1.209 + 2.074 Profiled Customers

The Y intercept, b_0, is -1.2088. The Y intercept represents the predicted value of Y when X equals 0. Because the number of profiled customers of the store cannot be 0, this Y intercept has little or no practical interpretation. Also, the Y intercept for this example is outside the range of the observed values of the X variable, and therefore interpretations of the value of b_0 should be made cautiously. Figure 13.5 displays the actual values and the prediction line.

FIGURE 13.5

Excel scatter plot and prediction line for Sunflowers Apparel data

Scatter Plot of Profiled Customers and Annual Sales

y = 2.0742x - 1.2088
R² = 0.8479

Example 13.1 illustrates a situation in which there is a direct interpretation for the Y intercept, b_0.

EXAMPLE 13.1

Interpreting the *Y* Intercept, b_0, and the Slope, b_1

A statistics professor wants to use the number of absences from class during the semester (X) to predict the final exam score (Y). A regression model is fit based on data collected from a class during a recent semester, with the following results:

$$\hat{Y}_i = 85.0 - 5X_i$$

What is the interpretation of the *Y* intercept, b_0, and the slope, b_1?

SOLUTION The *Y* intercept $b_0 = 85.0$ indicates that when the student does not have any absences from class during the semester, the predicted mean final exam score is 85.0. The slope $b_1 = -5$ indicates that for each increase of one absence from class during the semester, the predicted change in the mean final exam score is -5.0. In other words, the final exam score is predicted to decrease by a mean of 5 points for each increase of one absence from class during the semester.

Return to the Sunflowers Apparel scenario on page 484. Example 13.2 illustrates how you use the prediction line to predict the annual sales.

EXAMPLE 13.2

Predicting Annual Sales Based on Number of Profiled Customers

Use the prediction line to predict the annual sales for a store with 4 million profiled customers.

SOLUTION You can determine the predicted value of annual sales by substituting $X = 4$ (millions of profiled customers) into the simple linear regression equation:

$$\hat{Y}_i = -1.2088 + 2.0742X_i$$
$$\hat{Y}_i = -1.2088 + 2.0742(4) = 7.0879 \text{ or } \$7,087,900$$

Thus, a store with 4 million profiled customers has predicted mean annual sales of $7,087,900.

Predictions in Regression Analysis: Interpolation Versus Extrapolation

You use only the **relevant range** of the independent variable to make predictions. This relevant range represents all values from the smallest to the largest X used in developing the regression model. Hence, when predicting Y for a given value of X, you cannot extrapolate beyond this range of X values.

For example, in the Sunflowers Apparel scenario the number of profiled customers to predict annual sales varies from 2.2 to 5.8 million (see Table 13.1 on page 487). Therefore, you should predict annual sales *only* for stores that have between 2.2 and 5.8 million profiled customers. Any prediction of annual sales for stores outside this range wrongly assumes that the observed relationship between sales and the number of profiled customers for stores that have between 2.2 and 5.8 million profiled customers would be the same. For example, it would be improper to use the prediction line to forecast the sales for a new store that has 8 million profiled customers. The relationship between sales and the number of profiled customers might, for example, have a point of diminishing returns. If that was true, the effect that the number of profiled customers has on sales would be less, leading to an overestimation of the predicted sales.

Computing the Y Intercept, b_0 and the Slope, b_1

For small data sets, you can use a hand calculator to compute the least-squares regression coefficients. Equations (13.3) and (13.4) give the values of b_0 and b_1, which minimize

$$\sum_{i=1}^{n}(Y_i - \hat{Y}_i)^2 = \sum_{i=1}^{n}[Y_i - (b_0 + b_1 X_i)]^2$$

COMPUTATIONAL FORMULA FOR THE SLOPE, b_1

$$b_1 = \frac{SSXY}{SSX} \qquad\qquad\qquad \textbf{(13.3)}$$

where

$$SSXY = \sum_{i=1}^{n}(X_i - \overline{X})(Y_i - \overline{Y}) = \sum_{i=1}^{n}X_i Y_i - \frac{\left(\sum_{i=1}^{n}X_i\right)\left(\sum_{i=1}^{n}Y_i\right)}{n}$$

$$SSX = \sum_{i=1}^{n}(X_i - \overline{X})^2 = \sum_{i=1}^{n}X_i^2 - \frac{\left(\sum_{i=1}^{n}X_i\right)^2}{n}$$

COMPUTATIONAL FORMULA FOR THE Y INTERCEPT, b_0

$$b_0 = \overline{Y} - b_1\overline{X} \qquad\qquad\qquad \textbf{(13.4)}$$

where

$$\overline{Y} = \frac{\sum_{i=1}^{n}Y_i}{n}$$

$$\overline{X} = \frac{\sum_{i=1}^{n}X_i}{n}$$

EXAMPLE 13.3

Computing the Y Intercept, b_0, and the Slope, b_1

▶(continued)

Compute the Y intercept, b_0, and the slope, b_1, for the Sunflowers Apparel data.

SOLUTION Use Equations (13.3) and (13.4). To use those equations, note the sample size $n = 14$ and compute the following: $\sum_{i=1}^{n}X_i$, the sum of the Profiled Customers X values; $\sum_{i=1}^{n}Y_i$, the sum of the Annual Sales Y values; $\sum_{i=1}^{n}X_i^2$, the sum of the squared X values; and $\sum_{i=1}^{n}X_i Y_i$, the sum of the product of X and Y. Table 13.2 presents calculations necessary to determine these four quantities for the Sunflowers Apparel example. The table also includes $\sum_{i=1}^{n}Y_i^2$, the sum of the squared Y values that will be used to compute SST in Section 13.3.

TABLE 13.2

Computations for the Sunflowers Apparel Data

Store	X	Y	X^2	Y^2	XY
1	3.7	5.7	13.69	32.49	21.09
2	3.6	5.9	12.96	34.81	21.24
3	2.8	6.7	7.84	44.89	18.76
4	5.6	9.5	31.36	90.25	53.20
5	3.3	5.4	10.89	29.16	17.82
6	2.2	3.5	4.84	12.25	7.70
7	3.3	6.2	10.89	38.44	20.46
8	3.1	4.7	9.61	22.09	14.57
9	3.2	6.1	10.24	37.21	19.52
10	3.5	4.9	12.25	24.01	17.15
11	5.2	10.7	27.04	114.49	55.64
12	4.6	7.6	21.16	57.76	34.96
13	5.8	11.8	33.64	139.24	68.44
14	3.0	4.1	9.00	16.81	12.30
Totals	52.9	92.8	215.41	693.90	382.85

student TIP

Although examples in this chapter show the manual evaluation of formulas to provide insight, best practice is usually to use software for all regression-related calculations.

Using Equations (13.3) and (13.4), you can compute b_0 and b_1:

$$SSXY = \sum_{i=1}^{n}(X_i - \overline{X})(Y_i - \overline{Y}) = \sum_{i=1}^{n}X_iY_i - \frac{\left(\sum_{i=1}^{n}X_i\right)\left(\sum_{i=1}^{n}Y_i\right)}{n}$$

$$= 382.85 - \frac{(52.9)(92.8)}{14} = 382.85 - 350.65142$$

$$= 32.19858$$

$$SSX = \sum_{i=1}^{n}(X_i - \overline{X})^2 = \sum_{i=1}^{n}X_i^2 - \frac{\left(\sum_{i=1}^{n}X_i\right)^2}{n}$$

$$= 215.41 - \frac{(52.9)^2}{14} = 215.41 - 199.88642$$

$$= 15.52358$$

With these values, compute b_1:

$$b_1 = \frac{SSXY}{SSX} = \frac{32.19858}{15.52358} = 2.07417$$

and:

$$\overline{Y} = \frac{\sum_{i=1}^{n}Y_i}{n} = \frac{92.8}{14} = 6.62857$$

$$\overline{X} = \frac{\sum_{i=1}^{n}X_i}{n} = \frac{52.9}{14} = 3.77857$$

With these values, compute b_0:

$$b_0 = \overline{Y} - b_1\overline{X}$$

$$= 6.62857 - 2.07417(3.77857)$$

$$= -1.2088265$$

VISUAL EXPLORATIONS

Exploring Simple Linear Regression Coefficients

Open the **VE-Simple Linear Regression add-in workbook** to explore the coefficients. (For Excel technical requirements, see Appendix D). When this workbook opens properly, it adds a **Simple Linear Regression** menu in either the Add-ins tab (Microsoft Windows) or the Apple menu bar (OS X).

To explore the effects of changing the simple linear regression coefficients, select **Simple Linear→ Regression→Explore Coefficients**. In the Explore Coefficients floating control panel (shown inset below),

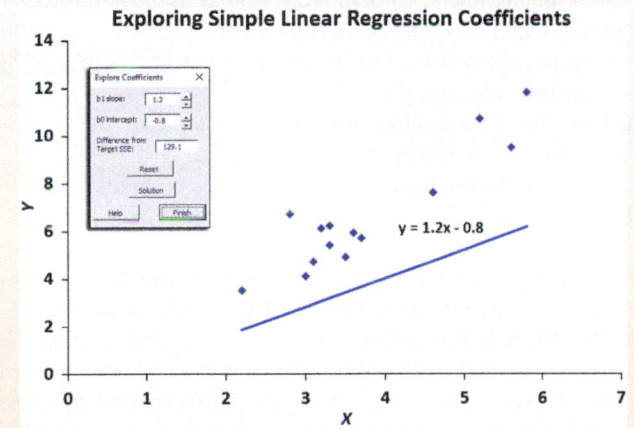

Exploring Simple Linear Regression Coefficients

click the spinner buttons for b_1 **slope** (the slope of the prediction line) and b_0 **intercept** (the Y intercept of the prediction line) to change the prediction line. Using the visual feedback of the chart, try to create a prediction line that is as close as possible to the prediction line defined by the least-squares estimates. In other words, try to make the **Difference from Target SSE** value as small as possible. (See page 496 for an explanation of *SSE*.)

At any time, click **Reset** to reset the b_1 and b_0 values or **Solution** to reveal the prediction line defined by the least-squares method. Click **Finish** when you are finished with this exercise.

Using Your Own Regression Data

Open to the worksheet that contains your data and uses row 1 for variable names. Select **Simple Linear Regression using your worksheet data** from the **Simple Linear Regression** menu. In the procedure's dialog box, enter the cell range of your Y variable as the **Y Variable Cell Range** and the cell range of your X variable as the **X Variable Cell Range**. Click **First cells in both ranges contain a label**, enter a **Title**, and click **OK**. After the scatter plot appears, continue with the Explore Coefficients floating control panel.

PROBLEMS FOR SECTION 13.2

LEARNING THE BASICS

13.1 Fitting a straight line to a set of data yields the following prediction line:

$$\hat{Y}_i = 2 + 5X_i$$

a. Interpret the meaning of the Y intercept, b_0.
b. Interpret the meaning of the slope, b_1.
c. Predict the value of Y for $X = 3$.

13.2 If the values of X in Problem 13.1 range from 2 to 25, should you use this model to predict the mean value of Y when X equals
a. 3? **b.** −3? **c.** 0? **d.** 24?

13.3 Fitting a straight line to a set of data yields the following prediction line:

$$\hat{Y}_i = 16 - 0.5X_i$$

a. Interpret the meaning of the Y intercept, b_0.
b. Interpret the meaning of the slope, b_1.
c. Predict the value of Y for $X = 6$.

APPLYING THE CONCEPTS

 13.4 The production of wine is a multibillion-dollar worldwide industry. In an attempt to develop a model of

wine quality as judged by wine experts, data were collected from red wine variants of Portuguese "Vinho Verde" wine.

Source: Data extracted from Cortez, P., Cerdeira, A., Almeida, F., Matos, T., and Reis, J., "Modeling Wine Preferences by Data Mining from Physicochemical Properties," *Decision Support Systems*, 47, 2009, pp. 547–553 and **bit.ly/9xKIEa**.

A sample of 50 wines is stored in VinhoVerde . Develop a simple linear regression model to predict wine quality, measured on a scale from 0 (very bad) to 10 (excellent), based on alcohol content (%).
a. Construct a scatter plot.
  For these data, $b_0 = -0.3529$ and $b_1 = 0.5624$.
b. Interpret the meaning of the slope, b_1, in this problem.
c. Predict the mean wine quality for wines with a 10% alcohol content.
d. What conclusion can you reach based on the results of (a)–(c)?

13.5 Zagat's publishes restaurant ratings for various locations in the United States. The file Restaurants contains the Zagat rating for food, décor, service, and the cost per person for a sample of 100 restaurants located in the center of New York City and in an outlying area of New York City. Develop a regression model to predict the cost per person, based on a variable that represents the sum of the ratings for food, décor, and service.

Source: Extracted from *Zagat Survey 2016, New York City*

a. Construct a scatter plot.

b. Assuming a linear relationship, use the least-squares method to compute the regression coefficients b_0 and b_1.

c. Interpret the meaning of the Y intercept, b_0, and the slope, b_1, in this problem.

d. Predict the mean cost per person for a restaurant with a summated rating of 50.

e. What should you tell the owner of a group of restaurants in this geographical area about the relationship between the summated rating and the cost of a meal?

13.6 Is an MBA a golden ticket? Pursuing an MBA is a major personal investment. Tuition and expenses associated with business school programs are costly, but the high costs come with hopes of career advancement and high salaries. A prospective MBA student would like to examine the factors that impact starting salary upon graduation and decides to develop a model that uses program per-year tuition as a predictor of starting salary. Data were collected for 37 full-time MBA programs offered at private universities. The data are stored in FTMBA .

Source: Data extracted from "U.S. News Business School Compass," available at **premium.usnews.com/best-graduate-schools/top-business-schools/mba-rankings**.

a. Construct a scatter plot.

b. Assuming a linear relationship, use the least-squares method to determine the regression coefficients b_0 and b_1.

c. Interpret the meaning of the slope, b_1, in this problem.

d. Predict the mean starting salary upon graduation for a program that has a per-year tuition cost of $50,450.

e. What insights do you gain about the relationship between program per-year tuition and starting salary upon graduation?

13.7 Starbucks Coffee Co. uses a data-based approach to improving the quality and customer satisfaction of its products. When survey data indicated that Starbucks needed to improve its package-sealing process, an experiment was conducted to determine the factors in the bag-sealing equipment that might be affecting the ease of opening the bag without tearing the inner liner of the bag.

Source: Data extracted from L. Johnson and S. Burrows, "For Starbucks, It's in the Bag," *Quality Progress*, March 2011, pp. 17–23.

One factor that could affect the rating of the ability of the bag to resist tears was the plate gap on the bag-sealing equipment. Data were collected on 19 bags in which the plate gap was varied. The results are stored in Starbucks .

a. Construct a scatter plot.

b. Assuming a linear relationship, use the least-squares method to determine the regression coefficients b_0 and b_1.

c. Interpret the meaning of the slope, b_1, in this problem.

d. Predict the mean tear rating when the plate gap is equal to 0.

e. What should you tell management of Starbucks about the relationship between the plate gap and the tear rating?

13.8 The value of a sports franchise is directly related to the amount of revenue that a franchise can generate. The file BBValues represents the value in 2017 (in $millions) and the annual revenue (in $millions) for the 30 Major League Baseball franchises.

Source: Data extracted from **www.forbes.com/mlb-valuations/list**.

Suppose you want to develop a simple linear regression model to predict franchise value based on annual revenue generated.

a. Construct a scatter plot.

b. Use the least-squares method to determine the regression coefficients b_0 and b_1.

c. Interpret the meaning of b_0 and b_1 in this problem.

d. Predict the mean value of a baseball franchise that generates $250 million of annual revenue.

e. What would you tell a group considering an investment in a major league baseball team about the relationship between revenue and the value of a team?

13.9 An agent for a residential real estate company in a suburb located outside of Washington, DC, has the business objective of developing more accurate estimates of the monthly rental cost for apartments. Toward that goal, the agent would like to use the size of an apartment, as defined by square footage to predict the monthly rental cost. The agent selects a sample of 57 one-bedroom apartments and collects and stores the data in RentSilverSpring .

a. Construct a scatter plot.

b. Use the least-squares method to determine the regression coefficients b_0 and b_1.

c. Interpret the meaning of b_0 and b_1 in this problem.

d. Predict the mean monthly rent for an apartment that has 800 square feet.

e. Why would it not be appropriate to use the model to predict the monthly rent for apartments that have 1,500 square feet?

f. Your friends Jim and Jennifer are considering signing a lease for a one-bedroom apartment in this residential neighborhood. They are trying to decide between two apartments, one with 800 square feet for a monthly rent of $1,130 and the other with 830 square feet for a monthly rent of $1,410. Based on (a) through (d), which apartment do you think is a better deal?

13.10 A box office analyst seeks to predict opening weekend box office gross for movies. Toward this goal, the analyst plans to use YouTube trailer views as a predictor. For each of 66 movies, the YouTube trailer view count, the number of YouTube trailer views from the release of the trailer through the Saturday before a movie opens, and the opening weekend box office gross (in $millions) are collected and stored in Movie .

Source: Data extracted from "Box Office Report," available at **bit.ly/2srM34F**.

For these data,

a. Construct a scatter plot.

b. Assuming a linear relationship, use the least-squares method to determine the regression coefficients b_0 and b_1.

c. Interpret the meaning of the slope, b_1, in this problem.

d. Predict the mean weekend box office gross for a movie that had 20 million YouTube trailer views.

e. What conclusions can you reach about predicting weekend box office gross from YouTube trailer views?

13.3 Measures of Variation

When using the least-squares method to determine the regression coefficients you need to compute three measures of variation. The first measure, the **total sum of squares (SST)**, is a measure of variation of the Y_i values around their mean, $\overline{Y}$. The **total variation**, or total sum of squares, is subdivided into **explained variation** and **unexplained variation**. The explained variation, or **regression sum of squares (SSR)**, represents variation that is explained by the relationship between X and Y, and the unexplained variation, or **error sum of squares (SSE)**, represents variation due to factors other than the relationship between X and Y. Figure 13.6 shows the different measures of variation for a single Y_i value.

FIGURE 13.6
Measures of variation

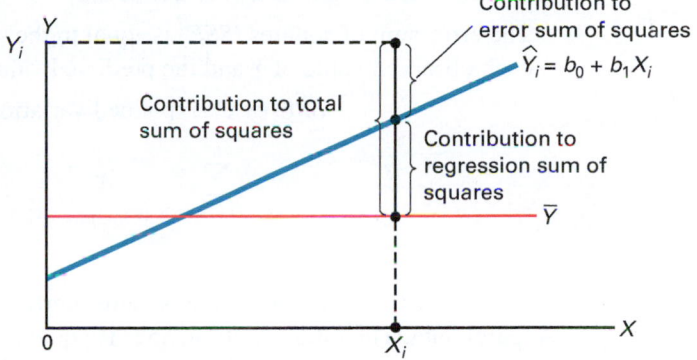

Computing the Sum of Squares

The regression sum of squares (SSR) is based on the difference between $\hat{Y}_i$ (the predicted value of Y from the prediction line) and $\overline{Y}$ (the mean value of Y). The error sum of squares (SSE) represents the part of the variation in Y that is not explained by the regression. It is based on the difference between Y_i and $\hat{Y}_i$. The total sum of squares (SST) is equal to the regression sum of squares (SSR) plus the error sum of squares (SSE). Equations (13.5), (13.6), (13.7), and (13.8) define these measures of variation and the total sum of squares (SST).

MEASURES OF VARIATION IN REGRESSION

The total sum of squares (SST) is equal to the regression sum of squares (SSR) plus the error sum of squares (SSE).

$$SST = SSR + SSE \tag{13.5}$$

TOTAL SUM OF SQUARES (SST)

The total sum of squares (SST) is equal to the sum of the squared differences between each observed value of Y and the mean value of Y.

$$SST = \text{Total sum of squares}$$

$$= \sum_{i=1}^{n}(Y_i - \overline{Y})^2 \tag{13.6}$$

REGRESSION SUM OF SQUARES (SSR)

The regression sum of squares (SSR) is equal to the sum of the squared differences between each predicted value of Y and the mean value of Y.

$$SSR = \text{Explained variation or regression sum of squares}$$

$$= \sum_{i=1}^{n} (\hat{Y}_i - \bar{Y})^2 \tag{13.7}$$

ERROR SUM OF SQUARES (SSE)

The error sum of squares (SSE) is equal to the sum of the squared differences between each observed value of Y and the predicted value of Y.

$$SSE = \text{Unexplained variation or error sum of squares}$$

$$= \sum_{i=1}^{n} (Y_i - \hat{Y}_i)^2 \tag{13.8}$$

Figure 13.7 shows the sum of squares portion of the Figure 13.4 results for the Sunflowers Apparel data. The total variation, SST, is equal to 78.7686. This amount is subdivided into the sum of squares explained by the regression (SSR), equal to 66.7854, and the sum of squares unexplained by the regression (SSE), equal to 11.9832. From Equation (13.5) on page 495:

$$SST = SSR + SSE$$

$$78.7686 = 66.7854 + 11.9832$$

FIGURE 13.7

Sum of squares portion of the Figure 13.4 Excel results

	A	B	C	D	E	F	G
10	ANOVA						
11		df	SS	MS	F	Significance F	
12	Regression	1	66.7854	66.7854	66.8792	0.0000	
13	Residual	12	11.9832	0.9986			
14	Total	13	78.7686				
15							
16		Coefficients	Standard Error	t Stat	P-value	Lower 95%	Upper 95%
17	Intercept	-1.2088	0.9949	-1.2151	0.2477	-3.3765	0.9588
18	Profiled Customers	2.0742	0.2536	8.1780	0.0000	1.5216	2.6268

The Coefficient of Determination

By themselves, SSR, SSE, and SST provide little information. However, the ratio of the regression sum of squares (SSR) to the total sum of squares (SST) measures the proportion of variation in Y that is explained by the linear relationship of the independent variable X with the dependent variable Y in the regression model. This ratio, called the coefficient of determination, r^2, is defined in Equation (13.9).

COEFFICIENT OF DETERMINATION

The coefficient of determination is equal to the regression sum of squares (i.e., explained variation) divided by the total sum of squares (i.e., total variation).

$$r^2 = \frac{\text{Regression sum of squares}}{\text{Total sum of squares}} = \frac{SSR}{SST} \tag{13.9}$$

studentTIP

r^2 must be a value between 0 and 1 inclusive. It cannot be negative.

The **coefficient of determination** measures the proportion of variation in Y that is explained by the variation in the independent variable X in the regression model. The range of r^2 is from 0 to 1 and the greater the value, the more the variation in Y in the regression model can be explained by the variation in X.

For the Sunflowers Apparel data, with $SSR = 66.7854$, $SSE = 11.9832$, and $SST = 78.7686$,

$$r^2 = \frac{66.7854}{78.7686} = 0.8479$$

Therefore, the variability in the number of profiled customers explains 84.79% of the variation in annual sales. This large r^2 indicates a strong linear relationship between these two variables because the regression model has explained 84.79% of the variability in predicting annual sales. (Only 15.21% of the sample variability in annual sales is due to factors not considered by the regression model.)

Figure 13.8 presents the regression statistics table portion of the Figure 13.4 results for the Sunflowers Apparel data. This table contains the coefficient of determination.

FIGURE 13.8

Regression statistics portion of the Figure 13.4 Excel results

	A	B
3	*Regression Statistics*	
4	Multiple R	0.9208
5	R Square	0.8479
6	Adjusted R Square	0.8352
7	Standard Error	0.9993
8	Observations	14

EXAMPLE 13.4

Computing the Coefficient of Determination

Compute the coefficient of determination, r^2, for the Sunflowers Apparel data.

SOLUTION You can compute SST, SSR, and SSE, which are defined in Equations (13.6), (13.7), and (13.8) on pages 495 and 496, by using Equations (13.10), (13.11), and (13.12).

COMPUTATIONAL FORMULA FOR SST

$$SST = \sum_{i=1}^{n}(Y_i - \bar{Y})^2 = \sum_{i=1}^{n}Y_i^2 - \frac{\left(\sum_{i=1}^{n}Y_i\right)^2}{n} \tag{13.10}$$

COMPUTATIONAL FORMULA FOR SSR

$$SSR = \sum_{i=1}^{n}(\hat{Y}_i - \bar{Y})^2$$

$$= b_0\sum_{i=1}^{n}Y_i + b_1\sum_{i=1}^{n}X_iY_i - \frac{\left(\sum_{i=1}^{n}Y_i\right)^2}{n} \tag{13.11}$$

COMPUTATIONAL FORMULA FOR SSE

$$SSE = \sum_{i=1}^{n}(Y_i - \hat{Y}_i)^2 = \sum_{i=1}^{n}Y_i^2 - b_0\sum_{i=1}^{n}Y_i - b_1\sum_{i=1}^{n}X_iY_i \tag{13.12}$$

Using the summary results from Table 13.2 on page 492,

$$SST = \sum_{i=1}^{n}(Y_i - \bar{Y})^2 = \sum_{i=1}^{n}Y_i^2 - \frac{\left(\sum_{i=1}^{n}Y_i\right)^2}{n}$$

$$= 693.9 - \frac{(92.8)^2}{14}$$

$$= 693.9 - 615.13142$$

$$= 78.76858$$

▶*(continued)*

$$SSR = \sum_{i=1}^{n}(\hat{Y}_i - \bar{Y})^2$$

$$= b_0\sum_{i=1}^{n}Y_i + b_1\sum_{i=1}^{n}X_iY_i - \frac{\left(\sum_{i=1}^{n}Y_i\right)^2}{n}$$

$$= (-1.2088265)(92.8) + (2.07417)(382.85) - \frac{(92.8)^2}{14}$$

$$= 66.7854$$

Using something other than the Excel that was used to calculate these coefficients may result in slightly different results. Those results will be consistent to the conclusion that there is a strong linear relationship between the two variables.

$$SSE = \sum_{i=1}^{n}(Y_i - \hat{Y}_i)^2$$

$$= \sum_{i=1}^{n}Y_i^2 - b_0\sum_{i=1}^{n}Y_i - b_1\sum_{i=1}^{n}X_iY_i$$

$$= 693.9 - (-1.2088265)(92.8) - (2.07417)(382.85)$$

$$= 11.9832$$

Therefore,

$$r^2 = \frac{66.7854}{78.7686} = 0.8479$$

Standard Error of the Estimate

Although the least-squares method produces the line that fits the data with the minimum amount of prediction error, unless all the observed data points fall on a straight line, the prediction line is not a perfect predictor. Just as all data values cannot be expected to be exactly equal to their mean, neither can all the values in a regression analysis be expected to be located exactly on the prediction line. Figure 13.5 on page 489 illustrates the variability around the prediction line for the Sunflowers Apparel data. Notice that many of the observed values of Y fall near the prediction line, but none of the values are exactly on the line.

The **standard error of the estimate** measures the variability of the observed Y values from the predicted Y values in the same way that the standard deviation in Chapter 3 measures the variability of each value around the sample mean. In other words, the standard error of the estimate is the standard deviation *around* the prediction line, whereas the standard deviation in Chapter 3 is the standard deviation *around* the sample mean. Equation (13.13) defines the standard error of the estimate, represented by the symbol S_{YX}.

STANDARD ERROR OF THE ESTIMATE

$$S_{YX} = \sqrt{\frac{SSE}{n-2}} = \sqrt{\frac{\sum_{i=1}^{n}(Y_i - \hat{Y}_i)^2}{n-2}} \tag{13.13}$$

where

Y_i = observed value of Y for a given X_i

$\hat{Y}_i$ = predicted value of Y for a given X_i

SSE = error sum of squares

From Equation (13.8) and Figure 13.4 or Figure 13.7 on pages 489 or 496, $SSE = 11.9832$. Thus,

$$S_{YX} = \sqrt{\frac{11.9832}{14 - 2}} = 0.9993$$

This standard error of the estimate, equal to 0.9993 millions of dollars (i.e., $999,300), is labeled Standard Error in the Figure 13.8 Excel results, Root Mean Square Error in the JMP results, and S in the Minitab results. The standard error of the estimate represents a measure of the variation around the prediction line. It is measured in the same units as the dependent variable Y. The interpretation of the standard error of the estimate is similar to that of the standard deviation. Just as the standard deviation measures variability around the mean, the standard error of the estimate measures variability around the prediction line. For Sunflowers Apparel, the typical difference between actual annual sales at a store and the predicted annual sales using the regression equation is approximately $999,300.

PROBLEMS FOR SECTION 13.3

LEARNING THE BASICS

13.11 How do you interpret a coefficient of determination, r^2, equal to 0.80?

13.12 If $SSR = 36$ and $SSE = 4$, determine SST and then compute the coefficient of determination, r^2, and interpret its meaning.

13.13 If $SSR = 66$ and $SST = 88$, compute the coefficient of determination, r^2, and interpret its meaning.

13.14 If $SSE = 10$ and $SSR = 30$, compute the coefficient of determination, r^2, and interpret its meaning.

13.15 If $SSR = 120$, why is it impossible for SST to equal 110?

APPLYING THE CONCEPTS

✓**SELF TEST** **13.16** In Problem 13.4 on page 493, the percentage of alcohol was used to predict wine quality (stored in VinhoVerde). For those data, $SSR = 21.8677$ and $SST = 64.0000$.
a. Determine the coefficient of determination, r^2, and interpret its meaning.
b. Determine the standard error of the estimate.
c. How useful do you think this regression model is for predicting sales?

13.17 In Problem 13.5 on page 493, you used the summated rating to predict the cost of a restaurant meal (stored in Restaurants).
a. Determine the coefficient of determination, r^2, and interpret its meaning.
b. Determine the standard error of the estimate.
c. How useful do you think this regression model is for predicting the cost of a restaurant meal?

13.18 In Problem 13.6 on page 494, a prospective MBA student wanted to predict starting salary upon graduation, based on program per-year tuition (stored in FTMBA). Using the results of that problem,
a. determine the coefficient of determination, r^2, and interpret its meaning.
b. determine the standard error of the estimate.
c. How useful do you think this regression model is for predicting starting salary?

13.19 In Problem 13.7 on page 494, you used the plate gap on the bag-sealing equipment to predict the tear rating of a bag of coffee (stored in Starbucks). Using the results of that problem,
a. determine the coefficient of determination, r^2, and interpret its meaning.
b. determine the standard error of the estimate.
c. How useful do you think this regression model is for predicting the tear rating based on the plate gap in the bag-sealing equipment?

13.20 In Problem 13.8 on page 494, you used annual revenues to predict the value of a baseball franchise (stored in BBValues). Using the results of that problem,
a. determine the coefficient of determination, r^2, and interpret its meaning.
b. determine the standard error of the estimate.
c. How useful do you think this regression model is for predicting the value of a baseball franchise?

13.21 In Problem 13.9 on page 494, an agent for a real estate company wanted to predict the monthly rent for one-bedroom apartments, based on the size of the apartment (stored in RentSilverSpring). Using the results of that problem,
a. determine the coefficient of determination, r^2, and interpret its meaning.
b. determine the standard error of the estimate.
c. How useful do you think this regression model is for predicting the monthly rent?
d. Can you think of other variables that might explain the variation in monthly rent?

13.22 In Problem 13.10 on page 494, you used YouTube trailer views to predict movie weekend box office gross (stored in Movie). Using the results of that problem,
a. determine the coefficient of determination, r^2, and interpret its meaning.
b. determine the standard error of the estimate.
c. How useful do you think this regression model is for predicting movie weekend box office gross?
d. Can you think of other variables that might explain the variation in movie weekend box office gross?

13.4 Assumptions of Regression

When hypothesis testing and the analysis of variance were discussed in Chapters 9 through 12, the importance of the assumptions to the validity of any conclusions reached was emphasized. The assumptions necessary for regression are similar to those of the analysis of variance because both are part of the general category of *linear models* (reference 4).

The four **assumptions of regression** (known by the acronym LINE) are:

- Linearity
- Independence of errors
- Normality of error
- Equal variance

The first assumption, **linearity**, states that the relationship between variables is linear. Relationships between variables that are not linear are discussed in Chapter 15.

The second assumption, **independence of errors**, requires that the errors (ε_i) be independent of one another. This assumption is particularly important when data are collected over a period of time. In such situations, the errors in a specific time period are sometimes correlated with those of the previous time period.

The third assumption, **normality**, requires that the errors (ε_i) be normally distributed at each value of X. Like the *t* test and the ANOVA *F* test, regression analysis is fairly robust against departures from the normality assumption. As long as the distribution of the errors at each level of X is not extremely different from a normal distribution, inferences about β_0 and β_1 are not seriously affected.

The fourth assumption, **equal variance**, or **homoscedasticity**, requires that the variance of the errors (ε_i) be constant for all values of X. In other words, the variability of Y values is the same when X is a low value as when X is a high value. The equal-variance assumption is important when making inferences about β_0 and β_1. If there are serious departures from this assumption, you can use either data transformations (see Section 15.2) or weighted least-squares methods (see reference 4).

13.5 Residual Analysis

Sections 13.2 and 13.3 developed a regression model using the least-squares method for the Sunflowers Apparel data. Is this the correct model for these data? Are the assumptions presented in Section 13.4 valid? **Residual analysis** visually evaluates these assumptions and helps you determine whether the regression model that has been selected is appropriate.

The **residual**, or estimated error value, e_i, is the difference between the observed (Y_i) and predicted ($\hat{Y}_i$) values of the dependent variable for a given value of X_i. A residual appears on a scatter plot as the vertical distance between an observed value of Y and the prediction line. Equation (13.14) defines the residual.

> RESIDUAL
>
> The residual is equal to the difference between the observed value of Y and the predicted value of Y.
>
> $$e_i = Y_i - \hat{Y}_i \tag{13.14}$$

student TIP

When there is no apparent pattern in the residual plot, the plot of the residuals will look like a random scattering of points.

Evaluating the Assumptions

Recall from Section 13.4 that the four assumptions of regression (known by the acronym LINE) are linearity, independence, normality, and equal variance.

Linearity   To evaluate linearity, you plot the residuals on the vertical axis against the corresponding X_i values of the independent variable on the horizontal axis. If the linear model is appropriate for the data, you will not see any apparent pattern in the residual plot. However, if the linear model is not appropriate, in the residual plot, there will be a relationship between the X_i values and the residuals, e_i.

You can see such a pattern in the residuals in Figure 13.9. Panel A shows a situation in which, although there is an increasing trend in Y as X increases, the relationship seems curvilinear because the upward trend decreases for increasing values of X. This effect is even more apparent in Panel B, where there is a clear relationship between X_i and e_i. By removing the linear trend of X with Y, the residual plot has exposed the lack of fit in the simple linear model more clearly than the scatter plot in Panel A. For these data, a curvilinear model such as a quadratic model (see Section 15.1) is a better fit and should be used instead of the simple linear model.

FIGURE 13.9

Studying the appropriateness of the simple linear regression model

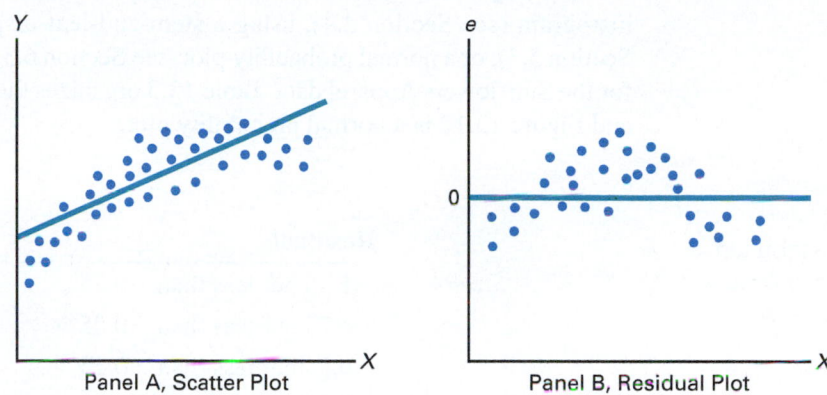

Panel A, Scatter Plot　　　　Panel B, Residual Plot

To determine whether the simple linear regression model for the Sunflowers Apparel data is appropriate, you need to determine the residuals. Figure 13.10 displays the predicted annual sales values and residuals for the Sunflowers Apparel data.

FIGURE 13.10

Table of residuals for the Sunflowers Apparel data

	A	B	C	D	E
1	Observation	Profiled Customers	Predicted Annual Sales	Annual Sales	Residuals
2	1	3.7	6.4656	5.7	-0.7656
3	2	3.6	6.2582	5.9	-0.3582
4	3	2.8	4.5988	6.7	2.1012
5	4	5.6	10.4065	9.5	-0.9065
6	5	3.3	5.6359	5.4	-0.2359
7	6	2.2	3.3543	3.5	0.1457
8	7	3.3	5.6359	6.2	0.5641
9	8	3.1	5.2211	4.7	-0.5211
10	9	3.2	5.4285	6.1	0.6715
11	10	3.5	6.0508	4.9	-1.1508
12	11	5.2	9.5769	10.7	1.1231
13	12	4.6	8.3324	7.6	-0.7324
14	13	5.8	10.8214	11.8	0.9786
15	14	3	5.0137	4.1	-0.9137

To assess linearity, you plot the residuals versus the independent variable (number of profiled customers, in millions) in Figure 13.11. Although there is widespread scatter in the residual plot, there is no clear pattern or relationship between the residuals and X_i. The residuals appear to be evenly spread above and below 0 for different values of X. You can conclude that the linear model is appropriate for the Sunflowers Apparel data.

FIGURE 13.11

Excel and Minitab plots of residuals versus the profiled customers of a store for the Sunflowers Apparel data

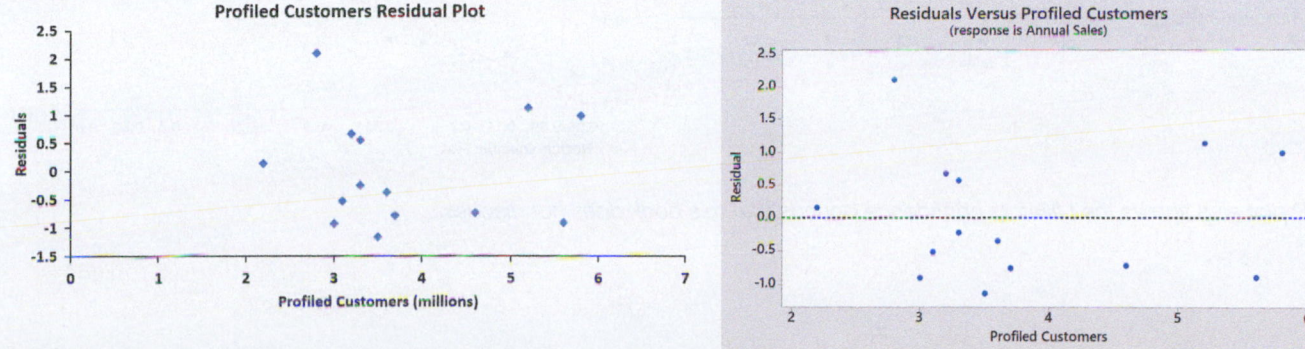

Independence   You can evaluate the assumption of independence of the errors by plotting the residuals in the order or sequence in which the data were collected. If the values of *Y* are part of a time series (see Section 2.5), a residual may sometimes be related to the residual that precedes it. If this relationship exists between consecutive residuals (which violates the assumption of independence), the plot of the residuals versus the time variable will often show a cyclical pattern. If it does, you would then need to use the alternative approaches that reference 4 discusses. (Because the Sunflowers Apparel data are not time-series data, you may not need to evaluate the independence assumption in the Sunflowers Apparel example.)

Normality   You can evaluate the assumption of normality in the errors by constructing a histogram (see Section 2.4), using a stem-and-leaf display (see Section 2.4), a boxplot (see Section 3.3), or a normal probability plot (see Section 6.3). To evaluate the normality assumption for the Sunflowers Apparel data, Table 13.3 organizes the residuals into a frequency distribution and Figure 13.12 is a normal probability plot.

TABLE 13.3

Frequency Distribution of 14 Residual Values for the Sunflowers Apparel Data

Residuals	Frequency
−1.25 but less than −0.75	4
−0.75 but less than −0.25	3
−0.25 but less than +0.25	2
+0.25 but less than +0.75	2
+0.75 but less than +1.25	2
+1.25 but less than +1.75	0
+1.75 but less than +2.25	1
	14

Although the small sample size makes it difficult to evaluate normality, from the normal probability plot of the residuals in Figure 13.12, the data do not appear to depart substantially from a normal distribution. The robustness of regression analysis with modest departures from normality enables you to conclude that you should not be overly concerned about departures from this normality assumption in the Sunflowers Apparel data.

FIGURE 13.12

Excel and JMP (quantile–quantile) normal probability plot of the residuals for the Sunflowers Apparel data

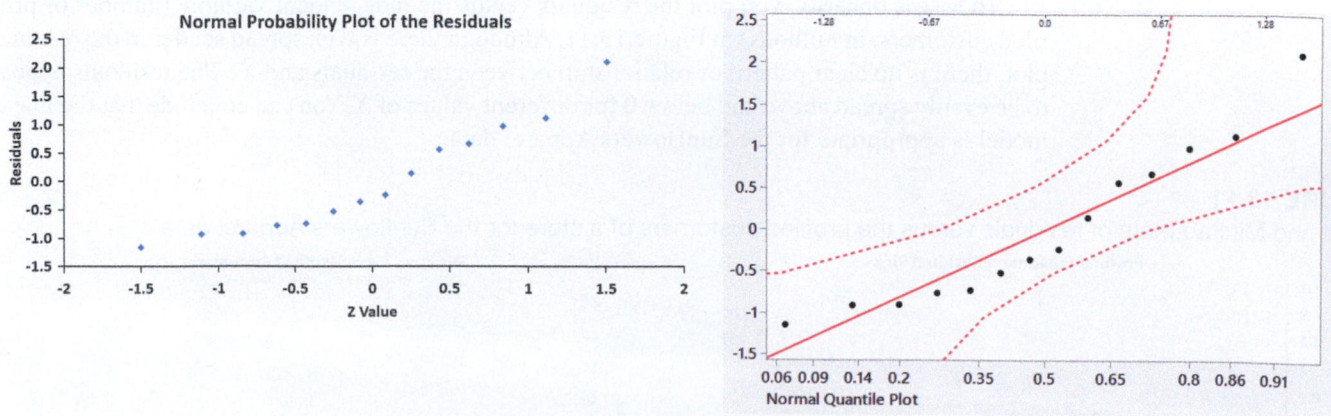

The JMP plot also shows the Lilliefors confidence bounds that this book does not discuss.

Equal Variance   You can evaluate the assumption of equal variance from a plot of the residuals with X_i. You examine the plot to see if there is approximately the same amount of variation in the residuals at each value of X. For the Sunflowers Apparel data of Figure 13.11 on page 501, there do not appear to be major differences in the variability of the residuals for different X_i values. Thus, you can conclude that there is no apparent violation in the assumption of equal variance at each level of X.

To examine a case in which the equal-variance assumption is violated, observe Figure 13.13, which is a plot of the residuals with X_i for a hypothetical set of data. This plot is fan shaped because the variability of the residuals increases dramatically as X increases. Because this plot shows unequal variances of the residuals at different levels of X, the equal-variance assumption is invalid and you would need to use the alternative approaches that reference 4 discusses.

FIGURE 13.13
Violation of equal variance

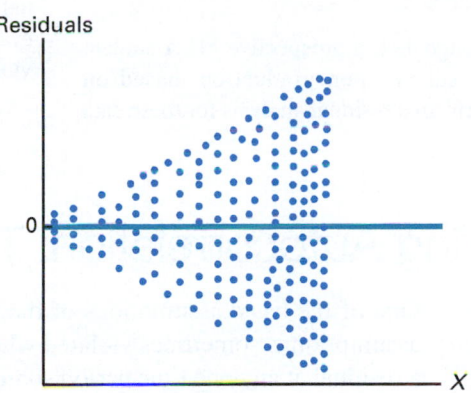

PROBLEMS FOR SECTION 13.5

LEARNING THE BASICS

13.23 The following results provide the X values, residuals, and a residual plot from a regression analysis:

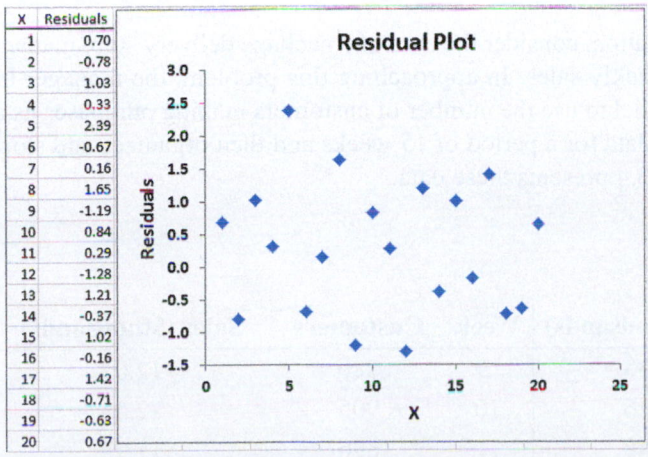

X	Residuals
1	0.70
2	-0.78
3	1.03
4	0.33
5	2.39
6	-0.67
7	0.16
8	1.65
9	-1.19
10	0.84
11	0.29
12	-1.28
13	1.21
14	-0.37
15	1.02
16	-0.16
17	1.42
18	-0.71
19	-0.63
20	0.67

Is there any evidence of a pattern in the residuals? Explain.

13.24 The following results show the X values, residuals, and a residual plot from a regression analysis:

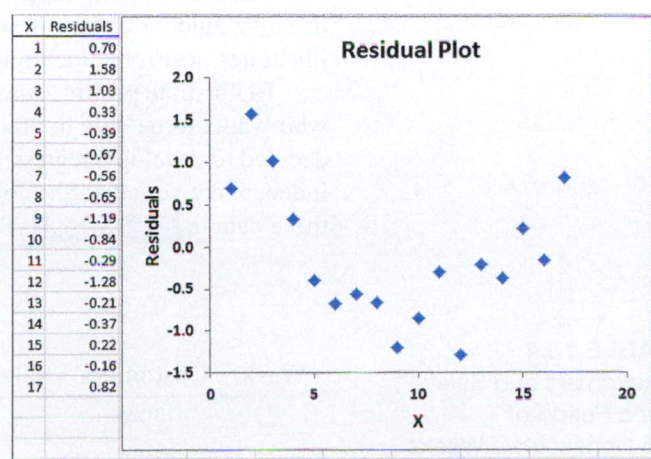

X	Residuals
1	0.70
2	1.58
3	1.03
4	0.33
5	-0.39
6	-0.67
7	-0.56
8	-0.65
9	-1.19
10	-0.84
11	-0.29
12	-1.28
13	-0.21
14	-0.37
15	0.22
16	-0.16
17	0.82

Is there any evidence of a pattern in the residuals? Explain.

APPLYING THE CONCEPTS

13.25 In Problem 13.5 on page 493, you used the summated rating to predict the cost of a restaurant meal. Perform a residual analysis for these data (stored in Restaurants). Evaluate whether the assumptions of regression have been seriously violated.

✓**SELF** **13.26** In Problem 13.4 on page 493, you used the
 TEST percentage of alcohol to predict wine quality. Perform a residual analysis for these data (stored in VinhoVerde). Evaluate whether the assumptions of regression have been seriously violated.

13.27 In Problem 13.7 on page 494, you used the plate gap on the bag-sealing equipment to predict the tear rating of a bag of coffee. Perform a residual analysis for these data (stored in Starbucks). Based on these results, evaluate whether the assumptions of regression have been seriously violated.

13.28 In Problem 13.6 on page 494, a prospective MBA student wanted to predict starting salary upon graduation, based on program per-year tuition. Perform a residual analysis for these data (stored in FTMBA). Based on these results, evaluate whether the assumptions of regression have been seriously violated.

13.29 In Problem 13.9 on page 494, an agent for a real estate company wanted to predict the monthly rent for one-bedroom apartments, based on the size of the apartments. Perform a residual analysis for these data (stored in RentSilverSpring). Based on these results, evaluate whether the assumptions of regression have been seriously violated.

13.30 In Problem 13.8 on page 494, you used annual revenues to predict the value of a baseball franchise. Perform a residual analysis for these data (stored in BBValues). Based on these results, evaluate whether the assumptions of regression have been seriously violated.

13.31 In Problem 13.10 on page 494, you used YouTube trailer views to predict movie weekend box office gross. Perform a residual analysis for these data (stored in Movie). Based on these results, evaluate whether the assumptions of regression have been seriously violated.

13.6 Measuring Autocorrelation: The Durbin-Watson Statistic

One of the basic assumptions of the regression model is the independence of the errors. This assumption is sometimes violated when data are collected over sequential time periods because a residual at any one time period sometimes is similar to residuals at adjacent time periods. This pattern in the residuals is called **autocorrelation**. When a set of data has substantial autocorrelation, the validity of a regression model is in serious doubt.

Residual Plots to Detect Autocorrelation

As mentioned in Section 13.5, one way to detect autocorrelation is to plot the residuals in time order. If a positive autocorrelation effect exists, there will be clusters of residuals with the same sign, and you will readily detect an apparent pattern. If negative autocorrelation exists, residuals will tend to jump back and forth from positive to negative to positive, and so on. Because negative autocorrelation is very rarely seen in regression analysis, the example in this section illustrates positive autocorrelation.

To illustrate positive autocorrelation, consider the case of a package delivery store manager who wants to be able to predict weekly sales. In approaching this problem, the manager has decided to develop a regression model to use the number of customers making purchases as an independent variable. She collects data for a period of 15 weeks and then organizes and stores these data in FifteenWeeks . Table 13.4 presents these data.

TABLE 13.4
Customers and Sales
for a Period of
15 Consecutive Weeks

Week	Customers	Sales ($thousands)	Week	Customers	Sales ($thousands)
1	794	9.33	9	880	12.07
2	799	8.26	10	905	12.55
3	837	7.48	11	886	11.92
4	855	9.08	12	843	10.27
5	845	9.83	13	904	11.80
6	844	10.09	14	950	12.15
7	863	11.01	15	841	9.64
8	875	11.49			

Because the data are collected over a period of 15 consecutive weeks at the same store, you need to determine whether there is autocorrelation. First, you can develop the simple linear regression model you can use to predict sales based on the number of customers assuming there is no autocorrelation in the residuals. Figure 13.14 presents results for these data.

FIGURE 13.14

Excel and JMP regression results for the Table 13.4 package delivery store data

From Figure 13.14, observe that r^2 is 0.6574, indicating that 65.74% of the variation in sales is explained by variation in the number of customers. In addition, the Y intercept, b_0, is -16.0322 and the slope, b_1, is 0.0308. However, before using this model for prediction, you must perform a residual analysis. Because the data have been collected over a consecutive period of 15 weeks, in addition to checking the linearity, normality, and equal-variance assumptions, you must investigate the independence-of-errors assumption. To do this, you plot the residuals versus time in Figure 13.15 in order to examine whether a pattern in the residuals exists. In Figure 13.15, you can see that the residuals tend to fluctuate up and down in a cyclical pattern. This cyclical pattern provides strong cause for concern about the existence of autocorrelation in the residuals and, therefore, a violation of the independence-of-errors assumption.

FIGURE 13.15

Excel residual plot for the Table 13.4 package delivery store data

Package Delivery Store Sales Analysis Residual Plot

The Durbin-Watson Statistic

The **Durbin-Watson statistic** is used to measure autocorrelation. This statistic measures the correlation between each residual and the residual for the previous time period. Equation (13.15) defines the Durbin-Watson statistic.

DURBIN-WATSON STATISTIC

$$D = \frac{\sum_{i=2}^{n}(e_i - e_{i-1})^2}{\sum_{i=1}^{n}e_i^2}$$

(13.15)

where

e_i = residual at the time period i

In Equation (13.15), the numerator, $\sum_{i=2}^{n}(e_i - e_{i-1})^2$, represents the squared difference between two successive residuals, summed from the second value to the nth value and the denominator, $\sum_{i=1}^{n} e_i^2$, represents the sum of the squared residuals. This means that the value of the Durbin-Watson statistic, D, will approach 0 if successive residuals are positively autocorrelated. If the residuals are not correlated, the value of D will be close to 2. (If the residuals are negatively autocorrelated, D will be greater than 2 and could even approach its maximum value of 4.)

From Figure 13.16, the Durbin-Watson statistic, D, is 0.8830 for the package delivery store data.

FIGURE 13.16
Excel, JMP, and Minitab Durbin-Watson statistic results for the package delivery store data

	A	B
1	Durbin-Watson Statistic	
2		
3	Sum of Squared Difference of Residuals	10.0575
4	Sum of Squared Residuals	11.3901
5		
6	Durbin-Watson Statistic	0.8830

Durbin-Watson

Durbin-Watson	Number of Obs.	AutoCorrelation
0.8830026	15	0.5181

Durbin-Watson Statistic
Durbin-Watson Statistic = 0.883003

You need to determine when the autocorrelation is large enough to conclude that there is significant positive autocorrelation. To do so, you compare D to the critical values of the Durbin-Watson statistic found in Table E.8, a portion of which is presented in Table 13.5. The critical values depend on α, the significance level chosen, n, the sample size, and k, the number of independent variables in the model (in simple linear regression, $k = 1$).

TABLE 13.5
Finding Critical Values of the Durbin-Watson Statistic

$\alpha = .05$

	$k = 1$		$k = 2$		$k = 3$		$k = 4$		$k = 5$	
n	d_L	d_U	d_L	d_U	d_L	d_U	d_L	d_U	d_L	d_U
15	1.08	1.36	.95	1.54	.82	1.75	.69	1.97	.56	2.21
16	1.10	1.37	.98	1.54	.86	1.73	.74	1.93	.62	2.15
17	1.13	1.38	1.02	1.54	.90	1.71	.78	1.90	.67	2.10
18	1.16	1.39	1.05	1.53	.93	1.69	.82	1.87	.71	2.06

In Table 13.5, two values are shown for each combination of α (level of significance), n (sample size), and k (number of independent variables in the model). The first value, d_L, represents the lower critical value. If D is below d_L, you conclude that there is evidence of positive autocorrelation among the residuals. If this occurs, the least-squares method used in this chapter is inappropriate, and you should use alternative methods (see reference 4). The second value, d_U, represents the upper critical value of D, above which you would conclude that there is no evidence of positive autocorrelation among the residuals. If D is between d_L and d_U, you are unable to arrive at a definite conclusion.

For the package delivery store data, with one independent variable ($k = 1$) and 15 values ($n = 15$), $d_L = 1.08$ and $d_U = 1.36$. Because $D = 0.8830 < 1.08$, you conclude that there is positive autocorrelation among the residuals. The least-squares regression analysis of the data shown in Figure 13.14 on page 505 is inappropriate because of the presence of significant positive autocorrelation among the residuals. In other words, the independence-of-errors assumption is invalid. You need to use alternative approaches, discussed in reference 4.

PROBLEMS FOR SECTION 13.6

LEARNING THE BASICS

13.32 The residuals for 10 consecutive time periods are as follows:

Time Period	Residual	Time Period	Residual
1	−5	6	+1
2	−4	7	+2
3	−3	8	+3
4	−2	9	+4
5	−1	10	+5

a. Plot the residuals over time. What conclusion can you reach about the pattern of the residuals over time?

b. Based on (a), what conclusion can you reach about the autocorrelation of the residuals?

13.33 The residuals for 15 consecutive time periods are as follows:

Time Period	Residual	Time Period	Residual
1	+4	9	+6
2	−6	10	−3
3	−1	11	+1
4	−5	12	+3
5	+2	13	0
6	+5	14	−4
7	−2	15	−7
8	+7		

a. Plot the residuals over time. What conclusion can you reach about the pattern of the residuals over time?

b. Compute the Durbin-Watson statistic. At the 0.05 level of significance, is there evidence of positive autocorrelation among the residuals?

c. Based on (a) and (b), what conclusion can you reach about the autocorrelation of the residuals?

APPLYING THE CONCEPTS

13.34 In Problem 13.7 on page 494 concerning the bag-sealing equipment at Starbucks, you used the plate gap to predict the tear rating.

a. Is it necessary to compute the Durbin-Watson statistic in this case? Explain.

b. Under what circumstances is it necessary to compute the Durbin-Watson statistic before proceeding with the least-squares method of regression analysis?

13.35 What is the relationship between the price of crude oil and the price you pay at the pump for gasoline? The file Oil & Gasoline contains the price ($) for a barrel of crude oil (Cushing, Oklahoma, spot price) and a gallon of gasoline (U.S. average conventional spot price) for 388 weeks, ending June 2, 2017.

Source: Data extracted from **www.eia.gov**.

a. Construct a scatter plot with the price of oil on the horizontal axis and the price of gasoline on the vertical axis.

b. Use the least-squares method to develop a simple linear regression equation to predict the price of a gallon of gasoline using the price of a barrel of crude oil as the independent variable.

c. Interpret the meaning of the slope, b_1, in this problem.

d. Plot the residuals versus the time period.

e. Compute the Durbin-Watson statistic.

f. At the 0.05 level of significance, is there evidence of positive autocorrelation among the residuals?

g. Based on the results of (d) through (f), is there reason to question the validity of the model?

h. What conclusions can you reach concerning the relationship between the price of a barrel of crude oil and the price of a gallon of gasoline?

✓ SELF TEST **13.36** A mail-order catalog business that sells personal computer supplies, software, and hardware maintains a centralized warehouse for the distribution of products ordered. Management is currently examining the process of distribution from the warehouse and has the business objective of determining the factors that affect warehouse distribution costs. Currently, a handling fee is added to the order, regardless of the amount of the order. Data that indicate the warehouse distribution costs and the number of orders received have been collected over the past 24 months and are stored in Warecost.

a. Assuming a linear relationship, use the least-squares method to find the regression coefficients b_0 and b_1.

b. Predict the monthly warehouse distribution costs when the number of orders is 4,500.

c. Plot the residuals versus the time period.

d. Compute the Durbin-Watson statistic. At the 0.05 level of significance, is there evidence of positive autocorrelation among the residuals?

e. Based on the results of (c) and (d), is there reason to question the validity of the model?

f. What conclusions can you reach concerning the factors that affect distribution costs?

13.37 A freshly brewed shot of espresso has three distinct components: the heart, body, and crema. The separation of these three components typically lasts only 10 to 20 seconds. To use the espresso shot in making a latte, a cappuccino, or another drink, the shot must be poured into the beverage during the separation of the heart, body, and crema. If the shot is used after the separation occurs, the drink becomes excessively bitter and acidic, ruining the final drink. Thus, a longer separation time allows the drink-maker more time to pour the shot and ensure that the beverage will meet expectations. An employee at a coffee shop hypothesized that the harder the espresso grounds were tamped down into the portafilter before brewing, the longer the separation time would be. An experiment using 24 observations was conducted to test this relationship. The independent variable Tamp measures the distance, in inches, between the espresso grounds and the top of the portafilter (i.e., the harder the tamp, the greater the distance). The dependent variable Time is the number of seconds the heart, body, and crema are separated (i.e., the amount of time after the shot is poured before it must be used for the customer's beverage). The data are stored in Espresso.

a. Use the least-squares method to develop a simple regression equation with Time as the dependent variable and Tamp as the independent variable.

b. Predict the separation time for a tamp distance of 0.50 inch.

c. Plot the residuals versus the time order of experimentation. Are there any noticeable patterns?

d. Compute the Durbin-Watson statistic. At the 0.05 level of significance, is there evidence of positive autocorrelation among the residuals?

e. Based on the results of (c) and (d), is there reason to question the validity of the model?

f. What conclusions can you reach concerning the effect of tamping on the time of separation?

13.38 The owners of a chain of ice cream stores have the business objective of improving the forecast of daily sales so that staffing shortages can be minimized during the summer season. As a starting point, the owners decide to develop a simple linear regression model to predict daily sales based on atmospheric temperature.

They select a sample of 21 consecutive days and store the results in IceCream . (Hint: Determine which are the independent and dependent variables.)

a. Assuming a linear relationship, use the least-squares method to compute the regression coefficients b_0 and b_1.

b. Predict the sales for a day in which the temperature is 83°F.

c. Plot the residuals versus the time period.

d. Compute the Durbin-Watson statistic. At the 0.05 level of significance, is there evidence of positive autocorrelation among the residuals?

e. Based on the results of (c) and (d), is there reason to question the validity of the model?

f. What conclusions can you reach concerning the relationship between sales and atmospheric temperature?

13.7 Inferences About the Slope and Correlation Coefficient

Sections 13.1 through 13.3 use regression solely for descriptive purposes. These sections discuss how to determine the regression coefficients using the least-squares method and how to predict Y for a given value of X. In addition, these sections discuss how to calculate and interpret the standard error of the estimate and the coefficient of determination.

When the residual analysis that Section 13.5 discusses indicates that the assumptions of a least-squares regression model are not seriously violated and that the straight-line model is appropriate, you can make inferences about the linear relationship between the variables in the population.

t Test for the Slope

To determine the existence of a significant linear relationship between the X and Y variables, you test whether β_1 (the population slope) is equal to 0. The null and alternative hypotheses are as follows:

$$H_0: \beta_1 = 0 \text{ [There is no linear relationship (the slope is zero).]}$$
$$H_1: \beta_1 \neq 0 \text{ [There is a linear relationship (the slope is not zero).]}$$

If you reject the null hypothesis, you conclude that there is evidence of a linear relationship. Equation (13.16) defines the test statistic for the slope, which is based on the sampling distribution of the slope.

TESTING A HYPOTHESIS FOR A POPULATION SLOPE, β_1, USING THE *t* TEST

The t_{STAT} test statistic equals the difference between the sample slope and hypothesized value of the population slope divided by S_{b_1}, the standard error of the slope.

$$t_{STAT} = \frac{b_1 - \beta_1}{S_{b_1}} \tag{13.16}$$

where

$$S_{b_1} = \frac{S_{YX}}{\sqrt{SSX}}$$

$$SSX = \sum_{i=1}^{n}(X_i - \bar{X})^2$$

The t_{STAT} test statistic follows a t distribution with $n - 2$ degrees of freedom.

Figure 13.17 presents the t test results for the Sunflowers Apparel scenario at the level of significance $\alpha = 0.05$.

FIGURE 13.17

Excel t test for the slope results for the Sunflowers Apparel data

	A	B	C	D	E	F	G
16		Coefficients	Standard Error	t Stat	P-value	Lower 95%	Upper 95%
17	Intercept	-1.2088	0.9949	-1.2151	0.2477	-3.3765	0.9588
18	Profiled Customers	2.0742	0.2536	8.1780	0.0000	1.5216	2.6268

From Figure 13.4 or Figure 13.17,

$$b_1 = +2.0742 \quad n = 14 \quad S_{b_1} = 0.2536$$

and

$$t_{STAT} = \frac{b_1 - \beta_1}{S_{b_1}}$$

$$= \frac{2.0742 - 0}{0.2536} = 8.178$$

Using the 0.05 level of significance, the critical value of t with $n - 2 = 12$ degrees of freedom is 2.1788. Because $t_{STAT} = 8.178 > 2.1788$ or because the p-value is 0.0000, which is less than $\alpha = 0.05$, you reject H_0 (see Figure 13.18). Hence, you conclude that there is a significant linear relationship between mean annual sales and the number of profiled customers.

FIGURE 13.18

Testing a hypothesis about the population slope at the 0.05 level of significance, with 12 degrees of freedom

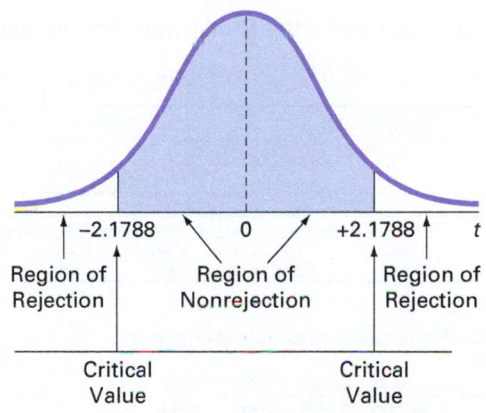

F Test for the Slope

As an alternative to the t test, in simple linear regression, you can use an F test to determine whether the slope is statistically significant. In previous chapters, Section 10.4 uses the F distribution to test the ratio of two variances and Sections 11.1 and 11.2 use the F distribution as part of the analysis of variance. Equation (13.17) defines the F test for the slope as the ratio of the variance that is due to the regression (MSR) divided by the error variance $(MSE = S_{YX}^2)$.

TESTING A HYPOTHESIS FOR A POPULATION SLOPE, β_1, USING THE F TEST

The F_{STAT} test statistic is equal to the regression mean square (MSR) divided by the mean square error (MSE).

$$F_{STAT} = \frac{MSR}{MSE} \tag{13.17}$$

where

$$MSR = \frac{SSR}{1} = SSR$$

$$MSE = \frac{SSE}{n - 2}$$

The F_{STAT} test statistic follows an F distribution with 1 and $n - 2$ degrees of freedom.

Using a level of significance α, the decision rule is

$$\text{Reject } H_0 \text{ if } F_{STAT} > F_\alpha;$$

otherwise, do not reject H_0.

Table 13.6 organizes the complete set of results into an analysis of variance (ANOVA) table.

TABLE 13.6

ANOVA Table for Testing the Significance of a Regression Coefficient

Source	df	Sum of Squares	Mean Square (variance)	F
Regression	1	SSR	$MSR = \dfrac{SSR}{1} = SSR$	$F_{STAT} = \dfrac{MSR}{MSE}$
Error	$n - 2$	SSE	$MSE = \dfrac{SSE}{n - 2}$	
Total	$n - 1$	SST		

Figure 13.19, the completed ANOVA table for the Sunflowers Apparel sales data (and part of Figure 13.4), shows that the computed F_{STAT} test statistic is 66.8792 (66.88 in Minitab) and the p-value is 0.0000 (or less than 0.0001).

FIGURE 13.19

Excel, JMP, and Minitab F test results for the Sunflowers Apparel data

	A	B	C	D	E	F	G
10	ANOVA						
11		df	SS	MS	F	Significance F	
12	Regression	1	66.7854	66.7854	66.8792	0.0000	
13	Residual	12	11.9832	0.9986			
14	Total	13	78.7686				
15							
16		Coefficients	Standard Error	t Stat	P-value	Lower 95%	Upper 95%
17	Intercept	-1.2088	0.9949	-1.2151	0.2477	-3.3765	0.9588
18	Profiled Customers	2.0742	0.2536	8.1780	0.0000	1.5216	2.6268

Analysis of Variance

Source	DF	Sum of Squares	Mean Square	F Ratio
Model	1	66.785405	66.7854	66.8792
Error	12	11.983167	0.9986	Prob > F
C. Total	13	78.768571		<.0001*

Regression Analysis: Annual Sales versus Profiled Customers
Analysis of Variance

Source	DF	Adj SS	Adj MS	F-Value	P-Value
Regression	1	66.7854	66.7854	66.88	0.000
Profiled Customers	1	66.7854	66.7854	66.88	0.000
Error	12	11.9832	0.9986		
Lack-of-Fit	11	11.6632	1.0603	3.31	0.406
Pure Error	1	0.3200	0.3200		
Total	13	78.7686			

Using a level of significance of 0.05, from Table E.5, the critical value of the F distribution, with 1 and 12 degrees of freedom, is 4.75 (see Figure 13.20). Because $F_{STAT} = 66.8792 > 4.75$ or because the p-value $= 0.0000 < 0.05$, you reject H_0 and conclude that there is a significant linear relationship between the number of profiled customers and annual sales. Because the F test in Equation (13.17) on page 509 is equivalent to the t test in Equation (13.16) on page 508, you reach the same conclusion.

In simple linear regression, $t^2 = F$.

FIGURE 13.20

Regions of rejection and nonrejection when testing for the significance of the slope at the 0.05 level of significance, with 1 and 12 degrees of freedom

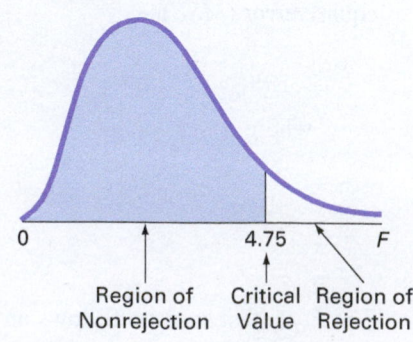

0   4.75   F

Region of   Critical   Region of
Nonrejection   Value   Rejection

Confidence Interval Estimate for the Slope

In addition to testing for the existence of a linear relationship between the variables, you can construct a confidence interval estimate of β_1 using Equation (13.18).

CONFIDENCE INTERVAL ESTIMATE OF THE SLOPE, β_1

The confidence interval estimate for the population slope can be constructed by taking the sample slope, b_1, and adding and subtracting the critical t value multiplied by the standard error of the slope.

$$b_1 \pm t_{\alpha/2}S_{b_1}$$

$$b_1 - t_{\alpha/2}S_{b_1} \le \beta_1 \le b_1 + t_{\alpha/2}S_{b_1} \tag{13.18}$$

where

$t_{\alpha/2}$ = critical value corresponding to an upper-tail probability of $\alpha/2$ from the t distribution with $n - 2$ degrees of freedom (i.e., a cumulative area of $1 - \alpha/2$)

From the Figure 13.17 results on page 509,

$$b_1 = 2.0742 \quad n = 14 \quad S_{b_1} = 0.2536$$

To construct a 95% confidence interval estimate, $\alpha/2 = 0.025$, and from Table E.3, $t_{\alpha/2} = 2.1788$. Thus,

$$b_1 \pm t_{\alpha/2}S_{b_1} = 2.0742 \pm (2.1788)(0.2536)$$

$$= 2.0742 \pm 0.5526$$

$$1.5216 \le \beta_1 \le 2.6268$$

Therefore, you have 95% confidence that the population slope is between 1.5216 and 2.6268. The confidence interval indicates that for each increase of 1 million profiled customers, predicted annual sales are estimated to increase by at least $1,521,600 but no more than $2,626,800. Because both of these values are above 0, you have evidence of a significant linear relationship between annual sales and the number of profiled customers. Had the interval included 0, you would have concluded that there is no evidence of a significant linear relationship between the variables.

t Test for the Correlation Coefficient

Section 3.5 notes that the strength of the relationship between two numerical variables can be measured using the **correlation coefficient**, r. The values of the coefficient of correlation range from -1 for a perfect negative correlation to $+1$ for a perfect positive correlation. You use the correlation coefficient to determine whether there is a statistically significant linear relationship between X and Y. To do so, you hypothesize that the population correlation coefficient, ρ, is 0. Thus, the null and alternative hypotheses are

$$H_0: \rho = 0 \text{ (no correlation)}$$

$$H_1: \rho \ne 0 \text{ (correlation)}$$

Equation (13.19) defines the test statistic for determining the existence of a significant correlation.

TESTING FOR THE EXISTENCE OF CORRELATION

$$t_{STAT} = \frac{r - \rho}{\sqrt{\dfrac{1 - r^2}{n - 2}}} \qquad (13.19a)$$

where

$$r = +\sqrt{r^2} \quad \text{if} \quad b_1 > 0$$
$$r = -\sqrt{r^2} \quad \text{if} \quad b_1 < 0$$

The t_{STAT} test statistic follows a t distribution with $n - 2$ degrees of freedom. r is calculated as in Equation (3.17) on page 509:

$$r = \frac{\text{cov}(X, Y)}{S_X S_Y} \qquad (13.19b)$$

where

$$\text{cov}(X, Y) = \frac{\displaystyle\sum_{i=1}^{n}(X_i - \bar{X})(Y_i - \bar{Y})}{n - 1}$$

$$S_X = \sqrt{\frac{\displaystyle\sum_{i=1}^{n}(X_i - \bar{X})^2}{n - 1}} \qquad S_Y = \sqrt{\frac{\displaystyle\sum_{i=1}^{n}(Y_i - \bar{Y})^2}{n - 1}}$$

In the Sunflowers Apparel example, $r^2 = 0.8479$ and $b_1 = +2.0742$ (see Figure 13.4 on page 489). Because $b_1 > 0$, the correlation coefficient for annual sales and profiled customers is the positive square root of r^2—that is, $r = +\sqrt{0.8479} = +0.9208$. Using Equation (13.19a) to test the null hypothesis that there is no correlation between these two variables results in the following t_{STAT} statistic:

$$t_{STAT} = \frac{r - 0}{\sqrt{\dfrac{1 - r^2}{n - 2}}} = \frac{0.9208 - 0}{\sqrt{\dfrac{1 - (0.9208)^2}{14 - 2}}} = 8.178$$

Using the 0.05 level of significance, because $t_{STAT} = 8.178 > 2.1788$, you reject the null hypothesis. You conclude that there is a significant correlation between annual sales and the number of profiled customers. This t_{STAT} test statistic is equivalent to the t_{STAT} test statistic found when testing whether the population slope, β_1, is equal to zero.

PROBLEMS FOR SECTION 13.7

LEARNING THE BASICS

13.39 You are testing the null hypothesis that there is no linear relationship between two variables, X and Y. From your sample of $n = 10$, you determine that $r = 0.80$.
a. What is the value of the t test statistic t_{STAT}?
b. At the $\alpha = 0.05$ level of significance, what are the critical values?
c. Based on your answers to (a) and (b), what statistical decision should you make?

13.40 You are testing the null hypothesis that there is no linear relationship between two variables, X and Y. From your sample of $n = 18$, you determine that $b_1 = +4.5$ and $S_{b_1} = 1.5$.
a. What is the value of t_{STAT}?
b. At the $\alpha = 0.05$ level of significance, what are the critical values?
c. Based on your answers to (a) and (b), what statistical decision should you make?
d. Construct a 95% confidence interval estimate of the population slope, β_1.

13.41 You are testing the null hypothesis that there is no linear relationship between two variables, X and Y. From your sample of $n = 20$, you determine that $SSR = 60$ and $SSE = 40$.

a. What is the value of F_{STAT}?

b. At the $\alpha = 0.05$ level of significance, what is the critical value?

c. Based on your answers to (a) and (b), what statistical decision should you make?

d. Compute the correlation coefficient by first computing r^2 and assuming that b_1 is negative.

e. At the 0.05 level of significance, is there a significant correlation between X and Y?

APPLYING THE CONCEPTS

✓**SELF TEST** **13.42** In Problem 13.4 on page 493, you used the percentage of alcohol to predict wine quality. The data are stored in VinhoVerde. From the results of that problem, $b_1 = 0.5624$ and $S_{b_1} = 0.1127$.

a. At the 0.05 level of significance, is there evidence of a linear relationship between the percentage of alcohol and wine quality?

b. Construct a 95% confidence interval estimate of the population slope, β_1.

13.43 In Problem 13.5 on page 493, you used the summated rating of a restaurant to predict the cost of a meal. The data are stored in Restaurants.

a. At the 0.05 level of significance, is there evidence of a linear relationship between the summated rating of a restaurant and the cost of a meal?

b. Construct a 95% confidence interval estimate of the population slope, β_1.

13.44 In Problem 13.6 on page 494, a prospective MBA student wanted to predict starting salary upon graduation, based on program per-year tuition. The data are stored in FTMBA. Use the results of that problem.

a. At the 0.05 level of significance, is there evidence of a linear relationship between the starting salary upon graduation and program per-year tuition?

b. Construct a 95% confidence interval estimate of the population slope, β_1.

13.45 In Problem 13.7 on page 494, you used the plate gap in the bag-sealing equipment to predict the tear rating of a bag of coffee. The data are stored in Starbucks. Use the results of that problem.

a. At the 0.05 level of significance, is there evidence of a linear relationship between the plate gap of the bag-sealing machine and the tear rating of a bag of coffee?

b. Construct a 95% confidence interval estimate of the population slope, β_1.

13.46 In Problem 13.8 on page 494, you used annual revenues to predict the value of a baseball franchise. The data are stored in BBValues. Use the results of that problem.

a. At the 0.05 level of significance, is there evidence of a linear relationship between annual revenue and franchise value?

b. Construct a 95% confidence interval estimate of the population slope, β_1.

13.47 In Problem 13.9 on page 494, an agent for a real estate company wanted to predict the monthly rent for one-bedroom apartments, based on the size of the apartment. The data are stored in RentSilverSpring. Use the results of that problem.

a. At the 0.05 level of significance, is there evidence of a linear relationship between the size of the apartment and the monthly rent?

b. Construct a 95% confidence interval estimate of the population slope, β_1.

13.48 In Problem 13.10 on page 494, you used YouTube trailer views to predict movie weekend box office gross from data stored in Movie. Use the results of that problem.

a. At the 0.05 level of significance, is there evidence of a linear relationship between YouTube trailer views and movie weekend box office gross?

b. Construct a 95% confidence interval estimate of the population slope, β_1.

13.49 The volatility of a stock is often measured by its beta value. You can estimate the beta value of a stock by developing a simple linear regression model, using the percentage weekly change in the stock as the dependent variable and the percentage weekly change in a market index as the independent variable. The S&P 500 Index is a common index to use. For example, if you wanted to estimate the beta value for Disney, you could use the following model, which is sometimes referred to as a *market model*:

$$(\% \text{ weekly change in Disney}) = \beta_0$$
$$+ \beta_1(\% \text{ weekly change in S \& P 500 index}) + \varepsilon$$

The least-squares regression estimate of the slope b_1 is the estimate of the beta value for Disney. A stock with a beta value of 1.0 tends to move the same as the overall market. A stock with a beta value of 1.5 tends to move 50% more than the overall market, and a stock with a beta value of 0.6 tends to move only 60% as much as the overall market. Stocks with negative beta values tend to move in the opposite direction of the overall market. The following table gives some beta values for some widely held stocks as of June 27, 2017:

Company	Ticker Symbol	Beta
Apple	AAPL	1.43
Disney	DIS	1.30
American Eagle Mines	AEM	−0.52
Marriott	MAR	1.35
Microsoft	MSFT	1.39
Procter & Gamble	PG	0.55

Source: Data extracted from finance.yahoo.com, June 27, 2017.

a. For each of the six companies, interpret the beta value.

b. How can investors use the beta value as a guide for investing?

13.50 Index funds are mutual funds that try to mimic the movement of leading indexes, such as the S&P 500 or the Russell 2000. The beta values (as described in Problem 13.49) for these funds are therefore approximately 1.0, and the estimated market models for these funds are approximately

$$(\% \text{ weekly change in index fund}) = 0.0 + 1.0$$

$$(\% \text{ weekly change in the index})$$

Leveraged index funds are designed to magnify the movement of major indexes. Direxion Funds is a leading provider of leveraged index and other alternative-class mutual fund products for investment advisors and sophisticated investors. Two of the company's funds are shown in the following table:

Name	Ticker Symbol	Description
Daily Small Cap Bull 3x Fund	TNA	300% of the Russell 2000 Index
Daily S&P 500 Bull 2x Fund	SPUU	200% of the S&P 500 Index

Source: Data extracted from **www.direxionfunds.com**.

The estimated market models for these funds are approximately

$$(\% \text{ daily change in TNA}) = 0.0 + 3.0$$

$$(\% \text{ daily change in the Russell 2000})$$

$$(\% \text{ daily change in SPUU}) = 0.0 + 2.0$$

$$(\% \text{ daily change in the S\&P 500 Index})$$

Thus, if the Russell 2000 Index gains 10% over a period of time, the leveraged mutual fund TNA gains approximately 30%. On the downside, if the same index loses 20%, TNA loses approximately 60%.

a. The objective of the Direxion Funds Bull 2x Fund, SPUU, is 200% of the performance of the S&P 500 Index. What is its approximate market model?

b. If the S&P 500 Index gains 10% in a year, what return do you expect SPUU to have?

c. If the S&P 500 Index loses 20% in a year, what return do you expect SPUU to have?

d. What type of investors should be attracted to leveraged index funds? What type of investors should stay away from these funds?

13.51 The file Cereals contains the calories and sugar, in grams, in one serving of seven breakfast cereals:

Cereal	Calories	Sugar
Kellogg's All Bran	80	6
Kellogg's Corn Flakes	100	2
Wheaties	100	4
Nature's Path Organic Multigrain Flakes	110	4
Kellogg's Rice Krispies	130	4
Post Shredded Wheat Vanilla Almond	190	11
Kellogg's Mini Wheats	200	10

a. Compute and interpret the coefficient of correlation, r.

b. At the 0.05 level of significance, is there a significant linear relationship between calories and sugar?

13.52 Movie companies need to predict the gross receipts of an individual movie once the movie has debuted. The following results (stored in PotterMovies) are the first weekend gross, the U.S. gross, and the worldwide gross (in $millions) of the eight Harry Potter movies that debuted from 2001 to 2011:

Title	First Weekend	U.S. Gross	Worldwide Gross
Sorcerer's Stone	90.295	317.558	976.458
Chamber of Secrets	88.357	261.988	878.988
Prisoner of Azkaban	93.687	249.539	795.539
Goblet of Fire	102.335	290.013	896.013
Order of the Phoenix	77.108	292.005	938.469
Half-Blood Prince	77.836	301.460	934.601
Deathly Hallows Part I	125.017	295.001	955.417
Deathly Hallows Part II	169.189	381.001	1,328.11

Source: Data extracted from **www.the-numbers.com/interactive/comp-Harry-Potter.php**.

a. Compute the coefficient of correlation between first weekend gross and U.S. gross, first weekend gross and worldwide gross, and U.S. gross and worldwide gross.

b. At the 0.05 level of significance, is there a significant linear relationship between first weekend gross and U.S. gross, first weekend gross and worldwide gross, and U.S. gross and worldwide gross?

13.53 The file MobileSpeed contains the overall download and upload speeds in mbps for nine carriers in the United States.

Source: Data extracted from "Best Mobile Network 2016," **bit.ly/1KGPrMm**, accessed November 10, 2016.

a. Compute and interpret the coefficient of correlation, r.

b. At the 0.05 level of significance, is there a significant linear relationship between download and upload speed?

13.54 A survey by the Pew Research Center found that social networking is popular in many nations around the world. The file GlobalSocialMedia contains the level of social media networking (measured as the percent of individuals polled who use social networking sites) and the GDP per capita based on purchasing power parity (PPP) for each of 28 emerging and developing countries.

Source: Data extracted from "2. Online Activities in Emerging and Developing Nations," **pewrsr.ch/1RX3Iqq**.

a. Compute and interpret the coefficient of correlation, r.

b. At the 0.05 level of significance, is there a significant linear relationship between GDP and social media usage?

c. What conclusions can you reach about the relationship between GDP and social media usage?

13.8 Estimation of Mean Values and Prediction of Individual Values

In Chapter 8, you studied the concept of the confidence interval estimate of the population mean. In Example 13.2 on page 490, you used the prediction line to predict the mean value of Y for a given X. The mean annual sales for stores that had 4 million profiled customers within a fixed radius was predicted to be 7.0879 millions of dollars ($7,087,900). This estimate, however, is a *point estimate* of the population mean. This section presents methods to develop a confidence interval estimate for the mean response for a given X and for developing a prediction interval for an individual response, Y, for a given value of X.

The Confidence Interval Estimate for the Mean Response

Equation (13.20) defines the **confidence interval estimate for the mean response** for a given X.

CONFIDENCE INTERVAL ESTIMATE FOR THE MEAN OF Y

$$\hat{Y}_i \pm t_{\alpha/2} S_{YX} \sqrt{h_i}$$

$$\hat{Y}_i - t_{\alpha/2} S_{YX} \sqrt{h_i} \le \mu_{Y|X=X_i} \le \hat{Y}_i + t_{\alpha/2} S_{YX} \sqrt{h_i} \tag{13.20}$$

where

$$h_i = \frac{1}{n} + \frac{(X_i - \overline{X})^2}{SSX}$$

$\hat{Y}_i$ = predicted value of Y; $\hat{Y}_i = b_0 + b_1 X_i$

S_{YX} = standard error of the estimate

n = sample size

X_i = given value of X

$\mu_{Y|X=X_i}$ = mean value of Y when $X = X_i$

$$SSX = \sum_{i=1}^{n} (X_i - \overline{X})^2$$

$t_{\alpha/2}$ = critical value corresponding to an upper-tail probability of $\alpha/2$ from the t distribution with $n - 2$ degrees of freedom (i.e., a cumulative area of $1 - \alpha/2$)

The width of the confidence interval in Equation (13.20) depends on several factors. Increased variation around the prediction line, as measured by the standard error of the estimate, results in a wider interval. As you would expect, increased sample size reduces the width of the interval. In addition, the width of the interval varies at different values of X. When you predict Y for values of X close to $\overline{X}$, the interval is narrower than for predictions for X values farther away from $\overline{X}$.

In the Sunflowers Apparel example, suppose you want to construct a 95% confidence interval estimate of the mean annual sales for the entire population of stores that have 4 million profiled customers ($X = 4$). Using the simple linear regression equation,

$$\hat{Y}_i = -1.2088 + 2.0742 X_i$$

$$= -1.2088 + 2.0742(4) = 7.0879 \text{ (millions of dollars)}$$

$$\hat{Y}_i \pm t_{\alpha/2} S_{YX} \sqrt{h_i}$$

given these:

$$\overline{X} = 3.7786 \quad S_{YX} = 0.9993 \quad SSX = \sum_{i=1}^{n} (X_i - \overline{X})^2 = 15.5236$$

and from Table E.3, $t_{\alpha/2} = 2.1788$. To compute the confidence interval estimate where

$$h_i = \frac{1}{n} + \frac{(X_i - \overline{X})^2}{SSX}$$

results in

$$\hat{Y}_i \pm t_{\alpha/2}S_{YX}\sqrt{\frac{1}{n} + \frac{(X_i - \overline{X})^2}{SSX}}$$

$$= 7.0879 \pm (2.1788)(0.9993)\sqrt{\frac{1}{14} + \frac{(4 - 3.7786)^2}{15.5236}}$$

$$= 7.0879 \pm 0.5946$$

Therefore, the confidence interval estimate is:

$$6.4932 \le \mu_{Y|X=4} \le 7.6825$$

Therefore, the 95% confidence interval estimate is that the population mean annual sales are between $6,493,200 and $7,682,500 for all stores with 4 million profiled customers.

The Prediction Interval for an Individual Response

In addition to constructing a confidence interval for the mean value of Y, you can also construct a prediction interval for an individual value of Y. Although the form of this interval is similar to that of the confidence interval estimate of Equation (13.20), the prediction interval is predicting an individual value, not estimating a mean. Equation (13.21) defines the **prediction interval for an individual response,** Y, at a given value, X_i, denoted by $Y_{X=X_i}$.

> **PREDICTION INTERVAL FOR AN INDIVIDUAL RESPONSE, Y**
>
> $$\hat{Y}_i \pm t_{\alpha/2}S_{YX}\sqrt{1 + h_i}$$
>
> $$\hat{Y}_i - t_{\alpha/2}S_{YX}\sqrt{1 + h_i} \le Y_{X=X_i} \le \hat{Y}_i + t_{\alpha/2}S_{YX}\sqrt{1 + h_i} \qquad \textbf{(13.21)}$$
>
> where
>
> $Y_{X=X_i}$ = future value of Y when $X = X_i$
>
> $t_{\alpha/2}$ = critical value corresponding to an upper-tail probability of $\alpha/2$ from the t distribution with $n - 2$ degrees of freedom (i.e., a cumulative area of $1 - \alpha/2$)
>
> Note: h_i, $\hat{Y}_i$, S_{YX}, n, and X_i are defined as in Equation (13.20) on page 515.

To construct a 95% prediction interval of the annual sales for an individual store that has 4 million profiled customers ($X = 4$), you first compute $\hat{Y}_i$. Using the prediction line:

$$\hat{Y}_i = -1.2088 + 2.0742X_i$$

$$= -1.2088 + 2.0742(4)$$

$$= 7.0879 \text{ (millions of dollars)}$$

To compute the prediction interval estimate given these

$$\overline{X} = 3.7786 \quad S_{YX} = 0.9993 \quad SSX = \sum_{i=1}^{n}(X_i - \overline{X})^2 = 15.5236$$

and, from Table E.3, $t_{\alpha/2} = 2.1788$, results in

$$\hat{Y}_i \pm t_{\alpha/2}S_{YX}\sqrt{1 + \frac{1}{n} + \frac{(X_i - \overline{X})^2}{SSX}}$$

$$= 7.0879 \pm (2.1788)(0.9993)\sqrt{1 + \frac{1}{14} + \frac{(4 - 3.7786)^2}{15.5236}}$$

$$= 7.0879 \pm 2.2570$$

Therefore, the prediction interval estimate is:

$$4.8308 \leq Y_{X=4} \leq 9.3449$$

With 95% confidence, you predict that the annual sales for an individual store with 4 million profiled customers is between $4,830,800 and $9,344,900.

    If you compare the results of the confidence interval estimate and the prediction interval, you see that the width of the prediction interval for an individual store is much wider than the confidence interval estimate for the mean. Remember that there is much more variation in predicting an individual value than in estimating a mean value. Figure 13.21 presents the Excel, JMP, and Minitab results for the confidence interval estimate and the prediction interval for the Sunflowers Apparel data.

FIGURE 13.21

Excel, JMP (partial), and Minitab results for the confidence interval estimate and prediction interval for the Sunflowers Apparel data

	A	B
1	Confidence Interval Estimate and Prediction Interval	
2		
3	Data	
4	X Value	4
5	Confidence Level	95%
6		
7	Intermediate Calculations	
8	Sample Size	14
9	Degrees of Freedom	12
10	t Value	2.1788
11	Sample Mean	3.7786
12	Sum of Squared Difference	15.5236
13	Standard Error of the Estimate	0.9993
14	h Statistic	0.0746
15	Predicted Y (YHat)	7.0879
16		
17	For Average Y	
18	Interval Half Width	0.5946
19	Confidence Interval Lower Limit	6.4932
20	Confidence Interval Upper Limit	7.6825
21		
22	For Individual Response Y	
23	Interval Half Width	2.2570
24	Prediction Interval Lower Limit	4.8308
25	Prediction Interval Upper Limit	9.3449

7/0 Cols 15/0	Store	Profiled Customers	Annual Sales	Lower 95% Mean Annual Sales	Upper 95% Mean Annual Sales	Lower 95% Indiv Annual Sales	Upper 95% Indiv Annual Sales
12	12	4.6	7.6	7.5943424425	9.0703702064	6.0333934032	10.631319246
13	13	5.8	11.8	9.5618235656	12.080904084	8.3060094385	13.336718211
14	14	3.0	4.1	4.2899917102	5.7373676051	2.7192755371	7.3080837782
15	•	4.0	•	6.4932226416	7.6824825072	4.8308300269	9.344875122

Prediction for Annual Sales

Regression Equation

  Annual Sales = -1.209 + 2.074 Profiled Customers

Settings

Variable	Setting
Profiled Customers	4

Prediction

Fit	SE Fit	95% CI	95% PI
7.08785	0.272915	(6.49322, 7.68248)	(4.83083, 9.34488)

PROBLEMS FOR SECTION 13.8

LEARNING THE BASICS

13.55 Based on a sample of $n = 20$, the least-squares method was used to develop the following prediction line: $\hat{Y}_i = 5 + 3X_i$. In addition,

$$S_{YX} = 1.0 \quad \bar{X} = 2 \quad \sum_{i=1}^{n}(X_i - \bar{X})^2 = 20$$

a. Construct a 95% confidence interval estimate of the population mean response for $X = 2$.

b. Construct a 95% prediction interval of an individual response for $X = 2$.

13.56 Based on a sample of $n = 20$, the least-squares method was used to develop the following prediction line: $\hat{Y}_i = 5 + 3X_i$. In addition,

$$S_{YX} = 1.0 \quad \bar{X} = 2 \quad \sum_{i=1}^{n}(X_i - \bar{X})^2 = 20$$

a. Construct a 95% confidence interval estimate of the population mean response for $X = 4$.

b. Construct a 95% prediction interval of an individual response for $X = 4$.

c. Compare the results of (a) and (b) with those of Problem 13.55 (a) and (b). Which intervals are wider? Why?

APPLYING THE CONCEPTS

13.57 In Problem 13.5 on page 493, you used the summated rating of a restaurant to predict the cost of a meal. The data are stored in Restaurants .

a. Construct a 95% confidence interval estimate of the mean cost of a meal for restaurants that have a summated rating of 50.

b. Construct a 95% prediction interval of the cost of a meal for an individual restaurant that has a summated rating of 50.

c. Explain the difference in the results in (a) and (b).

✓ SELF TEST **13.58** In Problem 13.4 on page 493, you used the percentage of alcohol to predict wine quality. The data are stored in VinhoVerde . For these data, $S_{YX} = 0.9369$ and $h_i = 0.024934$ when $X = 10$.

a. Construct a 95% confidence interval estimate of the mean wine quality rating for all wines that have 10% alcohol.

b. Construct a 95% prediction interval of the wine quality rating of an individual wine that has 10% alcohol.

c. Explain the difference in the results in (a) and (b).

13.59 In Problem 13.7 on page 494, you used the plate gap on the bag-sealing equipment to predict the tear rating of a bag of coffee. The data are stored in Starbucks .

a. Construct a 95% confidence interval estimate of the mean tear rating for all bags of coffee when the plate gap is 0.

b. Construct a 95% prediction interval of the tear rating for an individual bag of coffee when the plate gap is 0.

c. Why is the interval in (a) narrower than the interval in (b)?

13.60 In Problem 13.6 on page 494, a prospective MBA student wanted to predict starting salary upon graduation, based on program per-year tuition. The data are stored in FTMBA .

a. Construct a 95% confidence interval estimate of the mean starting salary upon graduation of an individual program with per-year tuition cost of $50,450.

b. Construct a 95% prediction interval of the starting salary upon graduation of an individual program with per-year tuition cost of $50,450.

c. Why is the interval in (a) narrower than the interval in (b)?

13.61 In Problem 13.9 on page 494, an agent for a real estate company wanted to predict the monthly rent for one-bedroom apartments, based on the size of an apartment. The data are stored in RentSilverSpring .

a. Construct a 95% confidence interval estimate of the mean monthly rental for all one-bedroom apartments that are 800 square feet in size.

b. Construct a 95% prediction interval of the monthly rental for an individual one-bedroom apartment that is 800 square feet in size.

c. Explain the difference in the results in (a) and (b).

13.62 In Problem 13.8 on page 494, you predicted the value of a baseball franchise, based on current revenue. The data are stored in BBValues .

a. Construct a 95% confidence interval estimate of the mean value of all baseball franchises that generate $250 million of annual revenue.

b. Construct a 95% prediction interval of the value of an individual baseball franchise that generates $250 million of annual revenue.

c. Explain the difference in the results in (a) and (b).

13.63 In Problem 13.10 on page 494, you used YouTube trailer views to predict movie weekend box office gross from data stored in Movie . A movie, about to be released, has 50 million YouTube trailer views.

a. What is the predicted weekend box office gross?

b. Which interval is more useful here, the confidence interval estimate of the mean or the prediction interval for an individual response? Explain.

c. Construct and interpret the interval you selected in (b).

13.9 Potential Pitfalls in Regression

There are several different types of potential pitfalls when using regression analysis. Regression analysis requires knowledge of the subject matter, which, in turn, requires proper definition of the problem being solved or the goal being sought, the first task of the DCOVA framework that the First Things First chapter introduces. Without knowledge of the subject matter, important variables may be omitted from the regression model or nonsensical relationships among variables wrongly explored.

Many potential pitfalls arise from overlooking the issues that this chapter discusses. A lack of awareness of the assumptions of least-squares regression, not knowing how to evaluate the assumptions of least-squares regression, or extrapolating outside the relevant range are all common errors. So, too, are not knowing what alternatives exist to least-squares regression if an assumption is violated or thinking that every relationship must be linear. Overlooking logical casuality, a basic principle of all statistics (see page 6), can also occur when a person gets too involved in the mechanics of performing a regression.

Exhibit 13.1 presents a seven-step strategy that helps avoid the potential pitfalls when using regression analysis.

EXHIBIT 13.1

Seven Steps for Avoiding the Potential Pitfalls

1. Be clear about the problem or goal being investigated and the variables that need to be examined.
2. Construct a scatter plot to observe the possible relationship between X and Y.
3. Perform a residual analysis to check the assumptions of regression (linearity, independence, normality, equal variance):
   a. Plot the residuals versus the independent variable to determine whether the linear model is appropriate and to check for equal variance.

(continued)

b. Construct a histogram, stem-and-leaf display, boxplot, or normal probability plot of the residuals to check for normality.

c. Plot the residuals versus time to check for independence. (This step is necessary only if the data are collected over time.)

4. If there are violations of the assumptions, use alternative methods to least-squares regression or alternative least-squares models (see reference 4 and Section 15.2).

5. If there are no violations of the assumptions, carry out tests for the significance of the regression coefficients and develop confidence and prediction intervals.

6. Refrain from making predictions and forecasts outside the relevant range of the independent variable.

7. Remember that the relationships identified in observational studies may or may not be due to cause-and-effect relationships. (While causation implies correlation, correlation does not imply causation.)

Someone not familiar with the assumptions of regression or how to evaluate those assumptions may reach wrong conclusions about the data being analyzed. For example, Table 13.7, stored in Anscombe , presents the Anscombe data set that illustrates the importance of using scatter plots and residual analysis to complement the calculation of the Y intercept, the slope, and r^2.

TABLE 13.7
Four Sets of Artificial Data

Data Set A		Data Set B		Data Set C		Data Set D	
X_i	Y_i	X_i	Y_i	X_i	Y_i	X_i	Y_i
10	8.04	10	9.14	10	7.46	8	6.58
14	9.96	14	8.10	14	8.84	8	5.76
5	5.68	5	4.74	5	5.73	8	7.71
8	6.95	8	8.14	8	6.77	8	8.84
9	8.81	9	8.77	9	7.11	8	8.47
12	10.84	12	9.13	12	8.15	8	7.04
4	4.26	4	3.10	4	5.39	8	5.25
7	4.82	7	7.26	7	6.42	19	12.50
11	8.33	11	9.26	11	7.81	8	5.56
13	7.58	13	8.74	13	12.74	8	7.91
6	7.24	6	6.13	6	6.08	8	6.89

Source: Data extracted from F. J. Anscombe, "Graphs in Statistical Analysis," *The American Statistician,* 27 (1973), pp. 17–21.

Anscombe (reference 1) showed that all four data sets given in Table 13.7 have the following identical results:

$$\hat{Y}_i = 3.0 + 0.5X_i \quad S_{YX} = 1.237 \quad S_{b_1} = 0.118 \quad r^2 = 0.667$$

$$SSR = 27.51 \quad SSE = 13.76 \quad SST = 41.27$$

If you stopped the analysis at this point, you would fail to observe the important differences among the four data sets that scatter plots and residual plots can reveal. The Figure 13.22 scatter plots and residual plots show how different the four data sets are!

FIGURE 13.22
Scatter plots and residual plots for the data sets A, B, C, and D

Scatter plots

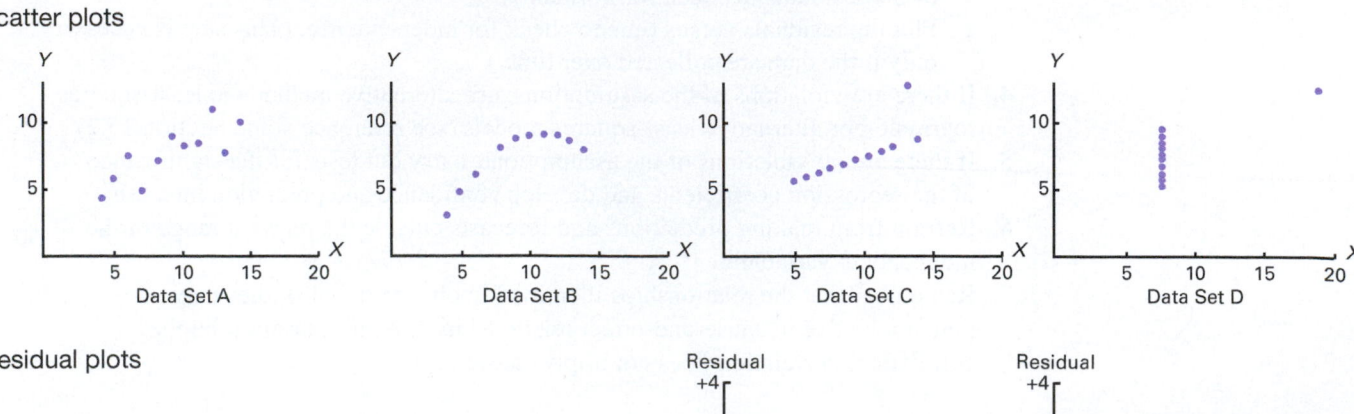

Residual plots

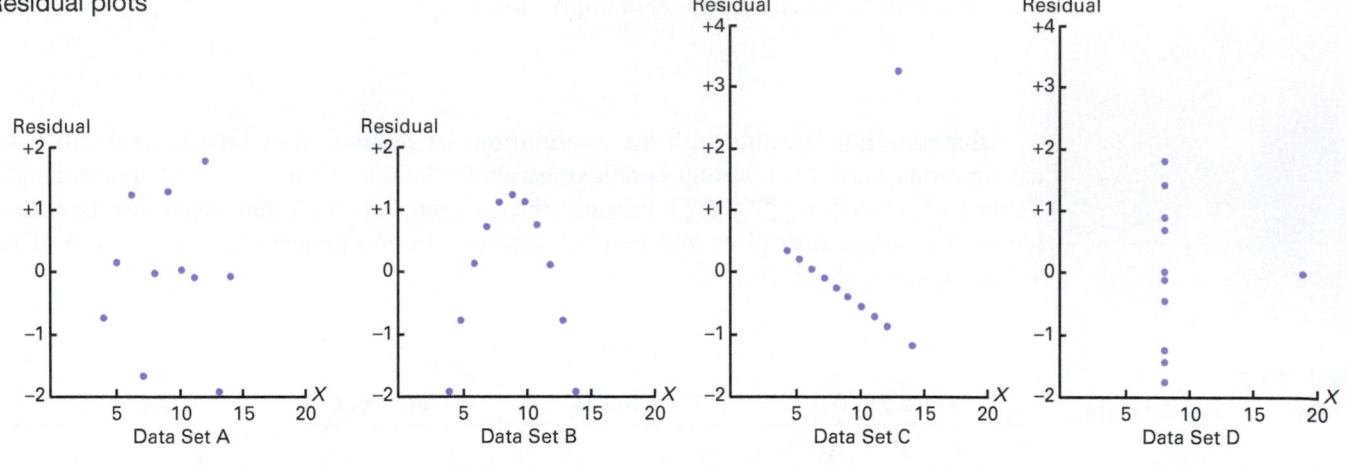

Each data set has a different relationship between X and Y. The only data set that seems to approximately follow a straight line is data set A. The residual plot for data set A does not show any obvious patterns or outlying residuals. This is certainly not true for data sets B, C, and D. The scatter plot for data set B shows that a curvilinear regression model is more appropriate. This conclusion is reinforced by the residual plot for data set B. The scatter plot and the residual plot for data set C clearly show an outlying observation. In this case, one approach used is to remove the outlier and reestimate the regression model (see reference 4). The scatter plot for data set D represents a situation in which the model is heavily dependent on the outcome of a single data point ($X_8 = 19$ and $Y_8 = 12.50$). Any regression model with this characteristic should be used with caution.

▼USING **STATISTICS**
Knowing Customers ..., Revisited

I n the Knowing Customers at Sunflowers Apparel scenario, you were the director of planning for a chain of upscale clothing stores for women. Until now, Sunflowers managers selected sites based on factors such as the availability of a good lease or a subjective opinion that a location seemed like a good place for a store. To make more objective decisions, you used the more systematic DCOVA approach to identify and classify groups of consumers and developed a regression model to analyze the relationship between the number of profiled customers who live within a fixed radius of a Sunflowers store and the annual sales of the store. The model indicated that about 84.8% of the variation in sales was explained by the number of profiled customers who live within a fixed radius of a Sunflowers store. Furthermore, for each increase of 1 million profiled customers, mean annual sales were estimated to increase by $2.0742 million. You can now use your model to help make better decisions when selecting new sites for stores as well as to forecast sales for existing stores.

▼ SUMMARY

This chapter develops the simple linear regression model and discusses the assumptions the model uses and how to evaluate them. Once you are assured that the model is appropriate, you can predict values by using the prediction line and test for the significance of the slope. Figure 13.23 provides a roadmap for navigating through the process of applying a simple linear regresssion model to a set of data. Chapters 14 and 15 extend regression analysis to models that include more than one independent variable or that have a categorical dependent variable as well as models that are nonlinear.

FIGURE 13.23
Roadmap for simple linear regression

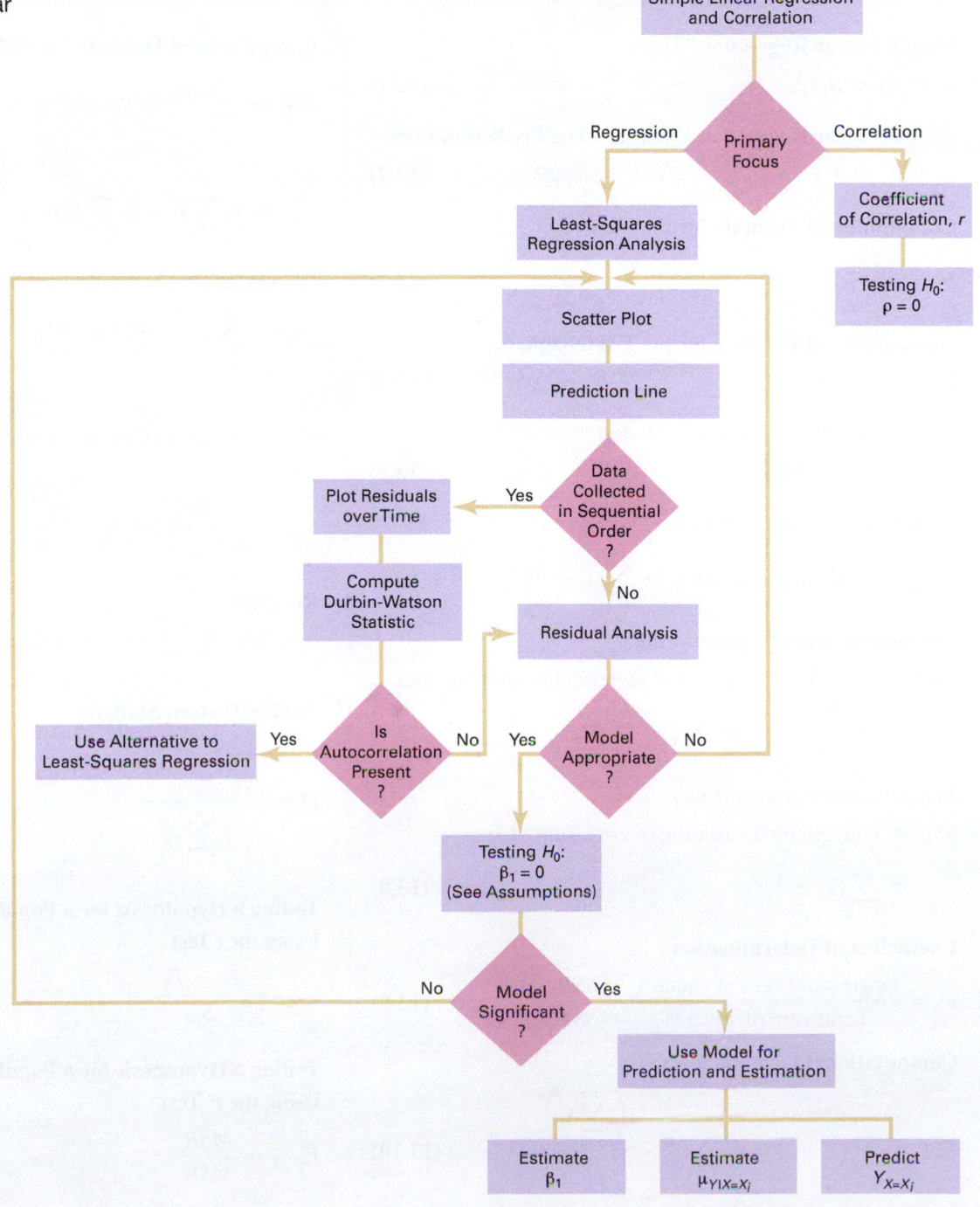

▼ REFERENCES

1. Anscombe, F. J. "Graphs in Statistical Analysis." *The American Statistician*, 27(1973): 17–21.
2. Hoaglin, D. C., and R. Welsch. "The Hat Matrix in Regression and ANOVA." *The American Statistician*, 32(1978): 17–22.
3. Hocking, R. R. "Developments in Linear Regression Methodology: 1959–1982." *Technometrics*, 25(1983): 219–250.
4. Kutner, M. H., C. J. Nachtsheim, J. Neter, and W. Li. *Applied Linear Statistical Models*, 5th ed. New York: McGraw-Hill/Irwin, 2005.
5. Montgomery, D. C., E. A. Peck, and G. G. Vining. *Introduction to Linear Regression Analysis*, 5th ed. New York, Wiley, 2012.

▼ KEY EQUATIONS

Simple Linear Regression Model

$$Y_i = \beta_0 + \beta_1 X_i + \varepsilon_i \tag{13.1}$$

Simple Linear Regression Equation: The Prediction Line

$$\hat{Y}_i = b_0 + b_1 X_i \tag{13.2}$$

Computational Formula for the Slope, b_1

$$b_1 = \frac{SSXY}{SSX} \tag{13.3}$$

Computational Formula for the Y Intercept, b_0

$$b_0 = \overline{Y} - b_1 \overline{X} \tag{13.4}$$

Measures of Variation in Regression

$$SST = SSR + SSE \tag{13.5}$$

Total Sum of Squares (SST)

$$SST = \text{Total sum of squares} = \sum_{i=1}^{n}(Y_i - \overline{Y})^2 \tag{13.6}$$

Regression Sum of Squares (SSR)

$SSR = $ Explained variation or regression sum of squares

$$= \sum_{i=1}^{n}(\hat{Y}_i - \overline{Y})^2 \tag{13.7}$$

Error Sum of Squares (SSE)

$SSE = $ Unexplained variation or error sum of squares

$$= \sum_{i=1}^{n}(Y_i - \hat{Y}_i)^2 \tag{13.8}$$

Coefficient of Determination

$$r^2 = \frac{\text{Regression sum of squares}}{\text{Total sum of squares}} = \frac{SSR}{SST} \tag{13.9}$$

Computational Formula for SST

$$SST = \sum_{i=1}^{n}(Y_i - \overline{Y})^2 = \sum_{i=1}^{n}Y_i^2 - \frac{\left(\sum_{i=1}^{n}Y_i\right)^2}{n} \tag{13.10}$$

Computational Formula for SSR

$$SSR = \sum_{i=1}^{n}(\hat{Y}_i - \overline{Y})^2$$

$$= b_0\sum_{i=1}^{n}Y_i + b_1\sum_{i=1}^{n}X_iY_i - \frac{\left(\sum_{i=1}^{n}Y_i\right)^2}{n} \tag{13.11}$$

Computational Formula for SSE

$$SSE = \sum_{i=1}^{n}(Y_i - \hat{Y}_i)^2 = \sum_{i=1}^{n}Y_i^2 - b_0\sum_{i=1}^{n}Y_i - b_1\sum_{i=1}^{n}X_iY_i \tag{13.12}$$

Standard Error of the Estimate

$$S_{YX} = \sqrt{\frac{SSE}{n-2}} = \sqrt{\frac{\sum_{i=1}^{n}(Y_i - \hat{Y}_i)^2}{n-2}} \tag{13.13}$$

Residual

$$e_i = Y_i - \hat{Y}_i \tag{13.14}$$

Durbin-Watson Statistic

$$D = \frac{\sum_{i=2}^{n}(e_i - e_{i-1})^2}{\sum_{i=1}^{n}e_i^2} \tag{13.15}$$

Testing a Hypothesis for a Population Slope, β_1, Using the t Test

$$t_{STAT} = \frac{b_1 - \beta_1}{S_{b_1}} \tag{13.16}$$

Testing a Hypothesis for a Population Slope, β_1, Using the F Test

$$F_{STAT} = \frac{MSR}{MSE} \tag{13.17}$$

Confidence Interval Estimate of the Slope, β_1

$$b_1 \pm t_{\alpha/2}S_{b_1}$$

$$b_1 - t_{\alpha/2}S_{b_1} \le \beta_1 \le b_1 + t_{\alpha/2}S_{b_1} \qquad \text{(13.18)}$$

Testing for the Existence of Correlation

$$t_{STAT} = \frac{r - \rho}{\sqrt{\dfrac{1 - r^2}{n - 2}}} \qquad \text{(13.19a)}$$

$$r = \frac{\text{cov}(X, Y)}{S_X S_Y} \qquad \text{(13.19b)}$$

Confidence Interval Estimate for the Mean of Y

$$\hat{Y}_i \pm t_{\alpha/2}S_{YX}\sqrt{h_i}$$

$$\hat{Y}_i - t_{\alpha/2}S_{YX}\sqrt{h_i} \le \mu_{Y|X=X_i} \le \hat{Y}_i + t_{\alpha/2}S_{YX}\sqrt{h_i} \quad \text{(13.20)}$$

Prediction Interval for an Individual Response, Y

$$\hat{Y}_i \pm t_{\alpha/2}S_{YX}\sqrt{1 + h_i}$$

$$\hat{Y}_i - t_{\alpha/2}S_{YX}\sqrt{1 + h_i} \le Y_{X=X_i} \le \hat{Y}_i + t_{\alpha/2}S_{YX}\sqrt{1 + h_i}$$
$$\text{(13.21)}$$

▼KEY TERMS

assumptions of regression   500
autocorrelation   504
coefficient of determination   496
confidence interval estimate for the
   mean response   515
correlation coefficient   511
dependent variable   485
Durbin-Watson statistic   505
equal variance   500
error sum of squares (*SSE*)   495
explained variation   495
explanatory variable   485
homoscedasticity   500
independence of errors   500

independent variable   485
least-squares method   488
linearity   500
model   485
normality   500
positive linear relationship   486
prediction interval for an individual
   response, Y 516
prediction line   487
regression analysis   485
regression coefficient   488
regression sum of squares (*SSR*)   495
relevant range   490

residual   500
residual analysis   500
response variable   485
scatter diagram   485
scatter plot   485
simple linear regression   485
simple linear regression equation   487
slope   487
standard error of the estimate   498
total sum of squares (*SST*)   495
total variation   495
unexplained variation   495
Y intercept   487

▼CHECKING YOUR UNDERSTANDING

13.64 What is the interpretation of the Y intercept and the slope in the simple linear regression equation?

13.65 What is the interpretation of the coefficient of determination?

13.66 When is the unexplained variation (i.e., error sum of squares) equal to 0?

13.67 When is the explained variation (i.e., regression sum of squares) equal to 0?

13.68 Why should you always carry out a residual analysis as part of a regression model?

13.69 What are the assumptions of regression analysis?

13.70 How do you evaluate the assumptions of regression analysis?

13.71 When and how do you use the Durbin-Watson statistic?

13.72 What is the difference between a confidence interval estimate of the mean response, $\mu_{Y|X=X_i}$, and a prediction interval of $Y_{X=X_i}$?

▼ CHAPTER REVIEW PROBLEMS

13.73 Can you use movie critics' opinions to forecast box office receipts on the opening weekend? The following data, stored in Tomatometer , indicate the Tomatometer rating, the percentage of professional critic reviews that are positive, and the receipts per theater ($thousands) on the weekend a movie opened for ten movies:

Movie	Tomatometer Rating	Receipts
The Mummy	16	7.8
Zookeeper's Wife	61	6.1
Beatriz at Dinner	80	28.4
The Hero	76	11.3
Wonder Woman	93	24.8
Baby Boss	52	13.3
The Circle	15	2.9
Dean	61	4.0
Baywatch	20	5.1
Churchill	38	1.9

Source: "Top Box Office Movies – Rotten Tomatoes," and "The Numbers – Weekend Box Office Chart for May 26th 2017," **bit.ly/2t0tqS6**.

a. Use the least-squares method to compute the regression coefficients b_0 and b_1.
b. Interpret the meaning of b_0 and b_1 in this problem.
c. Predict the mean receipts for a movie that has a Tomatometer rating of 55%.
d. Should you use the model to predict the receipts for a movie that has a Tomatometer rating of 5%? Why or why not?
e. Determine the coefficient of determination, r^2, and explain its meaning in this problem.
f. Perform a residual analysis. Is there any evidence of a pattern in the residuals? Explain.
g. At the 0.05 level of significance, is there evidence of a linear relationship between Tomatometer rating and receipts?
h. Construct a 95% confidence interval estimate of the mean receipts for a movie that has a Tomatometer rating of 55% and a 95% prediction interval of the receipts for a single movie that has a Tomatometer rating of 55%.
i. Based on the results of (a)–(h), do you think that Tomatometer rating is a useful predictor of receipts on the first weekend a movie opens? What issues about these data might make you hesitant to use Tomatometer rating to predict receipts?

13.74 Management of a soft-drink bottling company has the business objective of developing a method for allocating delivery costs to customers. Although one cost clearly relates to travel time within a particular route, another variable cost reflects the time required to unload the cases of soft drink at the delivery point. To begin, management decided to develop a regression model to predict delivery time based on the number of cases delivered. A sample of 20 deliveries within a territory was selected. The delivery times and the number of cases delivered were organized in the following table and stored in Delivery .

Customer	Number of Cases	Delivery Time (minutes)	Customer	Number of Cases	Delivery Time (minutes)
1	52	32.1	11	161	43.0
2	64	34.8	12	184	49.4
3	73	36.2	13	202	57.2
4	85	37.8	14	218	56.8
5	95	37.8	15	243	60.6
6	103	39.7	16	254	61.2
7	116	38.5	17	267	58.2
8	121	41.9	18	275	63.1
9	143	44.2	19	287	65.6
10	157	47.1	20	298	67.3

a. Use the least-squares method to compute the regression coefficients b_0 and b_1.
b. Interpret the meaning of b_0 and b_1 in this problem.
c. Predict the mean delivery time for 150 cases of soft drink.
d. Should you use the model to predict the delivery time for a customer who is receiving 500 cases of soft drink? Why or why not?
e. Determine the coefficient of determination, r^2, and explain its meaning in this problem.
f. Perform a residual analysis. Is there any evidence of a pattern in the residuals? Explain.
g. At the 0.05 level of significance, is there evidence of a linear relationship between delivery time and the number of cases delivered?
h. Construct a 95% confidence interval estimate of the mean delivery time for 150 cases of soft drink and a 95% prediction interval of the delivery time for a single delivery of 150 cases of soft drink.
i. What conclusions can you reach from (a) through (h) about the relationship between the number of cases and delivery time?

13.75 Measuring the height of a California redwood tree is very difficult because these trees grow to heights of over 300 feet. People familiar with these trees understand that the height of a California redwood tree is related to other characteristics of the tree, including the diameter of the tree at the breast height of a person. The data in Redwood represent the height (in feet) and diameter (in inches) at the breast height of a person for a sample of 21 California redwood trees.
a. Assuming a linear relationship, use the least-squares method to compute the regression coefficients b_0 and b_1. State the regression equation that predicts the height of a tree based on the tree's diameter at breast height of a person.
b. Interpret the meaning of the slope in this equation.
c. Predict the mean height for a tree that has a breast height diameter of 25 inches.
d. Interpret the meaning of the coefficient of determination in this problem.
e. Perform a residual analysis on the results and determine the adequacy of the model.

f. Determine whether there is a significant relationship between the height of redwood trees and the breast height diameter at the 0.05 level of significance.

g. Construct a 95% confidence interval estimate of the population slope between the height of the redwood trees and breast height diameter.

h. What conclusions can you reach about the relationship of the diameter of the tree and its height?

13.76 You want to develop a model to predict the asking price of homes based on their size. A sample of 61 single-family houses listed for sale in Silver Spring, Maryland, a suburb of Washington, DC, is selected to study the relationship between asking price (in $thousands) and living space (in square feet), and the data is collected and stored in SilverSpring . (Hint: First determine which are the independent and dependent variables.)

a. Construct a scatter plot and, assuming a linear relationship, use the least-squares method to compute the regression coefficients b_0 and b_1.

b. Interpret the meaning of the Y intercept, b_0, and the slope, b_1, in this problem.

c. Use the prediction line developed in (a) to predict the mean asking price for a house whose living space is 2,000 square feet.

d. Determine the coefficient of determination, r^2, and interpret its meaning in this problem.

e. Perform a residual analysis on your results and evaluate the regression assumptions.

f. At the 0.05 level of significance, is there evidence of a linear relationship between asking price and living space?

g. Construct a 95% confidence interval estimate of the population slope.

h. What conclusions can you reach about the relationship between the living space and asking price?

13.77 You want to develop a model to predict the taxes of houses, based on asking price. A sample of 61 single-family houses listed for sale in Silver Spring, Maryland, a suburb of Washington, DC, is selected. The taxes (in $) and the asking price of the houses (in $thousands) are recorded and stored in SilverSpring . (Hint: First determine which are the independent and dependent variables.)

a. Construct a scatter plot and, assuming a linear relationship, use the least-squares method to compute the regression coefficients b_0 and b_1.

b. Interpret the meaning of the Y intercept, b_0, and the slope, b_1, in this problem.

c. Use the prediction line developed in (a) to predict the mean taxes for a house whose asking price is $400,000.

d. Determine the coefficient of determination, r^2, and interpret its meaning in this problem.

e. Perform a residual analysis on your results and evaluate the regression assumptions.

f. At the 0.05 level of significance, is there evidence of a linear relationship between taxes and asking price?

g. What conclusions can you reach concerning the relationship between taxes and asking price?

13.78 An analyst has the objective of predicting the return on average tangible common equity (ROATCE) of banks. The analyst begins by using *efficiency ratio*, a measure of a bank's ability to turn resources into revenue. A sample of 100 American banks is selected and stored in AmericanBanks .

Source: Data extracted from K. Badenhausen, "America's Best Banks 2017," available at **bit.ly/2tpw1Er**.

a. Construct a scatter plot and, assuming a linear relationship, use the least-squares method to compute the regression coefficients b_0 and b_1.

b. Interpret the meaning of the Y intercept, b_0, and the slope, b_1, in this problem.

c. Use the prediction line developed in (a) to predict the mean ROATCE for a bank with an efficiency ratio of 60%.

d. Determine the coefficient of determination, r^2, and interpret its meaning in this problem.

e. Perform a residual analysis on your results and evaluate the regression assumptions.

f. At the 0.05 level of significance, is there evidence of a linear relationship between efficiency ratio and ROATCE?

g. Construct a 95% confidence interval estimate of the mean ROATCE of banks with an efficiency ratio of 60% and a 95% prediction interval of the ROATCE for a particular bank with an efficiency ratio of 60%.

h. Construct a 95% confidence interval estimate of the population slope.

i. What conclusions can you reach concerning the relationship between efficiency ratio and ROATCE?

13.79 An accountant for a large department store has the business objective of developing a model to predict the amount of time it takes to process invoices. Data are collected from the past 32 working days, and the number of invoices processed and completion time (in hours) are stored in Invoice . (Hint: First determine which are the independent and dependent variables.)

a. Assuming a linear relationship, use the least-squares method to compute the regression coefficients b_0 and b_1.

b. Interpret the meaning of the Y intercept, b_0, and the slope, b_1, in this problem.

c. Use the prediction line developed in (a) to predict the mean amount of time it would take to process 150 invoices.

d. Determine the coefficient of determination, r^2, and interpret its meaning.

e. Plot the residuals against the number of invoices processed and also against time.

f. Based on the plots in (e), does the model seem appropriate?

g. Based on the results in (e) and (f), what conclusions can you reach about the validity of the prediction made in (c)?

h. What conclusions can you reach about the relationship between the number of invoices and the completion time?

13.80 On January 28, 1986, the space shuttle *Challenger* exploded, and seven astronauts were killed. Prior to the launch, the predicted atmospheric temperature was for freezing weather at the launch site. Engineers for Morton Thiokol (the manufacturer of the rocket motor) prepared charts to make the case that the launch should not take place due to the cold weather. These arguments were rejected, and the launch tragically took place. Upon investigation after the tragedy, experts agreed that the disaster occurred because of leaky rubber O-rings that did not seal properly due to the cold temperature. Data indicating the atmospheric temperature at the time of 23 previous launches and the O-ring damage index are stored in O-Ring .

Note: Data from flight 4 is omitted due to unknown O-ring condition.

Sources: Data extracted from *Report of the Presidential Commission on the Space Shuttle Challenger Accident*, Washington, DC, 1986, Vol. II (H1–H3) and Vol. IV (664); and *Post-Challenger Evaluation of Space Shuttle Risk Assessment and Management*, Washington, DC, 1988, pp. 135–136.

a. Construct a scatter plot for the seven flights in which there was O-ring damage (O-ring damage index $\neq$ 0). What conclusions, if any, can you reach about the relationship between atmospheric temperature and O-ring damage?
b. Construct a scatter plot for all 23 flights.
c. Explain any differences in the interpretation of the relationship between atmospheric temperature and O-ring damage in (a) and (b).
d. Based on the scatter plot in (b), provide reasons why a prediction should not be made for an atmospheric temperature of 31°F, the temperature on the morning of the launch of the *Challenger*.
e. Although the assumption of a linear relationship may not be valid for the set of 23 flights, fit a simple linear regression model to predict O-ring damage, based on atmospheric temperature.
f. Include the prediction line found in (e) on the scatter plot developed in (b).
g. Based on the results in (f), do you think a linear model is appropriate for these data? Explain.
h. Perform a residual analysis. What conclusions do you reach?

13.81 A baseball analyst would like to study various team statistics for a recent season to determine which variables might be useful in predicting the number of wins achieved by teams during the season. He begins by using a team's earned run average (ERA), a measure of pitching performance, to predict the number of wins. He collects the team ERA and team wins for each of the 30 Major League Baseball teams and stores these data in Baseball . (Hint: First determine which are the independent and dependent variables.)
a. Assuming a linear relationship, use the least-squares method to compute the regression coefficients b_0 and b_1.
b. Interpret the meaning of the Y intercept, b_0, and the slope, b_1, in this problem.
c. Use the prediction line developed in (a) to predict the mean number of wins for a team with an ERA of 4.50.
d. Compute the coefficient of determination, r^2, and interpret its meaning.
e. Perform a residual analysis on your results and determine the adequacy of the fit of the model.
f. At the 0.05 level of significance, is there evidence of a linear relationship between the number of wins and the ERA?
g. Construct a 95% confidence interval estimate of the mean number of wins expected for teams with an ERA of 4.50.
h. Construct a 95% prediction interval of the number of wins for an individual team that has an ERA of 4.50.
i. Construct a 95% confidence interval estimate of the population slope.
j. The 30 teams constitute a population. In order to use statistical inference, as in (f) through (i), the data must be assumed to represent a random sample. What "population" would this sample be drawing conclusions about?
k. What other independent variables might you consider for inclusion in the model?
l. What conclusions can you reach concerning the relationship between ERA and wins?

13.82 Can you use the annual revenues generated by National Basketball Association (NBA) franchises to predict franchise values? Figure 2.17 on page 68 shows a scatter plot of revenue with

franchise value, and Figure 3.10 on page 148, shows the correlation coefficient. Now, you want to develop a simple linear regression model to predict franchise values based on revenues. (Franchise values and revenues are stored in NBAValues .)
a. Assuming a linear relationship, use the least-squares method to compute the regression coefficients b_0 and b_1.
b. Interpret the meaning of the Y intercept, b_0, and the slope, b_1, in this problem.
c. Predict the mean value of an NBA franchise that generates $150 million of annual revenue.
d. Compute the coefficient of determination, r^2, and interpret its meaning.
e. Perform a residual analysis on your results and evaluate the regression assumptions.
f. At the 0.05 level of significance, is there evidence of a linear relationship between the annual revenues generated and the value of an NBA franchise?
g. Construct a 95% confidence interval estimate of the mean value of all NBA franchises that generate $150 million of annual revenue.
h. Construct a 95% prediction interval of the value of an individual NBA franchise that generates $150 million of annual revenue.
i. Compare the results of (a) through (h) to those of baseball franchises in Problems 13.8, 13.20, 13.30, 13.46, and 13.62 and European soccer teams in Problem 13.83.

13.83 In Problem 13.82 you used annual revenue to develop a model to predict the franchise value of National Basketball Association (NBA) teams. Can you also use the annual revenues generated by European soccer teams to predict franchise values? (European soccer team values and revenues are stored in SoccerValues .)
a. Repeat Problem 13.82 (a) through (h) for the European soccer teams.
b. Compare the results of (a) to those of baseball franchises in Problems 13.8, 13.20, 13.30, 13.46, and 13.62 and NBA franchises in Problem 13.82.

13.84 During the fall harvest season in the United States, pumpkins are sold in large quantities at farm stands. Often, instead of weighing the pumpkins prior to sale, the farm stand operator will just place the pumpkin in the appropriate circular cutout on the counter. When asked why this was done, one farmer replied, "I can tell the weight of the pumpkin from its circumference." To determine whether this was really true, the circumference and weight of each pumpkin from a sample of 23 pumpkins were determined and the results stored in Pumpkin .
a. Assuming a linear relationship, use the least-squares method to compute the regression coefficients b_0 and b_1.
b. Interpret the meaning of the slope, b_1, in this problem.
c. Predict the mean weight for a pumpkin that is 60 centimeters in circumference.
d. Do you think it is a good idea for the farmer to sell pumpkins by circumference instead of weight? Explain.
e. Determine the coefficient of determination, r^2, and interpret its meaning.
f. Perform a residual analysis for these data and evaluate the regression assumptions.
g. At the 0.05 level of significance, is there evidence of a linear relationship between the circumference and weight of a pumpkin?
h. Construct a 95% confidence interval estimate of the population slope, β_1.

13.85 Refer to the discussion of beta values and market models in Problem 13.49 on page 513. The S&P 500 Index tracks the overall movement of the stock market by considering the stock prices of 500 large corporations. The file StockPrices2016 contains 2016 weekly data for the S&P 500 and three companies. The following variables are included:

> WEEK—Week ending on date given
> S&P—Weekly closing value for the S&P 500 Index
> GE—Weekly closing stock price for General Electric
> DISCA—Weekly closing stock price for Discovery Communications
> GOOG—Weekly closing stock price for Google

Source: Data extracted from **finance.yahoo.com**, June 11, 2017.

a. Estimate the market model for GE. (Hint: Use the percentage change in the S&P 500 Index as the independent variable and the percentage change in GE's stock price as the dependent variable.)
b. Interpret the beta value for GE.
c. Repeat (a) and (b) for Discovery Communications.
d. Repeat (a) and (b) for Google.
e. Write a brief summary of your findings.

13.86 The file CEO 2016 includes the total compensation (in $millions) for CEOs of 200 Standard & Poor's 500 companies and the investment return in 2016.

Source: Data extracted from R. Lightner and T. Francis, "How Much Do Top CEOs Make?" available at **bit.ly/1QqpEUZ**.)

a. Compute the correlation coefficient between compensation and the investment return in 2016.
b. At the 0.05 level of significance, is the correlation between compensation and the investment return in 2016 statistically significant?
c. Write a short summary of your findings in (a) and (b). Do the results surprise you?

REPORT WRITING EXERCISE

13.87 In Problems 13.8, 13.20, 13.30, 13.46, 13.62, 13.82, and 13.83, you developed regression models to predict franchise value of major league baseball, NBA basketball, and soccer teams. Now, write a report based on the models you developed. Append to your report all appropriate charts and statistical information.

CHAPTER 13

▾CASES

Managing Ashland MultiComm Services

To ensure that as many trial subscriptions to the *3-For-All* service as possible are converted to regular subscriptions, the marketing department works closely with the customer support department to accomplish a smooth initial process for the trial subscription customers. To assist in this effort, the marketing department needs to accurately forecast the monthly total of new regular subscriptions.

A team consisting of managers from the marketing and customer support departments was convened to develop a better method of forecasting new subscriptions. Previously, after examining new subscription data for the prior three months, a group of three managers would develop a subjective forecast of the number of new subscriptions. Livia Salvador, who was recently hired by the company to provide expertise in quantitative forecasting methods, suggested that the department look for factors that might help in predicting new subscriptions.

Members of the team found that the forecasts in the past year had been particularly inaccurate because in some months, much more time was spent on telemarketing than in other months. Livia collected data (stored in AMS13) for the number of new subscriptions and hours spent on telemarketing for each month for the past two years.

1. What criticism can you make concerning the method of forecasting that involved taking the new subscriptions data for the prior three months as the basis for future projections?

2. What factors other than number of telemarketing hours spent might be useful in predicting the number of new subscriptions? Explain.

3. a. Analyze the data and develop a regression model to predict the number of new subscriptions for a month, based on the number of hours spent on telemarketing for new subscriptions.

b. If you expect to spend 1,200 hours on telemarketing per month, estimate the number of new subscriptions for the month. Indicate the assumptions on which this prediction is based. Do you think these assumptions are valid? Explain.

c. What would be the danger of predicting the number of new subscriptions for a month in which 2,000 hours were spent on telemarketing?

Digital Case

Apply your knowledge of simple linear regression in this Digital Case, which extends the Sunflowers Apparel Using Statistics scenario from this chapter.

Leasing agents from the Triangle Mall Management Corporation have suggested that Sunflowers consider several locations in some of Triangle's newly renovated lifestyle malls that cater to shoppers with higher-than-mean disposable income. Although the locations are smaller than the typical Sunflowers location, the leasing agents argue that higher-than-mean disposable income in the surrounding community is a better predictor of higher sales than profiled customers. The leasing agents maintain that sample data from 14 Sunflowers stores prove that this is true.

Open **Triangle_Sunflower.pdf** and review the leasing agents' proposal and supporting documents. Then answer the following questions:

1. Should mean disposable income be used to predict sales based on the sample of 14 Sunflowers stores?

2. Should the management of Sunflowers accept the claims of Triangle's leasing agents? Why or why not?

3. Is it possible that the mean disposable income of the surrounding area is not an important factor in leasing new locations? Explain.

4. Are there any other factors not mentioned by the leasing agents that might be relevant to the store leasing decision?

Brynne Packaging

Brynne Packaging is a large packaging company, offering its customers the highest standards in innovative packaging solutions and reliable service. About 25% of the employees at Brynne Packaging are machine operators. The human resources department has suggested that the company consider using the Wesman Personnel Classification Test (WPCT), a measure of reasoning ability, to screen applicants for the machine operator job. In order to assess the WPCT as a predictor of future job performance, 25 recent applicants were tested using the WPCT; all were hired, regardless of their WPCT score. At a later time, supervisors were asked to rate the quality of the job performance of these 25 employees, using a 1-to-10 rating scale (where 1 = very low and 10 = very high). Factors considered in the ratings included the employee's output, defect rate, ability to implement continuous quality procedures, and contributions to team problem-solving efforts. The file BrynnePackaging contains the WPCT scores (WPCT) and job performance ratings (Ratings) for the 25 employees.

1. Assess the significance and importance of WPCT score as a predictor of job performance. Defend your answer.

2. Predict the mean job performance rating for all employees with a WPCT score of 6. Give a point prediction as well as a 95% confidence interval. Do you have any concerns using the regression model for predicting mean job performance rating given the WPCT score of 6?

3. Evaluate whether the assumptions of regression have been seriously violated.

▾EXCEL GUIDE

There are no Excel Guide instructions for Section 13.1.

EG13.2 DETERMINING the SIMPLE LINEAR REGRESSION EQUATION

Key Technique Use the **LINEST**(*cell range of Y variable, cell range of X variable*, **True, True**) array function to compute the b_1 and b_0 coefficients, the b_1 and b_0 standard errors, r^2 and the standard error of the estimate, the F test statistic and error *df*, and *SSR* and *SSE*.

Use the expression **T.INV.2T(1 − *confidence level, Error degrees of freedom*)** to compute the critical value for the *t* test.

Example Perform the Figure 13.4 analysis of the Sunflowers Apparel data on page 489.

PHStat Use **Simple Linear Regression**.

For the example, open to the **DATA worksheet** of the **Site Selection workbook**. Select **PHStat → Regression → Simple Linear Regression**. In the procedure's dialog box (shown below):

1. Enter **C1:C15** as the **Y Variable Cell Range**.
2. Enter **B1:B15** as the **X Variable Cell Range**.
3. Check **First cells in both ranges contain label**.
4. Enter **95** as the **Confidence level for regression coefficients.**
5. Check **Regression Statistics Table** and **ANOVA and Coefficients Table**.
6. Enter a **Title** and click **OK**.

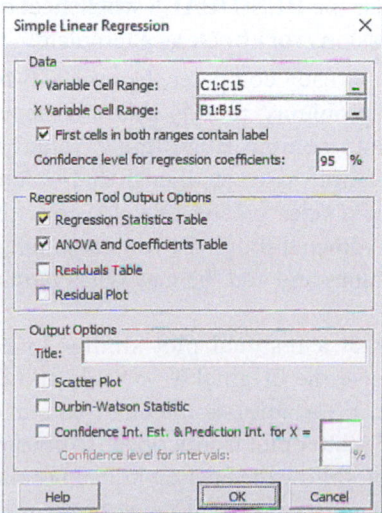

The procedure creates a worksheet that contains a copy of your data as well as the worksheet shown in Figure 13.4. For more information about these worksheets, read the following *Workbook* section.

To create a scatter plot that contains a prediction line and regression equation similar to Figure 13.5 on page 489, modify step 6 by checking **Scatter Plot** before clicking **OK**.

Workbook Use the **COMPUTE worksheet** of the **Simple Linear Regression workbook** as a template.

For the example, the worksheet uses the regression data already in the SLRData worksheet to perform the regression analysis. Worksheet columns A through I mimic the design of the Analysis ToolPak regression results even as the worksheet computes most values in columns L and M, unlike the ToolPak results, which do not include any cell formulas.

To perform simple linear regression for other data, paste the regression data into the SLRData worksheet, using column A for the X variable data and column B for the Y variable data. Then, open to the COMPUTE worksheet and:

1. Enter the confidence level in cell **L8**.
2. Select the gray-tinted cell range **L2:M6** (shown below).
3. In the formula bar, edit the **column A and B cell ranges** in the formula to reflect the range of the new regression data.
4. When finished editing, while holding down the **Control** and **Shift keys** (or **Command** on a Mac), press **Enter**.

Because the edited formula is an *array* formula (see Appendix Section B.2), the simple pressing of the Enter key without any other key being held down will not work as it would for entering simple formulas.

	K	L	M
1	Intermediate Calculations		
2	b1, b0 Coefficients	2.0742	-1.2088
3	b1, b0 Standard Error	0.2536	0.9949
4	R Square, Standard Error	0.8479	0.9993
5	F, Residual df	66.8792	12.0000
6	Regression SS, Residual SS	66.7854	11.9832
7			
8	Confidence level	95%	
9	t Critical Value	2.1788	
10	Half Width b0	2.1676	
11	Half Width b1	0.5526	

The gray-tinted cell range L2:M6 uses the LINEST function to compute the following statistics: the b_1 and b_0 coefficients in cells L2 and M2, the b_1 and b_0 standard errors in cells L3 and M3, r^2 and the standard error of the estimate in cells L4 and M4, the F test statistic and error *df* in cells L5 and M5, and SSR and SSE in cells L6 and M6.

Cell L9 uses the expression T.INV.2T(1 − confidence level, Error degrees of freedom) to compute the critical value for the t test. To see all of the formulas that the COMPUTE worksheet uses, open to the COMPUTE_FORMULAS worksheet.

529

Scatter Plot To create a scatter plot that contains both a prediction line and regression equation (similar to Figure 13.5 on page 489), first use the Section EG2.5 *Workbook* scatter plot instructions with the Table 13.1 Sunflowers Apparel data to create a scatter plot. Then select the chart and:

1. Select **Design** (or **Chart Design**)→ **Add Chart Element**→ **Trendline**→ **More Trendline Options**.
2. Check the **Display Equation on chart** and **Display R-squared value on chart** check boxes near the bottom of the pane (shown below).

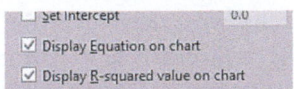

In Excel 2010, select **Layout**→ **Trendline**→ **More Trendline Options**. In the Format Trendline dialog box (similar to the Format Trendline pane), click **Trendline Options** in the left pane. In the Trendline Options right pane, check **Display Equation on chart**, check **Display R-squared value on chart**, and then click **Close**.

If the *X* axis of the scatter plot does not appear at the bottom of the plot, use the "Correcting the Display of the *X* Axis" instructions in Appendix Section B.5 to relocate the *X* axis to the bottom.

Analysis ToolPak Use **Regression**.

For the example, open to the **DATA worksheet** of the **SiteSelection workbook** and:

1. Select **Data**→ **Data Analysis**.
2. In the Data Analysis dialog box, select **Regression** from the **Analysis** Tools list and then click **OK**.

In the Regression dialog box (shown below):

3. Enter **C1:C15** as the **Input Y Range** and enter **B1:B15** as the **Input X Range**.
4. Check **Labels** and check **Confidence Level** and enter **95** in its box.
5. Click **New Worksheet Ply** and then click **OK**.

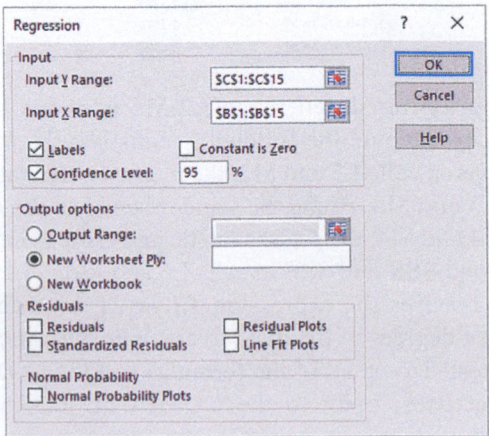

EG13.3   MEASURES of VARIATION

The measures of variation appear as part of the regression results worksheet that the Section EG13.2 instructions create.

If you use either Section EG13.2 *PHStat* or *Workbook* instructions, COMPUTE worksheet formulas compute these measures. The formulas in cells B5, B7, B13, C12, C13, D12, and E12 copy values computed by the array formula in cell range L2:M6.

EG13.4   ASSUMPTIONS of REGRESSION

There are no Excel Guide instructions for Section 13.4.

EG13.5   RESIDUAL ANALYSIS

Key Technique Use arithmetic formulas to compute the residuals. To evaluate assumptions, use the Section EG2.5 scatter plot instructions for constructing residual plots and the Section EG6.3 instructions for constructing normal probability plots.

Example Compute the Figure 13.10 residuals for the Table 13.1 Sunflowers Apparel on page 487.

PHStat Use the Section EG13.2 *PHStat* instructions to compute the residuals. Use the Section EG6.3 *PHStat* instructions to construct a normal probability plot.

For the example, modify step 5 of the EG13.2 *PHStat* instructions by checking **Residuals Table** and **Residual Plot** in addition to checking the two other check boxes. PHStat creates a residual plot and a worksheet containing the residuals in addition to the COMPUTE worksheet described earlier.

To construct a normal probability plot, open to the residuals worksheet and modify the EG6.3 *PHStat* instructions by using the cell range of the residuals as the **Variable Cell Range** in step 1.

Workbook Use the **RESIDUALS worksheet** of the **Simple Linear Regression workbook** as a template.

The worksheet already computes the residuals for the example. For other problems, modify this worksheet by pasting the *X* values into column B and the *Y* values into column D. Then, for sample sizes smaller than 14, delete the extra rows. For sample sizes greater than 14, copy the column C and E formulas down through the row containing the last pair and *X* and *Y* values and add the new observation numbers in column A.

To construct a residual plot similar to Figure 13.11 on page 501, use the original *X* variable and the residuals (plotted as the *Y* variable) as the chart data and follow the Section EG2.5 scatter plot instructions. To construct a normal probability plot, follow the Section EG6.3 normal probability plot instructions, using the cell range of the residuals as the **Variable Cell Range**.

Analysis ToolPak Use the Section EG13.2 *Analysis Tool-Pak* instructions.

Modify step 5 by checking **Residuals** and **Residual Plots** before clicking **New Worksheet Ply** and then **OK**. To construct a residual plot or normal probability plot, use the *Workbook* instructions.

EG13.6 MEASURING AUTOCORRELATION: the DURBIN-WATSON STATISTIC

Key Technique Use the **SUMXMY2(***cell range of the second through last residual*, *cell range of the first through the second-to-last residual***)** function to compute the sum of squared difference of the residuals.

Use the **SUMSQ(***cell range of the residuals***)** function to compute the sum of squared residuals.

Example Compute the Durbin-Watson statistic for the package delivery data shown in the Figure 13.16 on page 495.

PHStat Use the *PHStat* instructions at the beginning of Section EG13.2. Modify step 6 by checking the **Durbin-Watson Statistic** output option before clicking **OK**.

Workbook Use the **DURBIN_WATSON worksheet** of the **Simple Linear Regression** workbook as a template. The DURBIN_WATSON worksheet of the **Package Delivery workbook** already contains the proper cell formulas to compute the statistic for the example. (This workbook also uses the COMPUTE and RESIDUALS worksheet templates from the Simple Linear Regression workbook.)

To compute the Durbin-Watson statistic for other problems, first create the simple linear regression model and the residuals for the problem, using the Sections EG13.2 and EG13.5 *Workbook* instructions. Then open the DURBIN_WATSON worksheet and edit the formulas in cell B3 and B4 to point to the proper cell ranges of the new residuals.

EG13.7 INFERENCES ABOUT the SLOPE and CORRELATION COEFFICIENT

The t test for the slope, the F test for the slope, and the confidence interval estimate for the slope all appear in the worksheet created by using the Section EG13.2 instructions. The t test for the slope appears in cell D18, the F test for the slope appears in cell range E12:E13, and the confidence interval estimate for the slope appears in the cell range F18:G18 (and repeated in cell range H18:I18).

For the *PHStat* and *Workbook* worksheets (identical), cell D18 contains a formula that divides the cell B18 contents by cell C18 content. Cell E12 copies a value that the LINEST array function computes in cell L5. Cell F12 uses the F.DIST.RT function to compute the *p*-value for the F test for the slope. The cell range F18:G18 contains an arithmetic formula that uses the half-width of the b_1 that cell L11 computes.

EG13.8 ESTIMATION of MEAN VALUES and PREDICTION of INDIVIDUAL VALUES

Key Technique Use the **TREND(***Y variable cell range*, *X variable cell range*, *X value***)** function to compute the predicted Y value for the X value.

Use the **DEVSQ(***X variable cell range***)** function to compute the SSX value.

Example Compute the Figure 13.21 confidence interval estimate and prediction interval for the Sunflowers Apparel data that is shown on page 517.

PHStat Modify the Section EG13.2 *PHStat* instructions by replacing step 6 with these steps 6 and 7:

6. Check **Confidence Int. Est. & Prediction Int. for X =** and enter **4** in its box. Enter **95** as the percentage for **Confidence level for intervals**.
7. Enter a **Title** and click **OK**.

The additional worksheet created is discussed in the following *Workbook* instructions.

Workbook Use the **CIEandPI worksheet** of the **Simple Linear Regression workbook**, as a template.

The worksheet already contains the data and formulas for the example. To compute a confidence interval estimate and prediction interval for other problems:

1. Paste the regression data into the **SLRData worksheet**. Use column A for the X variable data and column B for the Y variable data.
2. Open to the **CIEandPI worksheet**.

In the CIEandPI worksheet:

3. Change values for the **X Value** and **Confidence Level**, as is necessary.
4. Edit the cell ranges used in the cell B15 formula that uses the TREND function to refer to the new cell ranges for the Y and X variables.

▼JMP GUIDE

There are no JMP Guide instructions for Section 13.1.

JG13.2 DETERMINING the SIMPLE LINEAR REGRESSION EQUATION

Use **Fit Model**.

For example, to perform Figure 13.4 analysis of the Sunflowers Apparel data on page 489, open to the **Site Selection data table**. Select **Analyze → Fit Model** and in the Fit Model dialog box (partially shown below):

1. Click **Annual Sales** in the columns list and then click **Y** to add Annual Sales to the Y box.
2. Click **Profiled Customers** in the columns list and then click **Add** to add Profiled Customers to the Construct Model Effects box.
3. Click **Run**.

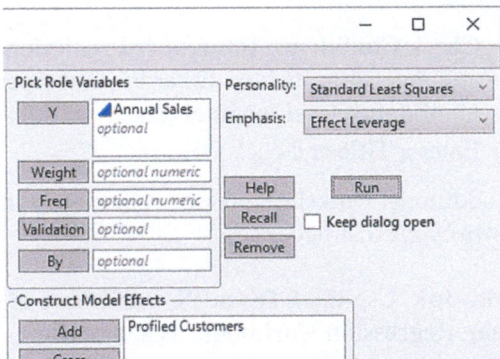

JMP displays results in a new window. Tabular regression results appear under the headings Summary of Fit, Analysis of Variance, and Parameter Estimates. Regression coefficients appear in the Estimate column of the Parameter Estimates table. Click the **Response Annual Sales red triangle** and select **Regression Reports** and check **Show All Confidence Intervals** in the submenu. Confidence interval estimate columns are added to the Parameter Estimates tabular summary.

To display the prediction expression for the regression analysis (not shown in Figure 13.4), click the **Response Annual Sales red triangle** and select **Estimates** and check **Show Prediction Expression** in the submenu.

If the values of Y are part of a time series, click the **Response Annual Sales red triangle** and select **Row Diagnostics** and check **Plot Residual by Rows** in the submenu to create a plot of the residuals versus the time variable.

JG13.3 MEASURES of VARIATION

The measures of variation appear in the Summary of Fit, Analysis of Variance, and Parameter Estimates tabular summaries.

JG13.4 ASSUMPTIONS of REGRESSION

There are no JMP Guide instructions for Section 13.4.

JG13.5 RESIDUAL ANALYSIS

The regression results in the JMP window that the Section JG13.2 instructions create include a residual plot of the residuals versus the predicted Annual Sales, equivalent to a residual plot of the residuals versus Profiled Customers, the independent X variable.

To save the residuals as a column variable in the current worksheet, click the **Response Annual Sales red triangle** and select **Save Columns → Residuals**. Use Graph Builder to create a scatter plot (see Section JG2.5) with that new column and the column variable of the independent X variable to create a residual plot of the residuals versus the independent X variable or a normal probability plot using the Section JG6.3 instructions.

JG13.6 MEASURING AUTOCORRELATION: the DURBIN-WATSON STATISTIC

Use the Section JG13.2 instructions to create the JMP window of regression results. Then click the **Response Annual Sales red triangle** and select **Row Diagnostics** and check **Durbin Watson Test** in the submenu. The Durbin-Watson statistic appears under the heading Durbin-Watson.

JG13.7 INFERENCES ABOUT the SLOPE and CORRELATION COEFFICIENT

The t test for the slope and the F test for the slope are included in the results that the Section JG13.2 instructions create.

JG13.8   ESTIMATION of MEAN VALUES and PREDICTION of INDIVIDUAL VALUES

Use **Fit Y by X** or **Profiler** (interactive, for confidence interval estimate only).

For example, to construct the Figure 13.21 confidence interval estimate and prediction interval for the Sunflowers data on page 517, open to the **Site Selection data table**. Select **Analyze➔Fit Y by X** and in the Fit Y by X - Contextual dialog box:

1. Click **Annual Sales** in the columns list and then click **Y, Response** to add Annual Sales to the Y, Response box.

2. Click **Profiled Customers** in the columns list and then click **X, Factor** to add Profiled Customers to the X, Factor box.

3. Click **OK**.

JMP displays results in a new window. In that window:

4. Click the **Bivariate Fit of Annual Sales By Profiled Customers Red triangle** and select **Fit Line** from its menu.

JMP adds tabular summaries and a Linear Fit red triangle to the results window.

5. Click the **Linear Fit Red triangle** and select **Mean Confidence Limit Formula** from its menu.

6. Click the **Linear Fit Red triangle** and select **Indiv Confidence Limit Formula** from its menu.

JMP adds two pairs of columns to the current data table that calculate the confidence interval estimate and prediction interval for each value of Profiled Customers. To have JMP compute these items for a specific X_i value, add the value to the Profiled Customers column. In Figure 13.21, the X value 4 has been added to the new row 15.

To estimate mean values using the interactive profiler, first use the Section JG13.2 instructions to create the JMP window of regression results. Then click the **Response Annual Sales red triangle** and select **Factor Profiling** and check **Profiler** in the submenu. JMP displays an interactive graph with the heading Prediction Profiler in the results window (shown below). Drag the crosshairs target until they align on the X value being used for constructing the interval estimate. The confidence interval estimate appears as part of the Y axis label. The profiler chart shown below is set to display that 95% confidence interval estimate of the mean annual sales for the entire population of stores that have 4 million profiled customers ($X = 4$) that page 517 calculates.

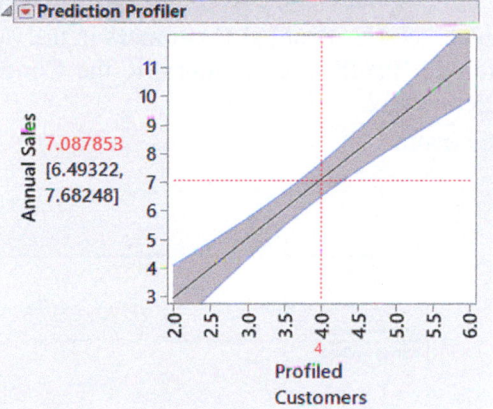

▾MINITAB GUIDE

There are no Minitab Guide instructions for Section 13.1.

MG13.2 DETERMINING the SIMPLE LINEAR REGRESSION EQUATION

Use **Regression** to perform a simple linear regression analysis.

For example, to perform the Figure 13.4 analysis of the Sunflowers Apparel data on page 489, open to the **Site Selection worksheet**. Select **Stat → Regression → Regression → Fit Regression Model**. In the Regression dialog box (shown below):

1. Double-click **C3 Annual Sales** in the variables list to add '**Annual Sales**' to the **Response** box and press **Tab**.
2. Double-click **C2 Profiled Customers** in the variables list to add '**Profiled Customers**' to the **Continuous predictors** box.
3. Click **Graphs**.

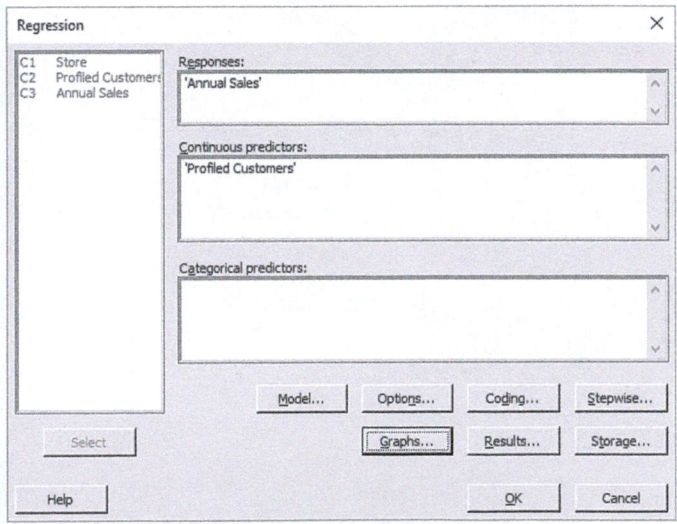

In the Regression: Graphs dialog box (shown at the top of the right column):

4. Select **Regular** from the **Residuals for plots** pull-down list.
5. Click **Individual plots**.
6. Check **Histogram of residuals, Normal plot of residuals,** and **Residuals versus fits** and then press **Tab** twice.
7. Double-click **C2 Profiled Customers** in the variables list to add '**Profiled Customers**' in the **Residuals versus the variables** box.
8. Click **OK**.

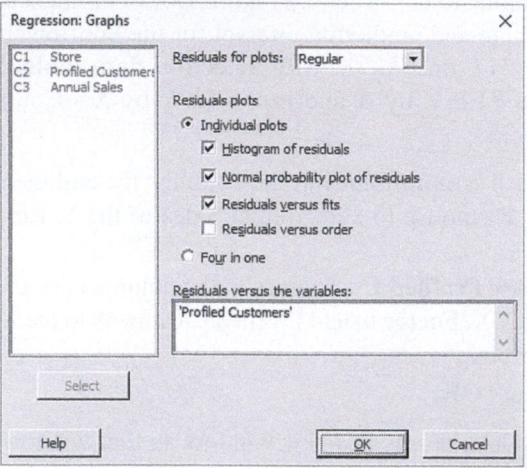

9. Back in the Regression dialog box, click **Results**.

In the Regression: Results dialog box (shown below):

10. Select **Simple tables** from the **Display of results** pull-down list.
11. Check all check boxes except **Durbin-Watson statistic**.
12. Select **For all observations** from the **Fits and diagnostics** pull down list.
13. Click **OK**.

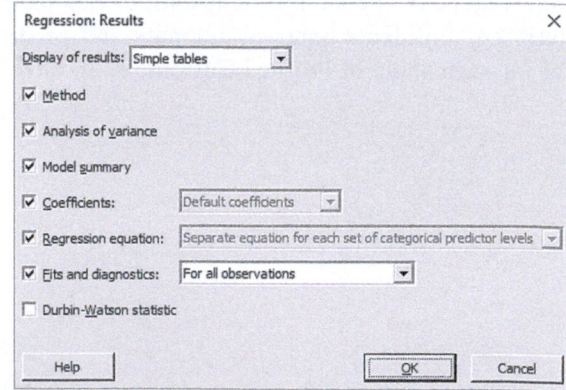

14. Back in the Regression dialog box, click **Options**.

In the Regression: Options dialog box (not shown):

15. Enter **95** in the **Confidence level for all intervals** box.
16. Click **OK**.
17. Back in the Regression dialog box, click **OK**.

To create a scatter plot that contains a prediction line and regression equation similar to Figure 13.5 on page 489, use the Section MG2.5 scatter plot instructions with the Table 13.1 Sunflowers Apparel data.

MG13.3 MEASURES OF VARIATION

The measures of variation appear in the Analysis of Variance table that is part of the regression results that the Section MG13.2 instructions create.

MG13.4 ASSUMPTIONS OF REGRESSION

There are no Minitab Guide instructions for Section 13.4.

MG13.5 RESIDUAL ANALYSIS

Steps 5, 6, 11, and 12 of the Section MG13.2 instructions create the list of residuals, residual plots, and normal probability plots necessary for residual analysis. To store the list of residual values in the current worksheet, replace steps 16 and 17 of the Section MG13.2 instructions with these steps 16 through 18:

16. Click **Storage**.
17. In the Regression: Storage dialog box (not shown), check **Residuals** and then click **OK**.
18. Back in the Regression dialog box, click **OK**.

MG13.6 MEASURING AUTOCORRELATION: the DURBIN-WATSON STATISTIC

To compute the Durbin-Watson statistic, modify the Section MG13.2 instructions by also checking **Durbin-Watson statistic** in step 12.

MG13.7 INFERENCES ABOUT the SLOPE and CORRELATION COEFFICIENT

The t test for the slope and F test for the slope are included in the results that the Section MG13.2 instructions create.

MG13.8 ESTIMATION of MEAN VALUES and PREDICTION of INDIVIDUAL VALUES

Use **Predict**.

For example, to create the Figure 13.21 confidence interval estimate and prediction interval for the Sunflowers Apparel data, open to the **Site Selection worksheet**. Select **Stat → Regression → Predict**. In the Predict dialog box (shown below):

1. Select **Annual Sales** from the **Response** pull-down list.
2. Select **Enter individual values** from the unlabeled pull-down list.
3. Enter **4** in the first cell of the **'Profiled Customers'** list.

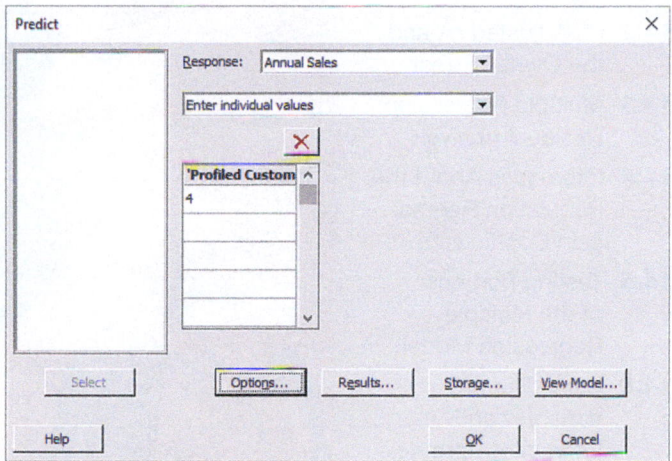

4. Click **Options**.
5. In the Predict: Options dialog box, verify that **95** is the **Confidence level** and **Two-sided** is the **Type of interval** and then click **OK**.
6. Back in the original dialog box, click **Results**.
7. In the Predict: Results dialog box, check both check boxes and then click **OK**.
8. Back in the original dialog box, click **OK**.

14

Introduction to Multiple Regression

OBJECTIVES

- Develop multiple regression models
- Interpret the regression coefficients
- Determine which independent variables to include in a model
- Identify the independent variables most important to predicting the dependent variable

▼ USING **STATISTICS**
The Multiple Effects of OmniPower Bars

Y ou are a marketing manager for OmniFoods, with oversight for nutrition bars and similar snack items. You seek to revive the sales of OmniPower, the company's primary product in this category. Originally marketed as a high-energy bar to runners, mountain climbers, and other athletes, OmniPower reached its greatest sales during an earlier time when high-energy bars were one of the most popular snack items with consumers. Now, you seek to reposition the product as a nutrition bar to benefit from the booming market for such bars.

Because the marketplace already contains several successful nutrition bars, you need to develop an effective marketing strategy. In particular, you need to determine the effect that price and in-store promotional expenses (special in-store coupons, signs, and displays as well as the cost of free samples) will have on sales of OmniPower. Before marketing the bar nationwide, you plan to conduct a test-market study of OmniPower sales, using a sample of 34 stores in a supermarket chain.

How can you extend the linear regression methods discussed in Chapter 13 to incorporate the effects of price *and* promotion into the same model? How can you use this model to improve the success of the nationwide introduction of OmniPower?

- Use categorical independent variables in a regression model
- Use logistic regression to predict a categorical dependent variable

Chapter 13 discusses simple linear regression models that use *one* numerical independent variable, X, to predict the value of a numerical dependent variable, Y. Often you can make better predictions by using *more than one* independent variable. This chapter introduces you to **multiple regression models** that use two or more independent variables to predict the value of a dependent variable.

14.1 Developing a Multiple Regression Model

In the OmniPower Bars scenario, your business objective, to determine the effect that price and in-store promotional expenses will have on sales, calls for examining a multiple regression model in which the price of an OmniPower bar in cents (X_1) and the monthly budget for in-store promotional expenses in dollars (X_2) are the independent variables and the number of Omni Power bars sold in a month (Y) is the dependent variable.

To develop this model, you collect data from a sample of 34 stores in a supermarket chain selected for a test-market study of OmniPower. You choose stores in a way to ensure that they all have approximately the same monthly sales volume. You organize and store the data collected in OmniPower . Table 14.1 presents these data.

TABLE 14.1
Monthly OmniPower Sales, Price, and Promotional Expenditures

Store	Sales	Price	Promotion	Store	Sales	Price	Promotion
1	4,141	59	200	18	2,730	79	400
2	3,842	59	200	19	2,618	79	400
3	3,056	59	200	20	4,421	79	400
4	3,519	59	200	21	4,113	79	600
5	4,226	59	400	22	3,746	79	600
6	4,630	59	400	23	3,532	79	600
7	3,507	59	400	24	3,825	79	600
8	3,754	59	400	25	1,096	99	200
9	5,000	59	600	26	761	99	200
10	5,120	59	600	27	2,088	99	200
11	4,011	59	600	28	820	99	200
12	5,015	59	600	29	2,114	99	400
13	1,916	79	200	30	1,882	99	400
14	675	79	200	31	2,159	99	400
15	3,636	79	200	32	1,602	99	400
16	3,224	79	200	33	3,354	99	600
17	2,295	79	400	34	2,927	99	600

When there are two independent variables in the multiple regression model, a three-dimensional (3D) scatter plot, which visualizes data as points inside a cube, may suggest a starting point for regression analysis. Figure 14.1 on page 538 presents JMP and Minitab 3D scatter plots of the OmniPower data. In these plots, points are plotted at a height equal to their sales and have drop lines down to their corresponding price and promotion expense values. Three-dimensional scatter plots can be interactively rotated to view the data from various perspectives, some of which may reveal the relationships among variables better than others. In Figure 14.1, the plots have rotated such that the Price and Promotion axes form the "floor" of the cube. This perspective suggests that a negative linear relationship between sales and price (sales decrease as price increases) and a positive linear relationship between sales and promotional expenses (sales increase as those expenses increase) may exist.

FIGURE 14.1

JMP and Minitab 3D scatter plots of the monthly OmniPower sales, price, and promotional expenses

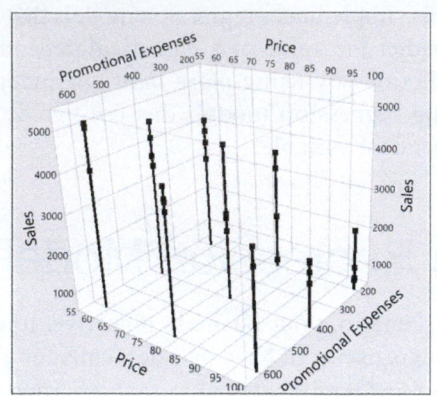
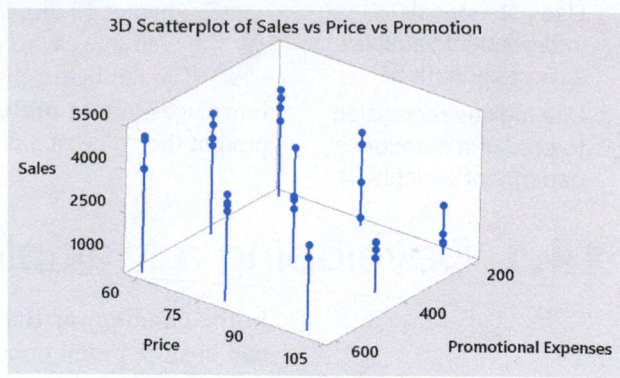

Interpreting the Regression Coefficients

When there are several independent variables, you can extend the simple linear regression model of Equation (13.1) on page 486 by assuming a linear relationship between each independent variable and the dependent variable. Equation (14.1) defines the general case of a multiple regression model with k independent variables. Equation (14.2) defines the specific case of the multiple regression model with two independent variables, the simplest case.

MULTIPLE REGRESSION MODEL WITH k INDEPENDENT VARIABLES

$$Y_i = \beta_0 + \beta_1 X_{1i} + \beta_2 X_{2i} + \beta_3 X_{3i} + \ldots + \beta_k X_{ki} + \varepsilon_i \qquad (14.1)$$

where

$\beta_0 = Y$ intercept

$\beta_1 = $ slope of Y with variable X_1, holding variables $X_2, X_3, \ldots, X_k$ constant

$\beta_2 = $ slope of Y with variable X_2, holding variables $X_1, X_3, \ldots, X_k$ constant

$\beta_3 = $ slope of Y with variable X_3, holding variables $X_1, X_2, \ldots, X_k$ constant

$\vdots$

$\beta_k = $ slope of Y with variable X_k holding variables $X_1, X_2, X_3, \ldots, X_{k-1}$ constant

$\varepsilon_i = $ random error in Y for observation i

MULTIPLE REGRESSION MODEL WITH TWO INDEPENDENT VARIABLES

$$Y_i = \beta_0 + \beta_1 X_{1i} + \beta_2 X_{2i} + \varepsilon_i \qquad (14.2)$$

Equation (14.2) has three **net regression coefficients**: β_0, β_1 and β_2. As in simple linear regression, β_0 represents the Y intercept, the value of Y when $X = 0$. The other two terms are slopes defined as follows:

- β_1: the change in Y per unit change in X_1, taking into account the effect of X_2.
- β_2: the change in Y per unit change in X_2, taking into account the effect of X_1.

Each independent X variable always has its own β term. Therefore, a multiple regression model that has j X variables will always have $j+1$ β terms, β_1 through β_j plus the Y intercept, β_0.

student TIP

Use software to calculate multiple regression results due to the complexitity of the calculations.

As you would do for simple linear regression, you use the least-squares method to calculate the sample regression coefficients b_0, b_1, and b_2 as estimates of the population parameters β_0, β_1, and β_2. Equation (14.3) defines the regression equation for a multiple regression model with two independent variables.

MULTIPLE REGRESSION EQUATION WITH TWO INDEPENDENT VARIABLES

$$\hat{Y}_i = b_0 + b_1X_{1i} + b_2X_{2i} \tag{14.3}$$

Figure 14.2 shows Excel, JMP, and Minitab results for the OmniPower sales data multiple regression model. In these results, the b_0 coefficient is labeled Intercept by Excel and JMP and labeled Constant by Minitab.

FIGURE 14.2

Excel, JMP, and Minitab results for the OmniPower sales multiple regression model

	A	B	C	D	E	F	G
1	Regression Analysis						
2							
3	*Regression Statistics*						
4	Multiple R	0.8705					
5	R Square	0.7577					
6	Adjusted R Square	0.7421					
7	Standard Error	638.0653					
8	Observations	34					
9							
10	ANOVA						
11		*df*	*SS*	*MS*	*F*	*Significance F*	
12	Regression	2	39472730.7730	19736365.3865	48.4771	0.0000	
13	Residual	31	12620946.6682	407127.3119			
14	Total	33	52093677.4412				
15							
16		*Coefficients*	*Standard Error*	*t Stat*	*P-value*	*Lower 95%*	*Upper 95%*
17	Intercept	5837.5208	628.1502	9.2932	0.0000	4556.3999	7118.6416
18	Price	-53.2173	6.8522	-7.7664	0.0000	-67.1925	-39.2421
19	Promotional Expenses	3.6131	0.6852	5.2728	0.0000	2.2155	5.0106

	I	J	K	L
1	Intermediate Calculations			
2	*b2, b1, b0* intercepts	3.6131	-53.2173	5837.5208
3	*b2, b1, b0* Standard Error	0.6852	6.8522	628.1502
4	R Square, Standard Error	0.7577	638.0653	#N/A
5	*F*, Residual *df*	48.4771	31	#N/A
6	Regression *SS*, Residual *SS*	39472730.77	12620946.67	#N/A
7				
8	Confidence level	95%		
9	*t* Critical Value	2.0395		
10	Half Width *b0*	1281.1208		
11	Half Width *b1*	13.9752		
12	Half Width *b2*	1.3975		

Summary of Fit

RSquare	0.757726
RSquare Adj	0.742095
Root Mean Square Error	638.0653
Mean of Response	3098.676
Observations (or Sum Wgts)	34

Analysis of Variance

Source	DF	Sum of Squares	Mean Square	F Ratio
Model	2	39472731	19736365	48.4771
Error	31	12620947	407127.31	Prob > F
C. Total	33	52093677		<.0001*

Parameter Estimates

Term	Estimate	Std Error	t Ratio	Prob>|t|	Lower 95%	Upper 95%
Intercept	5837.5208	628.1502	9.29	<.0001*	4556.3999	7118.6416
Price	-53.21734	6.852221	-7.77	<.0001*	-67.19253	-39.24214
Promotional Expenses	3.613058	0.685222	5.27	<.0001*	2.2155384	5.0105776

Regression Analysis: Sales versus Price, Promotional Expenses

Analysis of Variance

Source	DF	Adj SS	Adj MS	F-Value	P-Value
Regression	2	39472731	19736365	48.48	0.000
Price	1	24556917	24556917	60.32	0.000
Promotional Expenses	1	11319245	11319245	27.80	0.000
Error	31	12620947	407127		
Lack-of-Fit	6	673389	112232	0.23	0.961
Pure Error	25	11947558	477902		
Total	33	52093677			

Model Summary

S	R-sq	R-sq(adj)	R-sq(pred)
638.065	75.77%	74.21%	71.64%

Coefficients

Term	Coef	SE Coef	T-Value	P-Value	VIF
Constant	5838	628	9.29	0.000	
Price	-53.22	6.85	-7.77	0.000	1.01
Promotional Expenses	3.613	0.685	5.27	0.000	1.01

Regression Equation

Sales = 5838 - 53.22 Price + 3.613 Promotional Expenses

student TIP

Multiple regression coefficients are conditional on holding constant the effect of the other independent variables. The slope b_1 holds constant the effect of variable X_2. The slope b_2 holds constant the effect of variable X_1.

From Figure 14.2, the computed values of the net regression coefficients are

$$b_0 = 5{,}837.5208 \quad b_1 = -53.2173 \quad b_2 = 3.6131$$

Therefore, the multiple regression equation is

$$\hat{Y}_i = 5{,}837.5208 - 53.2173X_{1i} + 3.6131X_{2i}$$

where

$\hat{Y}_i$ = predicted monthly sales of OmniPower bars for store i

X_{1i} = price of OmniPower bar (in cents) for store i

X_{2i} = monthly in-store promotional expenses (in \$) for store i

The sample Y intercept, b_0, estimates the number of OmniPower bars sold in a month if the price was zero cents and the total amount spent on promotional expenses was $0.00. Because the price and promotion values are outside the range of price and promotion used in the test-market study, and because they make no logical sense for this problem, the value of b_0 has no useful interpretation.

Using the net regression coefficients b_1 and b_2, the effects of adding one cent to the price of OmniPower bars (X_1) or adding $1 to monthly promotion expenditures (X_2) can be summarized for management in Table 14.2, which explains the effect of changing one independent variable while holding the value of the all other independent variables constant.

TABLE 14.2

Net effects table for the OmniPower sales multiple regression model

Independent Variable Change	Net Effect
A price increase of one cent	Predict mean OmniPower monthly sales to decrease by 53.2173 bars, holding constant the promotional expenditures.
An increase of $1 in monthly promotional expenditures	Predict mean OmniPower monthly sales to increase by 3.6131 bars, holding constant the price.

The Table 14.2 estimates will allow OmniFoods decision makers to better understand how pricing and promotional expenditures decisions are predicted to affect OmniPower sales. Using the tables, managers could predict that a 10-cent decrease in price would result in the mean monthly sales increasing by about 532 bars, holding promotional costs constant, or that a $100 increase in promotional expenditures would increase mean monthly sales by about 361 bars, holding price constant.

Because net regression coefficients always estimate the predicted mean change in Y per unit change in a specific X, holding constant the effect of the other X variables, net effects tables are always a good way to summarize multiple regression results for decision-making purposes.

Predicting the Dependent Variable Y

Use the multiple regression equation to predict values of the dependent variable. For example, what are the predicted mean sales for a store charging 79 cents during a month in which promotional expenses are $400? Using the multiple regression equation,

$$\hat{Y}_i = 5{,}837.5208 - 53.2173X_{1i} + 3.6131X_{2i}$$

with $X_{1i} = 79$ and $X_{2i} = 400$,

student TIP

You should only predict within the range of the values of all the independent variables.

$$\hat{Y}_i = 5{,}837.5208 - 53.2173(79) + 3.6131(400)$$

$$= 3{,}078.57$$

Thus, you predict that stores charging 79 cents and spending $400 in promotional expenses will sell a mean of 3,078.57 OmniPower bars per month.

After developing the regression equation, doing a residual analysis (see Section 14.3), and determining the significance of the overall fitted model (see Section 14.2), you can construct a confidence interval estimate of the mean value and a prediction interval for an individual value. Figure 14.3 presents Excel, JMP, and Minitab confidence interval estimates and a prediction interval for the OmniPower sales data.

FIGURE 14.3
Excel, JMP, and Minitab confidence interval estimate and prediction interval results for the OmniPower sales data

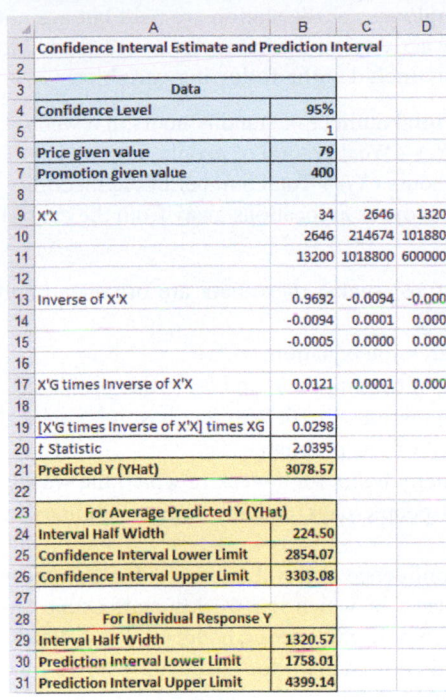

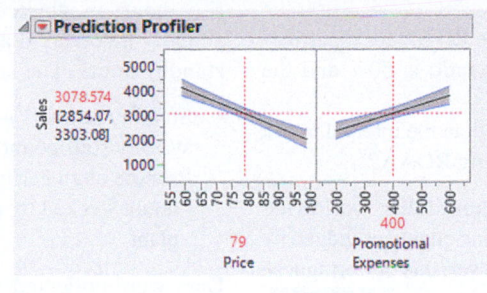

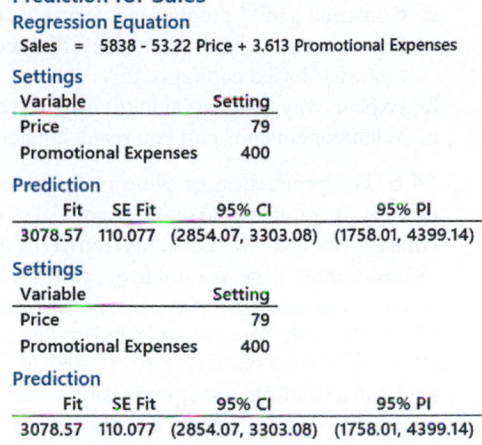

The 95% confidence interval estimate of the mean OmniPower sales for all stores charging 79 cents and spending $400 in promotional expenses is 2,854.07 to 3,303.08 bars. The prediction interval for an individual store is 1,758.01 to 4,399.14 bars.

PROBLEMS FOR SECTION 14.1

LEARNING THE BASICS

14.1 For this problem, use the following multiple regression equation:

$$\hat{Y}_i = 10 + 5X_{1i} + 3X_{2i}$$

a. Interpret the meaning of the slopes.
b. Interpret the meaning of the Y intercept.

14.2 For this problem, use the following multiple regression equation:

$$\hat{Y}_i = 50 - 2X_{1i} + 7X_{2i}$$

a. Interpret the meaning of the slopes.
b. Interpret the meaning of the Y intercept.

APPLYING THE CONCEPTS

14.3 A nonprofit analyst seeks to determine which variables should be used to predict nonprofit charitable commitment, a nonprofit organization commitment to its charitable purpose. Two independent variables under consideration are Revenue, a measurement of total revenue, in billions of dollars, as a measure of nonprofit size X_1 and Efficiency, a measurement of the percent of private donations remaining after fundraising expenses as a measure of nonprofit fundraising efficiency X_2. The dependent variable Y is Commitment, a measurement of the percent of total expenses that are allocated directly to charitable services. Data are collected from a random sample of 98 nonprofit organizations, with the following results:

Variable	Coefficients	Standard Error	T Statistic	p-Value
Intercept	11.002079	7.127101	1.54	0.1260
Revenue	0.6683647	0.320077	2.09	0.0395
Efficiency	0.8317339	0.077736	10.70	0.0001

a. State the multiple regression equation.
b. Interpret the meaning of the slopes, b_1 and b_2, in this problem.
c. What conclusions can you reach concerning nonprofit charitable commitment?

✓ SELF TEST **14.4** Profitability remains a challenge for banks and thrifts with less than $2 billion of assets. The business problem facing a bank analyst relates to the factors that affect return on average assets (ROAA), an indicator of how profitable a company is relative to its total assets. Data collected on a sample of 199 community banks and stored in CommunityBanks include the ROAA (%), the efficiency ratio (%) as a measure of bank productivity, and total risk-based capital (%) as a measure of capital adequacy.

Source: Data extracted from "What the Top 200 Publicly Traded Community Banks Do Better Than Peers," **bit.ly/2tKX9in**.

a. State the multiple regression equation.
b. Interpret the meaning of the slopes, b_1 and b_2, in this problem.
c. Predict the mean ROAA when the efficiency ratio is 60% and the total risk-based capital is 15%.

d. Construct a 95% confidence interval estimate for the mean ROAA when the efficiency ratio is 60% and the total risk-based capital is 15%.

e. Construct a 95% prediction interval for the ROAA for a particular community bank when the efficiency ratio is 60% and the total risk-based capital is 15%.

f. Explain why the interval in (d) is narrower than the interval in (e).

g. What conclusions can you reach concerning ROAA?

14.5 The production of wine is a multibillion-dollar worldwide industry. In an attempt to develop a model of wine quality as judged by wine experts, data was collected from red wine variants of Portuguese "Vinho Verde" wine. A sample of 50 wines is stored in VinhoVerde .

Source: Data extracted from P. Cortez, Cerdeira, A., Almeida, F., Matos, T., and Reis, J., "Modeling Wine Preferences by Data Mining from Physiochemical Properties," *Decision Support Systems*, 47, 2009, pp. 547–553 and **bit.ly/9xKIEa**.

Develop a multiple linear regression model to predict wine quality, measured on a scale from 0 (very bad) to 10 (excellent) based on alcohol content (%) and the amount of chlorides.

a. State the multiple regression equation.

b. Interpret the meaning of the slopes, b_1 and b_2, in this problem.

c. Explain why the regression coefficient, b_0, has no practical meaning in the context of this problem.

d. Predict the mean wine quality rating for wines that have 10% alcohol and chlorides of 0.08.

e. Construct a 95% confidence interval estimate for the mean wine quality rating for wines that have 10% alcohol and chlorides of 0.08.

f. Construct a 95% prediction interval for the wine quality rating for an individual wine that has 10% alcohol and chlorides of 0.08.

g. What conclusions can you reach concerning this regression model?

14.6 Human resource managers face the business problem of assessing the impact of factors on full-time job growth. A human resource manager is interested in the impact of full-time voluntary turnover and total worldwide revenues on the number of full-time job openings at the beginning of a new year. Data are collected from a sample of 63 "best companies to work for." The total number of full-time job openings as of February 2017, the full-time voluntary turnover in the past year (in %), and the total worldwide revenue (in $billions) are recorded and stored in BestCompanies .

Source: Data extracted from *Best Companies to Work For*, 2017, **fortune.com/best-companies**.

a. State the multiple regression equation.

b. Interpret the meaning of the slopes, b_1 and b_2, in this problem.

c. Interpret the meaning of the regression coefficient, b_0.

d. Which factor has the greatest effect on the number of full-time jobs added in the last year? Explain.

14.7 The business problem facing the director of broadcasting operations for a television station was the issue of standby hours (i.e., hours in which employees at the station are paid but are not actually involved in any activity) and what factors were related to standby hours. The study included the following variables:

Standby hours (Y)—Total number of standby hours in a week
Weekly staff count (X_1)—Weekly total of people-days
Remote engineering hours (X_2)—Total number of engineering hours worked by employees at locations away from the central plant

Data were collected for 26 weeks; these data are organized and stored in Nickels26Weeks .

a. State the multiple regression equation.

b. Interpret the meaning of the slopes, b_1 and b_2, in this problem.

c. Explain why the regression coefficient, b_0, has no practical meaning in the context of this problem.

d. Predict the mean standby hours for a week in which the weekly staff count was 310 people-days and the remote engineering hours total was 400.

e. Construct a 95% confidence interval estimate for the mean standby hours for weeks in which the weekly staff count was 310 people-days and remote engineering hours total was 400.

f. Construct a 95% prediction interval for the standby hours for a single week in which the weekly staff count was 310 people-days and the engineering remote hours total was 400.

g. What conclusions can you reach concerning standby hours?

14.8 Nassau County is located approximately 25 miles east of New York City. The data organized and stored in GlenCove include the fair market value (in $thousands), land area of the property in acres, and age, in years, for a sample of 30 single-family homes located in Glen Cove, a small city in Nassau County. Develop a multiple linear regression model to predict the fair market value based on land area of the property (in acres) and age, in years.

a. State the multiple regression equation.

b. Interpret the meaning of the slopes, b_1 and b_2, in this problem.

c. Explain why the regression coefficient, b_0, has no practical meaning in the context of this problem.

d. Predict the mean fair market value for a house that has a land area of 0.25 acre and is 55 years old.

e. Construct a 95% confidence interval estimate for the mean fair market value for houses that have a land area of 0.25 acre and are 55 years old.

f. Construct a 95% prediction interval estimate for the fair market value for an individual house that has a land area of 0.25 acre and is 55 years old.

14.2 r^2, Adjusted r^2, and the Overall F Test

This section discusses three methods you can use to evaluate the overall multiple regression model: the coefficient of multiple determination, r^2, the adjusted r^2, and the overall F test.

Coefficient of Multiple Determination

Section 13.3 explains that the coefficient of determination, r^2, measures the proportion of the variation in Y that is explained by the variability in the independent variable X in the simple linear regression model. In multiple regression, the **coefficient of multiple determination** represents the proportion of the variation in the dependent variable Y that is explained by all the variability in the independent

X variables that the model includes. Equation (14.4) defines the coefficient of multiple determination for a multiple regression model with two or more independent variables.

COEFFICIENT OF MULTIPLE DETERMINATION

The coefficient of multiple determination is equal to the regression sum of squares (SSR) divided by the total sum of squares (SST).

$$r^2 = \frac{\text{Regression sum of squares}}{\text{Total sum of squares}} = \frac{SSR}{SST} \tag{14.4}$$

In the OmniPower example, from Figure 14.2 on page 539, $SSR = 39,472,730.77$ and $SST = 52,093,677.44$. Thus,

$$r^2 = \frac{SSR}{SST} = \frac{39,472,730.77}{52,093,677.44} = 0.7577$$

The coefficient of multiple determination, $r^2 = 0.7577$, indicates that 75.77% of the variation in sales is explained by the variation in the price and in the promotional expenses. In Figure 14.2 on page 539, Excel labels the coefficient of multiple determination as R Square, JMP labels the coefficient as RSquare, and Minitab labels the coefficient as R-sq.

Adjusted r^2

When considering multiple regression models, some statisticians suggest using the **adjusted r^2** to take into account both the number of independent variables in the model and the sample size. Because a model that has additional independent variables will always have the same or higher regression sum of squares and r^2, using the adjusted r^2 provides a more appropriate interpretation when comparing models. Equation (14.5) defines the adjusted r^2.

ADJUSTED r^2

$$r_{\text{adj}}^2 = 1 - \left[(1 - r^2) \frac{n - 1}{n - k - 1} \right] \tag{14.5}$$

where
   k is the number of independent variables in the regression equation.

For the OmniPower sales data, because $r^2 = 0.7577$, $n = 34$, and $k = 2$,

$$r_{\text{adj}}^2 = 1 - \left[(1 - 0.7577) \frac{34 - 1}{34 - 2 - 1} \right] = 1 - \left[(0.2423) \frac{33}{31} \right]$$
$$= 1 - 0.2579$$
$$= 0.7421$$

Therefore, 74.21% of the variation in sales is explained by the multiple regression model—adjusted for the number of independent variables and sample size. In Figure 14.2 on page 539, Excel labels the adjusted r^2 as Adjusted R Square, JMP labels this statistic RSquare Adj, and Minitab labels it R-sq(adj).

Test for the Significance of the Overall Multiple Regression Model

You use the **overall F test** to determine whether there is a significant relationship between the dependent variable and the entire set of independent variables (the overall multiple regression model). Because there is more than one independent variable, you use the following null and alternative hypotheses:

H_0: $\beta_1 = \beta_2 = \cdots = \beta_k = 0$ (There is no linear relationship between the dependent variable and the independent variables.)

H_1: At least one $\beta_j \neq 0$, $j = 1, 2, \cdots, k$ (There is a linear relationship between the dependent variable and at least one of the independent variables.)

This test determines whether at least one independent variable has a linear relationship with the dependent variable. If you reject H_0, you are *not* concluding that all the independent variables have a linear relationship with the dependent variable, only that *at least one* independent variable does. Equation (14.6) defines the overall F test statistic. Table 14.3 presents the ANOVA summary table.

OVERALL *F* TEST

The F_{STAT} test statistic is equal to the regression mean square (*MSR*) divided by the mean square error (*MSE*).

$$F_{STAT} = \frac{MSR}{MSE}$$

(14.6)

The F_{STAT} test statistic follows an F distribution with k and $n - k - 1$ degrees of freedom, where k is the number of independent variables in the regression model.

TABLE 14.3
ANOVA Summary Table
for the Overall *F* Test

Source	Degrees of Freedom	Sum of Squares	Mean Squares (Variance)	F
Regression	k	SSR	$MSR = \dfrac{SSR}{k}$	$F_{STAT} = \dfrac{MSR}{MSE}$
Error	$n - k - 1$	SSE	$MSE = \dfrac{SSE}{n - k - 1}$	
Total	$n - 1$	SST		

The decision rule is

Reject H_0 at the α level of significance if $F_{STAT} > F_\alpha$;
otherwise, do not reject H_0.

If you fail to reject the null hypothesis, you conclude that the model fit is not appropriate. If you reject the null hypothesis, you use methods that Sections 14.4 and 14.5 discuss to determine which independent variables should be included in the model.

For the OmniPower sales study, using a level of significance, $\alpha = 0.05$, and Table E.5, the critical value of the F distribution with 2 and 31 degrees of freedom is approximately 3.32. Figure 14.4 visualizes the regions of nonrejection and rejection using this critical value.

FIGURE 14.4
Testing for the significance of a set of regression coefficients at the 0.05 level of significance, with 2 and 31 degrees of freedom

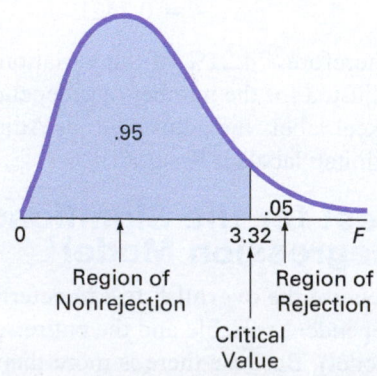

Figure 14.2 multiple regression results on page 539 includes the F_{STAT} test statistic in the ANOVA tables. Table 14.4 summarizes the results of the test for the set of regression coefficients. Based on the results, you conclude that either price or promotional expenses or both variables can be used to help predict mean monthly sales.

TABLE 14.4
Overall F test results
and conclusions

Result	Conclusions
$F_{STAT} = 48.4771$ is greater than the F critical value, 3.32	1. Reject the null hypothesis H_0.
p-value $= 0.0000$ is less than the level of significance, $\alpha = 0.05$	2. Conclude that evidence exists for claiming that at least one of the independent X variables (price or promotional expenses) is related to the dependent Y variable, sales.
	3. The probability is 0.0000 that $F_{STAT} > 48.4771$.

PROBLEMS FOR SECTION 14.2

LEARNING THE BASICS

14.9 The following ANOVA summary table is for a multiple regression model with two independent variables:

Source	Degrees of Freedom	Sum of Squares	Mean Squares	F
Regression	2	60		
Error	18	120		
Total	20	180		

a. Determine the regression mean square (MSR) and the mean square error (MSE).
b. Compute the overall F_{STAT} test statistic.
c. Determine whether there is a significant relationship between Y and the two independent variables at the 0.05 level of significance.
d. Compute the coefficient of multiple determination, r^2, and interpret its meaning.
e. Compute the adjusted r^2.

14.10 The following ANOVA summary table is for a multiple regression model with two independent variables:

Source	Degrees of Freedom	Sum of Squares	Mean Squares	F
Regression	2	30		
Error	10	120		
Total	12	150		

a. Determine the regression mean square (MSR) and the mean square error (MSE).
b. Compute the overall F_{STAT} test statistic.
c. Determine whether there is a significant relationship between Y and the two independent variables at the 0.05 level of significance.
d. Compute the coefficient of multiple determination, r^2, and interpret its meaning.
e. Compute the adjusted r^2.

APPLYING THE CONCEPTS

14.11 A financial analyst engaged in business valuation obtained financial data on 60 drug companies (Industry Group SIC 3 code: 283). The file **BusinessValuation** contains the following variables:

Company—Drug Company name
PB fye—Price-to-book-value ratio (fiscal year ending)
ROE—Return on equity
SGrowth—Growth (GS5)

a. Develop a regression model to predict price-to-book-value ratio based on return on equity.
b. Develop a regression model to predict price-to-book-value ratio based on growth.
c. Develop a regression model to predict price-to-book-value ratio based on return on equity and growth.
d. Compute and interpret the adjusted r^2 for each of the three models.
e. Which of these three models do you think is the best predictor of price-to-book-value ratio?

✓SELF TEST **14.12** In Problem 14.3 on page 541, you predicted nonprofit charitable commitment, based on nonprofit revenue and fundraising efficiency. The regression analysis resulted in this ANOVA table:

Source	Degrees of Freedom	Sum of Squares	Mean Squares	F	p-Value
Regression	2	3529.0718	1764.54	57.9410	<.0001
Error	95	2893.1323	30.45		
Total	97	6422.2041			

Determine whether there is a significant relationship between commitment and the two independent variables at the 0.05 level of significance.

14.13 In Problem 14.5 on page 542, you used the percentage of alcohol and chlorides to predict wine quality (stored in **VinhoVerde**). Use the results from that problem to do the following:
a. Determine whether there is a significant relationship between wine quality and the two independent variables (percentage of alcohol and chlorides) at the 0.05 level of significance.

b. Interpret the meaning of the p-value.
c. Compute the coefficient of multiple determination, r^2, and interpret its meaning.
d. Compute the adjusted r^2.

14.14 In Problem 14.4 on page 541, you used efficiency ratio and total risk-based capital to predict ROAA at a community bank (stored in CommunityBanks). Using the results from that problem,
a. determine whether there is a significant relationship between ROAA and the two independent variables (efficiency ratio and total risk-based capital) at the 0.05 level of significance.
b. interpret the meaning of the p-value.
c. compute the coefficient of multiple determination, r^2, and interpret its meaning.
d. compute the adjusted r^2.

14.15 In Problem 14.7 on page 542, you used the weekly staff count and remote engineering hours to predict standby hours (stored in Nickels26Weeks). Using the results from that problem,
a. determine whether there is a significant relationship between standby hours and the two independent variables (total staff present and remote engineering hours) at the 0.05 level of significance.
b. interpret the meaning of the p-value.
c. compute the coefficient of multiple determination, r^2, and interpret its meaning.
d. compute the adjusted r^2.

14.16 In Problem 14.6 on page 542, you used full-time voluntary turnover (%) and total worldwide revenue ($billions) to predict number of full-time jobs added (stored in BestCompanies). Using the results from that problem,
a. determine whether there is a significant relationship between number of full-time jobs added and the two independent variables (full-time voluntary turnover and total worldwide revenue) at the 0.05 level of significance.
b. interpret the meaning of the p-value.
c. compute the coefficient of multiple determination, r^2, and interpret its meaning.
d. compute the adjusted r^2.

14.17 In Problem 14.8 on page 542, you used the land area of a property and the age of a house to predict the fair market value (stored in GlenCove). Using the results from that problem,
a. determine whether there is a significant relationship between fair market value and the two independent variables (land area of a property and age of a house) at the 0.05 level of significance.
b. interpret the meaning of the p-value.
c. compute the coefficient of multiple determination, r^2, and interpret its meaning.
d. compute the adjusted r^2.

14.3 Multiple Regression Residual Analysis

As with simple linear regression, an analysis of the residuals, differences between the actual and predicted Y values, determines whether a fitted model is the most appropriate model and can also assist in determining whether the assumptions of regression have been violated. Residual analyses for all multiple regression models requires these residual plots:

student TIP

A residual plot that does not contain any apparent patterns will look like a random scattering of points.

- residuals versus the predicted value of Y
- for each independent X variable, residuals versus the independent variable

Models that contain data that have been collected in time order additionally require a residual plot of the residuals versus time. Table 14.5 summarizes the significance of discovering a pattern in the three types of residual plots.

TABLE 14.5
Interpreting Multiple Regression Residual Plots

Residual Plot	Significance of Discovered Pattern
Residuals versus the predicted value of Y	Evidence of a possible curvilinear effect in at least one independent variable, a possible violation of the assumption of equal variance, and/or the need to transform the Y variable
Residuals versus an independent X variable	Suggests evidence of a curvilinear effect and, therefore, indicates the need to add a curvilinear independent variable to the multiple regression model (see Section 15.1)
Residuals versus data collected in time order	Evidence that the independence of errors assumption has been violated. Associated with this residual plot, as in Section 13.6, you can compute the Durbin-Watson statistic to determine the existence of positive autocorrelation among the residuals.

Figure 14.5 presents the residual plots for the OmniPower sales example. There is very little or no pattern in the relationship between the residuals and the predicted value of Y, the value of X_1, price, or the value of X_2, promotional expenses. Thus, you conclude that the multiple regression model is appropriate for predicting sales. There is no need to plot the residuals versus time because the data were not collected in time order.

FIGURE 14.5
Residual plots for the OmniPower sales data:
residuals versus predicted Y, residuals versus price, and residuals versus promotional expenses

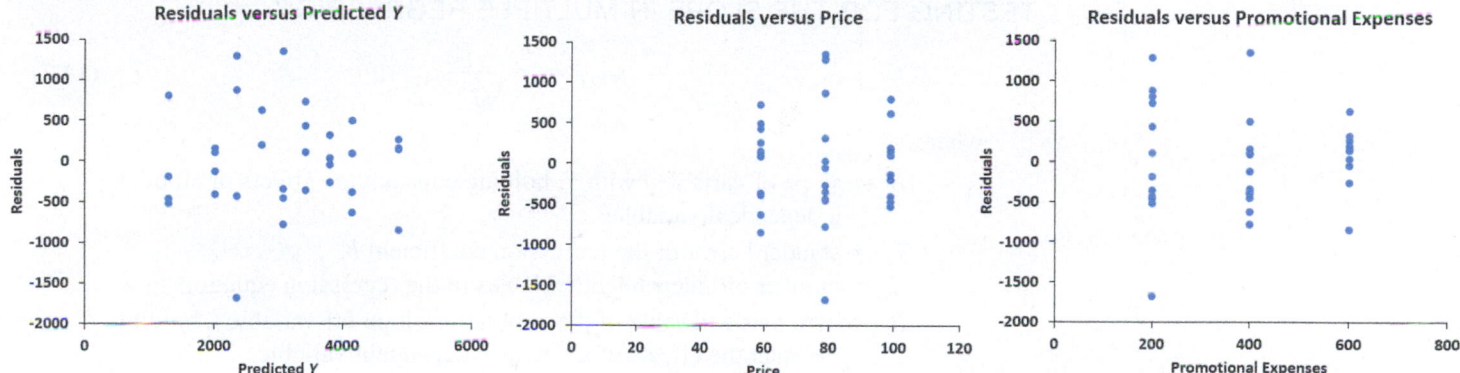

PROBLEMS FOR SECTION 14.3

APPLYING THE CONCEPTS

14.18 In Problem 14.4 on page 541, you used efficiency ratio and total risk-based capital to predict ROAA at a community bank (stored in CommunityBanks).

a. Plot the residuals versus $\hat{Y}_i$.
b. Plot the residuals versus X_{1i}.
c. Plot the residuals versus X_{2i}.
d. In the residual plots created in (a) through (c), is there any evidence of a violation of the regression assumptions? Explain.

14.19 In Problem 14.5 on page 542, you used the percentage of alcohol and chlorides to predict wine quality (stored in VinhoVerde).
a. Plot the residuals versus $\hat{Y}_i$
b. Plot the residuals versus X_{1i}.
c. Plot the residuals versus X_{2i}.
d. In the residual plots created in (a) through (c), is there any evidence of a violation of the regression assumptions? Explain.
e. Should you compute the Durbin-Watson statistic for these data? Explain.

14.20 In Problem 14.6 on page 542, you used full-time voluntary turnover (%), and total worldwide revenue ($billions) to predict number of full-time jobs added (stored in BestCompanies).
a. Perform a residual analysis on your results.
b. If appropriate, perform the Durbin-Watson test, using $\alpha = 0.05$.
c. Are the regression assumptions valid for these data?

14.21 In Problem 14.7 on page 542, you used the weekly staff count and remote engineering hours to predict standby hours (stored in Nickels26Weeks).
a. Perform a residual analysis on your results.
b. If appropriate, perform the Durbin-Watson test, using $\alpha = 0.05$.
c. Are the regression assumptions valid for these data?

14.22 In Problem 14.8 on page 542, you used the land area of a property and the age of a house to predict the fair market value (stored in GlenCove).
a. Perform a residual analysis on your results.
b. If appropriate, perform the Durbin-Watson test, using $\alpha = 0.05$.
c. Are the regression assumptions valid for these data?

14.4 Inferences About the Population Regression Coefficients

Section 13.7 explains how the t test for the slope in a simple linear regression model can determine the significance of the relationship between the X and Y variables. That Section also constructed a confidence interval estimate of the population slope. This section extends those procedures to multiple regression.

Tests of Hypothesis

In a simple linear regression model, to test a hypothesis concerning the population slope, β_1, you used Equation (13.16) on page 508:

$$t_{STAT} = \frac{b_1 - \beta_1}{S_{b_1}}$$

Equation (14.7) generalizes this equation for multiple regression.

TESTING FOR THE SLOPE IN MULTIPLE REGRESSION

$$t_{STAT} = \frac{b_j - \beta_j}{S_{b_j}} \tag{14.7}$$

where

b_j = slope of variable j with Y, holding constant the effects of all other independent variables

S_{b_j} = standard error of the regression coefficient b_j

k = number of independent variables in the regression equation

β_j = hypothesized value of the population slope for variable j, holding constant the effects of all other independent variables

t_{STAT} = test statistic for a t distribution with $n - k - 1$ degrees of freedom

---

To determine whether variable X_2 (amount of promotional expenses) has a significant effect on sales, after taking into account the effect of the price of OmniPower bars, the null and alternative hypotheses are

$$H_0 : \beta_2 = 0$$

$$H_1 : \beta_2 \neq 0$$

From Equation (14.7) and Figure 14.2 on page 539,

$$t_{STAT} = \frac{b_2 - \beta_2}{S_{b_2}}$$

$$= \frac{3.6131 - 0}{0.6852} = 5.2728$$

If you select a level of significance of 0.05, the critical values of t for 31 degrees of freedom from Table E.3 are -2.0395 and $+2.0395$ as Figure 14.6 illustrates.

FIGURE 14.6
Testing for significance of a regression coefficient at the 0.05 level of significance, with 31 degrees of freedom

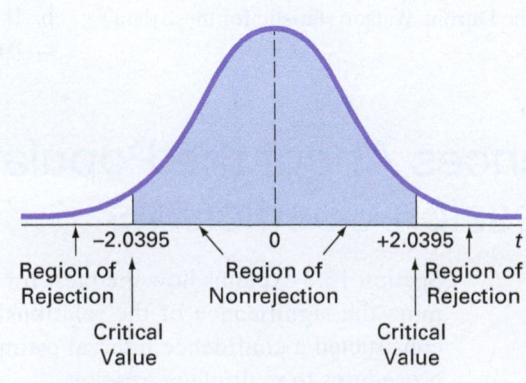

Table 14.6 summarizes the results of the test for the regression coefficient for promotional expenses (b_1) that appears as part of the Figure 14.2 OmniPower sales multiple regression results on page 539. Based on these conclusions, you conclude that promotional expenses has a significant effect on mean monthly sales.

TABLE 14.6

t Test for the Slope Results and Conclusions

Result	Conclusions
$t_{STAT} = 5.2728$ is greater than 2.0395 *p*-value $= 0.0000$ is less than the level of significance, $\alpha = 0.05$	1. Reject the null hypothesis H_0. 2. Conclude that strong evidence exists for claiming that promotional expenses is related to the dependent *Y* variable, sales, taking into account the price. 3. The probability is 0.0000 that t_{STAT} 5.2728 $t_{STAT} < -5.2728$.

Example 14.1 presents the test for the significance of β_1, the slope of sales with price.

EXAMPLE 14.1

Testing for the Significance of the Slope of Sales with Price

At the 0.05 level of significance, is there evidence that the slope of sales with price is different from zero?

SOLUTION From Figure 14.2 on page 539, $t_{STAT} = -7.7664 < -2.0395$, the critical value for $\alpha = 0.05$, or the *p*-value $= 0.0000 < 0.05$. Thus, there is a significant relationship between price, X_1, and sales, taking into account the promotional Expenses, X_2.

As shown with these two independent variables, the test of significance for a specific regression coefficient in multiple regression is a test for the significance of adding that variable into a regression model, given that the other variable is included. In other words, the *t* test for the regression coefficient is actually a test for the contribution of each independent variable.

Confidence Interval Estimation

Instead of testing the significance of a population slope, you may want to estimate the value of a population slope. Equation (14.8) defines the confidence interval estimate for a population slope in multiple regression.

CONFIDENCE INTERVAL ESTIMATE FOR THE SLOPE

$$b_j \pm t_{\alpha/2} S_{b_j} \tag{14.8}$$

where

$t_{\alpha/2}$ = the critical value corresponding to an upper-tail probability of $\alpha/2$ (a cumulative area of $1 - \alpha/2$) from the *t* distribution with $n - k - 1$ degrees of freedom

k = the number of independent variables

To construct a 95% confidence interval estimate of the population slope, β_1 (the effect of price, X_1, on sales, Y, holding constant the effect of promotional expenses, X_2), the critical value of *t* at the 95% confidence level with 31 degrees of freedom is 2.0395 (see Table E.3). Then, using Equation (14.8) and Figure 14.2 on page 539,

$$b_1 \pm t_{\alpha/2} S_{b_1}$$
$$-53.2173 \pm (2.0395)(6.8522)$$
$$-53.2173 \pm 13.9752$$
$$-67.1925 \leq \beta_1 \leq -39.2421$$

Taking into account the effect of promotional expenses, the estimated effect of a 1-cent increase in price is to reduce mean sales by approximately 39.2 to 67.2 bars. You have 95% confidence that this interval correctly estimates the relationship between these variables. From a hypothesis-testing viewpoint, because this confidence interval does not include 0, you conclude that the regression coefficient, for price, has a significant effect.

Example 14.2 constructs and interprets a confidence interval estimate for the slope of sales with promotional expenses.

EXAMPLE 14.2

Constructing a Confidence Interval Estimate for the Slope of Sales with Promotional Expenses

Construct a 95% confidence interval estimate of the population slope of sales with promotional expenses.

SOLUTION The critical value of t at the 95% confidence level, with 31 degrees of freedom, is 2.0395 (see Table E.3). Using Equation (14.8) and Figure 14.2 on page 539,

$$b_2 \pm t_{\alpha/2}S_{b_2}$$
$$3.6131 \pm (2.0395)(0.6852)$$
$$3.6131 \pm 1.3975$$
$$2.2156 \le \beta_2 \le 5.0106$$

Thus, taking into account the effect of price, the estimated effect of each additional dollar of promotional expenses is to increase mean sales by approximately 2.22 to 5.01 bars. You have 95% confidence that this interval correctly estimates the relationship between these variables. From a hypothesis-testing viewpoint, because this confidence interval does not include 0, you can conclude that the regression coefficient, β_2, has a significant effect.

PROBLEMS FOR SECTION 14.4

LEARNING THE BASICS

14.23 Use the following information from a multiple regression analysis:

$$n = 25 \quad b_1 = 5 \quad b_2 = 10 \quad S_{b_1} = 2 \quad S_{b_2} = 8$$

a. Which variable has the largest slope, in units of a t statistic?
b. Construct a 95% confidence interval estimate of the population slope, β_1.
c. At the 0.05 level of significance, determine whether each independent variable makes a significant contribution to the regression model. On the basis of these results, indicate the independent variables to include in this model.

14.24 Use the following information from a multiple regression analysis:

$$n = 20 \quad b_1 = 4 \quad b_2 = 3 \quad S_{b_1} = 1.2 \quad S_{b_2} = 0.8$$

a. Which variable has the largest slope, in units of a t statistic?
b. Construct a 95% confidence interval estimate of the population slope, β_1.
c. At the 0.05 level of significance, determine whether each independent variable makes a significant contribution to the regression model. On the basis of these results, indicate the independent variables to include in this model.

APPLYING THE CONCEPTS

14.25 In Problem 14.3 on page 541, you predicted nonprofit charitable commitment, based on nonprofit revenue (Revenue) and

fundraising efficiency (Efficiency) for a sample of 98 nonprofit organizations. Use the following results:

Variable	Coefficients	Standard Error	t Statistic	p-Value
Intercept	11.002079	7.127101	1.54	0.1260
Revenue	0.6683647	0.320077	2.09	0.0395
Efficiency	0.8317339	0.077736	10.70	<.0001

a. Construct 95% confidence interval estimates of the population slope between commitment and revenue and between commitment and efficiency.
b. At the 0.05 level of significance, determine whether each independent variable makes a significant contribution to the regression model. On the basis of these results, indicate the independent variables to include in this model.

✓**SELF TEST** **14.26** In Problem 14.4 on page 541, you used efficiency ratio and total risk-based capital to predict ROAA at a community bank (stored in **CommunityBanks**). Using the results from that problem,

a. construct a 95% confidence interval estimate of the population slope between ROAA and efficiency ratio.
b. at the 0.05 level of significance, determine whether each independent variable makes a significant contribution to the regression model. On the basis of these results, indicate the independent variables to include in this model.

14.27 In Problem 14.5 on page 542, you used the percentage of alcohol and chlorides to predict wine quality (stored in VinhoVerde). Using the results from that problem,
a. construct a 95% confidence interval estimate of the population slope between wine quality and the percentage of alcohol.
b. at the 0.05 level of significance, determine whether each independent variable makes a significant contribution to the regression model. On the basis of these results, indicate the independent variables to include in this model.

14.28 In Problem 14.6 on page 542, you used full-time voluntary turnover (%) and total worldwide revenue ($billions) to predict the number of full-time job openings (stored in BestCompanies). Using the results from that problem,
a. construct a 95% confidence interval estimate of the population slope between number of full-time job openings and total worldwide revenue.
b. at the 0.05 level of significance, determine whether each independent variable makes a significant contribution to the regression model. On the basis of these results, indicate the independent variables to include in this model.

14.29 In Problem 14.7 on page 542, you used the weekly staff present and remote engineering hours to predict standby hours (stored in Nickels26Weeks). Using the results from that problem,
a. construct a 95% confidence interval estimate of the population slope between standby hours and weekly staff present.
b. at the 0.05 level of significance, determine whether each independent variable makes a significant contribution to the regression model. On the basis of these results, indicate the independent variables to include in this model.

14.30 In Problem 14.8 on page 542, you used land area of a property and age of a house to predict the fair market value (stored in GlenCove). Using the results from that problem,
a. construct a 95% confidence interval estimate of the population slope between fair market value and land area of a property.
b. at the 0.05 level of significance, determine whether each independent variable makes a significant contribution to the regression model. On the basis of these results, indicate the independent variables to include in this model.

14.5 Testing Portions of the Multiple Regression Model

In developing a multiple regression model, you want to use only those independent variables that significantly reduce the error in predicting the value of a dependent variable. If an independent variable does not improve the prediction, you can delete it from the multiple regression model and use a model with fewer independent variables.

The **partial F test** is an alternative to the t test that Section 14.4 discusses for determining the contribution of an independent variable. The partial F test determines the contribution to the regression sum of squares made by each independent variable after all the other independent variables have been included in the model. An independent variable is included only if it significantly improves the model.

To conduct partial F tests for the OmniPower sales example, you need to evaluate the contribution of promotional expenses (X_2) after price (X_1) has been included in the model and also evaluate the contribution of price (X_1) after promotional expenses (X_2) has been included in the model.

In general, if there are several independent variables, you determine the contribution of each independent variable by taking into account the regression sum of squares of a model that includes all independent variables except the one of interest, j. This regression sum of squares is denoted SSR (all Xs except j). Equation (14.9) determines the contribution of variable j, assuming that all other variables are already included.

DETERMINING THE CONTRIBUTION OF AN INDEPENDENT VARIABLE TO THE REGRESSION MODEL

$$SSR(X_j \mid \text{All } Xs \text{ except } j) = SSR(\text{All } Xs) - SSR(\text{All } Xs \text{ except } j) \qquad \textbf{(14.9)}$$

If there are two independent variables, you use Equations (14.10a) and (14.10b) to determine the contribution of each variable.

CONTRIBUTION OF VARIABLE X_1, GIVEN THAT X_2 HAS BEEN INCLUDED

$$SSR(X_1 \mid X_2) = SSR(X_1 \text{ and } X_2) - SSR(X_2) \qquad \textbf{(14.10a)}$$

CONTRIBUTION OF VARIABLE X_2, GIVEN THAT X_1 HAS BEEN INCLUDED

$$SSR(X_2 \mid X_1) = SSR(X_1 \text{ and } X_2) - SSR(X_1) \qquad \textbf{(14.10b)}$$

The term $SSR(X_2)$ represents the sum of squares due to regression for a model that includes only the independent variable X_2 (promotional expenses). Similarly, $SSR(X_1)$ represents the sum of squares due to regression for a model that includes only the independent variable X_1 (price). Figures 14.7 and 14.8 present results for these two models.

FIGURE 14.7
Excel, Minitab, and JMP results for the simple linear regression model of sales with promotional expenses, $SSR(X_2)$

	A	B	C	D	E	F	G
1	Sales and Promotional Expenses Analysis						
2							
3	Regression Statistics						
4	Multiple R	0.5351					
5	R Square	0.2863					
6	Adjusted R Square	0.2640					
7	Standard Error	1077.8721					
8	Observations	34					
9							
10	ANOVA						
11		df	SS	MS	F	Significance F	
12	Regression	1	14915814.1025	14915814.1025	12.8384	0.0011	
13	Residual	32	37177863.3387	1161808.2293			
14	Total	33	52093677.4412				
15							
16		Coefficients	Standard Error	t Stat	P-value	Lower 95%	Upper 95%
17	Intercept	1496.0161	483.9789	3.0911	0.0041	510.1843	2481.8480
18	Promotional Expenses	4.1281	1.1521	3.5831	0.0011	1.7813	6.4748

Regression Analysis: Sales versus Promotional Expenses

Analysis of Variance

Source	DF	Adj SS	Adj MS	F-Value	P-Value
Regression	1	14915814	14915814	12.84	0.001
Promotional Expenses	1	14915814	14915814	12.84	0.001
Error	32	37177863	1161808		
Lack-of-Fit	1	432048	432048	0.36	0.550
Pure Error	31	36745815	1185349		
Total	33	52093677			

Model Summary

S	R-sq	R-sq(adj)	R-sq(pred)
1077.87	28.63%	26.40%	19.52%

Coefficients

Term	Coef	SE Coef	T-Value	P-Value	VIF
Constant	1496	484	3.09	0.004	
Promotional Expenses	4.13	1.15	3.58	0.001	1.00

Regression Equation

Sales = 1496 + 4.13 Promotional Expenses

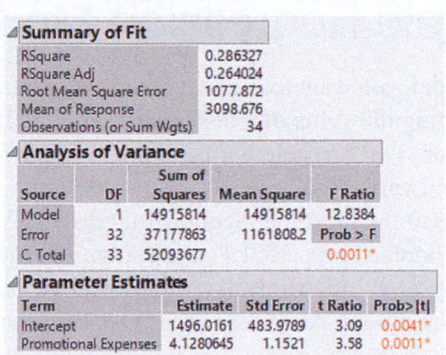

Summary of Fit

RSquare	0.286327
RSquare Adj	0.264024
Root Mean Square Error	1077.872
Mean of Response	3098.676
Observations (or Sum Wgts)	34

Analysis of Variance

Source	DF	Sum of Squares	Mean Square	F Ratio
Model	1	14915814	14915814	12.8384
Error	32	37177863	1161808.2	Prob > F
C. Total	33	52093677		0.0011*

Parameter Estimates

Term	Estimate	Std Error	t Ratio	Prob>|t|
Intercept	1496.0161	483.9789	3.09	0.0041*
Promotional Expenses	4.1280645	1.1521	3.58	0.0011*

FIGURE 14.8
Excel, Minitab, and JMP results for the simple linear regression model of sales with price, $SSR(X_1)$

	A	B	C	D	E	F	G
1	Sales and Price Analysis						
2							
3	Regression Statistics						
4	Multiple R	0.7351					
5	R Square	0.5404					
6	Adjusted R Square	0.5261					
7	Standard Error	864.9457					
8	Observations	34					
9							
10	ANOVA						
11		df	SS	MS	F	Significance F	
12	Regression	1	28153486.1482	28153486.1482	37.6318	0.0000	
13	Residual	32	23940191.2930	748130.9779			
14	Total	33	52093677.4412				
15							
16		Coefficients	Standard Error	t Stat	P-value	Lower 95%	Upper 95%
17	Intercept	7512.3480	734.6189	10.2262	0.0000	6015.9796	9008.7164
18	Price	-56.7138	9.2451	-6.1345	0.0000	-75.5455	-37.8822

Regression Analysis: Sales versus Price

Analysis of Variance

Source	DF	Adj SS	Adj MS	F-Value	P-Value
Regression	1	28153486	28153486	37.63	0.000
Price	1	28153486	28153486	37.63	0.000
Error	32	23940191	748131		
Lack-of-Fit	1	15602	15602	0.02	0.888
Pure Error	31	23924589	771761		
Total	33	52093677			

Model Summary

S	R-sq	R-sq(adj)	R-sq(pred)
864.946	54.04%	52.61%	48.79%

Coefficients

Term	Coef	SE Coef	T-Value	P-Value	VIF
Constant	7512	735	10.23	0.000	
Price	-56.71	9.25	-6.13	0.000	1.00

Regression Equation

Sales = 7512 - 56.71 Price

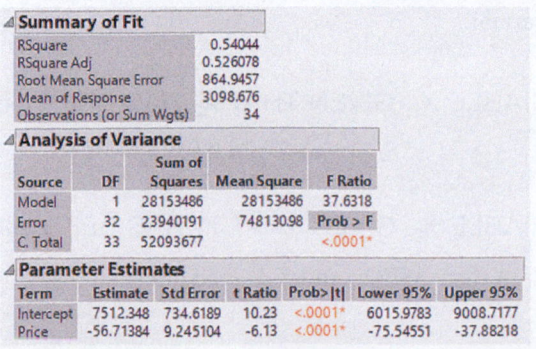

Summary of Fit

RSquare	0.54044
RSquare Adj	0.526078
Root Mean Square Error	864.9457
Mean of Response	3098.676
Observations (or Sum Wgts)	34

Analysis of Variance

Source	DF	Sum of Squares	Mean Square	F Ratio
Model	1	28153486	28153486	37.6318
Error	32	23940191	74813098	Prob > F
C. Total	33	52093677		<.0001*

Parameter Estimates

Term	Estimate	Std Error	t Ratio	Prob>|t|	Lower 95%	Upper 95%
Intercept	7512.348	734.6189	10.23	<.0001*	6015.9783	9008.7177
Price	-56.71384	9.245104	-6.13	<.0001*	-75.54551	-37.88218

From Figure 14.7, $SSR(X_2) = 14,915,814.10$ and from Figure 14.2 on page 539 $SSR(X_1 \text{ and } X_2) = 39,472,730.77$. Then, using Equation (14.10a),

$$SSR(X_1 | X_2) = SSR(X_1 \text{ and } X_2) - SSR(X_2)$$

$$= 39,472,730.77 - 14,915,814.10$$

$$= 24,556,916.67$$

To determine whether X_1 significantly improves the model after X_2 has been included, divide the regression sum of squares into two component parts, as shown in Table 14.7.

TABLE 14.7
ANOVA Table Dividing the Regression Sum of Squares into Components to Determine the Contribution of Variable X_1

Source	Degrees of Freedom	Sum of Squares	Mean Square (Variance)	F
Regression	2	39,472,730.77	19,736,365.39	
$\left\{\begin{array}{c} X_2 \\ X_1 \| X_2 \end{array}\right\}$	$\left\{\begin{array}{c} 1 \\ 1 \end{array}\right\}$	$\left\{\begin{array}{c} 14,915,814.10 \\ 24,556,916.67 \end{array}\right\}$	24,556,916.67	60.32
Error	31	12,620,946.67	407,127.31	
Total	33	52,093,677.44		

The null and alternative hypotheses to test for the contribution of X_1 to the model are:

H_0: Variable X_1 does not significantly improve the model after variable X_2 has been included.
H_1: Variable X_1 significantly improves the model after variable X_2 has been included.

Equation (14.11) defines the partial F test statistic for testing the contribution of an independent variable.

PARTIAL *F* TEST STATISTIC

$$F_{STAT} = \frac{SSR(X_j | \text{All Xs } except\, j)}{MSE} \tag{14.11}$$

The partial F test statistic follows an F distribution with 1 and $n - k - 1$ degrees of freedom.

From Table 14.7,

$$F_{STAT} = \frac{24,556,916.67}{407,127.31} = 60.32$$

The partial F_{STAT} test statistic has 1 and $n - k - 1 = 34 - 2 - 1 = 31$ degrees of freedom. Using a level of significance of 0.05, the critical value from Table E.5 is approximately 4.17 as Figure 14.9 illustrates.

FIGURE 14.9
Testing for the contribution of a regression coefficient to a multiple regression model at the 0.05 level of significance, with 1 and 31 degrees of freedom

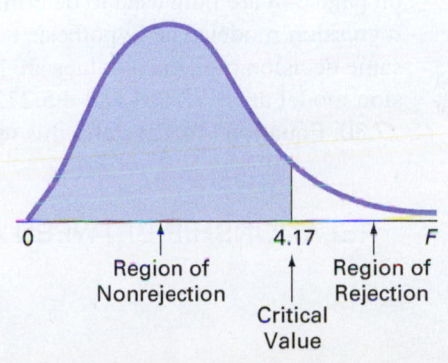

Because the computed partial F_{STAT} test statistic (60.32) is greater than the critical F value, 4.17, you reject H_0. You conclude that the addition of variable X_1, price, significantly improves a regression model that already contains variable X_2, promotional expenses.

To evaluate the contribution of variable X_2, promotional expenses, to a model in which variable X_1, price, has been included, use Equation (14.10b). First, from Figure 14.8 on page 552, observe that $SSR(X_1) = 28,153,486.15$. Second, from Table 14.7, observe that $SSR(X_1 \text{ and } X_2) = 39,472,730.77$. Then, using Equation (14.10b) on page 551,

$$SSR(X_2|X_1) = 39,472,730.77 - 28,153,486.15$$
$$= 11,319,244.62$$

To determine whether X_2 significantly improves a model after X_1 has been included, you can divide the regression sum of squares into two component parts, as shown in Table 14.8.

TABLE 14.8
ANOVA Table Dividing the Regression Sum of Squares into Components to Determine the Contribution of Variable X_2

Source	Degrees of Freedom	Sum of Squares	Mean Square (Variance)	F
Regression	2	39,472,730.77	19,736,365.39	
$\left\{ \begin{array}{c} X_1 \\ X_2\|X_1 \end{array} \right\}$	$\left\{ \begin{array}{c} 1 \\ 1 \end{array} \right\}$	$\left\{ \begin{array}{c} 28,153,486.15 \\ 11,319,244.62 \end{array} \right\}$	11,319,244.62	27.80
Error	31	12,620,946.67	407,127.31	
Total	33	52,093,677.44		

The null and alternative hypotheses to test for the contribution of X_2 to the model are:

H_0: Variable X_2 does not significantly improve the model after variable X_1 has been included.

H_1: Variable X_2 significantly improves the model after variable X_1 has been included.

Using Equation (14.11) and Table 14.8,

$$F_{STAT} = \frac{11,319,244.62}{407,127.31} = 27.80$$

Again, using a 0.05 level of significance, the critical value of F, with 1 and 31 degrees of freedom, is approximately 4.17. Because the computed partial F_{STAT} test statistic (27.80) is greater than this critical value (4.17), you reject H_0. You conclude that the addition of variable X_2, promotional expenses, significantly improves the multiple regression model already containing X_1, price.

By testing for the contribution of each independent variable after the other independent variable has been included in the model, you determine that each of the two independent variables significantly improves the model. Therefore, the multiple regression model should include both X_1, price, and X_2, promotional expenses.

The partial F test statistic that Section 14.4 discusses and the t test statistic of Equation (14.7) on page 548 are both used to determine the contribution of an independent variable to a multiple regression model. The hypothesis tests associated with these two statistics always result in the same decision (i.e., the p-values are identical). The t_{STAT} test statistics for the OmniPower regression model are -7.7664 and $+5.2728$, and the corresponding F_{STAT} test statistics are 60.32 and 27.80. Equation (14.12) states this relationship between t and F.[1]

[1] This relationship holds only when the F_{STAT} statistic has 1 degree of freedom in the numerator.

RELATIONSHIP BETWEEN A t STATISTIC AND AN F STATISTIC

$$t^2_{STAT} = F_{STAT} \qquad \textbf{(14.12)}$$

Coefficients of Partial Determination

Section 14.2 explains that the coefficient of multiple determination, r^2, measures the proportion of the variation in Y that is explained by variation in the independent variables. The **coefficients of partial determination** ($r^2_{Y1.2}$ and $r^2_{Y2.1}$) measure the proportion of the variation in the dependent Y variable that is explained by each independent X variable while controlling for, or holding constant, the other independent variable. These coefficients are different from the *coefficient of multiple determination* that measures the proportion of the variation in the dependent variable explained by the entire set of independent variables included in the model.

Equation (14.13) defines the coefficients of partial determination for a multiple regression model with two independent variables.

> **COEFFICIENTS OF PARTIAL DETERMINATION FOR A MULTIPLE REGRESSION MODEL CONTAINING TWO INDEPENDENT VARIABLES**
>
> $$r^2_{Y1.2} = \frac{SSR(X_1 | X_2)}{SST - SSR(X_1 \text{ and } X_2) + SSR(X_1 | X_2)} \qquad \text{(14.13a)}$$
>
> $$r^2_{Y2.1} = \frac{SSR(X_2 | X_1)}{SST - SSR(X_1 \text{ and } X_2) + SSR(X_2 | X_1)} \qquad \text{(14.13b)}$$
>
> where
>
> $SSR(X_1 | X_2)$ = sum of squares of the contribution of variable X_1 to the regression model, given that variable X_2 has been included in the model
>
> SST = total sum of squares for Y
>
> $SSR(X_1 \text{ and } X_2)$ = regression sum of squares when variables X_1 and X_2 are both included in the multiple regression model
>
> $SSR(X_2 | X_1)$ = sum of squares of the contribution of variable X_2 to the regression model, given that variable X_1 has been included in the model

For the OmniPower sales example, the coefficient of partial determination, $r^2_{Y1.2}$, of variable Y with X_1 while holding X_2 constant is 0.6605. For a given (constant) amount of promotional expenses, 66.05% of the variation in OmniPower sales is explained by the variation in the price.

$$r^2_{Y1.2} = \frac{24{,}556{,}916.67}{52{,}093{,}677.44 - 39{,}472{,}730.77 + 24{,}556{,}916.67}$$
$$= 0.6605$$

For the OmniPower sales example, the coefficient of partial determination, $r^2_{Y2.1}$, of variable Y with X_2 while holding X_1 constant is 0.4728. For a given (constant) price, 47.28% of the variation in OmniPower sales is explained by variation in the amount of promotional expenses.

$$r^2_{Y2.1} = \frac{11{,}319{,}244.62}{52{,}093{,}677.44 - 39{,}472{,}730.77 + 11{,}319{,}244.62}$$
$$= 0.4728$$

Equation (14.14) defines the coefficient of partial determination for the jth variable in a multiple regression model containing several (k) independent variables.

> **COEFFICIENT OF PARTIAL DETERMINATION FOR A MULTIPLE REGRESSION MODEL CONTAINING k INDEPENDENT VARIABLES**
>
> $$r^2_{Yj.(\text{All variables } except\, j)} = \frac{SSR(X_j | \text{All Xs } except\, j)}{SST - SSR(\text{All Xs}) + SSR(X_j | \text{All Xs } except\, j)} \qquad \text{(14.14)}$$

PROBLEMS FOR SECTION 14.5

LEARNING THE BASICS

14.31 The following is the ANOVA summary table for a multiple regression model with two independent variables:

Source	Degrees of Freedom	Sum of Squares	Mean Squares	F
Regression	2	60		
Error	18	120		
Total	20	180		

If $SSR(X_1) = 45$ and $SSR(X_2) = 25$,
a. determine whether there is a significant relationship between Y and each independent variable at the 0.05 level of significance.
b. compute the coefficients of partial determination, $r^2_{Y1.2}$ and $r^2_{Y2.1}$, and interpret their meaning.

14.32 The following is the ANOVA summary table for a multiple regression model with two independent variables:

Source	Degrees of Freedom	Sum of Squares	Mean Squares	F
Regression	2	30		
Error	10	120		
Total	12	150		

If $SSR(X_1) = 20$ and $SSR(X_2) = 15$,
a. determine whether there is a significant relationship between Y and each independent variable at the 0.05 level of significance.
b. compute the coefficients of partial determination, $r^2_{Y1.2}$ and $r^2_{Y2.1}$, and interpret their meaning.

APPLYING THE CONCEPTS

14.33 In Problem 14.5 on page 542, you used alcohol percentage and chlorides to predict wine quality (stored in VinhoVerde). Using the results from that problem,
a. at the 0.05 level of significance, determine whether each independent variable makes a significant contribution to the regression model. On the basis of these results, indicate the most appropriate regression model for this set of data.
b. compute the coefficients of partial determination, $r^2_{Y1.2}$ and $r^2_{Y2.1}$, and interpret their meaning.

✓ SELF TEST **14.34** In Problem 14.4 on page 541, you used efficiency ratio and total risk-based capital to predict ROAA at a community bank (stored in CommunityBanks). Using the results from that problem,
a. at the 0.05 level of significance, determine whether each independent variable makes a significant contribution to the regression model. On the basis of these results, indicate the most appropriate regression model for this set of data.
b. compute the coefficients of partial determination, $r^2_{Y1.2}$ and $r^2_{Y2.1}$, and interpret their meaning.

14.35 In Problem 14.7 on page 542, you used the weekly staff count and remote engineering hours to predict standby hours (stored in Nickels26Weeks). Using the results from that problem,
a. at the 0.05 level of significance, determine whether each independent variable makes a significant contribution to the regression model. On the basis of these results, indicate the most appropriate regression model for this set of data.
b. compute the coefficients of partial determination, $r^2_{Y1.2}$ and $r^2_{Y2.1}$, and interpret their meaning.

14.36 In Problem 14.6 on page 542, you used full-time voluntary turnover (%), and total worldwide revenue ($billions) to predict the number of full-time job openings (stored in BestCompanies). Using the results from that problem,
a. at the 0.05 level of significance, determine whether each independent variable makes a significant contribution to the regression model. On the basis of these results, indicate the most appropriate regression model for this set of data.
b. compute the coefficients of partial determination, $r^2_{Y1.2}$ and $r^2_{Y2.1}$, and interpret their meaning.

14.37 In Problem 14.8 on page 542, you used land area of a property and age of a house to predict the fair market value (stored in GlenCove). Using the results from that problem,
a. at the 0.05 level of significance, determine whether each independent variable makes a significant contribution to the regression model. On the basis of these results, indicate the most appropriate regression model for this set of data.
b. compute the coefficients of partial determination, $r^2_{Y1.2}$ and $r^2_{Y2.1}$, and interpret their meaning.

14.6 Using Dummy Variables and Interaction Terms

The multiple regression models that Sections 14.1 through 14.5 discuss assumed that each independent variable is a numerical variable. For example, in Section 14.1, you used price and promotional expenses, two numerical independent variables, to predict the monthly sales of OmniPower nutrition bars. However, for some models, you need to examine the effect of a categorical independent variable. In such cases, you use a **dummy variable** to include a categorical independent variable in a regression model.

Dummy variables use the numeric values 0 and 1 to recode two categories of a categorical independent variable in a regression model. In general, the number of dummy variables you need to define equals the number of categories – 1. If a categorical independent variable has only two categories, you define one dummy variable, X_d, and use the values 0 and 1 to represent the two categories. When the two categories represent the presence or absence of a characteristic, use 0 to represent the absence and 1 to represent the presence of the characteristic.

For example, to predict the monthly sales of the OmniPower bars, you might include the categorical variable location in the model to explore the possible effect on sales caused by displaying the OmniPower bars in the two different sales locations, a special front location and in the snack aisle, analogous to the locations used in the Chapter 10 Arlingtons scenario to sell streaming media players. In this case for the categorical variable location, the dummy variable, X_d, would have these values:

$$X_d = 0 \text{ if the value is the first category (special front location)}$$

$$X_d = 1 \text{ if the value is the second category (in-aisle location)}$$

To illustrate using dummy variables in regression, consider the business problem that seeks to develop a model for predicting the asking price of houses listed for sale ($thousands) in Silver Spring, Maryland, based on living space in the house (square feet) and whether the house has a fireplace. To include the categorical variable for the presence of a fireplace, the dummy variable X_2 is defined as

$$X_2 = 0 \text{ if the house does not have a fireplace}$$

$$X_2 = 1 \text{ if the house has a fireplace}$$

Assuming that the slope of asking price with living space is the same for houses that have and do not have a fireplace, the multiple regression model is

$$Y_i = \beta_0 + \beta_1 X_{1i} + \beta_2 X_{2i} + \varepsilon_i$$

where

Y_i = asking price, in thousands of dollars, for house i
β_0 = Y intercept
X_{1i} = living space, in thousands of square feet, for house i
β_1 = slope of asking price with living space, holding constant the presence or absence of a fireplace
X_{2i} = dummy variable that represents the absence or presence of a fireplace for house i
β_2 = net effect of the presence of a fireplace on asking price, holding constant the living space
ε_i = random error in Y for house i

Student Tip

The software guides for this Chapter explain how to create dummy variables from categorical variables not already coded with the values 0 and 1.

Figure 14.10 presents the regression results for this model, using a sample of 61 Silver Spring houses listed for sale that was extracted from trulia.com and stored in SilverSpring . In these results, the dummy variable X_2 is labeled as Fireplace.

FIGURE 14.10

Excel, JMP, and Minitab results for the regression model that includes Living Space and Fireplace

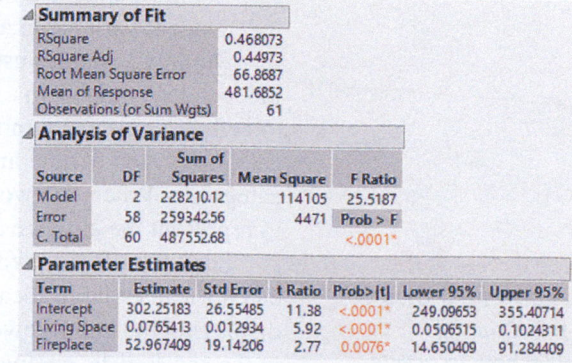

	A	B	C	D	E	F	G
1	Asking Price Analysis						
2							
3	*Regression Statistics*						
4	Multiple R	0.6842					
5	R Square	0.4681					
6	Adjusted R Square	0.4497					
7	Standard Error	66.8687					
8	Observations	61					
9							
10	ANOVA						
11		*df*	*SS*	*MS*	*F*	*Significance F*	
12	Regression	2	228210.1161	114105.0581	25.5187	0.0000	
13	Residual	58	259342.5606	4471.4235			
14	Total	60	487552.6767				
15							
16		*Coefficients*	*Standard Error*	*t Stat*	*P-value*	*Lower 95%*	*Upper 95%*
17	Intercept	302.2518	26.5548	11.3822	0.0000	249.0965	355.4071
18	Living Space	0.0765	0.0129	5.9179	0.0000	0.0507	0.1024
19	Fireplace	52.9674	19.1421	2.7671	0.0076	14.6504	91.2844

Summary of Fit

RSquare	0.468073
RSquare Adj	0.44973
Root Mean Square Error	66.8687
Mean of Response	481.6852
Observations (or Sum Wgts)	61

Analysis of Variance

Source	DF	Sum of Squares	Mean Square	F Ratio
Model	2	228210.12	114105	25.5187
Error	58	259342.56	4471	Prob > F
C. Total	60	487552.68		<.0001*

Parameter Estimates

Term	Estimate	Std Error	t Ratio	Prob>|t|	Lower 95%	Upper 95%
Intercept	302.25183	26.55485	11.38	<.0001*	249.09653	355.40714
Living Space	0.0765413	0.012934	5.92	<.0001*	0.0506515	0.1024311
Fireplace	52.967409	19.14206	2.77	0.0076*	14.650409	91.284409

Regression Analysis: Asking Price versus Living Space, Fireplace

Analysis of Variance

Source	DF	Adj SS	Adj MS	F-Value	P-Value
Regression	2	228210	114105	25.52	0.000
Living Space	1	156598	156598	35.02	0.000
Fireplace	1	34236	34236	7.66	0.008
Error	58	259343	4471		
Total	60	487553			

Model Summary

S	R-sq	R-sq(adj)	R-sq(pred)
66.8687	46.81%	44.97%	41.55%

Coefficients

Term	Coef	SE Coef	T-Value	P-Value	VIF
Constant	302.3	26.6	11.38	0.000	
Living Space	0.0765	0.0129	5.92	0.000	1.04
Fireplace	53.0	19.1	2.77	0.008	1.04

Regression Equation

Asking Price = 302.3 + 0.0765 Living Space + 53.0 Fireplace

From Figure 14.10, the regression equation is

$$\hat{Y}_i = 302.2518 + 0.0765X_{1i} + 52.9674X_{2i}$$

For houses without a fireplace, you substitute $X_2 = 0$ into the regression equation:

$$\hat{Y}_i = 302.2518 + 0.0765X_{1i} + 52.9674X_{2i}$$
$$= 302.2518 + 0.0765X_{1i} + 52.9674(0)$$
$$= 302.2518 + 0.0765X_{1i}$$

For houses with a fireplace, you substitute $X_2 = 1$ into the regression equation:

$$\hat{Y}_i = 302.2518 + 0.0765X_{1i} + 52.9674X_{2i}$$
$$= 302.2518 + 0.0765X_{1i} + 52.9674(1)$$
$$= 355.2192 + 0.0765X_{1i}$$

Table 14.9 summarizes the results of the test for the regression coefficient for living space (b_1) and the regression coefficient for presence or absence of a fireplace (b_2) that appears as part of Figure 14.10, the Silver Spring houses multiple regression results on page 558. Based on these results, you can conclude that living space has a significant effect on mean asking price and the presence of a fireplace also has a significant effect.

TABLE 14.9

t Test for the Slope results and conclusions for the Silver Spring houses multiple regression model

Result	Conclusions
$t_{STAT} = 5.9179$ is greater than 2.0017 p-value $= 0.0000$ is less than the level of significance, $\alpha = 0.05$	1. Reject the null hypothesis H_0. 2. Conclude that strong evidence exists for claiming that living space is related to the dependent Y variable, asking price, taking into account the presence or absence of a fireplace. 3. The probability is 0.0000 that $t_{STAT} < -5.9179$ or $t_{STAT} > 5.9179$
$t_{STAT} = 2.7671$ is greater than 2.0017 p-value $= 0.0076$ is less than the level of significance, $\alpha = 0.05$	1. Reject the null hypothesis H_0. 2. Conclude that strong evidence exists for claiming that presence of a fireplace is related to the dependent Y variable, asking price, taking into account the living space. 3. The probability is 0.0076 that $t_{STAT} < -2.7671$ or $t_{STAT} > 2.7671$.
$r^2 = 0.4681$	46.81% of the variation in the asking price can be explained by variation in living space and whether the house has a fireplace.

Using the net regression coefficients b_1 and b_2, the Table 14.10 net effects table summarizes the effects of adding one square foot of living space (X_1) or the presence of a fireplace (X_2).

TABLE 14.10

Net effects table for the Silver Spring houses multiple regression model

Independent Variable Change	Net Effect
An increase of one square foot in living space	Predict mean asking price to increase by 0.0765 ($000) or $76.50 holding presence of a fireplace constant.
Presence of a fireplace	Predict mean asking price to increase by $52.9674 ($000) or $52,967.40 holding living space constant.

studentTIP

Remember that an independent variable does not always make a significant contribution to a regression model.

In some situations, the categorical independent variable has more than two categories. When this occurs, two or more dummy variables are needed. Example 14.3 on page 560 illustrates such a situation.

EXAMPLE 14.3

Modeling a Three-
Level Categorical
Variable

Define a multiple regression model to predict the asking price of houses as the dependent variable, as was done in the previous example for the Silver Spring houses, and use Living Space and House Type as independent variables. House Type is a three-level categorical variable with the values colonial, ranch, and other.

SOLUTION To model the three-level categorical variable House Type, two dummy variables, X_1 and X_2, are needed:

$$X_{1i} = 1 \text{ if the House Type is colonial for house } i; 0 \text{ otherwise}$$

$$X_{2i} = 1 \text{ if the House Type is ranch for house } i; 0 \text{ otherwise}$$

Thus, if house i is a colonial then $X_{1i} = 1$ and $X_{2i} = 0$; if house i is a ranch, then $X_{1i} = 0$ and $X_{2i} = 1$; and if house i is other (neither colonial nor ranch), then $X_{1i} = X_{2i} = 0$. Thus, House Type other becomes the baseline category to which the effect of being a colonial or ranch House Type is compared. A third independent variable is used for Living Space:

$$X_{3i} = \text{Living Space for observation } i$$

Thus, the regression model for this example is

$$Y_i = \beta_0 + \beta_1 X_{1i} + \beta_2 X_{2i} + \beta_3 X_{3i} + \varepsilon_i$$

where

Y_i = Asking Price for house i

β_0 = Y intercept

β_1 = slope of Asking Price with Living Space, holding the House Type constant

β_2 = difference between the predicted Asking Price of House Type colonial and the predicted Asking Price of House Type other holding Living Space constant

β_3 = difference between the predicted Asking Price of House Type ranch and the predicted Asking Price of House Type other holding Living Space constant

ε_i = random error in Y for observation i

Interactions

In the regression models discussed so far, the effect an independent variable has on the dependent variable has been assumed to be independent of the other independent variables in the model. An **interaction** occurs if the effect of an independent variable on the dependent variable changes according to the *value* of a second independent variable. For example, it is possible that advertising will have a large effect on the sales of a product when the price of a product is low. However, if the price of the product is too high, increases in advertising will not dramatically change sales. In this case, price and advertising are said to interact. In other words, you cannot make general statements about the effect of advertising on sales. The effect that advertising has on sales is *dependent* on the price. You use an **interaction term** (sometimes referred to as a **cross-product term**) to model an interaction effect in a regression model.

To illustrate the concept of interaction and use of an interaction term, return to the example concerning the asking price of homes discussed on pages 557–559. In the regression model, you assumed that the effect that Living Space has on the Asking Price is independent of whether the house has a fireplace. In other words, you assumed that the slope of Asking Price with Living Space is the same for all houses, regardless of whether the house contains a fireplace. If these two slopes are different, an interaction exists between the Living Space and the presence or absence of a fireplace.

To evaluate whether an interaction exists, you first define an interaction term that is the product of the independent variable X_1 (Living Space) and the dummy variable X_2 (Fireplace). You then test whether this interaction variable makes a significant contribution to the regression model. If the interaction is significant, you cannot use the original model for prediction. For these data you define the following:

$$X_3 = X_1 \times X_2$$

Figure 14.11 presents regression results for the model that includes the Living Space, X_1, the presence of a fireplace, X_2, and the interaction of X_1 and X_2 (defined as X_3 and labeled Living Space*Fireplace).

FIGURE 14.11

Excel, JMP, and Minitab results for the regression model that includes Living Space, Fireplace, and interaction of Living Space and Fireplace

▲	A	B	C	D	E	F	G
1	Asking Price Analysis						
2							
3	Regression Statistics						
4	Multiple R	0.6849					
5	R Square	0.4691					
6	Adjusted R Square	0.4411					
7	Standard Error	67.3907					
8	Observations	61					
9							
10	ANOVA						
11		df	SS	MS	F	Significance F	
12	Regression	3	228686.7174	76228.9058	16.7849	0.0000	
13	Residual	57	258865.9593	4541.5081			
14	Total	60	487552.6767				
15							
16		Coefficients	Standard Error	t Stat	P-value	Lower 95%	Upper 95%
17	Intercept	316.2350	50.7878	6.2266	0.0000	214.5341	417.9359
18	Living Space	0.0681	0.0292	2.3319	0.0233	0.0096	0.1265
19	Fireplace	34.8926	59.0359	0.5910	0.5568	-83.3248	153.1101
20	Living Space*Fireplace	0.0106	0.0326	0.3239	0.7472	-0.0548	0.0759

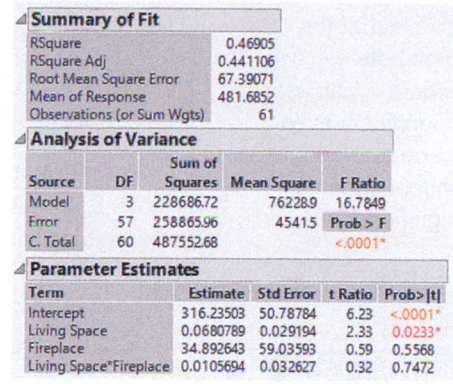

Summary of Fit

RSquare	0.46905
RSquare Adj	0.441106
Root Mean Square Error	67.39071
Mean of Response	481.6852
Observations (or Sum Wgts)	61

Analysis of Variance

Source	DF	Sum of Squares	Mean Square	F Ratio
Model	3	228686.72	76228.9	16.7849
Error	57	258865.96	4541.5	Prob > F
C. Total	60	487552.68		<.0001*

Parameter Estimates

Term	Estimate	Std Error	t Ratio	Prob>|t|
Intercept	316.23503	50.78784	6.23	<.0001*
Living Space	0.0680789	0.029194	2.33	0.0233*
Fireplace	34.892643	59.03593	0.59	0.5568
Living Space*Fireplace	0.0105694	0.032627	0.32	0.7472

Regression Analysis: Asking Price versus Living Space, Fireplace

Analysis of Variance

Source	DF	Adj SS	Adj MS	F-Value	P-Value
Regression	3	228687	76228.9	16.78	0.000
Living Space	1	24696	24696.4	5.44	0.023
Fireplace	1	1586	1586.5	0.35	0.557
Living Space*Fireplace	1	477	476.6	0.10	0.747
Error	57	258866	4541.5		
Total	60	487553			

Model Summary

S	R-sq	R-sq(adj)	R-sq(pred)
67.3907	46.91%	44.11%	38.95%

Coefficients

Term	Coef	SE Coef	T-Value	P-Value	VIF
Constant	316.2	50.8	6.23	0.000	
Living Space	0.0681	0.0292	2.33	0.023	5.22
Fireplace	34.9	59.0	0.59	0.557	9.74
Living Space*Fireplace	0.0106	0.0326	0.32	0.747	16.23

Regression Equation

Asking Price = 316.2 + 0.0681 Living Space + 34.9 Fireplace + 0.0106 Living Space*Fireplace

To test for the existence of an interaction, you use the null hypothesis:

$$H_0: \beta_3 = 0$$

versus the alternative hypothesis:

$$H_1: \beta_3 \neq 0.$$

Table 14.10 summarizes the results of the test for the interaction for living space (b_1) and presence of a fireplace (b_2) that appears as part of Figure 14.11. Based on these conclusions, you can conclude that interaction of living space (b_1) and presence of a fireplace (b_2) is not significant. The interaction term should not be included in the regression model to predict asking price.

TABLE 14.10

t Test for the interaction for living space and presence of a fireplace results and conclusions

Result	Conclusions
$t_{STAT} = 0.3239$ is less than 2.0025 *p*-value $= 0.7472$ is greater than the level of significance, $\alpha = 0.05$	1. Do not reject the null hypothesis H_0. 2. Conclude that there is insufficient evidence of an interaction of living space (b_1) and presence of a fireplace (b_2). 3. The probability is 0.7472 that $t_{STAT} < -0.3239$ or $t_{STAT} > 0.3239$.

student TIP

It is possible that the interaction between two independent variables will be significant even though one of the independent variables is not significant.

Regression models can have several numerical independent variables along with a dummy variable. Example 14.4 illustrates a regression model in which there are two numerical independent variables and a categorical independent variable.

EXAMPLE 14.4

Studying a Regression Model That Contains a Dummy Variable and Two Numerical Independent Variables

The business problem facing a real estate developer involves predicting heating oil consumption in single-family houses. The independent variables considered are atmospheric temperature (°F), X_1, Insulation, the amount of attic insulation, inches, X_2 and Ranch-style, whether the house is ranch-style, X_3. Data are collected from a sample of 15 single-family houses and stored in HeatingOil. Develop and analyze an appropriate regression model, using these three independent variables X_1, X_2, and X_3.

SOLUTION Define X_3, Ranch-style, a dummy variable for ranch-style house, as follows:

$$X_3 = 0 \text{ if not a Ranch-style house}$$

$$X_3 = 1 \text{ if a Ranch-style house}$$

Assuming that the slope between heating oil consumption and temperature, X_1, and between heating oil consumption and Insulation, X_2, is the same for both styles of houses, the regression model is

$$Y_i = \beta_0 + \beta_1 X_{1i} + \beta_2 X_{2i} + \beta_3 X_{3i} + \varepsilon_i$$

where

Y_i = monthly Heating Oil Consumption, in gallons, for house i

β_0 = Y intercept

β_1 = slope of Heating Oil Consumption with Temperature, holding constant the effect of Insulation and Ranch-style

β_2 = slope of Heating Oil Consumption with Insulation holding constant the effect of Temperature and Ranch-style

β_3 = incremental effect of Heating Oil Consumption the presence of a ranch-style house, holding constant the effect of Temperature and Insulation

ε_i = random error in Y for house i

Figure 14.12 presents results for this regression model.

▶*(continued)*

FIGURE 14.12

Excel, JMP, and Minitab results for the regression model that includes Temperature, Insulation, and Style for the heating oil data

	A	B	C	D	E	F	G
1	Heating Oil Consumption Analysis						
2							
3	Regression Statistics						
4	Multiple R	0.9942					
5	R Square	0.9884					
6	Adjusted R Square	0.9853					
7	Standard Error	15.7489					
8	Observations	15					
9							
10	ANOVA						
11		df	SS	MS	F	Significance F	
12	Regression	3	233406.9094	77802.3031	313.6822	0.0000	
13	Residual	11	2728.3200	248.0291			
14	Total	14	236135.2293				
15							
16		Coefficients	Standard Error	t Stat	P-value	Lower 95%	Upper 95%
17	Intercept	592.5401	14.3370	41.3295	0.0000	560.9846	624.0956
18	Temperature	-5.5251	0.2044	-27.0267	0.0000	-5.9751	-5.0752
19	Insulation	-21.3761	1.4480	-14.7623	0.0000	-24.5632	-18.1891
20	Ranch-style	-38.9727	8.3584	-4.6627	0.0007	-57.3695	-20.5759

Summary of Fit

RSquare	0.988446
RSquare Adj	0.985295
Root Mean Square Error	15.74894
Mean of Response	216.4933
Observations (or Sum Wgts)	15

Analysis of Variance

Source	DF	Sum of Squares	Mean Square	F Ratio
Model	3	233406.91	77802.3	313.6822
Error	11	2728.32	248.0	Prob > F
C. Total	14	236135.23		<.0001*

Parameter Estimates

Term	Estimate	Std Error	t Ratio	Prob>|t|	Lower 95%	Upper 95%
Intercept	592.54012	14.33698	41.33	<.0001*	560.98468	624.09561
Temperature	-5.525101	0.204431	-27.03	<.0001*	-5.975051	-5.075151
Insulation	-21.37613	1.448019	-14.76	<.0001*	-24.5632	-18.18906
Ranch-style	-38.97267	8.358437	-4.66	0.0007*	-57.36946	-20.57587

Regression Analysis: Gallons versus Temperature, ... lation, Ranch-style

Analysis of Variance

Source	DF	Adj SS	Adj MS	F-Value	P-Value
Regression	3	233407	77802	313.68	0.000
Temperature	1	181171	181171	730.44	0.000
Insulation	1	54052	54052	217.93	0.000
Ranch-style	1	5392	5392	21.74	0.001
Error	11	2728	248		
Total	14	236135			

Model Summary

S	R-sq	R-sq(adj)	R-sq(pred)
15.7489	98.84%	98.53%	97.63%

Coefficients

Term	Coef	SE Coef	T-Value	P-Value	VIF
Constant	592.5	14.3	41.33	0.000	
Temperature	-5.525	0.204	-27.03	0.000	1.01
Insulation	-21.38	1.45	-14.76	0.000	1.04
Ranch-style	-38.97	8.36	-4.66	0.001	1.05

Regression Equation

Gallons = 592.5 - 5.525 Temperature - 21.38 Insulation - 38.97 Ranch-style

From the results in Figure 14.12, the regression equation is

$$\hat{Y}_i = 592.5401 - 5.5251X_{1i} - 21.3761X_{2i} - 38.9727X_{3i}$$

For houses that are not ranch style, because $X_3 = 0$, the regression equation reduces to

$$\hat{Y}_i = 592.5401 - 5.5251X_{1i} - 21.3761X_{2i}$$

For houses that are ranch style, because $X_3 = 1$, the regression equation reduces to

$$\hat{Y}_i = 553.5674 - 5.5251X_{1i} - 21.3761X_{2i}$$

Table 14.11 on page 564 summarizes the results of the tests for the regression coefficient for Temperature (b_1), Insulation (b_2), and the regression coefficient for Ranch-style, the presence or absence of a ranch-style house (b_3) that appears as part of Figure 14.12. Based on these results, you can conclude that Temperature, Insulation, and Ranch-style each has a significant effect on mean monthly heating oil consumption.

►(continued)

TABLE 14.11

t Test for the Slope Results and Conclusions for the Example 14.4 Multiple Regression Model

Result	Conclusions
$t_{STAT} = -27.0267$ is less than -2.2010 *p*-value $= 0.0000$ is less than the level of significance, $\alpha = 0.05$	1. Reject the null hypothesis H_0. 2. Conclude that strong evidence exists for claiming that Temperature is related to the dependent *Y* variable, Heating Oil Consumption, holding Insulation and Ranch-style constant. 3. The probability is 0.0000 that $t_{STAT} < -27.0267$ or $t_{STAT} > 27.0267$
$t_{STAT} = -14.7623$ is less than -2.2010 *p*-value $= 0.0000$ is less than the level of significance, $\alpha = 0.05$	1. Reject the null hypothesis H_0. 2. Conclude that strong evidence exists for claiming that Insulation is related to the dependent *Y* variable, Heating Oil Consumption, holding Temperature and Ranch-style constant. 3. The probability is 0.0000 that $t_{STAT} < -14.7623$ or $t_{STAT} > 14.7623$
$t_{STAT} = -4.6627$ is less than -2.2010 *p*-value $= 0.0007$ is less than the level of significance, $\alpha = 0.05$	1. Reject the null hypothesis H_0. 2. Conclude that strong evidence exists for claiming that whether the house is a ranch-style is related to the dependent *Y* variable, Heating Oil Consumption, holding Temperature and Attic Insulation Amount constant. 3. The probability is 0.0007 that $t_{STAT} < -4.6627$ or $t_{STAT} > 4.6627$
$r^2 = 0.9884$	98.84% of the variation in the heating oil consumption can be explained by variation in Temperature, Attic Insulation Amount, and whether the house is a ranch-style.

Using the net regression coefficients b_1, b_2, and b_3, the Table 14.12 net effect effects summarizes the effects of an increase one degree of Temperature (X_1), adding one inch to the Attic Insulation Amount (X_2), and whether the house is a ranch-style (X_3). If the cost of adding one inch in attic insulation was equivalent to about 21 gallons of heating oil, a home owner could predict that the new insulation would "pay for itself" by lowering heating oil consumption in about one month.

TABLE 14.12

Net Effects Table for the Example 14.4 Multiple Regression Model

Independent Variable Change	Net Effect
An increase of one degree in temperature (°F)	Predict mean monthly heating oil consumption to decrease by 5.5251 gallons holding Attic Insulation Amount and Ranch-style constant.
An increase of one inch in attic insulation	Predict mean monthly heating oil consumption to decrease by 21.3761 gallons for each additional inch of attic insulation holding Temperature and Ranch-style constant.
Presence of a ranch-style house	Predict mean monthly heating oil consumption to decrease by 38.9727 gallons for a ranch style house holding Temperature and Attic Insulation Amount constant.

Before you can use the model in Example 14.4, you need to determine whether the independent variables interact with each other. In Example 14.5, three interaction terms are added to the model.

EXAMPLE 14.5

Evaluating a Regression Model with Several Interactions

For the Example 14.4 data, determine whether adding interaction terms makes a significant contribution to the regression model.

SOLUTION To evaluate possible interactions between the independent variables, three interaction terms are constructed as follows: $X_4 = X_1 \times X_2$, $X_5 = X_1 \times X_3$, and $X_6 = X_2 \times X_3$. The regression model is now

$$Y_i = \beta_0 + \beta_1 X_{1i} + \beta_2 X_{2i} + \beta_3 X_{3i} + \beta_4 X_{4i} + \beta_5 X_{5i} + \beta_6 X_{6i} + \varepsilon_i$$

where X_1 is Temperature, X_2 is Insulation, X_3 is the dummy variable Ranch-style, X_4 is the interaction between Temperature and Insulation, X_5 is the interaction between Temperature and Ranch-style, and X_6 is the interaction between Insulation and Ranch-style. Figure 14.13 presents the results for this regression model.

FIGURE 14.13

Excel, Minitab, and JMP results for the regression model that includes Temperature, X_1; Insulation, X_2; the dummy variable Ranch-style, X_3; the interaction of Temperature and Insulation, X_4; the interaction of Temperature and Ranch-style, X_5; and the interaction of Insulation and Ranch-style, X_6

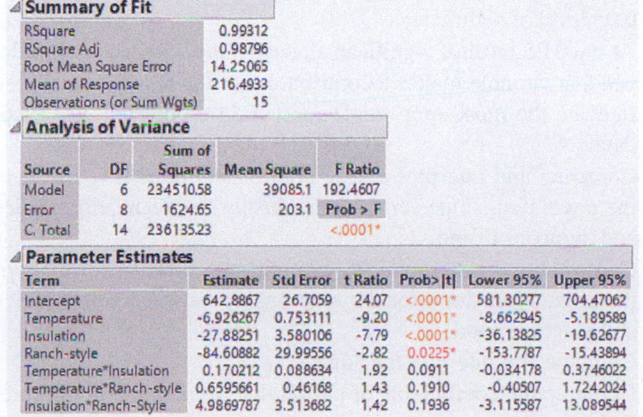

To test whether the three interactions significantly improve the regression model, you use the partial F test. The null and alternative hypotheses are

$$H_0: \beta_4 = \beta_5 = \beta_6 = 0 \text{ (There are no interactions among } X_1, X_2, \text{ and } X_3.)$$
$$H_1: \beta_4 \neq 0 \text{ and/or } \beta_5 \neq 0 \text{ and/or } \beta_6 \neq 0 \text{ (} X_1 \text{ interacts with } X_2,$$
$$\text{and/or } X_1 \text{ interacts with } X_3, \text{ and/or } X_2 \text{ interacts with } X_3.)$$

From Figure 14.13,

▶(*continued*)

$$SSR(X_1, X_2, X_3, X_4, X_5, X_6) = 234,510.5818 \text{ with 6 degrees of freedom}$$

and from Figure 14.12 on page 563, $SSR(X_1, X_2, X_3) = 233,406.9094$ with 3 degrees of freedom. Thus,

$$SSR(X_1, X_2, X_3, X_4, X_5, X_6) - SSR(X_1, X_2, X_3) = 234,510.5818 - 233,406.9094 = 1,103.6724$$

[2]In general, if a model has several independent variables and you want to test whether additional independent variables contribute to the model, the numerator of the F test is SSR (for all independent variables) minus SSR (for the initial set of variables) divided by the number of independent variables whose contribution is being tested.

The difference in degrees of freedom is $6 - 3 = 3$.

To use the partial F test for the simultaneous contribution of three variables to a model, you use an extension of Equation (14.11) on page 554.[2] The partial F_{STAT} test statistic is

$$F_{STAT} = \frac{[SSR(X_1, X_2, X_3, X_4, X_5, X_6) - SSR(X_1, X_2, X_3)]/3}{MSE(X_1, X_2, X_3, X_4, X_5, X_6)} = \frac{1,103.6724/3}{203.0809} = 1.8115$$

You compare the computed F_{STAT} test statistic to the critical F value for 3 and 8 degrees of freedom. Using a level of significance of 0.05, the critical F value from Table E.5 is 4.07. Because $F_{STAT} = 1.8115 < 4.07$, you conclude that the interactions do not make a significant contribution to the model, given that the model already includes Temperature, X_1; Insulation, X_2; and whether the house is ranch style, X_3. Therefore, you state the multiple regression model using X_1, X_2, and X_3 without any interaction terms is the better model. Had you rejected this null hypothesis, you would then have tested the contribution of each interaction separately in order to determine which interaction terms to include in the model.

PROBLEMS FOR SECTION 14.6

LEARNING THE BASICS

14.38 Suppose X_1 is a numerical variable and X_2 is a dummy variable with two categories and the regression equation for a sample of $n = 20$ is

$$\hat{Y}_i = 6 + 4X_{1i} + 2X_{2i}$$

a. Interpret the regression coefficient associated with variable X_1.
b. Interpret the regression coefficient associated with variable X_2.
c. Suppose that the t_{STAT} test statistic for testing the contribution of variable X_2 is 3.27. At the 0.05 level of significance, is there evidence that variable X_2 makes a significant contribution to the model?

APPLYING THE CONCEPTS

14.39 The chair of the accounting department plans to develop a regression model to predict the grade point average in accounting for those students who are graduating and have completed the accounting major, based on a student's SAT score and whether the student received a grade of B or higher in the introductory statistics course (0 = no and 1 = yes).
a. Explain the steps involved in developing a regression model for these data. Be sure to indicate the particular models you need to evaluate and compare.
b. Suppose the regression coefficient for the variable whether the student received a grade of B or higher in the introductory statistics course is +0.30. How do you interpret this result?

14.40 A real estate association in a suburban community would like to study the relationship between the size of a single-family house (as measured by the number of rooms) and the selling price of the house (in $thousands). Two different neighborhoods are included in the study, one on the east side of the community (=0) and the other on the west side (=1). A random sample of 20 houses was selected, with the results stored in Neighbor . For (a) through (k), do not include an interaction term.

a. State the multiple regression equation that predicts the selling price, based on the number of rooms and the neighborhood.
b. Interpret the regression coefficients in (a).
c. Predict the mean selling price for a house with nine rooms that is located in an east-side neighborhood. Construct a 95% confidence interval estimate and a 95% prediction interval.
d. Perform a residual analysis on the model and determine whether the regression assumptions are valid.
e. Is there a significant relationship between selling price and the two independent variables (rooms and neighborhood) at the 0.05 level of significance?
f. At the 0.05 level of significance, determine whether each independent variable makes a contribution to the regression model. Indicate the most appropriate regression model for this set of data.
g. Construct and interpret a 95% confidence interval estimate of the population slope for the relationship between selling price and number of rooms.
h. Construct and interpret a 95% confidence interval estimate of the population slope for the relationship between selling price and neighborhood.
i. Compute and interpret the adjusted r^2.
j. Compute the coefficients of partial determination and interpret their meaning.
k. What assumption do you need to make about the slope of selling price with number of rooms?
l. Add an interaction term to the model and, at the 0.05 level of significance, determine whether it makes a significant contribution to the model.
m. On the basis of the results of (f) and (l), which model is most appropriate? Explain.
n. What conclusions can the real estate association reach about the effect of the number of rooms and neighborhood on the selling price of homes?

14.41 In Problem 14.5 on page 542, you developed a multiple regression model to predict wine quality for red wines. Now, you wish to determine whether there is an effect on wine quality due to whether the wine is white (0) or red (1). These data are organized and stored in RedandWhite . Develop a multiple regression model to predict wine quality based on the percentage of alcohol and the type of wine.

For (a) through (m), do not include an interaction term.
a. State the multiple regression equation that predicts wine quality based on the percentage of alcohol and the type of wine.
b. Interpret the regression coefficients in (a).
c. Predict the mean quality for a red wine that has 10% alcohol. Construct a 95% confidence interval estimate and a 95% prediction interval.
d. Perform a residual analysis on the model and determine whether the regression assumptions are valid.
e. Is there a significant relationship between wine quality and the two independent variables (percentage of alcohol and the type of wine) at the 0.05 level of significance?
f. At the 0.05 level of significance, determine whether each independent variable makes a contribution to the regression model. Indicate the most appropriate regression model for this set of data.
g. Construct and interpret 95% confidence interval estimates of the population slope for the relationship between wine quality and the percentage of alcohol and between wine quality and the type of wine.
h. Compare the slope in (b) with the slope for the simple linear regression model of Problem 13.4 on page 493. Explain the difference in the results.
i. Compute and interpret the meaning of the coefficient of multiple determination, r^2.
j. Compute and interpret the adjusted r^2.
k. Compare r^2 with the r^2 value computed in Problem 13.16 (a) on page 499.
l. Compute the coefficients of partial determination and interpret their meaning.
m. What assumption about the slope of type of wine with wine quality do you need to make in this problem?
n. Add an interaction term to the model and, at the 0.05 level of significance, determine whether it makes a significant contribution to the model.
o. On the basis of the results of (f) and (n), which model is most appropriate? Explain.
p. What conclusions can you reach concerning the effect of alcohol percentage and type of wine on wine quality?

14.42 In mining engineering, holes are often drilled through rock, using drill bits. As a drill hole gets deeper, additional rods are added to the drill bit to enable additional drilling to take place. It is expected that drilling time increases with depth. This increased drilling time could be caused by several factors, including the mass of the drill rods that are strung together. The business problem relates to whether drilling is faster using dry drilling holes or wet drilling holes. Using dry drilling holes involves forcing compressed air down the drill rods to flush the cuttings and drive the hammer. Using wet drilling holes involves forcing water rather than air down the hole. Data have been collected from a sample of 50 drill holes that contains measurements of the time to drill each additional 5 feet (in minutes), the depth (in feet), and whether the hole was a dry drilling hole or a wet drilling hole. The data are organized and stored in Drill .

Source: Data extracted from R. Penner and D. G. Watts, "Mining Information," *The American Statistician*, 45, 1991, pp. 4–9.

Develop a model to predict additional drilling time, based on depth and type of drilling hole (dry or wet). For (a) through (k) do not include an interaction term.
a. State the multiple regression equation.
b. Interpret the regression coefficients in (a).
c. Predict the mean additional drilling time for a dry drilling hole at a depth of 100 feet. Construct a 95% confidence interval estimate and a 95% prediction interval.
d. Perform a residual analysis on the model and determine whether the regression assumptions are valid.
e. Is there a significant relationship between additional drilling time and the two independent variables (depth and type of drilling hole) at the 0.05 level of significance?
f. At the 0.05 level of significance, determine whether each independent variable makes a contribution to the regression model. Indicate the most appropriate regression model for this set of data.
g. Construct a 95% confidence interval estimate of the population slope for the relationship between additional drilling time and depth.
h. Construct a 95% confidence interval estimate of the population slope for the relationship between additional drilling time and the type of hole drilled.
i. Compute and interpret the adjusted r^2.
j. Compute the coefficients of partial determination and interpret their meaning.
k. What assumption do you need to make about the slope of additional drilling time with depth?
l. Add an interaction term to the model and, at the 0.05 level of significance, determine whether it makes a significant contribution to the model.
m. On the basis of the results of (f) and (l), which model is most appropriate? Explain.
n. What conclusions can you reach concerning the effect of depth and type of drilling hole on drilling time?

14.43 The owner of a moving company typically has his most experienced manager predict the total number of labor hours that will be required to complete an upcoming move. This approach has proved useful in the past, but the owner has the business objective of developing a more accurate method of predicting labor hours. In a preliminary effort to provide a more accurate method, the owner has decided to use the number of cubic feet moved and whether there is an elevator in the apartment building as the independent variables and has collected data for 36 moves in which the origin and destination were within the borough of Manhattan in New York City and the travel time was an insignificant portion of the hours worked. The data are organized and stored in Moving . For (a) through (k), do not include an interaction term.
a. State the multiple regression equation for predicting labor hours, using the number of cubic feet moved and whether there is an elevator.
b. Interpret the regression coefficients in (a).
c. Predict the mean labor hours for moving 500 cubic feet in an apartment building that has an elevator and construct a 95% confidence interval estimate and a 95% prediction interval.
d. Perform a residual analysis on the model and determine whether the regression assumptions are valid.
e. Is there a significant relationship between labor hours and the two independent variables (cubic feet moved and whether there is an elevator in the apartment building) at the 0.05 level of significance?

f. At the 0.05 level of significance, determine whether each independent variable makes a contribution to the regression model. Indicate the most appropriate regression model for this set of data.

g. Construct a 95% confidence interval estimate of the population slope for the relationship between labor hours and cubic feet moved.

h. Construct a 95% confidence interval estimate for the relationship between labor hours and the presence of an elevator.

i. Compute and interpret the adjusted r^2.

j. Compute the coefficients of partial determination and interpret their meaning.

k. What assumption do you need to make about the slope of labor hours with cubic feet moved?

l. Add an interaction term to the model, and at the 0.05 level of significance, determine whether it makes a significant contribution to the model.

m. On the basis of the results of (f) and (l), which model is most appropriate? Explain.

n. What conclusions can you reach concerning the effect of the number of cubic feet moved and whether there is an elevator on labor hours?

✓ SELF TEST **14.44** In Problem 14.4 on page 541, you used efficiency ratio and total risk-based capital to predict ROAA at a community bank (stored in CommunityBanks). Develop a regression model to predict ROAA that includes efficiency ratio, total risk-based capital, and the interaction of efficiency ratio and total risk-based capital.

a. At the 0.05 level of significance, is there evidence that the interaction term makes a significant contribution to the model?

b. Which regression model is more appropriate, the one used in (a) or the one used in Problem 14.4? Explain.

14.45 Zagat's publishes restaurant ratings for various locations in the United States. The file Restaurants contains the Zagat rating for food, décor, service, and cost per person for a sample of 50 center city restaurants and 50 metro area restaurants.

Source: Data extracted from *Zagat Survey 2016, New York City Restaurants.*

Develop a regression model to predict the cost per person, based on a variable that represents the sum of the ratings for food, décor, and service and a dummy variable concerning location (center city versus metro area). For (a) through (m), do not include an interaction term.

a. State the multiple regression equation.

b. Interpret the regression coefficients in (a).

c. Predict the mean cost for a center city restaurant with a summated rating of 60 and construct a 95% confidence interval estimate and a 95% prediction interval.

d. Perform a residual analysis on the model and determine whether the regression assumptions are satisfied.

e. Is there a significant relationship between price and the two independent variables (summated rating and location) at the 0.05 level of significance?

f. At the 0.05 level of significance, determine whether each independent variable makes a contribution to the regression model. Indicate the most appropriate regression model for this set of data.

g. Construct a 95% confidence interval estimate of the population slope for the relationship between cost and summated rating.

h. Compare the slope in (b) with the slope for the simple linear regression model of Problem 13.5 on page 493. Explain the difference in the results.

i. Compute and interpret the meaning of the coefficient of multiple determination.

j. Compute and interpret the adjusted r^2.

k. Compare r^2 with the r^2 value computed in Problem 13.17 (b) on page 499.

l. Compute the coefficients of partial determination and interpret their meaning.

m. What assumption about the slope of cost with summated rating do you need to make in this problem?

n. Add an interaction term to the model and, at the 0.05 level of significance, determine whether it makes a significant contribution to the model.

o. On the basis of the results of (f) and (n), which model is most appropriate? Explain.

p. What conclusions can you reach about the effect of the summated rating and the location of the restaurant on the cost of a meal?

14.46 In Problem 14.6 on page 542, you used full-time voluntary turnover (%), and total worldwide revenue ($billions) to predict number of full-time job openings (stored in BestCompanies). Develop a regression model to predict the number of full-time job openings that includes full-time voluntary turnover, total worldwide revenue, and the interaction of full-time voluntary turnover and total worldwide revenue.

a. At the 0.05 level of significance, is there evidence that the interaction term makes a significant contribution to the model?

b. Which regression model is more appropriate, the one used in this problem or the one used in Problem 14.6? Explain.

14.47 In Problem 14.5 on page 542, the percentage of alcohol and chlorides were used to predict the quality of red wines (stored in VinhoVerde). Develop a regression model that includes the percentage of alcohol, the chlorides, and the interaction of the percentage of alcohol and the chlorides to predict wine quality.

a. At the 0.05 level of significance, is there evidence that the interaction term makes a significant contribution to the model?

b. Which regression model is more appropriate, the one used in this problem or the one used in Problem 14.5? Explain.

14.48 In Problem 14.7 on page 542, you used weekly staff count and remote hours to predict standby hours (stored in Nickels26Weeks). Develop a regression model to predict standby hours that includes total staff present, remote hours, and the interaction of total staff present and remote hours.

a. At the 0.05 level of significance, is there evidence that the interaction term makes a significant contribution to the model?

b. Which regression model is more appropriate, the one used in this problem or the one used in Problem 14.7? Explain.

14.49 The director of a training program for a large insurance company has the business objective of determining which training method is best for training underwriters. The three methods to be evaluated are classroom, online, and courseware app. The 30 trainees are divided into three randomly assigned groups of 10. Before the start of the training, each trainee is given a proficiency exam that measures mathematics and computer skills. At the end of the training, all students take the same end-of-training exam. The results are organized and stored in Underwriting .

Develop a multiple regression model to predict the score on the end-of-training exam, based on the score on the proficiency exam and the method of training used. For (a) through (k), do not include an interaction term.

a. State the multiple regression equation.
b. Interpret the regression coefficients in (a).
c. Predict the mean end-of-training exam score for a student with a proficiency exam score of 100 who had courseware app-based training.
d. Perform a residual analysis on the model and determine whether the regression assumptions are valid.
e. Is there a significant relationship between the end-of-training exam score and the independent variables (proficiency score and training method) at the 0.05 level of significance?
f. At the 0.05 level of significance, determine whether each independent variable makes a contribution to the regression model. Indicate the most appropriate regression model for this set of data.

g. Construct and interpret a 95% confidence interval estimate of the population slope for the relationship between the end-of-training exam score and the proficiency exam score.
h. Construct and interpret 95% confidence interval estimates of the population slope for the relationship between the end-of-training exam score and type of training method.
i. Compute and interpret the adjusted r^2.
j. Compute the coefficients of partial determination and interpret their meaning.
k. What assumption about the slope of proficiency score with end-of-training exam score do you need to make in this problem?
l. Add interaction terms to the model and, at the 0.05 level of significance, determine whether any interaction terms make a significant contribution to the model.
m. On the basis of the results of (f) and (l), which model is most appropriate? Explain.

14.7 Logistic Regression

The discussion of the simple linear regression model in Chapter 13 and the multiple regression models in Sections 14.1 through 14.6 only considered *numerical* dependent variables. However, in many applications, the dependent variable is a *categorical* variable that takes on one of only two possible values, such as a customer purchases a product or a customer does not purchase a product. Using a categorical dependent variable violates the normality assumption of the least-squares method and can also result in predicted Y values that are impossible.

An alternative approach to least-squares regression originally applied to survival data in the health sciences (see reference 5), **logistic regression**, enables you to use regression models to predict the probability of a particular categorical response for a given set of independent variables. The logistic regression model uses the **odds ratio**, which represents the probability of an event of interest compared with the probability of not having an event of interest. Equation (14.15) defines the odds ratio.

ODDS RATIO

$$\text{Odds ratio} = \frac{\text{probability of an event of interest}}{1 - \text{probability of an event of interest}} \tag{14.15}$$

Using Equation (14.15), if the probability of an event of interest is 0.50, the odds ratio is

$$\text{Odds ratio} = \frac{0.50}{1 - 0.50} = 1.0, \text{ or 1 to 1}$$

If the probability of an event of interest is 0.75, the odds ratio is

$$\text{Odds ratio} = \frac{0.75}{1 - 0.75} = 3.0, \text{ or 3 to 1}$$

The logistic regression model is based on the natural logarithm of the odds ratio, ln(odds ratio).

Equation (14.16) defines the logistic regression model for k independent variables.

LOGISTIC REGRESSION MODEL

$$\ln(\text{Odds ratio}) = \beta_0 + \beta_1 X_{1i} + \beta_2 X_{2i} + \ldots + \beta_k X_{ki} + \varepsilon_i \qquad (14.16)$$

where

$$k = \text{number of independent variables in the model}$$
$$\varepsilon_i = \text{random error in observation } i$$

In Sections 13.2 and 14.1, the method of least squares was used to develop a regression equation. In logistic regression, a mathematical method called *maximum likelihood estimation* is typically used to develop a regression equation to predict the natural logarithm of this odds ratio. Equation (14.17) defines the logistic regression equation.

LOGISTIC REGRESSION EQUATION

$$\ln(\text{Estimated odds ratio}) = b_0 + b_1 X_{1i} + b_2 X_{2i} + \ldots + b_k X_{ki} \qquad (14.17)$$

Once you have determined the logistic regression equation, you use Equation (14.18) to compute the estimated odds ratio.

ESTIMATED ODDS RATIO

$$\text{Estimated odds ratio} = e^{\ln(\text{Estimated odds ratio})} \qquad (14.18)$$

Once you have computed the estimated odds ratio, you use Equation (14.19) to compute the estimated probability of an event of interest.

ESTIMATED PROBABILITY OF AN EVENT OF INTEREST

$$\text{Estimated probability of an event of interest} = \frac{\text{estimated odds ratio}}{1 + \text{estimated odds ratio}} \qquad (14.19)$$

To illustrate the use of logistic regression, consider the case of the sales and marketing manager for the credit card division of a major financial company. The manager wants to conduct a campaign to persuade existing holders of the bank's standard credit card to upgrade, for a nominal annual fee, to the bank's platinum card. The manager wonders, "Which of the existing standard credit cardholders should we target for this campaign?"

The manager has access to the results from a sample of 30 cardholders who were targeted during a pilot campaign last year. These results have been organized as three variables and stored in CardStudy. The three variables are Upgraded, whether a cardholder upgraded to a premium card, Y ($0 = $ no, $1 = $ yes); and two independent variables, Purchases, the prior year's credit card purchases (in \$thousands), X_1; and Extra Cards, whether the cardholder ordered additional credit cards for other authorized users, X_2 ($0 = $ no, $1 = $ yes). Figure 14.14 presents the Excel, JMP, and Minitab results for the logistic regression model using these data.

FIGURE 14.14

Excel, JMP, and Minitab logistic regression results for the credit card pilot study data

Logistic Regression

	Predictor	Coefficients	SE Coef	Z	p-Value
	Intercept	-6.9394	2.9471	-2.3547	0.0185
	Purchases	0.1395	0.0681	2.0490	0.0405
	Extra Cards:1	2.7743	1.1927	2.3261	0.0200
	Deviance	20.0769			

Lack Of Fit

Source	DF	-LogLikelihood	ChiSquare
Lack Of Fit	27	10.038451	20.0769
Saturated	29	0.000000	Prob>ChiSq
Fitted	2	10.038451	0.8275

Parameter Estimates

Term	Estimate	Std Error	ChiSquare	Prob>ChiSq
Intercept[0]	6.93983883	2.9472319	5.54	0.0185*
Purchases	-0.1394685	0.0680662	4.20	0.0405*
Extra Cards	-2.7743352	1.1927003	5.41	0.0200*

Effect Likelihood Ratio Tests

Source	Nparm	DF	L-R ChiSquare	Prob>ChiSq
Purchases	1	1	6.52797922	0.0106*
Extra Cards	1	1	6.80611313	0.0091*

*The JMP results (above) predict the probability of **not** upgrading. Therefore the coefficients in the results have the opposite signs to the signs found in the Excel and Minitab results*

Binary Logistic Regression: Upgraded versus Purchases, Extra Cards

Method

Link function   Logit
Rows used   30

Response Information

Variable	Value	Count	
Upgraded	1	13	(Event)
	0	17	
	Total	30	

Deviance Table

Source	DF	Adj Dev	Adj Mean	Chi-Square	P-Value
Regression	2	20.977	10.4885	20.98	0.000
Purchases	1	6.528	6.5280	6.53	0.011
Extra Cards	1	6.806	6.8061	6.81	0.009
Error	27	20.077	0.7436		
Total	29	41.054			

Model Summary

Deviance R-Sq	Deviance R-Sq(adj)	AIC
51.10%	46.22%	26.08

Coefficients

Term	Coef	SE Coef	VIF
Constant	-6.94	2.95	
Purchases	0.1395	0.0681	1.07
Extra Cards	2.77	1.19	1.07

Odds Ratios for Continuous Predictors

	Odds Ratio	95% CI
Purchases	1.1497	(1.0061, 1.3137)
Extra Cards	16.0280	(1.5476, 165.9988)

Regression Equation

$P(1) = \exp(Y')/(1 + \exp(Y'))$

$Y' = -6.94 + 0.1395 \text{ Purchases} + 2.77 \text{ Extra Cards}$

Using the net regression coefficients b_1 and b_2, the Table 14.13 net effects table summarizes the effects of the regression constant, Purchases (X_1) and Extra Cards (X_2) for management.

TABLE 14.13

Net Effects Table for the Credit Card Study Multiple Regression Model

Net Effect	Interpretation
The regression constant −6.9394	The estimated natural logarithm of the odds ratio of purchasing the premium card is −6.9394 for a credit cardholder who did not charge any purchases last year and who does not have additional cards.
Each additional $1,000 in credit card purchases last year	The estimated natural logarithm of the odds ratio of purchasing the premium card increases by 0.1395 for each increase of $1,000 in annual credit card spending using the company's card, holding constant the effect of whether the credit cardholder has additional cards for other authorized users.
Whether additional credit cards are ordered for a member of the household	The estimated natural logarithm of the odds ratio of purchasing the premium card increases by 2.7743 for a credit cardholder who has additional cards for other authorized users compared with one who does not have additional cards, holding constant the annual credit card spending.

The Table 14.13 estimates will allow the financial company decision-makers to better understand how spending and additional credit card ordering decisions are predicted to affect whether the cardholder will upgrade to a premium card. Managers can conclude that cardholders who charged more last year and possess additional cards for other authorized users are much more likely to upgrade to a premium credit card.

As is the case with least-squares regression models, a main purpose of performing logistic regression analysis is to provide predictions of a dependent variable. For example, consider a cardholder who charged \$36,000 last year and possesses additional cards for members of the household. What is the probability the cardholder will upgrade to the premium card during the marketing campaign? Using $X_1 = 36$, $X_2 = 1$, Equation (14.17) on page 570, and the results displayed in Figure 14.14 on page 571,

$$\ln(\text{estimated odds of purchasing versus not purchasing}) = -6.9394 + (0.1395)(36) + (2.7743)(1)$$

$$= 0.8569$$

Then, using Equation (14.18) on page 570,

$$\text{estimated odds ratio} = e^{0.8569} = 2.3558$$

Therefore, the odds are 2.3558 to 1 that a credit cardholder who spent \$36,000 last year and has additional cards will purchase the premium card during the campaign. Using Equation (14.19) on page 570, you can convert this odds ratio to a probability:

$$\text{estimated probability of purchasing premium card} = \frac{2.3558}{1 + 2.3558}$$

$$= 0.702$$

Thus, the estimated probability is 0.702 that a credit cardholder who spent \$36,000 last year and has additional cards will purchase the premium card during the campaign. In other words, you predict 70.2% of such individuals will purchase the premium card.

Now that you have used the logistic regression model for prediction, you need to determine whether or not the model is a good-fitting model. The **deviance statistic** is frequently used to determine whether the current model provides a good fit to the data. This statistic measures the fit of the current model compared with a model that has as many parameters as there are data points (what is called a *saturated* model). The deviance statistic follows a chi-square distribution with $n - k - 1$ degrees of freedom, where n is the sample size and k is the number of independent variables. The null and alternative hypotheses are

$$H_0: \text{The model is a good-fitting model.}$$

studentTIP

Unlike other hypothesis tests, rejecting the null hypothesis for this test means that the model is *not* a good fit.

$$H_1: \text{The model is not a good-fitting model.}$$

When using the deviance statistic for logistic regression, the null hypothesis represents a good-fitting model, which is the opposite of the null hypothesis when using the overall F test for the multiple regression model (see Section 14.2). Using the α level of significance, the decision rule is

$$\text{Reject } H_0 \text{ if deviance} > \chi_\alpha^2;$$

$$\text{otherwise, do not reject } H_o.$$

The critical value for a χ^2 statistic with $n - k - 1 = 30 - 2 - 1 = 27$ degrees of freedom is 40.113 (see Table E.4). From Figure 14.14 on page 571, the deviance (labeled Chi-Square in JMP and Minitab) $= 20.0769 < 40.113$. Thus, you do not reject H_0, and you conclude that there is insufficient evidence that the model is not a good-fitting one.

With evidence that the model is a good-fitting one, you need to evaluate whether each of the independent variables makes a significant contribution to the model in the presence of others. Do that evaluation by examining either the Z test statistic (called the **Wald statistic** in this context) or the chi-square test statistic.

Table 14.14 summarizes the results of the test for the regression coefficients for Purchases (b_1) and Extra Cards (b_2) that appears as part of Figure 14.14. Based on these results, you can conclude that both the amount of purchases and whether the cardholder has additional cards for members of the household have a significant effect on whether the cardholder will upgrade to a premium card.

TABLE 14.14

Evaluating Whether Each of the Independent Variables Makes a Significant Contribution

Result	Conclusions
$Z = 2.049$ is greater than 1.96 or chi-square (JMP) $= 4.20 > 3.8416$ p-value $= 0.0405$ is less than the level of significance, $\alpha = 0.05$	1. Reject the null hypothesis H_0. 2. Conclude that evidence exists for claiming that the amount of purchases is related to whether the cardholder will upgrade to a premium card holding constant whether the cardholder has additional cards for members of the household. 3. The probability is 0.0405 that $Z < -2.049$ or $Z > 2.049$.
$Z = 2.3261$ is greater than 1.96 or chi-square (JMP) $= 5.41 > 3.8416$ p-value $= 0.02$ is less than the level of significance, $\alpha = 0.05$	1. Reject the null hypothesis H_0. 2. Conclude that evidence exists for claiming that whether the cardholder will upgrade to a premium card is related to whether the cardholder has additional cards for members of the household holding constant the amount of purchases. 3. The probability is 0.02 that $Z < -2.3261$ or $Z > 2.3261$.

PROBLEMS FOR SECTION 14.7

LEARNING THE BASICS

14.50 Interpret the meaning of a slope coefficient equal to 2.2 in logistic regression.

14.51 Given an estimated odds ratio of 2.5, compute the estimated probability of an event of interest.

14.52 Given an estimated odds ratio of 0.75, compute the estimated probability of an event of interest.

14.53 Consider the following logistic regression equation:

$$\ln(\text{Estimated odds ratio}) = 0.1 + 0.5X_{1i} + 0.2X_{2i}$$

a. Interpret the meaning of the logistic regression coefficients.
b. If $X_1 = 2$ and $X_2 = 1.5$, compute the estimated odds ratio and interpret its meaning.
c. On the basis of the results of (b), compute the estimated probability of an event of interest.

APPLYING THE CONCEPTS

✓SELF TEST **14.54** Refer to Figure 14.14 on page 571.
a. Predict the probability that a cardholder who charged $36,000 last year and does not have any additional credit cards for other authorized users will purchase the platinum card during the marketing campaign.
b. Compare the results in (a) with those for a person with additional credit cards.
c. Predict the probability that a cardholder who charged $18,000 and does not have any additional credit cards for other authorized users will purchase the platinum card during the marketing campaign.
d. Compare the results of (a) and (c) and indicate what implications these results might have for the strategy for the marketing campaign.

14.55 A study was conducted to determine the factors involved in the rate of participation of discharged cardiac patients in a rehabilitation program. Data were collected from 516 treated patients.

Source: Data extracted from F. Van Der Meulen, T. Vermaat, and P. Williams, "C.ase Study: An Application of Logistic Regression in a Six Sigma Project in Health Care," *Quality Engineering*, 2011, pp. 113–124.

Among the variables used to predict participation ($0 = $ no, $1 = $ yes) were the distance traveled to rehabilitation in kilometers, whether the person had a car ($0 = $ no, $1 = $ yes), and the age of the person in years. The summarized data are:

	Estimate	Standard Error	Z Value	p-value
Intercept	5.7765	0.8619	6.702	0.0000
Distance	−0.0675	0.0111	−6.113	0.0000
Car	1.9369	0.2720	7.121	0.0000
Age	−0.0599	0.0119	−5.037	0.0000

a. State the logistic regression model.
b. Using the model in (a), predict the probability that a patient will participate in rehabilitation if he or she travels 20 km to rehabilitation, has a car, and is 65 years old.
c. Using the model in (a), predict the probability that a patient will participate in rehabilitation if he or she travels 20 km to rehabilitation, does not have a car, and is 65 years old.
d. Compare the results of (b) and (c).
e. At the 0.05 level of significance, is there evidence that the distance traveled, whether the patient has a car, and the age of the patient each make a significant contribution to the model?
f. What conclusions can you reach about the likelihood of a patient participating in the rehabilitation program?

14.56 Referring to Problem 14.41 on page 567, you have decided to analyze whether there are differences in fixed acidity, chlorides, and pH between white wines and red wines ($0 =$ white $1 =$ red). Using the data stored in RedandWhite,

a. Develop a logistic regression model to predict whether the wine is red based on the fixed acidity, chlorides, and pH.
b. Explain the meaning of the regression coefficients in the model developed in (a).
c. Predict the probability that a wine is red if it has a fixed acidity of 7.0, chlorides of 0.04, and pH of 3.5.
d. At the 0.05 level of significance, is there evidence that the logistic regression model developed in (a) is a good fitting model?
e. At the 0.05 level of significance, is there evidence that fixed acidity, chlorides, and pH each make a significant contribution to the model?
f. What conclusions concerning the probability of a wine selected being red can you reach?

14.57 Undergraduate students at Miami University in Oxford, Ohio, were surveyed in order to evaluate the effect of price on the purchase of a pizza from Pizza Hut. Students were first asked to imagine a situation in which they were planning to call and order for delivery a large two-topping pizza. Then they were asked to select from either Pizza Hut or another pizzeria of their choice. The price they would have to pay to get a Pizza Hut pizza differed from survey to survey. For example, some surveys used the price $11.49. Other prices investigated were $8.49, $9.49, $10.49, $12.49, $13.49, and $14.49. The dependent variable for this study is whether or not a student will select Pizza Hut. Possible independent variables are the price of a Pizza Hut pizza and the gender of the student. The file PizzaHut contains responses from 220 students and includes these three variables:

Gender: $1 =$ male, $0 =$ female

Price: 8.49, 9.49, 10.49, 11.49, 12.49, 13.49, or 14.49

Purchase: $1 =$ the student selected Pizza Hut, $0 =$ the student selected another pizzeria

a. Develop a logistic regression model to predict the probability that a student selects Pizza Hut based on the price of the pizza. Is price an important indicator of purchase selection?
b. Develop a logistic regression model to predict the probability that a student selects Pizza Hut based on the price of the pizza and the gender of the student. Is price an important indicator of purchase selection? Is gender an important indicator of purchase selection?
c. Compare the results from (a) and (b). Which model would you choose? Discuss.
d. Using the model selected in (c), predict the probability that a student will select Pizza Hut if the price is $8.99.
e. Using the model selected in (c), predict the probability that a student will select Pizza Hut if the price is $11.49.
f. Using the model selected in (c), predict the probability that a student will select Pizza Hut if the price is $13.99.

14.58 An automotive insurance company wants to predict which filed stolen vehicle claims are fraudulent, based on the mean number of claims submitted per year by the policy holder and whether the policy is a new policy, that is, is one year old or less (coded as $1 =$ yes, $0 =$ no). Data from a random sample of 98 automotive insurance claims, organized and stored in InsuranceFraud, show that 49 are fraudulent (coded as 1) and 49 are not (coded as 0).

Source: Data extracted from A. Gepp *et al.*, "A Comparative Analysis of Decision Trees vis-à-vis Other Computational Data Mining Techniques in Automotive Insurance Fraud Detection," *Journal of Data Science*, 10 (2012), pp. 537–561.

a. Develop a logistic regression model to predict the probability of a fraudulent claim, based on the number of claims submitted per year by the policy holder and whether the policy is new.
b. Explain the meaning of the regression coefficients in the model in (a).
c. Predict the probability of a fraudulent claim given that the policy holder has submitted a mean of one claim per year and holds a new policy.
d. At the 0.05 level of significance, is there evidence that a logistic regression model that uses the mean number of claims submitted per year by the policy holder and whether the policy is new to predict the probability of a fraudulent claim is a good fitting model?
e. At the 0.05 level of significance, is there evidence that the mean number of claims submitted per year by the policy holder and whether the policy is new each makes a significant contribution to the logistic model?
f. Develop a logistic regression model that includes only the number of claims submitted per year by the policy holder to predict the probability of a fraudulent claim.
g. Develop a logistic regression model that includes only whether the policy is new to predict a fraudulent claim.
h. Compare the models in (a), (f), and (g). Evaluate the differences among the models.

14.59 A marketing manager wants to predict customers with the risk of churning (switching their service contracts to another company) based on the number of calls the customer makes to the company call center and the number of visits the customer makes to the local service center. Data from a random sample of 30 customers, organized and stored in Churn show that 15 have churned (coded as 1) and 15 have not (coded as 0)

a. Develop a logistic regression model to predict the probability of churn, based on the number of calls the customer makes to the company call center and the number of visits the customer makes to the local service center.
b. Explain the meaning of the regression coefficients in the model in (a).
c. Predict the probability of churn for a customer who called the company call center 10 times and visited the local service center once.
d. At the 0.05 level of significance, is there evidence that a logistic regression model that uses the number of calls the customer makes to the company call center and the number of visits the customer makes to the local service center is a good fitting model?
e. At the 0.05 level of significance, is there evidence that the number of calls the customer makes to the company call center and the number of visits the customer makes to the local service center each make a significant contribution to the logistic model?
f. Develop a logistic regression model that includes only the number of calls the customer makes to the company call center to predict the probability of churn.
g. Develop a logistic regression model that includes only the number of visits the customer makes to the local service center to predict churn.
h. Compare the models in (a), (f), and (g). Evaluate the differences among the models.

14.60 A local supermarket manager wants to use two independent variables, customer age (in years) and whether the customer subscribes to the supermarket chain's health/wellness e-newsletters (coded as 1 = yes and 0 = no) to predict which customers are likely to purchase a new line of organic products. Data from a random sample of 100 loyalty program customers, organized and stored in `OrganicFood`, show that 65 have purchased the organic products (coded as 1) and 35 have not (coded as 0).

a. Develop a logistic regression model to predict the probability that a customer purchases the organic products, based on age and whether the customer subscribes to the supermarket chain's health/wellness e-newsletters.

b. Explain the meaning of the regression coefficients in the model in (a).

c. Predict the probability of purchasing the organic products for a 35-year-old customer who subscribes to the supermarket chain's health/wellness e-newsletters.

d. At the 0.05 level of significance, is there evidence that a logistic regression model that uses customer age and whether the customer subscribes to the supermarket chain's health/wellness e-newsletters to predict the probability of purchasing the organic products is a good fitting model?

e. At the 0.05 level of significance, is there evidence that customer age and whether the customer subscribes to the supermarket chain's health/wellness e-newsletters each make a significant contribution to the logistic model?

f. What conclusions can you reach about which variables are affecting purchase of organic foods?

14.8 Influence Analysis

Sections 13.5 and 14.3 use residual analysis to evaluate regression assumptions. The **Section 14.8 online topic** discusses several measures of the influence of individual values.

▼USING **STATISTICS**
The Multiple Effects..., Revisited

In the Using Statistics scenario, you were a marketing manager for OmniFoods, responsible for nutrition bars and similar snack items.

At the end of the one-month test-market study, you performed a multiple regression analysis on the data. Two independent variables were considered: the price of an OmniPower bar and the monthly budget for in-store promotional expenses. The dependent variable was the number of OmniPower bars sold in a month. The coefficient of determination indicated that 75.8% of the variation in sales was explained by knowing the price charged and the amount spent on in-store promotions. The model indicated that the predicted sales of OmniPower are estimated to decrease by 532 bars per month for each 10-cent increase in the price, and the predicted sales are estimated to increase by 361 bars for each additional $100 spent on promotions.

After studying the relative effects of price and promotion, OmniFoods needs to set price and promotion standards for a nationwide introduction (obviously, lower prices and higher promotion budgets lead to more sales, but they do so at a lower profit margin). You determined that if stores spend $400 a month for in-store promotions and charge 79 cents, the 95% confidence interval estimate of the mean monthly sales is 2,854 to 3,303 bars. OmniFoods can multiply the lower and upper bounds of this confidence interval by the number of stores included in the nationwide introduction to estimate total monthly sales. For example, if 1,000 stores are in the nationwide introduction, then total monthly sales should be between 2.854 million and 3.308 million bars.

▼SUMMARY

In this chapter, you learned how to develop and fit multiple regression models that use two or more independent variables to predict the value of a dependent variable. You also learned how to include categorical independent variables and interaction terms in regression models and learned the logistic regression model that is used to predict a categorical dependent variable. Figure 14.15 summarizes how to apply a multiple regression model to a set of data.

FIGURE 14.15
Roadmap for multiple regression

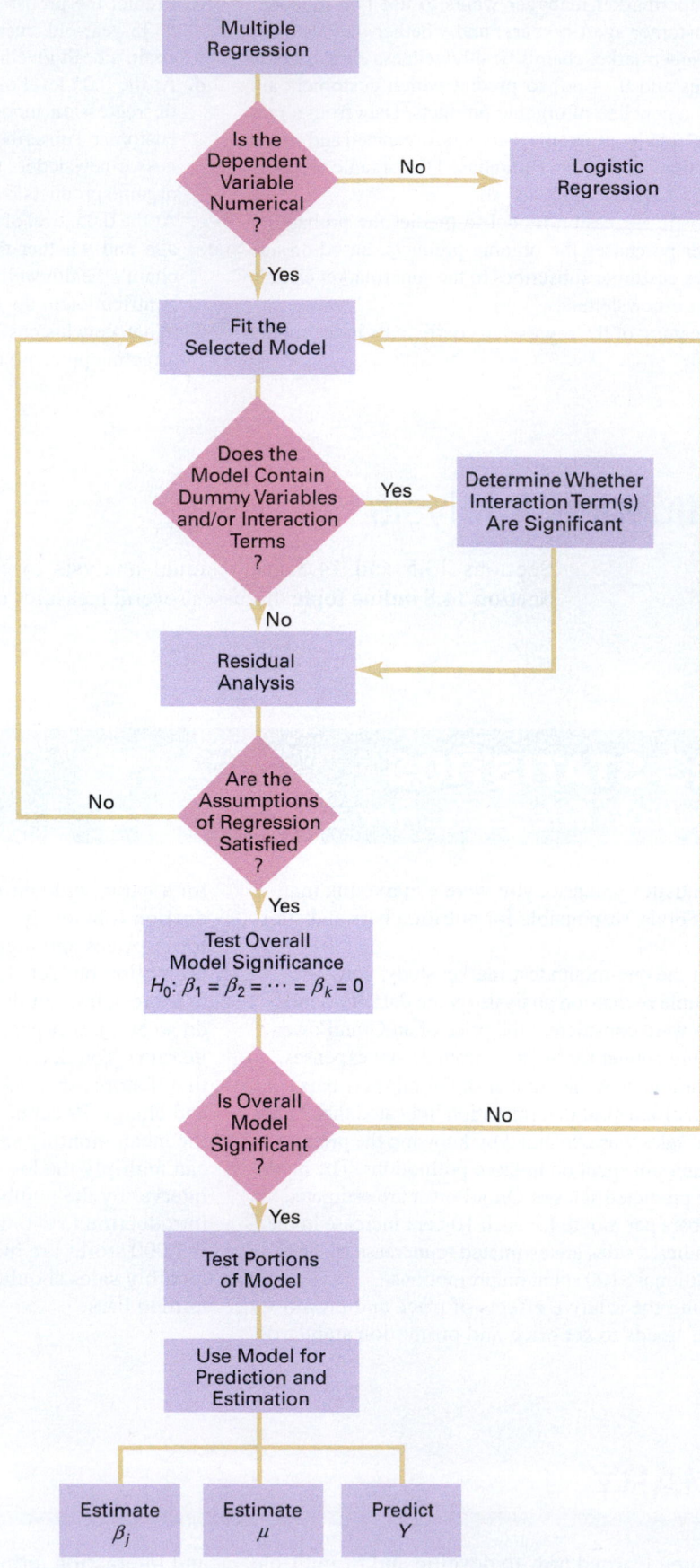

▼REFERENCES

1. Andrews, D. F., and D. Pregibon. "Finding the Outliers that Matter." *Journal of the Royal Statistical Society* 40 (Ser. B., 1978): 85–93.
2. Atkinson, A. C. "Robust and Diagnostic Regression Analysis." *Communications in Statistics* 11 (1982): 2559–2572.
3. Belsley, D. A., E. Kuh, and R. Welsch. *Regression Diagnostics: Identifying Influential Data and Sources of Collinearity.* New York: Wiley, 1980.
4. Cook, R. D., and S. Weisberg. *Residuals and Influence in Regression.* New York: Chapman and Hall, 1982.
5. Hosmer, D. W., and S. Lemeshow. *Applied Logistic Regression,* 2nd ed. New York: Wiley, 2001.
6. Hoaglin, D. C., and R. Welsch. "The Hat Matrix in Regression and ANOVA," *The American Statistician,* 32, (1978), 17–22.
7. Kutner, M., C. Nachtsheim, J. Neter, and W. Li. *Applied Linear Statistical Models,* 5th ed. New York: McGraw-Hill/Irwin, 2005.
8. Montgomery, D. C., E. A. Peck, and G. G. Vining. *Introduction to Linear Regression Analysis,* 5th ed. New York: Wiley, 2012.

▼KEY EQUATIONS

Multiple Regression Model with k Independent Variables

$$Y_i = \beta_0 + \beta_1 X_{1i} + \beta_2 X_{2i} + \beta_3 X_{3i} + \ldots + \beta_k X_{ki} + \varepsilon_i \tag{14.1}$$

Multiple Regression Model with Two Independent Variables

$$Y_i = \beta_0 + \beta_1 X_{1i} + \beta_2 X_{2i} + \varepsilon_i \tag{14.2}$$

Multiple Regression Equation with Two Independent Variables

$$\hat{Y}_i = b_0 + b_1 X_{1i} + b_2 X_{2i} \tag{14.3}$$

Coefficient of Multiple Determination

$$r^2 = \frac{\text{Regression sum of squares}}{\text{Total sum of squares}} = \frac{SSR}{SST} \tag{14.4}$$

Adjusted r^2

$$r^2_{\text{adj}} = 1 - \left[(1 - r^2)\frac{n-1}{n-k-1} \right] \tag{14.5}$$

Overall F Test

$$F_{STAT} = \frac{MSR}{MSE} \tag{14.6}$$

Testing for the Slope in Multiple Regression

$$t_{STAT} = \frac{b_j - \beta_j}{S_{b_j}} \tag{14.7}$$

Confidence Interval Estimate for the Slope

$$b_j \pm t_{\alpha/2} S_{b_j} \tag{14.8}$$

Determining the Contribution of an Independent Variable to the Regression Model

$$SSR(X_j | \text{All } Xs \text{ except } j) = SSR(\text{All } Xs) - SSR(\text{All } Xs \text{ except } j) \tag{14.9}$$

Contribution of Variable X_1, Given That X_2 Has Been Included

$$SSR(X_1 | X_2) = SSR(X_1 \text{ and } X_2) - SSR(X_2) \tag{14.10a}$$

Contribution of Variable X_2, Given That X_1 Has Been Included

$$SSR(X_2 | X_1) = SSR(X_1 \text{ and } X_2) - SSR(X_1) \tag{14.10b}$$

Partial F Test Statistic

$$F_{STAT} = \frac{SSR(X_j | \text{All } Xs \text{ except } j)}{MSE} \tag{14.11}$$

Relationship Between a t Statistic and an F Statistic

$$t^2_{STAT} = F_{STAT} \tag{14.12}$$

Coefficients of Partial Determination for a Multiple Regression Model Containing Two Independent Variables

$$r^2_{Y1.2} = \frac{SSR(X_1 | X_2)}{SST - SSR(X_1 \text{ and } X_2) + SSR(X_1 | X_2)} \tag{14.13a}$$

and

$$r^2_{Y2.1} = \frac{SSR(X_2 | X_1)}{SST - SSR(X_1 \text{ and } X_2) + SSR(X_2 | X_1)} \tag{14.13b}$$

Coefficient of Partial Determination for a Multiple Regression Model Containing k Independent Variables

$$r^2_{Yj.(\text{All variables except } j)} = \frac{SSR(X_j | \text{All } Xs \text{ except } j)}{SST - SSR(\text{All } Xs) + SSR(X_j | \text{All } Xs \text{ except } j)} \tag{14.14}$$

Odds Ratio

$$\text{Odds ratio} = \frac{\text{probability of an event of interest}}{1 - \text{probability of an event of interest}} \tag{14.15}$$

Logistic Regression Model

$$\ln(\text{Odds ratio}) = \beta_0 + \beta_1 X_{1i} + \beta_2 X_{2i} + \cdots + \beta_k X_{ki} + \varepsilon_i \tag{14.16}$$

Logistic Regression Equation

$$\ln(\text{Estimated odds ratio}) = b_0 + b_1 X_{1i} + b_2 X_{2i} + \cdots + b_k X_{ki} \tag{14.17}$$

Estimated Odds Ratio

$$\text{Estimated odds ratio} = e^{\ln(\text{Estimated odds ratio})} \tag{14.18}$$

Estimated Probability of an Event of Interest

Estimated probability of an event of interest

$$= \frac{\text{estimated odds ratio}}{1 + \text{estimated odds ratio}} \tag{14.19}$$

▼ KEY TERMS

adjusted r^2 543
coefficient of multiple determination   542
coefficient of partial determination   555
cross-product term   560
deviance statistic   572

dummy variable   557
interaction   560
interaction term   560
logistic regression   569
multiple regression model   537

net regression coefficient   538
odds ratio   569
overall F test   543
partial F test   551
Wald statistic   572

▼ CHECKING YOUR UNDERSTANDING

14.61 What is the difference between r^2 and adjusted r^2?

14.62 How does the interpretation of the regression coefficients differ in multiple regression and simple linear regression?

14.63 How does testing the significance of the entire multiple regression model differ from testing the contribution of each independent variable?

14.64 How do the coefficients of partial determination differ from the coefficient of multiple determination?

14.65 Why and how do you use dummy variables?

14.66 How can you evaluate whether the slope of the dependent variable with an independent variable is the same for each level of the dummy variable?

14.67 Under what circumstances do you include an interaction term in a regression model?

14.68 When a dummy variable is included in a regression model that has one numerical independent variable, what assumption do you need to make concerning the slope between the dependent variable, Y, and the numerical independent variable, X?

14.69 When do you use logistic regression?

14.70 What is the difference between least squares regression and logistic regression?

▼ CHAPTER REVIEW PROBLEMS

14.71 Increasing customer satisfaction typically results in increased purchase behavior. For many products, there is more than one measure of customer satisfaction. In many, purchase behavior can increase dramatically with an increase in just one of the customer satisfaction measures. Gunst and Barry ("One Way to Moderate Ceiling Effects," *Quality Progress*, October 2003, pp. 83–85) consider a product with two satisfaction measures, X_1 and X_2, that range from the lowest level of satisfaction, 1, to the highest level of satisfaction, 7. The dependent variable, Y, is a measure of purchase behavior, with the highest value generating the most sales. Consider the regression equation:

$$\hat{Y}_i = -3.888 + 1.449 X_{1i} + 1.462 X_{2i} - 0.190 X_{1i} X_{2i}$$

Suppose that X_1 is the perceived quality of the product and X_2 is the perceived value of the product. (Note: If the customer thinks the product is overpriced, he or she perceives it to be of low value and vice versa.)

a. What is the predicted purchase behavior when $X_1 = 2$ and $X_2 = 2$?

b. What is the predicted purchase behavior when $X_1 = 2$ and $X_2 = 7$?

c. What is the predicted purchase behavior when $X_1 = 7$ and $X_2 = 2$?

d. What is the predicted purchase behavior when $X_1 = 7$ and $X_2 = 7$?

e. What is the regression equation when $X_2 = 2$? What is the slope for X_1 now?

f. What is the regression equation when $X_2 = 7$? What is the slope for X_1 now?

g. What is the regression equation when $X_1 = 2$? What is the slope for X_2 now?

h. What is the regression equation when $X_1 = 7$? What is the slope for X_2 now?

i. Discuss the implications of (a) through (h) in the context of increasing sales for this product with two customer satisfaction measures.

14.72 The owner of a moving company typically has his most experienced manager predict the total number of labor hours that will be required to complete an upcoming move. This approach has proved useful in the past, but the owner has the business objective of developing a more accurate method of predicting labor hours. In a preliminary effort to provide a more accurate method, the owner has decided to use the number of cubic feet moved and the number of pieces of large furniture as the independent variables and has collected data for 36 moves in which the origin and destination were within the borough of Manhattan in New York City and the travel time was an insignificant portion of the hours worked. The data are organized and stored in Moving .

a. State the multiple regression equation.
b. Interpret the meaning of the slopes in this equation.
c. Predict the mean labor hours for moving 500 cubic feet with two large pieces of furniture.
d. Perform a residual analysis on your model and determine whether the regression assumptions are valid.
e. Determine whether there is a significant relationship between labor hours and the two independent variables (the number of cubic feet moved and the number of pieces of large furniture) at the 0.05 level of significance.
f. Determine the p-value in (e) and interpret its meaning.
g. Interpret the meaning of the coefficient of multiple determination in this problem.
h. Determine the adjusted r^2.
i. At the 0.05 level of significance, determine whether each independent variable makes a significant contribution to the regression model. Indicate the most appropriate regression model for this set of data.
j. Determine the p-values in (i) and interpret their meaning.
k. Construct a 95% confidence interval estimate of the population slope between labor hours and the number of cubic feet moved.
l. Compute and interpret the coefficients of partial determination.
m. What conclusions can you reach concerning labor hours?

14.73 Professional basketball has truly become a sport that generates interest among fans around the world. More and more players come from outside the United States to play in the National Basketball Association (NBA). You want to develop a regression model to predict the number of wins achieved by each NBA team, based on field goal (shots made) percentage and three-point field goal percentage for a recent season. The data are stored in NBA .

a. State the multiple regression equation.
b. Interpret the meaning of the slopes in this equation.
c. Predict the mean number of wins for a team that has a field goal percentage of 45% and a three-point field goal percentage of 35%.
d. Perform a residual analysis on your model and determine whether the regression assumptions are valid.
e. Is there a significant relationship between the number of wins and the two independent variables (field goal percentage and three-point field goal percentage) at the 0.05 level of significance?
f. Determine the p-value in (e) and interpret its meaning.
g. Interpret the meaning of the coefficient of multiple determination in this problem.
h. Determine the adjusted r^2.
i. At the 0.05 level of significance, determine whether each independent variable makes a significant contribution to the regression model. Indicate the most appropriate regression model for this set of data.

j. Determine the p-values in (i) and interpret their meaning.
k. Compute and interpret the coefficients of partial determination.
l. What conclusions can you reach concerning field goal percentage and three-point field goal percentage in predicting the number of wins?

14.74 A sample of 61 houses recently listed for sale in Silver Spring, Maryland, was selected with the objective of developing a model to predict the asking price (in $thousands), using the living space of the house (in square feet) and age (in years). The results are stored in SilverSpring .

a. Fit a multiple regression model.
b. Interpret the meaning of the slopes in this model.
c. Predict the mean asking price for a house that has 2,000 square feet and is 55 years old.
d. Perform a residual analysis on your model and determine whether the regression assumptions are valid.
e. Determine whether there is a significant relationship between asking price and the two independent variables (house size and age) at the 0.05 level of significance.
f. Determine the p-value in (e) and interpret its meaning.
g. Interpret the meaning of the coefficient of multiple determination in this problem.
h. Determine the adjusted r^2.
i. At the 0.05 level of significance, determine whether each independent variable makes a significant contribution to the regression model. Indicate the most appropriate regression model for this set of data.
j. Determine the p-values in (i) and interpret their meaning.
k. Construct a 95% confidence interval estimate of the population slope between asking price and the living space of the house. How does the interpretation of the slope here differ from that in Problem 13.76 on page 525?
l. Compute and interpret the coefficients of partial determination.
m. What conclusions can you reach about the asking price?

14.75 Measuring the height of a California redwood tree is very difficult because these trees grow to heights over 300 feet. People familiar with these trees understand that the height of a California redwood tree is related to other characteristics of the tree, including the diameter of the tree at the breast height of a person (in inches) and the thickness of the bark of the tree (in inches). The file Redwood contains the height, diameter at breast height of a person, and bark thickness for a sample of 21 California redwood trees.

a. State the multiple regression equation that predicts the height of a tree, based on the tree's diameter at breast height and the thickness of the bark.
b. Interpret the meaning of the slopes in this equation.
c. Predict the mean height for a tree that has a breast height diameter of 25 inches and a bark thickness of 2 inches.
d. Interpret the meaning of the coefficient of multiple determination in this problem.
e. Perform a residual analysis on the model and determine whether the regression assumptions are valid.
f. Determine whether there is a significant relationship between the height of redwood trees and the two independent variables (breast-height diameter and bark thickness) at the 0.05 level of significance.
g. Construct a 95% confidence interval estimate of the population slope between the height of redwood trees and breast-height diameter and between the height of redwood trees and the bark thickness.

h. At the 0.05 level of significance, determine whether each independent variable makes a significant contribution to the regression model. Indicate the independent variables to include in this model.

i. Construct a 95% confidence interval estimate of the mean height for trees that have a breast-height diameter of 25 inches and a bark thickness of 2 inches, along with a prediction interval for an individual tree.

j. Compute and interpret the coefficients of partial determination.

k. What conclusions can you reach concerning the effect of the diameter of the tree and the thickness of the bark on the height of the tree?

14.76 A sample of 61 houses recently listed for sale in Silver Spring, Maryland, was selected with the objective of developing a model to predict the taxes (in $) based on the asking price of houses (in $thousands) and the age of the houses (in years) (stored in SilverSpring):

a. State the multiple regression equation.

b. Interpret the meaning of the slopes in this equation.

c. Predict the mean taxes for a house that has an asking price of $400,000 and is 50 years old.

d. Perform a residual analysis on the model and determine whether the regression assumptions are valid.

e. Determine whether there is a significant relationship between taxes and the two independent variables (asking price and age) at the 0.05 level of significance.

f. Determine the p-value in (e) and interpret its meaning.

g. Interpret the meaning of the coefficient of multiple determination in this problem.

h. Determine the adjusted r^2.

i. At the 0.05 level of significance, determine whether each independent variable makes a significant contribution to the regression model. Indicate the most appropriate regression model for this set of data.

j. Determine the p-values in (i) and interpret their meaning.

k. Construct a 95% confidence interval estimate of the population slope between taxes and asking price. How does the interpretation of the slope here differ from that of Problem 13.77 on page 525?

l. Compute and interpret the coefficients of partial determination.

m. The real estate assessor's office has been publicly quoted as saying that the age of a house has no bearing on its taxes. Based on your answers to (a) through (l), do you agree with this statement? Explain.

14.77 A baseball analytics specialist wants to determine which variables are important in predicting a team's wins in a given season. He has collected data related to wins, earned run average (ERA), and runs scored per game for a recent season (stored in Baseball). Develop a model to predict the number of wins based on ERA and runs scored per game.

a. State the multiple regression equation.

b. Interpret the meaning of the slopes in this equation.

c. Predict the mean number of wins for a team that has an ERA of 4.50 and has scored 4.6 runs per game.

d. Perform a residual analysis on the model and determine whether the regression assumptions are valid.

e. Is there a significant relationship between the number of wins and the two independent variables (ERA and runs scored per game) at the 0.05 level of significance?

f. Determine the p-value in (e) and interpret its meaning.

g. Interpret the meaning of the coefficient of multiple determination in this problem.

h. Determine the adjusted r^2.

i. At the 0.05 level of significance, determine whether each independent variable makes a significant contribution to the regression model. Indicate the most appropriate regression model for this set of data.

j. Determine the p-values in (i) and interpret their meaning.

k. Construct a 95% confidence interval estimate of the population slope between wins and ERA.

l. Compute and interpret the coefficients of partial determination.

m. Which is more important in predicting wins—pitching, as measured by ERA, or offense, as measured by runs scored per game? Explain.

14.78 Referring to Problem 14.77, suppose that in addition to using ERA to predict the number of wins, the analytics specialist wants to include the league (0 = American, 1 = National) as an independent variable. Develop a model to predict wins based on ERA and league. For (a) through (k), do not include an interaction term.

a. State the multiple regression equation.

b. Interpret the slopes in (a).

c. Predict the mean number of wins for a team with an ERA of 4.50 in the American League.

d. Perform a residual analysis on the model and determine whether the regression assumptions are valid.

e. Is there a significant relationship between wins and the two independent variables (ERA and league) at the 0.05 level of significance?

f. At the 0.05 level of significance, determine whether each independent variable makes a contribution to the regression model. Indicate the most appropriate regression model for this set of data.

g. Construct a 95% confidence interval estimate of the population slope for the relationship between wins and ERA.

h. Construct a 95% confidence interval estimate of the population slope for the relationship between wins and league.

i. Compute and interpret the adjusted r^2.

j. Compute and interpret the coefficients of partial determination.

k. What assumption do you have to make about the slope of wins with ERA?

l. Add an interaction term to the model and, at the 0.05 level of significance, determine whether it makes a significant contribution to the model.

m. On the basis of the results of (f) and (l), which model is most appropriate? Explain.

14.79 You are a real estate broker who wants to compare property values in Glen Cove and Roslyn (which are located approximately 8 miles apart). In order to do so, you will analyze the data in GCRoslyn, a file that includes samples of houses from Glen Cove and Roslyn. Making sure to include the dummy variable for location (Glen Cove or Roslyn), develop a regression model to predict fair market value, based on the land area of a property, the age of a house, and location. Be sure to determine whether any interaction terms need to be included in the model.

14.80 HR practitioners are increasing performing gender pay audits to understand whether a gender gap exists at their company. Practitioners examine payroll data for evidence of a gender pay gap. An HR practitioner collects data on base pay ($), gender

(0 = female and 1 = male), and age (years) for 405 employees at his company and stores these data in HR.

Source: Data extracted from Chamberlain, A., *How to Analyze Your Gender Pay Gap: An Employer's Guide*, available at **bit.ly/2td7h33**.

Develop a multiple regression model that uses gender and age to predict employee base pay. Be sure to perform a thorough residual analysis. The HR practitioner suspected that there was a significant interaction between gender and age. Is there evidence to support the HR practitioner's suspicion?

14.81 Starbucks Coffee Co. uses a data-based approach to improving the quality and customer satisfaction of its products. When survey data indicated that Starbucks needed to improve its package sealing process, an experiment was conducted to determine the factors in the bag-sealing equipment that might be affecting the ease of opening the bag without tearing the inner liner of the bag.

Source: Data extracted from L. Johnson and S. Burrows, "For Starbucks, It's in the Bag," *Quality Progress*, March 2011, pp. 17–23.

Among the factors that could affect the rating of the ability of the bag to resist tears were the viscosity, pressure, and plate gap on the bag-sealing equipment.

Data were collected on 19 bags in which the plate gap was varied and stored in Starbucks. Develop a multiple regression model that uses the viscosity, pressure, and plate gap on the bag-sealing equipment to predict the tear rating of the bag. Be sure to perform a thorough residual analysis. Do you think that you need to use all three independent variables in the model? Explain.

14.82 An experiment was conducted to study the extrusion process of biodegradable packaging foam.

Source: Data extracted from W. Y. Koh, K. M. Eskridge, and M. A. Hanna, "Supersaturated Split-Plot Designs," *Journal of Quality Technology*, 45, January 2013, pp. 61–72.

Among the factors considered for their effect on the unit density (mg/ml) were the die temperature (145°C versus 155°C) and the die diameter (3 mm versus 4 mm). The results were stored in PackagingFoam3. Develop a multiple regression model that uses die temperature and die diameter to predict the unit density (mg/ml). Be sure to perform a thorough residual analysis. Do you think that you need to use both independent variables in the model? Explain.

14.83 Referring to Problem 14.82, instead of predicting the unit density, you now wish to predict the foam diameter from results stored in PackagingFoam4. Develop a multiple regression model that uses die temperature and die diameter to predict the foam diameter (mg/ml). Be sure to perform a thorough residual analysis. Do you think that you need to use both independent variables in the model? Explain.

CHAPTER 14

▼CASES

Managing Ashland MultiComm Services

In its continuing study of the *3-For-All* subscription solicitation process, a marketing department team wants to test the effects of two types of structured sales presentations (personal formal and personal informal) and the number of hours spent on telemarketing on the number of new subscriptions. The staff has recorded these data for the past 24 weeks in AMS14.

Analyze these data and develop a multiple regression model to predict the number of new subscriptions for a week, based on the number of hours spent on telemarketing and the sales presentation type. Write a report, giving detailed findings concerning the regression model used.

Digital Case

Apply your knowledge of multiple regression models in this Digital Case, which extends the OmniFoods Using Statistics scenario from this chapter.

To ensure a successful test marketing of its OmniPower energy bars, the OmniFoods marketing department has contracted with In-Store Placements Group (ISPG), a merchandising consulting firm. ISPG will work with the grocery store chain that is conducting the test-market study. Using the same 34-store sample used in the test-market study, ISPG claims that the choice of shelf location and the presence of in-store OmniPower coupon dispensers both increase sales of the energy bars.

Open **Omni_ISPGMemo.pdf** to review the ISPG claims and supporting data. Then answer the following questions:

1. Are the supporting data consistent with ISPG's claims? Perform an appropriate statistical analysis to confirm (or discredit) the stated relationship between sales and the two independent variables of product shelf location and the presence of in-store OmniPower coupon dispensers.

2. If you were advising OmniFoods, would you recommend using a specific shelf location and in-store coupon dispensers to sell OmniPower bars?

3. What additional data would you advise collecting in order to determine the effectiveness of the sales promotion techniques used by ISPG?

▼EXCEL GUIDE

EG14.1 DEVELOPING a MULTIPLE REGRESSION MODEL

Interpreting the Regression Coefficients

Key Technique Use the **LINEST**(*cell range of Y variable, cell range of X variables*, **True, True**) function to compute the regression coefficients and related values.

Example Develop the Figure 14.2 multiple regression model for the OmniPower sales data on page 539.

PHStat Use **Multiple Regression**.

For the example, open to the **DATA worksheet** of the **OmniPower workbook**. Select **PHStat → Regression → Multiple Regression**, and in the procedure's dialog box (shown below):

1. Enter **A1:A35** as the **Y Variable Cell Range**.
2. Enter **B1:C35** as the **X Variables Cell Range**.
3. Check **First cells in both ranges contain label**.
4. Enter **95** as the **Confidence level for regression coefficients**.
5. Check **Regression Statistics Table** and **ANOVA and Coefficients Table**.
6. Enter a **Title** and click **OK**.

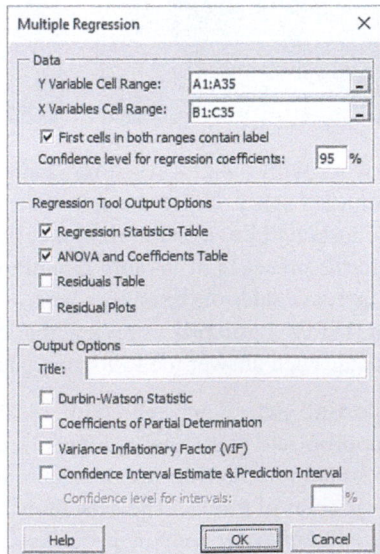

The procedure creates a worksheet that contains a copy of the data in addition to the Figure 14.2 worksheet.

Workbook Use the **COMPUTE worksheet** of the **Multiple Regression workbook** as a template.

For the example, the COMPUTE worksheet already uses the OmniPower sales data in the MRData worksheet to perform the regression analysis.

To perform multiple regression analyses for other data with two independent variables:

1. Paste the new regression data into the **MRData worksheet**, using column A for the *Y* variable data and subsequent columns, starting with B, for the *X* variable data.
2. Open to the **COMPUTE worksheet**.
3. Enter the **confidence level** in cell **L8**.
4. Edit the *array formula* in the cell range **L2:N6** to reflect the cell ranges of the data for the new *Y* and the new *X* variables.

These new cell ranges should start with row 2 so as to exclude the row 1 variable names, an exception to the usual practice in this book.

For problems with more than two independent variables, select, in step 4, a range wider than L2:N6, adding a column for each independent variable in excess of two. For example, with three independent variables, select the cell range **L2:O6**. Then continue with these steps 5 through 8:

5. Edit the labels in cells **K2** and **K3**.
6. Edit the ANOVA table formulas in columns **B** and **C**.
7. Select cell range **D18:I18**, right-click and select **Insert**. Repeat for as many times as necessary.
8. Select cell range **D17:I17** and copy down through all the rows of the ANOVA table (blank and nonblank).

The Short Takes for Chapter 14 explain more about this Intermediate Calculations area. Steps 5 through 8 may be difficult for Excel novices to complete. If you are an Excel novice, consider using the *PHStat* or *Analysis ToolPak* instructions when your problem includes more than two independent *X* variables.

Analysis ToolPak Use **Regression**.

For the example, open to the **DATA worksheet** of the **OmniPower workbook** and:

1. Select **Data → Data Analysis**.
2. In the Data Analysis dialog box, select **Regression** from the **Analysis Tools** list and then click **OK**.

In the Regression dialog box (shown on page 583):

3. Enter **A1:A35** as the **Input Y Range** and enter **B1:C35** as the **Input X Range**.
4. Check **Labels** and check **Confidence Level** and enter **95** in its box.
5. Click **New Worksheet Ply**.
6. Click **OK**.

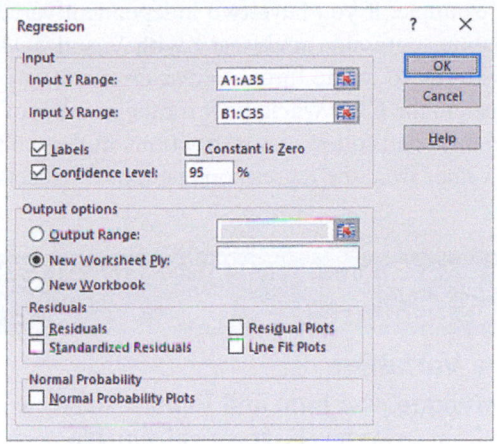

Predicting the Dependent Variable *Y*

Key Technique Use the **MMULT** array function and the **T.INV.2T** function to help compute intermediate values that determine the confidence interval estimate and prediction interval.

Example Compute the Figure 14.3 confidence interval estimate and prediction interval for the OmniPower sales data on page 541.

PHStat Use the *PHStat* "Interpreting the Regression Coefficients" instructions but replace step 6 with the following steps 6 through 8:

7. Check **Confidence Interval Estimate & Prediction Interval** and enter **95** as the percentage for **Confidence level for intervals**.
8. Enter a **Title** and click **OK**.
9. In the new worksheet, enter **79** in cell **B6** and enter **400** in cell **B7**.

These steps create a new worksheet that is similar to the CIEandPI worksheet that the following *Workbook* instructions discuss.

Workbook Use the **CIEandPI worksheet** of the **Multiple Regression workbook** as a template.
The worksheet already contains the data and formulas for the example. For other problems with two independent variables:

1. Paste the regression data for the independent variables into columns B and C of the **MRArray worksheet**.
2. Adjust the number of entries in column A, all of which are 1, to match the number of rows of the new data.
3. Use the "Interpreting the Regression Coefficients" *Worksheet* instructions to edit the COMPUTE worksheet to reflect the new data.
4. Open to the CIEandPI worksheet and edit the array formula in cell range **B9:D11** and the labels in cells **A6** and **A7** to reflect the new data.

Cell ranges in the array formula should start with row 2 so as to exclude the row 1 variable names, an exception to the usual practice in this book.

To learn more about the formulas that the CIEandPI worksheet uses, read the SHORT TAKES for Chapter 14.

EG14.2 r^2, ADJUSTED r^2, and the OVERALL *F* TEST

The coefficient of multiple determination, r^2, the adjusted r^2, and the overall *F* test appear as part of the multiple regression results that the Section EG14.1 instructions create.

PHStat and the *Workbook* instructions use formulas to compute these results in the **COMPUTE worksheet**. Formulas in cells B5, B7, B13, C12, C13, D12, and E12 copy values computed by the array formula in cell range L2:N6. In cell F12, the expression **F.DIST.RT(*F test statistic*, 1, *error degrees of freedom*)** computes the *p*-value for the overall *F* test.

EG14.3 MULTIPLE REGRESSION RESIDUAL ANALYSIS

Key Technique Use arithmetic formulas and some results from the multiple regression COMPUTE worksheet to compute residuals.

Example Perform the residual analysis for the OmniPower sales data shown in Figure 14.5, starting on page 547.

PHStat Use the Section EG14.1 "Interpreting the Regression Coefficients" *PHStat* instructions. Modify step 5 by checking **Residuals Table** and **Residual Plots** in addition to checking **Regression Statistics Table** and **ANOVA and Coefficients Table**.

Workbook Use the **RESIDUALS worksheet** of the **Multiple Regression workbook** as a template. Then construct residual plots for the residuals and the predicted value of *Y* and for the residuals and each of the independent variables.

For the example, the RESIDUALS worksheet uses the OmniPower sales data already in the **MRData worksheet** to compute the residuals. To compute residuals for other data, first use the EG14.1 "Interpreting the Regression Coefficients" *Workbook* instructions to modify the MRData and COMPUTE worksheets. Then, open to the **RESIDUALS worksheet** and:

1. If the number of independent variables is greater than 2, select column D, right-click, and click **Insert** from the shortcut menu. Repeat this step as many times as necessary to create the additional columns to hold all the *X* variables.
2. Paste the data for the *X* variables into columns, starting with column B and paste the *Y* values into the second-to-last column (column E if there are two *X* variables).

3. For sample sizes smaller than 34, delete the extra rows. For sample sizes greater than 34, copy the predicted Y and residuals formulas down through the row containing the last pair of X and Y values. Also, add the new observation numbers in column A.

To construct the residual plots, open to the RESIDUALS worksheet and select pairs of columns and then use the EG2.5 "The Scatter Plot" *Workbook* instructions. For example, to construct the residual plot for the residuals and the predicted value of Y, select columns D and F. (See Appendix B for help about selecting a noncontiguous cell range.)

To learn more about the formulas that the RESIDUAL worksheet uses, read the SHORT TAKES for Chapter 14.

Analysis ToolPak Use the Section EG14.1 *Analysis ToolPak* instructions. Modify step 5 by checking **Residuals** and **Residual Plots** before clicking **New Worksheet Ply** and then **OK**. The **Residuals Plots** option constructs residual plots only for each independent variable.

To construct a plot of the residuals and the predicted value of Y, select the predicted and residuals cells (in the RESIDUAL OUTPUT area of the regression results worksheet) and then apply the Section EG2.5 *Worksheet* "The Scatter Plot" instructions.

EG14.4 INFERENCES ABOUT the POPULATION REGRESSION COEFFICIENTS

The regression results worksheets that the Section EG14.1 instructions create include the information needed to make the inferences that Section 14.4 discusses.

EG14.5 TESTING PORTIONS of the MULTIPLE REGRESSION MODEL

Key Technique Adapt the Section EG14.1 "Interpreting the Regression Coefficients" instructions.

Example Test portions of the multiple regression model for the OmniPower sales data as discussed in Section 14.5, starting on page 551.

PHStat Use the Section EG14.1 *PHStat* "Interpreting the Regression Coefficients" instructions but modify step 6 by checking **Coefficients of Partial Determination** before you click **OK**.

Workbook Use one of the **CPD worksheets** of the **Multiple Regression workbook** as a template.

For the example, the **CPD_2 worksheet** already contains the data to compute the coefficients of partial determination. For other problems, first use the EG14.1 "Interpreting the Regression Coefficients" and EG13.2 *Worksheet* instructions to create all possible regression results worksheets.

For example, if you have two independent variables, you perform three regression analyses: Y with X_1 and X_2, Y with X_1, and Y with X_2, to create three regression results worksheets. Then, open to the **CPD worksheet** for the number of independent variables and follow the instructions in the worksheet to transfer values from the regression results worksheets you just created.

EG14.6 USING DUMMY VARIABLES and INTERACTION TERMS

Dummy Variables

Key Technique Use **Find and Replace** to create a dummy variable from a two-level categorical variable.

Example From the two-level categorical variable Has Fireplace, create the dummy variable Fireplace that the Figure 14.10 regression model on page 558 uses.

Workbook For the example, open to the **OriginalData worksheet** of the **SilverSpringUncoded workbook** and:

1. Copy and paste the **Has Fireplace** values in column **M** to **column N** (the first empty column).
2. Enter **Fireplace** in cell **N1** and then select **column N**.
3. Press **Ctrl+H** (the keyboard shortcut for **Find and Replace**).

In the Find and Replace dialog box:

4. Enter **Yes** in the **Find what** box and enter **1** in the **Replace with** box.
5. Click **Replace All**. If a message box to confirm the replacement appears, click **OK** to continue.
6. Enter **No** in the **Find what** box and enter **0** in the **Replace with** box.
7. Click **Replace All**. If a message box to confirm the replacement appears, click **OK** to continue.
8. Click **Close**.

Categorical variables that have more than two levels require the use of formulas in multiple columns. For example, to create the Example 14.3 dummy variables for Example 14.3 on page 560, two columns are needed. Assume that the three-level House Type variable in the example is in Column D. A first new column that contains formulas in the form =**IF(column D** *cell=first level*, **1, 0)** and a second new column that contains formulas in the form =**IF(column D** *cell=secondlevel*, **1, 0)** would properly create the two dummy variables that the example requires.

Interactions

To create an interaction term, add a column of formulas that multiply one independent variable by another. For example, if the first independent variable appeared in column B and the second independent variable appeared in column C, enter the formula =**B2*C2** in the row 2 cell of an empty new column and then copy the formula down through all rows of data to create the interaction.

EG14.7 LOGISTIC REGRESSION

Key Technique Use an automated process that incorporates the use of the Solver add-in to develop a logistic regression analysis model.

Example Develop the Figure 14.14 logistic regression model for the credit card pilot study data on page 571.

PHStat Use **Logistic Regression**.

For the example, open to the **DATA worksheet** of the **CardStudy workbook**. Select **PHStat → Regression → Logistic Regression**, and in the procedure's dialog box:

1. Enter **A1:A31** as the **Y Variable Cell Range**.
2. Enter **B1:C31** as the **X Variables Cell Range**.
3. Check **First cells in both ranges contain label**.
4. Enter a **Title** and click **OK**.

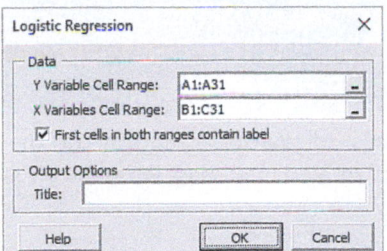

If the Solver add-in is not installed (see Appendix Section D.6), PHStat will display an error message instead of the Logistic Regression dialog box.

Workbook Use the **Logistic Regression add-in workbook**. *The Excel Solver add-in must be installed before using this add-in workbook* (see Appendix D).

For the example, the **COMPUTE worksheet** of the **Logistic Model workbook** already contains the logistic regression model. For other problems:

1. Open to the worksheet that contains the data for the problem. The worksheet *must* be part of a workbook saved in the current **.xlsx** format (not the older **.xls** format).
2. Open the Logistic Regression add-in workbook (as you would open any other Excel file).

If the add-in workbook opens properly, it adds a Logistic Add-in menu to the Add-ins tab in Microsoft Windows Excel or to the Apple menu bar in Excel for Mac.

3. Select **Logistic Add-in → Logistic Regression**.

In the Logistic Regression dialog box, (identical to the PHStat dialog box):

4. Use steps 1 through 4 of the *PHStat* instructions to complete the entries in the dialog box.

CHAPTER 14

▾ JMP GUIDE

JG14.1 DEVELOPING a MULTIPLE REGRESSION MODEL

Use **Scatterplot 3D** to create a three-dimensional plot for the special case of a regression model that contains two independent variables.

For example, to create the Figure 14.1 plot for the OmniPower sales data on page 538, open to the **OmniPower data table**. Select **Graph → Scatterplot 3D** and in the Scatterplot 3D dialog box (shown at right):

1. Click **Promotional Expenses** in the columns list and then click **Y, Columns** to add Promotional Expenses to the Y, Columns box.
2. Click **Sales** in the columns list and then click **Y, Columns** to add Sales to the Y, Columns box.
3. Click **Price** in the columns list and then click **Y, Columns** to add Price to the Y, Columns box.
4. Click **OK**.

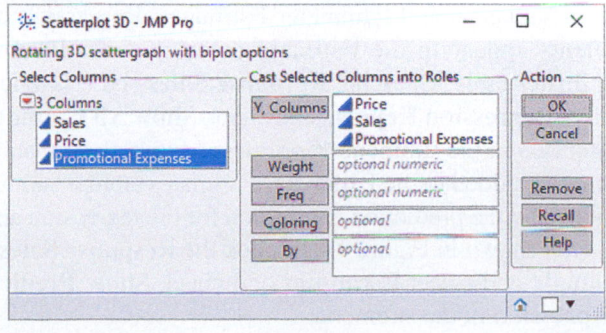

JMP displays the plot in a new results window. Drag the 3D cube to rotate the cube to better match the orientation of the Figure 14.1 plot.

5. Click the **Scatterplot 3D red triangle** and select **Drop Lines** from its menu.
6. Right-click on the cube and select **Settings**.
7. In the Settings panel, slide **Marker Size** until points appear on the drop lines, make any other adjustments necessary, and then click **Done**.

Interpreting the Regression Coefficients

Use **Fit Model**.

For example, to develop the Figure 14.2 multiple regression model for the OmniPower sales data on page 539, open to the **OmniPower data table**. Select **Analyze ➔ Fit Model** and in the Fit Model dialog box (partially shown below):

1. Click **Sales** in the columns list and then click **Y** to add Sales to the Y box.
2. Click **Price** in the columns list and then click **Add** to add Price to the Construct Model Effects box.
3. Click **Promotional Expenses** in the columns list and then click **Add** to add Promotional Expenses to the Construct Model Effects box.
4. Click **Run**.

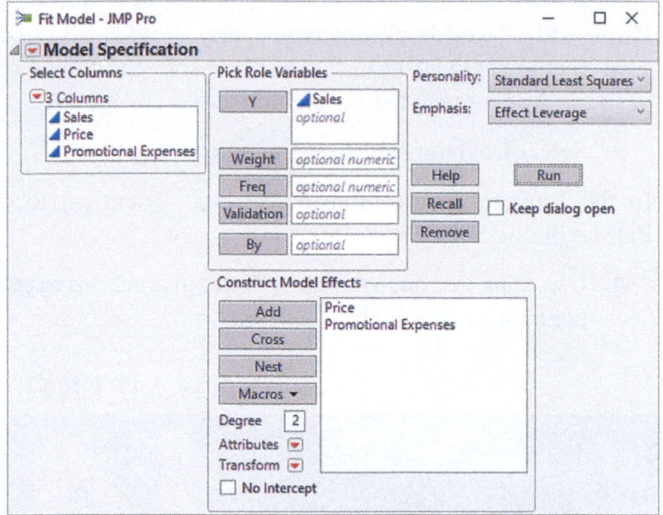

JMP displays results in a new window. Tabular regression results appear under the headings Summary of Fit, Analysis of Variance, and Parameter Estimates. Regression coefficients appear in the Estimate column of the Parameter Estimates table. Click the **Response Sales red triangle** and select **Regression Reports** and check **Show All Confidence Intervals** in the submenu. Confidence interval estimate columns are added to the Parameter Estimates tabular summary. To display the prediction expression for the regression analysis (not shown in Figure 14.2), click the **Response Sales red triangle** and select **Estimates** and check **Show Prediction Expression** in the submenu.

Predicting the Dependent Variable Y

Use **Profiler**.

For example, to construct the Figure 14.3 confidence interval estimate of the mean value for the OmniPower sales data on page 541, open to the **OmniPower data table**. Select **Analyze ➔ Fit Model** and follow Section JG14.1 steps 1 though 4 in the Interpreting the Regression Coefficients discussion above. In the results window, click the **Response Sales red triangle** and select **Factor Profiling**

and check **Profiler** in the submenu. JMP displays an interactive graph with the heading Prediction Profiler in the results window (shown below). Drag the crosshairs target until they align on the X values for the interval estimate. (Alternately, double-click on a red X value and enter a value.) The 95% confidence interval estimate appears as part of the Y axis label.

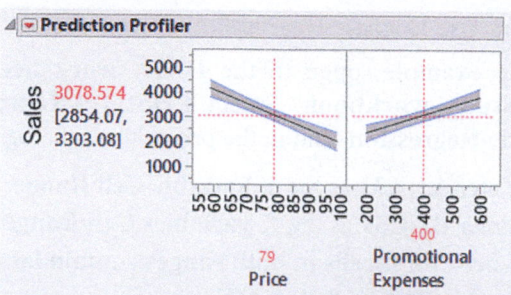

JG14.2 r^2, ADJUSTED r^2, and the OVERALL F TEST MEASURES of VARIATION

The measures of variation appear in the Summary of Fit, Analysis of Variance, and Parameter Estimates tabular summaries.

JG14.3 MULTIPLE REGRESSION RESIDUAL ANALYSIS

Use **Graph Builder**.

Create a plot of the residuals versus each of the independent X variables and the predicted Y variable values by adding columns of residuals and predicted values to a data table that JMP computes.

For example, to perform a residual analysis for the OmniPower sales multiple regression model, first follow the Section JG14.1 instructions to create a regression results window. Then, in the results window:

1. Click the **Response Sales red triangle** and select **Save Columns ➔ Residuals**.
2. Click the **Response Sales red triangle** and select **Save Columns ➔ Predicted Values**.

JMP adds residuals and predicted values columns to the original data table. Using that data table, select **Graph ➔ Graph Builder** and create scatter plots (see Section JG2.5) that correspond to the set of residual plots needed.

JG14.4 INFERENCES ABOUT the POPULATION

The regression results worksheets that the Section JG14.1 instructions created include the information needed to make the inferences that Section 14.4 discusses.

JG14.5   TESTING PORTIONS of the MULTIPLE REGRESSION MODEL

Compute the coefficients of partial determination by using a two-step process. First use the Section JG14.1 instructions to create all possible regression results and save them in the same project file. For example, with two independent variables, perform three regression analyses—Y with X_1 and X_2, Y with X_1, and Y with X_2—to create three sets of regression results. With those results compute the partial F test and the coefficients of partial determination using the method that Section 14.5 discusses.

JG14.6   USING DUMMY VARIABLES and INTERACTION TERMS

Dummy Variables

Use **Make Indicator Variables**.

For example, to create the dummy variable Fireplace from the categorical variable Has Fireplace with the categories yes and no, open to the **SilverSpringUncoded data table** and:

1. Select the **Has Fireplace column**.
2. Select **Cols → Utilities → Make Indicator Columns**.
3. In the Make Indicator Columns dialog box, check both check boxes and click **OK**.
4. Click **OK**.

JMP add two columns, Has **Fireplace_N**, in which the absence of a fireplace is coded as 1, and Has **Fireplace_Y**, in which the presence of a fireplace is coded as 1.

5. Delete the **Has Fireplace_N column**.
6. Rename the **Has Fireplace_Y column** as **Fireplace**.

Interaction Terms

Use **Fit Model**.

For example, to use the interaction term that is the product of the independent variable X_1 Living Space and the dummy variable X_2 Fireplace for the Silver Spring houses regression analysis, open to the **SilverSpring data table**. First, define a new column to hold the interaction term:

1. Double-click the first blank (fourteenth) column. JMP names the column Column 14.
2. Right-click the **Column 14 column heading** and select **Formula**.

In the Formula dialog box (see page 112):

3. Click **Living Space** in the columns list and then click ✕ (multiply button).
4. Click **Fireplace** in the columns list to complete the interaction term.
5. Click **OK**.

6. Rename Column 14 as **Living Space*Fireplace**.
7. Select **Analyze → Fit Model**.

In the Fit Model dialog box (partially shown below):

8. Click **Asking Price** in the columns list and then click **Y** to add Asking Price to the Y box.
9. Click **Living Space** in the columns list and then click **Add** to add Living Space to the Construct Model Effects box.
10. Click **Fireplace** in the columns list and then click **Add** to add Fireplace to the Construct Model Effects box.
11. Click **Living Space*Fireplace** in the columns list and then click **Add** to add LivingSpace*Fireplace to the Construct Model Effects box.
12. Uncheck **No Intercept**, if checked.
13. Click **Run**.

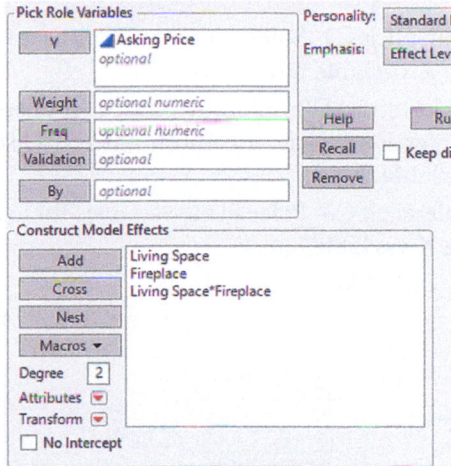

JG14.7   LOGISTIC REGRESSION

Use **Fit Model**.

For example, to perform the Figure 14.14 logistic regression analysis on page 571, open to **CardStudy data table**. Select **Analyze → Fit Model** and in the Fit Model dialog box:

1. Click **Upgraded** in the columns list and then click **Y** to add Upgraded to the Y box.
2. Click **Purchases** in the columns list and then click **Add** to add Purchases to the Construct Model Effects box.
3. Click **Extra Cards** in the columns list and then click **Add** to add Extra cards to the Construct Model Effects box.
4. Click **Run**.

JMP displays results in a new window. To perform a logistic regression analysis, the variable entered in the Y box must have the ordinal modeling type (as Upgraded does in the CardStudy data table).

MG14.1 DEVELOPING a MULTIPLE REGRESSION MODEL

Use **3D Scatterplot** for the special case of a regression model that contains two independent variables.

For example, to create the Figure 14.1 plot for the Omni Power sales data on page 538, open the **OmniPower worksheet**. Select **Graph ➔ 3D Scatterplot** and:

1. In the 3D Scatterplots dialog box (not shown), click **Simple** and then click **OK**.

In the 3D Scatterplot: Simple dialog box (shown below):

2. Double-click **C1 Sales** in the variables list to add **Sales** to the **Z variable** box.
3. Double-click **C2 Promotional Expenses** in the variables list to add **'Promotional Expenses'** to the **Y variable** box.
4. Double-click **C3 Price** in the variables list to add **Price** to the **X variable** box.
5. Click **Data View**.

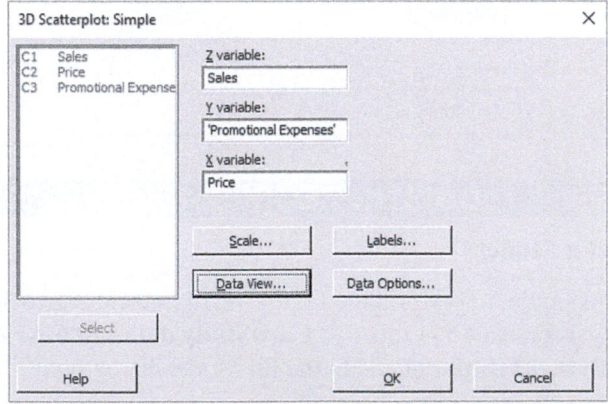

6. In the 3D Scatterplot: Data View dialog box, check **Symbols** and **Project lines** and then click **OK**.
7. Back in the 3D Scatterplot: Simple dialog box, click **OK**.

   Rotate the scatter plot using the icons to rotate the *X*, *Y*, and *Z* axes in the 3D Graph Tools toolbar. Select **Tools ➔ Toolbars ➔ 3D Graph Tools** if this toolbar is not visible in the Minitab window.

Interpreting the Regression Coefficients

Use **Fit Regression Model**.

For example, to perform the Figure 14.2 analysis of the OmniPower sales data on page 539, open to the **OmniPower**

worksheet. Select **Stat ➔ Regression ➔ Regression ➔ Fit Regression Model**. In the Regression dialog box (shown below):

1. Double-click **C1 Sales** in the variables list to add **Sales** to the **Responses** box and press **Tab**.
2. Double-click **C2 Price** in the variables list to add **Price** to the **Continuous predictors** box.
3. Double-click **C3 Promotional Expenses** in the variables list to add **'Promotional Expenses'** to the **Continuous predictors** box.
4. Click **Graphs**.

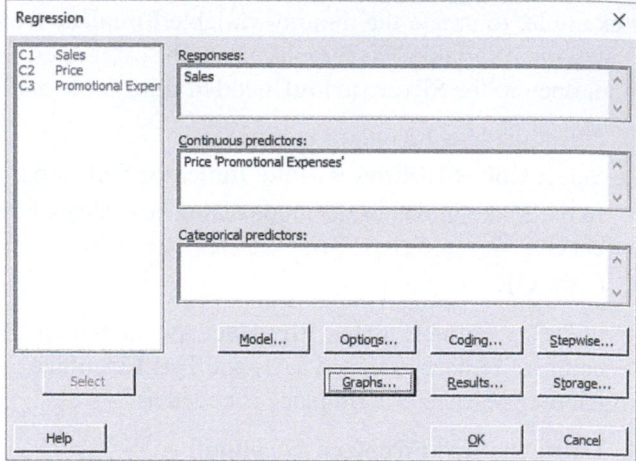

In the Regression: Graphs dialog box (shown below):

5. Select **Regular** from the **Residuals for plots** pull-down list.
6. Click **Individual Plots**.
7. Check **Histogram of residuals** and **Residuals versus fits** and clear the other check boxes.

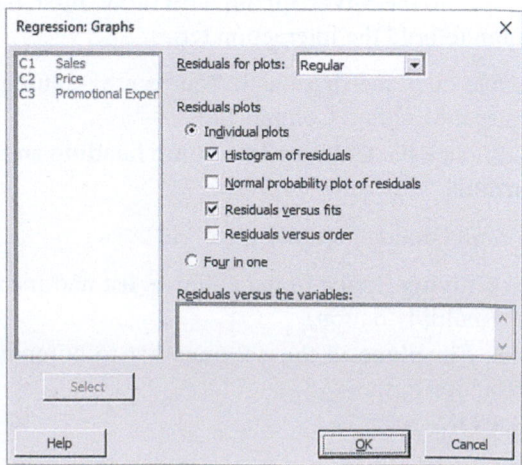

8. Click anywhere inside the **Residuals versus the variables** box.
9. Double-click **C2 Price** in the variables list to add **Price** in the **Residuals versus the variables** box.
10. Double-click **C3 Promotional Expenses** in the variables list to add **'Promotional Expenses'** in the **Residuals versus the variables** box.
11. Click **OK**.
12. Back in the Regression dialog box, click **Results**.

In the Regression: Results dialog box (shown below):

13. Select **Simple tables** from the **Display of results** pull-down list.
14. Check all check boxes except **Durbin-Watson statistic**.
15. Select **For all observations** from the **Fits and diagnostics** pull-down list and then click **OK**.

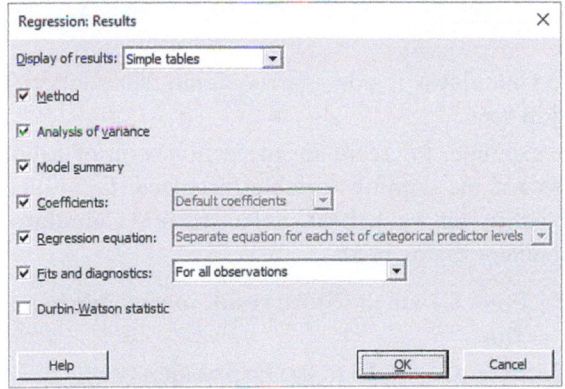

16. Back in the Regression dialog box, click **Options**.

In the Regression: Options dialog box (not shown):

17. Enter **95** in the **Confidence level for all intervals** box.
18. Verify that the **Type of confidence interval** is **Two-sided** and that the **Sum of squares for tests** is **Adjusted (Type III)**.
19. Click **OK**.
20. Back in the Regression dialog box, click **OK**.

Minitab displays residual plots in their own window as well as adding regression results and a list of residuals to the Session Window.

Predicting the Dependent Variable Y

Use **Predict**.

For example, to create the Figure 14.3 confidence interval estimate and prediction interval for the OmniPower sales data, open to the **OmniPower worksheet**. Select **Stat → Regression → Predict**. In the Predict dialog box:

1. Select **Sales** from the **Response** pull-down list.
2. Select **Enter individual values** from the unlabeled pull-down list.

3. Enter **79** in the first cell of the **Prices** list.
4. Enter **400** in the first cell of the **'Promotional Expenses'** list.
5. Click **Options** and in the Predict: Options dialog box, verify that **95** is the **Confidence level** and **Two-sided** is the **Type of interval** and then click **OK**.
6. Back in the original dialog box, click **Results**.
7. In the Predict: Results dialog box, check both check boxes and then click **OK**.
8. Back in the original dialog box, click **OK**.

MG14.2 r^2, ADJUSTED r^2, and the OVERALL F TEST

The coefficient of multiple determination, r^2, the adjusted r^2, and the overall F test appear as part of the multiple regression results that the Section MG14.1 instructions create.

MG14.3 MULTIPLE REGRESSION RESIDUAL ANALYSIS

The regression results that the Section MG14.1 instructions create include a residual analysis.

MG14.4 INFERENCES ABOUT the POPULATION REGRESSION COEFFICIENTS

The regression results that the MG14.1 instructions create include the information needed to make the inferences that Section 14.4 discusses.

MG14.5 TESTING PORTIONS of the MULTIPLE REGRESSION MODEL

Compute the coefficients of partial determination by using a two-step process. First use the Section MG14.1 instructions to create all possible regression results in the same project file. For example, with two independent variables, perform three regression analyses—Y with X_1 and X_2, Y with X_1, and Y with X_2—to create three sets of regression results. With those results compute the partial F test and the coefficients of partial determination using the method that Section 14.5 discusses.

MG14.6 USING DUMMY VARIABLES and INTERACTION TERMS in REGRESSION MODELS

Dummy Variables

Use **Make Indicator Variables**.

For example, to create the dummy variable Fireplace from the categorical variable Has Fireplace with the categories yes and no, open to the **SilverSpringUncoded worksheet.** Select **Calc → Make Indicator Variables.** In the Make Indicator Variables dialog box (shown below):

1. Double-click **C13 Has Fireplace** in the variables list to enter **'Has Fireplace'** in the **Indicator variables for** box.
2. Click **OK.**

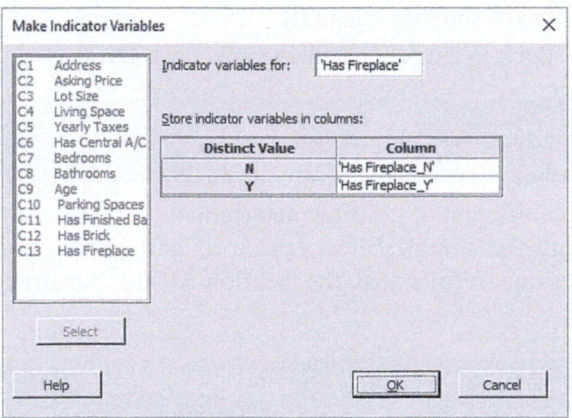

Minitab add two columns 'Has Fireplace_Y', in which the presence of a fireplace is coded as 1 and 'Has Fireplace_N' in which the absence of a fireplace is coded as 1:

3. Delete the **'Has Fireplace_N' column.**
4. Rename the **'Has Fireplace_Y' column** as **Fireplace.**

Column renaming can also be done in the Make Indicator Variables dialog box by changing the column name in the Column column.

Interactions

Use Model options of the Regression dialog box.

For example, to use the interaction term that is the product of the independent variable X_1 Living Space and the dummy variable X_2 Fireplace for the Silver Spring houses regression analysis, open to the **SilverSpring worksheet.** Select **Stat → Regression → Regression → Fit Regression Model.** In the Regression dialog box:

1. Double-click **C2 Asking Price** in the variables list to enter **'Asking Price'** in the **Responses** box and press **Tab.**
2. Double-click **C4 Living Space** in the variables list to enter **'Living Space'** in the **Continuous predictors** box.
3. Double-click **C13 Fireplace** in the variables list to enter **'Fireplace'** in the **Continuous predictors** box.
4. Click **Model.**

In the Regression: Model dialog box (shown at right):

5. Click **'Living Space'** in the **Predictors** list.
6. While holding down the **Ctrl key,** click **Fireplace** in the **Predictors** list.
7. Click **Add** that is to the right of **Interactions through order.**

Minitab adds **'Living Space'*Fireplace** to the **Terms in the model** list. Click **OK** to return to the Regression dialog box and then complete the regression analysis.

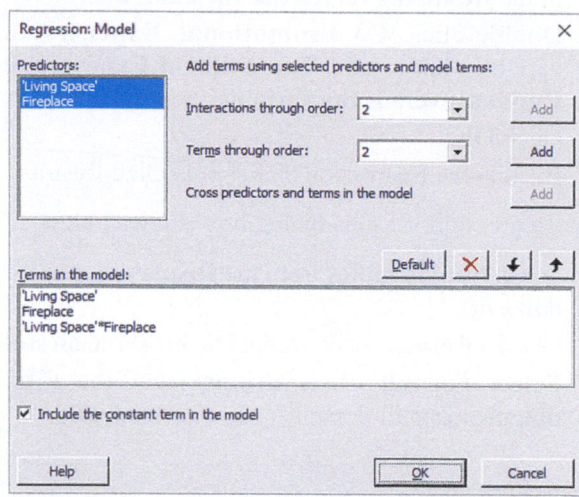

Use **Calculator** to add a new column that contains an interaction term.

For example, to create an interaction term of Living Space (C4) and the dummy variable Fireplace (C13), open to the **SilverSpring worksheet.** Select **Calc → Calculator.** In the Calculator dialog box:

1. Enter **C14** in the **Store result in variable** box and press **Tab.**
2. Enter **C4 * C13** in the **Expression** box.
3. Click **OK.**
4. Enter **Living Space*Fireplace** as the name for column **C14.**

MG14.7　LOGISTIC REGRESSION

Use **Binary Logistic Regression** to perform a logistic regression. For example, to perform the Figure 14.14 logistic regression analysis on page 571, open to **CardStudy worksheet.** Select **Stat → Regression → Binary Logistic Regression Fit Binary Logistic Regression Model.** In the Binary Logistic Regression dialog box (shown on page 591):

1. Select **Response in binary response/frequency format** from the pull-down list and press **Tab.**
2. Double-click **C1 Upgraded** in the variables list to add **Upgraded** in the **Response** box.
3. Keep **Response event** as **1.**
4. Click inside the **Continuous predictors** box.
5. Double-click **C2 Purchases** in the variables list to add **Purchases** to the **Continuous predictors** box.
6. Double-click **C3 Extra Cards** in the variables list to add **'Extra Cards'** to the **Categorical predictors** box and press **Tab.**
7. Click **OK.**

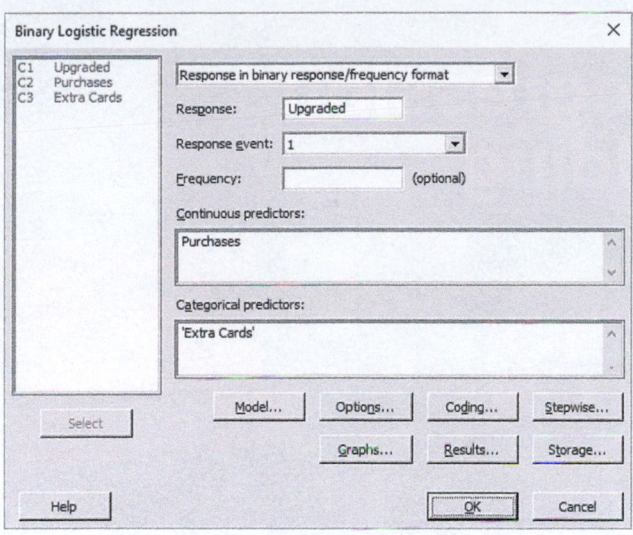

Use the Section MG14.1 "Interpreting the Regression Coefficients" instructions, replacing step 20 of those instructions with the steps 20 through 22 listed below.

For example, to perform the Figure 14.2 analysis of the OmniPower sales data on page 539, replace step 20 with these steps 20 through 22:

20. Back in the Regression dialog box, click **Storage**.
21. In the Regression: Storage dialog box, check **Deleted residuals**, **Leverages**, and **Cook's distance**, and then click **OK**.
22. Back in the Regression dialog box, click **OK**.

15

Multiple Regression Model Building

CONTENTS

OBJECTIVES

- Use quadratic terms in a regression model
- Use transformed variables in a regression model
- Measure the correlation among independent variables
- Build a regression model using either the stepwise or best subsets approach
- Avoid the pitfalls involved in developing a multiple regression model

▼USING **STATISTICS**
Valuing Parsimony at WSTA-TV

Nickels Broadcasting looks to minimize costs at its WSTA-TV News 37 broadcast center and has identified cutting *standby hours*, hours for which employees are scheduled but end up not being assigned any work, as a possible way to minimize costs. Nickels has already received an offer to move its broadcast center to Argleton, a locality that permits *on-call shifts*, a form of just-in-time scheduling. Using on-call shifts could eliminate many standby hours. However, relocating would create new costs and raise other concerns including the location of the proposed site, so management has deferred action on that offer.

Instead, Nickels management wonders if the numbers of staff hired each week and the number of weekly hours that the staff works in three job categories affects the weekly standby hours. Nickels hires you as an analyst and presents you with a 26-week sample of weekly standby hours as well as weekly staff count, remote engineering hours, graphics hours, and editorial production hours. You quickly establish that no single variable from the set of four independent variables can predict standby hours. How, then do you build a multiple regression model that uses some or all of the four variables? How can you determine a "best" regression model without examining all possible models?

The simple and multiple regression models that Chapters 13 and 14 discuss assume a linear relationship between the dependent Y variable and each independent X variable. This chapter extends the discussion of multiple regression to consider both nonlinear regression models as well as the methods that help efficiently develop the best model for any set of data, including those that have many independent X variables. Such methods can provide the means of identifying the "best" model for the WSTA-TV 26-week data.

15.1 The Quadratic Regression Model

One of the most common nonlinear relationships between variables is *curvilinear*. In the **curvilinear relationship**, the value of the dependent variable Y increases or decreases at a changing rate as the value of X changes. Figure 15.1 presents two scatter plots that illustrate two examples of curvilinear relationships.

FIGURE 15.1
Two curvilinear relationships

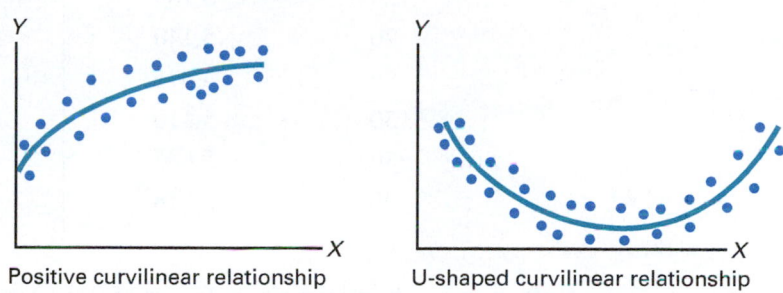

Positive curvilinear relationship   U-shaped curvilinear relationship

The simplest curvilinear relationship is a quadratic relationship in which there is a term in the regression model that is the square of the independent variable. Equation (15.1) defines this relationship as the **quadratic regression model**.

QUADRATIC REGRESSION MODEL

$$Y_i = \beta_0 + \beta_1 X_{1i} + \beta_2 X_{1i}^2 + \varepsilon_i \tag{15.1}$$

where

$\beta_0 = Y$ intercept

$\beta_1 = $ coefficient of the linear effect on Y

$\beta_2 = $ coefficient of the quadratic effect on Y

$\varepsilon_i = $ random error in Y for observation i

The quadratic regression model is similar to the multiple regression model with two independent variables that Equation (14.2) on page 538 defines. However, in a quadratic model, the square of the first independent variable that serves as the second independent variable is called the **quadratic term**. As with a multiple regression model, you use the least-squares method to compute sample regression coefficients (b_0, b_1, and b_2) as estimates of the population parameters (β_0, β_1, and β_2). Equation (15.2) defines the regression equation for the quadratic model with an independent variable (X_1) and a dependent variable (Y).

studentTIP

A quadratic regression model has an X term and an X squared term. Other curvilinear models can have additional X terms such as X cubed, X raised to the fourth power, and so on.

QUADRATIC REGRESSION EQUATION

$$\hat{Y}_i = b_0 + b_1 X_{1i} + b_2 X_{1i}^2 \tag{15.2}$$

In Equation (15.2), the first regression coefficient, b_0, represents the Y intercept; the second regression coefficient, b_1, represents the linear effect; and the third regression coefficient, b_2, represents the quadratic effect.

Finding the Regression Coefficients and Predicting *Y*

To illustrate the quadratic regression model, consider a study that examined the business problem facing a concrete supplier of how adding fly ash affects the strength of concrete. (Fly ash is an inexpensive industrial waste by-product that can be used as a substitute for Portland cement, a more expensive ingredient of concrete.) Batches of concrete were prepared in which the percentage of fly ash ranged from 0% to 60%. Data were collected from a sample of 18 batches and organized and stored in FlyAsh. Table 15.1 summarizes the results.

TABLE 15.1

Fly Ash Percentage and Strength of 18 Batches of 28-Day-Old Concrete

FlyAsh%	Strength (psi)	FlyAsh%	Strength (psi)
0	4,779	40	5,995
0	4,706	40	5,628
0	4,350	40	5,897
20	5,189	50	5,746
20	5,140	50	5,719
20	4,976	50	5,782
30	5,110	60	4,895
30	5,685	60	5,030
30	5,618	60	4,648

By creating the scatter plot in Figure 15.2 to visualize the relationship between the FlyAsh% and Strength variables, you will be better able to select the proper model for expressing the relationship between fly ash percentage and strength.

FIGURE 15.2

Scatter plot of fly ash percentage (*X*) and strength (*Y*)

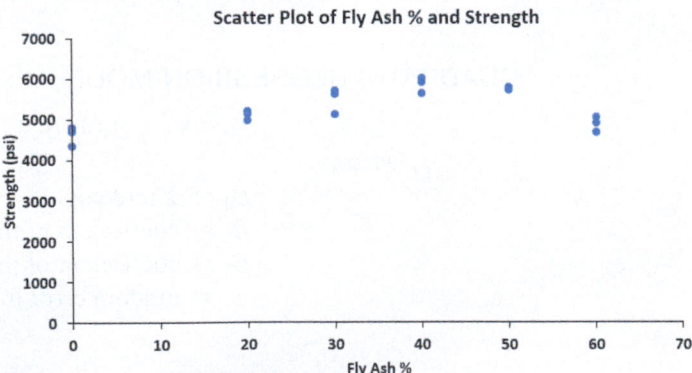

Figure 15.2 indicates an initial increase in the strength of the concrete as the percentage of fly ash increases. The strength appears to level off and then drop after achieving maximum strength at about 40% fly ash. Strength for 50% fly ash is slightly below strength at 40%, but strength at 60% fly ash is substantially below strength at 50%. Therefore, you should fit a quadratic model, not a linear model, to estimate strength based on fly ash percentage.

From Figure 15.3, which shows the Excel, JMP, and Minitab results for these data, the regression coefficients are

$$b_0 = 4{,}486.3611 \quad b_1 = 63.0052 \quad b_2 = -0.8765$$

Therefore, the quadratic regression equation is

$$\hat{Y}_i = 4{,}486.3611 + 63.0052X_{1i} - 0.8765X_{1i}^2$$

where

$$\hat{Y}_i = \text{predicted strength for sample } i$$

$$X_{1i} = \text{percentage of fly ash for sample } i$$

FIGURE 15.3

Excel, JMP, and Minitab multiple regression quadratic model results for the concrete strength data

	A	B	C	D	E	F	G
1	**Concrete Strength Analysis**						
2							
3	*Regression Statistics*						
4	Multiple R	0.8053					
5	R Square	0.6485					
6	Adjusted R Square	0.6016					
7	Standard Error	312.1129					
8	Observations	18					
9							
10	ANOVA						
11		*df*	*SS*	*MS*	*F*	*Significance F*	
12	Regression	2	2695473.4897	1347736.745	13.8351	0.0004	
13	Residual	15	1461217.0103	97414.4674			
14	Total	17	4156690.5000				
15							
16		*Coefficients*	*Standard Error*	*t Stat*	*P-value*	*Lower 95%*	*Upper 95%*
17	Intercept	4486.3611	174.7531	25.6726	0.0000	4113.8834	4858.8389
18	FlyAsh%	63.0052	12.3725	5.0923	0.0001	36.6338	89.3767
19	FlyAsh% ^2	-0.8765	0.1966	-4.4578	0.0005	-1.2955	-0.4574

Summary of Fit

RSquare	0.648466
RSquare Adj	0.601595
Root Mean Square Error	312.1129
Mean of Response	5271.833
Observations (or Sum Wgts)	18

Analysis of Variance

Source	DF	Sum of Squares	Mean Square	F Ratio
Model	2	2695473.5	1347737	13.8351
Error	15	1461217.0	97414	Prob > F
C. Total	17	4156690.5		0.0004*

Parameter Estimates

Term	Estimate	Std Error	t Ratio	Prob>|t|	Lower 95%	Upper 95%
Intercept	4486.3611	174.7531	25.67	<.0001*	4113.8836	4858.8386
FlyAsh%	63.005238	12.37255	5.09	0.0001*	36.633782	89.376694
FlyAsh%^2	-0.876468	0.196613	-4.46	0.0005*	-1.295538	-0.457398

Regression Analysis: Strength versus FlyAsh%, FlyAsh%^2

Analysis of Variance

Source	DF	Adj SS	Adj MS	F-Value	P-Value
Regression	2	2695473	1347737	13.84	0.000
FlyAsh%	1	2526147	2526147	25.93	0.000
FlyAsh%^2	1	1935855	1935855	19.87	0.000
Error	15	1461217	97414		
Lack-of-Fit	3	983965	327988	8.25	0.003
Pure Error	12	477252	39771		
Total	17	4156691			

Model Summary

S	R-sq	R-sq(adj)	R-sq(pred)
312.113	64.85%	60.16%	49.11%

Coefficients

Term	Coef	SE Coef	T-Value	P-Value	VIF
Constant	4486	175	25.67	0.000	
FlyAsh%	63.0	12.4	5.09	0.000	11.00
FlyAsh%^2	-0.876	0.197	-4.46	0.000	11.00

Regression Equation

Strength = 4486 + 63.0 FlyAsh% - 0.876 FlyAsh%^2

Figure 15.4 is a scatter plot of this quadratic regression equation that shows the fit of the quadratic regression model to the original data.

FIGURE 15.4

Scatter plot showing the quadratic relationship between fly ash percentage and strength for the concrete data

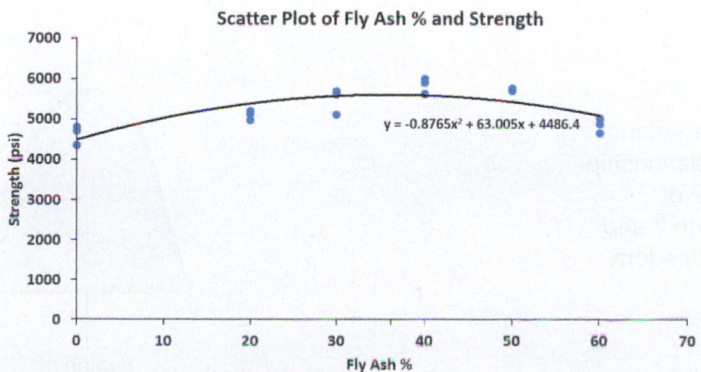

Scatter Plot of Fly Ash % and Strength

$y = -0.8765x^2 + 63.005x + 4486.4$

From the quadratic regression equation and Figure 15.4, the Y intercept, (4,486.3611) is the predicted strength when the percentage of fly ash is 0. To interpret the coefficients b_1 and b_2, observe that after an initial increase, strength decreases as fly ash percentage increases. This nonlinear relationship is further demonstrated by predicting the strength for fly ash percentages of 20, 40, and 60. Using the quadratic regression equation,

$$\hat{Y}_i = 4,486.3611 + 63.0052X_{1i} - 0.8765X_{1i}^2$$

for $X_{1i} = 20$,

$$\hat{Y}_i = 4{,}486.3611 + 63.0052(20) - 0.8765(20)^2 = 5{,}395.865$$

for $X_{1i} = 40$,

$$\hat{Y}_i = 4{,}486.3611 + 63.0052(40) - 0.8765(40)^2 = 5{,}604.169$$

and for $X_{1i} = 60$,

$$\hat{Y}_i = 4{,}486.3611 + 63.0052(60) - 0.8765(60)^2 = 5{,}111.273$$

Thus, the predicted concrete strength for 40% fly ash is 208.304 psi above the predicted strength for 20% fly ash, but the predicted strength for 60% fly ash is 492.896 psi below the predicted strength for 40% fly ash. The concrete supplier should consider using a fly ash percentage of 40% and not using fly ash percentages of 20% or 60% because those percentages lead to reduced concrete strength.

Testing for the Significance of the Quadratic Model

After you calculate the quadratic regression equation, you can test whether there is a significant overall relationship between strength, Y, and fly ash percentage, X_1. The null and alternative hypotheses are as follows:

$H_0: \beta_1 = \beta_2 = 0$ (There is no overall relationship between X_1 and Y.)

$H_1: \beta_1$ and/or $\beta_2 \neq 0$ (There is an overall relationship between X_1 and Y.)

Equation (14.6) on page 544 defines the overall F_{STAT} test statistic used for this test:

$$F_{STAT} = \frac{MSR}{MSE}$$

student TIP

If you reject H_0, you are *not* concluding that all the independent variables have a relationship with the dependent variable, only that *at least one* independent variable does.

From the Figure 15.3 results on page 595,

$$F_{STAT} = \frac{MSR}{MSE} = \frac{1{,}347{,}736.745}{97{,}414.4674} = 13.8351$$

Using a level of significance of 0.05 and Table E.5, the critical value of the F distribution, with 2 and 15 $(18 - 2 - 1)$ degrees of freedom, is 3.68 (see Figure 15.5).

FIGURE 15.5
Testing for the existence of the overall relationship at the 0.05 level of significance, with 2 and 15 degrees of freedom

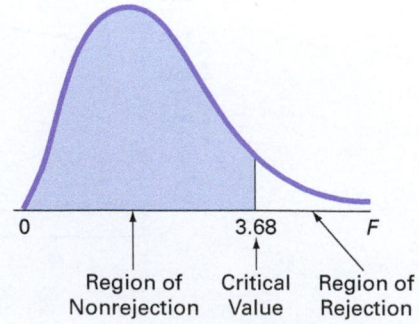

Table 15.2 summarizes the results of the test for the significance of the Figure 15.2 quadratic model on page 594. Based on the conclusions, there is strong evidence to conclude that strength is related to fly ash percentage. Therefore, you can state that fly ash percentage is useful in helping to determine the strength of the concrete.

TABLE 15.2

F Test Results for the Significance of the Quadratic Model and Conclusions

Result	Conclusions
$F_{STAT} = 13.8351$ is greater than 3.68 *p*-value $= 0.0004$ is less than the level of significance, $\alpha = 0.05$	1. Reject the null hypothesis H_0. 2. Conclude that evidence exists for claiming that fly ash percentage is related to the dependent Y variable, strength. 3. The probability is 0.0004 that $F_{STAT} > 13.8351$, given the null hypothesis is true.

Testing the Quadratic Effect

When using regression analysis to examine a relationship between two variables, the goal is to find the most accurate, as well as the *simplest*, model that expresses the relationship. Therefore, you need to examine whether there is a significant difference between the quadratic model:

$$Y_i = \beta_0 + \beta_1 X_{1i} + \beta_2 X_{1i}^2 + \varepsilon_i$$

and the linear model:

$$Y_i = \beta_0 + \beta_1 X_{1i} + \varepsilon_i$$

Section 14.4 discusses the *t* test to determine whether each independent variable makes a significant contribution to the regression model. To test the significance of the contribution of the quadratic effect, you use the following null and alternative hypotheses:

H_0: Including the quadratic effect does not significantly improve the model ($\beta_2 = 0$).

H_1: Including the quadratic effect significantly improves the model ($\beta_2 \neq 0$).

Equation (14.7) on page 548 defines the t_{STAT} test statistic for this test. The standard error of each regression coefficient and its corresponding t_{STAT} test statistic that this test needs appear in the regression results that Excel, JMP, or Minitab produce. For the fly ash example, using the values that appear in Figure 15.3:

$$t_{STAT} = \frac{b_2 - \beta_2}{S_{b_2}}$$

$$= \frac{-0.8765 - 0}{0.1966} = -4.4578$$

If you select the 0.05 level of significance, then from Table E.3, the critical values for the *t* distribution with 15 degrees of freedom are -2.1315 and $+2.1315$ (see Figure 15.6).

FIGURE 15.6

Testing for the contribution of the quadratic effect to a regression model at the 0.05 level of significance, with 15 degrees of freedom

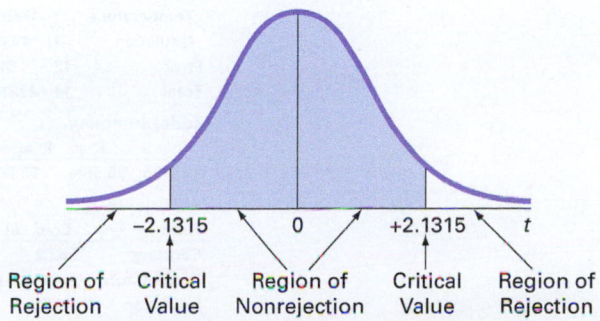

Table 15.3 summarizes the results of the test for the significance of the quadratic effect. Based on these conclusions, there is strong evidence to conclude that there is a quadratic effect of fly ash percentage and strength. Therefore, as part of the DCOVA framework, you can say that the quadratic effect of fly ash percentage can be used to help determine the strength of the concrete.

TABLE 15.3

t Test Results for the Significance of the Quadratic Model and Conclusions

Result	Conclusions
$t_{STAT} = -4.4578$ is less than -2.1315	1. Reject the null hypothesis H_0.
	2. Conclude that evidence exists for claiming that there is a quadratic effect of fly ash percentage with the dependent Y variable, strength.
p-value $= 0.0005$ is less than the level of significance, $\alpha = 0.05$	3. The probability is 0.0005 that $t_{STAT} = \ < -4.4578$ or > 4.4578, given the null hypothesis is true.

Example 15.1 provides an additional illustration of a possible quadratic effect.

EXAMPLE 15.1

Studying the Quadratic Effect in a Multiple Regression Model

A real estate developer studying the business problem of estimating the consumption of heating oil by single-family houses has decided to examine the effect of atmospheric temperature and the amount of attic insulation on heating oil consumption. Data are collected from a random sample of 15 single-family houses and stored in HeatingOil.

Figure 15.7 shows the regression results for a multiple regression model using the two independent variables: atmospheric temperature and attic insulation.

FIGURE 15.7

Excel, JMP, and Minitab multiple regression linear model results for predicting monthly consumption of heating oil

	A	B	C	D	E	F	G
1	Heating Oil Consumption Analysis						
2							
3	*Regression Statistics*						
4	Multiple R	0.9827					
5	R Square	0.9656					
6	Adjusted R Square	0.9599					
7	Standard Error	26.0138					
8	Observations	15					
9							
10	ANOVA						
11		df	SS	MS	F	Significance F	
12	Regression	2	228014.6263	114007.3132	168.4712	0.0000	
13	Residual	12	8120.6030	676.7169			
14	Total	14	236135.2293				
15							
16		Coefficients	Standard Error	t Stat	P-value	Lower 95%	Upper 95%
17	Intercept	562.1510	21.0931	26.6509	0.0000	516.1931	608.1089
18	Temperature	-5.4366	0.3362	-16.1699	0.0000	-6.1691	-4.7040
19	Insulation	-20.0123	2.3425	-8.5431	0.0000	-25.1162	-14.9084

Summary of Fit

RSquare	0.96561
RSquare Adj	0.959879
Root Mean Square Error	26.01378
Mean of Response	216.4933
Observations (or Sum Wgts)	15

Analysis of Variance

Source	DF	Sum of Squares	Mean Square	F Ratio
Model	2	228014.63	114007	168.4712
Error	12	8120.60	677	Prob > F
C. Total	14	236135.23		<.0001*

Parameter Estimates

Term	Estimate	Std Error	t Ratio	Prob>|t|	Lower 95%	Upper 95%
Intercept	562.15101	21.0931	26.65	<.0001*	516.19308	608.10894
Temperature	-5.436581	0.336216	-16.17	<.0001*	-6.169133	-4.704028
Insulation	-20.01232	2.342505	-8.54	<.0001*	-25.1162	-14.90844

Regression Analysis: Gallons versus Temperature, Insulation

Analysis of Variance

Source	DF	Adj SS	Adj MS	F-Value	P-Value
Regression	2	228015	114007	168.47	0.000
Temperature	1	176938	176938	261.47	0.000
Insulation	1	49390	49390	72.99	0.000
Error	12	8121	677		
Total	14	236135			

Model Summary

S	R-sq	R-sq(adj)	R-sq(pred)
26.0138	96.56%	95.99%	94.43%

Coefficients

Term	Coef	SE Coef	T-Value	P-Value	VIF
Constant	562.2	21.1	26.65	0.000	
Temperature	-5.437	0.336	-16.17	0.000	1.00
Insulation	-20.01	2.34	-8.54	0.000	1.00

Regression Equation

Gallons = 562.2 - 5.437 Temperature - 20.01 Insulation

The residual plot for attic insulation (not shown) contains some evidence of a quadratic effect. Therefore, the real estate developer reanalyzed the data by adding a quadratic term for attic insulation to the multiple regression model. At the 0.05 level of significance, is there evidence of a significant quadratic effect for attic insulation?

▶(continued)

SOLUTION Figure 15.8 shows the results for this regression model.

FIGURE 15.8

Excel results for the multiple regression model with a quadratic term for attic insulation

	A	B	C	D	E	F	G
1	Quadratic Effect for Insulation Variable?						
2							
3	*Regression Statistics*						
4	Multiple R	0.9862					
5	R Square	0.9725					
6	Adjusted R Square	0.9650					
7	Standard Error	24.2938					
8	Observations	15					
9							
10	ANOVA						
11		*df*	*SS*	*MS*	*F*	*Significance F*	
12	Regression	3	229643.1645	76547.7215	129.7006	0.0000	
13	Residual	11	6492.0649	590.1877			
14	Total	14	236135.2293				
15							
16		*Coefficients*	*Standard Error*	*t Stat*	*P-value*	*Lower 95%*	*Upper 95%*
17	Intercept	624.5864	42.4352	14.7186	0.0000	531.1872	717.9856
18	Temperature	-5.3626	0.3171	-16.9099	0.0000	-6.0606	-4.6646
19	Insulation	-44.5868	14.9547	-2.9815	0.0125	-77.5019	-11.6717
20	Insulation ^2	1.8667	1.1238	1.6611	0.1249	-0.6067	4.3401

The multiple regression equation is

$$\hat{Y}_i = 624.5864 - 5.3626X_{1i} - 44.5868X_{2i} + 1.8667X_{2i}^2$$

To test for the significance of the quadratic effect:

H_0: Including the quadratic effect of insulation does not significantly improve the model ($\beta_3 = 0$).

H_1: Including the quadratic effect of insulation significantly improves the model ($\beta_3 \neq 0$).

From Figure 15.8 and Table E.3 with $11\,(15 - 3 - 1)$ degrees of freedom, $-2.2010 < t_{STAT} = 1.6611 < 2.2010$ (or the p-value $= 0.1249 > 0.05$). Therefore, the developer does not reject the null hypothesis. The developer concludes that there is insufficient evidence that the quadratic effect for attic insulation is different from zero. In the interest of keeping the model as simple as possible, the developer should use the Figure 15.7 multiple regression equation:

$$\hat{Y}_i = 562.1510 - 5.4366X_{1i} - 20.0123X_{2i}$$

The Coefficient of Multiple Determination

studentTIP

For the case of quadratic regression, r^2 represents the proportion of the variation in the dependent variable Y that is explained by the linear term and the quadratic term.

In the multiple regression model, the coefficient of multiple determination, r^2, that Section 14.2 explains, represents the proportion of variation in Y that is explained by variation in the independent variables. You compute r^2 by using Equation (14.4) on page 543:

$$r^2 = \frac{SSR}{SST}$$

Consider the quadratic regression model that predicts the strength of concrete using fly ash and fly ash squared. From Figure 15.3 on page 595,

$$SSR = 2{,}695{,}473.4897 \qquad SST = 4{,}156{,}690.5$$

Thus,

$$r^2 = \frac{SSR}{SST} = \frac{2{,}695{,}473.4897}{4{,}156{,}690.5} = 0.6485$$

This coefficient of multiple determination indicates that 64.85% of the variation in strength is explained by the quadratic relationship between strength and the percentage of fly ash. You should also compute r_{adj}^2 to account for the number of independent variables and the sample size. In the quadratic regression model, $k = 2$ because there are two independent variables, X_1 and X_1^2. Thus, using Equation (14.5) on page 543,

$$r_{adj}^2 = 1 - \left[(1 - r^2)\frac{(n - 1)}{(n - k - 1)}\right] = 1 - \left[(1 - 0.6485)\frac{17}{15}\right]$$

$$= 1 - 0.3984$$

$$= 0.6016$$

PROBLEMS FOR SECTION 15.1

LEARNING THE BASICS

15.1 The following is the quadratic regression equation for a sample of $n = 25$:

$$\hat{Y}_i = 5 + 3X_{1i} + 1.5X_{1i}^2$$

a. Predict Y for $X_1 = 2$.

b. Suppose that the computed t_{STAT} test statistic for the quadratic regression coefficient is 2.35. At the 0.05 level of significance, is there evidence that the quadratic model is better than the linear model?

c. Suppose that the computed t_{STAT} test statistic for the quadratic regression coefficient is 1.17. At the 0.05 level of significance, is there evidence that the quadratic model is better than the linear model?

d. Suppose the regression coefficient for the linear effect is -3.0. Predict Y for $X_1 = 2$.

APPLYING THE CONCEPTS

15.2 Businesses actively recruit business students with well-developed higher-order cognitive skills (HOCS) such as problem identification, analytical reasoning, and content integration skills. Researchers conducted a study to see if improvement in students' HOCS was related to the students' GPA.

Source: Data extracted from R. V. Bradley, C. S. Sankar, H. R. Clayton, V. W. Mbarika, and P. K. Raju, "A Study on the Impact of GPA on Perceived Improvement of Higher-Order Cognitive Skills," *Decision Sciences Journal of Innovative Education*, January 2007, 5(1), pp. 151–168.

The researchers conducted a study in which business students were taught using the case study method. Using data collected from 300 business students, the following quadratic regression equation was derived:

$$\text{HOCS} = -3.48 + 4.53(\text{GPA}) - 0.68(\text{GPA})^2$$

where the dependent variable HOCS measured the improvement in higher-order cognitive skills, with 1 being the lowest improvement in HOCS and 5 being the highest improvement in HOCS.

a. Construct a table of predicted HOCS, using GPA equal to 2.0, 2.1, 2.2, ..., 4.0.

b. Plot the values in the table constructed in (a), with GPA on the horizontal axis and predicted HOCS on the vertical axis.

c. Discuss the curvilinear relationship between students' GPA and their predicted improvement in HOCS.

d. The researchers reported that the model had an r^2 of 0.07 and an adjusted r^2 of 0.06. What does this tell you about the scatter of individual HOCS scores around the curvilinear relationship plotted in (b) and discussed in (c)?

15.3 A study was conducted on automobile engines to examine the relationship between engine speed measured in revolutions per minute (RPM) and engine torque with the goal of predicting engine torque.

Source: Data extracted from Y. Chen et al., "Cluster-Based Profile Analysis in Phase I," *Journal of Quality Technology*, 47, January 2015, and stored in Engines .

a. Construct a scatter plot for RPM and torque.

b. Fit a quadratic regression model and state the quadratic regression equation.

c. Predict the mean torque for an RPM of 3,000.

d. Perform a residual analysis on the results and determine whether the regression assumptions are valid.

e. At the 0.05 level of significance, is there a significant quadratic relationship between torque and RPM?

f. At the 0.05 level of significance, determine whether the quadratic model is a better fit than the linear model.

g. Interpret the meaning of the coefficient of multiple determination.

h. Compute the adjusted r^2.

i. What conclusions can you reach concerning the relationship between RPM and torque?

15.4 Is the number of calories in a beer related to the number of carbohydrates and/or the percentage of alcohol in the beer? Data concerning 158 of the best-selling domestic beers in the United States are stored in DomesticBeer . The values for three variables are included: the number of calories per 12 ounces, the alcohol percentage, and the number of carbohydrates (in grams) per 12 ounces.

Source: Data extracted from **www.beer100.com/beercalories.htm**, December 1, 2016.

a. Perform a multiple linear regression analysis, using calories as the dependent variable and percentage alcohol and number of carbohydrates as the independent variables.

b. Add quadratic terms for alcohol percentage and the number of carbohydrates.

c. Which model is better, the one in (a) or (b)?

d. What conclusions can you reach concerning the relationship between the number of calories in a beer and the alcohol percentage and number of carbohydrates?

15.5 In the production of printed circuit boards, errors in the alignment of electrical connections are a source of scrap. The data in the file RegistrationError-HighCost contains the registration error and the temperature used in the production of circuit boards in an experiment in which higher cost material was used.

Source: Data extracted from C. Nachtsheim and B. Jones, "A Powerful Analytical Tool," *Six Sigma Forum Magazine*, August 2003, pp. 30–33.

a. Construct a scatter plot for temperature and registration error.

b. Fit a quadratic regression model to predict registration error and state the quadratic regression equation.

c. Perform a residual analysis on the results and determine whether the regression model is valid.

d. At the 0.05 level of significance, is there a significant quadratic relationship between temperature and registration error?

e. At the 0.05 level of significance, determine whether the quadratic model is a better fit than the linear model.

f. Interpret the meaning of the coefficient of multiple determination.

g. Compute the adjusted r^2.

h. What conclusions can you reach concerning the relationship between registration error and temperature?

✓**SELF TEST**   **15.6** An automotive sales manager wishes to examine the relationship between age (years) and sales price ($) for used Honda automobiles. The file HondaPrices contains data for a sample of Honda Civic LXs that were listed for sale at a car shopping website.

Source: Data extracted from **cargurus.com**.

a. Construct a scatter plot for age and price.

b. Fit a quadratic regression model to predict price and state the quadratic regression equation.

c. Predict the mean price of a Honda Civic LX that is five years old.

d. Perform a residual analysis on the results and determine whether the regression model is valid.

e. At the 0.05 level of significance, is there a significant quadratic relationship between age and price?

f. What is the p-value in (e)? Interpret its meaning.

g. At the 0.05 level of significance, determine whether the quadratic model is a better fit than the linear model.

h. What is the p-value in (g)? Interpret its meaning.

i. Interpret the meaning of the coefficient of multiple determination.

j. Compute the adjusted r^2.

k. What conclusions can you reach concerning the relationship between age and price?

15.7 Researchers wanted to investigate the relationship between employment and accommodation capacity in the European travel and tourism industry. The file EuroTourism contains a sample of 27 European countries. Variables included are the number of jobs generated in the travel and tourism industry in 2015 and the number of establishments that provide overnight accommodation for tourists.

Source: Data extracted from **www.marketline.com**.

a. Construct a scatter plot of the number of jobs generated in the travel and tourism industry in 2015 (Y) and the number of establishments that provide overnight accommodation for tourists (X).

b. Fit a quadratic regression model to predict the number of jobs generated and state the quadratic regression equation.

c. Predict the mean number of jobs generated in the travel and tourism industry for a country with 3,000 establishments that provide overnight accommodation for tourists.

d. Perform a residual analysis on the results and determine whether the regression model is valid.

e. At the 0.05 level of significance, is there a significant quadratic relationship between the number of jobs generated in the travel and tourism industry in 2015 and the number of establishments that provide overnight accommodation for tourists?

f. What is the p-value in (e)? Interpret its meaning.

g. At the 0.05 level of significance, determine whether the quadratic model is a better fit than the linear model.

h. Interpret the meaning of the coefficient of multiple determination.

i. Compute the adjusted r^2.

j. What conclusions can you reach concerning the relationship between the number of jobs generated in the travel and tourism industry in 2015 and the number of establishments that provide overnight accommodation for tourists?

15.2 Using Transformations in Regression Models

learnMORE

To learn more about logarithms, see Appendix Section A.3.

Transformations are mathematical alterations of data values made to either overcome violations of the assumptions of regression or to make a model whose form is not linear into a linear model. Transformations can be applied to the values of an independent X variable or the dependent Y variable or both. Among the many transformations available (see references 1 and 2), the square-root transformation and transformations involving the common logarithm (base 10) and the natural logarithm (base e) are the most commonly used.

The Square-Root Transformation

The **square-root transformation** often overcomes violations of the normality and equal-variance assumptions as well as transforms a model whose form is not linear into a linear model. When the error term is normally distributed and the errors are equal for all values of X, you use a square-root transformation of X to make the linear model appropriate. When the errors are not equal for all values of X or when the errors are not normally distributed, you use a square-root transformation of Y (see reference 1).

Equation (15.3) shows a regression model that uses a square-root transformation of the dependent variable.

REGRESSION MODEL WITH A SQUARE-ROOT TRANSFORMATION

$$\sqrt{Y_i} = \beta_0 + \beta_1 X_{1i} + \varepsilon_i \tag{15.3}$$

Example 15.2 illustrates the use of a square-root transformation of the *Y* variable.

EXAMPLE 15.2

Using the Square-Root Transformation of the *Y* Variable

Given the following values for *X* and *Y*, use a square-root transformation for the *Y* variable:

X	Y	X	Y
1	57.3	3	87.9
1	70.0	4	124.4
2	92.5	4	96.1
2	77.4	5	141.3
3	114.7	5	111.1

Construct a scatter plot and a residual plot for these *X* and *Y* values, stored in `Example15-2`, and for *X* and the square root of *Y*.

SOLUTION Figures 15.9 and 15.10 display the four plots.

Figure 15.9 contains a scatter plot of *X* and *Y* that has been fit for a linear model in which $b_0 = 52.15$, $b_1 = 15.04$, and $r^2 = 0.7518$. The Figure 15.9 residual plot indicates the variation in the residuals in this model is much greater when $X = 3$, 4, and 5, than when $X = 1$ or 2. To overcome this lack of homogeneity of variance of the residuals, you use a square-root transformation of the *Y* variable.

FIGURE 15.9

Scatter plot and residual plot for the *X* and *Y* values

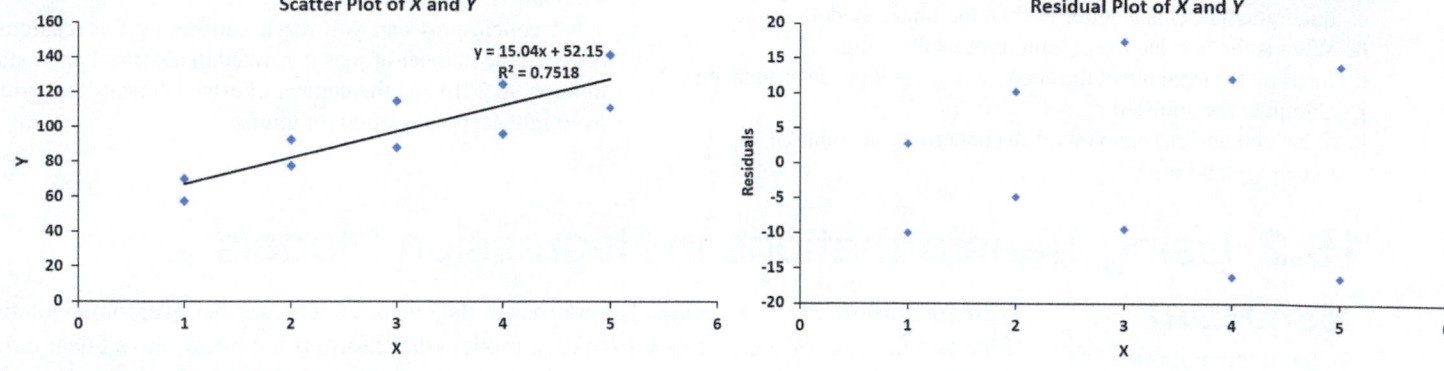

Figure 15.10 shows a scatter plot of *X* and the square root of *Y* that has been fit for a linear model in which $b_0 = 7.4536$, $b_1 = 0.7762$, and $r^2 = 0.7622$. The b_0 value $= 7.4536$ means that the predicted mean square root of *Y* when $X = 0$ is 7.4536. The b_1 value of 0.7762 means that for each increase of one unit of *X*, the predicted mean square root of *Y* increases by 0.7762.

FIGURE 15.10

Scatter plot and residual plot for *X* and the square root of *Y*

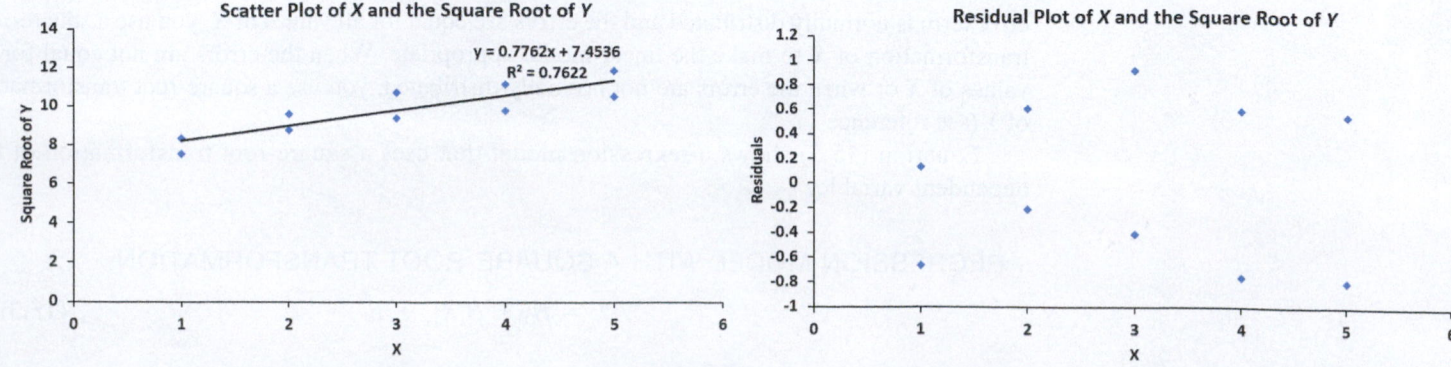

The Figure 15.10 residual plot shows much less variation in the residuals for different values of X, although the r^2 values of the two models are not very different. Because the residuals differ much less than the linear model to predict Y, the model that predicts the square root of Y is preferable to the model that predicts Y.

The Log Transformation

The **logarithmic transformation** often overcomes violations of the normality and equal-variance assumptions. You can also use the logarithmic transformation to change a nonlinear model into a linear model. Equation (15.4) shows a multiplicative model.

ORIGINAL MULTIPLICATIVE MODEL

$$Y_i = \beta_0 X_{1i}^{\beta_1} X_{2i}^{\beta_2} \varepsilon_i \tag{15.4}$$

By taking base 10 logarithms of both the dependent and independent variables, you can transform Equation (15.4) in to the model that Equation (15.5) defines.

TRANSFORMED MULTIPLICATIVE MODEL

$$\begin{aligned}
\log Y_i &= \log(\beta_0 X_{1i}^{\beta_1} X_{2i}^{\beta_2} \varepsilon_i) \\
&= \log \beta_0 + \log(X_{1i}^{\beta_1}) + \log(X_{2i}^{\beta_2}) + \log \varepsilon_i \\
&= \log \beta_0 + \beta_1 \log X_{1i} + \beta_2 \log X_{2i} + \log \varepsilon_i
\end{aligned} \tag{15.5}$$

The transformed model that Equation (15.5) defines is a *linear* model. Equations (15.6) and (15.7) illustrate that a similar transformation can be done for an exponential model using the natural logarithm of both sides of the equation. (The transformed exponential model that Equation 15.7 defines is a linear model.)

ORIGINAL EXPONENTIAL MODEL

$$Y_i = e^{\beta_0 + \beta_1 X_{1i} + \beta_2 X_{2i}} \varepsilon_i \tag{15.6}$$

TRANSFORMED EXPONENTIAL MODEL

$$\begin{aligned}
\ln Y_i &= \ln(e^{\beta_0 + \beta_1 X_{1i} + \beta_2 X_{2i}} \varepsilon_i) \\
&= \ln(e^{\beta_0 + \beta_1 X_{1i} + \beta_2 X_{2i}}) + \ln \varepsilon_i \\
&= \beta_0 + \beta_1 X_{1i} + \beta_2 X_{2i} + \ln \varepsilon_i
\end{aligned} \tag{15.7}$$

Example 15.3 illustrates the use of a natural log transformation.

EXAMPLE 15.3

Using the Natural Log Transformation

Given the following values for X and Y, use a natural logarithm transformation for the Y variable:

X	Y	X	Y
1	0.7	3	4.8
1	0.5	4	12.9
2	1.6	4	11.5
2	1.8	5	32.1
3	4.2	5	33.9

Construct a scatter plot and a residual plot for these X and Y values, stored in **Example15-3**, and for X and the natural logarithm of Y.

SOLUTION Figures 15.11 and 15.12 display the four plots.

Figure 15.11 contains a scatter plot of X and Y that has been fit for a linear model in which $b_0 = 12.19$, $b_1 = 7.53$, and $r^2 = 0.7854$ and shows an exponential relationship between X and Y. The Figure 15.11 residual plot shows a very clear curvilinear plot of the residuals. Therefore, you use the natural log transformation of the Y variable.

FIGURE 15.11

Scatter plot and residual plot for the X and Y values

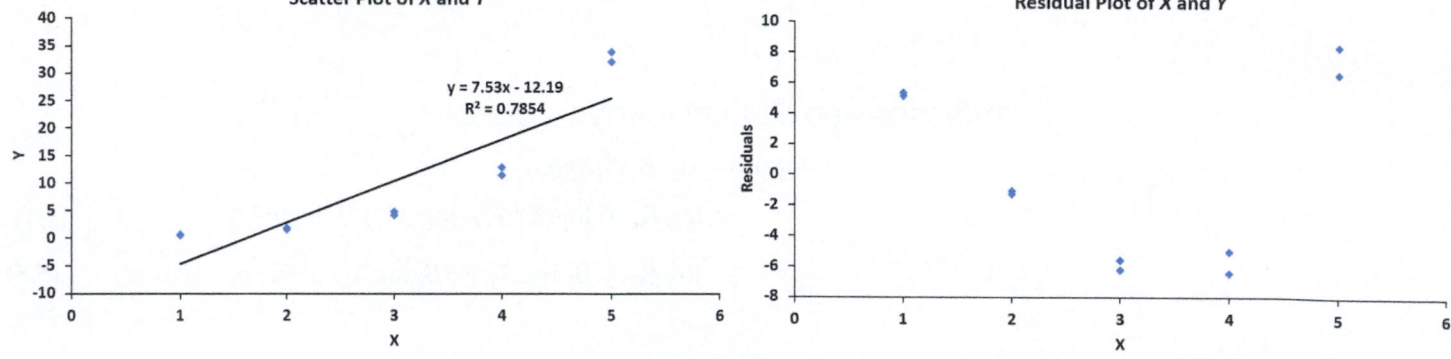

Figure 15.12 contains a scatter plot of X and the natural log of Y that has been fit for a linear model in which $b_0 = -1.5035$, $b_1 = 1.0013$, and $r^2 = 0.9959$. The b_0 value $= -1.5035$ means that the predicted mean natural log of Y when $X = 0$ is -1.5035. The b_1 value of 1.0013 means that for each increase of one unit of X, the predicted mean natural log of Y increases by 1.0013. The Figure 15.12 residual plot does not show a pattern, although there is some difference in the variation when $X = 1$ and $X = 5$. In addition, the r^2 of this natural log model is 0.9959 as compared to an r^2 of 0.7854 for the simple linear model. Because of these facts, the natural log model is preferable to the linear model.

FIGURE 15.12

Scatter plot and residual plot for X and the natural logarithm of Y

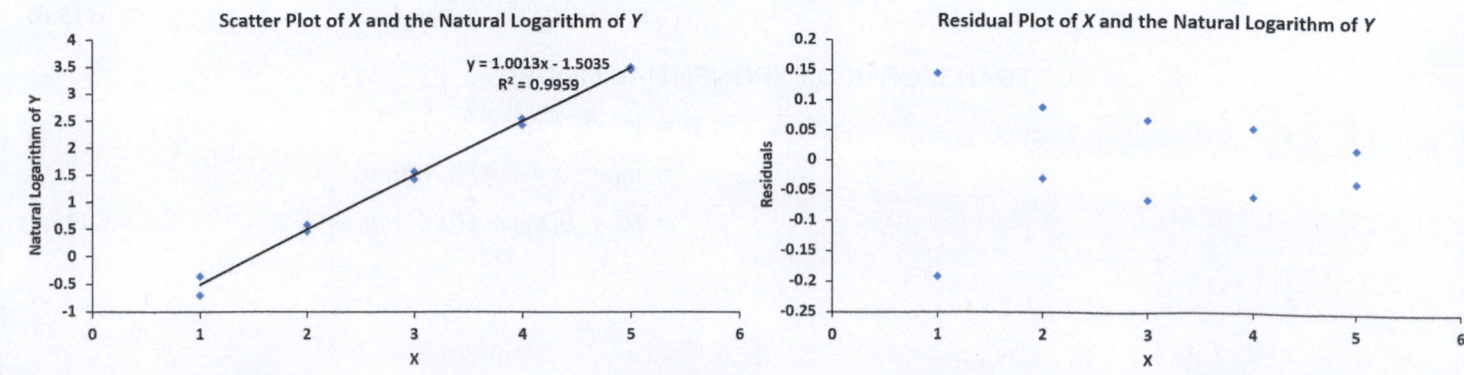

PROBLEMS FOR SECTION 15.2

LEARNING THE BASICS

15.8 Consider the following regression equation:

$$\log \hat{Y}_i = \log 3.07 + 0.9 \log X_{1i} + 1.41 \log X_{2i}$$

a. Predict the value of Y when $X_1 = 8.5$ and $X_2 = 5.2$.
b. Interpret the meaning of the regression coefficients b_0, b_1, and b_2.

15.9 Consider the following regression equation:

$$\ln \hat{Y}_i = 4.62 + 0.5X_{1i} + 0.7X_{2i}$$

a. Predict the value of Y when $X_1 = 8.5$ and $X_2 = 5.2$.
b. Interpret the meaning of the regression coefficients b_0, b_1, and b_2.

APPLYING THE CONCEPTS

✓ SELF TEST **15.10** Using the data of Problem 15.4 on page 600, stored in **DomesticBeer**, perform either a square-root transformation on the dependent variable (calories) or a square-root transformation on each of the independent variables (percentage alcohol and number of carbohydrates) depending on whether the residuals are normally distributed or vary across X values.
a. State the regression equation.
b. At the 0.05 level of significance, is there a significant relationship between calories and the percentage of alcohol and the number of carbohydrates?
c. Interpret the meaning of the coefficient of determination, r^2, in this problem.
d. Compute the adjusted r^2.
e. Compare your results with those in Problem 15.4. Which model is better? Why?

15.11 Using the data of Problem 15.4 on page 600, stored in **DomesticBeer**, perform a natural logarithmic transformation of the dependent variable (calories). Using the transformed dependent variable and the percentage of alcohol and the number of carbohydrates as the independent variables, perform a multiple regression analysis.
a. State the regression equation.
b. Perform a residual analysis of the results and determine whether regression assumptions are valid.

c. At the 0.05 level of significance, is there a significant relationship between the natural logarithm of calories and the percentage of alcohol and the number of carbohydrates?
d. Interpret the meaning of the coefficient of determination, r^2, in this problem.
e. Compute the adjusted r^2.
f. Compare your results with those in Problems 15.4 and 15.10. Which model is best? Why?

15.12 Using the data of Problem 15.6 on page 601, stored in **HondaPrices**, perform a natural logarithm transformation of the dependent variable (price). Using the transformed dependent variable and the age as the independent variable, perform a regression analysis.
a. State the regression equation.
b. Predict the mean price for a five-year-old Honda Civic LX.
c. Perform a residual analysis of the results and determine whether the regression assumptions are valid.
d. At the 0.05 level of significance, is there a significant relationship between the natural logarithm of price and age?
e. Interpret the meaning of the coefficient of determination, r^2, in this problem.
f. Compute the adjusted r^2.
g. Compare your results with those in Problem 15.6. Which model is better? Why?

15.13 Using the data of Problem 15.6 on page 601 stored in **HondaPrices**, perform a square-root transformation of the dependent variable (price). Using the square root of price as the dependent variable, perform a regression analysis.
a. State the regression equation.
b. Predict the mean price for a five-year-old Honda Civic LX.
c. Perform a residual analysis of the results and determine whether the regression model is valid.
d. At the 0.05 level of significance, is there a significant relationship between the square root of price and age?
e. Interpret the meaning of the coefficient of determination, r^2, in this problem.
f. Compute the adjusted r^2.
g. Compare your results with those of Problems 15.6 and 15.12. Which model is best? Why?

15.3 Collinearity

Collinearity of the independent variables exists when two or more of the independent variables are highly correlated with each other. When this occurs, collinear variables do not provide unique information, and it becomes difficult to separate the effects of such variables on the dependent variable. Collinearity may cause the values of the regression coefficients for the correlated variables to fluctuate drastically, depending on which independent variables are included in the model.

One method of measuring collinearity is to determine the **variance inflationary factor (VIF)** for each independent variable. Equation (15.8) defines VIF_j, the variance inflationary factor for variable j. The R_j^2 is the coefficient of multiple determination for a regression model, using variable X_j as the dependent variable and all other X variables as independent variables.

VARIANCE INFLATIONARY FACTOR

$$VIF_j = \frac{1}{1 - R_j^2} \tag{15.8}$$

If there are only two independent variables, R_1^2 is the coefficient of determination between X_1 and X_2. It is identical to R_2^2, which is the coefficient of determination between X_2 and X_1. If there are three independent variables, then R_1^2 is the coefficient of multiple determination of X_1 with X_2 and X_3; R_2^2 is the coefficient of multiple determination of X_2 with X_1 and X_3; and R_3^2 is the coefficient of multiple determination of X_3 with X_1 and X_2.

If a set of independent variables is uncorrelated, each VIF_j is equal to 1. If the set is highly correlated, then a VIF_j might even exceed 10. Snee (see reference 3) recommends using alternatives to least-squares regression if the maximum VIF_j exceeds 5.

Multiple regression models that have one or more large VIF values should be used with extreme caution. And because the independent variables contain overlapping information, you should always avoid interpreting the regression coefficient estimates separately because you cannot accurately estimate the individual effects of the independent variables. One approach in this situation is to delete the variable with the largest VIF value. The reduced model (the model with the independent variable with the largest VIF value deleted) is often free of collinearity problems. Keep eliminating and rerunning the regression analysis until no variables have a $VIF > 5$. If you determine that all the independent variables are needed in the model, you can use methods discussed in reference 1.

In the OmniPower sales data (see Section 14.1), the correlation between the two independent variables, price and promotional expenditure, is -0.0968. Because there are only two independent variables in the model, from Equation (15.8):

$$VIF_1 = VIF_2 = \frac{1}{1 - (-0.0968)^2}$$

$$= 1.009$$

Thus, you conclude that you should not be concerned with collinearity for the OmniPower sales data.

In models containing quadratic and interaction terms, collinearity is usually present. The linear and quadratic terms of an independent variable are usually highly correlated with each other, and an interaction term is often correlated with one or both of the independent variables making up the interaction. Thus, you cannot interpret individual regression coefficients separately. You need to interpret the linear and quadratic regression coefficients together in order to understand the nonlinear relationship. Likewise, you need to interpret an interaction regression coefficient in conjunction with the two regression coefficients associated with the variables comprising the interaction. In summary, large VIFs in quadratic or interaction models do not necessarily mean that the model is not a good one. They do, however, require you to carefully interpret the regression coefficients.

PROBLEMS FOR SECTION 15.3

LEARNING THE BASICS

15.14 If the coefficient of determination between two independent variables is 0.20, what is the VIF?

15.15 If the coefficient of determination between two independent variables is 0.50, what is the VIF?

APPLYING THE CONCEPTS

✓ **SELF TEST** **15.16** Refer to Problem 14.4 on page 541. Perform a multiple regression analysis using the data in CommunityBanks and determine the VIF for each independent variable in the model. Is there reason to suspect the existence of collinearity?

15.17 Refer to Problem 14.5 on page 542. Perform a multiple regression analysis using the data in VinhoVerde and determine the *VIF* for each independent variable in the model. Is there reason to suspect the existence of collinearity?

15.18 Refer to Problem 14.6 on page 542. Perform a multiple regression analysis using the data in BestCompanies and determine the *VIF* for each independent variable in the model. Is there reason to suspect the existence of collinearity?

15.19 Refer to Problem 14.7 on page 542. Perform a multiple regression analysis using the data in Nickels26Weeks and determine the *VIF* for each independent variable in the model. Is there reason to suspect the existence of collinearity?

15.20 Refer to Problem 14.8 on page 542. Perform a multiple regression analysis using the data in GlenCove and determine the *VIF* for each independent variable in the model. Is there reason to suspect the existence of collinearity?

15.4 Model Building

The techniques that Chapter 14 and this chapter discuss can be combined into a series of steps to identify the most appropriate regression model for a set of data.

Exhibit 15.1 lists these steps for successful model building.

EXHIBIT 15.1

Successful Model Building

1. Use the DCOVA framework to identify the business problem or goal to be examined, define variables and collect data. Identify the variables that will serve as candidate independent X variables for the multiple regression model.
2. Develop a regression model that includes all candidate independent X variables.
3. Compute the *VIF* for each of the X variables. Apply the decision-making process that Section 15.3 discusses until no X variable has a $VIF > 5$.
4. Perform a best subsets analysis with the remaining independent variables and compute the C_p statistic or the adjusted r^2 for each subset regression model as this section discusses later.
5. Choose a best model from the models that have C_p close to or less than k + 1 and/or a high adjusted r^2.
6. Perform a complete analysis of that best model chosen, including a residual analysis.
7. Review the results of the residual analysis. If necessary, add quadratic or interaction terms or transform variables. Repeat steps 3 through 6.
8. Validate the regression model.

As this section later explains, performing a stepwise regression can be an alternate to steps 4 and 5, although at the cost of not examining all possible regression models.

These steps ensure that an appropriate model will be selected. That model may not be the optimal model, but the model will be one that decision-makers can use for prediction and inference. The **principle of parsimony** should cause you to choose the model with the fewest independent X variables that can predict the dependent Y variable adequately, should several different models in step 5 have a C_p statistic close to or less than $k + 1$ and/or a high adjusted r^2. Regression models with fewer independent variables are easier to interpret, particularly because they are less likely to be affected by the collinearity problems that Section 15.3 discusses.

To illustrate the model-building process, return to the Nickels Broadcasting scenario in which you were asked to build a regression model that uses the Table 15.4 26-week sample that includes the weekly staff count (Staff), remote engineering hours (RemoteEng), graphics hours (Graphics), and editorial production (Production) hours as independent X variables to predict the dependent Y variable standby hours (Standby).

To begin analyzing the 26-week sample that Table 15.4 presents stored in Nickels26Weeks, calculate the variance inflationary factors (see Section 15.3) to measure the amount of collinearity among the independent variables. The four *VIF*s for four independent variables appear in Figure 15.13 along with the results for the regression model that uses those variables. Observe that all the *VIF* values are relatively small, ranging from a high of 1.9993 for Production to a low of 1.2333 for RemoteEng. Using criteria developed by Snee that all *VIF* values should be less than 5.0, there is little evidence of collinearity among the set of independent variables.

TABLE 15.4

Predicting Standby Hours Based on Staff, Remote Engineering Hours, Graphics Hours, and Production Hours

Week	Standby (Y)	Staff (X_1)	RemoteEng (X_2)	Graphics (X_3)	Production (X_4)
1	245	338	414	323	2001
2	177	333	598	340	2030
3	271	358	656	340	2226
4	211	372	631	352	2154
5	196	339	528	380	2078
6	135	289	409	339	2080
7	195	334	382	331	2073
8	118	293	399	311	1758
9	116	325	343	328	1624
10	147	311	338	353	1889
11	154	304	353	518	1988
12	146	312	289	440	2049
13	115	283	388	276	1796
14	161	307	402	207	1720
15	274	322	151	287	2056
16	245	335	228	290	1890
17	201	350	271	355	2187
18	183	339	440	300	2032
19	237	327	475	284	1856
20	175	328	347	337	2068
21	152	319	449	279	1813
22	188	325	336	244	1808
23	188	322	267	253	1834
24	197	317	235	272	1973
25	261	315	164	223	1839
26	232	331	270	272	1935

FIGURE 15.13

Excel, JMP, and Minitab multiple regression linear model results for predicting standby hours based on four independent variables (with Excel worksheets for Durbin-Watson statistic and *VIF*, inset)

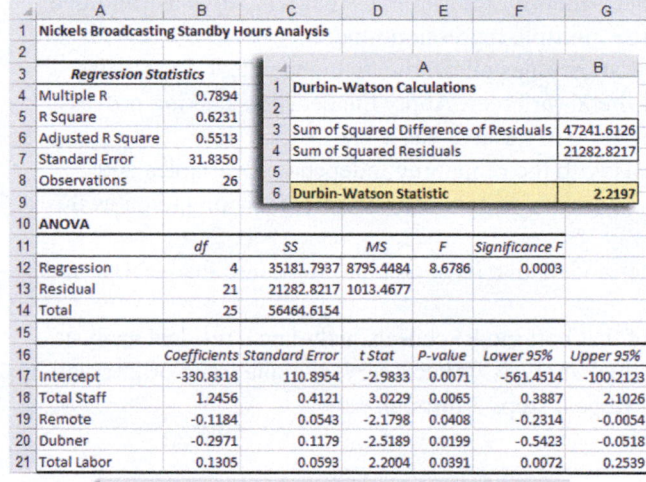

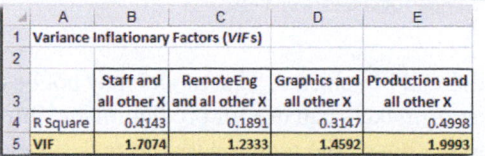

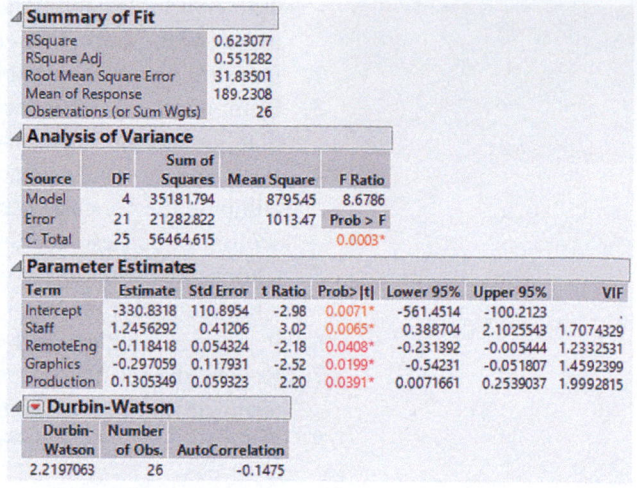

Regression Analysis: Standby versus Staff, RemoteEng, ... s, Production

Analysis of Variance

Source	DF	Adj SS	Adj MS	F-Value	P-Value
Regression	4	35182	8795	8.68	0.000
Staff	1	9261	9261	9.14	0.006
RemoteEng	1	4816	4816	4.75	0.041
Graphics	1	6430	6430	6.34	0.020
Production	1	4907	4907	4.84	0.039
Error	21	21283	1013		
Total	25	56465			

Model Summary

S	R-sq	R-sq(adj)	R-sq(pred)
31.8350	62.31%	55.13%	30.23%

Coefficients

Term	Coef	SE Coef	T-Value	P-Value	VIF
Constant	-331	111	-2.98	0.007	
Staff	1.246	0.412	3.02	0.006	1.71
RemoteEng	-0.1184	0.0543	-2.18	0.041	1.23
Graphics	-0.297	0.118	-2.52	0.020	1.46
Production	0.1305	0.0593	2.20	0.039	2.00

Regression Equation

Standby = -331 + 1.246 Staff - 0.1184 RemoteEng
          - 0.297 Graphics + 0.1305 Production

Durbin-Watson Statistic

Durbin-Watson Statistic = 2.21971

The Stepwise Regression Approach to Model Building

Whether a subset of all independent variables yields an adequate and appropriate model is the next step in model building. **Stepwise regression** is a model selection process that attempts to find the "best" regression model without examining all possible models.

The first step of stepwise regression is to find the best model that uses one independent variable. The next step is to find the best of the remaining independent variables to add to the model selected in the first step. An important feature of the stepwise approach is that an independent variable that has entered into the model at an early stage may subsequently be removed after other independent variables are considered. Therefore, in stepwise regression, variables are either added to or deleted from the regression model at each step of the model-building process. The t test for the slope (see Section 14.4) or the partial F_{STAT} test statistic (see Section 14.5) determines whether variables are added or deleted. The stepwise procedure terminates when no additional variables can be added to or deleted from the last model evaluated.

Figure 15.14 presents the stepwise regression results for the Nickels Broadcasting data.

FIGURE 15.14

PHStat (Excel), JMP, and Minitab stepwise regression results for the Nickels Broadcasting data

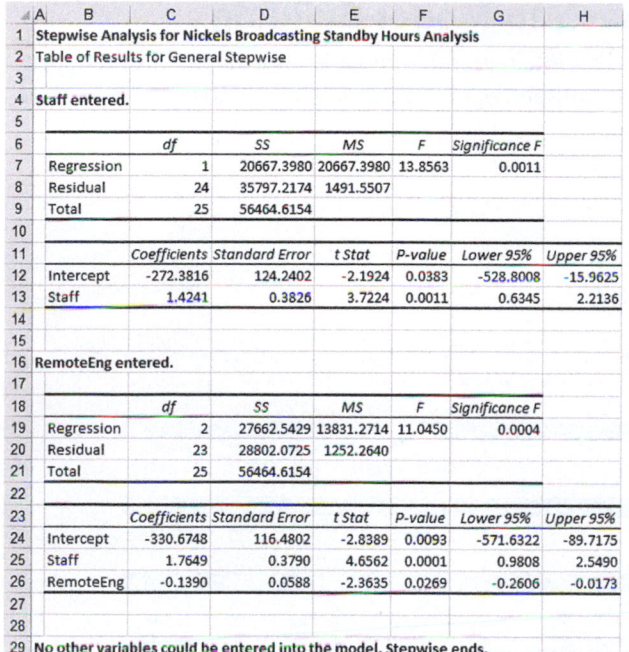

For this example, a significance level of 0.05 is used to enter a variable into the model or to delete a variable from the model. The first variable entered into the model is Staff, the variable that correlates most highly with the dependent variable Standby. Because the p-value = 0.0011 < 0.05, Staff is included in the regression model.

The next step involves selecting a second independent variable for the model. The second variable chosen is one that makes the largest contribution to the model, given that the first variable has been selected. For this model, the second variable is RemoteEng. Because the p-value for RemoteEng = 0.0269 < 0.05, RemoteEng is included in the regression model.

After RemoteEng has been entered into the model, the stepwise procedure determines whether Staff is still an important contributing variable or whether that variable can be eliminated from the model. Because the *p*-value of 0.0001 for Staff is less than 0.05, Staff remains in the regression model.

The next step involves selecting a third independent variable for the model. Because none of the other variables meets the 0.05 criterion for entry into the model, the stepwise procedure terminates with a model that includes the weekly staff count and the remote engineering hours.

This stepwise regression approach to model building was originally developed more than five decades ago, when regression computations were time-consuming and costly. Although stepwise regression limited the evaluation of alternative models, the method was deemed a good trade-off between evaluation and cost.

Given the ability of today's computers to perform regression computations at very low cost and high speed, stepwise regression has been superseded to some extent by the best subsets approach which evaluates a larger set of alternative models. Stepwise regression is not obsolete, however. Today, stepwise regression can play an important role in helping to analyze big data when used with certain predictive analytics methods.

The Best Subsets Approach to Model Building

The **best subsets approach** evaluates all possible regression models for a given set of independent variables. Figure 15.15 presents best subsets regression results of all possible regression models for the Nickels Broadcasting data.

FIGURE 15.15

Excel, JMP, and Minitab best subsets regression results for the Nickels Broadcasting data

Best Subsets Analysis for Standby Hours Analysis

Intermediate Calculations	
R 2T	0.6231
1 - R 2T	0.3769
n	26
T	5
n - T	21

Model	Cp	k+1	R Square	Adj. R Square	Std. Error
X1	13.3215	2	0.3660	0.3396	38.6206
X1X2	8.4193	3	0.4899	0.4456	35.3873
X1X2X3	7.8418	4	0.5362	0.4729	34.5029
X1X2X3X4	5.0000	5	0.6231	0.5513	31.8350
X1X2X4	9.3449	4	0.5092	0.4423	35.4921
X1X3	10.6486	3	0.4499	0.4021	36.7490
X1X3X4	7.7517	4	0.5378	0.4748	34.4426
X1X4	14.7982	3	0.3754	0.3211	39.1579
X2	33.2078	2	0.0091	-0.0322	48.2836
X2X3	32.3067	3	0.0612	-0.0205	48.0087
X2X3X4	12.1381	4	0.4591	0.3853	37.2608
X2X4	23.2481	3	0.2238	0.1563	43.6540
X3	30.3884	2	0.0597	0.0205	47.0345
X3X4	11.8231	3	0.4288	0.3791	37.4466
X4	24.1846	2	0.1710	0.1365	44.1619

All Possible Models

Ordered up to best 4 models up to 4 terms per model.

Model	Number	RSquare	RMSE	AICc	BIC	Cp
Staff	1	0.3660	38.6206	268.791	271.475	13.3215 ●
Production	1	0.1710	44.1619	275.763	278.447	24.1846 ○
Graphics	1	0.0597	47.0345	279.040	281.724	30.3884 ○
RemoteEng	1	0.0091	48.2836	280.403	283.087	33.2078 ○
Staff,RemoteEng	2	0.4899	35.3873	265.952	269.080	8.4193 ●
Staff,Graphics	2	0.4499	36.7490	267.916	271.043	10.6486 ○
Graphics,Production	2	0.4288	37.4466	268.894	272.021	11.8231 ○
Staff,Production	2	0.3754	39.1579	271.217	274.345	14.7982 ○
Staff,Graphics,Production	3	0.5378	34.4426	266.485	269.775	7.7517 ●
Staff,RemoteEng,Graphics	3	0.5362	34.5029	266.576	269.866	7.8418 ○
Staff,RemoteEng,Production	3	0.5092	35.4921	268.046	271.336	9.3449 ○
RemoteEng,Graphics,Production	3	0.4591	37.2608	270.574	273.865	12.1381 ○
Staff,RemoteEng,Graphics,Production	4	0.6231	31.8350	264.602	267.730	5.0000 ●

Best Subsets Regression: Standby versus Staff,
... Graphics, Production

Response is Standby

						S t a f f	R e m o t e E n g	G r a p h i c s	P r o d u c t i o n
Vars	R-Sq	R-Sq (adj)	R-Sq (pred)	Mallows Cp	S				
1	36.6	34.0	26.5	13.3	38.621	X			
1	17.1	13.7	4.1	24.2	44.162				X
1	6.0	2.1	0.0	30.4	47.035			X	
2	49.0	44.6	31.7	8.4	35.387	X	X		
2	45.0	40.2	27.0	10.6	36.749	X		X	
2	42.9	37.9	23.2	11.8	37.447			X	X
3	53.8	47.5	23.0	7.8	34.443	X		X	X
3	53.6	47.3	32.0	7.8	34.503	X	X	X	
3	50.9	44.2	22.9	9.3	35.492	X	X		X
4	62.3	55.1	30.2	5.0	31.835	X	X	X	X

A criterion often used in model building is the adjusted r^2, which adjusts the r^2 of each model to account for the number of independent variables in the model as well as for the sample size (see Section 14.2). Because model building requires you to compare models with different numbers of independent variables, the adjusted r^2 is more appropriate than r^2. In Figure 15.15, the adjusted r^2 reaches a maximum value of 0.5513 when all four independent variables plus the intercept term (for a total of five estimated parameters) are included in the model.

A second criterion often used in the evaluation of competing models is the C_p **statistic** developed by Mallows (see reference 1). The C_p statistic, defined in Equation (15.9), measures the differences between a fitted regression model and a *true* model, along with random error.

C_p STATISTIC

$$C_p = \frac{(1 - R_k^2)(n - T)}{1 - R_T^2} - [n - 2(k + 1)] \tag{15.9}$$

where

k = number of independent variables included in a regression model

T = total number of parameters (including the intercept) to be estimated in the full regression model

R_k^2 = coefficient of multiple determination for a regression model that has k independent variables

R_T^2 = coefficient of multiple determination for a full regression model that contains all T estimated parameters

Using Equation (15.9) to compute C_p for the model containing Staff and RemoteEng,

$$n = 26 \quad k = 2 \quad T = 4 + 1 = 5 \quad R_k^2 = 0.4899 \quad R_T^2 = 0.6231$$

so that

$$C_p = \frac{(1 - 0.4899)(26 - 5)}{1 - 0.6231} - \left[26 - 2(2 + 1)\right]$$

$$= 8.4193$$

When a regression model with k independent variables contains only random differences from a *true* model, the mean value of C_p is $k + 1$, the number of parameters. Thus, in evaluating many alternative regression models, the goal is to find models whose C_p is close to or less than $k + 1$. In Figure 15.15, you see that only the model that includes all four independent variables has a C_p value close to or below $k + 1$. Therefore, using the C_p criterion, you should choose that model.

With many data sets, the C_p statistic often provides several alternative models for you to evaluate in greater depth. Moreover, the best model or models using the C_p criterion might differ from the model selected using the adjusted r^2 and/or the model selected using the stepwise procedure. For example, the Nickels Broadcasting model that stepwise regression selects has a C_p value of 8.4193, which is substantially above the suggested criterion of $k + 1 = 3$ for that model. Remember that there may be several equally appropriate models and no one uniquely best model. Final model selection often involves using subjective criteria, such as parsimony, interpretability, and departure from model assumptions, as evaluated by residual analysis.

When you have finished selecting the independent variables to include in the model, you need to perform a residual analysis to evaluate the regression assumptions. For data collected in time order, such as the Nickels Broadcasting data, you also need to compute the Durbin-Watson statistic to determine whether there is autocorrelation in the residuals (see Section 13.6). For the Nickels Broadcasting data, the Durbin-Watson statistic, D, is 2.2197 (see Figure 15.13). Because D is greater than 2.0, there is no indication of positive correlation in the residuals. Figure 15.16 residual plots for the Nickels Broadcasting data (see page 612) reveal no apparent patterns. In addition, the Figure 15.17 plot of the residuals versus the predicted values of Y does not show evidence of unequal variance. Therefore, using the Figure 15.13 regression model results, you state the regression equation as

$$\hat{Y}_i = -330.8318 + 1.2456X_{1i} - 0.1184X_{2i} - 0.2971X_{3i} + 0.1305X_{4i}$$

FIGURE 15.16
Residual plots for the Nickels Broadcasting data

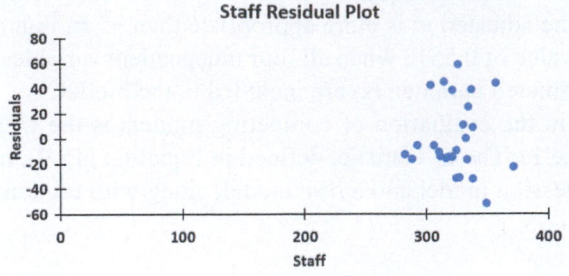

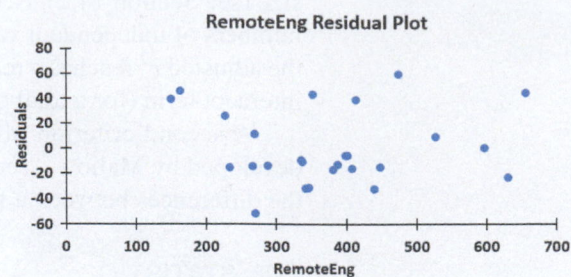

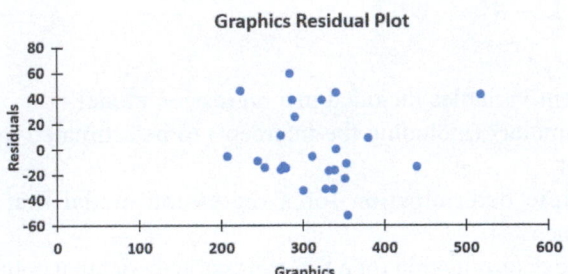

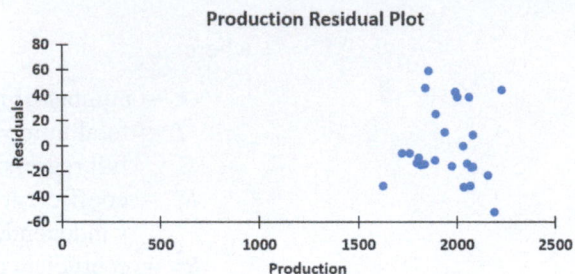

FIGURE 15.17
Scatter plot of the
residuals versus the
predicted values of Y

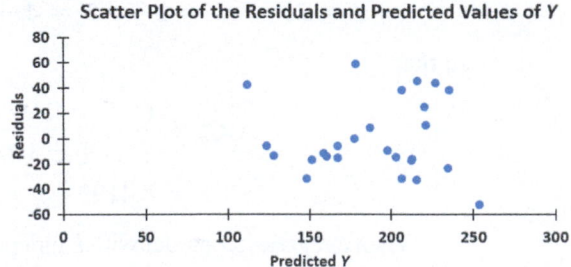

Example 15.4 presents a situation in which there are several alternative models in which the C_p statistic is close to or less than $k + 1$.

EXAMPLE 15.4

**Choosing Among
Alternative
Regression Models**

Table 15.5 shows results from a best subsets regression analysis of a regression model with seven independent variables. Determine which regression model you would choose as the *best* model.

▶*(continued)*

TABLE 15.5
Partial Results from Best-Subsets Regression

Number of Variables	r^2	Adjusted r^2	C_p	Variables Included
1	0.121	0.119	113.9	X_4
1	0.093	0.090	130.4	X_1
1	0.083	0.080	136.2	X_3
2	0.214	0.210	62.1	X_3, X_4
2	0.191	0.186	75.6	X_1, X_3
2	0.181	0.177	81.0	X_1, X_4
3	0.285	0.280	22.6	X_1, X_3, X_4
3	0.268	0.263	32.4	X_3, X_4, X_5
3	0.240	0.234	49.0	X_2, X_3, X_4
4	0.308	0.301	11.3	X_1, X_2, X_3, X_4
4	0.304	0.297	14.0	X_1, X_3, X_4, X_6
4	0.296	0.289	18.3	X_1, X_3, X_4, X_5
5	0.317	0.308	8.2	X_1, X_2, X_3, X_4, X_5
5	0.315	0.306	9.6	X_1, X_2, X_3, X_4, X_6
5	0.313	0.304	10.7	X_1, X_3, X_4, X_5, X_6
6	0.323	0.313	6.8	$X_1, X_2, X_3, X_4, X_5, X_6$
6	0.319	0.309	9.0	$X_1, X_2, X_3, X_4, X_5, X_7$
6	0.317	0.306	10.4	$X_1, X_2, X_3, X_4, X_6, X_7$
7	0.324	0.312	8.0	$X_1, X_2, X_3, X_4, X_5, X_6, X_7$

SOLUTION From Table 15.5, you need to determine which models have C_p values that are less than or close to $k + 1$. Two models meet this criterion. The model with six independent variables ($X_1, X_2, X_3, X_4, X_5, X_6$) has a C_p value of 6.8, which is less than $k + 1 = 6 + 1 = 7$, and the full model with seven independent variables ($X_1, X_2, X_3, X_4, X_5, X_6, X_7$) has a C_p value of 8.0.

One way you can choose between the two models is to select the model with the largest adjusted r^2, which is the model with six independent variables. Another way to select a final model is to determine whether the models contain a subset of variables that are common. Then you test whether the contribution of the additional variables is significant. In this case, because the models differ only by the inclusion of variable X_7 in the full model, you test whether variable X_7 makes a significant contribution to the regression model, given that the variables X_1, X_2, X_3, X_4, X_5, and X_6 are already included in the model. If the contribution is statistically significant, then you should include variable X_7 in the regression model. If variable X_7 does not make a statistically significant contribution, you should not include it in the model.

Model Validation

The final step in the model-building process is to validate the selected regression model. This step involves checking the model against data that were not part of the sample analyzed. The following are several ways of validating a regression model:

- Collect new data and compare the results.
- Compare the results of the regression model to previous results.
- If the data set is large, split the data into two parts and cross-validate the results.

Collecting new data is perhaps the best way of validating a regression model. If the results with new data are consistent with the selected regression model, you have strong reason to believe that the fitted regression model is applicable in a wide set of circumstances.

When collecting new data is impractical or impossible, for example, when working with very large data sets or big data, you can use cross-validation. **Cross-validation** first splits the existing data into two parts. You then use the first part of the data to *develop* the regression model and then use the second part of the data to *evaluate* the predictive ability of the model. Cross-validation is often used as a practical way of validating a model developed by predictive analytics methods (discussed in Section 17.5).

Figure 15.18 summarizes the model building process.

FIGURE 15.18
The model building process

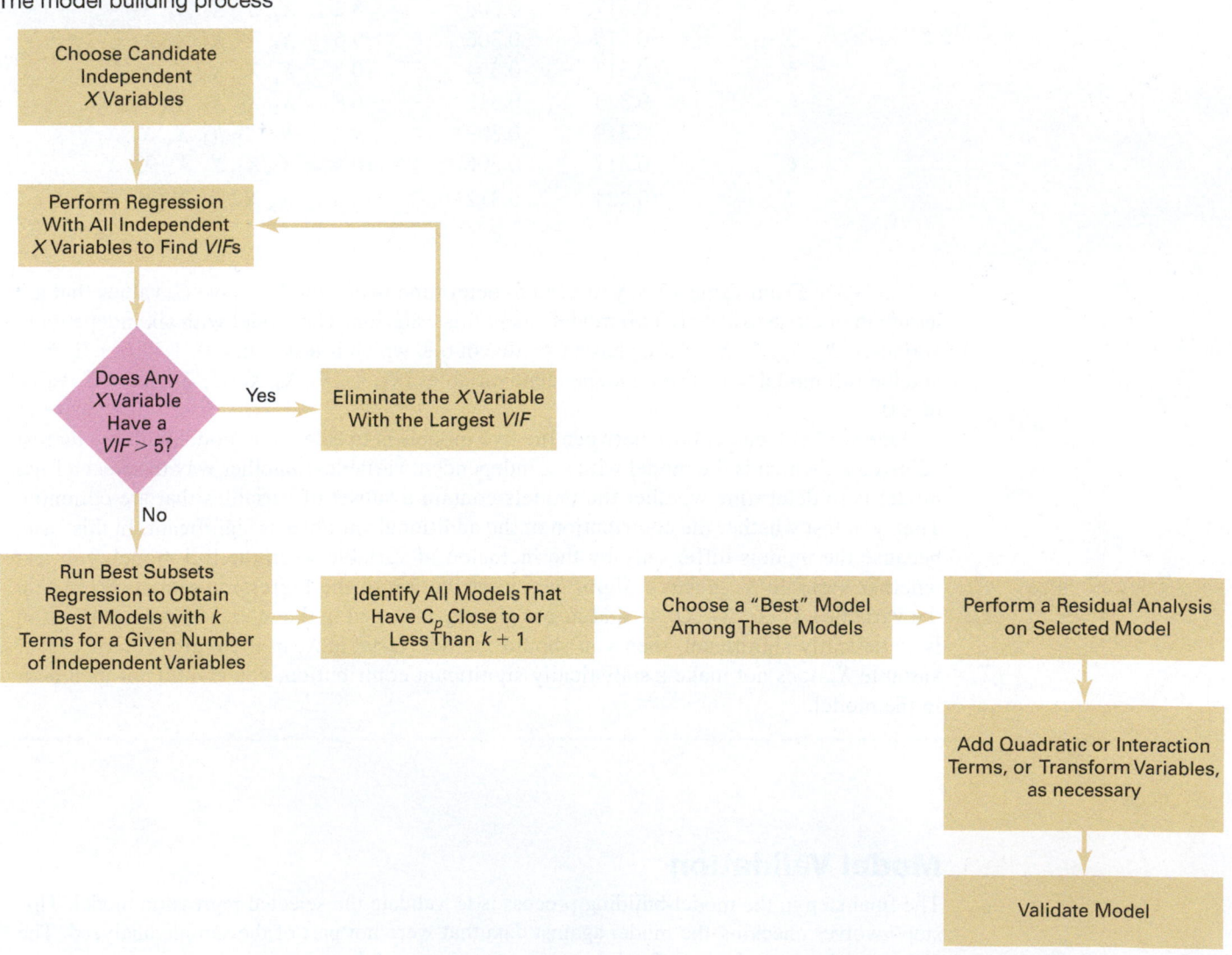

PROBLEMS FOR SECTION 15.4

LEARNING THE BASICS

15.21 You are considering four independent variables for inclusion in a regression model. You select a sample of $n = 30$, with the following results:

1. The model that includes independent variables A and B has a C_p value equal to 4.6.
2. The model that includes independent variables A and C has a C_p value equal to 2.4.
3. The model that includes independent variables A, B, and C has a C_p value equal to 2.7.
   a. Which models meet the criterion for further consideration? Explain.
   b. How would you compare the model that contains independent variables A, B, and C to the model that contains independent variables A and B? Explain.

15.22 You are considering six independent variables for inclusion in a regression model. You select a sample of $n = 40$, with the following results:

$$k = 2 \quad T = 6 + 1 = 7 \quad R_k^2 = 0.274 \quad R_T^2 = 0.653$$

a. Compute the C_p value for this two-independent-variable model.
b. Based on your answer to (a), does this model meet the criterion for further consideration as the best model? Explain.

APPLYING THE CONCEPTS

15.23 The file FTMBA contains data from a sample of full-time MBA programs offered by private universities. The variables collected for this sample are average starting salary upon graduation ($), the percentage of applicants to the full-time program who were accepted, the average GMAT test score of students entering the program, program per-year tuition ($), and percent of students with job offers at time of graduation.

Source: Data extracted from U.S. News & World Report Education, "Best Graduate Schools," **bit.ly/1E8MBcp**.

Develop the most appropriate multiple regression model to predict the mean starting salary upon graduation. Be sure to include a thorough residual analysis. In addition, provide a detailed explanation of the results, including a comparison of the most appropriate multiple regression model to the best simple linear regression model.

✓ **SELF TEST** **15.24** You need to develop a model to predict the asking price of houses listed for sale in Silver Spring, Maryland, based on the living space of the house, the lot size, and the age, whether it has a fireplace, the number of bedrooms, and the number of bathrooms. A sample of 61 houses is selected and the results are stored in SilverSpring. Develop the most appropriate multiple regression model to predict asking price. Be sure to perform a thorough residual analysis. In addition, provide a detailed explanation of the results.

15.25 *Accounting Today* identified top public accounting firms in ten geographic regions across the U.S. The file AccountingPartners6 contains data for public accounting firms in the Southeast, Gulf Coast, and Capital Regions. The variables are: revenue ($millions), number of partners in the firm, number of professionals in the firm, proportion of business dedicated to management advisory services (MAS%), whether the firm is located in the Southeast Region ($0 = $ no, $1 = $ yes), and whether the firm is located in the Gulf Coast Region ($0 = $ no, $1 = $ yes).

Source: Data extracted from *2017 Top 100 Firms*, **bit.ly/2sNGVqH**.

Develop the most appropriate multiple regression model to predict firm revenue. Be sure to perform a thorough residual analysis. In addition, provide a detailed explanation of the results.

15.5 Pitfalls in Multiple Regression and Ethical Issues

Pitfalls in Multiple Regression

Model building is an art as well as a science. Different individuals may not always agree on the best multiple regression model. To develop a good regression model, use the process that Exhibit 15.1 and Figure 15.18 on pages 607 and 614 summarize. As you follow that process, you must avoid certain pitfalls that can interfere with the development of a useful model. Section 13.9 discussed pitfalls in simple linear regression and strategies for avoiding them. Multiple regression models require the following additional precautions to avoid common pitfalls:

- Interpret the regression coefficient for a particular independent variable from a perspective in which the values of all other independent variables are held constant.
- Evaluate residual plots for each independent variable.
- Evaluate interaction and quadratic terms.
- Compute the *VIF* for each independent variable before determining which independent variables to include in the model.
- Examine several alternative models, using best subsets regression.
- Use logistic regression instead of least squares regression when the dependent variable is categorical.
- Validate the model before implementing it.

Ethical Issues

Ethical issues arise when a user who wants to make predictions manipulates the development process of the multiple regression model. The key here is intent. In addition to the situations that Section 13.9 discuss, unethical behavior occurs when someone uses multiple regression analysis and *willfully fails* to remove from consideration independent variables that exhibit a high collinearity with other independent variables or *willfully fails* to use methods other than least-squares regression when the assumptions necessary for least-squares regression are seriously violated.

▼USING **STATISTICS**
Valuing Parsimony..., Revisited

In the Using Statistics scenario, you were hired by Nickels Broadcasting to determine which variables have an effect on WSTA-TV standby hours. You were given a 26-week sample that contained the weekly standby hours, staff count, remote engineering hours, graphics hours, and production hours.

You performed a multiple regression analysis on the data. The coefficient of multiple determination indicated that 62.31% of the variation in standby hours can be explained by variation in the weekly staff count and the number of remote engineering, graphics, and editorial production hours. The model indicated that standby hours are estimated to increase by 1.2456 hours for each additional weekly staff member present, holding constant the other independent variables; to decrease by 0.1184 hour for each additional remote engineering hour, holding constant the other independent variables; to decrease by 0.2971 hour for each additional graphics hour, holding constant the other independent variables; and to increase by 0.1305 hour for each additional editorial production hour, holding constant the other independent variables.

Each of the four independent variables had a significant effect on Standby, holding constant the other independent variables. This regression model enables you to predict standby hours based on the weekly staff count, remote engineering hours, graphics hours, and editorial production hours. Any predictions developed by the model can then be carefully monitored, new data can be collected, and other variables may possibly be considered.

▾ SUMMARY

Figure 15.19 summarizes the several topics associated
with multiple regression model building.

FIGURE 15.19
Roadmap for multiple
regression

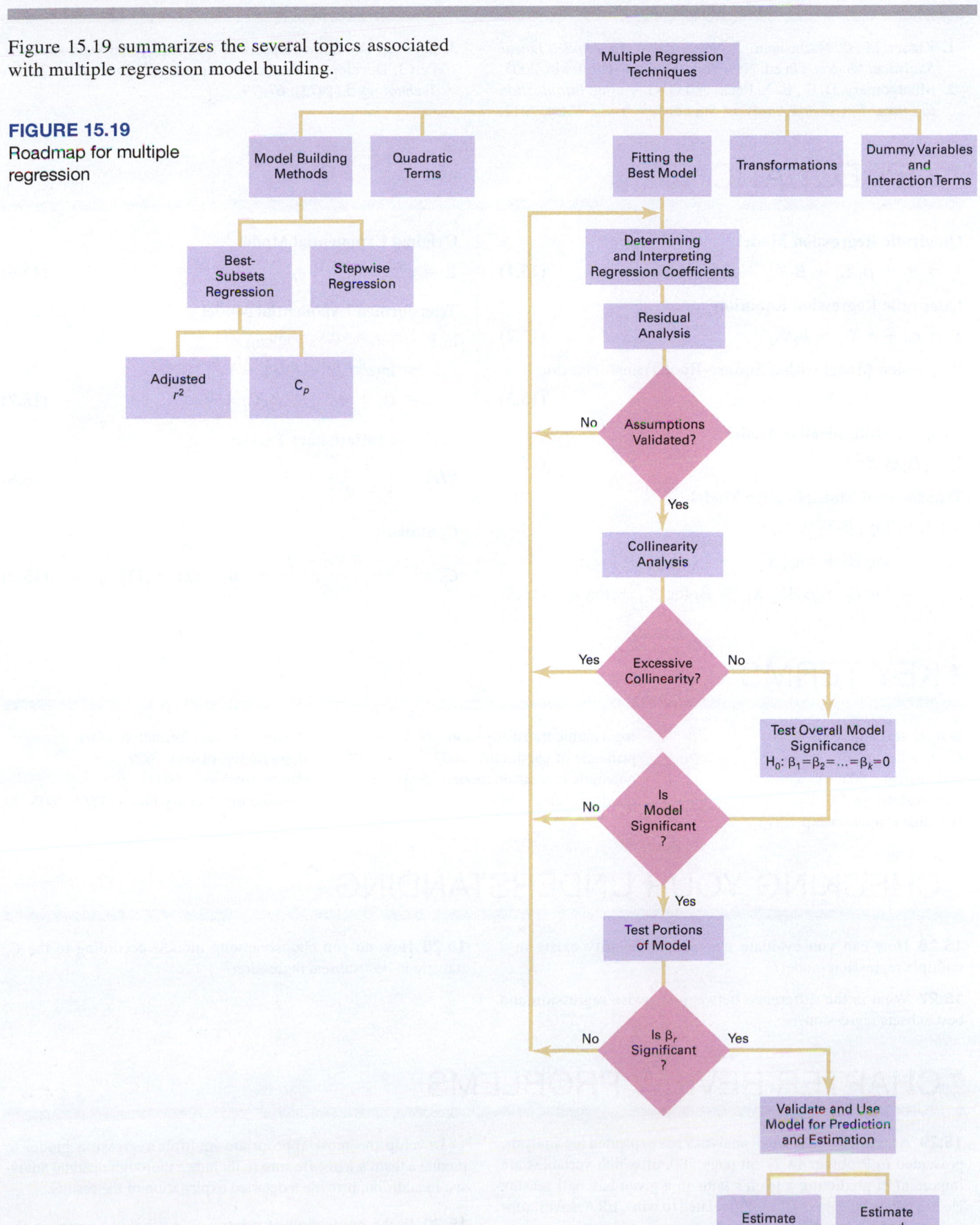

▼ REFERENCES

1. Kutner, M., C. Nachtsheim, J. Neter, and W. Li. *Applied Linear Statistical Models*, 5th ed. New York: McGraw-Hill/Irwin, 2005.
2. Montgomery, D. C., E. A. Peck, and G. G. Vining. *Introduction to Linear Regression Analysis*, 5th ed. New York: Wiley, 2012.
3. Snee, R. D. "Some Aspects of Nonorthogonal Data Analysis, Part I. Developing Prediction Equations." *Journal of Quality Technology* 5 (1973): 67–79.

▼ KEY EQUATIONS

Quadratic Regression Model

$$Y_i = \beta_0 + \beta_1 X_{1i} + \beta_2 X_{1i}^2 + \varepsilon_i \tag{15.1}$$

Quadratic Regression Equation

$$\hat{Y}_i = b_0 + b_1 X_{1i} + b_2 X_{1i}^2 \tag{15.2}$$

Regression Model with a Square-Root Transformation

$$\sqrt{Y_i} = \beta_0 + \beta_1 X_{1i} + \varepsilon_i \tag{15.3}$$

Original Multiplicative Model

$$Y_i = \beta_0 X_{1i}^{\beta_1} X_{2i}^{\beta_2} \varepsilon_i \tag{15.4}$$

Transformed Multiplicative Model

$$
\begin{aligned}
\log Y_i &= \log\left(\beta_0 X_{1i}^{\beta_1} X_{2i}^{\beta_2} \varepsilon_i\right) \\
&= \log \beta_0 + \log\left(X_{1i}^{\beta_1}\right) + \log(X_{2i}^{\beta_2}) + \log \varepsilon_i \\
&= \log \beta_0 + \beta_1 \log X_{1i} + \beta_2 \log X_{2i} + \log \varepsilon_i \tag{15.5}
\end{aligned}
$$

Original Exponential Model

$$Y_i = e^{\beta_0 + \beta_1 X_{1i} + \beta_2 X_{2i}} \varepsilon_i \tag{15.6}$$

Transformed Exponential Model

$$
\begin{aligned}
\ln Y_i &= \ln(e^{\beta_0 + \beta_1 X_{1i} + \beta_2 X_{2i}} \varepsilon_i) \\
&= \ln(e^{\beta_0 + \beta_1 X_{1i} + \beta_2 X_{2i}}) + \ln \varepsilon_i \\
&= \beta_0 + \beta_1 X_{1i} + \beta_2 X_{2i} + \ln \varepsilon_i \tag{15.7}
\end{aligned}
$$

Variance Inflationary Factor

$$VIF_j = \frac{1}{1 - R_j^2} \tag{15.8}$$

C_p Statistic

$$C_p = \frac{(1 - R_k^2)(n - T)}{1 - R_T^2} - \left[n - 2(k + 1) \right] \tag{15.9}$$

▼ KEY TERMS

best subsets approach 610
C_p statistic 611
collinearity 605
cross-validation 614
curvilinear relationship 593

logarithmic transformation 603
principle of parsimony 607
quadratic regression model 593
quadratic term 593

square-root transformation 601
stepwise regression 609
transformations 601
variance inflationary factor (*VIF*) 605

▼ CHECKING YOUR UNDERSTANDING

15.26 How can you evaluate whether collinearity exists in a multiple regression model?

15.27 What is the difference between stepwise regression and best subsets regression?

15.28 How do you choose among models according to the C_p statistic in best subsets regression?

▼ CHAPTER REVIEW PROBLEMS

15.29 A specialist in baseball analytics has expanded his analysis, presented in Problem 14.77 on page 580, of which variables are important in predicting a team's wins in a given baseball season. He has collected data in Baseball related to wins, ERA, saves, runs scored per game, batting average, home runs, and batting average against for a recent season.

Develop the most appropriate multiple regression model to predict a team's wins. Be sure to include a thorough residual analysis. In addition, provide a detailed explanation of the results.

15.30 In the production of printed circuit boards, errors in the alignment of electrical connections are a source of scrap. The file

RegistrationError contains the registration error, the temperature, the pressure, and the cost of the material (low versus high) used in the production of circuit boards.

Source: Data extracted from C. Nachtsheim and B. Jones, "A Powerful Analytical Tool," *Six Sigma Forum Magazine*, August 2003, pp. 30–33.

Develop the most appropriate multiple regression model to predict registration error.

15.31 Hemlock Farms is a community located in the Pocono Mountains area of eastern Pennsylvania. The file HemlockFarms contains information on homes that were recently for sale. The variables included were

List Price—Asking price of the house
Hot Tub—Whether the house has a hot tub, with 0 = No and 1 = Yes
Lake View—Whether the house has a lake view, with 0 = No and 1 = Yes
Bathrooms—Number of bathrooms
Bedrooms—Number of bedrooms
Loft/Den—Whether the house has a loft or den, with 0 = No and 1 = Yes
Finished basement—Whether the house has a finished basement, with 0 = No and 1 = Yes
Acres—Number of acres for the property

Develop the most appropriate multiple regression model to predict the asking price. Be sure to perform a thorough residual analysis. In addition, provide a detailed explanation of your results.

15.32 Nassau County is located approximately 25 miles east of New York City. The file GlenCove contains a sample of 30 single-family homes located in Glen Cove. Variables included are the fair market value, land area of the property (acres), interior size of the house (square feet), age (years), number of rooms, number of bathrooms, and number of cars that can be parked in the garage.

a. Develop the most appropriate multiple regression model to predict fair market value.
b. Compare the results in (a) with those of Problems 15.33 (a) and 15.34 (a).

15.33 Data similar to those in Problem 15.32 are available for homes located in Roslyn (approximately 8 miles from Glen Cove) and are stored in Roslyn.

a. Perform an analysis similar to that of Problem 15.32.
b. Compare the results in (a) with those of Problems 15.32 (a) and 15.34 (a).

15.34 Data similar to Problem 15.32 are available for homes located in Freeport (located approximately 20 miles from Roslyn) and are stored in Freeport.

a. Perform an analysis similar to that of Problem 15.32.
b. Compare the results in (a) with those of Problems 15.32 (a) and 15.33 (a).

15.35 You are a real estate broker who wants to compare property values in Glen Cove and Roslyn (which are located approximately 8 miles apart). Use the data in GCRoslyn. Make sure to include the dummy variable for location (Glen Cove or Roslyn) in the regression model.

a. Develop the most appropriate multiple regression model to predict fair market value.
b. What conclusions can you reach concerning the differences in fair market value between Glen Cove and Roslyn?

15.36 You are a real estate broker who wants to compare property values in Glen Cove, Freeport, and Roslyn. Use the data in GCFreeRoslyn.

a. Develop the most appropriate multiple regression model to predict fair market value.
b. What conclusions can you reach concerning the differences in fair market value between Glen Cove, Freeport, and Roslyn?

15.37 Financial analysts engage in business valuation to determine a company's value. A standard approach uses the multiple of earnings method: You multiply a company's profits by a certain value (average or median) to arrive at a final value. More recently, regression analysis has been demonstrated to consistently deliver more accurate predictions. A valuator has been given the assignment of valuing a drug company. She obtained financial data on 60 drug companies (Industry Group Standard Industrial Classification [SIC] 3 code 283), which included pharmaceutical preparation firms (SIC 4 code 2834), in vitro and in vivo diagnostic substances firms (SIC 4 code 2835), and biological products firms (SIC 4 2836). The file BusinessValuation2 contains these variables:

COMPANY—Drug company name
TS—Ticker symbol
SIC 3—Standard Industrial Classification 3 code (industry group identifier)
SIC 4—Standard Industrial Classification 4 code (industry identifier)
PB fye—Price-to-book value ratio (fiscal year ending)
PE fye—Price-to-earnings ratio (fiscal year ending)
NL Assets—Natural log of assets (as a measure of size)
ROE—Return on equity
SGROWTH—Growth (GS5)
DEBT/EBITDA—Ratio of debt to earnings before interest, taxes, depreciation, and amortization
D2834—Dummy variable indicator of SIC 4 code 2834 (1 if 2834, 0 if not)
D2835—Dummy variable indicator of SIC 4 code 2835 (1 if 2835, 0 if not)

Develop the most appropriate multiple regression model to predict the price-to-book value ratio. Perform a thorough residual analysis and provide a detailed explanation of your results.

15.38 The J. Conklin article, "It's a Marathon, Not a Sprint," *Quality Progress*, June 2009, pp. 46–49, discussed a metal deposition process in which a piece of metal is placed in an acid bath and an alloy is layered on top of it. The key quality characteristic is the thickness of the alloy layer. The file Thickness contains the following variables:

Thickness—Thickness of the alloy layer
Catalyst—Catalyst concentration in the acid bath
pH—pH level of the acid bath
Pressure—Pressure in the tank holding the acid bath
Temp—Temperature in the tank holding the acid bath
Voltage—Voltage applied to the tank holding the acid bath

Develop the most appropriate multiple regression model to predict the thickness of the alloy layer. Be sure to perform a thorough residual analysis. The article suggests that there is a significant interaction between the pressure and the temperature in the tank. Do you agree?

15.39 A molding machine that contains different cavities is used in producing plastic parts. The product characteristics of interest are the product length (in.) and weight (g). The mold cavities were filled with raw material powder and then vibrated during the experiment. The factors that were varied were the vibration time (seconds), the vibration pressure (psi), the vibration amplitude (%), the raw material density (g/mL), and the quantity of raw material (scoops). The experiment was conducted in two different cavities on the molding machine. The data are stored in Molding .

Source: Data extracted from M. Lopez and M. McShane-Vaughn, "Maximizing Product, Minimizing Costs," *Six Sigma Forum Magazine*, February 2008, pp. 18–23.

a. Develop the most appropriate multiple regression model to predict the product length in cavity 1. Be sure to perform a thorough residual analysis. In addition, provide a detailed explanation of your results.
b. Repeat (a) for cavity 2.
c. Compare the results for length in the two cavities.
d. Develop the most appropriate multiple regression model to predict the product weight in cavity 1. Be sure to perform a thorough residual analysis. In addition, provide a detailed explanation of your results.
e. Repeat (d) for cavity 2.
f. Compare the results for weight in the two cavities.

15.40 The file Cities contains a sample of 25 cities in the United States. Variables included are city average annual salary ($), unemployment rate (%), median home value ($thousands), number of violent crimes per 100,000 residents, average commuter travel time (minutes), and livability score, a rating on a scale of 0 to 100 that rates the overall livability of the city.

Source: Data extracted from "100 Best Places to Live in the USA," available at **bit.ly/2jYvtFz** and "AARP Livability Index," available at **bit.ly/1Qbd6oj**.

Develop the most appropriate multiple regression model to predict average annual salary ($). Be sure to perform a thorough residual analysis and provide a detailed explanation of the results as part of your answer.

REPORT WRITING EXERCISE

15.41 In Problems 15.32–15.36 you developed multiple regression models to predict the fair market value of houses in Glen Cove, Roslyn, and Freeport. Now write a report based on the models you developed. Append all appropriate charts and statistical information to your report.

CHAPTER

▼ CASES

15

The Mountain States Potato Company

Mountain States Potato Company sells a by-product of its potato-processing operation, called a filter cake, to area feedlots as cattle feed. The business problem faced by the feedlot owners is that the cattle are not gaining weight as quickly as they once were. The feedlot owners believe that the root cause of the problem is that the percentage of solids in the filter cake is too low.

Historically, the percentage of solids in the filter cakes ran slightly above 12%. Lately, however, the solids are running in the 11% range. What is actually affecting the solids is a mystery, but something has to be done quickly. Individuals involved in the process were asked to identify variables that might affect the percentage of solids. This review turned up the six variables (in addition to the percentage of solids) listed in the right column. Data collected by monitoring the process several times daily for 20 days are stored in Potato .

1. Thoroughly analyze the data and develop a regression model to predict the percentage of solids.

2. Write an executive summary concerning your findings to the president of the Mountain States Potato Company. Include specific recommendations on how to get the percentage of solids back above 12%.

Variable	Comments
SOLIDS	Percentage of solids in the filter cake.
PH	Acidity. This measure of acidity indicates bacterial action in the clarifier and is controlled by the amount of downtime in the system. As bacterial action progresses, organic acids are produced that can be measured using pH.
LOWER	Pressure of the vacuum line below the fluid line on the rotating drum.
UPPER	Pressure of the vacuum line above the fluid line on the rotating drum.
THICK	Filter cake thickness, measured on the drum.
VARIDRIV	Setting used to control the drum speed. May differ from DRUMSPD due to mechanical inefficiencies.
DRUMSPD	Speed at which the drum is rotating when collecting the filter cake. Measured with a stopwatch.

Sure Value Convenience Stores

You work in the corporate office for a nationwide convenience store franchise that operates nearly 10,000 stores. The per-store daily customer count (i.e., the mean number of customers in a store in one day) has been steady, at 900, for some time. To increase the customer count, the chain is considering cutting prices for coffee beverages. The question to be determined is how much prices should be cut to increase the daily customer count without reducing the gross margin on coffee sales too much. You decide to carry out an experiment in a sample of 24 stores where customer counts have been running almost exactly at the national average of 900. In six of the stores, the price of a small coffee will now be $0.59, in six stores the price of a small coffee will now be $0.69, in six stores, the price of a small coffee will now be $0.79, and in six stores, the price of a small coffee will now be $0.89. After four weeks at the new prices, the daily customer count in the stores is determined and is stored in CoffeeSales2 .

a. Construct a scatter plot for price and sales.

b. Fit a quadratic regression model and state the quadratic regression equation.

c. Predict the mean weekly sales for a small coffee priced at 79 cents.

d. Perform a residual analysis on the results and determine whether the regression model is valid.

e. At the 0.05 level of significance, is there a significant quadratic relationship between weekly sales and price?

f. At the 0.05 level of significance, determine whether the quadratic model is a better fit than the linear model.

g. Interpret the meaning of the coefficient of multiple determination.

h. Compute the adjusted r^2.

i. What price do you recommend the small coffee should be sold for?

Digital Case

Apply your knowledge of multiple regression model building in this Digital Case, which extends the Chapter 14 OmniPower Bars Using Statistics scenario.

Still concerned about ensuring a successful test marketing of its OmniPower bars, the marketing department of OmniFoods has contacted Connect2Coupons (C2C), another merchandising consultancy. C2C suggests that earlier analysis done by In-Store Placements Group (ISPG) was faulty because it did not use the correct type of data. C2C claims that its Internet-based viral marketing will have an even greater effect on OmniPower energy bar sales, as new data from the same 34-store sample will show. In response, ISPG says its earlier claims are valid and has reported to the OmniFoods marketing department that it can discern no simple relationship between C2C's viral marketing and increased OmniPower sales.

Open **OmniPowerForum15.pdf** to review all the claims made in a private online forum and chat hosted on the Omni-Foods corporate website. Then answer the following:

1. Which of the claims are true? False? True but misleading? Support your answer by performing an appropriate statistical analysis.

2. If the grocery store chain allowed OmniFoods to use an unlimited number of sales techniques, which techniques should it use? Explain.

3. If the grocery store chain allowed OmniFoods to use only one sales technique, which technique should it use? Explain.

The Craybill Instrumentation Company Case

The Craybill Instrumentation Company produces highly technical industrial instrumentation devices. The human resources (HR) director has the business objective of improving recruiting decisions concerning sales managers. The company has 45 sales regions, each headed by a sales manager. Many of the sales managers have degrees in electrical engineering, and due to the technical nature of the product line, several company officials believe that only applicants with degrees in electrical engineering should be considered.

At the time of their application, candidates are asked to take the Strong-Campbell Interest Inventory Test and the Wonderlic Personnel Test. Due to the time and money involved with the testing, some discussion has taken place about dropping one or both of the tests. To start, the HR director gathered information on each of the 45 current sales managers, including years of selling experience, electrical engineering background, and the scores from both the Wonderlic and Strong-Campbell tests. The HR director has decided to use regression modeling to predict a dependent variable of "sales index" score, which is the ratio of the regions' actual sales divided by the target sales. The target values are constructed each year by upper management, in consultation with the sales managers, and are based on past performance and market potential within each region. The file Managers contains information on the 45 current sales managers. The following variables are included:

Sales—Ratio of yearly sales divided by the target sales value for that region; the target values were mutually agreed-upon "realistic expectations"

Wonder—Score from the Wonderlic Personnel Test; the higher the score, the higher the applicant's perceived ability to manage

SC—Score on the Strong-Campbell Interest Inventory Test; the higher the score, the higher the applicant's perceived interest in sales

Experience—Number of years of selling experience prior to becoming a sales manager

Engineer—Dummy variable that equals 1 if the sales manager has a degree in electrical engineering and 0 otherwise

a. Develop the most appropriate regression model to predict sales.

b. Do you think that the company should continue administering both the Wonderlic and Strong-Campbell tests? Explain.

c. Do the data support the argument that electrical engineers outperform the other sales managers? Would you support the idea to hire only electrical engineers? Explain.

d. How important is prior selling experience in this case? Explain.

e. Discuss in detail how the HR director should incorporate the regression model you developed into the recruiting process.

More Descriptive Choices Follow-Up

Follow-up the Using Statistics scenario "More Descriptive Choices, Revisited" on page 159, by developing regression models to predict the one-year return, the three-year return, the five-year return, and the ten-year return based on the assets, turnover ratio, expense ratio, beta, standard deviation, type of fund (growth versus value), and risk (stored in Retirement Funds). (For this analysis, combine low and average risk into the new category "not high.") Be sure to perform a thorough residual analysis. Provide a summary report that explains your results in detail.

▾EXCEL GUIDE

EG15.1 The QUADRATIC REGRESSION MODEL

Key Technique Use the exponential operator (^) in a column of formulas to create the quadratic term.

Example Create the quadratic term for the Section 15.1 concrete strength analysis.

PHStat, Workbook, *and* Analysis ToolPak For the example, open to the **DATA worksheet** of the **FlyAsh workbook**, which contains the independent X variable FlyAsh% in column A and the dependent Y variable Strength in column B and:

1. Select column B, right-click, and click **Insert** from the shortcut menu. This creates a new, blank column B, and changes Strength to column C.
2. Enter the label **FlyAsh%^2** in cell **B1** and then enter the formula **=A2^2** in cell **B2**.
3. Copy this formula down column B through all the data rows (through row 19).

(Best practice places the quadratic term in a column that is contiguous to the columns of the other independent X variables.)

Adapt the Section EG14.1 instructions to perform a regression analysis using the quadratic term. For *PHStat*, use **C1:C19** as the **Y Variable Cell Range** and **A1:B19** as the **X Variables Cell Range**. For *Worksheet*, use **C2:C19** and **A2:B19** in step 4 as the new cell ranges. For *Analysis ToolPak*, use **C1:C19** as the **Input Y Range** and **A1:B19** as the **Input X Range**.

To create a scatter plot, adapt the EG2.5 "The Scatter Plot" instructions. For *PHStat*, use **C1:C19** as the **Y Variable Cell Range** and **A1:B19** as the **X Variable Cell Range**. For *Worksheet*, select the noncontiguous cell range **A1:A19, C1:C19** in step 1 and skip step 3. (Appendix B explains how to select a noncontiguous cell range.) Select the scatter chart and then:

1. Select **Design** (or **Chart Design**)➔ **Add Chart Element** ➔ **Trendline** ➔ **More Trendline Options**.

In the Format Trendline pane (parts shown below),

2. Click **Polynomial** (shown at top of right column).

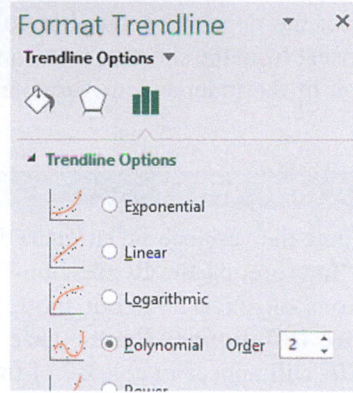

3. Check **Display Equation on chart** (shown below).

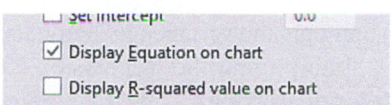

In older Excels, select **Layout** ➔ **Trendline** ➔ **More Trendline Options** in step 1 and in the Format Trendline dialog box, click **Trendline Options** in the left pane. In the Trendline Options right pane, click **Polynomial**, check **Display Equation on chart**, and click **OK**.

EG15.2 USING TRANSFORMATIONS in REGRESSION MODELS

The Square-Root Transformation

To the worksheet that contains your regression data, add a new column of formulas that computes the square root of the variable for which you want to create a square-root transformation. For example, to create a square-root transformation in a blank column D for a variable in a column, enter the formula **=SQRT(C2)** in cell D2 of that worksheet and copy the formula down through all data rows.

If the column to the immediate right of the variable to be transformed is not empty, first select that column, right-click, and click **Insert** from the shortcut menu. Then place the transformation in the newly inserted blank column.

The Log Transformation

To the worksheet that contains your regression data, add a new column of formulas that computes the common (base 10) logarithm or natural logarithm (base e) of the dependent variable to create a log transformation. For example, to create a common logarithm transformation in a blank column D for a variable in a column C, enter the formula **=LOG(C2)** in cell D2 of that worksheet and copy the formula down through all data rows. To create a natural logarithm transformation in a blank column D for a variable in column C, enter the formula **=LN(C2)** in cell D2 of that worksheet and copy the formula down through all data rows.

If the dependent variable appears in a column to the immediate right of the independent variable being transformed, first select the dependent variable column, right-click, and click **Insert** from the shortcut menu and then place the transformation of the independent variable in that new column.

EG15.3 COLLINEARITY

PHStat To compute the variance inflationary factor (*VIF*), use the EG14.1 "Interpreting the Regression Coefficients" *PHStat* instructions on page 582, but modify step 6 by checking **Variance Inflationary Factor** (*VIF*) before you click **OK**. The *VIF* will appear in cell B9 of the regression results worksheet, immediately following the Regression Statistics area.

Workbook To compute the variance inflationary factor, first use the EG14.1 "Interpreting the Regression Coefficients" *Workbook* instructions on page 582 to create regression results worksheets for every combination of independent variables in which one serves as the dependent variable. Then, in each of the regression results worksheets, enter the label *VIF* in cell **A9** and enter the formula **=1/(1 − B5)** in cell **B9** to compute the *VIF*.

EG15.4 MODEL BUILDING

The Stepwise Regression Approach to Model Building

Key Technique Use PHStat to perform a stepwise analysis.
Example Perform the Figure 15.14 stepwise analysis for the Nickels Broadcasting data on page 609.

PHStat Use **Stepwise Regression**.

For the example, open to the **DATA worksheet** of the **Nickels26Weeks workbook** and select **PHStat→ Regression→Stepwise Regression**. In the procedure's dialog box (shown at the top of the right column):

1. Enter **A1:A27** as the **Y Variable Cell Range**.
2. Enter **B1:E27** as the **X Variables Cell Range**.
3. Check **First cells in both ranges contain label**.
4. Enter **95** as the **Confidence level for regression coefficients**.
5. Click **p values** as the **Stepwise Criteria**.
6. Click **General Stepwise** and keep the pair of **.05** values as the **p value to enter** and the **p value to remove**.
7. Enter a **Title** and click **OK**.

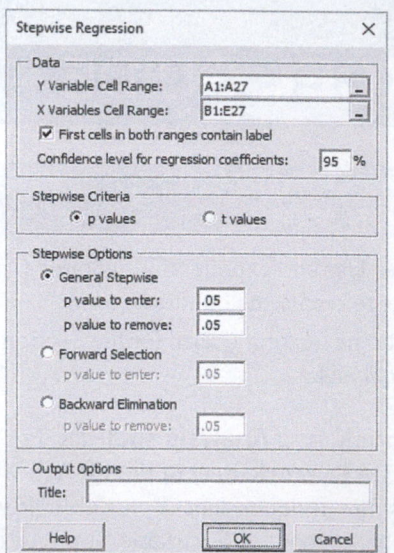

This procedure may take more than a few seconds to construct its results. The procedure finishes when the statement "Stepwise ends" is added to the stepwise regression results worksheet (in row 29 in Figure 15.14 on page 609).

The Best Subsets Approach to Model Building

Key Technique Use PHStat to perform a best subsets analysis.

Example Perform the Figure 15.15 best subsets analysis for the Nickels Broadcasting data on page 610.

PHStat Use **Best Subsets**.

For the example, open to the **DATA worksheet** of the **Nickels26Weeks workbook**. Select **PHStat→ Regression→Best Subsets**. In the procedure's dialog box (shown below):

1. Enter **A1:A27** as the **Y Variable Cell Range**.
2. Enter **B1:E27** as the **X Variables Cell Range**.
3. Check **First cells in each range contains label**.
4. Enter **95** as the **Confidence level for regression coefficients**.
5. Enter a **Title** and click **OK**.

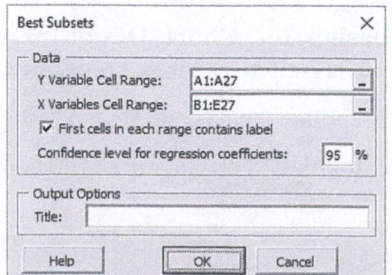

Because this procedure examines many different regression models, there may be a noticeable delay between when OK is clicked and results appear onscreen.

▼ JMP GUIDE

JG15.1 The QUADRATIC REGRESSION MODEL

Use **Formula**.

For example, to create a quadratic term for the Section 15.1 concrete strength analysis, open to the **FlyAsh data table** and:

1. Right-click the Strength column and select **Insert Columns** from the shortcut menu.
2. Right-click the new, blank Column 2 and select **Formula** from the shortcut menu.

In the Formula dialog box (see illustration on page 112):

3. Click **FlyAsh%** in the columns list. FlyAsh% appears in the formula workspace.
4. Click the **x^y icon.** Flyash%^{2} appears in the formula workspace.
5. Click **OK**.
6. Rename Column 2 as **FlyAsh%^2**.

To perform a regression analysis using this new variable, modify the Section JG14.1 instructions on page 585.

JG15.2 USING TRANSFORMATIONS in REGRESSION MODELS

Use **Formula**.

Open to the data table that contains your regression data and:

1. Double-click an empty column.
2. Right-click that column and select **Formula** from the shortcut menu.
3. Enter the transformation using the natural log (log base *e*), log base 10, or square-root transformation.
4. Select the column in the **Columns** list that contains the data to be transformed.
5. Click **OK**.

For a natural log (log base *e*) transformation, enter **ln** in the filter box above the list of formula functions, click **Ln**, and then complete the expression. For a log base 10 transformation, enter **log** in the filter box and then click **Log10**, and then complete the expression. For a square-root transformation, click the **square-root icon** (highlighted below) and complete the expression.

JG15.3 COLLINEARITY

Use **Fit Model** and then modify the Parameter Estimates table in the results window. For example, to compute the variance inflationary factors (*VIF*s) for the Nickels Broadcasting data, modify the Section JG14.1 instructions that use Fit Model to create the initial regression results in a new window. Right-click anywhere in the body of the Parameter Estimates table and select **Columns** from the shortcut menu and then check **VIF** in the submenu.

JG15.4 MODEL BUILDING

The Stepwise Regression Approach to Model Building

Use **Fit Model**.

For example, to create the Figure 15.14 stepwise analysis of the Nickels Broadcasting data, open to the **Nickels26Weeks data table**. Select **Analyze ➔ Fit Model** and in the Fit Model dialog box (partially shown below):

1. Click **Standby** in the columns list and then click **Y** to add Standby to the Y box.
2. While holding down the **Ctrl key**, select **Staff**, **RemoteEng**, **Graphics**, and **Production** in the columns list and then click **Add** to add these four columns to the Construct Model Effects box.
3. Select **Stepwise** from the **Personality** pull-down list.
4. Click **Run**.

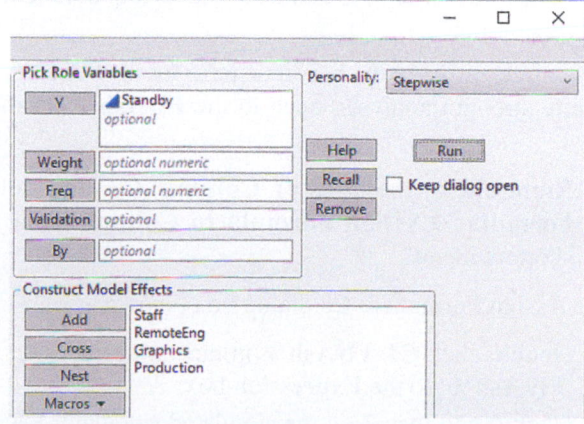

In the Fit Stepwise window partially (partially shown on page 626):

5. Select **P-value Threshold** from the **Stopping Rule** pull-down list.
6. Enter **0.05** in both the **Prob to Enter** and **Prob to Leave** boxes.

7. Select **Mixed** from the **Direction** pull-down list.
8. Click **Go**.

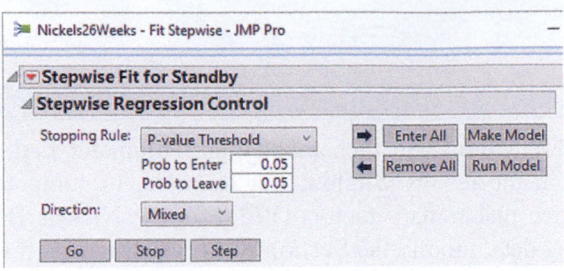

JMP displays the stepwise regression results in the bottom portion of the Fit Stepwise window (shown in Figure 15.14).

The Best Subsets Approach to Model Building

Modify the Stepwise Regression instructions.

For example, to create the Figure 15.15 best subsets analysis of the Nickels Broadcasting data, open to the **Nickels26Weeks data table** and follow steps 1 through 8 of the preceding stepwise regression instructions. Continue with these steps 9 through 12:

9. Click the **Stepwise Fit for Standby red triangle** and select **All Possible Models**.
10. In the Please Enter Values dialog box, verify that 4 appears in both the **Maximum number of terms in a model** and **Number of best models** to see boxes.
11. Click **OK**.
12. Right-click anywhere in the body of the All Possible Models table and select **Columns** from the shortcut menu and then check **Cp** in the submenu.

The All Possible Models table does not include the adjusted r^2 values for each model. However, clicking an open circle in the last column displays the adjusted r^2 for a row model in the summary area above the Current Estimates Table (which also changes as a circle is clicked). To use the adjusted r^2 evaluation, click the open circles in the last column one at a time and note the model with the best adjusted r^2 value.

CHAPTER

15

▼MINITAB GUIDE

MG15.1 The QUADRATIC REGRESSION MODEL

Use **Assign Formula to Column** to create a quadratic term in a new column.

For example, to create the quadratic term for the Section 15.1 concrete strength analysis, open to the **FlyAsh worksheet** and:

1. Right-click (the empty) **Column C3** and select **Formulas→Assign Formula to Column** from the shortcut menu.

In the Assign Formula to C3 dialog box (shown at right):

2. Double-click **C1 FlyAsh%** in the variables list to add **'Fly Ash%'** to the **Expression** box.
3. Click **^** and then **2** on the simulated calculator keypad to add **^2** to the **Expression** box to form the expression **'FlyAsh%'^2**.

4. Click **OK**.
5. Enter **FlyAsh%^2** as the name for column **C3**.

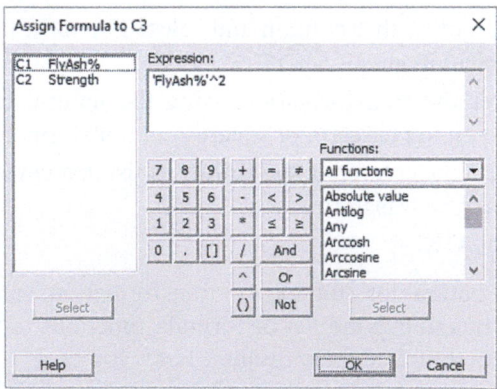

To perform a regression analysis using this new variable, adapt the Section MG14.1 instructions on page 588 to include the quadratic term.

MG15.2   USING TRANSFORMATIONS in REGRESSION MODELS

Use **Assign Formula to Column**.

Open to the worksheet that contains your regression data and:

1. Right-click an empty column and select **Formulas→ Assign Formula to Column** from the shortcut menu.
2. Select **All functions** from the **Functions** drop-down list.
3. In the list of functions, select one of these choices: **Square root**, **Log base 10**, or **Natural log (log base e)**. Selecting these choices enters **SQRT(number)**, **LOGTEN(number)**, or **LN(number)**, respectively, in the **Expression** box.
4. Double-click the name of the variable to be transformed in the variables list to replace **number** with the variable name in the **Expression** box.
5. Click **OK**.
6. Enter a name for the transformed values column.

MG15.3   COLLINEARITY

The variance inflationary factors appear as part of the results that the Section MG14.1 "Interpreting the Regression Coefficients" instructions on page 588 create.

MG15.4   MODEL BUILDING

The Stepwise Regression Approach to Model Building

Use **Fit Regression Model**.

For example, to create the Figure 15.14 stepwise analysis of the Nickels Broadcasting data on page 609, open to the **Nickels26Weeks worksheet**. Select **Stat→Regression→ Regression→Fit Regression Model**. In the Regression dialog box (shown at right):

1. Double-click **C1 Standby** in the variables list to add **Standby** in the **Response** box.
2. Enter **C2-C5** in the **Predictors** box. (Entering **C2-C5** is a shortcut way of referring to the columns 2 through 5 variables.)
3. Click **Stepwise**.

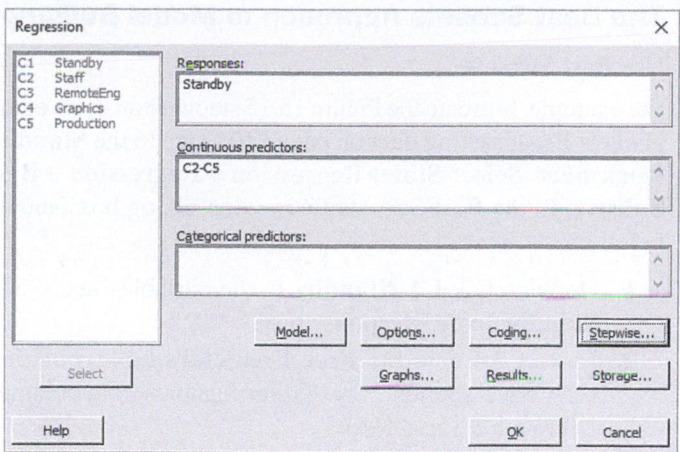

In the Regression: Stepwise dialog box (shown below):

4. Select **Stepwise** from the **Method** pull-down list.
5. Enter **0.05** in the **Alpha to enter** box and **0.05** in the **Alpha to remove** box.
6. Click **OK**.

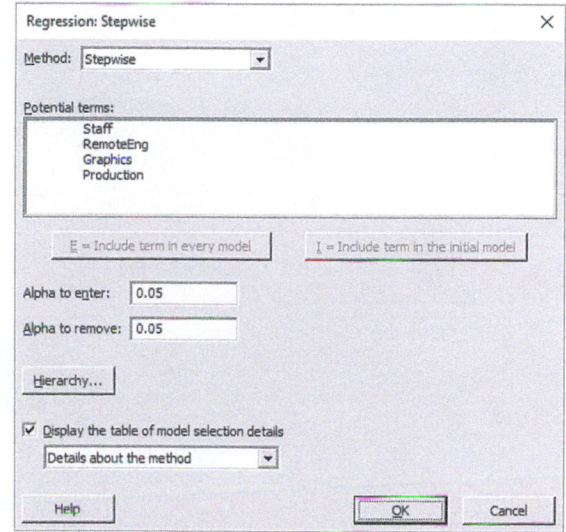

7. Back in the Regression dialog box, click **OK**.

Note that Method will remain as **Stepwise** (step 4 instruction) for other regressions done in the same Minitab session until the Method is reset. To reset Method, select **None** from the pull-down list in the Regression: Stepwise dialog box.

The Best Subsets Approach to Model Building

Use **Best Subsets**.

For example, to create the Figure 15.15 stepwise analysis of the Nickels Broadcasting data on page 610, open to the **Standby worksheet**. Select **Stat → Regression → Regression → Best Subsets**. In the Best Subsets Regression dialog box (shown below):

1. Double-click **C1 Standby** in the variables list to add **Standby** in the **Response** box.
2. Enter **C2-C5** in the **Free Predictors** box. (Entering **C2-C5** is a shortcut way of referring to the four columns 2 through 5 variables.)
3. Click **Options**.

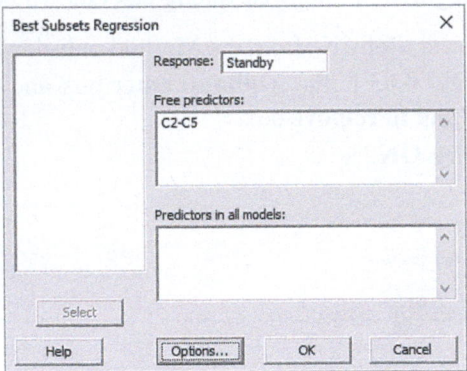

In the Best Subsets Regression: Options dialog box (shown below):

4. Enter **1** in the **Minimum box** and leave the **Maximum** box empty.
5. Enter **3** in the **Models of each size to print** box.
6. Check **Fit intercept**.
7. Click **OK**.
8. Back in the Best Subsets Regression dialog box, click **OK**.

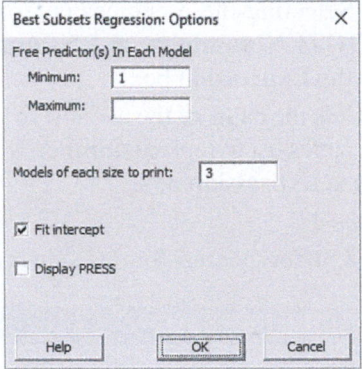

Time-Series Forecasting

OBJECTIVES

- Construct different time-series forecasting models for annual and seasonal data
- Choose the most appropriate time-series forecasting model

▼USING **STATISTICS**
Is the ByYourDoor Service Trending?

Senior managers at ByYourDoor, an online food delivery service, have asked you to analyze sales data. These managers would like to know if that sales data can be used to estimate future sales. They already know that their business is thriving, but sales seem to be subject to periodic dips that make it hard to accurately estimate short-term physical and labor resources requirements for the company.

One manager wondered if a regression technique might be useful, but another manager recalls that simple and multiple regression models can only predict inside the range of the X values used to create the model. Looking forward would require going beyond the values in such a range. Is it even possible to make a useful estimation about a *future* value of a dependent Y variable?

Forecasting estimates future business conditions by monitoring changes that occur over time. Managers must be able to develop forecasts to anticipate likely changes their businesses will face. For example, retail marketing executives might forecast product demand, sales revenues, consumer preferences, and inventory, among other things, to make decisions regarding product promotions and strategic planning. **Time-series forecasting**, the focus of this chapter, uses a **time series**, a set of numerical data collected over time at regular intervals as the basis for the estimation. Both government and business activities generate time series data. Some government examples include economic indicators such as a consumer price index or the quarterly gross domestic product (GDP) as well as measurements of real-world phenomena such as the mean monthly level of lakes, the levels of carbon dioxide in the air, or the daily high temperature for a locality. Businesses generate many types of time series and typically include annual measurements of sales revenues, net profits, and other accounting data in annual reports or similar documents.

Time-series forecasting is not the only type of forecasting that uses numerical data. **Causal forecasting methods**, beyond the scope of this book to explore, help determine the factors that relate to the variable being estimated. These methods include multiple regression analysis with lagged variables, econometric modeling, leading indicator analysis, and other economic barometers that are beyond the scope of this text (see references 3–5).

Although time-series forecasting shares the goal of prediction with the regression methods that previous chapters discuss, time-series forecasting seeks to estimate a *future* value, a goal very different than from the goals of the regression methods that Chapters 13, 14, and 15 discuss. For ByTheDoor, an initial complication would be to establish the time interval that most makes sense for estimating future sales. The time interval can affect both the perception of the data as well as the statistical methods used to analyze the time series. Because the company buys supplies monthly and because customers use the service once a month, on average, collecting monthly data might make best sense, but other time intervals might also be appropriate depending on the goal of the senior managers at the firm.

16.1 Time-Series Component Factors

As Section 2.5 notes, a time-series plot, in which the X axis represents units of time and the Y axis represents the values of a numerical variable, can help visualize trends in data that occur over time. A **trend**, an overall long-term upward or downward movement, that exists in a time series, is one possible pattern, or component of a time series. Establishing whether a trend exists in a time series is an important early step in time series analysis. Time-series plots can suggest whether a trend component exists in the time series. If a time series shows no trend, then the techniques of moving averages and exponential smoothing that Section 16.2 discusses can be used to analyze the time series. If a time series shows a trend, the various methods that Sections 16.3 through 16.5 discuss can be used if the time series represents annual data. Figure 16.1 Panel A shows a time series with a strong upward trend.

Time-series data may also show a combination of cyclical and irregular components. A **cyclical component** is up-and-down movement in the time series of medium duration, typically from two to ten years in length. Figure 16.1 Panel B shows a time series with two cycles of differing durations. These cycles often correlate with "business cycles" that are associated with certain types of economic activities.

Figure 16.1 Panel C visualizes a times series that has a strong irregular component. An **irregular component** reflects one-time changes to a time series that cannot be explained by the trend or cyclical components. For business decision makers, discovering an irregularity may signal an inflection point in which a significant business or economic change has occurred. Figure 16.2 shows the time series of houses sold in the United States over a fifty-year period. An irregular component centered on 2008 reflects the collapse of the U.S. housing market that led to the "Great Depression" of 2007–2009.

FIGURE 16.1
Trend, cyclical, and irregular components of time series

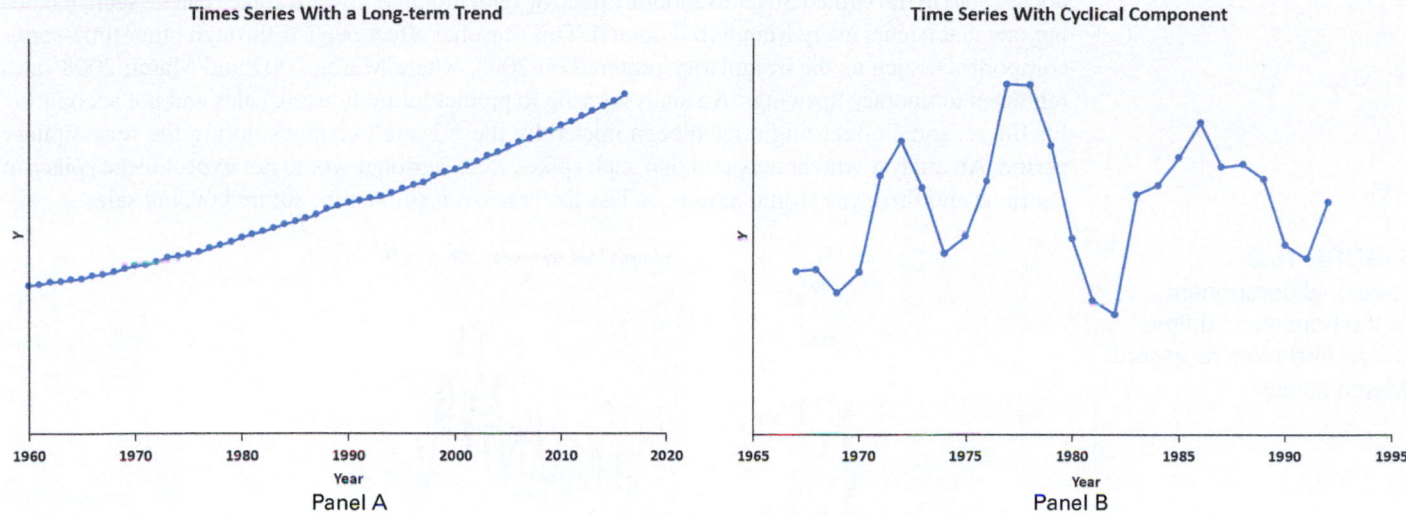

Panel A

Panel B

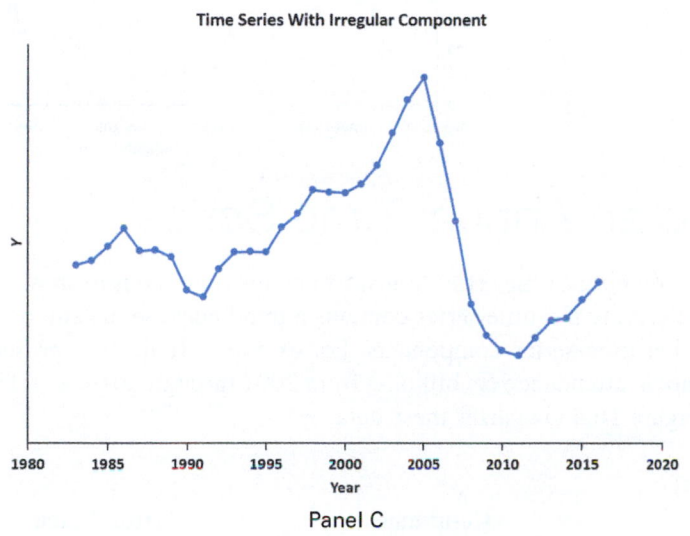

Panel C

FIGURE 16.2
Houses sold in the United States, 1963–2016

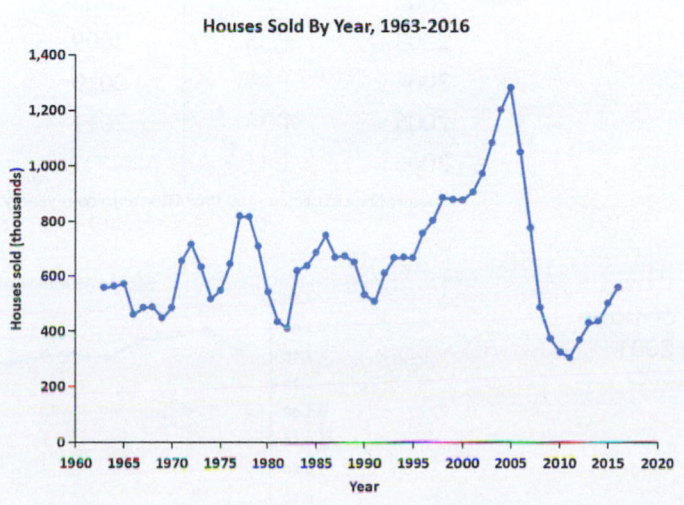

If a time series is collected at intervals less than year, such as monthly or quarterly, the time series may also have a **seasonal component**. Figure 16.3 shows the latter part of the time series of houses sold in the United States as monthly data. Several monthly upward spikes can be seen, including one that occurs every March (red points). This seasonal effect persists through other time-series components, such as the irregularity centered on 2008, where March 2007 and March 2008 sales represent temporary upswings. An analyst trying to predict future housing sales and not accounting for the seasonal effect might have been misled by these March changes during the recessionary period. An analyst who understood that such spikes were seasonal would not expect these spikes to continue and therefore would have been less likely to overestimate the future housing sales.

FIGURE 16.3
Seasonal component in the houses sold time series (red plots represent March sales)

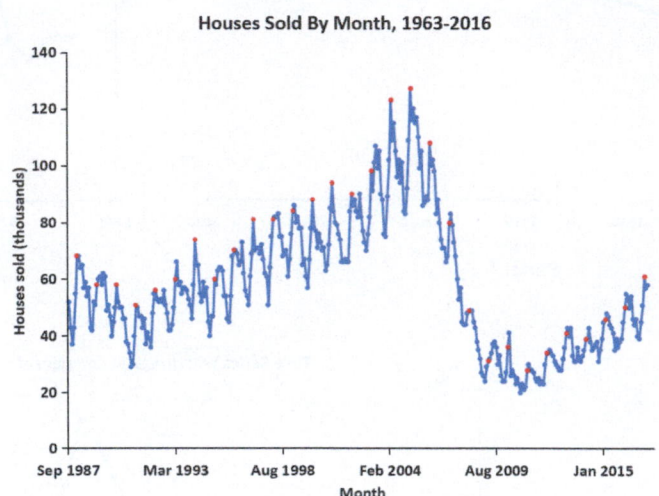

16.2 Smoothing an Annual Time Series

Smoothing a time series, transforming the time series to show small-scale fluctuations, can help determine if a time series contains a trend because the smoothing minimizes the effects of the other time-series components. For example, Table 16.1 presents the annual U.S. and Canada movie attendance (in billions) from 2001 through 2016, as reflected by number of tickets sold. Figure 16.4 visualizes these data.

TABLE 16.1
Annual Movie Attendance From 2001 Through 2016 (stored in Original Movie Attendance)

Year	Attendance (billions)	Year	Attendance (billions)	Year	Attendance (billions)
2001	1.44	2007	1.40	2012	1.36
2002	1.58	2008	1.34	2013	1.34
2003	1.55	2009	1.41	2014	1.27
2004	1.47	2010	1.34	2015	1.32
2005	1.38	2011	1.28	2016	1.32
2006	1.41				

Source: Data extracted from **boxofficemojo.com/yearly**.

FIGURE 16.4
Time-series plot of movie attendance from 2001 through 2016

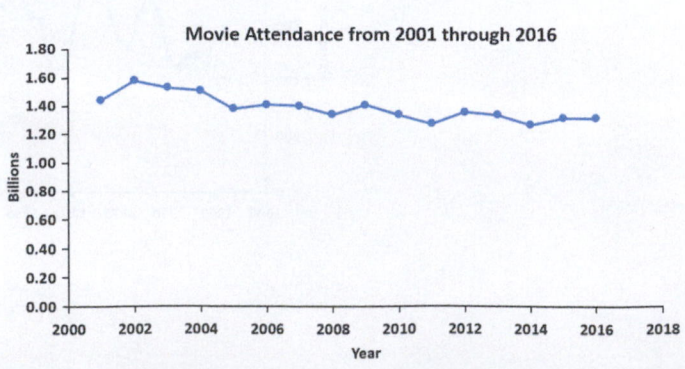

Figure 16.4 seems to show a slight downward trend in movie attendance especially in the beginning of the time series. However, the variation that exists from one time period to another can sometimes obscure a long-term trend which can make an existing trend hard to identify. Using *moving averages* or *exponential smoothing* can smooth the data and better visualize a long-term trend that may be present.

Moving Averages

The **moving averages** method calculates means for sequences of consecutive time-series values for a time duration L. The sequences each differ by one time-series value, as the moving average method "moves" through the time-series. For example, for a three-year moving average for an annual time series of eleven years, the first calculated mean would be the mean of the time-series values for years 1 through 3, the second calculated mean would be the mean for years 2 through 4, and the ninth calculated mean would be the mean for years 9 through 11.

The moving averages method always reduces the number of values because moving averages cannot be calculated for the first $(L - 1)/2$ years and the last $(L - 1)/2$ years of the time series. For the example, in which $L = 3$, a moving average cannot be calculated for either the first or last (eleventh) year. Although L could be any whole number, making L an odd number permits centering each moving average on a time value which simplifies preparing tabular and visual summaries of a moving average. For example, if $L = 3$, the first moving average for an annual time series of eleven years would be centered on year 2. If $L = 5$, the first moving average would be centered on year 3. However, if $L = 4$, the moving average would be centered on year "2.5," a time value that is not part of the original time series.

For annual time-series data that does not contain an obvious cyclical component, using 3, 5, or 7 as the value of L are reasonable choices. If a cyclical component exists in a time series, the value of L should be a number that corresponds to or is a multiple of the estimated length of a cycle. Example 16.1 illustrates calculating moving averages for $L = 5$.

student TIP

Remember that you cannot calculate moving averages at the beginning and at the end of the series.

EXAMPLE 16.1

Calculating Five-Year Moving Averages

The following data represent revenue (in $millions) for a casual dining restaurant over the 11-year period 2007 to 2017.

$$4.0 \quad 5.0 \quad 7.0 \quad 6.0 \quad 8.0 \quad 9.0 \quad 5.0 \quad 7.0 \quad 7.5 \quad 5.5 \quad 6.5$$

Compute the five-year moving averages for this annual time series.

SOLUTION Five-year moving averages take the mean of five consecutive time-series values. The first of the five-year moving averages is

$$MA(5) = \frac{Y_1 + Y_2 + Y_3 + Y_4 + Y_5}{5} = \frac{4.0 + 5.0 + 7.0 + 6.0 + 8.0}{5} = \frac{30.0}{5} = 6.0$$

The second of the five-year moving averages is:

$$MA(5) = \frac{Y_2 + Y_3 + Y_4 + Y_5 + Y_6}{5} = \frac{5.0 + 7.0 + 6.0 + 8.0 + 9.0}{5} = \frac{35.0}{5} = 7.0$$

The third, fourth, fifth, sixth, and seventh moving averages are:

$$MA(5) = \frac{Y_3 + Y_4 + Y_5 + Y_6 + Y_7}{5} = \frac{7.0 + 6.0 + 8.0 + 9.0 + 5.0}{5} = \frac{35.0}{5} = 7.0$$

$$MA(5) = \frac{Y_4 + Y_5 + Y_6 + Y_7 + Y_8}{5} = \frac{6.0 + 8.0 + 9.0 + 5.0 + 7.0}{5} = \frac{35.0}{5} = 7.0$$

$$MA(5) = \frac{Y_5 + Y_6 + Y_7 + Y_8 + Y_9}{5} = \frac{8.0 + 9.0 + 5.0 + 7.0 + 7.5}{5} = \frac{36.5}{5} = 7.3$$

$$MA(5) = \frac{Y_6 + Y_7 + Y_8 + Y_9 + Y_{10}}{5} = \frac{9.0 + 5.0 + 7.0 + 7.5 + 5.5}{5} = \frac{34.0}{5} = 6.8$$

$$MA(5) = \frac{Y_7 + Y_8 + Y_9 + Y_{10} + Y_{11}}{5} = \frac{5.0 + 7.0 + 7.5 + 5.5 + 6.5}{5} = \frac{31.5}{5} = 6.3$$

Using computerized methods avoids tedious hand calculations of moving averages. Figure 16.5 presents a worksheet that computes the five-year moving averages for the casual dining restaurant revenue time series. The figure also contains a time-series plot that visualizes the revenues and the computed five-year moving averages. The plot of the moving averages shows much less variation than the plot of the revenues because the moving averages method has smoothed the data.

FIGURE 16.5

Casual dining restaurant revenue and five-year moving average

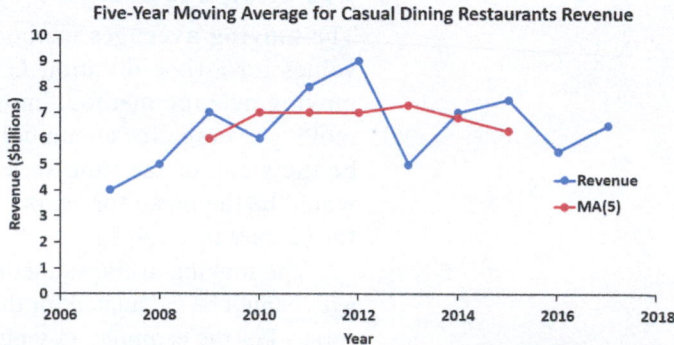

student TIP

Using a time duration *L* that is an odd number facilitates the comparison of the moving averages with the original time-series data.

Figure 16.6 (left) visualizes the three-year and five-year moving averages for the movie attendance data. The moving average plots show a downward trend, but, unlike the Figure 16.4 time-series plot, reveal that the trend has greatly slowed or stopped after 2004. Figure 16.6 (right), a redone plot that discards the time-series values for the early years 2001 through 2004 that show a strong trend, reveals a time series with no perceptible trend. This shorter time series may lead to a more accurate short-term forecast of future movie attendance.

FIGURE 16.6

Time-series plots for the three- and five-year moving averages for the movie attendance for two time series, 2001 through 2016 and 2005 through 2016

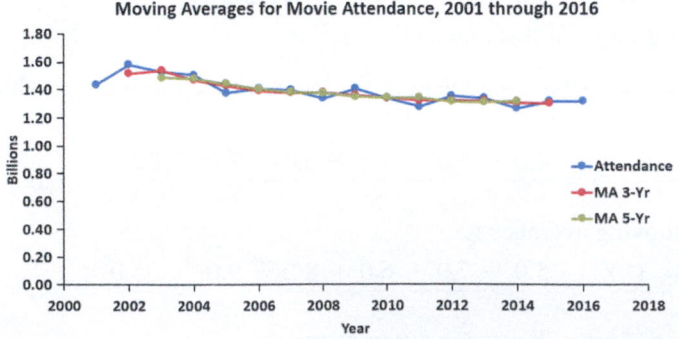
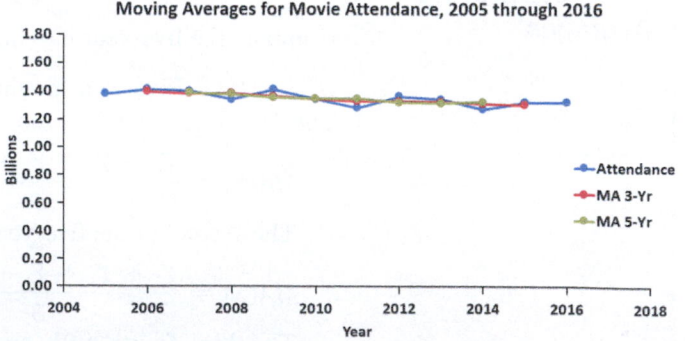

While discarding data is almost never allowed in the inferential methods that earlier chapters discuss, discarding consecutive time series is an example of the partially subjective nature of time-series forecasting. Determining the proper length of a time series to be used for forecasting can be a mix of business experience and awareness of external or one-time, irregular factors. For the U.S. and Canadian movie attendance time series, further investigation reveals that the year 2002 was unusual in being the only year in which the popular *Star Wars*, *Harry Potter*, and the *Lord of the Rings* movie series all had releases. (And those three films were *only* the second, third, and fourth most popular movies that year, as 2002 also saw the release of the first modern-day *Spider-Man* movie.)

Later movie attendance examples in this chapter use the shorter 2005 through 2016 time series for the reasons this passage discusses.

Because the shorter movie attendance time series shows no trend, the moving averages based on the shorter time series could be used for short-term forecasting. However, a second technique, *exponential smoothing*, typically offers better short-term forecasting.

Exponential Smoothing

Exponential smoothing consists of a series of *exponentially weighted* moving averages. The weights assigned to the values change so that the most recent (the last) value receives the highest weight, the previous value receives the second-highest weight, and so on, with the first value receiving the lowest weight. Therefore, the more recent a time-series value is, the more influence the value has on the smoothing function. Each exponentially smoothed value depends on all previous values that makes this method different from moving averages, which uses only a subset of the time series to determine each value.

Exponential smoothing also allows you to compute short-term (one period into the future) forecasts when the presence and type of long-term trend in a time series is difficult to determine. Equation (16.1) defines how to compute an exponentially smoothed value for any time period i. Note the special case that the smoothed value for time period 1 is the observed value for time period 1.

COMPUTING AN EXPONENTIALLY SMOOTHED VALUE IN TIME PERIOD i

$$E_1 = Y_1$$

$$E_i = WY_i + (1 - W)E_{i-1} \quad i = 2, 3, 4, \ldots \tag{16.1}$$

where

E_i = value of the exponentially smoothed series being computed in time period i

E_{i-1} = value of the exponentially smoothed series already computed in time period $i - 1$

Y_i = observed value of the time series in period i

W = subjectively assigned weight or smoothing coefficient, where $0 < W < 1$

---

studentTIP

Although *W* can approach 1.0, in virtually all business applications, $W \leq 0.5$.

Choosing the weight or smoothing coefficient, W, that you assign to the time series is both critical to the smoothing and somewhat subjective. If your goal is to smooth a series by eliminating unwanted cyclical and irregular variations in order to see the overall long-term tendency of the series, select a small value for W (close to 0). If your goal is forecasting future short-term directions, choose a large value for W (close to 0.5).

Figure 16.7 presents the exponentially smoothed values (with smoothing coefficients $W = 0.50$ and $W = 0.25$), the movie attendance from 2005 to 2016, and a plot of the original data and the two exponentially smoothed time series. Observe that exponential smoothing has smoothed some of the variation in the movie attendance.

FIGURE 16.7

Exponentially smoothed series ($W = 0.50$ and $W = 0.25$) worksheet and plot for the movie attendance data

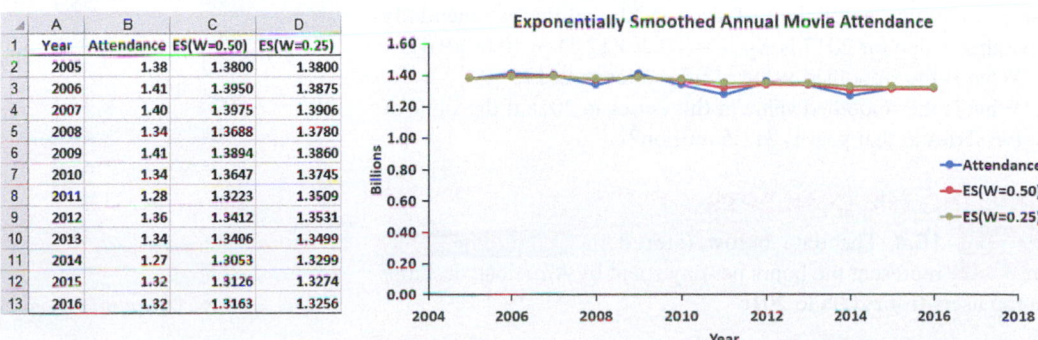

	A	B	C	D
1	Year	Attendance	ES(W=0.50)	ES(W=0.25)
2	2005	1.38	1.3800	1.3800
3	2006	1.41	1.3950	1.3875
4	2007	1.40	1.3975	1.3906
5	2008	1.34	1.3688	1.3780
6	2009	1.41	1.3894	1.3860
7	2010	1.34	1.3647	1.3745
8	2011	1.28	1.3223	1.3509
9	2012	1.36	1.3412	1.3531
10	2013	1.34	1.3406	1.3499
11	2014	1.27	1.3053	1.3299
12	2015	1.32	1.3126	1.3274
13	2016	1.32	1.3163	1.3256

To illustrate these exponential smoothing caculations for a smoothing coefficient of $W = 0.25$, begin with the initial value $Y_{2005} = 1.38$ as the first smoothed value ($E_{2005} = 1.38$). Then, using the value of the time series for 2006 ($Y_{2006} = 1.41$), smooth the series for 2006 as follows:

$$E_{2006} = WY_{2006} + (1 - W)E_{2005}$$
$$= (0.25)(1.41) + (0.75)(1.38) = 1.3875$$

To smooth the series for 2007:

$$E_{2007} = WY_{2007} + (1 - W)E_{2006}$$
$$= (0.25)(1.40) + (0.75)(1.3875) = 1.3906$$

This smoothing would continue for each of the remaining years in the time series. (Figure 16.7 also contains results of this smoothing operation.)

Exponential smoothing is a weighted average of all previous time periods. Therefore, when you use exponential smoothing for forecasting, you use the smoothed value in the current time period as the forecast of the value in the following period $\left(\hat{Y}_{i+1} \right)$.

FORECASTING TIME PERIOD $i + 1$

$$\hat{Y}_{i+1} = E_i \tag{16.2}$$

To forecast the movie attendance in 2017, using a smoothing coefficient of $W = 0.25$, you use the smoothed value for 2016 as its estimate.

$$\hat{Y}_{2016+1} = E_{2016}$$

$$\hat{Y}_{2017} = E_{2016}$$

$$\hat{Y}_{2017} = 1.3256$$

The exponentially smoothed forecast for 2017 is 1.3256 billion.

PROBLEMS FOR SECTION 16.2

LEARNING THE BASICS

16.1 If you are using exponential smoothing for forecasting an annual time series of revenues, what is your forecast for next year if the smoothed value for this year is $32.4 million?

16.2 Consider a nine-year moving average used to smooth a time series that was first recorded in 1984.
a. Which year serves as the first centered value in the smoothed series?
b. How many years of values in the series are lost when computing all the nine-year moving averages?

16.3 You are using exponential smoothing on an annual time series concerning total revenues (in $millions). You decide to use a smoothing coefficient of $W = 0.20$, and the exponentially smoothed value for 2017 is $E_{2017} = (0.20)(12.1) + (0.80)(9.4)$.
a. What is the smoothed value of this series in 2017?
b. What is the smoothed value of this series in 2018 if the value of the series in that year is $11.5 million?

APPLYING THE CONCEPTS

✓SELF TEST **16.4** The data below (stored in `DesktopLaptop`) represent the hours per day spent by American desktop/laptop users from 2008 to 2016.

Year	Hours per Day	Year	Hours per Day
2008	2.2	2013	2.3
2009	2.3	2014	2.2
2010	2.4	2015	2.2
2011	2.6	2016	2.2
2012	2.5		

Source: Data extracted from M. Meeker, Internet Trends 2017-Code Conference, available at **bit.ly/2vW8Nej**.

a. Plot the time series.
b. Fit a three-year moving average to the data and plot the results.

c. Using a smoothing coefficient of $W = 0.50$, exponentially smooth the series and plot the results.
d. What is your exponentially smoothed forecast for 2017?
e. Repeat (c) and (d), using $W = 0.25$.
f. Compare the results of (d) and (e).
g. What conclusions can you reach about desktop/laptop use by American users?

16.5 The following data, stored in `CoreAppliances` provide the total number of shipments of core major household appliances in the U.S. from 2000 to 2016 (in millions).

Year	Shipments	Year	Shipments
2000	38.4	2009	36.5
2001	38.2	2010	38.2
2002	40.8	2011	36.0
2003	42.5	2012	35.8
2004	46.1	2013	39.2
2005	47.0	2014	41.5
2006	46.7	2015	42.9
2007	44.1	2016	44.7
2008	39.8		

Source: Data extracted from **www.statistica.com**.

a. Plot the time series.
b. Fit a three-year moving average to the data and plot the results.
c. Using a smoothing coefficient of $W = 0.50$, exponentially smooth the series and plot the results.
d. What is your exponentially smoothed forecast for 2017?
e. Repeat (c) and (d), using $W = 0.25$.
f. Compare the results of (d) and (e).
g. What conclusions can you reach concerning the total number of shipments of core major household appliances in the U.S. from 2000 to 2016 (in millions)?

16.6 How have stocks performed in the past? The following table presents the data stored in Stock Performance , which show the performance of a broad measure of stock performance (by percentage) for each decade from the 1830s through the 2000s:

Decade	Performance (%)	Decade	Performance (%)
1830s	2.8	1920s	13.3
1840s	12.8	1930s	−2.2
1850s	6.6	1940s	9.6
1860s	12.5	1950s	18.2
1870s	7.5	1960s	8.3
1880s	6.0	1970s	6.6
1890s	5.5	1980s	16.6
1900s	10.9	1990s	17.6
1910s	2.2	2000s*	−0.5

* Through December 15, 2009.

Source: T. Lauricella, "Investors Hope the '10s Beat the '00s," *The Wall Street Journal*, December 21, 2009, pp. C1, C2.

a. Plot the time series.
b. Fit a three-period moving average to the data and plot the results.
c. Using a smoothing coefficient of $W = 0.50$, exponentially smooth the series and plot the results.
d. What is your exponentially smoothed forecast for the 2010s?
e. Repeat (c) and (d), using $W = 0.25$.

f. Compare the results of (d) and (e).
g. What conclusions can you reach concerning how stocks have performed in the past?

16.7 The data (stored in CoffeeExports) represent the coffee exports (in thousands of 60 kg bags) by Costa Rica from 2004 to 2016:
a. Plot the data.
b. Fit a three-year moving average to the data and plot the results.
c. Using a smoothing coefficient of $W = 0.50$, exponentially smooth the series and plot the results.
d. What is your exponentially smoothed forecast for 2017?
e. Repeat (c) and (d), using a smoothing coefficient of $W = 0.25$.
f. Compare the results of (d) and (e).
g. What conclusions can you reach about the exports of coffee in Costa Rica?

16.8 The file IPOs contains the number of initial public offerings (IPOs) issued from 2001 through 2016.

Source: Data extracted from K.W. Hanley, "The Economics of Primary Markets," available at **bit.ly/2vWb6hv**.

a. Plot the data.
b. Fit a three-year moving average to the data and plot the results.
c. Using a smoothing coefficient of $W = 0.50$, exponentially smooth the series and plot the results.
d. What is your exponentially smoothed forecast for 2017?
e. Repeat (c) and (d), using a smoothing coefficient of $W = 0.25$.
f. Compare the results of (d) and (e).

16.3 Least-Squares Trend Fitting and Forecasting

To make intermediate and long-range forecasts requires identifying the trend component in a time series. Identifying the trend means being able to develop the most appropriate model that fits the trend. As with regression models that previous chapters discuss, time series data might fit a linear trend model (see Section 13.2), a quadratic trend model (see Section 15.1), or, if the time-series data increase at a rate such that the percentage difference from value to value is constant, an exponential trend model.

The Linear Trend Model

The **linear trend model**:

$$Y_i = \beta_0 + \beta_1 X_i + \varepsilon_i$$

is the simplest forecasting model. Equation (16.3) defines the linear trend forecasting equation.

LINEAR TREND FORECASTING EQUATION

$$\hat{Y}_i = b_0 + b_1 X_i \qquad (16.3)$$

Recall that in linear regression analysis, you use the method of least squares to compute the sample slope, b_1, and the sample Y intercept, b_0. You then substitute the values for X into Equation (16.3) to predict Y.

When using the least-squares method for fitting trends in a time series, you can simplify the interpretation of the coefficients by assigning coded values to the X (time) variable. You assign consecutively numbered integers, starting with 0, as the coded values for the time periods. For example, in time-series data that have been recorded annually for 19 years, you assign the coded value 0 to the first year, the coded value 1 to the second year, the coded value 2 to the third year, and so on, concluding by assigning 18 to the nineteenth year.

To illustrate model fitting, consider the Table 16.2 time series that lists The Coca-Cola Company's annual revenues (in $billions) from 1998 to 2016 (stored in Coca-Cola).

TABLE 16.2
Annual Revenues for The Coca-Cola Company, 1998–2016

Founded in 1886 and headquartered in Atlanta, Georgia, Coca-Cola manufactures, distributes, and markets more than 500 beverage brands in over 200 countries worldwide.

Year	Revenues ($billions)	Year	Revenues ($billions)
1998	18.8	2008	31.9
1999	19.8	2009	31.0
2000	20.5	2010	35.1
2001	20.1	2011	46.5
2002	19.6	2012	48.0
2003	21.0	2013	46.7
2004	21.9	2014	45.9
2005	23.1	2015	44.3
2006	24.1	2016	41.9
2007	28.9		

Source: Data extracted from *Mergent's Handbook of Common Stocks*, 2006; and The Coca-Cola Company, "Archive of Annual and Other Reports," **bit.ly/1XYa2Ai**.

Figure 16.8 presents the regression results for the simple linear regression model that uses the consecutive coded values 0 through 18 as the X (coded year) variable. These results produce the linear trend forecasting equation:

$$\hat{Y}_i = 14.45 + 1.8395X_i$$

FIGURE 16.8
Excel, Minitab, and JMP regression results for the linear trend model to forecast revenues (in $billions) for The Coca-Cola Company

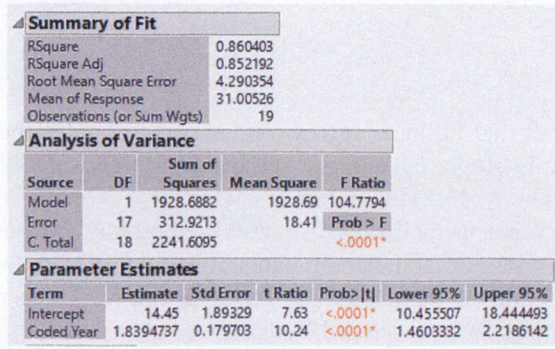

For this regression model, $X_1 = 0$ represents the year 1998 and the regression coefficients are interpreted as follows:

- The Y intercept, $b_0 = 14.45$, is the predicted mean revenues (in \$billions) at The Coca-Cola Company during the origin, or base, year, 1998.
- The slope, $b_1 = 1.8395$, indicates that mean revenues are predicted to increase by \$1.8395 billion per year.

To project the trend in the revenues at Coca-Cola to 2017, you substitute $X_{20} = 19$, the code for 2017 into the linear trend forecasting equation:

$$\hat{Y}_i = 14.45 + 1.8395(19) = 49.4005 \text{ billions of dollars}$$

Figure 16.9 presents the linear trendline plotted with the time-series values. There is a strong upward linear trend, and r^2 is 0.8604, indicating that more than 86% of the variation in revenues is explained by the linear trend of the time series. However, observe that the early years are slightly above the trend line, but the middle years are below the trend line and many of the later years are also above the trend line but the last two years are below the trend line. To investigate whether a different trend model might provide a better fit, a *quadratic* trend model and an *exponential* trend model can be fitted.

FIGURE 16.9

Plot of the linear trend forecasting equation for The Coca-Cola Company annual revenue data

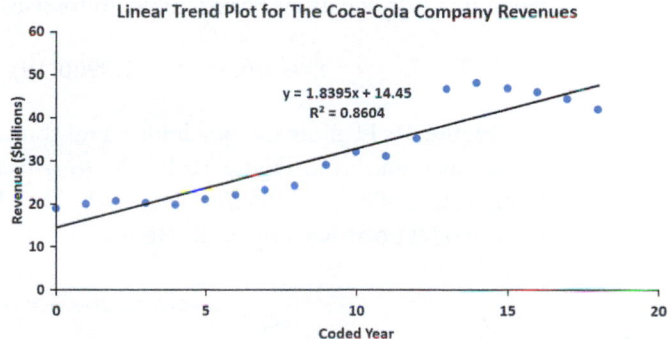

The Quadratic Trend Model

A **quadratic trend model**:

$$Y_i = \beta_0 + \beta_1 X_i + \beta_2 X_i^2 + \varepsilon_i$$

is a nonlinear model that contains a linear term and a curvilinear term in addition to a Y intercept. Using the least-squares method for a quadratic model that Section 15.1 describes, Equation (16.4) defines a quadratic trend forecasting equation.

QUADRATIC TREND FORECASTING EQUATION

$$\hat{Y}_i = b_0 + b_1 X_i + b_2 X_i^2 \tag{16.4}$$

where

$$b_0 = \text{estimated } Y \text{ intercept}$$
$$b_1 = \text{estimated } linear \text{ effect on } Y$$
$$b_2 = \text{estimated } quadratic \text{ effect on } Y$$

Figure 16.10 presents the regression results for the quadratic trend model to forecast annual revenues at The Coca-Cola Company.

FIGURE 16.10

Excel regression results worksheet for the quadratic trend model to forecast annual revenues (in $billions) for The Coca-Cola Company

	A	B	C	D	E	F	G
1	Quadratic Trend Model for The Coca-Cola Company Revenues						
2							
3	*Regression Statistics*						
4	Multiple R	0.9331					
5	R Square	0.8707					
6	Adjusted R Square	0.8546					
7	Standard Error	4.2560					
8	Observations	19					
9							
10	ANOVA						
11		*df*	*SS*	*MS*	*F*	*Significance F*	
12	Regression	2	1951.7965	975.8983	53.8774	0.0000	
13	Residual	16	289.8130	18.1133			
14	Total	18	2241.6095				
15							
16		*Coefficients*	*Standard Error*	*t Stat*	*P-value*	*Lower 95%*	*Upper 95%*
17	Intercept	16.5549	2.6458	6.2571	0.0000	10.9461	22.1637
18	Coded Year	1.0966	0.6815	1.6092	0.1271	-0.3480	2.5412
19	Coded Year Squared	0.0413	0.0365	1.1295	0.2753	-0.0362	0.1187

In Figure 16.10,

$$\hat{Y}_i = 16.5549 + 1.0966X_i + 0.0413X_i^2$$

where the year coded 0 is 1998.

To compute a forecast using the quadratic trend equation, substitute the appropriate coded X value into this equation. For example, to forecast the trend in revenues for 2017 (i.e., $X = 19$),

$$\hat{Y}_i = 16.5549 + 1.0966(19) + 0.0413(19)^2 = 52.2996$$

Figure 16.11 plots the quadratic trend forecasting equation along with the time series for the actual data. From Figure 16.10, the t_{STAT} test statistic for the contribution of the quadratic term to the model is 1.1295 (p-value = 0.2753). Having an adjusted $r^2 = 0.8546$, this quadratic trend model provides a fit similar to the fit of the linear trend model.

FIGURE 16.11

Plot of the quadratic trend forecasting equation for The Coca-Cola Company annual revenue data

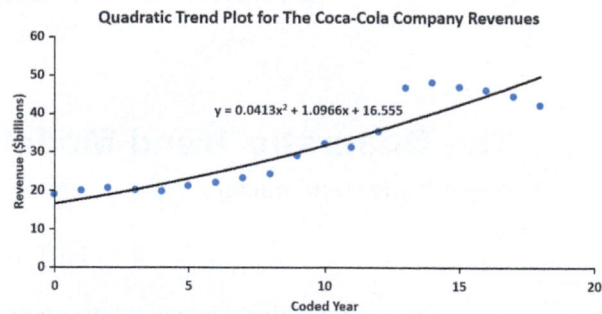

The Exponential Trend Model

When a time series increases at a rate such that the percentage difference from value to value is constant, an exponential trend is present. Equation (16.5) defines the **exponential trend model**.

EXPONENTIAL TREND MODEL

$$Y_i = \beta_0 \beta_1^{X_i} \varepsilon_i \tag{16.5}$$

where

$$\beta_0 = Y \text{ intercept}$$
$$(\beta_1 - 1) \times 100\% = \text{annual compound growth rate (\%)}$$

The model in Equation (16.5) is not in the form of a linear regression model. To transform this nonlinear model to a linear model, you use a base 10 logarithm transformation.[1] Taking the logarithm of each side of Equation (16.5) results in the transformed model that Equation (16.6) defines.

[1]Alternatively, you can use base e logarithms. For more information on logarithms, see Section A.3 in Appendix A.

TRANSFORMED EXPONENTIAL TREND MODEL

$$\begin{aligned}\log(Y_i) &= \log(\beta_0\beta_1^{X_i}\varepsilon_i)\\ &= \log(\beta_0) + \log(\beta_1^{X_i}) + \log(\varepsilon_i)\\ &= \log(\beta_0) + X_i\log(\beta_1) + \log(\varepsilon_i)\end{aligned} \quad \textbf{(16.6)}$$

student TIP

Log is the symbol used for base 10 logarithms. The log of a number is the power that 10 needs to be raised to equal that number.

Using the transformed model and the least-squares method, with $\log(Y_i)$ as the dependent variable and X_i as the independent variable produces the Equation (16.7a) forecasting equation.

EXPONENTIAL TREND FORECASTING EQUATION

$$\log(\hat{Y}_i) = b_0 + b_1X_i \quad \textbf{(16.7a)}$$

where

$$b_0 = \text{estimate of } \log(\beta_0) \text{ and thus } 10^{b_0} = \hat{\beta}_0$$

$$b_1 = \text{estimate of } \log(\beta_1) \text{ and thus } 10^{b_1} = \hat{\beta}_1$$

therefore,

$$\hat{Y}_i = \hat{\beta}_0\hat{\beta}_1^{X_i} \quad \textbf{(16.7b)}$$

where

$$(\hat{\beta}_i - 1) \times 100\% \text{ is the estimated annual compound growth rate } (\%)$$

Figure 16.12 shows the Excel regression results for an exponential trend model to forecast annual revenues at The Coca-Cola Company.

Using Equation (16.7a) and the results from Figure 16.12,

$$\log(\hat{Y}_i) = 1.2299 + 0.0261X_i$$

where the year coded 0 is 1998.

FIGURE 16.12
Excel regression results for the exponential trend model to forecast annual revenues (in $billions) for The Coca-Cola Company

	A	B	C	D	E	F	G
1	Exponential Trend Model for The Coca-Cola Company Revenues						
2							
3	*Regression Statistics*						
4	Multiple R	0.9494					
5	R Square	0.9013					
6	Adjusted R Square	0.8955					
7	Standard Error	0.0501					
8	Observations	19					
9							
10	ANOVA						
11		*df*	*SS*	*MS*	*F*	*Significance F*	
12	Regression	1	0.3892	0.3892	155.3247	0.0000	
13	Residual	17	0.0426	0.0025			
14	Total	18	0.4318				
15							
16		*Coefficients*	*Standard Error*	*t Stat*	*P-value*	*Lower 95%*	*Upper 95%*
17	Intercept	1.2299	0.0221	55.6730	0.0000	1.1833	1.2765
18	Coded Year	0.0261	0.0021	12.4629	0.0000	0.0217	0.0306

Compute the values for $\hat{\beta}_0$ and $\hat{\beta}_1$ by taking the antilog of the regression coefficients (b_0 and b_1):

$$\hat{\beta}_0 = \text{antilog}(b_0) = \text{antilog}(1.2299) = 10^{1.2299} = 16.9785$$

$$\hat{\beta}_1 = \text{antilog}(b_1) = \text{antilog}(0.0261) = 10^{0.0261} = 1.0619$$

Thus, using Equation (16.7b), the exponential trend forecasting equation is

$$\hat{Y}_i = (16.9785)(1.0619)^{X_i}$$

where the year coded 0 is 1998.

The Y intercept, $\hat{\beta}_0 = 16.9785$ billions of dollars, is the revenue forecast for the base year 1998. The value $(\hat{\beta}_1 - 1) \times 100\%, = 6.19\%$, is the annual compound growth rate in revenues at The Coca-Cola Company.

For forecasting purposes, substitute the appropriate coded X values into either Equation (16.7a) or Equation (16.7b). For example, to forecast revenues for 2017 ($X = 19$) using Equation (16.7a),

$$\log(\hat{Y}_i) = 1.2299 + 0.0261(19) = 1.7258$$

$$\hat{Y}_i = \text{antilog}(1.7258) = 10^{1.7258} = 53.1863 \text{ billion of dollars}$$

Figure 16.13 plots the exponential trend forecasting equation, along with the time-series data. The adjusted r^2 for the exponential trend model (0.8955) is greater than the adjusted r^2 for the linear trend model (0.8522) and for the quadratic model (0.8546).

FIGURE 16.13

Plot of the exponential trend forecasting equation for The Coca-Cola Company annual revenue data

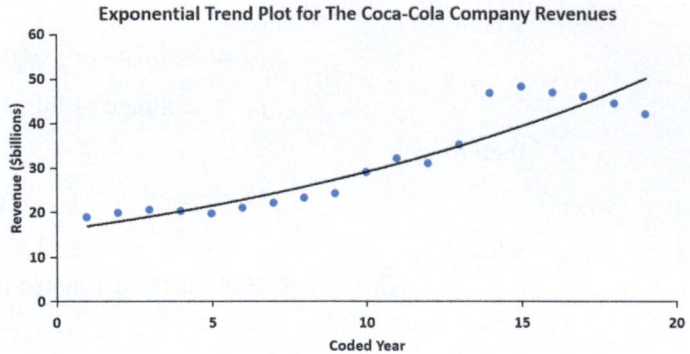

Model Selection Using First, Second, and Percentage Differences

Examining the first, second, and percentage differences in a time series helps determine which type of model is most appropriate for the time series. Exhibit 16.1 summarizes how these differences identify the most appropriate model.

EXHIBIT 16.1

Model Selection Using First, Second, and Percentage Differences

- If a linear trend model provides a perfect fit to a time series, then the first differences are constant. Thus, the first differences will be constant:

$$(Y_2 - Y_1) = (Y_3 - Y_2) = \cdots = (Y_n - Y_{n-1})$$

- If a quadratic trend model provides a perfect fit to a time series, then the second differences will be constant:

$$[(Y_3 - Y_2) - (Y_2 - Y_1)] = [(Y_4 - Y_3) - (Y_3 - Y_2)] = \cdots = [(Y_n - Y_{n-1}) - (Y_{n-1} - Y_{n-2})]$$

- If an exponential trend model provides a perfect fit to a time series, then the percentage differences between consecutive values will be constant:

$$\frac{Y_2 - Y_1}{Y_1} \times 100\% = \frac{Y_3 - Y_2}{Y_2} \times 100\%, = \cdots = \frac{Y_n - Y_{n-1}}{Y_{n-1}} \times 100\%$$

Although most time-series data will not perfectly fit any of the models, consider the first differences, second differences, and percentage differences as guides in choosing an appropriate model. Examples 16.2, 16.3, and 16.4 illustrate linear, quadratic, and exponential trend models that have perfect (or nearly perfect) fits to their respective data sets.

EXAMPLE 16.2	
A Linear Trend Model with a Perfect Fit	The following time series represents the number of customers per year (in thousands) at a branch of a fast-food chain:

	Year									
	2008	**2009**	**2010**	**2011**	**2012**	**2013**	**2014**	**2015**	**2016**	**2017**
Customers Y	200	205	210	215	220	225	230	235	240	245

Using first differences, show that the linear trend model provides a perfect fit to these data.

SOLUTION The following table shows the solution:

	Year									
	2008	**2009**	**2010**	**2011**	**2012**	**2013**	**2014**	**2015**	**2016**	**2017**
Customers Y	200	205	210	215	220	225	230	235	240	245
First differences		5.0	5.0	5.0	5.0	5.0	5.0	5.0	5.0	5.0

The differences between consecutive values in the series are the same throughout. Thus, the number of customers at the branch of the fast-food chain shows a linear growth pattern.

EXAMPLE 16.3	
A Quadratic Trend Model with a Perfect Fit	The following time series represents the number of customers per year (in thousands) at another branch of a fast-food chain:

	Year									
	2008	**2009**	**2010**	**2011**	**2012**	**2013**	**2014**	**2015**	**2016**	**2017**
Customers Y	200	201	203.5	207.5	213	220	228.5	238.5	250	263

Using second differences, show that the quadratic trend model provides a perfect fit to these data.

SOLUTION The following table shows the solution:

	Year									
	2008	**2009**	**2010**	**2011**	**2012**	**2013**	**2014**	**2015**	**2016**	**2017**
Customers Y	200	201	203.5	207.5	213	220	228.5	238.5	250	263
First differences		1.0	2.5	4.0	5.5	7.0	8.5	10.0	11.5	13.0
Second differences			1.5	1.5	1.5	1.5	1.5	1.5	1.5	1.5

The second differences between consecutive pairs of values in the series are the same throughout. Thus, the number of customers at the branch of the fast-food chain shows a quadratic growth pattern. Its rate of growth is accelerating over time.

EXAMPLE 16.4	
An Exponential Trend Model with an Almost Perfect Fit	The following time series represents the number of customers per year (in thousands) for another branch of the fast-food chain:

	Year									
	2008	**2009**	**2010**	**2011**	**2012**	**2013**	**2014**	**2015**	**2016**	**2017**
Customers Y	200	206	212.18	218.55	225.11	231.86	238.82	245.98	253.36	260.96

▶(*continued*)

Using percentage differences, show that the exponential trend model provides almost a perfect fit to these data.

SOLUTION The following table shows the solution:

					Year					
	2008	2009	2010	2011	2012	2013	2014	2015	2016	2017
Customers Y	200	206	212.18	218.55	225.11	231.86	238.82	245.98	253.36	260.96
Percentage differences		3.0	3.0	3.0	3.0	3.0	3.0	3.0	3.0	3.0

The percentage differences between consecutive values in the series are approximately the same throughout. Thus, this branch of the fast-food chain shows an exponential growth pattern. Its rate of growth is approximately 3% per year.

Figure 16.14 shows a worksheet that compares the first, second, and percentage differences for the The Coca-Cola Company revenues. Neither the first differences, second differences, nor percentage differences are constant across the series. Therefore, other models (including those considered in Section 16.5) may be more appropriate.

FIGURE 16.14
Excel, JMP, and Minitab templates that compute first, second, and percentage differences in revenues (in $billions) for The Coca-Cola Company

	A	B	C	D	E
			First	Second	Percentage
1	Year	Revenues	Difference	Difference	Difference
2	1998	18.8	#N/A	#N/A	#N/A
3	1999	19.8	1.0	#N/A	5.32%
4	2000	20.5	0.7	-0.3	3.54%
5	2001	20.1	-0.4	-1.1	-1.95%
6	2002	19.6	-0.5	-0.1	-2.49%
7	2003	21.0	1.4	1.9	7.14%
8	2004	21.9	0.9	-0.5	4.29%
9	2005	23.1	1.2	0.3	5.48%
10	2006	24.1	1.0	-0.2	4.33%
11	2007	28.9	4.8	3.8	19.92%
12	2008	31.9	3.0	-1.8	10.38%
13	2009	31.0	-0.9	-3.9	-2.82%
14	2010	35.1	4.1	5.0	13.23%
15	2011	46.5	11.4	7.3	32.48%
16	2012	48.0	1.5	-9.9	3.23%
17	2013	46.7	-1.3	-2.8	-2.71%
18	2014	45.9	-0.8	0.5	-1.71%
19	2015	44.3	-1.6	-0.8	-3.49%
20	2016	41.9	-2.4	-0.8	-5.42%

5/0 ▼			First	Second	Percentage
19/0	Year	Revenues	Difference	Difference	Difference
1	1998	18.8	.	.	.
2	1999	19.8	1.0	.	5.32%
3	2000	20.5	0.7	-0.3	3.54%
4	2001	20.1	-0.4	-1.1	-1.95%
5	2002	19.6	-0.5	-0.1	-2.49%
6	2003	21.0	1.4	1.9	7.14%
7	2004	21.9	0.9	-0.5	4.29%
8	2005	23.1	1.2	0.3	5.48%
9	2006	24.1	1.0	-0.2	4.33%
10	2007	28.9	4.8	3.8	19.92%
11	2008	31.9	3.0	-1.8	10.38%
12	2009	31.0	-0.9	-3.9	-2.82%
13	2010	35.1	4.1	5.0	13.23%
14	2011	46.5	11.4	7.3	32.48%
15	2012	48.0	1.5	-9.9	3.23%
16	2013	46.7	-1.3	-2.8	-2.71%
17	2014	45.9	-0.8	0.5	-1.71%
18	2015	44.3	-1.6	-0.8	-3.49%
19	2016	41.9	-2.4	-0.8	-5.42%

↓	C1	C2	C3 ✓	C4 ✓	C5 ✓
	Year	Revenues	First Differences	Second Differences	Percentage Differences
1	1998	18.8	*	*	*
2	1999	19.8	1.0	*	5.32%
3	2000	20.5	0.7	-0.3	3.54%
4	2001	20.1	-0.4	-1.1	-1.95%
5	2002	19.6	-0.5	-0.1	-2.49%
6	2003	21.0	1.4	1.9	7.14%
7	2004	21.9	0.9	-0.5	4.29%
8	2005	23.1	1.2	0.3	5.48%
9	2006	24.1	1.0	-0.2	4.33%
10	2007	28.9	4.8	3.8	19.92%
11	2008	31.9	3.0	-1.8	10.38%
12	2009	31.0	-0.9	-3.9	-2.82%
13	2010	35.1	4.1	5.0	13.23%
14	2011	46.5	11.4	7.3	32.48%
15	2012	48.0	1.5	-9.9	3.23%
16	2013	46.7	-1.3	-2.8	-2.71%
17	2014	45.9	-0.8	0.5	-1.71%
18	2015	44.3	-1.6	-0.8	-3.49%
19	2016	41.9	-2.4	-0.8	-5.42%

PROBLEMS FOR SECTION 16.3

LEARNING THE BASICS

16.9 If you are using the method of least squares for fitting trends in an annual time series containing 25 consecutive yearly values,
a. what coded value do you assign to X for the first year in the series?
b. what coded value do you assign to X for the fifth year in the series?
c. what coded value do you assign to X for the most recent recorded year in the series?
d. what coded value do you assign to X if you want to project the trend and make a forecast five years beyond the last observed value?

16.10 The linear trend forecasting equation for an annual time series containing 22 values (from 1996 to 2017) on total revenues (in $millions) is

$$\hat{Y}_i = 4.0 + 1.5X_i$$

a. Interpret the Y intercept, b_0.
b. Interpret the slope, b_1.
c. What is the fitted trend value for the fifth year?
d. What is the fitted trend value for the most recent year?
e. What is the projected trend forecast three years after the last value?

16.11 The linear trend forecasting equation for an annual time series containing 42 values (from 1976 to 2017) on net sales (in $billions) is

$$\hat{Y}_i = 1.2 + 0.5X_i$$

a. Interpret the Y intercept, b_0.
b. Interpret the slope, b_1.
c. What is the fitted trend value for the tenth year?
d. What is the fitted trend value for the most recent year?
e. What is the projected trend forecast two years after the last value?

APPLYING THE CONCEPTS

✓**SELF TEST** **16.12** There has been much publicity about bonuses paid to workers on Wall Street. Just how large are these bonuses? The file Bonuses contains the bonuses paid (in $000) from 2000 to 2016.

Source: Data extracted from J. Spector, "Wall Street bonuses rise 1% to average $138,210," *USA Today*, March 15, 2017.

a. Plot the data.
b. Compute a linear trend forecasting equation and plot the results.
c. Compute a quadratic trend forecasting equation and plot the results.
d. Compute an exponential trend forecasting equation and plot the results.
e. Using the forecasting equations in (b) through (d), what are your annual forecasts of the bonuses for 2017 and 2018?
f. How can you explain the differences in the three forecasts in (e)? What forecast do you think you should use? Why?

16.13 Gross domestic product (GDP) is a major indicator of a nation's overall economic activity. It consists of personal consumption expenditures, gross domestic investment, net exports of goods and services, and government consumption expenditures. The file GDP contains the GDP (in billions of current dollars) for the United States from 1980 to 2016.

Source: Data extracted from Bureau of Economic Analysis, U.S. Department of Commerce, **www.bea.gov**.

a. Plot the data.
b. Compute a linear trend forecasting equation and plot the trend line.
c. What are your forecasts for 2017 and 2018?
d. What conclusions can you reach concerning the trend in GDP?

16.14 The data in FedReceipt represent federal receipts from 1978 through 2016, in billions of current dollars, from individual and corporate income tax, social insurance, excise tax, estate and gift tax, customs duties, and federal reserve deposits.

Source: Data extracted from "Historical Federal Receipt and Outlay Summary," Tax Policy Center, **tpc.io/1JMFKpo**.

a. Plot the series of data.
b. Compute a linear trend forecasting equation and plot the trend line.
c. What are your forecasts of the federal receipts for 2017 and 2018?
d. What conclusions can you reach concerning the trend in federal receipts?

16.15 The file HouseSales contains the number of new, single-family houses sold in the U.S. from 1992 through 2016.
a. Plot the data.
b. Compute a linear trend forecasting equation and plot the trend line.
c. Compute a quadratic trend forecasting equation and plot the results.
d. Compute an exponential trend forecasting equation and plot the results.
e. Which model is the most appropriate?
f. Using the most appropriate model, forecast the number of new, single-family houses sold in the U.S. in 2017.

16.16 The data shown in the following table and stored in Solar Power represent the yearly amount of solar power generated by utilities (in millions of kWh) in the United States from 2002 through 2016:

Year	Solar Power Generated (millions of kWh)	Year	Solar Power Generated (millions of kWh)
2002	555	2010	1,212
2003	534	2011	1,818
2004	575	2012	4,327
2005	550	2013	9,253
2006	508	2014	18,321
2007	612	2015	26,473
2008	864	2016	36,754
2009	892		

Source: Data extracted from **en.wikipedia.org/wiki/Solar_power_in__the_United_States**.

a. Plot the data.
b. Compute a linear trend forecasting equation and plot the trend line.
c. Compute a quadratic trend forecasting equation and plot the results.
d. Compute an exponential trend forecasting equation and plot the results.
e. Using the models in (b) through (d), what are your annual trend forecasts of the yearly amount of solar power generated by utilities (in millions of kWh) in the United States in 2017 and 2018?

16.17 The file CarProduction contains the number of passenger cars produced in the U.S. (in thousands) from 1999 to 2016.

Source: Data extracted from **www.statista.com**.

a. Plot the data.
b. Compute a linear trend forecasting equation and plot the trend line.
c. Compute a quadratic trend forecasting equation and plot the results.
d. Compute an exponential trend forecasting equation and plot the results.
e. Which model is the most appropriate?
f. Using the most appropriate model, forecast the U.S. car production for 2017.

16.18 The average salary of Major League Baseball players on opening day from 2000 to 2017 is stored in BBSalaries and shown below.

Year	Salary ($millions)	Year	Salary ($millions)
2000	1.99	2009	3.26
2001	2.29	2010	3.27
2002	2.38	2011	3.32
2003	2.58	2012	3.38
2004	2.49	2013	3.62
2005	2.63	2014	3.81
2006	2.83	2015	4.25
2007	2.92	2016	4.40
2008	3.13	2017	4.70

Source: Data extracted from "Baseball Salaries," *USA Today*, April 6, 2009, p. 6C; **mlb.com**, and *USA Today*, April 2, 2017.

a. Plot the data.

b. Compute a linear trend forecasting equation and plot the trend line.

c. Compute a quadratic trend forecasting equation and plot the results.

d. Compute an exponential trend forecasting equation and plot the results.

e. Which model is the most appropriate?

f. Using the most appropriate model, forecast the average salary for 2018.

16.19 The file Silver contains the following prices in London for an ounce of silver (in US$) on the last day of the year from 1999 to 2016:

Year	Price (US$/ounce)	Year	Price (US$/ounce)
1999	5.330	2008	10.790
2000	4.570	2009	16.990
2001	4.520	2010	30.630
2002	4.670	2011	28.180
2003	5.965	2012	29.950
2004	6.815	2013	19.500
2005	8.830	2014	15.970
2006	12.900	2015	13.820
2007	14.760	2016	15.990

Source: Data extracted from JM Bullion, "Silver Spot Price & Charts," **bit.ly/2w4YPYI**.

a. Plot the data.

b. Compute a linear trend forecasting equation and plot the trend line.

c. Compute a quadratic trend forecasting equation and plot the results.

d. Compute an exponential trend forecasting equation and plot the results.

e. Which model is the most appropriate?

f. Using the most appropriate model, forecast the price of silver at the end of 2017.

16.20 The data in CPI-U reflect the annual values of the consumer price index (CPI) in the United States over the 52-year period 1965 through 2016, using 1982 through 1986 as the base period. This index measures the average change in prices over time in a fixed "market basket" of goods and services purchased by all urban consumers, including urban wage earners (i.e., clerical, professional, managerial, and technical workers; self-employed individuals; and short-term workers), unemployed individuals, and retirees.

Soruce: Data extracted from Bureau of Labor Statistics, U.S. Department of Labor, **www.bls.gov**.)

a. Plot the data.

b. Describe the movement in this time series over the 52-year period.

c. Compute a linear trend forecasting equation and plot the trend line.

d. Compute a quadratic trend forecasting equation and plot the results.

e. Compute an exponential trend forecasting equation and plot the results.

f. Which model is the most appropriate?

g. Using the most appropriate model, forecast the CPI for 2017 and 2018.

16.21 Although you should not expect a perfectly fitting model for any time-series data, you can consider the first differences, second differences, and percentage differences for a given series as guides in choosing an appropriate model.

Year	Series I	Series II	Series III
2005	10.0	30.0	60.0
2006	15.1	33.1	67.9
2007	24.0	36.4	76.1
2008	36.7	39.9	84.0
2009	53.8	43.9	92.2
2010	74.8	48.2	100.0
2011	100.0	53.2	108.0
2012	129.2	58.2	115.8
2013	162.4	64.5	124.1
2014	199.0	70.7	132.0
2015	239.3	77.1	140.0
2016	283.5	83.9	147.8

For this problem, use each of the time series presented in the table above and stored in TSModel1:

a. Determine the most appropriate model.

b. Compute the forecasting equation.

c. Forecast the value for 2017.

16.22 A time-series plot often helps you determine the appropriate model to use. For this problem, use each of the time series presented in the following table and stored in TSModel2:

Year	Series I	Series II
2005	100.0	100.0
2006	115.2	115.2
2007	130.1	131.7
2008	144.9	150.8
2009	160.0	174.1
2010	175.0	200.0
2011	189.8	230.8
2012	204.9	266.1
2013	219.8	305.5
2014	235.0	351.8
2015	249.8	403.0
2016	264.9	469.2

a. Plot the observed data Y over time X and plot the logarithm of the observed data (log Y) over time X to determine whether a linear trend model or an exponential trend model is more appropriate. (Hint: If the plot of log Y versus X appears to be linear, an exponential trend model provides an appropriate fit.)

b. Compute the appropriate forecasting equations.

c. Forecast the values for 2017.

16.4 Autoregressive Modeling for Trend Fitting and Forecasting

Frequently, the values of a time series at particular points in time are highly correlated with the values that precede and succeed them. This type of correlation is called *autocorrelation*. When the autocorrelation exists between values that are in consecutive periods in a time series, the time series displays **first-order autocorrelation**. When the autocorrelation exists between values that are two periods apart, the time series displays **second-order autocorrelation**. For the general case in which the autocorrelation exists between values that are p periods apart, the time series displays ***p*th-order autocorrelation**.

Autoregressive modeling uses a set of *lagged predictor variables* to overcome the problems that autocorrelation causes with other models. A **lagged predictor variable** takes its value from the value of a predictor variable for a previous time period. To analyze pth-order autocorrelation, you create a set of p lagged predictor variables. The first lagged predictor variable takes its value from the value of a predictor variable that is one time period away, the *lag*; the second lagged predictor variable takes its value from the value of a predictor variable that is two time periods away; and so on until the pth lagged predictor variable that takes its value from the value of a predictor variable that is p time periods away. Note that each subsequent lagged predictor variable contains one less time-series value. In the general case, a p lagged variable will contain p less values.

Equation (16.8) defines the ***p*th-order autoregressive model**. In the equation, $A_0, A_1, \ldots, A_p$ represent the parameters and $a_0, a_1, \ldots, a_p$ represent the corresponding regression coefficients. This is similar to the multiple regression model, Equation (14.1) on page 538, in which $\beta_0, \beta_1, \ldots, \beta_k$, represent the regression parameters and $b_0, b_1, \ldots, b_k$ represent the corresponding regression coefficients.

learnMORE

The exponential smoothing model that Section 16.3 describes and the autoregressive models that Section 16.4 describes are special cases of autoregressive integrated moving average (ARIMA) models developed by Box and Jenkins. To learn more about such models, see references 1, 3, and 6.

---

pTH-ORDER AUTOREGRESSIVE MODELS

$$Y_i = A_0 + A_1 Y_{i-1} + A_2 Y_{i-2} + \cdots + A_p Y_{i-p} + \delta_i \tag{16.8}$$

where

Y_i = observed value of the series at time i

Y_{i-1} = observed value of the series at time $i - 1$

Y_{i-2} = observed value of the series at time $i - 2$

Y_{i-p} = observed value of the series at time $i - p$

p = number of autoregression parameters (not including a Y intercept) to be estimated from least-squares regression analysis

$A_0, A_1, A_2, \ldots, A_p$ = autoregression parameters to be estimated from least-squares regression analysis

δ_i = a nonautocorrelated random error component (with mean = 0 and constant variance)

studentTIP

δ is the Greek letter delta.

Equations (16.9) and (16.10) define two specific autoregressive models. Equation (16.9) defines the **first-order autoregressive model** and is similar in form to the simple linear regression model, Equation (13.1) on page 486. Equation (16.10) defines the **second-order autoregressive model** and is similar to the multiple regression model with two independent variables, Equation (14.2) on page 538.

FIRST-ORDER AUTOREGRESSIVE MODEL

$$Y_i = A_0 + A_1 Y_{i-1} + \delta_i \tag{16.9}$$

SECOND-ORDER AUTOREGRESSIVE MODEL

$$Y_i = A_0 + A_1 Y_{i-1} + A_2 Y_{i-2} + \delta_i \tag{16.10}$$

Selecting an Appropriate Autoregressive Model

Selecting an appropriate autoregressive model can be complicated. You must weigh the advantages of using a simpler model against the concern of using a model that does not take into account important autocorrelation in the data. On the other hand, selecting a higher-order model that requires estimates of numerous parameters may contain some unnecessary parameters, especially if the time series is short (n is small). Recall that when computing an estimate of A_p, p out of the n time series values are lost due to the lagging of values. Examples 16.5 and 16.6 illustrate this loss.

EXAMPLE 16.5

Comparison Schema for a First-Order Autoregressive Model

Consider the following series of $n = 7$ consecutive annual values:

				Year			
	1	2	3	4	5	6	7
Series	31	34	37	35	36	43	40

Show the comparisons needed for a first-order autoregressive model.

SOLUTION

Year i	First-Order Autoregressive Model (Lag1: Y_i versus Y_{i-1})
1	$31 \leftrightarrow \ldots$
2	$34 \leftrightarrow 31$
3	$37 \leftrightarrow 34$
4	$35 \leftrightarrow 37$
5	$36 \leftrightarrow 35$
6	$43 \leftrightarrow 36$
7	$40 \leftrightarrow 43$

Because Y_1 is the first value and there is no value prior to it, Y_1 is not used in the regression analysis. Therefore, the first-order autoregressive model would be based on six pairs of values.

EXAMPLE 16.6

Comparison Schema for a Second-Order Autoregressive Model

Consider the following series of $n = 7$ consecutive annual values:

				Year			
	1	2	3	4	5	6	7
Series	31	34	37	35	36	43	40

Show the comparisons needed for a second-order autoregressive model.

SOLUTION

Year i	Second-Order Autoregressive Model Lag2: Y_i vs. Y_{i-1} and Y_i vs. Y_{i-2}
1	$31 \leftrightarrow \ldots$ and $31 \leftrightarrow \ldots$
2	$34 \leftrightarrow 31$ and $34 \leftrightarrow \ldots$
3	$37 \leftrightarrow 34$ and $37 \leftrightarrow 31$
4	$35 \leftrightarrow 37$ and $35 \leftrightarrow 34$
5	$36 \leftrightarrow 35$ and $36 \leftrightarrow 37$
6	$43 \leftrightarrow 36$ and $43 \leftrightarrow 35$
7	$40 \leftrightarrow 43$ and $40 \leftrightarrow 36$

Because no value is recorded prior to Y_1, the first two comparisons, each of which requires a value prior to Y_1, cannot be used when performing regression analysis. Therefore, the second-order autoregressive model would be based on five pairs of values.

Determining the Appropriateness of a Selected Model

After selecting a model and using the least-squares method to compute the regression coefficients, you need to determine the appropriateness of the model. You either select a particular *p*th-order autoregressive model based on previous experiences with similar data or start with a model that contains several autoregressive parameters and then eliminate the higher-order parameters that do not significantly contribute to the model. In this latter approach, you use a *t* test for the significance of A_p, the highest-order autoregressive parameter in the current model under consideration. The null and alternative hypotheses are:

$$H_0: A_p = 0$$

$$H_1: A_p \neq 0$$

Equation (16.11) defines the test statistic.

---

t TEST FOR SIGNIFICANCE OF THE HIGHEST-ORDER AUTOREGRESSIVE PARAMETER, A_P

$$t_{STAT} = \frac{a_p - A_p}{S_{a_p}} \tag{16.11}$$

where

A_p = hypothesized value of the highest-order parameter, A_p, in the autoregressive model

a_p = regression coefficient that estimates the highest-order parameter, A_p, in the autoregressive model

S_{a_p} = standard deviation of a_p

The t_{STAT} test statistic follows a *t* distribution with $n - 2p - 1$ degrees of freedom.

In addition to the degrees of freedom lost for each of the *p* population parameters being estimated, *p* additional degrees of freedom are lost because there are *p* fewer comparisons to be made from the original *n* values in the time series.

For a given level of significance, α, you reject the null hypothesis if the t_{STAT} test statistic is greater than the upper-tail critical value from the *t* distribution or if the t_{STAT} test statistic is less than the lower-tail critical value from the *t* distribution. Thus, the decision rule is

$$\text{Reject } H_0 \text{ if } t_{STAT} < -t_{\alpha}/2 \text{ or if } t_{STAT} > t_{\alpha/2};$$

otherwise, do not reject H_0.

Figure 16.15 illustrates the decision rule and regions of rejection and nonrejection.

FIGURE 16.15

Rejection regions for a two-tail test for the significance of the highest-order autoregressive parameter A_p

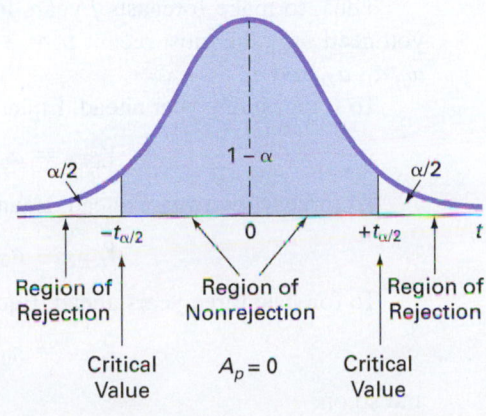

If you do not reject the null hypothesis that $A_p = 0$, you conclude that the selected model contains too many estimated autoregressive parameters. You then discard the highest-order term and develop an autoregressive model of order $p - 1$, using the least-squares method. You then repeat the test of the hypothesis that the new highest-order parameter is 0. This testing and modeling continues until you reject H_0. When this occurs, you can conclude that the remaining highest-order parameter is significant, and you can use that model for forecasting purposes.

Equation (16.12) defines the fitted pth-order autoregressive equation.

FITTED pTH-ORDER AUTOREGRESSIVE EQUATION

$$\hat{Y}_i = a_0 + a_1 Y_{i-1} + a_2 Y_{i-2} + \ldots + a_p Y_{i-p} \tag{16.12}$$

where

$$\hat{Y}_i = \text{fitted values of the series at time } i$$
$$Y_{i-1} = \text{observed value of the series at time } i - 1$$
$$Y_{i-2} = \text{observed value of the series at time } i - 2$$
$$Y_{i-p} = \text{observed value of the series at time } i - p$$
$$p = \text{number of autoregression parameters (not including a } Y \text{ intercept) to}$$
$$\text{be estimated from least-squares regression analysis}$$
$$a_0, a_1, a_2, \ldots, a_p = \text{regression coefficients}$$

You use Equation (16.13) to forecast j years into the future from the current nth time period.

pTH-ORDER AUTOREGRESSIVE FORECASTING EQUATION

$$\hat{Y}_{n+j} = a_0 + a_1 \hat{Y}_{n+j-1} + a_2 \hat{Y}_{n+j-2} + \ldots + a_p \hat{Y}_{n+j-p} \tag{16.13}$$

where

$$a_0, a_1, a_2, \ldots, a_p = \text{regression coefficients that estimate the parameters}$$
$$p = \text{number of autoregression parameters (not including a } Y \text{ intercept)}$$
$$\text{to be estimated from least-squares regression analysis}$$
$$j = \text{number of years into the future}$$
$$\hat{Y}_{n+j-p} = \text{forecast of } Y_{n+j-p} \text{ from the current year for } j - p > 0$$
$$\hat{Y}_{n+j-p} = \text{observed value for } Y_{n+j-p} \text{ for } j - p \leq 0$$

Thus, to make forecasts j years into the future, using a third-order autoregressive model, you need only the most recent $p = 3$ values (Y_n, Y_{n-1}, and Y_{n-2}) and the regression estimates $a_0, a_1, a_2,$ and a_3.

To forecast one year ahead, Equation (16.13) becomes

$$\hat{Y}_{n+1} = a_0 + a_1 Y_n + a_2 Y_{n-1} + a_3 Y_{n-2}$$

To forecast two years ahead, Equation (16.13) becomes

$$\hat{Y}_{n+2} = a_0 + a_1 \hat{Y}_{n+1} + a_2 Y_n + a_3 Y_{n-1}$$

To forecast three years ahead, Equation (16.13) becomes

$$\hat{Y}_{n+3} = a_0 + a_1 \hat{Y}_{n+2} + a_2 \hat{Y}_{n+1} + a_3 Y_n$$

and so on.

Autoregressive modeling is a powerful forecasting technique for time series that have auto-correlation. Exhibit 16.2 summarizes the steps to construct an autoregressive model.

student TIP

Remember that in an autoregressive model, the independent variable(s) are equal to the dependent variable lagged by a certain number of time periods.

EXHIBIT 16.2

Autoregressive Modeling Steps

1. Choose a value for p, the highest-order parameter in the autoregressive model to be evaluated, remembering that the t test for significance is based on $n - 2p - 1$ degrees of freedom.
2. Create a set of p lagged predictor variables. (See Figure 16.16 for an example.)
3. Perform a least-squares analysis of the multiple regression model containing all p lagged predictor variables.
4. Test for the significance of A_p, the highest-order autoregressive parameter in the model.
5. If you do not reject the null hypothesis, discard the pth variable and repeat steps 3 and 4 with a revised degrees of freedom that correspond to the revised number of predictors.

   If you reject the null hypothesis, select the autoregressive model with all p predictors for fitting [see Equation (16.12)] and forecasting [see Equation (16.13)].

To demonstrate the autoregressive modeling approach, consider the Table 16.2 annual revenues for The Coca-Cola Company on page 638. Figure 16.16 presents a worksheet that uses that 19-year times series to compute three lagged predictor variables, Lag1, Lag2, and Lag3, that can be used for the first-order, second-order, and third-order autoregressive models.

FIGURE 16.16

Excel and JMP templates for computing lagged predictor variables for the first-order, second-order, and third-order autoregressive models of the revenues for The Coca-Cola Company (1998–2016)

	A	B	C	D	E
1	Year	Revenues	Lag1	Lag2	Lag3
2	1998	18.8	#N/A	#N/A	#N/A
3	1999	19.8	18.8	#N/A	#N/A
4	2000	20.5	19.8	18.8	#N/A
5	2001	20.1	20.5	19.8	18.8
6	2002	19.6	20.1	20.5	19.8
7	2003	21.0	19.6	20.1	20.5
8	2004	21.9	21.0	19.6	20.1
9	2005	23.1	21.9	21.0	19.6
10	2006	24.1	23.1	21.9	21.0
11	2007	28.9	24.1	23.1	21.9
12	2008	31.9	28.9	24.1	23.1
13	2009	31.0	31.9	28.9	24.1
14	2010	35.1	31.0	31.9	28.9
15	2011	46.5	35.1	31.0	31.9
16	2012	48.0	46.5	35.1	31.0
17	2013	46.7	48.0	46.5	35.1
18	2014	45.9	46.7	48.0	46.5
19	2015	44.3	45.9	46.7	48.0
20	2016	41.9	44.3	45.9	46.7

	Year	Revenues	Lag1	Lag2	Lag3
1	1998	18.8	•	•	•
2	1999	19.8	18.8	•	•
3	2000	20.5	19.8	18.8	•
4	2001	20.1	20.5	19.8	18.8
5	2002	19.6	20.1	20.5	19.8
6	2003	21.0	19.6	20.1	20.5
7	2004	21.9	21.0	19.6	20.1
8	2005	23.1	21.9	21.0	19.6
9	2006	24.1	23.1	21.9	21.0
10	2007	28.9	24.1	23.1	21.9
11	2008	31.9	28.9	24.1	23.1
12	2009	31.0	31.9	28.9	24.1
13	2010	35.1	31.0	31.9	28.9
14	2011	46.5	35.1	31.0	31.9
15	2012	48.0	46.5	35.1	31.0
16	2013	46.7	48.0	46.5	35.1
17	2014	45.9	46.7	48.0	46.5
18	2015	44.3	45.9	46.7	48.0
19	2016	41.9	44.3	45.9	46.7

To fit the third-order autoregressive model, all three lagged predictor variables are used. To fit the second-order autoregressive model, only the Lag1 and Lag2 variables are used. To fit the first-order autoregressive model, only the Lag1 variable is used.

Selecting an autoregressive model that best fits the annual time series begins with the *highest-order* autoregressive model being considered. For The Coca-Cola Company time-series revenues, the highest-order model being considered is the third-order autoregressive model. This choice of $p = 3$ arises from both past experience using the time series and because the third-order model is often used as a starting point when no other insights into the time series exist.

From Figure 16.17, the fitted third-order autoregressive equation is

$$\hat{Y}_i = 2.9184 + 1.3795Y_{i-1} - 0.7180Y_{i-2} + 0.2829Y_{i-3}$$

where the first year in the series is 2001.

FIGURE 16.17
Excel, Minitab, and JMP regression results for a third-order autoregressive model for The Coca-Cola Company revenues

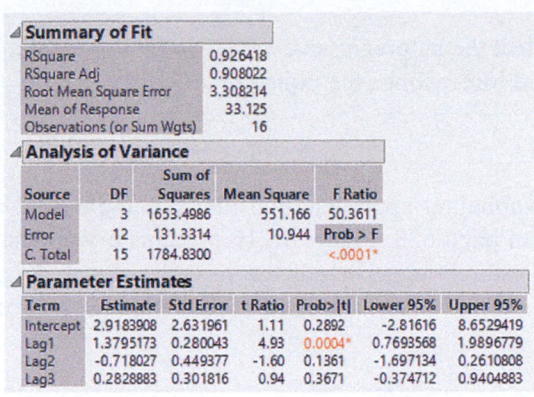

	A	B	C	D	E	F	G
1	Third-Order Autoregressive Model for The Coca-Cola Company Revenues						
2							
3		*Regression Statistics*					
4	Multiple R	0.9625					
5	R Square	0.9264					
6	Adjusted R Square	0.9080					
7	Standard Error	3.3082					
8	Observations	16					
9							
10	ANOVA						
11		*df*		*SS*	*MS*	*F*	*Significance F*
12	Regression	3		1653.4986	551.1662	50.3611	0.0000
13	Residual	12		131.3314	10.9443		
14	Total	15		1784.8300			
15							
16		*Coefficients*	*Standard Error*	*t Stat*	*P-value*	*Lower 95%*	*Upper 95%*
17	Intercept	2.9184	2.6320	1.1088	0.2892	-2.8162	8.6529
18	Lag1	1.3795	0.2800	4.9261	0.0004	0.7694	1.9897
19	Lag2	-0.7180	0.4494	-1.5978	0.1361	-1.6971	0.2611
20	Lag3	0.2829	0.3018	0.9373	0.3671	-0.3747	0.9405

Summary of Fit

RSquare	0.926418
RSquare Adj	0.908022
Root Mean Square Error	3.308214
Mean of Response	33.125
Observations (or Sum Wgts)	16

Analysis of Variance

Source	DF	Sum of Squares	Mean Square	F Ratio
Model	3	1653.4986	551.166	50.3611
Error	12	131.3314	10.944	Prob > F
C. Total	15	1784.8300		<.0001*

Parameter Estimates

Term	Estimate	Std Error	t Ratio	Prob>|t|	Lower 95%	Upper 95%
Intercept	2.9183908	2.631961	1.11	0.2892	-2.81616	8.6529419
Lag1	1.3795173	0.280043	4.93	0.0004*	0.7693568	1.9896779
Lag2	-0.718027	0.449377	-1.60	0.1361	-1.697134	0.2610808
Lag3	0.2828883	0.301816	0.94	0.3671	-0.374712	0.9404883

Regression Analysis: Revenues versus Lag1, Lag2, Lag3

Method

Rows unused 3

Analysis of Variance

Source	DF	Adj SS	Adj MS	F-Value	P-Value
Regression	3	1653.50	551.166	50.36	0.000
Lag1	1	265.58	265.579	24.27	0.000
Lag2	1	27.94	27.941	2.55	0.136
Lag3	1	9.61	9.615	0.88	0.367
Error	12	131.33	10.944		
Total	15	1784.83			

Model Summary

S	R-sq	R-sq(adj)	R-sq(pred)
3.30821	92.64%	90.80%	82.83%

Coefficients

Term	Coef	SE Coef	T-Value	P-Value	VIF
Constant	2.92	2.63	1.11	0.289	
Lag1	1.380	0.280	4.93	0.000	13.17
Lag2	-0.718	0.449	-1.60	0.136	33.00
Lag3	0.283	0.302	0.94	0.367	13.56

Regression Equation

Revenues = 2.92 + 1.380 Lag1 - 0.718 Lag2 + 0.283 Lag3

Next, you test for the significance of A_3, the highest-order parameter. The highest-order regression coefficient, a_3, for the fitted third-order autoregressive model is 0.2829, with a standard error of 0.3018.

To test the null hypothesis:

$$H_0: A_3 = 0$$

against the alternative hypothesis:

$$H_1: A_3 \neq 0$$

using Equation (16.11) on page 649 and the worksheet results given in Figure 16.17,

$$t_{STAT} = \frac{a_3 - A_3}{S_{a_3}} = \frac{0.2829 - 0}{0.3018} = 0.9373$$

Using a 0.05 level of significance, the two-tail t test with 12 degrees of freedom has critical values of ± 2.1788. Because $-2.1788 < t_{STAT} = 0.9373 < 2.1788$ or because the p-value $= 0.3671 > 0.05$, you do not reject H_0. You conclude that the third-order parameter of the autoregressive model is not significant and should not remain in the model. You continue by fitting the Figure 16.18 second-order autoregressive model.

The fitted second-order autoregressive equation is

$$\hat{Y}_i = 3.0263 + 1.3066Y_{i-1} - 0.3805Y_{i-2}$$

where the first year of the series is 2000.

FIGURE 16.18

Excel regression results worksheet for the second-order autoregressive model for The Coca-Cola Company revenues data

	A	B	C	D	E	F	G
1	Second-Order Autoregressive Model for The Coca-Cola Company Revenues						
2							
3	*Regression Statistics*						
4	Multiple R	0.9624					
5	R Square	0.9262					
6	Adjusted R Square	0.9157					
7	Standard Error	3.1927					
8	Observations	17					
9							
10	ANOVA						
11		*df*	*SS*	*MS*	*F*	*Significance F*	
12	Regression	2	1792.1346	896.0673	87.9050	0.0000	
13	Residual	14	142.7101	10.1936			
14	Total	16	1934.8447				
15							
16		*Coefficients*	*Standard Error*	*t Stat*	*P-value*	*Lower 95%*	*Upper 95%*
17	Intercept	3.0263	2.3648	1.2798	0.2214	-2.0456	8.0982
18	Lag1	1.3066	0.2569	5.0864	0.0002	0.7557	1.8576
19	Lag2	-0.3805	0.2610	-1.4578	0.1670	-0.9403	0.1793

From Figure 16.18, the highest-order parameter estimate is $a_2 = -0.3805$, with a standard error of 0.2610.

To test the null and alternative hypotheses:

$$H_0: A_2 = 0$$

$$H_1: A_2 \neq 0$$

using Equation (16.11) on page 649,

$$t_{STAT} = \frac{a_2 - A_2}{S_{a_2}} = \frac{-0.3805 - 0}{0.2610} = -1.4578$$

Using the 0.05 level of significance, the two-tail t test with 14 degrees of freedom has critical values of ± 2.1448. Because $-2.1448 < t_{STAT} = -1.4578 < 2.1488$ or because the p-value $= 0.1670 > 0.05$, you do not reject H_0. You conclude that the second-order parameter of the autoregressive model is not significant and should be deleted from the model. You then continue by fitting the Figure 16.19 first-order autoregressive model.

FIGURE 16.19

Excel regression results worksheet for the first-order autoregressive model for The Coca-Cola Company revenues data

	A	B	C	D	E	F	G
1	First-Order Autoregressive Model for The Coca-Cola Company Revenues						
2							
3	*Regression Statistics*						
4	Multiple R	0.9596					
5	R Square	0.9208					
6	Adjusted R Square	0.9158					
7	Standard Error	3.2129					
8	Observations	18					
9							
10	ANOVA						
11		*df*	*SS*	*MS*	*F*	*Significance F*	
12	Regression	1	1919.1973	1919.1973	185.9150	0.0000	
13	Residual	16	165.1677	10.3230			
14	Total	17	2084.3650				
15							
16		*Coefficients*	*Standard Error*	*t Stat*	*P-value*	*Lower 95%*	*Upper 95%*
17	Intercept	2.7337	2.2542	1.2127	0.2428	-2.0449	7.5124
18	Lag1	0.9523	0.0698	13.6351	0.0000	0.8042	1.1003

The fitted first-order autoregressive equation is

$$\hat{Y}_i = 2.7337 + 0.9523Y_{i-1}$$

From Figure 16.19, the highest-order parameter estimate is $a_1 = 0.9523$, with a standard error of 0.0698.

To test the null and alternative hypotheses:

$$H_0: A_1 = 0$$

$$H_1: A_1 \neq 0$$

using Equation (16.11) on page 649,

$$t_{STAT} = \frac{a_2 - A_1}{S_{a_1}} = \frac{0.9523 - 0}{0.0698} = 13.6351$$

Using the 0.05 level of significance, the two-tail t test with 16 degrees of freedom has critical values of ± 2.1199. Because $t_{STAT} = 13.6351 > 2.1199$ or because the p-value $= 0.0000 < 0.05$, you reject H_0. You conclude that the first-order parameter of the autoregressive model is significant and should remain in the model.

The model-building approach has led to the selection of the first-order autoregressive model as the most appropriate for these data. Using the estimates $a_0 = 2.7337$, and $a_1 = 0.9523$, as well as the most recent data value $Y_{17} = 41.9$, the forecasts of revenues at The Coca-Cola Company for 2017 and 2018 from Equation (16.13) on page 650 are

$$\hat{Y}_{n+j} = 2.7337 + 0.9523\hat{Y}_{n+j-1}$$

Therefore,

2017: 1 year ahead, $\hat{Y}_{18} = 2.7337 + 0.9523(41.9) = 42.6351$ billions of dollars

2018: 2 years ahead, $\hat{Y}_{19} = 2.7337 + 0.9523(42.6351) = 43.3351$ billions of dollars

Figure 16.20 displays the actual and predicted Y values from the first-order autoregressive model.

FIGURE 16.20

Plot of actual and predicted revenues from a first-order autoregressive model at The Coca-Cola Company

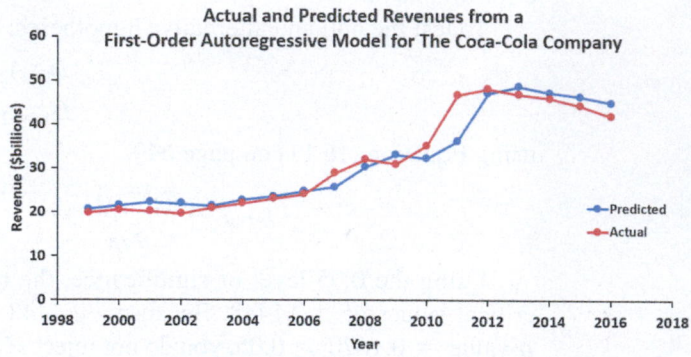

Actual and Predicted Revenues from a First-Order Autoregressive Model for The Coca-Cola Company

PROBLEMS FOR SECTION 16.4

LEARNING THE BASICS

16.23 You are given an annual time series with 40 consecutive values and asked to fit a fifth-order autoregressive model.
a. How many comparisons are lost in developing the autoregressive model?
b. How many parameters do you need to estimate?
c. Which of the original 40 values do you need for forecasting?
d. State the fifth-order autoregressive model.
e. Write an equation to indicate how you would forecast j years into the future.

16.24 A third-order autoregressive model is fitted to an annual time series with 17 values and has the following estimated parameters and standard errors:

$$a_0 = 4.50 \quad a_1 = 1.80 \quad a_2 = 0.80 \quad a_3 = 0.24$$
$$S_{a_1} = 0.50 \quad S_{a_2} = 0.30 \quad S_{a_3} = 0.10$$

At the 0.05 level of significance, test the appropriateness of the fitted model.

16.25 Refer to Problem 16.24. The three most recent values are
$$Y_{15} = 23 \quad Y_{16} = 28 \quad Y_{17} = 34$$
Forecast the values for the next year and the following year.

16.26 Refer to Problem 16.24. Suppose, when testing for the appropriateness of the fitted model, the standard errors are

$$S_{a_1} = 0.45 \quad S_{a_2} = 0.35 \quad S_{a_3} = 0.15$$

a. What conclusions can you reach?
b. Discuss how to proceed if forecasting is still your main objective.

APPLYING THE CONCEPTS

16.27 Using the data for Problem 16.15 on page 645 that represent the number of new, single-family houses sold in the U.S. from 1992 through 2016 (stored in HouseSales),
a. fit a third-order autoregressive model to the new single-family homes sold and test for the significance of the third-order autoregressive parameter. (Use $\alpha = 0.05$.)
b. if necessary, fit a second-order autoregressive model to the new single-family homes sold and test for the significance of the second-order autoregressive parameter. (Use $\alpha = 0.05$.)
c. if necessary, fit a first-order autoregressive model to the new single-family homes sold and test for the significance of the first-order autoregressive parameter. (Use $\alpha = 0.05$.)
d. if appropriate, forecast the new single-family homes sold in 2017.

16.28 Using the data for Problem 16.12 on page 645 concerning the bonuses paid to workers on Wall Street from 2000 to 2016 (stored in Bonuses),

a. fit a third-order autoregressive model to the bonuses paid and test for the significance of the third-order autoregressive parameter. (Use $\alpha = 0.05$.)

b. if necessary, fit a second-order autoregressive model to the bonuses paid and test for the significance of the second-order autoregressive parameter. (Use $\alpha = 0.05$.)

c. if necessary, fit a first-order autoregressive model to the bonuses paid and test for the significance of the first-order autoregressive parameter. (Use $\alpha = 0.05$.)

d. if appropriate, forecast the bonuses paid in 2017 and 2018.

16.29 Using the data for Problem 16.17 on page 645 concerning the number of passenger cars produced in the United States from 1999 to 2016 (stored in CarProduction),

a. fit a third-order autoregressive model to the number of passenger cars produced in the United States and test for the significance of the third-order autoregressive parameter. (Use $\alpha = 0.05$.)

b. if necessary, fit a second-order autoregressive model to the number of passenger cars produced in the United States and test for the significance of the second-order autoregressive parameter. (Use $\alpha = 0.05$.)

c. if necessary, fit a first-order autoregressive model to the number of passenger cars produced in the United States and test for the significance of the first-order autoregressive parameter. (Use $\alpha = 0.05$.)

d. forecast the U.S. car production for 2017.

16.30 Using the average baseball salary from 2000 through 2017 data for Problem 16.18 on page 645 (stored in BBSalaries),

a. fit a third-order autoregressive model to the average baseball salary and test for the significance of the third-order autoregressive parameter. (Use $\alpha = 0.05$.)

b. if necessary, fit a second-order autoregressive model to the average baseball salary and test for the significance of the second-order autoregressive parameter. (Use $\alpha = 0.05$.)

c. if necessary, fit a first-order autoregressive model to the average baseball salary and test for the significance of the first order autoregressive parameter. (Use $\alpha = 0.05$.)

d. forecast the average baseball salary for 2018.

16.31 Using the yearly amount of solar power generated by utilities (in millions of kWh) in the United States from 2002 through 2016 data for Problem 16.16 on page 645 (stored in SolarPower),

a. fit a third-order autoregressive model to the amount of solar power installed and test for the significance of the third-order autoregressive parameter. (Use $\alpha = 0.05$.)

b. if necessary, fit a second-order autoregressive model to the amount of solar power installed and test for the significance of the second-order autoregressive parameter. (Use $\alpha = 0.05$.)

c. if necessary, fit a first-order autoregressive model to the amount of solar power installed and test for the significance of the first-order autoregressive parameter. (Use $\alpha = 0.05$.)

d. forecast the yearly amount of solar power generated by utilities (in millions of kWh) in the United States in 2017 and 2018.

16.5 Choosing an Appropriate Forecasting Model

The previous two sections discuss six time-series methods for forecasting: the linear trend model, the quadratic trend model, and the exponential trend model (Section 16.3) and the first-order, second-order, and pth-order autoregressive models (Section 16.4). To choose which one of the six models should be used for forecasting, you consider these four criteria:

- The results from a residual analysis.
- The magnitude of the residuals through squared differences.
- The magnitude of the residuals through absolute differences.
- The principle of parsimony.

Residual Analysis

Sections 13.5 and 14.3 define residuals as the differences between observed and predicted values. After fitting a particular model to a time series, you plot the residuals over the n time periods. As shown in Figure 16.21 Panel A, if the particular model fits adequately, the residuals represent the irregular component of the time series. Therefore, they should be randomly distributed throughout the series. However, as illustrated in the three remaining panels of Figure 16.21, if the particular model does not fit adequately, the residuals may show a systematic pattern, such as a failure to account for trend (Panel B), a failure to account for cyclical variation (Panel C), or, with monthly or quarterly data, a failure to account for seasonal variation (Panel D).

FIGURE 16.21

Residual analysis for studying patterns of errors in regression models

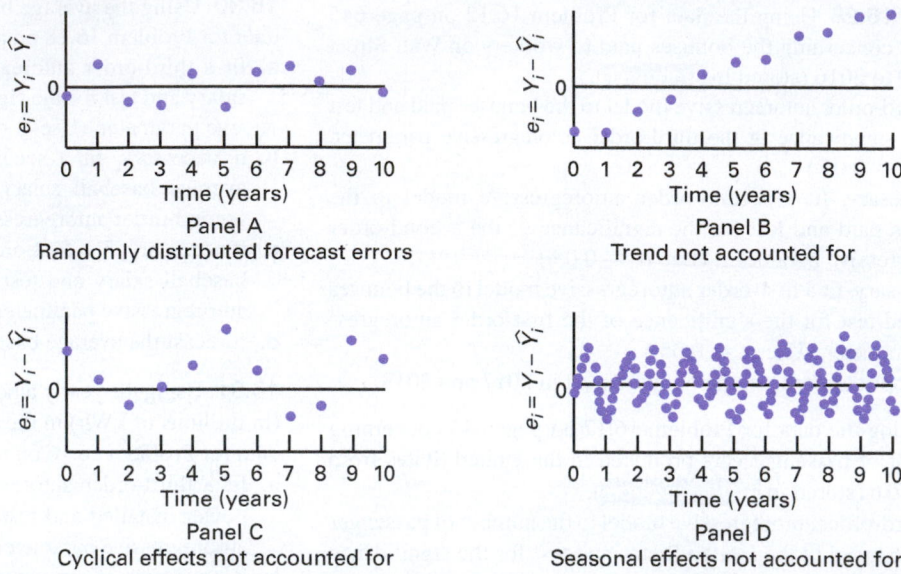

Panel A
Randomly distributed forecast errors

Panel B
Trend not accounted for

Panel C
Cyclical effects not accounted for

Panel D
Seasonal effects not accounted for

The Magnitude of the Residuals Through Squared or Absolute Differences

If, after performing a residual analysis, you still believe that two or more models appear to fit the data adequately, you can use additional methods for model selection. Numerous measures based on the residuals are available (see references 2 and 3).

In regression analysis (see Section 13.3), you have already used the standard error of the estimate S_{YX} as a measure of variation around the predicted values. For a particular model, this measure is based on the sum of squared differences between the actual and predicted values in a time series. If a model fits the time-series data perfectly, then the standard error of the estimate is zero. If a model fits the time-series data poorly, then S_{YX} is large. Thus, when comparing the adequacy of two or more forecasting models, you can select the model with the smallest S_{YX} as most appropriate.

However, a major drawback to using S_{YX} when comparing forecasting models is that whenever there is a large difference between even a single Y_i and $\hat{Y}_i$, the value of S_{YX} becomes overly inflated because the differences between Y_i and $\hat{Y}_i$ are squared. For this reason, many statisticians prefer the **mean absolute deviation (*MAD*)**. Equation (16.14) defines the *MAD* as the mean of the absolute differences between the actual and predicted values in a time series.

MEAN ABSOLUTE DEVIATION

$$MAD = \frac{\sum_{i=1}^{n} |Y_i - \hat{Y}_iq|}{n}$$

(16.14)

If a model fits the time-series data perfectly, the *MAD* is zero. If a model fits the time-series data poorly, the *MAD* is large. When comparing two or more forecasting models, you can select the one with the smallest *MAD* as the most appropriate model.

The Principle of Parsimony

If, after performing a residual analysis and comparing the S_{YX} and *MAD* measures, you still believe that two or more models appear to adequately fit the data, you can use the principle of parsimony for model selection. As Section 15.4 first explains, **parsimony** guides you to select the regression model with the fewest independent variables that can predict the dependent variable adequately. In general, the principle of parsimony guides you to select the least complex regression model. Among the six forecasting models studied in this chapter, most statisticians consider the least-squares linear and quadratic models and the first-order autoregressive model as simpler than the second and pth-order autoregressive models and the least-squares exponential model.

A Comparison of Four Forecasting Methods

To illustrate the model selection process, you can compare four of the forecasting models that Sections 16.3 and 16.4 discuss: the linear model, the quadratic model, the exponential model, and the first-order autoregressive model. Figure 16.22 shows the residual plots for the four models for The Coca-Cola Company revenues. In reaching conclusions from these residual plots, you must use caution because there are only 19 values for the linear model, the quadratic model, and the exponential model and only 18 values for the first-order autoregressive model.

In Figure 16.22, observe that the residuals in the linear model, quadratic model, and exponential model are positive for the early years, negative for the intermediate years, and positive again for the latest years. For the first-order autoregressive models the residuals do not exhibit any clear systematic pattern although the residual for 2010 is highly positive.

FIGURE 16.22

Residual plots for four forecasting models

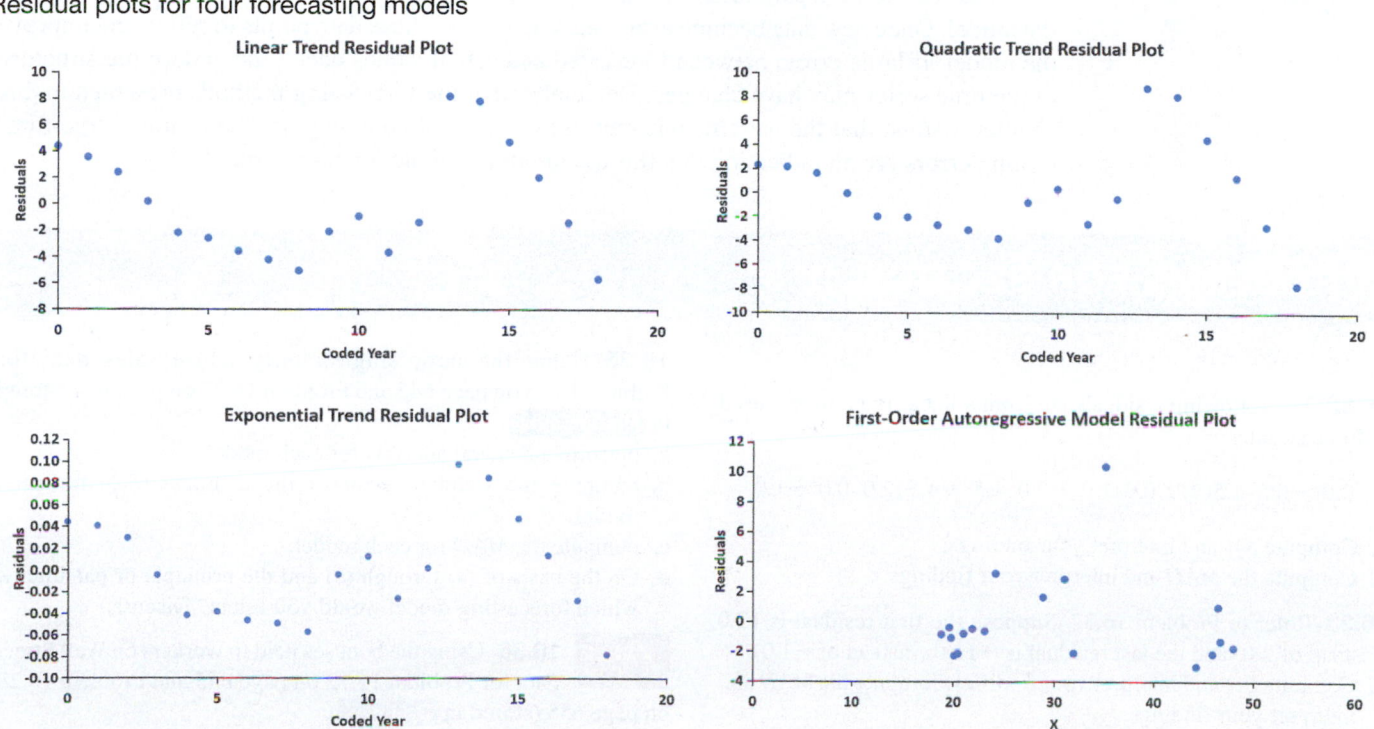

To summarize, on the basis of the residual analysis of all four forecasting models, it appears that the first-order autoregressive model is the most appropriate, and the linear, quadratic, and exponential models are not appropriate. For further verification, you can compare the magnitude of the residuals in the four models. Figure 16.23 shows the actual values (Y_i) along with the predicted values $\hat{Y}_i$, the residuals (e_i), the error sum of squares (SSE), the standard error of the estimate (S_{YX}), and the mean absolute deviation (MAD) for each of the four models.

For the Coca-Cola time series, the first-order autoregressive model provides the smallest *SSE*, followed by the quadratic, exponential, and the linear model. The first-order autoregressive model also contains the smallest S_{YX}. The *MAD* for the first-order autoregressive model is also less than the *MAD* for the other three models. Therefore, based on these results and the residual plots, you would select the first-order autoregressive model.

FIGURE 16.23

Comparison of four forecasting models using SSE, S_{YX}, and *MAD*

Year	Revenues	Linear		Quadratic		Exponential		First-Order AR	
		Predicted	Residual	Predicted	Residual	Predicted	Residual	Predicted	Residual
1998	18.8	14.4500	4.3500	16.5549	2.2451	16.9774	1.8226	#N/A	#N/A
1999	19.8	16.2895	3.5105	17.6927	2.1073	18.0303	1.7697	20.6368	-0.8368
2000	20.5	18.1289	2.3711	18.9131	1.5869	19.1485	1.3515	21.5891	-1.0891
2001	20.1	19.9684	0.1316	20.2161	-0.1161	20.3361	-0.2361	22.2557	-2.1557
2002	19.6	21.8079	-2.2079	21.6015	-2.0015	21.5973	-1.9973	21.8747	-2.2747
2003	21.0	23.6474	-2.6474	23.0696	-2.0696	22.9367	-1.9367	21.3986	-0.3986
2004	21.9	25.4868	-3.5868	24.6201	-2.7201	24.3592	-2.4592	22.7318	-0.8318
2005	23.1	27.3263	-4.2263	26.2532	-3.1532	25.8699	-2.7699	23.5889	-0.4889
2006	24.1	29.1658	-5.0658	27.9689	-3.8689	27.4743	-3.3743	24.7316	-0.6316
2007	28.9	31.0053	-2.1053	29.7671	-0.8671	29.1782	-0.2782	25.6839	3.2161
2008	31.9	32.8447	-0.9447	31.6478	0.2522	30.9878	0.9122	30.2549	1.6451
2009	31.0	34.6842	-3.6842	33.6111	-2.6111	32.9096	-1.9096	33.1118	-2.1118
2010	35.1	36.5237	-1.4237	35.6570	-0.5570	34.9506	0.1494	32.2547	2.8453
2011	46.5	38.3632	8.1368	37.7853	8.7147	37.1182	9.3818	36.1591	10.3409
2012	48.0	40.2026	7.7974	39.9963	8.0037	39.4202	8.5798	47.0152	0.9848
2013	46.7	42.0421	4.6579	42.2897	4.4103	41.8650	4.8350	48.4436	-1.7436
2014	45.9	43.8816	2.0184	44.6658	1.2342	44.4614	1.4386	47.2057	-1.3057
2015	44.3	45.7211	-1.4211	47.1243	-2.8243	47.2189	-2.9189	46.4438	-2.1438
2016	41.9	47.5605	-5.6605	49.6654	-7.7654	50.1473	-8.2473	44.9202	-3.0202
		SSE	312.9213	*SSE*	289.8130	*SSE*	309.3745	*SSE*	165.1677
		S_{YX}	4.2904	S_{YX}	4.2560	S_{YX}	4.2660	S_{YX}	3.2129
		MAD	3.4709	*MAD*	3.0057	*MAD*	2.9667	*MAD*	2.1147

After you select a particular forecasting model, you need to continually monitor and update the model. Once new data become available, you can use these data points to refine and improve the model. If large errors between forecasted and actual values occur, the underlying structure of the time series may have changed. Remember that the forecasting methods presented in this chapter assume that the patterns inherent in the past will continue into the future. Large forecasting errors are an indication that this assumption may no longer be true.

PROBLEMS FOR SECTION 16.5

LEARNING THE BASICS

16.32 The following residuals are from a linear trend model used to forecast sales:

2.0 −0.5 1.5 1.0 0.0 1.0 −3.0 1.5 −4.5 2.0 0.0 −1.0

a. Compute S_{YX} and interpret your findings.
b. Compute the *MAD* and interpret your findings.

16.33 Refer to Problem 16.32. Suppose the first residual is 12.0 (instead of 2.0) and the last residual is −11.0 (instead of −1.0).
a. Compute S_{YX} and interpret your findings Compute the *MAD* and interpret your findings.

APPLYING THE CONCEPTS

16.34 Using the yearly amount of solar power generated by utilities (in millions of kWh) in the United States data for Problem 16.16 on page 645 and Problem 16.31 on page 655 (stored in SolarPower),
a. perform a residual analysis.
b. compute the standard error of the estimate (S_{YX}).
c. compute the *MAD*.
d. On the basis of (a) through (c), and the principle of parsimony, which forecasting model would you select? Discuss.

16.35 Using the new, single-family house sales data for Problem 16.15 on page 645 and Problem 16.27 on page 654 (stored in HouseSales),
a. perform a residual analysis for each model.
b. compute the standard error of the estimate (S_{YX}) for each model.
c. compute the *MAD* for each model.
d. On the basis of (a) through (c) and the principle of parsimony, which forecasting model would you select? Discuss.

✓**SELF TEST** **16.36** Using the bonuses paid to workers on Wall Street data for Problem 16.12 on page 645 and Problem 16.28 on page 655 (stored in Bonuses),
a. perform a residual analysis for each model.
b. compute the standard error of the estimate (S_{YX}) for each model.
c. compute the *MAD* for each model.
d. On the basis of (a) through (c) and the principle of parsimony, which forecasting model would you select? Discuss.

16.37 Using the number of passenger cars produced in the U.S. data for Problem 16.17 on page 645 and Problem 16.29 on page 655 (stored in CarProduction),
a. perform a residual analysis for each model.
b. compute the standard error of the estimate (S_{YX}) for each model.

c. compute the *MAD* for each model.

d. On the basis of (a) through (c) and the principle of parsimony, which forecasting model would you select? Discuss.

16.38 Using the average baseball salary data for Problem 16.18 on page 645 and Problem 16.30 on page 655 (stored in BBSalaries),

a. perform a residual analysis for each model.

b. compute the standard error of the estimate (S_{YX}) for each model.

c. compute the *MAD* for each model.

d. On the basis of (a) through (c) and the principle of parsimony, which forecasting model would you select? Discuss.

16.39 Refer to the results for Problem 16.13 on page 645 that used the file GDP ,

a. perform a residual analysis.

b. compute the standard error of the estimate (S_{YX}).

c. compute the *MAD*.

d. On the basis of (a) through (c), are you satisfied with your linear trend forecasts in Problem 16.13? Discuss.

16.6 Time-Series Forecasting of Seasonal Data

As Section 16.1 first mentions, time-series data that are collected in intervals more frequently than annually, such as quarterly, monthly, weekly, or daily time series, may contain a seasonal component. To illustrate forecasting with seasonal data, consider the Table 16.3 time series that represents quarterly revenues for Wal-Mart Stores, Inc., a general retailer whose sales are very seasonal. Figure 16.24 visualizes this time series.

TABLE 16.3

Quarterly Revenues (in $billions) for Wal-Mart Stores, Inc., 2011–2016 (stored in Walmart)

As of 2017, Wal-Mart Stores, Inc., operates 11,695 stores under 59 banners in 20 countries and e-commerce websites in 11 countries that over 260 million customers and club members visit each week.

| | **Year** | | | | | |
Quarter	2011	2012	2013	2014	2015	2016
1	104.19	113.01	114.07	114.96	114.83	115.90
2	109.37	114.28	116.83	120.12	120.23	120.85
3	110.23	113.80	115.69	119.00	117.41	118.18
4	123.17	127.78	129.71	131.56	129.67	130.94

Source: Data extracted from **ycharts.com/companies/WMT/revenues**. Because the company ends its fiscal year on January 31st, quarters are offset by one month such that the first quarter starts on February 1st and the fourth quarter starts on November 1st.

FIGURE 16.24

Plot of quarterly revenues ($billions) for Wal-Mart Stores, Inc., 2011–2016

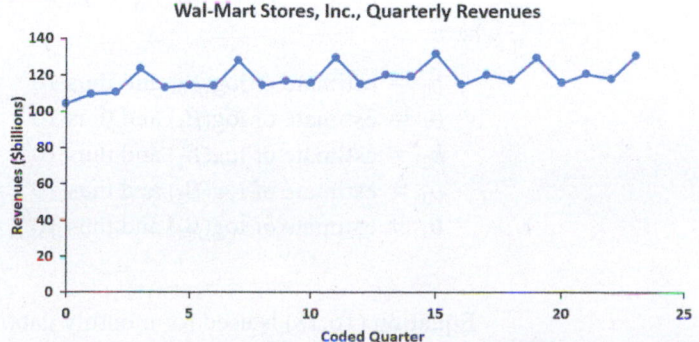

Least-Squares Forecasting with Monthly or Quarterly Data

To develop a least-squares regression model that includes a seasonal component, the least-squares exponential trend fitting method used in Section 16.3 is combined with dummy variables to represent the quarters (see Section 14.6) to model the seasonal component.

Equation (16.15) defines the exponential trend model for quarterly data.

EXPONENTIAL MODEL WITH QUARTERLY DATA

$$Y_i = \beta_0 \beta_1^{X_i} \beta_2^{Q_1} \beta_3^{Q_2} \beta_4^{Q_3} \varepsilon_i \tag{16.15}$$

where

X_i = coded quarterly value, $i = 0, 1, 2, \ldots$

Q_1 = 1 if first quarter, 0 if not first quarter

Q_2 = 1 if second quarter, 0 if not second quarter

Q_3 = 1 if third quarter, 0 if not third quarter

β_0 = Y intercept

$(\beta_1 - 1) \times 100\%$ = quarterly compound growth rate (in %)

β_2 = multiplier for first quarter relative to fourth quarter

β_3 = multiplier for second quarter relative to fourth quarter

β_4 = multiplier for third quarter relative to fourth quarter

ε_i = value of the irregular component for time period i

---

[2] Alternatively, you can use base e logarithms. For more information on logarithms, see Appendix Section A.3.

The model in Equation (16.15) is not in the form of a linear regression model. To transform this nonlinear model to a linear model, you use a base 10 logarithmic transformation.[2] Taking the logarithm of each side of Equation (16.15) results in Equation (16.16).

TRANSFORMED EXPONENTIAL MODEL WITH QUARTERLY DATA

$$\log(Y_i) = \log\left(\beta_0 \beta_1^{X_i} \beta_2^{Q_1} \beta_3^{Q_2} \beta_4^{Q_3} \varepsilon_i\right) \tag{16.16}$$

$$= \log(\beta_0) + \log(\beta_1^{X_i}) + \log(\beta_2^{Q_1}) + \log(\beta_3^{Q_2}) + \log(\beta_4^{Q_3}) + \log(\varepsilon_i)$$

$$= \log(\beta_0) + X_i \log(\beta_1) + Q_1 \log(\beta_2) + Q_2 \log(\beta_3) + Q_3 \log(\beta_4) + \log(\varepsilon_i)$$

Equation (16.16) is a linear model that you can estimate using least-squares regression. Performing the regression analysis using $\log(Y_i)$ as the dependent variable and X_i, Q_1, Q_2, and Q_3 as the independent variables results in Equation (16.17).

EXPONENTIAL GROWTH WITH QUARTERLY DATA FORECASTING EQUATION

$$\log(\hat{Y}_i) = b_0 + b_1 X_i + b_2 Q_1 + b_3 Q_2 + b_4 Q_3 \tag{16.17}$$

where

b_0 = estimate of $\log(\beta_0)$ and thus $10^{b_0} = \hat{\beta}_0$

b_1 = estimate of $\log(\beta_1)$ and thus $10^{b_1} = \hat{\beta}_1$

b_2 = estimate of $\log(\beta_2)$ and thus $10^{b_2} = \hat{\beta}_2$

b_3 = estimate of $\log(\beta_3)$ and thus $10^{b_3} = \hat{\beta}_3$

b_4 = estimate of $\log(\beta_4)$ and thus $10^{b_4} = \hat{\beta}_4$

Equation (16.18) is used for monthly data.

EXPONENTIAL MODEL WITH MONTHLY DATA

$$Y_i = \beta_0 \beta_1^{X_i} \beta_2^{M_1} \beta_3^{M_2} \beta_4^{M_3} \beta_5^{M_4} \beta_6^{M_5} \beta_7^{M_6} \beta_8^{M_7} \beta_9^{M_8} \beta_{10}^{M_9} \beta_{11}^{M_{10}} \beta_{12}^{M_{11}} \varepsilon_i \tag{16.18}$$

where

X_i = coded monthly value, $i = 0, 1, 2, \ldots$

M_1 = 1 if January, 0 if not January

M_2 = 1 if February, 0 if not February

$$M_3 = 1 \text{ if March, } 0 \text{ if not March}$$
$$\vdots$$
$$M_{11} = 1 \text{ if November, } 0 \text{ if not November}$$
$$\beta_0 = Y \text{ intercept}$$
$$(\beta_1 - 1) \times 100\% = \text{monthly compound growth rate (in \%)}$$
$$\beta_2 = \text{multiplier for January relative to December}$$
$$\beta_3 = \text{multiplier for February relative to December}$$
$$\beta_4 = \text{multiplier for March relative to December}$$
$$\vdots$$
$$\beta_{12} = \text{multiplier for November relative to December}$$
$$\varepsilon_i = \text{value of the irregular component for time period } i$$

The model in Equation (16.18) is not in the form of a linear regression model. To transform this nonlinear model into a linear model, you can use a base 10 logarithm transformation. Taking the logarithm of each side of Equation (16.18) results in Equation (16.19).

TRANSFORMED EXPONENTIAL MODEL WITH MONTHLY DATA

$$
\begin{aligned}
\log(Y_i) &= \log(\beta_0 \beta_1^{X_i} \beta_2^{M_1} \beta_3^{M_2} \beta_4^{M_3} \beta_5^{M_4} \beta_6^{M_5} \beta_7^{M_6} \beta_8^{M_7} \beta_9^{M_8} \beta_{10}^{M_9} \beta_{11}^{M_{10}} \beta_{12}^{M_{11}} \varepsilon_i) \quad \textbf{(16.19)} \\
&= \log(\beta_0) + X_i \log(\beta_1) + M_1 \log(\beta_2) + M_2 \log(\beta_3) \\
&\quad + M_3 \log(\beta_4) + M_4 \log(\beta_5) + M_5 \log(\beta_6) + M_6 \log(\beta_7) \\
&\quad + M_7 \log(\beta_8) + M_8 \log(\beta_9) + M_9 \log(\beta_{10}) + M_{10} \log(\beta_{11}) \\
&\quad + M_{11} \log(\beta_{12}) + \log(\varepsilon_i)
\end{aligned}
$$

Equation (16.19) is a linear model that you can estimate using the least-squares method. Performing the regression analysis using $\log(Y_i)$ as the dependent variable and $X_i, M_1, M_2, \ldots,$ and M_{11} as the independent variables results in Equation (16.20).

EXPONENTIAL GROWTH WITH MONTHLY DATA FORECASTING EQUATION

$$
\begin{aligned}
\log(\hat{Y}_i) &= b_0 + b_1 X_i + b_2 M_1 + b_3 M_2 + b_4 M_3 + b_5 M_4 + b_6 M_5 + b_7 M_6 \\
&\quad + b_8 M_7 + b_9 M_8 + b_{10} M_9 + b_{11} M_{10} + b_{12} M_{11} \quad \textbf{(16.20)}
\end{aligned}
$$

where

$$b_0 = \text{estimate of } \log(\beta_0) \text{ and thus } 10^{b_0} = \hat{\beta}_0$$
$$b_1 = \text{estimate of } \log(\beta_1) \text{ and thus } 10^{b_1} = \hat{\beta}_1$$
$$b_2 = \text{estimate of } \log(\beta_2) \text{ and thus } 10^{b_2} = \hat{\beta}_2$$
$$b_3 = \text{estimate of } \log(\beta_3) \text{ and thus } 10^{b_3} = \hat{\beta}_3$$
$$\vdots$$
$$b_{12} = \text{estimate of } \log(\beta_{12}) \text{ and thus } 10^{b_{12}} = \hat{\beta}_{12}$$

$Q_1, Q_2,$ and Q_3 are the three dummy variables needed to represent the four quarter periods in a quarterly time series. $M_1, M_2, M_3, \ldots, M_{11}$ are the 11 dummy variables needed to represent the 12 months in a monthly time series. In building the model, you use $\log(Y_i)$ instead of Y_i values and then find the regression coefficients by taking the antilog of the regression coefficients developed from Equations (16.17) and (16.20).

Although at first glance these regression models look imposing, when fitting or forecasting for any one time period, the values of all or all but one of the dummy variables in the model are equal to zero, and the equations simplify dramatically. In establishing the dummy variables for quarterly time-series data, the fourth quarter is the base period and has a coded value of zero for each dummy variable. With a quarterly time series, Equation (16.17) reduces as follows:

For any first quarter: $\log(\hat{Y}_i) = b_0 + b_1 X_i + b_2$

For any second quarter: $\log(\hat{Y}_i) = b_0 + b_1 X_i + b_3$

For any third quarter: $\log(\hat{Y}_i) = b_0 + b_1 X_i + b_4$

For any fourth quarter: $\log(\hat{Y}_i) = b_0 + b_1 X_i$

When establishing the dummy variables for each month, December serves as the base period and has a coded value of 0 for each dummy variable. For example, with a monthly time series, Equation (16.20) reduces as follows:

For any January: $\log(\hat{Y}_i) = b_0 + b_1 X_i + b_2$

For any February: $\log(\hat{Y}_i) = b_0 + b_1 X_i + b_3$

For any November: $\log(\hat{Y}_i) = b_0 + b_1 X_i + b_{12}$

For any December: $\log(\hat{Y}_i) = b_0 + b_1 X_i$

To demonstrate the process of model building and least-squares forecasting with a quarterly time series, return to the Wal-Mart Stores, Inc., revenue data (in billions of dollars) originally displayed in Table 16.3 page 659. The data are from the first quarter of 2011 through the last quarter of 2016. Figure 16.25 shows the regression results for the quarterly exponential trend model.

FIGURE 16.25
Excel, Minitab, and JMP regression results for the quarterly revenue data for Wal-Mart Stores, Inc.

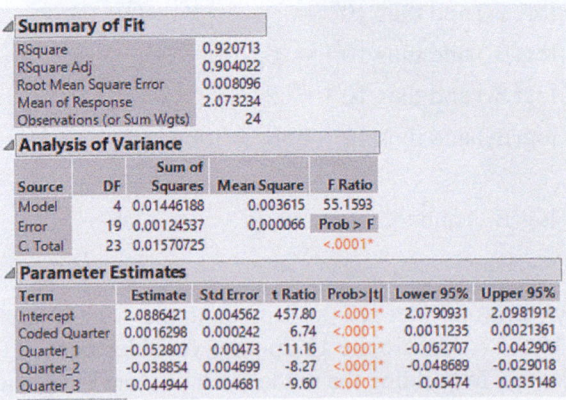

	A	B	C	D	E	F	G
1	Quarterly Exponential Trend Model for Wal-Mart Stores, Inc., Revenues						
2							
3	*Regression Statistics*						
4	Multiple R	0.9595					
5	R Square	0.9207					
6	Adjusted R Square	0.9040					
7	Standard Error	0.0081					
8	Observations	24					
9							
10	ANOVA						
11		df	SS	MS	F	Significance F	
12	Regression	4	0.0145	0.0036	55.1593	0.0000	
13	Residual	19	0.0012	0.0001			
14	Total	23	0.0157				
15							
16		Coefficients	Standard Error	t Stat	P-value	Lower 95%	Upper 95%
17	Intercept	2.0886	0.0046	457.8028	0.0000	2.0791	2.0982
18	Coded Quarter	0.0016	0.0002	6.7370	0.0000	0.0011	0.0021
19	Q1	-0.0528	0.0047	-11.1636	0.0000	-0.0627	-0.0429
20	Q2	-0.0389	0.0047	-8.2681	0.0000	-0.0487	-0.0290
21	Q3	-0.0449	0.0047	-9.6024	0.0000	-0.0547	-0.0351

Summary of Fit

RSquare	0.920713
RSquare Adj	0.904022
Root Mean Square Error	0.008096
Mean of Response	2.073234
Observations (or Sum Wgts)	24

Analysis of Variance

Source	DF	Sum of Squares	Mean Square	F Ratio
Model	4	0.01446188	0.003615	55.1593
Error	19	0.00124537	0.000066	Prob > F
C. Total	23	0.01570725		<.0001*

Parameter Estimates

Term	Estimate	Std Error	t Ratio	Prob>|t|	Lower 95%	Upper 95%
Intercept	2.0886421	0.004562	457.80	<.0001*	2.0790931	2.0981912
Coded Quarter	0.0016298	0.000242	6.74	<.0001*	0.0011235	0.0021361
Quarter_1	-0.052807	0.00473	-11.16	<.0001*	-0.062707	-0.042906
Quarter_2	-0.038854	0.004699	-8.27	<.0001*	-0.048689	-0.029018
Quarter_3	-0.044944	0.004681	-9.60	<.0001*	-0.05474	-0.035148

Regression Analysis: Log(Revenues) versus ... r_1, Quarter_2, Quarter_3

Analysis of Variance

Source	DF	Adj SS	Adj MS	F-Value	P-Value
Regression	4	0.014462	0.003615	55.16	0.000
Coded_Quarter	1	0.002975	0.002975	45.39	0.000
Quarter_1	1	0.008169	0.008169	124.63	0.000
Quarter_2	1	0.004481	0.004481	68.36	0.000
Quarter_3	1	0.006044	0.006044	92.21	0.000
Error	19	0.001245	0.000066		
Total	23	0.015707			

Model Summary

S	R-sq	R-sq(adj)	R-sq(pred)
0.0080960	92.07%	90.40%	86.83%

Coefficients

Term	Coef	SE Coef	T-Value	P-Value	VIF
Constant	2.08864	0.00456	457.80	0.000	
Coded_Quarter	0.001630	0.000242	6.74	0.000	1.03
Quarter_1	-0.05281	0.00473	-11.16	0.000	1.54
Quarter_2	-0.03885	0.00470	-8.27	0.000	1.52
Quarter_3	-0.04494	0.00468	-9.60	0.000	1.50

Regression Equation

Log(Revenues) = 2.08864 + 0.001630 Coded_Quarter - 0.05281 Quarter_1 - 0.03885 Quarter_2 - 0.04494 Quarter_3

From Figure 16.25, the model fits the data very well. The coefficient of determination $r^2 = 0.9207$, the adjusted $r^2 = 0.9040$, and the overall F test results in an F_{STAT} test statistic of 55.1593 (p-value = 0.000). At the 0.05 level of significance, each regression coefficient is highly statistically significant and contributes to the model. The following summary includes the antilogs of all the regression coefficients:

Regression Coefficient	$b_i = \log \hat{\beta}_i$	$\hat{\beta}_i = \text{antilog}\,(b_i) = 10^{b_i}$
b_0: Y intercept	2.0886	122.6428
b_1: coded quarter	0.0016	1.0038
b_2: first quarter	−0.0528	0.8855
b_3: second quarter	−0.0389	0.9144
b_4: third quarter	−0.0449	0.9017

The interpretations for $\hat{\beta}_0$, $\hat{\beta}_1$, $\hat{\beta}_2$, $\hat{\beta}_3$, and $\hat{\beta}_4$ are as follows:

- The Y intercept, $\hat{\beta}_0 = 122.6428$ (in $billions), is the *unadjusted* forecast for quarterly revenues in the first quarter of 2011, the initial quarter in the time series. *Unadjusted* means that the seasonal component is not incorporated in the forecast.
- The value $(\hat{\beta}_1 - 1) \times 100\%$, $= 0.0038$, or 0.38%, is the estimated *quarterly compound growth rate* in revenues, after adjusting for the seasonal component.
- $\hat{\beta}_2 = 0.8855$ is the seasonal multiplier for the first quarter relative to the fourth quarter; it indicates that there is $1 - 0.8855 = 11.45\%$ less revenue for the first quarter than for the fourth quarter.
- $\hat{\beta}_3 = 0.9144$ is the seasonal multiplier for the second quarter relative to the fourth quarter; it indicates that there is $1 - 0.9144 = 8.56\%$ less revenue for the second quarter than for the fourth quarter.
- $\hat{\beta}_4 = 0.9017$ is the seasonal multiplier for the third quarter relative to the fourth quarter; it indicates that there is $1 - 0.9017 = 9.83\%$ less revenue for the third quarter than for the fourth quarter. Thus, the fourth quarter, which includes the holiday shopping season, has the strongest sales.

Using the regression coefficients b_0, b_1, b_2, b_3, and b_4, and Equation (16.17) on page 660, you can make forecasts for selected quarters. As an example, to predict revenues for the fourth quarter of 2016 ($X_i = 23$),

$$\log(\hat{Y}_i) = b_0 + b_1 X_i$$

$$= 2.0886 + (0.0016)(23)$$

$$= 2.1254$$

Thus,

$$\log(\hat{Y}_i) = 10^{2.1254} = 133.4750$$

The predicted revenue for the fourth quarter of fiscal 2016 is $133.4750 billion. To make a forecast for a future time period, such as the first quarter of fiscal 2017 ($X_i = 24$, $Q_1 = 1$),

$$\log(\hat{Y}_i) = b_0 + b_1 X_i + b_2 Q_1$$

$$= 2.0886 + (0.0016)(24) + (-0.0528)(1)$$

$$= 2.0742$$

Thus,

$$\hat{Y}_i = 10^{2.0742} = 118.6315$$

The predicted revenue for the first quarter of fiscal 2017 is $118.6315 billion.

PROBLEMS FOR SECTION 16.6

LEARNING THE BASICS

16.40 In forecasting a monthly time series over a five-year period from January 2013 to December 2017, the exponential trend forecasting equation for January is

$$\log \hat{Y}_i = 2.0 + 0.01X_i + 0.10 \text{ (January)}$$

Take the antilog of the appropriate coefficient from this equation and interpret the
a. Y intercept, $\hat{b}_0$.
b. monthly compound growth rate.
c. January multiplier.

16.41 In forecasting daily time-series data, how many dummy variables are needed to account for the seasonal component day of the week?

16.42 In forecasting a quarterly time series over the five-year period from the first quarter of 2013 through the fourth quarter of 2017, the exponential trend forecasting equation is given by

$$\log \hat{Y}_i = 3.0 + 0.10X_i - 0.25Q_1 + 0.20Q_2 + 0.15Q_3$$

where quarter zero is the first quarter of 2013. Take the antilog of the appropriate coefficient from this equation and interpret the
a. Y intercept, $\hat{b}_0$.
b. quarterly compound growth rate.
c. second-quarter multiplier.

16.43 Refer to the exponential model given in Problem 16.42.
a. What is the fitted value of the series in the fourth quarter of 2017?
b. What is the fitted value of the series in the first quarter of 2017?
c. What is the forecast in the fourth quarter of 2017?
d. What is the forecast in the first quarter of 2018?

APPLYING THE CONCEPTS

✓ SELF TEST **16.44** The data in **Toys R Us** are quarterly revenues (in $millions) for Toys R Us from 1996-Q1 through 2017-Q1.

Source: Data extracted from *Standard & Poor's Stock Reports*, November 1995, November 1998, and April 2002, and Toys R Us, Inc., **www.toysrus.com**.

a. Do you think that the revenues for Toys R Us are subject to seasonal variation? Explain.
b. Plot the data. Does this chart support your answer in (a)?
c. Develop an exponential trend forecasting equation with quarterly components.
d. Interpret the quarterly compound growth rate.
e. Interpret the quarterly multipliers.
f. What are the forecasts for 2017-Q2, 2017-Q3, 2017-Q4, and all four quarters of 2018?

16.45 Are gasoline prices higher during the height of the summer vacation season than at other times? The file **GasPrices** contains the mean monthly prices (in $/gallon) for unleaded gasoline in the United States from January 2006 to June 2017.

Source: Data extracted from U.S. Energy Information Administration, "Monthly Energy Review," **bit.ly/2wYUEtV**.

a. Construct a time-series plot.
b. Develop an exponential trend forecasting equation with monthly components.

c. Interpret the monthly compound growth rate.
d. Interpret the monthly multipliers.
e. Write a short summary of your findings.

16.46 The file **Freezer** from January 2012 to December 2016 contains the number (in thousands) of freezer shipments in the United States from January 2012 to December 2016.

Source: Data extracted from **www.statista.com** and "Forecasts/Shipments Archives," **bit.ly/2fGtULf**.

a. Plot the time-series data.
b. Develop an exponential trend forecasting equation with monthly components.
c. What is the fitted value in December 2016?
d. What are the forecasts for the last four months of 2016?
e. Interpret the monthly compound growth rate.
f. Interpret the July multiplier.

16.47 The file **CallCenter** contains the monthly call volume for an existing product.

Source: Data extracted from S. Madadevan and J. Overstreet, "Use of Warranty and Reliability Data to Inform Call Center Staffing," *Quality Engineering* 24 (2012): 386–399.

a. Construct the time-series plot.
b. Describe the monthly pattern in the data.
c. In general, would you say that the overall call volume is increasing or decreasing? Explain.
d. Develop an exponential trend forecasting equation with monthly components.
e. Interpret the monthly compound growth rate.
f. Interpret the January multiplier.
g. What is the predicted call volume for month 60?
h. What is the predicted call volume for month 61?
i. How can this type of time-series forecasting benefit the call center?

16.48 The file **Silver-Q** contains the price in London for an ounce of silver (in US$) at the end of each quarter from 2004 through 2016.

Source: Data extracted from USAGold, "Daily Silver Price History," **bit.ly/2w8iBSl**.

a. Plot the data.
b. Develop an exponential trend forecasting equation with quarterly components.
c. Interpret the quarterly compound growth rate.
d. Interpret the first quarter multiplier.
e. What is the fitted value for the last quarter of 2016?
f. What are the forecasts for all four quarters of 2017?
g. Are the forecasts in (f) accurate? Explain.

16.49 The file **Gold** contains the price in London for an ounce of gold (in US$) at the end of each quarter from 2004 through 2016.
Source: Data extracted from USAGold, "Daily Gold Price History," **bit.ly/2w8iBSl**.
a. Plot the data.
b. Develop an exponential trend forecasting equation with quarterly components.
c. Interpret the quarterly compound growth rate.
d. Interpret the first quarter multiplier.
e. What is the fitted value for the last quarter of 2016?
f. What are the forecasts for all four quarters of 2017?
g. Are the forecasts in (f) accurate? Explain.

16.7 Index Numbers

An index number measures the value of an item (or group of items) at a particular point in time as a percentage of the value of an item (or group of items) at another point in time. The **Section 16.7 online topic** discusses this concept and illustrates its application.

Let the Model User Beware

When using a model, you must always review the assumptions built into the model and think about how novel or changing circumstances may render the model less useful.

Implicit in the time-series models developed in this chapter is that past data can be used to help predict the future. While using past data in this way is a legitimate application of time-series models, every so often, a crisis in financial markets illustrates that using models that rely on the past to predict the future is not without risk.

For example, during August 2007, many hedge funds suffered unprecedented losses. Apparently, many hedge fund managers used models that based their investment strategy on trading patterns over long time periods. These models did not—and could not—reflect trading patterns contrary to historical patterns (G. Morgenson, "A Week When Risk Came Home to Roost," *The New York Times*, August 12,

2007, pp. B1, B7). When fund managers in early August 2007 needed to sell stocks due to losses in their fixed income portfolios, stocks that were previously stronger became weaker, and weaker ones became stronger—the reverse of what the models expected. Making matters worse, many fund managers were using similar models and rigidly made investment decisions solely based on what those models said. These similar actions multiplied the effect of the selling pressure, an effect that the models had not considered and that therefore could not be seen in the models' results.

This example illustrates that using models does not absolve you of the responsibility of being a thoughtful decision maker. Go ahead and use models—when appropriately used, they will enhance your decision making. But always remember that no model can completely remove the risk involved in making a business decision.

▾USING **STATISTICS**
Is the ByYourDoor Service Trending? Revisited

In the ByYourDoor scenario, you were asked to analyze time-series sales data for the online food delivery service. You researched time-series forecasting methods and learned how to make short-term estimates of future time-series values.

You learned when to use moving averages and exponential smoothing methods to develop forecasts. You predicted that the movie attendance in 2017 would be 1.3256 billion.

For The Coca-Cola Company, you used least-squares linear, quadratic, and exponential models and autoregressive models to develop revenue forecasts. You evaluated these alternative models and determined that the first-order autoregressive model gave the best forecast, according to several

criteria. You predicted that the revenue of The Coca-Cola Company would be $42.6351 billion in 2017.

You realized that the ByYourDoor time series has a seasonal component and helped managers decide that you should be analyzing monthly data. You practiced for your task by using a least-squares regression model with a seasonal component to forecast revenues for Wal-Mart Stores, Inc. You predicted that Wal-Mart Stores would have revenues of $118.6315 billion in the first quarter of fiscal 2017.

▾SUMMARY

This chapter discusses smoothing techniques, least-squares trend fitting, autoregressive models, and forecasting of seasonal data. Figure 16.26 summarizes the time-series methods discussed in this chapter.

When using time-series forecasting, plot the time series and answer the following question: Is there a trend in the data? If there is a trend, then you can use the autoregressive model or the linear, quadratic, or exponential trend models. If there is no obvious trend in the time-series plot, then you should use moving averages or exponential smoothing to smooth out the effect of random effects and possible cyclical effects. After smoothing the data, if a trend is still not present, then you can use exponential smoothing to forecast short-term future values. If smoothing the data reveals a trend, then you can use the autoregressive model, or the linear, quadratic, or exponential trend models.

FIGURE 16.26
Summary chart of time-series forecasting methods

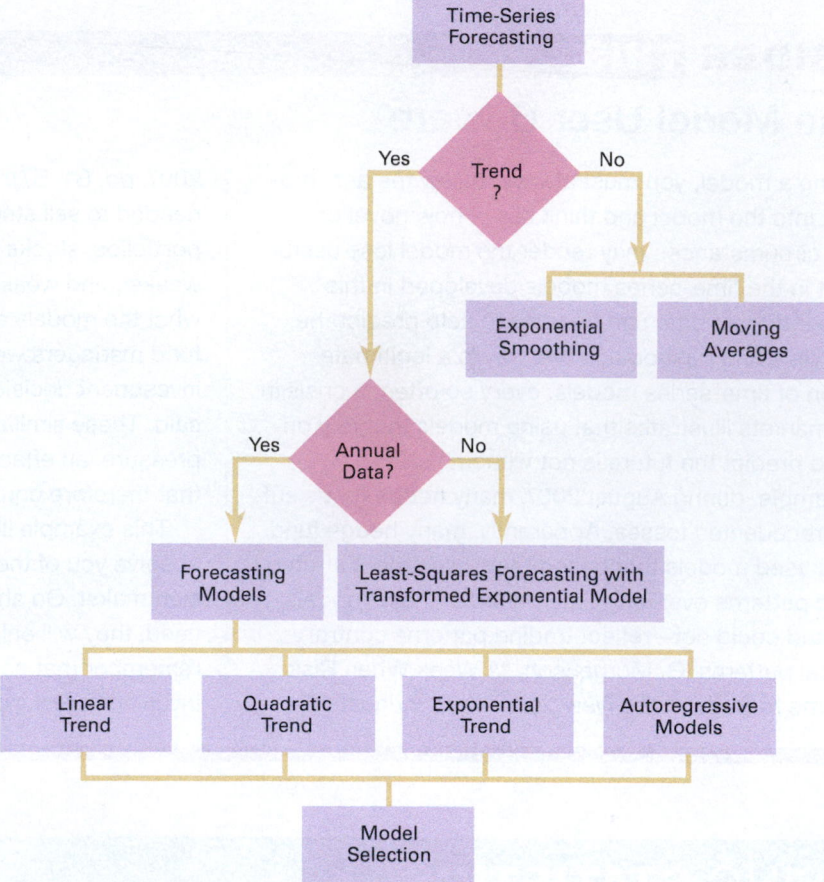

▼ REFERENCES

1. Bisgaard, S., and M. Kulahci. *Time Series Analysis and Forecasting by Example*. Hoboken, NJ: John Wiley and Sons, 2011.
2. Bowerman, B. L., R. T. O'Connell, and A. Koehler. *Forecasting, Time Series, and Regression*, 4th ed. Belmont, CA: Duxbury Press, 2005.
3. Box, G. E. P., G. M. Jenkins, G. C. Reinsel, and G. M. Leung. *Time Series Analysis: Forecasting and Control*, 4th ed. Hoboken, NJ: John Wiley and Sons, 2015.
4. Hanke, J. E., D. W. Wichern, and A. G. Reitsch. *Business Forecasting*, 7th ed. Upper Saddle River, NJ: Prentice Hall, 2001.
5. Montgomery, D. C., C. L. Jenning, and M. Kulahci. *Introduction to Time Series Analysis and Forecasting*, 2nd ed. Hoboken, NJ: John Wiley and Sons,
6. Pecar, B. *Box-Jenkins ARIMA Modelling in Excel*. Seattle: Amazon Digital Services, 2017.
7. *Wal-Mart Stores, Inc. Fact Book–Fiscal 2017*, available at **bit.ly/2ttCArb**.

▼ KEY EQUATIONS

Computing an Exponentially Smoothed Value in Time Period i

$$E_1 = Y_1$$

$$E_i = WY_i + (1 - W)E_{i-1} \quad i = 2, 3, 4, \ldots \quad (16.1)$$

Forecasting Time Period $i + 1$

$$\hat{Y}_{i+1} = E_i \quad (16.2)$$

Linear Trend Forecasting Equation

$$\hat{Y}_i = b_0 + b_1 X_i \quad (16.3)$$

Quadratic Trend Forecasting Equation

$$\hat{Y}_i = b_0 + b_1 X_i + b_2 X_i^2 \qquad (16.4)$$

Exponential Trend Model

$$Y_i = \beta_0 \beta_1^{X_i} \varepsilon_i \qquad (16.5)$$

Transformed Exponential Trend Model

$$
\begin{aligned}
\log(Y_i) &= \log(\beta_0 \beta_1^{X_i} \varepsilon_i) \\
&= \log(\beta_0) + \log(\beta_1^{X_i}) + \log(\varepsilon_i) \\
&= \log(\beta_0) + X_i \log(\beta_1) + \log(\varepsilon_i)
\end{aligned} \qquad (16.6)
$$

Exponential Trend Forecasting Equation

$$\log(\hat{Y}_i) = b_0 + b_1 X_i \qquad (16.7a)$$

$$\hat{Y}_i = \hat{\beta}_0 \hat{\beta}_1^{X_i} \qquad (16.7b)$$

***p*th-Order Autoregressive Models**

$$Y_i = A_0 + A_1 Y_{i-1} + A_2 Y_{i-2} + \cdots + A_p Y_{i-p} + \delta_i \qquad (16.8)$$

First-Order Autoregressive Model

$$Y_i = A_0 + A_1 Y_{i-1} + \delta_i \qquad (16.9)$$

Second-Order Autoregressive Model

$$Y_i = A_0 + A_1 Y_{i-1} + A_2 Y_{i-2} + \delta_i \qquad (16.10)$$

***t* Test for Significance of the Highest-Order Autoregressive Parameter, A_p**

$$t_{STAT} = \frac{a_p - A_p}{S_{a_p}} \qquad (16.11)$$

Fitted *p*th-Order Autoregressive Equation

$$\hat{Y}_i = a_0 + a_1 Y_{i-1} + a_2 Y_{i-2} + \cdots + a_p Y_{i-p} \qquad (16.12)$$

***p*th-Order Autoregressive Forecasting Equation**

$$\hat{Y}_{n+j} = a_0 + a_1 \hat{Y}_{n+j-1} + a_2 \hat{Y}_{n+j-2} + \cdots + a_p \hat{Y}_{n+j-p} \qquad (16.13)$$

Mean Absolute Deviation

$$MAD = \frac{\sum_{i=1}^{n} |Y_i - \hat{Y}_i|}{n} \qquad (16.14)$$

Exponential Model with Quarterly Data

$$Y_i = \beta_0 \beta_1^{X_i} \beta_2^{Q_1} \beta_3^{Q_2} \beta_4^{Q_3} \varepsilon_i \qquad (16.15)$$

Transformed Exponential Model with Quarterly Data

$$
\begin{aligned}
\log(Y_i) &= \log(\beta_0 \beta_1^{X_i} \beta_2^{Q_1} \beta_3^{Q_2} \beta_4^{Q_3} \varepsilon_i) \\
&= \log(\beta_0) + \log(\beta_1^{X_i}) + \log(\beta_2^{Q_1}) + \log(\beta_3^{Q_2}) \\
&\quad + \log(\beta_4^{Q_3}) + \log(\varepsilon_i) \\
&= \log(\beta_0) + X_i \log(\beta_1) + Q_1 \log(\beta_2) \\
&\quad + Q_2 \log(\beta_3) + Q_3 \log(\beta_4) + \log(\varepsilon_i)
\end{aligned} \qquad (16.16)
$$

Exponential Growth with Quarterly Data Forecasting Equation

$$\log(\hat{Y}_i) = b_0 + b_1 X_i + b_2 Q_1 + b_3 Q_2 + b_4 Q_3 \qquad (16.17)$$

Exponential Model with Monthly Data

$$Y_i = \beta_0 \beta_1^{X_i} \beta_2^{M_1} \beta_3^{M_2} \beta_4^{M_3} \beta_5^{M_4} \beta_6^{M_5} \beta_7^{M_6} \beta_8^{M_7} \beta_9^{M_8} \beta_{10}^{M_9} \beta_{11}^{M_{10}} \beta_{12}^{M_{11}} \varepsilon_i \qquad (16.18)$$

Transformed Exponential Model with Monthly Data

$$
\begin{aligned}
\log(Y_i) &= \log(\beta_0 \beta_1^{X_i} \beta_2^{M_1} \beta_3^{M_2} \beta_4^{M_3} \beta_5^{M_4} \beta_6^{M_5} \beta_7^{M_6} \beta_8^{M_7} \beta_9^{M_8} \beta_{10}^{M_9} \beta_{11}^{M_{10}} \beta_{12}^{M_{11}} \varepsilon_i) \\
&= \log(\beta_0) + X_i \log(\beta_1) + M_1 \log(\beta_2) + M_2 \log(\beta_3) \\
&\quad + M_3 \log(\beta_4) + M_4 \log(\beta_5) + M_5 \log(\beta_6) + M_6 \log(\beta_7) \\
&\quad + M_7 \log(\beta_8) + M_8 \log(\beta_9) + M_9 \log(\beta_{10}) + M_{10} \log(\beta_{11}) \\
&\quad + M_{11} \log(\beta_{12}) + \log(\varepsilon_i)
\end{aligned} \qquad (16.19)
$$

Exponential Growth with Monthly Data Forecasting Equation

$$
\begin{aligned}
\log(\hat{Y}_i) &= b_0 + b_1 X_i + b_2 M_1 + b_3 M_2 + b_4 M_3 + b_5 M_4 + b_6 M_5 \\
&\quad + b_7 M_6 + b_8 M_7 + b_9 M_8 + b_{10} M_9 + b_{11} M_{10} + b_{12} M_{11}
\end{aligned} \qquad (16.20)
$$

▼ KEY TERMS

▼CHECKING YOUR UNDERSTANDING

16.50 What is a time series?

16.51 What are the different components of a time-series model?

16.52 What is the difference between moving averages and exponential smoothing?

16.53 Under what circumstances is the exponential trend model most appropriate?

16.54 How does the least-squares linear trend forecasting model developed in this chapter differ from the least-squares linear regression model considered in Chapter 13?

16.55 How does autoregressive modeling differ from the other approaches to forecasting?

16.56 What are the different approaches to choosing an appropriate forecasting model?

16.57 What is the major difference between using S_{YX} and MAD for evaluating how well a particular model fits the data?

16.58 How does forecasting for monthly or quarterly data differ from forecasting for annual data?

▼CHAPTER REVIEW PROBLEMS

16.59 The data in the following table, stored in Polio , represent the annual incidence rates (per 100,000 persons) of reported acute poliomyelitis recorded over five-year periods from 1915 to 1955:

Year	1915	1920	1925	1930	1935	1940	1945	1950	1955
Rate	3.1	2.2	5.3	7.5	8.5	7.4	10.3	22.1	17.6

Source: Data extracted from B. Wattenberg, Ed., *The Statistical History of the United States: From Colonial Times to the Present*, ser. B303.

a. Plot the data.
b. Compute the linear trend forecasting equation and plot the trend line.
c. What are your forecasts for 1960, 1965, and 1970?
d. Using a library or the Internet, find the actually reported incidence rates of acute poliomyelitis for 1960, 1965, and 1970. Record your results.
e. Why are the forecasts you made in (c) not useful? Discuss.

16.60 The U.S. Department of Labor gathers and publishes statistics concerning the labor market. The file Workforce contains data on the size of the U.S. civilian noninstitutional population of people 16 years and over (in thousands) and the U.S. civilian noninstitutional workforce of people 16 years and over (in thousands) for 1984–2016. The workforce variable reports the number of people in the population who have a job or are actively looking for a job.

Source: Data extracted from Bureau of Labor Statistics, U.S. Department of Labor, **www.bls.gov**.

a. Plot the time series for the U.S. civilian noninstitutional population of people 16 years and older.
b. Compute the linear trend forecasting equation.
c. Forecast the U.S. civilian noninstitutional population of people 16 years and older for 2017 and 2018.
d. Repeat (a) through (c) for the U.S. civilian noninstitutional workforce of people 16 years and older.

16.61 The monthly commercial and residential prices for natural gas (dollars per thousand cubic feet) in the United States from January 2008 through December 2016 are stored in Natural Gas .

Source: Data extracted from Energy Information Administration, U.S. Department of Energy, **www.eia.gov**, *Natural Gas Monthly*, March 1, 2015.

For the commercial price and the residential price,

a. do you think the price for natural gas has a seasonal component?
b. plot the time series. Does this chart support your answer in (a)?
c. compute an exponential trend forecasting equation for monthly data.
d. interpret the monthly compound growth rate.
e. interpret the monthly multipliers. Do the multipliers support your answers in (a) and (b)?
f. compare the results for the commercial prices and the residential prices.

16.62 The data stored in McDonalds represent the gross revenues (in billions of current dollars) of McDonald's Corporation from 1975 through 2016:
a. Plot the data.
b. Compute the linear trend forecasting equation.
c. Compute the quadratic trend forecasting equation.
d. Compute the exponential trend forecasting equation.
e. Determine the best-fitting autoregressive model, using $\alpha = 0.05$.
f. Perform a residual analysis for each of the models in (b) through (e).
g. Compute the standard error of the estimate (S_{YX}) and the MAD for each corresponding model in (f).
h. On the basis of your results in (f) and (g), along with a consideration of the principle of parsimony, which model would you select for purposes of forecasting? Discuss.
i. Using the selected model in (h), forecast gross revenues for 2017.

16.63 Teachers' Retirement System of the City of New York offers several types of investments for its members. Among the choices are investments with fixed and variable rates of return. There are several categories of variable-return investments. The Diversified Equity Fund consists of investments that are primarily made in stocks, and the Stable-Value Fund consists of investments in corporate bonds and other types of lower-risk instruments. The data in TRSNYC represent the value of a unit of each type of variable-return investment at the beginning of each year from 1984 to 2017.

Source: Data extracted from "Historical Data-Unit Values, Teachers' Retirement System of the City of New York," **bit.ly/SESJF5**.

For each of the two time series,
a. plot the data.
b. compute the linear trend forecasting equation.
c. compute the quadratic trend forecasting equation.
d. compute the exponential trend forecasting equation.
e. determine the best-fitting autoregressive model, using $\alpha = 0.05$.
f. Perform a residual analysis for each of the models in (b) through (e).
g. Compute the standard error of the estimate (S_{YX}) and the *MAD* for each corresponding model in (f).

h. On the basis of your results in (f) and (g), along with a consideration of the principle of parsimony, which model would you select for purposes of forecasting? Discuss.
i. Using the selected model in (h), forecast the unit values for 2018.
j. Based on the results of (a) through (i), what investment strategy would you recommend for a member of the Teachers' Retirement System of the City of New York? Explain.

REPORT WRITING EXERCISE

16.64 As a consultant to an investment company trading in various currencies, you have been assigned the task of studying long-term trends in the exchange rates of the Canadian dollar, the Japanese yen, and the English pound. Data from 1980 to 2016 are stored in Currency , where the Canadian dollar, the Japanese yen, and the English pound are expressed in units per U.S. dollar.

Develop a forecasting model for the exchange rate of each of these three currencies and provide forecasts for 2017 and 2018 for each currency. Write an executive summary for a presentation to be given to the investment company. Append to this executive summary a discussion regarding possible limitations that may exist in these models.

CHAPTER 16

▾CASES

Managing Ashland MultiComm Services

As part of the continuing strategic initiative to increase subscribers to the *3-For-All* cable/phone/Internet services, the marketing department is closely monitoring the number of subscribers. To help do so, forecasts are to be developed for the number of subscribers in the future. To accomplish this task, the number of subscribers for the most recent 24-month period has been determined and is stored in AMS16 .

1. Analyze these data and develop a model to forecast the number of subscribers. Present your findings in a report that includes the assumptions of the model and its limitations. Forecast the number of subscribers for the next four months.

2. Would you be willing to use the model developed to forecast the number of subscribers one year into the future? Explain.

3. Compare the trend in the number of subscribers to the number of new subscribers per month stored in AMS13 . What explanation can you provide for any differences?

Digital Case

Apply your knowledge about time-series forecasting in this Digital Case.

The *Ashland Herald* competes for readers in the Tri-Cities area with the newer *Oxford Glen Journal (OGJ)*. Recently, the circulation staff at the *OGJ* claimed that their newspaper's circulation and subscription base is growing faster than that of the *Herald* and that local advertisers would do better if they transferred their advertisements from the *Herald* to the *OGJ*. The circulation department of the *Herald* has complained to the Ashland Chamber of Commerce about *OGJ*'s claims and has asked the chamber to investigate, a request that was welcomed by *OGJ*'s circulation staff.

Open **ACC_Mediation216.pdf** to review the circulation dispute information collected by the Ashland Chamber of Commerce. Then answer the following:

1. Which newspaper would you say has the right to claim the fastest-growing circulation and subscription base? Support your answer by performing and summarizing an appropriate statistical analysis.

2. What is the single most positive fact about the *Herald*'s circulation and subscription base? What is the single most positive fact about the *OGJ*'s circulation and subscription base? Explain your answers.

3. What additional data would be helpful in investigating the circulation claims made by the staffs of each newspaper?

▾EXCEL GUIDE

There are no Excel Guide instructions for Section 16.1.

EG16.2 SMOOTHING an ANNUAL TIME SERIES

Moving Averages

Key Technique Use the **AVERAGE**(*cell range of L consecutive values*) function to compute a moving average. Use the special value **#N/A** (not available) for time periods in which no moving average can be computed.

Example Calculate the Figure 16.6 three- and five-year moving averages for the movie attendance data on page 634.

Workbook Use the **COMPUTE worksheet** of the **Moving Averages workbook** as a template.

The worksheet already contains the data and formulas for the example. For other problems, paste the time-series data into columns A and B and:

1. For data that contain more than 12 time periods, copy the formulas in cell range **C13:D13** down through the new table rows; otherwise, delete rows as necessary.
2. Enter the special value **#N/A** in columns C and D for the first and last time periods.
3. Enter **#N/A** in the second and second-to-last time periods in column D.

To construct a moving average plot for other problems, open to the adjusted COMPUTE worksheet and:

1. Select the cell range of the time-series and the moving averages (**A1:D13** for the example).
2. Select **Insert → Scatter (X, Y) or Bubble Chart** and select the **Scatter** gallery item. (In Excel 2010, select **Insert → Scatter.**)
   Select **Insert → X Y (Scatter)** and select the **Scatter** gallery item.
3. Relocate the chart to a chart sheet, turn off the gridlines, add axis titles, and modify the chart title by using the instructions in Appendix Section B.5.

Exponential Smoothing

Key Technique Use arithmetic formulas to compute exponentially smoothed values.

Example Calculate the Figure 16.7 exponentially smoothed series ($W = 0.50$ and $W = 0.25$) for the movie attendance data on page 635.

Workbook Use the **COMPUTE worksheet** of the **Exponential Smoothing workbook**, as a template.

The worksheet already contains the data and formulas for the example. In this worksheet, cells C2 and D2 contain the formula **=B2** that copies the initial value of the time series. The exponential smoothing begins in row 3, with cell C3 formula **= 0.5 * B3 + 0.75 * C2**, and cell D3 formula **= 0.25 * B3 + 0.75 * D2**. Note that these formulas simplify the Equation (16.1) expression $1 - W$ as the values 0.5 and 0.75.

For other problems, paste the time-series data into columns A and B and adjust the entries in columns C and D. For problems with fewer than 12 time periods, delete the excess rows. For problems with more than 12 time periods, select cell range **C13:D13** and copy down through the new table rows.

To construct a plot of exponentially smoothed values for other problems, open to the adjusted COMPUTE worksheet and:

1. Select the cell range of the time-series data and the exponentially smoothed values (**A1:D13** for the example).
2. Select **Insert → Scatter (X, Y) or Bubble Chart** (or **Scatter**) and select the Scatter gallery item.
   Select **Insert → X Y (Scatter)** and select the **Scatter** gallery item.
3. Relocate the chart to a chart sheet, turn off the gridlines, add axis titles, and modify the chart title by using the instructions in Appendix Section B.5.

Analysis ToolPak Use **Exponential Smoothing.**

For the example, open to the **DATA worksheet** of the **Movie Attendance workbook** and:

1. Select **Data → Data Analysis.**
2. In the Data Analysis dialog box, select **Exponential Smoothing** from the **Analysis Tools** list and then click **OK.**

In the Exponential Smoothing dialog box (shown below):

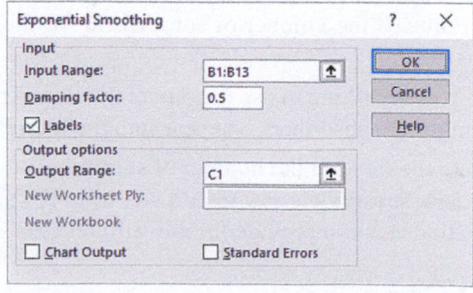

3. Enter **B1:B13** as the **Input Range.**
4. Enter **0.5** as the **Damping factor**. (The damping factor is equal to $1 - W$.)
5. Check **Labels**, enter **C1** as the **Output Range**, and click **OK.**

In the new column C:

6. Copy the last formula in cell **C12** to cell **C13**.
7. Enter the column heading **ES(W=.50)** in cell **C1**, replacing the **#N/A** value.

To create the exponentially smoothed values that use a smoothing coefficient of $W = 0.25$, repeat steps 1 through 7 but, enter **0.75** as the **Damping factor** in step 4, enter **D1** as the **Output Range** in step 5, and enter **ES(W=.25)** as the column heading in step 7.

EG16.3 LEAST-SQUARES TREND FITTING and FORECASTING

The Linear Trend Model

Key Technique Modify the Section EG13.2 instructions on page 529.

Use the cell range of the coded variable as the X variable cell range (called the **X Variable Cell Range** in the *PHStat* instructions, called the *cell range of X variable* in the *Workbook* instructions, and called the **Input X Range** in the *Analysis ToolPak* instructions).

To enter many coded values, use **Home → Fill** (in the Editing group) **→ Series** and in the Series dialog box, click **Columns** and **Linear**, and select appropriate values for **Step value** and **Stop value**.

The Quadratic Trend Model

Key Technique Modify the Section EG15.1 instructions on page 623.

Use the cell range of the coded variable and the squared coded variable as the X variables cell range, called the **X Variables Cell Range** in the *PHStat* instructions and the **Input X Range** in the *Analysis ToolPak* instructions.

The Exponential Trend Model

Key Technique Modify the Section EG15.2 instructions on page 623 and the EG13.5 instructions on page 530.

Use the **POWER(10, *predicted log(Y)*)** function to compute the predicted Y values from the predicted $\log(Y)$ results.

To create an exponential trend model, first convert the values of the dependent variable Y to $\log(Y)$ values using the Section EG15.2 instructions. Then perform a simple linear regression analysis with residual analysis using the $\log(Y)$ values. Modify the Section EG13.5 instructions using the cell range of the $\log(Y)$ values as the Y variable cell range and the cell range of the coded variable as the X variable cell range.

If you use the *PHStat* or *Workbook* instructions, residuals will appear in a residuals worksheet. If you use the Analysis ToolPak instructions, residuals will appear in the RESIDUAL OUTPUT area of the regression results worksheet. Because you use $\log(Y)$ values for the regression, the predicted Y and residuals listed are *log values* that need to be converted. [The Analysis ToolPak incorrectly labels the new column for the logs of the residuals *Residuals*, and not *LOG(Residuals)*.]

In an empty column in the residuals worksheet (*PHStat* or *Workbook*) or an empty column range to the right of RESIDUALS OUTPUT area (*Analysis ToolPak*):

1. Add a column of formulas that use the POWER function to compute the predicted Y values.
2. Copy the original Y values to the next empty column.
3. In the next empty (third new) column, enter formulas in the form **=Y value cell-predicted Y cell** to compute the residuals.

Use columns G through I of the **RESIDUALS worksheet** of the **Exponential Trend workbook** as a model for these three columns. The worksheet already contains the values and formulas needed to create the Figure 16.13 plot that fits an exponential trend forecasting equation for The Coca-Cola Company revenues.

To construct an exponential trend plot, first select the cell range of the time-series data and then use the Section EG2.5 instructions to construct a scatter plot. (For The Coca-Cola Company revenue example, use the cell range is **B1:B18** in the **Data worksheet** of the **Coca-Cola workbook**.) Select the chart and

1. Select **Design** (or **Chart Design) → Add Chart Element → Trendline → More Trendline Options**.
2. In the Format Trendline pane, click **Exponential**.

In Excel 2010, select **Layout → Trendline → More Trendline Options**. In the Format Trendline dialog box, click **Trendline Options** in the left pane and in the Trendline Options right pane, click **Exponential** and click **OK**.

Model Selection Using First, Second, and Percentage Differences

Key Technique Use the **COMPUTE worksheet** of the **Differences workbook** (see Figure 16.14 page 644), as a model for developing a differences worksheet.

Use arithmetic formulas to compute the first, second, and percentage differences. Use division formulas to compute the percentage differences and use subtraction formulas to compute the first and second differences. Open to the **COMPUTE_FORMULAS worksheet** to review the formulas the COMPUTE worksheet uses.

EG16.4 AUTOREGRESSIVE MODELING for TREND FITTING and FORECASTING

Creating Lagged Predictor Variables

Key Technique Use the **COMPUTE worksheet** of the **Lagged Predictors workbook** as a model for developing lagged predictor variables for the first-order, second-order, and third-order autoregressive models.

Create lagged predictor variables by creating a column of formulas that refer to a previous row's (previous time period's) Y value. Enter the special worksheet value **#N/A** (not available) for the cells in the column to which lagged values do not apply.

When specifying cell ranges for a lagged predictor variable, you include only rows that contain lagged values. Contrary to the usual practice in this book, you do not include rows that contain **#N/A**, nor do you include the row 1 column heading.

Open to the **COMPUTE_FORMULAS** worksheet to review the formulas that the Figure 16.16 COMPUTE worksheet on page 651 uses.

Autoregressive Modeling

Key Technique To create a third-order or second-order autoregressive model, modify the Section EG14.1 instructions on page 582. Use the cell range of the first-order, second-order, and third-order lagged predictor variables as the X variables cell range for the third-order model. Use the cell range of the first-order and second-order lagged predictor variables as the X variables cell range for the second-order model.

If you use the *PHStat* instructions, modify step 3 to *clear* not *check* **First cells in both ranges contain label.** If using the *Workbook* instructions, use the **COMPUTE3 worksheet** in lieu of the COMPUTE worksheet for the third-order model. If using the *Analysis ToolPak* instructions, do not check **Labels** in step 4.

To create a first-order autoregressive model, modify the Section EG13.2 instructions on page 529. Use the cell range of the first-order lagged predictor variable as the X variable cell range (called the **X Variable Cell Range** in the *PHStat* instructions, the *cell range of X variable* in the *Workbook* instructions, and the **Input X Range** in the *Analysis ToolPak* instructions). If using the *PHStat* instructions, modify step 3 to *clear* not *check* **First cells in both ranges contain label.** If using the *Analysis ToolPak* instructions, do not check **Labels** in step 4.

EG16.5   CHOOSING an APPROPRIATE FORECASTING MODEL

Performing a Residual Analysis

To create residual plots for the linear trend model or the first-order autoregressive model, use the Section EG13.5 instructions on page 530.

To create residual plots for the quadratic trend model or second-order autoregressive model, use the Section EG14.3 instructions on page 583.

To create residual plots for the exponential trend model, use the instructions Section EG16.4 on page 671.

To create residual plots for the third-order autoregressive model, use the Section EG14.3 instructions on page 583 but use the **RESIDUALS3** worksheet instead of the RESIDUALS worksheet if you use the *Workbook* instructions.

Measuring the Magnitude of the Residuals Through Squared or Absolute Differences

Key Technique Use the functions **SUMPRODUCT** and **COUNT** to compute the mean asolute deviation (*MAD*).

To compute the mean absolute deviation (*MAD*), first perform a residual analysis. Then, in an empty cell, add the formula **=SUMPRODUCT(ABS(*residuals cell range*)) / COUNT(*residuals cell range*)**. When entering the *residuals cell range,* do not include the column heading in the cell range. (See Appendix Section F.2 to learn more about the application of **SUMPRODUCT** function in this formula.)

Cell I19 of the **RESIDUALS_FORMULAS worksheet** of the **Exponential Trend workbook** contains the *MAD* formula for The Coca-Cola Company revenues example.

A Comparison of Four Forecasting Methods

Key Technique Use the **COMPARE** worksheet of the **Forecasting Comparison workbook** as a model.

Construct a model comparison worksheet similar to the Figure 16.23 worksheet on page 658 by using **Paste Special values** (see Appendix Section B.5) to transfer results from the regression results worksheets. For the *SSE* values (row 22 in Figure 16.23), copy the regression results worksheet cell C13, the *SS* value for Residual in the ANOVA table. For the S_{YX} values (row), copy the regression results worksheet cell B7, labeled Standard Error, for all but the exponential trend model. For the *MAD* values, add formulas as discussed in the previous section.

For the S_{YX} value for the exponential trend model, enter a formula in the form **=SQRT(*exponential SSE cell* / (COUNT(*cell range of exponential residuals*) - 2))**. In the COMPARE worksheet, this formula is **=SQRT(H22/ (COUNT(H3: H21) - 2))**.

Open to the **COMPARE_FORMULAS** worksheet to discover how the COMPARE worksheet uses the SUMSQ function as an alternate way of displaying the *SSE* values.

EG16.6   TIME-SERIES FORECASTING of SEASONAL DATA

Least-Squares Forecasting with Monthly or Quarterly Data

To develop a least-squares regression model for monthly or quarterly data, add columns of formulas that use the **IF** function (see Appendix Section F.2) to create dummy variables for the quarterly or monthly data. Enter all formulas in the form **=IF(*comparison*,1, 0)**.

Shown at right are the first five rows of columns F through K of a data worksheet that contains dummy variables. In the first illustration, columns F, G, and H contain the quarterly dummy variables Q1, Q2, and Q3 that are based on column B coded quarter values (not shown). In the second illustration, columns J and K contain the two monthly variables M1 and M6 that are based on column C month values (also not shown).

	F	G	H
1	Q1	Q2	Q3
2	=IF(B2 = 1, 1, 0)	=IF(B2 = 2, 1, 0)	=IF(B2 = 3, 1, 0)
3	=IF(B3 = 1, 1, 0)	=IF(B3 = 2, 1, 0)	=IF(B3 = 3, 1, 0)
4	=IF(B4 = 1, 1, 0)	=IF(B4 = 2, 1, 0)	=IF(B4 = 3, 1, 0)
5	=IF(B5 = 1, 1, 0)	=IF(B5 = 2, 1, 0)	=IF(B5 = 3, 1, 0)

	J	K
1	M1	M6
2	=IF(C2 ="January", 1, 0)	=IF(C2 = "June", 1, 0)
3	=IF(C3 ="January", 1, 0)	=IF(C3 = "June", 1, 0)
4	=IF(C4 ="January", 1, 0)	=IF(C4 = "June", 1, 0)
5	=IF(C5 ="January", 1, 0)	=IF(C5 = "June", 1, 0)

CHAPTER 16

▼ JMP GUIDE

There are no JMP Guide instructions for Section 16.1.

JG16.2 SMOOTHING an ANNUAL TIME SERIES

Moving Averages

Use **Time Series**.

For example, to compute the three and five-year moving averages for the original movie attendance time series that Figure 16.6 (left) uses on page 634, open to the **Original Movie Attendance data table**. Select **Analyze → Specialized Modeling → Times Series** and in the Time Series - Autocorrelations dialog box (shown below):

1. Click **Attendance** in the columns list and then click **Y, Time Series** to add Attendance to the Y, Time Series box.

2. Click **OK**.

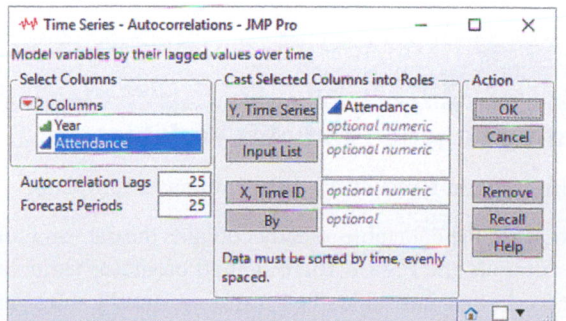

3. In the Please Enter a Number dialog box (not shown), enter **2** in the box and click **OK**.

4. In the new JMP results window, click the **Time Series Attendance red triangle** and select **Smoothing Model → Simple Smoothing Average** (**Simple Moving Average** in JMP 14) from the submenu.

In the Simple Smoothing Average Specification dialog box (shown below):

5. Enter **3** in the Enter smoothing window width box.

6. Click **Centered**.

7. Click **OK**.

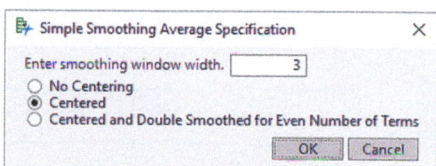

JMP displays a Simple Moving Average plot as part of the results window. To add a column of five-year moving averages:

8. Click the **Simple Moving Average red triangle** and select **Add Model** from its menu.

9. In the Simple Smoothing Average Specification dialog box, enter **5** in the Enter smoothing window width box, click **Centered**, and click **OK**.

10. Click the **Simple Moving Average red triangle** and select **Save to Data Table** from its menu.

JMP creates a duplicate of the original data table and adds the new columns SMA(3, Centered) and SMA(5, Centered) to the original data. Change these new column names to **MA 3-Yr** and **MA 5-Yr** and optionally save the data table.

As a by-product of steps 1 through 10, JMP creates a time-series plot of the movie attendance, similar to Figure 16.4, and a time-series plot of the moving averages, similar to Figure 16.6 (left). However, the Y axes of these charts will not begin at 0 (and can be adjusted using Appendix B instructions).

The SHORT TAKES for Chapter 16 describe a second method to compute moving averages using data table formulas, analogous to the Excel moving average worksheets and similar to the Exponential Smoothing data table template. This second method does not create any time-series plot as a by-product of the instructions.

Exponential Smoothing

Use the **Exponential Smoothing data table** as a template.

For example, the data table already contains the data and formulas to compute the Figure 16.7 exponentially smoothed series ($W = 0.50$ and $W = 0.25$) for the 12-year movie attendance time series on page 635. In this data table, the third and fourth columns contain formulas that compute the smoothed values. Because no smoothing is done for the first time-series value, each formula checks for the special case of a column cell being in row 1 of the data table. If the cell is in row 1, then the Attendance value is copied to the cell, otherwise an arithmetic formula computes the cell value.

For the *ES(W=0.25)* column, the arithmetic formula that computes cell values is $0.25 \times$ *Attendance-column-cell* $+ 0.75 \times$ *previous-cell-in-ES(W=0.25)-column*. Shown below is the JMP formula. Note the use of the If-else function to test the special case, the expression Row()==1 to test for the special case of being in the first row, and the expression Lag (*ES(W=0.25)*, 1) to select the value in the previous row of the column.

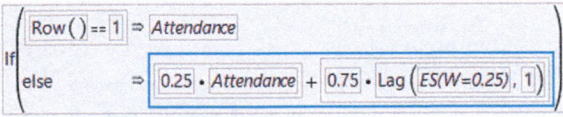

For other problems, paste the time-series data into the first two columns A and B, rename those columns, and, if necessary, adjust the smoothing coefficient in column formulas. For problems with fewer than 12 time periods, delete the excess rows.

JG16.3   LEAST-SQUARES TREND FITTING and FORECASTING

The Linear Trend Model

Modify the Section JG13.2 instructions on page 532.

Add the column that contains the coded variable to the **Construct Model Effects** box in step 2. To enter many coded values, select **Sequence Data** from the **Initialize Data** pull-down list in the New Column dialog box when creating the column for the coded values.

The Quadratic Trend Model

Modify the Section JG15.1 instructions on page 625.

Add the column that contains the coded variable and the newly-created squared coded variable to the **Construct Model Effects** box in steps 2 and 3 of the multiple regression (Section JG14.1 "Interpreting the Regression Coefficients") instructions.

The Exponential Trend Model

Modify the Section JG15.2 instructions on page 625 and the Sections JG13.2 and JG13.5 instructions that begin on page 532.

To create an exponential trend model, first convert the values of the dependent Y variable to log Log10(Y) values using the Section EG15.2 instructions. Then perform a simple linear regression analysis with residual analysis adding the column that contains the Log10(Y) values to the **Construct Model Effects** box in step 2 of the Section JG13.2 instructions. Then complete the Section JG13.5 instructions.

Model Selection Using First, Second, and Percentage Differences

Use the **Differences data table** as a template.

For example, the data table already contains the data and formulas to compute the Figure 16.14 The Coca-Cola Company revenues first, second, and percentage differences on page 644. In this data table, the second, third, and fourth columns contain formulas that compute the differences using the Dif function. This function assigns a missing value to cells for which no difference can be computed.

The First Differences column uses the function Dif (*Revenues*, 1) and the Second Differences column uses Dif(*First Difference*, 1). The Percentage Difference column uses the expression Dif(*Revenues*, 1) divided by Lag(*Revenues*, 1) to divide the first difference by the value in the previous time period. To explore the formulas, right-click a difference column and select **Formula** from the shortcut menu to display the formula workspace that contains the formula.

For other problems, paste the time-series data into the first two columns A and B, rename those columns, and, if necessary, adjust the smoothing coefficient in column formulas. For problems with fewer than 19 time periods, delete the excess rows.

JG16.4   AUTOREGRESSIVE MODELING for TREND FITTING and FORECASTING

Creating Lagged Predictor Variables

Use the **Lagged Predictors data table** as a template.

For example, the data table already contains the data and formulas to compute the Figure 16.16 lagged predictor variables on page 651. In this data table, the Lag1, Lag2, and Lag3 columns contain formulas that use the Lag function to select the value in a prior row of the Revenues column. The Lag1 column uses Lag(*Revenues*, 1) and the Lag2 column uses Lag(*Revenues*, 2), and the Lag3 column uses Lag(*Revenues*, 3). To explore the formulas, right-click a difference column and select **Formula** from the shortcut menu to display the formula workspace that contains the formula.

For other problems, paste the time-series data into the first two columns A and B and rename those columns. For problems with fewer than 19 time periods, delete the excess rows.

Autoregressive Modeling

To create a third-order or second-order autoregressive model, modify the Section JG14.1 instructions on page 585. Add the names of the columns containing the first-order, second-order, and third-order lagged predictor variables to the **Construct Model Effects** box for the third-order model. Add the names of the columns containing the first-order, and second-order lagged predictor variables to the **Construct Model Effects** box for the second-order model.

Modify the Section JG13.2 instructions on page 532 to create a first-order autoregressive model. Add the name of the column containing the first-order lagged predictor variable to the **Construct Model Effects** box.

JG16.5 CHOOSING an APPROPRIATE FORECASTING MODEL

A Comparison of Four Forecasting Methods

To compare the four forecasting models, use residual analysis to examine the models. Use the Section JG13.5 instructions on page 532 to create residual plots for the linear trend model or first-order autoregressive models. Use the Section JG14.1 instructions on page 585 to create residual plots for the quadratic and the exponential trend models.

JG16.6 TIME-SERIES FORECASTING of SEASONAL DATA

Least-Squares Forecasting with Monthly or Quarterly Data

Use **Make Indicator Columns**.

To develop a least-squares regression model for monthly or quarterly data, add columns of dummy variables (which JMP call indicator variables). For example, to make the quarterly dummy variables for the Table 16.3 Walmart quarterly revenues, open to the **Walmart data table** and

1. Select the **Quarter** column.
2. Select **Cols → Utilities → Make Indicator Variables**.
3. In the Make Indicator Variables dialog box (not shown), check **Append Column Name** and click **OK**.

JMP inserts four new columns name Quarter_1, Quarter_2, Quarter_3, and Quarter_4. Delete the Quarter_4 column as this column is unnecessary. (A fourth quarter is represented when the first three dummy variables are all zero.) Using this procedure, JMP will always create an unnecessary column that should be deleted for analysis.

For other problems, the column selected in step 1 must be the Nominal modeling type. Change the column to this model type, if necessary, before using steps 1 through 3.

CHAPTER 16

▼MINITAB GUIDE

There are no Minitab Guide instructions for Section 16.1.

MG16.2 SMOOTHING an ANNUAL TIME SERIES

Moving Averages

Use **Moving Average.**

For example, to compute the three- and five-year moving averages for the original movie attendance time series that Figure 16.6 (left) uses on page 634, open to the **Original Movie Attendance worksheet**. Select **Stat → Time Series → Moving Average**. In the Moving Average dialog box (shown at right):

1. Double-click **C2 Attendance** in the variables list to add **Attendance** to the **Variable** box.
2. Enter **3** in the **MA length** box.
3. Check **Center the moving averages**.
4. Click **Storage**.

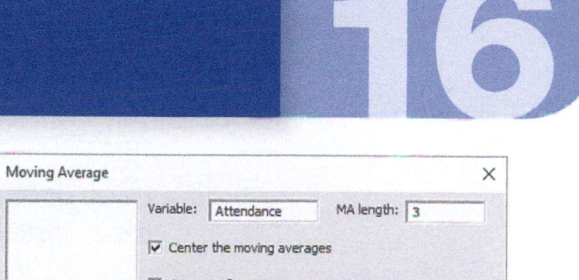

5. In the Moving Average: Storage dialog box (not shown), check **Moving Averages** and then click **OK**.
6. Back in the Moving Average dialog box, click **Graphs**.
7. In the Moving Average: Graphs dialog box (not shown), click **Plot smoothed vs. actual**, clear all check boxes, and then click **OK**.
8. Back in the Moving Average dialog box, click **Results**.

9. In the Moving Average: Results dialog box (not shown), click **Summary table and results table** and then click **OK**.

10. Back in the Moving Average dialog box, click **OK**.

11. Enter **MA 3-Yr** as the name for **column C3** (replacing AVER1).

To add the five-year moving averages, repeat steps 1 through 10, entering **5** in the **MA length** box in step 2. Enter **MA 5-Yr** as the name for **column C4** (replacing AVER1).

As a by-product of steps 1 through 11, Minitab creates a time-series plot of the moving average. After repeating those steps a second time, Minitab will have created two time-series plots that taken together are similar to Figure 16.6 (left).

Exponential Smoothing

Use **Single Exp Smoothing**.

For example, to compute the Figure 16.7 exponential smoothed values shown on page 635, open to the **Movie Attendance worksheet**. Select **Stat → Time Series → Single Exp Smoothing**. In the Single Exponential Smoothing dialog box (shown below):

1. Double-click **C2 Attendance** in the variables list to add **Attendance** to the **Variable** box.

2. Click **Use** and enter **0.50** in its box (for a W value of 0.50).

3. Click **Options**.

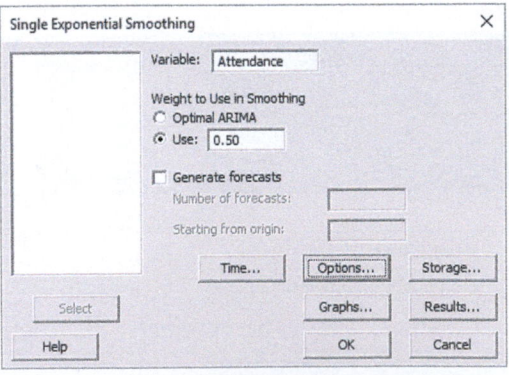

4. In the Single Exponential Smoothing: Options dialog box (not shown), enter **1** in the **Use average of first K observations K =** box and then click **OK**.

5. Back in the original dialog box, click **Storage**.

6. In the Single Exponential Smoothing: Storage dialog box (not shown), check **Smoothed data** and then click **OK**.

7. Back in the original dialog box, click **Graphs**.

8. In the Moving Average: Graphs dialog box (not shown), click **Plot smoothed vs. actual** and clear all check boxes, and then click **OK**.

9. Back in the original dialog box, click **Results**.

10. In the Single Exponential Smoothing: Results dialog box (not shown), click **Summary table and results table** and then click **OK**.

11. Back in the original dialog box, click **OK**.

12. Enter **ES(W=0.50)** as the name for **column C3** (replacing SMOO1).

For a W value of 0.25, repeat steps 1 through 11, entering **0.25** in step 2. Then enter **ES(W=0.25)** as the name for **column C4** (replacing SMOO1).

MG16.3 LEAST-SQUARES TREND FITTING and FORECASTING

The Linear Trend Model

Modify the Section MG13.2 instructions on page 534.

Enter the name of the column that contains the coded variable in the **Continuous predictors** box. To enter many coded values, enter zero in the first cell of a column, select that cell and move the mouse pointer to the lower right corner, and when the mouse pointer changes to a plus sign, drag the mouse down through the column while holding down the **Ctrl key**.

The Quadratic Trend Model

Modify the Section MG15.1 instructions on page 626.

Enter the names of the column that contains the coded variable and the squared coded variable in the **Continuous predictors** box in the multiple regression (Section MG14.1) instructions.

The Exponential Trend Model

Modify the Section MG15.2 instructions on page 627 and the Sections MG13.2 and MG13.5 instructions that begin on page 534.

To create an exponential trend model, first convert the values of the dependent Y variable to log LOGTEN(Y) values using the Section EG15.2 instructions. Then perform a simple linear regression analysis with residual analysis using the LOGTEN(Y) values using the Section MG13.2 instructions and complete the Section MG13.5 instructions.

Model Selection Using First, Second, and Percentage Differences

Use the **Differences worksheet** as a template.

For example, the data table already contains the data and formulas to compute the Figure 16.14 Coca-Cola Company revenues first, second, and percentage differences on page 644. In this data table, the second, third, and fourth columns contain formulas that compute the differences using the Differences function. This function assigns a missing value to cells for which no difference can be computed.

The First Differences column uses the function DIFFERENCES(Revenues, 1) and the Second Differences column uses DIFFERENCES('First Differences', 1). The Percentage Difference column uses the expression DIFFERENCES(Revenues, 1) divided by LAG(Revenues, 1) to divide the first difference by the value in the previous time period. To explore the formulas, right-click a difference column and select **Formula➔Assign Formula to Column** from the shortcut menu to display the Assign Formula dialog box.

For other problems, paste the time-series data into the first two columns A and B, rename those columns, and, if necessary, adjust the smoothing coefficient in column formulas. For problems with fewer than 19 time periods, delete the excess rows.

MG16.4 AUTOREGRESSIVE MODELING for TREND FITTING and FORECASTING

Creating Lagged Predictor Variables

Use **Lag** to create lagged predictor variables for autoregressive models.

For example, to create the Figure 16.16 lagged variables worksheet on page 651, open to the **Coca-Cola worksheet**. Select **Stat➔Time Series➔Lag**. In the Lag dialog box (shown below):

1. Double-click **C2 Revenues** in the variables list to add **Revenues** to the **Series** box.
2. Enter **C3** in the **Store lags in** box and press **Tab**.
3. Enter **1** in the **Lag** box (for a one-period lag).
4. Click **OK**.

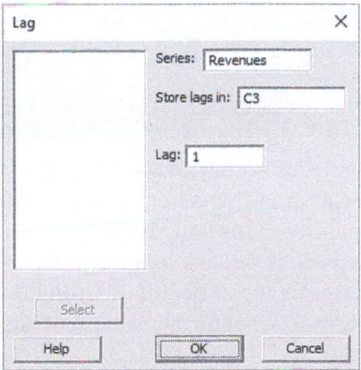

5. In the worksheet, enter **Lag1** as the name for **column C3**.
6. Again select **Stat➔Time Series➔Lag**. In the Lag dialog box, enter **C4** in the **Store lags in** box, press **Tab**, and enter **2** in the **Lag** box (for a 2-period lag). Click **OK**.
7. Enter **Lag2** as the name for **column C4**.
8. Reselect **Stat➔Time Series➔Lag**. In the Lag dialog box, enter **C5** in the **Store lags in** box, press **Tab**, and enter **3** in the **Lag** box (for a 3-period lag). Click **OK**.
9. Enter **Lag3** as the name for **column C5**.

Autoregressive Modeling

Modify the Section MG14.1 "Interpreting the Regression Coefficients" instructions on page 588 to create a third-order or second-order autoregressive model. Add the names of the columns containing the first-order, second-order, and third-order lagged predictor variables to the **Continuous predictors** box for the third-order model. Add the names of the columns containing the first-order, and second-order lagged predictor variables to the **Predictors** box for the second-order model.

Modify the Section MG13.2 instructions on page 534 to create a first-order autoregressive model. In step 2, add the name of the column containing the first-order lagged predictor variable to the **Continuous predictors** box.

MG16.5 CHOOSING an APPROPRIATE FORECASTING MODEL

A Comparison of Four Forecasting Methods

To compare the four forecasting models, use residual analysis to examine the models. Use the Section MG13.5 instructions on page 535 to create residual plots for the linear trend model or first-order autoregressive models. Use the Section MG14.1 instructions on page 588 to create residual plots for the quadratic and the exponential trend models.

MG16.6 TIME-SERIES FORECASTING of SEASONAL DATA

Least-Squares Forecasting with Monthly or Quarterly Data

Use **Make Indicator Variables**.

To develop a least-squares regression model for monthly or quarterly data, add columns of dummy variables. For example, to make the quarterly dummy variables for the Table 16.3 Wal-Mart quarterly revenues, open to the **Walmart worksheet** and

1. Select **Calc➔Make Indicator Variables**.
2. In the Make Indicator Variables dialog box (not shown), double-click **C2 Quarter** in the variables list to add **Quarter** to the **Indicator variables for** box and then click **OK**.

Minitab inserts four new columns name Quarter_1, Quarter_2, Quarter_3, and Quarter_4. Delete the Quarter_4 column as this column is unnecessary. (A fourth quarter is represented when the first three dummy variables are all zero.)

Using this procedure, Minitab will always create an unnecessary column that should be deleted for analysis. Note that for alphabetic values, such as the names of months, the Minitab procedure is case-sensitive. The values Jan and JAN in the same column will result in two dummy variables.

17

Business Analytics

OBJECTIVES

- Understand fundamental business analytics concepts
- Identify the the major business analytics categories
- Gain experience with selected analytics methods
- Understand the variety of predictive analytics methods

▼USING **STATISTICS**
Back to Arlingtons for the Future

Through sales experiments that the Using Statistics scenarios for Chapters 10 and 11 describe, Arlingtons discovered how the location of items in a store can affect the in-store sales. While making store placement decisions and charging varying store placement fees based on those experiments did increase revenues, long-term retailing trends toward online commerce continued to hurt the overall financial health of Arlingtons. When a private equity firm made an unsolicited bid for Arlingtons, senior management and the board of directors at Arlingtons reluctantly agreed to a buyout.

The new owners believe that with advanced data analysis, they can grow the business, especially in the online marketplace where Arlingtons has been a weak competitor. Just as multiple regression allows consideration of several independent variables, they believe that methods associated with *business analytics* will allow them to analyze many more relevant variables. For example, the new owners look to track customer buying habits and to be able to answer questions such as "Who were those customers that were most likely to buy the VLABGo players from the special front of store sales location?" and "What else could one expect those customers to buy at Arlingtons?" The new owners also believe that they will be able to start getting answers to more fundamental questions such as "Should we even be selling mobile electronics?" and "Should we invest more in online sales and less in brick-and-mortar (physical) stores?"

To introduce business analytics to existing store managers, the new owners have hired you to prepare notes for a management seminar that would introduce business analytics to these managers, each of whom already have a knowledge of introductory business statistics. What do you say to such a group?

Business statistics first gained widespread usage in an age of manual filing systems and limited computerization. The first wave of business computers made practical the calculations of advanced inferential methods that previous chapters discuss but data handling and storage was often limited or clumsy or both. As information technology and management matured, the application of business statistics grew within organizations and was applied to larger and larger sets of data. In today's world, where even mobile devices surpass the functionality of supercomputers that existed 30 years ago, much more can be done to support fact-based decision making.

This "much more" is the practical realization of techniques long imagined but that could not be implemented due to the limitations of information technology in the past. This much more combines statistics, information systems, and management science. This much more often uses well-known methods but extends those methods into more functional areas or provides the means to analyze large volumes of data. This much more is business analytics that Section FTF.2 on page 4 first defines.

Section FTF.2 describes business analytics as "the changing face of statistics," but these sets of techniques could also be called "the changing face of business." Just as business students today typically take at least one course in business statistics, business students of tomorrow (and some even today) will be taking at least one course in business analytics. This chapter serves as an introduction and bridge to that future.

17.1 Business Analytics Categories

Business analytics methods help management decision makers answer what has happened or has been happening in the business, what could happen in the business, or what should happen based on a recommended course of action. These three kinds of management questions define the three main categories of business analytics (see Table 17.1).

TABLE 17.1

Three Types of Business Analytics and the Questions They Answer

Question	Business analytics category
What has happened or has been happening?	*Descriptive analytics*
What could happen?	*Predictive analytics*
What should happen?	*Prescriptive analytics*

Descriptive analytics answer "What has happened or has been happening?" questions. **Descriptive analytics** methods summarize historical data to identify patterns to the data that might be worthy of investigation or provide decision makers with new insights about business operations. Many methods contain the ability for decision makers to *drill down*, or reveal, the details of data that were summarized and are related to or extensions of methods that Chapter 2 discusses.

Predictive analytics answer "What could happen?" questions. Several subtypes of this category exist. **Prediction methods** use historical data to predict a numerical target such as the likelihood of a business event occurring such as a specific type of customer behavior. **Classification methods** assign items in a collection to target categories or classes. **Clustering methods** find groupings in data being analyzed. **Association methods** find items that tend to occur together or specify the rules that explain such co-occurrences.

Prescriptive analytics answer "What should happen?" questions. Prescriptive methods seek to optimize the performance of a business and offer decision making recommendations for how to respond to and manage business circumstances in the future. These methods evaluate models that predictive analytics methods build to determine new ways to operate a business while balancing constraints and considering business objectives. Prescriptive methods blur the lines between operations research/management science and business analytics and "can take processes that were once expensive, arduous, and difficult, and complete them in a cost-effective and effortless manner." (see reference 3)

Table 17.2 summarizes the examples of descriptive and predictive analytics that Sections 17.2 through 17.6 present.

TABLE 17.2

Chapter 17 Business Analytics Examples

Method	Analytics Category	Section
Dashboards	Descriptive	17.2
Dynamic bubble chart	Descriptive	17.2
Regression tree	Prediction	17.3
Classification tree	Classification	17.4
k-means clustering	Clustering	17.5
Multiple correspondence analysis	Association	17.6
Multidimensional scaling	Association	17.6

Inferential Statistics and Predictive Analytics

On page 5, the opening chapter defines inferential statistics as "methods that use data collected from a small group to reach conclusions about a larger group." Chapter 13 introduces regression methods that seek to *predict* values of a dependent Y variable from one or more independent X variables as an example of inferential statistics. Section 14.7 discusses logistic regression stating that this method uses the *odds ratio* to represent *the probability of an event of interest*. That predicted probability serves to classify items. Therefore, logistic regression can be properly called a classification method in addition to being considered an example of regression.

In fact, predictive analytics often relies on inferential methods such as regression, methods that are sometimes "disguised" under other names, as the foundation and starting point for analysis. Decision makers using predictive analytics need to first understand how inferential methods help separate out real patterns from chance occurrences and help deal with uncertainty in results as well as assumptions and other requirements of such methods. Using business analytics without a knowledge of inferential statistics can be ruinous for a decision maker.

studentTIP

With good reason, this chapter appears as Chapter 17, after the book discusses inferential statistics and regression analysis. Not forgetting about those intervening pages is the first lesson of business analytics that you should remember.

Supervised and Unsupervised Methods

Predictive and prescriptive analytics differs from inferential statistics in that predictive analytics methods can be either supervised or unsupervised. **Supervised methods** begin with explicit facts that the methods use to understand relationships among variables and build models. These facts **train** the method, help the method develop the model. All inferential statistics methods that other chapters discuss are supervised methods because all those methods use data sets that are the basis of creating the inferential model. For example, the file `CardStudy` supplies historical data that contains how much a credit card holder charged in the past year, whether the cardholder ordered additional cards, and whether the cardholder upgraded to a premium card, a *known result* for the values of the other two variables, for the supervised method logistic regression.

The explicit facts used for training are more formally known as the **training data** or "labeled data." Using training data creates the possibility of *overfitting* a model. Regression chapters in the book discuss how all regression models, such as the simple linear model that Equation (13.1) defines or the multiple regression model that Equation (14.1) defines, contain a random error term ε_i. **Overfitting** in a supervised model occurs when the model begins to describe the random error found in the training data. Overfitting adds unnecessary terms to the model and violates the principle of parsimony. And because overfitting reflects *random* error, overfitting will produce a model that may work poorly for other data, which does not contain the same random error.

Several techniques guard against overfitting. In one technique, called **cross-validation**, the original data is first divided into training and test subsets. The model gets trained with the former and evaluated ("tested") with the latter. Then the training and test subsets are rearranged in a systematic way and another model produced. This rearrangement and model production continues until all data has had equal chances to be part of the training and test subsets. Then the evaluations are compared and a best model is chosen.

In contrast, **unsupervised methods** build models without training data and, in the general case, work without a business decision maker establishing a specific goal. Overfitting can occur in models that unsupervised methods create, but arises through a different means. If the decision maker starts with too many variables, unsupervised methods will start to produce models that too much reflect the random error of those variables. This means that choosing variables for the model, a task sometimes called *feature selection*, becomes a critical task for a decision maker. Unsupervised methods are typically run repeatedly but for a different reason: There is no guarantee that an unsupervised method will produce a model that will be useful for a decision maker. "Useful" means a model that can be mapped to business processes and decision making. Note that usefulness of supervised models is never in doubt *if* a decision maker has properly applied a problem-solving framework such as DCOVA and created an explicit target or goal aligned with the decision maker's needs.

Some predicative analytics methods can act as either supervised or unsupervised methods, depending on how a decision maker uses those methods. For example, the algorithms that clustering or association methods use are intrinsically unsupervised, but a decision maker that applies constraints on the method or supplies the method with example data is using the method in a supervised way, or, at least, in a *semi*-supervised way. Confusion arises because computer and data scientists may use the terms supervised and unsupervised to refer to algorithmic attributes of a model, while a business decision maker may use the terms to describe how a method is being applied.

CONSIDER THIS

What's My Major if I Want to be a Data Miner?

One often hears the term *data mining* when people discuss business analytics. **Data mining** is the process of extracting useful information from the data resources of a business, analogous to how "real" mining extracts natural resources from the earth. Data analysis software and service providers have defined and redefined the term over the past decade to the point that no one clear definition exists. The most common usage of data mining means the application of predictive analytics to big data. A software company marketing a suite of data mining tools is most likely marketing applications that perform the function of one or more of the predictive analytics subtypes that Section 17.1 identifies.

Applying predictive analytics to big data begins with sifting through a greater number of variables than the inferential statistics methods that other chapters discuss. That sifting is typically done on a semiautomated process that uses regression techniques to learn more about collections of variables. Understanding possible regression pitfalls (see Sections 13.9 and 15.5) becomes important in data mining as the chance of encountering such a pitfall increases. And because dumping every variable into the mining can be impractical as well as unwise because of resulting problems such as overfitting, choosing variables becomes critical. This choosing may include data preprocessing tasks that Chapter 1 discusses as well as other type of data access and manipulation that an information systems course might review.

Therefore, to be a data miner, you need a broad base of business skills, as one would get majoring in any business subject. Most critically, you need to know how to define problems and requirements using a problem-solving framework such as the DCOVA model and have an awareness for basic concepts of statistics, goals of this book. You might supplement your knowledge with a course that builds on the introduction to business analytics that this chapter provides. But, you do not need to major in data mining to be a data miner, just as you do not need to major in statistics to apply statistical methods to fact-based decision making.

If you are or plan to be a graduate student, consider a concentration in business analytics that more closely examines the application of data mining to a functional area. Whatever choices you make, the points made in Section FTF.1 about using a framework and understanding that analytical skills are more important than arithmetic (and other mathematical) skills will always hold. Ironically, as data mining/business analytics software gets more capable and gains the ability to analyze more and more data in ever increasing sophisticated ways, the points that Section FTF.1 emphasizes will become increasing important.

17.2 Descriptive Analytics

Chapters 2 and 3 discuss descriptive methods that organize and visualize previously collected data. What if current data could be organized and visualized as it gets collected? That would change descriptive methods from being summaries of the status of a business at some point in the past into a tool that could be used for day-to-day, if not minute-by-minute, business monitoring. Giving decision makers this ability is one of the goals of descriptive analytics.

Descriptive analytics provide the means to monitor business activities in *near real time*, very quickly after a transaction or other business event has occurred. Being able to do this monitoring can be useful for a business that handles perishable inventory. As the First Things First Chapter Using Statistics scenario notes, empty seats on an airplane or in a concert hall or theater cannot be sold after a certain time. Descriptive analytics allows for a continuously updated display of the inventory, informing late-to-buy customers of the current availability of seats as well as visualizing patterns of sold and unsold seats for managers.

Descriptive analytics can help manage sets of interrelated flows of people or objects as those flows occur. For example, managers of large sports complexes use descriptive analytics to monitor the flow of cars in parking facilities, the flow of arriving patrons into the stadium, as well as the flow of patrons inside the stadium. Summaries generated by descriptive methods can highlight trends as they occur, such as points of growing congestion. By being provided with such information in a timely manner, stadium managers can redirect personnel to trouble spots in the complex and redirect patrons to entrances or facilities that are underused.

Dashboards

Dashboards are comprehensive summary displays that enable decision makers to monitor a business or business activity. Dashboards present the most important pieces of information, typically, in a visual format that allows decision makers to quickly perceive the overall status of an activity. Dashboards present these key indicators in a way that provides drill-down abilities that can reveal progressive levels of detail interactively.

Dashboards can be of any size, from a single desktop computer display, to wall-mounted displays or even larger, such as the nearly 800-square-foot NASDAQ MarketSite Video Wall at Times Square which can be configured as a NASDAQ stock market dashboard that provides current stock market trends for passersby and viewers of financial programming (see reference 10).

Figure 17.1 presents a Microsoft Power BI dashboard that the new managers at Arlingtons might use to monitor national sales. The dashboard uses word tiles and clickable tabular summaries to present sales summaries at different levels of detail: by store category and then by the

FIGURE 17.1

National sales dashboard for the Arlingtons retail chain

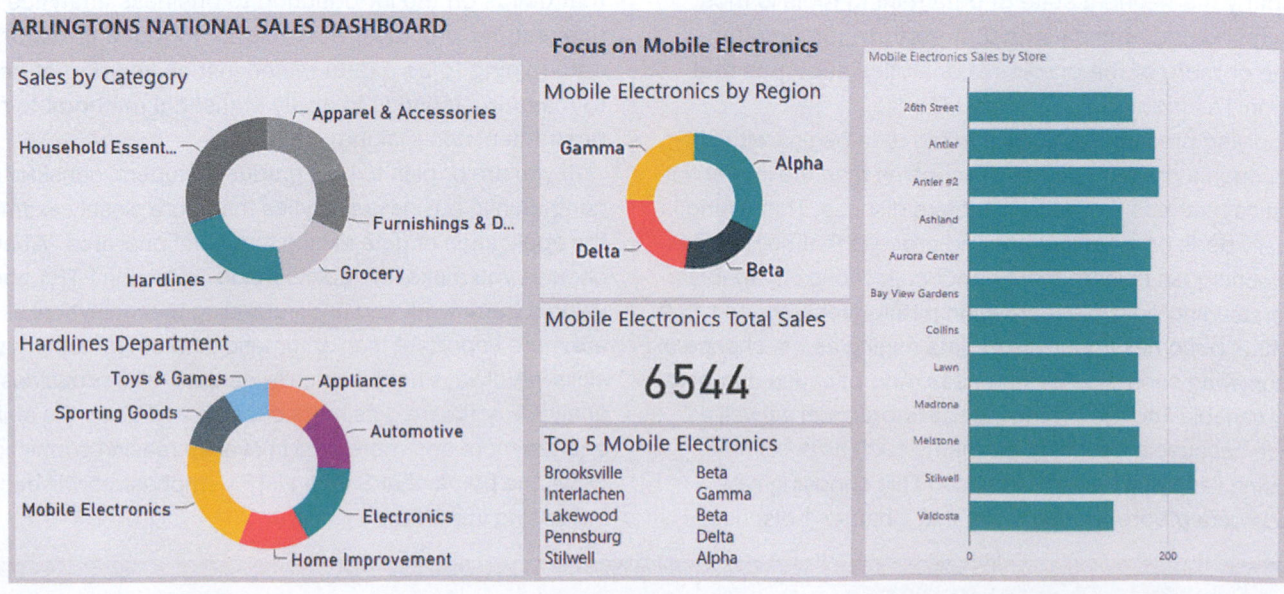

subcategories of the hardlines department that include mobile electronics sales, the subject of Chapter 10 and 11 sales experiments. In Figure 17.1, managers have decided to focus on mobile electronics sales and are currently viewing mobile electronics sales from one of the four national sales regions, while monitoring total mobile electronics sales nationwide (6544). By viewing a dashboard, the new owners of Arlingtons have a clearer and more immediate picture of current sales throughout the Arlingtons chain. That may help them better react to changes as they seek to manage the retailer to better success.

Figure 17.1 illustrates that dashboards can visually present drilled down data and act as complements to the data exploration techniques that organize and visualize a mix of variables that Sections 2.6 and 2.7 summarize. While Figure 17.1 contains simple visual summaries, visualizations that Section 2.7 describe, such as treemaps and colored scatter plots can also appear in dashboards. For dashboards designed for individual users, multidimensional contingency tables that permit drill-down (see Section 2.6) are also found.

Data Dimensionality and Descriptive Analytics

The newer types of visualizations associated with descriptive analytics typically have a higher **data dimensionality**, the ability to visualize a greater number of variables. This higher dimensionality overcomes the limits of standard business display technologies, such as screens and paper, that are two-dimensional surfaces. Although the Figure 14.1 3D scatterplots on page 538 (or the Figure 17.9 multidimensional scaling plots) uses perspective to represent a third data dimension inside a cube, such plots often require manipulation of the perspective and can be hard to interpret if many values are visualized. Better are visualizations that use color, size, or motion to represent multiple, additional dimensions.

Figure 17.9 (left) adds color to represent a third dimension that represents the Market Cap categorical variable in a colored scatter plot of Expense Ratio versus 3YrReturn for the sample of 306 growth retirement funds. Figure 17.2 (right) adds size to represent a fourth data dimension for Risk Level. Funds with low risk appear as the largest filled circles, funds with high risk appear as dots, and funds with average risk appear as smaller-sized filled circles. A client of The Choice *Is* Yours investment service (see Chapters 2 and 3) who is considering low-risk growth funds might find the second scatter plot useful for understanding the interplay between Expense Ratio and 3YrReturn in the growth funds sample.

Figure 17.2 (right) is an example of a bubble chart that uses filled-in circles called bubbles, the color and size (diameter) of which add additional data dimensions. Typically, color represents a categorical variable and size represents a numerical variable, but either of these attributes can be used differently, as Figure 17.2 illustrates. **Dynamic bubble charts**, also known as motion charts, extend bubble charts by using motion to represent one additional data dimension,

FIGURE 17.2
Colored scatter plots for the sample of 306 growth retirement funds:
Left: Expense Ratio, 3YrReturn, and Market Cap. Right: Expense Ratio, 3YrReturn, Market Cap, and Risk Level (size).

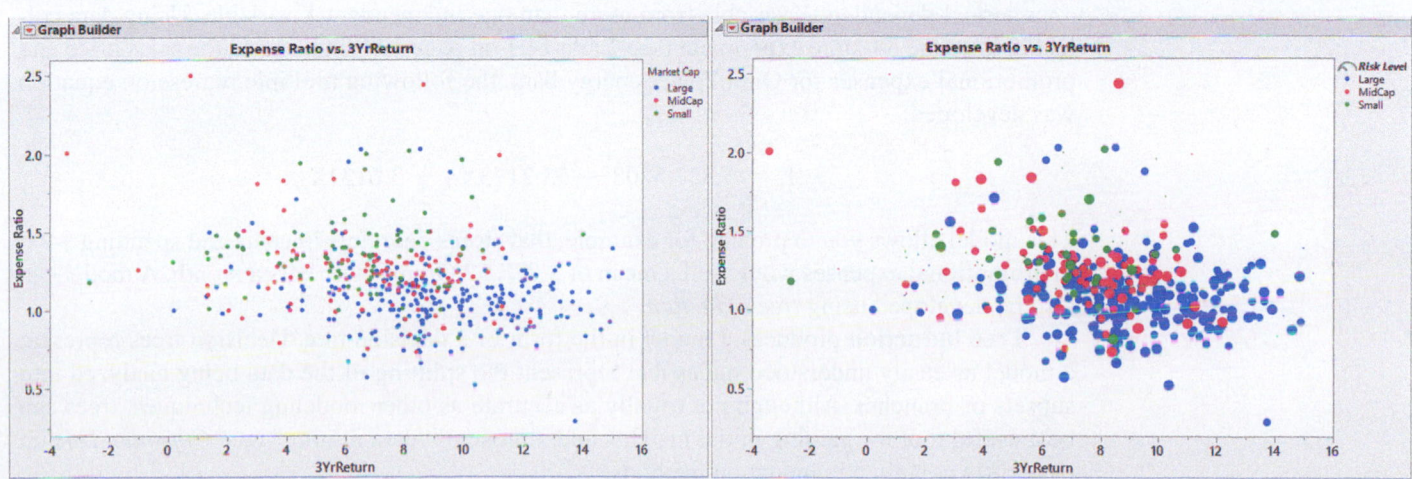

typically time. These charts take the form as animations in which bubbles change over time. The changing position of bubbles over time often reveal complex trends and interactions better than an equivalent time-series plot of the data.

Figure 17.3 shows a time-lapse image from a dynamic bubble chart animation that visualizes domestic movie revenues, by the MPAA ratings G, PG, PG-13, and R, for the years 2002 through 2016. The time-lapse image shows only the animation for the odd years in this time series. The animation reveals that as revenues of G-rated movies increase in a year, those revenues tend to depress the revenues of PG-rated movies, suggesting some relationship. The animation also shows how revenues for G-rated movies shrink over time.

FIGURE 17.3

Time-lapse of dynamic bubble chart for domestic movie revenues by MPPA rating, for the years 2002 through 2016

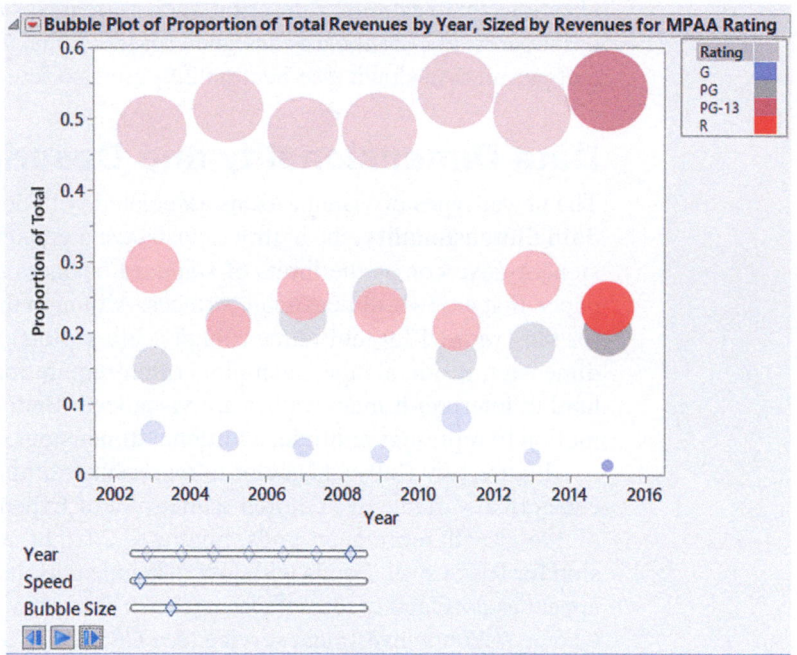

View the entire animation in any current browser by using the **DynamicBubbleChart.htm** *file. This file does not require the use of JMP. In some browsers, the interactive functionality of the file may be limited.*

For the new owners of Arlingtons, a dynamic bubble chart might reveal how store, region, merchandise department, or merchandise category sales have changed over time. Such a chart might be used as part of an executive summary that introduces changes in merchandising or geographical focus that the new owners may decide to undertake as well as serve as the starting point for deciding to make such changes.

17.3 Predictive Analytics for Prediction

Chapter 14 discusses multiple regression methods that seek to *predict*, or estimate, values of a numerical dependent Y variable from more than one independent X variable. Using data collected from the 34-store experiment (see Table 14.1 on page 537) that varied the sales price and promotional expenses for OmniPower energy bars, the following multiple regression equation was developed:

$$\hat{Y}_i = 5{,}837.5208 - 53.2173X_{1i} + 3.6131X_{2i}$$

This model allows you to predict, for example, that stores charging 79 cents and spending $400 in promotional expenses would sell a mean of 3,078.57 OmniPower bars a month. A model can also be developed using *tree induction*.

Tree induction produces a model in the form of a decision tree. Decision trees represent a model as easily understood nodes that represent the splitting of the data being analyzed into subsets or branches. Although not usually as accurate as other modeling techniques, trees can be a useful tool for gaining initial insights and almost all "data mining" (see *Consider This* on page 681) contain tree induction methods.

Splitting occurs based on specific values or ranges of a variable and at every node, beginning with the **root node**, the node that represents all the data. At each node, the method examines all possible splits and selects the best partition. Every split creates two new nodes for which a partitioning evaluation is done. Objective criteria determine which split is best at any node or whether no more splits can be done. Criteria useful for splitting decisions include the Akaike information criterion, AIC, its variant that corrects for sample size, AIC_c, and the LogWorth statistic.

The **Akaike information criterion** measures the relative quality of a model. Equations (17.1a) and (17.1b) define the two variants. Generally, the smaller the value of the AIC is, the better the model.

AKAIKE INFORMATION CRITERION (AIC)

$$AIC = 2k - 2\ln(L) \tag{17.1a}$$

AKAIKE INFORMATION CRITERION CORRECTED (AIC_C)

$$AIC_c = AIC + \frac{2k(k + 1)}{n - k - 1} \tag{17.1b}$$

where

$k =$ the number of parameters in the model

$L =$ is the maximum value of the likelihood function for the model

$n =$ sample size

The **LogWorth statistic** provides a basis for splitting a node. Generally, a value greater than 2 means that a split should be made. Equation (17.2) defines the Logworth statistic.

LOGWORTH STATISTIC

$$LogWorth = -\log(p\text{-value}) \tag{17.2}$$

where the adjusted p-value is based on the number of ways that splits can occur.

Independent of objective criteria, trees formed by tree induction methods may have branches that represent subsets that a decision maker will not find useful for the business problem or goal under study. In such cases, a decision maker can **prune** the tree to eliminate unwanted branches.

For the OmniPower sales experience, regression tree analysis could be used to predict sales. A **regression tree** is a tree induction method that predicts a numerical dependent Y variable, in this example sales. Figure 17.4 presents the JMP regression tree analysis for predicting the sales of OmniPower bars.

FIGURE 17.4

Regression tree results for predicting the sales of OmniPower bars

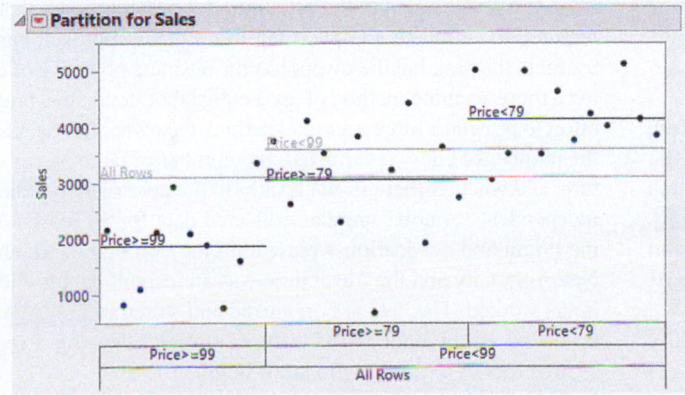

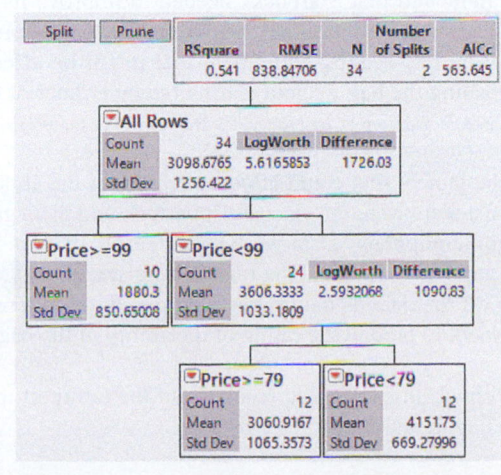

The tree model contains two splits and an AIC_c value of 563.65. At the root node, the data has been split based on whether the value of the Price variable is less than 99 cents or not. The less-than-99-cents subset of 24 stores is further split into two groups: Price less than 79 cents or not, each containing 12 stores. Note the LogWorth statistic for the first split is 5.62 and for the second split is 2.59.

The tree results also report the mean sales for each subset. Recall from Table 14.1 that the sample contains only three values for price: 59, 79, and 99 cents. At the first split, the less-than-99-cents subset of 24 stores has mean sales of about $3,606, nearly double the mean sales of the stores that sold the bars at or more than 99 cents, the 99-cent subset. At the second split, the less-than-79-cents subset, the 59-cent subset, had mean sales of about $4,152, nearly $1,500 more than the subset of stores that sold the bars for at least 79 cents but less than 99 cents, the 79-cent subset.

OmniFoods managers would note that the regression tree method did not base any split on the Promotional Expenses variable and that lower prices increase sales of OmniPower bars. They might decide to conduct additional sales experiments that contain prices greater than 59 cents but less than 79 cents to see the effects of such prices on sales.

As a supervised method, regression tree analysis is subject to overfitting that, for the sake of simplicity, this example overlooks. However, OmniFoods managers would need to make sure a technique, such as cross-validation that Section 17.1 explains, was used as part of the analysis.

PROBLEMS FOR SECTION 17.3

17.1 The business problem facing a consumer products company is to measure the effectiveness of different types of advertising media in the promotion of its products. Specifically, the company is interested in the effectiveness of radio advertising and newspaper advertising (including the cost of discount coupons). During a one-month test period, data were collected from a sample of 22 cities with approximately equal populations. Each city is allocated a specific expenditure level for radio advertising and for newspaper advertising. The sales of the product (in thousands of dollars) and also the levels of media expenditure (in thousands of dollars) during the test month are recorded and stored in Advertise .
a. Using all the data as the training sample, develop a regression tree model to predict the sales of the product.
b. What conclusions can you reach about the sales of the product?

17.2 Starbucks Coffee Co. uses a data-based approach for improving the quality and customer satisfaction of its products. When survey data indicated that Starbucks needed to improve its package sealing process, an experiment was conducted to determine the factors in the bag-sealing equipment that might be affecting the ease of opening the bag without tearing the inner liner of the bag.
Source: Data extracted from L. Johnson and S. Burrows, "For Starbucks, It's in the Bag," *Quality Progress*, March 2011, pp. 17–23.
Among the factors that could affect the rating of the ability of the bag to resist tears were the viscosity, pressure, and plate gap on the bag-sealing equipment. Data were collected on 19 bags in which the plate gap was varied and the results were stored in Starbucks .
a. Using all the data as the training sample, develop a regression tree model to predict the rating of the ability of the bag to resist tears.
b. What conclusions can you reach about the rating of the ability of the bag to resist tears?

17.3 In mining engineering, holes are often drilled through rock using drill bits. As a drill hole gets deeper, additional rods are added to the drill bit to enable additional drilling to take place. It is expected that drilling time increases with depth. This increased drilling time could be caused by several factors, including the mass of the drill rods that are strung together. The business problem relates to whether drilling is faster using dry drilling holes or wet drilling holes. Using dry drilling holes involves forcing compressed air down the drill rods to flush the cuttings and drive the hammer. Using wet drilling holes involves forcing water rather than air down the hole. Data have been collected from a sample of 50 drill holes that contains measurements of the time to drill each additional 5 feet (in minutes), the depth (in feet), and whether the hole was a dry drilling hole or a wet drilling hole. The data are organized and stored in Drill .
a. Using half the data as the training sample and the other half of the data as the test sample, develop a regression tree model to predict the drilling time.
b. What conclusions can you reach about the drilling time?

17.4 The owner of a moving company typically has his most experienced manager predict the total number of labor hours that will be required to complete an upcoming move. This approach has proved useful in the past, but the owner has the business objective of developing a more accurate method of predicting labor hours. In a preliminary effort to provide a more accurate method, the owner has decided to use the number of cubic feet moved, the number of large pieces of furniture, and whether there is an elevator in the apartment building as the independent variables and has collected data for 36 moves in which the origin and destination were within the borough of Manhattan in New York City and the travel time was an insignificant portion of the hours worked. The data are organized and stored in Moving .
a. Using all the data as the training sample, develop a regression tree model to predict the labor hours.
b. What conclusions can you reach about the labor hours?

17.4 Predictive Analytics for Classification

While a regression tree predicts a numerical dependent Y variable, a **classification tree** predicts a *categorical* dependent Y variable. Although a method that predicts something sounds like a *prediction* method, classification trees use rules and relationships to classify items into one of several groups, making this tree induction method useful for classification.

In the Section 14.7 credit card study, managers sought to ask, "What is the probability that a cardholder would upgrade to a premium card?" based on the cardholder's prior year credit card purchases and whether the cardholder had ordered additional cards for other authorized users. Classification tree analysis could ask a different type of question: "What type (subset) of credit card customers are likely to upgrade?" Figure 17.5 presents the JMP classification tree useful for such a classification task. For classification trees, JMP computes a LogWorth statistic that uses the value in conjunction with the likelihood ratio chi-square statistic, G^2, beyond the scope of this book to explain, to determine splits.

FIGURE 17.5

JMP classification tree results for the credit card upgrade study

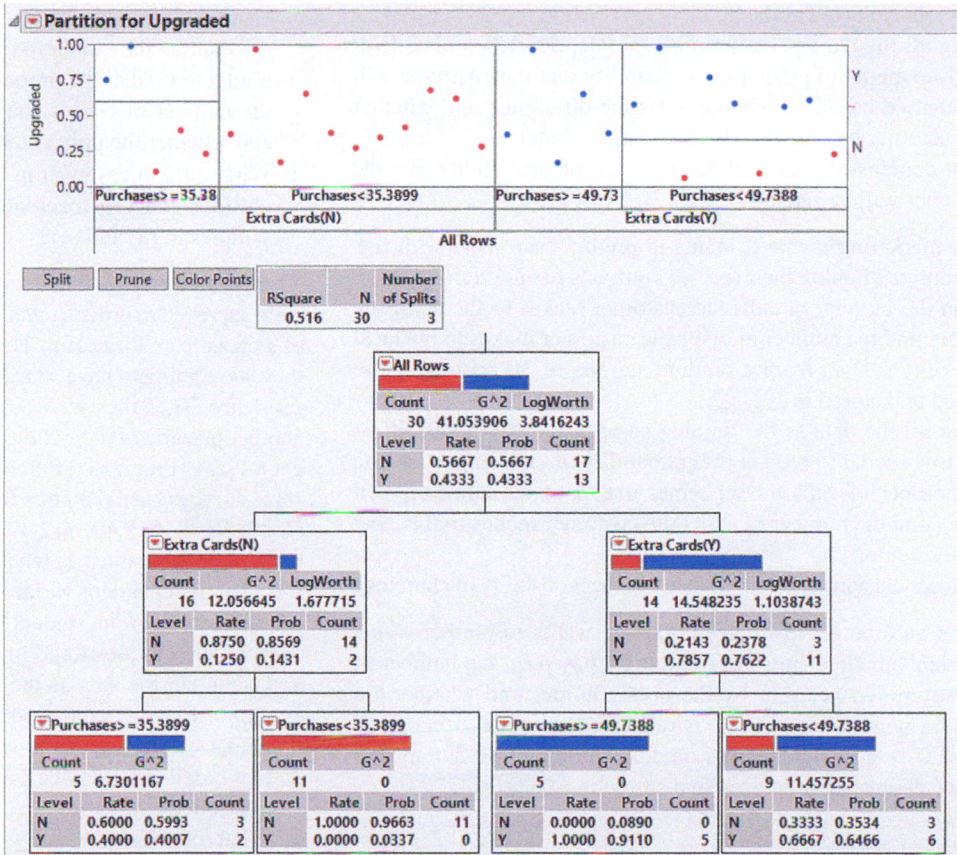

The tree model splits the root node and then splits each branch once. At the root node, the data has been split based on whether the cardholder ordered additional cards, represented by the Extra Cards variable with the categories Y and N. In each branch, splits have been made on specific values of the Purchases variable. Rate values in node boxes report the proportion of responses in the sample in a node.

The tree reveals that cardholders who have ordered additional cards and have prior year charged purchases that total $49,738.80 or more are most likely to upgrade to a premium card, while those with no additional cards and who have prior year charges of less than $35,389.90 are least likely to upgrade. These observations could lead to better targeting of campaigns that offer a premium card or similar services. Managers at the financial institution can focus on current regular cardholders or future cardholders that charged tens of thousands of dollars or who have ordered additional cards or both in future offers for upgrading to a premium card. In this way, the classification tree permits managers to classify their cardholders into one of two groups: more likely to upgrade and less likely to upgrade.

As a supervised method, classification tree analysis is subject to overfitting that, for the sake of simplicity, this example overlooks. However, managers overseeing this experiment would need to make sure that a technique, such as cross-validation that Section 17.1 explains, was used as part of the analysis.

PROBLEMS FOR SECTION 17.4

17.5 A hotel has designed a new system for room service delivery of breakfast that allows the customer to select a specific delivery time. The file `Satisfaction` contains the difference between the actual and requested delivery times (a negative time means that the breakfast was delivered before the requested time) recorded for 30 deliveries on a particular day along with whether the customer had previously stayed at the hotel.

a. Using all the data as the training sample, develop a classification tree model to predict the probability that the customer will be satisfied based on the delivery time difference and whether the customer had previously stayed at the hotel.

b. What conclusions can you reach about the probability that the customer will be satisfied?

17.6 A marketing manager wants to predict customers with risk of churning (switching their service contracts to another company) based on the number of calls the customer makes to the company call center and the number of visits the customer makes to the local service center. Data from a random sample of 30 customers are organized and stored in `Churn`.

a. Using all the data as the training sample, develop a classification tree model to predict the probability of churning, based on the number of calls the customer makes to the company call center and the number of visits the customer makes to the local service center.

b. What conclusions can you reach about the probability of churning?

17.7 An automotive insurance company wants to predict which filed stolen vehicle claims are fraudulent, based on the number of claims submitted per year by the policy holder and whether the policy is a new policy, that is, is one year old or less (coded as 1 = yes, 0 = no). Data from a random sample of 98 automotive insurance claims are organized and stored in `InsuranceFraud`.

Source: Data extracted from Gelp et al., "A Comparative Analysis of Decision Trees vis-à-vis Other Computational Data Mining Techniques in Automotive Insurance Fraud Detection," *Journal of Data Science*, 10 (2012), pp. 537–561.

a. Using all the data as the training sample, develop a classification tree model to predict the probability of a fraudulent claim, based on the number of claims submitted per year by the policy holder and whether the policy is new.

b. What conclusions can you reach about the probability of a fraudulent claim?

c. Using half the data as the training sample and the other half of the data as the validation sample, develop a classification tree model to predict the probability of a fraudulent claim, based on the number of claims submitted per year by the policy holder and whether the policy is new.

d. What differences exist in the results of (a) and (c)? What conclusions can you reach about the models fit from the training samples in (a) and (c)?

17.8 Undergraduate students at Miami University in Oxford, Ohio, were surveyed in order to evaluate the effect of price on the purchase of a pizza from Pizza Hut. The students were asked to suppose that they were going to have a large two-topping pizza delivered to their residence. Then they were asked to select from either Pizza Hut or another pizzeria of their choice. The price they would have to pay to get a Pizza Hut pizza differed from survey to survey. For example, some surveys used the price $11.49. Other prices investigated were $8.49, $9.49, $10.49, $12.49, $13.49, and $14.49. The dependent variable for this study is whether or not a student will select Pizza Hut. The independent variables are the price of a Pizza Hut pizza and the gender of the student (1 = male, 0 = female). The results of these surveys are stored in `PizzaHut`.

a. Using half the data as the training sample and the other half of the data as the validation sample, develop a classification tree model to predict the probability the student will select Pizza Hut based on the price of a Pizza Hut pizza and the gender of the student.

b. What conclusions can you reach about the probability the student will select Pizza Hut?

17.5 Predictive Analytics for Clustering

Whereas classification takes individual items and assigns the items to one of several groups that have been defined by rules such as "has ordered additional cards" for the credit card study example in the previous section, clustering methods take all items and form several groups based on similarity of individual items. Clustering methods vary based on how they compute similarity and how they form clusters, the groups into which all items are being organized. Some methods such as **k-means clustering** work best with purely numerical variables, while others such as **hierarchical clustering** work equally with a mix of numerical and categorical variables.

A calculated "distance" between items determines similarity. Equation (17.3) defines the **Euclidean distance** that calculates the square root of the sum of the squared differences among items as the distance. Euclidean distance is the most common technique for calculating distance and is often paired with transforming all variables to a common scale to make sure all variable values share a common magnitude.

Various measures of distance between clusters exist including complete linkage, single linkage, average linkage, and Ward's minimum variance method. **Complete linkage** bases the distance between clusters on the maximum distance between objects in one cluster and another cluster. **Single linkage** bases the distance between clusters on the minimum distance between objects in one cluster and another cluster. **Average linkage** bases the distance between clusters on the mean distance between objects in one cluster and another cluster. **Ward's minimum variance method** bases the distance between clusters on the sum of squares over all variables between objects in one cluster and another cluster.

EUCLIDEAN DISTANCE

$$d_{ij} = \sqrt{\sum_{k=1}^{r}(X_{ik} - X_{jk})^2} \tag{17.3}$$

where

d_{ij} = distance between object i and object j

X_{ik} = value of object i in dimension k

X_{jk} = value of object j in dimension k

r = number of data dimensions

In the The Choice *Is* Yours investment service scenarios (Chapters 2 and 3), the business objective was to help prospective clients learn more about a sample of 479 retirement funds. For a client interested in the 306 growth funds in that sample, clustering may find a group of funds that would appeal to that client and the investment service uses *k-means* clustering set to three clusters as an initial exploration of the growth funds. Figure 17.6 shows this clustering. (Minitab generates a different set of clusters than JMP because of differences in the random starting point for clustering and computing distances.)

FIGURE 17.6

JMP and Minitab *k-means* cluster summary and JMP cluster means table for $k=3$ for the sample of growth funds

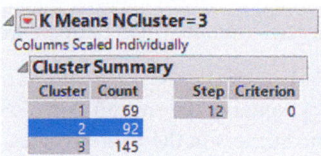

K Means NCluster=3			
Columns Scaled Individually			
Cluster Summary			
Cluster	Count	Step	Criterion
1	69	12	0
2	92		
3	145		

Cluster Means

Cluster	Assets	Turnover Ratio	SD	Sharpe Ratio	Beta	1YrReturn	3YrReturn	5YrReturn	10YrReturn	Expense Ratio
1	390.819565	81.4237681	15.6330435	0.29111594	1.0373913	-8.4985507	4.66666667	7.5526087	6.23521739	1.40217391
2	3761.19467	53.9119565	12.7490217	0.91076087	1.03576087	1.19456522	11.646413	12.4203261	8.92847826	1.02597826
3	783.18131	64.0147586	12.7916552	0.66564138	0.96096552	-0.9565517	8.34689655	10.0764828	7.54062069	1.23924138

K-means Cluster Analysis: Assets, Turnover Ratio, SD, ... Expense Ratio

Method

Number of clusters	3
Standardized variables	Yes

Final Partition

	Number of observations	Within cluster sum of squares	Average distance from centroid	Maximum distance from centroid
Cluster1	39	274.447	2.511	4.360
Cluster2	103	881.396	2.696	7.437
Cluster3	164	797.515	2.073	5.242

The method discovers that cluster #2 has higher means for the Sharpe Ratio, 3YrReturn, 5YrReturn, and 10YrReturn, and the lowest mean Expense Ratio, all important items for the client. Because the size of the cluster found 92 retirement funds, and because the optimal clustering was not sought, the investment service reruns the clustering to examine the range of 3 through 25 clusters.

Figure 17.7 shows parts of the JMP results window for the clustering analysis from 3 through 25 clusters. Using the **CCC statistic**, JMP determines that the optimal clustering in the range of 3 through 25 is 16 clusters. In the $k=16$ clustering, funds in the original cluster #2 for $k=3$ are distributed among 8 clusters (#1–5, 7, 9, and 10). In this new grouping of 16 clusters, the new cluster #2, a group of 25 funds, has the characteristics most sought by the client. The client could start a selection process with this group of funds or explore the real-world commonalities that the funds in the group possess. (Later investigation reveals that the funds in this group tend to be of low or average risk and have assets in the midrange of all growth funds in the sample.)

FIGURE 17.7
Partial cluster comparison table for the *k-means* clustering for $k=3$ through 25 and cluster means table for the *k-means* clustering for $k=16$

Cluster Comparison

Method	NCluster	CCC	Best
K-Means Clustering	3	-4.2479	
K-Means Clustering	16	-0.4033	Optimal CCC
K-Means Clustering	25	-2.452	

Columns Scaled Individually

Cluster Means

Cluster	Assets	Turnover Ratio	SD	Sharpe Ratio	Beta	1YrReturn	3YrReturn	5YrReturn	10YrReturn	Expense Ratio
1	1172.63875	85.00625	15.27375	0.5375	1.08625	-5.705	8.455	9.6875	5.96625	2.02875
2	2048.9812	45.806	12.1948	1.0568	1.0016	3.6316	12.9124	13.6116	9.4036	1.036
3	10516.4685	41.3175	12.642	0.8205	1.016	0.227	10.342	11.6365	8.986	0.946
4	1444.1275	161.436667	12.68	0.87583333	1.00166667	-0.3133333	11.165	12.2591667	9.26	1.06333333
5	1062.20754	77.3950877	12.6936842	0.65491228	1.01210526	-2.752807	7.90736842	9.57192982	7.56052632	1.19754386
6	71.015	249.5	14.005	0.25	0.945	-13.505	3.35	6.91	8.415	1.56
7	934.76037	51.5762963	11.8974074	0.85444444	0.99185185	1.67222222	10.2011111	10.8433333	6.69074074	1.0637037
8	262.701818	54.8372727	15.1254545	0.16245455	1.10272727	-12.029091	2.51272727	5.21272727	4.62818182	1.24818182
9	1277.39821	48.1189744	13.5133333	0.8174359	1.11	-0.975641	11.2779487	11.7620513	8.45076923	1.13051282
10	874.091111	24.7555556	11.3483333	0.87222222	0.85666667	3.80722222	9.66555556	11.4955556	8.2	1.16111111
11	504.648261	66.3947826	14.793913	0.48991304	0.90521739	-0.2778261	7.78391304	10.6595652	8.20043478	1.31130435
12	5.495	137.25	14.975	-0.09	0.945	-16.19	-1.315	1.195	0.965	2.255
13	86.72	262	13.98	0.225	1.02	-7.615	3.21	3.3	2.17	1.475
14	563.403871	65.4387097	14.5206452	0.33064516	0.94774194	-6.3406452	4.83612903	8.21096774	6.78677419	1.30612903
15	325.121111	48.8933333	12.3044444	0.45	0.71888889	-0.64	5.64444444	7.99	7.39888889	1.54666667
16	587.099	62.437	17.241	0.3325	1.117	-8.21	5.7325	8.574	7.15	1.3085

PROBLEMS FOR SECTION 17.5

17.9 Movie companies need to predict the gross receipts of individual movies once the movie has debuted. The following results, stored in 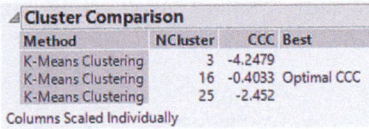, are the first weekend gross, the U.S. gross, and the worldwide gross (in $millions) of the Harry Potter movies.
a. Perform a cluster analysis using the complete linkage method on the Harry Potter movies based on the first weekend gross, the U.S. gross, and the worldwide gross (in $millions).
b. What conclusions can you reach about which Harry Potter movies are most similar?

17.10 The file Cereals contains the calories, carbohydrates, and sugar, in grams, in one serving of seven breakfast cereals.
a. Perform a cluster analysis using the complete linkage method on the cereals based on the calories, carbohydrates, and sugar in grams.
b. What conclusions can you reach about which cereals are most similar?

17.11 The file Protein contains calorie and cholesterol information for popular protein foods (fresh red meats, poultry, and fish) compiled by the U.S. Department of Agriculture.
a. Perform a cluster analysis using the complete linkage method on the protein foods based on the calories and cholesterol, in grams.
b. What conclusions can you reach about which protein foods are most similar?
c. Perform a cluster analysis using Ward's method on the protein foods based on the calories and cholesterol in grams.
d. What conclusions can you reach about which protein foods are most similar?
e. Compare the results of (a) and (c). Are there any differences in your conclusions? Explain

17.12 A Pew Research Center survey found that social networking is popular in many nations around the world. The file GlobalSocialMedia contains the level of social media networking (measured as the percent of individuals polled who use social networking sites) and the GDP at purchasing power parity (PPP) per capita for each of 28 selected countries.

Source: Data extracted from "Global Digital Communication: Texting, Social Networking Popular Worldwide," Pew Research Center, **bit.ly/sNjsmq**.

a. Perform a cluster analysis using the complete linkage method on the nations based on the level of social media networking (measured as the percent of individuals polled who use social networking sites) and the GDP at purchasing power parity (PPP) per capita.
b. What conclusions can you reach about which nations are most similar?

17.13 The file MobileSpeed contains the overall download and upload speeds in mbps for nine carriers in the United States.

Source: Data extracted from "Best Mobile Network 2016," **bit.ly/1KGPrMm**, accessed November 10, 2016.

a. Perform a cluster analysis using the complete linkage method on the U.S. carriers based on the download and upload speeds.
b. What conclusions can you reach about which carriers are most similar?

17.14 Have you wondered how Internet connection speed varies around the globe? The file ConnectionSpeed contains the mean connection speed, the mean peak connection speed, the percent of the time the connection speed is above 4 mbps, and the percent of the time the connection speed is above 10 Mbps for various countries.

Source: Data extracted from **bit.ly/2vPmifV**.

a. Perform a cluster analysis using the complete linkage method on the various countries based on the mean connection speed, the mean peak connection speed, the percent of the time the speed is above 4 Mbps, and the percent of the time the connection speed is above 10 Mbps.
b. What conclusions can you reach about which countries are most similar?

17.6 Predictive Analytics for Association

While clustering uses similarity to form groups, association methods look to use the similarity of items to uncover patterns to the items. Association methods support many of the currently most-discussed applications of business analytics such as text analytics, the extracting of meaning from unstructured text, market-basket analysis, a technique that can identify buying patterns and habits of different categories of consumers, and recommendation services, whether from a streaming media company such as Netflix, an online retailer such as Amazon, or, even, dating resource websites. As with clustering, some association methods, such as **multiple correspondence analysis (MCA)** best analyze categorical variables, while other methods, such as **multidimensional scaling (MDS)** best analyze numerical variables.

Managers in the T.C. Resort Properties scenario (see Chapter 12) might use multiple correspondence analysis (MCA) to provide additional insights into guest satisfaction. MCA examines similarity of items, as reflected in underlying contingency tables of items, to discover associations among categories of multiple categorical variables. Table 12.11 on page 455 summarizes guest satisfaction survey responses for the primary reason for not returning to a hotel by hotel. For a simple contingency table, MCA is not needed to uncover such associations as the Golden Palm Resort is associated with the quality-of-room reason for not returning. The survey also asked guests their booking source (T.C. Resorts website, travel site or agent, or walk-in) and their relationship status (single, couple, or family).

Figure 17.8 shows the JMP and Minitab biplots that summarizes these variables as well as the primary reason for not returning variable and reveals a number of associations. Those who gave the quality-of-room reason for not returning were associated with those who booked a room on the company's website. Using a third-party travel site or agent to book a room is associated with guests who stayed at the Palm Princess. Couples are more closely associated with the dining options reason for not returning than either families or single people.

Biplots are graphs that plot the relationships among the rows and columns of a contingency table. Distances between points in biplots are not linear. In Figure 17.8, saying that because the Palm Princess Resort (PP) is at twice the distance to the quality-of-room reason than the Palm Royale Resort (PR), the Palm Princess is only "half as associated" with this reason as the Palm Royale would be incorrect. Likewise, assigning meanings to the two dimensions is pointless as they are mathematical abstractions.

These associations could raise new questions for the managers to explore such as what attributes of the Palm Princess cause this hotel to be associated with the use of third-party agents. The associations might result in business changes such as revising room descriptions on the company's website to see if complaints about the room quality decrease over time.

FIGURE 17.8
JMP and Minitab multiple correspondence analysis for the T.C. Resorts guest satisfaction survey for the primary reason for not returning to a hotel.

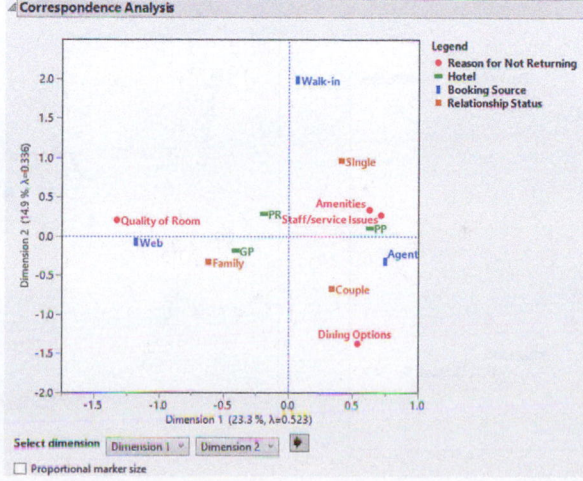

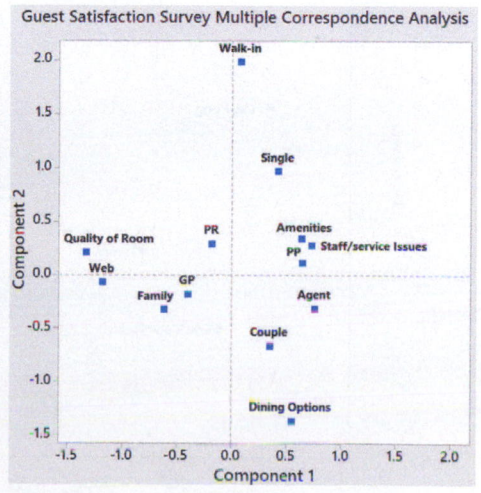

Multidimensional Scaling (MDS)

Multidimensional scaling (MDS) visualizes associations in a plot that contains two or more dimensions. Metric and nonmetric versions of this method exist, with ordinal-scale data requiring the use of nonmetric MDS. MDS uses the distance between items to determine the similarity of items. As with clustering methods, MDS methods commonly use Euclidean distance to compute distances.

Multidimensional scaling can be done in any number of abstract dimensions, usually no more than five. When using MDS, minimizing the number of dimensions used to interpret the results while maximizing the goodness of fit of the results to the original data is a primary goal. The **stress statistic** measures the goodness of fit, with the smaller the value, the better the fit. The stress statistic can vary as the number of dimensions change and a best practice is to increase dimensions as long as the stress statistic decreases substantially. (Typically, the decrease in the stress statistic will level off after the second or third dimension is considered.)

In marketing, a common problem is to identify how people's perceptions of similar items, such as competing brands or products, differ. While perceptional questions can be asked directly, asking a series of questions about the attributes of the set of similar items and then using MDS to plot the similarity can often be a more effective approach. For example, suppose a sports marketer wanted to better understand people's perceptions of nine sports: basketball, skiing, baseball, ping pong, hockey, track and field, bowling, tennis, and U.S. football. By asking people to use a seven-point ordinal scale to assign the degree of movement speed, the type of rules, the degree that a sport is team-oriented, or the amount of physical contact in the sport, a MDS method can transform those responses and visualize associations among sports.

Figure 17.9 contains two- and three-dimensional JMP plots from a MDS analysis of the sports survey data. Both plots show that those surveyed perceive basketball (1), baseball (3), hockey (5), and U.S. football (9) as more similar to each other than the other five. The 3D plot better reveals that relationship while also placing U.S. football on the "floor" of the cube, very far away from basketball. (The stress statistic for this analysis, not shown in Figure 17.9, is a small decimal amount that approximates zero.)

FIGURE 17.9

JMP two-dimensional and 3D MDS plots of the sports survey data

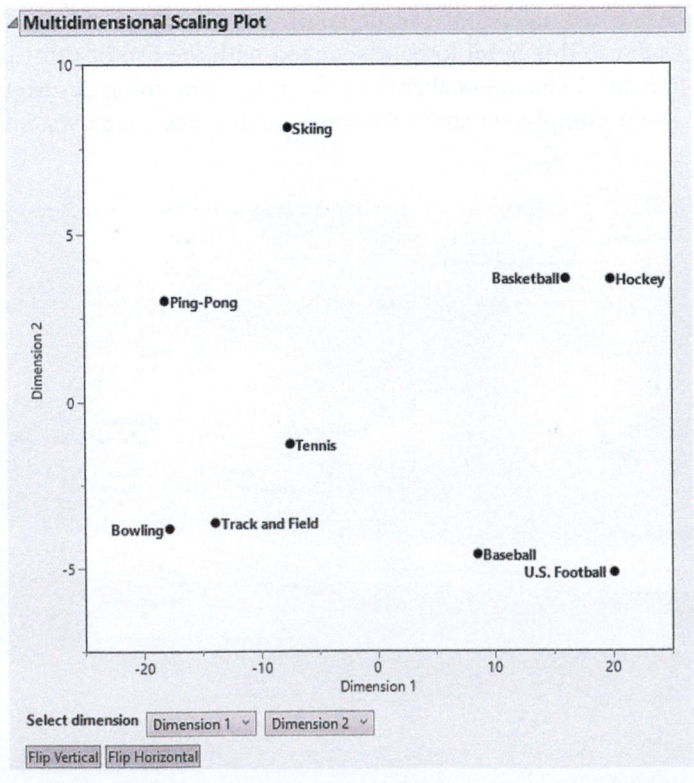

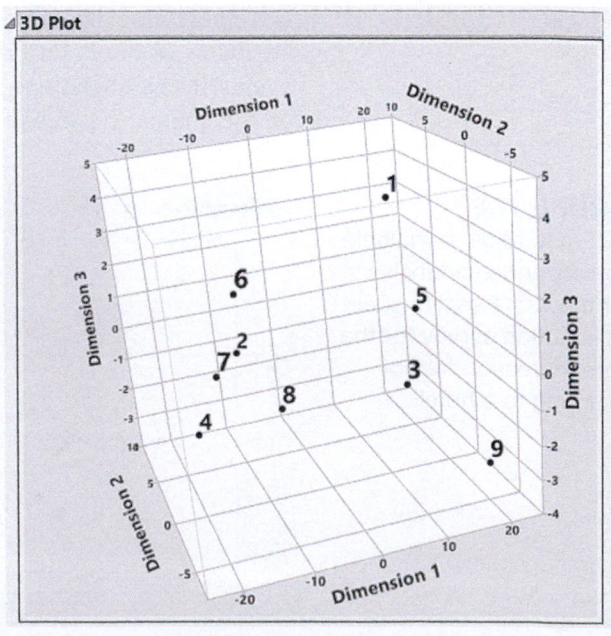

PROBLEMS FOR SECTION 17.6

17.15 The restaurant owner in Problem 2.91 continues to learn more about the weekend patterns of patron demand. For each patron, the owner has collected and stored in Patrons the gender, the entrée ordered, the dessert ordered, and payment method.
a. Conduct a multiple correspondence analysis of the patron data.
b. What observations can you make about the weekend patron patterns?

17.16 The file Social Response contains the product category, sentiment rating, and customer type and frequency of posting (low, average, high) for 300 recently posted comments to a retailer's community website.
a. Conduct a multiple correspondence analysis of the posted comments data.
b. What customer patterns does the analysis suggest?

17.17 Movie companies need to predict the gross receipts of individual movies once the movie has debuted. The following results, stored in PotterMovies, are the first weekend gross, the U.S. gross, and the worldwide gross (in $millions) of the Harry Potter movies.
a. Perform a multidimensional scaling analysis on the Harry Potter movies based on the first weekend gross, the U.S. gross, and the worldwide gross (in $millions).
b. What conclusions can you reach about which Harry Potter movies are most similar?

17.18 The file Cereals contains the calories, carbohydrates, and sugar, in grams, in one serving of seven breakfast cereals.
a. Perform a multidimensional scaling analysis on the cereals based on the calories, carbohydrates, and sugar in grams.
b. What conclusions can you reach about which cereals are most similar?

17.19 The file Protein contains calorie and cholesterol information for popular protein foods (fresh red meats, poultry, and fish) compiled by the U.S. Department of Agriculture.
a. Perform a multidimensional scaling analysis on the protein foods based on the calories and cholesterol, in grams.
b. What conclusions can you reach about which protein foods are most similar?

17.20 A Pew Research Center survey found that social networking is popular in many nations around the world. The file GlobalSocialMedia contains the level of social media networking (measured as the percent of individuals polled who use social networking sites) and the GDP at purchasing power parity (PPP) per capita for each of 28 selected countries.

Source: Data extracted from "Global Digital Communication: Texting, Social Networking Popular Worldwide," Pew Research Center, **bit.ly/sNjsmq**.

a. Perform a multidimensional scaling analysis on the nations based on the level of social media networking (measured as the percent of individuals polled who use social networking sites) and the GDP at purchasing power parity (PPP) per capita.
b. What conclusions can you reach about which nations are most similar?

17.21 The file MobileSpeed contains the overall download and upload speeds in mbps for nine carriers in the United States.

Source: Data extracted from "Best Mobile Network 2016," **bit.ly/1KGPrMm**, accessed November 10, 2016.

a. Perform a multidimensional scaling analysis on the United States carriers based on the download and upload speeds.
b. What conclusions can you reach about which carriers are most similar?

17.22 Have you wondered how Internet connection speed varies around the globe? The file ConnectionSpeed contains the mean connection speed, the mean peak connection speed, the percent of the time the connection speed is above 4 mbps, and the percent of the time the connection speed is above 10 Mbps for various countries.

Source: Data extracted from **bit.ly/2vPmifV**.

a. Perform a multidimensional scaling analysis on the various countries based on the mean connection speed, the mean peak connection speed, the percent of the time the speed is above 4 Mbps, and the percent of the time the connection speed is above 10 Mbps.
b. What conclusions can you reach about which countries are most similar?

17.7 Text Analytics

The First Things First Chapter defines *unstructured data* as data that are not comprehensible without additional interpretation. In the past, the interpretation of such data was done manually, limiting the effectiveness and timeliness of such data. Today, business analytics (and related techniques) can automate as well as analyze such data. While fictional portrayals of applications such as facial or voice processing systems sometimes exaggerate the capabilities of current technology, every day many customer response centers use voice-related statistical and analytics techniques to recognize and respond to language spoken by customers calling a help line—without the need for human intervention.

Techniques that use *unstructured text* are among the methods most evolved for business use today. The first business information systems used *structured* text, which can be translated in a row and column entries. Entries in standard business forms are structured text because each form can be represented easily as a row of data whose column values correspond to a filled-in response. **Unstructured text** are words, phrases, passages, or any type of writing that cannot be made to fit a template easily. Sending a text message, posting a comment to a social media website, or writing answers to an essay test are examples of unstructured text. Collections of big data typically contain unstructured text that results from trying to combine data in different forms from different sources.

While unstructured text has always existed, the growing use of big data and the growing influence of social media has made being able to interpret and analyze this form of unstructured data increasingly important. **Text analytics** is the blend of descriptive and prescriptive analytics that automates that interpretation and makes analysis possible. Text analytics takes many forms, including some techniques related to the application of Bayes' theorem that the Consider This feature in Chapter 4 explores.

As an example, consider an online retailer that allows customers to post reviews of products bought. Table 17.3 contains three such reviews about an unspecified product.

TABLE 17.3
Three Reviews
of a Product

Customer	Comment
Jill from Wynnewood	Great—I love this product and highly recommend it.
Bill from Woodwynn	Great—if you love a product that breaks after its first use!
Bryn from Billwood	Seller shipped fast. Five Stars!

learnMORE

Because of the complexity of text analytics, a practical demonstration of the concepts in this section is beyond the scope of this book. To learn how to use JMP to demonstrate some of text analytics techniques that this section discusses, read the **Text Analytics and JMP** online document.

With manual interpretation, most would recognize that Jill is positive about the product and Bill is not, while most would suspect that Bryn reviewed the seller of the product and not the product itself. Using methods known as **sentiment analysis**, frequencies of words that an analyst has classified as being positive words could be tallied and comments that have many positive terms separated and *classified*. Newer techniques called **semantic analysis** use *clustering* methods that operate on word *associations*. Semantic analysis combines predictive analytics with computer science natural language processing methods and does not rely on an analyst's classification of words as being positive, negative, or neutral.

One current focus of managers and researchers alike is *latent semantic analysis*. **Latent semantic analysis** creates clusters based on the "latent," dimensions of similarity in the unstructured text that exist implicitly. In an analogous way, in Section 17.6, the Figure 17.9 multidimensional scaling (MDS) of the sports survey data reveals dimensions of association such as that survey respondents perceive basketball, baseball, hockey, and U.S. football as more similar to each other than to the other five other sports mentioned in the survey. Respondents never mentioned that similarity explicitly; that similarity was *latent* in the ratings they assign to each sport.

Note that latent semantic analysis (LSA) discovers clusters—not meanings of words. LSA calculations are complex and only fairly recently practical in business computing. As with clustering in general, using LSA does not guarantee creating clusters that have practical use for a decision maker.

17.8 Prescriptive Analytics

Prescriptive analytics seek to optimize the performance of a business and offer decision-making recommendations for how to respond to and manage business circumstances in the future. Prescriptive analytics most directly illustrates the combining "traditional statistical methods with methods from management science and information systems to form an inter-disciplinary tool that supports fact-based decision making" that Section FTF.2 presents as the definition of business analytics. Prescriptive analytics builds on the results of predictive analytics methods, which themselves are built on inferential statistics and combines those results with management science techniques while using data handling and processing capabilities of current information systems to access large data sets or run multiple analyses.

To fully understand prescriptive analytics requires exposure to management science or a mastery of predictive analytics, both of which are beyond the scope of this book. Generally, prescriptive methods are based on one of two approaches: optimization or simulation. In **optimization**, a decision maker sets constraints, which reflect resource limitations that a business process faces, or numerical goals, to learn how the process can work most effectively. Prescriptive optimization methods result in a single solution, known as the *decision model*, that represents the best way to manage the business process. Managers in the T.C. Resort Properties scenario, using the results of multiple correspondence analysis (see Section 17.6) and other predictive analytics methods, might assign spending allocations for such items as room improvements, staff training, dining facilities, website expenses, travel agent payments, or reception services, or any combination of these items and see how best to allocate the rest of their budget.

In contrast, in **simulation**, a decision maker repeatedly runs a predictive analytics model while varying the assumptions or data of the model to create a set of results that offer choices about the business process being modeled. A decision maker then uses decision criteria to choose a specific run of the model, which is not guaranteed to be optimal, to guide decision-making. Simulation offers an alternative to optimization when the business process under study is not well understand or is subject to the unforeseen. Prescriptive simulation methods, sometimes called *simulation optimization*, automates this process of choosing and sometimes enhances the choice by examining varying analytics technique itself, such as varying the value of k or the measure of distance used in a clustering analysis (see Section 17.5).

▼USING **STATISTICS**
Back to Arlingtons ..., Revisited

In the Using Statistics scenario, you were asked to prepare notes for a management seminar that would introduce business analytics to store managers at Arlingtons. You decide to explain how descriptive analytics can help managers know the status of current business activities and how dashboards, specifically, can be the mode of presentation for such information. You decide to explain that business analytics also includes the categories of predictive and prescriptive analytics and that methods of predictive analytics can be further classified as methods involving prediction, classification, clustering, or association. You decide that the managers should understand how predictive analytics extends and builds on inferential methods such as regression. You also realize that managers should appreciate how clustering and association methods can help identify groups of customers of interest and gain insights into customer buying habits. You decide that the concluding section of your notes should explain how prescriptive analytics builds on the results of predictive analytics to start to answer questions about what *should* happen that can guide future managerial decision making.

▼REFERENCES

1. Breiman, L., J. Friedman, C. J. Stone, and R. A. Olshen. *Classification and Regression Trees*. London: Chapman and Hall, 1984.
2. Cox, T. F., and M. A. Cox. *Multidimensional Scaling*, 2nd ed. Boca Raton, FL: CRC Press, 2010.
3. Doron Cohen, as quoted in Morgan, L. "8 Smart Ways to Use Prescriptive Analytics." *InformationWeek* 6/28/2016, available at **ubm.io/293ZMoy**.
4. Everitt, B. S., S. Landau, and M. Leese. *Cluster Analysis*, 5th ed. New York: John Wiley, 2011.

5. Few, S. *Information Dashboard Design: Displaying Data for At-a-Glance Monitoring*, 2nd ed. Burlingame, CA: Analytics Press, 2013.

6. Koren, Y. "The BellKor Solution to the Netflix Grand Prize," available at **bit.ly/2vZVAkZ**.

7. Levine, D., D. Stephan, and K. Szabat. *Business Analytics Using JMP and Microsoft Office Tools*. Boston: Pearson, forthcoming 2018.

8. Loh, W. Y. "Fifty Years of Classification and Regression Trees." *International Statistical Review*, 2013.

9. "NASDAQ Wall Capabilities," **bit.ly/1ubnLGQ**.

10. Paczkowski, W. *Market Data Analysis Using JMP*. Cary, NC: SAS institute, 2016.

11. Provost, F., and T. Fawcett. *Data Science for Business*. Sebastopol, CA: O'Reilly Media, 2013.

▼ KEY EQUATIONS

Akaike Information Criterion (AIC)

$$\text{AIC} = 2k - 2\ln(L) \tag{17.1a}$$

Akaike Information Criterion corrected (AIC_c)

$$\text{AIC}_c = \text{AIC} + \frac{2k(k+1)}{n-k-1} \tag{17.1b}$$

LogWorth

$$\text{LogWorth} = -\log_{10}(p\text{-value}) \tag{17.2}$$

Euclidean Distance

$$d_{ij} = \sqrt{\sum_{k=1}^{r}(X_{ik} - X_{jk})^2} \tag{17.3}$$

▼ KEY TERMS

Akaike information criterion (AIC) 685
association methods 679
average linkage 689
biplot 691
CCC statistic 689
classification methods 679
classification tree 687
clustering methods 679
complete linkage 689
cross-validation 680
dashboard 682
data dimensionality 683
data mining 681
descriptive analytics 679
dynamic bubble charts 683

Euclidean distance 688
hierarchical clustering 688
k-means clustering 688
latent semantic analysis 695
LogWorth statistic 685
multidimensional scaling (MDS) 691
multiple correspondence analysis (MCA) 691
optimization 695
overfitting 680
prediction methods 679
predictive analytics 679
prescriptive analytics 679
prune 685
regression tree 685

root node 685
semantic analysis 694
sentiment analysis 694
simulation 695
single linkage 689
supervised methods 680
stress statistic 692
text analytics 694
training data 680
tree induction 684
unstructured text 694
unsupervised methods 681
Ward's minimum variance method 689

▼ CHECKING YOUR UNDERSTANDING

17.23 What is the difference between supervised and unsupervised analytics methods?

17.24 How do classification trees differ from regression trees?

17.25 How does multiple correspondence analysis differ from multidimensional scaling?

17.26 How does cluster analysis differ from multidimensional scaling?

▼ CHAPTER REVIEW PROBLEMS

17.27 The production of wine is a multibillion-dollar worldwide industry. In an attempt to develop a model of wine quality as judged by wine experts, data were collected from red and white wine variants of Portuguese "Vinho Verde" wine.

Source: Data extracted from P. Cortez et. al., "Modeling Wine Preferences by Data Mining from Physiochemical Properties," *Decision Support Systems*, 47, 2009, pp. 547–553 and **bit.ly/9xKlEa**.

The population of 6,497 wines is stored in VinhoVerde Population .

a. Using half the data as the training sample and the other half of the data as the validation sample, develop a classification tree model to predict the probability that the wine is red. (Consider the entire set of variables in your analysis.)

b. What conclusions can you reach about the probability that the wine is red.

17.28 Using to the data in Problem 17.27,

a. Use half the data as the training sample and the other half of the data as the validation sample to develop a regression tree model to predict wine quality. (Consider the entire set of variables in your analysis.)

b. What conclusions can you reach about wine quality?

17.29 The file FTMBA contains a sample of top-ranked full-time MBA programs. Variables included are mean starting salary upon graduation ($), percentage of students with job offers within three months of graduation, program cost ($), and total number of students per program. Source: Data extracted from **bit.ly/1E8MBcp**.

a. Using all the data as the training sample, develop a regression tree model to predict the mean starting salary upon graduation.

b. What conclusions can you reach about the mean starting salary upon graduation?

c. Using half the data as the training sample and the other half of the data as the validation sample, develop a regression tree model to predict the mean starting salary upon graduation.

d. What differences exist in the results of (a) and (c)?

17.30 A specialist in baseball analytics is interested in determining which variables are important in predicting a team's wins in a given baseball season. He has collected data in Baseball that includes the number of wins, ERA, saves, runs scored, hits allowed, walks allowed, and errors for a recent season.

a. Using all the data as the training sample, develop a regression tree model to predict the number of wins.

b. What conclusions can you reach about the number of wins?

17.31 Nassau County is located approximately 25 miles east of New York City. Data in GlenCove are from a sample of 30 single-family homes located in Glen Cove. Variables included are the fair market value, land area of the property (acres), interior size of the house (square feet), age (years), number of rooms, number of bathrooms, and number of cars that can be parked in the garage.

a. Using all the data as the training sample, develop a regression tree model to predict the fair market value.

b. What conclusions can you reach about the fair market value?

c. Using half the data as the training sample and the other half of the data as the validation sample, develop a regression tree model to predict the fair market value.

d. What differences exist in the results of (a) and (c)?

17.32 A market research study has been conducted by a travel website that specializes in restaurants with the business objective to determine which food cuisines are perceived to be similar and which are perceived to be different. The following cuisine types were studied:

Japanese	Mandarin	Cantonese	American
Szechuan	Spanish	French	Italian
Greek	Mexican		

The mean values of each cuisine on the scales of

Bland (1) to Spicy (7)
Light (1) to Heavy (7)
Low calorie (1) to High calories (7)

are stored in Foods .

a. Perform a cluster analysis on the types of cuisines.

b. Perform a multidimensional scaling analysis on the types of cuisines.

c. What conclusions can you reach about which types of cuisines are most similar?

17.33 A specialist in baseball analytics seeks to study which baseball teams were most similar in a recent season. The specialist has collected data in Baseball related to ERA, saves, runs scored, hits allowed, walks allowed, and errors for that recent season.

a. Perform a cluster analysis on the baseball teams.

b. Perform a multidimensional scaling analysis on the baseball teams.

c. What conclusions can you reach about which baseball teams were similar for that recent season?

17.34 Develop a model to predict the asking price of houses in Silver Spring, Maryland, based on living space, lot size, whether the has a fireplace, the number of bedrooms, the number of bathrooms, age, whether it has central air conditioning, the number of parking spaces, and whether the house has a brick exterior. Use the sample of 61 houses that is stored in SilverSpring as the data for this analysis.

a. Using all the data as a training sample, develop a regression tree model to predict the asking price of the house.

b. What conclusions can you reach about the asking price of the house?

c. Using half the data as the training sample and the other half of the data as the validation sample, develop a regression tree model to predict the asking price of the house.

d. What differences exist in the results of (a) and (c)?

17.35 With an assist from *Moneyball: The Art of Winning an Unfair Game*, a book by Michael Lewis, published in 2003 (and later adapted for the movie *Moneyball*), the management of professional teams in sports such as baseball, football, basketball, and hockey have turned to business analytics to help support decision making. In football, the most important position is the quarterback. The file Quarterback contains various attributes of 35 quarterbacks in a recent season.

a. Perform a cluster analysis on the quarterbacks.

b. Perform a multidimensional scaling analysis on the quarterbacks.

c. What conclusions can you reach about the quarterbacks?

17.36 In recent years, the share of Greek yogurts in the U.S. yogurt market has grown from 1% to over 50%, greatly increasing the variety of Greek yogurts available for sale. The file Yogurt contains the attributes of 17 regular plain, Greek plain, and regular berry yogurts.

a. Perform a cluster analysis on the yogurts.

b. Perform a multidimensional scaling analysis on the yogurts.

c. What conclusions can you reach about the yogurts?

▾ CASES

The Mountain States Potato Company

On page 620, you studied the Mountain States Potato Company which needed to determine why the percentage of solids in the filter cake that it sells was below its historical value. Construct a regression tree model for the percentage of solids in the filter cake and include the results in the report that is to be submitted to the president of the company.

The Craybill Instrumentation Company

On page 621, you studied the Craybill Instrumentation Company that sought to develop a multiple regression model to predict sales. Using the file Managers to construct a regression tree model for the sales and include the results in a report.

▼SOFTWARE GUIDE

INTRODUCTION

This software guide combines Excel, JMP, and Minitab instructions into one guide. Chapter 17 discusses methods that JMP includes but are either not included or weakly supported by Microsoft Excel and Minitab. Table SG.1 summarizes which programs do which methods.

TABLE SG.1

Method	Excel	JMP	Minitab
Dashboards	1	•	2
Dynamic bubble chart		•	
Regression tree		•	
Classification tree		•	
k-means clustering		•	•
Multiple correspondence analysis		•	•
Multidimensional scaling		•	

Notes:
(1) Using additional download available from Microsoft.
(2) Using report feature to simulate dashboard.

The **Software Guide Extended online topic** presents instructions for using other examples of business analytics software. (This online topic will also update guide instructions, as necessary, during the lifetime of the edition.)

SG17.2   DESCRIPTIVE ANALYTICS

Dashboards

Excel Use copy-and-paste commands or the PowerBI Desktop program.

Selecting Excel visualizations, copying them, and then pasting them into Word documents, PowerPoint slides, or other compatible formats can create results that mimic a dashboard. For a more professional result that includes the ability to interact with results use Power BI Desktop, a Microsoft business analytics program which can be downloaded at **powerbi.microsoft.com/desktop**.

With the Power BI Desktop installed and opened, open the **Arlingtons National Sales Power BI file (.pbix)** that contains the Figure 17.1 dashboard. The Power BI Desktop display includes a panel in which visualizations can be selected, formatted, and assigned data, as well as a Fields panel which lists the tables that provide the source data for the visualizations in the dashboard (shown in next column).

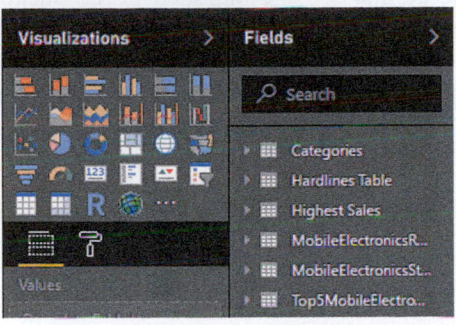

For the Arlingtons dashboard, the tables correspond to worksheets in the Arlingtons Dashboard Data workbook that were imported to Power BI Desktop. Some tables are linked. For example, clicking the Alpha sector in the "Mobile Electronics by Region" doughnut chart, selects only those stores that are in the Alpha region, which changes the "Top 5 Mobile Electronics" list. Such interactions can also drill down data, although the dashboard does not illustrate that feature.

To create a new dashboard, select **File ➔ New**. To import Excel data, select **Home ➔ Get Data** and in the Get Data dialog box, select **All** from the left list, **Excel** from the right list, and click **Connect**. In the standard Open dialog box, select the Excel workbook to import and click **Open**. PowerBI Desktop displays a Navigator dialog box that lists the names of the worksheets in the selected workbook. Check the worksheets to be imported and then click **Load**. PowerBI Desktop imports the worksheets as additional tables and lists them in the Fields panel.

Click the icon for a visualization to insert that visualization. Visualizations can be resized and repositioned in the dashboard report. Visualizations can be associated with data by dragging fields from the Fields pane into various field boxes that appear in the Visualization pane. Clicking the paint roller icon allows custom formatting of a selected visualization.

Power BI Desktop is one part of the Power BI family that includes online service and mobile components. The Power BI website (**powerbi.microsoft.com/desktop**) provides a complete summary as well as complete documentation for using Power BI and several worked-out business analytics examples. Note that Power BI considers Power BI files as reports and reserves the term dashboard for descriptive reports that can be *shared* by many users. In spite of that distinction, a Power BI file fully demonstrates the concept of a descriptive analytics dashboard.

JMP Use **Combine Windows** or **Dashboard**.

The Combine Windows method offers an efficient way to create a simple dashboard for pre-existing results windows. To use this method, first open the JMP results windows that contain the elements to be included in the dashboard. For example, to combine the Figures 17.8 and 17.9 (left) results windows that contain examples of association analysis, open those JMP results windows. Select **Window ➔ Combine Windows** and in the Combine Windows dialog box (shown below):

1. Enter **Association Examples** in the **Name** box.
2. Check **Figure 17.8** and **Figure 17.9 (left)**.
3. Click **OK**.

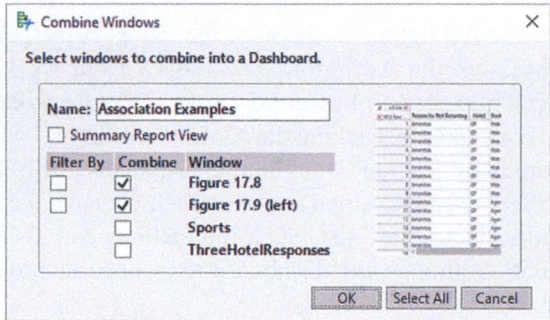

JMP creates a new window that contains the report dashboard which can also serve other presentation purposes. In the windows, click the **Report red triangle** and select **Edit Dashboard** to open the Dashboard Builder window (explained next).

   In the Dashboard method, JMP displays a new window that contains a gallery of stored design templates or sample dashboards that the Dashboard builder uses as the design for the new dashboard. By default, dashboards are saved as **.jmpappsource** files that permit later editing, but can be saved in several different formats, some which facilitate distribution of a dashboard to other users, including users *without* access to JMP.

   For example, to combine the Figures 17.8 and 17.9 (left) results windows that contain examples of association analysis (as well as other information), open those JMP results windows. Select **File ➔ New ➔ Dashboard** and in the template and samples gallery window:

1. Select the **2 × 2 Dashboard**.

JMP displays a new Dashboard Builder window that lists the opened reports and box types in the Sources panel (shown at the top of the next column).

2. Drag the **Text Box icon** and drop it on the upper left square. Double-click the text box and enter **Figure 17.8**.
3. Drag the **Text Box icon** and drop it on the upper right square. Double-click the text box and enter **Figure 17.9 (left)**.

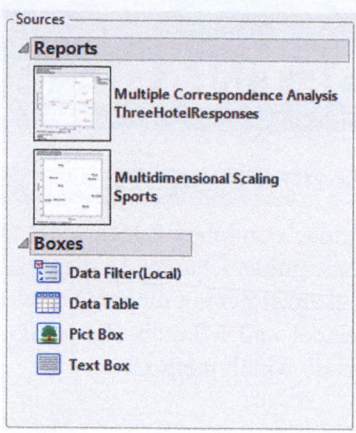

4. Drag the **Multiple Correspondence Analysis** and the **Multidimensional Scaling** reports to the second row.
5. Save the dashboard.

The completed dashboard is shown below.

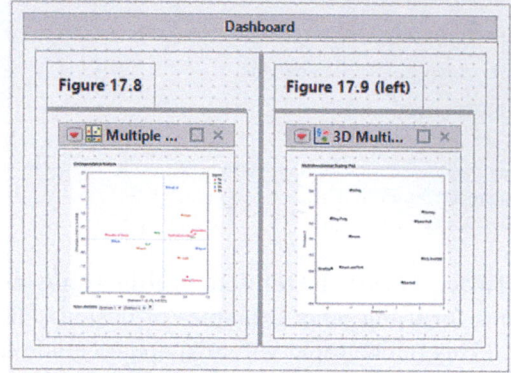

Minitab Use **ReportPad**.

Although Minitab does not contain a dashboard feature, the Minitab ReportPad can simulate a simple dashboard report. To use this method, create or open previously saved Minitab results. Select **Window ➔ Project Manager**. In the left panel of the Project Manager window, click the folder that represents the type of result (Session, Graphs, or Worksheets) to be included.

   For example, to include the Figure 17.8 column plot that Section SG17.6 multiple correspondence Minitab instructions create, click the Graphs folder in the left panel. Minitab displays a list of currently opened graphs in the right Panel. Right-click the Column Plot for the MCA analysis and select **Append to ReportPad** from the shortcut menu.

   To save a ReportPad, right-click the ReportPad folder in the left pane of the Project Manager window and select either **Save ReportPad As** or **Copy to Word Processor**. Either selection can save the contents of the ReportPad as a rich text format (**.rtf** file) and the Save As choice can also save the ReportPad as a **.html** (web page) file.

Dynamic Bubble Charts

Example Create a dynamic bubble chart for domestic movie revenues by MPPA rating, for the years 2002 through 2016, that is the basis of the Figure 17.3 time-lapse illustration on page 684.

JMP Use **Bubble Plot**.

For the example, open the **Movie Revenues by MPAA Rating data table**. Select **Graph ➔ Bubble Plot** and in the procedure's dialog box:

1. Click **Revenues** in the columns list and then click **Y** to add Revenues to the Y box. Click **Sizes** to also add Revenues to the Sizes box.
2. Click **Year** in the columns list and then click **X** to add Year to the X box. Click **Time** to also add Time to the Time box.
3. Click **Rating** in the columns list and then click **ID** to add Rating to the ID box. Click **Coloring** to also add Rating to the Coloring box.
4. Click **OK**.

JMP displays the dynamic bubble chart in a new window that contains sliders for year, speed (of animation), and bubble size and video play and step forward and backward buttons. For best effect, slide the **Bubble Size slider** to the right so that slider vertically aligns with the halfway point between 2002 and 2003 on the *X* axis of the chart. Click the **video play button** to continuously play the time-series animation. Click the **video pause button** to stop the animation.

SG17.3 PREDICTIVE ANALYTICS for PREDICTION

Example Create a regression tree similar to the Figure 17.4 OmniPower sales regression tree on page 685.

JMP Use **Partition**.

For example, to perform the Figure 17.4 regression tree analysis for predicting the sales of OmniPower bars, open the **OmniPower data table**. Select **Analyze ➔ Predictive Modeling ➔ Partition**. In the Partition dialog box:

1. Drag **Sales** to the **Y, Response** box.
2. Drag **Price** to the **X, Factor** box.
3. Drag **Promotion** to the **X, Factor** box.
4. Click **OK**.

In the new JMP results window:

5. Click **Split**. Repeat this step until clicking **Split** no longer has any effect on the tree diagram.

At any point, click **Prune** to remove the last split operation.

SG17.4 PREDICTIVE ANALYTICS for CLASSIFICATION

Example Create a classification tree similar to the Figure 17.5 credit card upgrade classification tree on page 687.

JMP Use **Partition**.

For the example, open the **CardStudy data table**. Select **Analyze ➔ Predictive Modeling ➔ Partition**. In the Partition dialog box (shown below):

1. Drag **Upgraded** to the **Y, Response** box.
2. Drag **Purchases** to the **X, Factor** box.
3. Drag **Extra Cards** to the **X, Factor** box.
4. Click **OK**.

In the new JMP results window:

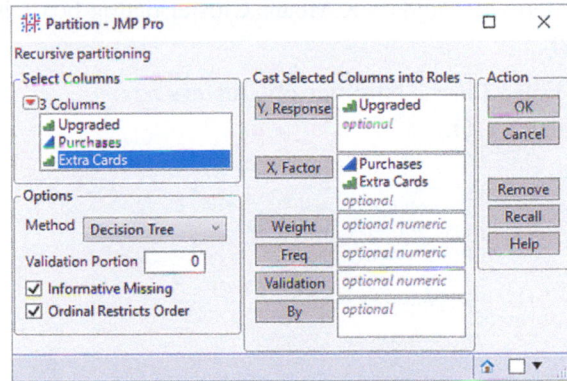

5. Click **Split**. Repeat this step until clicking **Split** no longer has any effect on the tree diagram.
6. If the contents of the diagram do not match Figure 17.5, click the **Partition for Upgraded red triangle** and then select **Display Options** from its menu. To match Figure 17.5, all choices on the Display Options submenu should be checked, except the last two choices, **Show Split Candidates** and **Sort Split Candidates**.

If necessary, click the **Partition for Upgraded red triangle** a second time and select **Color Points** from its menu to color points according to the colors that the tree uses to distinguish groups.

At any point, click **Prune** to remove the last split operation. To enhance the display of the points in the plot, right-click a point, then click **Marker Size** from the shortcut menu and click one of the size choices.

SG17.5 PREDICTIVE ANALYTICS for CLUSTERING

Example Perform the Figure 17.6 *k*-means clustering for $k = 3$ for the sample of growth funds on page 689.

JMP Use **Cluster**.

For the example, open the **Growth Funds data table**. Select **Analyze➔Clustering➔K Means Cluster** and in the Clustering dialog box:

1. Click **Assets** in the columns list.
2. While holding down the **Shift key**, click **Expense Ratio** to select the 10 numerical column names.
3. Click **Y, Columns** to enter the 10 numerical column names in the Y, Columns box.
4. Click **OK**.

In the Growth Funds – K Means Cluster dialog box (shown below):

5. Enter **3** in the **Number of Clusters** box.
6. Click **GO**.

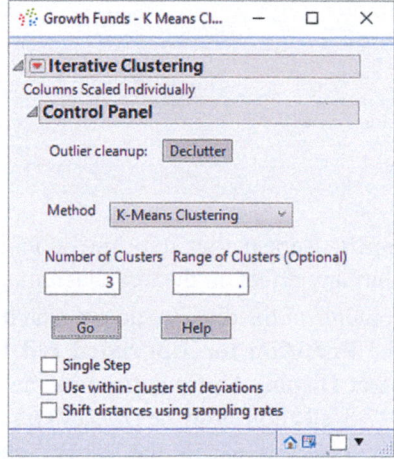

JMP displays the clustering summary in a new results window. To have JMP perform a series of *k*-means clustering for a range of *k*, enter the first value in the range in the Number of Clusters box and enter the last value in the range in the Range of Clusters (Optional) box.

To perform a hierarchical clustering (less useful for the example), select **Analyze➔Clustering➔Hierarchical Cluster** and in the Clustering dialog box, click **Complete** (under the Method heading) and then continue with steps 1 through 4. In the new JMP results window, click the **Hierarchical Clustering red triangle** and select **Color Clusters** from its menu. Drag the diamond-shaped handle at the top of the chart to change the number of clusters. (JMP recolors the dendrogram chart as the number of clusters selected changes.)

Minitab Use **Cluster K-Means**.

For the example, open the **Growth Funds worksheet**. Select **Stat➔Multivariate➔Cluster K-Means** and in the procedure's dialog box (shown below):

1. Enter **C5–C14** in the **Variables** box.
2. Click **Number of clusters** and enter **3** in its box.
3. Check **Standardize variables**.
4. Click **Storage**.
5. In the Cluster K-Means: Storage dialog box, enter **C16** in the **Cluster membership column** box and click **OK**.
6. Back in the original dialog box, click **OK**.

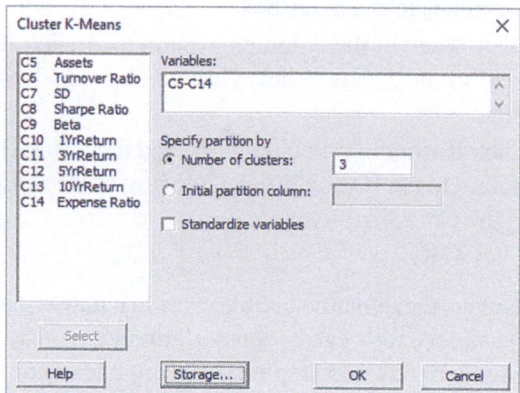

Minitab places a cluster number in column C16 as well as lists results in the Session window. Enter a name for column C16, which Minitab leaves unlabeled.

SG17.6 PREDICTIVE ANALYTICS for ASSOCIATION

Example Perform the Figure 17.8 multiple correspondence analysis for the T.C. Resorts guest satisfaction survey on page 692.

JMP Use **Multiple Correspondence Analysis**.

For the example, open the **ThreeHotelResponses data table**. Select **Analyze➔Consumer Research (Multivariate Methods** in JMP 14)**➔Multiple Correspondence Analysis**. In the procedure's dialog box:

1. While holding down the **Ctrl** key, click **Reason for Not Returning, Hotel, Booking Source**, and **Relationship Status** in the columns list and then click **Y, Response** to add the four column names to the Y, Response box.
2. Click **OK**.

JMP displays results in a new window. To examine another pair of dimensions, select a dimension from the **Select dimensions** pull-down lists. Click the **right arrow button** to the right of the pull-down list to step through every combination of dimensions.

Minitab Use **Multiple Correspondence Analysis**.

For the example, open the **ThreeHotelResponses worksheet**. This worksheet has columns for the four variables under study as well as a Categories column. Categories contains the list of categorical values for all four variables. The values in this special column appear in order by column variable, with the categorical values in column C1 appearing first and the categorical values for column C4 appearing last. Each set of values for a column appear in alphabetical order (and not in order or appearance in a column) and Minitab uses the values for chart labeling purposes. Select **Stat → Multivariate → Multiple Correspondence Analysis** and in the procedure's dialog box (shown below):

1. Enter **C1–C4** in the **Categorical Variables** box and press **Tab**.
2. Double-click **Categories** in the variables list to enter **Categories** in the **Category names** box.
3. Enter **4** in the **Number of components** box.
4. Click **Graphs**.
5. In the Multiple Correspondence Analysis: Graphs dialog box, check **Display column plot** and click **OK**.
6. Back in the original dialog box, click **OK**.

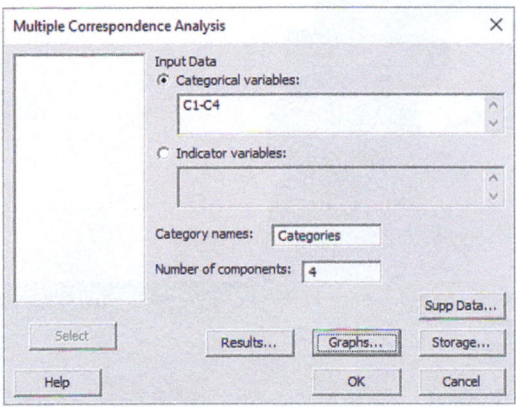

Minitab lists analysis results in the Session window and displays a graph of the analysis in a separate window.

Multidimensional Scaling (MDS)

Example Perform the Figure 17.9 multidimensional scaling for the perception of sports data on page 693.

JMP Use **Multidimensional Scaling**.

For the example, open the **Sports data table**. Select **Analyze → Consumer Research → Multidimensional Scaling** and in the procedure's dialog box:

3. While holding down the **Ctrl** key, click **Movement Speed**, **Rules**, **Team Oriented**, and **Amount of Contact** in the columns list and then click **Y, Columns** to add the four column names to the Y, Columns box.
4. Select **Attribute List** from the **Data Format** pull-down list.
5. Select **Ordinal** from the **Transformation** pull-down list.
6. Enter **3** in the **Set Dimensions** box.
7. Click **OK**.
8. In the new results window, click the **3D Multidimensional Scaling red triangle** and select **3D Plot** from its menu.

JMP adds a 3D plot to the results window. If points cannot be seen clearly in the 3D cube, right-click the cube and select **Settings** from the shortcut menu. Adjust graph settings in the Settings panel and click **OK** when finished.

For other problems, modify step 5 to select **None**, **Ratio**, **Interval**, or **Ordinal**, as appropriate, from the **Transformation** pull-down list.

CONTENTS

OBJECTIVES

- Identify the questions to ask when choosing which statistical methods to use to conduct data analysis
- Generate rules for applying statistics in future studies and analyses

▼USING **STATISTICS**
Mounting Future Analyses

Learning and applying business statistics methodology has some similarities with planning and executing a mountain climbing expedition. Initially, what might seem intimidating, or even overwhelming, can be conquered by applying methods and techniques using a framework that identifies and guides you through a series of tasks. In Section FTF.1, you first learned how the **DCOVA framework** can help apply statistical methods to business problems. After learning methods in early chapters to Define, Collect, and Organize data, you have spent most of your time studying ways to Visualize and Analyze data.

Determining which methods to use to organize, visualize, and analyze your data may have seemed straightforward when you worked out examples or problems from a particular chapter in which the data had already been defined and collected (and perhaps even organized) for you. The defined and possibly organized data gave clues about which methods to choose, as did the chapter itself. For example, while studying the descriptive statistics chapter, you could deduce properly that applying the inferential methods of other chapters would not be part of any example or problem.

But what should you do when you find yourself in new situations such as needing to analyze data for another course or to help solve a problem in a real business setting? You will not be studying a chapter of this book, so the methods to choose and apply will not necessarily be as obvious to you as they may have been when working out a specific problem from a specific chapter. How then can you guide yourself to choosing appropriate statistical methods as you seek to mount future analyses?

electing the appropriate methods to use with data turns out to be the single most difficult thing you do when you apply business statistics to real situations. This is also the single most important task you face. Recall that when using the DCOVA approach, you first define the variables that you want to study in order to solve a business problem or meet a business objective. To do this, you identify the type of business problem, such as trying to describe a group or trying to make inferences about a group, and then determine the type of variable—*numerical* or *categorical*—you will be analyzing.

That act of defining a variable provides the starting point for selecting appropriate statistical methods to use. Once you know the type of variable, you can ask yourself a series of questions about what you seek to do with that variable. The questions can guide you to the appropriate methods to select as surely as a mountain guide can help you to the summit of a mountain. Therefore, the *answer* to the question "How can you guide yourself to choosing appropriate statistical methods as you seek to mount future analyses?" is "Ask more questions."

In the following two sections, this chapter presents two sets of questions, one for numerical variables and the other for categorical variables, that you can ask yourself once you have defined your variable. Unlike other chapters, this chapter introduces a Using Statistics scenario to raise a completely different type of question.

studentTIP

Recall that *numerical variables* have values that represent quantities, while *categorical variables* have values that represent categories.

18.1 Analyzing Numerical Variables

To analyze a numerical variable, choose the appropriate Exhibit 18.1 question and then read the answer to the question in this section.

> **EXHIBIT 18.1**
>
> **Questions to Ask When Analyzing Numerical Variables**
>
> Do you want to
>
> - describe the characteristics of the variable (possibly broken down into several groups)?
> - reach conclusions about the mean or the standard deviation of the variable in a population?
> - determine whether the mean and/or standard deviation of the variable differs depending on the group?
> - determine which factors affect the value of a variable?
> - predict the value of the variable based on the values of other variables?
> - classify items into groups or look for patterns of association among items?
> - determine whether the values of the variable are stable over time?

Describe the Characteristics of a Numerical Variable?

You develop tables and charts and compute descriptive statistics to describe characteristics such as central tendency, variation, and shape. Specifically, you can create a stem-and-leaf display, percentage distribution, histogram, polygon, boxplot, normal probability plot, gauge, and treemap (see Sections 2.2, 2.4, 3.3, and 6.3), and you can compute statistics such as the mean, median, mode, quartiles, range, interquartile range, standard deviation, variance, coefficient of variation, skewness, and kurtosis (see Sections 3.1, 3.2, and 3.3).

Reach Conclusions About the Population Mean or the Standard Deviation?

You have several different choices, and you can use any combination of these choices. To estimate the mean value of the variable in a population, you construct a confidence interval estimate of the mean (see Section 8.2). To determine whether the population mean is equal to a specific value, you conduct a *t* test of hypothesis for the mean (see Section 9.2). To determine whether the population standard deviation or variance is equal to a specific value, you conduct a χ^2 test of hypothesis for the standard deviation or variance (see online Section 12.7).

Determine Whether the Mean and/or Standard Deviation Differs Depending on the Group?

When examining differences between groups, you first need to establish which categorical variable to use to divide your data into groups. You then need to know whether this grouping variable divides your data into two groups (such as male and female groups for a gender variable) or whether the variable divides your data into more than two groups (such as the four in-store locations for mobile electronics discussed in Section 11.1). Finally, you must ask whether your data set contains independent groups or whether your data set contains matched or repeated measurements.

If the Grouping Variable Defines Two Independent Groups and You Are Interested in Central Tendency   Which hypothesis tests you use depends on the assumptions you make about your data.

If you assume that your numerical variable is normally distributed and that the variances are equal, you conduct a pooled *t* test for the difference between the means (see Section 10.1). If you cannot assume that the variances are equal, you conduct a separate-variance *t* test for the difference between the means (see Section 10.1). In either case, if you believe that your numerical variables are not normally distributed, you can perform a Wilcoxon rank sum test (see Section 12.4) and compare the results of this test to those of the *t* test.

To evaluate the assumption of normality that the pooled *t* test and separate-variance *t* test include, you can construct boxplots and normal probability plots for each group.

If the Grouping Variable Defines Two Groups of Matched Samples or Repeated Measurements and You Are Interested in Central Tendency   If you can assume that the paired differences are normally distributed, you conduct a paired *t* test (see Section 10.2). If you cannot assume that the paired differences are normally distributed, you conduct a Wilcoxon signed rank test (see online Section 12.8).

If the Grouping Variable Defines Two Independent Groups and You Are Interested in Variability   If you can assume that your numerical variable is normally distributed, you conduct an *F* test for the difference between two variances (see Section 10.4).

If the Grouping Variable Defines More Than Two Independent Groups and You Are Interested in Central Tendency   If you can assume that the values of the numerical variable are normally distributed, you conduct a one-way analysis of variance (see Section 11.1); otherwise, you conduct a Kruskal-Wallis rank test (see Section 12.5). You can use the Levene test (see Section 11.1) to test for the homogeneity of variance between the groups.

If the Grouping Variable Defines More Than Two Groups of Matched Samples or Repeated Measurements and You Are Interested in Central Tendency   Suppose that you have a design where the rows represent the blocks and the columns represent the levels of a factor. If you can assume that the values of the numerical variable are normally distributed, you conduct a randomized block design *F* test (see online Section 11.3). If you cannot assume that the paired differences are normally distributed, you conduct a Friedman rank test (see online Section 12.9).

Determine Which Factors Affect the Value of a Variable?

If there are two factors to be examined to determine their effect on the values of a variable, you develop a two-factor factorial design (see Section 11.2).

Predict the Value of a Variable Based on the Values of Other Variables?

When predicting the values of a numerical dependent variable, you conduct least-squares regression analysis. The least-squares regression model you develop depends on the number of independent variables in your model. If there is only one independent variable being used to predict the numerical dependent variable of interest, you develop a simple linear regression model (see Chapter 13); otherwise, you develop a multiple regression model (see Chapters 14 and 15) and/or a regression tree (see Section 17.4).

If you have values over a period of time and you want to forecast the variable for future time periods, you can use moving averages, exponential smoothing, least-squares forecasting, and autoregressive modeling (see Chapter 16). If you want to visualize many variables simultaneously, you can use sparklines (see Section 2.7).

Classify or Associate Items?

If you are classifying items into groups, you can use cluster analysis. If you are looking for patterns of association among items, you can use multidimensional scaling.

Determine Whether the Values of a Variable Are Stable Over Time?

If you are studying a process and have collected data on the values of a numerical variable over a time period, you construct R and $\overline{X}$ charts (see online Section 19.5). If you have collected data in which the values are counts of the number of nonconformities, you construct a c chart (see online Section 19.4).

18.2 Analyzing Categorical Variables

To analyze a categorical variable, choose the appropriate Exhibit 18.2 question and then read the answer to the question in this section.

EXHIBIT 18.2

Questions to Ask When Analyzing Categorical Variables

Do you want to

- describe the proportion of items of interest in each category (possibly broken down into several groups)?
- reach conclusions about the proportion of items of interest in a population?
- determine whether the proportion of items of interest differs depending on the group?
- predict the proportion of items of interest based on the values of other variables?
- classify items into groups or look for patterns of association among items?
- determine whether the proportion of items of interest is stable over time?

Describe the Proportion of Items of Interest in Each Category?

You create summary tables and use these charts: bar chart, pie chart, doughnut chart, Pareto chart, or side-by-side bar chart (see Sections 2.1 and 2.3).

Reach Conclusions About the Proportion of Items of Interest?

You have two different choices. You can estimate the proportion of items of interest in a population by constructing a confidence interval estimate of the proportion (see Section 8.3). Or, you can determine whether the population proportion is equal to a specific value by conducting a Z test of hypothesis for the proportion (see Section 9.4).

Determine Whether the Proportion of Items of Interest Differs Depending on the Group?

When examining this difference, you first need to establish the number of categories associated with your categorical variable and the number of groups in your analysis. If your data contain two groups, you must also ask if your data contain independent groups or if your data contain matched samples or repeated measurements.

For Two Categories and Two Independent Groups You conduct either the Z test for the difference between two proportions (see Section 10.3) or the χ^2 test for the difference between two proportions (see Section 12.1).

For Two Categories and Two Groups of Matched or Repeated Measurements You conduct the McNemar test (see online Section 12.6).

For Two Categories and More Than Two Independent Groups You conduct a χ^2 test for the difference among several proportions (see Section 12.2).

For More Than Two Categories and More Than Two Groups You develop contingency tables, use multidimensional contingency tables to drill down to examine relationships among two or more categorical variables, and map the categories of several categorical variables (Sections 2.1, 2.6, and 17.6). When you have two categorical variables, you conduct a χ^2 test of independence (see Section 12.3).

Predict the Proportion of Items of Interest Based on the Values of Other Variables?

You develop a logistic regression model (see Section 14.7) or a classification tree (see Section 17.4).

Classify or Associate Items?

If you are classifying items into groups, you can use hierarchical cluster analysis. If you are looking for patterns of association among items, you can use multiple correspondence analysis.

Determine Whether the Proportion of Items of Interest Is Stable Over Time?

If you are studying a process and have collected data over a time period, you can create the appropriate control chart. If you have collected the proportion of items of interest over a time period, you develop a p chart (see online Section 19.2).

▼USING STATISTICS

The Future to Be Visited

This chapter summarizes the statistical methods that the book discusses in previous chapters as exhibits that list questions that help you determine the appropriate methods with which to analyze your data. As the First Things First Chapter notes, business statistics is an important part of your business education. Your business statistics education cannot end with this page, but must continue to keep you abreast of new developments such as business analytics becoming the changing face of statistics, which the initial chapter also notes.

▼CHAPTER REVIEW PROBLEMS

18.1 In many manufacturing processes, the term *work-in-process* (often abbreviated WIP) is used. At the LSS Publishing book manufacturing plants, WIP represents the time it takes for sheets from a press to be folded, gathered, sewn, tipped on end sheets, and bound together to form a book, and the book placed in a packing carton. The operational definition of the variable of interest, processing time, is the number of days (measured in hundredths) from when the sheets come off the press to when the book is placed in a packing carton. The company has the business objective of determining whether there are differences in the WIP between plants. Data have been collected from samples of 20 books at each of two production plants. The data, stored in WIP, are as follows:

Plant A

5.62	5.29	16.25	10.92	11.46	21.62	8.45	8.58	5.41	11.42
11.62	7.29	7.50	7.96	4.42	10.50	7.58	9.29	7.54	8.92

Plant B

9.54	11.46	16.62	12.62	25.75	15.41	14.29	13.13	13.71	10.04
5.75	12.46	9.17	13.21	6.00	2.33	14.25	5.37	6.25	9.71

Completely analyze the data.

18.2 Many factors determine the attendance at Major League Baseball games. These factors can include when the game is played, the weather, the opponent, whether the team is having a good season, and whether a marketing promotion is held. Popular promotions during a recent season included the traditional hat days and poster days and the newer craze, bobble-heads of star players.

Source: Data extracted from T. C. Boyd and T. C. Krehbiel, "An Analysis of the Effects of Specific Promotion Types on Attendance at Major League Baseball Games," *Mid-American Journal of Business*, 2006, 21, pp. 21–32.

The file BaseballTeams includes the following variables during a Major League Baseball season:

TEAM—Kansas City Royals, Philadelphia Phillies, Chicago Cubs, or Cincinnati Reds

ATTENDANCE—Paid attendance for the game

TEMP—High temperature for the day

WIN%—Team's winning percentage at the time of the game

OPWIN%—Opponent team's winning percentage at the time of the game

WEEKEND—1 if game played on Friday, Saturday, or Sunday; 0 otherwise

PROMOTION—1 if a promotion was held; 0 if no promotion was held

You want to predict attendance and determine the factors that influence attendance. Completely analyze the data for the Kansas City Royals.

18.3 Repeat Problem 17.2 for the Philadelphia Phillies.

18.4 Repeat Problem 17.2 for the Chicago Cubs.

18.5 Repeat Problem 17.2 for the Cincinnati Reds.

18.6 The file EuroTourism2 contains a sample of 28 European countries. Variables included are the number of jobs generated in the travel and tourism industry in 2015, the spending on business travel within the country by residents and international visitors in 2015, the total number of international visitors who visited the country in 2015, and the number of establishments that provide overnight accommodation for tourists.

Source: Data extracted from **www.marketline.com**.

Using the data, you seek to predict the number of jobs generated in the travel and tourism industry. Completely analyze the data.

18.7 The file Philly contains a sample of 25 neighborhoods in Philadelphia. Variables included are neighborhood population, median sales price of homes in the second quarter of 2017, mean number of days homes were on the market in the second quarter of 2017, number of homes sold in the second quarter of 2017, median neighborhood household income, percentage of residents in the neighborhood with a bachelor's degree or higher, and whether the neighborhood is considered "hot" (coded as 1 = yes, 0 = no).

Data extracted from **bit.ly/2wlcJWs**, **bit.ly/2smOyVu**, **bit.ly/2v4mqZd**, and **bit.ly/2n0RNPW**.

Using this data, you seek to predict median sales price of homes. Completely analyze the data.

18.8 Professional basketball has truly become a sport that generates interest among fans around the world. More and more players come from outside the United States to play in the National Basketball Association (NBA). Many factors could impact the number of wins achieved by each NBA team. In addition to the number of wins, the file NBA contains team statistics for points per game (for team, opponent, and the difference between team and opponent), field goal (shots made) percentage (for team and opponent), turnovers (losing the ball before a shot is taken) per game, and rebounds per game. You want to be able to predict the number of wins. Completely analyze the data.

18.9 The file UsedCars contains attributes of cars that are currently part of an inventory of a used car dealership. The variables included are car, year, age, price ($), mileage, power (hp), and fuel (mpg).

Source: Data extracted from **www.truecar.com/used-cars-for-sale/** and **www.cargurus.com/Cars/inventorylisting/**.

You want to describe each of these variables, and you would like to predict the price of the used cars. Analyze the data.

18.10 A study was conducted to determine whether any gender bias existed in an academic science environment. Faculty from several universities were asked to rate candidates for the position of undergraduate laboratory manager based on their application. The gender of the applicant was given in the applicant's materials. The raters were from either biology, chemistry, or physics departments. Each rater was to give a competence rating to the applicant's materials on a seven point scale with 1 being the lowest and 7 being the highest. In addition, the rater supplied a starting salary that should be offered to the applicant. These data (which have been altered from an actual study to preserve the anonymity of the respondents) are stored in Candidate Assessment.

Analyze the data. Do you think that there is any gender bias in the evaluations? Support your point of view with specific references to your data analysis.

18.11 Zagat's publishes restaurant ratings for various locations in the United States. The file Restaurants2 contains the Zagat rating for food, décor, service, cost per person, and popularity index (popularity points the restaurant received divided by the number of people who voted for that restaurant) for various types of restaurants in a large city.

You want to study differences in the cost of a meal for the different types of cuisines and also want to be able to predict the cost of a meal. Completely analyze the data.

18.12 The data in the file BankMarketing are from a direct marketing campaign conducted by a Portuguese banking institution.

Source: Data extracted from S. Moro, R. Laureano, and P. Cortez, "Using Data Mining for Bank Direct Marketing: An Application of the CRISP-DM Methodology," in P. Novais et al. (Eds.), *Proceedings of the European Simulation and Modeling Conference—ESM'2011*, pp. 117–121.

The variables included were age, type of job, marital status, education, whether credit is in default, average yearly balance in account in Euros, whether there is a housing loan, whether there is a personal loan, last contact duration in seconds, number of contacts performed during this campaign, and has the client purchased a term deposit.

Analyze the data and assess the likelihood that the client will purchase a term deposit.

18.13 A mining company operates a large heap-leach gold mine in the western United States. The gold mined at this location consists of ore that is very low grade, having about 0.0032 ounce of gold in 1 ton of ore. The process of heap-leaching involves the mining, crushing, stacking, and leaching of millions of tons of gold ore per year. In the process, ore is placed in a large heap on an impermeable pad. A weak chemical solution is sprinkled over the heap and is collected at the bottom after percolating through the ore. As the solution percolates through the ore, the gold is dissolved and is later recovered from the solution. This technology, which has been used for more than 30 years, has made the operation profitable. Due to the large amount of ore that is handled, the company is continually exploring ways to improve the process. As part of an expansion several years ago, the stacking process was automated with the construction of a computer-controlled stacker. This stacker was designed to load 35,000 tons of ore per day at a cost that was less than the previous process that used manually operated trucks and bulldozers. However, since its installation, the stacker has not been able to achieve these results consistently. Data for a recent 35-day period that indicate the amount stacked (tons) and the downtime (minutes) are stored in the file Mining. Other data that indicate the causes for the downtime are stored in Mining2.

Analyze the data, making sure to present conclusions about the daily amount stacked and the causes of the downtime. In addition, be sure to develop a model to predict the amount stacked based on downtime.

18.14 A survey was conducted on the characteristics of households in the United States. The data (which have been altered from an actual study to preserve the anonymity of the respondents) are stored in Households. The variables are gender, age, Hispanic origin, type of dwelling, age of dwelling in years, years living at dwelling, number of bedrooms, number of vehicles kept at dwelling, fuel type at dwelling, monthly cost of fuel at dwelling ($), U.S. citizenship, college degree, marital status, work for pay in previous week, mode of transportation to work, commuting time in minutes, hours worked per week, type of organization, annual earned income ($), and total annual income ($).

Analyze these data and prepare a report describing your conclusions.

18.15 The file HybridSales contains the number of domestic and imported hybrid vehicles sold in the United States from 1999 to 2016.

Source: Data extracted from Oak Ridge National Laboratory, "Vehicle Technologies Market Report," **bit.ly/2xrcrtO**.

You want to be able to predict the number of domestic and imported hybrid vehicles sold in the United States in 2017 and 2018. Completely analyze the data.

APPENDICES

Basic Math Concepts and Symbols

A.1 Operators

Operators express a calculation or a logical comparison. Operators are building blocks for the equations that define statistical concepts and for formulas, statements that process data in Excel and Minitab worksheets and JMP data tables.

$+$	add	$=$	equal to	$>$	greater than
$-$	subtract	$\neq$	not equal to	$\geq$	greater than or equal to
$\times$	multiply	$\cong$	approximately equal to	$<$	less than
$\div$	divide			$\leq$	less than or equal to

A.2 Rules for Arithmetic Operations

Rule	Example
1. $a + b = c$ and $b + a = c$	$2 + 1 = 3$ and $1 + 2 = 3$
2. $a + (b + c) = (a + b) + c$	$5 + (7 + 4) = (5 + 7) + 4 = 16$
3. $a - b = c$ but $b - a \neq c$	$9 - 7 = 2$ but $7 - 9 \neq 2$
4. $(a)(b) = (b)(a)$	$(7)(6) = (6)(7) = 42$
5. $(a)(b + c) = ab + ac$	$(2)(3 + 5) = (2)(3) + (2)(5) = 16$
6. $a \div b \neq b \div a$	$12 \div 3 \neq 3 \div 12$
7. $\dfrac{a + b}{c} = \dfrac{a}{c} + \dfrac{b}{c}$	$\dfrac{7 + 3}{2} = \dfrac{7}{2} + \dfrac{3}{2} = 5$
8. $\dfrac{a}{b + c} \neq \dfrac{a}{b} + \dfrac{a}{c}$	$\dfrac{3}{4 + 5} \neq \dfrac{3}{4} + \dfrac{3}{5}$
9. $\dfrac{1}{a} + \dfrac{1}{b} = \dfrac{b + a}{ab}$	$\dfrac{1}{3} + \dfrac{1}{5} = \dfrac{5 + 3}{(3)(5)} = \dfrac{8}{15}$
10. $\left(\dfrac{a}{b}\right)\left(\dfrac{c}{d}\right) = \left(\dfrac{ac}{bd}\right)$	$\left(\dfrac{2}{3}\right)\left(\dfrac{6}{7}\right) = \left(\dfrac{(2)(6)}{(3)(7)}\right) = \dfrac{12}{21}$
11. $\dfrac{a}{b} \div \dfrac{c}{d} = \dfrac{ad}{bc}$	$\dfrac{5}{8} \div \dfrac{3}{7} = \left(\dfrac{(5)(7)}{(8)(3)}\right) = \dfrac{35}{24}$

A.3 Rules for Algebra: Exponents and Square Roots

Rule	Example
1. $(X^a)(X^b) = X^{a+b}$	$(4^2)(4^3) = 4^5$
2. $(X^a)^b = X^{ab}$	$(2^2)^3 = 2^6$
3. $(X^a/X^b) = X^{a-b}$	$\dfrac{3^5}{3^3} = 3^2$
4. $\dfrac{X^a}{X^a} = X^0 = 1$	$\dfrac{3^4}{3^4} = 3^0 = 1$
5. $\sqrt{XY} = \sqrt{X}\sqrt{Y}$	$\sqrt{(25)(4)} = \sqrt{25}\sqrt{4} = 10$
6. $\sqrt{\dfrac{X}{Y}} = \dfrac{\sqrt{X}}{\sqrt{Y}}$	$\sqrt{\dfrac{16}{100}} = \dfrac{\sqrt{16}}{\sqrt{100}} = 0.40$

A.4 Rules for Logarithms

Base 10

Log is the symbol used for base-10 logarithms:

Rule	Example
1. $\log(10^a) = a$	$\log(100) = \log(10^2) = 2$
2. If $\log(a) = b$, then $a = 10^b$	If $\log(a) = 2$, then $a = 10^2 = 100$
3. $\log(ab) = \log(a) + \log(b)$	$\log(100) = \log[(10)(10)] = \log(10) + \log(10)$
	$= 1 + 1 = 2$
4. $\log(a^b) = (b)\log(a)$	$\log(1{,}000) = \log(10^3) = (3)\log(10) = (3)(1) = 3$
5. $\log(a/b) = \log(a) - \log(b)$	$\log(100) = \log(1{,}000/10) = \log(1{,}000) - \log(10)$
	$= 3 - 1 = 2$

EXAMPLE

Take the base-10 logarithm of each side for the equation: $Y = \beta_0 \beta_1^X \varepsilon$

SOLUTION Apply rules 3 and 4:

$$\log(Y) = \log(\beta_0 \beta_1^X \varepsilon)$$
$$= \log(\beta_0) + \log(\beta_1^X) + \log(\varepsilon)$$
$$= \log(\beta_0) + X\log(\beta_1) + \log(\varepsilon)$$

Base e

ln is the symbol used for base e logarithms, commonly referred to as natural logarithms. e is Euler's number, and $e \cong 2.718282$:

Rule	Example
1. $\ln(e^a) = a$	$\ln(7.389056) = \ln(e^2) = 2$
2. If $\ln(a) = b$, then $a = e^b$	If $\ln(a) = 2$, then $a = e^2 = 7.389056$
3. $\ln(ab) = \ln(a) + \ln(b)$	$\ln(100) = \ln[(10)(10)]$
	$= \ln(10) + \ln(10)$
	$= 2.302585 + 2.302585 = 4.605170$
4. $\ln(a^b) = (b)\ln(a)$	$\ln(1{,}000) = \ln(10^3) = 3\ln(10)$
	$= 3(2.302585) = 6.907755$
5. $\ln(a/b) = \ln(a) - \ln(b)$	$\ln(100) = \ln(1{,}000/10) = \ln(1{,}000) - \ln(10)$
	$= 6.907755 - 2.302585 = 4.605170$

EXAMPLE

Take the base e logarithm of each side for the equation: $Y = \beta_0 \beta_1^X \varepsilon$

SOLUTION Apply rules 3 and 4:

$$\ln(Y) = \ln(\beta_0 \beta_1^X \varepsilon)$$
$$= \ln(\beta_0) + \ln(\beta_1^X) + \ln(\varepsilon)$$
$$= \ln(\beta_0) + X\ln(\beta_1) + \ln(\varepsilon)$$

A.5 Summation Notation

The symbol Σ, the Greek capital letter sigma, represents "taking the sum of." Consider a set of n values for variable X. The expression $\sum_{i=1}^{n} X_i$ means to take the sum of the X_i values from X_1 through X_n:

$$\sum_{i=1}^{n} X_i = X_1 + X_2 + X_3 + \cdots + X_n$$

To illustrate the use of the symbol Σ, consider five values of a variable X: $X_1 = 2$, $X_2 = 0$, $X_3 = -1$, $X_4 = 5$, and $X_5 = 7$. Thus:

$$\sum_{i=1}^{5} X_i = X_1 + X_2 + X_3 + X_4 + X_5 = 2 + 0 + (-1) + 5 + 7 = 13$$

In statistics, the squared values of a variable are often summed. Thus:

$$\sum_{i=1}^{n} X_i^2 = X_1^2 + X_2^2 + X_3^2 + \cdots + X_n^2$$

and, in the example above:

$$\sum_{i=1}^{5} X_i^2 = X_1^2 + X_2^2 + X_3^2 + X_4^2 + X_5^2$$

$$= 2^2 + 0^2 + (-1)^2 + 5^2 + 7^2 = 4 + 0 + 1 + 25 + 49 = 79$$

$\sum_{i=1}^{n} X_i^2$, the summation of the squares, is *not* the same as $\left(\sum_{i=1}^{n} X_i\right)^2$, the square of the sum:

$$\sum_{i=1}^{n} X_i^2 \neq \left(\sum_{i=1}^{n} X_i\right)^2$$

In the example given above, the summation of squares is equal to 79. This is not equal to the square of the sum, which is $13^2 = 169$.

Another frequently used operation involves the summation of the product. Consider two variables, X and Y, each having n values. Then:

$$\sum_{i=1}^{n} X_i Y_i = X_1 Y_1 + X_2 Y_2 + X_3 Y_3 + \cdots + X_n Y_n$$

Continuing with the previous example, suppose there is a second variable, Y, whose five values are $Y_1 = 1$, $Y_2 = 3$, $Y_3 = -2$, $Y_4 = 4$, and $Y_5 = 3$. Then,

$$\sum_{i=1}^{n} X_i Y_i = X_1 Y_1 + X_2 Y_2 + X_3 Y_3 + X_4 Y_4 + X_5 Y_5$$

$$= (2)(1) + (0)(3) + (-1)(-2) + (5)(4) + (7)(3)$$

$$= 2 + 0 + 2 + 20 + 21$$

$$= 45$$

In computing $\sum_{i=1}^{n} X_i Y_i$, you need to realize that the first value of X is multiplied by the first value of Y, the second value of X is multiplied by the second value of Y, and so on. These products are then summed in order to compute the desired result. However, the summation of products is *not* equal to the product of the individual sums:

$$\sum_{i=1}^{n} X_i Y_i \neq \left(\sum_{i=1}^{n} X_i\right)\left(\sum_{i=1}^{n} Y_i\right)$$

In this example,

$$\sum_{i=1}^{5} X_i = 13$$

and

$$\sum_{i=1}^{5} Y_i = 1 + 3 + (-2) + 4 + 3 = 9$$

so that

$$\left(\sum_{i=1}^{5} X_i\right)\left(\sum_{i=1}^{5} Y_i\right) = (13)(9) = 117$$

However,

$$\sum_{i=1}^{5} X_i Y_i = 45$$

The following table summarizes these results:

Value	X_i	Y_i	$X_i Y_i$
1	2	1	2
2	0	3	0
3	−1	−2	2
4	5	4	20
5	7	3	21
	$\sum_{i=1}^{5} X_i = 13$	$\sum_{i=1}^{5} Y_i = 9$	$\sum_{i=1}^{5} X_i Y_i = 45$

Rule 1 The summation of the values of two variables is equal to the sum of the values of each summed variable:

$$\sum_{i=1}^{n}(X_i + Y_i) = \sum_{i=1}^{n} X_i + \sum_{i=1}^{n} Y_i$$

Thus,

$$\sum_{i=1}^{5}(X_i + Y_i) = (2 + 1) + (0 + 3) + (-1 + (-2)) + (5 + 4) + (7 + 3)$$

$$= 3 + 3 + (-3) + 9 + 10$$

$$= 22$$

$$\sum_{i=1}^{5} X_i + \sum_{i=1}^{5} Y_i = 13 + 9 = 22$$

Rule 2 The summation of a difference between the values of two variables is equal to the difference between the summed values of the variables:

$$\sum_{i=1}^{n}(X_i - Y_i) = \sum_{i=1}^{n} X_i - \sum_{i=1}^{n} Y_i$$

Thus,

$$\sum_{i=1}^{5}(X_i - Y_i) = (2 - 1) + (0 - 3) + (-1 - (-2)) + (5 - 4) + (7 - 3)$$

$$= 1 + (-3) + 1 + 1 + 4$$

$$= 4$$

$$\sum_{i=1}^{5} X_i - \sum_{i=1}^{5} Y_i = 13 - 9 = 4$$

Rule 3 The sum of a constant times a variable is equal to that constant times the sum of the values of the variable:

$$\sum_{i=1}^{n} cX_i = c\sum_{i=1}^{n} X_i$$

where c is a constant. Thus, if $c = 2$,

$$\sum_{i=1}^{5} cX_i = \sum_{i=1}^{5} 2X_i = (2)(2) + (2)(0) + (2)(-1) + (2)(5) + (2)(7)$$

$$= 4 + 0 + (-2) + 10 + 14$$

$$= 26$$

$$c\sum_{i=1}^{5} X_i = 2\sum_{i=1}^{5} X_i = (2)(13) = 26$$

Rule 4 A constant summed n times will be equal to n times the value of the constant.

$$\sum_{i=1}^{n} c = nc$$

where c is a constant. Thus, if the constant $c = 2$ is summed 5 times,

$$\sum_{i=1}^{5} c = 2 + 2 + 2 + 2 + 2 = 10$$

$$nc = (5)(2) = 10$$

EXAMPLE

Suppose there are six values for the variables X and Y, such that $X_1 = 2$, $X_2 = 1$, $X_3 = 5$, $X_4 = -3$, $X_5 = 1$, $X_6 = -2$ and $Y_1 = 4$, $Y_2 = 0$, $Y_3 = -1$, $Y_4 = 2$, $Y_5 = 7$, and $Y_6 = -3$. Compute each of the following:

a. $\sum_{i=1}^{6} X_i$ **b.** $\sum_{i=1}^{6} Y_i$

c. $\sum_{i=1}^{6} X_i^2$ **d.** $\sum_{i=1}^{6} Y_i^2$

e. $\sum_{i=1}^{6} X_i Y_i$ **f.** $\sum_{i=1}^{6} (X_i + Y_i)$

g. $\sum_{i=1}^{6} (X_i - Y_i)$ **h.** $\sum_{i=1}^{6} \left(X_i - 3Y_i + 2X_i^2 \right)$

i. $\sum_{i=1}^{6} (cX_i)$, where $c = -1$ **j.** $\sum_{i=1}^{6} (X_i - 3Y_i + c)$, where $c = +3$

Answers

a. 4   **b.** 9   **c.** 44   **d.** 79   **e.** 10   **f.** (13)   **g.** −5   **h.** 65   **i.** −4   **j.** −5

▼ REFERENCES

1. Bashaw, W. L., *Mathematics for Statistics* (New York: Wiley, 1969).
2. Lanzer, P., *Basic Math: Fractions, Decimals, Percents* (Hicksville, NY: Video Aided Instruction, 2006).
3. Levine, D. and A. Brandwein, *The MBA Primer: Business Statistics*, 3rd ed. (Cincinnati, OH: Cengage Publishing, 2011).
4. Levine, D., *Statistics* (Hicksville, NY: Video Aided Instruction, 2006).
5. Shane, H., *Algebra 1* (Hicksville, NY: Video Aided Instruction, 2006).

A.6 Greek Alphabet

Greek Letter		Name	Greek Letter		Name
A	α	alpha	N	ν	nu
B	β	beta	Ξ	ξ	xi
Γ	γ	gamma	O	o	omicron
Δ	δ	delta	Π	π	pi
E	ε	epsilon	P	ρ	rho
Z	ζ	zeta	Σ	σ	sigma
H	η	eta	T	τ	tau
Θ	θ	theta	Y	υ	upsilon
I	ι	iota	Φ	ϕ	phi
K	κ	kappa	X	χ	chi
Λ	λ	lambda	Ψ	ψ	psi
M	μ	mu	Ω	ω	omega

Important Software Skills and Concepts

B.1 Identifying the Software Version

Using the wrong version of Microsoft Excel, JMP, or Minitab with this book can make learning about business statistics harder and confound a reader following Guide instructions. Programs change over time in both their functionality and user interfaces, so using an out-of-date version of one of the programs that the book discusses could result in frustration or failure to complete tasks. This problem is most acute when using Microsoft Excel because even within a specific version such as Excel 2016 significant differences can arise due to periodic updates. Use this section to determine the version number of the software being used. Having a properly updated current version of Excel, JMP, or Minitab is the best way to proceed with this book.

Excel

Excel Guide instructions in this book work best with Microsoft Windows Excel 2016 and 2013, and Excel for Mac 2016, the versions of Excel that Microsoft fully supported at the time of publication. Subscribers to all but the most basic Office 365 plans have access to the most current full Excel version (Excel 2016 at the time of publication). The Excel Guide instructions also support the deprecated Microsoft Windows Excel 2010 but readers using Excel 2010 should consider upgrading as Excel 2010 does not contain all the Excel functionality that this book describes.

When slight variations among versions occur, the variations appear in parentheses or explanatory sentences that identify those variations. For example, a number of charting instructions begin **Design** (or **Chart Design**)→**Add Chart Element** because the Design tab is called Chart Design in Excel for Mac 2016. When Excel for Mac 2016 differs greatly from its Windows counterpart, Excel for Mac 2016 instructions appear in this color.

Identify the build number Excel has both a version number and a build number which identifies the extent to which the Excel copy has been updated. Knowing both can identify if an Excel copy is up-to-date and can also be helpful if technical support is needed. To identify the build number, open Excel and follow the appropriate instructions.

In Microsoft Windows Excel 2016 or 2013, select **File**→**Account** and, in the Account pane that appears, click the **About Excel icon**. In the dialog box that appears, note the build number that follows the words Microsoft Excel 2016 (or 2013). The Account pane may contain an

Update Options pull-down list from which **Update Now** can be selected to have Excel check for updates.

In Excel 2010, select **File**→**Help** and, in the information pane, note the build number that appears under the heading "About Microsoft Excel." Click **Check for Updates** in that pane to have Excel check for updates.

In Excel for Mac 2016, select **Excel**→**About Excel** and in the dialog box that appears, note the build number. Check for updates by selecting **Help**→**Check for Updates**.

JMP

JMP Guide instructions in this book work best with JMP or JMP Pro version 13 and were tested with the preliminary releases of JMP and JMP Pro 14 (the versions of which were being finalized at the time of publication).

To identify the JMP version being used, open JMP and select **Help**→**About JMP**. In the About JMP dialog box, JMP lists the name, version number, and software type under the JMP log, for example, "JMP Pro 13.1.0 (64-bit)," and provides a link to check for updates. The About JMP dialog box also contains licensing information that may be needed when asking for assistance from the SAS Institute, the publishers of JMP.

Minitab

Minitab Guide instructions in this book work best with Minitab version 18, but can also be used with Minitab 17, which Minitab, Inc., plans to stop supporting during the lifetime of this book. (Readers using Minitab 17 will experience occasional minor differences in menu selection sequences or in dialog box labels or items.)

To identify the Minitab version being used, open Minitab and select **Help**→**About Minitab**. In the About Minitab dialog box, Minitab lists the license information and the product version such as "Minitab 18.1." To check for updates, select **Help**→**Check for Updates**.

B.2 Formulas

Formulas are programming-like instructions that process data found in worksheets and data tables. Formulas can compute intermediate calculations, generate new data or statistics, retrieve data from other cells, or use a logical comparison to make a decision, among other things. In Excel, each worksheet cell can have its own formula, while in JMP and Minitab formulas are defined only for entire columns. Cells that contain formulas show the result of their formulas and not the formulas themselves.

Minitab places a green check mark by the column number for any column that contains a formula, but in Excel and JMP there is no visual signal that a cell or column contains a formula—the cell or column needs to be examined. In Excel, the keyboard shortcut **Ctrl+`** (grave accent) acts as a toggle to turn on and off the display of formulas. In JMP, the Column Information dialog box indicates if the column contains a formula.

Formulas make possible reusable templates such as the Figure 6.16 normal probabilities Excel, JMP, and Minitab templates on page 234. Users of the Excel Guide workbooks will discover that most workbooks contain one or more worksheets that present the formulas that the workbook uses to calculate results.

Entering a Formula

Guide instructions discuss the specifics of entering a formula as the need arises. For the general case in Excel, typing an equals sign (=) followed by the combination of arithmetic operators and cell references and the pressing of the **Enter key**, enters a formula for a specific cell. Unlike Excel, JMP or Minitab formulas do not begin with an equals signs. In Minitab, formulas are constructed in the calculator-like Assign Formulas dialog box. In JMP, formulas are constructed in the formulas dialog shown on page 112.

Functions simplify arithmetic operations or provide access to advanced processing or statistical calculations. Functions can simplify formulas. In Excel, formulas often contain cell ranges, a shorthand way to refer to a group of cells. For example, in Excel, the formula **=A1+A2+A3+A4+A5+A6+A7** that sums the first seven cells in column A can be simplified using the SUM function **=SUM(A1:A7)** that uses the cell range A1:A7. (Section B.3 further explains cell ranges.) In JMP and Minitab, formulas often contain column names. JMP presents column names in italics such as **COL SUM(*Frequency*)** that sums the column Frequency. Minitab presents column names, enclosed in a pair of single quotes if the name contains special characters, even if the column number was used to define the formula. For example, if column C2 was named Expense Ratio, the formula entered as **2*C2** would appear as 2 * 'Expense Ratio'.

Entering an Array Formula (Excel)

In Excel, an array formula defines a formula for a rectangular group of cells (the "array" of cells). To enter an array formula, first select the cell range and then type the formula, and then, while holding down the **Ctrl** and **Shift** keys, press **Enter** to enter the array formula into all of the cells of the cell range. (In Excel for Mac, pressing **Command+Enter** also enters an array formula.)

To edit an array formula, first select the cells that contain the array formula, then edit the formula and then press **Enter** while holding down **Ctrl+Shift** (or press **Command+Enter**). When selecting a cell that contains an array formula, Excel adds a pair of curly braces {} to the display of the formula in the formula bar to indicate that the formula is an array formula. These curly braces disappear when the formula is being edited. (Never type the curly braces when entering an array formula.)

Pasting with Paste Special (Excel)

While the keyboard shortcuts **Ctrl+C** and **Ctrl+V** to copy and paste cell contents will often suffice, pasting data from one worksheet to another can sometimes cause unexpected side effects when the source worksheet contains formulas. When the two worksheets are in different workbooks, a simple paste creates an external link to the original workbook that can lead to possible errors at a later time. Even pasting between worksheets in the same workbook can lead to problems if what is being pasted is a cell range of formulas. Use **Paste Special** to avoid these complications.

To use this command, copy the source cell range using **Ctrl+C** and then right-click the cell (or cell range) that is the target of the paste and click **Paste Special** from the shortcut menu.

In the Paste Special dialog box (shown below), click **Values** and then click **OK**. Paste Special Values pastes the current values of the cells in the first workbook and not formulas that use cell references to the first workbook.

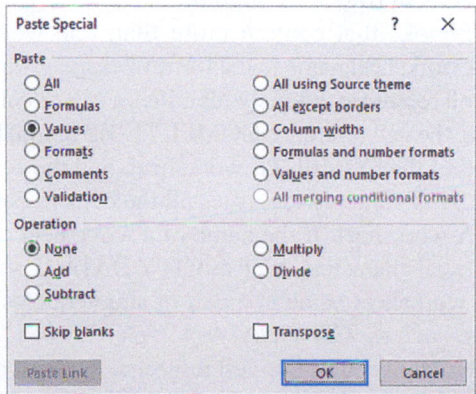

Paste Special can paste other types of information, including cell formatting information. In some copying contexts, placing the mouse pointer over Paste Special in the shortcut menu will reveal a gallery of shortcuts to the choices presented in the Paste Special dialog box.

To use PHStat with data in the form of formulas, first copy your data and then use Paste Special to paste columns of equivalent *values*. (Click **Values** in the Paste Special dialog box to create the values.) PHStat will not function properly if the data for a procedure are in the form of formulas.

Verifying Formulas

After entering all formulas or before using a worksheet or data table template that contains formulas, best practice suggests verifying the formulas for accuracy. In JMP and Minitab, the verification can be as simple as temporarily adding new data rows that contain simple numbers to verify that all formulas compute the correct results.

In Excel, additionally, relationships among cells can be examined visually. Selecting **Formulas → Trace Precedents** reveals relationships between a formula and its *precedents*, the cells that a formula references. Selecting **Formulas → Trace Dependents** reveals the relationship between a cell and its *dependents* cells that contain formulas that reference that cell.

B.3 Excel Cell References

Every Excel worksheet cell has its own **cell reference**, an address that identifies the cell based on the lettered column and numbered row of the cell. For example, the cell A1 is the cell in the first column and first row, A3 is the cell in in the first column and third row, and C1 is the cell in the third column and first row.

Cell references can be a **cell range** that refers to a rectangular group of cells. A cell range names the upper-left cell and the lower-right cell of the group, using the form *UpperLeftCell:LowerRightCell*. For example, the cell range C1:C12 refers to the first 12 cells in column C while the cell range A1:D3 refers to all the cells in columns A through D in rows 1 through 3. Cell ranges can also name one or more columns or rows such as A:A, all the cells in column A, and 4:6, all the cells in rows 4 through 6.

In workbooks that contain more than one worksheet, appending a worksheet name in the form *WorksheetName*! as a prefix to a cell reference uniquely identifies a cell or cell range. For example, the cell reference COMPUTE!B8 uniquely identifies cell B8 of the COMPUTE worksheet, and the cell reference DATA!A:A uniquely identifies all the cells in column A of the DATA worksheet. If the name of a worksheet contains spaces or special characters, such as CITY DATA_1, you must enclose the worksheet name in a pair of single quotes as part of the prefix, such as 'CITY DATA_1'!A2.

When Excel encounters a cell reference without a worksheet prefix, Excel assumes that the cells are in the same worksheet as the formula being entered, a helpful data entry shortcut that Excel Guide instructions use. Occasionally, an Excel feature requires that you use a worksheet prefix and instructions note these exceptions as you encounter them.

Although this book does not use them, cell references can include a workbook prefix in the form *[WorkbookName]WorksheetName*! If you discover workbook prefixes in the formulas you create using the instructions in this book, you may have committed an inadvertent error when transferring data from one workbook to another. Review your work and make sure you intended to include a workbook name prefix in your formula.

Absolute and Relative Cell References

To avoid the drudgery of typing many similar formulas, a formula can be entered once and then copied to other cells. For example, to copy a formula that has been entered in cell C2 down the column through row 12:

1. Right-click cell C2 and press **Ctrl+C** to copy the formula. A movie marquee–like highlight appears around cell C2.
2. Select the cell range **C3:C12**.
3. With the cell range highlighted, press **Ctrl+V** to paste the formula into the cells of the cell range.

During this copy-and-paste operation, Excel adjusts these **relative cell references** in formulas so that copying the formula =A2+B2 from cell C2 to cell C3 results in the formula =A3+B3 being pasted into cell C3, the formula =A4+B4 being pasted into cell C4, and so on.

Sometimes, this automatic adjustment is unwanted. For example, when copying the cell C2 formula =(A2+B2)/B15, if cell B15 contained the divisor to be used in all formulas, that reference should not be adjusted to B16, B17, and so on. To prevent Excel from adjusting a cell reference, use **absolute cell references** by inserting dollar signs ($) before the column and row references of a relative cell reference. For example, the absolute cell reference $B$15 in the copied cell C2 formula =(A2+B2)/$B$15 will cause Excel to paste the formula =(A3+B3)/$B$15 into cell C3.

Do not confuse the use of the dollar sign symbol with the worksheet formatting operation that displays numbers as dollar currency amounts.

Selecting Cell Ranges for Charts

Cell ranges can be entered in Excel dialog boxes in one of several ways. Cell ranges can be typed (most Excel Guide instructions use this method) or cell ranges can be selected using the mouse pointer. Likewise, most of the time cell ranges can be entered using either relative or absolute references. Two important exceptions to these general rules are the Axis Labels and Edit Series dialog boxes, associated with chart labels and data series.

To enter a cell range into these two dialog boxes, enter the cell range as a *formula* that uses absolute cell references in the form *WorksheetName!UpperLeftCell: LowerRightCell*, as the examples on page 721 illustrate. Entering these cell ranges is best done using the mouse-pointer method. Typing the cell range in these dialog boxes will often be frustrating as keys such as the cursor keys do not function as they do in other dialog boxes.

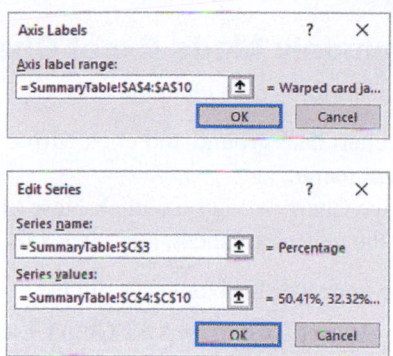

Selecting Non-contiguous Cell Ranges

In the general case, enter a non-contiguous cell range such as the cells A1:A11 and C1:C11 by typing the each cell range, separated by commas. For the example, type **A1:A11, C1:C11**. To enter a non-contiguous cell range for the Axis Labels and Edit Series dialog boxes that the previous section discusses, use the mouse pointer method. To use the mouse-pointer method with such ranges, first, select the cell range of the first group of cells and then, while holding down **Ctrl**, select the cell range of the other groups of cells that form the non-contiguous cell range.

B.4 Excel Worksheet Formatting

Format the contents of worksheet cells by either making entries in the Format Cells dialog box or clicking shortcut icons in the Home tab.

Format Cells Method

To use the Format Cells dialog box method, right-click a cell or cell range and click Format Cells in the shortcut menu. In the Format Cells dialog box, select the **Number** tab. Clicking a **Category** changes the panel to the right of the list. For example, clicking **Number** displays a panel (shown below) in which the number of decimal places to display can be specified.

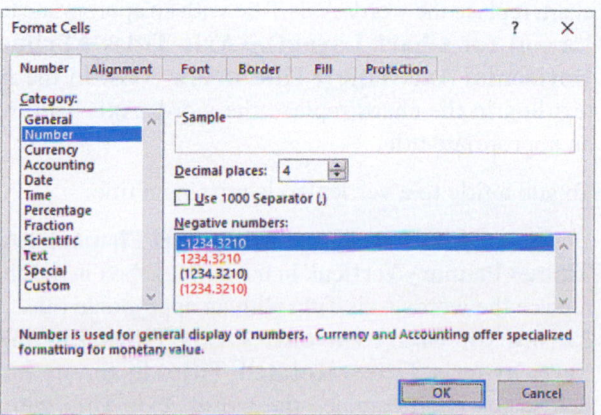

Click the **Alignment** tab of the Format Cells dialog box (partially shown below), to display a panel in which the horizontal and vertical positioning of cell contents can be specified as well as whether the cell contents can be wrapped to a second line if the contents are longer than the cell width.

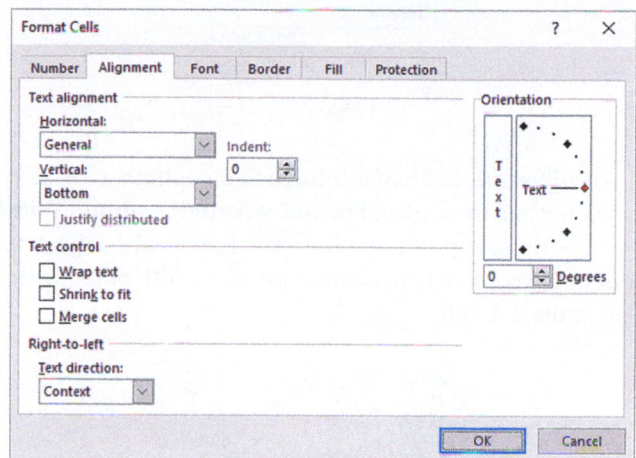

Home Tab Shortcuts Method

You can also format the contents of worksheets by using shortcuts on the Home tab. In Microsoft Windows Excels, these shortcuts are divided into the groups that the following instructions name. In Excel for Mac, the groups are implicit and group names are not shown on the Home tab.

Use the Font **group** shortcuts (shown at top below) to change the typeface, point size, color, and styling such as roman, bold, or italic of the text a cell displays or the background color of a cell. Use the **fill icon** in the same group to change the background color for a cell (shown as yellow in the illustration below). Click the drop-down button to the right of the fill icon to display a gallery of colors from which you can select a color or click **More Colors** for more choices.

Click the **A icon** drop-down button (not in Excel for Mac) to display a palette of color choices for changing the color of the text being displayed (shown at bottom below).

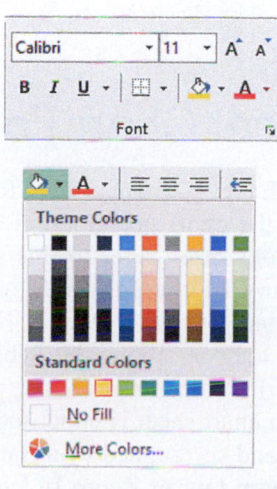

Use the shortcuts in the **Number** group (shown below) to change the formatting of numeric values, including the formatting changes the discussion of the Format Cells dialog box mentions.

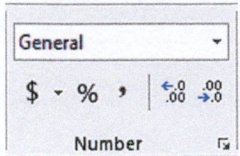

To adjust the width of a column to an optimal size, select the column and then select **Format→Autofit Column Width** in the Cells group (shown below). Excel will adjust the width of the column to accommodate the width of the widest value in the column.

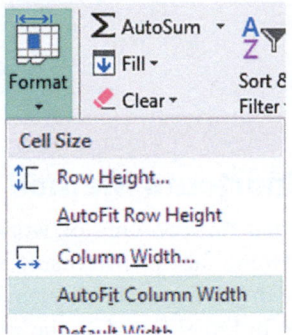

Many Home tab shortcuts contain a drop-down arrow that, when clicked, displays a gallery of choices. For **Merge & Center**, the gallery (shown below) displays all cell merging operations.

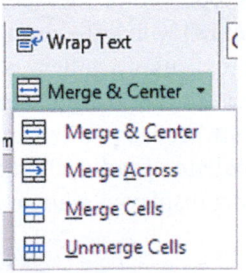

B.5E Excel Chart Formatting

Many charts that Excel constructs need formatting corrections to enhance the chart presentation and Excel Guide charting instructions often refer to this section as a final step. To apply any of the following corrections, first select the chart that is to be corrected. (If Chart Tools or PivotChart Tools appears above the Ribbon tabs, a chart has been selected.)

If a chart on a chart sheet is either too large to be fully seen or too small and surrounded by a frame mat that is too large, click the **Zoom Out** or **Zoom In icons**, located in the lower-right of the Excel window frame, to adjust the chart display.

For many chart formatting operations, instructions vary among current Excel versions. Minor differences among Microsoft Windows and Excel for Mac are noted in parenthetical phrases.

Most Commonly Made Excel Changes

To relocate a chart to its own chart sheet:

1. Click the chart background and click **Move Chart** from the shortcut menu.
2. In the Move Chart dialog box, click **New Sheet**, enter a name for the new chart sheet, and click **OK**.

To turn off the improper horizontal gridlines:

> **Design** (or **Chart Design**)**→Add Chart Element→ Gridlines→Primary Major Horizontal**
>
> **Layout** (or **Chart Layout**)**→Gridlines→Primary Horizontal Gridlines→None**

To turn off the improper vertical gridlines:

> **Design** (or **Chart Design**)**→Add Chart Element→ Gridlines→Primary Major Vertical**
>
> **Layout** (or **Chart Layout**)**→Gridlines→ Primary Vertical Gridlines→None**

To turn off the chart legend:

> **Design** (or **Chart Design**)**→Add Chart Element→ Legend→None**
>
> **Layout** (or **Chart Layout**)**→ Legend→None** (or **No Legend**)

Chart and Axis Titles

To add a chart title to a chart missing a title:

1. Select **Design** (or **Chart Design**)**→Add Chart Element→Chart Title→Above Chart**. Otherwise, click on the chart and then select **Layout** (or **Chart Layout**)**→ Chart Title→Above Chart**.
2. In the box that is added to the chart, select the words "Chart Title" and enter an appropriate title.

To add a title to a horizontal axis missing a title:

1. **Design** (or **Chart Design**)**→Add Chart Element→Axis Titles→Primary Horizontal**. In the new text box in the chart, replace the words Axis Title with an appropriate title.
2. **Layout** (or **Chart Layout**)**→Axis Titles→Primary Horizontal Axis Title→Title Below Axis**. In the new text box in the chart, replace the words Axis Title with an appropriate title.

To add a title to a vertical axis missing a title:

1. **Design** (or **Chart Design**)**→Add Chart Element→Axis Titles→Primary Vertical**. In the new text box in the chart, replace the words Axis Title with an appropriate title.
2. **Layout** (or **Chart Layout**)**→Axis Titles→Primary Vertical Axis Title→Rotated Title**. In the new text box in the chart, replace the words Axis Title with an appropriate title.

Chart Axes

To turn on the display of the *X* axis, if not already shown:

> **Design (or Chart Design)→Add Chart Element→ Axes→Primary Horizontal**

> **Layout (or Chart Layout)→Axes→Primary Horizontal Axis→Show Left to Right Axis (or Show Default Axis or Primary Default Axis)**

To turn on the display of the *Y* axis, if not already shown:

> **Design (or Chart Design)→Add Chart Element→ Axes→Primary Vertical**

> **Layout (or Chart Layout)→Axes→Primary Vertical Axis→Show Default Axis**

For a chart that contains secondary axes, to turn off the secondary horizontal axis title:

> **Design (or Chart Design)→Add Chart Element→ Axis Titles→Secondary Horizontal**

> **Layout (or Chart Layout)→Axis Titles→Secondary Horizontal Axis Title→None (or No Axis Title)**

For a chart that contains secondary axes, to turn on the secondary vertical axis title:

> **Design (or Chart Design)→Add Chart Element→ Axis Titles→Secondary Vertical**

> **Layout (or Chart Layout)→Axis Titles→Secondary Vertical Axis Title→Rotated Title**

Correcting the Display of the *X* Axis

In scatter plots and related line charts, Microsoft Excel displays the *X* axis at the *Y* axis origin ($Y = 0$). When plots have negative values, this causes the *X* axis not to appear at the bottom of the chart.

To relocate the *X* axis to the bottom of a scatter plot or line chart, open to the chart sheet that contains the chart, right-click the *Y* **axis**, and click **Format Axis** from the shortcut menu. In the Format Axis pane click **Axis value** and, in its box, enter the value shown in the **Minimum box** in the same pane.

Emphasizing Histogram Bars

To better emphasize each bar in a histogram, open to the chart sheet containing the histogram, right-click over one of the histogram bars, and click **Format Data Series** in the shortcut menu. In the Format Data Series pane, click the bucket icon. In the Border group, click **Solid line** (Click **Border** to reveal settings, if necessary.). From the **Color drop-down list**, select the darkest color in the same column as the currently selected (highlighted) color. Then, enter **2** (for 2 pt) as the **Width**.

B.5J JMP Chart Formatting

JMP often produces charts with titles and axis scales and titles that are too small for presentation purposes. While text attributes of titles and scales can be set by using the Preferences dialog box that Section D.2 discusses, changing text attributes there can have unintended consequences as that section explains. Better practice changes the text attributes of individual charts.

To change the text attributes of a chart or axis title

1. Right-click the title and select **Font** in the shortcut menu.
2. In the Font dialog box, change the type font, font style, and text size of the chart element and click **OK**.

To change the color of the text:

1. Right-click the title and select **Font Color** in the shortcut menu.
2. Click a color from the gallery of color choices displayed.

To change the text attributes of an axis scale:

1. Right-click the axis and select **Axis Settings** in the shortcut menu.
2. In the (X or Y) Axis Settings dialog box, click **Font**.
3. In the Font dialog box, change the type font, font style, and text size of the chart element and click **OK**.
4. Back in the original dialog box, click **OK**.

To change the formatting of an axis scale values:

1. Right-click the axis and select **Axis Settings** in the shortcut menu.
2. In the (X or Y) Axis Settings dialog box (partially shown below), make changes in the Scale group and/or Tick/Bin Increment group and then click **OK**.

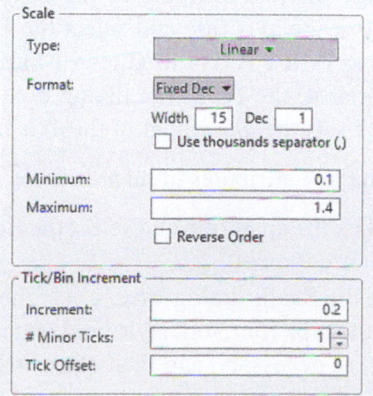

Generally, to change the formatting of other chart elements, right-clicking that element will display a shortcut menu from which changes can be made to the object. For advanced charts, some chart formatting choices may appear in a red triangle shortcut menu.

B.5M Minitab Chart Formatting

Minitab often produces charts with titles and axis scales and titles that are too small for presentation purposes. For these and other chart elements, right-clicking the chart element displays a shortcut menu that will include an Edit choice that when selected displays a dialog box that is appropriate for the chart element. Discussing the full capabilities of these edit dialog boxes is beyond the scope of this text. Examples for editing the chart title and axis titles and scale follow.

To change the text attributes or the contents of a chart title:

1. Right-click the chart title and select **Edit Title: *current title*** in the shortcut menu.
2. In the Edit Title dialog box, edit the ***current title*** in the **Text** box and change the type font, font style, and text size of the chart element, as necessary, and then click **OK**.

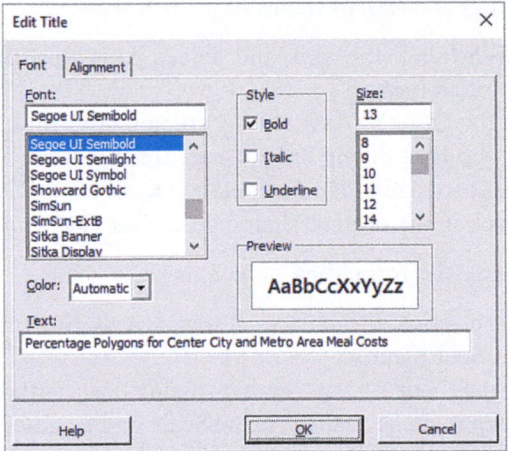

To change the text attribute or the contents of an axis title, right-click the axis title and select the Edit Axis Label choice, such as **Edit Y Axis Label** for a *Y* axis. The Edit Axis Label is similar to the Edit Title dialog box, but contains a Show tab that sets the placement of the axis title on the axis.

To change the text attributes of an axis scale:

1. Right-click the chart title and select the Edit Scale choice in the shortcut menu.
2. In the Edit Scale dialog box, click the **Font** tab and change the type font, font style, and text size of the chart element, as necessary, and then click **OK**.

The Edit Scale dialog box contains other tabs that control other attributes of the axis scale and that Minitab Guide instructions occasionally mention.

B.6 Creating Histograms for Discrete Probability Distributions (Excel)

Create a histogram for a discrete probability distribution based on a discrete probabilities table. For example, to create the Figure 5.3 histogram of the binomial probability distribution on page 207, open to the **COMPUTE worksheet** of the **Binomial workbook**. Select the cell range **B14:B18**, the probabilities in the Binomial Probabilities Table, and:

1. Select **Insert** (or **Charts**)➜**Column** and select the **Clustered Column** gallery item.
2. Right-click the chart and click **Select Data** in the shortcut menu.

In the Select Data Source dialog box:

3. Click **Edit** under the **Horizontal (Categories) Axis Labels** heading. In the Axis Labels display, drag the mouse to select and enter the cell range A14:A18 with a worksheet prefix (see Section B.3), *as a formula* in the **Axis label range** box.
   In Excel for Mac, in the Select Data Source display, click the icon inside the **Horizontal (Category) axis labels** [or **Category (X) axis labels**] box and drag the mouse to select and enter the same cell range, A14:A18.
4. Click **OK**.

In the chart:

5. Right-click inside a bar and click **Format Data Series** in the shortcut menu.
6. In the Format Data Series display, click **Series Options**. In the Series Options, click **Series Options**, enter **0** as the **Gap Width** and then close the display. (To see the second Series Options, you may have to first click the chart [third] icon near the top of the task pane.)

In Excel for Mac 2016 there is only one Series Options label and the Gap Width setting is displayed without having to click Series Options.

Relocate the chart to a chart sheet and adjust the chart formatting by using the instructions in Section B.5.

B.7 Deleting the "Extra" Histogram Bar (Excel)

As "Classes and Excel Bins" on page 49 explains, in Excel bins approximate classes. This approximation creates an "extra" bin that will have a frequency of zero. To delete the histogram bar associated with this extra bin, edit the cell range that Excel uses to construct the histogram.

Right-click the histogram background and click **Select Data**. In the Select Data Source dialog box in Microsoft Windows Excels:

1. Click **Edit** under the **Legend Entries (Series)** heading.
2. In the Edit Series dialog box, edit the **Series values** cell range formula to begin with the second cell of the original cell range and click OK.

3. Click **Edit** under the **Horizontal (Categories) Axis Labels** heading.
4. In the Axis Labels dialog box, edit the **Axis label range** formula to begin with the second cell of the original cell range and click **OK**.

In the Select Data Source dialog box in Excel for Mac:

1. Edit the **Y values** cell range formula to begin with the second cell of the original cell range and click OK.
2. Edit the **Horizontal (Category) axis labels** [or **Category (X) axis labels**] formula.
3. In the Axis Labels dialog box, edit the **Axis label range** formula to begin with the second cell of the original cell range and click **OK**.

Online Resources

C.1 About the Online Resources for This Book

Online resources complement and extend the study of business statistics and support the content of this book. Some resources, such as the collection of data files, are integral to learning with this book, while other resources, such as online sections and chapters are optional and can be skipped without loss of comprehension about the concepts and methods that this book discusses. For readers using Microsoft Excel, this book fully integrates the following: a set of Excel Guide Workbooks that contain templates or model solutions for applying Excel to specific statistical methods; the Visual Explorations Workbooks that interactively demonstrate selected statistical concepts; and PHStat, the Pearson statistics add-in for Excel, that the authors designed and which Appendix H discusses.

In addition to the data files and integrated Excel resources, online resources include documents that support the end-of-chapter cases and the optional online chapters, online topics, and chapter "Short Takes," all as PDF format files, and the data files for the optional materials and several online pamphlets for computing novices.

Access the Online Resources

To access the online resources for this book, visit the public download page for this book:

1. Open a web browser and go to www.pearsonhighered.com/levine.
2. In that web page, locate this book, *Basic Business Statistics, 14/e*, and click **Student Download Page** that appears below the title.
3. In the student download page, click the links of interest.

Registered users of a MyLab Statistics course for this book can also use the MyLab Statistics Tools for Success page:

1. Open the MyLab Statistics course for this book.
2. Click **Tools for Success** in the left pane.
3. In the Tools for Success page, click the links of interest.

Note that the Tools for Success page contains a number of items that were not prepared by the authors of this book but which Pearson offers MyLab Statistics users as additional supplements. Those additional supplements do not appear on the student download page.

In either method, clicking most item links will trigger a prompt to save a file. Some files are zip archives, collections of files, that need to be "unzipped" or expanded before use. Clicking the PHStat link will redirect a browser to a separate PHStat home page, from which the PHStat add-in can be obtained. Appendix H discusses obtaining PHStat in detail.

C.2 Data Files

As Section FTF.4 first explains, the names of data files that examples and problems use appear in a special inverted color typeface such as Retirement Funds. This section contains an alphabetized list of the data files that defines the variables for each file, the chapters that reference the file, and category definitions for categorical variables. Unless otherwise noted, data files are provided in ways that Excel, JMP, and Minitab can directly use without translation: as Excel workbooks, as Minitab worksheets or projects, and as JMP data tables or projects. Data files that can be used with only one or two of the programs also contain trailing single-letter codes E(xcel), J(MP), or M(initab) that identify which program or programs use the file.

311CALLCENTER Day and abandonment rate (%) (Chapter 3)

311CALLDURATION Call duration in seconds (Chapter 2)

ACCOUNTINGPARTNERS Firm and number of partners (Chapter 3)

ACCOUNTINGPARTNERS2 Region and number of partners (Chapter 10)

ACCOUNTINGPARTNERS6 Region, revenue ($millions), number of partners, number of professionals, MAS (%), southeast (0 = no, 1 = yes), and Gulf coast southeast (0 = no, 1 = yes) (Chapter 15)

ACT Method (online or traditional), ACT scores for condensed course, and ACT scores for regular course (Chapter 11)

ACT-ONEWAY Group 1 ACT scores, group 2 ACT scores, group 3 ACT scores, and group 4 ACT scores (Chapter 11)

ADINDEX Respondent, cola A Adindex, and cola B Adindex (Chapter 10)

ADVERTISE Sales ($thousands), radio ads ($thousands), and newspaper ads ($thousands) for 22 cities (Chapter 17)

AIRLINES Destination, Southwest airlines fare ($), and US Airways fare ($) (Chapter 10)

AIRPORTRATING Size (medium and large) and rating (Chapters 3 and 8)

AMERICANBANKS ROATCE(%) and efficiency rating(%) (Chapter 13)

AMS2-1 Types of errors and frequency, types of errors and cost, and types of wrong billing errors and cost (as three separate worksheets) (Chapter 2)

AMS2-2 Days and number of calls (Chapter 2)

AMS8 Rate willing to pay ($) (Chapter 8)

AMS9 Upload speed (Chapter 9)

AMS10 Update times for email interface 1 and email interface 2 (Chapter 10)

AMS11-1 Update time for system 1, system 2, and system 3 (Chapter 11)

AMS11-2 Technology (cable or fiber) and interface (system 1, system 2, or system 3) (Chapter 11)

AMS13 Number of hours spent telemarketing and number of new subscriptions (Chapter 13)

AMS14 Week, number of new subscriptions, hours spent tele-marketing, and type of presentation (formal or informal) (Chapter 14)

AMS16 Month and number of home delivery subscriptions (Chapter 16)

ANSCOMBE Data sets A, B, C, and D, each with 11 pairs of X and Y values (Chapter 13)

ARLINGTONS DASHBOARD DATA nine worksheets containing table data about Arlingtons stores and sales (Chapter 17) (E)

ATM TRANSACTIONS Cause, frequency, and percentage (Chapter 2)

BANK1 Waiting time (in minutes) of 15 customers at a bank located in a commercial district (Chapters 3, 9, 10, and 12)

BANK2 Waiting time (in minutes) of 15 customers at a bank located in a residential area (Chapters 3, 10, and 12)

BANKMARKETING Age, type of job, marital status (divorced, married, or single), education (primary, secondary, tertiary, or unknown), is credit in default, mean yearly balance in account, is there a housing loan, is there a personal loan, last contact duration in seconds, number of contacts performed during this campaign, and has the client purchased a term deposit (also contains the Binary-LogisticDATA worksheet that contains recoded variables) (Chapter 17)

BASEBALL Team, league (0 = American, 1 = National) wins, earned run average, runs scored per game, saves, batting average, HRs, and WHIP (walks plus hits per inning) (Chapters 13, 14, 15, and 17)

BASEBALLTEAMS Team, attendance, high temperature on game day, winning percentage of home team; opponentw's winning percentage, game played on weekend day (0 = no, 1 = yes), and promotion held (0 = no, 1 = yes) (Chapter 18)

BBCOST2016 Team and total cost ($) for two people (Chapter 2)

BBSALARIES Year and average major league baseball salary ($millions) (Chapter 16)

BBVALUES Team, revenue ($millions), and value ($millions) (Chapter 13)

BESTCOMPANIES Company, full-time jobs job openings, total worldwide revenues ($billions), and total voluntary turnover (%) (Chapters 14 and 15)

BONUSES Year and bonuses ($000) (Chapter 16)

BRANDZTECHFIN Brand, brand value in 2014 ($millions), % change in brand value from 2013, region, and sector (Chapters 10 and 12)

BREAKFAST Type (Continental or American), delivery time difference for early time period, and delivery time difference for late time period (Chapter 11)

BREAKFAST2 Type (Continental or American), delivery time difference for early time period, and delivery time difference for late time period (Chapter 11)

BRYNNEPACKAGING WPCT score and rating (Chapter 13)

BULBS Manufacturer (1 = A, 2 = B) and length of life (hours) (Chapters 2, 10, and 12)

BUNDLE Restaurant, bundle score, and typical cost ($) (Chapter 2)

BUSINESSVALUATION Drug company name, price to book value ratio, return on equity (ROE), and growth% (Chapter 14)

BUSINESSVALUATION2 Company, ticker symbol, Standard Industrial Classification 3 (SIC3) code, Standard Industrial Classification 4 (SIC4) code, price to book value ratio, price to earnings ratio, natural log of assets (as a measure of size), return on equity (ROE), growth percentage (GS5), debt to EBITDA ratio, dummy variable indicator of SIC 4 code 2834 (1 = 2834, 0 = not 2824), and dummy variable indicator of SIC 4 code 2835 (1 = 2835, 0 = not 2835) (Chapter 15)

CABERNET California wine rating, Washington wine rating, California wine ranking, and Washington wine ranking (Chapter 12)

CALLCENTER Month and call volume (Chapter 16)

CANDIDATE ASSESSMENT Salary, competence rating, gender of candidate (F or M), gender of rater (F or M), rater/candidate gender (F to F, F to M, M to M, M to M), school (Private, Public), department (Biology, Chemistry, Physics), and age of rater (Chapter 18)

CARDIOGOODFITNESS Product purchased (TM195, TM498, TM798), age in years, gender (Male or Female), education in years, relationship status (Single or Partnered), average number of times the customer plans to use the treadmill each week, self-rated fitness on a 1-to-5 ordinal scale (1 = poor to 5 = excellent), annual household income ($), and average number of miles the customer expects to walk/run each week (Chapters 2, 3, 6, 8, 10, 11, and 12)

CARDSTUDY Upgraded (0 = no, 1 = yes), purchases ($thousands), and extra cards (0 = no, 1 = yes) (Chapters 14 and 17)

CARPRODUCTION Year, coded year, and number of units produced (Chapter 16)

CATFOOD Ounces eaten of kidney, shrimp, chicken liver, salmon, and beef cat food (Chapters 11 and 12)

CATFOOD2 Piece size (F = fine, C = chunky), coded weight for low fill height, and coded weight for current fill height (Chapter 11)

CDRATE Bank, 1-year CD rate, and 5-year CD rate (Chapters 2, 3, 6, and 8)

CELLPHONEPROVIDERS Name of provider, type (tradional or prepaid), and rating (Chapter 2)

CEO2016 Company, CEO compensation ($millions), and return in 2016 (Chapter 2)

CEREALS Cereal, calories, carbohydrates, and sugar (Chapters 3, 13, and 17)

CHURN Customer ID, churn coded (0 = no, 1 = yes), churn, calls, and visits(Chapters 14 and 17)

CIGARETTETAX State and cigarette tax ($) (Chapters 2 and 3)

CITIES City, average annual salary ($), unemployment rate (%), median home value ($000), violent crime rate per 100,000 residents, average commuting time (minutes), livability score (Chapter 15)

COCA-COLA Year, coded year, and revenues ($billions) (Chapter 16)

COFFEE Expert and rating of coffees by brand A, B, C, and D (Chapter 10)

COFFEEEXPORTS Year and exports in thousands of 60-kg bags (Chapter 16)

COFFEESALES Coffee sales at $0.59, $0.69, $0.79, and $0.89 (Chapters 11 and 12)

COFFEESALES2 Coffee sales and price (Chapter 15)

COLLEGEDEBT Option and average debt at graduation ($) (Chapter 10)

COMMUNITYBANKS Institution, location, ROA(%), efficiency ratio(%), and total risk based capital(%) (Chapters 14 and 15)

COMMUTINGTIME City and average weekly commuting time (minutes) (Chapters 2 and 3)

CONCRETE1 Sample number and compressive strength after two days and seven days (Chapter 10)

CONGESTIONLEVEL Asia, Europe, and North America increase (%) in overall travel time compared to a free flow situation (Chapters 11 and 12)

CONNECTIONSPEED Country, average connection speed in mbps, average peak connection speed, percent above 4 mbps, percent above 10 mbps (Chapters 3 and 17)

COREAPPLIANCES Year and shipments in millions (Chapter 16)

CORNFLAKES thickness (mm) for four different toasting times (seconds) (Chapter 11)

CPI-U Year, coded year, and value of CPI-U (the consumer price index) (Chapter 16)

CREDIT SCORES City, state, and average credit score (Chapters 2 and 3)

CURRENCY Year, coded year, and exchange rates (against the U.S. dollar) for the Canadian dollar, Japanese yen, and English pound sterling (Chapters 2 and 16)

DELIVERY Customer, number of cases, and delivery time (Chapter 13)

DESKTOPLAPTOP Year and hours (Chapter 16)

DEVICE percentage used % (Chapter 2)

DIFFERENCES Year, revenues, first difference, second difference, and percentage difference (Chapter 16)

DIRTY DATA ID, gender (male or female), age (years), class (Sophomore, Junior, or Senior), Major (Accounting, CIS, Economics/Finance, International Business, Management, Retailing/Marketing, and Other (Chapter 1)

DOMESTICBEER Brand, alcohol percentage, calories, and carbohydrates (Chapters 2, 3, 6, and 15)

DOWDOGS Stock and 1-year return (Chapter 3)

DOWMARKETCAP Company and market capitalization ($billions) (Chapters 3 and 6)

DRILL Depth, time to drill additional 5 feet, and type of hole (dry or wet) (Chapters 14 and 17)

DRINK Amount of soft drink filled in 2-liter bottles (Chapters 2 and 9)

ENERGY State and per capita kilowatt hour use (Chapter 3)

ENGINES RPM and torque (Chapter 15)

ENTREE Type and number served (Chapter 2)

ERWAITING Emergency room waiting time (in minutes) at the main facility and at satellite 1, satellite 2, and satellite 3 (Chapters 11 and 12)

ESPRESSO Tamp (inches) and time (seconds) (Chapter 13)

EUROTOURISM Country, employment in tourism 2014, and tourism establishments (Chapter 15)

EUROTOURISM2 Country, employment in tourism 2015, business travel & tourism spending 2014 (US$millions), international visitors 2015, and tourism establishments (Chapter 17)

EXAMPLE15-2 X and Y (Chapter 15)

EXAMPLE15-3 X and Y (Chapter 15)

FASTFOOD Amount spent on fast food ($) (Chapters 2, 8, and 9)

FASTFOODCHAIN Mean sales per unit ($thousands) at burger, chicken, sandwich, and snack chains (Chapters 11 and 12)

FEDRECEIPT Year, coded year, and federal receipts ($billions current) (Chapter 16)

FIFTEENWEEKS Week number, number of customers, and sales ($thousands) over a period of 15 consecutive weeks (Chapter 13)

FLYASH Fly ash percentage and strength (PSI) (Chapter 15)

FOODS Type, blandspicy, lightheavy, and lowhighcalories rating (Chapter 17)

FORCE Force required to break an insulator (Chapters 2, 3, 8, and 9)

FOREIGNMARKET Country, level of development (Emerging or Developed), and time required to start a business (days) (Chapter 10)

FOREIGNMARKET2 Country, region, cost to export container (US$), and cost to import container (US$) (Chapters 11 and 12)

FREEPORT Address, fair market value ($thousands), property size (acres), house size, age, number of rooms, number of bathrooms, and number of cars that can be parked in the garage (Chapter 15)

FREEZER Month and shipments in thousands (Chapter 16)

FTMBA School number, tuition per year ($), GMAT score, acceptance rate (%), graduates employed at graduation (%), and mean starting salary and bonus ($) (Chapters 13, 15, and 17)

FURNITURE Days between receipt and resolution of complaints regarding purchased furniture (Chapters 2, 3, 8, and 9)

GASPRICES Month and price per gallon ($) (Chapter 16)

GCFREEROSLYN Address, location (Glen Cove, Freeport, or Roslyn), fair market value ($thousands), property size (acres), age, house size (sq. ft.), number of rooms, number of bathrooms, and number of cars that can be parked in the garage (Chapter 15)

GCROSLYN Address, location (Glen Cove or Roslyn), fair market value ($thousands), property size (acres), age, house size (sq. ft.), number of rooms, number of bathrooms, and number of cars that can be parked in the garage (Chapters 14 and 15)

GDP Year and gross domestic product (Chapter 16)

GLASS1 Breakoff pressure, percentage of chips breaking off at stopper height of 20, percentage of chips breaking off at stopper height of 25 (Chapter 11)

GLASS2 Zone 1 lower, effect on imprint at temperature of 695, effect on imprint at temperature of 715 (Chapter 11)

GLENCOVE Address, fair market value ($thousands), property size (acres), age, house size (sq. ft.), number of rooms, number of bathrooms, and number of cars that can be parked in the garage (Chapters 14 and 15)

GLOBALINTERNETUSAGE Country, GDP per capita ($thousands), and Internet use percentage (Chapters 2 and 3)

GLOBALSOCIALMEDIA Country, GDP, and social media usage (%) (Chapters 2, 3 and 13)

GOLD Quarter, coded quarter, price ($), Q1, Q2, and Q3 (Chapter 16)

GRANULE Granule loss in Boston and Vermont shingles (Chapters 3, 8, 9, and 10)

GROWTH FUNDS Subset of RETIREMENT FUNDS where type is growth (Chapter 17)

HEATINGOIL Monthly consumption of heating oil (gallons), temperature (degrees Fahrenheit), attic insulation (inches), and ranch-style (0 = not ranch-style, 1 = ranch-style) (Chapters 14 and 15)

HEMLOCKFARMS Asking price, hot tub (0 = no, 1 = yes), rooms, lake view (0 = no, 1 = yes), bathrooms, bedrooms, loft/den (0 = no, 1 = yes), finished basement (0 = no, 1 = yes), and number of acres (Chapter 15)

HHINCOME Median home value (000), violent crime rate/100,000 residents, average commuting time in minutes, and livability score (Chapter 15)

HONDAPRICES Age in years and price ($) (Chapter 15)

HOTELAWAY Nationality and cost (British pounds sterling) (Chapter 3)

HOTELPRICES City and average price (US$) of a hotel room at a 2-star price, 3-star price, and 4-star hotel (Chapters 2 and 3)

HOUSEHOLDS ID, Gender, age, Hispanic origin (N or Y), dwelling type (AB, AH, DH, or Other), age of dwelling (years), years living at dwelling, number of bedrooms, number of vehicles kept at dwelling, fuel type at dwelling (Electric, Gas, Oil, or Other), monthly cost of fuel at dwelling ($), U.S. citizenship (N or Y), college degree (N or Y), marital status (D, M, NM, S, or W), work for pay in previous week (N or Y), mode of transportation to work (Bus, Car, Home, Subway/Rail, Taxi, Other, or NA), commuting time (minutes), hours worked per week, type of organization(GOV, NA, PP, PNP, or SE), annual earned income ($), and total annual income ($) (Chapter 18)

HOUSESALES Year, coded year, total sales (Chapter 16)

HYBRIDSALES Year and number sold (Chapter 18)

ICECREAM Daily temperature (in degrees Fahrenheit) and sales ($thousands) for 21 days (Chapter 13)

INDICES Year, change in DJIA, S&P500, and NASDAQ (Chapter 3)

INSURANCE Processing time in days for insurance policies (Chapters 3, 8, and 9)

INSURANCECLAIMS Claims, buildup (0 = buildup not = indicated, 1 = buildup indicated), and excess payment ($) (Chapter 8)

INSURANCEFRAUD ID, fraud coded (0 = no, 1 = yes), fraud (No or Yes), new business coded (0 = no, 1 = yes), new business (No or Yes), and claims/year (Chapters 14 and 17)

INTERNETMOBILETIME time in minutes spent per day using the Internet from a mobile device (Chapter 9)

INTERNETMOBILETIME2 time in minutes spent per day using the Internet from a mobile device (Chapter 10)

INVOICE Number of invoices processed and amount of time (hours) for 30 days (Chapter 13)

INVOICES Amount recorded (in dollars) from sales invoices (Chapter 9)

IPOS Year and number of IPOs (Chapter 16)

LAGGED PREDICTORS Year, Coded Year, Revenues, Lag1, Lag2, and Lag3 (Chapter 16) (E, J)

LTE Download speed (Mbps) on LTE connections of AT&T and Verizon providers (Chapter 10)

LUGGAGE Delivery time (in minutes) for luggage in Wing A and Wing B of a hotel (Chapters 10 and 12)

MANAGERS Sales (ratio of yearly sales divided by the target sales value for that region), Wonderlic Personnel Test score, Strong-Campbell Interest Inventory Test score, number of years of selling experience prior to becoming a sales manager, and whether the sales manager has a degree in electrical engineering (No or Yes) (Chapter 15)

MARKETBASKET Product, Costco cost, and Walmart cost (Chapter 10)

MCDONALDS Year, coded year, and annual total revenues ($billions) at McDonald's Corporation (Chapter 16)

MCDONALDSSTORES State and number of stores (Chapter 3)

MEDICALWIRES1 Machine type, narrow, and wide (Chapter 11)

MEDICALWIRES2 Narrow, and wide (Chapter 11)

METALS Year and the total rate of return (in percentage) for platinum, gold, and silver (Chapter 3)

MINING Day, amount stacked, and downtime (Chapter 18)

MINING2 Day; hours of downtime due to mechanical, electrical, tonnage restriction, operator, and no feed; and total hours (Chapter 18)

MOBILE ELECTRONICS In-aisle sales, front sales, kiosk sales, and expert area sales (Chapter 11)

MOBILE ELECTRONICS STACKED Stacked version of Mobile Electronics (Chapter 11 and 12) (J, M)

MOBILE ELECTRONICS2 Mobile payments (No or Yes), in-aisle sales, front sales, kiosk sales, and expert area sales (Chapter 11)

MOBILECOMMERCE Country and mobile commerce penetration (%) (Chapters 3 and 8)

MOBILESPEED Carrier, download speed in mbps, upload speed in mbps (Chapters 2, 3, 13, and 17)

MOISTURE Moisture content of Boston shingles and Vermont shingles (Chapter 9)

MOLDING Vibration time (seconds), vibration pressure (psi), vibration amplitude (%), raw material density (g/ mL), quantity of raw material (scoops), product length in cavity 1 (in.), product length in cavity 2 (in.), product weight in cavity 1 (gr.), and product weight in cavity 2 (gr.) (Chapter 15)

MONTHLYMOVIEREVENUES Month and monthly revenues from 2005 through 2016 (Chapter 2) (E)

MOVIE Title, box office gross ($millions), and DVD revenue ($millions) (Chapter 13)

MOVIE ATTENDANCE Year and movie attendance (billions) (Chapters 2 and 16)

MOVIE ATTENDANCE16 Year and movie attendance (billions) (Chapter 2)

MOVIE REVENUES Year and revenue ($billions) (Chapter 2)

MOVIE REVENUES by MPAA RATING Year, rating (G, PG, PG-13, or R), and revenues (Chapter 16) (J)

MOVING Labor hours, cubic feet, number of large pieces of furniture, and availability of an elevator (Chapters 13 14, and 17)

MYELOMA Patient, before transplant measurement, and after transplant measurement (Chapter 10)

NATURAL GAS Month, wellhead price ($/thousands cu. ft.), and residential price ($/thousands cu. ft.) (Chapters 2 and 16)

NBA Team, number of wins, field goal %, 3-point field goal %, points per game for team, points per game for opponent, difference in points per game between team and opponent, rebounds per game, and turnovers per game (Chapters 14 and 17)

NBACOST Team and cost ($) (Chapters 2 and 6)

NBAVALUES Team, team code, annual revenue ($millions), and value ($millions) and 1-year change in value (%) (Chapters 2, 3 and 13)

NICKELS26WEEKS Standby hours, staff present, remote engineering hours, graphics hours, and production labor hours (Chapters 14 and 15)

NEIGHBOR Selling price ($thousands), number of rooms, and neighborhood location (0 = east, 1 = west) (Chapter 14)

NEWHOMESALES Month, sales in thousands, and mean price ($thousands) (Chapter 2)

NORMAL PROBABILITIES1 Normal probabilities template (Chapter 6) (J, M)

NORMAL PROBABILITIES2 Normal probabilities template (Chapter 6) (J, M)

OIL&GASOLINE Week, price of a gallon of gasoline ($), and price of oil per barrel, ($) (Chapter 13)

OMNIPOWER Bars sold, price (cents), and promotion expenses ($) (Chapters 14 and 17)

ORDER Time in minutes to fill orders for a population of 200 (Chapter 8)

ORGANICFOOD Customer, organic food purchaser (0 = no, 1 = yes), age, and online health wellness e-newsletters subscriber (0 = no, 1 = yes), (Chapter 14)

ORIGINAL MOVIE ATTENDANCE Year and attendance (millions) (Chapter 16)

O-RING Flight number, temperature, and O-ring damage index (Chapter 13)

PACKAGINGFOAM1 Die temperature, 3 mm. diameter, and 4 mm. diameter (Chapter 11)

PACKAGINGFOAM2 Die temperature, 3 mm. diameter, and 4 mm. diameter (Chapter 11)

PACKAGINGFOAM3 Die temperature, die diameter, and foam density (Chapter 14)

PACKAGINGFOAM4 Die temperature, die diameter, and foam diameter (Chapter 14)

PALLET Weight of Boston shingles and weight of Vermont shingles (Chapters 2, 8, 9, and 10)

PARACHUTE1WAY Tensile strength of parachutes from suppliers 1, 2, 3, and 4 (Chapter 11)

PARACHUTE2WAY Loom and tensile strength of parachutes from suppliers 1, 2, 3, and 4 (Chapter 11)

PATRONS Gender, entrée ordered, dessert ordered, and payment method (cash, credit/debit card, or mobile payment) (Chapter 17)

PAYMENT Method and percentage (Chapter 2)

PEN Ad and product rating (Chapters 11, 12)

PHILLY Zip code, population, median sales price 2012 ($000), average days on market 2012, units sold 2012, median household income ($), percentage of residents with a BA or higher, and hotness (0 = not hot, 1 = hot) (Chapter 17)

PHONE Time (in minutes) to clear telephone line problems and location (1 = I, 2 = II) (Chapters 10 and 12)

PIZZAHUT Gender coded (0 = Female, 1 = Male), gender (Female or Male), price ($), and purchase (0 = student selected another pizzeria, 1 = student selected Pizza Hut) (Chapter 14)

PIZZATIME Time period, delivery time for local restaurant, and delivery time for national chain (Chapter 10)

POLIO Year and incidence rates per 100,000 persons of reported poliomyelitis (Chapter 16)

POTATO Percentage of solids content in filter cake, acidity (pH), lower pressure, upper pressure, cake thickness, varidrive speed, and drum speed setting for 54 measurements (Chapter 15)

POTTERMOVIES Title, first weekend gross ($millions), U.S. gross ($millions), and worldwide gross ($millions) (Chapters 2, 3, and 13)

PROPERTYTAXES State and property taxes per capita ($) (Chapters 2, 3, and 6)

PROTEIN Type of food, calories (in grams), protein, percentage of calories from fat, percentage of calories from saturated fat, and cholesterol (mg) (Chapters 2, 3, and 17)

PUMPKIN Circumference and weight of pumpkins (Chapter 13)

QUARTERBACK Name, accuracy, arm strength, athleticism, pocket presence, field vision, and pre-snap (Chapter 17)

REDANDWHITE Fixed acidity, volatile acidity, citric acid, residual sugar, chlorides, free sulfur dioxide, total sulfur dioxide, density, pH, sulphates, alcohol, wine type coded (0 = White, 1 = Red), and wine type (Red or White), quality (Chapter 14)

REDWOOD Height (ft.), breast height diameter (in.), and bark thickness (in.) (Chapters 13 and 14)

REGISTRATIONERROR Registration error, temperature, pressure, and supplier (Chapter 15)

REGISTRATIONERROR-HIGHCOST Registration error and temperature (Chapter 15)

RENTSILVERSPRING Apartment size (sq. ft.) and monthly rental cost ($) (Chapter 13)

RESTAURANTS Location (City or Suburban), food rating, decor rating, service rating, summated rating, coded location (0 = Center City, 1 = Metro Area), and cost of a meal (Chapters 2, 3, 10, 12, 13 and 14)

RESTAURANTS2 Location, food rating, decor rating, service rating, cost of a meal, popularity index, and cuisine [American (New), Chinese, French, Indian, Italian, Japanese, or Mexican] (Chapter 17)

RETIREMENT FUNDS Fund number, market cap (Small, Mid-Cap, or Large), type (Growth or Value), assets ($millions), turnover ratio, beta (measure of the volatility of a stock), standard deviation (measure of returns relative to 36-month average), risk (Low, Average, or High), 1-year return, 3-year return, 5-year return, 10-year return, expense ratio, and star rating (Chapters 2, 3, 6, 8, 10, 11, 12, and 15)

ROSLYN Address, fair market value ($thousands), property size (acres), house size (sq. ft.), age, number of rooms, number of bathrooms, and number of cars that can be parked in the garage (Chapter 15)

SATISFACTION Satisfaction code (0 = not satisfied, 1 = satisfied), Satisfaction (No or Yes), delivery time difference (minutes), previous coded (0 = no, 1 = yes), and previous (No or Yes) (Chapter 17)

SECOND EXPERIMENT In-aisle sales, front sales, kiosk sales, and expert area sales (Chapter 12)

SERVICELEVEL Time to answer (Chapters 2, 8, and 9)

SILVER Year and price of silver ($) (Chapter 16)

SILVER-Q Quarter, coded quarter, price of silver ($), Q1, Q2, and Q3 (Chapter 16)

SILVERSPRING Address, asking price ($000), lot size (acres), yearly taxes ($), central a/c (0 = no, 1 = yes), number of bedrooms, number of bathrooms, age (years), number of parking spaces, finished basement (0 = no, 1 = yes), brick (0 = no, 1 = yes), and fireplace (0 = no, 1 = yes) (Chapters 13, 14, 15, and 17)

SILVERSPRINGUNCODED SilverSpring version with these uncoded variables: has central a/c, has finished basement, has brick, and has fireplace (all Y or N) (Chapter 14)

SITE SELECTION Store number, profiled customers, and sales ($millions) (Chapter 13)

SMARTPHONE SALES Type, and market share percentage for the years 2010 through 2014 (Chapter 2)

SMARTPHONES Price ($) (Chapter 3)

SOCCERVALUES Team, country, revenue ($millions), and value ($millions) (Chapter 13)

SOCIAL RESPONSE Product category (apparel, hardlines, household, furnishings, or grocery), sentiment rating (positive, neutral, or negative), customer type (online guest, online member, or in-store), and customer frequency of posting (low, average, or high) (Chapter 17)

SOLARPOWER Year and amount of solar power generated (megawatts) (Chapter 16)

STARBUCKS Tear, viscosity, pressure, and plate gap (Chapters 13 and 14)

STEEL Error in actual length and specified length (Chapters 2, 6, 8, and 9)

STOCK PERFORMANCE Decade and stock performance (%) (Chapters 2 and 16)

STOCKINDEX Stock index and percentage change for 2009 through 2013 (Chapter 2)

STOCKPRICES2016 Date, S&P 500 value, and closing weekly stock price for GE, Discovery Communications, and Google (Chapter 13)

STUDENTSURVEY ID, gender (Female or Male), age (as of last birthday), class designation (Sophomore, Junior, or Senior), major (Accounting, CIS, Economics/Finance, International Business, Management, Retail/Marketing, Other, or Undecided), graduate school intention (No, Yes, or Undecided), cumulative GPA, current employment status (Full-Time, Part-Time, or Unemployed), expected starting salary ($thousands), number of social networking sites registered for, satisfaction with student advisement services on campus, amount spent on books and supplies this semester, type of computer preferred (Desktop, Laptop, or Tablet), text messages per week, and wealth accumulated to feel rich (Chapters 2, 3, 6, 8, 10, 11, and 12)

SUPERBOWLADS Season, number of ads, and elapsed time (Chapter 2)

SUPERBOWLADSCORE Brand advertised, time of ad, and score (Chapters 3, 6, 8, 10, and 12)

TABLE 5.1 Interruptions per day and probability (Chapter 5) (J,M)

TAXIDELAYS Delay time in minutes for driver A and delay time in minutes for driver B (Chapter 10)

TEABAGS Teabag weight (ounces) (Chapters 3, 8, and 9)

TECHNOLOGIES Technologies and frequency (Chapter 2)

TELECOM Provider, TV rating, and phone rating (Chapter 10)

TESTRANK Rank scores and training method (0 = traditional, 1 = experimental) for 10 people (Chapter 12)

TEXTBOOKCOSTS Revenue category and percentage (Chapter 2)

THICKNESS Thickness, catalyst, pH, pressure, temperature, and voltage (Chapters 14 and 15)

THREE HOTEL REASONS STACKED Reason (amenities, quality or of room, dining options, or staff/service issues), hotel, and frequency (Chapter 12) (J)

THREE-HOTEL SURVEY Choose again (Yes or No), Golden Palm, Palm Royale, and Palm Princess (Chapter 12) (M)

THREE-HOTEL SURVEY STACKED Stacked version of Three-Hotel Survey (Chapter 12) (J)

THREEHOTELRESPONSES Reason for not returning, hotel (GP, PR, or PP), booking source (agent, walk-in, or web), relationship status (couple, family, or single (Chapter 17)

TIMES Get-ready times (Chapter 3)

TOMATOMETER Movie, tomato meter rating, and receipts ($K) (Chapter 13) receipts ($K) (Chapter 13)

TOYS R US Quarter, coded quarter, revenue, and the dummy variables Q1, Q2, and Q3 (Chapter 16)

TROUGH Width of trough (Chapters 2, 3, 8, and 9)

TRSNYC Year, unit value of Diversified Equity funds, and unit value of Stable Value funds (Chapter 16)

TSMODEL1 Year, coded year, and three time series (I, II, and III) (Chapter 16)

TSMODEL2 Year, coded year, and two time series (I and II) (Chapter 16)

TVREMOTE Filling time, 60, 72.5, and 85 degrees (Chapter 11)

TWITTERMOVIES Movie, Twitter activity, and receipts ($) (Chapter 13)

TWO-HOTEL SURVEY STACKED Choose again (Yes or No), hotel, and frequency (Chapter 12) (J, M)

UNDERWRITING End-of-training exam score, proficiency exam score, and training method (classroom, courseware app, or online) (Chapter 14)

UNSTACKED RESTAURANTS Center City meal cost and metro area meal cost (Chapter 2) (J)

UNSTACKED 3YRRETURN Three-year return for growth funds, three-year return for value funds (Chapter 2) (M)

USEDCARS Car, year, age, price ($), mileage, and power (hp), fuel (mpg) (Chapter 17)

UTILITY Utilities charges ($) for 50 one-bedroom apartments (Chapters 2 and 6)

VB Time to complete program (Chapter 10)

VINHOVERDE Fixed acidity, volatile acidity, citric acid, residual sugar, chlorides, free sulfur dioxide, total sulfur dioxide, density, pH, sulphates, alcohol, and quality (Chapters 13, 14 and 15)

VINHOVERDEPOPULATION see VINHOVERDE (Chapter 17)

VLABGO Storefront and in-aisle sales (E, M) or location and sales (J) (Chapters 10 and 12)

VLABGO STACKED Location and sales (Chapters 12 (J)

WAIT Waiting time and seating time (Chapter 6)

WALMART Quarter and Wal-Mart Stores quarterly revenues ($billions) (Chapter 16)

WARECOST Distribution cost ($thousands), sales ($thousands), and number of orders (Chapter 13)

WIP Processing times at each of two plants (1 = A, 2 = B) (Chapter 18)

WORKFORCE Year, population, and size of the workforce (Chapter 16)

YARN Side-by-side aspect and breaking strength scores for 30 psi, 40 psi, and 50 psi (Chapter 11)

YOGURT Name, type, calories, fat (g), sat. fat (g), protein (g), carbohydrates (g), sugar (g), sodium (mg), and calcium (%DV) (Chapter 17)

C.3 Files Integrated With Microsoft Excel

This book fully integrates a set of Excel Guide Workbooks that contain templates or model solutions for applying Excel to specific statistical methods, the Visual Explorations Workbooks that interactively demonstrate selected statistical concepts, and PHStat, the Pearson statistics add-in for Excel, that Appendix H discusses.

Excel Guide Workbooks

Excel Guide workbooks contain templates or model solutions for applying Excel to a particular statistical method. Chapter examples and the Excel Guide *Workbook* instructions feature worksheets from these workbooks.

Most workbooks include a **COMPUTE worksheet** (often shown in this book) and a **COMPUTE_FORMULAS worksheet** that allows you to examine all of the formulas that the worksheet uses. The Excel Guide workbooks (with chapter references) are:

Dirty Data (1)	**CIE Proportion (8)**
Recoded (1)	**Sample Size Mean (8)**
Challenging (2)	**Sample Size Proportion (8)**
Summary Table (2)	**Z Mean (9)**
Contingency Table (2)	**T Mean (9)**
Distributions (2)	**Z Proportion (9)**
Pareto (2)	**Pooled-Variance T (10)**
Histogram (2)	**Separate-Variance T (10)**
Polygons (2)	**Paired T (10)**
Scatter Plot (2)	**Z Two Proportions (10)**
Time Series (2)	**F Two Variances (10)**
MCT (2)	**One-Way ANOVA (11)**
Slicers (2)	**Levene (11)**
Sparklines (2)	**Two-Way ANOVA (11)**
Central Tendency (3)	**Randomized Block (11)**
Descriptive (3)	**Chi-Square (12)**
Quartiles (3)	**Chi-Square Worksheets (12)**
Boxplot (3)	**Wilcoxon (12)**
Parameters (3)	**Kruskal-Wallis Worksheets (12)**
Covariance (3)	
Correlation (3)	**Simple Linear Regression (13)**
Probabilities (4)	
Bayes (4)	**Package Delivery (13)**
Discrete Variable (5)	**Multiple Regression (14)**
Binomial (5)	**Logistic Regression add-in (14)**
Poisson (5)	
Portfolio (5)	**Moving Averages (16)**
Hypergeometric (5)	**Exponential Smoothing (16)**
Normal (6)	**Exponential Trend (16)**
NPP (6)	**Differences (16)**
Exponential (6)	**Lagged Predictors (16)**
SDS (7)	**Forecasting Comparison (16)**
CIE sigma known (8)	**Arlingtons National Sales**
CIE sigma unknown (8)	**.pbix (17)**

Visual Explorations

Visual Explorations are add-in workbooks that interactively demonstrate various key statistical concepts. To use these workbooks with Microsoft Windows Excel, first verify the Excel security settings (see step 4 in Appendix Section D.1). The Visual Explorations workbooks are:

VE-Normal Distribution
VE-Sampling Distribution
VE-Simple Linear Regression

PHStat

PHStat is the Pearson Education statistics add-in for Microsoft Excel that simplifies the task of using Excel as you learn business statistics. PHStat comes packaged as a zip file archive that you download and unzip to the folder of your choice. The archive contains:

PHStat.xlam, the main add-in workbook.
PHStat readme.pdf Explains the technical requirements, and setup and troubleshooting procedures for PHStat (PDF format).
PHStatHelp.chm The integrated help system for users of Microsoft Windows Excel.
PHStatHelp.pdf The help system as a PDF format file.
PHStatHelp.epub The help system in Open Publication Structure eBook format.

For more information about PHStat, see Appendix H.

C.4 Supplemental Files

Over three dozen online supplemental files provide opportunities for additional learning with this book. This set of files include two additional chapters and numerous additional sections that customize learning and which are optional to the main content of this book. Supplemental files also include the SHORT TAKES that expand on in-chapter explanations and the files that support the end-of-chapter cases.

All supplemental files use the Portable Document Format (PDF) that are best viewed using the latest version of Adobe Acrobat Reader (get.adobe.com/reader/) or Acrobat Pro. Files that support the Digital Cases use advanced PDF features and *require* the use of Acrobat Reader or Pro.

Configuring Software

Taking the time to properly configure software for use helps avoid technical issues that interfere with using that software with this book. Of Microsoft Excel, JMP, and Minitab, Excel requires the most set up and the other two minimal set up.

D.1 Microsoft Excel Configuration

Step 1: Update Excel

Proper configuration begins by ensuring the copy of Excel to be used with this book has been properly updated. For Microsoft Windows Excel, with any workbook open (even a blank one), select **File➔Account** and in the Account panel select **Update Now** from the **Update Options** pull-down list. For Excel for Mac, select **Help➔Check for Updates** to load the separate Microsoft AutoUpdate program that handles the downloading and installation of Office updates.

Step 2: Verify Microsoft Add-Ins

To use the *Analysis ToolPak* Excel Guide instructions, requires the Analysis ToolPak add-in. To use the Excel Guide instructions for logistic regression (Section EG14.7), requires the Solver add-in. Microsoft supplies these add-ins as part of any Excel installation, but the add-ins may not have been previously activated. (Readers who will not be using the Analysis ToolPak instructions and the Section EG14.7 instructions should skip to step 3.)

To check for the presence of the Analysis ToolPak or Solver add-ins in Microsoft Windows Excel:

1. Select **File➔Options**.

In the Excel Options dialog box:

2. Click **Add-Ins** in the left pane and look for the entry **Analysis ToolPak** (or **Solver Add-in**) in the right pane, under **Active Application Add-ins**.
3. If the entry appears, click **OK**.
4. If the entry does not appear in the **Active Application Add-ins** list, select **Excel Add-ins** from the **Manage** drop-down list and then click **Go**.
5. In the Add-Ins dialog box, check **Analysis ToolPak** (or **Solver Add-in**) in the **Add-Ins available** list and click **OK**.

If the Add-Ins available list does not include a Microsoft-supplied add-in that you need, rerun the Microsoft Office setup program to install the missing add-in.

To check for the presence of the Analysis ToolPak or Solver add-ins in Excel for Mac 2016:

1. Select **Tools➔Options**.
2. In the Adds-Ins dialog box, check **Analysis ToolPak** (or **Solver Add-In**) in the **Add-Ins available** list and click **OK**.

If the Add-Ins available list does not include a Microsoft-supplied add-in that you need, click **Browse** to locate the add-in. If a message appears that states that the add-in is not currently installed on your Mac, click **Yes** to install the add-in. Then exit Excel and restart Excel.

Step 3: Verify Excel Security Settings

Using Microsoft Windows Excel requires verifying Excel security settings to use any of the following: PHStat, one of the Visual Explorations add-in workbooks (see Section C.3), or the logistic regression add-in that Section EG14.7 requires. (Excel for Mac has no security settings and readers using Excel for Mac should skip to step 4.)

To properly configure the Microsoft Windows Excel security settings:

1. Select **File➔Options**.

In the Excel Options dialog box (shown below):

2. Click **Trust Center** in the left pane and then click **Trust Center Settings** in the right pane.

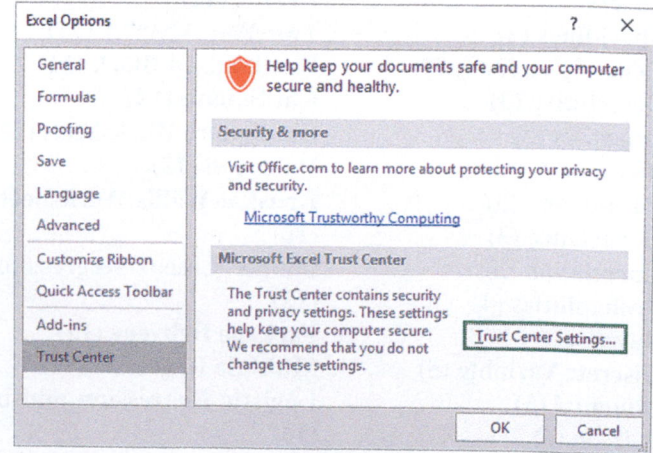

In the Trust Center dialog box:

3. Click **Add-ins** in the next left pane, and in the Add-ins right pane, clear all of the checkboxes (shown below).

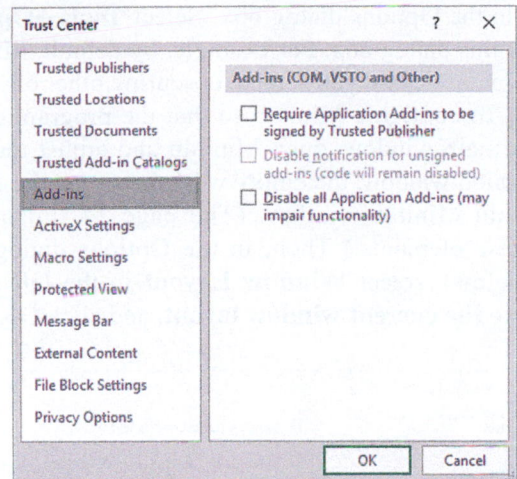

4. Click **Macro Settings** in the left pane, and in the Macro Settings right pane (shown below), click **Disable all macros with notification** and check **Trust access to the VBA object model**.

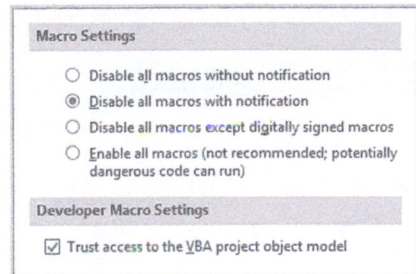

5. Click **OK** to close the Trust Center dialog box.

Back in the Excel Options dialog box:

6. Click **OK** to finish.

On some systems that have stringent security settings, you might need to modify step 4. For such systems, in step 4, also click **Trusted Locations** in the left pane and then, in the Trusted Locations right pane, click **Add new location** to add the folder path that you chose to store the PHStat or Visual Explorations add-in files.

Step 4: Opening Add-ins

Opening any of the following: PHStat, one of the Visual Explorations add-in workbooks (see Section C.3), or the logistic regression add-in that Section EG14.7 requires, will cause Excel to display a security notice that will be similar to the security notices for Microsoft Windows Excel and Excel for Mac notices shown below.

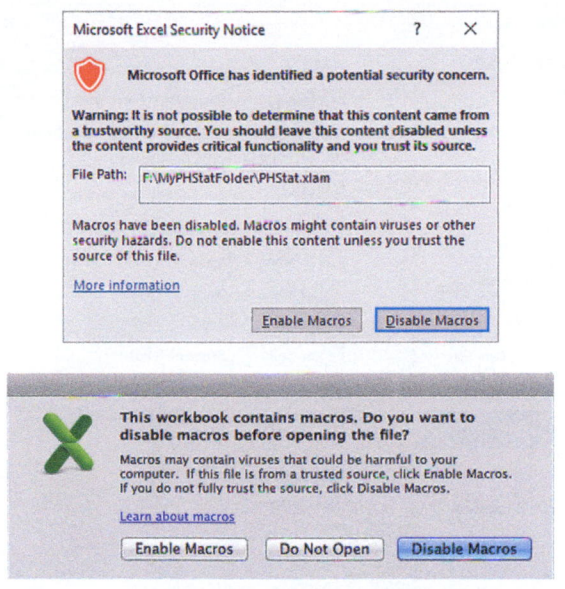

In these dialog boxes, click **Enable Macros**, which is *not* the default choice, to enable and use the add-in.

(Because Microsoft supplies the Analysis ToolPak and Solver add-ins, using either of those add-ins will *not* cause Excel to display a security notice.)

D.2 JMP Configuration

To use JMP with the JMP Guide instructions requires no special initial set up. However, for some analyses, changing certain global preferences may enhance the presentation of results. Select **File→Preferences** to display the Preferences dialog box. Selecting the Fonts Preference Group (shown below) changes the global preferences for textual displays and labels, such as chart titles and axis labels. Note that changes to a preference group are always global changes and may have unintended consequences in other displays and results. Best practice records current settings to any preference group before making changes so that the changes can be undone and the original settings restored.

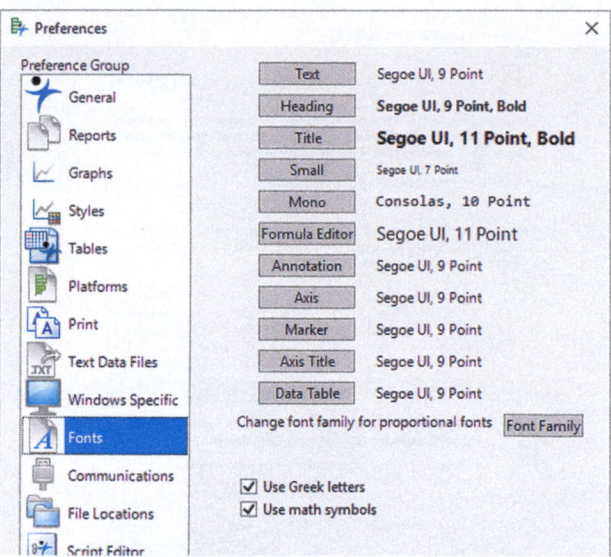

D.3 Minitab Configuration

To use Minitab with the Minitab Guide instructions requires no special initial set up. Configuration options can be changed in the Options dialog box. Select **Tools→Options** to display this dialog box. For example, by default, Minitab opens its main window full screen, obscuring other onscreen windows. To configure Minitab so that the program opens a smaller main window, open Minitab and adjust the size of the Session window, the empty worksheet, and the frame of the main Minitab window. (The page 14 illustration shows these elements.) Then, in the Options dialog box (shown below), select **Window Layout** in the left pane, check **Save the current window layout**, and click **OK**.

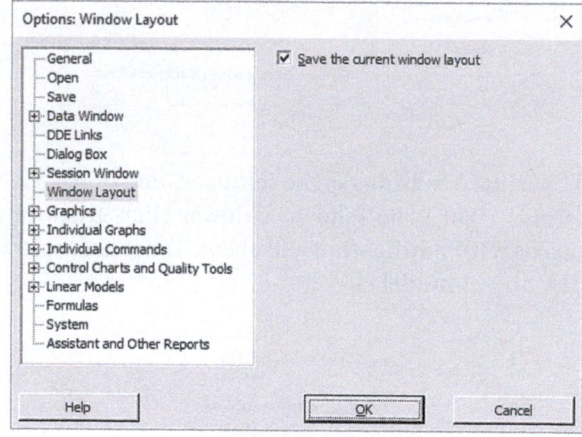

APPENDIX E

Table

TABLE E.1
Table of Random Numbers

	Column							
Row	**00000 12345**	**00001 67890**	**11111 12345**	**11112 67890**	**22222 12345**	**22223 67890**	**33333 12345**	**33334 67890**
01	49280	88924	35779	00283	81163	07275	89863	02348
02	61870	41657	07468	08612	98083	97349	20775	45091
03	43898	65923	25078	86129	78496	97653	91550	08078
04	62993	93912	30454	84598	56095	20664	12872	64647
05	33850	58555	51438	85507	71865	79488	76783	31708
06	97340	03364	88472	04334	63919	36394	11095	92470
07	70543	29776	10087	10072	55980	64688	68239	20461
08	89382	93809	00796	95945	34101	81277	66090	88872
09	37818	72142	67140	50785	22380	16703	53362	44940
10	60430	22834	14130	96593	23298	56203	92671	15925
11	82975	66158	84731	19436	55790	69229	28661	13675
12	30987	71938	40355	54324	08401	26299	49420	59208
13	55700	24586	93247	32596	11865	63397	44251	43189
14	14756	23997	78643	75912	83832	32768	18928	57070
15	32166	53251	70654	92827	63491	04233	33825	69662
16	23236	73751	31888	81718	06546	83246	47651	04877
17	45794	26926	15130	82455	78305	55058	52551	47182
18	09893	20505	14225	68514	47427	56788	96297	78822
19	54382	74598	91499	14523	68479	27686	46162	83554
20	94750	89923	37089	20048	80336	94598	26940	36858
21	70297	34135	53140	33340	42050	82341	44104	82949
22	85157	47954	32979	26575	57600	40881	12250	73742
23	11100	02340	12860	74697	96644	89439	28707	25815
24	36871	50775	30592	57143	17381	68856	25853	35041
25	23913	48357	63308	16090	51690	54607	72407	55538
26	79348	36085	27973	65157	07456	22255	25626	57054
27	92074	54641	53673	54421	18130	60103	69593	49464
28	06873	21440	75593	41373	49502	17972	82578	16364
29	12478	37622	99659	31065	83613	69889	58869	29571
30	57175	55564	65411	42547	70457	03426	72937	83792
31	91616	11075	80103	07831	59309	13276	26710	73000
32	78025	73539	14621	39044	47450	03197	12787	47709
33	27587	67228	80145	10175	12822	86687	65530	49325
34	16690	20427	04251	64477	73709	73945	92396	68263
35	70183	58065	65489	31833	82093	16747	10386	59293
36	90730	35385	15679	99742	50866	78028	75573	67257
37	10934	93242	13431	24590	02770	48582	00906	58595
38	82462	30166	79613	47416	13389	80268	05085	96666
39	27463	10433	07606	16285	93699	60912	94532	95632
40	02979	52997	09079	92709	90110	47506	53693	49892
41	46888	69929	75233	52507	32097	37594	10067	67327
42	53638	83161	08289	12639	08141	12640	28437	09268
43	82433	61427	17239	89160	19666	08814	37841	12847
44	35766	31672	50082	22795	66948	65581	84393	15890
45	10853	42581	08792	13257	61973	24450	52351	16602
46	20341	27398	72906	63955	17276	10646	74692	48438
47	54458	90542	77563	51839	52901	53355	83281	19177
48	26337	66530	16687	35179	46560	00123	44546	79896
49	34314	23729	85264	05575	96855	23820	11091	79821
50	28603	10708	68933	34189	92166	15181	66628	58599

TABLE E.1
Table of Random
Numbers (*continued*)

	Column							
Row	00000 12345	00001 67890	11111 12345	11112 67890	22222 12345	22223 67890	33333 12345	33334 67890
51	66194	28926	99547	16625	45515	67953	12108	57846
52	78240	43195	24837	32511	70880	22070	52622	61881
53	00833	88000	67299	68215	11274	55624	32991	17436
54	12111	86683	61270	58036	64192	90611	15145	01748
55	47189	99951	05755	03834	43782	90599	40282	51417
56	76396	72486	62423	27618	84184	78922	73561	52818
57	46409	17469	32483	09083	76175	19985	26309	91536
58	74626	22111	87286	46772	42243	68046	44250	42439
59	34450	81974	93723	49023	58432	67083	36876	93391
60	36327	72135	33005	28701	34710	49359	50693	89311
61	74185	77536	84825	09934	99103	09325	67389	45869
62	12296	41623	62873	37943	25584	09609	63360	47270
63	90822	60280	88925	99610	42772	60561	76873	04117
64	72121	79152	96591	90305	10189	79778	68016	13747
65	95268	41377	25684	08151	61816	58555	54305	86189
66	92603	09091	75884	93424	72586	88903	30061	14457
67	18813	90291	05275	01223	79607	95426	34900	09778
68	38840	26903	28624	67157	51986	42865	14508	49315
69	05959	33836	53758	16562	41081	38012	41230	20528
70	85141	21155	99212	32685	51403	31926	69813	58781
71	75047	59643	31074	38172	03718	32119	69506	67143
72	30752	95260	68032	62871	58781	34143	68790	69766
73	22986	82575	42187	62295	84295	30634	66562	31442
74	99439	86692	90348	66036	48399	73451	26698	39437
75	20389	93029	11881	71685	65452	89047	63669	02656
76	39249	05173	68256	36359	20250	68686	05947	09335
77	96777	33605	29481	20063	09398	01843	35139	61344
78	04860	32918	10798	50492	52655	33359	94713	28393
79	41613	42375	00403	03656	77580	87772	86877	57085
80	17930	00794	53836	53692	67135	98102	61912	11246
81	24649	31845	25736	75231	83808	98917	93829	99430
82	79899	34061	54308	59358	56462	58166	97302	86828
83	76801	49594	81002	30397	52728	15101	72070	33706
84	36239	63636	38140	65731	39788	06872	38971	53363
85	07392	64449	17886	63632	53995	17574	22247	62607
86	67133	04181	33874	98835	67453	59734	76381	63455
87	77759	31504	32832	70861	15152	29733	75371	39174
88	85992	72268	42920	20810	29361	51423	90306	73574
89	79553	75952	54116	65553	47139	60579	09165	85490
90	41101	17336	48951	53674	17880	45260	08575	49321
91	36191	17095	32123	91576	84221	78902	82010	30847
92	62329	63898	23268	74283	26091	68409	69704	82267
93	14751	13151	93115	01437	56945	89661	67680	79790
94	48462	59278	44185	29616	76537	19589	83139	28454
95	29435	88105	59651	44391	74588	55114	80834	85686
96	28340	29285	12965	14821	80425	16602	44653	70467
97	02167	58940	27149	80242	10587	79786	34959	75339
98	17864	00991	39557	54981	23588	81914	37609	13128
99	79675	80605	60059	35862	00254	36546	21545	78179
100	72335	82037	92003	34100	29879	46613	89720	13274

Source: Partially extracted from the Rand Corporation, *A Million Random Digits with 100,000 Normal Deviates* (Glencoe, IL, The Free Press, 1955).

TABLE E.2
The Cumulative Standardized Normal Distribution

Entry represents area under the cumulative standardized
normal distribution from $-\infty$ to Z

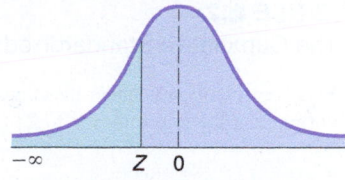

Z	\multicolumn{10}{c}{Cumulative Probabilities}
	0.00	0.01	0.02	0.03	0.04	0.05	0.06	0.07	0.08	0.09
−6.0	0.000000001									
−5.5	0.000000019									
−5.0	0.000000287									
−4.5	0.000003398									
−4.0	0.000031671									
−3.9	0.00005	0.00005	0.00004	0.00004	0.00004	0.00004	0.00004	0.00004	0.00003	0.00003
−3.8	0.00007	0.00007	0.00007	0.00006	0.00006	0.00006	0.00006	0.00005	0.00005	0.00005
−3.7	0.00011	0.00010	0.00010	0.00010	0.00009	0.00009	0.00008	0.00008	0.00008	0.00008
−3.6	0.00016	0.00015	0.00015	0.00014	0.00014	0.00013	0.00013	0.00012	0.00012	0.00011
−3.5	0.00023	0.00022	0.00022	0.00021	0.00020	0.00019	0.00019	0.00018	0.00017	0.00017
−3.4	0.00034	0.00032	0.00031	0.00030	0.00029	0.00028	0.00027	0.00026	0.00025	0.00024
−3.3	0.00048	0.00047	0.00045	0.00043	0.00042	0.00040	0.00039	0.00038	0.00036	0.00035
−3.2	0.00069	0.00066	0.00064	0.00062	0.00060	0.00058	0.00056	0.00054	0.00052	0.00050
−3.1	0.00097	0.00094	0.00090	0.00087	0.00084	0.00082	0.00079	0.00076	0.00074	0.00071
−3.0	0.00135	0.00131	0.00126	0.00122	0.00118	0.00114	0.00111	0.00107	0.00103	0.00100
−2.9	0.0019	0.0018	0.0018	0.0017	0.0016	0.0016	0.0015	0.0015	0.0014	0.0014
−2.8	0.0026	0.0025	0.0024	0.0023	0.0023	0.0022	0.0021	0.0021	0.0020	0.0019
−2.7	0.0035	0.0034	0.0033	0.0032	0.0031	0.0030	0.0029	0.0028	0.0027	0.0026
−2.6	0.0047	0.0045	0.0044	0.0043	0.0041	0.0040	0.0039	0.0038	0.0037	0.0036
−2.5	0.0062	0.0060	0.0059	0.0057	0.0055	0.0054	0.0052	0.0051	0.0049	0.0048
−2.4	0.0082	0.0080	0.0078	0.0075	0.0073	0.0071	0.0069	0.0068	0.0066	0.0064
−2.3	0.0107	0.0104	0.0102	0.0099	0.0096	0.0094	0.0091	0.0089	0.0087	0.0084
−2.2	0.0139	0.0136	0.0132	0.0129	0.0125	0.0122	0.0119	0.0116	0.0113	0.0110
−2.1	0.0179	0.0174	0.0170	0.0166	0.0162	0.0158	0.0154	0.0150	0.0146	0.0143
−2.0	0.0228	0.0222	0.0217	0.0212	0.0207	0.0202	0.0197	0.0192	0.0188	0.0183
−1.9	0.0287	0.0281	0.0274	0.0268	0.0262	0.0256	0.0250	0.0244	0.0239	0.0233
−1.8	0.0359	0.0351	0.0344	0.0336	0.0329	0.0322	0.0314	0.0307	0.0301	0.0294
−1.7	0.0446	0.0436	0.0427	0.0418	0.0409	0.0401	0.0392	0.0384	0.0375	0.0367
−1.6	0.0548	0.0537	0.0526	0.0516	0.0505	0.0495	0.0485	0.0475	0.0465	0.0455
−1.5	0.0668	0.0655	0.0643	0.0630	0.0618	0.0606	0.0594	0.0582	0.0571	0.0559
−1.4	0.0808	0.0793	0.0778	0.0764	0.0749	0.0735	0.0721	0.0708	0.0694	0.0681
−1.3	0.0968	0.0951	0.0934	0.0918	0.0901	0.0885	0.0869	0.0853	0.0838	0.0823
−1.2	0.1151	0.1131	0.1112	0.1093	0.1075	0.1056	0.1038	0.1020	0.1003	0.0985
−1.1	0.1357	0.1335	0.1314	0.1292	0.1271	0.1251	0.1230	0.1210	0.1190	0.1170
−1.0	0.1587	0.1562	0.1539	0.1515	0.1492	0.1469	0.1446	0.1423	0.1401	0.1379
−0.9	0.1841	0.1814	0.1788	0.1762	0.1736	0.1711	0.1685	0.1660	0.1635	0.1611
−0.8	0.2119	0.2090	0.2061	0.2033	0.2005	0.1977	0.1949	0.1922	0.1894	0.1867
−0.7	0.2420	0.2388	0.2358	0.2327	0.2296	0.2266	0.2236	0.2206	0.2177	0.2148
−0.6	0.2743	0.2709	0.2676	0.2643	0.2611	0.2578	0.2546	0.2514	0.2482	0.2451
−0.5	0.3085	0.3050	0.3015	0.2981	0.2946	0.2912	0.2877	0.2843	0.2810	0.2776
−0.4	0.3446	0.3409	0.3372	0.3336	0.3300	0.3264	0.3228	0.3192	0.3156	0.3121
−0.3	0.3821	0.3783	0.3745	0.3707	0.3669	0.3632	0.3594	0.3557	0.3520	0.3483
−0.2	0.4207	0.4168	0.4129	0.4090	0.4052	0.4013	0.3974	0.3936	0.3897	0.3859
−0.1	0.4602	0.4562	0.4522	0.4483	0.4443	0.4404	0.4364	0.4325	0.4286	0.4247
−0.0	0.5000	0.4960	0.4920	0.4880	0.4840	0.4801	0.4761	0.4721	0.4681	0.4641

TABLE E.2
The Cumulative Standardized Normal Distribution (*continued*)

Entry represents area under the cumulative standardized
normal distribution from $-\infty$ to Z

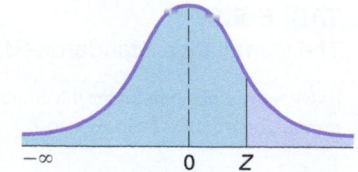

	Cumulative Probabilities									
Z	0.00	0.01	0.02	0.03	0.04	0.05	0.06	0.07	0.08	0.09
0.0	0.5000	0.5040	0.5080	0.5120	0.5160	0.5199	0.5239	0.5279	0.5319	0.5359
0.1	0.5398	0.5438	0.5478	0.5517	0.5557	0.5596	0.5636	0.5675	0.5714	0.5753
0.2	0.5793	0.5832	0.5871	0.5910	0.5948	0.5987	0.6026	0.6064	0.6103	0.6141
0.3	0.6179	0.6217	0.6255	0.6293	0.6331	0.6368	0.6406	0.6443	0.6480	0.6517
0.4	0.6554	0.6591	0.6628	0.6664	0.6700	0.6736	0.6772	0.6808	0.6844	0.6879
0.5	0.6915	0.6950	0.6985	0.7019	0.7054	0.7088	0.7123	0.7157	0.7190	0.7224
0.6	0.7257	0.7291	0.7324	0.7357	0.7389	0.7422	0.7454	0.7486	0.7518	0.7549
0.7	0.7580	0.7612	0.7642	0.7673	0.7704	0.7734	0.7764	0.7794	0.7823	0.7852
0.8	0.7881	0.7910	0.7939	0.7967	0.7995	0.8023	0.8051	0.8078	0.8106	0.8133
0.9	0.8159	0.8186	0.8212	0.8238	0.8264	0.8289	0.8315	0.8340	0.8365	0.8389
1.0	0.8413	0.8438	0.8461	0.8485	0.8508	0.8531	0.8554	0.8577	0.8599	0.8621
1.1	0.8643	0.8665	0.8686	0.8708	0.8729	0.8749	0.8770	0.8790	0.8810	0.8830
1.2	0.8849	0.8869	0.8888	0.8907	0.8925	0.8944	0.8962	0.8980	0.8997	0.9015
1.3	0.9032	0.9049	0.9066	0.9082	0.9099	0.9115	0.9131	0.9147	0.9162	0.9177
1.4	0.9192	0.9207	0.9222	0.9236	0.9251	0.9265	0.9279	0.9292	0.9306	0.9319
1.5	0.9332	0.9345	0.9357	0.9370	0.9382	0.9394	0.9406	0.9418	0.9429	0.9441
1.6	0.9452	0.9463	0.9474	0.9484	0.9495	0.9505	0.9515	0.9525	0.9535	0.9545
1.7	0.9554	0.9564	0.9573	0.9582	0.9591	0.9599	0.9608	0.9616	0.9625	0.9633
1.8	0.9641	0.9649	0.9656	0.9664	0.9671	0.9678	0.9686	0.9693	0.9699	0.9706
1.9	0.9713	0.9719	0.9726	0.9732	0.9738	0.9744	0.9750	0.9756	0.9761	0.9767
2.0	0.9772	0.9778	0.9783	0.9788	0.9793	0.9798	0.9803	0.9808	0.9812	0.9817
2.1	0.9821	0.9826	0.9830	0.9834	0.9838	0.9842	0.9846	0.9850	0.9854	0.9857
2.2	0.9861	0.9864	0.9868	0.9871	0.9875	0.9878	0.9881	0.9884	0.9887	0.9890
2.3	0.9893	0.9896	0.9898	0.9901	0.9904	0.9906	0.9909	0.9911	0.9913	0.9916
2.4	0.9918	0.9920	0.9922	0.9925	0.9927	0.9929	0.9931	0.9932	0.9934	0.9936
2.5	0.9938	0.9940	0.9941	0.9943	0.9945	0.9946	0.9948	0.9949	0.9951	0.9952
2.6	0.9953	0.9955	0.9956	0.9957	0.9959	0.9960	0.9961	0.9962	0.9963	0.9964
2.7	0.9965	0.9966	0.9967	0.9968	0.9969	0.9970	0.9971	0.9972	0.9973	0.9974
2.8	0.9974	0.9975	0.9976	0.9977	0.9977	0.9978	0.9979	0.9979	0.9980	0.9981
2.9	0.9981	0.9982	0.9982	0.9983	0.9984	0.9984	0.9985	0.9985	0.9986	0.9986
3.0	0.99865	0.99869	0.99874	0.99878	0.99882	0.99886	0.99889	0.99893	0.99897	0.99900
3.1	0.99903	0.99906	0.99910	0.99913	0.99916	0.99918	0.99921	0.99924	0.99926	0.99929
3.2	0.99931	0.99934	0.99936	0.99938	0.99940	0.99942	0.99944	0.99946	0.99948	0.99950
3.3	0.99952	0.99953	0.99955	0.99957	0.99958	0.99960	0.99961	0.99962	0.99964	0.99965
3.4	0.99966	0.99968	0.99969	0.99970	0.99971	0.99972	0.99973	0.99974	0.99975	0.99976
3.5	0.99977	0.99978	0.99978	0.99979	0.99980	0.99981	0.99981	0.99982	0.99983	0.99983
3.6	0.99984	0.99985	0.99985	0.99986	0.99986	0.99987	0.99987	0.99988	0.99988	0.99989
3.7	0.99989	0.99990	0.99990	0.99990	0.99991	0.99991	0.99992	0.99992	0.99992	0.99992
3.8	0.99993	0.99993	0.99993	0.99994	0.99994	0.99994	0.99994	0.99995	0.99995	0.99995
3.9	0.99995	0.99995	0.99996	0.99996	0.99996	0.99996	0.99996	0.99996	0.99997	0.99997
4.0	0.999968329									
4.5	0.999996602									
5.0	0.999999713									
5.5	0.999999981									
6.0	0.999999999									

TABLE E.3
Critical Values of t

For a particular number of degrees of freedom, entry represents the critical value of t corresponding to the cumulative probability $(1 - \alpha)$ and a specified upper-tail area (α).

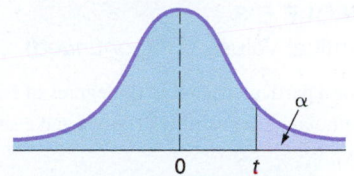

Degrees of Freedom	Cumulative Probabilities					
	0.75	0.90	0.95	0.975	0.99	0.995
	Upper-Tail Areas					
	0.25	0.10	0.05	0.025	0.01	0.005
1	1.0000	3.0777	6.3138	12.7062	31.8207	63.6574
2	0.8165	1.8856	2.9200	4.3027	6.9646	9.9248
3	0.7649	1.6377	2.3534	3.1824	4.5407	5.8409
4	0.7407	1.5332	2.1318	2.7764	3.7469	4.6041
5	0.7267	1.4759	2.0150	2.5706	3.3649	4.0322
6	0.7176	1.4398	1.9432	2.4469	3.1427	3.7074
7	0.7111	1.4149	1.8946	2.3646	2.9980	3.4995
8	0.7064	1.3968	1.8595	2.3060	2.8965	3.3554
9	0.7027	1.3830	1.8331	2.2622	2.8214	3.2498
10	0.6998	1.3722	1.8125	2.2281	2.7638	3.1693
11	0.6974	1.3634	1.7959	2.2010	2.7181	3.1058
12	0.6955	1.3562	1.7823	2.1788	2.6810	3.0545
13	0.6938	1.3502	1.7709	2.1604	2.6503	3.0123
14	0.6924	1.3450	1.7613	2.1448	2.6245	2.9768
15	0.6912	1.3406	1.7531	2.1315	2.6025	2.9467
16	0.6901	1.3368	1.7459	2.1199	2.5835	2.9208
17	0.6892	1.3334	1.7396	2.1098	2.5669	2.8982
18	0.6884	1.3304	1.7341	2.1009	2.5524	2.8784
19	0.6876	1.3277	1.7291	2.0930	2.5395	2.8609
20	0.6870	1.3253	1.7247	2.0860	2.5280	2.8453
21	0.6864	1.3232	1.7207	2.0796	2.5177	2.8314
22	0.6858	1.3212	1.7171	2.0739	2.5083	2.8188
23	0.6853	1.3195	1.7139	2.0687	2.4999	2.8073
24	0.6848	1.3178	1.7109	2.0639	2.4922	2.7969
25	0.6844	1.3163	1.7081	2.0595	2.4851	2.7874
26	0.6840	1.3150	1.7056	2.0555	2.4786	2.7787
27	0.6837	1.3137	1.7033	2.0518	2.4727	2.7707
28	0.6834	1.3125	1.7011	2.0484	2.4671	2.7633
29	0.6830	1.3114	1.6991	2.0452	2.4620	2.7564
30	0.6828	1.3104	1.6973	2.0423	2.4573	2.7500
31	0.6825	1.3095	1.6955	2.0395	2.4528	2.7440
32	0.6822	1.3086	1.6939	2.0369	2.4487	2.7385
33	0.6820	1.3077	1.6924	2.0345	2.4448	2.7333
34	0.6818	1.3070	1.6909	2.0322	2.4411	2.7284
35	0.6816	1.3062	1.6896	2.0301	2.4377	2.7238
36	0.6814	1.3055	1.6883	2.0281	2.4345	2.7195
37	0.6812	1.3049	1.6871	2.0262	2.4314	2.7154
38	0.6810	1.3042	1.6860	2.0244	2.4286	2.7116
39	0.6808	1.3036	1.6849	2.0227	2.4258	2.7079
40	0.6807	1.3031	1.6839	2.0211	2.4233	2.7045
41	0.6805	1.3025	1.6829	2.0195	2.4208	2.7012
42	0.6804	1.3020	1.6820	2.0181	2.4185	2.6981
43	0.6802	1.3016	1.6811	2.0167	2.4163	2.6951
44	0.6801	1.3011	1.6802	2.0154	2.4141	2.6923
45	0.6800	1.3006	1.6794	2.0141	2.4121	2.6896
46	0.6799	1.3002	1.6787	2.0129	2.4102	2.6870
47	0.6797	1.2998	1.6779	2.0117	2.4083	2.6846
48	0.6796	1.2994	1.6772	2.0106	2.4066	2.6822
49	0.6795	1.2991	1.6766	2.0096	2.4049	2.6800
50	0.6794	1.2987	1.6759	2.0086	2.4033	2.6778

TABLE E.3
Critical Values of *t* (continued)

For a particular number of degrees of freedom, entry represents the critical value of *t* corresponding to the cumulative probability $(1 - \alpha)$ and a specified upper-tail area (α).

	Cumulative Probabilities					
	0.75	0.90	0.95	0.975	0.99	0.995
Degrees of	Upper-Tail Areas					
Freedom	0.25	0.10	0.05	0.025	0.01	0.005
51	0.6793	1.2984	1.6753	2.0076	2.4017	2.6757
52	0.6792	1.2980	1.6747	2.0066	2.4002	2.6737
53	0.6791	1.2977	1.6741	2.0057	2.3988	2.6718
54	0.6791	1.2974	1.6736	2.0049	2.3974	2.6700
55	0.6790	1.2971	1.6730	2.0040	2.3961	2.6682
56	0.6789	1.2969	1.6725	2.0032	2.3948	2.6665
57	0.6788	1.2966	1.6720	2.0025	2.3936	2.6649
58	0.6787	1.2963	1.6716	2.0017	2.3924	2.6633
59	0.6787	1.2961	1.6711	2.0010	2.3912	2.6618
60	0.6786	1.2958	1.6706	2.0003	2.3901	2.6603
61	0.6785	1.2956	1.6702	1.9996	2.3890	2.6589
62	0.6785	1.2954	1.6698	1.9990	2.3880	2.6575
63	0.6784	1.2951	1.6694	1.9983	2.3870	2.6561
64	0.6783	1.2949	1.6690	1.9977	2.3860	2.6549
65	0.6783	1.2947	1.6686	1.9971	2.3851	2.6536
66	0.6782	1.2945	1.6683	1.9966	2.3842	2.6524
67	0.6782	1.2943	1.6679	1.9960	2.3833	2.6512
68	0.6781	1.2941	1.6676	1.9955	2.3824	2.6501
69	0.6781	1.2939	1.6672	1.9949	2.3816	2.6490
70	0.6780	1.2938	1.6669	1.9944	2.3808	2.6479
71	0.6780	1.2936	1.6666	1.9939	2.3800	2.6469
72	0.6779	1.2934	1.6663	1.9935	2.3793	2.6459
73	0.6779	1.2933	1.6660	1.9930	2.3785	2.6449
74	0.6778	1.2931	1.6657	1.9925	2.3778	2.6439
75	0.6778	1.2929	1.6654	1.9921	2.3771	2.6430
76	0.6777	1.2928	1.6652	1.9917	2.3764	2.6421
77	0.6777	1.2926	1.6649	1.9913	2.3758	2.6412
78	0.6776	1.2925	1.6646	1.9908	2.3751	2.6403
79	0.6776	1.2924	1.6644	1.9905	2.3745	2.6395
80	0.6776	1.2922	1.6641	1.9901	2.3739	2.6387
81	0.6775	1.2921	1.6639	1.9897	2.3733	2.6379
82	0.6775	1.2920	1.6636	1.9893	2.3727	2.6371
83	0.6775	1.2918	1.6634	1.9890	2.3721	2.6364
84	0.6774	1.2917	1.6632	1.9886	2.3716	2.6356
85	0.6774	1.2916	1.6630	1.9883	2.3710	2.6349
86	0.6774	1.2915	1.6628	1.9879	2.3705	2.6342
87	0.6773	1.2914	1.6626	1.9876	2.3700	2.6335
88	0.6773	1.2912	1.6624	1.9873	2.3695	2.6329
89	0.6773	1.2911	1.6622	1.9870	2.3690	2.6322
90	0.6772	1.2910	1.6620	1.9867	2.3685	2.6316
91	0.6772	1.2909	1.6618	1.9864	2.3680	2.6309
92	0.6772	1.2908	1.6616	1.9861	2.3676	2.6303
93	0.6771	1.2907	1.6614	1.9858	2.3671	2.6297
94	0.6771	1.2906	1.6612	1.9855	2.3667	2.6291
95	0.6771	1.2905	1.6611	1.9853	2.3662	2.6286
96	0.6771	1.2904	1.6609	1.9850	2.3658	2.6280
97	0.6770	1.2903	1.6607	1.9847	2.3654	2.6275
98	0.6770	1.2902	1.6606	1.9845	2.3650	2.6269
99	0.6770	1.2902	1.6604	1.9842	2.3646	2.6264
100	0.6770	1.2901	1.6602	1.9840	2.3642	2.6259
110	0.6767	1.2893	1.6588	1.9818	2.3607	2.6213
120	0.6765	1.2886	1.6577	1.9799	2.3578	2.6174
∞	0.6745	1.2816	1.6449	1.9600	2.3263	2.5758

TABLE E.4
Critical Values of χ^2

For a particular number of degrees of freedom, entry represents the critical value of χ^2 corresponding to the cumulative probability $(1 - \alpha)$ and a specified upper-tail area (α).

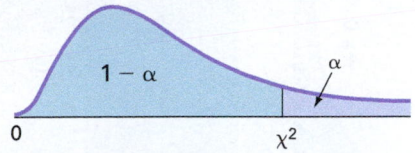

	Cumulative Probabilities											
	0.005	0.01	0.025	0.05	0.10	0.25	0.75	0.90	0.95	0.975	0.99	0.995
Degrees of Freedom	Upper-Tail Areas (α)											
	0.995	0.99	0.975	0.95	0.90	0.75	0.25	0.10	0.05	0.025	0.01	0.005
1			0.001	0.004	0.016	0.102	1.323	2.706	3.841	5.024	6.635	7.879
2	0.010	0.020	0.051	0.103	0.211	0.575	2.773	4.605	5.991	7.378	9.210	10.597
3	0.072	0.115	0.216	0.352	0.584	1.213	4.108	6.251	7.815	9.348	11.345	12.838
4	0.207	0.297	0.484	0.711	1.064	1.923	5.385	7.779	9.488	11.143	13.277	14.860
5	0.412	0.554	0.831	1.145	1.610	2.675	6.626	9.236	11.071	12.833	15.086	16.750
6	0.676	0.872	1.237	1.635	2.204	3.455	7.841	10.645	12.592	14.449	16.812	18.548
7	0.989	1.239	1.690	2.167	2.833	4.255	9.037	12.017	14.067	16.013	18.475	20.278
8	1.344	1.646	2.180	2.733	3.490	5.071	10.219	13.362	15.507	17.535	20.090	21.955
9	1.735	2.088	2.700	3.325	4.168	5.899	11.389	14.684	16.919	19.023	21.666	23.589
10	2.156	2.558	3.247	3.940	4.865	6.737	12.549	15.987	18.307	20.483	23.209	25.188
11	2.603	3.053	3.816	4.575	5.578	7.584	13.701	17.275	19.675	21.920	24.725	26.757
12	3.074	3.571	4.404	5.226	6.304	8.438	14.845	18.549	21.026	23.337	26.217	28.299
13	3.565	4.107	5.009	5.892	7.042	9.299	15.984	19.812	22.362	24.736	27.688	29.819
14	4.075	4.660	5.629	6.571	7.790	10.165	17.117	21.064	23.685	26.119	29.141	31.319
15	4.601	5.229	6.262	7.261	8.547	11.037	18.245	22.307	24.996	27.488	30.578	32.801
16	5.142	5.812	6.908	7.962	9.312	11.912	19.369	23.542	26.296	28.845	32.000	34.267
17	5.697	6.408	7.564	8.672	10.085	12.792	20.489	24.769	27.587	30.191	33.409	35.718
18	6.265	7.015	8.231	9.390	10.865	13.675	21.605	25.989	28.869	31.526	34.805	37.156
19	6.844	7.633	8.907	10.117	11.651	14.562	22.718	27.204	30.144	32.852	36.191	38.582
20	7.434	8.260	9.591	10.851	12.443	15.452	23.828	28.412	31.410	34.170	37.566	39.997
21	8.034	8.897	10.283	11.591	13.240	16.344	24.935	29.615	32.671	35.479	38.932	41.401
22	8.643	9.542	10.982	12.338	14.042	17.240	26.039	30.813	33.924	36.781	40.289	42.796
23	9.260	10.196	11.689	13.091	14.848	18.137	27.141	32.007	35.172	38.076	41.638	44.181
24	9.886	10.856	12.401	13.848	15.659	19.037	28.241	33.196	36.415	39.364	42.980	45.559
25	10.520	11.524	13.120	14.611	16.473	19.939	29.339	34.382	37.652	40.646	44.314	46.928
26	11.160	12.198	13.844	15.379	17.292	20.843	30.435	35.563	38.885	41.923	45.642	48.290
27	11.808	12.879	14.573	16.151	18.114	21.749	31.528	36.741	40.113	43.194	46.963	49.645
28	12.461	13.565	15.308	16.928	18.939	22.657	32.620	37.916	41.337	44.461	48.278	50.993
29	13.121	14.257	16.047	17.708	19.768	23.567	33.711	39.087	42.557	45.722	49.588	52.336
30	13.787	14.954	16.791	18.493	20.599	24.478	34.800	40.256	43.773	46.979	50.892	53.672

For larger values of degrees of freedom (df) the expression $Z = \sqrt{2\chi^2} - \sqrt{2(df)} - 1$ may be used and the resulting upper-tail area can be found from the cumulative standardized normal distribution (Table E.2).

TABLE E.5
Critical Values of F

For a particular combination of numerator and denominator degrees of freedom, entry represents the critical values of F corresponding to the cumulative probability $(1 - \alpha)$ and a specified upper-tail area (α).

Cumulative Probabilities = 0.95

Upper-Tail Areas = 0.05

Denominator, df_2	\multicolumn{19}{c}{Numerator, df_1}
	1	**2**	**3**	**4**	**5**	**6**	**7**	**8**	**9**	**10**	**12**	**15**	**20**	**24**	**30**	**40**	**60**	**120**	**∞**
1	161.40	199.50	215.70	224.60	230.20	234.00	236.80	238.90	240.50	241.90	243.90	245.90	248.00	249.10	250.10	251.10	252.20	253.30	254.30
2	18.51	19.00	19.16	19.25	19.30	19.33	19.35	19.37	19.38	19.40	19.41	19.43	19.45	19.45	19.46	19.47	19.48	19.49	19.50
3	10.13	9.55	9.28	9.12	9.01	8.94	8.89	8.85	8.81	8.79	8.74	8.70	8.66	8.64	8.62	8.59	8.57	8.55	8.53
4	7.71	6.94	6.59	6.39	6.26	6.16	6.09	6.04	6.00	5.96	5.91	5.86	5.80	5.77	5.75	5.72	5.69	5.66	5.63
5	6.61	5.79	5.41	5.19	5.05	4.95	4.88	4.82	4.77	4.74	4.68	4.62	4.56	4.53	4.50	4.46	4.43	4.40	4.36
6	5.99	5.14	4.76	4.53	4.39	4.28	4.21	4.15	4.10	4.06	4.00	3.94	3.87	3.84	3.81	3.77	3.74	3.70	3.67
7	5.59	4.74	4.35	4.12	3.97	3.87	3.79	3.73	3.68	3.64	3.57	3.51	3.44	3.41	3.38	3.34	3.30	3.27	3.23
8	5.32	4.46	4.07	3.84	3.69	3.58	3.50	3.44	3.39	3.35	3.28	3.22	3.15	3.12	3.08	3.04	3.01	2.97	2.93
9	5.12	4.26	3.86	3.63	3.48	3.37	3.29	3.23	3.18	3.14	3.07	3.01	2.94	2.90	2.86	2.83	2.79	2.75	2.71
10	4.96	4.10	3.71	3.48	3.33	3.22	3.14	3.07	3.02	2.98	2.91	2.85	2.77	2.74	2.70	2.66	2.62	2.58	2.54
11	4.84	3.98	3.59	3.36	3.20	3.09	3.01	2.95	2.90	2.85	2.79	2.72	2.65	2.61	2.57	2.53	2.49	2.45	2.40
12	4.75	3.89	3.49	3.26	3.11	3.00	2.91	2.85	2.80	2.75	2.69	2.62	2.54	2.51	2.47	2.43	2.38	2.34	2.30
13	4.67	3.81	3.41	3.18	3.03	2.92	2.83	2.77	2.71	2.67	2.60	2.53	2.46	2.42	2.38	2.34	2.30	2.25	2.21
14	4.60	3.74	3.34	3.11	2.96	2.85	2.76	2.70	2.65	2.60	2.53	2.46	2.39	2.35	2.31	2.27	2.22	2.18	2.13
15	4.54	3.68	3.29	3.06	2.90	2.79	2.71	2.64	2.59	2.54	2.48	2.40	2.33	2.29	2.25	2.20	2.16	2.11	2.07
16	4.49	3.63	3.24	3.01	2.85	2.74	2.66	2.59	2.54	2.49	2.42	2.35	2.28	2.24	2.19	2.15	2.11	2.06	2.01
17	4.45	3.59	3.20	2.96	2.81	2.70	2.61	2.55	2.49	2.45	2.38	2.31	2.23	2.19	2.15	2.10	2.06	2.01	1.96
18	4.41	3.55	3.16	2.93	2.77	2.66	2.58	2.51	2.46	2.41	2.34	2.27	2.19	2.15	2.11	2.06	2.02	1.97	1.92
19	4.38	3.52	3.13	2.90	2.74	2.63	2.54	2.48	2.42	2.38	2.31	2.23	2.16	2.11	2.07	2.03	1.98	1.93	1.88
20	4.35	3.49	3.10	2.87	2.71	2.60	2.51	2.45	2.39	2.35	2.28	2.20	2.12	2.08	2.04	1.99	1.95	1.90	1.84
21	4.32	3.47	3.07	2.84	2.68	2.57	2.49	2.42	2.37	2.32	2.25	2.18	2.10	2.05	2.01	1.96	1.92	1.87	1.81
22	4.30	3.44	3.05	2.82	2.66	2.55	2.46	2.40	2.34	2.30	2.23	2.15	2.07	2.03	1.98	1.94	1.89	1.84	1.78
23	4.28	3.42	3.03	2.80	2.64	2.53	2.44	2.37	2.32	2.27	2.20	2.13	2.05	2.01	1.96	1.91	1.86	1.81	1.76
24	4.26	3.40	3.01	2.78	2.62	2.51	2.42	2.36	2.30	2.25	2.18	2.11	2.03	1.98	1.94	1.89	1.84	1.79	1.73
25	4.24	3.39	2.99	2.76	2.60	2.49	2.40	2.34	2.28	2.24	2.16	2.09	2.01	1.96	1.92	1.87	1.82	1.77	1.71
26	4.23	3.37	2.98	2.74	2.59	2.47	2.39	2.32	2.27	2.22	2.15	2.07	1.99	1.95	1.90	1.85	1.80	1.75	1.69
27	4.21	3.35	2.96	2.73	2.57	2.46	2.37	2.31	2.25	2.20	2.13	2.06	1.97	1.93	1.88	1.84	1.79	1.73	1.67
28	4.20	3.34	2.95	2.71	2.56	2.45	2.36	2.29	2.24	2.19	2.12	2.04	1.96	1.91	1.87	1.82	1.77	1.71	1.65
29	4.18	3.33	2.93	2.70	2.55	2.43	2.35	2.28	2.22	2.18	2.10	2.03	1.94	1.90	1.85	1.81	1.75	1.70	1.64
30	4.17	3.32	2.92	2.69	2.53	2.42	2.33	2.27	2.21	2.16	2.09	2.01	1.93	1.89	1.84	1.79	1.74	1.68	1.62
40	4.08	3.23	2.84	2.61	2.45	2.34	2.25	2.18	2.12	2.08	2.00	1.92	1.84	1.79	1.74	1.69	1.64	1.58	1.51
60	4.00	3.15	2.76	2.53	2.37	2.25	2.17	2.10	2.04	1.99	1.92	1.84	1.75	1.70	1.65	1.59	1.53	1.47	1.39
120	3.92	3.07	2.68	2.45	2.29	2.17	2.09	2.02	1.96	1.91	1.83	1.75	1.66	1.61	1.55	1.50	1.43	1.35	1.25
∞	3.84	3.00	2.60	2.37	2.21	2.10	2.01	1.94	1.88	1.83	1.75	1.67	1.57	1.52	1.46	1.39	1.32	1.22	1.00

$\alpha = 0.05$

TABLE E.5
Critical Values of F (continued)

For a particular combination of numerator and denominator degrees of freedom, entry represents the critical values of F corresponding to the cumulative probability $(1 - \alpha)$ and a specified upper-tail area (α).

Cumulative Probabilities = 0.975

Upper-Tail Areas = 0.025

Denominator, df_2	Numerator, df_1																		
	1	2	3	4	5	6	7	8	9	10	12	15	20	24	30	40	60	120	∞
1	647.80	799.50	864.20	899.60	921.80	937.10	948.20	956.70	963.30	968.60	976.70	984.90	993.10	997.20	1,001.00	1,006.00	1,010.00	1,014.00	1,018.00
2	38.51	39.00	39.17	39.25	39.30	39.33	39.36	39.39	39.39	39.40	39.41	39.43	39.45	39.46	39.46	39.47	39.48	39.49	39.50
3	17.44	16.04	15.44	15.10	14.88	14.73	14.62	14.54	14.47	14.42	14.34	14.25	14.17	14.12	14.08	14.04	13.99	13.95	13.90
4	12.22	10.65	9.98	9.60	9.36	9.20	9.07	8.98	8.90	8.84	8.75	8.66	8.56	8.51	8.46	8.41	8.36	8.31	8.26
5	10.01	8.43	7.76	7.39	7.15	6.98	6.85	6.76	6.68	6.62	6.52	6.43	6.33	6.28	6.23	6.18	6.12	6.07	6.02
6	8.81	7.26	6.60	6.23	5.99	5.82	5.70	5.60	5.52	5.46	5.37	5.27	5.17	5.12	5.07	5.01	4.96	4.90	4.85
7	8.07	6.54	5.89	5.52	5.29	5.12	4.99	4.90	4.82	4.76	4.67	4.57	4.47	4.42	4.36	4.31	4.25	4.20	4.14
8	7.57	6.06	5.42	5.05	4.82	4.65	4.53	4.43	4.36	4.30	4.20	4.10	4.00	3.95	3.89	3.84	3.78	3.73	3.67
9	7.21	5.71	5.08	4.72	4.48	4.32	4.20	4.10	4.03	3.96	3.87	3.77	3.67	3.61	3.56	3.51	3.45	3.39	3.33
10	6.94	5.46	4.83	4.47	4.24	4.07	3.95	3.85	3.78	3.72	3.62	3.52	3.42	3.37	3.31	3.26	3.20	3.14	3.08
11	6.72	5.26	4.63	4.28	4.04	3.88	3.76	3.66	3.59	3.53	3.43	3.33	3.23	3.17	3.12	3.06	3.00	2.94	2.88
12	6.55	5.10	4.47	4.12	3.89	3.73	3.61	3.51	3.44	3.37	3.28	3.18	3.07	3.02	2.96	2.91	2.85	2.79	2.72
13	6.41	4.97	4.35	4.00	3.77	3.60	3.48	3.39	3.31	3.25	3.15	3.05	2.95	2.89	2.84	2.78	2.72	2.66	2.60
14	6.30	4.86	4.24	3.89	3.66	3.50	3.38	3.29	3.21	3.15	3.05	2.95	2.84	2.79	2.73	2.67	2.61	2.55	2.49
15	6.20	4.77	4.15	3.80	3.58	3.41	3.29	3.20	3.12	3.06	2.96	2.86	2.76	2.70	2.64	2.59	2.52	2.46	2.40
16	6.12	4.69	4.08	3.73	3.50	3.34	3.22	3.12	3.05	2.99	2.89	2.79	2.68	2.63	2.57	2.51	2.45	2.38	2.32
17	6.04	4.62	4.01	3.66	3.44	3.28	3.16	3.06	2.98	2.92	2.82	2.72	2.62	2.56	2.50	2.44	2.38	2.32	2.25
18	5.98	4.56	3.95	3.61	3.38	3.22	3.10	3.01	2.93	2.87	2.77	2.67	2.56	2.50	2.44	2.38	2.32	2.26	2.19
19	5.92	4.51	3.90	3.56	3.33	3.17	3.05	2.96	2.88	2.82	2.72	2.62	2.51	2.45	2.39	2.33	2.27	2.20	2.13
20	5.87	4.46	3.86	3.51	3.29	3.13	3.01	2.91	2.84	2.77	2.68	2.57	2.46	2.41	2.35	2.29	2.22	2.16	2.09
21	5.83	4.42	3.82	3.48	3.25	3.09	2.97	2.87	2.80	2.73	2.64	2.53	2.42	2.37	2.31	2.25	2.18	2.11	2.04
22	5.79	4.38	3.78	3.44	3.22	3.05	2.93	2.84	2.76	2.70	2.60	2.50	2.39	2.33	2.27	2.21	2.14	2.08	2.00
23	5.75	4.35	3.75	3.41	3.18	3.02	2.90	2.81	2.73	2.67	2.57	2.47	2.36	2.30	2.24	2.18	2.11	2.04	1.97
24	5.72	4.32	3.72	3.38	3.15	2.99	2.87	2.78	2.70	2.64	2.54	2.44	2.33	2.27	2.21	2.15	2.08	2.01	1.94
25	5.69	4.29	3.69	3.35	3.13	2.97	2.85	2.75	2.68	2.61	2.51	2.41	2.30	2.24	2.18	2.12	2.05	1.98	1.91
26	5.66	4.27	3.67	3.33	3.10	2.94	2.82	2.73	2.65	2.59	2.49	2.39	2.28	2.22	2.16	2.09	2.03	1.95	1.88
27	5.63	4.24	3.65	3.31	3.08	2.92	2.80	2.71	2.63	2.57	2.47	2.36	2.25	2.19	2.13	2.07	2.00	1.93	1.85
28	5.61	4.22	3.63	3.29	3.06	2.90	2.78	2.69	2.61	2.55	2.45	2.34	2.23	2.17	2.11	2.05	1.98	1.91	1.83
29	5.59	4.20	3.61	3.27	3.04	2.88	2.76	2.67	2.59	2.53	2.43	2.32	2.21	2.15	2.09	2.03	1.96	1.89	1.81
30	5.57	4.18	3.59	3.25	3.03	2.87	2.75	2.65	2.57	2.51	2.41	2.31	2.20	2.14	2.07	2.01	1.94	1.87	1.79
40	5.42	4.05	3.46	3.13	2.90	2.74	2.62	2.53	2.45	2.39	2.29	2.18	2.07	2.01	1.94	1.88	1.80	1.72	1.64
60	5.29	3.93	3.34	3.01	2.79	2.63	2.51	2.41	2.33	2.27	2.17	2.06	1.94	1.88	1.82	1.74	1.67	1.58	1.48
120	5.15	3.80	3.23	2.89	2.67	2.52	2.39	2.30	2.22	2.16	2.05	1.94	1.82	1.76	1.69	1.61	1.53	1.43	1.31
∞	5.02	3.69	3.12	2.79	2.57	2.41	2.29	2.19	2.11	2.05	1.94	1.83	1.71	1.64	1.57	1.48	1.39	1.27	1.00

$\alpha = 0.025$

(continued)

TABLE E.5
Critical Values of F (continued)

For a particular combination of numerator and denominator degrees of freedom, entry represents the critical values of F corresponding to the cumulative probability $(1 - \alpha)$ and a specified upper-tail area (α).

$\alpha = 0.01$

Cumulative Probabilities = 0.99

Upper-Tail Areas = 0.01

| Denominator, df_2 | \multicolumn{19}{c}{Numerator, df_1} |
	1	2	3	4	5	6	7	8	9	10	12	15	20	24	30	40	60	120	∞
1	4,052.00	4,999.50	5,403.00	5,625.00	5,764.00	5,859.00	5,928.00	5,982.00	6,022.00	6,056.00	6,106.00	6,157.00	6,209.00	6,235.00	6,261.00	6,287.00	6,313.00	6,339.00	6,366.00
2	98.50	99.00	99.17	99.25	99.30	99.33	99.36	99.37	99.39	99.40	99.42	99.43	99.45	99.46	99.47	99.47	99.48	99.49	99.50
3	34.12	30.82	29.46	28.71	28.24	27.91	27.67	27.49	27.35	27.23	27.05	26.87	26.69	26.60	26.50	26.41	26.32	26.22	26.13
4	21.20	18.00	16.69	15.98	15.52	15.21	14.98	14.80	14.66	14.55	14.37	14.20	14.02	13.93	13.84	13.75	13.65	13.56	13.46
5	16.26	13.27	12.06	11.39	10.97	10.67	10.46	10.29	10.16	10.05	9.89	9.72	9.55	9.47	9.38	9.29	9.20	9.11	9.02
6	13.75	10.92	9.78	9.15	8.75	8.47	8.26	8.10	7.98	7.87	7.72	7.56	7.40	7.31	7.23	7.14	7.06	6.97	6.88
7	12.25	9.55	8.45	7.85	7.46	7.19	6.99	6.84	6.72	6.62	6.47	6.31	6.16	6.07	5.99	5.91	5.82	5.74	5.65
8	11.26	8.65	7.59	7.01	6.63	6.37	6.18	6.03	5.91	5.81	5.67	5.52	5.36	5.28	5.20	5.12	5.03	4.95	4.86
9	10.56	8.02	6.99	6.42	6.06	5.80	5.61	5.47	5.35	5.26	5.11	4.96	4.81	4.73	4.65	4.57	4.48	4.40	4.31
10	10.04	7.56	6.55	5.99	5.64	5.39	5.20	5.06	4.94	4.85	4.71	4.56	4.41	4.33	4.25	4.17	4.08	4.00	3.91
11	9.65	7.21	6.22	5.67	5.32	5.07	4.89	4.74	4.63	4.54	4.40	4.25	4.10	4.02	3.94	3.86	3.78	3.69	3.60
12	9.33	6.93	5.95	5.41	5.06	4.82	4.64	4.50	4.39	4.30	4.16	4.01	3.86	3.78	3.70	3.62	3.54	3.45	3.36
13	9.07	6.70	5.74	5.21	4.86	4.62	4.44	4.30	4.19	4.10	3.96	3.82	3.66	3.59	3.51	3.43	3.34	3.25	3.17
14	8.86	6.51	5.56	5.04	4.69	4.46	4.28	4.14	4.03	3.94	3.80	3.66	3.51	3.43	3.35	3.27	3.18	3.09	3.00
15	8.68	6.36	5.42	4.89	4.56	4.32	4.14	4.00	3.89	3.80	3.67	3.52	3.37	3.29	3.21	3.13	3.05	2.96	2.87
16	8.53	6.23	5.29	4.77	4.44	4.20	4.03	3.89	3.78	3.69	3.55	3.41	3.26	3.18	3.10	3.02	2.93	2.81	2.75
17	8.40	6.11	5.18	4.67	4.34	4.10	3.93	3.79	3.68	3.59	3.46	3.31	3.16	3.08	3.00	2.92	2.83	2.75	2.65
18	8.29	6.01	5.09	4.58	4.25	4.01	3.84	3.71	3.60	3.51	3.37	3.23	3.08	3.00	2.92	2.84	2.75	2.66	2.57
19	8.18	5.93	5.01	4.50	4.17	3.94	3.77	3.63	3.52	3.43	3.30	3.15	3.00	2.92	2.84	2.76	2.67	2.58	2.49
20	8.10	5.85	4.94	4.43	4.10	3.87	3.70	3.56	3.46	3.37	3.23	3.09	2.94	2.86	2.78	2.69	2.61	2.52	2.42
21	8.02	5.78	4.87	4.37	4.04	3.81	3.64	3.51	3.40	3.31	3.17	3.03	2.88	2.80	2.72	2.64	2.55	2.46	2.36
22	7.95	5.72	4.82	4.31	3.99	3.76	3.59	3.45	3.35	3.26	3.12	2.98	2.83	2.75	2.67	2.58	2.50	2.40	2.31
23	7.88	5.66	4.76	4.26	3.94	3.71	3.54	3.41	3.30	3.21	3.07	2.93	2.78	2.70	2.62	2.54	2.45	2.35	2.26
24	7.82	5.61	4.72	4.22	3.90	3.67	3.50	3.36	3.26	3.17	3.03	2.89	2.74	2.66	2.58	2.49	2.40	2.31	2.21
25	7.77	5.57	4.68	4.18	3.85	3.63	3.46	3.32	3.22	3.13	2.99	2.85	2.70	2.62	2.54	2.45	2.36	2.27	2.17
26	7.72	5.53	4.64	4.14	3.82	3.59	3.42	3.29	3.18	3.09	2.96	2.81	2.66	2.58	2.50	2.42	2.33	2.23	2.13
27	7.68	5.49	4.60	4.11	3.78	3.56	3.39	3.26	3.15	3.06	2.93	2.78	2.63	2.55	2.47	2.38	2.29	2.20	2.10
28	7.64	5.45	4.57	4.07	3.75	3.53	3.36	3.23	3.12	3.03	2.90	2.75	2.60	2.52	2.44	2.35	2.26	2.17	2.06
29	7.60	5.42	4.54	4.04	3.73	3.50	3.33	3.20	3.09	3.00	2.87	2.73	2.57	2.49	2.41	2.33	2.23	2.14	2.03
30	7.56	5.39	4.51	4.02	3.70	3.47	3.30	3.17	3.07	2.98	2.84	2.70	2.55	2.47	2.39	2.30	2.21	2.11	2.01
40	7.31	5.18	4.31	3.83	3.51	3.29	3.12	2.99	2.89	2.80	2.66	2.52	2.37	2.29	2.20	2.11	2.02	1.92	1.80
60	7.08	4.98	4.13	3.65	3.34	3.12	2.95	2.82	2.72	2.63	2.50	2.35	2.20	2.12	2.03	1.94	1.84	1.73	1.60
120	6.85	4.79	3.95	3.48	3.17	2.96	2.79	2.66	2.56	2.47	2.34	2.19	2.03	1.95	1.86	1.76	1.66	1.53	1.38
∞	6.63	4.61	3.78	3.32	3.02	2.80	2.64	2.51	2.41	2.32	2.18	2.04	1.88	1.79	1.70	1.59	1.47	1.32	1.00

TABLE E.5
Critical Values of F

For a particular combination of numerator and denominator degrees of freedom, entry represents the critical values of F corresponding to the cumulative probability $(1 - \alpha)$ and a specified upper-tail area (α).

$\alpha = 0.005$

Cumulative Probabilities = 0.995

Upper-Tail Areas = 0.005

Denominator, df_2	Numerator, df_1																		
	1	2	3	4	5	6	7	8	9	10	12	15	20	24	30	40	60	120	∞
1	16,211.00	20,000.00	21,615.00	22,500.00	23,056.00	23,437.00	23,715.00	23,925.00	24,091.00	24,224.00	24,426.00	24,630.00	24,836.00	24,910.00	25,044.00	25,148.00	25,253.00	25,359.00	25,465.00
2	198.50	199.00	199.20	199.20	199.30	199.30	199.40	199.40	199.40	199.40	199.40	199.40	199.40	199.50	199.50	199.50	199.50	199.50	199.50
3	55.55	49.80	47.47	46.19	45.39	44.84	44.43	44.13	43.88	43.69	43.39	43.08	42.78	42.62	42.47	42.31	42.15	41.99	41.83
4	31.33	26.28	24.26	23.15	22.46	21.97	21.62	21.35	21.14	20.97	20.70	20.44	20.17	20.03	19.89	19.75	19.61	19.47	19.32
5	22.78	18.31	16.53	15.56	14.94	14.51	14.20	13.96	13.77	13.62	13.38	13.15	12.90	12.78	12.66	12.53	12.40	12.27	12.11
6	18.63	14.54	12.92	12.03	11.46	11.07	10.79	10.57	10.39	10.25	10.03	9.81	9.59	9.47	9.36	9.24	9.12	9.00	8.88
7	16.24	12.40	10.88	10.05	9.52	9.16	8.89	8.68	8.51	8.38	8.18	7.97	7.75	7.65	7.53	7.42	7.31	7.19	7.08
8	14.69	11.04	9.60	8.81	8.30	7.95	7.69	7.50	7.34	7.21	7.01	6.81	6.61	6.50	6.40	6.29	6.18	6.06	5.95
9	13.61	10.11	8.72	7.96	7.47	7.13	6.88	6.69	6.54	6.42	6.23	6.03	5.83	5.73	5.62	5.52	5.41	5.30	5.19
10	12.83	9.43	8.08	7.34	6.87	6.54	6.30	6.12	5.97	5.85	5.66	5.47	5.27	5.17	5.07	4.97	4.86	4.75	4.61
11	12.23	8.91	7.60	6.88	6.42	6.10	5.86	5.68	5.54	5.42	5.24	5.05	4.86	4.75	4.65	4.55	4.44	4.34	4.23
12	11.75	8.51	7.23	6.52	6.07	5.76	5.52	5.35	5.20	5.09	4.91	4.72	4.53	4.43	4.33	4.23	4.12	4.01	3.90
13	11.37	8.19	6.93	6.23	5.79	5.48	5.25	5.08	4.94	4.82	4.64	4.46	4.27	4.17	4.07	3.97	3.87	3.76	3.65
14	11.06	7.92	6.68	6.00	5.56	5.26	5.03	4.86	4.72	4.60	4.43	4.25	4.06	3.96	3.86	3.76	3.66	3.55	3.41
15	10.80	7.70	6.48	5.80	5.37	5.07	4.85	4.67	4.54	4.42	4.25	4.07	3.88	3.79	3.69	3.58	3.48	3.37	3.26
16	10.58	7.51	6.30	5.64	5.21	4.91	4.69	4.52	4.38	4.27	4.10	3.92	3.73	3.64	3.54	3.44	3.33	3.22	3.11
17	10.38	7.35	6.16	5.50	5.07	4.78	4.56	4.39	4.25	4.14	3.97	3.79	3.61	3.51	3.41	3.31	3.21	3.10	2.98
18	10.22	7.21	6.03	5.37	4.96	4.66	4.44	4.28	4.14	4.03	3.86	3.68	3.50	3.40	3.30	3.20	3.10	2.99	2.87
19	10.07	7.09	5.92	5.27	4.85	4.56	4.34	4.18	4.04	3.93	3.76	3.59	3.40	3.31	3.21	3.11	3.00	2.89	2.78
20	9.94	6.99	5.82	5.17	4.76	4.47	4.26	4.09	3.96	3.85	3.68	3.50	3.32	3.22	3.12	3.02	2.92	2.81	2.69
21	9.83	6.89	5.73	5.09	4.68	4.39	4.18	4.02	3.88	3.77	3.60	3.43	3.24	3.15	3.05	2.95	2.84	2.73	2.61
22	9.73	6.81	5.65	5.02	4.61	4.32	4.11	3.94	3.81	3.70	3.54	3.36	3.18	3.08	2.98	2.88	2.77	2.66	2.55
23	9.63	6.73	5.58	4.95	4.54	4.26	4.05	3.88	3.75	3.64	3.47	3.30	3.12	3.02	2.92	2.82	2.71	2.60	2.48
24	9.55	6.66	5.52	4.89	4.49	4.20	3.99	3.83	3.69	3.59	3.42	3.25	3.06	2.97	2.87	2.77	2.66	2.55	2.43
25	9.48	6.60	5.46	4.84	4.43	4.15	3.94	3.78	3.64	3.54	3.37	3.20	3.01	2.92	2.82	2.72	2.61	2.50	2.38
26	9.41	6.54	5.41	4.79	4.38	4.10	3.89	3.73	3.60	3.49	3.33	3.15	2.97	2.87	2.77	2.67	2.56	2.45	2.33
27	9.34	6.49	5.36	4.74	4.34	4.06	3.85	3.69	3.56	3.45	3.28	3.11	2.93	2.83	2.73	2.63	2.52	2.41	2.29
28	9.28	6.44	5.32	4.70	4.30	4.02	3.81	3.65	3.52	3.41	3.25	3.07	2.89	2.79	2.69	2.59	2.48	2.37	2.25
29	9.23	6.40	5.28	4.66	4.26	3.98	3.77	3.61	3.48	3.38	3.21	3.04	2.86	2.76	2.66	2.56	2.45	2.33	2.21
30	9.18	6.35	5.24	4.62	4.23	3.95	3.74	3.58	3.45	3.34	3.18	3.01	2.82	2.73	2.63	2.52	2.42	2.30	2.18
40	8.83	6.07	4.98	4.37	3.99	3.71	3.51	3.35	3.22	3.12	2.95	2.78	2.60	2.50	2.40	2.30	2.18	2.06	1.93
60	8.49	5.79	4.73	4.14	3.76	3.49	3.29	3.13	3.01	2.90	2.74	2.57	2.39	2.29	2.19	2.08	1.96	1.83	1.69
120	8.18	5.54	4.50	3.92	3.55	3.28	3.09	2.93	2.81	2.71	2.54	2.37	2.19	2.09	1.98	1.87	1.75	1.61	1.43
∞	7.88	5.30	4.28	3.72	3.35	3.09	2.90	2.74	2.62	2.52	2.36	2.19	2.00	1.90	1.79	1.67	1.53	1.36	1.00

TABLE E.6

Lower and Upper Critical Values, T_1, of the Wilcoxon Rank Sum Test

n_2	One-tail	Two-tail	4	5	6	7	8	9	10
	α					n_1			
4	0.05	0.10	11,25						
	0.025	0.05	10,26						
	0.01	0.02	—,—						
	0.005	0.01	—,—						
5	0.05	0.10	12,28	19,36					
	0.025	0.05	11,29	17,38					
	0.01	0.02	10,30	16,39					
	0.005	0.01	—,—	15,40					
6	0.05	0.10	13,31	20,40	28,50				
	0.025	0.05	12,32	18,42	26,52				
	0.01	0.02	11,33	17,43	24,54				
	0.005	0.01	10,34	16,44	23,55				
7	0.05	0.10	14,34	21,44	29,55	39,66			
	0.025	0.05	13,35	20,45	27,57	36,69			
	0.01	0.02	11,37	18,47	25,59	34,71			
	0.005	0.01	10,38	16,49	24,60	32,73			
8	0.05	0.10	15,37	23,47	31,59	41,71	51,85		
	0.025	0.05	14,38	21,49	29,61	38,74	49,87		
	0.01	0.02	12,40	19,51	27,63	35,77	45,91		
	0.005	0.01	11,41	17,53	25,65	34,78	43,93		
9	0.05	0.10	16,40	24,51	33,63	43,76	54,90	66,105	
	0.025	0.05	14,42	22,53	31,65	40,79	51,93	62,109	
	0.01	0.02	13,43	20,55	28,68	37,82	47,97	59,112	
	0.005	0.01	11,45	18,57	26,70	35,84	45,99	56,115	
10	0.05	0.10	17,43	26,54	35,67	45,81	56,96	69,111	82,128
	0.025	0.05	15,45	23,57	32,70	42,84	53,99	65,115	78,132
	0.01	0.02	13,47	21,59	29,73	39,87	49,103	61,119	74,136
	0.005	0.01	12,48	19,61	27,75	37,89	47,105	58,122	71,139

Source: Adapted from TABLE 1 of F. Wilcoxon and R. A. Wilcox, *Some Rapid Approximate Statistical Procedures* (Pearl River, NY: Lederle Laboratories, 1964), with permission of the American Cyanamid Company.

TABLE E.7

Critical Values of the Studentized Range, Q

Upper 5% Points ($\alpha = 0.05$)

Denominator, df	\multicolumn{19}{c}{Numerator, df}
	2	3	4	5	6	7	8	9	10	11	12	13	14	15	16	17	18	19	20
1	18.00	27.00	32.80	37.10	40.40	43.10	45.40	47.40	49.10	50.60	52.00	53.20	54.30	55.40	56.30	57.20	58.00	58.80	59.60
2	6.09	8.30	9.80	10.90	11.70	12.40	13.00	13.50	14.00	14.40	14.70	15.10	15.40	15.70	15.90	16.10	16.40	16.60	16.80
3	4.50	5.91	6.82	7.50	8.04	8.48	8.85	9.18	9.46	9.72	9.95	10.15	10.35	10.52	10.69	10.84	10.98	11.11	11.24
4	3.93	5.04	5.76	6.29	6.71	7.05	7.35	7.60	7.83	8.03	8.21	8.37	8.52	8.66	8.79	8.91	9.03	9.13	9.23
5	3.64	4.60	5.22	5.67	6.03	6.33	6.58	6.80	6.99	7.17	7.32	7.47	7.60	7.72	7.83	7.93	8.03	8.12	8.21
6	3.46	4.34	4.90	5.31	5.63	5.89	6.12	6.32	6.49	6.65	6.79	6.92	7.03	7.14	7.24	7.34	7.43	7.51	7.59
7	3.34	4.16	4.68	5.06	5.36	5.61	5.82	6.00	6.16	6.30	6.43	6.55	6.66	6.76	6.85	6.94	7.02	7.09	7.17
8	3.26	4.04	4.53	4.89	5.17	5.40	5.60	5.77	5.92	6.05	6.18	6.29	6.39	6.48	6.57	6.65	6.73	6.80	6.87
9	3.20	3.95	4.42	4.76	5.02	5.24	5.43	5.60	5.74	5.87	5.98	6.09	6.19	6.28	6.36	6.44	6.51	6.58	6.64
10	3.15	3.88	4.33	4.65	4.91	5.12	5.30	5.46	5.60	5.72	5.83	5.93	6.03	6.11	6.20	6.27	6.34	6.40	6.47
11	3.11	3.82	4.26	4.57	4.82	5.03	5.20	5.35	5.49	5.61	5.71	5.81	5.90	5.99	6.06	6.14	6.20	6.26	6.33
12	3.08	3.77	4.20	4.51	4.75	4.95	5.12	5.27	5.40	5.51	5.62	5.71	5.80	5.88	5.95	6.03	6.09	6.15	6.21
13	3.06	3.73	4.15	4.45	4.69	4.88	5.05	5.19	5.32	5.43	5.53	5.63	5.71	5.79	5.86	5.93	6.00	6.05	6.11
14	3.03	3.70	4.11	4.41	4.64	4.83	4.99	5.13	5.25	5.36	5.46	5.55	5.64	5.72	5.79	5.85	5.92	5.97	6.03
15	3.01	3.67	4.08	4.37	4.60	4.78	4.94	5.08	5.20	5.31	5.40	5.49	5.58	5.65	5.72	5.79	5.85	5.90	5.96
16	3.00	3.65	4.05	4.33	4.56	4.74	4.90	5.03	5.15	5.26	5.35	5.44	5.52	5.59	5.66	5.72	5.79	5.84	5.90
17	2.98	3.63	4.02	4.30	4.52	4.71	4.86	4.99	5.11	5.21	5.31	5.39	5.47	5.55	5.61	5.68	5.74	5.79	5.84
18	2.97	3.61	4.00	4.28	4.49	4.67	4.82	4.96	5.07	5.17	5.27	5.35	5.43	5.50	5.57	5.63	5.69	5.74	5.79
19	2.96	3.59	3.98	4.25	4.47	4.65	4.79	4.92	5.04	5.14	5.23	5.32	5.39	5.46	5.53	5.59	5.65	5.70	5.75
20	2.95	3.58	3.96	4.23	4.45	4.62	4.77	4.90	5.01	5.11	5.20	5.28	5.36	5.43	5.49	5.55	5.61	5.66	5.71
24	2.92	3.53	3.90	4.17	4.37	4.54	4.68	4.81	4.92	5.01	5.10	5.18	5.25	5.32	5.38	5.44	5.50	5.54	5.59
30	2.89	3.49	3.84	4.10	4.30	4.46	4.60	4.72	4.83	4.92	5.00	5.08	5.15	5.21	5.27	5.33	5.38	5.43	5.48
40	2.86	3.44	3.79	4.04	4.23	4.39	4.52	4.63	4.74	4.82	4.91	4.98	5.05	5.11	5.16	5.22	5.27	5.31	5.36
60	2.83	3.40	3.74	3.98	4.16	4.31	4.44	4.55	4.65	4.73	4.81	4.88	4.94	5.00	5.06	5.11	5.16	5.20	5.24
120	2.80	3.36	3.69	3.92	4.10	4.24	4.36	4.48	4.56	4.64	4.72	4.78	4.84	4.90	4.95	5.00	5.05	5.09	5.13
∞	2.77	3.31	3.63	3.86	4.03	4.17	4.29	4.39	4.47	4.55	4.62	4.68	4.74	4.80	4.85	4.89	4.93	4.97	5.01

(*continued*)

TABLE E.7

Critical Values of the Studentized Range, Q (continued)

Upper 1% Points ($\alpha = 0.01$)

Denominator, df	\\ Numerator, df																		
	2	3	4	5	6	7	8	9	10	11	12	13	14	15	16	17	18	19	20
1	90.03	135.00	164.30	185.60	202.20	215.80	227.20	237.00	245.60	253.20	260.00	266.20	271.80	277.00	281.80	286.30	290.40	294.30	298.00
2	14.04	19.02	22.29	24.72	26.63	28.20	29.53	30.68	31.69	32.59	33.40	34.13	34.81	35.43	36.00	36.53	37.03	37.50	37.95
3	8.26	10.62	12.17	13.33	14.24	15.00	15.64	16.20	16.69	17.13	17.53	17.89	18.22	18.52	18.81	19.07	19.32	19.55	19.77
4	6.51	8.12	9.17	9.96	10.58	11.10	11.55	11.93	12.27	12.57	12.84	13.09	13.32	13.53	13.73	13.91	14.08	14.24	14.40
5	5.70	6.98	7.80	8.42	8.91	9.32	9.67	9.97	10.24	10.48	10.70	10.89	11.08	11.24	11.40	11.55	11.68	11.81	11.93
6	5.24	6.33	7.03	7.56	7.97	8.32	8.61	8.87	9.10	9.30	9.49	9.65	9.81	9.95	10.08	10.21	10.32	10.43	10.54
7	4.95	5.92	6.54	7.01	7.37	7.68	7.94	8.17	8.37	8.55	8.71	8.86	9.00	9.12	9.24	9.35	9.46	9.55	9.65
8	4.75	5.64	6.20	6.63	6.96	7.24	7.47	7.68	7.86	8.03	8.18	8.31	8.44	8.55	8.66	8.76	8.85	8.94	9.03
9	4.60	5.43	5.96	6.35	6.66	6.92	7.13	7.32	7.50	7.65	7.78	7.91	8.03	8.13	8.23	8.33	8.41	8.50	8.57
10	4.48	5.27	5.77	6.14	6.43	6.67	6.87	7.06	7.21	7.36	7.49	7.60	7.71	7.81	7.91	7.99	8.08	8.15	8.23
11	4.39	5.15	5.62	5.97	6.25	6.48	6.67	6.84	6.99	7.13	7.25	7.36	7.47	7.56	7.65	7.73	7.81	7.88	7.95
12	4.32	5.04	5.50	5.84	6.10	6.32	6.51	6.67	6.81	6.94	7.06	7.17	7.26	7.36	7.44	7.52	7.59	7.66	7.73
13	4.26	4.96	5.40	5.73	5.98	6.19	6.37	6.53	6.67	6.79	6.90	7.01	7.10	7.19	7.27	7.35	7.42	7.49	7.55
14	4.21	4.90	5.32	5.63	5.88	6.09	6.26	6.41	6.54	6.66	6.77	6.87	6.96	7.05	7.13	7.20	7.27	7.33	7.40
15	4.17	4.84	5.25	5.56	5.80	5.99	6.16	6.31	6.44	6.56	6.66	6.76	6.85	6.93	7.00	7.07	7.14	7.20	7.26
16	4.13	4.79	5.19	5.49	5.72	5.92	6.08	6.22	6.35	6.46	6.56	6.66	6.74	6.82	6.90	6.97	7.03	7.09	7.15
17	4.10	4.74	5.14	5.43	5.66	5.85	6.01	6.15	6.27	6.38	6.48	6.57	6.66	6.73	6.81	6.87	6.94	7.00	7.05
18	4.07	4.70	5.09	5.38	5.60	5.79	5.94	6.08	6.20	6.31	6.41	6.50	6.58	6.66	6.73	6.79	6.85	6.91	6.97
19	4.05	4.67	5.05	5.33	5.55	5.74	5.89	6.02	6.14	6.25	6.34	6.43	6.51	6.59	6.65	6.72	6.78	6.84	6.89
20	4.02	4.64	5.02	5.29	5.51	5.69	5.84	5.97	6.09	6.19	6.29	6.37	6.45	6.52	6.59	6.65	6.71	6.77	6.82
24	3.96	4.55	4.91	5.17	5.37	5.54	5.69	5.81	5.92	6.02	6.11	6.19	6.26	6.33	6.39	6.45	6.51	6.56	6.61
30	3.89	4.46	4.80	5.05	5.24	5.40	5.54	5.65	5.76	5.85	5.93	6.01	6.08	6.14	6.20	6.26	6.31	6.36	6.41
40	3.83	4.37	4.70	4.93	5.11	5.27	5.39	5.50	5.60	5.69	5.76	5.84	5.90	5.96	6.02	6.07	6.12	6.17	6.21
60	3.76	4.28	4.60	4.82	4.99	5.13	5.25	5.36	5.45	5.53	5.60	5.67	5.73	5.79	5.84	5.89	5.93	5.97	6.02
120	3.70	4.20	4.50	4.71	4.87	5.01	5.12	5.21	5.30	5.38	5.44	5.51	5.56	5.61	5.66	5.71	5.75	5.79	5.83
∞	3.64	4.12	4.40	4.60	4.76	4.88	4.99	5.08	5.16	5.23	5.29	5.35	5.40	5.45	5.49	5.54	5.57	5.61	5.65

Source: Extracted from H. L. Harter and D. S. Clemm, "The Probability Integrals of the Range and of the Studentized Range—Probability Integral, Percentage Points, and Moments of the Range," *Wright Air Development Technical Report 58–484, Vol. 1, 1959.*

TABLE E.8

Critical Values, d_L and d_U, of the Durbin-Watson Statistic, D (Critical Values Are One-Sided)[a]

$\alpha = 0.05$

n	k=1 d_L	k=1 d_U	k=2 d_L	k=2 d_U	k=3 d_L	k=3 d_U	k=4 d_L	k=4 d_U	k=5 d_L	k=5 d_U
15	1.08	1.36	.95	1.54	.82	1.75	.69	1.97	.56	2.21
16	1.10	1.37	.98	1.54	.86	1.73	.74	1.93	.62	2.15
17	1.13	1.38	1.02	1.54	.90	1.71	.78	1.90	.67	2.10
18	1.16	1.39	1.05	1.53	.93	1.69	.82	1.87	.71	2.06
19	1.18	1.40	1.08	1.53	.97	1.68	.86	1.85	.75	2.02
20	1.20	1.41	1.10	1.54	1.00	1.68	.90	1.83	.79	1.99
21	1.22	1.42	1.13	1.54	1.03	1.67	.93	1.81	.83	1.96
22	1.24	1.43	1.15	1.54	1.05	1.66	.96	1.80	.86	1.94
23	1.26	1.44	1.17	1.54	1.08	1.66	.99	1.79	.90	1.92
24	1.27	1.45	1.19	1.55	1.10	1.66	1.01	1.78	.93	1.90
25	1.29	1.45	1.21	1.55	1.12	1.66	1.04	1.77	.95	1.89
26	1.30	1.46	1.22	1.55	1.14	1.65	1.06	1.76	.98	1.88
27	1.32	1.47	1.24	1.56	1.16	1.65	1.08	1.76	1.01	1.86
28	1.33	1.48	1.26	1.56	1.18	1.65	1.10	1.75	1.03	1.85
29	1.34	1.48	1.27	1.56	1.20	1.65	1.12	1.74	1.05	1.84
30	1.35	1.49	1.28	1.57	1.21	1.65	1.14	1.74	1.07	1.83
31	1.36	1.50	1.30	1.57	1.23	1.65	1.16	1.74	1.09	1.83
32	1.37	1.50	1.31	1.57	1.24	1.65	1.18	1.73	1.11	1.82
33	1.38	1.51	1.32	1.58	1.26	1.65	1.19	1.73	1.13	1.81
34	1.39	1.51	1.33	1.58	1.27	1.65	1.21	1.73	1.15	1.81
35	1.40	1.52	1.34	1.58	1.28	1.65	1.22	1.73	1.16	1.80
36	1.41	1.52	1.35	1.59	1.29	1.65	1.24	1.73	1.18	1.80
37	1.42	1.53	1.36	1.59	1.31	1.66	1.25	1.72	1.19	1.80
38	1.43	1.54	1.37	1.59	1.32	1.66	1.26	1.72	1.21	1.79
39	1.43	1.54	1.38	1.60	1.33	1.66	1.27	1.72	1.22	1.79
40	1.44	1.54	1.39	1.60	1.34	1.66	1.29	1.72	1.23	1.79
45	1.48	1.57	1.43	1.62	1.38	1.67	1.34	1.72	1.29	1.78
50	1.50	1.59	1.46	1.63	1.42	1.67	1.38	1.72	1.34	1.77
55	1.53	1.60	1.49	1.64	1.45	1.68	1.41	1.72	1.38	1.77
60	1.55	1.62	1.51	1.65	1.48	1.69	1.44	1.73	1.41	1.77
65	1.57	1.63	1.54	1.66	1.50	1.70	1.47	1.73	1.44	1.77
70	1.58	1.64	1.55	1.67	1.52	1.70	1.49	1.74	1.46	1.77
75	1.60	1.65	1.57	1.68	1.54	1.71	1.51	1.74	1.49	1.77
80	1.61	1.66	1.59	1.69	1.56	1.72	1.53	1.74	1.51	1.77
85	1.62	1.67	1.60	1.70	1.57	1.72	1.55	1.75	1.52	1.77
90	1.63	1.68	1.61	1.70	1.59	1.73	1.57	1.75	1.54	1.78
95	1.64	1.69	1.62	1.71	1.60	1.73	1.58	1.75	1.56	1.78
100	1.65	1.69	1.63	1.72	1.61	1.74	1.59	1.76	1.57	1.78

$\alpha = 0.01$

n	k=1 d_L	k=1 d_U	k=2 d_L	k=2 d_U	k=3 d_L	k=3 d_U	k=4 d_L	k=4 d_U	k=5 d_L	k=5 d_U
15	.81	1.07	.70	1.25	.59	1.46	.49	1.70	.39	1.96
16	.84	1.09	.74	1.25	.63	1.44	.53	1.66	.44	1.90
17	.87	1.10	.77	1.25	.67	1.43	.57	1.63	.48	1.85
18	.90	1.12	.80	1.26	.71	1.42	.61	1.60	.52	1.80
19	.93	1.13	.83	1.26	.74	1.41	.65	1.58	.56	1.77
20	.95	1.15	.86	1.27	.77	1.41	.68	1.57	.60	1.74
21	.97	1.16	.89	1.27	.80	1.41	.72	1.55	.63	1.71
22	1.00	1.17	.91	1.28	.83	1.40	.75	1.54	.66	1.69
23	1.02	1.19	.94	1.29	.86	1.40	.77	1.53	.70	1.67
24	1.04	1.20	.96	1.30	.88	1.41	.80	1.53	.72	1.66
25	1.05	1.21	.98	1.30	.90	1.41	.83	1.52	.75	1.65
26	1.07	1.22	1.00	1.31	.93	1.41	.85	1.52	.78	1.64
27	1.09	1.23	1.02	1.32	.95	1.41	.88	1.51	.81	1.63
28	1.10	1.24	1.04	1.32	.97	1.41	.90	1.51	.83	1.62
29	1.12	1.25	1.05	1.33	.99	1.42	.92	1.51	.85	1.61
30	1.13	1.26	1.07	1.34	1.01	1.42	.94	1.51	.88	1.61
31	1.15	1.27	1.08	1.34	1.02	1.42	.96	1.51	.90	1.60
32	1.16	1.28	1.10	1.35	1.04	1.43	.98	1.51	.92	1.60
33	1.17	1.29	1.11	1.36	1.05	1.43	1.00	1.51	.94	1.59
34	1.18	1.30	1.13	1.36	1.07	1.43	1.01	1.51	.95	1.59
35	1.19	1.31	1.14	1.37	1.08	1.44	1.03	1.51	.97	1.59
36	1.21	1.32	1.15	1.38	1.10	1.44	1.04	1.51	.99	1.59
37	1.22	1.32	1.16	1.38	1.11	1.45	1.06	1.51	1.00	1.59
38	1.23	1.33	1.18	1.39	1.12	1.45	1.07	1.52	1.02	1.58
39	1.24	1.34	1.19	1.39	1.14	1.45	1.09	1.52	1.03	1.58
40	1.25	1.34	1.20	1.40	1.15	1.46	1.10	1.52	1.05	1.58
45	1.29	1.38	1.24	1.42	1.20	1.48	1.16	1.53	1.11	1.58
50	1.32	1.40	1.28	1.45	1.24	1.49	1.20	1.54	1.16	1.59
55	1.36	1.43	1.32	1.47	1.28	1.51	1.25	1.55	1.21	1.59
60	1.38	1.45	1.35	1.48	1.32	1.52	1.28	1.56	1.25	1.60
65	1.41	1.47	1.38	1.50	1.35	1.53	1.31	1.57	1.28	1.61
70	1.43	1.49	1.40	1.52	1.37	1.55	1.34	1.58	1.31	1.61
75	1.45	1.50	1.42	1.53	1.39	1.56	1.37	1.59	1.34	1.62
80	1.47	1.52	1.44	1.54	1.42	1.57	1.39	1.60	1.36	1.62
85	1.48	1.53	1.46	1.55	1.43	1.58	1.41	1.60	1.39	1.63
90	1.50	1.54	1.47	1.56	1.45	1.59	1.43	1.61	1.41	1.64
95	1.51	1.55	1.49	1.57	1.47	1.60	1.45	1.62	1.42	1.64
100	1.52	1.56	1.50	1.58	1.48	1.60	1.46	1.63	1.44	1.65

[a] n = number of observations; k = number of independent variables.

Source: Computed from TSP 4.5 based on R. W. Farebrother, "A Remark on Algorithms AS106, AS153, and AS155: The Distribution of a Linear Combination of Chi-Square Random Variables," *Journal of the Royal Statistical Society*, Series C (Applied Statistics), (1984), 29, p. 323–333.

TABLE E.9

Control Chart Factors

Number of Observations in Sample/Subgroup (n)	d_2	d_3	D_3	D_4	A_2
2	1.128	0.853	0	3.267	1.880
3	1.693	0.888	0	2.575	1.023
4	2.059	0.880	0	2.282	0.729
5	2.326	0.864	0	2.114	0.577
6	2.534	0.848	0	2.004	0.483
7	2.704	0.833	0.076	1.924	0.419
8	2.847	0.820	0.136	1.864	0.373
9	2.970	0.808	0.184	1.816	0.337
10	3.078	0.797	0.223	1.777	0.308
11	3.173	0.787	0.256	1.744	0.285
12	3.258	0.778	0.283	1.717	0.266
13	3.336	0.770	0.307	1.693	0.249
14	3.407	0.763	0.328	1.672	0.235
15	3.472	0.756	0.347	1.653	0.223
16	3.532	0.750	0.363	1.637	0.212
17	3.588	0.744	0.378	1.622	0.203
18	3.640	0.739	0.391	1.609	0.194
19	3.689	0.733	0.404	1.596	0.187
20	3.735	0.729	0.415	1.585	0.180
21	3.778	0.724	0.425	1.575	0.173
22	3.819	0.720	0.435	1.565	0.167
23	3.858	0.716	0.443	1.557	0.162
24	3.895	0.712	0.452	1.548	0.157
25	3.931	0.708	0.459	1.541	0.153

Source: Reprinted from *ASTM-STP 15D* by kind permission of the American Society for Testing and Materials. Copyright ASTM International, 100 Barr Harbor Drive, Conshohocken, PA 19428.

TABLE E.10

The Standardized Normal Distribution

Entry represents area under the standardized normal
distribution from the mean to Z

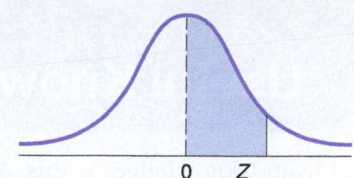

Z	.00	.01	.02	.03	.04	.05	.06	.07	.08	.09
0.0	.0000	.0040	.0080	.0120	.0160	.0199	.0239	.0279	.0319	.0359
0.1	.0398	.0438	.0478	.0517	.0557	.0596	.0636	.0675	.0714	.0753
0.2	.0793	.0832	.0871	.0910	.0948	.0987	.1026	.1064	.1103	.1141
0.3	.1179	.1217	.1255	.1293	.1331	.1368	.1406	.1443	.1480	.1517
0.4	.1554	.1591	.1628	.1664	.1700	.1736	.1772	.1808	.1844	.1879
0.5	.1915	.1950	.1985	.2019	.2054	.2088	.2123	.2157	.2190	.2224
0.6	.2257	.2291	.2324	.2357	.2389	.2422	.2454	.2486	.2518	.2549
0.7	.2580	.2612	.2642	.2673	.2704	.2734	.2764	.2794	.2823	.2852
0.8	.2881	.2910	.2939	.2967	.2995	.3023	.3051	.3078	.3106	.3133
0.9	.3159	.3186	.3212	.3238	.3264	.3289	.3315	.3340	.3365	.3389
1.0	.3413	.3438	.3461	.3485	.3508	.3531	.3554	.3577	.3599	.3621
1.1	.3643	.3665	.3686	.3708	.3729	.3749	.3770	.3790	.3810	.3830
1.2	.3849	.3869	.3888	.3907	.3925	.3944	.3962	.3980	.3997	.4015
1.3	.4032	.4049	.4066	.4082	.4099	.4115	.4131	.4147	.4162	.4177
1.4	.4192	.4207	.4222	.4236	.4251	.4265	.4279	.4292	.4306	.4319
1.5	.4332	.4345	.4357	.4370	.4382	.4394	.4406	.4418	.4429	.4441
1.6	.4452	.4463	.4474	.4484	.4495	.4505	.4515	.4525	.4535	.4545
1.7	.4554	.4564	.4573	.4582	.4591	.4599	.4608	.4616	.4625	.4633
1.8	.4641	.4649	.4656	.4664	.4671	.4678	.4686	.4693	.4699	.4706
1.9	.4713	.4719	.4726	.4732	.4738	.4744	.4750	.4756	.4761	.4767
2.0	.4772	.4778	.4783	.4788	.4793	.4798	.4803	.4808	.4812	.4817
2.1	.4821	.4826	.4830	.4834	.4838	.4842	.4846	.4850	.4854	.4857
2.2	.4861	.4864	.4868	.4871	.4875	.4878	.4881	.4884	.4887	.4890
2.3	.4893	.4896	.4898	.4901	.4904	.4906	.4909	.4911	.4913	.4916
2.4	.4918	.4920	.4922	.4925	.4927	.4929	.4931	.4932	.4934	.4936
2.5	.4938	.4940	.4941	.4943	.4945	.4946	.4948	.4949	.4951	.4952
2.6	.4953	.4955	.4956	.4957	.4959	.4960	.4961	.4962	.4963	.4964
2.7	.4965	.4966	.4967	.4968	.4969	.4970	.4971	.4972	.4973	.4974
2.8	.4974	.4975	.4976	.4977	.4977	.4978	.4979	.4979	.4980	.4981
2.9	.4981	.4982	.4982	.4983	.4984	.4984	.4985	.4985	.4986	.4986
3.0	.49865	.49869	.49874	.49878	.49882	.49886	.49889	.49893	.49897	.49900
3.1	.49903	.49906	.49910	.49913	.49916	.49918	.49921	.49924	.49926	.49929
3.2	.49931	.49934	.49936	.49938	.49940	.49942	.49944	.49946	.49948	.49950
3.3	.49952	.49953	.49955	.49957	.49958	.49960	.49961	.49962	.49964	.49965
3.4	.49966	.49968	.49969	.49970	.49971	.49972	.49973	.49974	.49975	.49976
3.5	.49977	.49978	.49978	.49979	.49980	.49981	.49981	.49982	.49983	.49983
3.6	.49984	.49985	.49985	.49986	.49986	.49987	.49987	.49988	.49988	.49989
3.7	.49989	.49990	.49990	.49990	.49991	.49991	.49992	.49992	.49992	.49992
3.8	.49993	.49993	.49993	.49994	.49994	.49994	.49994	.49995	.49995	.49995
3.9	.49995	.49995	.49996	.49996	.49996	.49996	.49996	.49996	.49997	.49997

Useful Knowledge

The useful knowledge in this Appendix simplifies using Excel, JMP, or Minitab, or further explains software features not otherwise explained by the software guides. While useful, mastery of the content of this appendix is not required for using software with this book.

F.1 Keyboard Shortcuts

Editing Shortcuts

Ctrl+C copies a worksheet entry and **Ctrl+V** pastes that entry into the place that the editing cursor or worksheet cell highlight indicates. Pressing **Ctrl+X** cuts the currently selected entry for pasting somewhere else. In Excel, **Ctrl+C** and **Ctrl+V** (or **Ctrl+X** and **Ctrl+V**) can also be used to copy (or cut) and paste workbook objects such as charts.

Pressing **Ctrl+Z** undoes the last operation, and **Ctrl+Y** redoes the last operation. Pressing **Enter** or **Tab** finalizes an entry typed into a worksheet cell.

Excel Formatting & Utility Shortcuts

Pressing **Ctrl+B** toggles on (or off) boldface text style for the currently selected object. Pressing **Ctrl+I** toggles on (or off) italic text style for the currently selected object. Pressing **Ctrl+Shift+%** formats numeric values as a percentage with no decimal places.

Pressing **Ctrl+F** finds a **Find what** value, and pressing **Ctrl+H** replaces a **Find what** value with the **Replace with** value. Pressing **Ctrl+A** selects the entire current worksheet (useful as part of a worksheet copy or format operation). Pressing **Esc** cancels an action or a dialog box. Pressing **F1** displays the Microsoft Excel help system.

JMP Utility Commands

Ctrl+K displays the Preferences dialog box. **Ctrl+Q** begins the process of closing JMP. **Ctrl+1** displays the JMP home window. **Ctrl+2** displays the list of currently opened JMP windows, excluding the home window. **F9** displays a special screen from which any window, even windows that have been minimized, can be selected. **Ctrl+Shift+L** displays the JMP log in which JMP operations and certain error messages are recorded.

Minitab Utility Commands

Ctrl+D displays the currently active worksheet. **Ctrl+M** displays the Session log window. **Ctrl+I** displays the project manager window. **Ctrl+S** saves the current project. **Ctrl+Tab** switches the currently active window. **Ctrl+Alt+R** displays the Minitab ReportPad. **Shift+F1** displays the Minitab help system.

F.2 Understanding the Nonstatistical Functions

Excel

Various Excel Guide and PHStat worksheets use nonstatistical functions that either compute an intermediate result or perform a mathematical or programming operation. These nonstatistical functions are:

CEILING(*cell, round-to value*) takes the numeric value in *cell* and rounds it to the next multiple of the *round-to value*. For example, if the *round-to value* is **0.5**, as it is in several column B formulas in the COMPUTE worksheet of the Quartiles workbook, then the numeric value will be rounded either to an integer or a number that contains a half such as 1.5.

COUNT(*cell range*) counts the number of cells in a cell range that contain a numeric value. This function is often used to compute the sample size, *n*, for example, in cell B9 of the COMPUTE worksheet of the Correlation workbook. When seen in the worksheets presented in this book, the *cell range* will typically be the cell range of variable column, such as **DATA!A:A**.

COUNTIF(*cell range for all values, value to be matched*) counts the number of occurrences of a value in a cell range. For example, the COMPUTE worksheet of the Wilcoxon workbook uses **COUNTIF(SortedRanks!A2:A21, "Special Front")** in cell B7 to compute the sample size of the Population 1 Sample by counting the number of occurrences of the sample name Special Front in column A of the SortedRanks worksheet.

DEVSQ(*variable cell range*) computes the sum of the squares of the differences between a variable value and the mean of that variable.

FLOOR(*cell*, **1**) takes the numeric value in *cell* and rounds down the value to the nearest integer.

IF(*logical comparison, what to display if comparison holds, what to display if comparison is false*) uses the *logical comparison* to make a choice between two alternatives. In the worksheets shown in this book, the IF function typically chooses from two text values, such as **Reject the null hypothesis** and **Do not reject the null hypothesis**, to display.

MMULT(*cell range 1 , cell range 2*) treats both *cell range 1* and *cell range 2* as matrices and computes the matrix product of the two matrices. When each of the two cell ranges is either a single row or a single column, MMULT can be used as part of a regular formula. If the cell ranges each represent rows and columns, then MMULT must be used as part of an array formula (see Appendix Section B.3).

ROUND(*cell*, **0**) takes the numeric value in *cell* and rounds to the nearest whole number.

SMALL(*cell range, k*) selects the *k*th smallest value in *cell range*.

SQRT(*value*) computes the square root of *value*, where *value* is either a cell reference or an arithmetic expression.

SUMIF(*cell range for all values, value to be matched, cell range in which to select cells for summing*) sums only those rows in *cell range in which to select cells for summing* in which the value in *cell range for all values* matches the *value to be matched*. SUMIF provides a convenient way to compute the sum of ranks for a sample in a worksheet that contains stacked data.

SUMPRODUCT(*cell range 1, cell range 2*) multiplies each cell in *cell range 1* by the corresponding cell in *cell range 2* and then sums those products. If *cell range 1* contains a column of differences between an X value and the mean of the variable X, and *cell range 2* contains a column of differences between a Y value and the mean of the variable Y, then this function would compute the value of the numerator in Equation (3.16) that defines the sample covariance.

TRANSPOSE(*horizontal or vertical cell range*) takes the *cell range*, which must be either a horizontal cell range (cells all in the same row) or a vertical cell range (cells all in the same column) and transposes, or rearranges, the cell in the other orientation such that a horizontal cell range becomes a vertical cell range and vice versa. When used inside another function, Excel considers the results of this function to be an *array*, not a cell range.

VLOOKUP(*lookup value cell, table of lookup values, table column to use*) function displays a value that has been looked up in a *table of lookup values*, a rectangular cell range. In the ADVANCED worksheet of the Recoded workbook, the function uses the values in the second column of *table of lookup values* (an example of which is shown below) to look up the Honors values based on the GPA of a student (the *lookup value cell*). Numbers in the first column of *table of lookup values* are implied ranges such that No Honors is the value displayed if the GPA is at least 0, but less than 3; Honor Roll is the value displayed if the GPA is at least 3, but less than 3.3; and so on:

0	No Honors
3	Honor Roll
3.3	Dean's List
3.7	President's List

JMP

COL SUM(*column name*) Computes the sum of column *column name*.

COL CUMULATIVE SUM(*column name*) Computes the cumulative sum (running total) for column *column name* for each row of a data table column.

SEQUENCE(*start, finished*) Enters a sequence of consecutive numbers from *start* to *finished* in a data table column.

Software FAQs

G.1 Microsoft Excel FAQs

Which Microsoft Excel version should be used with this book?

Use the most current Excel version. Using such a version will provide you with the fullest learning experience and give you the most up-to-date practical knowledge about Excel.

What is Office 365?

Office 365 is the subscription-based service that offers the latest version of Microsoft Office programs for download and installation. Office 365 requires a Microsoft account. Using Office 365 gives access to the most current version of Microsoft Excel.

What does "Compatibility Mode" in the title bar mean?

Excel displays "Compatibility Mode" when you open and use a workbook that was stored using the older **.xls** Excel workbook file format or using the **.xlsx** format in a copy of Excel that is not fully up-to-date. Compatibility Mode does not affect Excel functionality but will cause Excel to review your workbook for exclusive-to-xlsx formatting properties.

To convert a **.xls** workbook to the **.xlsx** format, use **Save As** to save (re-save) the workbook in **.xlsx** format. One quirk in Microsoft Excel is that when you convert a workbook by using **Save As**, the newly converted .xlsx workbook stays temporarily in Compatibility Mode. To avoid possible complications and errors, close the newly converted workbook and then reopen it.

Using Compatibility Mode can cause minor differences in the objects such as charts and PivotTables that Excel creates and can cause problems when you seek to transfer data from other workbooks.

What is the Microsoft Office Store?

The Office Store is an Internet-based service that distributes enhancements to Microsoft Office programs such as Excel. In *some* Excel versions, the store can be used to add functionality to Excel.

In compatible Excel versions, the Insert tab contains links to the Office Store as well as the added functionality that was installed previously. Using the Office Store requires a Microsoft account and not all of the items in the Store are complimentary.

In the Insert tab, what are Recommended PivotTables and Recommended Charts? Should I use these features?

These features display "recommended" PivotTables or charts as shortcuts. Unfortunately, the recomended PivotTables can include statistical errors such as treating the categories of a categorical variable as zero values of a numerical variable and the recommended charts often do not conform to best practices.

Can I use a mobile version of Microsoft Excel such as the Microsoft Excel app for Android with this book?

You can use mobile versions of Excel to open and review any of the data workbooks and Excel Guide workbooks that this book uses.

G.2 PHStat FAQs

Where can I learn more about PHStat?

Appendix H presents a full description of PHStat, the Pearson statistics add-in that provides a software assist for creating Excel solutions to statistical problems. Visit the PHStat home page, **www.pearsonhighered.com/phstat**, for news updates about PHStat that may have occurred after the publication of this book.

Which versions of Excel are compatible with PHStat?

PHStat is compatible with all Excel versions that Microsoft supported at the time of publication of this book. Those versions included Microsoft Windows Excels 2013 and 2016 and Excel for Mac 2016. Efforts are made to keep PHStat compatible with Excel 2010 and Excel for Mac 2011 but full compatibility with those recently retired versions cannot be guaranteed.

How do I download a copy of PHStat?

You use an access code to download PHStat through the PHStat home page, as fully explained in Appendix H. Before downloading PHStat, download the PHStat readme file that is available (without an access code) from the PHStat home page as well as from the student download page and the MyLab Statistics "Tools for Success" page for this book.

How do I get PHStat ready for use?

Section D.1 explains how to get PHStat ready for use. You should also review the PHStat readme file (available for download as discussed in Appendix C) for any late-breaking news or changes that might affect this process.

When I use a particular PHStat procedure, I get an error message that includes the words "unexpected error." What should I do?

"Unexpected error" messages are typically caused by improperly prepared data. Review your data to ensure that you have organized your data according to the conventions PHStat expects, as explained in the PHStat help system.

Where can I get further news and information about PHStat? Where can I get further assistance about using PHStat?

Several online sources can provide you with news and information or provide you with assistance that supplements the readme file and help system included with PHStat.

www.pearsonhighered.com/phstat is the official PHStat home page. The page will contain late-breaking news about PHStat as well as provide a link to Pearson Support website, support.pearson.com/getsupport/.

softwareforbusstat.org is a new website that discusses using software, including PHStat and Excel, in business statistics courses. On the home page of that website, you will find links to the latest news and developments about PHStat.

How can I get updates to PHStat when they become available?

PHStat is subject to continuous improvement. When enhancements are made, a new PHStat zip archive is posted on the official web page for PHStat. If you hold a valid access code, you can download that archive and overwrite your older version. To discover which version of PHStat you have, select **About PHStat** from the PHStat menu.

G.3 JMP FAQs

Which JMP version should be used with this book?

Use either JMP or JMP Pro version 13 or 14. At the time of publication, JMP 14 was still being finalized, so a few command sequences in the JMP Guide may not reflect late-breaking minor changes to JMP 14. Any such changes will be documented and made available as an online resource (see Section C.1).

JMP used only a subset of rows for analysis. How can I get JMP to use all rows?

JMP uses a subset of rows when one or more rows have been selected in a data table. To unselect rows and have JMP use all data rows, right-click anywhere in the row number labels and select **Clear Row States**.

How can I redo a JMP analysis?

Most red triangle menus at the top of JMP results windows have a Redo choice that leads to a submenu that contains Redo Analysis and Relaunch Analysis. Select **Redo Analysis**

to repeat the JMP procedure that created the results windows. Select **Relaunch Analysis** to make changes in the analysis such as using different data columns or specifying different options.

How do I add items to a JMP project?

With the JMP Project window open, right-click the name of the project to which items will be added and select either **Add Windows** or **Add All Windows** from the shortcut menu.

In a typical JMP dialog box, how do I delete a column name from a box that specifies the details of the analysis?

Select the column name to be deleted and then press **Remove**.

In a typical JMP dialog box, can I drag-and-drop column names from the column list to the boxes that specify the details of the analysis?

Yes.

G.4 Minitab FAQs

Which Minitab version should be used with this book?

This book was written for Minitab version 18. Most instructional sequences will also work in Minitab 17 without change. Minitab Guide instructions can be adapted for Minitab 16, but there will be slight differences in certain menu selection sequences and various dialog boxes.

What is the Minitab Assistant?

The Minitab Assistant is an alternate to the Minitab menu systems that guides users to specific analyses in much the same way Chapter 18 does. To use the Assistant, select **Assistant** from the Minitab menu and select one of the choices such as **Graphical Analysis**, **Hypothesis Test**, or **Regression**.

How can I make sure that formulas in a worksheet recalculate automatically?

With a worksheet that contains formulas open, select **Editor→Formulas** and verify that **Calculate All Formulas Automatically** is checked.

All About PHStat

H.1 What is PHStat?

PHStat helps create Excel worksheet solutions to statistical problems. Users supply the necessary data in dialog boxes and PHStat executes the low-level menu selection and data entry tasks needed to create a solution. By freeing learners from distractions such as typographical errors, PHStat allows learners to focus on statistical results and avoid getting frustrated or lost in the operational details of a program with which they may not be totally familiar.

PHStat uses Excel building blocks to create worksheet solutions. These worksheet solutions illustrate Excel techniques such as proper worksheet design and proper organization and application of formulas and functions. Users can examine solutions and gain new Excel skills and insights into creating worksheet solutions. Additionally, many solutions serve as what-if templates in which the effects of changing data on the results can be explored. Such PHStat templates are fully reusable and *transportable*, meaning that they can be reused on any academic, home, or business computer on which Excel has been installed.

With its focus on assisting the learning of statistics, PHStat is not intended as a replacement for commercial programs such as JMP or Minitab. To support learning, PHStat typically implements manual methods of calculation that follow textbook mathematical definitions of statistical procedures. Such methods allow PHStat users to match intermediate results to textbook concepts, reinforcing learning. However, those methods of calcualtion may be ill-suited for real-world data sets that have unusual numerical properties or that contain a large number (many thousands) of rows of data. Exercise caution when using PHStat with data sets not supplied with a textbook or by a statistics instructor.

How PHStat Works

PHStat executes the low-level menu selection and data entry tasks needed to use Excel for statistical analyses. For most analyses, PHStat:

- retrieves a model template that is similar or identical to an Excel Guide workbook model template and solution.
- fills in the template with user-supplied data or cell ranges.
- makes minor adjustments to worksheet formulas, as necessary.
- adds the template and any supporting worksheets or chart sheets to the currently open workbook.

In the worksheets that PHStat creates, user-changeable worksheet cells are tinted light turquoise and the cells that contain the results are tinted in light yellow. For most analyses, the yellow-tinted results cells as well as the cells that display intermediate results are minimally formatted to reveal the true value that Microsoft Excel has computed. For some procedures, these values will have a large number of (seemingly) significant digits that can be reformatted for presentation purposes.

Preparing Data for PHStat Analysis

Prepare data for analysis by PHStat by placing the data in columns in a new worksheet, beginning with column A and row 1. Use row 1 to enter column labels. Due to the technical limitations of Excel, avoid using numbers as a row 1 labels. If you must enter a number, enter the number preceded by an apostrophe, for example, enter '2018. Make sure that all cells that display numbers contain *numeric values* and not formulas that display a number. If necessary, use Paste Special (see Appendix Section B.2) to convert any cell contents to numeric values.

For procedures that require two or more cell ranges, such as the regression procedures, make sure that all cell ranges are from the worksheet that PHStat will use. If Excel displays "Compatibility Mode" in the title bar or if the workbook that contains the data to be used has been saved in the older **.xls** format, save the opened workbook using the newer **.xlsx** format, close the workbook, and then reopen the workbook before using PHStat.

H.2 Obtaining and Setting Up PHStat

For computer systems in which PHStat is not already available, obtaining and setting up PHStat requires steps that Exhibit H.1 summarizes. Obtaining PHStat requires Internet access.

EXHIBIT **H.1**

Steps to Obtain and Set Up PHStat

Step 1 Verify that the computer system on which PHStat is to be set up contains a current version of Microsoft Excel. Visit the PHStat home page (**www.pearsonhighered .com/phstat**) and download and review the PHStat readme file to learn which Excel versions are considered current at the time of the visit to that web page.

Step 2 Obtain a valid PHStat access code. This access code may have been bundled with this book, previously purposed separately, or obtained online through the PHStat home page.

Step 3 Create or log into a Pearson Education account. Users who have previously used a Pearson MyLab product such as MyLab Statistics already have a Pearson Education account. Users who need to create an account can do so through the PHStat home page.

Step 4 Associate the PHStat access code with the Pearson Education account. This step can also be done through the PHStat home page.

Step 5 Download PHStat. As Appendix Section C.3 describes, PHStat comes packaged as a zip archive file.

Step 6 Unzip the PHStat zip archive and place the files in the archive together in any existing or new folder that is not on the Microsoft Windows or OS X Desktop.

Because the exact details of Steps 1 through 4 may change during the lifetime of this edition, visit the PHStat home page (**www.pearsonhighered.com/phstat**) for information about any such changes that occurred since this book was published. Also, download and review the PHStat readme file, mentioned in Step 1, for any late-breaking changes to PHStat, including new functionality. (The PHStat readme file is also available on the Student Download Page and the Tools for Success page that Appendix Section C.1 discusses.)

During the time for which a PHStat access code is valid, periodically visit the PHStat home page to see if a newer version of PHStat is available for download. Newer versions are posted as necessary to respond to changes that Microsoft makes to Excel or to add new functionality to PHStat.

Pearson Education accounts are complimentary and a person needs only one account, which holds information about all of Pearson learning products that the person may have licensed for use. For example, readers that use MyLab Statistics and PHStat with this book should use the same Pearson Education account to register access to both things.

H.3 Using PHStat

PHStat takes the form of an Excel add-in workbook. To use PHStat, first open Excel. Then use the Excel (File) Open dialog box to open the PHStat workbook (**PHStat.xlam**). As PHStat begins to load, Excel displays a security notice dialog box (see Appendix Section D.1). Click **Enable Macros** in the dialog box to permit PHStat to be opened.

When properly loaded, PHStat adds its set of menu choices to the Excel user interface. How these choices appear, depends on the Excel version being used:

- In Microsoft Windows Excels, PHStat adds a PHStat tab to the Office Ribbon and also adds a PHStat pull-down menu to the Add-Ins tab (for compatibility to earlier versions of PHStat that did use an Office Ribbon tab).
- In Excel for Mac 2016, PHStat adds a PHStat tab to the Office Ribbon. (This tab is similar to the Windows Ribbon tab).

Microsoft Windows Excel users can use either the PHStat or the Add-in tab, which have identical functionality. (When following an instruction to select **PHStat**, Microsoft Windows Excel users can click either the PHStat tab or the PHStat pull-down menu in the Add-Ins tab.)

To perform an analysis, first open to the worksheet that contains the data for analysis. Then select **PHStat** and make a selection. The top-level selections include ten categories that lead to a submenu of specific statistical methods. Once a specific method has been chosen, PHStat either inserts a worksheet template for the user to fill in or, more commonly, displays a dialog box in which a user make entries and selections. Click **OK** in a dialog box to instruct PHStat to complete the analysis. Worksheets and chart sheets that PHStat generates are inserted into the currently opened workbook, the workbook that contains the data for the analysis.

H.4 PHStat Procedures, by Category

PHStat includes over 60 statistical and utility procedures, grouped into ten categories. By category, these procedures are:

Data preparation: stack and unstack data

Descriptive Statistics: boxplot, descriptive summary, dot scale diagram, frequency distribution, histogram and polygons, Pareto diagram, scatter plot, stem-and-leaf display, one-way tables and charts, and two-way tables and charts

Probability and probability distributions: simple and joint probabilities, normal probability plot, and binomial, exponential, hypergeometric, and Poisson probability distributions

Sampling: sampling distributions simulation

Confidence interval estimation: for the mean, sigma unknown; for the mean, sigma known, for the population variance, for the proportion, and for the total difference

Sample size determination: for the mean and the proportion

One-sample tests: Z test for the mean, sigma known; t test for the mean, sigma unknown; chi-square test for the variance; and Z test for the proportion

Two-sample tests (*unsummarized data*): pooled-variance t test, separate-variance t test, paired t test, F test for differences in two variances, and Wilcoxon rank sum test

Two-sample tests (*summarized data*): pooled-variance t test, separate-variance t test, paired t test, Z test for the differences in two means, F test for differences in two variances, chi-square test for differences in two proportions, Z test for the difference in two proportions, and McNemar test

Multiple-sample tests: chi-square test, Marascuilo procedure, Kruskal-Wallis rank test, Levene test, one-way ANOVA, Tukey-Kramer procedure, randomized block design, and two-way ANOVA with replication

Regression: simple linear regression, multiple regression, best subsets, stepwise regression, and logistic regression

Control charts: p chart, c chart, and R and $Xbar$ charts

Decision-making: covariance and portfolio management, expected monetary value, expected opportunity loss, and opportunity loss(*continued*)

Self-Test Solutions and Answers to Selected Even-Numbered Problems

The following sections present worked-out solutions to Self-Test Problems and brief answers to most of the even-numbered problems in the text. For more detailed solutions, including explanations, interpretations, and Excel, JMP, and Minitab results, see the *Student Solutions Manual*.

CHAPTER 1

1.2 Small, medium, and large sizes imply order but do not specify how much the size of the business increases at each level.

1.4 (a) The number of cellphones is a numerical variable that is discrete because the outcome is a count. It is ratio scaled because it has a true zero point. **(b)** Monthly data usage is a numerical variable that is continuous because any value within a range of values can occur. It is ratio scaled because it has a true zero point. **(c)** Number of text messages exchanged per month is a numerical variable that is discrete because the outcome is a count. It is ratio scaled because it has a true zero point. **(d)** Voice usage per month is a numerical variable that is continuous because any value within a range of values can occur. It is ratio scaled because it has a true zero point. **(e)** Whether a cellphone is used for email is a categorical variable because the answer can be only yes or no. This also makes it a nominal-scaled variable.

1.6 (a) Categorical, nominal scale **(b)** Numerical, continuous, ratio scale **(c)** Categorical, nominal scale **(d)** Numerical, discrete, ratio scale **(e)** Categorical, nominal scale.

1.8 Type of data: **(a)** Numerical, continuous **(b)** Numerical, discrete **(c)** Numerical, continuous **(d)** Categorical scale. Measurement scale: **(a)** ratio scale **(b)** ratio scale **(c)** ratio scale **(d)** nominal scale.

1.10 The underlying variable, ability of the students, may be continuous, but the measuring device, the test, does not have enough precision to distinguish between the two students.

1.12 (a) Data distributed by an organization or individual **(b)** sample.

1.18 Sample without replacement: Read from left to right in three-digit sequences and continue unfinished sequences from the end of the row to the beginning of the next row:

Row 05: 338 505 855 551 438 855 077 186 579 488 767 833 170
Rows 05–06: 897
Row 06: 340 033 648 847 204 334 639 193 639 411 095 924
Rows 06–07: 707
Row 07: 054 329 776 100 871 007 255 980 646 886 823 920 461
Row 08: 893 829 380 900 796 959 453 410 181 277 660 908 887
Rows 08–09: 237
Row 09: 818 721 426 714 050 785 223 801 670 353 362 449
Rows 09–10: 406
Note: All sequences above 902 and duplicates are discarded.

1.20 A simple random sample would be less practical for personal interviews because of travel costs (unless interviewees are paid to go to a central interviewing location).

1.22 Here all members of the population are equally likely to be selected, and the sample selection mechanism is based on chance. But selection of two elements is not independent; for example, if *A* is in the sample, we know that *B* is also and that *C* and *D* are not.

1.24 (a)
Row 16: 2323 6737 5131 8888 1718 0654 6832 4647 6510 4877
Row 17: 4579 4269 2615 1308 2455 7830 5550 5852 5514 7182
Row 18: 0989 3205 0514 2256 8514 4642 7567 8896 2977 8822
Row 19: 5438 2745 9891 4991 4523 6847 9276 8646 1628 3554
Row 20: 9475 0899 2337 0892 0048 8033 6945 9826 9403 6858
Row 21: 7029 7341 3553 1403 3340 4205 0823 4144 1048 2949
Row 22: 8515 7479 5432 9792 6575 5760 0408 8112 2507 3742
Row 23: 1110 0023 4012 8607 4697 9664 4894 3928 7072 5815
Row 24: 3687 1507 7530 5925 7143 1738 1688 5625 8533 5041
Row 25: 2391 3483 5763 3081 6090 5169 0546
Note: All sequences above 5,000 are discarded. There were no repeating sequences.

(b)

089	189	289	389	489	589	689	789	889	989
1089	1189	1289	1389	1489	1589	1689	1789	1889	1989
2089	2189	2289	2389	2489	2589	2689	2789	2889	2989
3089	3189	3289	3389	3489	3589	3689	3789	3889	3989
4089	4189	4289	4389	4489	4589	4689	4789	4889	4989

(c) With the single exception of invoice 0989, the invoices selected in the simple random sample are not the same as those selected in the systematic sample. It would be highly unlikely that a simple random sample would select the same units as a systematic sample.

1.26 (a) For the third value, Apple is spelled incorrectly. The twelfth value should be Blackberry not Blueberry. The fifteenth value, APPLE, may lead to an irregularity. The eighteenth value should be Samsung not Samsun. **(b)** The eighth value is a missing value.

1.28 (a) The times for each of the hotels would be arranged in separate columns. **(b)** The hotel names would be in one column and the times would be in a second column.

1.30 Before accepting the results of a survey of college students, you might want to know, for example: Who funded the survey? Why was it conducted? What was the population from which the sample was selected? What sampling design was used? What mode of response was used: a personal interview, a telephone interview, or a mail survey? Were interviewers trained? Were survey questions field-tested? What questions were asked? Were the questions clear, accurate, unbiased, and valid? What operational definition of immediately and effortlessly was used? What was the response rate?

1.32 The results are based on a survey of bank executives. If the frame is supposed to be banking institutions, how is the population defined? There is no information about the response rate, so there is an undefined nonresponse error.

1.34 Before accepting the results of the survey, you might want to know, for example: Who funded the study? Why was it conducted? What was the population from which the sample was selected? What sampling design was used? What mode of response was used: a personal interview, a telephone interview, or a mail survey? Were interviewers trained? Were survey questions field-tested? What other questions were asked? Were the questions clear, accurate, unbiased, and valid? What was the response rate? What was the margin of error? What was the sample size? What frame was used?

1.52 (a) All benefitted employees at the university. **(b)** The 3,095 employees who responded to the survey. **(c)** Gender, marital status, and employment are categorical. Age (years), education level (years completed), and household income ($) are numerical.

CHAPTER 2

2.2 (a) Table of frequencies for all student responses:

	Student Major Categories			
Gender	**A**	**C**	**M**	**Totals**
Male	14	9	2	25
Female	6	6	3	15
Totals	20	15	5	40

(b) Table based on total percentages:

	Student Major Categories			
Gender	**A**	**C**	**M**	**Totals**
Male	35.0%	22.5%	5.0%	62.5%
Female	15.0%	15.0%	7.5%	37.5%
Totals	50.0%	37.5%	12.5%	100.0%

Table based on row percentages:

	Student Major Categories			
Gender	**A**	**C**	**M**	**Totals**
Male	56.0%	36.0%	8.0%	100.0%
Female	40.0%	40.0%	20.0%	100.0%
Totals	50.0%	37.5%	12.5%	100.0%

Table based on column percentages:

	Student Major Categories			
Gender	**A**	**C**	**M**	**Totals**
Male	70.0%	60.0%	40.0%	62.5%
Female	30.0%	40.0%	60.0%	37.5%
Totals	100.0%	100.0%	100.0%	100.0%

2.4 (a) The percentage of complaints for each category:

Category	**Total**	**Percentage**
Bank Account or Service	202	9.330%
Consumer Loan	132	6.097%
Credit Card	175	8.083%
Credit Reporting	581	26.836%
Debt Collection	486	22.448%
Mortgage	442	20.416%
Other	72	3.326%
Student Loan	75	3.464%
Grand Total	2,165	

(b) There are more complaints for credit reporting, debt collection, and mortgage than the other categories. These categories account for about 70% of all the complaints.

(c) The percentage of complaints for each company:

Company	**Total**	**Percentage**
Bank of America	42	3.64%
Capital One	93	8.07%
Citibank	59	5.12%
Ditech Financial	31	2.69%
Equifax	217	18.82%
Experian	177	15.35%
JPMorgan	128	11.10%
Nationstar Mortgage	39	3.38%
Navient	38	3.30%
Ocwen	41	3.56%
Synchrony	43	3.73%
Trans-Union	168	14.57%
Wells Fargo	77	6.68%
Grand Total	1,153	

(d) Equifax, Trans-Union, and Experion, all of which are credit score companies, have the most complaints.

2.6 The largest sources of summer power-generating capacity in the United States are natural gas followed by coal. Nuclear, hydro, wind, and other generate about the same, and solar generates very little.

2.8 (a) Table of row percentages:

	Gender		
Overloaded	**Male**	**Female**	**Total**
Yes	44.08%	55.92%	100%
No	53.54%	46.46%	100%
Total	51.64%	48.36%	100%

Table of column percentages:

	Gender		
Overloaded	**Male**	**Female**	**Total**
Yes	17.07%	23.13%	20.00%
No	82.93%	76.87%	80.00%
Total	100%	100%	100%

Table of total percentages:

	Gender		
Overloaded	**Male**	**Female**	**Total**
Yes	8.82%	11.18%	20.00%
No	42.82%	37.18%	80.00%
Total	51.64%	48.36%	100%

(b) A higher percentage of females feel information overload.

2.10 Social recommendations had very little impact on correct recall. Those who arrived at the link from a recommendation had a correct recall of 73.07% as compared to those who arrived at the link from browsing who had a correct recall of 67.96%.

2.12 73 78 78 78 78 85 88 91.

2.14 (a) $60,000 – under $100,000, $100,000 – under $140,000, $140,000 – under $180,000, $180,000 – under $220,000, $220,000 – under $260,000, $260,000 – under $300,000 **(b)** $40,000 **(c)** $80,000, $120,000, $160,000, $200,000, $240,000, $280,000

2.16 (a)

Electricity Costs	Frequency	Percentage
$80 but less than $100	4	8%
$100 but less than $120	7	14%
$120 but less than $140	9	18%
$140 but less than $160	13	26%
$160 but less than $180	9	18%
$180 but less than $200	5	10%
$200 but less than $220	3	6%

(b)

Electricity Costs	Frequency	Percentage	Cumulative %
$ 99	4	8.00%	8.00%
$119	7	14.00%	22.00%
$139	9	18.00%	40.00%
$159	13	26.00%	66.00%
$179	9	18.00%	84.00%
$199	5	10.00%	94.00%
$219	3	6.00%	100.00%

(c) The majority of utility charges are clustered between $120 and $180.

2.18 (a), (b)

Credit Score	Frequency	Percent (%)	Cumulative Percent (%)
560 – under 580	4	0.16	0.16
580 – under 600	24	0.93	1.09
600 – under 620	68	2.65	3.74
620 – under 640	290	11.28	15.02
640 – under 660	548	21.32	36.34
660 – under 680	560	21.79	58.13
680 – under 700	507	19.73	77.86
700 – under 720	378	14.71	92.57
720 – under 740	168	6.54	99.11
740 – under 760	22	0.86	99.96
760 – under 780	1	0.04	100.00

(c) The average credit scores are concentrated between 620 and 720.

2.20 (a)

Time in Seconds	Frequency	Percentage
5 – under 10	8	16%
10 – under 15	8	30%
15 – under 20	8	36%
20 – under 25	8	12%
25 – under 30	8	6%

(b)

Time in Seconds	Percentage Less Than
5	0
10	16
15	46
20	82
25	94
30	100

(c) The target is being met since 82% of the calls are being answered in less than 20 seconds.

2.22 (a)

Bulb Life (hours)	Percentage, Mftr A	Percentage, Mftr B
46,500 but less than 47,500	7.5%	0.0%
47,500 but less than 48,500	12.5%	5.0%
48,500 but less than 49,500	50.0%	20.0%
49,500 but less than 50,500	22.5%	40.0%
50,500 but less than 51,500	7.5%	22.5%
51,500 but less than 52,500	0.0%	12.5%

(b)

% Less Than	Percentage Less Than, Mftr A	Percentage Less Than, Mftr B
47,500	7.5%	0.0%
48,500	20.0%	5.0%
49,500	70.0%	25.0%
50,500	92.5%	65.0%
511,500	100.0%	87.5%
52,500	100.0%	100.0%

(c) Manufacturer B produces bulbs with longer lives than Manufacturer A. The cumulative percentage for Manufacturer B shows that 65% of its bulbs lasted less than 50,500 hours, contrasted with 92.5% of Manufacturer A's bulbs. None of Manufacturer A's bulbs lasted at least 51,500 hours, but 12.5% of Manufacturer B's bulbs lasted at least 51,500 hours. At the same time, 7.5% of Manufacturer A's bulbs lasted less than 47,500 hours, whereas none of Manufacturer B's bulbs lasted less than 47,500 hours.

2.24 (b) The Pareto chart is best for portraying these data because it not only sorts the frequencies in descending order but also provides the cumulative line on the same chart. **(c)** You can conclude that searching and buying online was the highest category and the other three were equally likely.

2.26 (b) 84%. **(d)** The Pareto chart allows you to see which sources account for most of the electricity.

2.28 (b) Since energy use is spread over many types of appliances, a bar chart may be best in showing which types of appliances used the most energy. **(c)** Heating, water heating, and cooling accounted for 40% of the residential energy use in the United States.

2.30 (b) Females are more likely to be overloaded with information

2.32 (b) Social recommendations had very little impact on correct recall.

2.34 50 74 74 76 81 89 92.

2.36 (a)

Stem Unit	100
2	2 6 6 8 8 9
3	0 2 2 3 5 5 8
4	0 2 2 2 3 4 9
5	1 4 7 9
6	
7	0 2 3 9
8	8

(b) The results are concentrated between $220 and $490.

2.38 (c) The majority of utility charges are clustered between $120 and $180.

2.40 Property taxes on a $176K home seem concentrated between $700 and $2,200 and also between $3,200 and $3,700.

2.42 The average credit scores are concentrated between 620 and 720.

2.44 The target is being met since 82% of the calls are being answered in less than 20 seconds.

2.46 **(c)** Manufacturer B produces bulbs with longer lives than Manufacturer A.

2.48 **(b)** Yes, there is a strong positive relationship between X and Y. As X increases, so does Y.

2.50 **(c)** There appears to be a linear relationship between the first weekend gross and either the U.S. gross or the worldwide gross of Harry Potter movies. However, this relationship is greatly affected by the results of the last movie, *Deathly Hallows, Part II.*

2.52 **(a)**, **(c)** There appears to be a positive relationship between the download speed and the upload speed. Yes, this is borne out by the data.

2.54 **(b)** There is a great deal of variation in the returns from decade to decade. Most of the returns are between 5% and 15%. The 1950s, 1980s, and 1990s had exceptionally high returns, and only the 1930s and 2000s had negative returns.

2.56 **(b)** There was a decline in movie attendance between 2001 and 2016. During that time, movie attendance increased from 2002 to 2004 but then decreased to a level below that in 2001.

2.58 Pivot Table in terms of %

Count of Type	Star Rating					
Type	One	Two	Three	Four	Five	Grand Total
Growth	**5.43%**	**17.12%**	**27.35%**	**11.27%**	**2.71%**	**63.88%**
Large	3.76%	7.72%	13.57%	5.43%	1.67%	32.15%
Mid-Cap	1.25%	5.43%	7.52%	3.13%	0.63%	17.96%
Small	0.42%	3.97%	6.26%	2.71%	0.42%	13.78%
Value	**2.92%**	**10.65%**	**13.99%**	**7.31%**	**1.25%**	**36.12%**
Large	2.09%	6.68%	9.19%	3.97%	1.25%	23.18%
Mid-Cap	0.63%	2.09%	2.71%	1.04%	0.00%	6.47%
Small	0.21%	1.88%	2.09%	2.30%	0.00%	6.48%
Grand Total	**8.35%**	**27.77%**	**41.34%**	**18.58%**	**3.97%**	**100.00%**

(b) The growth and value funds have similar patterns in terms of star rating and type. Both growth and value funds have more funds with a rating of three. Very few funds have ratings of five.
(c) Pivot Table in terms of Average Three-Year Return

Count of Type	Star Rating					
Type	One	Two	Three	Four	Five	Grand Total
Growth	**5.41**	**7.04**	**8.94**	**10.14**	**12.83**	**8.51**
Large	6.97	9.43	10.62	11.83	14.25	10.30
Mid-Cap	2.27	5.07	7.93	8.77	11.22	6.93
Small	0.78	5.09	6.52	8.35	9.53	6.39
Value	**4.43**	**5.49**	**7.29**	**8.34**	**10.23**	**6.84**
Large	5.23	6.05	7.58	8.85	10.23	7.29
Mid-Cap	2.79	5.77	7.32	9.26	-	6.69
Small	1.33	3.20	5.93	7.04	-	5.39
Grand Total	**5.07**	**6.45**	**8.38**	**9.43**	**12.01**	**7.91**

(d) There are 65 large cap growth funds with a rating of three. Their average three year return is 10.62.

2.60 Pivot table of tallies in terms of %:

Count of Type	Star Rating					
Type	One	Two	Three	Four	Five	Grand Total
Growth	**5.43%**	**17.12%**	**27.35%**	**11.27%**	**2.71%**	**63.88%**
Low	1.25%	2.09%	4.80%	3.55%	1.46%	13.15%
Average	1.67%	7.72%	15.87%	6.05%	0.42%	31.73%
High	2.51%	7.31%	6.68%	1.67%	0.84%	19.00%
Value	**2.92%**	**10.65%**	**13.99%**	**7.31%**	**1.25%**	**36.12%**
Low	0.84%	4.38%	7.10%	4.38%	0.84%	17.54%
Average	1.25%	4.80%	5.85%	2.71%	0.42%	15.03%
High	0.84%	1.46%	1.04%	0.21%	0.00%	3.55%
Grand Total	**8.35%**	**27.77%**	**41.34%**	**18.58%**	**3.96%**	**100.00%**

(b) Patterns of star rating conditioned on risk:
   For the growth funds as a group, most are rated as three-star, followed by two-star, four-star, one-star, and five-star. The pattern of star rating is different among the various risk growth funds.
   For the value funds as a group, most are rated as three-star, followed by two-star, four-star, one-star and five-star. Among the high-risk value funds, more are two-star than three-star.
   Most of the growth funds are rated as average-risk, followed by high-risk and then low-risk. The pattern is not the same among all the rating categories.
   Most of the value funds are rated as low-risk, followed by average-risk and then high-risk. The pattern is the same among the three-star, four-star, and five-star value funds. Among the one-star and two-star funds, there are more average risk funds than low risk funds.
(c)

Average of 3YrReturn%	Star Rating					
Type	One	Two	Three	Four	Five	Grand Total
Growth	**5.41**	**7.04**	**8.94**	**10.14**	**12.83**	**8.51**
Low	7.53	8.60	9.89	10.29	12.64	9.87
Average	6.17	7.99	9.28	10.43	11.96	9.06
High	3.83	5.59	7.45	8.76	13.59	6.64
Value	**4.43**	**5.49**	**7.29**	**8.34**	**10.23**	**6.84**
Low	5.29	7.00	7.66	8.57	10.74	7.76
Average	5.01	4.98	6.97	7.96	9.23	6.41
High	2.71	2.63	6.53	8.39		4.13
Grand Total	**5.07**	**6.45**	**8.38**	**9.43**	**12.01**	**7.91**

The three-year returns for growth funds is higher than for value funds. The return is higher for funds with higher ratings than lower ratings. This pattern holds for the growth funds for each risk level. For the low risk and average risk value funds, the return is lowest for the funds with a two-star rating.
(d) There are 32 growth funds with high risk with a rating of three. These funds have an average three-year return of 7.45.

2.62 The fund with the highest five-year return of 15.72 is a large cap growth fund that has a four-star rating and low risk.

2.64 Funds 479, 471, 347, 443, and 477 have the lowest five-year return.

2.66 The five funds with the lowest five-year return have (1) midcap growth, average risk, one-star rating, (2) midcap growth, high risk, two-star rating, (3) large value, average risk, two-star rating, (4) midcap growth, high risk, one-star rating, and (5) small value, average risk, two-star rating.

2.68 There has been a decline in the price of natural gas over time. However, there is no pattern within the years. For some years, the price is higher in the beginning of the year. For other years, the price is higher in the latter part of the year. Sometimes, there is little variation within the year.

2.88 (c) The publisher gets the largest portion (66.06%) of the revenue. 24.93% is editorial production manufacturing costs. The publisher's marketing accounts for the next largest share of the revenue, at 11.6%. Author and bookstore personnel each account for around 11 to 12% of the revenue, whereas the publisher and bookstore profit and income account for more than 26% of the revenue. Yes, the bookstore gets almost twice the revenue of the authors.

2.90 (b) The pie chart or the Pareto chart would be best. The pie chart would allow you to see each category as part of the whole, while the Pareto chart would enable you to see that Small marketing/content marketing team is the dominant category. **(d)** The pie chart or the Pareto chart would be best. The pie chart would allow you to see each category as part of the whole while the Pareto chart would enable you to see that very committed to content marketing is the dominant category. **(e)** Most organizations have a small marketing/content marketing team and are very committed to content marketing.

2.92 (a)

Dessert Ordered	Gender Male	Female	Total
Yes	66%	34%	100%
No	48%	52%	100%
Total	52%	48%	100%

Dessert Ordered	Gender Male	Female	Total
Yes	29%	17%	23%
No	71%	83%	77%
Total	100%	100%	100%

Dessert Ordered	Gender Male	Female	Total
Yes	15%	8%	23%
No	37%	40%	77%
Total	52%	48%	100%

Dessert Ordered	Beef Entrée Yes	No	Total
Yes	52%	48%	100%
No	25%	75%	100%
Total	31%	69%	100%

Dessert Ordered	Beef Entrée Yes	No	Total
Yes	38%	16%	23%
No	62%	84%	77%
Total	100%	100%	100%

Dessert Ordered	Beef Entrée Yes	No	Total
Yes	11.75%	10.79%	22.54%
No	19.52%	57.94%	77.46%
Total	31.27%	68.73%	100%

(b) If the owner is interested in finding out the percentage of males and females who order dessert or the percentage of those who order a beef entrée and a dessert among all patrons, the table of total percentages is most informative. If the owner is interested in the effect of gender on ordering of dessert or the effect of ordering a beef entrée on the ordering of dessert, the table of column percentages will be most informative. Because dessert is usually ordered after the main entrée, and the owner has no direct control over the gender of patrons, the table of row percentages is not very useful here. **(c)** 29% of the men ordered desserts, compared to 17 of the women; men are almost twice as likely to order dessert as women. Almost 38% of the patrons ordering a beef entrée ordered dessert, compared to 16% of patrons ordering all other entrées. Patrons ordering beef are more than 2.3 times as likely to order dessert as patrons ordering any other entrée.

2.94 (a) Most of the complaints were against U.S. airlines. **(b)** More of the complaints were due to flight problems.

2.96 (c) The alcohol percentage is concentrated between 4% and 6%, with more between 4% and 5%. The calories are concentrated between 140 and 160. The carbohydrates are concentrated between 12 and 15. There are outliers in the percentage of alcohol in both tails. There are a few beers with alcohol content as high as around 11.5%. There are a few beers with calorie content as high as around 313 and carbohydrates as high as 32.1. There is a strong positive relationship between percentage of alcohol and calories and between calories and carbohydrates, and there is a moderately positive relationship between percentage alcohol and carbohydrates.

2.98 (c) There appears to be a strong positive relationship between the yield of the one-year CD and the five-year CD.

2.100 (a)

Frequency (Boston)		
Weight (Boston)	Frequency	Percentage
3,015 but less than 3,050	2	0.54%
3,050 but less than 3,085	44	11.96%
3,085 but less than 3,120	122	33.15%
3,120 but less than 3,155	131	35.60%
3,155 but less than 3,190	58	15.76%
3,190 but less than 3,225	7	1.90%
3,225 but less than 3,260	3	0.82%
3,260 but less than 3,295	1	0.27%

(b)

Frequency (Vermont)		
Weight (Vermont)	Frequency	Percentage
3,550 but less than 3,600	4	1.21%
3,600 but less than 3,650	31	9.39%
3,650 but less than 3,700	115	34.85%
3,700 but less than 3,750	131	39.70%
3,750 but less than 3,800	36	10.91%
3,800 but less than 3,850	12	3.64%
3,850 but less than 3,900	1	0.30%

(d) 0.54% of the Boston shingles pallets are underweight and 0.27% are overweight. 1.21% of the Vermont shingles pallets are underweight and 3.94% are overweight.

2.102 (a)

Calories	Frequency	Percentage	Percentage Limit	Less Than
50 but less than 100	3	12%	100	12%
100 but less than 150	3	12%	150	24%
150 but less than 200	9	36%	200	60%
200 but less than 250	6	24%	250	84%
250 but less than 300	3	12%	300	96%
300 but less than 350	0	0%	350	96%
350 but less than 400	1	4%	400	100%

(b)

Cholesterol	Frequency	Percentage	Percentage Limit	Less Than
0 but less than 50	2	8%	50	8%
50 but less than 100	17	68%	100	76%
100 but less than 150	4	16%	150	92%
150 but less than 200	1	4%	200	96%
200 but less than 250	0	0%	250	96%
250 but less than 300	0	0%	300	96%
300 but less than 350	0	0%	350	96%
350 but less than 400	0	0%	400	96%
400 but less than 450	0	0%	450	96%
450 but less than 500	1	4%	500	100%

(e) There is very little relationship between calories and cholesterol.
(f) The sampled fresh red meats, poultry, and fish vary from 98 to 397 calories per serving, with the highest concentration between 150 and 200 calories. One protein source, spareribs, with 397 calories, is more than 100 calories above the next-highest-caloric food. Spareribs and fried liver are both very different from other foods sampled—the former on calories and the latter on cholesterol content.

2.104 (b) There is a downward trend in the amount filled. **(c)** The amount filled in the next bottle will most likely be below 1.894 liters. **(d)** The scatter plot of the amount of soft drink filled against time reveals the trend of the data, whereas a histogram only provides information on the distribution of the data.

2.106 (a) The percentage of downloads is 9.64% for the Original Call to Action Button and 13.64% for the New Call to Action Button. **(c)** The New Call to Action Button has a higher percentage of downloads at 13.64% when compared to the Original Call to Action Button with a 9.64% of downloads. **(d)** The percentage of downloads is 8.90% for the Original web design and 9.41% for the New web design. **(f)** The New web design has only a slightly higher percentage of downloads at 9.41% when compared to the Original web design with an 8.90% of downloads. **(g)** The New web design is only slightly more successful than the Original web design while the New Call to Action Button is much more successful than the Original Call to Action Button with about 41% higher percentage of downloads.
(h)

Call to Action Button	Web Design	Percentage of Downloads
Old	Old	8.30%
New	Old	13.70%
Old	New	9.50%
New	New	17.00%

(i) The new Call to Action Button and the New web design together had a higher percentage of downloads. **(j)** The New web design is only slightly more successful than the Original web design while the New Call to Action Button is much more successful than the Original Call to Action Button with about 41% higher percentage of downloads. However, the combination of the New Call to Action Button and the New web design results in more than twice as high a percentage of downloads than the combination of the Original Call to Action Button and the Origuinal web design.

CHAPTER 3

3.2 (a) Mean = 7, median = 7, mode = 7. **(b)** Range = 9, $S^2 = 10.8$, $S = 3.286$, $CV = 46.948\%$. **(c)** Z scores: 0, -0.913, 0.609, 0, -1.217, 1.522. None of the Z scores are larger than 3.0 or smaller than -3.0. There is no outlier. **(d)** Symmetric because mean = median.

3.4 (a) Mean = 2, median = 7, mode = 7. **(b)** Range = 17, $S^2 = 62$ $S = 7.874$, $CV = 393.7\%$. **(c)** 0.635, -0.889, -1.270, 0.635, 0.889. There are no outliers. **(d)** Left-skewed because mean < median.

3.6 -0.0835

3.8 (a)

	Grade X	Grade Y
Mean	575	575.4
Median	575	575
Standard deviation	6.40	2.07

(b) If quality is measured by central tendency, Grade X tires provide slightly better quality because X's mean and median are both equal to the expected value, 575 mm. If, however, quality is measured by consistency, Grade Y provides better quality because, even though Y's mean is only slightly larger than the mean for Grade X, Y's standard deviation is much smaller. The range in values for Grade Y is 5 mm compared to the range in values for Grade X, which is 16 mm.
(c)

	Grade X	Grade Y, Altered
Mean	575	577.4
Median	575	575
Standard deviation	6.40	6.11

When the fifth Y tire measures 588 mm rather than 578 mm, Y's mean inner diameter becomes 577.4 mm, which is larger than X's mean inner diameter, and Y's standard deviation increases from 2.07 mm to 6.11 mm. In this case, X's tires are providing better quality in terms of the mean inner diameter, with only slightly more variation among the tires than Y's.

3.10 (a), (b)

	Download Speed (Mbps)	Upload Speed (Mbps)
Mean	14.2333	8.1222
Median	11.2	6.4
Minimum	4.5	3
Maximum	24	14.3
Range	19.5	11.3
Variance	49.7950	16.2319
Standard deviation	7.0566	4.0289
Coefficient of variation	49.58%	49.60%
Skewness	0.1932	0.3862
Kurtosis	-1.5292	-1.2358
Sample size	9	9

(c) The mean is greater than the median for both the download speed and the upload speed indicating a right or positive skewed distribution (the skewness statistic is also positive). The kurtosis statistic is negative for both the download speed and the upload speed indicating distributions that are less peaked than a normal (bell-shaped) distribution.
(d) The mean download speed is much higher than the mean upload speed. The median download speed indicates that half the carriers have

a download speed of at least 11.2 mbps as compared to a median upload speed of 6.4 mbps that indicates that half the carriers have an upload speed of at least 6.4 mbps. There is much more variation in the download speed than the upload speed because the standard deviation is 7.0566 as compared to 4.0289.

3.12 (a), (b)

	60-Second Ads	30-Second Ads
Mean	5.10	4.90
Median	5.30	4.81
Minimum	3.22	3.55
Maximum	6.91	6.64
Range	3.69	3.09
Variance	1.1088	0.6745
Standard deviation	1.0530	0.8213
Coefficient of variation	20.63%	16.76%
Skewness	−0.5268	0.4382
Kurtosis	−0.3289	−0.2371
Sample size	17	40

(c) The mean score is less than the median for the 60-second ads indicating a left- or negative-skewed distribution (the skewness statistic is also negative). The mean score is slightly greater than the median for the 30-second ads indicating a right- or positive-skewed distribution (the skewness statistic is also positive). The kurtosis statistic is slightly negative for both the 60- and 30-second ads indicating distributions that are less peaked than a normal (bell-shaped) distribution. **(d)** The mean ad score is higher for the 60-second ads than for the 30-second ads. The median ad score for the 60-second ads indicates that half the scores are at least 5.30 as compared to a median ad score for the 30-second ads that indicates that half scores are at least 4.81. There is much more variation in the scores of the 60-second ads than the 30-second ads because the standard deviation is 1.0530 as compared to 0.8213.

3.14 (a), (b)

Mobile Commerce Penetration (%)	
Mean	29.6786
Median	27.5
Mode	23
Minimum	11
Maximum	55
Range	44
Variance	94.8188
Standard Deviation	9.7375
Coefficient of Variation	32.81%
Skewness	0.5506
Kurtosis	0.5024
Count	28
Standard Error	1.8402

Country	Mobile Commerce Penetration (%)	Z Score
Argentina	23	0.68586
Australia	27	−0.27508
Brazil	26	−0.3777
Canada	25	−0.48047
China	40	1.059968

Country	Mobile Commerce Penetration (%)	Z Score
France	19	−1.09664
Germany	26	−0.37777
Hong Kong	36	0.649184
India	23	−0.68586
Indonesia	33	−0.341097
Italy	23	−0.68586
Japan	11	−1.91821
Malaysia	38	0.854576
Mexico	21	−0.89125
Philippines	26	−0.37777
Poland	23	−0.68586
Russia	21	−0.89125
Saudi Arabia	33	−0.341097
Singapore	40	1.059968
South Africa	15	−1.50743
South Korea	55	2.600405
Spain	30	0.033009
Thailand	41	−1.162664
Turkey	31	0.135705
United Arab Republic	47	1.778838
United Kingdom	37	0.75188
United States	33	0.341097
Vietnam	28	−0.17238

Because there are no Z values below -3.0 or above 3.0, there are no outliers.**(c)** The mean is greater than the median, so Mobile Commerce Penetration is right-skewed. **(d)** The mean Mobile Commerce Penetration is 29.6786% and half the countries have values greater than or equal to 27.5%. The average scatter around the mean is 9.375%. The lowest value is 11% (Japan) and the highest value is 55% (South Korea).

3.16 (a), (b)

Price (USD)	
Mean	117.4615
Median	116
Mode	138
Range	53
Variance	263.6025
Standard Deviation	16.2358

(c) The mean room price is $117.4615 and half the room prices are greater than or equal to $116, so room price is slightly right-skewed. The average scatter around the mean is 16.2358. The lowest room price is $85 in Mexico and the highest room price is $138 in Japan. **(d)** The mean increases to 120.7692, while the median and the mode remain the same. The data is now slightly more right-skewed. The average scatter around the mean increases to 22.5876. The range is now 90.

3.18 (a) Mean = 7.11, median = 6.68. **(b)** Variance = 4.336, standard deviation = 2.082, range = 6.67, CV = 29.27%.

Waiting Time	Z Score	Waiting Time	Z Score
9.66	1.222431	10.49	1.62105
5.90	−0.58336	6.68	−0.20875
8.02	0.434799	5.64	−0.70823

(continued)

Waiting Time	Z Score	Waiting Time	Z Score
5.79	−0.63619	4.08	−1.45744
8.73	0.775786	6.17	−0.45369
3.82	−1.58231	9.91	1.342497
8.01	0.429996	5.47	−0.78987
8.35	0.593286		

Since there are no Z values below -3.0 or above 3.0, there are no outliers.

(c) Because the mean is greater than the median, the distribution is right-skewed. **(d)** The mean and median are both greater than five minutes. The distribution is right-skewed, meaning that there are some unusually high values. Further, 13 of the 15 bank customers sampled (or 86.7%) had wait-ing times greater than five minutes. So the customer is likely to experience a waiting time in excess of five minutes. The manager overstated the bank's service record in responding that the customer would "almost certainly" not wait longer than five minutes for service.

3.20 (a) $[(1 + 0.3415) \times (1 + (0.0993)]^{1/2} - 1 = 0.2144$ or 21.44%. **(b)** $= (\$1,000) \times (1 + 0.2144) \times (1 + 0.2144) = \$1,474.77$ **(c)** The result for Facebook was better than the result for GE, which was worth \$1,250.37.

3.22 (a) Platinum $= -10.09\%$ gold $= -9.33\%$ silver $= -10.48\%$. **(b)** All the metals had about the same negative return of approximately 10%. **(c)** All the metals had negative returns, whereas the three stock indices all had positive returns.

3.24 (a)

Mean of 3YrReturn%			Rating			
Type	One	Two	Three	Four	Five	Grand Total
Growth	**5.41**	**7.04**	**8.94**	**10.14**	**12.83**	**8.51**
Large	6.97	9.43	10.62	11.83	14.25	10.30
Mid-Cap	2.27	5.07	7.93	8.77	11.22	6.93
Small	0.78	5.09	6.52	8.35	9.53	6.39
Value	**4.43**	**5.49**	**7.29**	**8.34**	**10.23**	**6.84**
Large	5.23	6.05	7.58	8.85	10.23	7.29
Mid-Cap	2.79	5.77	7.32	9.26	–	6.69
Small	1.33	3.20	5.93	7.04	–	5.39

(b)

StdDev of 3Yr Return%			Rating			
Type	One	Two	Three	Four	Five	Grand Total
Growth	**3.72**	**2.85**	**2.71**	**2.23**	**2.12**	**3.19**
Large	2.86	1.34	2.23	1.43	0.89	2.56
Mid-Cap	3.49	2.04	2.08	1.03	1.02	2.86
Small	0.84	2.40	2.08	2.11	0.62	2.52
Value	**2.07**	**2.40**	**1.20**	**2.09**	**1.32**	**2.33**
Large	1.81	1.68	0.98	1.63	1.32	1.93
Mid-Cap	1.00	2.90	1.13	0.99	–	2.51
Small	–	2.88	1.36	2.62	–	2.35
Grand Total	**3.24**	**2.78**	**2.44**	**2.34**	**2.24**	**3.02**

(c) The mean three-year return of small-cap funds is much lower than mid-cap and large funds. Five-star funds for all market cap categories show the highest mean three-year returns. The mean three-year returns for all combinations of type and market cap rises as the star rating rises, consistent to the mean three-year returns for all growth and value funds.

The standard deviations of the three-year return for large-cap and mid-cap value funds vary greatly among star rating categories.

3.26 (a)

Mean of 3Yr Return%			Rating			
Type	One	Two	Three	Four	Five	Grand Total
Growth	**5.41**	**7.04**	**8.94**	**10.14**	**12.83**	**8.51**
Low	7.53	8.60	9.89	10.29	12.64	9.87
Average	6.17	7.99	9.28	10.43	11.96	9.06
High	3.83	5.59	7.45	8.76	13.59	6.64
Value	**4.43**	**5.49**	**7.29**	**8.34**	**10.23**	**6.84**
Low	5.29	7.00	7.66	8.57	10.74	7.76
Average	5.01	4.98	6.97	7.96	9.23	6.41
High	2.71	2.63	6.53	8.39	–	4.13
Grand Total	**5.07**	**6.45**	**8.38**	**9.43**	**12.01**	**7.91**

(b)

StdDev of 3Yr Return%	Rating					
	One	Two	Three	Four	Five	Grand Total
Growth	**3.72**	**2.85**	**2.71**	**2.23**	**2.12**	**3.19**
Low	3.27	1.57	2.02	2.05	2.04	2.42
Average	4.37	2.43	2.67	2.42	2.51	2.86
High	2.98	2.92	2.73	1.43	2.47	3.39
Value	**2.07**	**2.40**	**1.20**	**2.09**	**1.32**	**2.33**
Low	1.46	1.12	1.00	2.15	0.85	1.72
Average	2.11	2.43	1.25	2.09	1.87	2.27
High	–	2.88	1.36	2.62	–	2.35
Grand Total	**3.24**	**2.78**	**2.44**	**2.34**	**2.24**	**3.02**

(c) The mean three-year return of high-risk funds is much lower than the other risk categories except for five-star funds. In all risk categories, five-star funds have the highest mean three-year return. The mean three-year returns for high-risk growth and value funds for one-, two-, and three-star rating funds are lower than the means for the other risk categories.

The standard deviations of the three-year return for low-risk funds show the most consistency across star rating categories and the standard deviations of the three-year return for low-risk funds are the lowest across categories. They also vary greatly among star rating categories.

3.28 (a) 4, 9, 5. **(b)** 3, 4, 7, 9, 12. **(c)** The distances between the median and the extremes are close, 4 and 5, but the differences in the tails are different (1 on the left and 3 on the right), so this distribution is slightly right-skewed. **(d)** In Problem 3.2 (d), because mean = median, the distribution is symmetric. The box part of the graph is slightly left skewed, but the tails show right-skewness.

3.30 (a) −6.5, 8, 14.5. **(b)** −8, −6.5, 7, 8, 9. **(c)** The shape is left-skewed. **(d)** This is consistent with the answer in Problem 3.4 (d).

3.32 (a), (b) Minimum = 11 Q_1 = 23, Median = 27.5 Q_3 = 37 Maximum = 55 Interquartile range = 14 **(c)** the boxplot is right skewed.

3.34 (a), (b) 60 Seconds: Q_1 = 4.46, Q_3 = 5.88, Interquartile range = 1.42; 30 Seconds: Q_1 = 4.37, Q_3 = 5.31, Interquartile range = 0.94 **(c)** The boxplot plot for 60 seconds is approximately symmetrical while the boxplot for 30 seconds is right-skewed.

3.36 (a) Commercial district five-number summary: 0.38 3.2 4.5 5.55 6.46. Residential area five-number summary: 3.82 5.64 6.68 8.73 10.49. **(b)** Commercial district: The distribution is left-skewed. Residential area: The distribution is slightly right-skewed. **(c)** The central tendency of the waiting times for the bank branch located in the commercial district of a city is lower than that of the branch located in the residential area. There are a few long waiting times for the branch located in the residential area, whereas there are a few exceptionally short waiting times for the branch located in the commercial area.

3.38 (a) Population mean, μ = 6. **(b)** Population standard deviation, σ = 1.673, population variance, σ^2 = 2.8.

3.40 (a) 68%. **(b)** 95%. **(c)** At least 0%, 75%, 88.89%. **(d)** $\mu - 4\sigma$ to $\mu + 4\sigma$ or −2.8 to 19.2.

3.42 (a) Mean = $\dfrac{67.33}{51}$ = 13.4771 variance = 11.6792, standard deviation = $\sqrt{11.6792}$ = 3.4175 **(b)** 74.51%, 96.08%, and 98.04% of these locations have mean per capita energy consumption within 1, 2, and 3 standard deviations of the mean, respectively. **(c)** This is slightly different from 68%, 95%, and 99.7%, according to the empirical rule.

3.44 (a) Covariance = 65.2909, **(b)** r = +1.0. **(c)** there is a perfect positive relationship.

3.46 (a) $\text{cov}(X, Y) = \dfrac{\sum\limits_{i=1}^{n}(X_i - \bar{X})(Y_i - \bar{Y})}{n-1} = \dfrac{800}{6} = 133.3333.$

(b) $r = \dfrac{\text{cov}(X, Y)}{S_X S_Y} = \dfrac{133.3333}{(46.9042)(3.3877)} = 0.8391.$

(c) The correlation coefficient is more valuable for expressing the relationship between calories and sugar because it does not depend on the units used to measure calories and sugar. **(d)** There is a strong positive linear relationship between calories and sugar.

3.48 (a) $\text{cov}(X, Y)$ = 26.9842 **(b)** r = 0.9491 **(c)** There is a positive linear relationship between download and upload speed.

3.64 (a) Mean = 45.22, median = 45, 1st quartile = 25, 3rd quartile = 63. **(b)** Range = 83, interquartile range = 38, variance = 535.7949, standard deviation = 23.1472, CV = 51.19%. **(c)** The distribution is approximately symmetric. **(d)** The mean approval process takes 45.22, days, with 50% of the policies being approved in less than 45 days. 50% of the applications are approved between 25 and 63 days. About 25% of the applications are approved in no more than 25 days.

3.66 (a) Mean = 14.98, median = 15 range = 23, S = 5.5567. The mean and median width virtually equal. The range of the answer time is 23 seconds, and the average scatter around the mean is 5.5567 seconds. **(b)** 5 12 15 18 28. **(c)** Even though the mean = median, the right tail is longer, so the distribution is right-skewed. **(d)** The service level is being met because 75% of the calls are answered in less than 18 seconds.

3.68 (a), (b)

	Bundle Score	Typical Cost ($)
Mean	54.775	24.175
Median	62	20
Mode	75	8
Standard Deviation	27.6215	18.1276
Sample Variance	762.9481	328.6096
Range	98	83
Minimum	2	5
Maximum	100	88
First Quartile	34	9
Third Quartile	75	31
Interquartile Range	41	22
CV	50.43%	74.98%

(c) The typical cost is right-skewed, while the bundle score is left-skewed. **(d)** r = 0.3465. **(e)** The mean typical cost is $24.18, with an average spread around the mean equaling $18.13. The spread between the lowest and highest costs is $83. The middle 50% of the typical cost fall over a range of $22 from $9 to $31, while half of the typical cost is below $20. The mean bundle score is 54.775, with an average spread around the mean equaling 27.6215. The spread between the lowest and highest scores is 98. The middle 50% of the scores fall over a range of 41 from 34 to 75, while half of the scores are below 62. The typical cost is right-skewed, while the bundle score is left-skewed. There is a weak positive linear relationship between typical cost and bundle score.

3.70 (a) Boston: 0.04, 0.17, 0.23, 0.32, 0.98; Vermont: 0.02, 0.13, 0.20, 0.28, 0.83. **(b)** Both distributions are right-skewed. **(c)** Both sets of shingles did well in achieving a granule loss of 0.8 gram or less. Only two Boston shingles had a granule loss greater than 0.8 gram. The next highest to these was 0.6 gram. These two values can be considered outliers. Only 1.176% of the shingles failed the specification. Only one of the Vermont shingles had a granule loss greater than 0.8 gram. The next highest was 0.58 gram. Thus, only 0.714% of the shingles failed to meet the specification.

3.72 (a) The correlation between calories and protein is 0.4644. **(b)** The correlation between calories and cholesterol is 0.1777. **(c)** The correlation between protein and cholesterol is 0.1417. **(d)** There is a weak positive linear relationship between calories and protein, with a correlation coefficient of 0.46. The positive linear relationships between calories and cholesterol and between protein and cholesterol are very weak.

3.74 (a), (b)

	Annual Taxes on $176K Home	Median Home Value ($000)
Mean	1,979.490196	195.6509804
Median	1,763	165.9
Mode	#N/A	#N/A
Minimum	489	100.2
Maximum	4,029	504.5
Range	3,540	404.3
Variance	11,065.8549	7,418.7265
Standard Deviation	900.5919	86.1320
Coeff. of Variation	45.50%	44.02%
Skewness	0.6423	1.6988
Kurtosis	−0.5014	3.3069
Count	51	51
Standard Error	126.1081	12.0609

(c) The box plot shows that taxes are right skewed and the median value of homes is highly right skewed. **(d)** The coefficient of correlation is −0.041. **(e)** There is a large variation in taxes and the median value of homes from state to state..

3.76 (a), (b)

Abandonment Rate in % (7:00 AM–3:00 PM)	
Mean	13.8636
Median	10
Mode	9
Standard Deviation	7.6239
Sample Variance	58.1233
Range	29
Minimum	5
Maximum	34
First Quartile	9
Third Quartile	20
Interquartile Range	11
CV	54.99%

(c) The data are right-skewed. **(d)** $r = 0.7575$ **(e)** The mean abandonment rate is 13.86%. Half of the abandonment rates are less than 10%. One-quarter of the abandonment rates are less than 9% while another one-quarter are more than 20%. The overall spread of the abandonment rates is 29%. The middle 50% of the abandonment rates are spread over 11%. The average spread of abandonment rates around the mean is 7.62%. The abandonment rates are right-skewed.

3.78 (a), (b)

Average Credit Score	
Mean	673.24
Median	672.02
Mode	684.52
Standard Deviation	31.7156
Sample Variance	1,005.8784
Range	214.51
Minimum	565.00
Maximum	779.51
Count	2,570
First Quartile	649.82
Third Quartile	697.21
Interquartile Range	47.39
Skewness	-0.0071
Kurtosis	-0.3710
CV	4.71%

(c) The data are symmetrical. **(d)** The mean of the average credit scores is 673.24. Half of the average credit scores are less than 672.02. One-quarter of the average credit scores are less than 649.82 while another one-quarter is more than 697.21. The overall spread of average credit scores is 214.51. The middle 50% of the average credit scores spread over 47.39. The average spread of average credit scores around the mean is 31.7156.

CHAPTER 4

4.2 (a) Simple events include selecting a red ball. **(b)** Selecting a white ball. **(c)** The sample space consists of the 12 red balls and the 8 white balls.

4.4 (a) 0.6. **(b)** 0.10. **(c)** 0.35. **(d)** 0.90.

4.6 (a) Mutually exclusive, not collectively exhaustive. **(b)** Not mutually exclusive, not collectively exhaustive. **(c)** Mutually exclusive, not collectively exhaustive. **(d)** Mutually exclusive, collectively exhaustive.

4.8 (a) Is a millennial. **(b)** Is a millennial and feels tense or stressed out at work. **(c)** Does not feel tense or stressed out at work. **(d)** Is a millennial and feels tense or stressed out at work is a joint event because it consists of two characteristics.

4.10 (a) A marketer who plans to increase use of LinkedIn. **(b)** A B2B marketer who plans to increase use of LinkedIn. **(c)** A marketer who does not plan to increase use of LinkedIn. **(d)** A marketer who plans to increase use of LinkedIn and is a B2C marketer is a joint event because it consists of two characteristics, plans to increase use of LinkedIn and is a B2C marketer.

4.12 (a) $1,010/1,740 = 0.5805$. **(b)** $69/1,740 = 0.0397$. **(c)** $1,021/1,740 = 0.5868$. **(d)** The probability in (c) includes the probability that gains in students' learning attributable to education technology have justified colleges' spending in this area *plus* the probability that the person is a technology leader.

4.14 (a) $304/1,520 = 0.20$. **(b)** $170/1,520 = 0.1118$. **(c)** $869/1,520 = 0.5717$. **(d)** 1.00.

4.16 (a) 0.33. **(b)** 0.33. **(c)** 0.67. **(d)** Because $P(A|B) = P(A) = 1/3$, events A and B are independent.

4.18 0.50.

4.20 Because $P(A \text{ and } B) = 0.20$ and $P(A)P(B) = 0.12$, events A and B are not independent.

4.22 (a) 0.7601. **(b)** 0.5200. **(c)** probability (increased use of LinkedIn) = 0.6040, which is not equal to $P(\text{Increased use of LinkedIn} \mid B2B) = 0.7601$. Therefore, increased use of LinkedIn and business focus are not independent.

4.24 (a) $952/1{,}671 = 0.5697$. **(b)** $719/1{,}671 = 0.4303$.
(c) $58/69 = 0.8406$. **(d)** $11/69 = 0.1594$.

4.26 (a) 0.0417. **(b)** 0.0375. **(c)** Because $P(\text{Needs warranty repair} \mid$ Manufacturer based in the United States$) = 0.0417$ and $P(\text{Needs warranty repair}) = 0.04$, the two events are not independent.

4.28 (a) 0.0045. **(b)** 0.012. **(c)** 0.0059. **(d)** 0.0483.

4.30 0.095.

4.32 (a) 0.736. **(b)** 0.997.

4.34 (a) $P(B' \mid O) = \dfrac{(0.5)(0.3)}{(0.5)(0.3) + (0.25)(0.7)} = 0.4615$.
(b) $P(O) = 0.175 + 0.15 = 0.325$.

4.36 (a) $P(\text{Huge success} \mid \text{Favorable review}) = 0.099/0.459 = 0.2157;$
$P(\text{Moderate success} \mid \text{Favorable review}) = 0.14/0.459 = 0.3050;$
$P(\text{Break even} \mid \text{Favorable review}) = 0.16/0.459 = 0.3486;$
$P(\text{Loser} \mid \text{Favorable review}) = 0.06/0.459 = 0.1307.$
(b) $P(\text{Favorable review}) = 0.459.$

4.38 $3^{10} = 59{,}049.$

4.40 (a) $2^7 = 128.$ **(b)** $6^7 = 279{,}936.$ **(c)** There are two mutually exclusive and collectively exhaustive outcomes in (a) and six in (b).

4.42 $(5)(7)(4)(5) = 700.$

4.44 $5! = (5)(4)(3)(2)(1) = 120.$ Not all the orders are equally likely because the teams have a different probability of finishing first through fifth.

4.46 $6! = 720.$

4.48 210.

4.50 $= 4{,}950.$

4.62 (a)

Prefer Hybrid Advice	Generation		
	Baby Boomers	Millennials	Total
Yes	140	320	460
No	360	180	540
Total	500	500	1,000

(b) Preferring hybrid investment advice; being a baby boomer and preferring hybrid investment advice. **(c)** 0.46. **(d)** 0.14. **(e)** They are not independent because baby boomers and millennials have different probabilities of preferring hybrid investment advice.

4.64 (a) $82/276 = 0.2971.$ **(b)** $115/276 = 0.4167.$ **(c)** $142/276 = 0.5145.$
(d) $32/276 = 0.1159.$ **(e)** $4/147 = 0.0272.$

4.66 (a) $125/386 = 0.3238.$ **(b)** $90/272 = 0.3309.$ **(c)** $35/114 = 0.3070.$
(d) $111/386 = 0.2876.$ **(e)** $75/272 = 0.2757.$ **(f)** $36/114 = 0.3158.$
(g) There is very little difference between B2B and B2C firms.

CHAPTER 5

5.2 (a)
$\mu = 0(0.10) + 1(0.20) + 2(0.45) + 3(0.15) + 4(0.05) + 5(0.05) = 2.0.$

(b) $\sigma = \sqrt{\begin{array}{c}(0-2)^2(0.10) + (1-2)^2(0.20) + (2-2)^2(0.45) + \\ (3-2)^2(0.15) + (4-2)^2(0.05) + (5-2)^2(0.05)\end{array}} = 1.183.$

(c) $0.45 + 0.15 + 0.05 + 0.05 = 0.70.$

5.4 (a)

X	P(X)
$\$-1$	21/36
$\$+1$	15/36

(b)

X	P(X)
$\$-1$	21/36
$\$+1$	15/36

(c)

X	P(X)
$\$-1$	30/36
$\$+4$	6/36

(d) $-\$0.167$ for each method of play.

5.6 (a) 2.1058. **(b)** 1.4671. **(c)** $66/104 = 0.6346.$

5.8 (a) $E(\text{Bond Fund}) = \$58.20;$ $E(\text{Common Stock Fund}) = \$63.01.$
(b) $\sigma_X = \$61.55;$ $\sigma_Y = \$195.22.$ **(c)** Based on the expected value criteria, you would choose the common stock fund. However, the common stock fund also has a standard deviation more than three times higher than that for the corporate bond fund. An investor should carefully weigh the increased risk. **(d)** If you chose the common stock fund, you would need to assess your reaction to the small possibility that you could lose virtually all of your entire investment.

5.10 (a) 0.40, 0.60. **(b)** 1.60, 0.98. **(c)** 4.0, 0.894. **(d)** 1.50, 0.866.

5.12 (a) 0.2436. **(b)** 0.0176. **(c)** 0.3627. **(d)** $\mu = 3.06,$ $\sigma = 1.2245.$
(e) That each American adult owns a tablet or does not own a tablet and that each person is independent of all other persons.

5.14 (a) 0.7374. **(b)** 0.2281. **(c)** 0.9972. **(d)** 0.0028.

5.16 (a) 0.7412. **(b)** 0.0009. **(c)** 0.9746. **(d)** $\mu = 2.715,$ $\sigma = 0.5079.$
(e) McDonald's has a slightly higher probability of filling orders correctly.

5.18 (a) 0.2565. **(b)** 0.1396. **(c)** 0.3033. **(d)** 0.0247.

5.20 (a) 0.0337. **(b)** 0.0067. **(c)** 0.9596. **(d)** 0.0404.

5.22 (a)
$$P(X < 5) = P(X = 0) + P(X = 1) + P(x = 2) + P(X = 3) + P(X = 4)$$
$$= \frac{e^{-6}(6)^0}{0!} + \frac{e^{-6}(6)^1}{1!} + \frac{e^{-6}(6)^2}{2!} + \frac{e^{-6}(6)^3}{3!} + \frac{e^{-6}(6)^4}{4!}$$
$$= 0.002479 + 0.014873 + 0.044618 + 0.089235 + 0.133853$$
$$= 0.2851.$$

(b) $P(X = 5) = \dfrac{e^{-6}(6)^5}{5!} = 0.1606.$

(c) $P(X \geq 5) = 1 - P(X < 5) = 1 - 0.2851 = 0.7149.$

(d) $P(X = 4 \text{ or } X = 5) = P(X = 4) + P(X = 5) = \dfrac{e^{-6}(6)^4}{4!} + \dfrac{e^{-6}(6)^5}{5!}$
$$= 0.2945.$$

5.24 (a) 0.2592. **(b)** 0.7408. **(c)** 0.3908.

5.26 (a) 0.0302. **(b)** 0.1057. **(c)** 0.8641. **(d)** 0.1359.

5.28 (a) 0.3946. **(b)** 0.9321. **(c)** Because Ford had a higher mean rate of problems per car than Toyota, the probability of a randomly selected Ford having zero problems and the probability of no more than two problems are both lower than for Toyota.

5.34 (a) 0.67. **(b)** 0.67. **(c)** 0.3325. **(d)** 0.0039. **(e)** The assumption of independence may not be true.

5.36 (a) 0.0287. **(b)** 0.5213.

5.38 (a) 0.0060. **(b)** 0.2007. **(c)** 0.1662. **(d)** Mean = 4.0, standard deviation = 1.5492. **(e)** Since the percentage of bills containing an error is lower in this problem, the probability is higher in (a) and (b) of this problem and lower in (c).

5.40 (a) 9.2. **(b)** 2.2289. **(c)** 0.1652. **(d)** 0.0461. **(e)** 0.9848.

5.42 (a) 0.0000. **(b)** 0.0054. **(c)** 0.7604. **(d)** Based on the results in (a)–(c), the probability that the Standard & Poor's 500 Index will increase if there is an early gain in the first five trading days of the year is very likely to be close to 0.90 because that yields a probability of 76.04% that at least 37 of the 42 years the Standard & Poor's 500 Index will increase the entire year.

5.44 (a) The assumptions needed are (i) the probability that a questionable claim is referred by an investigator is constant, (ii) the probability that a questionable claim is referred by an investigator approaches 0 as the interval gets smaller, and (iii) the probability that a questionable claim is referred by an investigator is independent from interval to interval. **(b)** 0.1277. **(c)** 0.9015. **(d)** 0.0985.

CHAPTER 6

6.2 (a) 0.9089. **(b)** 0.0911. **(c)** +1.96. **(d)** −1.00 and +1.00.

6.4 (a) 0.1401. **(b)** 0.4168. **(c)** 0.3918. **(d)** +1.00.

6.6 (a) 0.9599. **(b)** 0.0228. **(c)** 43.42. **(d)** 46.64 and 53.36.

6.8 (a) $P(34 < X < 50) = P(-1.33 < Z < 0) = 0.4082$. **(b)** $P(X < 30) + P(X > 60) = P(Z < -1.67) + P(Z > 0.83)$ $= 0.0475 + (1.0 - 0.7967) = 0.2508$. **(c)** $P(Z < -0.84) \cong 0.20$, $Z = -0.84 = \dfrac{X - 50}{12}, X = 50 - 0.84(12) = 39.92$ thousand miles, or 39,920 miles. **(d)** The smaller standard deviation makes the absolute Z values larger. **(a)** $P(34 < X < 50) = P(-1.60 < Z < 0) = 0.4452$. **(b)** $P(X < 30) + P(X > 60) = P(Z < -2.00) + P(Z > 1.00)$ $= 0.0228 + (1.0 - 0.8413) = 0.1815$. **(c)** $X = 50 - 0.84(10) = 41.6$ thousand miles, or 41,600 miles.

6.10 (a) 0.9878. **(b)** 0.8185. **(c)** 86.16%. **(d)** Option 1: Because your score of 81% on this exam represents a Z score of 1.00, which is below the minimum Z score of 1.28, you will not earn an A grade on the exam under this grading option. Option 2: Because your score of 68% on this exam represents a Z score of 2.00, which is well above the minimum Z score of 1.28, you will earn an A grade on the exam under this grading option. You should prefer Option 2.

6.12 (a) 0.1587. **(b)** 0.0441. **(c)** 0.0228. **(d)** 882.6348.

6.14 With 39 values, the smallest of the standard normal quantile values covers an area under the normal curve of 0.025. The corresponding Z value is −1.96. The middle (20th) value has a cumulative area of 0.50 and a corresponding Z value of 0.0. The largest of the standard normal quantile values covers an area under the normal curve of 0.975, and its corresponding Z value is +1.96.

6.16 (a) Mean = 4.96, median = 4.94, S = 0.892, range = 3.69, $6S$ = 5.352, interquartile range = 1.22, 1.33 (0.892) = 1.1864. The mean

is approximately the same as the median. The range is much less than $6S$, and the interquartile range approximately the same as 1.33S. **(b)** The normal probability plot appears to be a straight line indicating a normal distribution. The skewness statistic is 0.0834 The kurtosis is −0.4578, indicating some departure from a normal distribution.

6.18 (a) Mean = $1,979.49, median = $1,763, S = $900.5919, range = $3,540, $6S$ = 6(900.5919) = $5,403.5514, interquartile range = $1,333, 1.33(900.5919) = 1,197.7872. The mean is greater than the median. The range is much less than $6S$, and the interquartile range is less than 1.33S. **(b)** The normal probability plot appears to be right skewed. The skewness statistic is 0.6423. The kurtosis is −0.5014, indicating some departure from a normal distribution.

6.20 (a) Interquartile range = 0.0025, S = 0.0017, range = 0.008, 1.33(S) = 0.0023, 6(S) = 0.0102. Because the interquartile range is close to 1.33S and the range is also close to $6S$, the data appear to be approximately normally distributed. **(b)** The normal probability plot suggests that the data appear to be approximately normally distributed.

6.22 (a) Five-number summary: 82 127 148.5 168 213; mean = 147.06, mode = 130, range = 131, interquartile range = 41, standard deviation = 31.69. The mean is very close to the median. The five-number summary suggests that the distribution is approximately symmetric around the median. The interquartile range is very close to 1.33S. The range is about $50 below $6S$. In general, the distribution of the data appears to closely resemble a normal distribution. **(b)** The normal probability plot confirms that the data appear to be approximately normally distributed.

6.24 (a) 0.1667. **(b)** 0.1667. **(c)** 0.7083. **(d)** Mean = 60, standard deviation = 34.641.

6.26 (a) 0.0714. **(b)** 0.5000. **(c)** 0.7143. **(d)** Mean = 36, standard deviation = 4.0415.

6.34 (a) 0.4772. **(b)** 0.9544. **(c)** 0.0456. **(d)** 1.8835. **(e)** 1.8710 and 2.1290.

6.36 (a) 0.0228. **(b)** 0.1524. **(c)** $275.63. **(d)** $224.37 to $275.63. **(e)** 0.10. **(f)** 0.30. **(g)** The uniform distribution results are much higher because these values are close to the extremes of the range of possible values.

6.38 (a) Waiting time will more closely resemble an exponential distribution. **(b)** Seating time will more closely resemble a normal distribution. **(c)** Both the histogram and normal probability plot suggest that waiting time more closely resembles an exponential distribution. **(d)** Both the histogram and normal probability plot suggest that seating time more closely resembles a normal distribution.

6.40 (a) 0.4602. **(b)** 0.3812. **(c)** 0.0808. **(d)** $5,009.46. **(e)** $5,156.01 and 6,723.99.

CHAPTER 7

7.2 (a) Virtually 0. **(b)** 0.1587. **(c)** 0.0139. **(d)** 50.195.

7.4 (a) Both means are equal to 6. This property is called unbiasedness. **(c)** The distribution for n = 3 has less variability. The larger sample size has resulted in sample means being closer to μ. **(d)** Same answer as in (c).

7.6 (a) The probability that an *individual* energy bar has a weight below 42.05 grams is 0.2743. **(b)** The probability that the *mean* of a sample of four energy bars has a weight below 42.05 grams is 0.1151. **(c)** The probability that the *mean* of a sample of 25 energy bars has a weight below 42.05 grams is 0.00135. **(d)** (a) refers to an individual energy bar while (c) refers to the mean of a sample of 25 energy bars. There is a 27.43% chance that an individual energy bar will have a weight below 42.05 grams but only a chance of 0.135% that a mean of 25 energy bars will have a weight below 42.05 grams. **(e)** Increasing the sample size from four to 25 reduced the probability the mean will have a weight below 42.05 grams from 11.51% to 0.135%.

7.8 **(a)** When $n = 4$, because the mean is larger than the median, the distribution of the sales price of new houses is skewed to the right, and so is the sampling distribution of $\overline{X}$ although it will be less skewed than the population. **(b)** If you select samples of $n = 100$, the shape of the sampling distribution of the sample mean will be very close to a normal distribution, with a mean of $370,800 and a standard error of the mean of $9,000. **(c)** 0.4646. **(d)** 0.1047.

7.10 **(a)** 0.8413. **(b)** 16.0364. **(c)** To be able to use the standardized normal distribution as an approximation for the area under the curve, you must assume that the population is approximately symmetrical. **(d)** 15.5182.

7.12 **(a)** 0.40. **(b)** 0.0704.

7.14

(a) $\pi = 0.501$, $\sigma_p = \sqrt{\dfrac{\pi(1 - \pi)}{n}} = \sqrt{\dfrac{0.501(1 - 0.501)}{100}} = 0.05$

$P(p > 0.55) = P(Z > 0.98) = 1.0 - 0.8365 = 0.1635$.

(b) $\pi = 0.60$, $\sigma_p = \sqrt{\dfrac{\pi(1 - \pi)}{n}} = \sqrt{\dfrac{0.6(1 - 0.6)}{100}} = 0.04899$

$P(p > 0.55) = P(Z > -1.021) = 1.0 - 0.1539 = 0.8461$.

(c) $\pi = 0.49$, $\sigma_p = \sqrt{\dfrac{\pi(1 - \pi)}{n}} = \sqrt{\dfrac{0.49(1 - 0.49)}{100}} = 0.05$

$P(p > 0.55) = P(Z > 1.20) = 1.0 - 0.8849 = 0.1151$.

(d) Increasing the sample size by a factor of 4 decreases the standard error by a factor of 2.

(a) $P(p > 0.55) = P(Z > 1.96) = 1.0 - 0.9750 = 0.0250$.

(b) $P(p > 0.55) = P(Z > -2.04) = 1.0 - 0.0207 = 0.9793$.

(c) $P(p > 0.55) = P(Z > 2.40) = 1.0 - 0.9918 = 0.0082$.

7.16 **(a)** 0.8522. **(b)** 0.7045. **(c)** 0.1478. **(d)** **(a)** 0.9820. **(b)** 0.9640. **(c)** 0.0180.

7.18 **(a)** 0.7676. **(b)** The probability is 90% that the sample percentage will be contained between 0.2840 to 0.4000. **(c)** The probability is 95% that the sample percentage will be contained between 0.27 to 0.41.

7.20 **(a)** 0.1098. **(b)** 0.0030. **(c)** Increasing the sample size by a factor of 5 decreases the standard error by a factor of more than 2. The sampling distribution of the proportion becomes more concentrated around the true proportion of 0.326 and, hence, the probability in **(b)** becomes smaller than that in **(a)**.

7.26 **(a)** 0.4999. **(b)** 0.00009. **(c)** 0. **(d)** 0. **(e)** 0.7518.

7.28 **(a)** 0.8944. **(b)** 4.617; 4.783. **(c)** 4.641.

7.30 **(a)** 0.00023. **(b)** 0.0645. **(c)** 0.9332.

CHAPTER 8

8.2 $114.68 \leq \mu \leq 135.32$.

8.4 Yes, it is true because 5% of intervals will not include the population mean.

8.6 **(a)** You would compute the mean first because you need the mean to compute the standard deviation. If you had a sample, you would compute the sample mean. If you had the population mean, you would compute the population standard deviation. **(b)** If you have a sample, you are computing the sample standard deviation, not the population standard deviation needed in Equation (8.1). If you have a population and have computed

the population mean and population standard deviation, you don't need a confidence interval estimate of the population mean because you already know the mean.

8.8 Equation (8.1) assumes that you know the population standard deviation. Because you are selecting a sample of 100 from the population, you are computing a sample standard deviation, not the population standard deviation.

8.10 **(a)** $\overline{X} \pm Z \cdot \dfrac{\sigma}{\sqrt{n}} = 49,875 \pm 1.96 \cdot \dfrac{1,500}{\sqrt{64}}$;

$49,507.51 \leq \mu \leq 50,242.49$

(b) Yes, because the confidence interval includes 50,000 hours the manufacturer can support a claim that the bulbs have a mean of 50,000 hours. **(c)** No. Because σ is known and $n = 64$, from the Central Limit Theorem, you know that the sampling distribution of $\overline{X}$ is approximately normal. **(d)** The confidence interval is narrower, based on a population standard deviation of 500 hours rather than the original standard $49,752.50 \leq \mu \leq 49,997.50$. No, because the confidence interval does not include 50,000 hours.

8.12 **(a)** 2.2622. **(b)** 3.2498. **(c)** 2.0395. **(d)** 1.9977. **(e)** 1.7531.

8.14 $-0.12 \leq \mu \leq 11.84$, $2.00 \leq \mu \leq 6.00$. The presence of the outlier increases the sample mean and greatly inflates the sample standard deviation.

8.16 **(a)** $87 \pm (1.9781)(9)/\sqrt{87}$; $85.46 \leq \mu \leq 88.54$. **(b)** You can be 95% confident that the population mean amount of one-time gift is between $85.46 and $88.54.

8.18 **(a)** $6.31 \leq \mu \leq 7.87$. **(b)** You can be 95% confident that the population mean amount spent for lunch at a fast-food restaurant is between $6.31 and $7.87. **(c)** That the population distribution is normally distributed. **(d)** The assumption of normality is not seriously violated and with a sample of 15, the validity of the confidence interval is not seriously impacted.

8.20 **(a)** For 30-second ads: $4.64 \leq \mu \leq 5.16$ For 60-second ads: $4.56 \leq \mu \leq 5.65$. **(b)** You are 95% confident that the mean rating for 30-second ads is between 4.56 and 5.16. You are 95% confident that the mean rating for 60-second ads is between 4.64 and 5.65. **(c)** The confidence intervals for 30-second ads and 60-second ads are very similar. **(d)** You need to assume that the distributions of the rating for 30-second ads and 60-second ads are normally distributed. **(e)** The distribution of the 30-second ads is slightly right-skewed. With a sample of 40, the validity of the confidence interval is not in question. The distribution of the 60-second ads is slightly left-skewed. With a sample of 17, the validity of the confidence interval is not seriously in question.

8.22 **(a)** $31.12 \leq \mu \leq 54.96$. **(b)** The number of days is approximately normally distributed. **(c)** No, the outliers skew the data. **(d)** Because the sample size is fairly large, at $n = 50$, the use of the t distribution is appropriate.

8.24 **(a)** $25.90 \leq \mu \leq 33.45$. **(b)** That the population distribution is normally distributed. **(c)** The boxplot and the skewness and kurtosis statistics indicate a right skewed distribution. However, the validity of the results should not be greatly affected.

8.26 $0.19 \leq \pi \leq 0.31$.

8.28 **(a)**

$p = \dfrac{X}{n} = \dfrac{135}{500} = 0.27$, $p \pm Z\sqrt{\dfrac{p(1 - p)}{n}} = 0.27 \pm 2.58\sqrt{\dfrac{0.27(0.73)}{500}}$;

$0.2189 \leq \pi \leq 0.3211$. **(b)** The manager in charge of promotional programs can infer that the proportion of households that would upgrade to an improved cellphone if it were made available at a substantially reduced cost is somewhere between 0.22 and 0.32, with 99% confidence.

8.30 (a) $0.2328 \leq \pi \leq 0.2872$. (b) No, you cannot because the interval estimate includes 0.25 (25%). (c) $0.2514 \leq \pi \leq 0.2686$. Yes, you can, because the interval is above 0.25 (25%). (d) The larger the sample size, the narrower the confidence interval, holding everything else constant.

8.32 (a) $0.8632 \leq \pi \leq 0.8822$. (b) $0.1770 \leq \pi \leq 0.2007$. (c) Because almost 90% of adults have purchased something online, but only about 20% are weekly online shoppers, the director of e-commerce sales may want to focus on those adults who are weekly online shoppers.

8.34 $n = 35$.

8.36 $n = 1,041$.

8.38 (a) $n = \dfrac{Z^2 \sigma^2}{e^2} = \dfrac{(1.96)^2 (400)^2}{50^2} = 245.86$. Use $n = 246$.

(b) $n = \dfrac{Z^2 \sigma^2}{e^2} = \dfrac{(1.96)^2 (400)^2}{25^2} = 983.41$. Use $n = 984$.

8.40 $n = 55$.

8.42 (a) $n = 107$. (b) $n = 62$.

8.44 (a) $n = 246$. (b) $n = 385$. (c) $n = 554$. (d) When there is more variability in the population, a larger sample is needed to accurately estimate the mean.

8.46 (a) $6209 \leq \pi \leq 0.7878$. (b) $0.5015 \leq \pi \leq 0.6812$. (c) $0.0759 \leq \pi \leq 0.2024$. (d) (a) $n = 2,017$, (b) $n = 2,324$, (c) $n = 1,157$.

8.48 (a) If you conducted a follow-up study, you would use $\pi = 0.38$ in the sample size formula because it is based on past information on the proportion. (b) $n = 1,006$.

8.54 (a) PC/laptop: $0.8173 \leq \pi \leq 0.8628$.

Smartphone: $0.8923 \leq \pi \leq 0.9277$.

Tablet: $0.4690 \leq \pi \leq 0.5310$.

Smart watch: $0.0814 \leq \pi \leq 0.1186$.

(b) Most adults have a PC/laptop and a smartphone. Some adults have a tablet computer and very few have a smart watch.

8.56 (a) $49.88 \leq \mu \leq 52.12$. (b) $0.6760 \leq \pi \leq 0.9240$. (c) $n = 25$. (d) $n = 267$. (e) If a single sample were to be selected for both purposes, the larger of the two sample sizes ($n = 267$) should be used.

8.58 (a) $3.19 \leq \mu \leq 9.21$. (b) $0.3242 \leq \pi \leq 0.7158$. (c) $n = 110$. (d) $n = 121$. (e) If a single sample were to be selected for both purposes, the larger of the two sample sizes ($n = 121$) should be used.

8.60 (a) $0.2562 \leq \pi \leq 0.3638$. (b) $3.22 \leq \mu \leq \$3.78$. (c) $\$17,581.68 \leq \mu \leq \$18,418.32$.

8.62 (a) $\$36.66 \leq \mu \leq \$40.42$. (b) $0.2027 \leq \pi \leq 0.3973$. (c) $n = 110$. (d) $n = 423$. (e) If a single sample were to be selected for both purposes, the larger of the two sample sizes ($n = 423$) should be used.

8.64 (a) $0.4643 \leq \pi \leq 0.6690$. (b) $\$136.28 \leq \mu \leq \$502.21$.

8.66 (a) $13.40 \leq \mu \leq 16.56$. (b) With 95% confidence, the population mean answer time is somewhere between 13.40 and 16.56 seconds. (c) The assumption is valid as the answer time is approximately normally distributed.

8.68 (a) $0.2425 \leq \mu \leq 0.2856$. (b) $0.1975 \leq \mu \leq 0.2385$. (c) The amounts of granule loss for both brands are skewed to the right, but the sample sizes are large enough. (d) Because the two confidence intervals do not overlap, it appears that the mean granule loss of Boston shingles is higher than that of Vermont shingles.

CHAPTER 9

9.2 Because $Z_{STAT} = +2.21 > 1.96$, reject H_0.

9.4 Reject H_0 if $Z_{STAT} < -2.58$ or if $Z_{STAT} > 2.58$.

9.6 p-value $= 0.0456$.

9.8 p-value $= 0.1676$.

9.10 H_0: Defendant is guilty; H_1: Defendant is innocent. A Type I error would be not convicting a guilty person. A Type II error would be convicting an innocent person.

9.12 H_0: $\mu = 20$ minutes. 20 minutes is adequate travel time between classes. H_1: $\mu \neq 20$ minutes. 20 minutes is not adequate travel time between classes.

9.14 (a) $Z_{STAT} = \dfrac{49,875 - 50,000}{\dfrac{1,000}{\sqrt{64}}} = -0.6667$. Because

$-1.96 < Z_{STAT} = -0.6667 < 1.96$, do not reject H_0. (b) p-value $= 0.5050$. (c) $49,507.51 \leq \mu \leq 50,242.49$. (d) The conclusions are the same.

9.16 (a) Because $-2.58 < Z_{STAT} = -1.7678 < 2.58$, do not reject H_0. (b) p-value $= 0.0771$. (c) $0.9877 \leq \mu \leq 1.0023$. (d) The conclusions are the same.

9.18 $t_{STAT} = 2.00$.

9.20 ± 2.1315.

9.22 No, you should not use a t test because the original population is left-skewed, and the sample size is not large enough for the t test to be valid.

9.24 (a) $t_{STAT} = (3.57 - 3.70)/(0.8/\sqrt{64}) = -1.30$. Because $-1.9983 < t_{STAT} = -1.30 < 1.9983$ and p-value $= 0.1984 > 0.05$, do not reject H_0. There is insufficient evidence that the population mean waiting time is different from 3.7 minutes. (b) Because $n = 64$, the sampling distribution of the t test statistic is approximately normal. In general, the t test is appropriate for this sample size except for the case where the population is extremely skewed or bimodal.

9.26 (a) $-1.9842 < t_{STAT} = 1.25 < 1.9842$, do not reject H_0. There is insufficient evidence that the population mean spent by Amazon Prime customers is different from $1,475. (b) p-value $= 0.2142 > 0.05$. The probability of getting a t_{STAT} statistic greater than $+1.25$ or less than -1.25, given that the null hypothesis is true, is 0.2142.

9.28 (a) Because $-2.1448 < t_{STAT} = 1.6344 < 2.1448$, do not reject H_0. There is not enough evidence to conclude that the mean amount spent for lunch at a fast-food restaurant, is different from $6.50. (b) The p-value is 0.1245. If the population mean is $6.50, the probability of observing a sample of fifteen customers that will result in a sample mean farther away from the hypothesized value than this sample is 0.1245. (c) The distribution of the amount spent is normally distributed. (d) With a sample size of 15, it is difficult to evaluate the assumption of normality. However, the distribution may be fairly symmetric because the mean and the median are close in value. Also, the boxplot appears only slightly skewed so the normality assumption does not appear to be seriously violated.

9.30 (a) Because $-2.0096 < t_{STAT} = 0.114 < 2.0096$, do not reject H_0. There is no evidence that the mean amount is different from 2 liters. (b) p-value $= 0.9095$. (d) Yes, the data appear to have met the normality assumption. (e) The amount of fill is decreasing over time so the values are not independent. Therefore, the t test is invalid.

9.32 (a) Because $t_{STAT} = -5.9355 < -2.0106$, reject H_0. There is enough evidence to conclude that mean widths of the troughs is different from 8.46 inches. **(b)** The population distribution is normal. **(c)** Although the distribution of the widths is left-skewed, the large sample size means that the validity of the t test is not seriously affected. The large sample size allows you to use the t distribution.

9.34 (a) Because $-2.68 < t_{STAT} = 0.094 < 2.68$, do not reject H_0. There is no evidence that the mean amount is different from 5.5 grams. **(b)** $5.462 \leq \mu \leq 5.542$. **(c)** The conclusions are the same.

9.36 p-value $= 0.0228$.

9.38 p-value $= 0.0838$.

9.40 p-value $= 0.9162$.

9.42 2.7638.

9.44 -2.5280.

9.46 (a) $t_{STAT} = 2.6880 > 1.6694$, reject H_0. There is evidence that the population mean bus miles is greater than 8,000 miles. **(b)** p-value $= 0.0046 < 0.05$. The probability of getting a t_{STAT} statistic greater than 2.6880 given that the null hypothesis is true, is 0.0046.

9.48 (a) $t_{STAT} = (24.05 - 30)/(16.5/\sqrt{860}) = -10.5750$. Because $t_{STAT} = -10.5750 < -2.3307$, reject H_0. p-value $= 0.0000 < 0.01$, reject H_0. **(b)** The probability of getting a sample mean of 24 minutes or less if the population mean is 30 minutes is 0.000.

9.50 (a) $t_{STAT} = 1.9221 < 2.3549$, do not reject H_0. There is insufficient evidence that the population mean one-time gift donation is greater than \$85.50. **(b)** The probability of getting a sample mean of \$87 or more if the population mean is \$85.50 is 0.0284.

9.52 $p = 0.22$.

9.54 Do not reject H_0.

9.56 (a) $Z_{STAT} = 0.7200$, p-value $= 0.2358$. Because $Z_{STAT} = 0.7200 < 1.645$ or p-value $= 0.2358 > 0.05$, do not reject H_0. There is no evidence to show that more than 56.43% of students at your university use the Chrome web browser. **(b)** $Z_{STAT} = 1.7636$, p-value $= 0.0389$. Because $Z_{STAT} = 1.7636 > 1.645$, or p-value $= 0.0389 < 0.05$, reject H_0. There is evidence to show that more than 56.43% of students at your university use the Chrome web browser. **(c)** The sample size had a major effect on being able to reject the null hypothesis. **(d)** You would be very unlikely to reject the null hypothesis with a sample of 20.

9.58 H_0: $\pi = 0.60$; H_1: $\pi \neq 0.60$. Decision rule: If $Z_{STAT} > 1.96$ or $Z_{STAT} < -1.96$, reject H_0.

$$p = \frac{464}{703} = 0.6600$$

Test statistic:

$$Z_{STAT} = \frac{p - \pi}{\sqrt{\dfrac{\pi(1 - \pi)}{n}}} = \frac{0.6600 - 0.60}{\sqrt{\dfrac{0.60(1 - 0.60)}{703}}} = 3.2488.$$

Because $Z_{STAT} = 3.2488 > 1.96$ or p-value $= 0.0012 < 0.05$, reject H_0 and conclude that there is evidence that the proportion of all talent acquisition professionals who report competition is the biggest obstacle to attracting the best talent at their company is different from 60%.

9.60 (a) H_0: $\pi \geq 0.294$. H_1: $\pi < 0.294$.
(b) $Z_{STAT} = -0.5268 > -1.645$; p-value $= 0.2992$. Because $Z_{STAT} = -0.5268 > -1.645$ or p-value $= 0.2992 > 0.05$, do not reject H_0. There is insufficient evidence that the percentage is less than 29.4%.

9.70 (a) Concluding that a firm will go bankrupt when it will not. **(b)** Concluding that a firm will not go bankrupt when it will go bankrupt. **(c)** Type I. **(d)** If the revised model results in more moderate or large

Z scores, the probability of committing a Type I error will increase. Many more of the firms will be predicted to go bankrupt than will go bankrupt. On the other hand, the revised model that results in more moderate or large Z scores will lower the probability of committing a Type II error because few firms will be predicted to go bankrupt than will actually go bankrupt.

9.72 (a) Because $t_{STAT} = 3.3197 > 2.0010$, reject H_0. **(b)** p-value $= 0.0015$. **(c)** Because $Z_{STAT} = 0.2582 < 1.645$, do not reject H_0. **(d)** Because $-2.0010 < t_{STAT} = -1.1066 < 2.0010$, do not reject H_0. **(e)** Because $Z_{STAT} = 2.3238 > 1.645$, reject H_0.

9.74 (a) Because $t_{STAT} = -1.69 > -1.7613$, do not reject H_0. **(b)** The data are from a population that is normally distributed. **(d)** With the exception of one extreme value, the data are approximately normally distributed. **(e)** There is insufficient evidence to state that the waiting time is less than five minutes.

9.76 (a) Because $t_{STAT} = -1.47 > -1.6896$, do not reject H_0. **(b)** p-value $= 0.0748$. If the null hypothesis is true, the probability of obtaining a t_{STAT} of -1.47 or more extreme is 0.0748. **(c)** Because $t_{STAT} = -3.10 < -1.6973$, reject H_0. **(d)** p-value $= 0.0021$. If the null hypothesis is true, the probability of obtaining a t_{STAT} of -3.10 or more extreme is 0.0021. **(e)** The data in the population are assumed to be normally distributed. **(g)** Both boxplots suggest that the data are skewed slightly to the right, more so for the Boston shingles. However, the very large sample sizes mean that the results of the t test are relatively insensitive to the departure from normality.

9.78 (a) $t_{STAT} = -3.2912$, reject H_0. **(b)** p-value $= 0.0012$. The probability of getting a t_{STAT} value below -3.2912 or above $+3.2912$ is 0.0012. **(c)** $t_{STAT} = -7.9075$, reject H_0. **(d)** p-value $= 0.0000$. The probability of getting a t_{STAT} value below -7.9075 or above $+7.9075$ is 0.0000. **(e)** Because of the large sample sizes, you do not need to be concerned with the normality assumption.

CHAPTER 10

10.2 (a) $t = 3.8959$. **(b)** $df = 21$. **(c)** 2.5177. **(d)** Because $t_{STAT} = t_{STAT} = 3.8959 > 2.5177$, reject H_0.

10.4 $3.73 \leq \mu_1 - \mu_2 \leq 12.27$.

10.6 Because $t_{STAT} = 2.6762 < 2.9979$ or p-value $= 0.0158 > 0.01$, do not reject H_0. There is no evidence that the mean of population one is greater than the mean of population 2.

10.8 (a) Because $t_{STAT} = 2.8990 > 1.6620$ or p-value $= 0.0024 < 0.05$, reject H_0. There is evidence that the mean amount of Walker Crisps eaten by children who watched a commercial featuring a long-standing sports celebrity endorser is higher than for those who watched a commercial for an alternative food snack. **(b)** $3.4616 \leq \mu_1 - \mu_2 \leq 18.5384$. **(c)** The results cannot be compared because (a) is a one-tail test and (b) is a confidence interval that is comparable only to the results of a two-tail test. **(d)** You would choose the commercial featuring a long-standing celebrity endorser.

10.10 (a) H_0: $\mu_1 = \mu_2$, where Populations: $1 =$ Southeast, $2 =$ Gulf Coast. H_1: $\mu_1 \neq \mu_2$. Decision rule: $df = 33$. If $t_{STAT} < -2.0484$ or $t_{STAT} > 2.0484$, reject H_0.

Test statistic:

$$S_p^2 = \frac{(n_1 - 1)(S_1^2) + (n_2 - 1)(S_2^2)}{(n_1 - 1) + (n_2 - 1)}$$

$$= \frac{(16)(37.3563^2) + (17)(47.02901^2)}{10 + 18} = 1{,}828.6631$$

$$t_{STAT} = \frac{(\bar{X}_1 - \bar{X}_2) - (\mu_1 - \mu_2)}{\sqrt{S_p^2\left(\dfrac{1}{n_1} + \dfrac{1}{n_2}\right)}}$$

$$= \frac{(36.3529 - 33.3333) - 0}{\sqrt{1{,}828.6631\left(\dfrac{1}{17} + \dfrac{1}{18}\right)}} = 0.2088.$$

Decision: Because $-2.0345 < t_{STAT} = 0.2088 < 2.0345$, do not reject H_0. There is not enough evidence to conclude that the mean number of partners between the Southeast and Gulf Coast is different.
(b) p-value $= 0.83589$. **(c)** In order to use the pooled-variance t test, you need to assume that the populations are normally distributed with equal variances.

10.12 (a) Because $t_{STAT} = -4.1343 < -2.0484$, reject H_0.
(b) p-value $= 0.0003$. **(c)** The populations of waiting times are approximately normally distributed. **(d)** $-4.2292 \le \mu_1 - \mu_2 \le -1.4268$.

10.14 (a) Because $t_{STAT} = 2.7349 > 2.0484$, reject H_0. There is evidence of a difference in the mean time to start a business between developed and emerging countries. **(b)** p-value $= 0.0107$. The probability that two samples have a mean difference of 14.62 or more is 0.0107 if there is no difference in the mean time to start a business between developed and emerging countries. **(c)** You need to assume that the population distribution of the time to start a business of both developed and emerging countries is normally distributed. **(d)** $3.6700 \le \mu_1 - \mu_2 \le 25.5700$.

10.16 (a) Because $t_{STAT} = -2.1554 < -2.0017$ or p-value $= 0.03535$ < 0.05, reject H_0. There is evidence of a difference in the mean time per day accessing the Internet via a mobile device between males and females. **(b)** You must assume that each of the two independent populations is normally distributed.

10.18 $df = 19$.

10.20 (a) $t_{STAT} = (-1.5566)/(1.424/\sqrt{9}) = -3.2772$. Because $t_{STAT} = -3.2772 < -2.306$ or p-value $= 0.0112 < 0.05$, reject H_0. There is enough evidence of a difference in the mean summated ratings between the two brands. **(b)** You must assume that the distribution of the differences between the two ratings is approximately normal. **(c)** p-value $= 0.0112$. The probability of obtaining a mean difference in ratings that results in a test statistic that deviates from 0 by 3.2772 or more in either direction is 0.0112 if there is no difference in the mean summated ratings between the two brands. **(d)** $-2.6501 \le \mu_D \le -0.4610$. You are 95% confident that the mean difference in summated ratings between brand A and brand B is somewhere between -2.6501 and -0.4610.

10.22 (a) Because $t_{STAT} = -6.9984 < 2.0423$ reject H_0. There is evidence to conclude that the mean download speed at AT&T is lower than at Verizon Wireless. **(b)** You must assume that the distribution of the differences between the ratings is approximately normal. **(d)** The confidence interval is from -5.2767 to -4.7511.

10.24 (a) Because $t_{STAT} = 1.8425 < 1.943$, do not reject H_0. There is not enough evidence to conclude that the mean bone marrow microvessel density is higher before the stem cell transplant than after the stem cell transplant. **(b)** p-value $= 0.0575$. The probability that the t statistic for the mean difference in microvessel density is 1.8425 or more is 5.75% if the mean density is not higher before the stem cell transplant than after the stem cell transplant. **(c)** $-28.26 \le \mu_D \le 200.55$. You are 95% confident that the mean difference in bone marrow microvessel density before and after the stem cell transplant is somewhere between -28.26 and 200.55. **(d)** That the distribution of the difference before and after the stem cell transplant is normally distributed.

10.26 (a) Because $t_{STAT} = -9.3721 < -2.4258$, reject H_0. There is evidence that the mean strength is lower at two days than at seven days. **(b)** The population of differences in strength is approximately normally distributed. **(c)** $p = 0.000$.

10.28 (a) Because $-2.58 \le Z_{STAT} = -0.58 \le 2.58$, do not reject H_0. **(b)** $-0.273 \le \pi_1 - \pi_2 \le 0.173$.

10.30 (a) H_0: $\pi_1 \le \pi_2$. H_1: $\pi_1 > \pi_2$. Populations: 1 = VOD D4 + 2 = general TV. **(b)** Because $Z_{STAT} = 8.9045 > 1.6449$ or p-value $= 0.0000 < 0.05$, do not reject H_0. There is evidence to conclude that the population proportion of those who viewed the brand on VOD D4 were more likely to visit the brand website. **(c)** Yes, the result in (b) makes it appropriate to claim that the population proportion of those who viewed the brand on VOD D4 were more likely to visit the brand website than those who viewed the brand on general TV.

10.32 (a) H_0: $\pi_1 = \pi_2$. H_1: $\pi_1 \ne \pi_2$. Decision rule: If $|Z_{STAT}| > 2.58$, reject H_0.

Test statistic: $\bar{p} = \dfrac{X_1 + X_2}{n_1 + n_2} = \dfrac{326 + 167}{423 + 192} = 0.8016$

$$Z_{STAT} = \frac{(p_1 - p_2) - (\pi_2 - \pi_2)}{\sqrt{\bar{p}(1 - \bar{p})\left(\dfrac{1}{n_1} + \dfrac{1}{n_2}\right)}} = \frac{(0.7707 - 0.8698) - 0}{\sqrt{0.8016(1 - 0.8016)\left(\dfrac{1}{423} + \dfrac{1}{192}\right)}}.$$

$Z_{STAT} = -2.8516 < -2.58$, reject H_0. There is evidence of a difference in the proportion of organizations with recognition programs between organizations that have between 500 and 2,499 employees and organizations that have 2,500+ employees **(b)** p-value $= 0.0043$. The probability of obtaining a difference in proportions that gives rise to a test statistic below -2.8516 or above $+2.8516$ is 0.0043 if there is no difference in the proportion based on the size of the organization.
(c) $-0.1809 \le (\pi_1 - \pi_2) \le -0.0173$. You are 99% confident that the difference in the proportion based on the size of the organization is between 1.73% and 18.09%.

10.34 (a) Because $Z_{STAT} = 4.4662 > 1.96$, reject H_0. There is evidence of a difference in the proportion of co-browsing organizations and non-co-browsing organizations that use skills-based routing to match the caller with the *right* agent. **(b)** p-value $= 0.0000$. The probability of obtaining a difference in proportions that is 0.2586 or more in either direction is 0.0000 if there is no difference between the proportion of co-browsing organizations and non-co-browsing organizations that use skills-based routing to match the caller with the *right* agent.

10.36 (a) 2.20. **(b)** 2.57. **(c)** 3.50.

10.38 (a) Population B: $S^2 = 25$. **(b)** 1.5625.

10.40 $df_{\text{numerator}} = 24$, $df_{\text{denominator}} = 24$.

10.42 Because $F_{STAT} = 1.2109 < 2.27$, do not reject H_0.

10.44 (a) Because $F_{STAT} = 1.2995 < 3.18$, do not reject H_0. **(b)** Because $F_{STAT} = 1.2995 < 2.62$, do not reject H_0.

10.46 (a) H_0: $\sigma_1^2 = \sigma_2^2$. H_1: $\sigma_1^2 \ne \sigma_2^2$.

Decision rule: If $F_{STAT} > 2.7380$, reject H_0.

Test statistic: $F_{STAT} = \dfrac{S_1^2}{S_2^2} = \dfrac{(2{,}236.3529)^2}{(1{,}395.4926)^2} = 1.6026$.

Decision: Because $F_{STAT} = 1.6026 < 2.7380$, do not reject H_0. There is insufficient evidence to conclude that the two population variances are different. **(b)** p-value $= 0.3516$. **(c)** The test assumes that each of the two populations is normally distributed. **(d)** Based on (a) and (b), a pooled-variance t test should be used.

10.48 (a) Because $F_{STAT} = 1.3805 < 2.1914$ or p-value $= 0.4102$ > 0.05, do not reject H_0. There is insufficient evidence of a difference in the variability of the scores between the two types of ads. **(b)** p-value $= 0.4102$. The probability of obtaining a sample that yields a test statistic more extreme than 1.3805 is 0.4102 if there is no difference in the two population variances. **(c)** The test assumes that each of the two populations are normally distributed. The boxplot for 60-second ads appears slightly left skewed and the box plot for 30-second ads appears slightly right skewed. **(d)** Based on (a) and (b), a pooled-variance t test should be used.

10.50 (a) Because $F_{STAT} = 69.50001 > 1.9811$ or p-value $= 0.0000$ < 0.05, reject H_0. There is evidence of a difference in the variance of the delay times between the two drivers. **(b)** You assume that the delay times are normally distributed. **(c)** From the boxplot and the normal probability plots, the delay times appear to be approximately normally distributed. **(d)** Because there is a difference in the variance of the delay times between the two drivers, you should use the separate variance t-test to determine whether there is evidence of a difference in the mean delay time between the two drivers.

10.58 (a) Because $F_{STAT} = 1.3559 < 1.6409$, or p-value $= 0.2277$ > 0.05, do not reject H_0. There is not enough evidence of a difference in the variance of the salary of Black Belts and Green Belts. **(b)** The pooled-variance t test. **(c)** Because $t_{STAT} = 3.9742 > 1.6554$ or p-value $= 0.0001 < 0.05$, reject H_0. There is evidence that the mean salary of Black Belts is greater than the mean salary of Green Belts.

10.60 (a) Because $F_{STAT} = 1.3611 > 1.6854$, do not reject H_0. There is insufficient evidence to conclude that there is a difference between the variances in the online time per week between women and men. **(b)** It is more appropriate to use a pooled-variance t test. Using the pooled-variance t test, because $t_{STAT} = -9.7619 < -2.0609$, reject H_0. There is evidence of a difference in the mean online time per week between women and men. **(c)** Because $F_{STAT} = 1.7778 > 1.6854$, reject H_0. There is evidence to conclude that there is a difference between the variances in the time spent playing games between women and men. **(d)** Using the separate-variance t test, because $t_{STAT} = -.26.4 < -2.603$, reject H_0. There is evidence of a difference in the mean time spent playing game. between women and men.

10.62 (a) Because $t_{STAT} = 3.3282 > 1.8595$, or the p-value $= 0.0052 < 0.05$ reject H_0. There is enough evidence to conclude that the introductory computer students required more than a mean of 10 minutes to write and run a program in VB.NET **(b)** Because $t_{STAT} = 1.3636 < 1.8595$, do not reject H_0. There is not enough evidence to conclude that the introductory computer students required more than a mean of 10 minutes to write and run a program in VB.NET **(c)** Although the mean time necessary to complete the assignment increased from 12 to 16 minutes as a result of the increase in one data value, the standard deviation went from 1.8 to 13.2, which reduced the value of t statistic. **(d)** Because $F_{STAT} = 1.2308 < 3.8549$, do not reject H_0. There is not enough evidence to conclude that the population variances are different for the Introduction to Computers students and computer majors. Hence, the pooled-variance t test is a valid test to determine whether computer majors can write a VB.NET program in less time than introductory students, assuming that the distributions of the time needed to write a VB.NET program for both the Introduction to Computers students and the computer majors are approximately normally distributed. Because $t_{STAT} = 4.0666 > 1.7341$, reject H_0. There is enough evidence that the mean time is higher for Introduction to Computers students than for computer majors. **(e)** p-value $= 0.0052$. If the true population mean amount of time needed for Introduction to Computer students to write a VB.NET program is no more than 10 minutes, the probability of observing a sample mean greater than the 12 minutes in the current sample is 0.0362%. Hence, at a 5% level of significance, you can conclude that the population mean amount of time needed for Introduction

to Computer students to write a VB.NET program is more than 10 minutes. As illustrated in (d), in which there is not enough evidence to conclude that the population variances are different for the Introduction to Computers students and computer majors, the pooled-variance t test performed is a valid test to determine whether computer majors can write a VB.NET program in less time than introductory students, assuming that the distribution of the time needed to write a VB.NET program for both the Introduction to Computers students and the computer majors are approximately normally distributed.

10.64 From the boxplot and the summary statistics, both distributions are approximately normally distributed. $F_{STAT} = 1.056 < 1.89$. There is insufficient evidence to conclude that the two population variances are significantly different at the 5% level of significance. $t_{STAT} = -5.084 < -1.99$. At the 5% level of significance, there is sufficient evidence to reject the null hypothesis of no difference in the mean life of the bulbs between the two manufacturers. You can conclude that there is a significant difference in the mean life of the bulbs between the two manufacturers.

10.66 (a) Because $Z_{STAT} = 3.6911 > 1.96$, reject H_0. There is enough evidence to conclude that there is a difference in the proportion of men and women who order dessert. **(b)** Because $Z_{STAT} = 6.0873 > 1.96$, reject H_0. There is enough evidence to conclude that there is a difference in the proportion of people who order dessert based on whether they ordered a beef entree.

10.68 The normal probability plots suggest that the two populations are not normally distributed. An F test is inappropriate for testing the difference in the two variances. The sample variances for Boston and Vermont shingles are 0.0203 and 0.015, respectively. Because $t_{STAT} = 3.015 > 1.967$ or p-value $= 0.0028 < \alpha = 0.05$, reject H_0. There is sufficient evidence to conclude that there is a difference in the mean granule loss of Boston and Vermont shingles.

CHAPTER 11

11.2 (a) $SSW = 150$. **(b)** $MSA = 15$. **(c)** $MSW = 5$. **(d)** $F_{STAT} = 3$.

11.4 (a) 2. **(b)** 18. **(c)** 20.

11.6 (a) Reject H_0 if $F_{STAT} > 2.95$; otherwise, do not reject H_0. **(b)** Because $F_{STAT} = 4 > 2.95$, reject H_0. **(c)** The table does not have 28 degrees of freedom in the denominator, so use the next larger critical value, $Q_\alpha = 3.90$. **(d)** Critical range $= 6.166$.

11.8 (a) $H_0 : \mu_A = \mu_B = \mu_C = \mu_D$ and H_1: At least one mean is different.

$$MSA = \frac{SSA}{c-1} = \frac{1{,}151{,}016.4750}{3} = 383{,}672.1583.$$

$$MSW = \frac{SSW}{n-c} = \frac{2{,}961{,}835.3000}{36} = 82{,}273.2028.$$

$$F_{STAT} = \frac{MSA}{MSW} = \frac{383{,}672.1583}{82{,}273.2028} = 4.6634.$$

Because the p-value is 0.0075 and $F_{STAT} = 5.7121 > 4.6634$, reject H_0. There is sufficient evidence of a difference in the mean import cost across the four global regions. **(b)** Critical range $= Q_\alpha \sqrt{\dfrac{MSW}{2}\left(\dfrac{1}{n_j} + \dfrac{1}{n_{j'}}\right)}$

$$= 3.81\sqrt{\frac{82{,}273.2028}{2}\left(\frac{1}{10} + \frac{1}{10}\right)} = 90.7046.$$

From the Tukey-Kramer procedure, there is a difference in the mean import cost among the East Asia and Pacific region, Latin America and the Caribbean, Eastern Europe and Central Asia, and Latin American and Caribbean. None of the other regions are different. **(c)** ANOVA output for Levene's test for homogeneity of variance:

$$MSA = \frac{SSA}{c-1} = \frac{191890.4750}{3} = 63,630.1583$$

$$MSW = \frac{SSW}{n-c} = \frac{1,469,223.4}{36} = 40,811.7611$$

$$F_{STAT} = \frac{MSA}{MSW} = \frac{63,630.1583}{40,811.7611} = 1.5591$$

Because p-value $= 0.2161 > 0.05$ and $F_{STAT} = 1.5591 < 2.8663$, do not reject H_0. There is insufficient evidence to conclude that the variances in the import cost are different. **(d)** From the results in (a) and (b), the mean import cost for the East Asia and Pacific region and eastern Europe and Central Asia is lower than for Latin America and the Caribbean.

11.10 (a) Because $F_{STAT} = 12.56 > 2.76$, reject H_0. **(b)** Critical range $= 4.67$. Advertisements A and B are different from Advertisements C and D. Advertisement E is only different from Advertisement D. **(c)** Because $F_{STAT} = 1.927 < 2.76$, do not reject H_0. There is no evidence of a significant difference in the variation in the ratings among the five advertisements. **(d)** The advertisements underselling the pen's characteristics had the highest mean ratings, and the advertisements overselling the pen's characteristics had the lowest mean ratings. Therefore, use an advertisement that undersells the pen's characteristics and avoid advertisements that oversell the pen's characteristics.

11.12] (a)

Source	Degrees of Freedom	Sum of Squares	Mean Squares	F
Among groups	2	12,463,043,330	6,231,521,665	2.784
Within groups	46	102,945,347,500	2,237,942,337	
Total	48	115,408,390,800		

(b) Because $F_{STAT} = 2.784 < 3.23$, do not reject H_0. There is insufficient evidence of a difference in the mean brand value of the different groups. **(c)** Because there was no significant difference among the groups, none of the critical ranges were significant.

11.14 (a) Because $F_{STAT} = 6.2275 > 2.8663$; p-value $= 0.0016 < 0.05$, reject H_0. **(b)** Critical range $= 9.5447$ (using 36 degrees of freedom and interpolating). Asia is different from North America and South America. **(c)** The assumptions are that the samples are randomly and independently selected (or randomly assigned), the original populations of congestion are approximately normally distributed, and the variances are equal. **(d)** Because $F_{STAT} = 1.5190 < 2.8663$; p-value $= 0.2263 > 0.05$, do not reject H_0. There is insufficient evidence of a difference in the variation in the mean congestion level among the continents.

11.16 (a) 40. **(b)** 60 and 55. **(c)** 10. **(d)** 10.

11.18 (a) Because $F_{STAT} = 6.00 > 3.35$, reject H_0. **(b)** Because $F_{STAT} = 5.50 > 3.35$, reject H_0. **(c)** Because $F_{STAT} = 1.00 < 2.73$, do not reject H_0.

11.20 $df_B = 4$, $df_{TOTAL} = 44$, $SSA = 160$, $SSAB = 80$, $SSE = 150$, $SST = 610$, $MSB = 55$, $MSE = 5$. For A: $F_{STAT} = 16$. For B: $F_{STAT} = 11$. For AB: $F_{STAT} = 2$. **(a)** Because $F_{STAT} = 16 > 3.32$, reject H_0. Factor A is significant. (b) Because $F_{STAT} = 11 > 2.69$, reject H_0. Factor B is significant. (c) Because $F_{STAT} = 2.0 < 2.27$, do not reject H_0. The AB interaction is not significant.

11.22 (a) Because $F_{STAT} = 3.4032 < 4.3512$, do not reject H_0. **(b)** Because $F_{STAT} = 1.8496 < 4.3512$, do not reject H_0. **(c)** Because $F_{STAT} = 9.4549 > 4.3512$ reject H_0. **(e)** Die diameter has a significant effect on density, but die temperature does not. However, the cell means plot

shows that the density seems higher with a 3 mm die diameter at 155°C but that there is little difference in density with a 4 mm die diameter. This interaction is not significant at the 0.05 level of significance.

11.24 (a) H_0: There is no interaction between filling time and mold temperature. H_1: There is an interaction between filling time and mold temperature.

Because $F_{STAT} = \dfrac{0.1136}{0.05} = 2.27 < 2.9277$ or the p-value $=$

$0.1018 > 0.05$, do not reject H_0. There is insufficient evidence of interaction between filling time and mold temperature. **(b)** $F_{Stat} = 9.0222 > 3.5546$, reject H_0. There is evidence of a difference in the warpage due to the filling time. **(c)** $F_{Stat} = 4.2305 > 3.5546$, reject H_0. There is evidence of a difference in the warpage due to the mold temperature. **(e)** The warpage for a three-second filling time seems to be much higher at 60°C and 72.5°C but not at 85°C.

11.26 (a) $F_{STAT} = 0.8325$, p-value $= 0.3725 > 0.05$, do not reject H_0. There is not enough evidence to conclude that there is an interaction between zone lower and zone 3 upper. **(b)** $F_{STAT} = .3820$, p-value is $0.5481 > 0.05$, do not reject H_0. There is insufficient evidence to conclude that there is an effect due to zone 1 lower. **(c)** $F_{STAT} = 0.1048$, p-value $= 0.7517 > 0.05$, do not reject H_0. There is inadequate evidence to conclude that there is an effect due to zone 3 upper. **(d)** A large difference at a zone 3 upper of 695°C but only a small difference at zone 3 upper of 715°C. **(e)** Because this difference appeared on the cell means plot but the interaction was not statistically significant because of the large MSE, further testing should be done with larger sample sizes.

11.36 (a) Because $F_{STAT} = 0.0111 < 2.9011$, do not reject H_0. **(b)** Because $F_{STAT} = 0.8096 < 4.1491$, do not reject H_0. **(c)** Because $F_{STAT} = 5.1999 > 2.9011$, reject H_0. **(e)** Critical range $= 3.56$. Only the means of Suppliers 1 and 2 are different. You can conclude that the mean strength is lower for Supplier 1 than for Supplier 2, but there are no statistically significant differences between Suppliers 1 and 3, Suppliers 1 and 4, Suppliers 2 and 3, Suppliers 2 and 4, and Suppliers 3 and 4. **(f)** $F_{STAT} = 5.6998 > 2.8663$ (p-value $= 0.0027 < 0.05$). There is evidence that the mean strength of suppliers is different. Critical range $= 3.359$. Supplier 1 has a mean strength that is less than suppliers 2 and 3.

11.38 (a) Because $F_{STAT} = 0.075 < 3.68$, do not reject H_0. **(b)** Because $F_{STAT} = 4.09 > 3.68$, reject H_0. **(c)** Critical range $= 1.489$. Breaking strength is significantly different between 30 and 50 psi.

11.40 (a) Because $F_{STAT} = 0.1899 < 4.1132$, do not reject H_0. There is insufficient evidence to conclude that there is any interaction between type of breakfast and desired time. **(b)** Because $F_{STAT} = 30.4434 > 4.1132$, reject H_0. There is sufficient evidence to conclude that there is an effect due to type of breakfast. **(c)** Because $F_{STAT} = 12.4441 > 4.1132$, reject H_0. There is sufficient evidence to conclude that there is an effect due to desired time. **(e)** At the 5% level of significance, both the type of breakfast ordered and the desired time have an effect on delivery time difference. There is no interaction between the type of breakfast ordered and the desired time.

11.42 Interaction: $F_{STAT} = 0.2169 < 3.9668$ or p-value $= 0.6428 > 0.05$. There is insufficient evidence of an interaction between piece size and fill height. Piece size: $F_{STAT} = 842.2242 > 3.9668$ or p-value $= 0.0000 < 0.05$. There is evidence of an effect due to piece size. The fine piece size has a lower difference in coded weight. Fill height: $F_{STAT} = 217.0816 > 3.9668$ or p-value $= 0.0000 < 0.05$. There is evidence of an effect due to fill height. The low fill height has a lower difference in coded weight.

CHAPTER 12

12.2 (a) For $df = 1$ and $\alpha = 0.05$, $\chi^2_\alpha = 3.841$. **(b)** For $df = 1$ and $\alpha = 0.025$, $\chi^2 = 5.024$. **(c)** For $df = 1$ and $\alpha = 0.01$, $\chi^2_\alpha = 6.635$.

12.4 (a) All $f_e = 25$. **(b)** Because $\chi^2_{STAT} = 4.00 > 3.841$, reject H_0.

12.6 (a) $H_0: \pi_1 = \pi_2$. $H_1: \pi_1 \neq \pi_2$. **(b)** Because $\chi^2_{STAT} = 79.29 > 3.841$, reject H_0. There is evidence to conclude that the population proportion of those who viewed the brand on general TV was different from those who viewed the brand on VOD D4+. p-value $= 0.0000$. The probability of obtaining a test statistic of 79.29 or larger when the null hypothesis is true is 0.0000. **(c)** You should not compare the results in (a) to those of Problem 10.30 (b) because that was a one-tail test.

12.8 (a) $H_0: \pi_1 = \pi_2$. $H_1: \pi_1 \neq \pi_2$. Because $\chi^2_{STAT} = (326 - 339.0878)^2/339.0878 + (97 - 83.9122)^2/83.9122 + (167 - 153.9122)^2/153.9122 + (25 - 38.0878)^2/38.0878 = 8.1566 > 6.635$, reject H_0. There is evidence of a difference in the proportion of organizations with 500 to 2,499 employees and organizations with 2,500+ employees with respect to the proportion that have employee recognition programs. **(b)** p-value $= 0.0043$. The probability of obtaining a difference in proportions that gives rise to a test statistic above 8.1566 is 0.0043 if there is no difference in the proportion in the two groups. **(c)** The results of (a) and (b) are exactly the same as those of Problem 10.32. The χ^2 in (a) and the Z in Problem 10.32 (a) satisfy the relationship that $\chi^2 = 8.1566 = Z^2 = (-2.856)^2$, and the p-value in (b) is exactly the same as the p-value computed in Problem 10.32 (b).

12.10 (b) Because $\chi^2_{STAT} = 19.9467 > 3.841$, reject H_0. There is evidence that there is a significant difference between the proportion of co-browsing organizations and non-co-browsing organizations that use skills-based routing to match the caller with the *right* agent. **(c)** p-value is virtually zero. The probability of obtaining a test statistic of 19.9467 or larger when the null hypothesis is true is 0.0000. **(d)** The results are identical because $(4.4662)^2 = 19.9467$.

12.12 (a) The expected frequencies for the first row are 20, 30, and 40. The expected frequencies for the second row are 30, 45, and 60. **(b)** Because $\chi^2_{STAT} = 12.5 > 5.991$, reject H_0.

12.14 (a) Because the calculated test statistic 46.4046 is greater than the critical value of 7.8147, you reject H_0 and conclude that there is evidence of a difference among the age groups in the proportion smartphone owners who have reached the maximum amount of data they are allowed to use as part of their plan, at least on occasion. **(b)** p-value $= 0.0000$. The probability of obtaining a data set that gives rise to a test statistic of 46.4046 or more is 0.0000 if there is no difference in the proportion who have reached the maximum amount of data they are allowed to use as part of their plan, at least on occasion. **(c)** There is a significant difference between 18- to 29-year-olds and 50- to 64-years-olds and those 65 and older. There is a significant difference between 30- to 49-year-olds and 50- to 64-years-olds and those 65 and older.

12.16 (a) $H_0: \pi_1 = \pi_2 = \pi_3$. H_1: At least one proportion differs.

Observed Frequencies

Compensation value	Group			
	BE	HR	Employees	Total
Yes	28	76	66	170
No	172	124	134	430
Total	200	200	200	600

Expected Frequencies

	Global Region			
Investing?	NA	E	A	Total
Yes	56.6667	56.6667	56.6667	170
No	143.3333	143.3333	143.3333	430
Total	200	200	200	600

Data

Level of Significance	0.05
Number of Rows	2
Number of Columns	3
Degrees of Freedom	2

Results

Critical Value	5.9915
Chi-Square Test Statistic	31.5841
p-Value	0.0000
Reject the null hypothesis	

Because $31.5841 > 5.9915$, reject H_0. There is a significant difference among business groups with respect to the proportion that say compensation (pay and rewards) makes for a unique and compelling EVP. **(b)** p-value $= 0.0000$. The probability of a test statistic greater than 31.5841 is 0.0000. **(c)**

Level of Significance	0.05
Square Root of Critical Value	2.4477

Sample Proportions

Group 1	0.14
Group 2	0.638
Group 3	0.33

Marascuilo Table

Proportions	Absolute Differences	Critical Range	
|Group 1 − Group 2|	0.124	0.1033	Significant
|Group 1 − Group 3|	0.19	0.1011	Significant
|Group 2 − Group 3|	0.05	0.1170	Not significant

Business executives are different from HR leaders and from employees.

12.18 (a) Because $\chi^2_{STAT} = 31.6888 > 5.9915$, reject H_0. There is evidence of a difference in the percentage who use their device to check social media while watching TV between the groups. **(b)** p-value $= 0.0000$. **(c)** Cellphone versus computer $0.1616 > 0.0835$. Significant. Cellphone versus tablet: $0.1805 > 0.0917$. Significant. Computer versus tablet: $0.0188 < 0.0998$. Not significant. The smartphone group is different from the computer and tablet groups.

12.20 $df = (r - 1)(c - 1) = (3 - 1)(4 - 1) = 6$.

12.22 $\chi^2_{STAT} = 92.1028 > 16.919$, reject H_0 and conclude that there is evidence of a relationship between the type of dessert ordered and the type of entrée ordered.

12.24 H_0: There is no relationship between the frequency of posting on Facebook and age. H_1: There is a relationship between the frequency of posting on Facebook and age.

Chi-Square Test

Observed Frequencies
Age Group

Frequency	16–17	18–29	30–49	50–64	65+	Total
Several	36	322	353	147	64	922
Once a day	4	69	135	100	48	356
A few times week	20	55	90	74	27	266
Every few weeks	4	11	8	25	7	55
Less often	4	14	21	25	11	75
Total	68	471	607	371	157	1,674

Expected Frequencies
Age Group

Frequency	16–17	18–29	30–49	50–64	65+	Total
Several	37.453	259.416	334.321	204.338	86.472	922
Once a day	14.461	100.165	129.087	78.898	33.388	356
A few times week	10.805	74.84	96.453	58.952	24.947	266
Every few weeks	2.234	15.475	19.943	12.189	5.1583	55
Less often	3.0466	21.102	27.195	16.622	7.034	75
Total	68	471	607	371	157	1,674

Data

Level of Significance	0.01
Number of Rows	5
Number of Columns	5
Degrees of Freedom	16

Results

Critical Value	31.99993
Chi-Square Test Statistic	119.7494
p-Value	6.14E-18

Reject the null hypothesis

Expected frequency assumption is met.

Decision: Because $\chi^2_{STAT} = 119.7494 > 31.9999$ reject H_0. There is evidence to conclude that there is a relationship between the frequency of Facebook posts and age.

12.26 Because $\chi^2_{STAT} = 81.6061 > 47.3999$ reject H_0. There is evidence of a relationship between identified main opportunity and geographic region.

12.28 (a) 31. **(b)** 29. **(c)** 27. **(d)** 25.

12.30 40 and 79.

12.32 (a) The ranks for Sample 1 are 1, 2, 4, 5, and 10. The ranks for Sample 2 are 3, 6.5, 6.5, 8, 9, and 11. **(b)** 22. **(c)** 44.

12.34 Because $T_1 = 22 > 20$, do not reject H_0.

12.36 (a) The data are ordinal. **(b)** The two-sample t test is inappropriate because the data can only be placed in ranked order. **(c)** Because $Z_{STAT} = -2.2054 < -1.96$, reject H_0. There is evidence of a significance difference in the median rating of California Cabernets and Washington Cabernets.

12.38 (a) H_0: $M_1 = M_2$, where Populations: $1 = $ Wing A, $2 = $ Wing B. H_1: $M_1 \neq M_2$.

Population 1 sample: Sample size 20, sum of ranks 561

Population 2 sample: Sample size 20, sum of ranks 259

$$\mu_{T_1} = \frac{n_1(n + 1)}{2} = \frac{20(40 + 1)}{2} = 410$$

$$\sigma_{T_1} = \sqrt{\frac{n_1 n_2(n + 1)}{12}} = \sqrt{\frac{20(20)(40 + 1)}{12}} = 36.9685$$

$$Z_{STAT} = \frac{T_1 - \mu_{T_1}}{S_{T_1}} = \frac{561 - 410}{36.9685} = 4.0846$$

Decision: Because $Z_{STAT} = 4.0846 > 1.96$ (or p-value $= 0.0000 < 0.05$), reject H_0. There is sufficient evidence of a difference in the median delivery time in the two wings of the hotel. **(b)** The results of (a) are consistent with the results of Problem 10.65.

12.40 (a) Because $Z_{STAT} = 2.1342 > 1.96$, reject H_0. There is evidence to conclude that there is a difference in the median brand value between the two sectors. **(b)** You must assume approximately equal variability in the two populations. **(c)** using the pooled-variance t test you rejected the null hypothesis and the separate-variance t test rejected the null hypothesis so you conclude in Problem 10.17 that the mean brand value is different between the two sectors. In this test, using the Wilcoxon rank sum test with large-sample Z approximation you rejected the null hypothesis and concluded that the median brand value differs between the two sectors.

12.42 (a) Because $-1.96 < Z_{STAT} = 1.1687 < 1.96$ (or the p-value $= 0.2425 > 0.05$), do not reject H_0. There is not enough evidence to conclude that there is a difference in the median rating of 60-second and 30-second ads. **(b)** You must assume approximately equal variability in the two populations. **(c)** Using the pooled-variance t-test, you do not reject the null hypothesis ($t = -2.0040 < t_{STAT} = 0.7949 < 2.0040$; p-value $= 0.4301 > 0.05$) and conclude that there is insufficient evidence of a difference in the mean rating of 60-second and 30-second ads in Problem 10.11 (a).

12.44 (a) Decision rule: If $H > \chi^2_U = 15.086$, reject H_0. **(b)** Because $H = 13.77 < 15.806$, do not reject H_0.

12.46 (a) $H = 13.517 > 7.815$, p-value $= 0.0036 < 0.05$, reject H_0. There is sufficient evidence of a difference in the median waiting time in the four locations. **(b)** The results are consistent with those of Problem 11.9.

12.48 (a) $H = 19.3269 > 9.488$, reject H_0. There is evidence of a difference in the median ratings of the ads. **(b)** The results are consistent with those of Problem 11.10. **(c)** Because the combined scores are not true continuous variables, the nonparametric Kruskal-Wallis rank test is more appropriate because it does not require that the scores are normally distributed.

12.50 (a) Because $H = 13.0522 > 7.815$ or the p-value is 0.0045, reject H_0. There is sufficient evidence of a difference in the median cost associated with importing a standardized cargo of goods by sea transport across the global regions. **(b)** The results are the same.

12.56 (a) Because $\chi^2_{STAT} = 0.412 < 3.841$, do not reject H_0. There is insufficient evidence to conclude that there is a relationship between a student's gender and pizzeria selection. **(b)** Because $\chi^2_{STAT} = 2.624 < 3.841$, do not reject H_0. There is insufficient evidence to conclude that there is a relationship between a student's gender and pizzeria selection. **(c)** Because $\chi^2_{STAT} = 4.956 < 5.991$, do not reject H_0. There is insufficient evidence to conclude that there is a relationship between price and pizzeria selection. **(d)** p-value $= 0.0839$. The probability of a sample that gives a test statistic equal to or greater than 4.956 is 8.39% if the null hypothesis of no relationship between price and pizzeria selection is true.

12.58 (a) Because $\chi^2_{STAT} = 7.4298 < 9.4877$; p-value $= 0.1148 > 0.05$ do not reject H_0. There is not enough evidence to conclude that there is evidence of a difference in the proportion of organizations that have embarked on digital transformation on the basis of industry sector. **(b)** Because $\chi^2_{STAT} = 38.09 > 21.0261$; p-value $= 0.0001 < 0.05$ reject H_0. There is evidence of a relationship between digital transformation progress and industry sector.

CHAPTER 13

13.2 (a) Yes. **(b)** No. **(c)** No. **(d)** Yes.

13.4 (a) The scatter plot shows a positive linear relationship. **(b)** For each increase in alcohol percentage of 1.0, mean predicted mean wine quality is estimated to increase by 0.5624. **(c)** $\hat{Y} = 5.2715$. **(d)** Wine quality appears to be affected by the alcohol percentage. Each increase of 1% in alcohol leads to a mean increase in wine quality of a little more than half a unit.

13.6 (b) $b_0 = -13,130.6592$, $b_1 = 2.4218$. **(c)** For each increase of \$1,000 in tuition, the mean starting salary is predicted to increase by \$2,421.80. **(d)** \$109,047.01 **(e)** Starting salary seems higher for those schools that have a higher tuition.

13.8 (b) $b_0 = -1,039.5317$, $b_1 = 8.5816$. **(c)** For each additional million-dollar increase in revenue, the mean value is predicted to increase by an estimated \$8.5816 million. Literal interpretation of b_0 is not meaningful because an operating franchise cannot have zero revenue. **(d)** \$1,105.864 million. **(e)** That the value of the franchise can be expected to increase as revenue increases.

13.10 (b) $b_0 = -0.7744$, $b_1 = 1.4030$. **(c)** For each increase of million YouTube trailer views, the predicted weekend box office gross is estimated to increase by \$1.4030 million. **(d)** \$27.2847 million. **(e)** You can conclude that the mean predicted increase in weekend box office gross is \$1.4030 million for each million increase in YouTube trailer views.

13.12 $SST = 40$, $r^2 = 0.90$. 90% of the variation in the dependent variable can be explained by the variation in the independent variable.

13.14 $r^2 = 0.75$. 75% of the variation in the dependent variable can be explained by the variation in the independent variable.

13.16 (a) $r^2 = \dfrac{SSR}{SST} = \dfrac{21.8677}{64.0000} = 0.3417$, 34.17% of the variation in wine quality can be explained by the variation in the percentage of alcohol.

(b) $S_{YX} = \sqrt{\dfrac{SSE}{n-2}} = \sqrt{\dfrac{\sum\limits_{i=1}^{n}(Y_i - \hat{Y}_i)^2}{n-2}} = \sqrt{\dfrac{42.1323}{48}} = 0.9369$.

(c) Based on (a) and (b), the model should be somewhat useful for predicting wine quality.

13.18 (a) $r^2 = 0.7665$. 76.65% of the variation in starting salary can be explained by the variation in tuition. **(b)** $S_{YX} = 15,944.3807$. **(c)** Based on (a) and (b), the model should be very useful for predicting the starting salary.

13.20 (a) $r^2 = 0.9612$, 96.12% of the variation in the value of a baseball franchise can be explained by the variation in its annual revenue. **(b)** $S_{YX} = 140.8188$. **(c)** Based on (a) and (b), the model should be very useful for predicting the value of a baseball franchise.

13.22 (a) $r^2 = 0.6676$, 66.76% of the variation in weekend box office gross can be explained by the variation in YouTube trailer views. **(b)** $S_{YX} = 19.4447$. **(c)** Based on (a) and (b), the model should be useful for predicting weekend box office gross. **(d)** Other variables that might

explain the variation in weekend box office gross could be the amount spent on advertising, the timing of the release of the movie, and the type of movie.

13.24 A residual analysis of the data indicates a pattern, with sizable clusters of consecutive residuals that are either all positive or all negative. This pattern indicates a violation of the assumption of linearity. A curvilinear model should be investigated.

13.26 There does not appear to be a pattern in the residual plot. The assumptions of regression do not appear to be seriously violated.

13.28 Based on the residual plot, the assumption of equal variance may be violated.

13.30 Based on the residual plot, there is no evidence of a pattern.

13.32 (a) An increasing linear relationship exists. **(b)** There is evidence of a strong positive autocorrelation among the residuals.

13.34 (a) No, because the data were not collected over time. **(b)** If data were collected at a single store had been selected and studied over a period of time, you would compute the Durbin-Watson statistic.

13.36 (a)
$$b_1 = \dfrac{SSXY}{SSX} = \dfrac{201,399.05}{12,495,626} = 0.0161$$
$$b_0 = \bar{Y} - b_1\bar{X} = 71.2621 - 0.0161\,(4,393) = 0.4576.$$

(b) $\hat{Y} = 0.458 + 0.0161X = 0.4576 + 0.0161(4,500) = 72.9867$, or \$72,987. **(c)** There is no evidence of a pattern in the residuals over time.

(d) $D = \dfrac{\sum\limits_{i=2}^{n}(e_i - e_{i-1})^2}{\sum\limits_{i=1}^{n} e_i^2} = \dfrac{1,243.2244}{599.0683} = 2.08 > 1.45$. There is no evidence of positive autocorrelation among the residuals. **(e)** Based on a residual analysis, the model appears to be adequate.

13.38 (a) $b_0 = -2.535$, $b_1 = 0.06073$. **(b)** \$2,505.40. **(d)** $D = 1.64 > d_U = 1.42$, so there is no evidence of positive autocorrelation among the residuals. **(e)** The plot shows some nonlinear pattern, suggesting that a nonlinear model might be better. Otherwise, the model appears to be adequate.

13.40 (a) 3.00. **(b)** ± 2.1199. **(c)** Reject H_0. There is evidence that the fitted linear regression model is useful. **(d)** $1.32 \le \beta_1 \le 7.68$.

13.42 (a) $t_{STAT} = \dfrac{b_1 - \beta_1}{S_{b_1}} = \dfrac{0.5624}{0.1127} = 4.9913 > 2.0106$. Reject H_0.

There is evidence of a linear relationship between the percentage of alcohol and wine quality.
(b) $b \pm t_{\alpha/2}S_{b_1} = 0.5624 \pm 2.0106\,(0.1127)$ $0.3359 \le \beta_1 \le 0.7890$.

13.44 (a) $t_{STAT} = 10.7174 > 2.0301$; p-value $= 0.0000 < 0.05$ reject H_0. There is evidence of a linear relationship between tuition and starting salary. **(b)** $1.963 \le \beta_1 \le 2.8805$.

13.46 (a) $t_{STAT} = 26.3347 > 2.0484$ or because the p-value is 0.0000, reject H_0 at the 5% level of significance. There is evidence of a linear relationship between annual revenue and franchise value. **(b)** $7.9141 \le \beta_1 \le 9.2491$.

13.48 (a) $t_{STAT} = 11.3381 > 1.9977$ or because the p-value $= 0.0000 < 0.05$; reject H_0. There is evidence of a linear relationship between YouTube trailer views and weekend box office gross. **(b)** $1.1558 \le \beta_1 \le 1.6501$.

13.50 (a) (% daily change in SPUU) $= b_0 + 2.0$ (% daily change in S&P 500 index). **(b)** If the S&P 500 gains 10% in a year, SPUU is expected to gain an estimated 20%. (c) If the S&P 500 loses 20% in a year, SPUU is expected to lose an estimated 40%. (d) Risk takers will be attracted to leveraged funds, and risk-averse investors will stay away.

13.52 (a), (b) First weekend and U.S. gross: $r = 0.7284$, $t_{STAT} = 2.6042 > 2.4469$, p-value $= 0.0404 < 0.05$. reject H_0. At the 0.05 level of significance, there is evidence of a linear relationship between first weekend sales and U.S. gross. First weekend and worldwide gross: $r = 0.8233$, $t_{STAT} = 3.5532 > 2.4469$, p-value $= 0.0120 < 0.05$. reject H_0. At the 0.05 level of significance, there is evidence of a linear relationship between first weekend sales and worldwide gross. U.S. gross and worldwide gross: $r = 0.9642$, $t_{STAT} = 8.9061 > 2.4469$, p-value $= 0.0001 < 0.05$. Reject H_0. At the 0.05 level of significance, there is evidence of a linear relationship between U.S gross and worldwide gross.

13.54 (a) $r = 0.3002$. There is an insignificant linear relationship between social media networking and the GDP per capita.
(b) $t_{STAT} = 1.6048$, p-value $= 0.1206 > 0.05$. Do not reject H_0. At the 0.05 level of significance, there is insufficient evidence of a linear relationship between social media networking and the GDP per capita. **(c)** There does not appear to be a linear relationship.

13.56 (a) $15.95 \le \mu_{Y|X=4} \le 18.05$. **(b)** $14.651 \le Y_{X=4} \le 19.349$.
(c) The intervals in this problem are wider than in Problem 13.55 because they involve X values that are different from the mean.

13.58 (a) $\hat{Y} = -0.3529 + (0.5624)(10) = 5.2715 \ \hat{Y} \pm t_{\alpha/2}S_{YX}\sqrt{h_i}$

$$= 5.2715 \pm 2.0106(0.9369)\sqrt{0.0249}$$
$$4.9741 \le \mu_{Y|X=10} \le 5.5690.$$

(b) $\hat{Y} \pm t_{\alpha/2}S_{YX}\sqrt{1 + h_i}$

$$= 5.2715 \pm 2.0106(0.9369)\sqrt{1 + 0.0249}$$
$$3.3645 \le Y_{X=10} \le 7.1786.$$

(c) Part (b) provides a prediction interval for the individual response given a specific value of the independent variable, and part (a) provides a confidence interval estimate for the mean value, given a specific value of the independent variable. Because there is much more variation in predicting an individual value than in estimating a mean value, a prediction interval is wider than a confidence interval estimate.

13.60 (a) $\$103,638.95 \le \mu_{Y|X=50,450} \le \$114,455.06$.
(b) $\$76,229.52 \le Y_{X=50,450} \le \$141,864.49$. **(c)** You can estimate a mean more precisely than you can predict a single observation.

13.62 (a) $1,043.1911 \le \mu_{Y|X=250} \le 1,168.5370$. **(b)** $810.6799 \le Y_{X=250} \le 1,401.0480$ **(c)** Because there is much more variation in predicting an individual value than in estimating a mean, the prediction interval is wider than the confidence interval.

13.74 (a) $b_0 = 24.84$, $b_1 = 0.14$. **(b)** For each additional case, the predicted delivery time is estimated to increase by 0.14 minute. The interpretation of the Y intercept is not meaningful because the number of cases delivered cannot be 0. **(c)** 45.84. **(d)** No, 500 is outside the relevant range of the data used to fit the regression equation. **(e)** $r^2 = 0.972$. **(f)** There is no obvious pattern in the residuals, so the assumptions of regression are met. The model appears to be adequate. **(g)** $t_{STAT} = 24.88 > 2.1009$; reject H_0.
(h) $44.88 \le \mu_{Y|X=150} \le 46.80$. $41.56 \le Y_{X=150} \le 50.12$.
(i) The number of cases explains almost all of the variation in delivery time.

13.76 (a) $b_0 = 326.5935$, $b_1 = 0.0835$. **(b)** For each additional square foot of living space in the house, the mean asking price is predicted to increase by \$83.50. The estimated asking price of a house with 0 living space is 326.5935 thousand dollars. However, this interpretation is not meaningful because the living space of the house cannot be 0. **(c)** $\hat{Y} = 493.6769$ thousand dollars. **(d)** $r^2 = 0.3979$. So 39.79% of the variation in asking price is explained by the variation in living space. **(e)** Neither the residual plot nor the normal probability plot reveals any potential violation of the linearity, equal variance, and normality

assumptions. **(f)** $t_{STAT} = 6.2436 > 2.0010$, p-value is 0.0000. Because p-value < 0.05, reject H_0. There is evidence of a linear relationship between asking price and living space. **(g)** $0.0568 \le \beta_1 \le 0.1103$.
(h) The living space in the house is somewhat useful in predicting the asking price, but because only 39.79% of the variation in asking price is explained by variation in living space, other variables should be considered.

13.78 (a) $b_0 = 21.2034$, $b_1 = -0.1517$. **(b)** For each additional point on the efficiency ratio, the predicted mean tangible common equity (ROATCE) is estimated to decrease by 0.1517. For an efficiency of 0, the predicted mean tangible common equity (ROATCE) is 21.2034. **(c)** 12.0989.
(d) $r^2 = 0.1882$. **(e)** There is no obvious pattern in the residuals, so the assumptions of regression are met. The model appears to be adequate.
(f) $t_{STAT} = -4.7662 < -1.9845$; reject H_0. There is evidence of a linear relationship between efficiency ratio and tangible common equity (ROATCE).
(g) $11.4060 \le \mu_{Y|X=60} \le 12.7918$, $5.1534 \le Y_{X=60} \le 19.0444$.
(h) $-0.2149 \le \beta_1 \le -0.0886$. **(i)** There is a small relationship between efficiency ratio and tangible common equity (ROATCE).

13.80 (a) There is no clear relationship shown on the scatter plot.
(c) Looking at all 23 flights, when the temperature is lower, there is likely to be some O-ring damage, particularly if the temperature is below 60 degrees. **(d)** 31 degrees is outside the relevant range, so a prediction should not be made. **(e)** Predicted $Y = 18.036 - 0.240X$, where $X =$ temperature and $Y =$ O-ring damage. **(g)** A nonlinear model would be more appropriate. **(h)** The appearance on the residual plot of a nonlinear pattern indicates that a nonlinear model would be better. It also appears that the normality assumption is invalid.

13.82 (a) $b_0 = -893.4994$, $b_1 = 12.3871$. **(b)** For each additional million-dollar increase in revenue, the franchise value will increase by an estimated 12.3871 million. Literal interpretation of b_0 is not meaningful because an operating franchise cannot have zero revenue. **(c)** \$964.5599 million. **(d)** $r^2 = 0.8251$. 82.51% of the variation in the value of an NBA franchise can be explained by the variation in its annual revenue.
(e) There does not appear to be a pattern in the residual plot. The assumptions of regression do not appear to be seriously violated.
(f) $t_{STAT} = 11.493 > 2.0484$ or because the p-value is 0.0000, reject H_0 at the 5% level of significance. There is evidence of a linear relationship between annual revenue and franchise value.
(g) $852.6812 \le \mu_{Y|X=150} \le 1,076.439$. **(h)** $405.1897 \le Y_{X=150} \le 1,523.93$. **(i)** The strength of the relationship between revenue and value is approximately the same for NBA franchises and for European soccer teams but lower than for Major League Baseball teams.

13.84 (a) $b_0 = -2,629.222$, $b_1 = 82.472$. **(b)** For each additional centimeter in circumference, the weight is estimated to increase by 82.472 grams. **(c)** 2,319.08 grams. **(d)** Yes, because circumference is a very strong predictor of weight. **(e)** $r^2 = 0.937$. **(f)** There appears to be a nonlinear relationship between circumference and weight. **(g)** p-value is virtually $0 < 0.05$; reject H_0. **(h)** $72.7875 \le \beta_1 \le 92.156$.

13.86 (a) The correlation between compensation and stock performance is 0.0550. **(b)** $t_{STAT} = 0.7757$; p-value $= 0.4388 > 0.05$. The correlation between compensation and stock performance is not significant, only 0.3% of the variation in compensation can be explained by return.
(c) The small correlation between compensation and stock performance was surprising (or maybe it shouldn't have been!).

CHAPTER 14

14.2 (a) For each one-unit increase in X_1, you estimate that the mean of Y will decrease 2 units, holding X_2 constant. For each one-unit increase in X_2, you estimate that the mean of Y will increase 7 units, holding X_1 constant. **(b)** The Y intercept, equal to 50, estimates the value of Y when both X_1 and X_2 are 0.

14.4 (a) $\hat{Y} = 1.3960 - 0.0117X_1 + 0.0286X_2$. **(b)** For a given capital adequacy, for each increase of 1% in efficiency ratio, ROAA decreases by 0.0117%. For a given efficiency ratio, for each increase of 1% in capital adequacy, ROAA increases by 0.0286% **(c)** $\hat{Y} = 1.1214$ **(d)** $1.0798 \leq \mu_{Y|X} \leq 1.1629$. **(e)** $0.5679 \leq Y_X \leq 1.6749$ **(f)** The interval in (e) is narrower because it is estimating the mean value, not an individual value. **(g)** The model uses both the efficiency ratio and capital adequacy to predict ROA. This may produce a better model than if only one of these independent variables is included.

14.6 (a) $\hat{Y} = 301.78 + 3.4771X_1 + 41.041X_2$. **(b)** For a given amount of voluntary turnover, for each increase of \$1 billion in worldwide revenue, the mean number of full-time jobs added is predicted to increase by 3.4771. For a given \$1 billion in worldwide revenue, for each increase of 1% in voluntary turnover, the mean number of full-time jobs added is predicted to increase by 41.041. **(c)** The Y intercept has no meaning in this problem. **(d)** Holding the other independent variable constant, voluntary turnover has a higher slope than worldwide revenue

14.8 (a) $\hat{Y} = 532.2883 + 407.1346X_1 - 2.8257X_2$, where $X_1 =$ land area, $X_2 =$ age. **(b)** For a given age, each increase by one acre in land area is estimated to result in an increase in the mean fair market value by \$407.1346 thousands. For a given land area, each increase of one year in age is estimated to result in a decrease in the mean fair market value by \$2.8257 thousands. **(c)** The interpretation of b_0 has no practical meaning here because it would represent the estimated fair market value of a new house that has no land area. **(d)** $\hat{Y} = \$478.6577$ thousands. **(e)** $446.8367 \leq \mu_{Y|X} \leq 510.4788$. **(f)** $307.2577 \leq Y_X \leq 650.0577$.

14.10 (a) $MSR = 15$, $MSE = 12$. **(b)** 1.25. **(c)** $F_{STAT} = 1.25 < 4.10$; do not reject H_0. **(d)** 0.20. 20% of the variation in Y is explained by variation in X. **(e)** 0.04.

14.12 p-value for revenue is $0.0395 < 0.05$ and the p-value for efficiency is less than $0.0001 < 0.05$. Reject H_0 for each of the independent variables. There is evidence of a significant linear relationship with each of the independent variables.

14.14 (a) $F_{STAT} = 37.8384 > 3.00$; reject H_0. **(b)** p-value $= 0.0000$. The probability of obtaining an F_{STAT} value > 37.8384 if the null hypothesis is true is 0.0000. **(c)** $r^2 = 0.2785$. 27.85% of the variation in ROA can be explained by variation in efficiency ratio and variation in risk-based capital. **(d)** $r^2_{adj} = 0.2712$.

14.16 (a) $F_{STAT} = 1.95 < 3.15$; Do not reject H_0. There is insufficient evidence of a significant linear relationship. **(b)** p-value $= 0.1512$. The probability of obtaining an F_{STAT} value > 1.95 if the null hypothesis is true is 0.1512. **(c)** $r^2 = 0.0610$. 6.10% of the variation in full-time jobs added can be explained by variation in worldwide revenue and variation in full-time voluntary turnover. **(d)** $r^2_{adj} = 0.0297$.

14.18 (a) – (e) Based on a residual analysis, there is no evidence of a violation of the assumptions of regression.

14.20 (a) There is no evidence of a violation of the assumptions **(b)** Because the data are not collected over time, the Durbin-Watson test is not appropriate. **(c)** They are valid

14.22 (a) The residual analysis reveals no patterns. **(b)** Because the data are not collected over time, the Durbin-Watson test is not appropriate. **(c)** There are no apparent violations in the assumptions.

14.24 (a) Variable X_2 has a larger slope in terms of the t statistic of 3.75 than variable X_1, which has a smaller slope in terms of the t statistic of 3.33. **(b)** $1.46824 \leq \beta_1 \leq 6.53176$. **(c)** For $X_1 : t_{STAT} = 3.33 > 2.1098$. Reject H_0. There is evidence that X_1 contributes to a model already containing X_2. For $X_2 : t_{STAT} = 3.75 > 2.1098$. Reject H_0. There is evidence that X_2 contributes to a model already containing X_1. Both X_1 and X_2 should be included in the model.

14.26 (a) 95% confidence interval on $\beta_1 : b_1 \pm t S_{b_1}$, -0.0117 ± 1.98 (0.0022), $-0.0161 \leq \beta_1 \leq -0.0074$. **(b)** For $X_1 : t_{STAT} = b_1/S_{b_1} = -0.0177/0.0022 = -5.3415 < -1.98$. Reject H_0. There is evidence that X_1 contributes to a model already containing X_2. For $X_2 : t_{STAT} = b_2/S_{b_2} = 0.0286/0.0054 = 5.2992 > 1.98$. Reject H_0. There is evidence that X_2 contributes to a model already containing X_1. Both X_1 (efficiency ratio) and X_2 (total risk-based capital) should be included in the model.

14.28 (a) $-5.8682 \leq \beta_1 \leq 12.8225$. **(b)** For $X_1 : t_{STAT} = 0.7443 < 2.0003$. Don't reject H_0. There is insufficient evidence that X_1 contributes to a model already containing X_2. For $X_2 : t_{STAT} = 1.8835 < 2.0003$. Do not reject H_0. There is insufficient evidence that X_2 contributes to a model already containing X_1. Neither variable contributes to a model that includes the other variable. You should consider using only a simple linear regression model.

14.30 (a) $274.1702 \leq \beta_1 \leq 540.0990$. **(b)** For $X_1 : t_{STAT} = 6.2827$ and p-value $= 0.0000$. Because p-value < 0.05, reject H_0. There is evidence that X_1 contributes to a model already containing X_2. For $X_2 : t_{STAT} = -4.1475$ and p-value $= 0.0003$. Because p-value < 0.05 reject H_0. There is evidence that X_2 contributes to a model already containing X_1. Both X_1 (land area) and X_2 (age) should be included in the model.

14.32 (a) For $X_1 : F_{STAT} = 1.25 < 4.96$; do not reject H_0. For $X_2 : F_{STAT} = 0.833 < 4.96$; do not reject H_0. **(b)** 0.1111, 0.0769.

14.34 (a) For $X_1 : SSR(X_1|X_2) = SSR (X_1 \text{ and } X_2) - SSR(X_2) =$

$$5.9271 - 3.6923 = 2.2348 \quad F_{STAT} = \frac{SSR(X_1|X_2)}{MSE} =$$

$$\frac{2.2348}{15.3521/196} = 28.5227 > 3.897. \text{ Reject } H_0.$$ There is evidence that X_1 contributes to a model already containing X_2. For $X_2 : SSR(X_2|X_1) = SSR (X_1 \text{ and } X_2) - SSR(X_1) = 5.9271 - 3.7275 = 2.1996$,

$$F_{STAT} = \frac{SSR(X_2|X_1)}{MSE} = \frac{2.1996}{15.3521/196} = 28.0823 > 3.897.$$

Reject H_0. There is evidence that X_2 contributes to a model already containing X_1. Because both X_1 and X_2 make a significant contribution to the model in the presence of the other variable, both variables should be included in the model.

(b) $r^2_{Y1.2} = \dfrac{SSR(X_1|X_2)}{SST - SSR(X_1 \text{ and } X_2) + SSR(X_1|X_2)}$

$$= \frac{2.2348}{21.2791 - 5.9271 + 2.2348} = 0.1271.$$

Holding constant the effect of the total risk based capital, 12.71% of the variation in ROAA can be explained by the variation in efficiency ratio.

$$r^2_{Y2.1} = \frac{SSR(X_2|X_1)}{SST - SSR(X_1 \text{ and } X_2) + SSR(X_2|X_1)}$$

$$= \frac{2.1996}{21.2791 - 5.9271 + 2.1996} = 0.1253$$

Holding constant the effect of efficiency ratio 12.53% of the variation in ROA can be explained by the variation in the total risk-based capital.

14.36 (a) For $X_1 : F_{STAT} = 0.554 < 4.00$; Don't reject H_0. There is insufficient evidence that X_1 contributes to a model containing X_2. For $X_2 : F_{STAT} = 3.5476 < 4.00$. Do not reject H_0. There is insufficient evidence that X_2 contributes to a model already containing X_1. Because only X_1 makes a significant contribution to the model in the presence of the other variable, only X_i should be included in the model. **(b)** $r^2_{Y1.2} = 0.0091$. Holding constant the effect of full-time voluntary turnover, 0.91% of the variation in full-time jobs added be explained by the variation in total worldwide revenue. $r^2_{Y2.1} = 0.0558$. Holding constant the effect of total worldwide revenue, 5.58% of the variation in full-time jobs created can be explained by the variation in full-time voluntary turnover.

14.38 (a) Holding constant the effect of X_2, for each increase of one unit of X_1, Y increases by 4 units. **(b)** Holding constant the effect of X_1, for each increase of one unit of X_2, Y increases by 2 units. **(c)** Because $t_{STAT} = 3.27 > 2.1098$, reject H_0. Variable X_2 makes a significant contribution to the model.

14.40 (a) $\hat{Y} = 243.7371 + 9.2189X_1 + 12.6967X_2$, where $X_1 =$ number of rooms and $X_2 =$ neighborhood (east = 0). **(b)** Holding constant the effect of neighborhood, for each additional room, the mean selling price is estimated to increase by 9.2189 thousands of dollars, or \$9,218.9. For a given number of rooms, a west neighborhood is estimated to increase the mean selling price over an east neighborhood by 12.6967 thousands of dollars, or \$12,696.7. **(c)** $\hat{Y} = 326.7076$, or \$326,707.6. $\$309,560.04 \le Y_X \le 343,855.1$. $\$321,471.44 \le \mu_{Y|X} \le \$331,943.71$. **(d)** Based on a residual analysis, the model appears to be adequate. **(e)** $F_{STAT} = 55.39$, the p-value is virtually 0. Because p-value < 0.05, reject H_0. There is evidence of a significant relationship between selling price and the two independent variables (rooms and neighborhood). **(f)** For X_1: $t_{STAT} = 8.9537$, the p-value is virtually 0. Reject H_0. Number of rooms makes a significant contribution and should be included in the model. For X_2: $t_{STAT} = 3.5913$, p-value $= 0.0023 < 0.05$. Reject H_0. Neighborhood makes a significant contribution and should be included in the model. Based on these results, the regression model with the two independent variables should be used. **(g)** $7.0466 \le \beta_1 \le 11.3913$. **(h)** $5.2378 \le \beta_2 \le 20.1557$. **(i)** $r_{adj}^2 = 0.851$. **(j)** $r_{Y1.2}^2 = 0.825$. Holding constant the effect of neighborhood, 82.5% of the variation in selling price can be explained by variation in number of rooms. $r_{Y2.1}^2 = 0.431$. Holding constant the effect of number of rooms, 43.1% of the variation in selling price can be explained by variation in neighborhood. **(k)** The slope of selling price with number of rooms is the same, regardless of whether the house is located in an east or west neighborhood. **(l)** $\hat{Y} = 253.95 + 8.032X_1 - 5.90X_2 + 2.089X_1X_2$. For $X_1 X_2$, p-value $= 0.330$. Do not reject H_0. There is no evidence that the interaction term makes a contribution to the model. **(m)** The model in (b) should be used. **(n)** The number of rooms and the neighborhood both significantly affect the selling price, but the number of rooms has a greater effect.

14.42 (a) Predicted time $= 8.01 + 0.00523$ Depth $- 2.105$ Dry. **(b)** Holding constant the effect of type of drilling, for each foot increase in depth of the hole, the mean drilling time is estimated to increase by 0.00523 minutes. For a given depth, a dry drilling hole is estimated to reduce the drilling time over wet drilling by a mean of 2.1052 minutes. **(c)** 6.428 minutes, $6.210 \le \mu_{Y|X} \le 6.646$, $4.923 \le Y_X \le 7.932$. **(d)** The model appears to be adequate. **(e)** $F_{STAT} = 111.11 > 3.09$; reject H_0. **(f)** $t_{STAT} = 5.03 > 1.9847$; reject H_0. $t_{STAT} = -14.03 < -1.9847$; reject H_0. Include both variables. **(g)** $0.0032 \le \beta_1 \le 0.0073$. **(h)** $-2.403 \le \beta_2 \le -1.808$. **(i)** 69.0%. **(j)** 0.207, 0.670. **(k)** The slope of the additional drilling time with the depth of the hole is the same, regardless of the type of drilling method used. **(l)** The p-value of the interaction term $= 0.462 > 0.05$, so the term is not significant and should not be included in the model. **(m)** The model in part (b) should be used. Both variables affect the drilling time. Dry drilling holes should be used to reduce the drilling time.

14.44 (a) $\hat{Y} = 1.1079 - 0.0070X_1 + 0.0448X_2 - 0.0003X_1X_2$, where $X_1 =$ efficiency ratio, $X_2 =$ total risk-based capital, p-vale $= 0.4593 > 0.05$. Do not reject H_0. There is not enough evidence that the interaction term makes a contribution to the model. **(b)** Because there is insufficient evidence of any interaction effect between efficiency ratio and total risk-based capital, the model in Problem 14.4 should be used.

14.46 (a) The p-value of the interaction term $= 0.1650 < 0.05$, so the term is not significant and should be not included in the model. **(b)** Use the model developed Problem 14.6.

14.48 (a) For $X_1 X_2$, p-value $= 0.2353 > 0.05$. Do not reject H_0. There is insufficient evidence that the interaction term makes a contribution to the model. **(b)** Because there is not enough evidence of an interaction effect

between total staff present and remote hours, the model in Problem 14.7 should be used.

14.50 Holding constant the effect of other variables, the natural logarithm of the estimated odds ratio for the dependent categorical response will increase by 2.2 for each unit increase in the particular independent variable.

14.52 0.4286.

14.54 (a) ln(estimated odds ratio) $= -6.9394 + 0.1395X_1 + 2.7743X_2 = -6.9394 + 0.1395(36) + 2.7743(0) = -1.91908$. Estimated odds ratio $= 0.1470$. Estimated Probability of Success $=$ Odds Ratio/(1 + Odds Ratio) $= 0.1470/(1 + 0.1470) = 0.1260$. **(b)** From the text discussion of the example, 70.2% of the individuals who charge \$36,000 per annum and possess additional cards can be expected to purchase the premium card. Only 12.60% of the individuals who charge \$36,000 per annum and do not possess additional cards can be expected to purchase the premium card. For a given amount of money charged per annum, the likelihood of purchasing a premium card is substantially higher among individuals who already possess additional cards than for those who do not possess additional cards. **(c)** ln(estimated odds ratio) $= -6.9394 + 0.13957X_1 + 2.7743X_2 = -6.9394 + 0.1395(18) + 2.7743(0) = -4.4298$. Estimated odds ratio $= e^{-4.4298} = 0.0119$. Estimated Probability of Success $=$ Odds Ratio/(1 + Odds Ratio) $= 0.0119/(1 + 0.0119) = 0.01178$. **(d)** Among individuals who do not purchase additional cards, the likelihood of purchasing a premium card diminishes dramatically with a substantial decrease in the amount charged per annum.

14.56 (a) ln(estimated odds) $= -47.4723 + 1.3099$ fixed acidity $+ 90.5722$ chlorides $+ 9.777$ pH. **(b)** Holding constant the effect of chlorides and pH, for each increase of one point in fixed acidity, ln (estimated odds) increases by an estimate of 1.3099. Holding constant the effect of fixed acidity and pH, for each increase of one point in chlorides, ln(estimated odds) increases by an estimate of 90.5722. Holding constant the effect of fixed acidity and chlorides, for each increase of one point in pH, ln(estimated odds) increases by an estimate of 9.777. **(c)** 0.3686. **(d)** Deviance $= 54.456$, p-value $= 1.0000$, do not reject H_0, so model is adequate. **(e)** For fixed acidity: $Z_{STAT} = 3.17 > 1.96$, reject H_0. For chlorides: $Z_{STAT} = 4.00 > 1.96$, reject H_0. For pH: $Z_{STAT} = 3.29 > 1.96$, reject H_0. Each variable makes a significant contribution to the model. **(f)** Fixed acidity, chlorides, and pH are all important factors in distinguishing between white and red wines.

14.58 (a) ln(estimated odds) $= -0.6048 + 0.0938$ claims/year $+ 1.8108$ new business **(b)** Holding constant the effects of whether the policy is new, for each increase of the number of claims submitted per year by the policy holder, ln(odds) increases by an estimate of 0.0938. Holding constant the number of claims submitted per year by the policy holder, ln(odds) is estimated to be 1.8108 higher when the policy is new as compared to when the policy is not new. **(c)** ln(estimated odds ratio) $= 1.2998$. Estimated odds ratio $= 3.6684$. Estimated probability of a fraudulent claim $= 0.7858$ **(d)** The deviance statistic is 119.4353 with a p-value $= 0.0457 < 0.05$. Reject H_0. The model is not a good fitting model. **(e)** For claims/year: $Z_{STAT} = 0.1865$, p-value $= 0.8521 > 0.05$. Do not reject H_0. There is insufficient evidence that the number of claims submitted per year by the policy holder makes a significant contribution to the logistic regression model. For new business: $Z_{STAT} = 2.2261$, p-value $= 0.0260 < 0.05$. Reject H_0. There is sufficient evidence that whether the policy is new makes a significant contribution to the logistic model regression. **(f)** ln(estimated odds) $= -1.0125 + 0.9927$ claims/year. **(g)** ln(estimated odds) $= -0.5423 + 1.9286$ new business. **(h)** The deviance statistic for (f) is 125.0102 with a p-value $= 0.0250 < 0.05$. Reject H_0. The model is not a good fitting model. The deviance statistic for (g) is 119.4702 with a p-value $= 0.0526 > 0.05$. Do not reject H_0. The model is a good fitting model. The model in (g) should be used to predict a fraudulent claim.

14.60 (a) ln(estimated odds) $= 1.252 - 0.0323$ Age $+ 2.2165$ subscribes to the wellness newsletters. **(b)** Holding constant the effect of subscribes to the wellness newsletters, for each increase of one year in age, ln(estimated odds) decreases by an estimate of 0.0323. Holding constant the effect of age, for a customer who subscribes to the wellness newsletters, ln(estimated odds) increases by an estimate of 2.2165. **(c)** 0.912. **(d)** Deviance $= 102.8762$, p-value $= 0.3264$. Do not reject H_0 so model is adequate. **(e)** For Age: $Z = -1.8053 > -1.96$, Do not reject H_0. For subscribes to the wellness newsletters: $Z = 4.3286 > 1.96$, Reject H_0. **(f)** Only subscribes to wellness newsletters is useful in predicting whether a customer will purchase organic food.

14.72 (a) $\hat{Y} = -3.9152 + 0.0319X_1 + 4.2228X_2$, where X_1 = number cubic feet moved and X_2 = number of pieces of large furniture. **(b)** Holding constant the number of pieces of large furniture, for each additional cubic foot moved, the mean labor hours are estimated to increase by 0.0319. Holding constant the amount of cubic feet moved, for each additional piece of large furniture, the mean labor hours are estimated to increase by 4.2228. **(c)** $\hat{Y} = 20.4926$. **(d)** Based on a residual analysis, the errors appear to be normally distributed. The equal-variance assumption might be violated because the variances appear to be larger around the center region of both independent variables. There might also be violation of the linearity assumption. A model with quadratic terms for both independent variables might be fitted. **(e)** $F_{STAT} = 228.80$, p-value is virtually $0 < 0.05$, reject H_0. There is evidence of a significant relationship between labor hours and the two independent variables (the amount of cubic feet moved and the number of pieces of large furniture). **(f)** The p-value is virtually 0. The probability of obtaining a test statistic of 228.80 or greater is virtually 0 if there is no significant relationship between labor hours and the two independent variables (the amount of cubic feet moved and the number of pieces of large furniture). **(g)** $r^2 = 0.9327$. 93.27% of the variation in labor hours can be explained by variation in the number of cubic feet moved and the number of pieces of large furniture. **(h)** $r^2_{adj} = 0.9287$. **(i)** For X_1: $t_{STAT} = 6.9339$, the p-value is virtually 0. Reject H_0. The number of cubic feet moved makes a significant contribution and should be included in the model. For X_2: $t_{STAT} = 4.6192$, the p-value is virtually 0. Reject H_0. The number of pieces of large furniture makes a significant contribution and should be included in the model. Based on these results, the regression model with the two independent variables should be used. **(j)** For X_1: $t_{STAT} = 6.9339$, the p-value is virtually 0. The probability of obtaining a sample that will yield a test statistic greater than 6.9339 is virtually 0 if the number of cubic feet moved does not make a significant contribution, holding the effect of the number of pieces of large furniture constant. For X_2: $t_{STAT} = 4.6192$, the p-value is virtually 0. The probability of obtaining a sample that will yield a test statistic greater than 4.6192 is virtually 0 if the number of pieces of large furniture does not make a significant contribution, holding the effect of the amount of cubic feet moved constant. **(k)** $0.0226 \leq \beta_1 \leq 0.0413$. **(l)** $r^2_{Y1.2} = 0.5930$. Holding constant the effect of the number of pieces of large furniture, 59.3% of the variation in labor hours can be explained by variation in the amount of cubic feet moved. $r^2_{Y2.1} = 0.3927$. Holding constant the effect of the number of cubic feet moved, 39.27% of the variation in labor hours can be explained by variation in the number of pieces of large furniture. **(m)** Both the number of cubic feet moved and the number of large pieces of furniture are useful in predicting the labor hours, but the cubic feet moved is more important.

14.74 (a) $\hat{Y} = 360.2158 + 0.0775X_1 - 0.4122X_2$, where X_1 = house size and X_2 = age. **(b)** Holding constant the age, for each additional

square foot in the size of the house, the mean asking price is estimated to increase by 77.50 thousand dollars. Holding constant the living space of the house, for each additional year in age, the asking price is estimated to decrease by 0.4122 thousand dollars. **(c)** $\hat{Y} = 492.5316$ thousand dollars. **(d)** Based on a residual analysis, the model appears to be adequate. **(e)** $F_{STAT} = 19.4909$, the p-value $= 0.0000 < 0.05$, reject H_0. There is evidence of a significant relationship between asking price and the two independent variables (size of the house and age). **(f)** The p-value is 0.0000. The probability of obtaining a test statistic of 19.4909 or greater is virtually 0 if there is no significant relationship between asking price and the two independent variables (living space of the house and age). **(g)** $r^2 = 0.4019$. 40.19% of the variation in asking price can be explained by variation in the size of the house and age. **(h)** $r^2_{adj} = 0.3813$. **(i)** For X_1: $t_{STAT} = 4.6904$, the p-value is 0.0000. Reject H_0. The living space of the house makes a significant contribution and should be included in the model. For X_2: $t_{STAT} = -0.6304$, p-value $= 0.5309 > 0.05$. Do not reject H_0. Age does not make a significant contribution and should not be included in the model. Based on these results, the regression model with only the size of the house should be used. **(j)** For X_1: $t_{STAT} = 4.6904$. The probability of obtaining a sample that will yield a test statistic farther away than 4.6904 is 0.0000 if the living space does not make a significant contribution, holding age constant. For X_2: $t_{STAT} = -0.6304$. The probability of obtaining a sample that will yield a test statistic farther away than 0.6304 is 0.5309 if the age does not make a significant contribution holding the effect of the living space constant. **(k)** $0.0444 \leq \beta_1 \leq 0.1106$. You are 95% confident that the asking price will increase by an amount somewhere between \$44.40 thousand and \$110.60 thousand for each additional thousand square foot increase in living space, holding constant the age of the house. In Problem 13.76, you are 95% confident that the assessed value will increase by an amount somewhere between \$56.8 thousand and \$110.30 thousand for each additional 1,000 square foot increase in living space, regardless of the age of the house. **(l)** $r^2_{Y1.2} = 0.2750$. Holding constant the effect of the age of the house, 27.50% of the variation in asking price can be explained by variation in the living space of the house. $r^2_{Y2.1} = 0.0068$. Holding constant the effect of the size of the house, 0.68% of the variation in asking price can be explained by variation in the age of the house. **(m)** only the living space of the house should be used to predict asking price.

14.76 (a) $\hat{Y} = -90.2166 + 9.2169X_1 + 2.5069X_2$, where X_1 = asking price and X_2 = age. **(b)** Holding age constant, for each additional \$1,000 in asking price, the taxes are estimated to increase by a mean of \$9.2169 thousand. Holding asking price constant, for each additional year, the taxes are estimated to increase by \$2.5069 **(c)** $\hat{Y} = \$3,721.90$. **(d)** Based on a residual analysis, the errors appear to be normally distributed. The equal-variance assumption appears to be valid. However, there is one very large residual that is from the house that is 107 years old. Removing this point, still leaves a residual for the house that has an asking price of \$550,000 and is 52 years old. However, because this model is an almost perfect fit, you may want to use this model. In this model, age is no longer significant. **(e)** $F_{STAT} = 1,677.8619$, p-value $= 0.0000 < 0.05$, reject H_0. There is evidence of a significant relationship between taxes and the two independent variables (asking price and age). **(f)** p-value $= 0.0000$. The probability of obtaining an F_{STAT} test statistic of 1,677.8619 or greater is virtually 0 if there is no significant relationship between taxes and the two independent variables (asking price and age). **(g)** $r^2 = 0.9830$, 98.30% of the variation in taxes can be explained by variation in asking price and age. **(h)** $r^2_{adj} = 0.9824$. **(i)** For X_1: $t_{STAT} = 53.7184$, p-value $= 0.0000 < 0.05$. Reject H_0. The asking price makes a significant contribution and should be included in the model. For X_2: $t_{STAT} = 2.7873$, p-value $= 0.0072 < 0.05$. Reject H_0. The age of a house makes a significant contribution and should be included in the model. Based on these results, the regression model with asking price and age should be used. **(j)** For X_1: p-value $= 0.0000$. The probability of obtaining a sample that will yield a test statistic greater than 53.7184 is 0.0000 if the asking price does not make a significant contribution, holding age constant. For X_2: p-value $= 0.0072$. The probability of obtaining a sample that will yield a test statistic greater than 2.7873 is 0.0072 if the age of a house does not make a significant contribution, holding the effect of the asking price constant. **(k)** $8.8735 \leq \beta_1 \leq 9.5604$. You are 95% confident that the mean taxes will increase by an amount somewhere between \$8.87 and \$9.56 for each additional \$1,000 increase in the asking price, holding constant the age. In Problem 13.77, you are 95% confident that the mean taxes will increase by an amount somewhere between \$5.968 and \$11.03 for each additional \$1,000 increase in asking price, regardless of the age. **(l)** $r^2_{Y1.2} = 0.9803$. Holding constant the effect of age, 98.03% of the variation in taxes can be explained by variation in the asking price. $r^2_{Y2.1} = 0.1181$. Holding constant the effect of the asking price, 11.81% of the variation in taxes can be explained by variation in the age. **(m)** Based on your answers to (b) through (k), the age of a house has an effect on its taxes. However, given the results when the 107-year-old house is not included, the assessor can state that for houses that are not that old, that age does not have an effect on taxes.

14.78 (a) $\hat{Y} = 160.6120 - 18.7181X_1 - 2.8903X_2$, where $X_1 = $ ERA and $X_2 = $ league (American $= 0$ National $= 1$). **(b)** Holding constant the effect of the league, for each additional earned run, the number of wins is estimated to decrease by 18.7181. For a given ERA, a team in the National League is estimated to have 2.8903 fewer wins than a team in the American League. **(c)** 76.3803 wins. **(d)** Based on a residual analysis, there is no pattern in the errors. There is no apparent violation of other assumptions. **(e)** $F_{STAT} = 24.306 > 3.35$, p-value $= 0.0000 < 0.05$, reject H_0. There is evidence of a significant relationship between wins and the two independent variables (ERA and league). **(f)** For X_1: $t_{STAT} = -6.9184 < -2.0518$, the p-value $= 0.0000$. Reject H_0. ERA makes a significant contribution and should be included in the model. For X_2: $t_{STAT} = -1.1966 > -2.0518$, p-value $= 0.2419 > 0.05$. Do not reject H_0. The league does not make a significant contribution and should not be included in the model. Based on these results, the regression model with only the ERA as the independent variable should be used. **(g)** $-24.2687 \leq \beta_1 \leq -13.1676$. **(h)** $-7.8464 \leq \beta_2 \leq 2.0639$. **(i)** $r^2_{adj} = 0.6165$. 61.65% of the variation in wins can be explained by variation in ERA and league after adjusting for number of independent variables and sample size. **(j)** $r^2_{Y1.2} = 0.6394$. Holding constant the effect of league, 63.94% of the variation in number of wins can be explained by the variation in ERA. $r^2_{Y2.1} = 0.0504$. Holding constant the effect of ERA, 5.04% of the variation in number of wins can be explained by the variation in league. **(k)** The slope of the number of wins with ERA is the same, regardless of whether the team belongs to the American League or the National League. **(l)** For X_1X_2: $t_{STAT} = 1.175 < 2.0555$ the p-value is $0.2506 > 0.05$. Do not reject H_0. There is no evidence that the interaction term makes a contribution to the model. **(m)** The model with one independent variable (ERA) should be used.

14.80 The multiple regression model is Predicted base salary $= 48,091.7853 + 8,249.2156$ (gender) $+ 1,061.4521$ (age). Holding constant the age of the person, the mean base salary is predicted to be \$8,249.22 higher for males than for females. Holding constant the gender of the person, for each addition year of age, the mean base salary is predicted to be \$1,061.45 higher. The regression model with the two independent variables has $F = 118.0925$ and a p-value $= 0.0000$. So, you can conclude that at least one of the independent variable makes a significant contribution to the model to predict base pay. Each independent variable makes a significant contribution to the regression model given that the other variable is included. ($t_{STAT} = 3.9937$, p-value $= 0.0001$ for gender and $t_{STAT} = 14.8592$, p-value $= 0.0000$ for age). Both independent variables should be included in the model. 37.01% of the variation in base salary can be explained by gender and age. There is no pattern in the residuals and no other violations of the assumptions, so the model appears to be appropriate. Including an interaction

term of gender and age does not significantly improve the model ($t_{stat} = -0.2371$, p-value $= 0.8127 > 0.05$). You can conclude that females are paid less than males holding constant the age of the person. Perhaps other variables such as department, seniority, and score on a performance evaluation can be included in the model to see if the model is improved.

14.82 $b_0 = 18.2892$ (die temperature), $b_1 = 0.5976$, (die diameter), $b_2 = -13.5108$. The r^2 of the multiple regression model is 0.3257 so 32.57% of the variation in unit density can be explained by the variation of die temperature and die diameter. The F test statistic for the combined significance of die temperature and die diameter is 5.0718 with a p-value of 0.0160. Hence, at a 5% level of significance, there is enough evidence to conclude that die temperature and die diameter affect unit density. The p-value of the t test for the significance of die temperature is 0.2117, which is greater than 5%. Hence, there is insufficient evidence to conclude that die temperature affects unit density holding constant the effect of die diameter. The p-value of the t test for the significance of die diameter is 0.0083, which is less than 5%. There is enough evidence to conclude that die diameter affects unit density at the 5% level of significance holding constant the effect of die temperature. After removing die temperature from the model, $b_0 = 107.9267$ (die diameter), $b_1 = -13.5108$. The r^2 of the multiple regression is 0.2724. So 27.24% of the variation in unit density can be explained by the variation of die diameter. The p-value of the t test for the significance of die diameter is 0.0087, which is less than 5%. There is enough evidence to conclude that die diameter affects unit density at the 5% level of significance. There is some lack of equality in the residuals and some departure from normality.

CHAPTER 15

15.2 (a) Predicted HOCS is 2.8600, 3.0342, 3.1948, 3.3418, 3.4752, 3.5950, 3.7012, 3.7938, 3.8728, 3.9382, 3.99, 4.0282, 4.0528, 4.0638, 4.0612, 4.045, 4.0152, 3.9718, 3.9148, 3.8442, and 3.76. **(c)** The curvilinear relationship suggests that HOCS increases at a decreasing rate. It reaches its maximum value of 4.0638 at GPA $= 3.3$ and declines after that as GPA continues to increase. **(d)** An r^2 of 0.07 and an adjusted r^2 of 0.06 tell you that GPA has very low explanatory power in identifying the variation in HOCS. You can tell that the individual HOCS scores are scattered widely around the curvilinear relationship.

15.4 (a) $\hat{Y} = -5.48730 - 21.5105X_1 + 3.9633X_2$ where $X_1 = $ alcohol % and $X_2 = $ carbohydrates. $F_{STAT} = 2,258.7579$ p-value $= 0.0000 < 0.05$, so reject H_0. At the 5% level of significance, the linear terms are significant together. **(b)** $\hat{Y} = 10.0421 + 15.0776X_1 + 4.5851X_2 + 0.4874X_1^2 - 0.0209X_2^2$, where $X_1 = $ alcohol % and $X_2 = $ carbohydrates. **(c)** $F_{STAT} = 1,154.1043$ p-value $= 0.0000 < 0.05$, so reject H_0. At the 5% level of significance, the model with quadratic terms are significant. $t_{STAT} = 2.2414$, and the p-value $= 0.0264$. Reject H_0. There is enough evidence that the quadratic term for alcohol % is significant at the 5% level of significance. $t_{STAT} = -1.2313$, p-value $= 0.2201$. Do not reject H_0. There is insufficient evidence that the quadratic term for carbohydrates is significant at the 5% level of significance. Hence, because the quadratic term for alcohol is significant, the model in **(b)** that includes this term is better. **(d)** The number of calories in a beer depends quadratically on the alcohol percentage but linearly on the number of carbohydrates. The alcohol percentage and number of carbohydrates explain about 96.79% of the variation in the number of calories in a beer.

15.6 (b) price $= 18,029.9837 - 1,812.9389$ age $+ 63.2116$ age^2. **(c)** $18,029.9837 - 1,812.9389(5) + 63.2116(5)^2 = \$10,545.58$. **(d)** There are no patterns in any of the residual plots. **(e)** $F_{STAT} = 243.5061 > 3.27$. Reject H_0. There is a significant quadratic relationship between age and price. **(f)** p-value $= 0.0000$. The probability of $F_{STAT} = 243.5061$ or higher is 0.0000, given the null hypothesis is true.

(g) $t_{STAT} = 4.8631 > 2.0281$. Reject H_0. **(h)** The probability of $t_{STAT} < -4.8631$ or > 4.8631 is 0.0000, given the null hypothesis is true. **(i)** $r^2 = 0.9312$. 93.12% of the variation in price can be explained by the quadratic relationship between age and price. **(j)** adjusted $r^2 = 0.9273$. **(k)** There is a strong quadratic relationship between age and price.

15.8 (a) 215.37. **(b)** For each additional unit of the logarithm of X_1, the logarithm of Y is estimated to increase by 0.9 unit, holding all other variables constant. For each additional unit of the logarithm of X_2, the logarithm of Y is estimated to increase by 1.41 units, holding all other variables constant.

15.10 (a) $\sqrt{\hat{Y}} = 6.2417 + 0.7768X_1 + 0.1683X_2$, where X_1 = alcohol % and X_2 = carbohydrates. **(b)** The normal probability plot of the linear model showed departure from a normal distribution, so a square-root transformation of calories was done. $F_{STAT} = 1,720.6801$. Because the p-value is 0.0000, reject H_0 at the 5% level of significance. There is evidence of a significant linear relationship between the square root of calories and the percentage of alcohol and the number of carbohydrates. **(d)** $r^2 = 0.9569$. So 95.69% of the variation in the square root of calories can be explained by the variation in the percentage of alcohol and the number of carbohydrates. **(e)** Adjusted $r^2 = 0.9563$. **(f)** The model in Problem 15.4 is slightly better because it has a higher r^2.

15.12 (a) Predicted ln(Price) $= 9.7771 - 0.10622$ Age. **(b)** \$10,573.4350. **(c)** The model is adequate. **(d)** $t_{STAT} = -19.4814 < -2.0262$; reject H_0. **(e)** 91.12%. 91.12% of the variation in the natural log of price can be explained by the age of the auto. **(f)** 90.88%. **(g)** Choose the model from Problem 15.6. That model has a higher adjusted r^2 of 92.73%.

15.14 1.25.

15.16 $R_1^2 = 0.0634$, $VIF_1 = \dfrac{1}{1 - 0.0634} = 1.0677$, $R_2^2 = 0.0634$,

$VIF_2 = \dfrac{1}{1 - 0.0634} = 1.0677$. There is no evidence of collinearity becasue both VIFs are < 5.

15.18 $VIF = 1.0066 < 5$. There is no evidence of collinearity.

15.20 $VIF = 1.0105$. There is no evidence of collinearity.

15.22 (a) 35.04. **(b)** $C_p > 3$. This does not meet the criterion for consideration of a good model.

15.24 Let Y = asking price, X_1 = lot size, X_2 = living space, and X_3 = number of bedrooms. X_4 = number of bathrooms, X_5 = age, and X_6 = fireplace (0 = No, 1 = Yes). Based on a full regression model involving all of the variables, all the VIF values (1.3953, 2.1175, 2.0878, 2.3537, 1.7807, and 1.0939, respectively) are less than 5. There is no reason to suspect the existence of collinearity. Based on a best-subsets regression and examination of the resulting C_p values, the best model appear to be a model with variables X_2 and X_6, which has $C_p = 0.8701$. Models that add other variables do not change the results very much. Based on a stepwise regression analysis with all the original variables, only variables X_2 and X_6 make a significant contribution to the model at the 0.05 level. Thus, the best model is the model using the living area of the house (X_2) and fireplace X_6 should be included in the model. This was the model developed in Section 14.6.

15.30 (a) An analysis of the linear regression model with all of the three possible independent variables reveals that the highest VIF is only 1.06. A stepwise regression model selects only the supplier dummy variable for inclusion in the model. A best-subsets regression produces only one model that has a C_p value less than or equal to $k + 1$ which is the model that includes pressure and the supplier dummy variable. This model is $\hat{Y} = -31.5929 + 0.7879X_2 + 13.1029X_3$. This model has $F = 5.1088$ with a p-value $= 0.027$. $r^2 = 0.4816$, $r_{adj}^2 = 0.3873$. A residual analysis

does not reveal any strong patterns. The errors appear to be normally distributed.

15.32 (a) Best model: $C_p = 2.1558$, predicted fair market value $= 260.6791 + 362.8318$ land $+ 0.1109$ house size (sq ft) $- 1.7543$ age. **(b)** The adjusted r^2 for the best model in 15.32(a), 15.33(a), and 15.34(a) are, respectively, 0.8242, 0.9047, and 0.8481. The model in 15.33(a) has the highest explanatory power after adjusting for the number of independent variables and sample size.

15.34 (a) Predicted fair maket value $= 145.1217 + 149.9337$ land $+ 0.0913$ house size (sq. ft.). **(b)** The adjusted r^2 for the best model in 15.32(a), 15.33(a), and 15.34(a) are, respectively, 0.8242, 0.9047, and 0.8481. The model in 15.33(a) has the highest explanatory power after adjusting for the number of independent variables and sample size.

15.36 Let Y = fair market value, X_1 = land area, X_2 = interior size, X_3 = age, X_4 = number of rooms, X_5 = number of bathrooms, X_6 = garage size, X_7 = 1 if Glen Cove and 0 otherwise, and X_8 = 1 if Roslyn and 0 otherwise. **(a)** The VIFs of X_2, X_3, and X_7 are greater than 5. Dropping X_2 with the largest VIF, X_3 still has a VIF greater than 5. After dropping X_2 and X_3, all remaining VIFs are less than 5 so there is no reason to suspect collinearity between any pair of variables. The following is the multiple regression model that has the smallest $C_p(4.3211)$ and the highest adjusted $r^2(0.6815)$:

Fair Market Value $= 49.2379 + 579.0105$ Land $+ 109.5767$ Baths $+ 48.2282$ Garage $+ 213.2326$ Roslyn

The individual t test for the significance of each independent variable at the 5% level of significance concludes that only property size, baths, and the dummy variable Roslyn are significant given that the others are in the model. The following is the multiple regression result for the model chosen by stepwise regression:

Fair Market Value $= 30.3016 + 611.6910$ Land $+ 130.7788$ Baths $+ 214.2567$ Roslyn

All the variables are significant individually at the 5% level of significance. Combining the stepwise regression and the best-subsets regression results along with the individual t test results, the most appropriate multiple regression model for predicting the fair market value is the stepwise regression model. **(b)** The estimated fair market value in Roslyn is \$214.2567 thousands above Glen Cove or Freeport for two otherwise identical properties.

15.38 In the multiple regression model with catalyst, pH, pressure, temperature, and voltage as independent variables, none of the variables has a VIF value of 5 or larger. The best-subsets approach showed that only the model containing X_1, X_2, X_3, X_4, and X_5 should be considered, where X_1 = catalyst, X_2 = pH, X_3 = pressure, X_4 = temp, and X_5 = voltage. Looking at the p-values of the t statistics for each slope coefficient of the model that includes X_1 through X_5 reveals that pH level is not significant at the 5% level of significance (p-value $= 0.2862$). The multiple regression model with pH level deleted shows that all coefficients are significant individually at the 5% level of significance. The best linear model is determined to be $\hat{Y} = 3.6833 + 0.1548X_1 - 0.04197X_3 - 0.4036X_4 + 0.4288X_5$. The overall model has $F = 77.0793$, with a p-value that is virtually 0. $r^2 = 0.8726$, $r_{adj}^2 = 0.8613$. The normal probability plot does not suggest possible violation of the normality assumption. A residual analysis reveals a potential nonlinear relationship in temperature. The p-value of the squared term for temperature (0.1273) in the following quadratic transformation of temperature does not support the need for a quadratic transformation at the 5% level of significance. The p-value of the interaction term between pressure and temperature (0.0780) indicates that there is not enough evidence of an interaction at the 5% level of significance. The best model is the one that includes catalyst, pressure, temperature, and voltage, which explains 87.26% of the variation in thickness.

15.40 Best subset regression produced several models that had $C_p \leq k + 1$. They were $X_2X_3 = 3.9$, $X_2X_3X_4 = 3.3$, and $X_1X_2X_3X_4 = 4.7$. Stepwise regression produced a model that included only X_2 (median home value) and X_4 (average commuting time). Because X_2 (median home value), X_3 (violent crime rate), and average commuting time (X_4) had a low C_p, this model was chosen for further analysis. The residual plot for all the independent variables showed only random patterns and no violations in the assumptions. The model is

$$\text{Median Average Annual Salary} = 16{,}830 + 38.256 \text{ Median}$$
$$\text{home value (\$000)} - 9.534$$
$$\text{Violent crime}/100{,}000 \text{ residents}$$
$$+ 1{,}053 \text{ average commuting}$$
$$\text{time in minutes}$$

The r^2 of this model is 0.847, meaning that 84.7% of the variation in Average Annual Salary can be explained by variation in median home value, variation in violent crime, and variation in average commuting time.

CHAPTER 16

16.2 (a) 1988. **(b)** The first four years and the last four years.

16.4 (b), (c), (e)

Year	Hours Per Day	MA(3)	ES(W = 0.5)	ES(W = 0.25)
2008	2.2	#N/A	2.2000	2.2000
2009	2.3	2.3000	2.2500	2.2250
2010	2.4	2.4333	2.3250	2.2688
2011	2.6	2.5000	2.4625	2.3516
2012	2.5	2.4667	2.4813	2.3887
2013	2.3	2.3333	2.3906	2.3665
2014	2.2	2.2333	2.2953	2.3249
2015	2.2	2.2000	2.2477	2.2937
2016	2.2	#N/A	2.2238	2.2702

(d) $W = 0.5$: $\hat{Y}_{2017} = E_{2016} = 2.2238$; $W = 0.25$: $\hat{Y}_{2017} = E_{2016} = 2.3249$. **(f)** The exponentially smoothed forecast for 2017 with $W = 0.5$ is slightly lower than that with $W = 0.25$. A smoothing coefficient of $W = 0.25$ smooths out the hours less than $W = 0.50$.

16.6 (b), (c), (e)

Decade	Performance (%)	MA(3)	ES(W = 0.5)	ES(W = 0.25)
1830s	2.8	#N/A	2.8000	2.8000
1840s	12.8	7.4000	7.8000	5.3000
1850s	6.6	10.6333	7.2000	5.6250
1860s	12.5	8.8667	9.8500	7.3438
1870s	7.5	8.6667	8.6750	7.3828
1880s	6.0	6.3333	7.3375	7.0371
1890s	5.5	7.4667	6.4188	6.6528
1900s	10.9	6.2000	8.6594	7.7146
1910s	2.2	8.8000	5.4297	6.3360
1920s	13.3	4.4333	9.3648	8.0770
1930s	-2.2	6.9000	3.5824	5.5077

Decade	Performance (%)	MA(3)	ES(W = 0.5)	ES(W = 0.25)
1940s	9.6	8.5333	6.5912	6.5308
1950s	18.2	12.0333	12.3956	9.4481
1960s	8.3	11.0333	10.3478	9.1611
1970s	6.6	10.5000	8.4739	8.5208
1980s	16.6	13.6000	12.5370	10.5406
1990s	17.6	11.2333	15.0685	12.3055
2000s	-0.5	#N/A	7.2842	9.1041

(d) $\hat{Y}_{2010} = E_{2000} = 7.2842$ **(e)** $\hat{Y}_{2010} = E_{2000} = 9.1041$. **(f)** The exponentially smoothed forecast for the 2010s with $W = 0.5$ is lower than that with $W = 0.25$. **(g)** According to the exponential smoothing with $W = 0.25$, there appears to be a general upward trend in the performance of the stocks in the past.

16.8 (b), (c), (e)

Year	IPOs	MA 3-Yr	ES(W = .50)	ES(W = .25)
2001	79	#N/A	79.0000	79.0000
2002	66	69.3333	72.5000	75.7500
2003	63	100.6667	67.7500	72.5625
2004	173	131.6667	120.3750	97.6719
2005	159	163.0000	139.6875	113.0039
2006	157	158.3333	148.3438	124.0029
2007	159	112.3333	153.6719	132.7522
2008	21	73.6667	87.3359	104.8141
2009	41	51.0000	64.1680	88.8606
2010	91	71.0000	77.5840	89.3955
2011	81	88.3333	79.2920	87.2966
2012	93	110.3333	86.1460	88.7224
2013	157	152.3333	121.5730	105.7918
2014	207	160.3333	164.2865	131.0939
2015	117	132.3333	140.6432	127.5704
2016	73	#N/A	106.8216	113.9278

(d) $W = 0.5$: $\hat{Y}_{2017} = E_{2016} = 106.8216$; $W = 0.25$: $\hat{Y}_{2017} = E_{2016} = 113.9278$. **(f)** The exponentially smoothed forecast for 2017 with $W = 0.5$ is lower than that with $W = 0.25$.

16.10 (a) The Y intercept $b_0 = 4.0$ is the fitted trend value reflecting the real total revenues (in millions of dollars) during the origin, or base year, 1994. **(b)** The slope $b_1 = 1.5$ indicates that the real total revenues are increasing at an estimated rate of $1.5 million per year. **(c)** Year is 2000, $X = 2000 - 1996 = 4$, $\hat{Y}_5 = 4.0 + 1.5(4) = 10.0$ million dollars. **(d)** Year is 2017, $X = 2017 - 1996 = 21$, $\hat{Y}_{20} = 4.0 + 1.5(21) = 35.5$ million dollars. **(e)** Year is 2020, $X = 2020 - 1996 = 24$, $\hat{Y}_{23} = 4.0 + 1.5(24) = 40$ million dollars.

16.12 (b) Linear trend: $\hat{Y} = 99.5412 + 3.7912X$, where X is relative to 2000. **(c)** Quadratic trend: $\hat{Y} = 75.922 + 13.2389X - 0.5905X^2$, where X is relative to 2000. **(d)** Exponential trend: $\log_{10}\hat{Y} = 1.9726 + 0.0154X$, where X is relative to 2000.
(e) Linear trend: $\hat{Y}_{2017} = 99.5412 + 3.7912(17) = 163.9912$
$$\hat{Y}_{2018} = 99.5412 + 3.7912(18) = 167.7824$$
Quadratic trend: $\hat{Y}_{2017} = 75.9220 + 13.2389(17) - 0.5905(17)^2$
$$= 130.1338$$
$\hat{Y}_{2018} = 75.9220 + 13.2389(18) - 0.5905(18)^2 = 122.9059$
Exponential trend: $\hat{Y}_{2017} = 10^{1.9726 + 0.0154(17)} = 171.4728$
$$\hat{Y}_{2018} = 10^{1.9726 + 0.0154(18)} = 177.6593$$

(f) The quadratic trend model fit the data better than the linear trend or exponential trend models and, hence, that forecast should be used.

16.14 (b) $\hat{Y} = 246.7986 + 71.0028X$ where $X =$ years relative to 1978. **(c)** $X = 39$, $\hat{Y} = 3,015.907$ billion $X = 40$ $\hat{Y} = 3,086.91$ billion **(d)** There is an upward trend in federal receipts between 1978 and 2016. The trend appears to be linear.

16.16 (b) Linear trend: $\hat{Y} = -6,786.2833 + 1,952X$, where X is relative to 2002. **(c)** Quadratic trend: $\hat{Y} = 4,667.05 - 3,333.361 + 377.5824X^2$, where X is relative to 2002. **(d)** Exponential trend: $\log_{10}\hat{Y} = 2.3228 + 0.1401X$, where X is relative to 2002. **(e)** Linear trend: $\hat{Y}_{2015} = 22,505.61$ million KWh $\hat{Y}_{2018} = 24,458.402$ million KWh
Quadratic trend: $\hat{Y}_{2017} = 39,622.68$ million KWh
$\hat{Y}_{2018} = 47,994.17$ millions of KWh
Exponential trend: $\hat{Y}_{2017} = 26,533.8946$ million KWh
$\hat{Y}_{2018} = 36,632.706$ million KWh.

16.18 (b) Linear trend: $\hat{Y} = 1.9998 + 0.1389X$, where X is relative to 2000. **(c)** Quadratic trend: $\hat{Y} = 2.1902 + 0.0675X - 0.0042X^2$, where X is relative to 2000. **(d)** Exponential trend: $\log_{10}\hat{Y} = 0.3289 + 0.0191X$, where X is relative to 2000.
The quadratic and exponential models appear to fit the data equally, so choose the quadratic model because it is simplest.
(f) The forecast using the quadratic model is:
Quadratic trend: $\hat{Y}_{2018} = 4.7663$ millions

16.20 (b) There has been an upward trend in the CPI in the United States over the 52-year period.
(c) Linear trend: $\hat{Y} = 16.5346 + 4.4751X$. **(d)** Quadratic trend: $\hat{Y} = 18.6219 + 4.2246X + 0.0049X^2$. **(e)** Exponential trend: $\log_{10}\hat{Y} = 1.5764 + 0.0180X$. **(f)** Choose the linear model because it is simplest. **(g)** Linear trend:
For 2017: $\hat{Y}_{2017} = 249.2405$
For 2018: $\hat{Y}_{2018} = 253.7156$

16.22 (a) For Time Series I, the graph of Y versus X appears to be more linear than the graph of log Y versus X, so a linear model appears to be more appropriate. For Time Series II, the graph of log Y versus X appears to be more linear than the graph of Y versus X, so an exponential model appears to be more appropriate.
(b) Time Series I : $\hat{Y} = 100.0731 + 14.9776X$, where $X =$ years relative to 2005
Time Series II: $\hat{Y} = 10^{1.9982 + 0.0609X}$, where $X =$ years relative to 2005.
(c) $X = 12$ for year 2017 in all models. Forecasts for the year 2017:
Time Series I: $\hat{Y} = 100.0731 + 14.9776(12) = 279.8045$
Time Series II: $\hat{Y} = 10^{1.9982 + 0.0609(12)} = 535.6886$.

16.24 $t_{STAT} = 2.40 > 2.2281$; reject H_0.

16.26 (a) $t_{STAT} = 1.60 < 2.2281$; do not reject H_0.

16.28 (a) Because the p-value $= 0.7509 > 0.05$ level of significance, the third-order term can be dropped. **(b)** Because the p-value $= 0.3448 > 0.05$, the second-order term can be dropped.
(c)

	Coefficients	Standard Error	t Stat	p-value
Intercept	56.5818	28.2785	2.0009	0.0652
YLag1	0.5808	0.2107	2.7564	0.0155

Because the p-value $= 0.0155 < 0.05$ the first-order term cannot be dropped.
(d) The most appropriate model for forecasting is the first-order autoregressive model:
$\hat{Y}_{2017} = 56.5818 + 0.5808Y_{2016} = 136.8484$.
$\hat{Y}_{2018} = 56.5818 + 0.5808\hat{Y}_{2017} = 136.0635$.

16.30 (a) Because the p-value $= 0.515 > 0.05$ level of significance, the third-order term can be dropped. **(b)** Because the p-value $= 0.594 > 0.05$ level of significance, the second-order term can be dropped. **(c)** Because the p-value is 0.0000, the first-order term is significant. **(d)** The most appropriate model for forecasting is the first-order autoregressive model:
$\hat{Y}_{2018} = 0.0132 + 1.0473Y_{2017} = \$4.9355$ million.

16.32 (a) 2.121. **(b)** 1.50.

16.34 (a) The residuals in the linear, quadratic, and exponential trend model show strings of consecutive positive and negative values. **(b), (c)**

	Linear	Quadratic	Exponential	AR2
Syx	7,449.3680	3,332.5112	6,481.891	1,484.3969
MAD	5,785.5073	2,612.3410	3,199.24	977.5796

(d) The residuals in the three trend models show strings of consecutive positive and negative values. The autoregressive model performs well for the historical data and has a fairly random pattern of residuals. It has the smallest values in MAD and S_{YX}. The autoregressive model would be the best model for forecasting.

16.36 (b), (c)

	Linear	Quadratic	Exponential	AR1
Syx	31.3035	29.2719	29.6198	30.1604
MAD	22.3806	21.2215	23.0246	22.3010

(d) The residuals in the linear and exponential trend models show strings of consecutive positive and negative values. The quadratic and autoregressive models have a fairly random pattern of residuals. There is very little difference in MAD and S_{YX} between the quadratic and autoregressive models. Either the quadratic or autoregressive model can be chosen for forecasting.

16.38 (b), (c)

	Linear	Quadratic	Exponential	AR1
Syx	0.1654	0.1305	0.1227	0.1245
MAD	0.1254	0.1009	0.1039	0.0935

(d) The residuals in the linear and exponential trend models show strings of consecutive positive and negative values. The quadratic and autoregressive models have a fairly random pattern of residuals. The MAD and S_{YX} values are similar in the quadratic, exponential, and autoregressive models. The quadratic or autoregressive model would be the best model for forecasting due to their fairly random pattern of residuals.

16.40 (a) log $\hat{\beta}_0 = 2$, $\hat{\beta}_0 = 100$. This is the fitted value for January 2011 prior to adjustment with the January multiplier.
(b) log $\hat{\beta}_1 = 0.01$, $\hat{\beta}_1 = 1.0233$. The estimated monthly compound growth rate is 2.33%.
(c) log $\hat{\beta}_2 = 0.1$, $\hat{\beta}_2 = 1.2589$. The January values in the time series are estimated to have a mean 25.89% higher than the December values.

16.42 (a) log $\hat{\beta}_0 = 3.0$, $\hat{\beta}_0 = 1,000$. This is the fitted value for the first quarter of 2013 prior to adjustment by the quarterly multiplier.
(b) log $\hat{\beta}_1 = 0.1$, $\hat{\beta}_1 = 1.2589$. The estimated quarterly compound growth rate is $(\hat{\beta}_1 - 1)100\% = 25.89\%$.
(c) log $\hat{\beta}_3 = 0.2$, $\hat{\beta}_3 = 1.5849$.

16.44 (a) The retail industry is heavily subject to seasonal variation due to the holiday seasons and so are the revenues for Toys R Us.
(b) There is obvious seasonal effect in the time series.
(c) $\log_{10}\hat{Y} = 3.6522 + 0.0014X - 0.3600Q_1 - 0.3604Q_2 - 0.3390Q_3$.
(d) $\log_{10}\hat{\beta}_1 = 0.0014$. $\hat{\beta}_1 = 1.0032$. The estimated quarterly compound growth rate is $(\hat{\beta}_1 - 1)100\% = 0.32\%$.
(e) $\log_{10}\hat{\beta}_2 = -0.3600$. $\hat{\beta}_2 = 0.4365$. $(\hat{\beta}_2 - 1)100\% = -56.35\%$. The 1st quarter values in the time series are estimated to have a mean 56.35%

below the 4th quarter values. $\log_{10}\hat{\beta}_3 = -0.3604$. $\hat{\beta}_3 = 0.4361$.
$(\hat{\beta}_3 - 1)100\% = -56.39\%$.

The 2nd quarter values in the time series are estimated to have a mean 56.39% below the 4th quarter values.

$\log_{10}\hat{\beta}_4 = -0.3390$. $\hat{\beta}_4 = 0.4581$. $(\hat{\beta}_4 - 1)100\% = -54.19\%$.
The 3rd quarter values in the time series are estimated to have a mean 54.19% below the 4th quarter values. **(f)** Forecasts for the last three quarters of 2017 and all of 2018 are 2,577.9471, 2,750.4706, 6,018.1637, 2,605.5535, 2,611.5299, 2,752.2508, and 6,026.7614 millions.

16.46 (b) $\log10(\text{Predicted } Y) = 2.2313 + 0.0007X - 0.1871M_1 - 0.1241M_2 - 0.0144M_3 - 0.1196M_4 - 0.0902M_5 + 0.0560M_6 - 0.0725M_7 - 0.0207M_8 + 0.0677M_9 - 0.0056M_{10} - 0.0802M_{11}$.
(c) 216.5938, 183.2386, 154.5297, 186.1607. **(e)** 0.1613%
(f) $0.8463(\hat{\beta}_8 - 1)100\% = -15.37\%$. The July values in the time series are estimated to have a mean 15.37% below the December values.

16.48 (b) $\log10(\text{Predicted } Y) = 0.9640 + 0.0087X + 0.045Q_1 + 0.0083Q_2 + 0.0130Q_3$
(c) 2.0234%, after adjusting for the seasonal component.
(d) 10.92% above the fourth-quarter values.
(e) Last quarter, 2016: $Y = \$25.4407$.
(f) 2017: 28.7858, 26.9885, 27.8299, 27.5524.

16.60 (b) Linear trend: $\hat{Y} = 173{,}789.3351 + 2{,}459.3332X$ where X is relative to 1984.
(c) 2017: $\hat{Y}_{2017} = 256{,}024.235$ thousands
2018: $\hat{Y}_{2018} = 257{,}406.665$.
(d) (b) Linear trend: $\hat{Y} = 116{,}723.2674 + 1{,}435.6197X$, where X is relative to 1984.
(c) 2017: $\hat{Y}_{2017} = 164{,}098.716$ thousands. 2018: $\hat{Y}_{2018} = 165{,}534.336$ thousands.

16.62 (b) Linear trend: $\hat{Y} = -2.6364 + 0.7247X$, where X is relative to 1975.
(c) Quadratic trend: $\hat{Y} = 0.2377 + 0.2935X + 0.0105X^2$, where X is relative to 1975.
Exponential trend: $\log_{10}\hat{Y} = 0.2115 + 0.0345X$, where X is relative to 1975.
Test of A_3: p-value $= 0.14 > 0.05$. Do not reject H_0 that $A_2 = 0$. Third-order term can be deleted. A third-order autoregressive model is not appropriate. Test of A_2: p-value $= 0.0042 < 0.05$ Reject H_0. The second-order term cannot be deleted. The second-order model is appropriate.
AR(2): $\hat{Y}_i = 0.3681 + 1.5164Y_{i-1} - 0.5249Y_{i-2}$

	Linear	Quadratic	Exponential	AR2
Syx	1.9955	1.4253	3.7962	0.7264
MAD	1.7133	0.8943	2.1893	0.4681

(h) The residuals in the first three models show strings of consecutive positive and negative values. The autoregressive model performs well for the historical data and has a fairly random pattern of residuals. It also has the smallest values in the standard error of the estimate and MAD. Based on the principle of parsimony, the autoregressive model would probably be the best model for forecasting.

(i) $\hat{Y}_{2015} = \$28.3149$ billions.

CHAPTER 17

17.2 The r^2 for the regression tree model is 0.373. The first split is based on a plate gap of 1.8. For those bags with a plate gap less than 1.8, the mean tear is 0.3107. For those bags with a plate gap at least 1.8, the mean tear is 1.98. For those bags with a plate gap less than 0.0, the mean tear is 0.06. For those bags with a plate gap less than 1.8 but greater than 0, the

mean tear is 0.45. Thus, you would recommend that a plate gap of less than 0 be used to minimize tears in the bag.

17.4 The r^2 for the regression tree model is 0.789. The first split is based on 831 square feet. Moves of at least 831 sq. ft. have a mean moving time of 51.1875 hours. Moves of less than 831 square feet have a mean moving time of 22.6071 hours. Among moves of less than 831 sq. ft., moves of less than 486 sq. ft., have a mean moving time of 15.7955 hours. Moves of less than 344 sq. ft. have a mean moving time of 12.75 hours. Moves of between 344 and 486 sq. ft. have a mean moving time of 18.3333 hours. Moves of between 486 and 830 sq. ft. have a mean moving time of 27.0147 hours. Moves between 486 and 599 sq. ft. have a mean moving time of 24.825 hours. Moves between 600 and 830 have a mean moving time of 30.1429 hours. Moves between 557 and 599 sq. ft. have a mean moving time of 24.05 hours. Moves between 486 and 557 sq. ft have a mean moving time of 25.6 hours.

17.6 (b) The r^2 for the classification tree model is 0.434. The first split is for the 8 customers who called 50 or more times. Among customers who called fewer than 50 times, those who called at least seven times and visited two or more times are more likely to churn.

17.8 Because half the data will be used for a validation sample, the results will differ depending on which values are in the training sample and which are in the validation sample.

17.10 (b) The first two cereals to cluster are Wheaties and Nature's Path Organic Multigrain Flakes followed by Post Shredded Wheat Vanilla Almond and Kellogg's Mini Wheats. At the two cluster level, one cluster contains Post Shredded Wheat Vanilla Almond and Kellogg's Mini Wheats and the other cluster contains the other five cereals.

17.12 The optimal number of clusters in the range between three and five is 3 (CCC $= -1.4223$). The first cluster consists of Russia, Poland, Lebanon, Malaysia, Argentina, Chile, Venezuela, Turkey, Brazil, and Mexico. The mean GDP per capita of this cluster is 21,085.4 and the social media usage % is 81.4. The second cluster consists of Ukraine, Jordan, Philippines, Vietnam, Peru, South Africa, Indonesia, Ghana, Kenya, Senegal, Tanzania, Uganda, Nigeria, and Ethiopia. The mean GDP per capita of this cluster is 6,613.36 and the social media usage % is 80.14. The third cluster consists of China, India, Pakistan, and Burkina Faso. The mean GDP per capita of this cluster is 6,768.75 and the social media usage % is 60. Thus, cluster 1 is characterized by high GDP and high social media usage. Cluster 2 is characterized by low GDP and high social media usage. Cluster 3 is characterized by low GDP and high social media usage.

17.14 The optimal number of clusters in the range between three and eight is 6 (CCC $= 2.4411$). The first cluster consists of Austria, Canada, Germany, Hungary, India, Ireland, Israel, New Zealand, Poland, Portugal, Russia, Slovakia, Spain, Taiwan, and Thailand. The mean connection speed is 10.44 Mbps, the mean peak connection speed is 54.9067 Mbps, 86% are above 4 Mbps, and 36.0667% are above 18.15 Mbps. The second cluster consists of Hong Kong and South Korea. The mean connection speed is 10.44 Mbps, the mean peak connection speed is 93.85 Mbps, 94% are above 4 Mbps, and 63.5% are above 10 Mbps. The third cluster consists only of Singapore. The mean connection speed is 12.5 Mbps, the mean peak connection speed is 13.5 Mbps, 87 % are above 4 Mbps, and 51% are above 10 Mbps.

The fourth cluster consists of Belgium, Czech Republic, Denmark, Finland, Japan, Netherlands, Norway, Rumania, Sweden, Switzerland, United Kingdom, and the United States. The mean connection speed is 14.6167 Mbps, the mean peak connection speed is 60.975 Mbps, 90.0833% are above 4 Mbps, and 52.75% are above 10 Mbps. The fifth cluster consists of Argentina, Bolivia, Brazil, China, Costa Rica, Ecuador, Philippines, South Africa, Venezuela, and VietNam. The mean connection speed is 3.4269 Mbps, the mean peak connection speed is 21.3538 Mbps,

66.25% are above 4Mbps, and 1.3692% are above 10 Mbps. The sixth cluster consists of Australia, Chile, Colombia, France, Italy, Malaysia, Mexico, Peru, Sri Lanka, Turkey, United Arab Republic, and Uruguay. The mean connection speed is 5.9333 Mbps, the mean peak connection speed is 37.9167 Mbps, 66.25% are above 4Mbps, and 8.15% are above 10 Mbps.

Cluster 1 is characterized by moderate mean connection speed, moderately high mean peak connection speed, high % are above 4 Mbps, and moderate % are above 10Mbps. Cluster 2 is characterized by very high mean connection speed, very high mean peak connection speed, very high % are above 4 Mbps, and very high % are above 10 Mbps. Cluster 3 (Singapore) is characterized by high mean connection speed, extremely high mean peak connection speed, high % are above 4 Mbps, and high % are above 10 Mbps.

Cluster 4 is characterized by high mean connection speed, moderately high mean peak connection speed, high % are above 4 Mbps, and moderate % are above 10 Mbps. Cluster 5 is characterized by very low mean connection speed, low mean peak connection speed, low % are above 4 Mbps, and very low % are above 10 Mbps. Cluster 6 is characterized by low mean connection speed, moderately low mean peak connection speed, moderate % are above 4 Mbps, and very low % are above 10Mbps.

17.16 The correspondence analysis plot shows that online guests are associated with purchasing household items while online members are strongly associated with grocery items and in-store customers more associated with hardlines and apparel than the two other categories. Positive comments are most associated with apparel items, while household items are associated with negative comments. Those that post most frequently tend to post positive comments. Managers may want to further examine the experience of online guests purchasing household items as such customers may be among the most disappointed by their shopping experience.

17.18 (b) Because the stress statistic is 0.0973 in three dimensions, 0.1308 in two dimensions, and 0.3147 in one dimension, it is reasonable to try to interpret a two-dimensional mapping of the cereals. Looking at a 45° rotation, one dimension separates Post Shredded Wheat Vanilla Almond and Kellogg's Mini Wheats based on their higher calorie and sugar content. A second dimension does not seem to be interpretable. In addition, All Bran, which has lower calories and higher sugar is separated from the other cereals.

17.20 The two-dimensional plot has a stress value of virtually 0.0000. One of the dimensions appears to separate countries with high GDP from those with low GDP. Many of the sub-Sahara African countries are grouped together.

17.22 The two-dimensional plot has a stress value of 0.0524. Singapore is separated from the other countries. The countries opposite Singapore low mean connection speed, moderately low mean peak connection speed, moderate % are above 4Mbps, and very low % are above 10Mbps. There appears to be a grouping of countries that have low mean connection speed, low mean peak connection speed, low % are above 4Mbps, and very low % are above 10Mbps. Many of the countries that are opposite these have moderate mean connection speed, moderately high mean peak connection speed, high % are above 4Mbps, and moderate % are above 10Mbps.

17.28 Because half the data will be used for a validation sample, the results will differ depending on which values are in the training sample and which are in the validation sample.

17.30 The r^2 of the regression tree model is 0.731. The prime determinant of wins is the ERA Teams with an ERA below 4.05 had a mean of 91.6667 wins while teams with an ERA above 4.05 had a mean of 76.2857 wins. Teams with an ERA above 4.05 who had at least 44 saves had a mean of 83.5 wins while teams with fewer than 44 saves had a mean of 71.8461 wins. Teams with an ERA above 4.05 who had fewer than 44 saves and an ERA below 4.33 had a mean of 77.4 wins. (Those that had an ERA above 4.33 had a mean of 68.375 wins.)

17.32 (c) The first two foods to cluster are Cantonese and American, followed by French and Mandarin, followed by Spanish and Greek. At the two cluster level, the first cluster includes Japanese, French, Mandarin, Szechuan, and Mexican. The second cluster includes Cantonese, American, Spanish, Greek, and Italian. Because the stress statistic is 0.0468 in four dimensions, 0.1164 in three dimensions, 0.2339 in two dimensions, and 0.4079 in one dimension, it is reasonable to try to first try interpret a two-dimensional mapping of the foods. There does not seem to be a clear interpretation of the dimensions along the lines of the three scales. The two spicy foods, Mexican and Szechuan are close to each other as are French and Greek, and Japanese and American. Italian is separated by itself as is Spanish.

17.34 The r^2 of the regression tree model is 0.727. The first split is based on the living space of 2,220 square feet. Houses with a living space < 2,220 square feet have a mean asking price of $558,678.95 while houses with a living space > 2,220 square feet have a mean asking price of $ $446,854.76. Houses with a living space > 2,220 square feet that have a brick exterior have a mean asking price of $499,616.67 while those without a brick exterior have a mean asking price of $585,938.46. Houses without a brick exterior that have a lot size greater than 0.46 (acres) have a mean asking price of $634,760 while houses that have a lot size less than 0.46 (acres) have a mean asking price of $555,425.

Houses with a living space < 2,220 square feet that have a living space > 1,197 square feet have a mean asking price of $463,741.18 while those with a living space below 1,197 square feet have a mean asking price of $375,087.50. Houses with a living space < 2,220 square feet that have a living space > 1,197 square feet that have a fireplace have a mean asking price of $484,643.48 while those that do not have a fireplace have a mean asking price of $420,036.36.

Houses with a living space < 2,220 square feet that have a living space > 1,197 square feet that have a fireplace and a lot size > 0.19 acres have a mean asking price of $448,128.57 (those with a brick exterior have a mean asking price of $463,928.57 while those without a brick exterior have a mean asking price of $432,328.57) while those that have a lot size < 0.19 acres have a mean asking price of $541,444.44.

Houses with a living space < 2,220 square feet that have a living space > 1,197 square feet that do not have a fireplace and have at least three bathrooms have a mean asking price of $444,100 while those that have fewer than three bathrooms have a mean asking price of $391,160.

17.36 The optimal number of clusters in the range between three and eight is 6 (CCC = 3.97273). The first cluster consists of Stonyfield Organic Greek. The second cluster consists of the six regular yogurts. The third cluster consists of the Great Value Greek only. The fourth cluster consists of the Organic Valley Greek only. The fifth cluster consists of the Trader Joe's Plain Whole Greek only. The sixth cluster consists of Dannon Oikos, Wallaby Organic, and Chobani Greek. You can conclude that the regular yogurts are different from the Greek yogurts and that many of the Greek yogurts are different from each other.

Index

Credits

Photos

Front Matter
Page viii, Courtesy of David Levine

First Things First
Page 1, Wallix/iStock/Getty Images

Chapter 1
Pages 16 and 31, Haveseen/YAY Micro/AGE Fotostock

Chapter 2
Pages 41 and 81, Scanrail/123RF

Chapter 3
Pages 120 and 153, Gitanna/Fotolia

Chapter 4
Pages 168 and 192 Vectorfusionart/Shutterstock

Chapter 5
Pages 199 and 215, Hongqi Zhang/123RF

Chapter 6
Pages 223 and 243, Ken Mellott/Shutterstock

Chapter 7
Pages 252 and 267, Bluecinema/E+/Getty Images

Chapter 8
Pages 275 and 298, Monkey Business Images/Shutterstock

Chapter 9
Pages 311 and 340, Ahmettozar/iStock/Getty Images

Chapter 10
Pages 351 and 381, Gundam_Ai/Shutterstock

Chapter 11
Page 398, Fotoinfot/Shutterstock

Chapter 12
Pages 440 and 471, Vibrant Image Studio/Shutterstock

Chapter 13
Pages 484 and 520, Pixfly/Shutterstock

Chapter 14
Pages 536 and 575, Maridav/123RF

Chapter 15
Pages 592 and 616, Anthony Brown/Fotolia

Chapter 16
Pages 629 and 665, Stylephotographs/123RF

Chapter 17
Pages 678 and 695, Rawpixel.com/Shutterstock

Online Chapter 19
Zest marina/Fotolia

Online Chapter 20
Cloki/Shutterstock

Text

Chapter 2
Page 44, Data Extracted from "Gartner Says Worldwide Smartphone Sales Grew 9.7 Percent in Fourth Quarter of 2015" Press Release, Egham, UK, February 18, 2016, www.gartner.com/newsroom/id/3215217; Data extracted from Consumer Financial Protection Bureau, bit.ly/2pR7ryO. **Page 45**, Data extracted from "Timetric: insurance product complexity the main barrier to online engagement" (Life Insurance International) By Ronan McCaughey, bit.ly/2qxMFRj; Data extracted from Pew Research Center, Internet & Technology, bit.ly/2pR5bHZ; Data extracted from Kickstarter Stats — Kickstarter, Successfully Funded Projects, Kickstarter.com, kickstarter.com/help/stats. **Page 53**, Data extracted from a blog "Which NBA Teams Offer the Most Affordable Home Games?" Sreekar Jasthi, www.nerdwallet.com/blog/which-nba-teams-mostaffordable. **Page 59**, U.S. Bureau of Labor Statistics, bit.ly/2qxIjcH, accessed February 3, 2017; Data extracted from Consumer Financial Protection Bureau, bit.ly/2pR7ryO. **Page 68**, Data extracted from Domestic Movie Theatrical Market Summary 1995 to 2017, The Numbers, www.the-numbers.com/market. **Page 69**, Data extracted from Box Office History for Harry Potter Movies, The Numbers, www.the-numbers.com/interactive/comp-Harry-Potter.php. **Page 70**, Data extracted from Yearly Box Office, Boxofficemojo, An IMDb company, boxofficemojo.com/yearly; Data extracted from U.S. Census Bureau New Residential Sales, bit.ly/2eEcIBR, accessed March 19, 2017. **Page 77**, Data extracted from U.S. Census Bureau New Residential Sales, bit.ly/2eEcIBR, March 19, 2017. **Page 83**, Data extracted from "Why Are Textbooks So Expensive?", bit.ly/2ppEetq. **Page 84**, Data extracted from Domestic Theatrical Market Summary for 2014, The Numbers, www.the-numbers.com/market/2016/summary; Data extracted from "B2B Content Marketing Trends—North America: Content Marketing Institute/MarketingProfs", bit.ly/2d98EaN. **Page 86**, Data extracted from "How many CALORIES IN BEER? Calories in Beer, Alcohol in Beer, Carbs in Beer ", www.beer100.com/beercalories.htm; Data extracted from "How Much Do Top CEOs Make?" By Renee Lightner and Theo Francis, bit.ly/1QqpEUZ.

Chapter 3

Page 147, Data extracted from Complete List of McDonald's US Locations, Aggdata, bit.ly/2qJjFpF. **Page 152**, Data extracted from Box Office Comparison Chart for Harry Potter Franchise, The Numbers, www.the-numbers.com/interactive/comp-Harry-Potter.php.

Chapter 5

Page 213, U.S. Department of Transportation, bit.ly/2pCTdBZ; Data extracted from Consumer Financial Protection Bureau, bit.ly/2nGDsc7. **Page 216**, Data extracted from Mobile Fact Sheet, Pew Research Center, www.pewinternet.org/fact-sheet/mobile/.

Chapter 6

Page 236, Data extracted from The Nielsen Comparable Metrics Report Q3 2016, bit.ly/2rj8GHm. **Page 240**, Data extracted from "Which NBA Teams Offer the Most Affordable Home Games?", Sreekar Jasthi, Nerd-Wallet, Inc., www.nerdwallet.com/blog/which-nba-teamsmost-affordable.

Page 245, Data extracted from "88% Of Shoppers Are Webrooming," Retail TouchPoints, bit.ly/1JEcmqh.

Chapter 7

Page 270, Data extracted from "Study shows cities with highest and lowest credit scores", *San Antonio Business Journal*, bit.ly/2oCgnbi;

Chapter 8

Page 289, Data extracted from "Digital in 2017 Global Overview" report from We Are Social, bit.ly/2jXeS3F.

Chapter 17

Page 690, Data extracted from https://en.wikipedia.org/wiki/List_of_countries_by_Internet_connection_speeds. **Page 693**, Data extracted from https://en.wikipedia.org/wiki/List_of_countries_by_Internet_connection_speeds. **Page 697**.